Red Gold

Red Gold

THE CONQUEST OF THE
BRAZILIAN INDIANS

John Hemming

Harvard University Press
Cambridge, Massachusetts 1978

Printed in the United States of America

Library of Congress Cataloging in Publication Data

Hemming, John, 1935-
  Red gold.

  Bibliography: p.
  Includes index.
  1. Indians of South America — Brazil — History.
2. Indians of South America — Brazil — Government re-
lations. 3. Brazil — Discovery and exploration.
  I.   Title.
F2519.H45   981'.01   77-22863
ISBN 0-674-75107-8

FOR LOUISA AND HER FAMILY

Contents

List of Illustrations

MAPS

Pages xviii to xxiii, drawn by K. C. Jordan.

Preface

MY FIRST contact with Brazilian Indians was in 1961. I was on an expedition to explore the headwaters of the Iriri river in the forests of central Brazil. We were supported by the Royal Geographical Society in London; and the Brazilian Geographical Institute sent three surveyors on our eleven-man expedition.

Before penetrating this unexplored region, we consulted two legendary figures of the Indian Protection Service – Orlando Villas Boas and Francisco Meirelles. Both assured us that no Indians lived in the Cachimbo hills which we would be penetrating. They were wrong: an uncontacted tribe laid an ambush on one of the paths we had cut into the forest and killed the expedition's leader, my friend Richard Mason. We brought out arrows and clubs used in the attack. Other Indians identified these as belonging to a tribe called Kreen-Akrore. It took many expeditions and ten years of attraction-campaigns before the Villas Boas brothers finally made contact with the Kreen-Akrore. It was my first glimpse of the Indian Service at work, and my first realisation that unknown tribes were still being contacted and conquered on the Amazon frontiers of Brazil.

My interest in Brazilian Indians developed during four later journeys into the interior of that vast country. In 1971 I visited many tribes, and joined Cláudio Villas Boas on an expedition to the Jarina river of the central Xingu. The following year I was on a team from the Aborigines Protection Society invited to report on the treatment of Brazilian Indians. We saw tribes in all parts of Brazil. In the course of those journeys I probably visited more Indian tribes than any other non-Brazilian.

During those years I helped create a charity, Survival International, whose purpose is to help tribal peoples in all parts of the world. I became aware of the terrible impact of our society on isolated tribes. I saw the many failings and occasional successes of the Brazilian Indian Protection Service and its successor Funai. We often debated the morality of integration or isolation of the few surviving Indians. And the more I researched into the subject, the more I realised that an understanding of the tragedy lay in its history. That history began in 1500, with the arrival of the first Europeans on the shores of Brazil. This book is therefore a history of Brazilian Indians or of the colonial conquest of Brazil in terms of its native peoples.

In the sixteenth century the history of Brazilian Indians was the history of Brazil itself. There were millions of natives living in the half of South America that is now Brazil. That continent may well have had a population as large as Africa's in 1500. But, while the native population of Africa has survived and multiplied and Africa is now being decolonised, the native peoples of South America have diminished and declined.

The first Europeans were fascinated by the newly discovered natives of Brazil. Vaz Caminha, Vespucci and other explorers wrote wide-eyed accounts of the Indians. When the Portuguese established their first colonies, chroniclers such as Gabriel Soares de Sousa and Pero de Magalhães Gandavo produced competent descriptions of the coastal Tupi tribes, and Vicente do Salvador wrote a fine history of the Portuguese conquest of the north coast of Brazil. But by far the best observers were from other European countries. The German Hans Staden wrote an enthralling account of his capture by the Tupinambá; and the splendid French missionaries Jean de Léry, André Thevet, Claude d'Abbeville and Yves d'Evreux gave the most vivid descriptions of Indian reactions to European invasion. The French prided themselves on their sympathy with the Indians, and this emerges in the writing of the French chroniclers. They alone bothered to translate and record Indian speech. Brazilian Indians are proud of their oratory, but the Portuguese never deigned to report Indian opinions, anxieties or wisdom.

After the sixteenth century Portuguese colonists lost all curiosity about the peoples they were subjugating. Expeditions into the interior and wars against Indians were waged by illiterate backwoodsmen intent only on killing or enslaving natives. Colonial administrators organised campaigns against groups of 'heathen' without recording even tribal names. The history of the protracted and dramatic Indian wars in the north-east emerges only from dry, voluminous official papers.

The great exception to Portuguese apathy about Indians was among the missionaries, and especially the Jesuits. The Society of Jesus attracted highly educated men to its missionary calling. The letters of Nóbrega, Anchieta and other early Jesuits are full of information about Indians – for missionaries had to understand native societies in order to transform them.

Jesuits were involved in the two great Portuguese thrusts into the interior, into the Paraná–Paraguay and Amazon basins. In the south, Spanish Jesuits were on the defensive, protecting their Paraguayan missions from bandeirante raiders from São Paulo. On the Amazon, Portuguese Jesuits collaborated in the colonial destruction of riverine tribes. Their 'descents' of forest Indians were unwittingly as destructive as the settlers' slave raids.

The colonial conquest of Brazil was often brutal. But the ultimate objective of both colonists and missionaries was to subdue rather than to destroy the Indians. The colonists wanted Indian labour, and the missionaries wanted converts. It was disease that annihilated the Indians. Native bravery and fighting skills were nullified by a lack of genetically inherited defences against European and African diseases. Decimation by disease has condemned Brazilian Indians to near-extinction. Instead of repossessing a decolonised country, they are now reduced to a pathetic minority on the fringe of a successful European society.

The Jesuits were in charge of Indian welfare for most of the centuries of Portuguese colonial rule. This book therefore ends with the expulsion of the Jesuits in the 1760s, by which time the balance of power between colonists and Indians had changed irretrievably. The main history of Brazil was by then enacted in the flourishing coastal cities. Their inhabitants were European settlers and their African slaves: the surviving Indians had been driven far inland to remote recesses of forest and savannah.

There have been many studies of individual tribes and much fine history of colonial Brazil. But this book is the first attempt at a history of all Brazilian Indians during those centuries of colonial conquest. I am working on a sequel, to bring the tragic story up to the present day. I hope that this record will increase awareness of the Indians' present plight and of the origins of modern Brazil.

Acknowledgements

THIS is an opportunity to thank the many organisations and individuals who helped me on my visits to Brazil. The Iriri River Expedition was supported by the Royal Geographical Society and by the Blue Star Line, Frigorífico Anglo, Shell and other firms. In Rio de Janeiro we were given great hospitality by John Hay-Edie and his family, and by Sir Geoffrey and Lady Wallinger at the British Embassy. My next journey to Brazil was made possible by a Miranda Scholarship, awarded by Celso da Rocha Miranda through the Anglo-Brazilian Society. The Brazilian Ambassador in London, Sérgio Corrêa da Costa, helped me with the introductions that are essential for permission to visit any Indians. In the field I was encouraged by the greatest Indianists, Orlando and Cláudio Villas Boas, and travelled with Dr Roberto Baruzzi and his splendid team of volunteer doctors from the Escola Paulista de Medicina who give so much devoted care to the Xingu Indians.

In 1972 I was fortunate to be included in the team sent to study Brazilian Indians by the Aborigines Protection Society (part of the Anti-Slavery Society). We wrote a report that augmented that made by my great friends Robin and Marika Hanbury-Tenison on behalf of Survival International. During this visit to all parts of Brazil we were often helped by the staff of Funai, the Fundação Nacional do Índio, and by various missionary orders. But all movement was made possible, on this and other trips to Amazonia, by the daring pilots of the transport wing, Correo Aéreo Nacional, of the Brazilian Air Force, F.A.B.

When it came to studying the history of Brazilian Indians, I was lent a delightful house outside São Paulo for six months by Dr João Batista Pereira de Almeida. His cousin Beatrice Almeida helped me to obtain a private room for study at the Biblioteca Municipal of São Paulo. In Rio de Janeiro, I spent many pleasant weeks working in the magnificent library of books about Brazilian Indians belonging to Carlos de Araújo Moreira Neto. J. Spencer Anderson and his colleagues at Samab were very kind to me. I am also very grateful to the staffs of various libraries:

those of the Museu do Índio and Museu Nacional in Rio de Janeiro, of Funai in Brasília, of the Biblioteca Nacional in Rio, Lisbon and Mexico City, the Instituto Indigenista Interamericano in Mexico, and of Canning House, the London Library, the British Library Reading Room and the Institute of Historical Research in London. Lastly my thanks go to Professor Charles Boxer for his comments on the typescript.

JOHN HEMMING

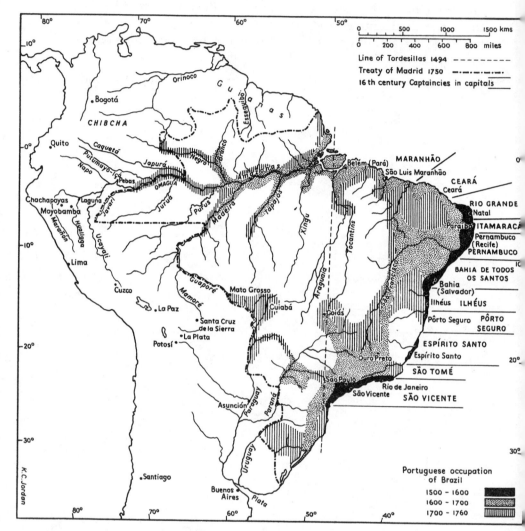

1   The Portuguese Occupation of Brazil

2   *Eastern Brazil*

| 0 | 100 | 200 | 300 | 400 kms. |
| 0 | 100 | 200 | 300 miles |

Tribal names in capitals   *PURI*
18th century gold mine   ●
Modern names in brackets...(Brasília)

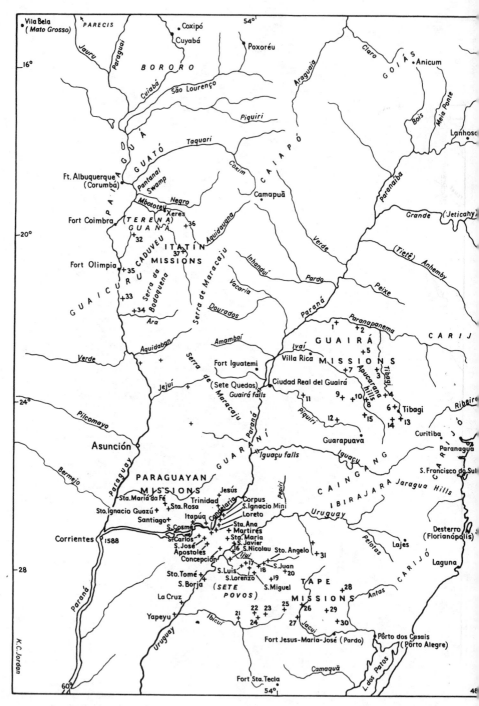

3   *The Paraguayan Missions*

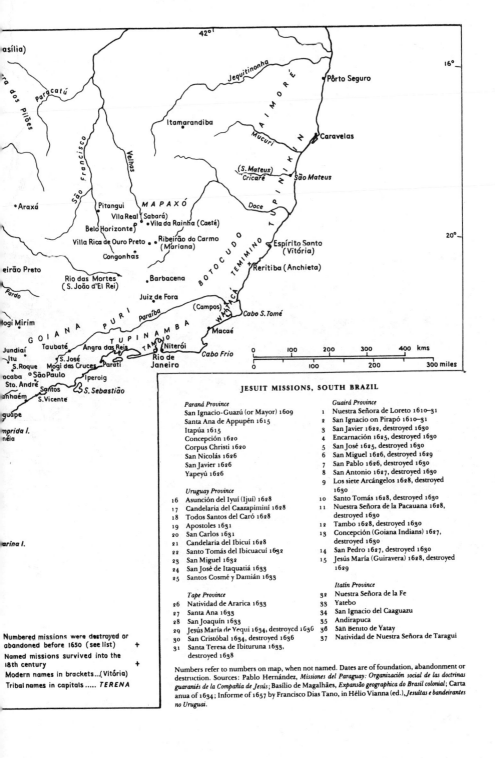

JESUIT MISSIONS, SOUTH BRAZIL

Paraná Province
San Ignacio-Guazú (or Mayor) 1609
Santa Ana de Appupén 1615
Itapúa 1615
Concepción 1620
Corpus Christi 1620
San Nicolás 1626
San Javier 1626
Yapeyú 1626

Uruguay Province
16 Asunción del Iyuí (Ijuí) 1628
17 Candelaria del Caazapiminí 1628
18 Todos Santos del Caró 1628
19 Apostoles 1631
20 San Carlos 1631
21 Candelaria del Ibicuí 1628
22 Santo Tomás del Ibicuacuí 1632
23 San Miguel 1632
24 San José de Itaquatiá 1633
25 Santos Cosmé y Damián 1633

Tape Province
26 Natividad de Ararica 1633
27 Santa Ana 1633
28 San Joaquín 1633
29 Jesús María de Yequi 1694, destroycd 1636
30 San Cristóbal 1634, destroyed 1636
31 Santa Teresa de Ibituruna 1633, destroyed 1638

Guairá Province
1 Nuestra Señora de Loreto 1610–31
2 San Ignacio on Pirapó 1610–31
3 San Javier 1622, destroyed 1630
4 Encarnación 1625, destroyed 1630
5 San José 1625, destroyed 1630
6 San Miguel 1626, destroyed 1629
7 San Pablo 1626, destroyed 1630
8 San Antonio 1627, destroyed 1630
9 Los siete Arcángelos 1628, destroyed 1630
10 Santo Tomás 1628, destroyed 1630
11 Nuestra Señora de la Pacauana 1628, destroyed 1630
12 Tambo 1628, destroyed 1630
13 Concepción (Goiana Indians) 1627, destroyed 1630
14 San Pedro 1627, destroyed 1630
15 Jesús María (Guiravera) 1628, destroyed 1629

Itatín Province
32 Nuestra Señora de la Fe
33 Yatebo
34 San Ignacio del Caaguazu
35 Andirapuca
36 San Benito de Yatay
37 Natividad de Nuestra Señora de Taragui

Numbers refer to numbers on map, when not named. Dates are of foundation, abandonment or destruction. Sources: Pablo Hernández, *Missiones del Paraguay: Organización social de las doctrinas guaraniés de la Compañía de Jesús*; Basílio de Magalhães, *Expansão geographica do Brasil colonial*; Carta anua of 1634; Informe of 1657 by Francisco Dias Tano, in Hélio Vianna (ed.), *Jesuítas e bandeirantes no Uruguai.*

Numbered missions were destroyed or abandoned before 1650 (see list) +
Named missions survived into the 18th century +
Modern names in brackets...(Vitória)
Tribal names in capitals ..... TERENA

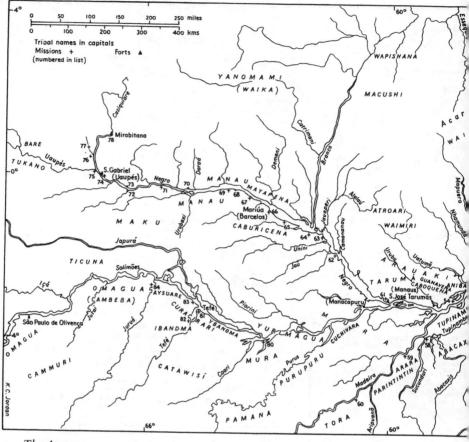

4   *The Amazon*

MISSIONS
(Names in brackets=new na

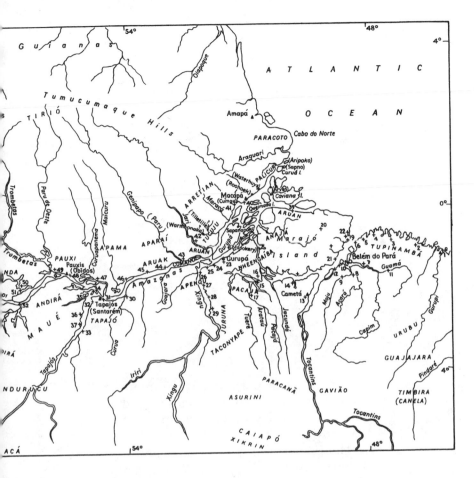

AMAZON
expulsion of Jesuits, 1759)

45 Urubucoara (Outeiro)
46 Gurupatuba (Monte Alegre)
47 Surubiú (Alenquer)
48 Pauxis (Óbidos) + Fort
49 Muruapig
50 Santa Cruz dos Aruaquis
51 Santa Cruz da Nhamundá (Faro)
52 Parintintin
53 Saracá (Silves)
54 Abacaxis (Serpa/Itacoatiara)
55 Abacaxis (Vila Bela da Imperatriz)
58 Canumã
59 Trocano (Borba)
60 Manicoré

Rio Negro
61 São José de Tarumãs (Manaus) + Fort (Barra do Rio Negro)
62 Jaú (Airão)
63 Pedreira (Moura)
64 Aracari (Carvoeiro)
65 Cumarú (Poyares)

66 Mariúa (Barcelos)
67 (Moreira)
68 (Lama Longa)
69 (Tomar)
70 Nossa Senhora do Loreto
71 Santo António do Castanheiro
72 São João Nepomuceno
73 Nossa Senhora de Nazareth
74 São Gabriel da Cachoeira (Uaupés) + Fort
75 São Joaquim do Coané
76 São Miguel do Iparaná
77 (Bamba)
78 São José de Mirabitena + Fort

Solimões (Upper Amazon)
80 Coari
81 Tefé (Ega or Tefé)
82 Nogueira
83 (Alvarães)
84 (Fonte Boa)
87 São Paulo de Olivença

RED GOLD

'. . . the . . . true purpose was to capture Indians: to draw from their veins the red gold which has always been the mine of that province!'

(The Jesuit António Vieira's comment, in 1656, on the many expeditions that plunged into central Brazil, nominally to seek gold mines, but in reality to enslave Indians.)

ONE

Noble Savages

THE first Portuguese sighting of Brazil was on 22 April 1500. A fleet of thirteen ships commanded by the young nobleman Pero Álvares Cabral was on its way to India around the recently discovered Cape of Good Hope, but was blown too far to the west, across the Atlantic towards Brazil. Its sailors realised that they were approaching land. They pressed on, and sighted a high round mountain which their commander named Mount Pascoal ('Easter Mountain'). They sailed closer and anchored in nine fathoms, a mile from the mouth of a forested river.

The first meeting between the Portuguese and Brazilian natives occurred immediately. 'We caught sight of men walking on the beaches. . . . The Admiral sent Nicolau Coelho ashore in a longboat to examine the river. As soon as he approached it, men began to assemble on the shore in twos and threes: by the time the boat reached the mouth of the river eighteen or twenty men were already there. They were dark and entirely naked, with nothing to cover their private parts, and carried bows and arrows in their hands. Nicolau Coelho made a sign to them to lay down their bows, and they laid them down. He could not speak with them there . . . because of the breaking of the sea on the shore. He merely threw them a [four-cornered] red hat, and a linen [conical cap] he was wearing on his head, and a black hat. One of them gave him a head-dress of long feathers with a small tuft of red and grey feathers like those

Indian canoes greet a Portuguese ship.

of a parrot. Another gave him a large string of very small white beads which looked like seed pearls.'*

Cabral's expedition spent only nine days sailing along the coast of Brazil before moving off towards India. But it fortunately contained a chronicler, Pero Vaz de Caminha, who described the thrilling discovery in a long letter to King Manoel I that was sent back by ship directly from Brazil. Caminha was a narrator equal to the magnitude of the event. He combined sharp observation with plenty of delightful detail, and has earned a place as Brazil's first ethnological observer. Every word in the letter carries information, all of it accurate; and yet Caminha managed to convey his excitement and wonder at the marvels of the new discovery. He also touched on many of the aspects of relations between European and Brazilian natives that were to become constants during the years ahead.

Even during its short visit, Cabral's expedition held the first Christian service in Brazil. Native Indians watched in fascination as the Portuguese celebrated mass on an empty beach. 'And when the mass was finished and we sat down for the sermon, many of them stood up and blew a horn or trumpet and began to leap and dance for a while.' Cabral later ordered two ship's carpenters to build a large cross. 'Many of them came there to be with the carpenters. I believe that they did this more to see the iron tools with which these were making it than to see the cross itself.' This was the intense thrill of Stone Age people at their first sight of the cutting power of metal. 'For they have nothing made of iron. They cut their wood and boards with wedge-shaped stones fixed into pieces of wood and firmly tied between two sticks.' Once the cross was made, Cabral had his men 'kneel down and kiss the cross so that [the Indians] might see our veneration for it. We did so, and motioned to them to do the same: they at once all went to kiss it.' When the cross was finally planted, the natives joined in the ceremony, kneeling for the prayers and imitating the Portuguese when they rose for the sermon. 'And at the elevation of the Host, when we knelt, they placed themselves as we were with hands uplifted, and so quietly that I assure Your Highness that they gave us much edification.'

It looked as though conversion to Christianity would be easy. 'They seem to be such innocent people that, if we could understand their speech and they ours, they would immediately become Christians. For it appears that they do not have or understand any faith. . . . May it please

---

* References for all quotations will be found in the Notes and References on pages 527–648, indicated by the page-number of the text and the last words of the quotation. Notes to other passages are indicated by an asterisk in the text and are likewise printed at the end of the book. A dagger (†) indicates an explanatory note.

God to bring them to a knowledge of [our holy religion]: for truly these people are good and of pure simplicity. Any belief we wish to give them may easily be stamped upon them, for the Lord has given them fine bodies and good faces, like good men. . . . Your Majesty who so greatly wishes to spread the holy Catholic faith may therefore look for their salvation. Pray God it may be accomplished with few difficulties.'

It was the Indians' simplicity and innocence that gave such high hopes of conversion. Such openness amazed men who had come from the tight moral confines of medieval Europe. They were enchanted by the vision of people living in apparent freedom in what seemed an earthly paradise, a place of abundant game and easy harvests.

The thing that most intrigued Caminha and his companions was their first sight of a naked people. At the first Brazilian anchorage, Cabral received two Indians on board his flagship. He evidently thought he was to meet the emissaries of some oriental potentate, and greeted them with all possible pomp. He was seated on a chair, on a carpet, wearing his finest clothes and a gold chain around his neck, with his officers seated at his feet, framed by lighted torches. But his visitors were two handsome native warriors, 'naked and without any covering: they pay no more attention to concealing or exposing their private parts than to showing their faces, and in this respect they are very innocent'. They disappointed the Europeans by making no gesture of courtesy and paying no attention to the Admiral – other than to ask in vain to be given his gold chain. The sailors showed them a series of strange objects from the far side of the Atlantic, and offered food and drink, which the Indians declined. 'Finally they lay on their backs on the carpet to sleep. They did not try to cover their private parts in any way; these were uncircumcised and the hair on them well shaved and arranged. The Admiral ordered one of his cushions to be put under the head of each one, and the man with a [feather] head-dress took special care that this should not be spoiled. They had a cloak spread over them. They consented to this and pulled it over themselves and slept.'

The excitement at the first sight of a totally naked people grew feverish when the fleet saw its first women, at a landing further down the coast. 'Three or four girls went among them, good and young and tender, with long very black hair hanging down their backs. And their privy parts were so high and tightly closed and so free from pubic hair that, even when we examined them very closely, they did not become embarrassed.' Caminha described the warriors looking magnificent in their plumage and painted in quarterings of black and red vegetable-dyes. But it was the women who really fascinated him. There were four or five among another group, 'just as naked as the men, and most pleasing to the eye. One of them had her thighs from knee to hip and her buttocks all painted with that black dye, but the rest of her in her own colour. Another had both knees and calves so painted, but her privy parts so naked and exposed with such innocence that there was no shame there. Another young woman was carrying an infant tied at her breasts by some sort of cloth so that only its little legs showed; but the legs of the mother, and the rest of her, were not concealed by any cloth.' Taking the King by the elbow, Caminha grew lyrical about another girl who was 'all dyed from head to foot in that paint; and indeed she was so well built and so well curved, and her privy part (what a one she had!) was so gracious that many women of our country, on seeing such charms, would be ashamed that theirs were not like hers'.

Caminha noticed that Brazil had no natural domestic animals – none of the cattle, sheep, pigs or chickens that provided protein and clothing for Europeans. Nor were there any rich cereals apart from fast-growing manioc. 'Despite this, they are stronger and better fed than we are with all the wheat and vegetables we eat.' 'I infer that they are bestial people, of very little knowledge. . . . And yet they are well cared for and very clean, and in this they seem to me rather like birds or wild animals, to which the air gives better plumage and fur than to tame ones. Their bodies are so clean and so plump and so beautiful that they could not be more so.'

The naked beauty of the Indians impressed Cabral's men, but it also offended their sense of morality; they at once tried to induce the Indians to wear clothing. Cabral sent his two visitors back ashore wearing new shirts, red hats and rosaries; but they reappeared later undressed. One young woman stayed throughout the mass, but her nudity disturbed the sailors in the congregation. 'She was given a cloth with which to cover herself, and we put it about her; but as she sat down she did not think to spread it much to cover herself. Thus, my Lord, the innocence of these people is such that Adam's cannot have been greater in respect of modesty.'

The Indians' hospitality was just as ingenuous as their dress. They accepted the sudden appearance of these strangers quite calmly, despite the Europeans' clothing and beards and remarkable possessions. Some were timid, but their welcome was generally warm and friendly. The two races managed to fraternise cheerfully. On one river the Portuguese came upon an Indian dance. Diogo Dias, who was revenue officer of the town of Sacavem near Lisbon, crossed the river to join them. 'He is an agreeable and pleasure-loving man, and he took with him one of our bagpipe-players with his bagpipe, and began to dance among them, taking them by the hands. They were delighted and laughed and accompanied him very well to the sound of the pipe. After they had danced he went along the level ground making many light turns and a remarkable leap which astonished them, and they laughed and enjoyed themselves greatly. But although he reassured and flattered them a great deal with this, they soon became sullen, like wild men, and moved off upstream.' Another group spent a day with the strangers, during which 'they continually skipped and danced with us to the sound of one of our tambours, in such a manner that they are far more our friends than we theirs. When we asked by signs whether they wished to come aboard the ships, they at once made ready to do so.'

Cabral's fleet was on a trading venture to India, and the Admiral therefore sought any possible trade in the land he had chanced upon. There seemed little potential in such a primitive place. The natives had no gold or other metals. Individual sailors traded for native artefacts and curios. 'The Indians traded some bows for sheets of paper or some worthless old cap or for anything else. . . . A good twenty or thirty of our people went with them to a place containing many more of them, including girls and women. They brought back many bows and head-dresses of birds' feathers, some green and some yellow. . . . And according to those who went there, they made merry with them.' One commercial possibility appeared to be decorative parrot and macaw feathers – and Venetian spies in Lisbon soon reported that Cabral had found 'a new land that they call Land of the Parrots', which appeared to be a continental mainland.* Another saleable commodity was timber, for the immense plains and hills of Brazil were covered in forests. Cabral sent the supply ship, *Lemos*, back to Portugal; which Indians helped him fill with dyewood logs. 'They loaded as much of that wood as they could, very willingly, and carried it to the boats. They were calmer and more at ease among us than we were among them.'

The ship that returned took Pero Vaz de Caminha's letter and the first favourable notices of the innocent natives of Brazil. The rest of the fleet sailed on towards the real India – as opposed to the 'Indies', as the Americas were known because of Columbus' conviction, when he first discovered them eight years previously, that he was at the edge of India and among 'Indians'. Some of Cabral's ships were lost in storms off the Cape of Good Hope. Pero Vaz de Caminha and many others were killed a few months later in a battle at Calicut. But enough ships returned to Portugal loaded with spices to make the venture a commercial success.

During its brief stop in Brazil, the fleet left behind two of the most potent weapons of colonialism. One was a first taste of alcohol, of which Caminha wrote: 'It seems to me that if they became accustomed to it they would drink it with great willingness.' The other was the first settlers themselves. Two convicts under sentence of death had been taken on the voyage with the intention of leaving them somewhere to begin intermarriage with any natives. Cabral decided to abandon them in Brazil. When the time came for departure, 'these began to weep, but the men of the land comforted them and showed that they pitied them'. The Portuguese thus resorted to miscegenation almost instinctively as the fastest way to spread themselves across the world.

The discovery of Brazil came in the midst of the amazing explosion of Portuguese maritime expansion. In 1527 Portugal had only 280,528 hearths or households. Reckoning four persons per hearth, the country's population would have been little over 1,120,000. Yet this small people was setting out with reckless daring and outrageous presumption to try to people the world.*

Portugal had an advantage over its neighbour Spain in that the Moors had been driven out of Portugal in the mid-thirteenth century, whereas Granada, the last Moorish kingdom in Spain, surrendered only in 1492, the year of Columbus' discovery of America. Portugal had been a separate kingdom since 1139, had successfully fought off Spanish attempts at domination, and had formed a vigorous national identity during three and a half centuries of independence. Its location at the south-western corner of Europe was also a help. Cut off from the rest of Europe by Spain, and heavily dependent on fishing, some Portuguese developed the sailing skills and adventurous outlook of an island people.

The fight against the Mohammedans was carried across the Straits of Gibraltar with campaigns against Tangiers and Ceuta. The booty from the Moors included geographical information about the coast of Africa to the south, and new knowledge of mathematics, cartography and astronomy. All this was developed by a great royal patron, Prince Henry the Navigator, son of King João I and grandson of England's John of Gaunt. He established himself at Sagres, in the south-western corner of Portugal, and dedicated his life to improvements in the arts of sailing and navigation. Portuguese ships sailed south, pushing their discoveries steadily down the west coast of Africa, spreading Christianity on the dark continent and bringing back the first lucrative cargoes of slaves and spices. Atlantic islands were colonised: Madeira; then the Azores; and in 1460, the year of Prince Henry's death, the Cape Verde Islands. In 1488 Bartolomeu Dias rounded the point that he himself called Cape of Torments but that his backer optimistically renamed the Cape of Good Hope – because it gave such high hopes of a maritime route to India. There may have been secret, undocumented expeditions beyond the newly discovered cape; but the next recorded voyage of discovery was

Vasco da Gama's, and it at last reached the promised land. His four ships sailed to Calicut in south India and returned to Lisbon in 1498 with the sought-after oriental spices – pepper, ginger, cinnamon and cloves, so prized in Europe in the days before refrigeration – and with dyes, medicines and exotic woods, including the rich red dye of a tree known as the brazilwood.

Vasco da Gama's voyage showed that India could be reached by sea. The small kingdom of Portugal feverishly sought to repeat that success. The King and nobility financed and assembled a great fleet of thirteen ships. It contained 1200 men – sailors, merchants, soldiers, friars and savants – with provisions for a year, arms and trade goods. The fleet sailed off down the Tagus on 8 March 1500. The ships were decked in bunting and their sails bore the great red cross of the Order of Christ. The people of Lisbon, from King Manoel down, were dressed in their holiday best and crowded on the shore near the turreted Tower of Belém to see them off. This was the fleet commanded by Pero Álvares Cabral, which was to sight the coast of Brazil six weeks later.

Cabral's objective was India, and his discovery of Brazil was apparently pure chance. It was a remarkable stroke of luck, for the newly discovered land fell within a sphere of discovery allotted to Portugal – to the east of a line drawn by Pope Alexander VI and negotiated between Spain and Portugal at the Treaty of Tordesillas on 7 June 1494. The Pope, as Vicar of Christ on earth, claimed the right to apportion among Christian monarchs the mission to occupy heathen lands. The Papacy accordingly assigned to Portugal the lands and islands to be discovered to the east of the Line of Tordesillas; while Spain received the lands to the west. Portugal's share included the coasts of Africa and the sea routes pioneered by Bartolomeu Dias and Vasco da Gama. But it also included the eastern bulge of Brazil.† Some historians have speculated that the canny and secretive kings of Portugal might have known of the existence of Brazil before negotiating the Treaty. But it seems more likely that, although they may have suspected the existence of some such land, its discovery was fortuitous.†

The Portuguese sent small fleets to explore the Brazilian coast during the years immediately after Cabral's discovery. It was only in 1513 that a Portuguese captain sailed south and found a silver knife – probably Inca – on a great river which he promptly named the Rio de la Plata ('River of Silver'). But it was the Spaniards who followed up his discovery and eagerly explored the tributaries of that river in search of the source of the Indian silver. In that same year, 1513, Balboa crossed the Isthmus of Panama and discovered the Pacific Ocean. Within a decade Cortés conquered the Aztec empire in Mexico and Pizarro was sailing down the

Pacific coast of South America towards the Incas in Peru. The Spaniards were now aware that a continental mass lay between them and India. They started sending expeditions to discover a sea route round its southern edge. As early as 1520 the Portuguese Fernão de Magalhães (Magellan), sailing in the service of Spain, succeeded in passing through the strait that bears his name, and his fleet went on to complete the first circumnavigation of the world. The Spaniards thus established themselves at Buenos Aires and upstream in Paraguay, and the Portuguese were left with the great curve of coast stretching north to the mouth of the Amazon (which had also been discovered by Spaniards a few months before Cabral's landing). Almost by chance, the two Iberian kingdoms divided the east coast of South America roughly along the Line of Tordesillas.†

Once the Portuguese had established that there were no obvious riches in Brazil, they paid little attention to the new land. The small kingdom was straining its resources to equip fleets of great galleons for the India trade and to man outposts along the coasts of Africa.

The only important commercial attraction in Brazil – and the origin of its name – was the magnificent great tree known as brazilwood. Ever since the twelfth century trees that yielded a red dye were known as *brasile*, from the Latin word for red. And a hardwood found in the new continent produced a powerful dye that ranged from maroon to ochre. This tree was therefore called *pau do brasil*, or brazilwood (*Caesalpinia echinata*). The brazilwood is a tall tree, with grey bark and perpetual pale-green leaves. It looks rather like an English oak, but has brilliant yellow blossoms.

The ship *Lemos* that Cabral sent back with Vaz de Caminha's letter carried some logs of this dyewood. In 1501 the King sent Captain André Gonçalves to investigate the potential utility of the new land. He reported that it contained nothing of use, apart from a quantity of these trees. The tree's wood is a creamy colour when first cut, but it soon blushes a deep red. Its logs were shipped back to Europe, where the hardwood was rasped into sawdust and soaked in water for a few weeks to form the red dye. The dye was not particularly stable, but reds were fashionable, especially at the French court, and the profits from the brazilwood trade were attractive enough to justify the risks involved in the ocean crossing.

In 1502 King Manoel awarded a monopoly of the brazilwood trade to a group of Lisbon merchants. They included Fernão de Noronha, who tried to colonise the island in the Atlantic that bears his name. The syndicate was to send six ships a year to Brazil, and pay a share of its profits to the Crown. By the following year French ships began to seek the wood for themselves. European sails started to become a familiar sight in the forested bays and inlets of the Brazilian coast. The early Portuguese wrote about the 'wood of brasil' or red-dye wood. Cabral had named his discovery the Land of the True Cross. But by 1530, to the disgust of the great Portuguese poet Camões, it was being called Land of Brazil.†

During the first thirty years after the discovery of Brazil, European visits consisted of a steady trickle of small ships seeking brazilwood and a few other commodities. The trees at first were close to the sea and river estuaries, and the Indians were content to barter the cut logs for trade goods. The visiting merchants were on their best behaviour, dependent as they were on Indian help, and in some awe of the large warrior tribes that they found inhabiting the Brazilian coast.

The profitable brazilwood trade depended entirely on the Brazilian Indians. Their lands produced the trees, and the natives themselves felled the brazilwoods, cut their hard wood into logs and transported these to the coast for loading on to European ships. 'The ships are sometimes far from the place where the cutting is done, perhaps four or five leagues [11–14 miles]. The only profit that these poor people derive from so much effort might be some miserable shirt or the lining from some clothing of little value. . . . After they have carried the logs to the ships during several journeys, you see their shoulders all bruised and torn by the weight of the wood – which is well known to be heavy and massive. This is hardly surprising, since they are naked and carry these loads so far. And yet they consider themselves very fortunate . . . to do this service for the Christians, whom they love, cherish and honour . . . because they showed them the way to cut wood with iron, with which they supply them.'

Metal axes and tools seemed miraculous to peoples who spent much of their year in the laborious business of clearing forest with stone axes. Indians had always made skilled artefacts but, as one chronicler explained, 'they took a very long time to make anything. This is why they value metal so greatly – because of the ease they experience in making things with it. For this reason they delight in communication with the whites.' It was a fatal fascination, the greatest weakness of Brazilian Indians. Throughout Brazilian history, knives and axes have always been the surest way of winning Indian friendship, and they are still the main instrument in the attraction and pacification of hostile tribes.

Other manufactured goods were almost as attractive as metal tools. Paulmier de Gonneville, a French captain from Normandy, spent six months among the Carijó of southern Brazil in 1503–4, and said that the

Indians never ceased to marvel at the contents of his ship. All this treasure was 'so coveted that for these things the Indians would willingly have let themselves be quartered, and they brought abundant meat and fish, fruits and food, and whatever they saw was agreeable to the Christians'. He had come well stocked with trade goods: 300 pieces of various cloths, 4000 axes, spades, scythes, cleavers and pitchforks, 2000 pikes, 50 dozen small mirrors, 6 hundredweight of beads, 8 hundredweight of Rouen ironmongery, 240 dozen knives and a ball of pins and needles.

The French organised their trading slightly differently from the Portuguese. The French sent interpreters to live in the midst of the Indians – blond Normans who settled in the native villages and organised the gathering of logs for the next ship from France. These men went native, living as naked sultans among the tribes that adopted them. 'I must record, to my great regret,' the French Protestant pastor Jean de Léry wrote in 1556, 'that some interpreters from Normandy who have lived eight or nine years in that country accommodated themselves to the savages and led the lives of atheists. They not only polluted themselves with all sorts of lewdness and villainy among the women and girls . . . but surpassed the savages in inhumanity: I have heard them boasting of having killed and eaten prisoners!' The Portuguese were more restrained and businesslike. They established small warehouses at half a dozen places along the coast. A few Portuguese lived in these, trading with the tribes and accumulating the precious wood.

The records of one Portuguese ship have survived – the *Bertoa*, which left Lisbon in February 1511 and spent three months in Brazil loading brazilwood. The *Bertoa* was a náo like Columbus' *Santa Maria*, a round-bellied ship with high bow and poop and perhaps five sails on three short masts and a bowsprit. She had a complement of thirty-six: five officers, thirteen able seamen, fourteen apprentices and four pages. She spent a month at a vast bay called Bahia de Todos os Santos ('Bay of All Saints'), on the north-eastern bulge of Brazil, where the land is low and flat with a coastline of beaches, dunes and wooded cliffs. She then sailed south to Cabo Frio ('Cold Cape'), not far from another enormous bay that the Indians called Guanabara, the site of the future city of Rio de Janeiro. At Cabo Frio three or four hundred fifty-pound logs were loaded every day, and the *Bertoa* sailed home with 5000 logs weighing about 125 tons.†

The *Bertoa* brought back some cargo besides brazilwood: parrots, pet animals, jaguar skins – and thirty-five Indian slaves. A German described another Portuguese ship a few years later: 'Below decks the ship is loaded with brazilwood and on deck it is full of young men and women who are being brought back. They cost the Portuguese little, for most are given freely; the people there think that their children are going to a promised land.' But a Spanish captain who spent some time among the Carijó at the Lagoa dos Patos ('Lagoon of Ducks') in south Brazil complained of Sebastian Cabot's slaving activity among them. Diego García wrote in 1526 that the Carijó 'are a good people who treat Christians very well. They gave us much food called corn and manioc flour and many calabash gourds, and many ducks and other foodstuffs, for they are good Indians. Sebastian Cabot arrived there dying of hunger during the time I was there. The Indians gave him food and all that his people needed for their voyage.' But Cabot repaid their hospitality by taking off four sons of the local chief and keeping them as his slaves in Seville. 'Because he took the sons of the chiefs of the island, he ruined that anchorage, which used to be the best and [located] among the nicest people in those parts.'

Other Indians sailed across to Europe more innocently. They were taken to impress on them the wonders of the sailors' mother country, and to be exhibited there as curiosities from the new continent. Amerigo Vespucci, the Florentine who gave his name to the Americas, sailed to Brazil on a voyage of exploration in the year after Cabral's discovery. He reported that his fleet took back three Indians who wished to visit Lisbon. In 1513 three Tupinikin Indians from Pôrto Seguro (near Cabral's landfall) were taken to visit King Manoel I. They went wearing their feather regalia and carrying bows and arrows, and the King conversed with them through an interpreter.* William Hawkins of Plymouth brought back a chief from Brazil in 1531. He was taken to see Henry VIII at Whitehall and spent a year in England.†

The French were as active as the Portuguese in bringing Brazilians back to Europe during those early years. Paulmier de Gonneville, the captain from Honfleur who so impressed the Carijó with his ship full of trade goods, took the son of the Carijó chief to France in 1505. He promised the father that he would teach the boy 'artillery, which they greatly desired to dominate their enemies, and also how to make mirrors, knives, axes and all that they saw and admired among the Christians. Promising them all this was like promising a Christian gold, silver and jewels, or to teach him about the philosopher's stone.' Back in France, the boy was 'well regarded in Honfleur and in all the places we passed: for there had never been in France a person from so distant a country'. Gonneville christened the boy Binot, gave him a good education, married him to his daughter Suzanne and bequeathed him some property and the name and arms of Gonneville. But Binot never returned to his people to teach them how to make the magical artillery, mirrors and knives.

Four years later, Captain Thomas Aubert brought seven Indians back from Brazil in his ship *La Pensée*. They were paraded through Rouen wearing feathers and loin-cloths and carrying bows and arrows and bark canoes. One Frenchman noted with disgust that they lacked the fundamentals of French culture: 'They speak with their lips and have no religion. . . . And they know nothing about bread, wine or money.'

Jean d'Ango, a Dieppe merchant who dominated the French brazilwood trade, spent his fortune on a magnificent palace built of different tropical woods. Ango entertained there prodigiously, with exotic animals running about the house and decorations that included carvings of Brazilian Indians. Francis I made Ango Viscount of Dieppe, and for a time his fleets filled the Atlantic; but he grew over-proud and was eventually deserted by his friends and attacked by creditors. He died in 1551 and was buried in the church of Saint-Jacques in Dieppe, below a stone frieze showing naked Brazilian men and women cavorting in their American paradise.†

By the middle of the century Brazilians brought back by French sailors were a familiar sight in Normandy. When the city of Rouen wished to stage a lavish welcome for Henry II and Catherine de' Medici when they visited the city with their court in 1550, someone thought of importing more Indians and using them in a tableau. A meadow beside the Seine was decked out to resemble Brazil. New trees and bushes were planted. Existing trees were made more luxuriant with extra branches and festooned with imitation fruit. Parrots, monkeys, coatis and other American animals clambered about in this jungle. Thatched cabins were built at either end of the meadow, each surrounded by a log palisade: these were intended to represent villages of the Tupinambá and Tobajara, two warring tribes from the northern coast of Brazil. 'All along this site as many as three hundred men busied themselves here and there. They were completely naked, tanned and shaggy, without in any way covering the parts that nature commands, and were decorated and equipped in the manner of those savages of America from whom brazilwood is brought. Among their number there were a good fifty natural savages freshly brought from that country. . . . The remainder of the company were French sailors who had frequented that country: they spoke the language as well, and expressed themselves as naïvely in the gestures and mannerisms of the savages, as if they were natives of that same country.'

The pageant opened with the real natives and the naked sailors going about their daily life, demonstrating archery, chasing game 'like troglodytes after water-fowl', swinging in hammocks, or loading wood on to a French ship anchored in the river (Plate 5). This peaceful scene was suddenly broken by an attack on the Tupinambá village by their Tobajara enemies. Norman sailors and real Indians staged a mock battle wielding clubs and bows and arrows; but the Tupinambá – traditional allies of the French – were victorious. The spectacle's climax was the burning of the Tobajara hut. The King and his court were enchanted by it all.

It was in such a world of fantasy that Europeans came to imagine the native peoples of Brazil. Pero Vaz de Caminha's letter to the King had been a sober description of the people he saw; but even he paused frequently to marvel at the Indians' simplicity, beauty and natural innocence. Cabral sent back one Tupinikin who 'was received with joy in Portugal by the King and kingdom. Great and small could never tire of seeing and hearing the gestures, talk or movements of that new individual of the human race. Some took him to be half-goat, others a faun or some kind of ancient monster.' Later visitors to Brazil were less objective than Caminha. A letter from a pilot on one of the first voyages was widely diffused through Europe: it depicted the Brazilians as beautiful naked people living innocently in a perfect climate surrounded by birds and animals.*

Amerigo Vespucci was the first to write a sensationalised description of Brazilian Indians. He sailed in some ships that investigated the Brazilian coast in 1501–2, and claimed this as his third visit to the New World. He described Brazil in a famous letter to his prince Piero Lorenzo de' Medici, written in 1503 and soon published in Latin, Italian, German and Dutch. Vespucci wanted to excite his readers by stressing anything outlandish about the natives; and he succeeded – for his letter was a bestseller in its day, and had a powerful impact on European thinking.

Vespucci was fascinated by the apparent freedom and innocence of these new peoples. He claimed that the Indians had no private property and shared everything in common. They lived without money, property or trade. They had complete social and moral freedom, and their communities functioned harmoniously without kings or religion, temples, palaces or idols. None of this was entirely true, for the Brazilians did have their own forms of laws, leaders and beliefs, even if these were rudimentary by European standards. Whether accurate or not, Vespucci's reports swept across Europe and rapidly gained currency among other early travellers.

Vespucci wrote in an earlier letter that he had lived with the Indians for twenty-seven days. He said that 'They have no laws or faith, and live according to nature. They do not recognise the immortality of the soul; they have among them no private property, because everything is common; they have no boundaries of kingdoms and provinces, and no king! They obey nobody, each is lord unto himself. '[They have] no justice and no gratitude, which to them is unnecessary because it is not part of their code. . . . They are a very prolific people, but have no heirs because they hold no property.'

Vespucci marvelled at the intricacy of the Indians' long-huts – 'truly wonderful . . . for people who have no iron or other metal'. He described their food as a succulent diet of fruits, herbs, game and 'an infinity of fish and great quantities of shellfish: crabs, oysters, lobsters, crayfish, and many other things which the sea produces'. He portrayed Brazil as a very delightful land, with evergreen trees yielding 'the sweetest aromatic perfumes and . . . an infinite variety of fruit', with so many flowers in the fields, brilliant songbirds and strange animals in the forests that 'I fancied myself to be near the terrestrial paradise'. He told his eager reader that Indian girls on reaching puberty were first corrupted by a close relative other than their father. He showed how Indian mothers gave birth without any fuss, merely washing the infant in a stream; and he calculated that they lived to the advanced age of 130 years.

The first known illustration of Brazilian Indians is a stiff woodcut, evidently inspired by Vespucci's letter. It shows five men and two women, modestly decked in feathers, with human meat on the rafters of their hut, and European ships visible in the distance (Plate 6). Its caption, in German, reads: 'This picture represents the people and island that have been discovered by the subjects of the Christian King of Portugal. The people are thus: naked, handsome, brown, with their heads, necks, arms, private parts and feet of men and women a little covered in feathers. . . . None possesses any thing, but all things are held in common. . . . They become a hundred and fifty years old. And have no government.'

Some travellers were shocked by the Indians. One Frenchman wrote to his friends from Brazil that 'this nation is, I believe, the most barbarous, the most remote from all honesty, that exists under heaven. For they live without any knowledge of God, without cares, without law or any religion – nothing more than brute beasts who are led by their sentiments alone.' One of the best Portuguese chroniclers, Pero de Magalhães de Gandavo, acknowledged that, although the Indians had no kings, each village did have a chief and a council of elders. Gandavo was the first to notice that the melodious Tupí language, spoken by most of the tribes living along the Brazilian coast, did not use the letters *F, L* or

R: this seemed to tally with their having no Faith, Law or Royalty, and many writers repeated this apparent link between the Indians' language and society.*

There was something almost subversive in the enthusiasm with which early travellers reported this absence of monarchy or church. When added to the Indians' lack of greed or possessiveness it formed a picture of noble savages living in a golden age. Pietro Martire d'Anghiera, writing in the year of Cabral's discovery, said that among American natives 'the land belonged to all, just like the sun and water. Mine and thine, the seeds of all evils, do not exist for those people. . . . They live in a golden age, and do not surround their properties with ditches, walls or hedges. They live in open gardens, without laws or books, without judges, and they naturally follow goodness and consider odious anyone who corrupts himself by practising evil. . . .' It was an obvious return to the golden age of Ovid's *Metamorphoses*, a book which was often read at the time. The idea of the noble savage antedated the discovery of America: the Belgian Mandeville said in the fifteenth century that savages were 'good people, loyal, full of all virtues, free from all vice and sin'. Marco Polo wrote praise of primitive men, and Dante's master Brunetto Latini said that Africans were innocent, naked and not greedy for gold. So, when Brazil was discovered and its people had so many of the requisite qualities, fact and legend blended to transform them into virtuous innocents living in a terrestrial paradise.

These natives were in fact very open and generous about their possessions. Lack of greed or material ambition have always characterised Brazilian Indians. Those qualities that so impressed sixteenth-century writers still frustrate attempts to draw present-day Indians into a competitive economy. Magalhães de Gandavo's description is typical: 'In every house they all live together in harmony, with no dissension between them. They are so friendly to one another that what belongs to one belongs to all. When one has something to eat, no matter how small, all his neighbours share it.'

The chroniclers soon started to draw comparisons between Indian generosity and European greed. 'Each man is able to provide for himself, without expecting any legacy in order to be rich, other than the growth which Nature universally bestows on all creatures. . . . They have no property and do not try to acquire it as other men do. So they live free from the greed and inordinate desire for riches that are so prevalent among other nations. . . . All the Indians live without owning property or tilled fields which would be a source of worry. They have no class distinctions or notions of dignity or ceremonial. And they do not need them. For all are equal in every respect, and so in harmony with their surroundings that they all live justly and in conformity with the laws of nature.' 'When it comes to the bother of dividing inheritances, of lawsuits or fixing markers, in short of the separation of property – they leave all that to the avaricious landowners and quarrellers of Europe.' The French Capuchin Yves d'Evreux said that Indians could not comprehend European values that rated jewels and precious metals above useful tools like knives.

Another French cleric, Jean de Léry, illustrated Indian logic with an anecdote. 'An old man once asked me, "Why do you people, French and Portuguese, come from so far away to seek wood to warm you? Don't you have wood in your country?" I answered that we had plenty, but not of that quality, and that we did not burn it as he supposed but extracted a dye from it for dyeing, just as they did to their cotton cords and their feathers. The old man immediately replied: "And I suppose that you need much of it?" "Yes," I answered, "for in our country there are traders who own more cloth, knives, scissors, mirrors and other goods than you can imagine. One single trader buys all the brazilwood carried back by many loaded ships." "Ah," said the old man, "you are telling me marvels. But this very rich man you are telling me about, does he not die?" "Yes," I said, "he dies like all the rest." But savages are great debaters and generally pursue any matter to its conclusion. He therefore asked me: "When he dies what becomes of what he leaves?" "It is for his children if he has them . . . or for his closest brothers and relatives." "Indeed," continued the old man, who as you can see was no fool, "I now see that you French are great madmen. You cross the sea and suffer great inconvenience, as you say when you arrive here, and work so hard to accumulate riches for your children or for those who survive you. Is the land that nourished you not sufficient to feed them too? We have fathers, mothers and children whom we love. But we are certain that after our death the land that nourished us will also feed them. We therefore rest without further cares."'

Léry could not resist drawing moral conclusions from his story: 'Although this tribe may be blind in attributing to nature . . . more than we do to the power of God's providence, yet it will rise up in judgement against the plunderers who bear the name of Christians. . . . May God let the Tupinambá act as demons and furies to torment our insatiable gluttons!'

This generosity and lack of worldliness made the Indians good hosts. Léry declared: 'I can tell you that there is no more liberal nation under heaven – provided [the visitors] are not their enemies. For as soon as they see someone from a distant country arrive in their land they . . . have the grace to present him with food, lodging and often a girl for his service.

What is more, the women and girls come and surround a stranger, sitting on the ground, to weep and cry as a sign of joy for your welcome.' The welcome was not entirely disinterested. The women 'would present us with fruits or some other native produce, with a manner full of flattery that they normally use – and drove us crazy by following us about continually, saying "Frenchman, you are good, give me some of your bracelets or glass beads!" . . . It always gave me great pleasure to see the little boys . . . who never failed to come out in troops and dance before us when they saw us arrive at their villages. Then, to be rewarded, they used to cajole us and follow close behind us, often repeating their little refrain . . . "My friend and ally, give me some fish-hooks!"' And the Protestant pastor Léry would amuse himself by throwing a few hooks into the dust to watch the children scrabble for them like conies.*

Much of the appeal of the Brazilian natives was the fantasy of a handsome naked people governed only by natural instincts, an adolescent's dream world where carefree single women had complete sexual liberty. The early visitors to Brazil made the most of this fascinating theme. The Italian Antonio Pigafetta, who sailed with Magellan, described how naked Indian women climbed aboard the ships and surrendered to the white men with natural innocence. He saw one girl take a large iron nail and calmly place it in her vagina – he admitted that he never discovered whether she wanted to steal the nail or to adorn herself in an original way. The French pilot Jean Alphonse de Saintonge described the docility and affability of the Indian girls towards Christians. His compatriot Jean Parmentier admired the girls' beauty and the way in which, although wives were strictly faithful, fathers would readily offer their daughters to the European strangers. They were like 'colts who have never experienced a rein'. The Bavarian, Ulrich Schmidel, who travelled among the tribes of Paraguay and southern Brazil in the years between 1534 and 1554, was more cautious. He said that native women had certain delights, especially when enjoyed in the dark.*

Other travellers excited their readers with tales of Indian refinements in love-making. 'The women are as voluptuous as *femmes du monde*. They are also cunning and highly experienced in whatever could help attract men to sleep with them. They know herbs which they use on their husbands and which arouse them so that they are constrained to go to the women or else suffer pain in their private parts.'

Amerigo Vespucci admired the Indians' agility and their beautiful features and robust bodies. 'The women go naked, and although libidinous they are pretty and well shaped. We were amazed that, among those we saw, we noticed none with fallen breasts. Those who had given birth, as seen by the shape and contraction of their stomachs, were no different from virgins and resembled them in other parts of their bodies. . . . When they can have relations with us Christians, impelled by desire, they show no trace of modesty. . . . They have another extravagant custom which seems incredible. Being libidinous, the women make their husbands' members swell so much that they look like those of animals: they do this by the artifice of the bite of certain poisonous insects. As a result many men lose them altogether, and are left as eunuchs.' Gabriel Soares de Sousa reported the same practice among the Potiguar. He said the swelling was caused by applying the fur of a poisonous insect. 'They suffer great pains from this during more than six months that they continue to corrode them. In the end their prick becomes so large and deformed that the women cannot wait for it, or endure it.'

These details were doubtless correct, but the impression they conveyed was misleading. For the Indians were less obsessed with sex than their European visitors, and the offer of girls to sleep with strangers was an act of hospitality. But sexual innocence was a necessary corollary to religious and political freedom in the mystique of the noble savage. A few more qualities completed that picture. One was cleanliness, a startling innovation for Renaissance Europeans who rarely washed. Yves d'Evreux remarked on the Indians' beautiful bodies and the firm breasts of the young women, and concluded that 'the reward always given to purity is integrity and purity accompanied by a good smell. . . . They are very careful to keep their bodies free of any filth. They bathe their entire bodies very often . . . rubbing all parts with their hands to remove dirt and other filth. The women never fail to comb themselves frequently. They are very afraid of becoming thin . . . and complain to their friends, saying, "I am thin", at which everyone commiserates . . . weeps for them and laments. . . .'

When the French later tried to found a colony at Rio de Janeiro, they did their utmost to make their Indian women dress as Europeans. 'But it was never within our power to make them dress. . . . As an excuse for always remaining naked, they cited their custom of crouching on the banks of any spring or clear stream they encountered, or plunging in and splashing water on their heads with both hands, or diving in with their entire bodies like ducks, more than a dozen times a day. They said it would be too much effort to undress so often! Isn't that a beautiful and cogent reason? . . . We forced female prisoners of war – whom we purchased and kept as slaves for the work of our fort – to cover themselves, but as soon as night fell they secretly removed the chemises and other rags we had given them. To be really happy they had to stroll about our island quite naked before going to bed. Had it been left to the choice of these poor wretches – and had we not constrained them to dress by whipping – they would have preferred to endure the burning heat of the sun, to have their arms and shoulders scorched, to withstand earth and stones, than to endure anything on themselves.' Brazilian Indians still love to bathe frequently. This is one of the Indians' legacies to modern Brazil, a nation whose people take frequent showers and are never without a comb. When José de Anchieta saw Indian women wearing their first dresses, he found them 'so modest, serene, virtuous and bewildered that they appear as statues leaning against their male companions; and when they walk their slippers fall off, for they are not accustomed to wearing them'.

Vespucci also started the idea that Brazilian Indians lived to be extremely old. He said that some aged Indians told him they had four successive generations of descendants. One old man indicated his age by stones, and Vespucci interpreted this sign language to mean that he had lived for 1700 lunar months or 132 years. Vespucci later rounded this dubious figure upwards to 150 years. Longevity had always been an article of faith among proponents of the earthly paradise, and it now attached to the Brazilians. Ten years after Vespucci a German said that they reached 140 years, and Magellan's companion Pigafetta said that they could live from 125 to 140 years. Even the more sober Jean de Léry, who spent some months among the Tupinambá of Guanabara in the 1550s, claimed that some lived to 100 or 120, thanks to the benign climate and their freedom from worries, 'for they all truly drink from the fountain of youth'. A few years later the Jesuit Fernão Cardim recorded that Piratininga – the site of the city of São Paulo – was full of old people aged over a hundred: 'four of them, who are all alive, add up to five hundred years'. These great ages were possible but unlikely. Anyone who has tried to question Indians knows how elusive and sometimes whimsical their answers can be. Arithmetic is unimportant in their world, and they cannot comprehend foreigners' obsessions with figures. What was more certain among the early accounts was that there were no cripples to be seen – deformed babies were probably killed at birth – and that the Indians seemed able to cure the few diseases that arose among them. Long life and perfect health thus joined the other blessings of the Brazilian paradise. 'They die only of old age and by natural default, rather than from any malady, and commonly live for a hundred, six score or seven score years.' A seventeenth-century author claimed that 'I know some centenarians on the coast of Brazil who don't have a tooth missing from their mouths and still enjoy perfect physical powers: some even have three or four wives with whom they have intercourse. They affirmed to me that they had never been ill throughout the course of their lives.' I myself can recall visiting a Kayabi village below Diauarum on the Xingu in 1971 and paying my respects to the very aged, dignified and naked old chief, while his young wife nursed their infant in the hammock behind.

Anything written about the new worlds in the early years of the sixteenth century had sensational impact. At no other time in history has there been such a rush of new discoveries. Many Renaissance Europeans were dazzled by the new continents' fascinating people, plants and animals. Reports of the conquest of the Aztecs and Incas did not come until the 1520s and 1530s; so for the first years of the century the excitement was about unsophisticated societies of innocent savages.

In 1508, shortly after the publication of Caminha's and Vespucci's letters, Erasmus of Rotterdam stayed with his friend Thomas More in London. While there he wrote *In Praise of Folly* whose heroine Folly was born in the Fortunate Islands – a place similar to Vespucci's Brazil where happy people lived in a state of nature and the land yielded food without effort. More's own *Utopia* appeared in 1516 and was rapidly translated from Latin into other languages. Its main character was a Portuguese described as being one of twenty-four persons left in an outpost at Cabo Frio by Vespucci's expedition: his name was Rafael Hythlodaeus – Greek for 'teller of tall stories'. More made it clear that Utopia lay in the New World, and was south of the equator, and his model may well have been Fernando de Noronha, an island in the Atlantic discovered by the first Portuguese voyagers. More declared that in Utopia man should live by nature and the voice of his instincts, and he praised the Indians' disdain for possessions. *Utopia* had a great impact when it appeared, and again when retranslated by Rousseau in 1780. It was read by both Marx and Lenin, who mentioned the Indians' indifference to gold.

Thomas More wrote that mothers in Utopia breast-fed their own babies without wet-nurses, and that infant Indians were washed in cold water after birth and allowed to run free without swaddling-clothes. Jean de Léry heard screaming one night in an Indian village and found that it was a woman in labour. 'I myself saw the father receive the infant in his arms, first put a knot in the umbilical cord and then cut it with a bite of his teeth.' The father washed and painted his son, placed him in a little hammock, and made him a miniature wooden sword, bow and arrows so that he would grow into a warrior. Yves d'Evreux noted that an Indian infant is not 'caressed, enveloped, warmed, overfed, well tended or put into the hands of a nurse. It is simply washed in a stream . . . and [left] with its little limbs completely free without any swaddling of any sort on its body or head. For food it is content with its mother's milk, and grains of corn . . . chewed in the mother's mouth . . . and put

into its little mouth the way birds feed their young, namely from mouth
to mouth. . . . . If the infant is thirsty it knows very well how to demand by
gestures its mother's breast.' These lessons from American natives
caused a revolution in infant care in Europe. They fascinated Jean-
Jacques Rousseau, who was a passionate advocate of breast-feeding – he
used to send knots of ribbon he had made himself to any mother who
promised to feed her own babies.*

It was in France, a country actively trading in Brazil, that the humanist
philosophers were most impressed by the Indians. Rabelais was strongly
influenced by both More and Erasmus, and knew both André Thevet
and Jean Alphonse de Saintonge personally. The first part of *Pantagruel*
(1533) was borrowed from *Utopia* and from whatever Rabelais learned
from friends who had visited Brazil. The poet Pierre de Ronsard
idealised the Tupinambá who lived near France's short-lived colony at
Rio de Janeiro 'in America, where the unknown people wander
innocently, all savage and all naked' and subject to no one: 'Mais suivant
sa nature et seul maistre do soy; soy-mesme est sa loy, son Sénat et son
Roy.' Ronsard was moved by the Indians' communism, by the way they
shared possessions as we do the air we breathe or the water of a stream.
He contrasted their freedom from the concept of property, of 'mine'
and 'thine', with the greed of the Europeans. And he begged that they be
left alone and not subjected to the yoke of a tyrant, judge or new set of
laws.

> Vivez, heureuse gent, sans peine et sans souci.
> Vivez joyeusement; je voudrais vivre ainsi.

The political theorist who became most closely involved with
Brazilian Indians was Michel de Montaigne. Montaigne had studied in
Bordeaux in a college whose principal was the Portuguese André de
Gouveia. This teacher surrounded himself with a group of brilliant
young student revolutionaries who sought to discover 'man' in 'nature'.
Montaigne studied and copied from the works of the two French
travellers Jean de Léry and André Thevet. He also talked at length with
one of his servants who had spent some years in Brazil; filled his house
with Indian artefacts; and interrogated three Tupinambá whom he met
in Rouen in 1562. All the Indian virtues appear in Montaigne's famous
essay 'Des Cannibales', which ends with his most subversive
revolutionary doctrines. He imagined a conversation between the
Tupinambá and King Charles IX. 'The King spoke to them for a long
time. They were shown our way of life, our pomp, and the form of a
beautiful city. After that, someone asked their opinion and wished to
know what they had found most admirable. They replied . . . that they

had noticed that there were among us men full and gorged with all sorts of commodities, but that their opposites were beggars at their gates, emaciated from hunger and poverty. They found it strange that those needy opposites should suffer such injustice, and that they did not take the others by the throat or set fire to their houses.' Montaigne also spoke to a Tupinambá prince, who indicated that he used to lead some four or five thousand men. Montaigne asked him what advantages he gained from his rank. He answered only 'to march first into battle'. But after expounding the doctrine of the noble savage so eloquently Montaigne concluded sarcastically: 'That is all very well. But, good God, they don't wear breeches!'

The ideals of the noble savage thus took firm hold of the imagination of the philosophers. Indians, especially Brazilian natives, were depicted as unselfish paragons, innocent, courteous, hospitable, honest, without greed or ambition, even peaceful. Montaigne copied Léry's description of fierce Indian battles – but he changed their reasons for fighting. Indian wars were generally vendettas against neighbouring tribes; but to Montaigne they became 'noble and generous . . . with no motive other than to emulate virtue': occasions for the warriors to demonstrate their valour.*

Sixteenth-century writers used the example of Indian virtue to edify their readers, in an effort to reform men and improve their character. In the following century the emphasis became more juridical: Indian societies were shown to have evolved their institutions to serve the community's needs. The Dutchman Hugo Grotius cited the simple, communal life of the American Indians as one of the basic ways of life, a foundation of his monumental *The Law of War and Peace* (1625). There were more utopias during the seventeenth century, all owing much to More's and to the reports about Brazilians: Thomas Campanella's *City of Sun* (1643), Bacon's *Nova Atlantida* (1627) and others. The year 1632 saw the birth of Pufendorf in Germany, Locke in England and Spinoza in Holland – all of whom referred to the simplicity and nobility of the Americans. Shakespeare read Montaigne, but did not entirely swallow the panegyrics about the Indians: in *The Tempest* Caliban, for all his goodness and innocence, was crude and servile, and when Gonzalo expounded the virtues of a primitive society, in Act II, scene 1, he was ridiculed by Sebastian and Antonio.

Montesquieu, in *The Spirit of Laws* (1748), stressed the freedom and equality of the Indians. Because they had no possessions there was no inequality, no cause for robbery or abuse of others for money. These ideas reappeared in the entry 'Sauvages' in Diderot's famous *Encyclopedia* published in Paris in 1761. Diderot also produced an essay on the character of savage man. He praised the Indians' love of liberty, their despair at being confined, and reluctance to leave forests for cities. He admired the Indians' spirit – being unprotected by laws they were quick to retaliate against injury – and their resignation to pain or death. In their innocence there was no false modesty about natural acts. All this made them more open-minded and better able to hear the voice of reason.

Messages that originated with the first travellers to Brazil thus became a political theory, a call to independence and revolution. The noble savage was described and his way of life eulogised by men who had never been near a Brazilian Indian.

Daniel Defoe's *Robinson Crusoe* (1719) opens in Bahia, and ends with an attack by Brazilian cannibals who kill Man Friday. And Voltaire's *Candide* (1759) travels from the territory of the Guaraní on the Paraguay across Brazil to the Guianas. But the man who believed most strongly in the ideal of the noble savage, and through whom it came to influence the French Revolution and the independence movements in the Americas themselves, was Jean-Jacques Rousseau. His models were the newly discovered Hottentots of southern Africa; but the ideas of natural goodness stem directly from Caminha, Vespucci and the other observers of Brazilian Indians. And those Indians earned their splendid reputation by the innocent hospitality they gave the strangers who appeared on their shores. 'If the Christians had been angels descended from heaven, they could not have been more cherished by those poor Indians.'

TWO

From Barter to Slavery

THE realities in Brazil were rather different from the philosophers'
ideals. The Indians themselves were more human, less perfect than
Montaigne's or Rousseau's noble savages. And the colonists soon began
to shatter any earthly paradise that may have existed in the New World.

When the Portuguese first visited Brazil its coast was being invaded by
the warlike Tupi-speaking nations, first the Tupinikin, then a wave of
Tupinambá. It was a situation slightly analogous to that of the Aztecs in
Mexico or Incas in Peru: the Europeans arrived soon after the land had
been conquered by an exceptionally aggressive tribe. The similarity ends
there, for the naked nomadic Brazilians were hunter-gatherers or
primitive farmers, in no way comparable with the sophisticated Aztecs
or Incas with their metal-working, art and architecture and their
elaborate economic, religious and political structures. The Tupi were
migrating, probably northwards from a nucleus in the Paraguay basin,
and were driving the tribes living along the coast to seek refuge inland.
The Tupi had since fragmented into a score of tribes along the vast curve
of the central coast of Brazil. These tribes were often at war with one
another, bitterly divided by ancient vendettas; but their language and
customs were so similar at the time of the conquest that they must have
separated only recently. They called anyone who did not speak their
language 'Tapuia' – 'people of strange tongue' – and there were still
many pockets of Tapuia who had not yet been driven from the coastal
forests or were living a short distance inland.

A naked Hans Staden watches Tamoio cooking human flesh.

For all its luxuriant vegetation and mild climate, Brazil provided meagre food for its inhabitants. There were no domestic animals whatsoever, and no cereal crops. Amerigo Vespucci described the wealth of wild animals in Brazil – 'so many that it would have been hard for them to have entered Noah's ark . . . but no domestic animals whatsoever, they do not have any'. The Brazilian Indians were therefore forced to hunt and fish for their protein. There was plenty of game, and Indians always love to recite the wealth of their land in wild pig, deer, tapir, monkeys, agouti, armadillos and many delicious game birds. Hunting forced the people to live in small groups, with enough men to hunt in packs, but never too many to exhaust an area's fish or game.

The Incas were able to develop an advanced civilisation partly because they had a source of protein in their thousands of domesticated llamas and guinea-pigs. They lived in the relatively open countryside of the Andes, and could easily cultivate maize and potatoes. Brazilian Indians had none of these advantages. Their immense lands were covered in either mighty rain forests or dense dry woods and scrublands. None of their animals could be reared in captivity. When they cleared forest – by slashing with crude stone axes and then burning away the undergrowth – the soil was surprisingly weak. Heavy rains leach away the accumulation of forest humus in a few years. The Indians learned that a clearing should soon be allowed to revert to forest vegetation. Brazil has a gentle climate with plenty of sun and rain; but it also has the world's richest insect life, with innumerable ants, termites and caterpillars attacking every crop.

The luxuriant growths of the forest survive in an almost closed cycle. Nutrients that fall to the ground decompose rapidly from the onslaughts of insects, rain and heat. They are quickly absorbed by the shallow root systems of the forest trees. Few nutrients penetrate downwards into the soil. If the forest is cleared, the weak soils deteriorate from the exposure to sun and rain: they lose their nutrients and soon turn into sterile pink dust and mud. The Indians understood this and developed an agricultural system based on slash-and-burn of temporary forest clearings. But this was another reason why they had to live in small, mobile communities. They could not develop the permanent agriculture or large plantations needed to support advanced civilisations.

The Amazon basin, which occupies half of Brazil, continues to defy and frustrate modern agriculturalists: unless clearings are rotated in the primitive Indian manner the topsoil is eroded. If wide areas are stripped of forest there is danger of drought. These very difficult conditions exist in the Amazon basin and on the central plateaux of Mato Grosso and

Goiás. But Brazil is a country covering half a continent. Many parts of it are more fertile and easier to farm, particularly on rivers flowing into the Atlantic or in the south, further from the equator, where the climate is more temperate and the land can be as rich as in Europe or the United States.

The same forests that prevented many Brazilian Indians from developing extensive agriculture discouraged them from leaving permanent monuments. With such an abundance of timber and thatch there was no reason to build in brick or stone. Hunting tribes were too small to mobilise the hundreds of workers needed to build monuments on the scale of the Inca cities or the Aztec or Maya pyramids. Brazilian tribes build fine huts, with intricate thatch and a subtle architecture of beams and rafters. But they have to be prepared to move on to new forest clearings and fresh areas of game. Their abandoned huts soon collapse or burn, and are rapidly consumed by the jungle.

Brazilian natives developed great skills within the limits of their difficult environment. Hunting and fighting were the chief male occupations. Every boy played and practised with his bow and arrow, and Indians became brilliant archers. They could draw their long bows of hard dark wood and fire a quick succession of arrows with deadly accuracy. The arrows varied slightly from tribe to tribe. The Tupi used a long straight bamboo or reed, feathered with two half-feathers tied to the end in a spiral to spin the arrow in flight. The heads were of different types – a sharp wooden leaf-shaped blade, a simple fire-hardened point, a barbed point of bone or sting-ray tail, a serrated series of barbs, or a knob for stunning birds and monkeys: each type of game or fish had its appropriate arrow.

The chroniclers were amazed by native hunting skills. 'These arrows might appear ludicrous, but they are a cruel weapon that can pierce cotton cuirasses or break a stick in two if they hit it, or sometimes pass clean through a man and plunge into the ground beyond him. They practise with these weapons from a very young age and are great archers, so accurate that no bird escapes them, however small.'

The Indians acquired a deep understanding of the wildlife of their forests. They felt at home there as no white man ever could: Indians can recognise individual trees of a forest in the way a city man recognises streets and houses. 'They can see exceptionally well, spotting something a league [four miles] away, and they hear equally well. They have an amazing sense of direction. They guide themselves by the sun and go wherever they wish, two or three hundred leagues through dense forests without missing their goal. They travel much and always at a trot, generally with loads: a man on a horse cannot catch them. They are great fishermen and swimmers and fear neither sea nor waves. They can endure a day and night of swimming, and do the same paddling, sometimes without eating.' 'Wherever they go, whether in the forest or on the water, they are never without their bows and arrows. When in the forest they are perpetually watching, with eyes raised towards the trees. When they hear the noise of birds, monkeys or other animals in the trees they are expert at shooting them, tracking them unceasingly until they succeed. It is rare for a man to return empty-handed from hunting. They catch fish on the sea shore in the same way: they have keen vision, and as soon as a fish jumps they shoot and seldom miss. When they have hit a fish they jump into the water to swim after it. Some big fish sink to the bottom when they feel the arrow; but the savages will dive to a depth of almost six fathoms to get them. . . . The man who catches the greatest number divides his catch with his fellows.'

Most of the skills that impressed the sixteenth-century chroniclers exist among any Indians at any period of Brazilian history. Expert hunters, in a land full of game, they were concerned only with immediate necessities. It was better to leave game and fish alive until it was needed than to dry or salt it for storage. This hunter's mentality produced the indifference to wealth that so enchanted the philosophers – and the improvidence and apparent laziness that so infuriated anyone who tried to make Indians work. The French Capuchin Claude d'Abbeville observed that the men spent most of their time in idleness, and even their hunting and fishing were 'more to feed and amuse themselves than to amass riches'.

The Indians also farmed the few domestic plants native to Brazil: manioc (cassava), maize, some gourds, pumpkins, broad beans and peanuts, and cotton for hammocks and cord. It was primitive slash-and-burn agriculture. The tribe moved its village periodically and made clearings (roças) in the forest. The Indians felled a few trees laboriously with their stone axes and then set fire to the patch a few months later.†
Once the men had made the clearing they returned to their hammocks and hunting, and left the actual farming to women, the fertile sex. Not that the farming was very intricate. Manioc cuttings and tubers, kernels of maize or beans were planted and left to grow, unattended apart from a little weeding. The clearings were not entirely communal as the political theorists imagined: 'each couple has a private plantation of roots which supplies both man and wife with food'.

The preparation of manioc is a legacy from the Indians to all modern Brazilians and it can be observed in almost any surviving tribe. The women dig up manioc roots as they need them, and then begin an elaborate process to make them edible. One form of manioc contains prussic acid. The Indians discovered how to extract this poison by grating and soaking the tubers, and squeezing them in a cunning invention called a tipiti: a plaited straw tube the size of a man, with a weight at the closed end, that stretches and squeezes the contents as the liquid drains off. The pulp is then roasted on large flat pottery platters. It produces either pancake-like beiju, rather like Biblical unleavened bread, or a tasty flour looking like sawdust – the inevitable farinha that has been a staple of every expedition in Brazil, and still appears on every table and on top of most dishes in the Brazilian interior.†

Besides their plentiful fish and game, and these few vegetables, the Indians varied their diet with what they could gather in the forests and on the shores – wild honey to provide their only sweetness, various nuts and fruits, palm hearts, some edible grubs and ants, oysters and the eggs of birds and turtles. Indians were naturally very skilful at finding these delicacies and knowing when to form expeditions to gather them. So the Indians never went hungry. Their tribes were relatively small for such a vast country, every member of the community helped provide food, and the land was luxuriantly fertile and teeming with wildlife. To that extent they lived in a carefree paradise.

Their idyll was spoiled by one great blemish. The Tupi were one of the most bellicose nations of Brazilian Indians, constantly at war with other tribes and with rival sections of their own people. These wars were not over territory, for there was plenty of land, nor over material possessions, for the Indians had so few. The fighting was to avenge past wrongs and to kill and capture members of the enemy tribe: endless, pointless vendettas that came to dominate much of the group's society and life-cycle. 'These Indians . . . are well set up, lusty and of good stature – a very brave people who regard death lightly; daring in war and with very little prudence. They are very ungrateful, inhuman and cruel, with a penchant for fighting, and are extremely vindictive. They live at their ease, with no preoccupation other than eating, drinking and killing people.' Much of the fighting was by stealth, with surprise attacks at dawn or dusk on enemy villages. 'There is no nation on earth so inclined to war and to making new voyages as these Brazilian savages. Four or five hundred leagues are nothing to them to go and attack their enemies and capture slaves. Although by nature fearful and timid, once they warm to combat they stand firm until they have no more weapons, and then use their teeth and nails against their enemies.'

Military expeditions would be undertaken on foot, with the naked warriors advancing across country in single file led by their chief, or in flotillas of long war-canoes paddling up the forested rivers. There was much attention to omens and dreams in planning an attack. 'They spy out the enemy's huts at night and attack at dawn. . . . They attack with loud yells, stamping on the ground and blowing blasts on gourd trumpets. They all carry cords bound about their bodies to tie up their prisoners, and adorn themselves with red feathers to distinguish their friends from their foes. They shoot very rapidly and send fire arrows into the enemy's huts to set them alight. And if they are wounded they have special herbs with them to heal their wounds.'

Some battles were set-piece affairs in open country. The timorous Calvinist missionary Jean de Léry had to go and watch one of these fights to please his Indian friends. Léry and his French companion stood at the rear with drawn swords, and fired pistols to encourage their side; but they risked certain death if their Tupinambá lost. 'One could scarcely believe how cruel and terrible the combat was. . . . As soon as they were two or three hundred yards apart they greeted one another with [a volley] of arrows. . . . Their bows are so much longer and stronger than those we have here [in France] that one of our men could scarcely draw one, far less shoot it. . . . Anyone who has seen them busy with their bows will agree with me that, naked as they are and without any armlet, they can draw and shoot them so fast that, with due respect to the good English bowmen, our savages, holding their supply of arrows in the hand with which they hold the bow, would have fired off a dozen while [the English] would have released six. . . . If any of them were hit, as several were, they tore [the arrows] from their bodies with marvellous courage, broke them and bit the pieces with their fine teeth like mad dogs. But this did not prevent them returning, all wounded, to the combat. . . . When they were finally in a mêlée with their great wooden swords and clubs, they charged one another with mighty two-handed blows. If they struck an enemy's head they did not just knock him to the ground, but slaughtered him as one of our butchers fells an ox. . . . These Americans are so furious in their wars that they fight on without stopping as long as they can move arms and legs, never retreating or turning tail. . . . Apart from the entertainment of watching them jump, whistle and wield their swords, circling and bobbing, it was also marvellous to see so many arrows with their great plumage of red, blue, green, scarlet and many other coloured feathers flying through the air and sparkling in the rays of sunlight, and also so many robes, head-dresses, bracelets and other ornaments all made of these natural feathers.'

Two Englishmen, both shipwrecked on the coast of Brazil in the late sixteenth century, found themselves living among Indians at different times and advising them how to win their battles. The Cornishman Peter Carder was with Drake on his circumnavigation, but his ship became separated from the others in the Pacific and its crew tried to row and sail home in a five-ton pinnace. Shipwrecked near the River Plate, Carder eventually spent about a year alone among the Tupinambá. Before his tribe set out on an expedition Carder had them make a hundred bark shields and two hundred clubs. He set out with seven hundred warriors and arranged that they should all paint one leg with red urucum dye from the knee downward, for easy recognition. After a three-day march they came upon the enemy village, and attacked at about four o'clock in the morning. Carder's shields and clubs gave an advantage and 'we immediately knocked down to the number of two hundred; the rest, except some twenty prisoners, escaped into the woods'.

A few years later Anthony Knivet sailed under Thomas Cavendish to raid the Brazilian coast. Knivet was captured and survived an amazing series of adventures that included periods of living with the Indians, a series of slaving raids on behalf of his Portuguese captors, life as a slave himself and various last-minute escapes from execution by both Indians and Portuguese. He was with the Tamoio tribe of Tupinambá when they were feuding with the related Temimino. Knivet took part in many battles and raids, including one campaign by five thousand Tamoio in which, in a ten-day pursuit, they 'took many old men and women, which as we took them we killed'. Knivet also tried to improve Tamoio fighting methods. 'When I saw the rusticall manner of their fight, that without any order they would set upon their enemies like Buls, I taught them how to set themselves in Battaile, and to lye in ambush, and how to retire and draw their enemies into a snare: by this meanes we had alwayes the upper hand of our enemies, and I was held in great accompt amongst them, for they would never goe to the field, except I went with them.'

Although there were great migrations when an entire Indian nation moved into a new region, inter-tribal wars were not primarily to conquer land. The wars did, however, achieve a territorial balance between tribes: each group knew that when it crossed a certain river or landmark it was entering the lands of its enemies. It sometimes managed to expel those enemies altogether. Knivet boasted that after he had improved the fighting techniques of his group of Tupinambá 'in a short time we gave so many battailes to the Temominos that we made them leave their Countrey and flye further from us; so wee lived in peace'.

The bloody battles also served to keep down the population, to a level that the land could easily support. War was 'the ordinary drain of such a multitude, without which they would not have fitted into that land'. Knivet once found himself near the Paraíba river among a group of Tapuia in which the women heavily outnumbered the men: they explained that their warriors had attempted a war against the

Tupinambá and been wiped out. Successful military expeditions occasionally destroyed the enemies' plantations or sacked the few belongings in their huts; but such pillage was of very little concern to the Indians.

All observers noted the true motive for Tupi wars: it was to capture prisoners so that these could be eaten in a special ceremony by the victorious tribe. The Tupi tribes of the Brazilian coast evolved a terrible cycle of vendettas. The eating of a prisoner was an intolerable insult that demanded revenge. Raid therefore followed raid interminably. The ritual cannibalism was surrounded by elaborate rules and ceremonies, from the moment of an enemy's capture until the final disposal of his flesh and bones months later. It was a subject that fascinated Europeans, and the chroniclers satisfied their readers' curiosity with pages of grisly details.

The most famous descriptions came from the German gunner Hans Staden. The Portuguese had employed Staden to manage the artillery in a fort called Bertioga on the island of Santo Amaro, near the port of Santos. One day in 1552 Staden went into the woods to collect some game shot by his Indian servant. 'As I was going through the forest I heard loud yells on either side of me. . . . Immediately a company of savages came running towards me, surrounded me on every side and shot at me with their bows and arrows. I cried out "Now may God preserve my soul!" I had scarcely uttered the words before they threw me to the ground and shot and stabbed at me. God be praised, they only wounded me in the leg. But they tore the clothes from my body: one tore off my jerkin, another my hat, a third my shirt and so forth. . . . At last two of them seized me and lifted me up, naked as I was, took me by the arms, some running in front and some behind, and carried me with them through the forest at a great pace towards the sea where they had their canoes.'

Staden's friends tried to rescue him, but his captors paddled too fast. They rushed him back to their village some thirty miles away.

The warriors disappeared into the huts, 'leaving me to the pleasure of the women who gathered around and accompanied me, in front and behind, dancing and singing the songs they usually sing to their own people when they are about to eat them. . . . They fell upon me and beat me with their fists, plucking at my beard and crying out in their speech . . . "With this blow I avenge my friend who was slain by your people." . . . A woman approached carrying a piece of crystal fastened to a kind of ring, and scraped off my eyebrows with it. She tried to scrape off my beard as well but I resisted, saying that I would die with my beard on. They answered that they were not ready to kill me yet and left me my beard; but they cut it off a few days later with some scissors a Frenchman had given them. . . . They made a ring around me – I was in the middle with two women – and tied my leg with strings of objects that rattled. They also bound me with sheaves of feathers, arranged in a square and fastened behind my neck so that they stood up above my head. . . . The women then began to sing together. I had to keep time with the rattles on my leg by stamping as they sang. But my wounded leg was so painful that I could hardly stand upright, for my wound had not been dressed.' On another occasion Staden had his legs bound together 'and I was forced to hop through the huts on both feet, at which they made merry, saying: "Here comes our food hopping towards us."'

The German somehow managed to survive, first by trying to deny that he was an ally of the Portuguese, then by having a toothache that stopped him eating and made him too thin to kill. He later made some daring prophecies – that a disease would strike the tribe, that the chief would not die, and that they would win a particular raid. When these all came true, Staden became a venerated oracle in the tribe.

Months later, Staden was on a fishing expedition that ended in a skirmish in which some of his friends, Christian half-castes born of Portuguese fathers and Indian mothers, were captured. Those who were badly wounded were killed at once and roasted. 'One was called Hieronymus. He had been captured by a native belonging to my hut, and this man spent the whole night roasting Hieronymus, scarcely a step from the spot where I lay. . . . Hieronymus's flesh remained in the hut where I was for three weeks, hanging in a pot in the smoke over the fire until it was as dry as wood.' Staden consoled the other prisoners. He even tried to intercede for them with the great chief Konyanbebe, but 'he had a great vessel full of human flesh in front of him and was eating a leg. He held this to my mouth inviting me to taste it. I replied that even beasts did not eat their own species. . . . But he took a bite saying . . . "I am a jaguar: it tastes good."'

A prisoner was normally kept for some months as a slave, almost a guest in the village. Hans Staden, who experienced all this, reported that 'they give him a woman who attends him and has intercourse with him. If the woman conceives, the child is reared until it is fully grown; then when the mood seizes them they kill and eat it.' A prisoner's temporary wife might even fall in love with him and help him escape: the chronicler Magalhães de Gandavo said 'there are a few Portuguese who have escaped that way and are still alive'.

The tribe would brew maize beer and prepare a great celebration for the ceremony of killing its prisoners. A special ceremonial club was used for the death blow, which was delivered from behind and stunned or killed the prisoner. Before his death the victim was taunted and was expected to conduct himself with calm defiance. 'The women run about him mocking him and boasting that they will eat him. . . . They then make a fire some two paces from the victim, which he has to tend. After this a woman brings the club, waving the tassels in the air, shrieking with joy, and running to and fro before the prisoner so that he may see it.'

The warrior designated as executioner arrives with his arms and face dyed red with urucum. 'He addresses the victim thus: "I am he that will kill you, since you and your people have slain and eaten many of my friends." To which the prisoner replies: "When I am dead I shall still have many to avenge *my* death."'

'Then the slayer strikes from behind and beats out his brains. The women seize the body at once and carry it to the fire.' 'They come forward with hot water that they have ready, rub and scald the dead body, remove the outer skin and leave it as white as our cooks know how to do with a sucking-pig ready to roast. They . . . then take this poor body, cleave it and instantly cut it into pieces, faster than any butcher in our country could dismember a sheep.' 'Then they cut off the head and give it to [the executioner]. They take the guts and give them to the women, after which they joint him, joint by joint, first hands, then elbowes, and so all the body. After which they send to every house a peece, then they fall a-dancing, and all the women make great store of Wine: the next day they boil every joint in a great pot of water, because their wives and children might eate of the broth; for the space of three days they do nothing but dance and drinke day and night.' 'They eat the innards, and also the flesh on the skin, and the tongue; and they let the children eat what they especially enjoy.' 'Although they all confess that this human flesh is marvellously good and delicate, nevertheless they feast on it more out of vengeance than taste. . . . Their main purpose in . . . gnawing the dead down to the bones in this way is to fill the living with fear and horror. . . . Everything that can be found in the bodies of these prisoners is completely eaten by them – from the extremities of the toes right up to the nose, ears and crown of the head. I except, however, the brain, which they do not touch.'

The executioner added the victim's name to his own, but did not eat any of his meat. Instead, he retired to his hammock and fasted to recover from delivering the death blow. Skulls were kept as trophies, leg and arm bones used to make flutes, and teeth strung into necklaces. It was then up to the relatives of the dead person to avenge him by a similar capture and ritual execution.

It was tragic that the Tupi tribes occupying the Brazilian coast at the time of the conquest – unlike most of the hundreds of tribes in the interior of the country – had evolved these cannibalistic rites. Such practices gave the colonists a fine moral excuse for their invasion. The Spaniards made similar capital out of the Aztecs' human sacrifices, and tried to find some such blemish among the Incas. Nicholas Durand de Villegagnon, who was in charge of the French attempt to colonise Rio de Janeiro, wrote to Calvin in Geneva in 1557: 'They are fierce and savage people far removed from any courtesy or humanity and quite different from us in their way of life and upbringing. . . . It even entered my thoughts whether we had fallen among beasts wearing a human aspect.' The inter-tribal vendettas fragmented the tribes and made them eager to enlist the Europeans as allies against their enemies. And the capture of prisoners for execution resulted in a form of slavery among the Indians, which gave the Europeans a convenient precedent – even a pretext – for enslaving Indians.

The early years of peaceful trading of metal tools for brazilwood logs soon degenerated into bloodshed and oppression. Rivalry between French and Portuguese traders grew violent and turned into undeclared war between the two powers. The Portuguese regarded Brazil as theirs, granted by the division of the unexplored world by the Treaty of Tordesillas. Portuguese kings protested to French kings, but the French could see no reason to restrain their subjects from this lucrative trade on a coast occupied only by Indians. The Portuguese were more pragmatic and tough than the far richer French. The government in Lisbon sent fleets of 'coastguards' to destroy any French ships caught off Brazil. This was done ruthlessly: French ships and warehouses were burned and their crews were not only killed but sometimes tortured to death. One French ship returning from Brazil was captured by a trick in the Mediterranean and its crew imprisoned in Lisbon. This was violent behaviour for two nations at peace with one another, but Francis I of France was too intent on preserving friendship with the Portuguese as potential allies against his Spanish enemies to make much protest.

French captains were furious. Jean Parmentier wrote of the Portuguese: 'Even though this people is the smallest of all the globe, that globe does not seem large enough to satisfy all its cupidity. The Portuguese must have drunk the dust of the heart of King Alexander to show such exaggerated ambition. . . . If it were within their power to close the seas from Cape Finisterre to Ireland they would have done so long ago. And yet the Portuguese have no right to prevent French merchants from landing in lands that they have abrogated, in which they have not planted the Christian faith and are neither loved nor obeyed. . . . As soon as they have sailed along a coast they take possession of it and consider it a conquest.'

Parmentier underestimated the 'smallest people of the globe'; the next coastguard expedition sent by the King of Portugal was to make a permanent colonial settlement. The fleet of five ships that sailed under Martím Afonso de Sousa in 1530 carried future colonists among its 400 crew and passengers, and took seeds, plants and domestic animals. It cruised for two years along the coast of Brazil, destroying French shipping, trading with Indians and investigating reports of rich mines in the interior. In March 1531 it called at the enormous Bay of All Saints – the Bahia de Todos os Santos – one of the finest anchorages on the coast of Brazil and a favourite port of call for French and Portuguese since the first discoveries.

A Portuguese sailor called Diogo Álvares had gone ashore at Bahia in the first decade of the century. He managed to preserve an arquebus, powder and shot, and used these to impress the natives with his supernatural powers. His charm and personality did the rest. The local Tupinambá adopted this castaway. They called him Caramuru after a fish that lives in the shallows around Bahia. Caramuru was soon married to Paraguaçu, the daughter of the paramount Tupinambá chief, and himself became an honoured leader. 'He was on very good terms with the Indians, who considered him their chief. They were very obedient to him and he had them well subjected. They treated him with as much respect as if he had been born as their lord.' His was not an easy situation, for the Bahia Tupinambá were fragmented and warlike.

When Martím Afonso de Sousa's fleet sailed into the Bay in March 1531, its men were delighted to find their compatriot so well established among the Indians. Caramuru's tribe brought the fleet large quantities of food and performed great dances of welcome. The Admiral's brother wrote that 'the people of this land are all pale skinned: the men very well disposed and the women very beautiful – they bear comparison with any from the Rua Nova in Lisbon. The men use only bows and arrows as weapons, and every two leagues they are at war with one another. When we were in this bay in the middle of the river, fifty war-canoes from one bank fought fifty from the other. Each canoe carries sixty men, all protected by shields painted like ours. They fought from midday till sunset. The fifty canoes of the bank on which we were anchored were the victors. They carried off many of the others as captives, and killed them, bound with cords, amid great ceremonies. After they were killed, they roasted and ate them.'

Two years later a Spanish fleet bound for the River Plate stopped at Bahia and found Caramuru presiding over a village of some 300 huts containing about a thousand warriors. The Spaniards gave him a longboat and two pipes of wine in exchange for food, and they were pleased to find him still well versed in the articles of the Christian faith. 'He gave them to understand that he was living on that coast and in isolation in order to save and succour Christians who passed by there. He said that he had saved Frenchmen, Portuguese and Spaniards who had been lost on that coast.'

Finally, in early 1532, Martím Afonso decided to plant his colony, not at Bahia, but a thousand miles further south at São Vicente, a few miles from the modern port of Santos, with another settlement nine leagues inland near modern São Paulo. Martím Afonso's brother wrote: 'This land seemed so good to us all that my brother, the Captain, determined to colonise it, and gave to all the men lands for them to make farms. . . . And he put everything into a good state of justice, to the great satisfaction of the men, for they saw towns being founded, with laws and discipline, the celebration of matrimony, and living in civilised communion, with each man as lord of his own property, and private injuries redressed, and all the other benefits of a secure and sociable life.'

It was an ominous moment for the natives already occupying these lands. But Portuguese ambition was vast. King João III now attempted nothing less than the colonisation of the entire 2500 miles of coastline east of the Line of Tordesillas. He divided it into fourteen 'captaincies', each ranging from a hundred to four hundred miles of coastline and awarded to one of his subjects. Each recipient was called a 'donatory'. He became hereditary lord of his huge stretch of territory, with considerable civil and criminal jurisdiction that included the death penalty for slaves, Indians and ordinary freemen. He was empowered to found towns and award grants of land, and could take a total of forty miles of coast as his private estate. He could export whatever he wished to the mother country, except for brazilwood and some spices which the King reserved as a royal monopoly.*

The donatory system worked reasonably well from the King's point of view. Some of the recipients never attempted to colonise their areas. But the majority did and, although some failed through shipwrecks, Indian wars or other disasters, enough managed to establish footholds to justify the Portuguese claim to Brazil. Two were particularly successful: Duarte Coelho at Pernambuco on the north-eastern bulge of the Brazilian coast; and the agents of Martím Afonso de Sousa around his new ports of Santos and São Vicente and the town of Piratininga.

The original awards to the donatories also restricted a human commodity. Royal patents specified that a donatory could use all the

Indian slaves he wished in Brazil or on his ships, but he might send only twenty-four a year back to Portugal.* Slaves had been sent back since the first ships visited Brazil, and slavery now became institutionalised as part of the colonial way of life in Brazil itself.

The barter of trade goods for Indian labour continued smoothly during the first generation after the discovery of Brazil. The Indians were so enchanted by the cutting edges of metal tools that they were prepared to work hard, felling and carrying logwood and feeding the European traders. The Indians would work for very little in those happy days. João Gonçalves, administrator of the captaincy of Itamaracá to the north of Pernambuco, treated the Indians well and they responded generously. They offered to serve the whites 'of their own free will, and cultivated their lands for nothing or next to nothing. . . . In this captaincy there was no white man, however poor, who did not have twenty or thirty of those darkies to use as slaves, and the rich had whole villages. And what shall I say of the trading? For one sickle, knife or comb [the Indians] would bring loads of hens, monkeys, parrots, honey, wax, cotton thread and whatever else those poor people had.'

But Indian wants were easily satisfied. Once they had enough tools to clear their roças they could see little reason to accumulate more imported riches, particularly as the trees were becoming scarcer and had to be carried from further inland. Duarte Coelho, donatory of Pernambuco, complained to the King in 1546 about the difficulty of persuading Indians to cut the royal brazilwood. 'To get your brazilwood [the traders] importune the Indians so much . . . that my country is all in disorder. For it is not enough, Sire, to give them tools as was customary. To make the Indians fetch brazilwood you now have to give them beads from Bahia, and feather caps and coloured clothing that a man could not afford to buy to clothe himself and, what is worse, swords and arquebuses. . . . For when the Indians were needy and wanted tools they used to come and, in return for what we gave them, they did the carrying and all the heavy work, and used to come and sell us food which we needed rather badly. But now that they have plenty of tools they are becoming more useless than usual, are growing restless and proud, and are rebelling.' One Jesuit complained that the natives 'have their houses full of metal tools. . . . Indians who formerly were nobodies and always dying of hunger through not having axes to clear roças now have as many tools and roças as they want, and eat and drink continually. They are always drinking wines in their villages, starting wars and doing much mischief.' He felt that there should be a ban on any supply of tools to heathen Indians. The country might then return to the good old days, for 'I once saw a time here in Brazil when the Indians had nothing with

which to clear roças . . . and were dying of hunger: they used to sell a
slave for a chisel containing about a pound of iron, and also used to sell
their sons and daughters and would even surrender themselves as
slaves.'

Trade goods might lose their appeal as payment for labour; but the
settlers' appetite for Indian workers grew steadily. Brazil yielded none of
the gold or silver of Mexico or Peru in those early years. But the colonists
found the climate excellent for growing sugar, which commanded good
prices in Europe. During the 1540s sugar mills were being organised at
the various places where Portuguese colonists were trying to settle. Each
mill involved heavy labour – clearing forest and undergrowth, raising
oxen or canalising water to drive the cane presses, and building the mills
themselves. Once the mills were functioning they continued to need a
large force to cut and press the cane and brew the molasses. This was
hard labour: drudgery that the Indians refused to do at any price.
Clearing the forest and preparing the sugar estate was one thing. But
cutting the cane, running the mills and boiling molasses were brutish
jobs. They used none of the Indian skills in hunting, forest lore or
archery. They were regarded as agriculture, which was women's work.
And they produced an incomprehensible and unnecessary surplus: far
more sugar than the colonists and Indians themselves needed.

Fernão Cardim wrote that each sugar mill used one or two hundred
slaves. 'The work is insufferable. The workers are always on the run and
because of this many slaves die.' The owners' profits were huge. 'This
sweet bears a heavy load of guilt, for the owners commit so many sins.'
The Indians refused to do this work for any form of payment or any
amount of trade goods. Everything about the work on the plantations
was alien to their nature. They had no interest in profit and no ambition
for material wealth. They disliked physical labour and were insulted by
being asked to perform women's work. Indians prided themselves on
generosity and hospitality, and shared what they had with members of
their family or tribe. The idea of working for someone else was therefore
abhorrent. The plant they were required to grow was unknown to them
– imported from the Caribbean – and of limited value. And the notion
of working for long hours, right through the heat of the day, with no
time to relax and enjoy the pleasures of hunting or community life was
intolerable. The colonists could therefore obtain labour for their
plantations only by force, and they resorted naturally to slavery in an age
that accepted it as one of the conditions of man.

The colonists used to buy slaves with trade goods from tribes that had
captured prisoners and would otherwise have eaten them. That was the
original justification for enslaving Indians. To European thinking it was

better to survive as an overworked slave than to be executed for ritual cannibalism. The Indians probably thought otherwise. One slave told Yves d'Evreux that 'he was little concerned about being eaten. For', he said, 'when you are dead you no longer feel anything. Whether they eat you or not is all the same to a dead man. But I should be angry to die in bed, and not to die in the manner of great men, surrounded by dances and drinking and swearing vengeance on those who would eat me before I died. For whenever I reflect that I am the son of one of the great men of my country and that my father was feared, and that everyone surrounded him to listen to him when he visited the men's hut, and seeing myself now a slave without paint and with no feathers fastened to my head or on my arms or wrists, as the sons of great men are normally accoutred in my country – when I think all this I wish I were dead . . . and can only regret my life.' But to the Europeans it seemed more charitable to save such a victim and work him to a lingering death.

It was considered legally correct for the captives of inter-tribal wars to be classified as slaves. An officer of Sebastian Cabot's fleet bought five natives at São Vicente and explained that they were slaves 'because the Indians of that country, who are called Tupi, go to capture them in wars against their enemies in other tribes, and then sell them to the Portuguese for barter. . . . The Portuguese later sell them to ships that reach that port, or send them to Portugal to be sold as slaves, which they are.'

The supply of captive prisoners was quite inadequate for the voracious demands of the new sugar industry. The Portuguese therefore incited Indians to attack their enemies in order to obtain more captives. Even this was not enough. The next step was therefore direct, forcible enslavement, unadorned by any pretence of rescue from a worse fate.

Slavers took to sailing along the coast to kidnap Indians and ship them to other captaincies. One donatory, Pero de Góis of São Tomé, complained bitterly to King João III in 1546 that his captaincy had been ruined because one Henrique Luís had sailed down from Espírito Santo to trade with the Indians. Luís had seized the most powerful chief in the area, who had been a good friend to the Christians, and held him on his ship. He demanded a large ransom in captives. But when the tribe paid this Luís took the chief and delivered him to an enemy tribe to be eaten. He gained slaves from both tribes in this way, and hoped to fuel a vendetta that would yield more prisoners.*

Another colonist told the King of a similar scandal: a man was shipwrecked and badly wounded but saved and cured in the house of an Indian chief. He left after some months as the guest of the tribe, but later returned and invited the chief on board his ship to thank him. Once the chief was on board, he seized him and his companions and took them for sale in Pôrto Seguro. But on another voyage off that coast the slaver 'lost his ship, and the fishes ate him, and the heathen ate the fishes that had eaten this man: it was divine justice'.

The King had been emptying the prisons of Lisbon and sending the most hardened criminals to Brazil. The energetic Duarte Coelho, donatory of Pernambuco, passionately begged the King to send no more murderers. 'They do no good or profit to the land, but much harm and damage. Because of them we have lost the esteem we had up to now with the Indians. If God and nature cannot remedy [such men] how can I do so, Sire, even if I keep ordering them to be hanged – which also does us great discredit in the eyes of the Indians. They are no good for any form of work, they arrive poor and naked, and cannot stop getting up to their old tricks. Your Highness must know that they are worse than a plague in this land. I beg you for the love of God not to send me any more such poison here.'

Coelho insisted that the other captaincies must stop 'allowing people to go raiding everywhere on anyone they can easily seize. They are destroying everything with this and we are about to lose it all. They are so bloodthirsty about it that they have caused that entire area to rebel.' He was furious about six large caravels that had sailed up to enslave Indians off his stretch of coast. He had managed to catch one of these, sent its victims back to their tribes and 'gave those raiders the punishment I saw fit'. The Tupinambá who captured Hans Staden poured out their hatred of the Portuguese – people who lured them on to their ships and enslaved them, sent frequent raids against them, and maimed and killed them with their guns. None of the chroniclers or authors of letters from Brazil tried to conceal the fact that 'the main reason why these heathen make war on the Christians was the raids made on them by ships sailing along this coast', and the King fully admitted this in his instructions to the first governor of Brazil. *

It was not only Indian men who interested the slavers. The first colonists arrived in Brazil without women and were eager to acquire plump and sensual Indian girls, the same naked beauties who had so delighted Pero Vaz de Caminha. Few Portuguese women went to Brazil – they were frightened of the rough crossing in ships full of sailors and convicts, and of the danger of attack by pirates. Brazil did not have the gold and silver that attracted Spanish women to seek rich marriages among the colonists of Mexico and Peru. Portugal itself suffered none of the conflicts of the Reformation that forced persecuted minorities from northern Europe to sail to the New World with their families. The only Portuguese equivalents were converted Jewish 'New Christians' or family groups from the overcrowded Azores who emigrated to Brazil.

Neither the Portuguese nor the native Brazilians were repelled by inter-racial unions. The Portuguese, living at the southern extremity of Europe and accustomed to close contact with Africa, had no inhibitions about sexual relations with coloured women. Brazilian women had pale coppery skin, straight black hair, and lovely Asiatic faces that were closer to European standards of beauty than the looks of any African women. Although Portuguese colonial societies were stratified by colour, there was no rigid colour bar. In the early colonies, miscegenation was almost official policy – the only way in which the small Portuguese nation could quickly expand over the immense territories it had discovered. Nor were the Indians opposed to unions between their women and the colonists. If a Portuguese or Frenchman befriended a tribe, the Indians wanted him to be surrounded by their women. It was the mark of important men in a tribe – chiefs, sorcerers or successful warriors – to have several wives. The first settlers, who arrived mysteriously from the sea and owned wonderful tools and firearms, were godlike figures who easily qualified for the many wives befitting their rank.

When the first members of the newly formed Society of Jesus arrived in Brazil in 1549, they were appalled by what they saw. Their leader Father Manoel da Nóbrega complained of the laxness of the clergy and friars of other orders already in Brazil. 'They publicly tell the men that it is lawful for them to live in sin with their coloured women since these are their slaves, and that they may raid [Indian men] since they are dogs.' 'The settlers use all their Indian women [slaves] as concubines. They also ask the Indians for free Indian women as wives, following the local custom of having many wives. And they abandon them when they please, which is a great scandal for the new church we wish to found.' 'Although Christians, they lived like heathen. Their sensual debauchery was extreme. They generally kept their own Indian women as concubines inside their houses whether they were married or single.' Even when they formally married one half-caste wife they continued to sleep with twenty or more slave girls. 'They established a custom in their houses that their own wives, whom they married at the church door, should bring whichever concubines they desired most to their bed. If their wives refused, they thrashed them. Not long ago I remember asking a half-caste woman, "What slave girls are those you have with you?" She answered that they were her husband's wives. She was escorting them about everywhere with her, keeping an eye on them like an abbess with her nuns!'

The founders of both **Bahia** and **São Paulo** were such patriarchs. When Martím Afonso made his first settlement at São Vicente in 1532 he found a Portuguese settler called João Ramalho already long established in the area. The Indians had found Ramalho on the beach in about 1510; no one knows whether he was the survivor of a shipwreck, or a deserter or a marooned criminal. They took him up to their chief Tibiriça on the plateau of Piratininga. 'By the grace of God, Tibiriça took a liking to him and gave him his daughter, who was later baptised as Isabel. When Martím Afonso de Sousa reached São Vicente [in 1532], João Ramalho went to talk to him, and he already had married children by then.' Ramalho won a reputation as a great fighter and became an honoured figure in the Goianá Tupinikin tribe that adopted him. He gave only guarded help to his compatriots when they arrived in his area; but to them he was indispensable – an interpreter, son-in-law of the most powerful chief in the area, and a man whom the Indians admired and trusted. Ramalho persuaded Martím Afonso to settle his colonists on the plateau as well as on the coast, and Chief Tibiriça welcomed them. Twenty years later, the King was told that Ramalho 'has so many children, grandchildren, great-grandchildren and descendants that I would not dare to tell Your Majesty how many. But he does not have a grey hair on his head or face, and he walks nine leagues on foot before dinner.'

Ramalho remained true to his one Indian wife, but his sons showed no such restraint. 'They have many women. They and their sons cohabit with their [wives'] sisters and have children by them. They go to war with the Indians, their festivals are Indian ones, and they live like them, as naked as the Indians themselves.' Tomé de Sousa ordered the settlers to gather together into the town of Santo André in 1553, and put Ramalho in charge of them. At his own expense, Ramalho 'built a wall surrounding the town, and within it formed four bulwarks in which were mounted artillery pieces to harass the repeated assults of the Tamoio of the Paraíba river'. A German adventurer visited the town at that time and was impressed by the good looks and toughness of Ramalho's offspring; but he found the place a bandits' lair. He reported that Ramalho 'had waged war and pacified the province, assembling five thousand Indians while the King of Portugal could assemble only two thousand'. Ramalho wanted to marry his Indian wife, but he was worried about a Portuguese wife called Catarina whom he had left in Portugal many years before. The Jesuits tried to discover whether she was still alive, and hoped that she was not: they wanted Ramalho to be in a state of grace, since he could be so helpful to them. Possibly because of her, or more probably because of his sons' wild behaviour and his own extensive slaving activities, Ramalho fell out with the Jesuits and obstructed their missionary activity. But when in 1562 the settlers moved across the valley from Santo André to a new town alongside the Jesuit college of São Paulo their military commander was still João Ramalho. It was he who led them on a punitive expedition against the Tupinikin two years later. When he died in 1580, aged over ninety, he was still concerned about the young wife he had deserted so long before: but his descendants were spread throughout the tribes of the Piratininga plateau.*

Other Portuguese were also isolated among the Indians. On the island of Cananéia, south of Santos, there was a mysterious white man who may have been the first of all European settlers in South America. This Portuguese was referred to only as the Bacharel (university graduate) of Cananéia. He helped supply food and Indian slaves to the Spaniards sailing towards the River Plate in 1527, and they wrote that he had lived there for 'about thirty years'. He and others were busily producing the first generation of mamelucos – half-castes born of European fathers and Indian mothers. Their children were a tough breed of frontiersmen who managed to combine the hardier characteristics of both races.†

The Portuguese had an amazing ability to adapt themselves to strange conditions. This was seen most strongly at São Paulo, where the two races and cultures blended to produce a tough mixed stock. The word Paulista, meaning an inhabitant of São Paulo, became almost synonymous with mameluco. Thanks to João Ramalho and his children, this transition happened quickly, with the mestizo class arising from the outset. The Paulistas learned all aspects of Indian life and forest lore. They spoke Tupi, the language of their Indian mothers. 'Almost all the Portuguese who come from the Kingdom [Portugal] and settle here and communicate with the Indians learn [Tupi] in a short while; and the children of Portuguese born here, both men and women, speak it better than [newly arrived] Portuguese, especially in the Captaincy of São Vicente.' A century later families in São Paulo were still closely linked to Indians: 'The language spoken in such families is that of the Indians; and children go to school to learn Portuguese.'

The Indian women were ready partners, and in the early days their men acquiesced because it was hospitable to offer women to strangers. The great Jesuit missionary José de Anchieta wrote to his Superior that 'the women go naked and are unable to say no to anyone. They themselves in fact provoke and importune the men, sleeping with them in hammocks; for they hold it to be an honour to sleep with the Christians.' Another shocked Jesuit reported that the women 'have little resistance against those who assault them. In fact, instead of resisting, they go and seek them out in their houses!' 'The women go naked and are so base that they go after the youths to sin with them and seduce them. And these readily allow themselves to be seduced.'

The great Brazilian historian João Capistrano de Abreu wrote: 'The work of the first decades can be summarised as brazilwood, parrots, slaves and mestizos.' During the first half of the sixteenth century, the attitudes of whites and natives changed. Barter – of trade goods for brazilwood – degenerated into slavery. Native hospitality was rebuffed and exploited by the uncouth strangers. And the Portuguese decided to make permanent settlements in this new world. The division of Brazil into captaincies under hereditary donatories was a deliberate act of colonisation. It was a daring move, one of the earliest European colonial adventures, made in a wild forested country that contained no obvious treasures or advanced civilisations. Brazil had no known gold or silver, and no cities and temples to be looted. Its only wealth was limitless land, and innumerable natives who might be made to farm it.

The Indians saw it all differently. An aged chief told the French missionary Claude d'Abbeville: 'In the beginning the Portuguese did nothing but trade with us, without wishing to live here in any other way. At that time they freely slept with our daughters, which our women . . . considered a great honour.' But the Europeans invariably began to insist that the Indians help them build settlements, and fortifications to dominate the surrounding country. 'And, after [exhausting] the slaves ransomed from [prisoners] of war, they wanted to have our own children.'

THREE

Origins and
Fantasies

THE new land of Brazil was so immense that it inspired the early travellers to talk in superlatives. Many wrote panegyrics of a terrestrial paradise with a perfect climate, bounteous soil, and handsome carefree natives. Others were cowed – dismayed by the endless forests and savannahs, the rivers so great that no expedition seemed able to reach their sources, and distant hills and plains that led into the heart of the continent. Such writers described the natives as brutish cannibals. They felt cheated by the lack of cities to plunder and saw the Indians only as a labour force with which to tame the forests.

No one knew what lay in the interior of this new world. It contained exotic wildlife – the manatee or sea-cow that might have inspired the mermaid legend, the peccary that looked like a boar with its navel on its spine, giant sloths, tapirs, toucans with great yellow beaks, electric eels and a panoply of unknown insects, birds and fishes. Spaniards found fossilised bones of giant mammals in what is now Ecuador, eastern Bolivia and the southern Argentine. These were the bones of extinct giant ostriches, cameloids and horses that had roamed the South American plains before the Ice Ages; but the conquistadores assumed they were the bones of human giants. In 1547 other Spaniards discovered a veritable mountain of silver at Potosí, in the most remote part of the Bolivian altiplano.

With so many fantastic discoveries, anything seemed possible. Some authors stated that Brazil contained the legendary curiosities that had

Indian men and women felling brazilwood.

fascinated medieval travel writers. There were men with eight toes; the Mutayus whose feet pointed backwards so that pursuers tracked them in the wrong direction; men born with white hair that turned black in old age; others with dogs' heads, or one cyclopean eye, or heads between their shoulders, or one leg on which they ran very fast. Medieval authors had spoken of people who ate only fish, and of others who ate aged members of their tribe before they died of old age. There were in fact tribes in Brazil who behaved in such ways. Then there was Upupiara, half man and half fish, the product of fish impregnated by the sperm of drowned men. The cruel and treacherous Upupiara caught men in the water, drowned them, and ate their eyes and genitals so that their bodies were recovered with these parts missing. Brazil was also thought to contain giants and pygmies.

Brazil seemed the logical place to look for Amazons, the female warriors whose advanced society functioned without men. Ulrich Schmidel was on an expedition searching for Amazons on the Paraguay river in the 1540s, and the French cosmographer André Thevet was sure that such women existed in Brazil. The first Spaniards who descended the Amazon river in 1542 brought back reports of Amazons, and the conviction grew that they existed near the river that now bears their name. There were so many fables of medieval monsters that accurate reporters despaired. Hans Staden was worried that none would accept his extraordinary story of surviving capture by cannibal Tupinambá. He wrote in the preface: 'There have been travellers who, with their lies and stories of false things, have caused honest and truthful men returning from distant lands not to be believed.'

Fervent Christians developed a different myth about Brazil. It came to be accepted that the land of brazilwood and Amazons had once been visited by the Apostle St Thomas. There had for many centuries been a group of Nestorian Christians living in India, and it was said that they were originally converted by St Thomas. King Alfred of England had sent the Bishop of Sherborne on an embassy to them in 883, and they were described in the writings of Vasco da Gama, Prester John and St Francis Xavier. Many of the first Portuguese to visit Brazil had also visited India. They wondered whether the Apostle Thomas might have preached in the American Indies as well as in India itself. They questioned the natives, and these associated the white men's Thomas with one of their own legendary creators called Sumé. This Sumé sounded very like Tomé, the Portuguese for Thomas. As early as 1514, a European visitor to Brazil reported: 'They have a recollection of St Thomas. . . . They wanted to show the Portuguese some footprints of St Thomas in the interior of the country. When they speak of St Thomas they call him the little god, but say that there was another greater god. . . . In the country they frequently call their sons Sumé.'

The legend of an earlier visit by a Christian holy man had a strong appeal to Catholic missionaries: it made them feel that they were continuing the work of an apostle. In their teaching they benefited from the idea that the natives' ancestors had been taught by an earlier Christian. A similar interpretation was given to the Inca legend of the creator Viracocha, who disappeared over the Pacific, and to the Aztecs' Quetzalcóatl, who was destined to reappear from the Caribbean.

The leader of the first Jesuits to reach Brazil, Manoel da Nóbrega, wrote in 1549 that he had been shown St Thomas' footprints on a rock beside a river near Bahia. 'I saw with my own eyes four footprints, very clearly marked, with their toes; the river sometimes covers them when it rises.' Other missionaries reported being shown similar footprints at no less than six different places. Anthony Knivet visited a huge outcrop of rock with a cave 'like any Hall in England' where St Thomas had once preached.* Hans Staden noted that Tupi men shaved the crowns of their heads, leaving 'a circle of hair around it like a monk', and concluded that they did this in imitation of an ancestor 'who had worked many miracles among them, and this man is thought to have been a prophet or one of the apostles'.

The Calvinist pastor Jean de Léry preached to the Tupinambá near Rio de Janeiro in the 1550s. An old man thanked Léry for his explanation of the marvels of Christianity, but said: 'Your sermon reminds me of what we have often heard our grandfathers relate. Namely, that long ago – so many moons that we could not keep count of them – a mair (which means "stranger"), clothed and bearded like some of your people, came to this land. He hoped to bring our ancestors to the obedience of your god, and addressed them in the same language that you have to us now. However, as we understand it from father to son, they would not believe. Another man then came, who, as a sign of malediction, presented them with a sword. As a result we have always killed one another since that time . . . to such an extent that . . . if we now abandoned this custom and desisted all the neighbouring tribes would mock us!'

When they considered that St Thomas might have visited Brazil shortly after the time of Christ, the Portuguese pondered the origin of the natives taught by that apostle. The two sources of accepted wisdom were the Holy Scriptures and Classical literature: it was to these that men turned to discover the origin of the Brazilian Indians. A Papal Bull of 1512 clearly stated that American natives were descended from Adam and Eve, as was the rest of mankind. Their ancestor must therefore have appeared in the Bible. That ancestor might have been Noah's descendant Jobab, since during the days of his father 'was the earth divided'; or Ham, the son whose descendants were cursed because he had seen Noah's nakedness. Some thought the Indians sprang from Jacob. But the most common theory was that they were one of the lost tribes of Israel. The Inquisitor Gregorio García assembled all the theories in a book published in 1607, but he himself had no doubts: 'The Indians are cowardly, do not recognise Jesus Christ, and give no thanks for good done to them': they must therefore be Jews. Another erudite author advanced the argument that the Spanish words for Indian and Jew – *indio* and *iudio* – were identical except that the *n* and *u* were inverted!*

The debate still rages. Almost every author to write about American Indians attempts a hypothesis about their place of origin.

Most theorists assumed that the Indians came from another continent. It might have been a vanished land, such as Plato's Atlantis that sank beneath the ocean in a night and a day, or a 'Pacific continent', or Lemuria that disappeared between Africa and India, or a southern land-mass called Antartida. But most assumed that the Americans originated in the Old World. They might have been Canaanites or Phoenicians, the great voyagers of the Biblical and Classical world, or Sumerians, Babylonians or Egyptians. Torquemada thought they were Carthaginians. Diego Andrés Rocha argued in 1681 for a Spanish origin; and Walter Ralegh ventured that the name of the first Inca – Inca Manco Capac – sounded just like 'Englishman Capac'. Grotius suggested in 1642 that the Indians came from Scandinavia, and there have been many later proponents of a Norse discovery of America. All these ideas were made before the application of serious archaeology, anthropology or palaeontology to the problem. They were based on research in Classical or Biblical sources, on cultural or linguistic similarities, or on mere nationalistic pride.*

One school argued that American man was autochthonous. Others claimed that mankind had originated simultaneously in different parts of the world, including one group native to America.* The most plausible theories saw the origin of the Americans in eastern Asia, the product of migrations of Mongols, Tartars, Chinese or Polynesians. There were obvious similarities in the skin colour and facial appearance of American Indians and the Mongoloid peoples of central Asia.

Once scientific methods were applied to the problem, the eastern Asian school was vindicated. In the early twentieth century, Aleš Hrdlička of the National Museum of Washington carefully analysed all the known American fossils and took thousands of anthropometric measurements of Indians in North and South America. Hrdlička and his collaborators recorded the skin and hair colour, shapes of noses and eyes, bone lengths, and particularly the skull measurements of many different tribes.

Hrdlička elaborated a theory that is generally accepted by anthropologists. He concluded that American Indians form a single race, both in the fossil remains and in the surviving Indians. The many differences between tribes are not sufficiently great to constitute separate races. Hrdlička's 'Average American Indian' is of Mongoloid origin. It is wrong to speak of 'red skins' as opposed to Asian 'yellow' races. American man was not autochthonous, but arrived relatively recently, probably not more than ten or twenty thousand years ago. The Americans came from the northern regions of eastern Asia, presumably accompanying migrations of animals across the Bering Strait that separates Siberia and Alaska.

The sea-bed under the Bering Strait is shallow and very level. It forms a vast plain, most of which was above present sea-level during the fifty million years of the Tertiary period. It had sunk to its present depth – 180 feet below sea-level at the Strait, and sloping gently towards the south – long before man reached the area. But, during the recent Pleistocene period, glaciation during the Ice Ages lowered the earth's sea-levels by as much as 400 feet. This would have exposed an enormous area, of continental proportions, between Siberia and Alaska. There was a land-bridge of flat tundra up to 700 miles wide between Asia and North America. This land would have been most exposed in about 17,000 B.C., and submerged for the last time in about 8000 B.C.

Many animals crossed this bridge: rodents, mammoths, musk oxen, bison, moose, elk, mountain sheep and goats, camels, foxes, bears, wolves and horses. Some of these, notably horses and camels, later became extinct in the Americas. It is now known that even during the Ice Ages parts of Alaska and the Mackenzie river leading into the heart of Canada were free of glaciation. Thus for thousands of years relatively warm-weather animals could have moved eastwards into America. Early man lived where there were animals to hunt. Excavations in Alaska have unearthed large deposits of man-made stone and flint tools. It would have been natural for groups of these early Americans to move towards warmer lands in the south. None of their movements would have been conscious migrations, and yet we know, from historical migrations in Brazil itself, that tribes of hunter-gatherers can be highly mobile. One group of Tupi from the Atlantic coast migrated right across Brazil to the Andes and back to the mouth of the Amazon, during only two generations in the late sixteenth century – a journey of some three thousand miles.

According to Hrdlička, there were various waves of migration from Asia to North America. The first was by dolichocephalic – 'long-headed' – people whose skulls showed a breadth of less than three-quarters the depth from front to back. More recent migrations were by brachycephalic types – 'short-headed' people with the breadth of skull eighty per cent or more of its depth. The most recent migration was that of the Eskimos.

The migrants reached America in a primitive cultural state and evolved their cultures after arrival. This has been verified by archaeologists. In Peru, for instance, the earliest strata are of simple shell-gatherers: only later did the early Peruvians start to cultivate maize, discover pottery and evolve their skills as potters, architects and weavers.*

The only important qualification to the Mongoloid theory is that some groups of American Indians may have arrived in different migrations, from Australia, Melanesia or Indonesia. Paul Rivet, the organiser of the Musée de l'Homme in Paris, argued that there was powerful evidence for such an influx, presumably by migrations from island to island across the south Pacific. Human fossil remains from lower California and from a famous series of caves known as Lagoa Santa in the state of Minas Gerais in Brazil were very similar to the race that dominated Melanesia and Australia. There are cultural and linguistic affinities between some tribes, such as the Chon of Patagonia, with Australian natives; and there are many cultural or ethnological similarities between American Indians and the peoples of Malay–Polynesian stock.*

Brazil contributed relatively little to the archaeology of pre-Columbian America. This was because Brazilian natives made their houses and artefacts of perishable materials from the abundant wood and vegetation of the Brazilian forests. Brazilian tribes failed to evolve advanced civilisations with lasting monuments. Brazilian palaeontology and archaeology may therefore be reduced to three elements: skeletons, shell mounds and ceramics.

The fossils of Lagoa Santa Man were discovered by the Danish archaeologist Peter Wilhelm Lund in the 1830s in caves in Minas Gerais. They caused great excitement because they were alongside bones of mammals of species thought to have become extinct in the Pleistocene age. But it is now thought that the extinct mammals survived longer in South America than in the Old World. Carbon dating has also helped to establish that Lagoa Santa Man is not more than some ten thousand years old.*

The other source of early Brazilian remains is a series of enormous mounds of mollusc shells, found on the southern coasts of Brazil and on the island of Marajó in the mouth of the Amazon. These are called sambaquis, which means 'hills of shells' in Tupi-Guaraní. A typical sambaqui on the Guaraí river near Rio de Janeiro is some 160 feet long and 6 feet high; but others are taller and more conical in shape. Excavations have shown that the mounds are of natural origin: accumulations of mollusc shells heaped together by marine action. Most also contain human remains. In their upper levels they were used as kitchen middens and even burial places by ancient Brazilians. It was once thought that there was a single sambaqui culture. But it is now known that the Indians who used sambaquis were coastal members of at least four cultures that stretched far inland. Their earliest artefacts were crude stone hammers, of about 5000 B.C., found in Maratuá near Santos. Fragments of pottery appeared in sambaquis at the mouth of the Amazon in about 500 B.C.; but in southern Brazil pottery begins only about A.D. 1000, evidently at the time of the first Tupi invasions.* Pottery was essential to people living in the humid climate of the Amazon, where stone was scarcer than in southern Brazil.

The Amazon is the world's largest river in the midst of the greatest area of forest. The mighty river was easily accessible from the crescent of lands from the Andes to the Guianas and Caribbean. River tribes could rapidly move along the river and its tributaries. A series of migrations clearly took place during the prehistory of the Amazon basin.

The problem is to decide the direction of these migrations. The orthodox view is that cultures moved into the Amazon, downstream from what is now Ecuador, Colombia and Venezuela. But Donald Lathrap has argued convincingly that the early cultures spread *outwards* from the Amazon. He postulates a centre of Aruak-speaking peoples flourishing on the flood plain near the modern city of Manaus in about 3000 B.C. By 800 B.C. a new pottery style known as Barrancoid appeared along huge stretches of river banks on the lower Orinoco. The pottery surfaces were smooth, but decorated with elegant cursive geometric incision. Sometimes appliqué and modelling techniques were used to emphasise key points of the design: the centres of curves and spirals might be allowed to bulge out from the pot. Variations of this distinctive style appeared during the next thousand years at different places along the Amazon – on the Ucayali high upstream inside Peru, on the Japurá and at Manacapuru upstream of Manaus, and on sites at Itacoatiara and near the mouth of the Tapajós and Trombetas rivers on the lower Amazon. The Barrancoid style may well have spread outwards from the central Amazon.

One version of these ceramic styles flourished on Marajó, the vast flat island the size of Switzerland in the mouth of the Amazon river. The tribes of Marajó island produced an elaborate culture now called Marajoara. Its remains suggest a stratified society, ruled by a powerful dominant class and with an occupational division of labour – there were, for instance, professional potters. Marajoara was more complex than any of the later tribal societies encountered by European colonists. Over a hundred mounds have been found on Marajó and excavated, generally with little scientific skill, since the 1870s. Some were dwelling-sites and others were house foundations also used for burials. The most famous is a mound 290 feet long that rises some 13 feet above the waters of Lake Arari on Marajó island.

Marajoara pottery is almost as fine as the pottery of the Andean civilisations. The clay is light grey, but turns orange-red in firing. Vessels are covered in graceful, flowing geometric patterns, painted on to the ceramic in red, white or brown paint and generally outlined by incisions. The pottery comes in many shapes: figurines, most of which are female; jars, bowls and tripods; and great funerary urns that stand three feet above ground and are ornamented with human faces. Some of the most frequent finds are tangas – triangular vessels that curve to cover women's pubic regions. These tangas are always made of very fine clay and are smooth and thin, with holes at each corner for the cords that held them in place. Their outer curve was decorated in symmetrical patterns of great beauty.*

Farther up the Amazon there was another advanced pottery style called Santarém. Little was known about this until 1922 when a cloudburst washed away the streets of Santarém and revealed a profusion of stone tools and pottery. Fortunately, Curt Nimuendajú, the greatest of all Brazilian anthropologists, was at hand. He managed to save much of this treasure and to excavate from mounds up the Tapajós river. Some Santarém pottery is of baroque elaboration – exotic shapes covered in bird and animal ornaments, volutes, foliation and bosses.* Santarém sites are generally small with few deposits – the dwelling-places of semi-nomadic tribes – and they contain many round vessels associated with the roasting of manioc flour. Burial was by cremation, or by secondary burial with the bones placed in urns. All this corresponds with historical accounts of the Aruak tribes found in the Guianas.

A series of polychrome pottery styles appeared along the entire length of the Amazon and flourished from roughly the tenth century A.D. to the European conquest. The complex and beautiful Caimito style is echoed on sites from the Ucayali and Napo rivers of the upper Amazon, inside

Peru, all the way down to Marajó and the Gurupi on the Atlantic coast. Once again, there is debate about the direction of spread of this style. Peter Hilbert, Clifford Evans and Betty Meggers all assumed that the movement was downstream from the Napo. But Lathrap noted that the polychrome vessel shapes were very similar to those of earlier Barrancoid-style pottery. He therefore argued that this style also spread outwards from the central Amazon, possibly carried upstream by the Omagua and Cocama tribes and their ancestors.

An even later migration or invasion of the Amazon produced the Aruan phase on Marajó island. The shapes and decoration of its pottery, and its burials in large urns, show links with the natives of the Caribbean. And after the European conquest Aruan Indians tended to flee from Marajó back along the Atlantic coast towards the Guianas.

The peoples who migrated along the Amazon also spread up its tributaries, settling along all the river banks. Indian tribes are highly mobile. They can gather up their children and few household belongings and travel very rapidly. They know that the forests and rivers will always provide food and building materials for new villages. Indians have a hunter's sense of direction, and the stamina to paddle or march for days and weeks on end. The waves of migration fragmented in this way. Tribal groups scattered throughout the forests of the Amazon. They fought one another, expanded, died out, moved to fresh hunting-grounds or merged to form a kaleidoscope of slowly shifting language and tribal patterns.

The land-mass that is now Brazil was covered in native tribes at the time of the conquest, and pockets of Indians survive into the twentieth century in many inaccessible sanctuaries. Investigators have sought to rationalise the confused map of Indian tribes. The earliest observers noted differences in language and customs, different styles of housing, ornament, weapons or food. Tribes wear their hair in different ways, and physical appearances are obvious enough for the most casual observer to distinguish between tribes. Such studies became more scientific in the nineteenth century. Tribes were carefully classified by language and by anthropological features – such as the use of hammocks, ceremonies and rituals, marriage customs, methods of hunting and fishing, and every detail of their daily lives. Recent studies in physical anthropology have measured biological differences, from skull dimensions to blood groups.

The picture that emerges from these studies is very complex. But there are broad divisions and it is possible to make some generalisations. A biological classification, first made by the Argentinian José Imbelloni and now somewhat dated, recognised four main biological types living within what is now Brazil. The Laguid type, named after Lagoa Santa Man, occupies the great plateaux that lie between the headwaters of the Paraná-Plate, São Francisco and Tocantins rivers – roughly the north-east and centre-east of Brazil. Laguid people have rather long and domed skulls, low stature but well-developed chests and shoulders, broad faces and small noses, and a marked difference in height between the sexes. Most Brazilian Indians are of Amazonid type, characterised by a skull tending to be rounded, robust body with long powerful arms but short and weak legs, and skin of different tones with a yellowish base. Amazonids occupy most of the forested parts of Brazil: the Amazon, Paraguay and Paraná basins. The Fuegid type, named after Tierra del Fuego, occupies the coastal region of the south-east. Such individuals have an elongated skull with a low crown, narrow forehead, fine nose, strong arches over the eye sockets, and small lower limbs. The fourth type, Pampids (named after the Argentine Pampas), are found only in the far south and centre-south of Brazil. These are tall and well-built people, with dark skin and strong smooth hair. Their skulls tend to be elongated and voluminous, with salient cheekbones, strong chins and fine noses.*

A more accurate and acceptable classification is by language. Linguists have found that Brazilian Indians can be divided into four main language trunks or groups: Gê, Tupi, Carib and Aruak. Each language group divides into various families, in the way that in Europe the Latin and German groups could be subdivided. There are also at least a dozen language families unrelated to the four main groups.

The four main language groups should probably begin with Gê, since tribes speaking this language are of the Laguid anthropological type. They are presumably descended from Lagoa Santa Man, whose fossils are the earliest human remains found in Brazil. Gê-speaking Indians occupy the relatively open plateau and scrublands of central and eastern Brazil and tend to avoid dense forests. The Gê probably occupied the Atlantic seaboard until they were evicted by Tupi-speaking tribes during the centuries before the arrival of the Portuguese. The Tupi apparently advanced northwards and north-eastwards from the Guaraní homeland of Paraguay and eastern Bolivia. Because the Tupi occupied most of the coastline at the time of the conquest, they were the Indians best known to the Europeans and most closely observed by the early chroniclers. Spanish Jesuits later established themselves among the Guaraní of Paraguay, and the Jesuits made Tupi-Guaraní the official language of all their missions. They called it the *lingua geral* or general language.

While the Gê and Tupi were contesting occupation of southern and eastern Brazil, the endless forests of the Amazon basin had long been occupied by Carib and Aruak. The Carib-speaking tribes are related linguistically to the original inhabitants of the Caribbean, while the Aruak- or Arawak-speaking peoples form part of a great language group stretching through central America as far as Florida.

Warfare and migration have caused the four main language groups to fragment, so that isolated tribes speaking these languages may be found in remote parts of Brazil. The cluster of tribes now living on the headwaters of the Xingu river closely resemble one another in customs and social structure; and yet they include tribes speaking each of the main languages, as well as two tribes using distinct isolated tongues. There are a number of such unrelated languages among the Brazilian Indians. In the forests of the western frontier adjoining Venezuela, Colombia and Peru are tribes speaking Xirianá, Makú, Tukano and Pano; while on the south-western frontiers with Bolivia and Paraguay are Indians speaking Txapakura, Nambikwara, Guató and Guaikuru – all languages apparently unrelated to the four more common language groups.*

White colonists and scientists have thus evolved theories on the origins of American natives. But what of the Indians' own views? Contrary to the early European notion that the Indians had no faith, each tribe was enveloped in a tapestry of legends, myths, ceremonies and spiritual beliefs. Far from being without beliefs, Indian societies were governed by the spirit world. Almost every ceremony, whether related to the agricultural calendar, hunting, warfare, or the life-cycle, was steeped in spiritual meaning. Every tribe had shamans to interpret the supernatural world, and to heal through the patient's faith in their special powers. Tribal elders loved to narrate the legends of their ancestors. They made decisions by interpreting portents or by divination. And each individual Indian was obsessed with superstitions, alternately buoyed up or terrified by the spirits that infested the forest or were incarnated in animals or members of their tribe, living and dead.

The chronicler who did most to record Tupinambá beliefs and legends was the French Franciscan André Thevet, who was at Guanabara from 1555 to 1556. 'The first awareness that these savages have of what surpasses the earth is of one whom they call Monan, to whom they attribute the same perfections that we do to God. They say that he is without end or beginning, being of all time, and that it was he who created the sky, the earth and the birds and animals that are in them. They do not, however, mention the sea, born of Aman Atoupave, which means "Showers of Water" in their language. They say that the sea was caused by an accident that happened on earth, which was previously united and flat, with no mountains whatsoever, producing all things for the use of mankind.' This Monan was a culture hero and not strictly a god, since he was not worshipped.

The Tupinambá legend was that early men abandoned themselves to pleasure and 'fell into such great folly that they began to despise Monan. . . . Monan saw the ingratitude of men and their disdain of him: he who had been so bounteous towards them [therefore] abandoned them. He then caused the descent of Tatá, the fire from heaven, which burned and consumed all that was on the face of the earth, and [caused it to crumple into valleys and mountains].' One man alone was saved: Irin-Magé, whom Monan took to heaven to escape the fury of the fire. 'Seeing everything destroyed, Irin-Magé addressed Monan, saying to him with tears and sighs: "Do you also wish to destroy the skies and their ornament? Hey, and where will our home be now? On what will I live, having no being similar to myself?" Monan was moved to compassion by these words. Wishing to remedy the harm he had done to earth because of the sins of men, he caused it to rain in such abundance that all the fire was extinguished.' Unable to return to heaven, the waters accumulated to form the ocean, which became saline from the salt of the fire's ashes. 'When Monan saw that the earth was restored to its first beauty, and that the sea embellished and surrounded it . . . he summoned Irin-Magé and gave him a wife, so that he might repeople the earth with better men.'

From Irin-Magé came a great caraíba (hero, or 'prophet') called Maira-Monan. Thevet called him the 'Transformer', because Maira-Monan changed all the animals into their species. He was a great medicine-man who lived in seclusion, and it was he who taught his descendants the essential skills: the use of fire and agriculture. In one legend, he changed himself into a child who, when beaten, dropped fruits, manioc and other tubers into the ground. In another tradition, Maira-Monan initiated a young girl into the secrets of agriculture. It was he who introduced social organisation to mankind, and imposed severe taboos and penalties on non-conformists.

Mankind began to fear this Maira-Monan, suspecting that he planned to turn them all into animals. They decided to kill this great pagé or shaman. He was invited to a hostile village and challenged to prove his supernatural powers by passing through three lighted fires. He passed the first, but fainted in the second. 'No sooner had he set foot in it than he was enveloped in fire and flame, and was instantly burned and consumed. They say, however, that this did not occur without a miracle. For his head burst, with such great explosion and hideous noise that the sound mounted to heaven, and to Tupan [spirit of thunder]. They say that this engendered thunder, and that the lightning that precedes the thunder-clap is simply the manifestation of the fire by which this Maira was consumed.'

Most present-day Indians call white people caraíba, the word for prophet. Monan meant an elder. And mair was the sixteenth-century word for Europeans, and particularly for the French. 'Any men who did something greater or more marvellous than the rest were generally called Maira, as heirs and successors of Maira-Monan. . . . Therefore, when they see that we know how to make more things than they, and that our skills seem to them admirable, they say that we are the successors and true children of Maira-Monan, and that his true race moved to our lands. They were deprived of it because of the flood and because they were wicked towards the second Maira-Monan.'

Another name for this great caraíba or pagé was Sumé. Thevet said that Sumé was a descendant of Maira-Monan, but other chroniclers spoke only of Sumé, the originator of agriculture and clearly the same culture hero. This seemed to Nóbrega and other missionaries confirmation that St Thomas had indeed visited Brazil and instructed its ungrateful people.*

Sumé or Maira-Monan had two sons, Tamendonar and Arikut. The many legends that surround these sons form a twin-cycle, so common throughout South American mythology and reminiscent of the Biblical Cain and Abel. There are many variations of these legends. Some involve meetings with animals, Jaguar and Opossum, who behave as men, ruling villages, fighting wars or sleeping with Maira-Monan's wife. In one legend the twins search for their father, who insists on a trial of strength before he will acknowledge them. One has to shoot arrows into the sky, so fast and accurately that each will pierce the butt of another, forming a long chain. In another ordeal the brothers pass between clashing rocks: one brother is crushed, but brought to life again by his twin. In another legend, the peaceful brother Tamendonar is insulted when Arikut throws the arm of a half-eaten victim at him. Tamendonar causes a spring to flow, so profusely that its waters flood the earth. But the brothers escape to repopulate mankind. André Thevet also told a story that is still popular among many South American tribes. It involved the evil brother, Maira-pochy ('Bad Maira'), a powerful shaman who appeared in a village disguised as a dirty, impoverished old man. He made the chief's daughter pregnant by giving her a fish. Her child later rejected all the warriors who claimed to be its father, and handed the aged Maira-pochy a bow and arrows to identify him as its parent.

These are a few of the best-known origin-myths of the Tupinambá. Every tribe in Brazil has similar legends about all the elements in its environment. These stories are told in the tribal councils, when the men sit around the fire or in the men's hut in the evenings, on canoe trips or hunting expeditions, and they are passed on from parents to children. Some legends inspired awe and almost formed the basis of a religious canon; others were simply good stories, taken no more seriously than that of Jonah and the whale by Christians.

A secondary figure in the early mythology was Tupan, demon of thunder, lightning and rain. The first missionaries evidently sought to identify their creator God with the roar of thunder. When the Indians told them that thunder was called Tupan, they adopted this name as the Tupi for God. Nóbrega, the leader of the first Jesuits, admitted that 'we have no other term more suitable for bringing them to an understanding of God than to call Him "Pai-Tupan".'

When the missionaries sought a native equivalent to the Christian devil, they had no difficulty. The Tupi were convinced that they were surrounded by supernatural powers. Many spirits or demons lurked in the darkest parts of the forest and were generally malevolent. These ghostly forces frightened the Indians, who often complained of being attacked or tormented by them. They caused diseases, droughts, floods and defeats. Some took the form of strange birds, bats or salamanders. 'This miserable people is often afflicted by several fantastic illusions and persecuted by the malignant spirit, which they perceive in various forms. It appears to them and chastises them beyond measure . . . keeping them so blinded that it torments their bodies both night and day. . . . When we were there we sometimes heard them cry out most terribly during the night, calling on us for help, saying in their language: "Can't you see . . . Anhan (their name for the malign spirit) who is beating and tormenting me? Defend me, if you wish me to serve you and cut wood for you!" . . . This is why these poor savages do not dare to emerge from their huts at night without torches: for, if they suddenly feel themselves beaten, fire is the sovereign remedy and defence against their enemy.' This Anhan was known as Jurupari among the Tupi of the northern coasts. He was an ogre or goblin that haunted the recesses of the forest. Whenever accidents happened to Indians in the forests they blamed Anhan or Jurupari. The missionaries adopted Anhan or Jurupari as their names for the Devil.

Missionaries were also eager to explore any Indian concepts of the after-life. Most tribes had a generalised fear of ghosts. The French Capuchin Yves d'Evreux wrote that Jurupari was a malicious being who inhabited abandoned villages and 'especially places where the bodies of their ancestors are buried'. The dead were believed to send messages by a species of cuckoo called *Matim tapirera*, whose name has been transformed into Sacipereré among people living along the Amazon today: its sonorous but piercing and repeated call seemed an incantation of the spirits. One nineteenth-century anthropologist recorded a rich series of legends about the Saci among Amazonian caboclos. Its haunting call sounds to Brazilians like 'sem-fin' ('without end').*

So great was the Indians' awe of the many spirits that they could easily be beguiled into suicidal migrations – crusading pilgrimages in search of a promised land. Chief Iacoupen of the Maranhão Caeté blamed evil spirits for the failure of one such messianic movement. He told Yves d'Evreux: 'I am reminded of the cruelty of Jurupari towards our nation. For he made us all die, and persuaded our shamans to lead us into the midst of an unknown forest, where we danced incessantly. We had nothing to eat but palm hearts and game, so that several died of weakness and debility. When we emerged from there . . . Jurupari prepared another ambush for us, inciting the Tupinambá, through a Frenchman, to massacre and eat several of our people. Had you Fathers not come, they would have finished by killing us all.'

There were many other spirits, just as there were innumerable legends. There was Corupira, another forest demon who protected game and was no friend of men: he hovered near the crossings of jungle trails, and would attack hunters who abused animals. Corupira was depicted as a gnome with upturned feet: the Europeans identified him with their medieval legends of people whose feet pointed backwards. Corupira is still alive in the folklore of the Brazilian interior. He is also known as Caapora or Caaguera ('Forest Dweller'), lord of the secrets of the forest. He sometimes deluded Indians, appearing to them in inoffensive disguises and asking for some simple service such as tobacco for his pipe: if refused, he thrashed the wretch who had failed to recognise him. There was also Macachera, a spirit who marched in front of travellers. The Potiguar considered Macachera as the messenger of all good news, whereas for the Tupinambá he was the enemy of human health. Upupiara was the spirit of the waters, and his name has contracted in modern folklore to Iara, the mother of water, who corresponds to Yemanjá of the African slaves imported into Brazil. The Tupinambá had a generic name for all water spirits. They called them Baetatá, and this has survived as the word for marsh fire, the will-o'-the-wisp or phosphorescence that appears in swamps and cemeteries. Transformed into Mboitatá, the same Tupinambá word, linked to the African root *mboi*, signifies the Fire Serpent, part of the Amazonian cycle of legends about a Giant Snake.

These and many more legends of spirits were handed down from generation to generation. Individuals told about their vivid experiences with the spirit world, and the myths were enacted and recounted in each village's men's hut. The Tupinambá religion was not as formalised as Christianity. But belief in the powers of the spirits was just as real as the superstitions and religious convictions of the Europeans.

The interpreters of the supernatural were the shamans or pagés. All chiefs and the old men and women of each tribe had some knowledge of magic. But only those who had demonstrated unusual powers were revered as true shamans: their reputations depended on the accuracy of their predictions and the success of their cures. The greatest pagés were known as caraíba ('prophets') or pagé-guaçu ('great medicine men').

'Our savages, devoid of all reason and abused by their pagés just as much as they are afflicted by [the spirit] Anhan, are intrigued by their dreams. They believe that what they dream will take place without fail. Thus, if they dream that they will defeat their enemies or will themselves succumb in battle, it is impossible to remove such fantasies from their heads. They regard them as fate which cannot happen otherwise.' As we have seen, Hans Staden, the German gunner captured by the Tupinambá, saved himself from ritual execution by the accuracy of his predictions: the tribe that had intended to eat him came to respect him as its greatest pagé.

'They are nourished in this folly by the pagés, whom they regard as men who never stray from the truth. They hold them in such esteem that those who are in the pagés' good graces, or who can make them some present, regard themselves as most fortunate.' 'There is no village where the people do not feed one or two of these caraíba, and honour them so greatly that they pray to them in their affliction. But, if a sick person develops differently from the pagé's prediction, it is certain that this prophet will be killed, as unworthy of the title and dignity of such a name.'

André Thevet described the ritual surrounding a pagé's predictions. 'Should something important happen, whose outcome they wish to know, these prophets practise certain invocations and ceremonies. . . . They first construct a new hut in which no man has ever lived, and suspend in it a [hammock] of clean white cotton. . . . They bring a great quantity of food into this hut – such as cauin, which is their usual drink, and manioc flour that they use as bread. When these arrangements are ready, the caraíba is solemnly led into the hut by the people. Before entering, he must have abstained from his wife for nine days; and as he enters he has to be washed by a virgin girl. Once he is in the chamber of mysteries, the people withdraw. He then lies prone on the prepared bed. He makes a thousand grimaces and invokes the spirit, which they call by its proper name Uiulsira, for some length of time. The spirit then comes to him, whistling and fluting, as the savages themselves describe it. Some of them have told me that Uiulsira often arrives when the people are still present – not that they see him, but rather hear some noise and howling. This poor deluded people then cry out in a most horrible voice, saying: "We beg you, please tell the truth to our pagé who is awaiting you in there!"' The Tupinambá were naturally most interested in predictions about the outcome of their battles. 'Whatever it may be, these savages do nothing without having had a reply from their prophet. When he has finished the mystery of these invocations, he emerges from the hut, all bewildered, as if transported from his senses. He is immediately surrounded by all the people, to whom he declares what he has heard from the gentle spirit Uiulsira – not without being caressed in every possible way by these foolish people, each of whom gives him whatever present he can afford, as if he had worked hard and done his duty.'

'After these caraíbas and pagés have done all these monkey tricks and foolery with the simple people, they spend two or three days in constant cauin-drinking and dancing with nut-rattles [on their legs], richly adorned in robes covered in natural feathers of diverse colours, and holding in their hands one or two maracá rattles, made of [gourd] fruits, oval in shape like ostrich eggs and as large as an average pumpkin. . . .' Maracá rattles have always been an essential part of Tupi ceremonial. Gourds would be painted or dyed, decorated with tufts of feathers, filled with pebbles and fitted with wooden handles. Pagés shook their maracás rhythmically, in time to the beat of the dance. And when they stamped their feet they rattled the bands of ahouai nuts tied round their ankles. These triangular fruits – now known as 'Napoleon's hats' – contain a stone that is highly poisonous. The pagés used ahouai poison, for 'these venerables act as murderers among this people. If some quarrel arises between neighbours, one approaches these pagés in order that they will make those who are detested die of poison.' 'And when the shells of the [ahouai] fruit are dried they make bells of them, which they wear on their legs, and which rattle briskly. . . . Men and women use them when they hold their cauin revels and their massacres – so much that you would sometimes not hear it thunder when they are dancing, accompanied by their various forms of instrument. And I myself', boasted Thevet, 'have a fine collection of these good bells in my cabinet, with some of their swords, and also various sorts of plucked birds' skins.' Thevet's book contains a woodcut of a pagé dancing, with his maracás and ahouai anklets; but he is shown prancing, hand on hip like a French courtier, not stamping, head forward, like a true Tupinambá shaman (Plate 4).

Yves d'Evreux wrote that pagés 'occupy among the savages the place of mediators between the spirits and the rest of the people'. Luís Figueira, a Jesuit who lived with the Tobajara of the Ibiapaba hills in northern Brazil, described some of the pagés' powers in protecting their people from the ever-present spirit world. 'One night, suddenly, we heard hands clapping in one hut, then in another, and then generally in all of them with a great din. We asked what that was. They answered that a sorcerer had heard the voice of a snake that came flying through the air: by clapping his hands in that way, he was giving a signal that they should all be alert, so that it would not fall upon someone and bite them.' 'They greatly fear that the sky will fall upon them. To prevent this disaster, some of them, when they awake in the morning, get up and brace their legs on the ground, with both hands towards the sky to support it with their hands so that it will not fall. They believe that in this way it will be all right throughout the day.'

'They are also greatly tormented by a fear that the land will open and the sea will flood them. The sorcerers among them frequently converse with the devil. He talks to them by night, in the dark. But they do not see him: they hear him, and give him tobacco to inhale. They can see the smoke in the air, but do not see who has it; they do, however, see the puffs he emits. He tells them some truth surrounded by many lies; and when they are going hunting he tells them where they will find game and where there is wild honey.'

Apart from divination, a shaman's reputation depended on his medical ability. He was the tribe's medicine-man, expected to cure the sick or at least predict the outcome of their illnesses. Pagés knew the properties of medicinal herbs, as did most Indians. But the pagé's usual method was by faith-healing. Indians believed that the shaman's breath was loaded with magical powers, especially when reinforced with the smoke of petun tobacco. By blowing on a patient, amid incantations, a pagé could transmit his own powers and virtues; and by sucking he could extract the cause of the ailment. Luís Figueira said that 'when we were in our hut one night we heard someone coughing to great effect and spitting, trying to vomit, and making a great racket. We sent to learn what it was. They came to tell us that it was a sick child and a witch-doctor who was curing him. The cure was to suck him in their usual way, [with the pagé] claiming that he was extracting the evil from within him. To heighten the pretence of the deception, they place a nail or similar object in their mouths, and with their spitting they pretend that they have sucked it and extracted it from the sick person, and that it was this which was causing him harm.' This was the classical ritual for faith-healing. I myself have seen pagés in action among widely different modern tribes, from the Canela of Maranhão to the Bororo of Mato

Grosso and the Yamomami of Roraima, and their ministrations follow similar patterns.

Faith-healing is still an important part of Brazilian life. Its devotees are numbered in millions, from the blacks and mestizos of the northeast to senior army officers. The weekly picture magazine *O Cruzeiro* specialises in stories about faith-healers, curandeiros, whose rallies attract immense crowds and who achieve spectacular cures if a patient's faith is sufficiently strong.

The pagés' breath and smoke were used to consecrate maracá rattles. Each Indian would bring his maracá, painted and adorned with feathers, for the pagé to pass before his mouth, blowing tobacco over it and conversing with the spirit within the gourd. Warriors received a similar blessing. The pagé would blow smoke over a warrior and exclaim: 'Receive the force of the spirit, so that you will overcome your enemies!'

These magical powers gave pagés the authority to enforce conformity in the tribe. The harmony and tranquillity that so enchanted foreign observers might conceal tensions and passions within the small tribal society. The success of a hunting community, constantly at war with its neighbours, depended on rigid conformity to established customs. The rules were easy enough. But anyone who was too eccentric and troublesome might find himself branded as an evil influence, a malignant sorcerer. Any disaster, such as the death of a chief's son, might be blamed on an unpopular nonconformist. The pagé could then pronounce a verbal condemnation. Gabriel Soares de Sousa wrote that the pagé would tell a transgressor: 'Go, for you must die!' The victim knew that nothing could save him or her. He would lie down in his hammock and refuse all further food. He would soon die of the fast, or be sewn up and buried half-alive in his hammock. Such rough justice, based on magical fears, is still a powerful force in many tribes.

So great was a tribe's faith in its pagés that entire villages would sometimes follow a spiritual leader in a disastrous messianic migration. 'There sometimes arises among them a sorcerer . . . who is usually some Indian of rotten life. This man performs some witchcraft and strange rituals in their manner – such as showing that he can revive a living person who made himself dead. With this and similar demonstrations, he leads them all behind him into the wilderness, deceiving them and telling them not to make clearings or plant their vegetables and food, or dig, or work, etc. For, with his arrival, a time has come when hoes will dig by themselves and baskets will go to the clearings and bring back food. With such falsehoods he leads them off, intoxicated and bewitched, ceasing to care for their lives or farm their foods. And so these congregations move onwards, dying of sheer hunger and slowly disintegrating, until the holy man is left alone or they kill him.'

Calm manners and gentle behaviour have always been the ideal among the Tupi: any outburst of anger was abhorred. People shunned temperamental persons. 'And if someone commits some cowardly or mean act they vituperate him for ever; just as they always praise the virtue and magnanimity of the most excellent of their ancestors.'

Pagés were often the chiefs of their tribes, but not necessarily. The chief of Tapuitapera told Yves d'Evreux: 'My witchcraft contributed less than the courage I have often demonstrated in battle to win the position I occupy.' Other chiefs were not pagés, and might even quarrel with them. A chief acquired his rank from military prowess, oratorical gifts, magical powers and wealth in wives and captive slaves. Gabriel Soares de Sousa said that 'a chief must be a man of courage. He has to belong to a large family and to be well liked by its members, so that they will be willing to help cultivate his plantations. But even when he opens a clearing with the help of his relatives he is the first to put his hand to the task.' A chief came into his own in wartime, when his authority was undisputed. This was why he was 'the most valiant captain, he who had done the greatest number of feats in battle, who had massacred the greatest number of enemies, who possessed the greatest number of wives, largest family and most slaves acquired by his personal valour'.

In peacetime the chief had few special powers and received no tribute. He was simply a leading member of the village council of elders. These met every evening to discuss the tribe's affairs. They sat outside the men's hut smoking evil-smelling yellow cheroots. 'And before undertaking some enterprise of great consequence, whether for war or otherwise, they hold an assembly of the oldest and wisest men, at which women and children are not permitted to attend. They call the old men morbicha. You would say that some of these lords were councillors of the Senate of Venice, for they show so much gravity and decorum in their consultations. You would never hear a confused cry by prattlers: for only one speaks at a time, with the grace and respect of the others. Each listens diligently to him. When he has spoken, another takes his place and says his opinion. The listeners are seated on the ground, except for some who, from pre-eminence of age or valour, are lying in their hammocks.'

The morbicha had little to show for their rank. They were naked like the rest of the tribe. All men had their body hair and eyebrows removed and the tops of their heads shaved like monks' tonsures. 'They say that if they had their hair long in front and wore a beard, they might be seized and captured by these if they fell into the hands of their enemies; and also that [their removal] gives them more strength and endurance. If their body hair grows, the women remove the men's with a certain reed-like grass that cuts like a razor. . . . As for the pubic hair, they pluck it reciprocally from one another . . . and the women pluck the men's beards.'

Tupinambá men also pierced their lower lips. As boys they wore seashells protruding from the holes. But when they reached a marriageable age they inserted finely polished plugs of green jadeite – precious objects passed from tribe to tribe in a complex chain of trading. André Thevet was fascinated by these lip plugs. 'These savages disfigure themselves with these stones, and delight and glory in them as much as Europeans who wear great chains of gold round their necks and precious jewels on their fingers. He who wears the greatest number and the most beautiful stones is as esteemed by the others as if he had the title of king or lord. Such men wear them not only in their lips, but also on both sides of their cheeks. These stones are sometimes as wide as – or wider than – a German thaler, and as thick as a good finger's breadth. This impedes their speech so much that it is as difficult to understand them as someone with his mouth full of flour. These stones and their cavities sometimes makes the mouths of these brutes thick as a fist. When the stone is removed and they want to speak, you see the saliva pour out of this hole, a most hideous thing to see. And if these barbarians wish to mock one another they push their tongues through there, like someone extracting a hog's tongue.'

Both sexes wore necklaces of shells as white as ivory, and ear or neck pendants of crescent-shaped fish-bones. Otherwise the women's ornaments were less exotic than the men's: they plucked but did not pierce their bodies, and let their shining black hair fall straight down their backs. They combed their hair frequently, with combs made from the spikes of a fruit tree; washed it in suds from the skins of another fruit; and, when working, tied it in two bundles held by cotton fillets.

Tupinambá warriors were tattooed with a scarred stripe for every enemy they had killed. The wound was made with a tooth or shell, and the mark fixed with charcoal or plant dyes. But the favourite body decoration of both sexes was painting with black genipapo or scarlet urucum. These vegetable-dyes stained the skin for a week or two, and their renewal was a cosmetic so elaborate that it became an art form. 'The women paint their men, and make a thousand delights on their bodies, such as figures of birds or waves of the sea . . . and the women paint their own legs, so that seen from a distance you would think that they were dressed in very fine black worsted stockings. . . .' Pero Vaz de

Caminha had been struck by the handsome black and red quarterings on the naked bodies of the first Indians he saw.

Brazil contains almost as many species of bird as the rest of the world combined. The Indians gloried in this profusion of brilliant plumage. There was every size and colour of feather: long red and blue macaw plumes, gleaming black feathers from the mutum wild turkey or anú cuckoo, scarlet from the guara ibis, reds, yellows and blacks from the toucan, bright yellows, greys and greens from the parrot and parakeet, tiny iridescents from the humming-bird, tawny browns from the various falcons and hawks, smoky blue from the kingfisher, lacy feathers from the siriema secretary-bird, and brilliant white plumes from the egret. Every Indian carries an arrow with a blunt head for stunning birds. I have often seen birds shot for their plumage, and the feathers eagerly plucked as soon as the bird falls. Many Indian villages have caged harpy eagles as their guardians. Others have half-plucked macaws and parakeets hopping about with their wings clipped, kept as pets for the feathers they produce.

The Tupinambá made many dazzling feather ornaments. The men wore high head-dresses of parrots' tail-feathers. There were bonnets of small feathers fastened into a cotton net, fixed together so finely that the fabric resembled velvet. Some of these bonnets had a fan of long plumes over the nape of the wearer's neck. There were delicate necklaces and fluffy anklets or armbands made of bright feathers. A few colourful feathers were used to decorate bows and arrows, clubs, maracá rattles or women's girdles. The most spectacular ornaments were broad, long cloaks entirely covered in scarlet ibis feathers. Such was the love of feathers that men and women glued them directly to their heads, or smeared their entire bodies with gum and sprinkled themselves with chopped feathers. At their most solemn ceremonies a Tupinambá would fasten a great circle of ostrich plumes at the small of his back.

All these head-dresses and diadems were carefully stored after use. A person's wealth consisted of his collection of feather ornaments. Men and women generally made their own featherwork, just as each individual made almost everything else he or she used. Artistic invention and manual dexterity were lavished on these handicrafts. Indians, who were themselves so creative and self-sufficient, marvelled at the splendid objects brought by the Europeans. But they could not understand how such clumsy people, such inept hunters, could have made themselves such fine possessions. Europeans loved to collect Indian head-dresses. Cabral's sailors sent some back to Portugal in 1500, and André Thevet said: 'I brought to France a rich and very handsome bonnet of this plumage. I presented it to the late King Henry II, as a rare and singular object, deserving admiration for the delicacy of the work-manship. These savages had made the feathered fabric so daintily with their fillet of barkwood that in Europe it could scarcely be better if made entirely of silk thread.'

The Indians also demonstrated their virtuosity in building stockaded villages. The thatch of the Tupinambá long-houses was mounted on an elaborate tracery of wooden beams and joists. The Cornishman Peter Carder described one village as 'built four square, with foure houses onely, every house containing above two bowe shot in length, and the houses made with small trees like an Arbour, being thatched over downe to the ground with palme tree leaves'. There were low doors at each end of these long-huts, and occasional other doors in the sides. Each hut contained thirty or more families, with their hammocks suspended from rows of wooden pillars. There was an open passage along the centre of the hut, but no partitions between the family areas.

Many chroniclers marvelled at the harmony within each hut, despite this total lack of privacy. Fernão Cardim wrote that 'two or three hundred people live inside, with each married couple in its section with no partitions of any kind . . . and all in view of one another. Since there are many people they generally have fires burning day and night, summer and winter: for fire is their clothing and without fire they are very wretched. The house seems like an inferno or labyrinth. Some are singing, others crying, others eating, others making manioc flour, wine, etc., and the entire hut is full of burning fires. Yet there is such conformity among them that there is never a quarrel all year long; and, since they have nothing locked, there are no thefts. No other nation could live like this without many quarrels, disagreements and even deaths – none of which happens among them.' Magalhães de Gandavo confirmed this: 'They are . . . in rows, with an open passage along the middle of the house, like the gangway in a galley, used by everybody to go to their sleeping-quarters. All live together in harmony in each house, with no dissension among them. They are so friendly to one another that what belongs to one belongs to all. When one has something to eat, no matter how small, all his neighbours share it.' Most chroniclers praised the calm and tranquillity within a Tupi long-house, or maloca. But one Jesuit, António Blásques, was less tolerant: to him they were 'dark, smelly and smoky houses', with some of the Indians inside 'laughing, others crying so persistently that they can spend a night at this without anyone stopping them. Their beds are hammocks, rotted with urine because they are so lazy that they are reluctant to get up at the call of nature.' My own experience of sleeping in Indian huts has been good: there is the cool and gloom of a cathedral, an agreeably exotic smell of wood-smoke and vegetable-dyes, and great calm – for Indians talk gently, the children are quiet, and there are few objects that can make a noise on the earth floor.

The entire village was a temporary place. It would be moved every few years, when the soil of the surrounding clearings began to be exhausted and the thatch became infested with ticks and fleas. The dry thatch burns very easily. It is quite common to see the charred remains of a maloca in an Indian village: one that caught fire from a stray spark, a cooking accident, or a child playing with fire. There were few possessions inside the huts – only hammocks, some gourds and cooking-pots, wooden stools, and wooden chests containing each person's bead, shell and feather ornaments. When a village was moved, the inhabitants took these belongings and the roof beams of their huts. And when the tribe went to war the Indians carried their hammocks and removed their possessions as a precaution against the village being burned in battle.

The Tupinambá village was thus a simple, transient home for people who lived in communal harmony with few possessions or cares. This was the vision that inspired the theories of the noble savage. But it concealed a more complex society, with elaborate rules of conduct and kinship, a rich mythology and ceremonial calendar, constant fears of enemy attack and spirit magic, and artistic expression in pottery, ornaments and architecture.

FOUR

The First Colonies

MARTÍM AFONSO DE SOUSA founded the first permanent Portuguese colony in Brazil on the island of São Vicente, near the modern port of Santos, in early 1532. Between 1534 and 1536 King João III divided the entire coast of Brazil into fourteen hereditary captaincies. The casual trading of the first third of the century now changed into permanent colonisation.

The coastal tribes soon became aware of the change. The godlike strangers with wonderful metal tools assumed a different aspect. They revealed themselves as uncouth invaders who were generally brutal, greedy and licentious. They violated all the codes of Indian behaviour, scorned tribal customs, abused hospitality and attacked Indian beliefs. They had arrived to occupy the land of Brazil, and were interested in its native men only as labourers and women as concubines.

The Tupi were warrior tribes, and the honourable course for them was to fight, to try to drive the invaders back into the sea. Warfare broke out all along the coast of Brazil, fragmentary and disjointed because the Indian tribes themselves were so divided and because the Portuguese and French formed alliances with rival tribes and incited them against one another. Most tribes were still obsessed with myopic hatreds of traditional enemies and often regarded the Europeans as useful allies rather than potential invaders.

These early struggles are worth examining. They illustrate the different situations that arose between the European colonists and

A battle between European ships and Indian canoes.

native peoples during the mid-sixteenth century. No two are quite alike. Each conflict depended on the personalities of the colonists, the attitudes of individual tribes, geographical conditions, and the fortunes of war.

The coast of Brazil is so immense that these colonial wars were separated by hundreds of miles of virgin forest. Pockets of settlers established their beachheads at places where brazilwood had been plentiful or sugar plantations seemed possible, where there was an anchorage, where the Indians were friendly or where an energetic donatory was prepared to spend his fortune financing a colony. The isolated colonies communicated with one another only by sea, and voyages along the coasts were dependent on prevailing winds and currents.

The coast of Brazil divides into two main regions. On the north-eastern bulge, from Paraíba to Espírito Santo, the land is flat and the nearest hills are a hundred miles or more inland. Sluggish brown rivers meander across the coastal plain, which at that time was forested and watered by abundant tropical rainfalls. All the early explorers described Brazil as a land of many trees. A belt of luxuriant tropical forest ran along the Atlantic seaboard, from São Paulo in the south to Pernambuco and Rio Grande in the north-east. This Zona da Mata ('Forest Zone') was only about fifty miles wide, and it was rapidly destroyed in the northern captaincies. Brazilwood trees were ruthlessly cut down for their dyes. Other woodlands were cleared to make way for sugar plantations, and the surviving trees were demolished to provide fuel for the molasses ovens. The shores are often sandy dunes protected by reefs, so that anchorages tended to be in river estuaries or the few bays and inlets. Sea breezes mitigate the tropical humidity. This part of Brazil is hot and dry and it proved to be perfect for sugar plantations.

Farther south, the hills run right along the coast. The scenery is more spectacular, with granite cliffs dropping sheer into the Atlantic. The coastal hills and thousands of islands are covered in luxuriant forests. There are feathery palms and garlands of creepers and mosses. For much of the year the jungles and beaches contrast with the tropical sea in the bright green, gold and blue of the Brazilian flag. At other times there are violent electrical storms and torrential rain, and the forested hills are shrouded in sea mists. No rivers are navigable, and settlers had to climb out of the narrow shore valley, over the coastal hills and on to the plateau beyond. Once across the hills, the colonists found the land sloping endlessly westwards towards the Paraná–Paraguay basin. It was cut by rivers full of rapids. The climate was more temperate, but the land was still covered by forest or immense stretches of mato – low dry woods – and campo – scrubland, with gnarled trees standing amid coarse grass and tall pink termite hills: desolate boring country that looks like an orchard struck by drought, overgrown and sadly abandoned.

All the chroniclers were struck by Brazil's forests. Pero de Magalhães de Gandavo wrote: 'This land is very fertile and luxuriant, all covered in very tall and leafy trees. The greenery remains during winter and summer. This causes it to rain often, and there is no cold to damage what the land produces. Beneath these forests there is great and very abundant undergrowth, and it is so dark and dense in places that the ground never feels the heat or light of the sun. It is thus constantly humid, producing water of its own accord.'

The northernmost of the new captaincies lay to the east of the mouth of the Amazon, in what is now the state of Maranhão. The King awarded this area to a historian, the erudite João de Barros. He formed a partnership with one of the richest Indian spice merchants, Aires da Cunha, and they assembled a mighty expedition. It contained 900 men, of whom 130 were knights with their horses, and was well armed with mortars and other firearms. The expedition was a disaster. Its ships were wrecked on the treacherous coast of Maranhão. Aires da Cunha drowned, and only a few of his men struggled ashore near the modern city of São Luís. These soldiers were veterans of wars in India, and they treated the Brazilian tribes with brutality and scorn, respecting neither their customs nor their possessions. French Normans also incited the local tribes against the Portuguese. The result was an attack that destroyed or evicted the survivors of Barros' expedition. João de Barros' sons tried to organise a relief expedition, by land and sea, in 1554, but was also repulsed and defeated.

The 'East–West Coast' that stretches for some 900 miles from the Amazon to the easternmost tip of South America was abandoned by Portuguese colonists after these failures. French traders and sailors moved in vigorously. The Portuguese settler Gabriel Soares de Sousa wrote in 1587 that many Frenchmen preferred to live there like heathen, surrounded by native women, than to return to France. 'These today have many descendants who are blond, milk-white and freckled, children borne by Tupinambá women.'

The north-eastern tip of Brazil was occupied by the most powerful and populous of all the Tupi tribes – the Potiguar, 'the largest and most warlike heathen in Brazil'. Their name meant 'Shrimp-eaters', for this tribe ate great quantities of shellfish. An English sailor, Anthony Knivet, found the Potiguar more civilised than other tribes, with large, settled villages. 'If you come as a Merchant unto them they will trafficke with you, if as a Warrier, they will fight very valiantly.'

The French wooed the Potiguar with boatloads of trade goods, for the brazilwood on the Paraíba river was of excellent quality, and the Indians were 'jolly and approachable fellows, people who take great trouble when they work for the merchants. They have the stamina to carry the wood on their necks for five or six long leagues' distance from the sea.' Their French alliance made the Potiguar enemies of the Portuguese, who were frustrated by their numbers and cohesion. They were not as fragmented as other Indian nations, and could not be provoked into internecine wars. 'This is the way in which we Portuguese contrive many fights in which tribes quarrel with one another. With this ruse we enter and defeat them. If all united we could do nothing with them and could not dominate them. This trick is of no use with the Potiguar . . . who are completely united and in harmony with one another.'

The Portuguese had a captaincy on the island of Itamaracá that started on good terms with the Potiguar. But relations soon deteriorated. The donatory was the chronicler Pero Lopes de Sousa, who neglected his grant and left it to be managed by agents. The colony was soon reduced to a precarious settlement at the southern end of the island, with the sea and mainland controlled by the Potiguar and French.† This change was the fault of the colonists, who antagonised the Potiguar with slave raids along their coast in the 1540s. The result was half a century of fierce fighting in which the Potiguar, armed and advised by the French, were generally victorious.*

Just south of Itamaracá and the Potiguar territory was the captaincy of Pernambuco, which rapidly became the most successful and richest of the colonies. This was New Lusitania, full of brazilwood and with flat fertile lands perfect for growing sugar-cane. It fell to the most energetic donatory, Duarte Coelho, who 'built a tower of stone and lime on a height where the town of Olinda now stands. Many lives were lost and he spent many thousands of cruzados he had acquired in India defending it against the Indians and French and clearing the coast, which was infested by Caeté.' Coelho started by using Indian labour to build a sugar mill and a settlement called Igaraçu. The Indians used to enter the town freely to trade with the settlers. One of the products they received was European alcohol, more potent than their own brews, and during one drinking session a quarrel broke out among the Indians. Coelho sent armed men to break up the disturbance; but the Indians resisted — 'they were always afraid of the whites, and concerned that they were going to seize and enslave them'. In the struggle a chief's son was killed, and his smashed skull was sent from village to village to recruit warriors for battle.

For two years the Caeté and Tupinambá besieged Igaraçu. They killed its commander Afonso Gonçalves with an arrow through the eye. 'Even the [Portuguese] women stood watch inside the fort during one quarter while the men slept. One night when they were at their posts the enemy noticed that it was very silent, as if no one was there. Some of them climbed up and began to crawl through the gun embrasures. But the women had heard them climbing up, and were waiting for them with halberds in their hands. When their bodies were already half-inside, they thrust these [halberds] through their chests, from one side to the other. One woman, not content with this, took a firebrand and fired a gun, which made the rest flee and awoke our men. It was a very heroic deed for women to remain so silent and show such spirit.'

The German artilleryman Hans Staden found himself among these besieged settlers in early 1548. Some ninety Christians and thirty negro slaves were defending the stockade of Igaraçu against eight thousand Indians. The native besiegers prepared breastworks and foxholes as protection against the defenders' guns, and they fired burning arrows to ignite the settlement houses. At one point, Staden and others took a boat down-river to get food from Itamaracá. They fought their way past a barrage of Indian arrows, and on the return journey the natives sent great trees crashing down in an attempt to crush the boat. They even tried to asphyxiate the Portuguese with 'a sort of pepper that grows there'.

The donatory Duarte Coelho was also besieged in his tower at Olinda. One of his men, Vasco Fernandes de Lucena, was married to a chief's daughter, and 'was feared and esteemed among the heathen. Their chief felt honoured to have him as a son-in-law because he considered him a great sorcerer.' His wife crept out during the siege and induced the women of her tribe to bring food and gourds of water for the besieged. Vasco Fernandes then went out alone and tried to persuade the Indians to abandon the French. He drew a line on the ground and said that anyone who crossed it would die. Eight Indians ran up to kill him but, when they crossed the line, legend has it that they *did* die. The chronicler Vicente do Salvador offered no explanation, but confessed that 'I would not have believed this . . . did I not know that on the very place where the line was drawn, in front of the tower, a sumptuous church of the Saviour was built' to commemorate the miracle. The demoralised Indians raised the siege.*

Duarte Coelho moved along the coast fighting or making peace agreements with the Indians. They came to fear him, but there was also respect, for Coelho did at least restrain the more unruly settlers. In a vigorous letter to the King asking for powder, shot and cannon to use against the Indians, he told of hanging colonists for illegal slave-raiding and other crimes. He excelled other donatories in founding a real colony, planting numerous sugar mills, building ships for coastal trade, and imposing some rough justice on his pioneer settlements.

When Coelho returned to Portugal the Indians 'saw that the man they feared was absent and started . . . to kill and eat all the whites and negroes they could catch along the roads'. The Portuguese wanted to retaliate, and also to divide the Indians for easier conquest. 'The entire kingdom would then be divided and desolate, and they would destroy one another without our waging war on them. When necessary we would fight, helping the other side. This was always the easiest way to wage war that we Portuguese used in Brazil.'

All the chiefs were invited to a banquet and made drunk on wine. The sorcerer Vasco Fernandes de Lucena offered to help them fight an enemy tribe if they would first reveal who had killed Christians. 'It must have been the influence of the wine – for they never speak the truth except when drunk – but they began to name the culprits. They thereupon came to blows, shooting arrows, wounding and killing one another. Finally Governor Jerónimo de Albuquerque [Coelho's brother-in-law] came up and arrested them. He ascertained which were the killers of white men. He ordered some of these to be placed at the mouths of cannon, and fired them in the sight of the rest, so that they could watch them fly through the air in pieces. He handed the others over to their accusers, who killed and ate them on the village squares and thus confirmed their enmity.' The resulting split among the Indians made it easy for the colonists to occupy the land of the faction friendly to them.

These were hard wars, in which the colonists had to fight fiercely to maintain the plantations they had founded and to preserve their foothold in Brazil. By 1555 Jerónimo de Albuquerque wrote to the King that, in two years of fighting, the captaincy's two largest sugar mills had been lost. The sugar crop was badly reduced, and the settlers were suffering financially. The captaincy of Pernambuco 'had to gain by inches what [the King of Portugal] had granted by leagues'. Potiguar to the north and Caeté to the south fought stubbornly, and they had French support. At the end of the 1550s the tribes of Pernambuco mounted another war against the Portuguese, and the settlers could venture only a few miles from the town of Olinda.

The two sons of the first donatory, Duarte Coelho de Albuquerque and Jorge de Albuquerque Coelho, eventually succeeded their father. They were fully occupied with Indian wars. When the twenty-year-old Jorge reached Pernambuco in 1560 he was immediately elected to lead a war against the many Indian chiefs opposing the Portuguese. He fought for five years, leading men largely paid and equipped by himself. They gradually advanced southwards from Olinda towards Cape St

Augustine. His expedition often lived in the forests. 'He had shelters of branches made by the many [Indian] slaves that he took in his company and who served to explore and scout the country and the sites where they would camp.' His men were often starving, reduced to eating forest crabs, flour and wild fruits. But their main source of food was the supplies they captured from Indian villages. 'And as soon as they finished taking one village they immediately moved against another, which they took easily, for [the Indians] did not have time to make ready.' By the time Jorge returned to Portugal in 1565 the colonists had extended their rule to control over 350 kilometres of the coast around Pernambuco.

Throughout these years, the Portuguese had the alliance of the Tobajara living near Olinda. This friendship was sealed by the marriage of the first donatory's brother-in-law Jerónimo de Albuquerque to the daughter of the Tobajara chief Green Bow. Jerónimo had many children by her – so many that he became known as the Adam of Pernambuco. With the support of this Tobajara tribe, and a steady influx of Portuguese men and supplies, the settlers gradually defeated enemy tribes and conquered Pernambuco.

Jorge's brother Duarte succeeded as donatory and continued the conquests. Between 1569 and 1571 he led a powerful expedition of six companies of Portuguese and 20,000 Indian allies against the natives of Cape St Augustine. All the nearby captaincies sent men; every settler went from Itamaracá, except for a few old men. The Indians of the Cape put up a heroic defence, but were defeated and their lands divided among the victors. The colonists moved on against the Indians of Serinhaém. A land force was led by Jerónimo de Albuquerque and a flotilla of ships by his son-in-law, the Florentine nobleman Filipe Cavalcante. It was a cruel and terrible campaign. The stunned victims let themselves be sold into slavery like sheep. But many thousands of them escaped, taking their wives and children on an exodus deep into the interior of Brazil.*

This was a time when the most successful colonists could convince the natives – and their fellow-Portuguese – of their supernatural powers. The second donatory of Pernambuco, the ferocious Duarte Coelho de Albuquerque, fell under the spell of one such magician, António de Gouveia. This man had been in trouble with the Inquisition for suspected witchcraft. But when he reached Pernambuco in 1568 he soon persuaded the donatory Duarte that he was an alchemist and great expert on gold mines. The settlers knew him as the Golden Father. He behaved like a Jesuit Father, preaching to settlers and Indians, releasing wrongly enslaved natives, and removing Indian concubines from colonists. But he also fought and killed many Indians, branded captives on the face, flogged peaceful chiefs, and kept his own slaves. When the numerous Viatan tribe, neighbours of the Potiguar, were struck by famine, Gouveia persuaded them with his sorcery to be trussed up and carted in boatloads to the Olinda slave markets. The Donatory was convinced that Gouveia could find gold, and set him off with an escort of thirty whites and 200 Indians. 'He did not want these or need them. For when he reached any heathen village, however large, strong or well populated, he would pluck a large hen or strip the leaves from a branch: however many feathers or leaves he threw into the air, that number of black demons would emerge from hell emitting flames from their mouths. At the mere sight of these, the heathen, males and females, started trembling at their hands and feet. They went up to the whites that the Father had with him, and these simply tied them up and carried them to the boats. And when these [boats] left others came.'

There were outraged protests by the Jesuits and the more level-headed colonists, but Duarte Coelho refused to stop the Golden Father, either because he was himself profiting too much from the slaves, or because he was bewitched. In October 1569 the Treasurer of Pernambuco issued an indictment against Gouveia, and on 19 February 1571 his friend Bishop Pero Leitão finally ordered his arrest. Duarte Coelho tried to prevent this taking place, but on 25 April 1571· King Sebastião ordered the Donatory to return to Portugal because of his involvement with the Golden Father and his excesses against the Indians. The Golden Father was shipped home to face the Inquisition. But when his ship stopped at the Cape Verde Islands 'he disappeared one night and nothing more was heard of him'.

The true victims of such scoundrels were the Indians. Duarte Coelho de Albuquerque 'waged so many wars on the Indians of Pernambuco, with the help of a cleric who was considered a necromantic, that he destroyed his entire captaincy. There is thus not a single Indian settlement left [in 1584] between the São Francisco river and Lua, a distance of ten leagues.' Pernambuco suffered a lack of manpower, and had no Indian allies to defend it from the Potiguar and French.

The cruellest destruction of the Indians of Pernambuco took place in the slavery of sugar mills rather than on the battlefield. The colony prospered despite – and because of – this terrible destruction. By 1570 the towns of Olinda and Igaraçu had over a thousand households, and there were twenty-three mills producing a large export of sugar. The entire system was built and worked by slaves, Indians at first and negroes from Guinea when the Indians died out or ran off. Even the poorest immigrant from Portugal was awarded a large allotment in the new land. From then on his prosperity depended on slaves. 'The first thing they try to obtain is slaves to work the farms. Anyone who succeeds in obtaining two pairs or half a dozen of them has the means to sustain his family in a respectable way, even though he may have no other earthly possessions. For one fishes for him, another hunts and the rest cultivate and till his fields. There is thus no expense in the maintenance of his slaves or his household. One may infer from this how very extensive are the estates of those who own two or three hundred slaves: for there are many colonists who have that number or more.' As soon as these settlers grow rich, 'they shed the humble manners that they were forced to use because of the necessity and poverty that they suffered back in the Kingdom [Portugal]. And their [mestizo] sons . . . shed their red skins like snakes and used the most honorific titles in all things.'

The richest of all the settlers lived in Pernambuco. They were lavish hosts to other Europeans. When Fernão Cardim travelled across the captaincy with a group of fellow-Jesuits in 1583, he 'marvelled at the great facility with which they welcome guests. For, at whatever hour of day or night we arrived, they gave us all food in the shortest time . . . every variety of meat, chickens, turkeys, ducks, sucking-pigs, kids and other meats all raised by them. . . . In their abundance they seem like counts, and spend lavishly.' 'Some of them are heavily in debt, because of the great losses they have had with slaves from Guinea, many of whom die on them, and because of the excesses and heavy expenditure they incur in their style of life. They and their wives and children dress in all sorts of velvets, damasks and other silks, and show great excess in this. The women behave as great ladies but are not very devout and do not frequent mass, sermons, confession, etc. The men are so smart that they buy horses costing 200 or 300 cruzados, and some have three or four thoroughbreds. They are very addicted to parties. If a girl of good family marries an [eligible] man the friends and relatives come dressed in crimson velvet, others in green, and others in damasks and other silks of various colours, and the pennants and saddlecloths of their horses are of the same silks that they are wearing. On the wedding day they have bullfights, play at cane jousting, ducks or hoop-la, and come to pay a visit to the Jesuit college so that the Father Superior can see them. . . . They are unduly fond of banquets, at which ten or twelve mill-owners generally spend a day eating together. They each entertain in turn, and spend all they have. Every year they commonly drink 50,000 cruzados' worth of wines from Portugal. . . . In short, there is more luxury to be found in Pernambuco than in Lisbon.'

The great Bay of All Saints was 450 miles south-west of Recife, but it was the next colony to be established by the Portuguese. It was here that

Diogo Álvares Caramuru had gained such influence with the local Tupinambá. French, Portuguese and Spanish ships frequently visited the Bay during the first decades of the century. When King João III divided Brazil into captaincies, Bahia was an obvious plum and it went to a veteran soldier called Francisco Pereira Coutinho. He landed in 1535 and immediately started distributing land to his men. The Tupinambá acquiesced for a few years. They helped the settlers build a couple of sugar mills, a fortified tower and a town for a hundred people. They even fed the newcomers because they were friends of Caramuru. Food cost very little: 'For a tapir, a vintém coin, for a deer the same vintém . . . fish is so abundant that it is given for nothing . . . hake, salmonets, lobsters, sardines. . . .' But those idyllic conditions could not last. It was the usual story of barter degenerating into slavery, and wary friendship into warfare. During the first decade the colonists fell out among themselves, and sided with hostile groups of Indians. A cleric called Bezerra incited some colonists against the Donatory. The Europeans were greedy about land and tried to exact labour from the natives, who were already suspicious and warlike. The Tupinambá decided to fight. They destroyed the invaders' mills and quickly drove them into the stockade of their fledgling settlement. Francisco Pereira Coutinho judged his position to be untenable, and in 1545 fled south to another captaincy with all his men. Pero Borges wrote that he was 'to blame for not knowing how to behave toward the people like a good Christian and for being weak in resisting the madnesses and excesses of the idiots and ill-educated who cause risings and conspiracies. . . .' The trouble was that the Donatory and many of his men were veterans of India, where abuse of the natives was commonplace. A contemporary book, Diogo de Couto's *Soldado practico*, described conditions in India; it is full of rapes, robbery, stabbings and adultery – the conduct of tough colonial troops.

The success of the Bahia Indians inspired those of other captaincies to try to expel their invaders. The Donatory of Pôrto Seguro wrote to the King in July 1546 begging for guns and ammunition. But the Bahia Tupinambá began to repent and relent. Their success had deprived them of their source of coveted knives and metal tools – the opium of the Brazilian Indian. With Caramuru acting as intermediary they actually invited the Portuguese to return.† Pereira Coutinho accepted the invitation and led his men back to try again. His flotilla was shipwrecked in 1547 on the island of Itaparica at the mouth of the Bay. The Indians may have planned treachery all along, or the colonists may have fallen among a hostile group; but all the shipwrecked colonists, except Caramuru, were ceremonially killed and eaten. The ritual death-blow to the Donatory himself was delivered by a five-year-old boy, the son of a chief he had killed.*

Although Caramuru had been spared from the massacre of his compatriots, he felt insecure among his Indian relatives. He seized an opportunity to sail to France on a French ship that called at Bahia in late 1547. The French were well aware of the importance of their visitor: they gave him and his wife a splendid reception and arranged for their marriage and her baptism as Catharina Álvares. A Portuguese emissary who was then in Paris – Pero Fernandes Sardinha, the future Bishop of Brazil – wrote to his king in alarm at this French manœuvre, particularly when the French refused Caramuru's request to stop in Portugal on his return journey. But Caramuru's patriotism was unshaken: as soon as he and his wife returned to Bahia, they encouraged her tribe to massacre the crew of the French ship that brought them.*

Although the attempt to settle Bahia had been a complete failure, the King of Portugal recognised the strategic importance of the Bay and the potential fertility of its hinterland. He chose it as the seat of the first royal government of Brazil, purchased the rights of the heir to the Donatory, and in 1549 sent out an energetic ex-soldier called Tomé de Sousa to be first governor of Brazil. Sousa sailed with a fleet containing some thousand persons – officials in charge of justice, revenue and warfare, soldiers and exiled convicts to act as colonists. There were many converted Jews and the first six Jesuits led by Manoel da Nóbrega. King João III wrote detailed instructions to his governor. These dealt with all aspects of land tenure, trade and defence of the proposed colony, and of course mentioned the native peoples who happened to be living there. The Indians were in fact used as the pretext for this colonial adventure. 'The principal thing that moved me to order the settlement of those lands of Brazil was that its people should be converted to our Holy Catholic faith. . . . Therefore treat all who are peaceful well, favour them always, and do not consent to any oppression or insult being done to them.' The King acknowledged that raiders along the coast were seizing Indians and selling them as slaves: he ordered the Governor to stop this traffic, 'for the heathen rebel because of this and make war on the Christians, and this has been the main cause of the damage done to us up to now'. He sought to control commerce with the natives by restricting it to weekly fairs. Ordinary colonists were not to visit Indian villages without permission – such visits could result in exploitation of natives unaware of the Portuguese monetary and legal systems that the Governor was to introduce to the colony. An exception was made for the owners of sugar mills, who were always allowed to visit villages that lay within their estates!

The royal instructions of 1548 dealt with the military situation in Bahia, for the first governor was being sent to an area from which the Portuguese had been successfully evicted. The King reckoned that the Tupinambá near Bahia numbered 5000–6000 warriors, and that some of these were still friendly to the Christians. Tomé de Sousa was therefore to begin by identifying the real enemies. He was to punish these, 'destroying their villages and settlements, and killing and enslaving whatever part of them you consider sufficient to act as a punishment and an example to them all. From then onwards, if they seek peace, concede it and pardon them. This, of course, would be on condition that they acknowledge subjection and vassalage, and pay annual tribute of some food for the people of your town. When they seek peace, do your best to get some of the chiefs involved in the rising into your power. You will then order these to be hanged by justices, in the villages of which they were chiefs.'

Tomé de Sousa's fleet of six ships reached the Bay of All Saints on 29 March 1549. The landing was in many ways a model colonial operation. It had been carefully planned and was smoothly executed. The King had written to ask Diogo Álvares Caramuru to help, 'because I am informed of the great practical experience you have of those lands and people and their customs'. Caramuru chose the site for the new city of Salvador, on high ground above a natural harbour. The Governor marched his men up to these heights and expelled three villages of Indians living on the sites of the future Jesuit, Carmelite and Desterro monasteries. Caramuru persuaded the Indians to help build the city and its defences. The Portuguese Government had had the foresight to send great quantities of merchandise – axes, scythes, hoes, scissors, fish-hooks, knives – to barter for native labour. Some of the payment registers have survived, and show that Indian artisans were well paid: António Gonçalves, 'Indian Labourer, of those who are involved in the works of this city', received 800 reis' worth of merchandise for two months' work, which was almost the pay of a European man-at-arms.* The Governor set an example by helping to carry logs and pound mud walls. Bulwarks were soon built, and bastions filled with artillery to repel corsairs or Indians. Stone houses were constructed for the town council, governor and religious orders. European cereals and fruits were planted and flourished; horses and cattle were bred, and were soon being exported to other captaincies. A yard was started to build ships for coastal traffic, using local woods, and native fibres and lianas for rigging. The King sent out a fleet of reinforcements each year, and even thought to include marriageable girls, many of them the orphaned daughters of men lost in Portugal's extraordinary trading, exploring and colonising efforts all over the world. The new capital of Portuguese Brazil was formally founded on 1 November 1549 and was named Salvador: but it has always also been known as Bahia.

Tomé de Sousa governed competently for four years: there was no friction with the local Indians, and the Governor found time to sail along the coast to impress royal government on the other captaincies. His successor, Duarte da Costa, was less successful. He and his sons antagonised many colonists with their arrogance, and there was a bitter quarrel between him and the first bishop of Brazil. Duarte da Costa's attitude to the Indians was harsh. On 26 May 1555 fifty Indians 'assaulted the sugar mill of António Cardoso, declaring that the land was theirs and that he must remove his mill. With these words, and others even more arrogant, they came to blows and fought for a while.' Costa reacted savagely, sending his son Álvaro at the head of a force of seventy-six Portuguese foot-soldiers and horsemen to attack and destroy three villages near the town. The mission was accomplished with the deaths of some Indian defenders, capture of a chief, release of white hostages and burning of the villages and their canoes.

Such aggression galvanised the Indians. Within a week, news came that a thousand warriors were besieging António Cardoso's mill. The Governor again sent his son, leading a large force. It burned five villages on the way to the mill and then had a fierce fight against the Indian besiegers. Various Portuguese were wounded by arrows. But the horses overpowered the enemy: 'Those on horseback overtook them and killed many including some chiefs; many were also wounded and were later found dead in the woods.'

The first Jesuits reached Brazil in 1549 with the first royal governor, Tomé de Sousa. More Jesuits arrived in the fleet bringing the second governor, Duarte da Costa. But the task of ministering to the growing number of settlers and the infinite tribes of natives was too great for these few missionaries. Their leader Nóbrega suggested that Brazil needed its own bishop, of the 'secular' clergy as opposed to the 'regulars' or 'religiouses' of the monastic or missionary orders. Pope Julius III approved the new diocese in 1551, and Pero Fernandes Sardinha (the envoy who had been alarmed by the appearance in France of Caramuru and his Indian wife) was sent as first bishop of Brazil. He proved to be an inflexible old man who quarrelled bitterly with Governor Duarte da Costa. He complained to the King that Costa and his unruly sons governed despotically and encouraged the most lawless settlers. The Governor complained that the Bishop was hindering his administration and had humiliated some settlers by having them stripped to the waist, gagged and forced to do penance for the terrible crime of imitating the Indians – by smoking tobacco. Neither Governor nor Bishop was concerned about the welfare of the Indians: the Governor prided himself on subduing them by force of arms, and the Bishop generally ignored them.

The quarrel grew so acute that Bishop Sardinha finally set sail with many outraged colonists to complain about the Governor to the King. But on 16 June 1556 the Bishop's ship *Nossa Senhora da Ajuda* was wrecked in shallows half-way between Bahia and Pernambuco, between the mouths of the Coruripe and São Francisco rivers. As the survivors staggered ashore they were all captured by the Caeté, implacable enemies of all Portuguese. They tried to tell the Indians 'that that man was the Great Prelate of the Portuguese, a consecrated priest of God who would take vengeance on their excesses. But nothing penetrated their hard hearts. They struck the holy prelate with a sacrificial club and split his head open in the middle. They did the same to his companions and carried them off to become the favourite provision for their stomachs, and their bones to be insignia of such a great deed. And that was the end of the first bishop of Brazil.' Along with the Bishop, the Caeté stripped, bound and sacrificed in turn 'António Cardoso de Barros, the Chief Treasurer, two canons and two honoured matrons, many noblemen and many other people: over a hundred whites in all, not counting slaves'.

The young colony was appalled. The Jesuit Manoel da Nóbrega saw the massacre as divine punishment for the excesses of the Bahia settlers, but reported with horror: 'There perished clergy and laity, married and single, women and children!'

During the 1550s the Portuguese controlled only small territories near their settlements of Olinda and Recife in Pernambuco, and Salvador at Bahia. The French were established through years of trading among the Indians of the Sergipe river. Otherwise the coast between Pernambuco and Bahia was occupied by a succession of Tupi-speaking tribes. Tupinambá controlled the coast to the north of the Bay. They occupied the south bank of the São Francisco river, and in some places both banks. One group of Tupinambá, called Amoipira after their chief, controlled a long stretch of the São Francisco, but far inland, some four hundred miles from the mouth of the great river. The Tupinambá had gained these territories at the expense of Tapuia (non-Tupi) tribes and a group called Tupina, who were earlier Tupi-speaking invaders of this coast. The Tupinambá were thus at war with the Gê-speaking Tapuia and the Tupina on their inland frontiers.

North of the São Francisco were the Caeté, friends of the French and enemies of both Tupinambá and Portuguese. 'In the first years of the conquest of this state of Brazil, [the Caeté] were lords of this coast from the mouth of the São Francisco river to the Paraíba river, where they always waged cruel war against the Potiguar.' Gabriel Soares de Sousa said that the Caeté made boats of periperi reeds capable of holding a dozen warriors. They used these to attack the Tupinambá on the São Francisco river and along the coast. The Caeté were also at war with the Portuguese of Pernambuco to the north and of Bahia to the south. After the execution of Bishop Sardinha it was all-out war: the settlers were determined to exact vengeance on the tribe that killed and ate their prelate.

The third royal governor of Brazil, Mem de Sá, was an experienced soldier who also held a diploma in jurisprudence. This tough but honourable official governed Brazil for fourteen years from 1558 to 1572. During his administration the fledgling colonies began to look like a colonial country, with military victories over native tribes and French rivals, and the imposition of some royal and ecclesiastical control of the settlers.

Mem de Sá found the Bahia Tupinambá thoroughly aroused. He decided that he must subdue or annihilate them. He proclaimed liberty for peaceful Indians and punished some settlers who continued illegal slave raids. But he also ordered that the Indians change their way of life and conform to Christian ethics: they must stop ritual eating of human flesh, must stop inter-tribal wars, and must gather into permanent settlements run by the Jesuits – an existence alien to hunter-gatherers, and one that meant the rapid extinction of tribal cultures.

Some tribal groups conformed and submitted to acculturation. One important chief, called Cururupeba ('Bloated Toad'), felt powerful enough to resist. 'He hurled great defiance at the Portuguese. He said they were cowards and did not dare to test his forces. He cared nothing for their orders and intended to preserve his ancient rites, to kill and eat his enemies in his village square. He would do the same to the Portuguese if they tried to impede such noble actions!' Governor Mem de Sá decided to make an example of Cururupeba. He led a force of picked men on a secret attack on the Indians' homes. 'They suddenly attacked their villages, filling the air with thunderous fire and musket shot. The Indians, who were carelessly sleeping, were thrown into confusion. By the time they tried to defend themselves their bows had been removed and their houses entered. Any who put up a resistance were killed. Most fled in the darkness of the night and hid in the forests, leaving poor Chief Toad alone and unprotected. He was discovered in the place where he tried to hide, taken into custody and placed in a confined prison, and brought to the town, where he no longer swelled or bit, nor puffed himself out with the wind of his native fantasies!'

Other tribes were cowed by the fall of Cururupeba, but an inter-tribal incident soon provoked Mem de Sá to take more savage reprisals. Three Indians who had accepted Christianity were killed while fishing. The tribe suspected of this crime refused to surrender those responsible. Many settlers felt it unnecessary to risk a war over an inter-tribal feud, but the Governor, backed by the Jesuits, insisted that an important principle was at stake: Indians who ceased fighting and accepted Christian ways must be protected. He landed a punitive force and cut inland, up the Paraguaçu river for a day and a night towards the natives' camp, which was on the crest of a hill and defended by palisades and ditches. It was manned by thousands of warriors, magnificent in war paint and feather ornaments. A long battle ensued, but native arrows and courage were no match for arquebuses. The defenders broke and fled, pursued by the Portuguese and their Indian allies: there was 'a pitiful slaughter that stained the foliage with blood'. Mem de Sá marched further inland and found warriors from two hundred villages massed in a fort at the summit of a forested hill with a lake at its foot. His men managed to climb this by roots and branches, covered by arquebus fire, and charged into the fort. 'There was a scene of bestial torment. Everyone was filled with fear and horror by the uncontrolled shouting of the barbarians and the booming of our arquebuses, all within those dense forests. A barrage of arrows obscured the sun, like clouds or hail. But when the enemy saw the square littered with dead bodies, so many that they impeded the living, they abandoned the fight and took to their heels into the undergrowth. It was in vain. They were pursued . . . and the slaughter was so great that the bodies could not be counted.' All chroniclers agreed that Mem de Sá and his military commander Vasco Rodrigues de Caldas thoroughly crushed the Indians living near Bahia. Gabriel Soares de Sousa wrote that he burned and razed over thirty villages, Vicente do Salvador said it was seventy villages and a Jesuit chronicler said 160 villages.*

The native survivors sued for peace. The campaigns had been so overwhelming that the Indians were terrified into accepting Christianity. One Jesuit wrote in 1558 that 'the Governor undertook, with many men, to subjugate them and make them appreciate the only path by which they can arrive at an understanding of their Creator. . . . In this way they all tremble with fear of the Governor, a fear which, although it may not last a lifetime, is enough for us to teach them. It serves us so that we can tell them about Christ and the kindness which Our Lord will show them. . . . This fear makes them better able to hear the word of God.' Many Tupinambá thus entered the chain of mission villages being founded by the Jesuits near Bahia.

Another section of the Tupinambá tribe remained undefeated on the stretch of coast north of Bahia, occupying the lands bounded by the Sergipe, Itapicuru and Real rivers. They survived there for a couple of decades, encouraged by the French, but were defeated by expeditions from Bahia, first in 1574 and finally in 1587–90. All were eventually killed or enslaved.

A third group of Tupinambá decided that their only hope lay in flight: taking their families and few possessions, they migrated for hundreds of miles into the interior. One Tupinambá told the Jesuit José de Anchieta of the panic that forced them to move. 'We must go, we must go, before these Portuguese arrive! . . . We are not fleeing from the Church or from your [Jesuit] Company: if you wish to go with us, we will live with you in the depths of the forest or bush. . . . But these Portuguese will not leave us in peace. You see how a few of them come among us and are seizing our brothers. What could we hope if the rest were to come? They would surely enslave us ourselves and our wives and children.' Once on the move, the Tupinambá marched and fought their way right across Brazil and back to the Amazon in one of the most remarkable migrations in history. Their descendants reappeared in the European orbit when the French and Portuguese invaded the lower Amazon at the beginning of the seventeenth century.

Diogo Álvares Caramuru died on 5 October 1557. He had been the Trojan Horse that introduced his compatriots to the area; but he also did much to help the two races understand one another. He was the colony's founder. The Jesuit leader Nóbrega called him 'the most renowned man in this land' and wanted to have him named 'father and governor' of the Indians.* In old age Caramuru was 'an honoured old man who goes about the villages with the Fathers' acting as a guide, ambassador and interpreter.* He left a legacy to the Jesuits, as well as very numerous offspring who married the most distinguished colonists. His native widow Catharina spent some years among her people and then returned to live in Salvador as 'a much honoured widow, fond of giving alms to the poor and other works of piety'. Her acculturation to Christian ways was so great that she built a chapel for a statue of the Virgin brought by a Spanish ship, and then applied to the Pope to have her chapel recognised as a sanctuary.

The Caeté had been warned of divine punishment for executing Bishop Sardinha. It came soon enough. An alliance of their traditional enemies the Tupinambá of Bahia with the Tupina living inland defeated them, forced them down to the seashore, and killed and ate all who could not escape to the hills. 'The victors . . . sold an infinite number of them as slaves to the settlers of Pernambuco and Bahia in exchange for goods. Slaving caravels regularly went there and returned laden with these people.' The Caeté fought back against the Portuguese to the north and south of them and their Tupinambá allies.

The settlers of Bahia were clamouring to be allowed to capture more Indians as slaves. Governor Mem de Sá decided to appease them by launching a campaign to eliminate the Caeté. He proclaimed an official war against them in 1562, with any prisoners liable to enslavement. The Jesuits had by then made many converts among the Caeté. But the delighted settlers regarded the proclamation as an open hunting licence against any Caeté. The Jesuits watched in horror while Portuguese carried off men, women and children from their missions and attacked any Indians they met on the roads on the pretext that they were Caeté. The Indians had no legal recourse, and those who had accepted Christianity were no longer organised for armed resistance. They dared not venture out to their plantations. Their only salvation was to flee to the forests, and four missions located between thirty and a hundred miles north of Bahia were rapidly depopulated. Mem de Sá saw that his war against the Caeté was being abused and revoked it. He managed to liberate a few wrongly enslaved Indians, including forty pupils of a Jesuit college. But by 1587 'these heathen have been so thoroughly consumed that the only survivors now are those who fled inland or mixed with their enemies as slaves or intermarried with them'.

With the Tupinambá crushed by Mem de Sá and the Caeté repelled or annihilated, Bahia flourished. Its land and climate were perfect for growing sugar. The hinterland was soon full of opulent mills and plantations worked by hundreds of Indian and imported African slaves. A Frenchman called François Pyrard de Laval visited Salvador in 1610 and noted that the administrative area of Bahia contained two thousand whites, three to four thousand black slaves, and a further seven thousand Indian and black slaves on the sugar plantations. There were also eight thousand free Indians on the missions. Salvador was already a flourishing handsome city, the seat of royal authority and the most orderly place in Brazil.*

South of the great Bay of All Saints lies a stretch of 750 miles of unpromising coastline before the next fine anchorage, the bay of Guanabara, site of the future city of Rio de Janeiro. The coastal hills are never far from the sea and are heavily wooded. Few of the rivers running into the sea are navigable. When a road was finally established between Bahia and Rio de Janeiro, it ran behind the hills: the hills themselves and much of the coastline remained an Indian sanctuary for centuries after the first conquest. The first navigators did not appreciate how badly this coastal range blocked expansion inland. They considered this coast good potential for colonisation, and its first settlements did in fact prosper.

King João III divided this coast into four captaincies: Ilhéus; Pôrto Seguro, the 'safe port' first discovered by Cabral; Espírito Santo ('Holy Spirit'); and São Tomé, named after the apostle Thomas who was thought to have visited the Brazilian Indians at the time of Christ.

Ilhéus and Pôrto Seguro were the home of a Tupi tribe called Tupinikin. They welcomed the Portuguese more warmly than almost any coastal tribe. They saw the Europeans as allies against the Tupinambá. With the help of Tupinikin labour and heavy investment by Portuguese capitalists, the young captaincy flourished and eight sugar plantations were soon established along its shore. When the Donatory of Bahia fled from the Tupinambá in 1545 he took refuge in Ilhéus; and when the King sent the first governor to Bahia four years later he suggested that he protect himself with a contingent of friendly Tupinikin.* Imported diseases and the attrition of hard work and slavery soon took their toll of the Tupinikin. The tribe began to realise its error in co-operating with the Portuguese. The inevitable reaction took place in the late 1550s. The Tupinikin moved to avenge the death of two Indians, but were content to kill an equal number of Christians even though they could have killed more. The settlers were caught off-guard, abandoned their sugar mills in panic and retreated into the town of Ilhéus. They moved too fast to take any stores of food and were forced to live off oranges while the Indians besieged the settlement.

The Tupinikin revolt came too late, for Governor Mem de Sá had just finished his devastating campaign against the Tupinambá of Bahia. He was free to sail south with his victorious men. He advanced into thick forests and delivered a classic night attack on a Tupinikin village. 'When those savages considered themselves most secure, our men charged in and fell upon them, beheading, wounding and throwing to the ground every living being, men, women and children. Some passed directly from the sleep of night to the sleep of death; others attempted to flee, but ran towards us and fell into our hands. . . . The forests burned for many leagues and the night was turned into clear day. But when the sun began its day the sad barbarians could see better the magnitude of the slaughter. Parents found their children and husbands their wives by following trails of blood. For all lay dead beside the paths and the shelter of their hiding-places was turned to ashes.'

The Tupinikin rallied and attempted an attack on the town of Ilhéus, but they fell into an ambush laid by Mem de Sá and the many Tupinambá allies he had brought from Bahia. The Portuguese attacked from behind, and the Indians 'felt the arquebuses at their backs and the swords of the Portuguese on their heads'. The Tupinikin tried to escape by jumping into a lagoon but were then at the mercy of their Tupinambá enemies, who were better swimmers. A furious battle took place in the lagoon. 'But our [Indians] were helped by divine favour – for some were already Christians. They showed great energy. They killed many there and brought others on to the beach badly wounded, to finish killing them there.' It is ironic that Mem de Sá was using the newly conquered Tupinambá against the Tupinikin. A decade earlier, King João had recommended to Governor Tomé de Sousa that he use the docile Tupinikin against the Bahia Tupinambá, and settle some of them near his new city.*

Mem de Sá's campaign against the Tupinikin was a bloodbath. He himself described it thus: 'I went with the few people who followed me, and on the very night I entered Ilhéus I went on foot to attack an aldeia that was seven leagues from the town. It was on a small hill all surrounded with water from flooding, which we crossed with much difficulty. Before morning, at two o'clock, I attacked the village and destroyed it and killed all who tried to resist. On the return I came burning and destroying all the villages that lay behind. The heathen assembled and were following me all along the beach. I made some ambushes against them in which I surrounded them, and they were forced to plunge swimming into the sea off the open coast. I ordered other Indians and chosen men to follow them for almost two leagues. They fought there in the sea in such a way that no Tupinikin remained alive. And they brought them all on to land and placed them along the beach in order, and their bodies occupied almost one league [four miles]. I made many other sorties in which I destroyed many strong villages, and I fought with them on other occasions on which many were killed or wounded. They now dared only to live in the hills and forests, where they ate dogs and cocks. Forced by necessity, they came to beg for mercy. I granted them peace on condition that they must be subjects of His Majesty and pay tribute and rebuild the mills. They accepted everything, and did so. . . .'

On one occasion the Portuguese left eight 'sick and sad' African slaves as decoys in a forest clearing. Sixty Tupinikin warriors charged out and killed the eight slaves, whereupon the settlers launched their ambush, killing forty Indians. The Tupinikin tried to form a federation of tribes to expel the Europeans, but this was crushed in another murderous battle at the edge of the sea that ended with 'the beaches covered with bodies without souls, and the ocean surf that washed them turned to the colour of blood'.

Three hundred villages had by now been destroyed, and the

Tupinikin sued for peace. Some fled far inland, but others agreed to settle in mission villages run by the Jesuits. Mem de Sá gave public thanks in the church of Our Lady in Ilhéus and was carried in triumph by the colonists. The Jesuit Provincial, Manoel da Nóbrega, wrote that these victories removed some of the settlers' dread of the Indians, showing that these were 'not serpents, but only naked people'. The Donatory was able to write to the King that 'the Indians are now safe, thank God, and the land is depopulated of them'. By 1570 Ilhéus had four or five hundred settler families and eight sugar mills.

The Tupi of the captaincy of Espírito Santo, farther to the south, were embroiled in inter-tribal wars when the Portuguese first came to occupy the area. The invaders saw this internecine fighting as a convenient opening for themselves. They incited tribes against one another, encouraging them to eat their prisoners or sell them into slavery, so that the vendetta would be intensified. The Jesuit Nóbrega was appalled. 'They praised and approved the heathen eating one another. It has even been known for Christians to chew human meat to give a good example to the heathen. Others kill ceremonially in the Indian manner, adopting the names [of their victims]. Not only lowly men and mamelucos [half-castes] do this, but the Captain himself at times! Oh, cruel custom, inhuman abomination! . . . Their hatred of the heathen makes them call them dogs and treat them like dogs. . . . Another sin . . . is for Christians to teach the heathen to seize one another and sell their own people as slaves. I found this custom more prevalent in Espírito Santo than in any other area and for that reason it is considered the best captaincy!'

Divine retribution followed: Waitacá and Tupinikin tribes formed an alliance that smashed Espírito Santo's colonists. The Indians killed the Donatory's lieutenants, first Jorge de Menezes who had survived years of fighting in India and the Far East, then Simão de Castello Branco. The Donatory spent his entire fortune trying to re-establish his settlement, and died a pauper, begging for food from his fellow-colonists. The sugar mills were burned, the town destroyed, and the Portuguese driven to take refuge on an island or retreat to other captaincies.*

By the mid-1550s only one group of settlers survived in Espírito Santo. The Indians threatened their lands on the Cricaré (now São Mateus) river, and they sent to beg for help from the authorities in Bahia. Governor Mem de Sá wrote later: 'Because the settlers [of Bahia] would not let me go in person, I sent my son Fernão de Sá, with six sail and almost two hundred men. On arriving at the captaincy of Espírito Santo he entered . . . up the Cricaré river and went to attack three very strong fortresses that were called Marerique, where the heathen were doing and had done much damage and killed many Christians. He took these, with the death of many heathen. . . .' But the expedition paused on the return journey to celebrate its victory. The Indians chose this moment to counter-attack. A sudden charge sent the Europeans running to the shore in such disorder that they came under fire from their own ships' guns. Fernão de Sá himself was killed by an Indian arrow. His death was watched by Portuguese on the ships, and during the confusion he was abandoned by some of Caramuru's half-caste grandsons. It was normal to flee when attacked by hordes of Indians; but the disconsolate Governor considered this cowardice. He refused to see the survivors of the expedition when they returned to Bahia.

The Governor's nephew Baltasar de Sá continued the campaign. The Indians broke off their siege of the settlement on the Cricaré and retreated to another stronghold. But Baltasar stormed this and killed most of its defenders. The Indians sued for peace and surrendered. The Queen of Portugal wrote to console Mem de Sá on the loss of his son. She said she was delighted that Espírito Santo was pacified and 'its heathen so punished with so many deaths of such important people that it would seem that they will not quickly raise their heads'.

Mem de Sá himself landed at Espírito Santo in 1567, and boasted that 'in a very short time I calmed the heathen who wanted peace; and those who did not want it were punished and many killed; and those who escaped left the land, and it remained more peaceful than ever'. Despite this, the captaincy never flourished. By 1570 there were only sixty-eight European settlers in all Espírito Santo.

South of Espírito Santo and in the small captaincy called São Tomé the hills gave way to marshy swamps and fertile plains bisected by watercourses. This is the outlet of the southern Paraíba river – not to be confused with the northern Paraíba, north of Pernambuco, the home of the Potiguar; nor with the Parnaíba on the Maranhão–Piauí frontier; nor with the Paranaíba, which forms the border between Goiás and Minas Gerais and is the main headwater of the mighty Paraná. All these names derived from *paraná*, the Tupi for a large river.

The swampy lands around the mouth of the southern Paraíba were the home of the Waitacá, one of the original tribes that occupied the coast before the arrival of the Tupi. Most chroniclers mentioned the Waitacá, but none lived with them, so that our knowledge of them is sketchy. Soares de Sousa described the Waitacá as strong tall people, lighter in colour than the Tupi. Some shaved the front of the head, but all had their hair hanging long at the back. Being plains Indians, the Waitacá were famous for their agility: they could outrun any enemy and even hunted by running down game. They farmed little, nothing more than some maize and root crops, but both sexes were fine archers. They were also masters of their watery environment – brilliant swimmers who attacked sharks armed with only a sharp stick that they thrust into the shark's jaw. They hunted sharks not for food, but to use their teeth as arrow-heads.

The Waitacá managed to survive the Tupi invasions, and they held off the Portuguese for a century. They survived because they were nomadic, mobile and elusive, and also because they were such formidable warriors. The French pastor Jean de Léry described the Waitacá as 'ferocious and strange savages who, unable to live at peace with one another, also maintain continual open war both against their neighbours and generally against all strangers. . . . They must be considered and placed in the rank of the most barbarous, cruel and redoubtable nations to be found in all the West Indies or land of Brazil.'

The Waitacá were voracious cannibals who enjoyed the taste of human meat. André Thevet wrote that 'when they take one of their enemies they immediately tear him to pieces and eat him half-cooked, as they do with all other meats'. And Anthony Knivet said: 'These canibals have no peace with any kinde of Nation, but doe eate all kinds of people, Frenchmen, Portugals, and Blackamoores. Many times whilest I was at the River of Januarie [Rio de Janeiro] some ships were cast away at this Cape [Cabo Frio], and all the Portugals and Blackamoores were eaten.'

The Waitacá were brave, resourceful and well-trained warriors. As proof of their toughness, Thevet wrote: 'I have seen Waitacá being executed, who, after having their head broken and being prostrate on the ground have got up and seized the club from him who executed them with such fury that they knocked him to the ground. I would never have believed this had I not learned it from my own eyes!' 'They train their children to manœuvre agilely, to resist and elude the flight of arrows, at first using little stunning arrows, then to train them better they shoot more dangerous arrows at them. If they sometimes wound some of them, they tell them: "I prefer that you should die at my hand than my enemy's."' The Waitacá piled the bones of dead enemies outside their huts, and a family gained prestige from the size of its pile.

The other great defence of the Waitacá was their marshy habitat. 'They are more expert at war than any other tribe, added to which they are in an almost impregnable place because of the rivers and swamps that surround it.' Simão de Vasconcellos said that 'their villages consisted of several huts which were built on a single post, like pigeon houses, because of the waters. These dwellings were very small and covered in straw thatch. . . . Their doors are so small that it is necessary to go on all fours to penetrate them. They had no hammocks nor beds nor furniture: for their entire wealth consisted of their bows.' It is normal for Gê tribes to sleep on the ground whereas Tupi invariably use hammocks. This disgusted Knivet: 'They doe not lie in Nets as the Tamoyes and other Canibals doe, but on the ground like Hogs, making a fire in the middle of their houses.' The Waitacá who lived on more open plains had longer huts, covered in bark or thatch.

King João awarded the captaincy of São Tomé to a relatively poor donatory called Pero de Góis. He made a promising start. The Indians were persuaded to fell some forests and help build sugar mills driven by water and oxen. There was a small settlement called Vila da Rainha ('Queen's Town'). But everything was ruined by the Portuguese trader called Henrique Luís. This was the man who invited the paramount chief of the Waitacá to visit his ship, then seized him and demanded ransom from his tribe. It paid a ransom of slaves. But the chief was never released: Luís handed him over to a rival tribe for ritual execution and eating. The enraged Waitacá destroyed the captaincy's small settlement, razed its sugar plantations, seized its artillery and defeated all expeditions sent against them. The donatory Pero de Góis complained bitterly to the King about Luís' insane behaviour. 'Because of this the Indians all rebelled, saying much evil of us and not trusting us. . . . I am left with the loss of one eye from which I cannot see, and fifteen years in this country wasted.' Pero de Góis attempted another settlement in the 1550s, but this failed, and his son was equally unsuccessful. The Waitacá had earned the enviable reputation of being ferocious, elusive and invincible. They were not molested again until the early seventeenth century.

There are no records of the native tribes' reactions to the first invasions of their country. The chroniclers gave only a meagre outline of events from the Portuguese side, and made no attempt to penetrate their adversaries' thinking. We can only guess at the anguished debates that must have taken place in every tribal council. In tribes dominated by shamans, the Europeans were probably identified as returning ancestors, as dreaded spirits from the tribal mythology, or as powerful sorcerers in their own right. Each tribe had to decide how to deal with these strangers of unknown identity or intentions. Most went through the same cycle of reactions: initial welcome and delight at the new tools that revolutionised tribal labour; growing disillusion as the strangers became more brutal and insulting, as they violated all accepted codes of conduct and as the labour they demanded came to outweigh the attractions of their trade goods; awareness that the strangers were invaders, intent on conquering the tribes' lands and enslaving its people; resort to arms to throw the invaders back to the ocean.

By the 1560s, sixty years after the discovery of Brazil and thirty after
the first serious efforts at colonisation, the native tribes of the Brazilian
coast had often held off the Portuguese invasion. They had at first
allowed the Europeans to gain a foothold and even helped them build
their settlements. They had been seduced by European goods and were
too naïve and hospitable to suspect the strangers' true motives or the
magnitude of the threat to their way of life. But when barter degenerated
into slavery, and the colonists' provocations became intolerable, each
tribe in turn mounted an honourable resistance.

All that can be said for the colonists is that they were brave and
adventurous pioneers. Crossing the Atlantic in small round-bodied
sailing-ships was a dangerous business, and the toll of shipwrecks was
very heavy. Once in Brazil the Portuguese had to adapt to more tropical
conditions and learn to fight forest Indians who were excellent
woodsmen and archers. They did this successfully enough, largely by
using Indian tribes to fight one another and by breeding half-caste
mamelucos who became expert woodsmen and Indian-fighters. They
were perhaps fortunate to have struck Tupi tribes along the Brazilian
coast. Although brave and warlike, these Indians offered battle in a
phalanx of naked warriors that was terribly vulnerable to European
swords, firearms and cavalry: and they lived in villages of thatch huts
that could be located and destroyed.

After the Portuguese had decimated the Tupinikin from Ilhéus and
Pôrto Seguro, they found themselves exposed to a wilder and more
elusive enemy: tribes of Gê-speaking Indians who had been driven
inland by the Tupi migrations. For half a century these primitive Tapuia
had the better of the Portuguese, and drove the terrified settlers to
abandon a vast stretch of coast. The Portuguese called these peoples the
Aimoré – a Tupi word meaning 'evil person', 'thief' or 'killer' – but the
Aimoré called themselves by a variety of tribal names, including
Guerem-Guerem and Cariri. They emerged from the dense forests of
the coastal hills in the 1550s and at once struck terror into the
Portuguese and their Tupi Indians.

The Aimoré were tall, powerful men, paler in colour than the bronze-
skinned Tupi. Aimoré women cut their hair and sometimes decorated it
with a resin paste covered in a wig of feathers; but the warriors let theirs
grow, and Knivet reported that they 'have long blacke haire like wilde
Irish'. They called the Portuguese *crenton* meaning 'people with ugly
hair'. Both sexes wore round white stones in their ear lobes, and stone
discs in their lower lips. The Jesuit Jacomé Monteiro described them as
very good-looking, some tall and 'others as lusty as Germans, and some
females as pale-skinned as any other nation'.

The Aimoré were true nomads, and their mobility made them formidable adversaries. They were so elusive that Knivet thought they had no homes, 'but runne up and downe the wildernesse like wilde Beasts'. It was later found that they did make crude huts of palm thatch, but these were scattered a musket-shot apart in the forest so that an entire village could not be attacked in a single ambush. They were continually on the move, the men carrying their bows and arrows and the women running through the woods with children hanging to their backs. They slept on the ground, on large leaves, close to the embers of their fires, and were cannibals who ate human flesh for nourishment rather than ritual vengeance. 'They feede verie greedily on mans flesh, and are verie filthie people, for their bodies are alwayes foule with dust and durt, lying on the ground and in the ashes.'

The Portuguese could do nothing against these formidable warriors. The men were the most deadly shots of all Indian tribes, deeply ashamed if they ever missed. 'They are excessively strong and carry very long bows that are thick in proportion to their strength and with arrows to match.' Worst of all, they never fought in the open but only in 'treacherous assaults and ambushes without any order, and they hide themselves easily under the little leaves' that cover the forest floor.* If attacked, they scattered, hid and fell upon their pursuers from the rear. 'They are extraordinarily agile and great runners' who 'are afraid of no sort of people or weapons'. 'They are verie resolute and desperate; as swifte of foote as any Horse. These Canibals . . . are so desperate that five or sixe of them will set upon a Sugar house, where there are at least one hundred persons; and I have seene one of them take a man alive and defende himselfe with his prisoner, as if one of us would defend our selves with a Target.'

Fernão Guerreiro wrote that the Aimoré moved only in small groups, 'and without being seen they shoot arrows at people and kill them. They run away so agilely and disappear into the forest as if they were wild goats, often running on hands and feet with their bows and arrows on their backs. . . . Our men cannot see them except when they feel themselves hit by arrows.' When the Jesuit João Azpilcueta Navarro explored inland from Pôrto Seguro in 1554 his expedition was well escorted by Tupinikin. 'We moved with scouts in front, in great danger. One Indian . . . went a gunshot's distance ahead of the whites. Suddenly a herd of [Aimoré] Tapuia came and tore him to pieces and carried him off in quarters. After that fright, neither whites nor Indians dared stray from the path from then onwards. As a result we suffered much want, even of water.'

The captaincy of Ilhéus had once flourished, with rich men from

Portugal investing heavily in the construction of eight or ten sugar plantations. It never recovered from the revolt of the Tupinikin and the raids of the Aimoré. At Pôrto Seguro the Governor repelled the Aimoré for a time, and one settler wrote to the Queen in 1561 that he hoped that the Tupinikin would act as a shield for the captaincy's defence.† He was wrong: by the end of the century the Aimoré were well in control. Jesuit records reveal steady depopulation of Ilhéus, and the Jesuit Pero Rodrigues reported in 1599 that it was impossible to have missions near the town. Attempts to convert the Aimoré had all failed because no one spoke their language.

All the mills on the southern shore of the Bay of All Saints were destroyed: the few remaining settlers huddled on the islands of Tinharé and Boipeba and on the Camamu river. 'They have infested the entire sea coast to such an extent . . . that estates of thirty, forty or fifty thousand cruzados have been evacuated and dismantled, because their owners saw themselves in daily danger of death, and because [the Aimoré] had eaten the slaves and serving people. Because of them the town of Santo Amaro has been abandoned, with four or five mills. The Captaincy of Ilhéus, which has excellent lands, is almost all lost.' Gabriel Soares de Sousa complained in 1587: 'There occurred in this land a plague of Aimoré, so that there are now only six mills and these produce no sugar. No settler dares to plant cane, for if the slaves or men go into the fields they cannot escape these brutes. From fear of them the people are fleeing to Bahia. . . . The Captaincy of Pôrto Seguro and that of Ilhéus are destroyed and almost depopulated from fear of these barbarians. . . . In the past twenty-five years these brutes have killed over three hundred Portuguese and three thousand slaves.' 'Up to now no means has been found to destroy this perfidious race. . . . All who live in the country, Portuguese and Indians alike, fear them greatly. In those parts infested with them no inhabitant will go overland to his ranch without taking fifteen or twenty slaves armed with bows and arrows for his protection. . . . They are so barbarous and intractable that we have never been able to tame them or force any of them into servitude like the other Indians of this land, who accept submission to captivity.'

At Ilhéus the settlers huddled behind their fortifications on a narrow strip of shore. Farther south at Pôrto Seguro the captaincy was purchased by the Duke of Aveiro, but the Aimoré smashed all but one of its seven mills and two of its three towns. The local Indians were too reduced to help the settlers defend the colony or grow crops, and the Europeans began to leave for lack of food. Even Espírito Santo still further south suffered from attacks by Aimoré, Temimino and Waitacá and had to be re-established three times.* The situation was so bad by the end of the

century that governors used to threaten that anyone who spoke of the
need to abandon Ilhéus or Espírito Santo would face a spell in the
pillory with a stone round his waist.*

The Aimoré succeeded because they were true guerrilla fighters, using
camouflage, surprise and mobility. They made full use of their forest
environment, and fought a determined total war. They fought to kill,
not to take prisoners; to destroy and evict the invaders, not to trade with
them or attempt traditional hospitality. These Aimoré were very
different from the Tupi, who went into battle gaudily plumed, in a
phalanx and shouting defiantly. The Tupi had refined their inter-tribal
wars to such an extent that their fighting became almost chivalrous, with
elaborate rituals and rules of conduct. For all its barbarity there was
something elegant about Tupi warfare, and this made them easy victims
of ruthless Europeans. The Aimoré and other Tapuia tribes had been
driven from the coast by the Tupi shortly before the arrival of the first
Portuguese. Had they still been there, colonisation would have been
very much more difficult.

FIVE

The Arrival of the Jesuits

THE fleet that brought the first Portuguese governor of Brazil, Tomé de Sousa, to Bahia in 1549 contained the two powers that gave the Indians any hope of protection in those turbulent times: royal officials and Jesuit missionaries. The Society of Jesus was less than a decade old. A Spaniard, Ignatius Loyola, had founded it in 1539 as a militant monastic order, an intellectual and moral élite pledged to defend the Papacy against the Protestant Reformation. Loyola organised his society on military lines, and himself became its first general in 1541. The Jesuits were to be active and international, not rooted in the cloistered calm of monasteries. They therefore found a sympathetic home in Portugal, a dynamic Catholic country that was expanding across the world with crusading fervour. The first Jesuit college was founded in Coimbra, the first Jesuit missionaries sailed to the east in Portuguese fleets, and in 1553 Brazil became the first foreign province of the Society.

As one would expect of a new order, the first Jesuit missionaries in Brazil were men of exceptional zeal and dedication. Their leader Manoel da Nóbrega travelled tirelessly, deploying his black-robed Fathers among the fledgling colonies. One settler described them: 'Oh! If you could see the Fathers . . . travelling among these forests and scrublands. If you could see Nóbrega, their Superior, you would see a man who does not look like one: a man of skin and bones [held together] by hinges; a face of yellow wax, although always cheerful and full of smiles; sunken

A cross erected beside a Tupinambá village.

eyes; with a vestment that you wouldn't know whether it had ever been one; bare feet flayed by the ground. . . .'

Nóbrega brought five other Jesuits in the fleet of the first governor, and twenty more arrived during the ensuing decade. They were not the first missionaries in Brazil. The Franciscans had appeared there in 1503 and again in 1515, and had established a convent in Olinda in 1543. But the Jesuits were bursting with physical and intellectual energy, and rapidly took charge of the moral welfare of both settlers and Indians. By the end of the century there were only 128 Jesuits in Brazil, but they controlled virtually all Indians under Portuguese rule there.

The Jesuits soon learned the Tupi language and were the first to make serious studies of the Indian way of life. Within a year of reaching Brazil, Nóbrega produced an *Information about Brazil*, which was translated into various languages. In 1556 he wrote the important *Dialogue about the Conversion of the Heathen*, the first true Brazilian literary work, an imaginary debate about the nature, customs and philosophy of the natives. All the Jesuits wrote letters filled with details of the early life of the Brazilian colonies and the habits of their Indians. Nóbrega's secretary and later Provincial was José de Anchieta, a saintly and dynamic man who produced the first account of Brazilian plants and animals, the first grammar of the Tupi language and a great mass of letters, reports and sermons. His colleague Fernão Cardim wrote important books on Brazilian natural sciences and ethnology.*

The first meetings between Indians and Jesuits were joyful affairs, with each side enthusiastic and delighted by what it saw of the other. The Indians found in the Jesuits the first Portuguese they could trust, men devoid of material greed, who returned Indian hospitality with honest friendship. The Indians were impressed by the respect enjoyed by these black-robed holy men among their compatriots. Some of their awe of the tribes' own sorcerers and pagés was transferred to the Jesuit Fathers. It immediately became clear that the Fathers were the Indians' main allies against colonial excesses, in those bewildering times when barter was degenerating into slavery and the settlers were imposing their barbaric notions of law, trade and morality.

The Jesuits were just as enchanted by the Indians' openness and zeal to learn about Christianity. They wrongly regarded them as an empty slate on which they could imprint their Christian religion. Immediately after landing, Nóbrega wrote: 'They are not certain about any god, and believe anyone who tells them he is a god. . . . A few letters will suffice here, for it is all a blank page. All we need do is to inscribe on it at will the necessary virtues, be zealous, and ensure that the Creator is known to these creatures of his.' Two years later he repeated this notion, but with less assurance. He wrote to the King that 'the conversion of these heathen is an easy matter. But they can be kept in good behaviour only with many workers. For they believe in nothing – they are a blank page on which one can write at will, provided one sustains them by example and continual converse.' 'All the heathen of this coast want to be Christians; but they find it harsh to abandon their customs.'

In his first enthusiasm, Nóbrega wrote that 'in many things [the Indians] are superior to Christians, for they live better morally and observe natural law better'. He described his first successes. 'We are beginning to visit their villages, we four companions, to converse familiarly and to promise them the kingdom of heaven if they will do what we are teaching them. We invite the children to read and write, and at the same time teach them Christian doctrine. . . . They are very eager to learn, and want to be Christians like us. They are prevented only by the great effort involved in abandoning their evil customs. . . . Wherever we go we are received with great kindness, particularly by the children whom we teach. . . . We normally baptise husbands and wives together and marry them immediately afterwards . . . at which they appear very content. They pay great attention to whatever we order.'

The Indians flocked to the Jesuits for mass conversions and huge ceremonies of baptism. Defeated Indians turned to the Jesuits as their best hope of protection. Jesuit policy was to form large mission settlements, known in Portuguese as aldeias (villages) and in Spanish as reductions. The missionaries rapidly filled these with the coastal tribes that were defeated in the first round of colonial wars. One Jesuit wrote in 1561 that chiefs were coming to his settlement near Bahia from distances of over a hundred miles. 'They come in such humility that it is something for which to praise the Lord. Our town is very prosperous with such honoured and important people. Fifteen villages will be joined to form one, which we have called Good Jesus. The great chief Caquiriacum, an eater of human flesh, has also come here to live with us and has built his house very happily. Other chiefs are also requesting sites to build their houses. . . . The people treat me with much reverence, humility and obedience. They are very regular about bringing their sick to the church and calling me to baptise them. . . . They are very simple people and well behaved and domesticated, and are becoming even more so. Whatever I teach them they accept. . . .'

Other Jesuits wrote excitedly about mass conversions. The Provincial Luís de Grã promised that 'every Father or Brother who comes from [Portugal] . . . will be entrusted with a settlement of at least a thousand souls'. Grã himself moved among the tribes near Bahia performing mass baptism and marriage ceremonies. In one aldeia he baptised nine hundred in a ceremony that lasted all night until cock crow, and then married seventy couples. The largest ceremony of all was at the aldeia of São Pedro, with 1150 baptisms and 150 marriages.

The Indians welcomed the Jesuit Superior with great festivities, doing him the special honour of clearing the paths leading to their villages and sending an escort of young men to carry him there in a litter. The Indians had been defeated by the third governor, Mem de Sá, and clearly thought that their salvation lay in conversion to Christianity. 'It was not necessary to use much force. The Governor ordered it all, and many aldeias were soon founded.' 'At the beginning it was a joy to see the fervour and devotion with which they came to church. When the bell was rung for instruction or mass they ran with such impetus and tumult that they seemed like horses.' If a tribe was reluctant, the Jesuits employed simple stratagems. Luís de Grã played hard to get with one hostile chief: he said that he had come for the benefit of all Indians and moved on to other tribes: the chief's wife persuaded him to hurry after the Fathers and beg them to return. When another chief hesitated, Grã told him to consult his people. These soon appeared, drunken and dancing, and readily accepted 'what the Father wanted, and appeared very content about it'.

The royal authorities, particularly the victorious Governor, Mem de Sá, ensured that the Jesuits were successful. One proud chief, 'the haughtiest of this land . . . disdained the laws and ate human flesh with his subjects at great feasts'. The Governor summoned him to appear before him, and received him so coolly that the chief begged for pardon and agreed to a Jesuit establishment in his village. Other chiefs submitted in the same way. 'These are the fruits that the Lord is harvesting from this field that was sterile until now.' The missionaries erected their church and started services and teaching, and the Governor 'made one of the principal Indians bailiff of the village, ordered him to be suitably dressed and handed him his staff of office – which caused considerable amazement among them because it was a novelty'.

Because the Governor exercised firm but temperate justice, the cowed Indians accepted Portuguese rule, and the Jesuit missionaries reaped their harvest. 'Thus, [the Indians] send requests from far away for priests to indoctrinate them, because they want friendship with Christians and to change their habits for ours. In this way four large settlements are already constructed for them. . . . Besides these, other settlements are being prepared in more remote parts where Christians never imagined it possible to enter and subjugate. . . . They all tremble with fear of the Governor, a fear which, though it may not last a lifetime, is enough for us to teach them. It is sufficient for us to tell them of Christ; and the kindness that Our Lord will show them will cause all human fear to flee, so that they will remain a strong and stable people. This fear makes them more capable of being able to hear the word of God. Their children are instructed; the innocent ones about to die are all baptised; they are forgetting their customs and exchanging them for good ones.'

In those early years when the tribes poured in to accept Christianity, the euphoric Jesuit Fathers performed prodigies. Father João de Azpilcueta Navarro described a missionary journey of a thousand miles in the interior of Espírito Santo and Ilhéus. 'We always moved along little-known paths, through very densely wooded hills. There were so many rivers that at some places in a space of four or five leagues we crossed the water fifty times in succession. Had I not been helped I would have drowned. For over three months we went through country that was very cold and humid because of the many trees and under-growth. . . . It often rained and on many nights we slept soaked. . . . Almost all of us were half dead from diseases, some in the villages and others in the wilderness. . . . We often had no food other than manioc flour and water. But no one died.' The expedition was also in considerable danger from the Aimoré, through whose territory it was passing, and survived a canoe journey down the rapids of the São Francisco river.

This Father João de Azpilcueta was one of the most successful early missionaries. He was an eloquent preacher who spoke perfect Tupi. He even had his own unorthodox times for preaching. He would wait for the Indians to return exhausted from their hunting expeditions, 'and when they were tired and satisfied and preparing for night, unrolling their blankets, he would begin to unleash the torrent of his eloquence, raising his voice and preaching the mysteries of the Faith to them. He walked around them, stamping his foot and clapping his hands. He made the same pauses, breaks and histrionics that they were accustomed to among their own preachers, in order to please them and persuade them the more.' The Indians enjoyed such oratory, and flocked to Azpilcueta for baptism.

It was not long before the Jesuits began to realise that their triumphs were superficial. The Indians were interested in Christianity for the immediate advantages it could offer: protection against the colonists, music and ceremonial, the attention of the Fathers, presents given by the missionaries, and the magic of the white man's cult. But they were not concerned with the missionaries' convoluted theology, based as it was on the experiences of the Hebrews on the far side of the world. Nor were they prepared to abandon their own tribal customs and their own beliefs. For each tribe *did* have beliefs, in the spiritual and magical properties of the natural world that surrounded it, and in the powers of its pagés or faith-healers and of its ancestors. The lingering notion that Brazilian Indians had no faith was based on mistaken European preconceptions and faulty observation.

Even the apparent lack of religion worried some of the first Jesuits. Pero Correia wrote in 1551: 'The Indians have so little awareness of God that I think they are going to give us much trouble.' His prediction soon proved all too correct. As fast as the missionaries imprinted their doctrines on the 'blank page' of the natives and performed the rituals of conversion, the teaching evaporated. It was like writing on the sand of a beach, washed clean by the first wave. Some missionaries hesitated. Afonso Braz wrote from Espírito Santo, 'I do not dare baptise the heathen here too readily, even though they continually request it. For I fear their inconstancy and instability, except when they are on the point of death. We have very little confidence in them here because they are so fickle.' If baptised after inadequate instruction, they 'return to the vomit of their ancient customs'.

Tribes that casually accepted Christianity did not appreciate that they were also supposed to change their way of life. In the eyes of the missionaries they lapsed, and 'fled back to the heathen, and were worse than before: they resumed their vices and the eating of human flesh'. José de Anchieta – the Jesuit who has remained a popular hero in modern Brazil – was especially disillusioned by the Indian boys, on whom the missionaries had concentrated their attentions. 'There are no results with the adult men and women – they do not wish to apply the Christian faith and doctrine. But there is not even success with the boys whom we rear almost at our breasts with the milk of Christian doctrine. After being well instructed they follow their parents, first into their houses and then in their customs.' 'All that I can say of them is that on reaching puberty they began to take charge of themselves. They then reached such a state of corruption that they now exceed their parents in evil by as much as they formerly did in good. They now abandon themselves to drunkenness and debauchery with greater shamelessness and recklessness, in proportion to the greater modesty and obedience they formerly devoted to the Christian way of life and to divine instruction.'

After six years of missionary effort, Nóbrega wrote his *Dialogue* between two Jesuits, one of whom was optimistic about the Indians and the other hostile. One of his characters complained: 'The worst thing of all with the Indians is that when they come to my tent by giving them one fish-hook I can convert them all, and with another I could unconvert them again, for they are inconstant. . . . We see that they are dogs because they kill and eat one another, and pigs in their vices and way of life. It must be for this reason that some Fathers who come from the mother country take a dim view of them. For they came hoping to convert all Brazil in an hour, and they see that they cannot convert it in a year, because of their primitive bestiality.' One of Nóbrega's Jesuits said that he was 'half in despair over their conversion. Working with these people, who are so bestial that nothing of God enters their hearts . . . is like preaching in a stony desert.' The other Jesuit agreed: 'Since these heathen worship nothing at all and believe in nothing, all that you say to them is worthless.' Nóbrega's characters debated whether the Indians were even true men, or whether they were descended from Ham, who was cursed for discovering his father Noah's nakedness. But they concluded that 'it is obvious that they have souls, for the soul has three properties – understanding, memory and will – all of which they have. . . . You will see that in matters within their sphere and which they practise they have just as good skills, inventions and discreet speech as anyone. The Fathers experience this daily with Indian children. They find them so intelligent that many are superior to Christian children.' And they ended their debate by recalling many devout Indians, some of whom had abandoned their tribes to follow the new religion, and chiefs who had brought their people from afar to have them instructed.

The Jesuits sought to explain their failure and to find solutions. Nóbrega had the idea of sending native boys back to Portugal for thorough indoctrination. But this was an expensive business, and the boys had a disconcerting way of reverting to tribal customs on their return. Such experiments have been attempted from the first discovery of Brazil until the present. The assumption is that young Indians will be dazzled by our civilisation and will relay it back to their people. In practice they make a choice – and almost invariably decide that the tribal way of life is preferable.†

Another theory was to attract Europeans to the Brazilian interior so that they could live near the Indians. Father Azpilcueta explained that his expedition inland from Pôrto Seguro was 'to discover whether there was any tribe of greater quality, or whether there was anything in the land to attract more Christians to colonise it, for this is of the utmost importance for the conversion of these heathen'. The first Jesuits used to travel inland, visit the Indians in their villages preaching to them there. But the conviction grew that conversion could take place only if the Indians were uprooted from their homes and moved to large new mission aldeias. To become civilised they had to live in cities. The Jesuits also deluded themselves that the natives would be inspired by closer contact with Europeans – despite the overwhelming evidence that most white men abused Indians. The Provincial Luís de Grã wrote to Ignatius Loyola, founder of the Society: 'These heathen, Father, will not be converted by simply telling them the things of the faith, nor by reasoning nor preaching.' What they needed was more exposure to the Christian way of life.* Another Jesuit said: 'As I see it, they *can* be converted by much discussion and contact. But they are people with very weak memories for the things of God.'

Nóbrega took the first step at Piratininga, the future city of São Paulo. He joined together three small Indian villages, and on the feast of St John the Baptist, 29 August 1553, performed a ceremony admitting fifty catechumens to the Jesuits' new church and convent there. This could be described as the act of foundation of what has become the largest city in South America.* He and other Jesuits explained the policy of 'reducing' Indians, congregating them in tidy new mission settlements: 'Some means are sought so that larger numbers of Indians can be taught and indoctrinated with greater ease in the matters of the Faith. . . . The first step, which is already a great success, is to concentrate the Indians from scattered villages into one large village. Whereas before many of us were needed to teach and indoctrinate them because they were scattered about, now that they are concentrated together fewer of us are needed. In this way it is also easier to correct their errors and sins which they committed because they were so inconveniently located.'

Settlement in these mission aldeias demanded a profound change in the Indians' way of life. Their own villages were moved periodically, and forest clearings near each village were changed even more frequently. With slash-and-burn farming a forest clearing lasted for only a few years, after which its weak soil began to be exhausted and the Indians allowed it to revert to jungle. In a land without any kind of domestic animal, the Indians were forced to hunt and fish for their protein. They moved their villages when game in the surrounding forests or fish in the streams began to run short. All this changed when tribes settled in fixed villages with permanent boundaries. Mission Indians had to change from being semi-nomadic hunters to subsistence farmers working permanent farms and rearing European livestock. They had to learn that the land was no longer a free commodity like air or water, something so abundant that men could roam and hunt across it at will. If they now moved outside the mission boundaries they were trespassing on estates awarded to Portuguese colonists. The loss of freedom must have been suffocating.

The move into mission villages involved more than a transformation of a tribe's farming and hunting. Mission Indians had to accept Jesuit tutelage in every aspect of their lives. The Fathers imposed a new discipline that occupied every hour of the day and controlled the life-cycle from cradle to grave. Most traditions had to cease. Almost all the ceremonies that delighted the people were altered or suppressed, from puberty rites to the ritual killing and eating of prisoners, from dances and drinking parties to the ministrations of the shamans. It was an abrupt and profound cultural shock.

Worst of all was the contact with European civilisation. Royal and ecclesiastical authorities always maintained that this was the justification for the new settlements. Only by living in close proximity with settlers could the natives assimilate the glories of European religion and civilisation. There was some normal contact, with Indians wandering into the new colonial towns or European traders visiting the Indian villages. There was occasional friendship and fellow-feeling. The King of Portugal ordered that Indians trade with colonists at regular markets. But in trading with the Indians it was all too easy for white men to drive bargains so hard that they amounted to exploitation. For the settlers the true purpose of the settlements was to provide a pool of native labour for the surrounding estates. Just as barter degenerated into slavery, this casual labour by mission Indians degenerated into forced labour in conditions indistinguishable from slavery. 'The greatest impediments to conversion arise from the Portuguese. . . . These have no zeal for the salvation of the Indians . . . but consider them as savages.'

Once decided on a policy of reducing Indians into mission aldeias, the Jesuits came to condone force as the only way to make Indians accept the move. Even the saintly Nóbrega gradually accepted the need for fear and force. In 1549 he wrote that 'they fear us very much, which also helps'. Next year he said: 'Perhaps they would be converted faster by fear than by love.' By 1557 he was convinced. 'By experience we see that their conversion by love is a very difficult business, whereas, being a servile people, they do anything from fear. . . . They are people with whom one can do whatever one wishes by custom and by upbringing with subjection – which would not be possible by reasoning and arguments.'

Nóbrega knew that mission aldeias benefited the colonists. 'If the heathen were subjected or evicted [from their homes into aldeias], which could be achieved with little effort or expense, and if they had a spiritual life, recognising their Creator, their vassalage to His Majesty and obedience to the Christians, everyone would live better and would be well provided. His Majesty would have a large income in this country. . . . If the heathen were subjected . . . men would have legiti-mate slaves captured in just wars, and would also have the service and vassalage of the [mission] Indians. The land would be populated [by colonists]. Our Lord would gain many souls, and His Majesty would have a large income from this land.'

The Jesuits were too intelligent to favour force except as a last resort when persuasion had failed. But for them the end justified the means: the saving of souls was all-important, something to be achieved even at the expense of the Indians' wishes, customs or freedom. Nóbrega wrote that he was constantly tormented by the desire to see the Indians accept Christian teaching and 'become capable of grace and entry into the church of God. . . . For this to take place, I also wish . . . to see the heathen subjugated and placed under the yoke of obedience to the Christians, so that we could imprint on them all that we desire. . . . Nothing can be done with them if they are left at liberty, for they are brutish people.'

When disillusioned and frustrated by the Indians' stubborn conservatism, the Jesuits themselves could become brutal. Anchieta echoed the Gospel of St Luke: 'compel them to come in'. He wrote in 1563: 'We now think that the gates are open for the conversion of the heathen in this captaincy, if Our Lord God would arrange that they be placed under the yoke. For these people there is no better preaching than by the sword and iron rod. Here more than anywhere, it is necessary to adopt the policy of compelling them to come in.'

When the Caeté killed and ate the first bishop of Brazil, Nóbrega, who normally championed Indians against the colonists, exploded in a burst of nationalistic fury. 'I do not understand how the Portuguese race, which is the most feared and obeyed in all the world, is patiently enduring and almost subjecting itself along this coastal region to the most vile and miserable heathen in all mankind.'

The instrument of force that the missionaries wanted came in 1557 in the person of Governor Mem de Sá. He crushed the natives of the Bahia region in a series of devastating campaigns. One Jesuit wrote home that this had 'amazed and frightened not only those Indians but those all along the coast because such a thing had never happened there before. The Governor then undertook with many people to subjugate them and make them understand the only path by which they can arrive at an understanding of their Creator. Therefore it is necessary that many labourers come to reap such a great harvest. . . .'

The first converts near Bahia were gathered into two mission parishes in 1557, one near the town of Salvador da Bahia and the other nearby on the Red River. These were Indians who had already accepted Christianity, and the move was partly to protect them from having their lands and plantations invaded by settlers' cattle. Mem de Sá arrived that year and issued stern edicts to stop the colonists molesting Indians. In 1559 Nóbrega founded the large aldeia of St Peter and St Paul a few miles from the Jesuit college. In its spacious church the Governor acted as godfather to the first mass baptisms. During the next few years the Jesuits went on to gather an estimated 34,000 Indians into eleven parishes near Bahia. Nóbrega 'persuaded the Governor Mem de Sá to use force with the Indians of Bahia to gather them into large aldeias with churches for them to hear the word of God – against the advice and wishes of all the settlers. This was then extended along all the coast and was the sole means of salvation of so many souls and propagation of the Faith.'

The Jesuits were naturally delighted to have a tough governor filling their missions with vanquished tribes. 'He began to rule the gentiles . . . making them join together in large villages. He began to punish some of them and to put them under the yoke. Another system is thus beginning, one not dared up to now, which is [to convert] by fear and subjection. By the indications this is giving at the outset, we can recognise the results that will follow later: for with this policy they all fear and obey, and become ready to accept the Faith.' When the missionaries discovered that their Indians were continuing to celebrate their old festivals, with drinking and dancing in huts outside the mission perimeter, the Governor ordered the Indians to desist or he would burn down their homes. Francisco Pires explained: 'I have always felt that success was impossible in these parts without one of two things: the mercy of the Lord or his justice. . . . Recently justice has entered here, with the naked sword and the war camp, through the good industry of Senhor Mem de Sá, Governor. Because of it they are all at peace. And, since they have physical peace, we are working to give it to them spiritually.'

Another Jesuit, Pero Rodrigues, enumerated the advantages of the aldeia system. His list was rather one-sided. There are 'advantages for the Indians, who have become civilised and are saved; temporal advantages for the Portuguese in their wars against foreigners who are more afraid of Indians' arrows than white men's arquebuses; advantages against the negroes [slaves], for there is a danger that the multitude of them might some day put some captaincies in danger; advantages for the settlers, whom [the Indians] serve for payment fixed by royal regulation'.

These Jesuit remarks now sound opportunist and hypocritical. It shocks us to hear priests of a gentle religion advocating conversion by fear and force with such relish. Renaissance Europe was convinced of its superiority over the rest of the world, a superiority apparently proved by its easy colonial conquests. Much of its arrogance arose from the conviction that Christianity was the true religion. Missionary fervour for Christianity was at its strongest among the Jesuits, the intellectual vanguard of the Counter Reformation. They collected the souls of their converts with the fanaticism of revolutionaries. The first Jesuits wrote home from Brazil boasting of the enthusiasm with which the natives were flocking to baptism and outward conversion. Their letters spoke of the ease of imprinting beliefs on the Indians' minds, and promised a rich harvest of converts to missionaries who came to Brazil. Success was measured in head-counts of the baptised. When the Indians proved to have spiritual beliefs and to cling stubbornly to their way of life, the Jesuits were loath to admit that their first judgements had been wrong. And, when the first converts lapsed or melted away, wounded pride made the missionary Fathers struggle to fill their aldeias with fresh levies and to win new converts.

By the 1560s Jesuit letters were showing frustration and disillusion. Anchieta wrote in 1561: '. . . at the outset, when they were all congregated, we had some success with them, particularly the women and children. . . . But now when we visit them in their villages, by river or overland with considerable difficulty, they receive us as they do other Portuguese Christians who go to trade with them: as friends, but with no respect for the salvation of their souls or the indoctrination of their children. They are completely engrossed in their ancient and diabolical customs. . . .' By the following year Anchieta was more angry. 'We now have no influence at all over the Brazilians, our former disciples whom we were rearing with so much toil and effort. They have become indisposed to any good, have scattered in various directions where they cannot be taught, and have thus all reverted to the customs of their fathers. . . . In truth, both Portuguese and Brazilian Indians are worse now, following the paths of the flesh and abandoning those of God.'

Gabriel Soares de Sousa, a shrewd settler with years of experience of Brazil, wrote in 1586 about the Jesuits' failures. 'The first fathers of the Society who came to Brazil found the Indians extremely easy in receiving the faith of Christ our saviour. Because of this they baptised thousands daily and wrote to Portugal about it. . . . But the Indians reverted to their heathen ways with the same facility with which they had become Christian. They all ran off to the sertão, fleeing from their doctrine.

'The Jesuits once governed more than fifty aldeias of these Christian Indians, but there are now no more than three aldeias, and these are largely full of new people – for [the Jesuits] go every year and fetch them.

'They have had no success with the Indians, because these are incapable of understanding the things of God or of believing them. [Indians] think that there is nothing more than living and dying. . . . The

Fathers work . . . in vain because these heathen are so barbarous that, up to the present, none of them [continues to] live as a Christian as soon as he spends a week away from contact with the Fathers.'

Missionary thinking was illogical: Indians who did not readily adhere to the new religion and a complete change in their way of life were considered fickle. They were, of course, stubbornly conservative in clinging to established tribal cultures.

Despite the frustrations and reverses, the Jesuits pressed ahead with the founding of mission aldeias. The Jesuits were in control of Brazilian Indians for two centuries. The discipline and routine that they established in the first aldeias varied little during this long period. Many thousands of Indians lived in the aldeias. In duration and scope these missions were the greatest attempt at co-existence between Europeans and Brazilian Indians. They evolved their own subculture, a curious world of detribalised Indians isolated and sheltered from the tough life of the colonies and subjected to incessant religious indoctrination.

Many missionaries and observers described the unchanging daily routine in the mission villages. Ruy Pereira wrote from Bahia in 1560: 'This is the order of the doctrine in a parish. A bell is rung at daybreak every day and the unmarried girls (and also many married women who accompany them without compulsion) come for religious instruction. When this is over the schoolboys come and spend some two hours in reading, writing and religion. Meanwhile, after their instruction, the girls and other women go to their tasks: to spin and produce cloth with which to cover themselves – many are already clothed from it. When the boys have finished school they go to fish to feed themselves – for these people have so little care for the morrow that on days when they do not hunt they generally have nothing.'

The routine was little changed a century later. 'When day breaks the bell summoning to mass is heard throughout the aldeia. All the boys go and assemble in the main chapel of the church. They then intone in loud voices and praise of Jesus and of the Virgin, on their knees, in two choirs. Those of one choir say: "Blessed and praised be the most holy name of Jesus." And those of the other choir respond: "And of the most holy Virgin Mary his mother, for ever more, Amen." And then all together: "Gloria Patri, et Filio, et Spiritui Sancto, Amen." They continue doing this until the start of mass, which they hear in silence.

'When this is over and most of the Indians have left, the Father waits for them in the same place where he tends them. He then teaches them the prayers of the Christian doctrine in a loud voice. After it he teaches the mysteries of our Holy Faith in the same way, in dialogues of questions and responses composed for this purpose in the Brazilian language, about the most holy Trinity, the creation of the world, first men, incarnation, death and passion, resurrection and the other mysteries of the Son of God, of the universal judgement, limbo, purgatory, hell, the Catholic Church, etc. [The boys] become so expert that they can teach. They do in fact teach their parents in their homes, for the parents are normally more rustic.

'When the doctrine is finished the boys again say their choir responses: "Praised be the most holy name of Jesus" and the others reply: "And of the most holy Virgin Mary his mother, for ever more, Amen." . . . All then go to their classes to read, write or sing. Others go to learn musical instruments, according to individual talent. They become so skilled in singing and playing instruments that they help officiate at masses and church processions with as much perfection as the Portuguese. . . . They spend two hours in these schools in the morning and two more in the afternoon. They return to them when the bell rings, to which they assemble punctually.

'When the bells ring for the evening Ave Marias they again assemble at the entrance to the church. From there they form a procession with a cross raised in front. Arranged in order, they progress through the streets singing holy canticles in a loud voice in their language. When they reach a cross that is their destination they kneel at its foot and pray for souls in Purgatory in their language. . . .'

It has always been the custom in many tribes for the chief or elders to go around the huts in the morning and evening, lecturing to the people and advising them what will be done each day. He tells them to prepare hunting or fishing trips, discusses dances or festivities and reports the tribe's news. It is a gentle but effective tradition, one of the bonds of tribal unity. The Jesuits adopted this and other native customs that could be useful for their mission. Nóbrega had the chiefs of his Bahia aldeias preach in the huts at dawn on Sundays and holy days, in the local manner.

In the early days of conversion the missionaries often worked through chiefs. Tribal leaders sometimes asked for missionaries or brought their people to be instructed. Once the tribes were dominated and settled in the aldeias, the Fathers ensured that their favourites, the most devout Indians, became chiefs. But when the Jesuits began to impose their rules – insisting on one wife for each man, forbidding ritual cannibalism and inter-tribal fighting, stopping most of the drinking and dancing, and attacking the shamans – it was the chiefs who suffered most and who naturally led the reaction against Christianity.

The Jesuit effort therefore concentrated on the young. Indian boys were bright and enthusiastic pupils. They had the innocence that the missionaries valued so highly. These boys would spend their childhood in Christian education rather than learning the skills of tribal hunters and warriors. They would become artificial righteous beings so dear to the Jesuits' hearts. They would also become accomplices in the emasculation of tribal culture.

Nóbrega wrote in 1551: 'We chiefly seek to teach the boys, for if these are well indoctrinated and accustomed to virtue they will be firm and constant.' In all the early aldeias there was a college for boys to live and study in, immediately alongside the house of the Jesuit Fathers. Boys had the innocence and ability to learn the Catechism and be baptised: children formed the greater part of the mass baptisms. Every aldeia had its boys' choir, 'singing in their language and in Portuguese canticles in their manner giving glory to God'. When Nóbrega visited an aldeia, the boys came to receive him, with crosses on their heads and in their hands. They all tried to kiss his hand, and accompanied him from house to house singing praises to Our Lord and 'looking like angels singing matins'.

The Jesuit Simão de Vasconcellos was frank about the way the system worked: 'the first stratagem that [the Fathers] employed was to make the Indian children household companions, even if it had to be accomplished through gifts and petting. For these boys are less deluded and more intelligent than grown Indians. In all the nations of Brazil they are easier to instruct. Once the sons are converted [the Fathers] begin to instruct their parents through them. This is a system that experience has shown to be heaven-sent.'

Some children used their European education to dominate and patronise their parents. They behaved like the youth organisations of modern totalitarian régimes. 'Those who were more advanced in education would go through the streets intoning hymns, prayers and the mysteries of the Faith, all composed in fitting style. All of this enormously delighted their fathers. . . . The Indians came to have an exaggerated opinion of these young ones, for they respected them as something sacred. No one dared do anything against their will, for the others believed what they said and were convinced that some divinity was lodged in them. They even strewed the roads along which they passed with boughs.'

By 1559 António Blásques was able to report to the General of the Society of Jesus that dedicated youths were denouncing the lapses of their elders. 'The boys are daily increasing in love and zeal for our law. They reprehend the customs of their fathers and reveal to the Brothers any abuses that these practise without our knowing. One . . . came and betrayed his own father who was secretly practising witchcraft. When [the father] found out he beat him terribly, but the boy suffered it patiently for the love of God.' That boy's father later came to church to seek pardon for the beating and the witchcraft. One old chief used to retell his battle exploits 'with such excessive boasting that it became insufferable. A child called Benedito – a Christian and very small – saw this and went to him. The chief was old and some of his relatives were with him who could harm [the boy], but notwithstanding he went and reprehended him terribly: "Why did he rave on like that to no purpose?" This, and other things that mortified the poor old man.'

The full fury of the Jesuits fell upon the tribal shamans. Nóbrega declared that 'these are the greatest enemies we have here. They sometimes make the sick believe that we have put knives, scissors and similar objects into their bodies and are killing them with this.' 'The witchdoctors are persecuted by us, and we are removing many of the abuses they had. . . .' When Nóbrega himself was confronted with a famous sorcerer, he demanded whether the man was performing his cures in the name of God or of Satan. 'The barbarian answered with the most diabolical pride . . . that he was God himself, and the son of him who reigned in heaven, by whom he was greatly loved, and who had often revealed himself in shining clouds and among terrifying thunder. Nóbrega roared at him as if the heavens were about to fall and intimidated him. The poor devil fell on his knees and begged to be made a Christian.'

Indian villages were then, and always have been, riddled with superstition and fear of sorcery. Without any formal religion the tribes invested the trees, animals and people of their world with spiritual properties. The beliefs differ from tribe to tribe, and vary in intensity. The Tupi tribes, with whom the Jesuits were working, have always been notably mystical. It was easy for old men and women to claim supernatural powers and lead messianic movements. When anything unusual occurred the people readily suspected witchcraft. The forces of magic must have seemed terrifyingly powerful in those turbulent years of the early colonies, a time of shattering cultural shock and physical devastation.

Nóbrega told about the brother of a chief who had gone and killed an old woman because he suspected her spirit of having made him ill. The Jesuits were trying to stop such killings. But because he was the chief's brother and 'it was his first offence . . . he was flogged and some fingers were cut off his hands in such a way that he could still work with the rest. [The Indians] became very frightened by this and did no more crimes that deserved more than a few days in prison.'

When suppressing shamans, the Jesuits' favourite weapon was

ridicule. Jesuit letters and reports are full of triumphs over spiritual rivals. António Ruíz de Montoya told how he came upon an old sorcerer who claimed to be the lord of death, of human beings and of plantations, and who danced like a madman, beating bone rattles. The missionaries furiously ordered that he be tied up and thrashed. 'The sorcerer soon cried out and admitted that, far from being God, he was nothing more than a poor old man whose breath could achieve nothing. Despite these retractions, the most robust neophytes continued to administer the beating until they had completed about a hundred strokes – all to the great delight of the children.' After two days of this, he abjured his errors and became a good convert.* Another pagé claimed that he conversed with the sun, which had established him as its son and as a god. He was brought back to the mission bound to a litter and gagged to stop his preaching. The converts pulled him to the ground and started to kick him, pull him about, and puncture him with their arrows to such an extent that the Fathers had to intervene to save him.*

Another sorcerer called Ieguacari, an old and twisted man, was forced to dance in front of the catechumens. The boys were frightened at first, but gradually lost their fear and finally 'came over and fell upon him, threw him to the ground, and mistreated him in every fashion'. He ended by becoming the missionaries' cook.*

The Jesuits attacked other aspects of Indian life with equal fervour. Manoel da Nóbrega set out the changes he demanded. 'The law which must be given to them is: (1) forbid them to eat human flesh or to make war without permission from the Governor; (2) make them keep only one wife; (3) dress them, for they have plenty of cotton, at least after they are Christians; (4) remove their sorcerers; (5) maintain justice between them and between them and the Christians; (6) make them live quietly without moving to another place unless they move in among Christians, having sufficient lands allocated to them and Fathers of the Society to instruct them.'

The Jesuits gave varying interpretations of Tupi anthropophagy. Azpilcueta said it was solely for vengeance; Cardim described the glory felt by the ritual executioner and the caters, but Anchieta dismissed it as pure cannibalism. One Jesuit pointed out that the execution was done by one blow with a club, 'which is a very easy death . . . if they do any cruelty, on rare occasions, it is from imitating the Portuguese and French'. But all Europeans naturally condemned the eating of human flesh as unnatural and disgusting. The Jesuits sometimes intervened bravely to try to rescue prisoners doomed to this death. But they were soon able to leave the suppression of ritual executions and cannibalism to the secular authorities. Such rites were considered murder and therefore punishable by a death sentence. They soon died out: only the coastal Tupi had evolved the cycle of ritual eating and vengeance, and such practices have rarely been found in other parts of Brazil since those coastal tribes were subdued.

The insistence that Indians keep only one wife was resented by the chiefs. Polygamy was a prerogative of tribal leaders, something that enhanced heroic old warriors. It also corrected any imbalance between the sexes resulting from losses of men in battle. Tupi tribes were controlled by the elders of both sexes. The old men had the pick of young girls. This produced surpluses of young men and of older women – either widows or elderly wives supplanted by younger ones. The result was unions between old women and young men, with the older women seeing the social and sexual education of the young men as their agreeable duty. All of which appalled the Jesuits. The Indians were equally baffled by the Jesuits: they were obviously respected by other colonists and seemed virile enough, but they rejected all women. It was difficult to reconcile this with the behaviour of ordinary settlers, who were obsessed with sex, surrounded themselves with concubines and taught the native women erotic refinements. Some Indians despised the Jesuits because of their celibacy. The Jesuits, for their part, hoped that monogamy would result from their education of the young. Sexual morality was one of the main lessons they drummed into their pupils, and they paired off and married boys and girls soon after puberty. The resident Father, as confessor and ruler of a mission, used all his powers to enforce complete marital fidelity.

When the missionaries arranged marriages and enforced monogamy they disrupted tribal marriage customs: among the Tupinambá the preferred matches were between cross-cousins or between a girl and her maternal uncle. Marriages were matrilocal, with the man moving in to his wife's hut. The Christian system also destroyed the long-houses in which families slung their hammocks in what the missionaries considered indecent proximity. In the new mission settlements each family had its own mud-and-wattle hut. Tribes used to move periodically and rebuild their long-houses or malocas – partly to destroy the vermin that infested their thatch; but the new missions huts were considered permanent.

These tidy rectangular houses were arranged on a grid of streets around a vast square plaza. Dominating the mission and the surrounding countryside was the church. It would be built of local materials – wood and thatch on the Amazon, plaster and tile on the coast, stone in the later missions in Paraguay and southern Brazil. It was an inspiration to the entire community, large enough to hold all its members, with a baroque façade flanked by towers, vaguely reminiscent of the Society's Church of the Jesu in Rome. The retables and altars inside were gilded or carved in fine Brazilian hardwoods, often by the Indians themselves. Their niches contained statues of the Holy Family and the saints of the Society of Jesus. Alongside the church were the handsome quarters of the missionaries, with their gardens, storehouses, workshops and the all-important college for Indian children.

The community was run entirely by two Jesuit Fathers, a vicar and a curate, always dressed in long black habits and four-cornered caps. They exercised all ecclesiastical functions, performed as doctors, managed the agricultural co-operative and administered justice. They appointed Indians to serve for life as chiefs, and annually as magistrates, bailiffs and other civil and ecclesiastical offices. All other members of the community, of both sexes, wore long trailing robes of white cotton. Children were removed from their parents and housed in colleges, with boys and girls rigidly segregated.

All this meant the complete overthrow and suppression of Indian culture. Such destruction is now called ethnocide, and its effect on the will to survive can be almost as deadly as genocide. Indian nudity had to be covered. Ornaments were replaced by impersonal robes. Father Azpilcueta was once teaching a group of children to make the sign of the cross; the green stones in their lips got in the way and one mother removed her child's stone; all then discarded theirs, to the delight of the missionaries. António Blásques reported that the Indians of his reduction near Bahia 'sold all the feather ornaments kept by themselves and their wives. . . . These feathers are the best finery they have: they use them when they kill and eat their enemies, and make capes and other ornaments out of them. They have now thrown all this out, whereas formerly anyone without such ornament was not honoured among them.' Indians were attracted by European clothing, but as a novel type of ornament rather than an essential covering. Anchieta said that 'when they marry they go to the wedding clothed. But in the afternoon they go out for a walk with only a bonnet on their heads, and no other clothing. They think they are stepping out right gallantly.' Anchieta was shocked when he and his companions were entertained by a settler called Barrufo at Bertioga, and 'at dinner-time they brought in to serve at table some Indian maids, immodestly nude'.

It was not long before the mission Indians outdid even Europeans in prudery. They gained little by adopting clothing. The climate was mild enough for the covering to be unnecessary, and the Indians had vegetable dyes to protect them against insects. When they were naked they could wash frequently, jumping into streams at all hours. But clothing had to be washed with soap and needed constant repair and renewal. It thus created new needs, for soap and cloth, that the Indians could not easily produce for themselves. Clothing remains one of the most striking differences between uncontacted and accultured tribes – the latter may look more modest, but the clothing does nothing for their appearance. Even when they do their best to patch their cheap shirts, trousers and dresses, and even when they manage to pound them clean with a little soap, the effect is threadbare and shabby. The sociologist Gilberto Freyre felt that the change was medically dangerous: 'The forced use of clothing . . . has played no small part in the development of those skin and pulmonary diseases that have competed with one another in decimating whole populations of savages. . . .'

The Jesuit mission system was by any measure the most important experiment in dealing with Brazilian Indians: it involved many more Indians, affected them more profoundly, and lasted far longer than any other attempt at co-existence between the races. The Jesuit Fathers were heroic and unselfish men, acting from high moral motives. The discipline and routine of their missions would strike a modern European as suffocating monotony; but this regimentation had more appeal to Indians accustomed to an uneventful communal existence devoid of individual competition. The Jesuits managed the lands and labour of their missions in such a way that their Society grew rich and they themselves lived comfortably. But their organisation and discipline also forced the Indians to change from being carefree improvident hunters to efficient farm labourers. Most of the Indians' labour went to keeping themselves well housed, clothed and fed.

The intellectual life on the missions was more controversial. The Jesuits were brilliant educators, the best in the Catholic world: they ran colleges for white boys in the Brazilian towns, as well as the Indian missions. But, after some disastrous failures in trying to ordain Indians, they decided that the natives were inherently inferior. They contented themselves with patronising tuition, sufficient for the mission Indians to recite and perform their religious offices but with no scope for intellectual stimulus or debate. Their aim was to turn out pious domesticated congregations, and they succeeded. Their education had nothing whatever to do with the Indians' environment. It deprived them of tribal skills without making them competitive in the harsh colonial world.

The Jesuits did at least expose their Indians to the glories of baroque church architecture and music. It was the only time in Brazilian history that the natives had been shown any of the finer points of our civilisation – I have visited enough Indian reserves in every part of Brazil to know that there is now no sign of western art or culture on any of them: nothing but the sterile and shoddy intellectual desert of the frontiersmen. The Indians responded eagerly, particularly to the music. The Jesuits immediately observed that the heathen 'are extremely fond of music and singing'. Jesuit letters are full of praise for their pupils' aptitude at playing musical instruments and singing in choirs. Governor Mem de Sá liked attending mass at mission churches because the boys sang so well. Music became a powerful weapon for the conversion of new tribes. Manoel Gomes told how he won over the tribes of Maranhão: 'We occupied ourselves with the conversion of souls, raising crosses and churches with music and oboes that I took with me, singing choral masses with organs on holy days and Sundays, with the Indian singers that I brought from Brazil in order to win the affection of the minds of the heathen to our Holy Faith.'

The Indians delighted in religious festivals that involved processions and ceremonial. When Fernão Cardim visited the Bahia aldeias in 1583 he found that 'they have their singing choir and flutes for their festivals. They do their dances in the Portuguese manner, with tambourines and viols, with as much grace as if they were Portuguese boys. When they do these dances, they put on their heads diadems of birds' feathers of various colours, and also make arches in this way, and plume and paint their bodies. Painted thus and very handsome in their manner they perform their festivals very adequately.'

Vicente do Salvador told of his own experience with a newly converted tribe of Potiguar. 'They all attend willingly only on feast days on which there is some ceremony, for they greatly love any novelties – for instance, St John the Baptist's Day, because of the fireworks and musicians; the day of General Remembrance of the Dead, to make offerings to them; the day of Ashes; and of Palms – and especially of Flagellation to discipline themselves, which they consider bravery.' One powerful chief called Iniaobba missed the flagellations of Holy Week and returned to the aldeia only on Easter Monday. Friar Vicente told him that it was now time for rejoicing, but he insisted that his dignity required that he undergo the ordeal of flagellation. The Friar relented, and 'he immediately went through the entire aldeia flagellating himself richly, spilling as much blood from his back as the others were putting wine into the jars for the festival'.

The trouble was that this music was unnatural and imported. Boys on the missions had to sing dry and mechanical hymns of devotion composed by the Jesuit Fathers. Any expression of their own culture that did not conform to Catholic morality was emasculated. Gilberto Freyre condemned Jesuit influence as 'quite as harmful as that of their antagonists, the colonists, who saw in the Indian only a voluptuous female to be taken or a rebellious slave to be subjugated and exploited. . . . While admirably efficient, it was a regime that destroyed any animal spirits, freshness or spontaneity, combativeness of mind, or *cultural potential* that the aboriginal may have possessed.'

SIX

Antarctic France

THE French had been visiting Brazil for almost as long as the Portuguese. French ships loaded brazilwood all along the coast, and Frenchmen were happily installed in many Indian villages to supervise the cutting and transportation of the logs. The French prided themselves on treating the Indians better than the Portuguese did. They were more generous with the presents they gave; they made much of friendly chiefs, lavishing fine clothing, swords and firearms on them, or taking them back to be received at the French court. Individual Frenchmen joined tribes very readily, shedding their clothes and their inhibitions when they did so. Above all, the French did not attempt permanent settlements: their merchants left agents in Indian villages but did not build their own forts or storehouses. It was the Portuguese who first claimed Brazil for their king, divided it into captaincies, and sent out shiploads of colonists.

This reticence changed in the middle of the sixteenth century. The French minister Admiral Coligny wanted to imitate the successes of Spain and Portugal in colonising the New World. He was therefore receptive when an enthusiast called Nicholas Durand de Villegagnon approached him with a dream of founding a French colony in Brazil. He proposed to occupy the great bay that the natives called Guanabara.

The Portuguese had first appreciated the potential of that magnificent natural harbour, with its entrance flanked by the towering granite outcrops of the Sugar Loaf, Corcovado and the cliffs and hills of Niterói.

France's ally, the Tamoio chief Cunhambebe.

Early in the century they built one of their towers and landed a few exiled criminals to garrison it. Because they started their settlement on New Year's Day, and because they thought that the bay must be the estuary of a great river, they called it Rio de Janeiro ('January River'). The convicts in the tower were supposed to 'mingle with the native inhabitants and learn their language. After a few years elapsed, these men behaved so badly towards those natives that the greater part of them were exterminated, destroyed and eaten. The survivors fled to sea in a boat. Since then the [Portuguese] have not dared to live there. Their name has remained so odious to this day that [the Indians] take voluptuous delight in eating the head of a Portuguese.' Anchieta confirmed that the Tamoio had once been good friends of the Portuguese 'but rebelled against them because of the great abuse and injustice that these did them, and welcomed the French from whom they received no abuse'.

Nicholas de Villegagnon seemed ideally qualified to lead a colonising expedition. He was an educated man who had studied theology at the Sorbonne, at the same time as Calvin. He was also a man of action. A fine swordsman, he had fought in Italy, Hungary and in the Emperor Charles V's attack on Algiers. But his greatest exploit had been to organise a mission to spirit the child Mary Queen of Scots out of Scotland in 1548 for betrothal to Francis II of France – Villegagnon sailed round the northern coasts of Scotland to elude the English fleet waiting to intercept him. When Villegagnon conceived the idea of colonising Guanabara Bay, he was in his mid-forties, a Knight of Malta, and Vice-Admiral of Brittany. He sailed out of Le Havre with three ships and a tough collection of potential settlers, and reached his destination on 10 November 1555.

The French fortified themselves on a small island at the mouth of the Bay, and gave their tiny colony the grandiose title of Antarctic France. They enlisted the natives to build strong forts on the outcrops of rock at either end of the island, and to build walls wherever there was a break in the cliffs around the island's shores. The only harbour was a narrow bay and this was defended with gun emplacements. A cave in one of the forts was made into a powder store. Mem de Sá called it one of the strongest fortresses in Christendom – but it lacked water.*

Antarctic France was not a success. In the first year the colonists suffered from disease and famine. Villegagnon wrote to Calvin asking him to send Protestant missionaries, but painted a gloomy description of his settlement. 'This country was all wilderness and wasteland. There were no houses or roofs nor any crops of cereals. On the contrary, there were fierce and savage people, strangers to any courtesy or humanity, totally different from us in their methods and education. They were without religion or any knowledge of honour or virtue, of what is right and what is unjust. It even entered my thoughts that we might have landed among beasts wearing human shapes.' This complaint was particularly unfair. The local Tamoio branch of the Tupinambá welcomed the French and treated them with traditional Indian hospitality. Other Frenchmen who wrote descriptions of the colony praised Tamoio generosity. 'They are very prompt to give pleasure and service for a small salary. . . . Thus, if you have to travel, they will conduct you for fifty or sixty leagues with all possible duty, fidelity and courtesy. . . . Once they have undertaken to guide you they will keep their promise, even if they have to shed their blood and their lives. . . . I can tell you that there is no nation under heaven more generous towards strangers with what grows in their country. . . . For as soon as they see someone from a distant country arrive in their land, far from rejecting or mistreating him, they have the grace to present him with food, lodging and often a girl for his service.' Such generosity was not enough for Villegagnon, who complained to Calvin that 'the people of the country live from one day to the next, not troubling to farm the land. We therefore found no food supplies assembled in one place, but had to go far, hither and thither, to gather and seek it.'

The French filled their small island with slaves. They bought captives from the local Tupinambá – prisoners captured from enemies such as the Maracaja Temimino. Villegagnon, who was so unsympathetic to the Indians, was also puritanically severe towards his own men. He ordered the women slaves to dress, and had them thrashed if they discarded superfluous clothes. And he 'forbade any Frenchman to have an affair with these savage bitches unless he took one of them as wife, on pain of death'. This was an impossible edict. Indians expected married women to be faithful, but offered unmarried girls to strangers as a gesture of hospitality or for some small reward. 'The worst thing I find among these people is that a father will prostitute his daughter for something of cheap value. . . . Thus, as soon as you arrive they ask you: "Come here, what will you give me if I present you with my daughter to serve you? She is beautiful and will serve you well in all your needs. She will provide you with fish, manioc flour and other produce of the land; and will come and go on your errands."'

One Norman had been among the Tupinambá since long before Villegagnon's arrival. He refused to marry or abandon his native woman 'with whom he had lived – as they all do – in the greatest abomination and epicurean manner . . . for seven years'. This man decided to do away with Villegagnon rather than lose his concubine. He incited the Indians by telling them that Villegagnon was responsible for the epidemic of fevers that had killed so many of them. He also enlisted some frustrated Normans with visions of the good life to be enjoyed among the native women. Villegagnon wrote to Calvin that 'twenty-six of our mercenaries, inspired by carnal desires, conspired to kill me. But on the day fixed for the execution one of the accomplices revealed the enterprise to me at the very instant that they were hurrying along to strike me down.' Villegagnon armed his retainers, including a bodyguard of three loyal Scots, overpowered the conspirators, hanged the ringleader and enslaved the others.

Shortly after this abortive revolt, Antarctic France was reinforced by three ships under Villegagnon's nephew, the Lord of Bois-le-Comte. This fleet brought three hundred colonists including some women, and two pastors sent from Geneva by Calvin. One was the incomparable Jean de Léry, who wrote one of the most sympathetic and accurate accounts of Brazilian Indians. The small colony already contained a fine chronicler, the Franciscan friar André Thevet, who later became Cosmographer Royal of France. Although Villegagnon had written to his friend Calvin asking for missionaries, he soon turned against the Protestants. The pastors may have been too militant. The small island was torn apart by a miniature war of religion. Villegagnon banished most Protestants to the mainland, and executed five of them in January 1558. He himself returned to France shortly after, leaving his young colony in terrible disarray.

There were two tribes of Indians around the bay of Guanabara: a group of Temimino under Chief Maracaja-guaçu ('Big Wild Cat'), living on the island now called Ilha do Governador ('Governor's Island') at the head of the Bay; and their enemies the Tamoio, a powerful federation of Tupinambá tribes occupying the lands between Cabo Frio and the Piratininga plateau, the site of modern São Paulo. The Temimino of Chief Big Wild Cat had been losing the war against the stronger Tamoio. In April 1555 they had appealed to the Portuguese Donatory of Espírito Santo to be given sanctuary in his area. The Portuguese rescued this group, transporting them up the coast to be settled in Jesuit aldeias alongside the Tupinikin of Espírito Santo.†

For all their good intentions, the French did nothing but harm to their Indian allies, the Tamoio. They decimated them with imported diseases, encouraged their wars against the Temimino and Waitacá, and sought to convince them of the advantages of a French alliance by stressing how much more powerful France was than Portugal. The only good to result from the colony of Antarctic France was the splendid writing of the rival chroniclers André Thevet and Jean de Léry. Each left vivid descriptions of Tupinambá life. Their books are the best ethnographic works of the sixteenth century. Léry loved visiting Indian villages. He revelled in the traditional weeping greeting of the women, and enjoyed watching the children scrabble for fish-hooks and the women teasingly beg for presents. He never forgot his first visit to a village. 'I immediately found myself surrounded by savages who demanded, "What is your name?" One of them took my hat, which he put on his head; another my sword and belt, which he strapped around his naked body; another my cassock, which he put on. Then, deafening me with their cries, they ran about their village in this way with my clothes.' Léry thought he had lost his possessions. But this was a normal greeting for a stranger, and everything was soon returned to him. 'By a fortunate coincidence my surname Léry means oyster in their language. I therefore told them that I was called Léry-guaçu, which means Big Oyster. They were highly satisfied by this, and said with admiration, "Teh!" and laughing, "That is a truly fine name! We have never before seen a mair [Frenchman] called that!"' Léry was deeply impressed by Indian generosity and natural goodness. He was an excellent observer of everything from the rites of cannibalism to the way in which mothers wiped their babies' bottoms. He had no prejudices about Indian barbarity – if anything, he was too sympathetic, often contrasting Indian virtue with European greed and hypocrisy.

Thevet left a portrait of the paramount chief Quoniambec or Cunhambebe of the Tamoio, and managed to record the repetitive bombastic style of Indian oratory. Cunhambebe was 'the most redoubtable devil of all the country. He came from eighty or a hundred leagues to see us face to face. By his wise remarks he showed us great rays of virtue hidden beneath that brutal upbringing – above all in his opinion about the immortality of the soul. This man ate with us, and drank of our most precious drink, which was vinegar mixed with water. He left still fairly sober, but felt his stomach heat up and rumble. He laughed and said that his soul was rejoicing inside him and in his body. Then striking his stomach, shoulders and thighs with his hands . . . he boasted that if at that moment he had caught the cleverest of his Maracaja Temimino enemies he would have made a fine fricassee of him. This man was big and strong-limbed, some eight feet tall, and the toughest, cruellest and most feared of all the other kings of the neighbouring provinces. He was also bellicose for that country, and very wise and experienced in matters of war, and full of good advice: for it was he who advised us to seize the rivers and islands alongside ours and to build forts on them for our defence.'

'If you could have seen his palace, it is a hut no richer than the others, all adorned and trimmed outside with the heads of the adversaries he had massacred and eaten. As soon as this warrior was advised of our arrival, he did not fail to come and visit us. We presented him with a two-handed sword and robes of red and green cloth and some billhooks and knives. He stayed with us for a full month, spending most of the time reciting his deeds and exploits to us. . . . He would make a discourse and harangue lasting two full hours, marching about quite naked, beating and slapping his chest and thighs, always interspersing it with menaces against his enemies the Peros (who were the Portuguese). He would say: "I have eaten so many of them, and Maracaja as well. I have slain so many of their wives and children. Having disposed of them at will, I caused myself, because of my heroic deeds, to take the title of the greatest morbicha [chief] there has ever been among us. Despite their cunning and caution my enemies have never been able to attack me without giving good warning. I have delivered many people from the jaws of my enemies. I am great. I am powerful. I am strong. Can any man be compared with me?" And a thousand other boasts [were] made by this venerable king while he walked about striking his shoulders or thighs, with such gestures that there was scarcely a man who did not tremble hearing him speak with a voice so great, hideous and terrible that you could hardly have heard had it thundered. Our Captain Villegagnon gave him an audience, putting on a good expression, as did all those of our company: there was not one who dared laugh for fear of irritating this valorous champion and those of his suite.' Cunhambebe would count his hundreds of victims on his fingers and toes. He used to love watching the French praying, and would himself kneel and raise his hands to heaven, asking Thevet to teach him Christian prayers.

'He was so strong that he could have carried a hogshead of wine in his arms. To demonstrate this better and to give courage to his men in battle, he once took two guns he had removed by force from a Portuguese ship (which could fire a ball as big as an ostrich egg) and put these over his shoulders, turning the mouths of the cannons towards his enemies. . . . When he heard the Maracaja approaching he ordered one of his troop to put fire to these pieces. And, when they were discharged, he immediately took two more to start firing again. When he then saw his enemies covering the ground and fleeing in terror, God knows how he mocked them! For they fear the noise of artillery or any other firearms above all else.'

Although most Tamoio customs were those of other Tupi tribes, the Tamoio were famous for their music and dancing. 'They are great composers of impromptu songs, for which they are greatly esteemed by the heathen wherever they go.'

The French colony was planted during the administration of the ineffectual Duarte da Costa, second governor of Portuguese Brazil. His successor Mem de Sá immediately saw that he must evict this intrusion into the country claimed by his king. He moved with characteristic energy, and the Portuguese fought with their usual determination and efficiency. Their professionalism made the French look almost amateurish, despite the friendship of the Tamoio and the bombast of Cunhambebe. Mem de Sá sailed south in 1560, bringing a force of the Bahia Tupinambá he had just subdued. His fleet entered the Bay and sailed off Fort Coligny for three weeks. The French refused to surrender, and were joined on the island by hundreds of their Tamoio allies. Mem de Sá told the Queen-Regent that Villegagnon 'is extremely liberal with the Indians and does them justice . . . because of which he is . . . loved by the heathen. He ordered that they be taught all forms of weapons drill, and helps them in their wars. His heathen are many, and among the most valiant of the coast.'

The Portuguese finally attacked on 15 March 1560. Villegagnon's fort seemed impregnable as they sailed towards it. The cliffs of the island fell sheer into the sea on all sides, and the only entrance was defended by French artillery. The forts were full of heavily armed Frenchmen and Tamoio, well supplied with food and munitions. But Mem de Sá was undaunted: 'We fought the fortress by sea from all sides . . . and on that day we entered the island on which the fortress was erected. We fought all that day and the next without resting day or night. . . .' The defenders 'twice came out against us and fought fiercely'. At the height of the battle two Portuguese managed to scale an almost inaccessible cliff and seized the French powder store. The battle raged for most of Friday and all Saturday. 'Many died on both sides, but most on ours. It came to a point where we had lost hope of victory and were planning how we could safely re-embark and remove the munitions that were on land.' The Portuguese ships were out of powder. Their men on the island were exhausted. But on the Saturday night the French and Tamoio gave up: they abandoned their fort and escaped to the mainland in canoes and rafts. They were equally short of powder and had run out of water – the great weakness of Villegagnon's Fort Coligny.*

The two sides gave wildly different versions of the numbers involved and their losses. Thevet claimed there were only 10 French defenders resisting 2000 attackers in 26 heavily armed ships and many war-canoes. But Mem de Sá said that the fort contained 116 Frenchmen 'and well over a thousand natives of the country, all picked men and just as good musketeers as the French; while we were only 120 Portuguese and 140 heathen, badly armed and with little will to fight'. Mem de Sá also boasted that 'Our Lord saw fit to have us enter the fort with much victory and death of the enemy and little of our men.' But Thevet said that for every Frenchman killed there were 120 dead among the attackers; and the Portuguese authors Anchieta and Soares de Sousa both admitted heavy losses by the Portuguese and their Indian allies.*

Mem de Sá wrote to the Queen with clumsy modesty: 'If this victory did not involve me so closely, I could affirm to Your Highness that it is many years since there has been a similar one between Christians. For, although I have seen much but read little, it seems to me that no other fortress has been seen in the world as strong as this. . . . The deed was done by Our Lord, who did not want . . . Lutherans and Calvinists to be planted in this land. . . .' He ended with a plea that was not answered: 'I beg Your Highness to order my departure for I am old and not long for this earth. I owe a lot of money, for wars cannot be waged in a niggardly way, and I will be ruined if I stay here longer.' The Portuguese thus destroyed Villegagnon's Antarctic France. They did not, however, feel strong enough to colonise Rio de Janeiro, even though the far-sighted Nóbrega recommended the foundation of another city as large as Bahia. He begged the King to 'send settlers rather than soldiers'.

Mem de Sá said that after the capture of Villegagnon's island 'I destroyed some strong villages, killing many Indians'. But the Tamoio were still very powerful. French ships continued to trade with them and encourage them against the Portuguese. The Jesuit Leonardo do Vale noted the presence of seven French ships at Rio de Janeiro, and Anchieta was sure that the Tamoio were determined 'to put all São Vicente to fire and blood'.

Anchieta claimed that all the French at Rio de Janeiro were Protestants. It was imperative that they be expelled. He himself did much to prepare a fresh attempt against the Tamoio – for even the most devout Jesuits could become militarily aggressive when they wanted to defeat hostile tribes or Lutheran enemies. Ignatius Loyola was a soldier, and had conceived his Society of Jesus on military lines as the militant defenders of the Papacy.

The Tamoio federation controlled most of the Paraíba valley and the coast south-westwards from Cabo Frio past Rio de Janeiro to the plateau of Piratininga. The Tamoio were therefore in conflict with the Portuguese settlers of São Paulo de Piratininga and their Tupinikin allies. The town council of that fledgling frontier community wrote to the King to ask for guns, oxen, two dozen good swords, and some exiled convicts to marry the local native women and help populate the land. They described a battle against the Tamoio in 1560. Thirty whites, thirty half-castes – most of them sons of João Ramalho – and their Tupinikin allies set out 'having confessed and taken communion and greatly trusting in Our Lord'. The Tamoio knew that they were coming 'and had fortified themselves so strongly that it was a thing of horror. They had assembled their most chosen men on the frontier, and had many strongholds, each with four very strong enclosures around them like walls, as if they had been white men, and besides this many arquebuses and powder and swords that the French gave them. But Our Lord in His mercy gave us victory. The enclosures were entered and all of them killed or captured. . . . It cost us the death of two good settlers and one half-caste, and we were almost all wounded or shot by arrows, and some of our Indians were killed.'

Settlers tended to write to their king only about victories. We learn from Jesuit letters that the Portuguese generally had the worst of the fighting against the Tamoio. There were times when the settlements – Santos and São Vicente on the coast and São Paulo on the plateau – looked as though they would not survive the Indian onslaughts.

The main defence of these colonial outposts was the friendship of the local Tupinikin, the tribe of Chief Tibiriça who had married his daughter to João Ramalho. For a variety of reasons the Portuguese now fell out with their native allies. The Indians were alarmed by the mortality from imported diseases. They concluded that white magic was neither powerful nor beneficial if it allowed such destruction of Indians who accepted Christianity. They were also influenced by the wild half-caste sons of João Ramalho. These men resented Jesuit strictures against their polygamy, slaving and other 'heathen' practices. They had the prestige of their European father and important Indian mother, so that the tribes listened to them rather than to the Fathers.

The first aggression came from the whites. Anchieta sailed down the Tietê in a punitive raid on the Tupinikin at Easter 1561.† The Indian counter-attack came next year. Disaffected Tupinikin joined the Tamoio in a combined attack on São Paulo. For once, hostile tribes joined forces in an effort to expel the colonists. José de Anchieta described the Indian attack – this young Jesuit had a way of being present whenever there was action, and had the literary ability to describe it. A great mass of Indians led by Chief Piquerobi attacked the young settlement on the morning of 9 July 1561. They dashed across the plain, shouting bloodcurdling war-cries, magnificently plumed and painted for battle. Native women huddled in the Jesuit church, praying before an altar of lighted candles and soaking the pews and walls with blood shed in their mortifications. São Paulo was saved not by prayer but because the paramount Chief Tibiriça remained loyal to the Jesuits. He rallied eight villages of converted Indians and rushed them in to defend the settlement. 'He moved the hearts of many Indians . . . to take up arms against their own people.' In the fighting, Christian Tupinikin were resisting their immediate relatives – brother against brother, even son against father. The Jesuits' 'disciples marched out under the banners of the church, and fighting like the first Saracens, in full belief that Paradise was to be their reward, their zeal was invincible'. After two days the attackers called off their siege, doubtless because of the opposition by their chief Tibiriça. Anchieta reported with satisfaction that one lapsed convert, Tibiriça's nephew Jaguanharo ('Wild Dog'), was killed by an arrow when he tried to get at the women and booty inside the Jesuit college. He also noted that Tibiriça stopped former Christians from appealing to the Jesuits for mercy. The old chief smashed their heads with a ceremonial execution club 'without telling us about it. . . . For with this sort of people there is no better preaching than the sword and iron rod.'

Anchieta admitted that, if Tibiriça had joined the attackers, most Christian Indians would have followed him. 'They would have had little difficulty in killing and eating us all.' But it was the great chief himself who died: he caught the dreaded epidemic that killed so many of his people. In December 1562 'our chief and great friend Martím Afonso [Tibiriça] died . . . of an illness of fluxes of blood. He had made himself the enemy of his own brothers and relatives for the love of God and his Church.' On his deathbed he confessed, 'with such brains and maturity that he did not seem like a Brazilian'. He was buried in the Jesuit college in a ceremony attended by all the Indians and with the Portuguese holding candles for their protégé. The Jesuits remembered Tibiriça as 'the benefactor and even the founder of the college of Piratininga and of our lives'.

The two great Jesuits, Nóbrega and Anchieta, now embarked on their most famous exploit. They plunged into the territory of their Tamoio enemies on a daring mission of personal diplomacy. The Portuguese were seriously worried that the Tamoio and French were going to drive them out of São Vicente. The road between the plateau of Piratininga and the coast was cut by constant Indian attack. It is one of the world's most spectacular roads, dropping off the plateau in a cascade of steep hairpins and tunnels, down forested cliffs with the narrow coastal plain lost in the haze far below. Indian raids on this supply line increased alarmingly. Tamoio war-canoes harassed the islands and inlets near São Vicente. 'No longer content with assaults, the enemy was now attempting to attack the entire land and take possession of it.' Plantations were not safe from Indians who ceaselessly 'seized the slaves, women and children of the Christians, killing and eating them', and would not be deterred by 'very serious tortures to stop their cruel business'. 'They killed many and carried off women and children into captivity – the latter as tender fodder for their bellies, the former for their licentiousness. There was no remedy for all these evils. For they moved in flying canoes with ten or twenty rowers on each side. They were very skilful paddlers and no one could catch or overtake them. We had no force to intimidate them.' Unless the coast north-east of São Vicente could be made safe for Portuguese shipping, there could never be a successful Portuguese invasion and settlement of Rio de Janeiro. Nóbrega decided upon his bold embassy to achieve this strategic purpose, and took the young Anchieta along as interpreter.

The two Jesuits set off from the fort of Bertioga near Santos in heavily armed boats on 23 April 1563. They camped on the island of São Sebastião, which was deserted and full of jaguars, and sailed on for seventy-five miles to the Tamoio settlements of Iperoig ('River of Sharks'). Indian canoes appeared but dared not approach the Portuguese ships for fear of being seized as slaves. An Indian woman who had lived among the Portuguese identified Nóbrega as the Jesuit leader, and assured her people that they 'could safely trust in us'. The Jesuits were received as guests and allowed to preach in the Tamoio villages. Indian hostages remained on the ships, and Nóbrega and Anchieta took up residence in an Indian hut. 'The Indians gave us all possible good treatment, considering their poverty and humble way of life.' They repeatedly offered girls to sleep with their guests and were amazed when the Jesuits declined. The temptation troubled young Anchieta. He wrote that a celibate needed special divine help 'when living among people for whom an essential element of happiness rests in [sex]. Their thoughts, words and actions all ultimately return to this subject – something that one can scarcely fail to hear and even see.'

The Tamoio explained why they were prepared to negotiate with the Portuguese. It was not from fear, 'for they have always conquered the [Portuguese] Christians and caused them much damage. Nor was it from a need for trade goods, for the French give them plenty of clothing and tools, arquebuses and swords.' The reason was the usual myopic tribal hatred. The Tamoio were impressed that the Portuguese had recently fallen out with their Tupinikin allies, and were longing for 'a good vengeance on [the Tupinikin], killing and eating them at will. . . . They wanted revenge on the Tupi and not on us [Portuguese], and wanted to direct our fury against the Tupi who had rebelled against us without reason.'

The Jesuits also recorded the reasons for Tamoio hatred of the Portuguese. They met one chief 'who had long ago been seized deceitfully by the Portuguese with many others. He had escaped, jumping from a ship with irons on his feet and fleeing all night.

Although he had cause for great hatred against us because of this, he decided to forget it and change it to love.' One of his wives had been seized and sold into slavery. But the Jesuits had refused absolution to her captor until he freed her. She now showed her gratitude by helping Nóbrega and Anchieta.

When Chief Pindobuçu ('Palm Leaf') arrived he was furious to find Jesuits in the village, and threw them out of his hut. Anchieta professed friendship, but Pindobuçu 'answered very angrily and proudly, "I want none of your company," and other harsh things'. Pindobuçu wanted to kill these enemies; but he admitted that he had always favoured making peace with the Portuguese. He reasoned with his people: 'If we fear our own shamans, how much more should we fear the Fathers. They must be true saints, for they have the power to inflict on us fluxes of blood, coughing, headaches, fevers and other calamities from which we all die!' Pindobuçu therefore accepted the Jesuits and became their staunch defender during the ensuing months. They often needed his help.

On one occasion Chief Ambiré arrived from Rio de Janeiro with ten canoes of warriors, determined to kill and eat the Jesuits. He was another chief who had been seized by the Portuguese during a truce and had escaped in shackles. He had married his daughter to a Frenchman, and 'was a tall man, dry and of a sad and troubled countenance, and we knew that he was very cruel'. He harangued the Jesuits, reminding them of Portuguese wrongs, while flexing his arms and brandishing his arrows. His warriors surrounded the Fathers, with their bows and clubs ready for the order to kill; but Pindobuçu intervened to save them.

Nóbrega and Anchieta were walking on the beach one day and were seen by a war-canoe from Guanabara. Nóbrega was too weak from disease to run back to the village. The canoe turned in towards the Jesuits and they had to plunge waistdeep into a stream, with Nóbrega still wearing shoes and stockings. Anchieta's back was too painful to carry his Superior. They crossed the stream as the canoe raced into it, and plunged into the forest beyond. Nóbrega removed his cassock, shoes and stockings while the warriors landed and began to search the undergrowth. The Fathers hurried inland in soaking shifts, and were finally rescued and half-carried to their village by some of Pindobuçu's men.*

During their stay at Iperoig, the two Jesuits spied out the strength of Tamoio military preparations. They saw 200 war-canoes, each made from the bark of a single tree, with bark bulwarks and liana strengthening – canoes that could carry twenty or thirty warriors with their weapons and could sail through rough seas. The Tamoio were determined to destroy the Portuguese in a series of raids by sea and a descent by all the tribes of the Paraíba. They hoped to drive the intruders out of the captaincy of São Vicente. Nóbrega and Anchieta 'considered the difficulties and dangers of their mission well spent, when they saw these preparations and compared them with those of our men who were so reduced in strength'.

A truce was arranged on 28 May 1563 and the terms sent to the Governor of São Vicente for ratification. One condition was that the Portuguese must surrender some Tupinikin chiefs to the Tamoio; but Nóbrega wrote secretly that this must not be done. By mid-June the two Jesuits were again in danger from anti-Portuguese Tamoio, and their saviour now was the same Cunhambebe who had been such a good friend of Villegagnon's Frenchmen. The Fathers moved to Cunhambebe's village and were warmly received by the great chief. He brewed cauin and gave a party in their honour. He ordered one of his women to bring the shin of an Indian slave captured from the Portuguese. 'And, asking for manioc flour, they began to gnaw at it like dogs, one on one side and another on the other.' The Tamoio now allowed Nóbrega to return to São Vicente, and Cunhambebe accompanied him. They moved on down the coast to the church of Itanhaém for a ceremony of reconciliation between the Tamoio of Iperoig and those Tupinikin who had remained allies of the Portuguese. But the purpose of this reconciliation was to destroy the Tupinikin who were in rebellion.

Chief Pindobuçu was with Nóbrega but hurried back to Iperoig to protect Anchieta. This Jesuit remained alone as a hostage among the Tamoio from 21 June to 14 September 1563. He preached to the Indian children and spent his time composing almost six thousand couplets in honour of the Virgin Mary. It was Cunhambebe who finally obtained the release of Anchieta, even though there were still Tamoio hostages at São Vicente. Anchieta's safe return caused rejoicing among the people of São Vicente. He described his adventures in fine letters, and his biographer Simão de Vasconcellos ensured that the brave mission passed into Brazilian legend. The truce saved São Vicente from a powerful Tamoio attack, and the Jesuit emissaries brought back details of Tamoio fighting strength. It ended years of fighting during which the Tamoio had killed forty Portuguese and many Tupinikin. It meant that the coast between São Vicente and Guanabara was safe for a Portuguese attack on Rio de Janeiro. The Tamoio of Iperoig remained at peace while the Portuguese attacked other groups of Tamoio. But in the end the promises of lasting friendship contained in the truce proved meaningless – for settlers soon enslaved even the Tamoio of Iperoig.

In 1563, the year of the truce of Iperoig, Mem de Sá's nephew Estácio de Sá reached Bahia with two large ships from Portugal. Estácio sailed south, picking up the Maracaja Temimino who had been taken to Espírito Santo and were eager to return to their homes at Guanabara. These were now led by a great warrior called Arariboia. Mem de Sá advised his nephew to consult Nóbrega, and Estácio sent a ship to fetch the Jesuit leader from São Vicente. Nóbrega and Anchieta sailed to the Bay and narrowly escaped capture by the Tamoio of Rio de Janeiro. On Easter Sunday 1564 they celebrated mass on Villegagnon's abandoned island. But the Jesuit leader advised Estácio de Sá to make better preparations before launching his attack on the Tamoio.

The Portuguese commander sailed on to São Vicente to recruit settlers, many of whom feared that they were too few to conquer the Tamoio and colonise Rio de Janeiro. The Jesuits from São Paulo sent contingents of Indian volunteers from their missions – these left their families and went out of love for the Jesuits and because they had been told that the Tamoio planned to attack them. Estácio de Sá then returned and landed his men on 1 March 1565 at the foot of the Sugar Loaf, in what is now the Urca district of Rio de Janeiro. He had a moment of panic before landing, and asked Nóbrega: '"Father Nóbrega! What report shall I give to God and the King if I go and lose this fleet?" [Nóbrega] replied with superhuman confidence: "Sir, *I* will account to God for everything. And if necessary I will go to the presence of the King and will answer for you there."'

The Portuguese dedicated their camp to St Sebastian and even started a rudimentary town administration. Everyone worked at felling trees and carrying logs. They fortified the camp with trenches, stockades, artillery redoubts and even tile roofs on their huts as protection against fire arrows. A two-year stalemate ensued. The Tamoio were powerfully fortified in their villages around the Bay. One of their strongest bases was on the Glória hill facing the Portuguese camp across the small bay of Botafogo. There were frequent battles on land and sea, but neither side was strong enough to dislodge the other.

No quarter was given in this fighting – there had been too much cruelty and merciless killing by both sides during the past decades. Thevet once tried to save the life of a Portuguese prisoner about to be eaten by the Tamoio. But the Indian chief turned on him angrily: 'Ha, you wretch! I would never have thought that you could forget so much or be so disloyal as to ask me to spare one who is the enemy of your name. Do you not know that his people and our enemies the Maracaja ask for nothing but the ruin of your captain and you, as well as of us who have always been your friends?' Another Portuguese prisoner who spoke good Tupi tried to save himself by skilful pleading. His captors were pitiless: 'He who held him prisoner, seeing him so downhearted and fearful of death, killed him on the spot with arrow shots, without awaiting the day of the ritual massacre. He said to him: "You are worthless and do not deserve to be done the honour of dying in good company as honourably as the others."'

Jean de Léry told a similar story. 'Our savages once surprised two Portuguese in an earthen hut in the woods near their fort called Morpion [São Vicente]. They defended themselves valiantly from morning until evening. When the ammunition for their arquebuses and bolts for their crossbows were exhausted, each emerged with a two-handed sword and caused such a check to their assailants that many were killed and others wounded. The savages, however, became increasingly stubborn and resolved all to be cut to pieces rather than retreat without winning. They finally took them and led the two Portuguese off as prisoners. The savages sold me some buffalo-hide clothes from the spoil. . . . On return to their village they tore the beards from these two Portuguese as an insult. They not only made them die cruelly, but the savages also mocked them because the wretches afflicted in this way felt sorrow and were complaining. The savages said to them: "What, can this be so? You defended yourselves bravely. But now that you must die with honour you show no more courage than women." They were then killed and eaten in the customary way.' Another group of Tamoio told Léry of a happy day when they surprised a Portuguese caravel. They slaughtered and ate the crew, and then tackled the cargo of barrels of brandy. 'We stood these up and broke open the ends to taste the contents. Well! . . . I do not know what sort of cauin they contained, or whether you have that sort in your country. But I can tell you: after we drank ourselves into intoxication we were so knocked out and soporific that we could not wake up for two or three days!'

In this savage fighting the Europeans rejoiced in the power of their firearms. Estácio de Sá addressed his troops as they marched against hordes of Tamoio: 'All their shouting deafens our ears but not our hearts. But our musketry silences both their hearing *and* their hearts! You will see them either fall dead or flee when they see our muskets. Their bows are no match for our arquebuses, nor their arrows for our shot. . . . We all know the arrogance of these licentious savages, the ancient and present hatreds . . . their intention to destroy us, and the assaults by sea and land with which they disturb our entire coast, robbing, enslaving, killing, eating the flesh of our men and drinking their blood like wild beasts. Our vengeance is amply justified. . . . Let us put an end to this plague once and for all and remove the settlers from its threat, clear the land and build a city on it. . . .' The Portuguese also had the advantage of a good leader, in the tenacious young Estácio de Sá. Anchieta described him as 'a great friend of God, gentle and affable. He never rests by day or night, attending to all and sundry and always the first in any labours.'

There were some great sea-battles during 1566. On one occasion Tamoio canoes were waiting in ambush behind the islands off Rio de Janeiro. A large bird flew across, and a Tamoio archer could not resist a shot. The ambush was thus betrayed when the bird glided in from seaward, transfixed by a Tamoio arrow. In mid-July the Tamoio assembled 180 war-canoes under the famous Chief Guaixara of Cabo Frio and lured the Portuguese into an ambush. These would certainly have been defeated, but a canoe full of gunpowder caught fire and exploded. The Tamoio commander's wife took fright and started screaming. The Indians fled in disorder, 'as if the fire of a Mount Etna were falling upon them'.

Both French and Portuguese sent to Europe for reinforcements to break the deadlock. Jesuits and royal officials wrote to beg for a new fleet. Once again, the government in Lisbon took Brazil more seriously than that in Paris. A fleet of three galleons under Cristóvão Cardoso de Barros reached Bahia in August 1566. It sailed south a few months later with more ships and men, Indian auxiliaries from the missions and plantations, six Jesuits including Anchieta and Luís de Grã, and the old governor Mem de Sá himself. Mem de Sá reached his nephew's camp on 18 January 1567, and the Portuguese immediately launched an offensive. On St Sebastian's Day, 20 January, they attacked the fortified village of Chief Ibiriguaçu-mirim on the Glória behind Flamengo beach. It was a hard battle, but the Portuguese and their Indian allies won. All the Tamoio defenders were killed, including a shaman who was promising them victory. Five Frenchmen who survived the fighting were hanged from trees. But Estácio de Sá was hit in the face by an arrow and died a month later from the wound. The man who had commanded the Portuguese camp at the foot of the Sugar Loaf was very young: one Jesuit wrote of him, 'When Estácio de Sá acted as governor he was seventeen years old, but very vigorous.'

Mem de Sá now attacked the redoubt of Paranapecu on the Temimino's former home, the Ilha do Governador. He wrote that 'there were over a thousand fighting men there and much artillery. Our men attacked it continuously for three days until they entered it with much effort and danger and the deaths of some whites. After defending themselves vigorously, [the Tamoio] surrendered and were all enslaved. We were about to march against another fortress stronger than all of them, in which there were many Frenchmen. It had three extremely strong enclosures and many bulwarks and strongholds. But they did not dare to await us, and abandoned the fortress. They then came to me to seek peace and I granted it them. . . .'

Mem de Sá decided to move the settlement of Rio de Janeiro to a level space, in what is now the business centre of the city. 'I chose a site . . . that was a great dense forest, full of many thick trees. It involved quite a lot of work cutting them down and clearing the site and building a large city surrounded by a rampart 20 palmos wide and as many high, all enclosed with a wall on top and many strong bastions full of artillery. . . . I ordered many settlers and much cattle to come and people the said city, which is going very well and is already a great creation.'

The Jesuits had been very active in the conquest of Rio de Janeiro, and Mem de Sá gave them a large site for their college. Manoel da Nóbrega arrived in July 1567 as its first rector. Anchieta wrote of him: 'During the past years at São Vicente he was already very weak from the many diseases he brought from Bahia. He slept little at night, and spent most nights in prayer, reciting the divine office, and he cared for and planned the affairs of government, not only that of the Society, but also of everything that he felt to be of concern to the common good. . . . Some serious persons said that he was fit to govern the entire world.' Nóbrega died at Rio de Janeiro in 1570, 'after leaving all that land subjected and pacific, with the Tamoio Indians subjected and vanquished, and everything subject to the King. It was he who did most in the settlement [of the city]. For through his counsel, fervour and aid was begun, continued and brought to conclusion the town of Rio de Janeiro.'

Mem de Sá settled a few Tamoio near the city and distributed others as slaves to the colonists. Some tried to resist but were crushed. Many were killed. But the majority fled inland or along the coast to the strongholds of other Tamoio at Cabo Frio. The most powerful of their abandoned villages were handed over to the returning Temimino of Chief Arariboia, together with some twenty-seven square miles of land. The return of this chief was a provocation to the Tamoio of Cabo Frio. They longed 'to lay their hands on him and make a merry banquet of him'. The French were still trading with the surviving Tamoio, and in 1568 these enlisted four French ships to help them attack Arariboia. They sailed past the Portuguese settlement of Rio de Janeiro and landed a mass of French and Tamoio alongside the Temimino village. Arariboia refused to surrender, evacuated non-combatants and attacked the Tamoio before dawn next morning. The French ships had gone aground on falling tide, and a falconet on Arariboia's ramparts pounded them with stones. The grounded French ships could not reply;

and, as soon as the tide refloated them, they hurried back to France. It was a fine victory for the Temiminos, with plenty of Tamoio and a few French killed. King Sebastião rewarded Arariboia with 'a habit of the Order of Christ with a pension, and a suit off his own body'.

Mem de Sá left his nephew Salvador Corrêa de Sá in command at Rio de Janeiro, and this Salvador made a successful attack on French shipping at Cabo Frio. By 1570 a Jesuit could write: 'Now at last, by the goodness of God, the Tamoio are beginning to beg for peace. The Captain has already given some [as slaves to colonists] and is scattering them among other settlers for the greater good.' The Tamoio of the Paraíba valley made peace in 1574. But the final destruction of the Tamoio came in 1575 with the arrival of Dr Antonio de Salema as governor of southern Brazil.

Salema was a lawyer, a hard man with little sympathy for Brazilian Indians. Soon after his arrival, Chief Arariboia was given an audience. The old warrior crossed his legs in the presence of the Governor and was rebuked by him. 'The Indian at once answered, without anger or arrogance: "If you knew how tired these legs of mine are from the wars in which I have served the King, you would not begrudge them this little rest. Since, however, you find me lacking in courtesy I shall return to my village, where we do not trouble about such details, and will never again return to your court."' In the mid-1570s Arariboia's Temiminos were moved from their choice site at the mouth of the Carioca river to the far side of Guanabara Bay, to ground now occupied by the thriving modern city of Niterói. Some descendant of the Temimino might even try to claim the land, which was given to Arariboia in perpetuity, 'for him and for all his heirs and successors who come after him'.

In 1575 the Tamoio from Cabo Frio raided some of the sugar plantations near Rio de Janeiro. The settlers clamoured for action by Governor Salema. He organised a powerful force of 400 Portuguese, including such famous captains as Jerónimo Leitão and Cristóvão Cardoso de Barros, almost every able-bodied citizen of Rio de Janeiro and many from São Vicente. They marched out on 27 August 1575 accompanied by 700 Indian allies – but not the disgruntled Arariboia himself. The Tamoio of Cabo Frio were 'very proud and strong, with many weapons from the French – swords, daggers, broadswords, arquebuses and cannons'. Salema besieged the fortified village of the Tamoio Chief Japuguaçu. He persuaded most Frenchmen in the area to desert their Indian friends and accept a separate peace. The native defenders were short of water and seemed about to launch a desperate sortie. The Portuguese commander therefore sent a Jesuit, Father Baltasar, to parley, and on 22 September Chief Japuguaçu emerged to

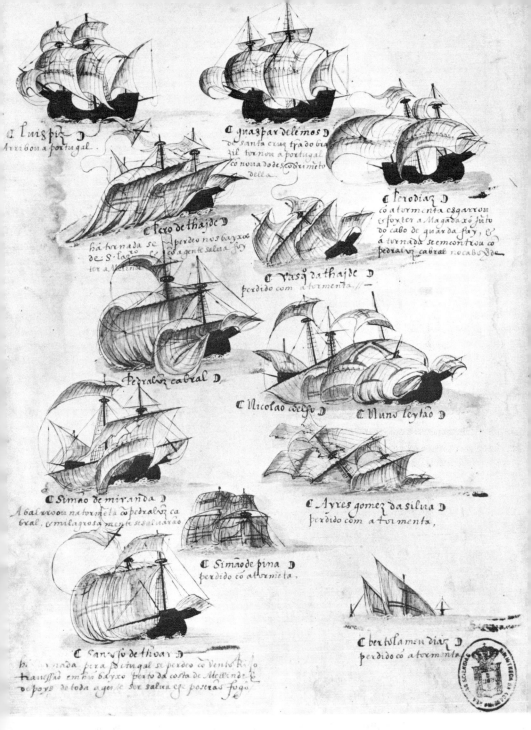

1 The fleet of 1500 that discovered Brazil: only three ships survived the voyage to India. The ship of Gaspar de Lemos (*top, centre*) returned to Portugal with news of the discovery of Brazil. Pero Álvares Cabral and Pero Vaz de Caminha drowned in the wreck of the flagship (*centre, left*), and the ship of Bartolomeu Dias, discoverer of the Cape of Good Hope, is shown sinking (*bottom, right*).

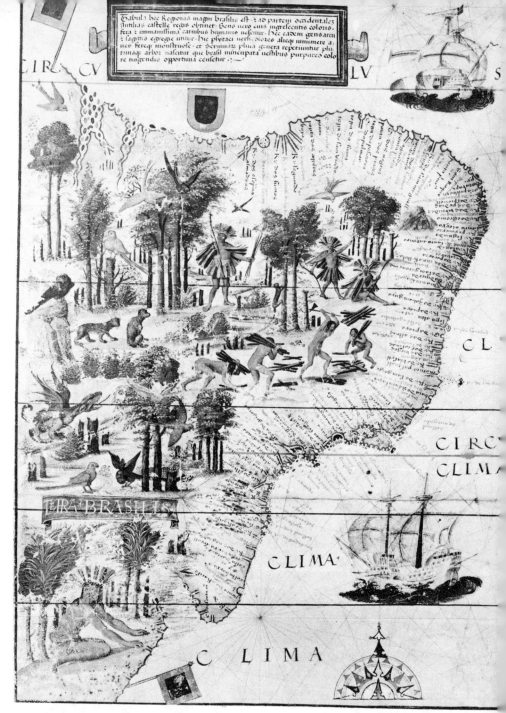

2 Lopo Homem's map of Brazil (1519) was the first to give an accurate impression of the mouths of the Amazon and **Pará** rivers. It shows Portuguese flags north of the Amazon and south of the Plate – a claim well beyond the Line of Tordesillas. Indians are shown cutting brazilwood with a metal axe, and the rich fauna includes parrots, macaws, monkeys, a jaguar and even a fantastic dragon.

3 The German gunner Hans Staden is captured by Tamoio at the fort of Bertioga near Santos, and taken (*right*) to be taunted by the women of their village, 1552.

4 Tupinambá shamans with maracá gourd rattles and anklets of ahouai nuts. They wear characteristic Tupinambá decoration – lip plugs, tonsured heads, a feathered headdress and a buttock ornament of ostrich feathers attached to a ball of gum.

5 The entertainment organised by the city of Rouen to greet
Henri II and Catherine de Medici in 1550. Brazilian Indians and
naked French sailors staged a mock battle on the banks of the Seine.

6 The oldest known woodcut of Brazilian Indians shows human flesh
hanging from a rafter and a man chewing a severed arm. Probably *c.* 1505.

7 Friars from Cabral's fleet say mass in newly discovered Brazil, watched by Indians of Bahia. A romantic nineteenth-century portrayal.

8 French Capuchins bring Christianity to the Indians of Maranhão in 1612.

9 A Tupinambá chief from Maranhão was baptised in Paris, with King Louis XIII as godfather. He wore white satin and carried a fleur-de-lys.

The family life of Brazilian Indians is notably harmonious, even in crowded communal huts. Tupi-speaking Kamayurá, upper Xingu, Mato Grosso: (*left*) a mother with baby and a pet bird, (*right*) a family resting on native and imported hammocks.

A recently contacted Tupi tribe: Asurini, lower Xingu, Pará.

10 These modern photographs, and those later in the book, show Brazilian Indians visited by the author; their appearance has changed little since their ancestors were first encountered by Europeans.

Warriors of a newly contacted Tupi tribe, the Suruí (or Cintas Largas, 'broad belts'), Aripuanã, Rondônia. They wear lip plugs and straw penis sheaths.

11 Indians from the north-east of Brazil brandish arrows and clubs in a war dance. The haircuts of these 'Tapuia', as painted by Albert Eckhout in *c.* 1640, is identical to that of modern Gê-speaking Canela from the same part of Brazil (*see* plate 25).

12 Brazilian Indians impressed Europeans with their brilliant archery.

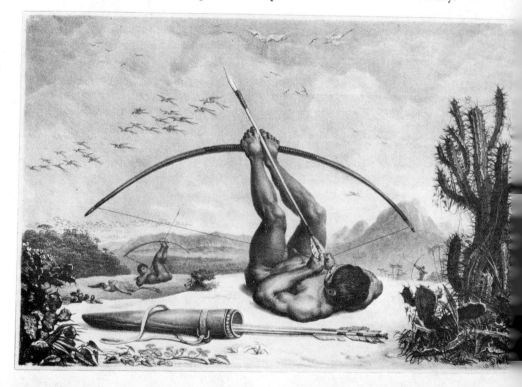

talk to the Governor. He came majestically clothed, proud and venerable. Salema insisted that he surrender two Frenchmen and one Englishman who were still directing the defence: this was done, and all three were summarily hanged after confessing to the Jesuits. Salema then ordered Japuguaçu to demolish his fortress, which he did. The old chief erected a cross in his village and asked to be allowed to remain there with his people, as loyal subjects of Portugal. Salema agreed on condition that 500 archers from the Paraíba Tamoio be surrendered to him. He considered that these had broken the peace of the previous year, and therefore massacred them or awarded them as slaves to his men.

'The first village was the strongest, with the best men in all that land. . . . But its chief heard and accepted the words of one of our [Jesuit] Fathers, and subjected himself and his entire village. . . . [Governor] Salema killed many Indians in the first village, which was the strongest, and after that all the rest surrendered almost without battle.' Two officers on the campaign wrote memoirs about it, and said that the Tamoio put up a good fight. 'Victory was in doubt for a long time. . . . We Portuguese were finally victorious, not because our courage was superior to our adversaries' but because of the advantages of firearms and discipline. These enabled us to make a great slaughter among them: for they had nothing but their fearlessness with which to oppose us.'

When the Tamoio of other villages heard of the slaughter of those who surrendered in the first, they panicked and fled inland. Salema pursued, killing two thousand and enslaving a further four thousand. He took care to split up families, separating wives and husbands, parents and children: some went to Rio, others far along the coast to São Vicente or Espírito Santo. Gabriel Soares de Sousa wrote that there were infinite dead and eight or ten thousand captives. Miguel Ayres Maldonado said that 'their settlements were abandoned. The Tamoio were totally annihilated, and the rest of the Tupinambá abandoned the coasts of Rio de Janeiro, set fire to their homes, took to the neighbouring forests and moved off to the north'. By the end of the century Jacomé Monteiro said that the Tamoio of Cabo Frio had been so devastated 'that there is now no trace of them'.

Anthony Knivet had some final glimpses of the Tamoio. In 1597 he left Rio de Janeiro on an expedition to help the Goiana of the Paraíba defend themselves against a village of Tamoio – 'the most mortall enemies that the Portugals have in all America'.

On a later expedition, Knivet and some Portuguese companions were captured by another village of Paraíba Tamoio. His companions were killed and eaten, but Knivet saved himself by saying that he was French –

just as Hans Staden had done when captured by these Indians half a century before. Knivet spent many months with his Tamoio, living among them 'all naked without any thing, onely a few leaves I tied before mee for shame'. He found them delightful people. 'These Tamoyes be as proper men as any bee in all Europe. . . . The men have their heads alwayes set with feathers of divers colours which showeth very prettily, they goe stark naked. The women are as proper as any Nation can be, tall, comly, well legd, cleane made of body, very small in the waste, very faire of complexion, fine handed, and very comly faces. They use a kind of carving over their breasts, which becommeth them very well.' But young Knivet persuaded his Tamoio to follow him on a disastrous migration to the coast far south of Santos. He claimed to have led thirty thousand on this pilgrimage back to their beloved ocean. The Portuguese soon attacked, killing ten thousand and taking twenty thousand prisoner. It is the last we hear of the great Tamoio branch of the Tupinambá, the tribe that had once controlled the lands between modern São Paulo and Rio de Janeiro.†

SEVEN

Disease and Slavery

THE Jesuits were never free to run their missionary world in the isolation they wanted. Throughout the two centuries of their administration, they fought losing battles against two forces from across the Atlantic: the European colonists, and their diseases.

The first Europeans were impressed by the numbers of Indians living along the coast of Brazil. Afonso Braz wrote home in 1551: 'There are so many of them and the land is so great and they are increasing so much that if they were not continuously at war and eating one another it could not contain them.' The first governor, Tomé de Sousa, said that there were so many Indians that 'they would never lack, even if we were to cut them up in slaughterhouses'. But Magalhães de Gandavo was to write, only twenty years later: 'All the country was full when the Portuguese began to settle it'; but the coasts of the captaincies were now depopulated because 'the governors and captains of the land destroyed [the natives] little by little and killed many, and others fled into the interior . . .'. Nor were the dense populations only along the Atlantic coast. The first expedition to descend the Amazon in 1542 spent three months sailing down the Brazilian part of the river. It reported that 'we continued to pass numerous and very large villages', and 'the farther we went the more thickly populated and better did we find the land'. And the Englishmen Anthony Knivet said that one could travel right across South America from Brazil to the mines of Potosí in the Andes 'and all the way as you goe, you shall have great townes of Indians. . . . You shall

Lamenting Indians greeting European visitors.

have five hundred of these Indians by the way as you travell readie with Nets [hammocks] to carry you. . . .'

Not only was the native population dense and growing, it was also remarkably healthy. The early chroniclers reported very few illnesses in this earthly paradise. Nóbrega wrote, 'I never heard it said that anyone here died of fever but only of old age, and many of the Gallic malady [venereal disease].' The Indian 'men and women have, I reckon, the best-proportioned bodies in all the world'. They were in magnificent condition and lived to a remarkable old age. But this fitness concealed a fatal weakness – the Indians had no immunity against a terrible range of Eurasian and African diseases. This factor more than any other has doomed American natives to probable extinction. Imported diseases have destroyed hundred of thousands of natives throughout the Americas, and reduced their populations to levels at which they could not mount effective resistance or claim their lands on demographic grounds.

European epidemics were reported from the outset of permanent colonisation. The Jesuit Francisco Pires noted in 1552 that disease struck the first batch of converts near Bahia. 'Almost none of these has survived and did not die. . . . Our Lord wished that these people's children, who were baptised in innocence, died in the same innocence. In this way the parents were punished but the children were saved.' An epidemic of violent fevers and 'bloody fluxes' appeared near São Paulo in 1554: 'It struck with such violence that as soon as it appeared it laid them low, unconscious, and within three or four days it carried them to the grave.' Two years later these fevers struck the French colony at Rio de Janeiro. 'This contagious malady ran everywhere so strangely that several of us died of it, and an infinite number of savages.'

The missionaries did what they could to cure or explain away the epidemics. At Bahia the Jesuits said it was punishment for lapses in devotion by the first converts. At Rio de Janeiro, André Thevet told the Indians that God was punishing them 'for the larceny they were doing in our lodgings, and for our disfavour with them'. At São Paulo the Jesuits resorted to blood-letting, using feathers as lancets; and at São Vicente 'we made nine processions of nine choirs of angels against all Hell, and the death at once ceased'.

The Indians were not deceived. They instinctively realised the origin of the disease. Eight thousand natives died at Rio de Janeiro. 'When the evil gathered force, they had the opinion that it was our Captain or I who was making them die. . . . They suddenly all cried out against us, and were convinced that we had brought them this illness to make them die. They therefore plotted together to massacre us and eat us.' Near Bahia, the tribal shamans tried to use the epidemics to discredit the Jesuits; but the Indian reaction was to fear the missionaries and therefore respect them the more. 'Because of this great mortality, and incited by the witchdoctors, other Indians seized opportunities to flee from the Fathers. They said that we brought them death and they feared us. Because of this fear they did whatever we asked them. . . . The heathen fled from the Fathers and Brothers as if from death: they abandoned their houses and fled into the forest. Others burned pepper to stop death entering their houses. They carried a cross raised on high, for they have a great fear of it. Some came out on the road to beg the Fathers not to harm them but to pass by – they showed them the road, trembling like twigs.' In the midst of this tragedy the natives understandably misinterpreted the ceremony of baptism – for people who washed several times a day it was a curious rite, and yet the Jesuits seemed to attach exaggerated importance to it. 'The sorcerers delude them with a thousand follies and lies . . . preaching that we kill them with baptism, and proving this because many of them *do* die.'

These epidemics were a shattering setback to the missionaries. As fast as they preached their ministry they saw their flocks suffer and die from diseases they were powerless to cure. Some must have suspected that they themselves had unwittingly imported the diseases. But they were at a loss to explain God's purpose in striking down these new converts.

The situation grew far worse. The fevers and haemorrhaging spread along the coast, striking Espírito Santo in 1559. Missionary priests worked hard to baptise and confess the dying. The disease swept inland and struck Bahia from the tribes of the interior. It raged at Bahia until 1561 and in that year reappeared at São Paulo. It killed many thousands, particularly children. They died of 'coughing and mortal catarrh' in four or five days, with terrible bloody fluxes and pleurisy. One Jesuit wrote that the epidemic was 'of some fevers that they say immediately attacked the hearts, and which quickly struck them down'.

António Blásques described the misery that resulted: 'You can imagine how one's heart was torn with pity at seeing so many children orphaned, so many women widowed, and the disease and epidemic so rife among them that it seemed like a pestilence. They were terrified and almost stunned by what was happening to them. They no longer performed their songs and dances. Everything was grief. In our aldeia there was nothing to be heard but weeping and groaning by the dying.'

This disease was clearly imported from across the Atlantic, for it attacked only native peoples. It seems to have been a form of haemorrhagic dysentery, combined with influenza or whooping cough. At its height it was killing three or four people a day in villages of a few thousand. But it was only a prelude for worse horrors.

In 1561 the plague struck Portugal, carrying off 40,000 in Lisbon alone. This plague and also the dreaded smallpox then crossed the Atlantic. The first outbreak started on Itaparica island and lasted for some three months in 1562. The second outbreak reached Ilhéus in a ship from Portugal and was carried from there to Bahia in another ship in January 1563. The effect of such deadly diseases on people with no immunity was devastating.

Contemporary medical descriptions were baffling: 'The disease began with serious pains inside the intestines which made the liver and the lungs rot. It then turned into pox that were so rotten and poisonous that the flesh fell off them in pieces full of evil-smelling beasties.'

The Jesuits valiantly tried to cure the victims. 'The skin and flesh of the sick often remained stuck to their hands; and the smell was too strong to endure.' Anchieta described how he found the Indians trying to cure their sick by heating them on beds of leaves and branches laid over trenches filled with fire. 'I pulled them by force off these fires, let their blood, and healed them by the goodness of God. With others who were ill from that evil pestilence, I peeled part of their legs and almost all their feet, cutting off the corrupt skin with scissors and exposing the live flesh – a pitiful thing to see – and washing that corruption with warm water. With which, by the goodness of the Lord, they were healed.' The Indians flocked to the Jesuit Fathers to be treated medically, and even to be fed. This charity embraced everyone in the young colony. Anchieta wrote that 'the Portuguese themselves seem unable to live without us in their illnesses and in those of their slaves. They find in us doctors, pharmacists and nurses.'

Leonardo do Vale also described the tremendous labours of the Jesuits during this crisis. His letter of 12 May 1563 from Bahia is a magnificent description of the horrors of an epidemic in an age of rudimentary medicine. He and his companions were left with no fixed times for sleep, eating or prayer: they were too busy day and night tending the dying and giving last rites and burial to the dead.

'When this tribulation was past and they wanted to raise their heads a little, another illness engulfed them, far worse than the other. This was a form of smallpox or pox so loathsome and evil-smelling that none could stand the great stench that emerged from them. For this reason many died untended, consumed by the worms that grew in the wounds of the pox and were engendered in their bodies in such abundance and of such great size that they caused horror and shock to any who saw them.'

In some huts there were 120 sick. The dead included many men and boys but, 'what is worse, the mothers, sisters and wives who are the ones who do everything, except felling the forest which is men's work: it is their task to plant, grind, roast and make the manioc flour for cooking. With them gone, there was no one to tend the sick or go to fetch them a gourd of water from the spring.' Pregnant women were particularly vulnerable. The disease exhausted them and they gave premature birth to babies who died immediately after a rushed baptism. But 'the afterbirth remained in them and gave rise to an insufferable smell, until they died'. 'In the end the thing grew so bad that there was no one to make graves and some were buried in dunghills and around the huts, but so badly that the pigs routed them up.'

There were an estimated 40,000 Indians working as slaves or forced labourers for the Bahia planters. The epidemic played havoc among these. It did not even spare those 'legally' enslaved. It killed 'Not only those seized in raids and wrongly "ransomed", but also those [enslaved] with good title, and accultured ones who prayed a lot, and [negro slaves] of Guinea. They died in two or three days, and bloodletting and medicines did them no good. In one household 190 slaves died, and there were others with none left to go and fetch water.'

In the confusion of defeat by Mem de Sá's expeditions, the cultural shock of contact with European civilisation, and the terrors of unknown diseases, the Indians turned to a messianic cult for consolation. They hoped for salvation from a prophetic sorcerer called Santo who was to appear in their midst. This movement, called Santidade, was an obvious distortion of Christianity and it infuriated the missionaries. 'It all redounds in carnalities and diabolical vices. They generally pay for it all with the famines and mortalities with which Our Lord God punishes them.' Father João Pereira was almost killed by his Indians in 1564 when he tried to stop them fleeing from the epidemics.

A further tragedy occurred because the Indians, believing in the salvation of the Santidade and struck down by disease, had failed to plant manioc. Those who survived the epidemic were faced with starvation. Leonardo do Vale wrote that, despite the natural fertility of Brazil, famine 'is almost universal among them. . . . They now come and enter the houses and plantations to eat their food. [They are] so miserable that many [settlers] do not have the heart to throw them out. But some happen to go to places where such kindness of heart is lacking, and . . . consent to be purchased and made slaves. There are some who were not even wanted as slaves. These had themselves shackled so that they would be taken: it seemed less likely that they would be rejected if already in irons.' 'Driven by necessity, some went so far as to sell themselves for something to eat. One man surrendered his liberty for only one gourd of flour to save his life. Others hired themselves out to work all or part of their lives, others sold their own children.'

These epidemics and famine came just after the Jesuits had filled their mission settlements with the vanquished of Mem de Sá's campaigns. Herded together in the new aldeias, demoralised and bewildered, these people were terribly vulnerable. The first outbreak carried off some 30,000 in three months. The second killed between a quarter and two-thirds of the survivors. In the aldeia of Our Lady of the Assumption 1080 persons died, 'and the Indians say this was nothing in comparison with the mortality raging through the forests' – the tribes of the interior beyond the reach of the missionaries.* The epidemic moved inexorably around the Bay of All Saints and then up the coast to Pernambuco. Most of the Jesuit settlements around Bahia and Olinda were destroyed or abandoned. In the early 1560s there were over 40,000 converts in the Jesuit villages near Bahia. By 1585 Anchieta reported that, despite infusions of thousands more from the interior, these were reduced to ten thousand. Another Jesuit reckoned that 60,000 were baptised near Bahia between 1559 and 1583. He reported that by the 1580s the aldeia of Santo António alone remained; and it had only 300 men.* 'If one asks about so many people they will tell you that they died. . . . The number of people who have died here in Bahia in the past twenty years seems unbelievable. No one ever imagined that so many people could ever be expended, far less in so short a time.'

The Jesuit António Blásques was appalled by the condition of the survivors. 'Anyone who saw them in this distress, remembering the time past and how many there were then and how few now, and how previously they had enough to eat but they now die of hunger, and how previously they used to live in freedom but they now found them-selves beyond misery, assaulted at every step and enslaved by force by the Christians – anyone who considered and pondered this sudden change cannot fail to grieve and weep many tears of compassion.'

The mortality was best recorded by the Jesuits of Bahia. But it raged with equal ferocity up and down the coast and deep into the interior. Leonardo do Vale talked to a boy who had returned from slave raids on the Pernambuco and Ilhéus coasts. 'He saw so much destruction along the coast that the people could not bury one another. Where previously there were 500 fighting men there would not now be twenty.'

In 1565 smallpox struck two Jesuit aldeias in Espírito Santo. 'It was a pitiful spectacle. The houses served equally as hospitals for the sick and cemeteries for the dead. . . . You did not know which to pity most – to attend to the healing of the living, or to give the dead the common piety of a burial. The former called you with their cries, the latter with their pestiferous smell, piled four by four on top of each other, rotting and corrupt.' Two Jesuits, Diogo Iacomé and Pero Gonçalves, were alone there. 'They were bloodletters, surgeons, doctors and also parish priests and porters.' There were few Indians to help them carry the dead to burial, 'either because they were all ill, or because those not ill had fled from the corruption and bad smell as from death itself. One man ran off in the midst of the journey, leaving the full weight of the corpse on the hands of the Fathers, who collapsed with it out of weakness.' Father Diogo caught a fever and eventually died. 'He had been exhausted by such excessive work and consumed with despair at such a sad outcome, watching a populous aldeia that he loved dearly so rapidly undone, ravaged and abandoned.'

The Jesuits did what they could to fight the diseases. They did their best as doctors, nurses and gravediggers. They gave spiritual help with deathbed confessions and Christian funeral rites. They organised special processions and prayed endlessly to exorcise the diseases. They blamed the Indians' heretical cults or the shallowness of Indian conversions for provoking God's wrath. But their final answer, when the epidemics were over and the missions were ravaged and empty, was simply to fill them with new levies of uncontacted Indians from the interior. A bishop of Brazil testified approvingly in 1582: 'Many Indians died and the aldeias remained denuded. On several occasions the Fathers of the Society [of Jesus] themselves sent Fathers into the sertão at their own expense, for the common good, to seek Indians. They brought these down [to the coast] and reconstituted those aldeias with them.' 'On certain occasions the Fathers sent Indians from their churches or went in person to the sertão, to descend people to replenish [the missions], so that their heathen would not die out completely, as happened around 1562. Chief Morrangão and other chiefs came. . . . Then Father Gaspar Lourenco went to Arabó and brought another batch of people. After that Father Diogo Nunes went to the Rari hills and also descended people, all of them descended without help from the Portuguese, who contributed nothing towards the expenses but were always against this.'

The Jesuits were intelligent enough to appreciate that the epidemics were probably imported by Europeans, and that they struck hardest at converts congregated into mission settlements. This did not deter them. Throughout the two centuries of their presence in Brazil, they always filled empty settlements by luring more innocents into them. Some may have believed that it was better for Indians to be baptised but dead than heathen but alive and free. But it often seemed that what really mattered was pride in maintaining the mission system. The Jesuits became obsessed with their personal soul-count.

It was hopelessly difficult for the Jesuits to explain such catastrophes to their congregations. Father Anchieta visited the Espírito Santo aldeias 'and wept with the Indians over their miseries. With his customary eloquence, and in the Brazilian language, he exhorted them to bear that scourge with patience.' It was God's will, possibly intended for the salvation of its victims. *

It was equally difficult for the missionaries to excuse the slaving and other excesses of their compatriots. They could, however, do something to oppose them. They used their great moral prestige to preach restraint to the colonists. While the regular clergy and the other monastic orders often compromised and condoned slavery, the Jesuits fought it inflexibly. They also used their influence in the mother country to obtain liberal legislation, and with the colonial administrators to see that this was enforced.

The Portuguese were slightly worse than the Spaniards in this respect. Portuguese laws permitted the enslavement of Indians under special circumstances, whereas the Spaniards almost never legalised it. The Spaniards were generally dealing with more settled and docile natives in Mexico and the Andes – they could force them to labour in the mines and encomiendas without resorting to enslavement. They instituted slavery only on the fringes of their empire, when dealing with indomitable tribes in southern Chile or northern Mexico.

Spanish theologians and lawyers had been debating the morality of conquest since the early sixteenth century. Men like Bartolomé de Las Casas, António de Montesinos, Matías de Paz and Francisco de Vitoria all championed American Indians in different ways; and Spanish kings like Charles I or Philip II worried about their own souls if their conquests were too brutal. The Brazilian historian Sérgio Buarque de Holanda suggested that there is no 'black legend' about Portuguese atrocities simply because the Portuguese gave no thought to the moral implications of colonialism. They did not produce impassioned defences of the Indians, such as the writings of Las Casas, that could be quoted against them by Protestant propagandists. * On 9 June 1537 the Farnese Pope Paul III issued the Bull *Veritas ipsa* which declared that American Indians were true men and not beasts, and were therefore capable of answering the call of Christ. Even tribes that were not yet converted to Christianity 'should not be deprived of their freedom or the enjoyment of their property, and should not be reduced to slavery'.

Almost nothing was done for the protection of Brazilian Indians in the half-century after Cabral's discovery. But the fleet that carried the first governor of Brazil and the first Jesuit missionaries also took the King's instructions to his governor, the Regimento of Tomé de Sousa of

17 December 1548. King João III declared in this Regimento that his main purpose in colonising Brazil was the conversion of its natives. This could best be achieved by protecting them and preventing illegal slaving. But the Regimento also permitted the issue of slaving licences to trustworthy persons in time of need, and it ordered wars on hostile tribes and the enslavement of captives in such wars. It was the start of a long series of confused and contradictory legislation concerning the liberty of Brazilian Indians.* The early governors tried to carry out the King's instructions, particularly Mem de Sá during his outstanding fifteen-year administration. Although he conquered the Bahia Tupinambá, he also tried to stop the indiscriminate slave-raiding that had provoked so many Indian wars. He gave full support to the Jesuits. Their mission settlements seemed the best alternative to enslavement of the Indians: they provided a pool of labour for hire, and they promised to turn Indians into Christian subjects of the King of Portugal.

Mem de Sá's very successes as governor undermined his protection of the Indians. The colony prospered. With the Governor's crushing victories the colonists lost some of their fear of the Indians. They occupied great expanses of Indian territory and enjoyed the security to develop enormous sugar plantations. More settlers sailed out from Europe, each intent on acquiring slave labour to make himself a fortune. Sugar was a labour-intensive business, with hundreds of workers needed to cut and crush the cane. It was also highly profitable. It thus caused powerful economic pressure to find labour, either by enslaving natives or by importing black slaves from Africa.

Mem de Sá reached Brazil in 1558 and soon conquered the tribes near Bahia. He treated the vanquished well, so that they entered the Jesuits' missions willingly enough, and hundreds of their warriors volunteered in 1560 to help the Governor against the Tupinikin of Espírito Santo and the French and Tamoio of Guanabara. Mem de Sá boasted to King Sebastião in March 1560 that he had brought peace and prosperity to the Indians.*

The Caeté Indians had killed and eaten Bishop Sardinha after his shipwreck in 1556. They continued to resist Portuguese expansion into the region of the São Francisco river between Bahia and Pernambuco. In 1562 Mem de Sá proclaimed a 'just' war against the Caeté and authorised perpetual enslavement of any prisoners. It was precisely the excuse the colonists had been waiting for. They launched an 'open season' against any Caeté, heathen or Christian, hostile or friendly, and were soon enslaving any Indians of any tribe on the grounds that they might be Caeté. 'In the churches of the Fathers there were many heathen of that [Caeté] stock – but born and raised in this part of Bahia, and who took no part in those killings [of Bishop Sardinha and his companions]. But, as the Devil knows, this was the best possible invention for destroying what had been done and impeding the progress of the conversion of the heathen. It was assisted by the Portuguese desire to get slaves. Thus, in a few days the entire land was depopulated. For when the heathen saw that their women and children, sisters and brothers were being seized and raided in their villages and when they journeyed along the roads, and were being carried off as slaves even though they were born natives of the land, with no legal recourse, since the Portuguese claimed they were also murderers in those killings', they fled. Four Jesuit missions near Caeté territory rapidly declined from twelve thousand to one thousand inhabitants. Mem de Sá eventually revoked the sentence on the Caeté, but it was too late.*

This was the time when the Bahia Tupinambá were decimated by epidemics and famine. It was also a time when the Portuguese monarchs were particularly devout. The Queen-Regent Dona Catarina urged the town council of Salvador: 'You will favour the Fathers of the Company of Jesus in everything necessary for the conversion of the heathen. . . . You will treat the heathen who become Christian well, and not vex them nor take their lands.' Her pious grandson King Sebastião made the same recommendations to Mem de Sá in 1566. 'I am informed that in those parts unjust enslavement is commonplace. Ransoms are conducted, under title of "extreme necessity", with the vendors being the fathers of those they sell. . . . I strongly commend to you to favour the newly converted. . . .' He urged the Governor to remedy illegal slavery, and suggested that he place honourable Portuguese colonists in each aldeia as protectors. Mem de Sá did attempt this, and also appointed a man called Diogo Zorrilla as Prosecutor for the Indians.†

The Jesuits protested at the injustice of Indians who faced starvation being forced to sell themselves into slavery. The matter was referred to the Mesa da Consciência ('Tribunal of Conscience') in Lisbon, but it ruled that, 'if forced by extreme necessity, a father may sell his children, and anyone may sell himself to enjoy the sale price'. King Sebastião sent this ruling back to Brazil, where the Governor called a special junta to debate the problem. This met in Bahia in 1566. Nóbrega was a member, but being far away in southern Brazil he wrote his opinion in a document discovered only recently. He argued eloquently that freedom was a natural right, not something that could be sold for mere money in times of need. An adult could lose his freedom only to save his life in extreme necessity. Any colonist who acquired slaves other than in such extreme necessity must free them. No confessor could ever absolve masters who owned slaves purchased in time of famine: they had violated natural and divine law. The junta decided that Indians who took refuge among the Jesuits would be protected. Settlers were not allowed to enter mission aldeias. And each slave was to be examined to confirm that he was legally enslaved, and freed if not.*

Mem de Sá strongly supported the Jesuits, but he was ambivalent about slavery. He was the veteran of many savage Indian wars. He himself owned two large plantations, one called Sant' Anna in Ilhéus and another on an island in the Sergipe river, as well as a stretch of fifteen miles of coast near Bahia and various ranches. The Sergipe plantation contained 250 slaves, and at the Ilhéus mill there were 95 male and 84 female Indian slaves, and 18 male and 2 female African slaves. These details emerged in a will written by Mem de Sá in 1569. The African slaves were valued at from 13 to 40 escudos each, whereas Indian men fetched only about 1 escudo, unless they were skilled – 10 escudos for a fisherman, 20 for a caulker, 30 for a box-maker. Mem de Sá also employed a converted Jew called Domingos Ribeiro to go and barter for Indian slaves in the interior of Sergipe. This agent fell foul of the Inquisition, not for slaving, but for having traded firearms to the Indians.*

The Governor was therefore sympathetic towards the settlers. He warned the Queen-Regent not to be too liberal to the natives. 'This land cannot and should not be regulated by the same laws and manners as the Kingdom. If Your Majesty is not very lenient in pardoning, there will be no [white] people in Brazil. And, since I have won it back, I want it to be preserved.'

In the harsh world of the sixteenth century, slavery was an accepted institution. It had been justified philosophically since Aristotle. Universities included slavery in the civil law inherited from the Romans. Most Europeans accepted slavery as a condition of certain inferior peoples. They were convinced of the superiority of Christianity and European civilisation over all others. Some theorists argued that Brazilian Indians were inferior, since they were less sophisticated than Europeans intellectually, technologically and politically. They were therefore natural slaves.

Fortunately, the idea of enslaving American natives ran counter to Christian and humanist doctrine. The Papacy had declared that these natives were descendants of Adam, with souls equal to those of other human beings in the sight of God. Renaissance humanists were impressed by the natural virtues of the Indians, and regarded freedom as a natural right. Missionaries wanted converts, and the activities of the slavers obstructed this work. 'When the Fathers saw the lunacy practised on them and the disservice to God that resulted, they attended to this matter, and forbade the many raids that the Portuguese were making along this coast. The Portuguese were loading their consciences by illegally enslaving many Indians and provoking unjust wars.'

None of this solved the acute labour problem in the new colonies. Sugar was the source of big profits in a country apparently devoid of other riches. This agricultural economy could not succeed without ample labour. The mother country Portugal was too small to supply enough settlers to work such immense territories. But free Indians were determined not to work for hire – for the meagre lengths of cloth or shoddy trade goods offered by the plantation-owners. Slavery seemed the only answer.

Legal and ecclesiastical authorities condoned slavery only in the case of 'extreme necessity' – in other words, as an alternative to immediate death. The only occasion when Indians faced death was if they were captured in battle, either by another tribe or by Europeans.

The first tribes encountered by the colonists were coastal Tupi who waged incessant wars on one another to capture prisoners for ritual execution. Any settler who found an 'Indian of the cord' tied up ready for sacrifice, and who bought him from his captors, had saved his life. It was argued that this rescue entitled the purchaser to perpetual service from the Indian he saved and from his descendants. The settler had paid to save the man from death. It was reminiscent of ransoms paid to recover captives from the Moors. 'Ransoming' thus became a euphemism for enslaving Indians.

The other legitimate form of slavery was capture in 'just' wars by the colonists. The moralists insisted that campaigns by Europeans must be legitimate or 'just' wars of self-defence or retaliation, not wars of aggression or mere slave raids. Just wars had to be approved by the royal and ecclesiastical authorities and officially proclaimed by the Governor.

The colonial authorities were not prepared to pay settlers who fought to defend or expand the colony. There was therefore nothing to lure settlers from their farms to face the hardships of the jungle and scrublands and possible death from starvation or an Indian arrow. The Brazilian jungles contained no booty for them to capture, cities to sack or important captives to ransom. The only income to finance such wars was the sale of prisoners into slavery. Any particularly troublesome tribe – the Caeté or Aimoré, for instance – became the object of a legitimate or 'just' war: a campaign whose objectives were the destruction of the tribe as a fighting force, the occupation of its territory, and the enslavement of its men and women. The victims' persons paid for the war that destroyed them. It was a return to the ancient code of war when defeat meant enslavement. *Vae victis!*

These were the principles behind the first law on Indian liberty, inspired by Mem de Sá and the Jesuits, and issued by the devout King Sebastião on 20 March 1570. The law started with the eloquent statement that Indians 'may on no account and in no way be enslaved'. It then became contradictory and made exceptions. It defined 'just' wars, and permitted enslavement of those 'who may be taken in a just war, and those who habitually attack the Portuguese and other Indians'. The Aimoré were singled out as a tribe so hostile that its members might always be enslaved.

Laws are only as good as those who enforce them. Nóbrega died in the year of the new law, 1570, and Mem de Sá two years later. The Jesuits who succeeded Nóbrega were less sure about the injustice of slavery, and lacked his influence in opposing it. The men sent to succeed Mem de Sá were hard reactionaries. The King tried dividing Brazil between two governors, but both were determined to accelerate the colony's growth by slavery if necessary and by wars of extinction on hostile tribes. The two governors met at Bahia on 6 January 1574 as members of another junta on Indian freedom. They dismissed all Nóbrega's scruples and declared that any adult Indian could sell himself into slavery if he wished. They broadened the definition of 'just' wars so far that almost anyone could go slave raiding with impunity. The northern Governor Luís de Brito de Almeida sent a seasoned Indian-hunter called Domingos Fernandes Nobre Tomacauna on at least three long expeditions to capture slaves in the forests of Arabó and inland Ilhéus. This governor led a ferocious campaign against the Caeté of Sergipe while his southern colleague Dr António de Salema was destroying the Tamoio of Cabo Frio.* Simão de Vasconcellos wrote that the decisions of this tribunal of 1574 served only as an excuse for greatly increased slavery. Slavers could now claim that their captives had been sold by their tribes, in addition to the usual pretexts of 'ransoming' from ritual execution, or just wars. The chronicler Gabriel Soares de Sousa, who was a rich landowner, shipped off boatloads of Indians for sale as slaves in other captaincies. Indians had previously been classed as legal minors. Settlers easily distorted this concept from minority to incapacity. Gabriel Soares wrote that Indians were incapable of living in freedom.

In 1578 King Sebastião led the flower of Portuguese chivalry on a quixotic crusade into Morocco. The young king vanished in the terrible defeat of Alcacer-Quibir. His great-uncle Cardinal Henrique succeeded, but on his death in 1580 the man with the best claim to the Portuguese throne was Philip II of Spain. Philip was the most powerful monarch in Europe, and the Spanish Empire was at its zenith. Portugal thus passed into subjection to Spain that was to last for sixty years.

Although the Spanish appear by nature crueller and more violent than the Portuguese, they very rarely legalised slavery in their American colonies. Their laws left the land nominally owned by the natives. Spanish settlers were granted encomiendas – large quotas of natives forced to provide labour and produce. With the discovery of great silver and gold mines in Mexico and Peru, the natives were further forced to work as miners for the State. By 1580, however, the encomienda system was failing and Spanish America was changing into a pattern of feudal land-ownership by white settlers. The Spaniards therefore saw no reason to change Portuguese policy towards Indians.

King Philip confirmed Sebastião's law of 1570 in 1587. This was partly because the Spaniards had promised not to change the Portuguese legal system, but also because Brazilian Indians were considered too primitive to enjoy the freedom proclaimed for the natives of Spanish America. Indian treatment in Brazil was almost entirely based on the Jesuits and it seemed to be working too well to alter. The first governor-general after the Spanish occupation, Manoel Teles Barreto, clashed with the Jesuits. He tried to remove them from administration of Indian aldeias and to install lay captains. But the Jesuits retained their control, after a meeting of church and state dignitaries in December 1583, at which the Bishop of Bahia championed the Jesuits.†

Slavery of Indians thus remained institutionalised. There were now so many ways in which Indians could legally be enslaved that laws about their freedom became almost academic. The sale of Indians had begun officially in the mid-1550s with an ordinance that ordered the natives 'that if by chance they captured prisoners they were either to sell them or use them as slaves'. Nóbrega protested that this order taught the natives to 'steal one another and sell them as slaves'.

With the reaction after Mem de Sá's death, trading for slaves became an organised traffic. Anchieta reckoned that slaving expeditions out of Bahia brought down an average of two or three thousand Indians a year. Vicente do Salvador told how António Dias Adorno was sent inland to search for minerals but returned with 7000 Tupiguen and how Luís Álvares Espinha, who marched out of Ilhéus on a punitive raid, 'was not content with capturing all those villages: he went on inland and brought down infinite heathen'. The Indians of the coast north of Sergipe became so terrified by Portuguese victories that 'they allowed themselves to be tied up by the whites like sheep or ewes. These therefore went along those rivers in boats which they sailed back loaded with Indians to sell for 2 cruzados or 1 milreis each, which is the price of a sheep.'

The Englishman Anthony Knivet went on many expeditions to buy slaves for the son of the Governor of Rio de Janeiro, towards the end of the sixteenth century. On one occasion he went to the Goiana 'which were in peace with the Portugals, and for knives and hatchets they sell their wives and children'. He moved on inland to the Puri, and heard a chief declare his hatred of the Portuguese. He managed to trade his merchandise with another chief for 70 slaves, and was provided with an escort of 300 bowmen for the return journey.

Knivet later tried to sail out to join John Hawkins, who was cruising off Brazil, but was caught and imprisoned. He himself then experienced the life of a slave, having once been a slaver. 'I was used like a dogge for the space of a fortnight: for I lay on the ground and had no meat given me, but cassavi [manioc] meal and water. After I had endured this miserie, I was condemned to be hanged for a runaway and a Lutheran, and as I was going by the Colledge of Jesus, all the Friars of the Colledge came forth with a great Crucifix, and falling on their knees before the Governour they craved pardon for me, and I was carried againe to prison. . . . Then I was brought forth on a market day, with my hands and feet bound, and there in publicke beaten with cordes, that I had not a whole spot of skin on all of my body. . . . After this the Governour commanded great hoopes of iron to bee clinched to my legge, of thirtie pound weight, the which I carried nine moneths, continually working in the sugar mill like a bond-slave. The Factor used me more like a Dogge than a Man, for his hatred was so much to me and to all strangers that I never came by him but I was sure of blowes.'

Knivet finally tried to stab the Factor, and fled back into the forest. His companion was another fugitive slave, a great chief in his own land, called Yellow Sun. 'Never man found truer friendship of any than I did of him.' They swam ashore from an island, and travelled for thirty-seven days to join Knivet's friend Chief Jawaripipo of the Puri. Knivet assembled his friends and incited them to rebel against the Portuguese. 'I began to rehearse unto them, how cruelly the Portugals did use their Nation, in making them bond-slaves, marking them like Dogs, whipping and tormenting them, as if they were not of flesh and bloud. . . . I encouraged them to bee valiant, and to pull up their spirits, and perswading them to defend themselves against such Tyrants, who under colour of friendship used them most villainously. . . . With that, many of them embraced me, all together giving a great hoope, saying, as long as their lives lasted and their bowes brake not, that they would defend themselves and me.' Knivet was with the Puri for nine months. But his exhortations were not as potent as Portuguese trade goods. His master Martím de Sá appeared among a neighbouring tribe, 'and giving them knives and Hatchets and Beades, hee won their hearts so much unto him that they gave him their Sonnes and Daughters to bee his slaves' – and also betrayed Knivet and his Indian companion. Knivet's own tribe promptly bound him and handed him and his friend over to the Portuguese. 'When the Canibals brought mee before Martin de Saa, all those that protested before most friendship unto mee, are now become my greatest and most mortall enemies, and with hooping and hallowing deride mee, striking mee on the head, and declaring to the Portugals, how I used great perswasions to have them become their enemies.' Sá offered Knivet the choice of returning to stand trial, or going on another expedition to the Paraíba 'to trafficke with the Canibals for Women, Boyes and Girles. . . . I chose, once againe, rather to stand to the Heathen mercy of savage Man-eaters then the bloudie crueltie of Christian Portugals.'

Knivet reached the Paraíba after a month's journey, built a canoe and descended in it to some villages of Tamoio. Although these were traditional enemies of the Portuguese, they received Knivet well, partly because he spoke their Tupi language and came accompanied by one of their own people. In the Tamoio village 'we were received with dancing and singing of great and small, and in every house I was received with great ceremonies and long speeches of the chiefest that were in the Towne. The next day I began to traffick with them for slaves, and I bought ninetie; all of which I brought to Martin de Saa at Ilha Grande.'

Knivet's adventures demonstrated the fatal fascination of European goods. 'Since these Indians covet certain things which come from the Kingdom of Portugal – namely shirts, jerkins, iron tools and similar objects – they sell one another in exchange for these articles. The Portuguese, on the other hand, capture as many as they want and do them many injuries without being restrained by anyone.'

It was often all too easy to lure tribes down to the coast without even bartering trade goods. All that was needed was someone whom the Indians trusted or admired. This was generally a mameluco, son of a white colonist and an Indian woman – sufficiently Indian to convince a tribe that he was one of them, and sufficiently white to be ruthless about luring them into slavery.

One Jesuit admitted that he was astounded by the 'boldness and impertinence with which [slavers] allow themselves to enter that great wilderness, at great cost, for two, three, four or more years. They go without God, without food, naked as the savages and subject to all the persecutions and miseries in the world. Such men venture two or three hundred leagues into the bush, serving the devil with such amazing martyrdom, just to barter or steal slaves.'

Some of these half-castes plunged inland to persuade Indians who had fled from the Portuguese to return to the coast. They 'were not so sure of their eloquence that they did not take many white soldiers and allied Indians armed with arrows and other weapons. . . . But the speech of a half-caste relative was generally sufficient. He described to them the abundance of fish and shellfish in the sea, and the freedom they would enjoy – which they would not have if it proved necessary to bring them by force. With such deceptions, and some gifts of clothing and tools to the chiefs . . . they roused up entire villages. But once they arrived with them in sight of the sea they separated children from parents, brother from brother and sometimes even husband from wife. The half-caste captain would take some and the soldiers others, those who had equipped the expedition took others, as did those who had petitioned for a licence [for the raid] from the Governor, and those who issued it. They all used them on their estates and some sold them. . . . Those who bought them used to brand them on the face at their first [attempted] flight or fault: they claimed that they had cost money and were their slaves. The preachers used to pound their pulpits about this, but they might as well have been preaching in a desert.'

'The Portuguese go 250 or 300 leagues to seek these heathen since they are now so far away. And because the land is now deserted most of them die of hunger on the return journey. There were some Portuguese who took a number of enemy heathen on a journey, killed them, and gave them to [their captives] to eat to sustain themselves.'

The Holy Inquisition first visited Brazil in 1591, and many of these woodsmen and slavers appeared to confess before it. Among them were Rodrigo Martins, who had gone on an expedition to the sertão of Hijuiuiba ('Baby Heron'), had smoked 'holy grass' with the Indians, and given them an arquebus (without powder or shot) and a sword; Manoel Branco, son of a French father, who had had himself scarred in the native manner with the permanent stripes that designated a valiant warrior; Tomas Ferreira, who had just returned from an eighteen-month expedition that had traded a sword, two arquebuses, powder, shot, a battle drum, banner, horse and mare to Chief Arataca in the Raripe sertão 'in exchange for heathen slaves'. The standards of the Holy Office were truly amazing. The Inquisition was not concerned that these raiders had illegally enslaved thousands of natives. The offences they were obliged to confess were: trading European weapons to Indians, practising Indian ceremonies and, most serious of all, eating meat during Lent while they were off on their long expeditions.

By far the most famous of these half-caste woodsmen was Domingos Fernandes Nobre, whom the Indians knew as Tomacauna. Born in Pernambuco to an Indian mother and white father, he himself had married a white woman. He admitted that for eighteen years, between the ages of eighteen and thirty-six, he had lived like an Indian and never prayed or confessed. He had taken part in a succession of expeditions, most of which were slave raids. In 1572 he was with António Dias Adorno in the hinterland of Pôrto Seguro, ostensibly in search of gold but in practice in search of Indians. They brought back most of the Tupiguen tribe: seven thousand people of all ages. The expedition moved slowly enough for this horde to feed itself on game and wild fruits and honey, so that all of them, even the aged and children, reached the slave markets fat and in good spirits.* In 1576 Tomacauna led a five-month expedition to the Arabó sertão inland of Bahia, on the orders of João Brito de Almeida; in 1577 he was back there leading a six-month expedition to capture slaves for Governor Luís de Brito de Almeida; and in the two following years he was in the Ilhéus sertão for that same governor on a fourteen-month slaving expedition. He later spent a year in the Bahia sertão on the orders of Governor Lourenço da Veiga. When he appeared before the Inquisition he had just returned from an expedition with Cristóvão da Rocha which had had an official licence to 'descend heathen'.

Tomacauna was clearly a superb woodsman who had spent most of his life scouting Indian trails into the heart of Brazil. His great success as a slaver came from his rapport with the Indians. He won their confidence by living as one of them. He scarred his thighs and buttocks with a paca tooth and filled the wound with black powder to leave permanent scars. These stripes were the sign of a warrior who had killed many enemies. He smoked the hallucinogenic 'holy grass' of the Indians. 'He sang and shook rattles and danced like them and went naked like them and wept and lamented just like them in their heathen manner . . . and he plumed his face with gum and dyed himself with the red dye urucum, and had seven Indian wives whom they gave him to keep in the Indian manner.' The Indians called him 'nephew'. They considered him a great sorcerer. If his convoys of tribespeople ever threatened to run off during the journey to the coast, he intimidated them with his magic. He thus enjoyed the best of both societies: respected as a slaver and woodsman among the colonists, and honoured as a great shaman among the natives. He confessed to the Inquisition that 'he often did not wish ever to return from the sertão, because in there he had many wives and ate meat on forbidden days and did everything else he wished without anyone paying attention'.

Tomacauna's most fascinating mission was to subvert and capture the members of the messianic movement called the Santidade. In their terror at the epidemics of 1562 and 1563, the Indians of Bahia turned to a vision of deliverance by this strange new cult. One girl who had been a devotee confessed to the Inquisition that the priests of the Santidade 'told [the Indians] not to work because food would grow itself; and anyone who did not believe in the Santidade would be turned into logs and stones; and white people would be turned into game for them to eat'. Belief in the Santidade spread throughout the Indians of Bahia, among both slaves and freemen. Those who could escaped from their masters and ran off into the wilds to join Santidade congregations in forest hideaways. Those who could not flee practised the rites secretly at night, in corners of plantation slave quarters well hidden from the white masters. Slaves clung to a pathetic belief that 'their god would free them from slavery and make them masters of the white people, who would become their slaves'.

By the 1580s the Santidade was so powerful that Governor Manoel Teles Barreto sent Tomacauna with a company of soldiers to destroy its base on the Jaguaribe river. The movement was now led by a Pope called António, a convert raised in the Jesuit establishment of Tinharé in Ilhéus. His wife called herself Mother of God, and there were various sacristans and other officers of the new church. The cult figure was a stone idol called Maria that was an abstract object unlike any man, woman, bird, fish or animal. 'They worshipped that idol and prayed certain things by means of beads, in a house they called church, in which they hung boards with markings they said were holy beads. Thus, in their own manner, they counterfeited the divine cult of the Christians.' The Pope said that he had survived the Flood in the heart of a palm-tree. The priests and congregation of the Santidade intoned their prayers in a language nobody understood.

Tomacauna's expedition was financed by a rich plantation-owner called Fernão Cabral de Ataide. Many members of the Santidade fled at Tomacauna's approach, but he did meet one group carrying the idol Maria. He raised his hat to this, to deceive them, and persuaded this contingent to settle on Cabral de Ataide's estate. The mill-owner and his wife allowed the sect to flourish on their land, and they themselves did reverence to the idol and made offerings of fish to it. They told the Inquisition that this worshipping was a bluff intended to lure down the Pope and the rest of his followers – but the Holy Office sentenced them to two years in prison for such sacrilege. Tomacauna travelled further and met Pope António. He was 'dressed in trousers of black cotton broadcloth and a green cassock, with a red biretta on his head'. Tomacauna knelt to this Pope and joined in his rituals, smoked 'holy grass' with him and gave him a sword and some fine clothing. Before long Tomacauna was himself being worshipped and was called St Louis.

But the Pope was too wily: he suspected treachery and ran off from Tomacauna's expedition.

The Bahia Santidade was still flourishing twenty years after the Inquisition's visitation. Diogo de Campos Moreno reported that in 1612 the interior was full of santidades of Indians practising garbled forms of Christianity. The biggest 'robbers' den' of such fugitives was far up the Paraguaçu river on the southern shore of the Bay of All Saints. 'It has grown so much that it is something worthy of consideration, about which His Majesty has been informed.' King Philip III wrote to order the Governor of Brazil to suppress these lairs of fugitives, either peacefully or else by force. Captured Indians were to be imprisoned, and negroes returned to their owners. The King suggested the use of one of Caramuru's descendants, Afonso Rodrigues Adorno, because of his skill as a woodsman and because his estate at Cachoeira ('Rapids') on the Paraguaçu was close to a santidade. 'He has some heathen whom his ancestors gathered together in times past, and continues to possess their administration. When necessary he rallies with 200 bowmen.' He used these to suppress one santidade in 1629.†

Not all Indians were so gullible that they marched off to slavery behind any persuasive mameluco. In the late 1580s the Tupinambá of the Raripe sertão of Sergipe and Pernambuco bartered captives with a 'ransoming' expedition of 200 whites and mamelucos. But, as the slavers were marching home with their booty, the Indians launched a surprise attack, killing fourteen and wounding many, recapturing the slaves and keeping the trade goods.*

There were also a few whites who sided with the Indians. Lázaro da Cunha lived for five years from 1585 among the Tupinambá of Pernambuco. He lived as one of them, naked and dyed. But he assured the Inquisition that when the time came to eat human meat he managed to substitute pork without the tribe noticing. He fought with his tribe against their enemies, and even helped them defeat an attack on their village by white slavers.*

There was the mameluco Pero Bastardo, who also lived for seven years among the Tupinambá of the Raripe sertão. The Indians called him Aratuam ('Macaw'). He confessed that he painted himself, had many wives, helped his tribe fight others, and practised heathen customs, 'telling them that he was also a heathen . . . and wanted to remain as a heathen and go with them for ever'.

Anthony Knivet found himself living among a group of Tamoio somewhere in the interior of São Paulo. This group had been driven inland after defeat by the Portuguese. The chiefs told Knivet how much they missed the coast and the days when they had traded with the French 'and wanted nothing, but now they had neither knives nor hatchets, nor nothing else, but lived in great necessitie'. Knivet proposed to lead this group to a stretch of uninhabited coast in what would now be Paraná. 'The old men went and told the people, which all desired to see the coast, so they resolved, and making provision, we departed from our abode, being thirty thousand of us.' After a long march they reached a coast inhabited by Carijó Indians. The Tamoio won the ensuing battle because of their superior numbers and better training, killing many Carijó and eating 300 prisoners. They occupied the Carijó town and enjoyed its large stores of food. But the Carijó appealed to their Portuguese friends along the coast. Martím de Sá sailed south with a fleet of caravels and canoes, and surrounded the town by night. At about three in the morning Sá's men shouted to the Tamoio to surrender or be massacred. At this Knivet's Indians 'began to russell with their Bowes and Arrowes, making a great noise, with that the Portugals shot of a Peece [cannon], then they all lay downe in their beds, like men without lives or soules; when the day was cleare . . . all the Indians were brought out of their houses, and being examined . . . the Portugals killed all the old men and women, and all those that had beene particular actors in Portugals' deaths, which were in all 10,000, and 20,000 were parted amongst them for their slaves'. It was a disastrously misguided migration, a tragic mistake for which Knivet made no apology in his memoirs.

It was almost impossible for the Jesuits to stop the activities of the slavers. Woodsmen like Tomacauna operated far beyond the reach of the civil or ecclesiastical authorities – and often went on behalf of the governors themselves. Portuguese colonists considered themselves very devout and loyal to their king. But their greed for slaves overruled any sanctions by church or royal laws. Even the Indians did not co-operate. Their passion for hunting and warfare was so great that they admired heroes like Tomacauna far more than the most pious Jesuit Father.

Despite the difficulties, the Jesuits did their best to oppose slavery. 'They suffer continual hardship defending [the Indians] against the many injuries and vexations that the Portuguese settlers do them. The Fathers seek the liberty of the same Indians by all possible means, defending them from the unjust slavery in which many wish to keep them.'

Many Jesuits eloquently described their despair at their impotence in stopping their compatriots' cruelty. Pero Correia wrote in 1553: 'When we Fathers came from Portugal word spread all along the coast that we were preaching an end to slave raids and raiders, that all who had been enslaved in raids or by deceit should be set free, and that the King ordered this. The heathen were very happy all along the coast and became good. Whenever they saw a Father of the Society they . . . believed whatever he told them. But they now say that they no longer believe us. Many came to our church and college begging us to help them, for they had been illegally enslaved. . . . But we cannot put these right, for the justice in this land is so remiss.' When the Jesuits tried to give sanctuary to illegally enslaved Indians, their owners invaded the convent with drawn swords to recover them. The Indians saw the Jesuits being threatened and insulted and 'they saw clearly that . . . we are no use in helping them and are creatures that even our own people despise'.

Manoel da Nóbrega wrote that Indian slaves felt that their only hope lay with the Jesuits. 'Their only knowledge of justice is to come to us, as to fathers and protectors, seeking the shelter of the Church. But we, because we have already learned our lesson and do not wish to cause scandals or get ourselves stoned, cannot help them and do not even dare to preach about it. As a result, because of the lack of justice, [the Indians] remain slaves and their masters remain in mortal sin, and we lose credit among all the heathen because of their [disappointed] hopes in us.' Nóbrega appealed to Governor Tomé de Sousa. But he took the advice of his council, which was full of slave-owners. 'It is his opinion that this matter should not be raised, because of the damage it would cause to many [white] men: and that it is better for [Indians] to be in subjection and to work on the plantations; that this is of greater service to the King and the good of the land and its settlers . . . and similar arguments. But I myself believe that we must not cease to do what is reasonable and just, equally to all. . . . For anything without justice is not favoured by Our Lord. I believe it would be of greater benefit to the land to give each person what is his, rather than to support it with sins from which [the colonists] can never escape!'

EIGHT

The Potiguar

THE other great tribe that continued to trade with the French was the Potiguar. This was the largest and most united of all the Tupi tribes on the coast of Brazil. Fearless warriors, they prevented Portuguese expansion along the 'East–West Coast' north of Pernambuco, and their presence was a constant threat to that rich captaincy.

The English sailor Anthony Knivet regarded the Potiguar as more civilised than other Indians. He was impressed that men, women and children washed themselves every morning – unlike most Europeans. He noted that they had populous great villages, in harmony with one another, and lived in long-huts with no apparent friction between families. Gabriel Soares de Sousa, himself a farmer, admired the Potiguar as 'great farmers of crops, with which they are always very well provided. They are good hunters, and an arrow shot by them never misses. . . . They are great line fishermen, both at sea and in fresh-water rivers. These Potiguar normally spare none of the enemies they capture: they kill and immediately eat them. . . . These heathen are very bellicose, warlike and treacherous.'

Although the Portuguese were avowed enemies of the coastal Potiguar, they managed to trade peacefully with the Potiguar living inland, west of Pernambuco. That peace came to an end in 1574, largely because of a powerful colonist called Diogo Dias. Dias had been granted some 80,000 acres in the rich plain of Goiana, forty miles north of Recife. He had a stone farmhouse defended by a stockade manned by

Indian warriors, with scars to show the number of their victims.

hundreds of armed Indian and African slaves. Not content with all this, he tried to extend his estate across the Capibaribe-mirim river into Potiguar territory.

One half-caste trader, the son of an important colonist and his Indian woman, now fell in love with the daughter of the Potiguar Chief Iniguaçu ('Big Hammock'). The Chief allowed him to live with her in the tribal village. But he wanted to return to the comforts of Olinda, and eventually tried to elope there with her. Iniguaçu sent his sons to recover his daughter. They saw the Governor and returned under safe conduct with the girl. The various sugar estates received them well until they reached the last, the stone farmhouse of Diogo Dias. Dias seized the Chief's daughter and sons. The provocation led to war. Iniguaçu joined the coastal Potiguar and their French allies. They marched against Diogo Dias, lured him and his retainers out of their stockade, and slaughtered them before they could run back inside. The killing of a powerful settler introduced another round of frontier wars.*

A large Portuguese expedition sailed north in 1574 and landed at the mouth of the northern Paraíba river: Its leader 'took possession of it in the name of the King with much solemnity, with deeds that he ordered to be carefully notarised. This done, he returned well satisfied to Pernambuco. . . . The Potiguar, however, understood no part of the judicial deeds and paid no attention to them. They saw no mortars and no one to fire them, and therefore returned to rule the land as before.' They also surprised and killed one of Diogo Dias' sons who tried to rebuild his father's mill. Portuguese replies to this were grandiose, expensive and largely ineffectual. For a decade nothing was achieved in the conquest of Paraíba. Successive expeditions gained little more than the destruction of some French shipping and the marooning of its crews among the Potiguar. The Governor of northern Brazil, Luís de Brito de Almeida, himself commanded a great fleet of twelve ships containing all the nobility and officials of Bahia. It sailed as far as Recife in September 1575, but no further.

A rich colonist called Fructuoso Barbosa was then named Captain-Major of Paraíba. During the ten years that he held the title, most of the supplies and funds sent out from Portugal for the conquest of Paraíba were dispersed. In 1579 he equipped four ships at Recife, but never reached Paraíba: a storm drove his ships to the West Indies, and he returned to Brazil via Portugal. The death of King Sebastião and the disaster in Morocco led to a lull, during which the Portuguese made peace and traded peacefully with the Potiguar. Barbosa's expedition finally sailed again in 1582. It destroyed five out of eight French ships surprised on the Paraíba, but returned after suffering heavy casualties in land battles against the Potiguar.*

The Potiguar achieved some notable successes during these years. They ambushed a Portuguese landing-party in 1582, killing forty Portuguese, including the commander's son, on the beach in full view of their compatriots' ships. When an expedition arrived overland that same year it fought a fierce battle in which many Europeans were killed. Both expeditions retreated when faced with large concentrations of Indians.

Portugal fell under the control of Spain in 1580. In April 1578 Francis Drake had sailed past Brazil at the start of his famous circumnavigation. In his account of the voyage, Drake pondered the fate of the Brazilian Indians. He noted that in Magellan's day these natives were described as having no religion and living 'only according to the instinct of nature', whereas they now worshipped many spirits. 'For then, they lived as a free people among themselves, but now are in most miserable bondage and slavery, both in body, goods, wife and children, and life itself to the Portugals, whose hard and most cruel dealings against them forceth them to fly into the more unfruitful parts of their own land, rather there to starve or at least live miserably with liberty, than to abide such intolerable bondage as they lay upon them. . . .'

Drake's voyage prompted King Philip of Spain to send a mighty fleet of 23 ships and 3500 men to plant a colony on the Straits of Magellan. This expedition, led by an admiral called Diego Flores de Váldez, was beset by storms from the moment it left Spain and lost most of its ships and passengers. In January 1583 it fought two English ships under Edward Fenton at São Vicente.† The Spaniards pursued Fenton towards England. But when they called at Bahia the Governor persuaded them to help fight the Potiguar and French of Paraíba.

A joint Luso-Spanish expedition destroyed more French ships in the Paraíba river, and by May 1584 it had built a fort called São Felipe a few miles up the river. The new fort was garrisoned by 110 fine Spanish arquebusiers and 50 Brazilian mamelucos. But when an expedition ventured upstream it fell into another Potiguar ambush. Its commander was killed, with 40 Portuguese and many Indian allies. 'Our defeat and disorder were so great that [the Indians] went on killing them right up to our camp.' 'No one can resist the fury of this nation of victorious heathen. They are personally more spirited than any others, and so brave that they do not fear death. Among them it is all-important to be considered brave. Only the fury of our artillery prevented them from seizing the fort in their clutches – for [the guns] smashed them cruelly when it caught them in the open.' Most of the Paraíba expedition returned to Recife 'completely defeated' having lost 50 whites and 400 Indians, 'which was the greatest loss suffered by these captaincies up till then: for almost all [the Indians] were slaves'.

The Potiguar besieged the fort between November 1584 and February of the following year. French engineers showed them how to build earthworks and trenches defended against artillery by palm-logs. The defenders counter-attacked, burning French ships. But the garrison was dying of hunger and dysentery. They were forced to eat their horses to survive.*

The Potiguar's traditional enemy was a tribe called Tobajara, led by Chief Pirajiba ('Fish Arm' or 'Fin').† As enemies of the Potiguar, the Tobajara were natural allies to the Portuguese and had been linked to them ever since the marriage of Jerónimo de Albuquerque to the daughter of Chief Green Bow. But in 1584, at this critical juncture of the Paraíba war, a treacherous slaver managed to infuriate this powerful ally. Francisco de Caldas led a big expedition from Pernambuco to the São Francisco river, and enlisted the help of Pirajiba and many Tobajara warriors. 'They later returned towards the sea with seven thousand captives, but decided to repay Fish Fin by tying up and bringing him and all his people as well.' Pirajiba learned of their plan. He kept supplying them with food and game; but he enlisted the help of his relative, Chief Guirajibe ('Bird's Perch'). There were two hundred Tobajara in the expedition's camp. At an agreed signal they turned on the slavers, 'caught them all sleeping very carelessly, and suddenly attacked with such fury that they gave them no chance to seize their arms or to flee: and they killed them all. . . . They freed the other heathen captives and helped them celebrate their liberty by eating the flesh of their masters. They then let them return to their homes.' There was much lamentation among the widows and orphans in Olinda. Furious at the treachery, Pirajiba led his Tobajara to join the Potiguar in a concerted attack on Fort São Felipe.

The Portuguese now produced another of their brilliant commanders, the tough soldiers who won Brazil for that small nation. He was Martím Leitão, a judge from Recife, and he had the advantage of a fine chronicler – an anonymous Jesuit who accompanied Leitão and described his campaigns with sparkling realism. This account of the Paraíba wars gives an impression of the fighting taking place, unrecorded, in Indian wars all over Brazil.

Leitão persuaded five hundred settlers in Pernambuco to join his 'large and brilliant' expedition, which Vicente do Salvador described as 'the most beautiful thing ever seen in Pernambuco, and I doubt if it will ever see the like'. The column of march was almost two miles long, with

Indian scouts ahead and cavalry in the van. After five days' march it reached the great plains of the Paraíba. It plunged into forests as night was falling on 5 March 1585 and came upon a stockaded camp of three thousand Indians, mostly Pirajiba's Tobajara. Leitão attacked at once, despite nightfall and the stockade. 'They killed many of the enemy – for their hatred was too great to permit them to take prisoners in this first attack.' They slept in the deserted camp, which was full of food, guns and powder ready for an attack on the Portuguese fort.

The great expedition spent three days cutting through the riverside forests towards the fort. They had to cut and burn their way, bridge swamps with logs, and remove the pits and traps with which the Potiguar had mined the jungle trails. When they finally reached the fort its soldiers were in a wretched state, sick and dying, and with rivalries between the Spaniards and Portuguese. The relief army went down with dysentery. By April 1585 it was back in Recife, and a few months later the Spanish commander abandoned Fort São Felipe, throwing its guns into the sea.

Martím Leitão now concentrated on winning over the Tobajara. Pirajiba's men had fallen out with the Potiguar, and the chief was ready for peace. The Portuguese sent to help him against the Potiguar. Hostages were exchanged and fine clothing was sent to the Tobajara chiefs. When Leitão reached the Indian villages 'they embraced one another with great rejoicing. Leitão made his own retainers dismount and let [the Indian chiefs] ride the horses. Some were shaking because of the time they had spent among the whites, and had to be supported in the saddle. He led them into the midst of their villages in this triumphant manner, well dressed in the clothes they had been given, at which some cried and others laughed – a sight well worth seeing!'

Leitão marched inland with masons and carpenters, oxen and domestic animals, to build a fort on the Jaguaribe river. In a few weeks his men had cleared the forest and built a square fort, with towers of stone and oyster-shell mortar, mounting eight heavy cannon. There was 'a tower for the captain above the fort's gate, with two verandas, a noble affair; and a great building for a storehouse'.

On the return journey, Leitão was leading three hundred men, eighty of them white and only eighteen on wretched horses. They came upon a horde of Potiguar 'who made the river bank thunder with their usual terrifying battle cry – enough to confound other armies. . . . But Martím Leitão's confidence was something for which to thank God. In the face of that howling, he turned cheerfully and said: "Now we have what we were seeking! At them!"' In a confused charge Leitão's men rushed right through the enemy and into their stockade. The Indians ran out the far side into the forest. The stockade was one of the strongest ever seen in Brazil, clearly the work of Frenchmen. It boasted three large towers, seven lines of trenches and a labyrinth of log obstacles. Great trees had been arranged in traps 'which, if a bird touched them, would crash down and crush twenty men. . . . The place would certainly have terrified us all had we seen it properly in the midst of the fighting. But at that time the smoke from continuous arquebus fire, the shouting and arrows gave no chance to worry. . . .'

The column was marching single file along a forest path a few days later when its vanguard fell into a Potiguar ambush. Indian archers opened fire from three sides. The Portuguese were about to run, but Leitão managed to press his horse forward through low forest. 'He began to upbraid them, asking whether they were determined to flee or to build homes in which to live and die as old men. "If so, our homes must be those of the enemy. Therefore", he shouted, "be at them!"' Leitão leaped off his horse and led an attack on the Indian flank. 'With this they carried the enemy before them. They drove them out of a thousand extremely well fortified labyrinths they had prepared there. Their enclosures were strewn with a thousand dead bodies.' There was a lull while the Portuguese hacked their way forward. 'The enemy thus had a respite in a rotten great swamp (such as they always tend to use as a refuge). . . . Many [Portuguese] refused to follow their commander, the Chief Judge [Leitão]. Although his horse fell with him, he pulled it up by the bridle and emerged very elegantly from all the mud, mounted very nimbly and pursued the enemy along a trail, with two other horsemen and Indian allies who were busily destroying them.'

They entered the Indian village, a place of 'barbarous poverty', and learned that the Potiguar chief Tejucupapo, a great shaman, had organised an army of twenty thousand men beyond the Rio Grande. 'Since [the Potiguar] are masters of over 400 leagues of this coast it was not possible to eliminate them. For these heathen have the fault of being the largest and most united of any in Brazil.'

The Potiguar regained the initiative in 1586, reinforced by seven shiploads of men, arms and powder from France. They attacked the village of the Portuguese' closest Indian ally, Chief Guirajibe. In December the Portuguese marched inland with every available man from Pernambuco. They attempted a crossing of the dry wilderness to attack the Potiguar villages in the Copaoba hills. 'There was infinite hardship on this expedition, especially concerning water. There were only very rotten wells with a little milky water that smelt so bad that one had to hold one's nose with one hand and drink with the other.' The expedition surprised one village. 'Some managed to flee because our

Indians gave their battle cry before entering. But [our men] still made an incredible slaughter. Seventy or eighty slaves were taken, against the wishes of the Judge [Leitão] who wanted only to kill them.' The pursuit continued for a few miles to another village filled with enemy dead. Pirajiba's Tobajara were with this expedition and they insisted on a two-day drinking celebration, which was their custom 'after large slaughters like this one'.

The expedition plunged deeper into Copaoba, a fertile region with deep valleys and steep hills. It contained fifty Potiguar villages, all within sight of one another. A joint action was planned, but it failed when Pirajiba attacked the wrong enemy force, leaving a contingent of Portuguese stranded behind the Potiguar. The Potiguar had the expedition surrounded, and were even firing muskets at it. Portuguese and Tobajara were 'overcome with fear and appalled to find themselves so remote: 140 men with 500 archers of our heathen, where no white man ever dreamed of going, in lands that no one knew'. The expedition was trapped inside a stockade, and could count four or five thousand camp-fires of enemy around them. But Leitão rallied his men, and the priest Baltasar Lopes preached to them. They improvised shields from chests and creepers, and charged out, 'leaving everything burning, as we always do to all enclosures and villages we take'. In a day of savage fighting the Portuguese managed to destroy three more villages and to extricate themselves from encirclement.

Leitão's expedition moved on against chief Tejucupapo, descending towards the coast. They came upon a large stockade. The quality of the powder and the shooting showed that there were Frenchmen inside, and this was confirmed by French flags and drums. The Portuguese were soon pinned down behind tree trunks. Horses were hit by arrows and shot. João Tavares was up against the main gate of the stockade with a handful of men, 'hugging the ground and surrounded by enemy. They rammed their swords into the embrasures or loopholes to cover them, and defended themselves desperately. They could not turn back or retreat in any direction.' Only a covering fire from Portuguese arquebuses prevented the Potiguar and French from charging out. Other Portuguese hacked their way towards them through dense undergrowth. 'In this confused labyrinth no one could understand one another or hear orders, because of the shouting of the enemy blacks [Indians] and of ours, the booming of the muskets, and the many wounded falling at every step.' Leitão himself managed to cut through dense jungle, slashing the defences of creepers with his sword. He rushed right into the village. Someone hit his hand with a club so that the blood gushed from the nails. His helmet was knocked back by arrows. Many arrows hit his arms and chest, but his fine armour protected him. His companion Manoel da Costa fell in a hail of arrows. Leitão knelt to cover his head and remove the arrows. Potiguar warriors rushed up to capture him – they recognised Leitão by his armour and the cutlass scar on his head. This attempt to catch him alive saved Leitão's life: the Indians struck his ribs rather than his head. Another Portuguese officer charged into the village just in time with a few more men. The village was full of smoke from burning huts and arquebus fire. The Portuguese leaders rushed through it shouting 'Victory!' – 'and there is no joy equal to that word in such crises'. The defenders fled, 'and our men could do nothing but embrace one another, rejoicing, with tears in their eyes at the mercy God had done them'.

For the fourth year running the Portuguese burned French brazilwood before it could be loaded. The Potiguar retreated beyond the Rio Grande, and the Portuguese built another fort on the Paraíba. Before long there were fifty married settlers and as many bachelors in Paraíba. The Tobajara of Guirajibe and Pirajiba were 'settled around the fort and live there, and are invariably very domestic towards the whites. They help them greatly in everything, building their houses and growing their food, and in short serving them like slaves.' But with the departure of Martím Leitão, who had conquered Paraíba, it was feared 'that we will start abusing them as we have already seen in many captaincies, which may lead to some great disaster . . .'.

Hard on the heels of each conquest came the missionaries. There were always missionaries on any military mission, acting as interpreters, trying to restrain the excesses of the soldiery, and using their reputation as shamans and their knowledge of native psychology to overawe Indian allies and enemies. The Jesuits established themselves at the new town of Filipeía a few miles up the Paraíba in 1585. They had soon converted many Tobajara, thanks to Chief Pirajiba. By 1591 there were 1100 people in their aldeia.

Other missionary orders also appeared: the Franciscans established a convent at Filipeía in 1589 and started converting the Potiguar. Franciscans were less intellectual than Jesuits, closer to nature and given to farming and manual labour. This made them more sympathetic to the Indians, and on the Paraíba they had a fine leader in Friar Melchior de Santa Catarina. The plantation-owner Gabriel Soares de Sousa commented that the Tupinambá were 'in a very good condition for Franciscan friars', and possessed 'great inclination for learning the trades . . . of carpenters, hewers and sawers of wood, pottery-makers . . . all the tasks of the sugar plantations . . . and the raising of cattle'.

After their initial successes, the Jesuits baffled Indians by not behaving like important men – indifferent to women and opposed to warfare, in marked contrast to the licentious and aggressive settlers. Tribes who accepted Jesuit discipline gained no prestige from association with such powerful shamans, but became meek and cowed. The Jesuits also worried the colonial authorities by their controversial defence of Indian liberties. In 1591 the Governor replaced them on the Paraíba by Carmelites, a more placid order that contented itself with catechising Indians and did not oppose the settlers' abuse of native women and labour.†

The battles in the Potiguar villages of the Paraíba were typical of similar frontier wars on other parts of the coast. The French were still strongly linked to the Potiguar, by many years of trade, friendship, military alliance and intermarriage. With the loss of the Paraíba, the Potiguar retreated north to the Rio Grande, and French ships traded with them on the estuary of the Potengi.

In 1597 the French and Potiguar made an unsuccessful attack on the Portuguese fort on the Paraíba. The Portuguese response was a powerful expedition against Rio Grande commanded by Captain-Major Manoel de Mascarenhas Homem. He sailed along the coast, while the Governor of Paraíba, Feliciano Coelho, marched overland. Coelho was leading '178 [Portuguese] foot and horse, besides our heathen: 90 bowmen from the Pernambuco aldeias and 730 from those of Paraíba, with their chiefs who led them, Fish Arm, Bird's Perch, Green Stone, Mangrove and Big Thistle'. Coelho's land expedition suffered a terrible epidemic of smallpox, losing ten or twelve men a day; but this proved a deadly weapon, one that annihilated the Potiguar more effectively than any arquebus.

The expeditions reached the Potengi at the end of 1597, and hastily built a stockade. They were soon under furious attack. 'Infinite' Potiguar appeared, 'accompanied by fifty Frenchmen, who had survived from [destroyed] ships or were living married to Potiguar. These surrounded our enclosure and wounded many of our men with mortars or arrows fired between the mangrove logs [of the stockade].' But the Portuguese rallied, 'like elephants who catch sight of blood', and broke the siege. There was a truce, but this soon ended in mutual suspicion. More fighting followed: ambushes in the mangrove swamps, skirmishes at the fort's walls, and one battle in which the Tobajara pursued some Potiguar down to the river 'and even went on killing them swimming in the water, leaving none alive, netting such a catch in this fishing that our boats had to go to fetch them back from beyond the bar of the river'.

In April 1598 Feliciano Coelho marched north with a reinforcement of 24 horsemen, 60 arquebusiers and 350 Indian bowmen with their chiefs. They decided to finish building the fort, working in shifts: Fish Arm's men working one day together with Coelho's whites, Bird's Perch the next day with other whites, and Green Stone the third, in rotation. 'Each company of heathen was also given a white man expert in their language to exhort them to work.' Other Tobajara and Brazilian-born Portuguese continued to raid the countryside. 'They went to attack one village where they killed over four hundred Potiguar and captured eighty. They learned from these that there were many Potiguar and French nearby, in six very strong enclosures, ready to attack and kill our people. They had not yet done so, because many had fallen sick and died from the smallpox epidemic.'

The fort was finished and named dos Reis Magos after the Magi. Feliciano Coelho marched back toward Paraíba in late 1598. The hero of his march was an Indian convert called Tavira. With only fourteen scouts Tavira managed to surprise and kill every Potiguar sentry. Coelho's force was thus able to surprise a large fortified village. During two hours' fighting the only man to enter was Tavira, 'who boldly scaled it and jumped inside with a sword and buckler. Shouting his name, he began to kill and wound the enemy, until his sword broke and he was left with only the buckler to ward off arrows. This was seen by Captain Ruy de Aveiro and his soldier Bento da Rocha. They fired two arquebuses through an embrasure, at which the enemy drew back. [Tavira] had a chance to climb the palisade again and emerge with the agility of a bird. This Indian gained such a reputation with this and similar feats that he had only to call his name, shouting, "I am Tavira!" for the enemy all to grow cowardly and timorous.' That night the expedition attacked again, in a barrage of arquebus and arrow fire, amid cries from the Potiguar women and children. They forced an entry, drove out the defending warriors and won a victory with over 1500 dead and captive. The fighting was harder at another village occupied only by Potiguar fighting-men. These included a dozen good arquebusiers: they and the Potiguar archers never missed, and killed or wounded many Portuguese.

The mameluco Jerónimo de Albuquerque was left in charge of the fort of the Magi.† He consulted with the Jesuit Gaspar de Samperes on how best to end the Potiguar war. Their solution was to release a captive called Big Island, a powerful chief and shaman. He informed his relatives that he came from the Portuguese to tell them: 'If you wish to remain alive and quiet and stay in your homes and lands with your wives and children, it is necessary that you go with me without further consultation, to the white men's fort to talk to their captain Jerónimo de Albuquerque and to the Fathers; and to make peace with them. Such peace will be firm and perpetual, like the peace they made with Fish Arm and the other Tobajara, and as they do throughout Brazil. For any who enter the Church are not enslaved, but are instructed and defended. This is something that the French never did for us, and will do even less now that their port is blocked by the fortress, so that they cannot enter without being killed and their ships sent to the bottom by the artillery.'

The peace overture was welcomed by the Potiguar, 'and most especially by the women who were fed up with marching with baggage continually on their backs, fleeing through the forests and unable to enjoy their homes or the vegetables they had planted. They brought their husbands, threatening them that they must go to the whites. They themselves preferred to be captives than to live in such fear of continual wars and surprise attacks.' Powerful chiefs, including Zorobabe ('Dry Wood'), went to the fort to negotiate.

The outcome was a peace treaty, approved by the Governor-General in Bahia, and signed at Paraíba on 11 June 1599, 'with the solemnity of law', in a ceremony attended by many Portuguese officials. The interpreter was the Franciscan friar Bernardino das Neves, 'who was very expert in the Brazilian language and very respected by the Potiguar, for that reason and because his father was Captain João Tavares, who had been very feared among them'. Jerónimo de Albuquerque became first captain-major of Rio Grande. A town called Natal was soon built near the fort. Settlers moved in. The soil was too sandy for sugar but proved ideal for raising cattle, and there were fine natural salt flats nearby.

The Potiguar made one last bid for freedom. In 1601 they besieged Coelho in the new town on the Rio Grande. He sent a desperate appeal to Manoel de Mascarenhas Homem that the town would be lost and its inhabitants slaughtered if they were not relieved. Mascarenhas set off with a force of 400 Portuguese and 3000 Indians. Anthony Knivet was with them and described the campaign. It took a week to reach the Rio Grande, 'having many a brave skirmish with divers Canibals in the way'.

Mascarenhas found an army of 40,000 Potiguar besieging the town, and attacked at once. 'The which was very bravely performed, for the Canibals the day before in a skirmish they had, did take two hundred prisoners, and having killed many of them to eate, not expecting our coming in the chiefest of their feast and their drinking, we set upon them. The people of the Towne on the other side, hearing the rumour, issued forth, thus taking them on the sudden, wee made much slaughter among them, that they were forced to remoove their siege, with the losse of three thousand prisoners, and five thousand that were slaine.'

The Potiguar were shaken at this defeat by a far smaller force of

Portuguese and their allies. The French seemed to have abandoned them. They therefore sued for peace again, surrendered their prisoners, submitted themselves to Portugal, agreed to baptism, and decided to transfer their loyalties and alliance to the successful Portuguese. Mascarenhas readily accepted, 'and thus one of the greatest Provinces of all the North part of Brasilia became subject to the King of Spaine'. Two forts were built to protect the new town. The army was paid off with precious stones and ambergris – since there were no prisoners to be sold as slaves. And Anthony Knivet at last managed to return to Portugal and thence to England.

Once the Potiguar had surrendered, it was decided to use them against the elusive Aimoré, who continued to intimidate the old captaincies of Ilhéus and Pôrto Seguro. This would disperse the Potiguar and keep them occupied, and they might even succeed in catching some Aimoré, since they were 'jungle beasts' like them.* In 1603 the Governor of Brazil, Diogo Botelho, 'personally persuaded them to go and serve His Majesty, which they did with goodwill because of his good treatment of them'. Some 1300 Tobajara and Potiguar bowmen under Chief Zorobabe sailed south in six caravels. They not only managed to catch and kill a good many Aimoré, but even induced part of that elusive tribe to accept a peace. It seemed miraculous to have persuaded the ferocious Potiguar to co-operate in this way, and even more miraculous that they succeeded.*

The resistance of the Aimoré was further weakened by the initiative of a settler from Cachoeira on the Paraguaçu river south of Bahia. His kind treatment of an Aimoré girl was the prototype of countless later pacifications of hostile tribes. Álvaro Rodrigues captured the girl in a raid with his Indian retainers. 'She was taught the language of our Tupinambá, and he made some of our men learn hers. He treated her well, showed her the mysteries of our holy Catholic faith . . . and baptised her as Margarida. After she was instructed and had grown fond of us, he dressed her in a cotton shift, which is the dress of our Indian women, gave her a hammock to sleep in, mirrors, combs, knives, wine and whatever else she could carry; and sent her to go and disabuse her people. She did this, showing them that we drank wine, and not their blood as they feared; that we ate the meat of cows and other animals and not human flesh; that we did not go about naked, or sleep on the ground like them but in hammocks. She then slung the hammock between two trees and every one of them tried lying in it, and combing himself, and looking in the mirror.' Some of the braver young men of the tribe returned with this girl to Rodrigues' house on the Paraguaçu, and he took them to Bahia. The military commander entertained them 'and at once ordered that they be dressed in red cloth and shown the city, where every single shop and tavern invited them in and gave them things'. Peace was made with the Aimoré. Many Potiguar were left to settle in Ilhéus and Pôrto Seguro, and colonists rapidly occupied much of the territory that had been defended by the Aimoré for the past forty years.

The King gave generous rewards to the Governor who persuaded the Potiguar to help subdue the Aimoré. The Potiguar chief who led the campaign was treated more shabbily. When Zorobabe returned with most of his men, he was sent off to subdue a mocambo – a hideaway of black slaves who had fled from the sugar mills of Bahia to the forests of the Itapicuru. The Potiguar had little difficulty in tracking down and crushing the Africans. 'But few slaves returned to their masters. The heathen Indians killed many, and Zorobabe removed some which he sold along his route to buy a battle standard, drum, horse and clothing with which to make a triumphal entry into his land.' The Potiguar gave their chief an enthusiastic welcome, lining the expedition's route for many miles. Zorobabe entered in his finery and riding his horse, preceded by the standard and drummer, and with 'an Indian brave with a drawn sword fencing in front of him, separating the crowd which was innumerable'. He asked the Jesuits for a welcome by a choir of schoolboys, and that the church should be decorated with branches in his honour. He celebrated the day of his return with heavy drinking but attended church next day together with four chiefs from neighbouring villages. He announced that he intended to march inland to attack the people of Chief Green Corn, until the Jesuits reminded him that royal permission was now required for campaigns against Indians. The missionaries advised him to plant manioc to feed the people, which he did. The Jesuits found Zorobabe obedient and manageable. He even promised to become Christian and to shed all but one wife – he was planning a great marriage feast of chicken and game birds. But the Portuguese authorities were suspicious of Zorobabe. They found him too arrogant and potentially rebellious. The Captain-Major of Pernambuco eventually arrested him and sent him to prison in Bahia. Vicente do Salvador, who was in the city at the time, wrote that 'in prison they often put poison into his water and wine' but he avoided drinking it. 'In the end they sent him to Lisbon. But [Lisbon] was a seaport from which ships were leaving daily for Brazil, in which he might return. They therefore sent him to lodge in the city of Évora. There he ended his life and the suspicions that he might rebel.'

There were a few last pockets of native resistance along the coast. The Sergipe river between Bahia and Pernambuco was the home of some

Tupinambá tribes, and formed a refuge for Caeté and other Indians that had escaped from Portuguese colonies. The area was still visited by the French – and worse still by Protestant Huguenots. 'They had made a La Rochelle of it, with the help of thirty villages that existed in that area in which were counted 25,000 fighting-men.' But the Indians decided that they could not survive for long with powerful Portuguese captaincies on either side of them. They reasoned that their only hope was to forestall a military attack by seeking ecclesiastical protection. They therefore sent a delegation to Bahia in January 1575 to request Jesuit missionaries. The Jesuits were delighted by this invitation, and at once sent Gaspar Lourenço and another Missionary. Everything went splendidly. Lourenço built a church with a cross twenty palmos high in one village, and then moved to the aldeia of Chief Surubi on the banks of the Vasa Barris and founded a mission called Santo Inácio. By June the Jesuits had built three churches, baptised hundreds of Indians and already had schools full of native boys. The usual choirs and processions were being organised. Twenty-eight villages on the Cirigi river had been visited and were about to be converted.

But the Jesuits were not allowed to operate in isolation. Governor Luís de Brito de Almeida sent a contingent of twenty soldiers to escort the missionaries. Although these remained camped at the mouth of the river, their presence alarmed the Indians. During the famines and epidemics of the 1560s many slaves had fled from Portuguese fazendas to join messianic santidades, some of which were in Sergipe. The colonists demanded their return, and sent mameluco agitators to the Sergipe tribes to tell them that the Jesuits planned to enslave them – why else would they have brought a military escort? The colonists managed to foment trouble 'for their interest was slaves, and they resolved everything with deceptions'. The Governor himself was not above some slaving, and decided to intervene in person. The Jesuits begged him to leave them alone, but he saw a tempting opportunity. He marched out of Bahia in November 1575 at the head of a powerful force, and by 22 December had reached Sergipe and was off in pursuit of Indians.

The Indians in the new Jesuit mission took fright. 'They preached in the streets: "Let us go! Let us go before the Portuguese arrive!"' A mameluco had seized a chief's wife, claiming she was a runaway slave. At that the entire mission village decided to flee to the forests, saying: 'Let us all go and wait no longer. For, if a mameluco has the power to do this to us inside our own houses, what will the Governor do when he comes?' Chief Surubi joined his people in flight. They allied themselves to Chief Aperipé, whose conquest was the excuse for the Governor's intervention. The army soon overtook them. Chief Surubi, the man who had just submitted to Portugal and requested Christianity, was killed by a musket shot in the ensuing battle. Gabriel Soares de Sousa took part in the campaign and gained some slaves on it. He wrote that Governor Brito de Almeida 'gave such punishment as had never before been seen in those parts. For he ordered the bravest and greatest of the corsair chiefs of that heathen to be destroyed. . . . Those chiefs were killed and those of their people who escaped alive were enslaved.'

The fugitive tribes surrendered when told they would return to their mission. 'But, when they reached the church of St Thomas, the Governor turned it into a prison into which he ordered all those people to be herded, so that they could be divided up as slaves for life.' 'One cannot describe all the abuse and fear done to the Indians of the St Thomas [mission] . . . during the time the Governor and the Portuguese were there. These left no food or vegetables, no hen, nor anything that they did not destroy. They even took [the Indians'] beads which are their only wealth, and left them no axe or hoe that they did not take. And with this that great conversion ceased . . . and the Cirigi Indians have remained at war until now [1587].' Even the Governor's Indian auxiliaries – men from the missions around Bahia who were pressed into unpaid military service – 'were scandalised at the bad treatment they received from the Portuguese in the war: for these used them as porters, or put them in front as a barrier against the enemy'.

The missionary Gaspar Lourenço managed to retain part of his new flock. He led an exodus of 1200 people back to the Jesuit missions around Bahia. It was a 200-mile march, on which parents carried their children and the young carried old members of the tribe. The pathetic column was harassed by settlers. The Fathers 'could not leave them for a moment, for before their eyes the whites were seizing them, tying them up and hiding them in the woods to be used as slaves'. The Bahia mission Indians welcomed the refugees, even though some were from traditionally enemy tribes. But the new arrivals joined the missions at a time when these were again being devastated by smallpox and measles, and most were soon dead. The Government in Portugal did not approve of the Sergipe campaign: it declared the war 'unjust' and ordered the captives taken on it be freed. But the Governor was easily able to circumvent this order in his execution of it. The settlers kept their illegal slaves.

Sergipe was not finally conquered until fifteen years later, when Cristóvão Cardoso de Barros – whose father had been eaten by the Caeté together with Bishop Sardinha – conquered the tribes of the Baepeba hills. He killed 1600 Indians and captured four thousand, and founded São Cristóvão at the mouth of the Sergipe river. The Jesuits were then able to develop vast cattle-ranches on the lands once inhabited by Surubi's people. And Sergipe, the last pocket of French influence on the central coast of Brazil, was successfully colonised.†

The Waitacá living on the swamps and plains of the southern Paraíba survived in isolation longer than the Aimoré. Many of their traditional enemies – the Tupinikin to the north and Tamoio to the south – had long been dispersed or annihilated. One group of Waitacá took refuge in a Jesuit mission at Cabo Frio in 1620. They said that they had come to escape a famine in their own lands, and because of an internecine war within the tribe. The missionary reported that 'we received them all with much joy and abundant fish, manioc flour and everything else there was in the aldeia'.

In 1627 the Waitacá territory was awarded to two old soldiers, Miguel Ayres Maldonado and José de Castilho Pinto, in recognition of their services against the Tamoio some fifty years previously. They sailed with fifteen friends past Macaé and Cape São Tomé, and marched inland. Their first meeting with a village of Waitacá was very friendly. The Waitacá offered them fish. 'At this Senhor Maldonado said: "These people are very fond of brandy. Let us therefore make them a present of some to win their affection." "Yes, let's do that," said Senhor Gonçalo. At that Senhor Castilho made himself barman, grabbed a gourd and started drinking toasts to them all. At this they all clapped their hands very happily as a form of thanks. We also gave the chief a small mirror, and when he saw his image in it he became amazed and delighted.' The Waitacá guided the expedition inland. They showed them a lake, which the colonists named Lagoa-Feia ('Ugly Lagoon'), and led them back towards Cape São Tomé. The King had awarded these colonists virtually unexplored land, the home of the Waitacá tribe. One evening, 'after we had pitched our tents and the cook was preparing the meal, we went out on to the open plain to see its vast size. Our hearts filled with joy, seeing that we had achieved such a rich property, for us to rear the horses and cattle we needed so greatly for use in our sugar mills. Our view did not reach to the end of the continuous plains. With that we returned to our camp highly satisfied.' They reached a large Indian village and were welcomed by its chief. The village was full of freshly caught game: 'deer and capivara and many birds large and small – an abundance!' The group of colonists returned in 1633 to mark out and explore the magnificent fertile plains. They travelled across them, happily giving names to streams and lakes, and impressed by the Indians' skills in hunting birds or making fishing-nets. 'Because they were reared in this life, out here on the plains, and because of its fertility in game and fish, their fathers declined to accompany the other Waitacá when they migrated north of the Paraíba.'

The colonists were not able to enjoy the Indian lands they had been awarded. 'Our discovery of the Waitacá Plains caused a sensation, and aroused the envy of various persons in the captaincy of Rio de Janeiro. We found ourselves stampeded to sell our lands. The Jesuit Provincial and Benedictine Abbot were the most insistent in this.' The Governor summoned the aged colonists. He insisted that the Waitacá were dangerous: 'My friends, these rabble never remain peaceful; they are so averse to us. . . . Force is necessary to oppose them properly. Your Honours do not have the resources for this.' The colonists tried to resist the Governor's intervention. 'Sir, there is not a great number of savages: we observe them very well, and they do not exceed some two hundred. Although of the Waitacá tribe, they are very peaceful . . . and have done us no harm, apart from [killing] one heifer.' But the Governor insisted on sending an expedition. 'The gentlemen Fathers of the Society [of Jesus] appeared in their black vestments with an image of the Lord crucified in their hands, accompanied by a large escort. They arrived at the village with their customary barriers against the Indians, assuming that they were wild when they were in fact so peaceful. What they did was to settle them in an aldeia. . . . This is how they expelled the savages. It is in the shadow of the image of Our Lord that these ambitious missionaries deploy their precepts and sophistries cloaked in fraud and malice . . . !' The Jesuits, Benedictines and other colonists thus gained possession of the Waitacá Plains.

A few years later, a governor-general wrote that 'the Waitacá nation, who were the most barbarous and formidable of Brazil . . . [are] now tractable'. Another governor wrote that experience had shown 'that only when they suffer stern discipline do the insolences of conquered barbarians subside. This has been seen with the Waitacá tribe of Cabo Frio and the southern Paraíba. Only after being completely destroyed do they become quiet.'

By the end of the sixteenth century the Portuguese were pushing westwards beyond the Rio Grande towards the mouth of the Amazon. Apart from some of the wilder stretches, such as the swamps at the mouth of the southern Paraíba inhabited by the Waitacá, and some parts of Ilhéus, Pôrto Seguro and Espírito Santo devastated by the Aimoré, the conquest of the eastern seaboard of Brazil was complete.

The conquest was an extraordinary achievement by the Portuguese, done at a time when that country was more concerned with rounding Africa and trading with the Orient. It involved displacing the French, a nation many times richer and more populous than Portugal, and driving off corsairs from other northern countries. Tough Portuguese colonists crushed tribe after tribe of native Brazilians, using every weapon available to them; gunfire, armour, seapower, cavalry to a limited extent, and their own determination and bravery. All the Indian wars exploited fatal rivalries between tribes. No Portuguese ever took the field without masses of native auxiliaries eager to attack their traditional enemies.

The conquests were consolidated by the persuasive religious indoctrination of the Jesuits and other missionaries. And the relatively few colonists swelled their numbers by fathering a race of half-castes. The number of intruders was increased by the terrible traffic in black slaves from Guinea: by the end of the century some 100,000 Africans had been imported, compared with about half that number of white immigrants.*

The Portuguese who occupied Brazil were no worse than other European colonists of their day. They fought ferociously in the frontier wars – struggles in which no quarter was given by either side. The colonists were convinced of the superiority of their religion and technology, and treated the Indians with scorn or at best condescension. They fought fiercely from fear of the Indians' numbers and fighting skills, possibly heightened by a sense of guilt at invading the lands of others. They feared the certain death that awaited prisoners, and the thought of their bodies being dissected, roasted and eaten by their captors.

Few Europeans ever feel really at home in the Brazilian forests. It is impossible to see an enemy lurking in the endless tapestry of tree-trunks and dappled foliage. There is no way of moving silently across the bed of dry leaves, clambering over fallen logs or cutting through tangles of undergrowth. I myself have been in forest knowing that there were hostile uncontacted Indians nearby. You try to move alertly with head high, not concentrating on any particular object, but relying on all-round vision both to warn of unfamiliar movement out of the corners of your eyes and to watch the obstacles underfoot. Birds warn of the approach of an intruder. Anyone not raised in the forest feels very vulnerable to ambush.

Once in control, the Portuguese were hard masters to the slaves on their plantations. 'The slaves are the hands and feet of the lord of a sugar mill: for without them it is impossible in Brazil to make, maintain or increase property, or keep a mill running.' The slaves worked without respite. One plantation-owner confessed to the Inquisition that he 'ordered his factors to grind with the mill, load wagons of wood and cane, and do the other work relating to milling on Sundays and holy days as if they were weekdays. . . . But so did all the owners and factors of sugar mills everywhere in this captaincy without exception.'

Colonial society was strongly colour-conscious, with the whites clearly at the top; but it was not obsessed with race prejudice. It was very rare for white settlers to marry coloured women, but they had no sexual scruples about colour. Mixed unions outside marriage were the rule – despite the fulminations of the clergy and the disapproval of the authorities. From the outset, colonists surrounded themselves with native women, and the families descended from pioneers such as Caramuru and Ramalho or Jerónimo de Albuquerque were proud of their Indian blood; such families even bolstered land claims by boasting descent from the original inhabitants of Brazil!

After the sixteenth century, miscegenation tended to be between white men and black women. The coastal Indians had died out or run off into the interior. Those who remained retreated to their tribes and shunned contact with whites; and the Jesuits kept their mission Indians carefully segregated from colonial society. It was far easier for slave-owners to exercise a *droit de seigneur* with their African slave girls. Brazil is a country where 'a drop of white blood makes a person white', but it is nonsense to pretend that its society was not concerned with colour. Discrimination against children of mixed blood was not severe, largely because there were so many, and because the mixed mamelucos and mulattos were a useful force in opening Brazil. But there *was* race prejudice, with society strongly stratified in favour of whiteness.*

The Portuguese Government hoped to involve the Indians as its subjects in Brazil. It hoped to integrate them into colonial society and turn them into God-fearing citizens. This was in contrast to the British and French in North America, where elaborate treaties were made with Indian nations, but the settlers wanted the land rid of Indian inhabitants.

The Government's policy of making the Indians useful subjects failed utterly. The Jesuits opposed it: they preferred to keep their congregations isolated, and to convert their disciples into pious élites that in practice became regimented curiosities. By the end of the century there were 128 Jesuit Fathers in Brazil administering about thirty mission aldeias.* The colonists had no intention of treating the Indians as social equals or of encouraging them to find a place in colonial society: they wanted the Indians only as workers, either slaves or 'free men' forced to work for measures of cotton cloth. The Government tacitly acquiesced by never completely forbidding enslavement of Indians, and by fixing shamefully low wages for Indian labourers. The Indians themselves did not co-operate – they were never given a chance. They were never gripped by the ambitions of a competitive society. They consistently preferred to shelter in the remnants of their tribes rather than struggle at the base of the colonial world.

By the end of the sixteenth century, the settlers were still clustered along the coast. Except in São Paulo and a few mining areas, they remained on the coast throughout the colonial period. Various expeditions were sent inland, but failed to find jewels or precious metals in abundance. Brazil produced only raw materials and crops: first brazilwood, then sugar, cotton, tobacco and hides. These were profitable only when exported to Europe, so that plantations had to be close to marine transport. Lopez Vaz, who wrote in 1587, said that there were about a dozen towns along the coast of Brazil in his day. Olinda and Pernambuco (Recife) was the largest town, with over 3000 houses and 70 sugar mills nearby. Salvador (Bahia) had a thousand houses; Ilhéus 150 houses; Pôrto Seguro 300 in four small towns; Espírito Santo two towns of 300 houses each; Rio de Janeiro 300 houses; São Vicente and Santos 400 houses.

The Indians left various legacies in colonial Brazil. Until the nineteenth century, a few Indians were still living along the coast in dozens of missions or shabby settlements far from the cities. They left their blood, visible in the high cheekbones and coppery skin of many Brazilians, or more often in a three-way mixture of white, black and Indian that produces the caboclos of the interior – tough wiry people with powers of endurance to match their leathery skins. Indian women who lived among the settlers taught their children personal neatness and cleanliness. The Brazilian sociologist Gilberto Freyre noted that 'the Brazilian of today, a lover of the bath and always with a comb and mirror in his pocket, his hair gleaming with lotion or coconut oil, is reflecting the influence of his remote grandmother'. Most place-names in eastern Brazil are of Tupi origin, a tribute to the Indians' sense of geography.

The colonists readily adopted Indian foods. The most famous was the ubiquitous cassava or manioc, which grew so quickly and easily all over Brazil. Manioc flour appears on every table in central Brazil and is the basis of many dishes. Native women taught the settlers how to grow and prepare manioc – the Indians had invented the tipiti, an ingenious tube of woven basketry that stretches and contracts to squeeze poisonous liquid out of manioc. Europeans ate Indian dishes made from manioc: mingau porridge, beiju cakes like unleavened bread, tapioca, and the sawdust-like roast flour or farinha. The first governors of Brazil all ate bread made from manioc. Gabriel Soares said that 'Governors Tomé de Sousa, D. Duarte [da Costa] and Mem de Sá did not eat wheat bread in Brazil because they found that it did not agree with them, and many other persons did likewise'. The men who explored central Brazil or marched inland to enslave Indians or seek gold all relied on manioc. They carried as much as they could, raided Indian plantations, or even paused long enough to grow a crop for themselves. This was the bulk food that supplemented game, fish, wild honey and fruit on the expeditions. Whenever a governor prepared a military expedition his correspondence was concerned with accumulating enough manioc flour to feed it.

Then there was tobacco, which the Tupi tribes loved to smoke or chew. Europeans were not sure about it. Father Nóbrega said it was good for the stomach and for his catarrh, but he thought that Jesuits and other Christians should avoid tobacco or they would resemble the heathen too closely. The first bishop of Brazil savagely attacked the vice of 'drinking smoke': he made one smoker do penance stripped to the waist in church, and threatened to excommunicate the Donatory of Espírito Santo unless he broke the habit. The Jesuit chronicler Fernão Cardim disapproved of smoking and the resulting 'drunkenness'; but his contemporary Gabriel Soares regarded it as something of a panacea – a cure for festering sores, asthma and heavy drinking. The Indians loved it. The council of elders in any Indian village can still be seen at night seated in the centre of the village enclosure, smoking powerful cheroots as they debate the tribe's affairs. The French Capuchin Yves d'Evreux tried a strong tobacco called petun and declared that it made his brain clearer and his voice stronger. He described its use by a victim of French justice: 'A savage sentenced to death at the mouth of a cannon . . . asked for a pipe of petun, saying: "Give me this last consolation in this life, so that I can give up the ghost strongly and joyously." . . . When the cannon ball had split his body in two, with one part carried out to sea and the other fallen at the foot of the rock . . . the pipe of tobacco was still found in the right hand attached to it.' Tobacco eventually became one of the main exports of Brazil, and was the principal commodity bartered for slaves in west Africa.

Other Indian vegetables had less immediate success. Only a few tribes grew maize corn, the staple of the Incas and Aztecs. Others grew pumpkins, broad beans, sweet potatoes and gourds. They gathered passion fruit, cashews, guavas, Brazil nuts, mangoes, palm-hearts and a wealth of other Amazonian nuts and fruits, many still unknown outside Brazil. The chronicler Gabriel Soares de Sousa was a plantation-owner who learned much from his Indians. His book is full of recipes, including a page extolling the midubi or peanut. There was also the red dye urucum – anatto – that has inspired women throughout the Brazilian interior to prefer red clothes.

The Indians possessed cotton, which was almost the only important plant to be found on both sides of the Atlantic before the conquest. They used it to make hammocks, another native invention eagerly adopted by the colonists. In a country so full of trees, hammocks were the lightest and most mobile form of bed, essential for expeditions into the wilds. Some fazendeiros in the north-east still prefer hammocks to beds, and the verandas of isolated farms may be festooned with visitors' hammocks. Any inn of the Brazilian interior has hammock hooks set into the walls of its bedrooms.

Many native products became current only after the Europeans had settled on the Amazon. There was a range of Amazonian spices and medicinal herbs – sarsaparilla, ipecac, copaiba balsam, quinine and cinnamon – and such useful commodities as cocoa, indigo and, in later centuries, rubber. The Indians showed settlers a profusion of dishes based on turtles, the oil from turtle eggs, and the many succulent Amazon fishes.

The Indians' greatest contribution to modern Brazil was the help they gave the settlers in penetrating the interior of the country. All expeditions into the heart of the continent relied on Indian skills as guides, hunters, woodsmen or canoers. But it was these expeditions that opened Brazil to the Europeans and ultimately doomed its native peoples to destruction.

NINE

The Discovery of the Amazon

Indian women and children.

DURING the century after its discovery, the mighty Amazon was a Spanish rather than a Portuguese river. It was discovered in January 1500 by a Spaniard, Vicente Yáñez Pinzón – a few months before the Portuguese Cabral discovered the southern part of Brazil.† Yáñez Pinzón's four small ships probably struck the coast of Brazil in Pernambuco. His men strode ashore and took possession of the land by carving their own names and those of their monarchs, Ferdinand and Isabella, on the trees and rocks. They then sailed north-westwards towards the mouth of the Amazon, and achieved many 'firsts': the first battle with Brazilian Indians, probably Potiguar; the first captives – thirty-six men 'bigger than large Germans'; and the first peaceful contacts 'with many painted people who flocked to the ships with as much love as if they had conversed with them all their lives'. But their most exciting achievement was to sail for 80–100 miles up a great river, which they named Santa María de la Mar Dulce ('St Mary of the Sweet [Freshwater] Sea'). They then recrossed the equator, seeing the Pole Star again, and sailed on to Columbus' discoveries in the West Indies. They had discovered part of the Amazon basin, probably the main stream of the Amazon itself.†

Once discovered, the great river was left undisturbed by Europeans. There were various reasons for this. The coasts on either side of the mouth of the Amazon were forbidding. To the north were the dense forests and swamps of what are now Brazilian Amapá and French

Guiana, areas still very thinly settled. To the south-east was the long 'East–West Coast' of Brazil, with winds and currents so difficult that coastal shipping was often swept up to the Caribbean, with dangerous reefs and shallows, and no easy anchorage apart from the inlet that later became São Luís do Maranhão. By a curious chance, the mouth of the Amazon lay inside the Spanish half of the world as defined by the Treaty of Tordesillas.† The Spaniards made one abortive attempt to colonise the river: Diego de Ordaz led two shiploads of colonists there in 1531, but the shoals and currents were too difficult – Ordaz' own ship managed to sail away, but the other was wrecked and some of its survivors intermarried with the Indians.*

The Portuguese were preoccupied with their voyages to India and the brazilwood trade in other parts of Brazil, and therefore tended to respect the Line of Tordesillas. When King João III divided the coasts of Brazil into captaincies in 1534, he dealt only with lands on the Portuguese side of the Line. The northernmost donation was Maranhão, granted to the navigator Aires da Cunha and the historian and government official João de Barros. They tried to exploit their grant in 1535 by assembling a great colonial enterprise of 900 men and all the necessary arms, trade goods and supplies in ten ships. But the coast of Maranhão was too treacherous. The leader, Aires da Cunha, was shipwrecked and drowned within sight of land. Some of his colonists managed to land but the colony never took root. A few Europeans intermarried with the local Indians. But the initial welcome soon deteriorated into warfare in which the Potiguar and Tupinambá destroyed the invaders and forced the last survivors to abandon the colony and return to Portugal in 1538.

The Portuguese colonists of 1535 did try to explore the great river discovered at the beginning of the century. They sailed up the Amazon for some hundreds of miles, until their seagoing ships began to run aground and could no longer manœuvre enough to sail against the current.* A son of the Donatory João de Barros made one further attempt to colonise Maranhão, but was defeated by the native inhabitants. Another failure by Luís de Melo da Silva in 1554 put an end to Portuguese endeavours in Maranhão or on the Amazon for the rest of the sixteenth century. The area had earned a bad reputation, with its difficult navigation, fierce inhabitants, and lack of obvious riches.

The Spaniards were also preoccupied elsewhere. During the first decades of the sixteenth century their conquistadores were exploring Central and South America with dazzling speed – first the coasts of the Caribbean, then Balboa's crossing of the Isthmus of Panama, Cortés' conquest of the Aztecs in Mexico, the explorations of the Plate and the Straits of Magellan, and in 1531 Francisco Pizarro's overthrow of the

Inca emperor Atahualpa. By 1540 Pizarro's conquistadores had overrun the entire Inca empire, in what is now Peru, Ecuador and parts of Bolivia, Chile and Argentina. His youngest brother, the dashing Gonzalo Pizarro, spent 1539 in an unsuccessful attempt to catch the last Inca ruler, Manco, who had retreated to the Vilcabamba forests north of Cuzco.

Peru was full of rumours of lands of great riches in the interior of South America, somewhere east of Quito. There was the land of El Dorado ('The Gilded Man'), a ruler whose kingdom was so full of gold that he had himself covered in gold dust each year in a ceremony in the middle of a lake. And there was La Canela, 'The Land of Cinnamon', one of the spices so highly valued in Europe that they inspired Columbus' voyages across the Atlantic and the Portuguese rounding of the Cape of Good Hope. It is easy for us to smile knowingly at the thought of fanatical explorers exhausting themselves in the Amazon forests in pursuit of the mythical El Dorado. But no one had suspected the wealth of Moctezuma when the Spaniards first sighted the mosquito-ridden forests of Central America; and Pizarro struggled for years along the harsh coasts of Colombia before he found and conquered the Inca empire, and became one of the richest men in the world. Pizarro's 170 men captured an empire; whereas many far larger expeditions – such as Cunha's 900 men in Maranhão – failed to establish even meagre colonies on the American shores.

One expedition left the eastern foothills of the Andes in 1538 and reached the Huallaga, one of the headwaters of the Amazon. The leader, Captain Alonso de Mercadillo, sent twenty-five horsemen to explore the country ahead. One of these was a Portuguese called Diogo Nunes. He reported that after twenty-five days the horsemen reached a land full of Indians who had gold ornaments. They fought these and moved on to the territory of a prosperous, well-organised people called Machifalo or Machiparo, whose many villages lay on the upper Amazon.*

Gonzalo Pizarro was fired by the idea of the discovery of El Dorado and La Canela. He persuaded his brother to appoint him Governor of Quito, marched north along the Andes, and reached Quito in December 1540. By February 1541 he was ready to march out of Quito at the head of an expedition of 220 Spaniards, many horses and four thousand manacled Andean Indian porters. Gonzalo wrote to the King that he was inspired by 'the many reports which I had received in Quito and elsewhere from prominent and very aged chiefs as well as from Spaniards, whose accounts agreed with one another, to the effect that the province of La Canela and Lake El Dorado were a very populous and rich land . . . [from which] would be obtained great treasures . . .'.

By the end of 1541 Gonzalo Pizarro's great expedition was near disaster. It had travelled at random in the valleys and forests east of Quito, pushing through savannahs and forests with the determination of seasoned conquistadores. The rains had set in. Much equipment and most of the horses were lost and, as Gonzalo wrote later, the greater part of their four thousand native porters had died of exhaustion, under-nourishment and the descent from their mountain homes into Amazon jungles. The expedition camped on the upper Napo, in the territory of Indians who plied the river in canoes and who wore long cotton shifts like the modern Jívaro. Gonzalo Pizarro decided to build a brigantine. He needed a vessel stronger than the canoes stolen from the Indians to transport the expedition's arquebuses, crossbows and heavy equipment. He also contemplated sailing downstream with the current until they found 'good country wherein to found colonies' or else 'of not stopping until I should come out in the North Sea [the Atlantic]'. The Spaniards already had a good idea of the outline of South America, and were fairly sure that the rivers rising on the eastern slopes of the Andes would flow into the Atlantic.

Pizarro's brigantine was built with nails scrounged from any metal found in the camp. Some of the expedition sailed in it, others in the canoes, and the rest marched through the forests on the banks. The jungle became increasingly dense. There were no villages of natives from whom the expedition could trade or seize food. The men were facing starvation. There was a report of a prosperous country up one of the rivers to the east. The second-in-command of the expedition, Captain Francisco de Orellana, volunteered to take the brigantine with some sixty men to try to find this land.

It was the turning-point in the expedition. For Orellana and his men did not find the food, but sailed on down the entire length of the Amazon to the Atlantic; and Gonzalo Pizarro was left to struggle back overland to Quito. Was it treachery on Orellana's part? Pizarro was convinced that it was. 'Being confident that Captain Orellana would do as he said, because he was my lieutenant, I told him that I was pleased at the idea of his going for the food . . . and gave him the brigantine and sixty men. . . . But instead of bringing food he went down the river without leaving any arrangements, leaving only signs and choppings showing that they had been on land and had stopped at the junctions of rivers and other places. . . . He thus displayed toward the whole expedition the greatest cruelty that ever faithless men have shown, aware that it was left unprovided with food and caught in a vast uninhabited region and among great rivers. He carried off all the arquebuses and crossbows and munitions and iron materials of the whole expedition.'

Orellana's excuse was that he was swept further and further downstream in search of food. His men were desperate from hunger. They were reduced to eating hides or the soles of their shoes cooked with herbs. Many were too weak to stand. When they crawled into the forest to search for food they often ended by eating poisonous roots. Seven died of starvation. 'They were like madmen, without sense.' They sailed for over a week 'and as the river flowed fast, we proceeded on at the rate of from twenty to twenty-five leagues [a day], for now the river was high and increased by many other rivers which emptied into it . . .'. Not surprisingly, an attempt to send a canoe back to Gonzalo Pizarro failed, and the crudely built brigantine could not possibly sail back against the current. 'Desirous though we were of returning to the expedition where Governor [Pizarro] had remained behind, it was impossible to go back because of the fact that the currents were too strong. . . .'

Orellana's men finally came upon a prosperous tribe of Indians, who loaded them with food when they claimed to be sons of the sun. They remained there a month, waiting to see whether Gonzalo might follow them, and building another boat. They were reasonably sure that by drifting downstream they would arrive safely at the Atlantic, and therefore wanted two ocean-going vessels. Orellana and his men were seized by the desire to explore the great river and win the credit for its discovery – even if it meant abandoning Gonzalo Pizarro and the rest of the expedition. None of them suspected that the journey would take eight months and cover thousands of miles of river.†

So Orellana and his fifty men set off in their two crude brigantines, down the Napo towards the Marañón and Amazon. Along most of their route they were the first white men seen by the natives. Tribe after tribe experienced the profound shock of first contact with men of another race. It was an experience in store for every tribe in South America, one to which each group of Indians reacted differently.

The first tribe on the Napo were Irimarai, possibly the Indians now called Ticuna. The expedition met four canoes of them paddling upstream. These turned round to warn their fellows, and Orellana ordered his men to row faster to overtake them. The Indians were drawn up ready to oppose these extraordinary strangers who presented themselves so unexpectedly on their river. But on seeing the Spaniards leap out on land and advance resolutely towards their village they lost heart, fled in terror and were soon out of sight in the forest. The starving Spaniards started greedily eating the food in the Indian village. In the afternoon, inquisitive Indians reappeared on the river bank. Orellana was a brilliant linguist who had already managed to learn a few words of the regional language: he therefore persuaded two of the most daring.

Indians to approach and asked them to summon their chief. This chief soon appeared in full regalia, and was delighted when Orellana embraced him and gave him a costume and other objects. In return the Indians fed the expedition for a month, and their chiefs submitted to a ceremony in which Orellana formally annexed their lands to Spain.

On 11 February 1542 Orellana's men sailed out of the Napo and on to the main stream of the Amazon.* Two weeks later they were met by canoes of Indians bearing gifts of food from another powerful chief called Aparia. These Indians also helped them gather resins to use as tar in the construction of another, better brigantine – a task that took over a month. They were treated like visiting gods or honoured guests throughout the passage through the territory of this tribe, which apparently occupied what is roughly modern Leticia. But in mid-May they moved on into the lands of Machiparo, close to what is now Brazil. This great warrior tribe did not welcome the strangers. Canoes attacked the Spanish boats, and a landing-party had a stiff fight to enter a fortified village. Machiparo canoes harassed them all night, and paddled out against them in relays throughout the following day and for a further two days and nights. The Spaniards were only just able to drive them off with their crossbows and arquebuses. They sailed on for days through Machiparo country, 'and the farther we went the more thickly populated and the better did we find the land'.

At the main Machiparo village Indians paddled out to inform the expedition that their chief wished to see them. He wanted to know their tribe, destination and purpose. The Spaniards landed and advanced towards the village in battle order, with the fuses of their arquebuses lit and the strings of their crossbows cranked back ready to fire. 'When the chief saw them to have different dress and aspect from all other people he had seen, and all bearded (for Indians are not), he revered them to some extent, and was courteous towards them.' He allowed them to occupy part of his village. But when the hungry Spaniards ran amok, pillaging the huts and trying to catch the thousands of turtles being reared in lagoons alongside each house, the Indians decided they were not deities but greedy mortals, and suddenly attacked. They came at the disorganised Spaniards with clubs and spears, and were themselves protected by long shields of crocodile and manatee skins. The Spaniards managed to rally and drive them off, capturing some of the shields and killing many natives; but they suffered sixteen wounded and two dead.†

Downstream lay the rich villages of the great Omagua tribe. The Spaniards were impressed by their 'numerous and very large settlements and very pretty country and very fruitful land', and by the great quantities of food and the fine roads radiating from a village they captured. What impressed them most was their first sight of fine glazed pottery, evidently similar to the Marajó pottery that is the pride of the museums of Belém and Rio de Janeiro. They saw huge jars capable of holding a hundred gallons, plates, bowls and candelabra, all magnificently decorated with drawings and paintings and expertly glazed: it seemed to Orellana's men to be equal to the finest porcelain in the world, better than Málaga-ware and comparable with Roman work. It was 'thin and smooth, glazed and with colours shading off into one another in the style of that made in China', according to Toribio de Ortigüera.* The village was abundantly stocked with cotton, maize, yucca, sweet potatoes and yams, beans and peanuts, peppers, gourds, quantities of fruits, game birds and dried fish.

The next tribe was ruled by a chief called Paguana. The first of its villages received the strangers hospitably and loaded them with food, including pineapples, avocado pears and chirimoya custard-apples. Although its main towns were inland from the river, one village stretched for some six miles along the banks of the Amazon. 'There was one day when we passed more than twenty villages.' Then came a very large, flourishing village with many landing-stages, each of them crowded with a great horde of Indians. Orellana decided to pass on without molesting them because of their numbers. But the Indians themselves came out in canoes and attacked the amazing craft sailing past them; they were driven back by arquebus and crossbow fire.

The Amazon here is as broad as a lake, a mass of gently swirling water the colour of an Indian's skin. The banks are unbroken lines of dark-green trees masked by a screen of undergrowth. These endless horizons of treetops are broken only by the occasional giant towering above the others, or by banks of mud or sand on which the Indians build their villages. Movement is in the sky, where immense formations of clouds soak up the moisture of the Amazon forests. The clouds pile up or race across the sky, and are reflected in the waters of the river. At dawn and sunset the surface of the Amazon mirrors a dazzling spectacle of colour, from silver to orange and deep purple. There is little else to break the monotony – occasional logs or islands of grasses floating with the current, a fish breaking the surface, tributaries or inlets making a brief opening in the walls of trees, or flights of birds, macaws, herons, or eagles watching the edges of the river. For most of the time, day after day, there is only the immensely broad, placid river and the unbroken lines of trees on its banks.

The Amazon basin, covering a third of the South American continent, is shaped like a gigantic funnel. In the remote geological past the river may have flowed in the opposite direction. The highlands of central

Brazil and the Guianas are of pre-Cambrian geological formation, and were probably joined. The lands of what is now the upper Amazon – the great triangle upstream of the Madeira and Japurá tributaries – rest on alluvial deposits of that era, when the river probably flowed westwards. Since then, continental drift has caused the upward folding of the Andes. The Amazon has reversed its direction, carrying the waters of the Andean snows eastwards to the Atlantic and slicing its way through the highland plateau near its present mouth. At one point, near modern Óbidos, the main Amazon still flows through a low gorge. The present mouth of the Amazon is not a true delta, but elevated land that has been drowned.

From the Indians' point of view there is a crucial geographical division between the flood plain of the Amazon rivers and the slightly higher forested land beyond. The flood plain is cut into the old alluvial deposits or through the highland shield. It consists of the flooded river banks and islands, side channels, ox-bow lakes and swamps. Its agricultural potential and protein resources are very attractive to man. The rivers teem with fish and their banks are full of turtles, rodents, birds and mammals. The recent alluvium of the flood plain is very fertile, particularly for growing manioc – the Omagua, for instance, learned to bury manioc tubers on Amazon islands and to recover them after the annual floods subsided. This is why the banks of the Amazon rivers were densely populated before the advent of European predators. All early accounts of journeys down these rivers confirm the populous villages along their edges.

The slightly higher ground between the rivers is, by contrast, far less hospitable. From the air the forests seem level and unbroken, stretching away to the horizons in an infinite green carpet. But movement through them is not easy. The ground beneath the tree canopy is surprisingly broken and hilly. There are swamps, steep hillsides of slippery pink laterite mud, tangles of lianas or patches of thorny scrub between the true rain forest, where the floor under the mighty trees is open and easier to cross. The earth beneath is unconsolidated sediment, a thick mantle of infertile muddy ground. Modern Brazilians who cut 'penetration roads' such as the Transamazônica, or try to clear and cultivate this land, are finding that it rapidly disintegrates and erodes when stripped of its forest cover.

In the sixteenth century the native population was very dense in the flood plain, or várzea. But the Amazon flood plain is relatively confined – probably less than a tenth of the area of the Amazon basin. The large populations seen by Orellana's expedition probably did not extend far inland. It is only in recent times that tribes have been forced to seek refuge in the depths of the forests and the upper headwaters of the rivers.

Downstream of the Omagua and Paguana, Orellana's expedition passed another populous province of people of medium stature, 'of very highly developed manners and customs', who used wooden shields and 'defended themselves in a very manly fashion'. On 2 June the expedition passed the mouth of the Rio Negro. They observed the way in which the black waters of the Negro flow into the main Amazon for miles before blending with it. They called it the Rio Negro ('Black River'), and the name has survived.† Below the Negro lived a fish-eating tribe, and Orellana's expedition fought its way into a stockade surrounding their village to steal fish.

Farther downstream lived a tribe whose villages contained totems of massive tree-trunks carved in the form of two jaguars supporting tower-like structures, with a central font for libations of chicha maize-beer. The Indians said that these remarkable altars were symbols of their allegiance to a tribe of female warriors. They also showed the expedition huts full of feathers and feather cloaks that were to be sent as tribute to these women.

News of the expedition's behaviour was evidently spreading down the river. Tribes no longer welcomed the strangers or allowed them to land without a fight. The two ships sailed past many villages in which the warriors were drawn up with their weapons and shields. Orellana let his men attempt to land only when they needed food. They seized one small village that was full of dried fish. It was occupied only by frightened women. Its men returned at nightfall and were amazed to find strangers from another civilisation occupying and pillaging their homes. 'They began to tell us to get out of them', but also prepared an attack.* Orellana's men had persuaded him, against his better judgement, to spend the night there in order to celebrate the important festival of Corpus Christi on land. They ended by spending the evening and the moonlit night repelling Indian attacks. Friar Carvajal, the author of the expedition's chronicle, dressed the wounded while Orellana directed the fighting. In the morning they withdrew to their boats. But, before leaving, Orellana 'ordered certain persons whom we had captured there to be hanged, and this was done. It was done in order that the Indians from here on might become afraid of us and not attack us.' News of the hangings spread only too well, for as long as the expedition passed the territory of that tribe they found hundreds of warriors shouting defiance from each village, and dared not sail near the shore. The warriors also attempted surprise attacks in their canoes.

On 10 June, Orellana's men passed the mouth of the Madeira, a river that seemed even larger than the one they were on. They were now sailing past the long island of Tupinambaranas, and the villages had posts festooned with trophy heads of enemies. Orellana's men called it Provincia de Picotas ('Province of the Gibbets'). When the Spaniards tried to land to capture food the Indians waited in ambush and attacked with great fury. Although a crossbowman managed to kill their chief, individual Indians retreated into the village and defended each hut 'like wounded dogs'. Orellana ordered that the village be set on fire, and in the confusion the expedition managed to escape with supplies of turtles, turkeys and parrots, and an Indian girl prisoner. She was an intelligent person, who told the Spaniards that there were other Christians, two of them with white wives, living in the interior to the north of her village. Carvajal assumed that they were survivors of Diego de Ordaz's expedition of 1531; or they might have been some of Cunha's Portuguese.

The expedition's looting and killing had by now thoroughly roused the riverine tribes. Flotillas of brightly decorated canoes sailed out against the Spaniards almost every day. The Spaniards were reduced to capturing and ransacking small villages for food, and finding deserted islands or forested banks on which to sleep.

Somewhere between the Madeira and the Tapajós the expedition passed gleaming white villages of what it understood to be 'the excellent land and dominion of the Amazons'. Orellana would have liked to have friendly relations, but these villages had been forewarned of the conduct of the Europeans. When Orellana called out to some canoes to make peace, 'they mocked us and came up close and told us to keep going, for farther downstream they were waiting for us and would seize us there and take us to the Amazons'. The Spaniards' reply was to fight, and before long they were trying to row the brigantines against a village defended by masses of warriors. The Spaniards' crossbows and guns took a heavy toll of the defenders, but these fought on, firing a barrage of arrows, dancing and shouting, heedless of their losses. The Spaniards defended themselves with shields captured from the Omagua. So many arrows were fired at the boats that they ended up looking like porcupines. Five Spaniards were hit before reaching the shore. One victim was the chronicler Friar Carvajal, who was hit by an arrow that penetrated his rib cage. 'Had it not been for the thickness of my habit that would have been the end of me.' The Spaniards jumped into chest-high water and fought for an hour, savagely holding off waves of native warriors. The Indians kept attacking despite their losses.

Carvajal was convinced that these Indians' determination was the result of their being subjects of the Amazons. 'We ourselves saw ten or twelve of these women, fighting there in front of all the Indian men as women captains. They fought so courageously that the Indian men did not dare turn their backs. They killed anyone who did turn back, with their clubs, right there in front of us; which is why the Indians kept up their defence for so long. These women are very white and tall, with very long hair braided and wound about their heads. They are very robust, and go naked with their private parts covered, with their bows and arrows in their hands, doing as much fighting as ten Indian men.' The Spaniards reckoned that they killed seven or eight of these Amazons before escaping to their boats. They drifted off with the current, too exhausted to row.

The expedition captured an Indian trumpeter during this battle. He stayed with them for the remainder of the voyage and they questioned him about the Amazons. He said that he had often visited their many villages, in the hills a week's march from the river. Prompted by the Spaniards' questioning, he drew a picture of the Amazons that sounds suspiciously like a blend of the Classical myth about the race of women warriors, and the explorers' knowledge of the recently conquered empire of the Incas. He said that the Amazons had no men living in their villages, but periodically went to war on a neighbouring tribe and forced its men to return with them. 'They kept them for the time that suited their caprice' and then sent them home unharmed. They themselves killed any male children but 'raised girls with great solemnity and instructed them in the arts of war'. Then, to whet the explorers' appetites, the Indian described the Amazons as having stone houses, temples to the sun, and a wealth of gold and silver – idols, table service and crowns of precious metals – dresses of llama wool, roads enclosed by walls and guarded by sentries, and animals like camels on which to ride. Their queen was called Conori and she ruled over many subject tribes.

Carvajal defended these extravagant stories by insisting that their informant 'was an Indian of much intelligence and very quick to comprehend' and that his account coincided with many other reports that the explorers had heard before leaving Quito. His contemporaries were more sceptical. Francisco López de Gómara wrote in 1552 that the idea of women fighting was nothing new in the Americas. 'But I do not believe either that any woman burns or cuts off her right breast in order to be able to shoot with a bow, for they shoot very well with [that breast]' – Carvajal never claimed that they did remove it; that notion came from the Classical legend of the Amazons of Asia Minor – ' . . . nor that they kill or exile their own sons; nor that they live without husbands, because they are very licentious. Others besides Orellana have proclaimed this same yarn about the Amazons ever since the Indies were discovered. No such thing has ever been seen along this river, and never will be seen.

Because of this imposture many already write and talk of the "River of the Amazons".' Even if the mysterious, sexually liberated Amazons were never discovered, the largest river in the world was named after them.

Orellana's weary men sailed on down the seemingly endless river. They were ambushed when trying to land at one village, and the only person hit by Indian arrows was Friar Carvajal. 'They planted an arrow shot right in one of my eyes, in such a way that the arrow went through to the other side. I have lost the eye from this wound, and am still not free of suffering or pain.'

The most striking aspect of their voyage was the vast numbers of Indian villages along the river. Whenever the expedition tried to find a deserted backwater in which to rest, there were more villages and more flotillas of hostile canoes. On 25 June they were attacked by over 200 canoes each carrying twenty or thirty Indians, probably Tapajós. Carvajal was impressed by the warriors' feather decorations, and by their music: they went into battle shouting and playing trumpets, drums, pipes and three-stringed rebecs, while their companions on shore leaped about, shouted and waved palm leaves at the passing ships. The territory of this tribe was thickly populated, and stretched for some 150 miles. Its Indians rejected the expedition's attempt to barter a few objects, and harassed it until it passed out of their territory.

The situation was no better downstream. On the north bank was the territory of a powerful and populous tribe – tall men with cropped hair and skin dyed black with genipapo. The expedition did not dare attack the larger villages, and when they tried to raid a small one a Spaniard was killed by an arrow tipped with curare poison. The expedition's Indian informant told them that this tribe was under a chief called Aripuna and that, unlike any of the other tribes on the Amazon, they ate human flesh.

There were populous tribes and battles against them throughout the islands and swamps of the lower Amazon. Time and again, Orellana's men were saved only by the tremendous shock effect of their firearms, particularly when a lucky shot managed to kill an Indian chief. The last half of July and first week of August were spent rebuilding the ships. The boats often ran aground, or dragged their stone anchors in the ocean tides. A docile tribe living near the mouth of the Amazon gave the Spaniards some food and on 26 August they sailed boldly out into the Atlantic. The two small improvised ships reached Spanish settlements off the coast of Venezuela on 9 and 11 September 1542, amid indescribable joy. They had accomplished one of the world's outstanding explorations, one that Fernández de Oviedo described as 'something more than a shipwreck, more a miraculous event'.

The next European presence on the Amazon was that of two Spaniards or Portuguese who accompanied a Tupi migration *up* rather than down the river. In 1549 the citizens of the Peruvian frontier town of Chachapoyas were amazed by the arrival of 'some three hundred Indians who said they were from Brazil and had left it in far greater numbers, led by two Spaniards who died on the journey. [They said] they were all fleeing from the vexations they suffered from the Portuguese conquerors of that province. . . . They told great news of their journey continually up-river, in which they had spent ten years. They emphasised the variety and multitude of tribes they had encountered, and particularly the wealth of a province they called Omagua.' Four Indians were taken to Lima with their chief Uiraraçu ('Big Bow') to see the President of Peru, Pero de la Gasca. Their arrival in Peru caused a sensation. Their report of great riches on the Amazon confirmed the legends of El Dorado that had beguiled Gonzalo Pizarro and so many other conquistadores. Everyone was impressed by their journey across the continent, moving up against the currents of the rivers. Various chroniclers told their story, including the Portuguese Pero de Magalhães de Gandavo, but he claimed that they had migrated because they lacked 'plantations to keep them in their homeland, and since it is their constant desire to seek new lands, in which they imagine that they will find immortality and perpetual ease'.

The thrilling reports of these Brazilian Indians inspired the last, greatest and most tragic Amazon expedition of the sixteenth century. In 1560 the Viceroy of Peru organised a vast expedition of 370 Spanish soldiers and two thousand Andean Indians under the command of Don Pedro de Ursúa. The objective was the conquest of the Omagua tribe on the upper Amazon. It was thought certain that the legendary El Dorado lay near their lands.

Ursúa's expedition crossed the Andes to Moyobamba and built a fleet of two brigantines, seven flatboats, twenty rafts and some canoes on the Huallaga tributary of the Amazon. All went well on the upper river, where the expedition was entertained by great villages of thousands of Indians. After three months it had descended to the lands of the Machiparo, close to the modern frontier between Peru and Brazil. An exploratory expedition marched inland for 150 miles along fine Indian trails, and found evidence of 'the richest and most populous country in the world'.

Ursúa's expedition contained the largest force of Europeans to appear on the upper Amazon throughout the sixteenth or seventeenth centuries – a force over twice the size of that with which Francisco Pizarro had conquered Peru. But its men were the dregs of that conquest. They took to massacring Indians, and the expedition was soon short of food and festering with revolt. Pedro de Ursúa was a poor leader, harsh and arbitrary, and he invited unrest by taking his beautiful mistress Doña Inéz de Atienza on the expedition. Ursúa spent more time in dalliance with her than leading his unruly men. The dissidents claimed that she was the expedition's real leader, and that they were liable to punishment at the whim of a whore.

Ursúa wanted to colonise the upper Amazon and then explore inland to discover El Dorado. He had his men spend a rainy season building a town. 'Where because it raineth much, and withall is very hot, sickness and want of victuals began to prevaile amongst them, whereupon the soldiers fell a murmuring among themselves. For coming out of Peru, which is one of the fruitfullest and richest countries in the world, they were more inclined to have their fill of bread and meat then to apply their bodies to labour.' The mutineers found a Spanish noble, Don Fernando de Guzmán, to act as their figurehead. But the instigator of their rebellion was Lope de Aguirre, a man of unmitigated evil, cruel, psychopathic and gripped by an obsessive grievance against the whole of Spanish society. Lopez Vaz described Aguirre as a Biscayan soldier, 'a very little man of bodie and lame of one of his legs, but very valiant and of good experience in the wars. . . . He asked his fellow-souldiers, what they went to seeke for in those wild deserts whither they were brought: For (said he) if you seeke riches, there are enough in Peru, and there is bread, wine, flesh, and faire women also; so it were better to conquer *that*. . . .'

The mutineers murdered Ursúa in his hammock near the mouth of the Putumayo, early in 1560. Aguirre persuaded the expedition that they must also rebel against the King of Spain: he proclaimed Guzmán 'Prince of Peru' and awarded members of the expedition great tracts of Amazon forest. Aguirre became captain of the militia, and surrounded himself with a corps of fifty Basque arquebusiers. The expedition moved down the Amazon and reached an intelligent and orderly tribe that wore cotton clothing. These were evidently the Omagua, near the Tefé river, for Aguirre's men recorded the same tanks containing thousands of turtles that had been raided by Orellana's expedition eighteen years previously. They were told that in ten days' journey up a tributary they would reach the El Dorado they were seeking, the province 'where there was more gold and silver than in Peru'. But, with Ursúa's murder, discipline was gone. There was a series of murders and brawls. Doña Inéz was stabbed to death. The expedition's chaplain was killed. Finally, after killing any man suspected of loyalty to Ursúa or to the King of Spain, Aguirre led his men in a massacre of the puppet leader Guzmán and all his closest followers.

Lope de Aguirre had no interest in exploring or conquering the upper Amazon. His sole ambition was to lead his rebels against the royal government of Peru. He forced the expedition to sail rapidly down the Amazon, forbidding his men to land for ten days at a time. When they did try to land to seize food, they were opposed by a tribe using poisoned arrows. But their greatest enemy was Aguirre's lust for blood: during the descent of the Amazon he killed over a hundred fellow-Spaniards. 'He determined not to carry with him any gentleman or persons of qualitie, and therefore slew all such persons; and then departing onely with the common souldiers, he left behind him all the Spanish women and sicke men. If I should rehearse all the cruell murthers of this wicked man one by one, I should be over tedious unto you.' But, during the descent, Aguirre reduced the Spaniards from 370 to 230 men. Aguirre was gripped with paranoia, 'because he ever stood in feare of his life: for had he seene at any time but two souldiers talking together, he would streight suspect that they were conspiring of his death . . .'. He was equally cruel to his Andean Indian followers. Most had died, but to clear the brigantines Aguirre ordered that the remaining 170 men and women be put ashore at the mercy of the local cannibal tribes. These victims were yanaconas, Christian Indians who had served Spanish masters throughout the conquest of Peru. They wept and complained bitterly at the injustice of their treatment. But when some Spaniards tried to intercede for them Aguirre had these immediately garrotted for insubordination.

The expedition reached the Atlantic and sailed up the coast to the island of Margarita off Venezuela. Aguirre terrorised some captured towns in Venezuela and then led his men overland towards Peru. They were quickly defeated. Aguirre returned to his tent and killed his own sixteen-year-old daughter, 'that she might not become a concubine to villaines, nor be called the daughter of a traytor'. The victors rushed in and shot Aguirre. His body was quartered and his head exposed for years in an iron cage.

Before he died, Lope de Aguirre wrote a letter to King Philip of Spain. It was an extraordinary document, a mixture of rebellious defiance, megalomania and self-pity. Aguirre told the King that he had no right to revenues from the Americas, since these lands had been conquered by others without danger to himself. Aguirre boasted that he and his men had travelled for eleven months to descend the Amazon. 'God knows how we got through that great mass of water. I advise you, O great King, never to send Spanish fleets to that cursed river.' The King followed this advice.

TEN

Maranhão

IT was the French who moved into the vacuum left by the Spanish and Portuguese near the Amazon. A French corsair landed many men among the Tupinambá of Maranhão after two of his three ships were wrecked there in 1594. Another Frenchman who had been captured by the Portuguese in Paraíba returned to France and promoted the idea of a French colony in Maranhão. Powerful courtiers became interested and obtained a royal charter. And in 1612 three ships sailed under the Lord of La Ravardière to colonise this northern coast of Brazil.†

Both French and Tupinambá were desperately eager for good relations with one another in Maranhão. Each saw the other as a protection against the Portuguese. The French took some Tupinambá to France, including Chief Big Ray of the Caeté. He returned after a year, speaking good French and duly impressed by the glories of France. He would often tell his people that the French were far more powerful than the Portuguese and would surely defeat them.

When the main French expedition arrived and started to build a fort called St Louis on the island of Maranhão, the Tupinambá helped enthusiastically. 'These savages came and set to work with incomparable ardour. . . . You would have thought they were going to a wedding rather than to work. They never stopped laughing and striving, each running with his load from the bottom of the ditch to the top of the rampart. There was considerable competition among them over who could make most journeys and carry the greatest number of baskets of

Tupinambá smoking and making fire.

earth. You will note from this that no people in the world are as indefatigable workers as these, when they undertake something in good heart. They do not bother to eat or drink provided they are enthusiastic about what they undertake. Faced with great difficulties they merely laugh, shout and sing to encourage one another. It is quite the opposite if you try to bully them or force them to work by threats: they will then do nothing worth while.' Even little children tried to help, and their parents encouraged them, explaining to the French that 'it is so that when they have reached old age they may say to their children and descendants: "Here are the fortresses that we and our fathers made for the French . . . who came to defend us against our enemies." '

The Tupinambá did their utmost to assimilate French ways. They loved the swords they obtained from the French and wore them constantly. They kept the blades sharp, and polished them lovingly with soft sand and palm-oil. Their fencing became so expert that one Frenchman compared them to Swiss swordsmen. Some even tried to grow moustaches and beards since they saw the French make such a fuss over theirs. They were fine mimics and soon acquired the trappings of French courtly manners. 'During the past two years the French have taught the Tupinambá to raise their hats and salute people, to kiss hands, make reverences, say good-day and good-bye, come to church, take holy water, kneel, clasp their hands, make the sign of the Cross on their hands and chests, beat their stomachs before God, listen to mass, hear the sermon even if they understand none of it, carry the Agnus Dei, help the priest say mass, sit down at table, put their napkins before them, wash their hands, take meat in three fingers, cut it on the plate, and drink a toast to the company. In short, they perform all the good manners and civilities that we who are so sophisticated practise among ourselves. They are so advanced in this that you would think they had been raised all their lives among the French.'

Each new Frenchman who reached Brazil linked himself with a Tupinambá in a close bond: they considered one another as compères or co-godfathers. The Capuchin friar Yves d'Evreux even wrote instructions to his compatriots. He advised them to bring plenty of wine and brandy (and to avoid drinking it during the sea crossing), the cheapest possible old swords and arquebuses, cheap cloth, plenty of knives with wooden handles, trinkets and jewellery. He described the Indians' excitement when fresh colonists arrived: ' "Here come the French ships! I shall get a good compère: he will give me axes, scythes, knives, swords and clothing! I will give him my daughter; I will go hunting and fishing for him and will make him plenty of cotton; I will hunt for egret feathers and amber to give him, and I shall be rich. For I will choose a good compère with plenty of merchandise!" And while they say this they beat their bottoms and chests as a sign of joy.' The missionary even described the conversation a newcomer could expect when he followed his compère to his village. This charmingly captures the repetitive elegance of Indian speech: Once in the village, 'the host offers his hand, with a certain gravity, as if he had never seen him, and says: "Have you come, my compère? A delightful and agreeable event."' After the women have performed the traditional weeping greeting, and the Frenchman has explained his choice of compère, the Indian gives the European a name and seats him in his hammock. 'The savage says to him, "That is excellent, I am infinitely pleased. You have honoured me greatly; you are welcome; you could find no better place to be received." . . . He then lights his pipe and, after inhaling five or six good draws, he enquires about your voyage, saying, "Did you leave your country to come here to see us, to visit us, to bring us merchandise?" You say to him: "Yes, I left it. I scorned my friends and my country to come and see you." Then, raising his head as a sign of admiration, he says, "You had compassion on us, you pitied us. The French have remembered us, they have not forgotten us. They leave their country to come and see us. How good the French are, and what good friends to us!"' The conversation then turns to the merchandise brought by the Frenchman, with the Indian eager to see and receive the trade goods and to establish his relationship with the stranger.

The French apparently understood and respected the Indians better than most Portuguese did. Two French Capuchins, Claude d'Abbeville and Yves d'Evreux, wrote about the Tupinambá with genuine sympathy. They were agreeably surprised by their first view of Brazilian natives. Many things about the Indians impressed them. Abbeville admitted that he had expected to be among ferocious savages, but found instead people of intelligence and sensibility. 'I have met no one nor heard of any nation that excels them.' He admired their good judgement. 'They are very susceptible to anything you wish to explain to them, and rapidly grasp whatever you wish to teach them – for they are eager to learn and be taught, and good at imitating anything they see done.' They were patient listeners who never interrupted – although they themselves loved delivering long speeches that could last for hours.

Abbeville noted the Indians' indifference to money. They 'lead happy and contented lives without greatly bothering to work'. Their hunting and fishing were for sport and to feed themselves rather than to amass riches. Yves d'Evreux gave the conventional judgement on this: 'They are unbelievably lazy and prefer to live wretchedly than to work and live fatly'. But he admired their generosity, lack of avarice, fairness to one another and absence of theft.

Both writers were impressed by the Indians' skills as hunters and trackers. 'They make a geography or natural description of whatever they are telling you with the tips of their fingers in the sand.' 'There are scarcely any stars in heaven that they do not know, and they can roughly judge the coming of the rains and other seasons of the year. They can distinguish the face of a Frenchman from a Portuguese. . . . They do nothing without deliberation, but weigh something in their judgement before giving an opinion on it. They remain quiet and reflective and are not precipitate in speaking. . . . They remember for ever what they have heard or seen once. They can explain to you all circumstances of place, time, persons and whatever was said or done.'

The French missionaries admired the graceful Indian girls with their smooth skins and well-rounded bodies. They were delighted to see them washing so frequently and combing their long black hair, and noted that they never smelled. The old women 'begin to be hideous and dirty, with breasts hanging down their flanks . . . which is a horrible sight. But when they are young they are quite the opposite, with firm breasts. I will not amuse myself more with this subject, except to say that the reward of purity is integrity and incorruption, accompanied by a good smell.' One French colonist described the embarrassment of the Capuchins when first confronted by these lovely girls. When the grey-robed friars arrived, the women 'assembled in great numbers to see them, but the Fathers would not open the door of their little cabin because the women were all naked. But these became impatient at a second refusal and broke down the door, which was not difficult to break. They crowded inside to regard and contemplate these prophets, and could not tire of watching them.' The Tupinambá then brought four hammocks and four beautiful girls for the Fathers; and were amazed when they refused. 'What, are these prophets not men like us? Why do they not accept these girls? How could a man possibly pass them by? Why do they do us such an affront?' The Capuchins had to explain their celibacy, which the Indians found unnatural and incomprehensible, but impressive.

The Tupinambá also tried to grasp the secrets of the Christians' successful religion. One shaman, the uncle of a friendly chief, came and told the French that he wanted to become Christian, to learn to read and write, speak French and behave in the European manner. He believed that such skills would initiate him in their magic. The missionaries were easily deceived: 'We believed this savage and several of us took great pains with him. After several months among us, he wanted to have vestments like the chasubles in which we said mass.' When this was refused, and the Christian magic proved illusory, the shaman turned against the French. He went about the villages claiming that they intended to enslave the Tupinambá, and uttered exquisite threats against them. 'He harangued them there in the lodges . . . beating his bottom with great slaps of his open hand, saying: "Me, me, me, I am furious and valiant! Me, me, me, I am a great sorcerer! It is I, I who kills the Fathers, I who made the Father die who is buried at Yuiret [St Louis] home of the Pai-guaçu, the Great Father [La Ravardière], to whom I sent all the troubles he has, and whom I will cause to die like the others. I will torment the French with maladies! I will give them so many worms in their feet and legs that they will be forced to return to their own country! I will make the roots in their garden die, so that they will die of hunger! I used to live among them and often ate with them. I watched how they performed when they served Tupan [God] – but I recognised that they knew nothing compared with us pagés, us sorcerers. Therefore we should not fear them. And if we must march out I wish to march at the head, for I am strong and valiant!"' Similar curses and challenges must have been shouted, in vain, by so many tribes confronted by European invasion. In the case of the Tupinambá pagé the defiance was short-lived. Other chiefs became alarmed by his behaviour and told him to stop; his nephew was sent to arrest him; and he hid in the woods, denied that he had ever made the speeches, and sent presents to the missionaries begging them not to believe the stories they heard about him.

The French Capuchins in Maranhão had the same initial success as the first Jesuits in Brazil. Immediately after his arrival, Claude d'Abbeville exulted that 'this is a people already acquired and won, a people great in truth, who love us and are infinitely fond of us. They call us the prophets of God.' Messengers came from the Indians of Pará near the Amazon 'where there are a hundred thousand men' begging for the missionaries to go and instruct them. The Indians enjoyed religious ceremonies, especially if they involved music or physical endurance – they prided themselves on the length of time they could remain kneeling or with their arms uplifted in prayer. The French were more lenient than the Jesuits over such matters as marriage: they told a man with several wives that he could marry one and keep the rest as 'servants'. The Indians also took readily to confession. 'Even the women confess things that the feminine sex over there [in France] has great difficulty in declaring to priests. . . . They very readily tell you the yes or no, the time, place, quality of persons, and the number, of their sins – with none of the silly *mondaine* shame that one sees over there.' It must have seemed another incomprehensible European idiosyncrasy that these grey-robed men, who refused women themselves, should have shown such interest in something as normal as the sex life of Indian women.

The French met a shrewd religious leader in Pacamont, the pagé of the Comma Tupinambá from Maranhão island. He was a small man, and when he paid his ceremonial visit to the French governor he made his wife carry him. 'Mounted on her thus, with his legs astride in the way that Indian women carry their children, he enters the fort and goes to find the Sieur [de la Ravardière]. His wife was as black as a fine devil, having painted herself from the soles of her feet to her head with genipapo juice. Just imagine the sight of one of the princes of Brazil mounted on such a fine nag.' But the small pagé disconcerted the French Capuchins by treating them as fellow-conspirators in exploiting the deceptions of priesthood. He explained that he had delayed his visit so as not to appear undignified and over-eager. He confided in them: 'You who speak to God will know that it is neither good nor expedient for us, who are esteemed for conversing with the spirits, to be light or facile. . . . Men like us are watched by our people, who imitate what we do. The power we have gained over our people is preserved by the gravity we show in our gestures and speech.'

Pacamont proposed a deal whereby the missionaries would instruct him in their magic and he would become their agent in propagating it among his tribe. '"I rejoice at your coming," he told them, "for I shall learn about God. I am more capable of understanding it than any of my people. . . . Once you have taught me what Tupan [God] is, I shall have more authority than I now have, and will be even more esteemed by my people than I was."' He explained how he had performed as pagé, washing people as in Christian baptism, blowing smoke on the sick to cure them and preventing the evil spirit Juripari from harming people. 'I used to cause good years to come; and on those who scorned me I avenged myself with sicknesses. I used to give people water that emerged from the floor of my hut. But I no longer do this and do not wish to. It was my cunning spirit that suggested all these things to me. I made a mockery of my people, who thought it was all a marvel, for they have no spirit. The truth is that it was a Frenchman who showed me how to make water spring up inside my hut.' He asked to be initiated as a pai, a Father. 'You pais are far greater than we are. For you speak to Toupan [God] and the spirits fear you. That is why I want to be a pai. I have been a pagé for a long time, and none was greater than me. . . . But I see that my people will pay attention only to you. I should like you to come to my province. It is a good land – there are plenty of wild pigs, deer and game, you will lack nothing, and I will always be with you.'

The missionary was shocked by Pacamont's taking him for an

accomplice. He reproved the pagé for seeking God for self-aggrandisement. Pacamont protested that he had welcomed the French and been a good friend to them. 'I have always encouraged my people to give them their daughters and produce in exchange for tools.' And on his next visit he left his followers at the door of the church and went to see Father Yves by himself. 'Approaching me, he whispered into my ear, "These people know nothing and are incapable of understanding how to talk to God. I want the two of us to talk together very handsomely."' Yves d'Evreux responded by arranging all his ornaments on the altar, and explaining the significance of each religious sculpture and painting. And Pacamont returned to his tribe with a wealth of fresh magic to bolster his reputation as the greatest pagé of the Maranhão Tupinambá.

The sensitive Yves d'Evreux observed some of the dilemmas of the Indians' deep cultural shock. Some were perplexed by the missionaries' claim that they alone knew the true god. They could not understand why the French were there; or why men who were so awkward, such poor hunters and woodsmen, should be so affluent. Chief Iacoupen told Yves: 'I observe that the French abound in riches, are valorous, have invented ships that cross the seas, cannon and powder to kill men invisibly, are well dressed and fed, and are feared and respected. We on the contrary have remained errant vagabonds, without axes, scythes, knives or other tools. What is the reason for this? Two infants are born at the same moment, one French and the other Tupinambá, both weak and feeble. Yet one is born to have all these commodities, and the other to spend his life poorly. . . . I cannot satisfy my mind when I ponder why you French have knowledge of God rather than we. . . . You tell us that God sent you. Why did he not send you sooner? Our fathers would not have been lost, as [you say] they were. The missionary Fathers are men like us: why are *they* rather than other men privileged to speak to God?'

Another chief, a tall, slender man with a modest and dignified manner, decided to have his children educated as Europeans. He offered his sons to Father Yves for him to convert them into caraíbas or white men. 'Ever since word spread in my country that you were telling marvels about Tupan and that you treated our people so gently, I would not rest. This fantasy bothered me incessantly: "When are you going to seek out the Father to learn from his mouth what your compatriots have told you?" . . . I have three small sons of whom you see the eldest. I want them to be kept near the Fathers so that they may sit at their feet, listening diligently to what emerges from their mouths and obeying them in whatever they command. They will go and hunt and fish for them.'

The French instituted stern justice in their fledgling colony. Any Indian who killed was condemned to execution by being fired from the mouth of a cannon. One old man came to the Capuchins to beg forgiveness for a son who was condemned to death. His speech revealed something of the teaching methods of the missionaries. 'You Fathers make us fill our meeting-huts at any hour you choose, and want young and old to be there to hear the reason that moved you to leave your homes and lands, which are far better than ours, to come and teach us the nature of God. You say that he is merciful and good, a lover of life and enemy of death, and wants no one to die, for which he died on a tree, to make those who were dead live. You also say that our children are no longer ours but are yours and that God gave them to you, and that you will keep them until death. Today you must show me that you spoke the truth.' The old man asked the missionary to take the condemned boy into his house and to obtain a pardon from the Governor; which the Indian's eloquence achieved.

The French planned to expand their colony by conquest. They began to explore the Amazon and to make war on the tribes near its mouth. All this delighted the Tupinambá, and galvanised them to leave their hammocks and prepare for the fighting expedition, 'for you should know that no nation on earth is so keen on war and making new voyages as these Brazilian savages. Four or five hundred leagues are nothing to them, if it means going to attack their enemies and capture slaves.' The Tupinambá mustered 1200 warriors and begged the French to wage merciless war on their enemies the Camarapin, a tribe living in huts built on stilts in the marshy islands at the mouth of the river. The expedition reached its objective in July 1613 and poured musket fire into the Camarapin village. The Indians defended themselves valiantly with their arrows. The French opened fire with a falconet, killing sixty Indians and setting fire to three huts. The Camarapin devised a ruse of propping dead bodies along their parapet and making them appear to move with cords: the French wasted much powder and shot peppering these corpses, 'at which the rabble hooted and jeered. Then one of their women appeared and signalled with a cotton cloth that she wanted to parley. All ceased firing. The woman then cried: "Vuac, vuac. Why have you brought these mouths-of-fire" – she meant the French, because of the flame that emerged from the musket barrels – "to ruin us and efface us from the earth? Do you think you will add us to your captives? Here are the bones of your friends and allies. I have eaten their flesh and I hope to eat you and your people as well! . . . No, no, we shall never surrender to the treacherous Tupinambá! Look at our chiefs who are dead, killed by these mouths-of-fire, by people we never saw before. If we must die, we will die willingly with our great warriors. Our nation is great enough to avenge our deaths!"'

The French also staged ceremonies to impress the Tupinambá and consolidate their rule in Maranhão. On 1 November 1612 they organised a procession in which six chiefs marched with the French royal standard at the foot of a great cross. They listened to the French leaders confirm French possession of their dominions. Six important Tupinambá were then sent back to France as ambassadors. They landed at Le Havre after a stormy crossing and were given a great reception, with a procession, gun salute, visit to the Governor and acclamation by the crowd. There were similar festivities in Rouen. But the greatest excitement was in Paris. A hundred priests greeted the Tupinambá party at the city gates, and escorted it to the Capuchin church for a mass attended by a galaxy of French nobility. The Tupinambá marched in the procession wearing their feathers and holding clubs. The Parisians were wild with curiosity: people poured in from the countryside, and the excited crowd burst the gates of the Capuchin convent housing the Indians. The Tupinambá were taken to the Louvre to visit King Louis XIII, and their leader made a speech in Tupi. But the inevitable European diseases struck these Americans – the sixty-year-old Carypira caught influenza and died, and two of his companions died soon after. They were buried in Franciscan habits. But the three survivors received the full panoply of French official hospitality. They were taken for baptism in the Capuchin church in the Faubourg Saint-Honoré, wearing long soutanes of white taffeta buttoned down the front with silk buttons and with small valois collars, and carrying tall hats with white plumes. Each carried a fleur-de-lys as a symbol of submission to the French (Plate 9). King Louis and his mother the Regent Marie de Médicis acted as godparents, and the Archbishop of Paris officiated. The leading Tupinambá was christened Louis-Marie, and he made a speech of acceptance. The three were then taken to the convent of Sainte-Claire to satisfy the curiosity of its nuns, who were desperate to see the exotic strangers.

When the Tupinambá returned to Maranhão in 1614 they took young French brides – girls convinced they were going to grace some oriental court. A Portuguese saw them a few months later, with the men 'dressed in the French manner with breeches and short jackets of crimson velvet garnished with fine gold braid, waistcoats of finely worked cloth-of-gold, gilded swords and daggers, sword belts of crimson velvet worked with gold and everything else of a similar nature, right up to beaver-fur hats with many white plumes and shining Paris ribbons worked with silver; and on their necks crosses of fine gold of Knights of St Louis.

They brought wives with them, white French girls dressed as ladies with such costly clothes and ornaments that everything was silk with gold garnishing.'

French and Tupinambá fear of the Portuguese was well justified. Portuguese colonists were advancing along the coast towards Maranhão before the French colonial experiment. By 1612 the lands of the Potiguar in Paraíba and Rio Grande do Norte had been thoroughly pacified. Franciscans, Benedictines and Carmelites were running eight populous mission villages in Paraíba. Chief Poti, known as Camarão ('Shrimp'), of the Rio Grande Potiguar welcomed Jesuit missionaries in 1606, and there were soon sixteen mission villages there. The Indians lived in the shadow of the Fort of the Magi, and were peaceful, helpful to travellers, and military allies of the Portuguese. As a result their lands were parcelled out to colonists, who started to organise vast cattle and sugar estates in Rio Grande.*

To the north-west of Rio Grande lay a stretch of some three hundred miles of relatively barren country called Ceará. A range of hills called Ibiapaba separated Ceará from Maranhão, a more fertile province watered by a series of great rivers. The Portuguese started advancing into Ceará during the first decade of the seventeenth century.

The first Portuguese in Ceará exemplified three different approaches to the Indians. There was a ruthless Indian-fighter, an intrepid Jesuit martyr, and one of those rare settlers who became a friend and intimate of the Indians.

The Indian-fighter was the first. Pero Coelho de Sousa left Paraíba in mid-1603 with a force of 65 tough whites – half-castes, exiled murderers, but all experienced woodsmen – and 200 Tobajara and Potiguar warriors under four chiefs. They won over one tribe on the Jaguaribe with presents of scythes, axes and knives. 'These were such simple and deprived heathen that they left their houses and plantations and came with many wives and children, saying that they wanted only peace with the white Christians, and would follow them wherever they went.' By January 1604 the expedition had led this mob of five thousand people right across Ceará to the Camocim. They plunged inland to the Ibiapaba hills, but were halted by the hill tribes of Tobajara. Seven Frenchmen added their arquebus fire to the Ibiapaba Indians' arrows. Coelho de Sousa's expedition had been living off nuts, and was suffering terribly from hunger and thirst. They were saved by the discovery of a cave with water, 'which our Christian Indians took to be a miracle. They all knelt down to give thanks to God, and the Captain in his joy ordered the last horse he had with him to be killed, to comfort the soldiers.'

There followed weeks of hard fighting, with a battle on the plain and

sieges of three strongly fortified villages. The last of these, the village of
Chief Irapuan ('Round Honey') was 'extremely strong, with two
palisades of very thick and strong logs, one inside the other, and three
bulwarks from which the French fought'. The Portuguese were
victorious, and peace was made with the paramount chief Ubaúna and
chiefs Juripari-guaçu ('Great Devil') and Irapuan. Thirty populous
villages submitted to the Portuguese.

By 1605 Coelho de Sousa was back in Rio Grande with hundreds of
prisoners to be sold as captive slaves. He had treacherously included
among his victims 'a large part of those who had been brave and faithful
companions in his dangers and victories'. The corrupt Governor-
General Diogo Botelho wanted to enjoy his share of these captives. But
there was an outcry about such flagrant disregard for the laws on Indian
slavery. Coelho de Sousa's prisoners were placed in a special village to
await a ruling from the King. Some legal authorities argued that they
were legitimate captives. But King Philip ruled that they must be freed
and sent home with compensation. It would prejudice the progress of
the colony if Indians were 'scandalised with captivities, which they fear
and hate so much'.

Pero Coelho de Sousa was in disgrace, but he was allowed to return to
Ceará in 1606 to attempt to colonise the lands he had explored. He
sailed to the Ceará river, where he had left some soldiers for the past
eighteen months. Ceará was struck by a terrible drought, and the would-
be colonists were soon clamouring to return home. Coelho de Sousa
had taken his wife Tomasina and his five children, the eldest of whom
was eighteen. They set out on foot with eighteen soldiers and one
Indian. 'The sand was so hot that none could put a foot on it. The crying
of the children, groans of the women and grief of the soldiers had
begun. . . .' The Captain had to carry his youngest children. Many of
the water-holes were dry or saline. By the fifth day soldiers started to die,
and others asked to be left to expire rather than continue the march.
Even Tomasina wished to die there rather than endure more thirst.
'Shedding two rivers of tears from her eyes (which could have quenched
her thirst had they not been salt), she told her husband to press on and
save his life, for she wished only to die in the company of her children.'
But they all marched on, past more dry water-holes, and through miles
of mangrove swamp in waist-high mud. They were saved by catching
some miniature crabs, and finally finding fresh water. The eldest child
died and the rest collapsed on a beach. In the end they came upon some
people on a deserted beach, led by the Jesuit Vicar of Rio Grande, who
had been sent to convert the Indians of Ceará. He sent water, food, and
Indians to carry the survivors in hammocks. Both groups wept with

emotion. Coelho de Sousa's family looked like figures from a dance of death. They returned to Paraíba and then to Portugal, with all hopes of colonising Ceará or enslaving its Indians forgotten.

The Jesuits who rescued Coelho de Sousa were charged with the conversion of the tribes of Ceará. The Jesuit Provincial therefore sent two of his most exceptional missionaries on this dangerous enterprise. One was the fifty-six-year-old Francisco Pinto, who had spent almost forty years in Brazil and was 'a truly religious man, of much prayer and familiar converse with God, experienced in the customs and languages of Brazil'. The other was Luís Figueira, aged thirty-two, who wrote a fine study of the tribes visited on this mission, and later published the best early dictionary of Tupi. Pinto and Figueira left in January 1607, taking some converted Indians and 'tools and clothing, a contribution from the Governor, to be given to the barbarians'. They also took some of the Indians seized by Coelho de Sousa, to return them to their homes. With these as a passport, they were welcomed, first by Chief Amauay of the Jaguaribe river and then, after an amazing journey through the Uruburetama hills, by the Tupinikin (Tobajara) of Ibiapaba.

The two Jesuits spent some months with the Tobajara of Ibiapaba, preaching their religion and observing the tribe's customs. Luís Figueira was particularly interested in the performance of the pagés: he watched them converse with spirits, minister to the sick with smoke and sucking, and make predictions.

The Jesuits then tried to spread their message to some Cariri tribes living beyond Ibiapaba. These were Gê-speaking or Tapuia peoples. Some were receptive, but the Tacariju either suspected the preachers' motives or identified them with their Tupi enemies. On 11 January 1608 the Tacariju attacked the Jesuits' camp. The few Christian Indians tried to defend the missionaries with bows and arrows. Pinto emerged from his tent and sought to reason with the attackers. His own Indians protested in vain that he was a good man. The Tacariju rushed forward and smashed Pinto's head with their jucá-wood clubs. Figueira was warned in time, and hid in the forest. He returned later to find his companion's 'body stretched out, its head broken and face disfigured, covered in blood and mud'. Father Figueira washed and buried Francisco Pinto, and made his way back to Rio Grande in another remarkable journey along the coast of Ceará. The martyr's body was later disinterred and given a church burial, and the bloodstained club became an object of veneration in the Jesuit college in Bahia. But the Jesuit attempt to penetrate Ceará had failed.

A young Portuguese officer called Martím Soares Moreno was to succeed where the Indian-fighters and missionaries had failed. Martím

Soares had arrived in Brazil in 1602 with his uncle, who was an official of Governor Diogo Botelho. He was sent on Pero Coelho de Sousa's expedition of 1603, to learn something of the Brazilian interior and its Indians. When that Captain retreated, 'only that youth Martím Soares Moreno retained the credit and friendship of the people of Jaguaribe. . . . [He had been] living with them and making himself a close friend and relative, or co-godparent as they say.' By 1609 Martím Soares Moreno was lieutenant of the Fort of the Magi beside Natal in Rio Grande. He was fascinated by Ceará, and made three more journeys there. He became a close friend of its Indians, and especially of Chief Jacaúna of the Potiguar. He respected the Indians, adopted many of their customs, and impressed them as a splendid warrior. His uncle boasted that he moved into Ceará 'with only five soldiers and a chaplain, trusting in the proximity and friendship he had made with all the Indian chiefs on both banks [of the Jaguaribe]'. He pushed Portuguese expansion to the Camocim river, only 250 miles from Maranhão, 'with no resources beyond those of good relations [with the Indians] and the reputation of his fortress'.

But Martím Soares' purpose was to open this vast territory for European settlement. He took a son born in Ceará back to the Governor-General of Brazil to prove that the area was peaceful enough for settlement. By 1611 Martím Soares was Captain of Ceará, and the Portuguese built a fort at the mouth of the Ceará river and established the first colonists at what is now the city of Fortaleza; and in 1613 Martím Soares built another fort close to the Camocim. He sailed along the coast of Maranhão and reported on French activity there. He gained the friendship of the Tremembé, a Tapuia tribe living on the coast of Maranháo near the mouth of the Paraíba. When a French ship landed on the coast of Ceará in 1611, he attacked it with his Indian friends. Martím Soares fought naked, scarred and dyed black with genipapo in the Indian manner 'like a Guinea negro, killing on land and in the ship 42 men, and capturing the ship' with its guns and powder at Mocuripe. *

These advances placed the Portuguese within striking distance of the new French colony of Maragnan. They determined to eliminate it, just as thoroughly as they had driven the French from Rio de Janeiro, Cabo Frio, Sergipe, Paraíba and Rio Grande. On 8 October 1612 King Philip of Spain and Portugal ordered the expulsion of the French.

Both sides felt that the attitude of the Indian tribes would be decisive. The French did their best to win the friendship of the Tupinambá by the attention paid to the chiefs they took to France. The Portuguese trained the Ceará Potiguar in the techniques of European warfare. Martím Soares Moreno's friend Chief Jacaúna and Jacaúna's relative Chief

Camarão of Rio Grande both sent contingents on the expedition now being organised against the French. The Jesuits contributed 370 archers from their mission villages and two Fathers, Manoel Gomes and Diogo Nunes. The Franciscans sent experienced friars called Cosmé de São Damião and Manoel da Piedade. The commander was the formidable sixty-five-year-old Jerónimo de Albuquerque. Being half-Indian, he understood native psychology. He toured the villages of Christian Indians recruiting volunteers; but he did so without force. In one village 'he placed a bundle of bows and arrows on one side, and distaffs and spindles on the other. He showed these to them and said: "My nephews, I am going to war. These are the arms of the stout and valiant men who are going to follow me. These are those of weak women who are going to remain at home spinning. I now wish to hear which of you is man or woman." His words were no sooner said than they all began to undo and grab the bows and arrows, saying that they were men and would immediately leave for war. He quieted them, chose those he wished to take, and told them to make more arrows and go to await his fleet at Rio Grande.'

Jerónimo de Albuquerque consolidated an alliance with the Tremembé, who had fond memories of the visit of Martím Soares Moreno; and he tried to make an alliance with the powerful chief Juripari-guaçu of the Ibiapaba Tobajara. He obtained food for the expedition by distributing to the Indians 'quantities of tools and ridiculous clothes, bribes that are so important [in winning] the esteem of those barbarians'.

The Portuguese completed their preparations and in August 1614 sailed to the bay of Maranhão. They boldly established a fort at Guaxenduba facing the island occupied by the French. The French commander François de Rasilly rose to the challenge with a powerful force of 400 excellently equipped French and 2000 Indians in 45 canoes. He called on the outnumbered Portuguese to surrender. But on 19 November these rushed from their defences in a devastating charge that caught the French by surprise. Ninety Frenchmen were killed in the first onslaught and many more as they tried to escape to their ships; 400 Indians were killed, mostly by drowning; all the canoes were burned; and 200 muskets and arquebuses captured. The Tupinambá were impressed with the ease of the Portuguese victory. Many listened to the eloquent preaching of the Jesuits in Tupi, and switched allegiance from French to Portuguese.

After a year's truce, the French still had 200 well-armed men in Fort St Louis, with 17 cannon and 514 cannonballs. But the Portuguese once again acted with more vigour than the French. They sent a powerful reinforcement from Pernambuco under Alexandre de Moura. In November 1615 La Ravardière decided to surrender the fort. The French abandoned their colony and withdrew from Brazil for ever.*

The French defeat was a disaster for the Tupinambá. They had trusted French boasts that their country was far more powerful than Portugal, and had helped build the French fort with desperate enthusiasm. Many had fled from the Portuguese in Pernambuco a generation earlier. They had performed a prodigious migration across hundreds of miles of savannah and forest, to seek sanctuary with their families in Maranhão. The Jesuit Manoel Gomes reported that 'some revealed their past knowledge of us, for they had descended from Pernambuco when the Portuguese began to colonise it. They could name the early settlers and told events as precisely as if they had happened in their own days. Old age does not dim their memories – for some were over a hundred.'

The Tupinambá hoped that they might find protection with the Jesuits. Father Gomes described how 'the Indian chiefs of the island received us with presents and refreshments. . . . They came to visit us again to ask if we would go to their villages to raise new crosses and churches and declare to them the mysteries of our holy faith in their language.' The Jesuits were impressed by the work of some French Franciscans who remained in Maranhão, but they soon took over the mission villages run by the French. There were twenty-seven populous aldeias on the island alone, containing ten or twelve thousand souls, and many more villages on the mainland. Father Luís Figueira, who had survived the killing of his colleague Pinto in the Ibiapaba hills, worked for years among the Ceará Indians, and then moved on to head the Jesuit effort in Maranhão. One governor, António Moniz Barreiros, followed Figueira's advice in everything.

Jesuit protection was not enough to save the Tupinambá. Immediately after expelling the French in November 1615, the Portuguese moved with characteristic vigour to explore, conquer and exploit the hinterland of Maranhão. In the following month, Francisco Caldeira de Castelo Branco was sent with 150 men in three ships to establish an outpost on the Amazon. They sailed for some 400 miles along the coast and into the estuary of the Pará river, which was also the southern mouth of the mighty Amazon. They landed on a low forested island, and on 11 January 1616 built a wooden fort. 'This was done without opposition from the heathen natives of the land. But they could not help fearing these, when they saw how many arrived to ask the first settlers for tools and other things they had brought. They soon had nothing to give them, nor even powder and shot to defend themselves when the gifts were exhausted.' The fort soon developed into a town that became the modern city of Belém do Pará ('Bethlehem of the Pará river').

The new Portuguese commander of Maranhão also sent Martím Soares Moreno – the officer who had established such close bonds with the Potiguar of Ceará – to be captain of the coast of Maranhão from Cumá to Caeté, half-way to Pará. He took six canoes, with twenty-seven soldiers and the Carmelite missionary Cosmé da Anunciação. With his skill as a linguist and sympathy with Indian ways, Martím Soares had no trouble in pacifying the mainland Tupinambá. They knew all about the Portuguese victory, and were eager to join the winning side. Friar Cosmé erected many crosses and built churches. Unfortunately for the Indians, Martím Soares soon developed a painful fistula and withdrew from his command.†

Other Portuguese expanded European control of Maranhão. Bento Maciel Parente, who was to become one of the most ferocious Indian-fighters, led an expedition up the Pindaré that slaughtered many Guajajara and 'reduced the others to the bosom of the Church'. (Of all the tribes mentioned so far in this book, the Guajajara is the only one to survive as a coherent tribe to the present day.) A captain called Francisco de Azevedo explored the Turiaçu and Gurupi rivers. And in March 1616 the new settlement of Belém do Pará sent a force of four whites and thirty Indians across country to Maranhão to beg for reinforcements. This group had the rare experience of making first contact with several tribes. 'On this journey they suffered much hunger and thirst, since most of the heathen were savages who had never seen white, clothed men. Some welcomed them with much festivity, others fled full of horror, and others would have killed them had their escort not defended them.' One of the Portuguese who made this remarkable journey was a young captain called Pedro Teixeira, who was later to become an outstanding Amazon explorer.

The fort at Belém do Pará was reinforced, but its commander quarrelled with his men. The Indians lost their respect for the newcomers. 'And so, for that reason and because of some extortions and injuries received from some men who went "ransoming" in their villages, they killed these men and remained in rebellion. They immediately placed the new settlement of Pará in a close siege.' The Tupinambá of Maranhão also began to suspect that they would be enslaved by the new conquerors. One Indian called Amaro, who had been trained by the Jesuits, claimed that he could read Portuguese despatches being carried by the Indians. He told his people that these described a plan to enslave the Tupinambá. The tribes of the Maranhão mainland decided that they must fight. One night in 1617 they stormed the fort at Tapuitapera or Cumá (modern Alcântara) and killed its thirty white defenders. They killed a further fourteen in a boat on the Pará. The Tupinambá of Maranhão Island refused to join the revolt, and the Portuguese moved to take savage reprisals on those of the mainland. The Governor's son Mathias de Albuquerque led a punitive expedition of fifty soldiers and 200 Indians, and pursued the Cumá Tupinambá deep into the forests. The Indians tried to attack his stockade on 3 February 1617 but were defeated. 'Despite the most desperate opposition, within a few hours he found himself with nothing more to do. His spoils of victory . . . were the greater part of those many lives' – Indian captives to be sold as slaves.*

Other groups of Tupinambá in Pará joined the war and tried to expel Francisco Caldeira de Castelo Branco's new settlement. That commander sent one of his officers, Diogo Botelho, to crush this 'rebellion' by people trying to defend their homeland from his invasion. Botelho moved against one of the largest villages, called Cuju, and within a few hours of his attack 'there was nothing but ashes and bodies to be seen in it'. The Tupinambá regrouped, and were joined by the tribes of the Guamá river.

The Tupinambá war continued for three years. During the latter half of 1618 Mathias de Albuquerque landed on the Gurupi with a force of fifty soldiers and 600 Tapuia who were only too eager to fight their Tupi enemies. Bernardo de Berredo, a later governor of Maranhão, commented on these inter-tribal animosities: 'All heathen tribes are generally kept separated by hatred that is usually based on causes so trivial as to be ridiculous. We can attribute this to the disposition of divine providence. For, if they united for the ruin of Christianity, its survival there would become virtually impossible.' Most Tupinambá fled before this expedition and escaped into the forests. Albuquerque's men did manage to catch one group and 'performed so well that almost every blow cost a life. . . . One who did not [manage to escape] was the famous interpreter Amaro . . . the principal instigator of the Tupinambá rebellion. He fell into the hands of the victors and found punishment for his presumption at the horrible mouth of a cannon.' 'This extravagant punishment in one instant . . . completely disintegrated his savage breast. . . .'

The Tupinambá rallied, and on 7 January 1619 attempted a bold frontal assault on the new fortress of Belém. They attacked with desperate courage and managed to kill or wound a few defenders. But the fort's gunfire was too powerful. An arquebus shot killed the Tupinambá chief, whose name meant Old Woman's Hair. The Indians called off the assault and melted into the forests.

The Portuguese were now ready for a war of annihilation on the Tupinambá. A new governor, Jerónimo Fragoso de Albuquerque, set out from Belém in June 1619 with a 'lucid fleet' of four ships and many canoes filled with a hundred white soldiers and many hundreds of native auxiliaries. His men stormed the defences of the Tupinambá's main redoubt of Iguapé, and then moved along the Guanapus and Carapi rivers burning villages and killing or capturing any Indians they could catch.

The tough woodsman Bento Maciel Parente saw a fine opportunity for legalised slaving. The Governor of Brazil authorised him to march overland from Pernambuco to attack the Tupinambá from the rear. He warned him not to antagonise other tribes by letting his men steal their women, and asked him to try not to make the war too bloody.* Bento Maciel raised a force of eighty soldiers and 600 Indian archers at his own expense, and spent most of the year 1619 in a devastating sweep across the Tupinambá territory. 'He started at Tapuitapera near São Luís and continued as far as Belém in his destruction of them, and extinguished the last relics of those barbarians in that area.' Bento Maciel's expedition was a financial success, with a great haul of slaves captured in this 'just' war.

Some Tupinambá escaped by migrating yet again to join other tribes of their nation far up the Tocantins. A few surrendered at Belém and were settled on the Separara river near the city to work for its settlers. Seven years later, in 1626, Bento Maciel Parente had succeeded in becoming governor of Pará. The Tupinambá were holding a drunken festival – one of their few consolations after the crushing defeat – and 'some of the chiefs became excited and wanted to show off their valour: they apparently argued how easily they could destroy the Portuguese and indicated a way to do it'. An old woman told Bento Maciel that the Tupinambá were planning to kill all the whites while they were celebrating the Thursday of Holy Week. The Governor at once seized twenty-four chiefs and had them summarily executed. Berredo said that he delivered them to their Tapuia enemies to be killed by clubs and knives: Jacinto de Carvalho said that he wanted to tear them in two, but 'since he lacked horses, their feet were secured to two canoes and these were driven by the force of rowers in opposite directions'. Bernardo Berredo said that this mass execution on such flimsy evidence scandalised even the settlers of Belém: it could have prejudiced the peace of that captaincy had not Bento Maciel been removed by royal patent in October 1626.

Even the island Tupinambá who avoided the war were not spared. In 1621 São Luís de Maranhão was struck 'by an epidemic of smallpox of such virulence that any who caught it – most of whom were Indians – did not survive for more than three days. The Governor was deeply distressed. He not only helped the poor generously from his private fortune, but also in person with a total disregard for the danger of his own life.' The Tupinambá were already gone from mainland Maranhão and Pará – either slaughtered, enslaved or fled. This epidemic now destroyed most of the twenty-seven populous villages of Tupinambá that had once filled the island of Maranhão. These were the people who had welcomed the Europeans only a decade earlier. It was they who had let their children help build the French fort to provide security for future generations.

ELEVEN

Anarchy on the Amazon

DIFFICULT winds and currents made communication between Maranhão and the rest of Brazil almost impossible in certain seasons of the year. It was actually easier to sail from the Amazon to Portugal than to southern Brazil. For this reason the new colonies of Maranhão and Pará, and the entire Amazon basin, were made into a separate state, answering to the King in Lisbon and with its own governor residing in São Luís.† This northern territory was in wilder country, and generally poorer and more lawless than the remainder of Brazil.

In the early Indian wars the fighting was fierce, and settlers exulted over the slaughter or enslavement of their enemies. Francisco Teixeira de Moraes was delighted that the Tupinambá 'remained, if not extinct, very well tamed; and their neighbours well and truly warned how to behave towards us. . . . Once mastered by the conquistadores by fire and sword, they began to provide them with servants and abundant food and repose.'

The colonists of southern and central Brazil insisted on the need for Indian slaves to fell brazilwood or labour on the vast sugar plantations. Those of Maranhão and Pará now argued that they must have Indians because their colonies were too poor to afford African slaves, and because none but Indians were really at home in the forests, rivers and rapids of the Amazon. 'All the sustenance of the settlers' farming and of their very lives depended on the Indians. For whites on no account wished to apply themselves to agriculture – not even those who had

Amazon warriors.

called themselves labourers a few months before in their own country. This was because the labour of American agriculture is very arduous. Even Indians born in the land can tolerate it only with difficulty.'

A few voices were raised on behalf of the Indians. One of the first explorers of the Amazon, Simão Estácio da Silveira, was impressed that the natives he saw there were 'spirited, ingenious and somewhat more polished than others in Brazil. They are very easy and tractable and wish to obtain our friendship and deliver their children to us to instruct. We should use all justice and charity with them, to edify them and conquer their souls . . . for wisdom teaches us that one conquers more through charity than by arms.' He was absolutely correct about the efficacy of good treatment. But he was crying in the wilderness of newly conquered Amazonia.

The new colonies were soon in a state of near-anarchy. Military leaders quarrelled over political offices and possession of the hereditary captaincies being established around the mouths of the Amazon. After a promising start, the Jesuits were slow to move out of the town of Maranhão itself. Despite Luís Figueira's intelligence and the saintliness of Benedito Amodei, there were not enough Jesuits in Maranhão to restrain its settlers or catechise many Indians. The colonists of Pará managed to exclude the black-gowned Jesuits altogether. There were some Franciscans there, but although they established missions around the lower Xingu they did not have the power to oppose the colonists' excesses.

Capuchins of St Anthony reached Pará with the first settlement and were soon 'held in great veneration by all the heathen, who love them as the only remedy for their distress'. They tried to enforce a royal order of 1624 that removed the Indians from colonists who had arbitrarily appointed themselves as captains of native villages. The Capuchin leader Friar Cristóvão de Lisboa issued a pastoral at Cametá on 3 October 1625 excommunicating any who tried to retain private administration of Indian villages. Uproar ensued. The town council of Belém protested stridently. It claimed that without administrators the Indians would revert to their primitive ways and would shun Christianity – not that the lay administrators were concerned with spiritual conversion: what they wanted was Indian labour. They said that if missionaries assumed control of Indian villages it would be the ruin of the colony, which relied on the natives for defence and work.

The answer to the labour shortage was the seizure of the dense populations of the Amazon rivers. There were two ways of doing this. One was to send slaving expeditions to purchase captives in exchange for trade goods or simply to seize them by brute force. The euphemism for slaving was 'ransoming', for the law permitted the purchase or ransom of a prisoner about to be eaten by another tribe. The eating of human flesh and all the attendant rituals were done by few tribes other than the coastal Tupi. But this did nothing to reduce the number of 'ransom' expeditions among Amazonian tribes that were not anthropophagous. The other means of acquiring Indian labour was to have missionaries persuade entire tribes to 'descend' to compounds close to European settlements. Once there these nominally free Indians could be forced to work for the settlers in return for wages of trifling lengths of coarse cotton cloth.

During the first decades after the Portuguese arrived on the Amazon there was an almost unrestrained 'open season' on its inhabitants. When Bento Maciel Parente was in charge at Pará in 1626 he sent his son on an expedition nominally to expel foreigners trying to settle in the Amazon. 'He entirely fulfilled his father's purpose, for he occupied himself only with ransoming many Tapuia, and thus for a time silenced most of the clamours of the people' for more slaves.* The next governor, Manoel de Sousa, 'was well aware of the needs of the captaincy and had no doubt that the most important was to ransom more Tapuia slaves for its service'. He sent Captain Pedro Teixeira off on an official ransom expedition to the powerful Tapajós tribe, who lived near the mouth of the river of that name. A Capuchin friar called Cristóvão de São José accompanied the expedition to lend respectability and ensure that correct procedures were observed. For once, the expedition returned almost empty-handed, for although the Tapajós were hospitable and relatively sophisticated they were not prepared to barter for human lives, and seemed too strong to be attacked. The same captain and friar were, however, more successful in the number of slaves they ransomed on officially licensed expeditions during the next few years. Enterprising individuals also mounted their own unofficial raids: it was impossible for the authorities or the ecclesiastics to know what was happening in the labyrinth of Amazon tributaries.

The next governor, Francisco Coelho de Carvalho, had a momentary revulsion against 'the atrocious crimes that were committed in the wilds', and forbade all forms of slaving, even the ransoming permitted by royal law. There was another anguished outcry. The city council of Belém warned the Governor that he would cause 'irreparable damage to the public utility' and asked whether 'he wished to bear on his shoulders the formidable burden of answering before both the Divine and Human Majesties for having impeded the reduction of so many souls, the unhappy slaves of paganism!' The Governor immediately capitulated. He increased the number of official ransom expeditions, and enthusiastically joined in the traffic himself. Bernard O'Brien, an Irishman in Belém at the time, told the King of Spain about the great chests of gold and silver that Coelho de Carvalho regularly shipped off to the Caribbean. His successor as governor accused him of ruining the colony with his greed. He and his son exploited Maranhão's settlers and Indians so voraciously that by 1636 it seemed depopulated. 'When he became Governor there were six villages of Indians between the island of Maranhão and the mainland of Tapuitapera and all were prosperous with people. There were almost two thousand bowmen, whereas today there would not be five hundred in them all.'

The Capuchins were at first compliant, co-operating with the authorities in the search for slaves. Friar Cristóvão de Lisboa's first action on reaching Pará was to tour the Indian villages and impress on the chiefs the importance of loyalty to Portugal. He then went up the Tocantins and converted the villages of Chief Tomagico, building churches, baptising hundreds of Indians and bringing boys back to Belém for further indoctrination. His colleague Cristóvão de São José accompanied official ransom expeditions. But, as the ransoming activities grew in intensity, the Capuchins became embarrassingly censorious. Cristóvão de Lisboa excommunicated settlers who usurped the administration of aldeias, and Cristóvão de São José eventually preached a fiery sermon against Governor Coelho de Carvalho. When another Capuchin appeared at a window of their convent, he was shot by a settler who mistook him for Friar Cristóvão. The Governor then removed the Capuchins of Santo Antonio from the administration of Indian villages.*

The wretched business of conquering tribes continued throughout the region of the Pará and lower Amazon. After the Portuguese had annihilated the warlike Tupinambá, 'the blades of their conquering swords were not blunted by too much cutting, their spirits were not satiated with conquest or their arms tired or sluggish from wounding. . . . Instead, they continued to defeat the Indian confederates of the conquered [Tupinambá] – who had killed over a hundred Portuguese. They conquered fifteen provinces with over two thousand inhabited villages.' Some of these campaigns involved hard fighting because of the difficulties of the forests and rivers. Some tribes, notably those of the great island of Marajó, managed to resist successfully. Others surrendered willingly, seduced by the Europeans' promises and trade goods.

One of the most ferocious wars was against the tribes of the Pacajá river between the Xingu and Tocantins. European firearms annihilated these Pacajá. 'There was a vast multitude of heathen living along this river. At the beginning of the conquest all the Portuguese and the Indians from the royal aldeias joined together to go and make war on them. One of the first conquistadores of Pará assured me that it was so cruel that the river was dyed with blood. For the Pacajá Indians not only put themselves in battle order to await the fighting, but even came out in over five hundred canoes to confront the Tupinambá and their other enemies. Almost all were killed, both the defeated and the victors, and in due course many were descended to form five aldeias in Cametá, Pará, Sergipe and Tapuitapera.'

The great Jesuit preacher António Vieira quoted his Capuchin predecessor Cristóvão de Lisboa on the horrors of these wars. Besides killing and enslaving, 'they razed and burned entire villages, which are generally made of dry palm-leaves, roasting alive in them those who refused to surrender as slaves. They overcame and subjected others peacefully, but by execrable deceit. They would promise them alliance and friendship in the name and good faith of the King. But, once they had them off guard and unarmed, they seized and bound them all, dividing them among themselves as slaves or selling them with the greatest cruelty. . . .' Vieira scornfully attacked the 'injustices, cruelties and tyrannies executed through the greed and ungodliness of the so-called "Conquerors of Maranhão" on the goods, sweat, blood, liberty, women, children, lives and, above all, souls of the wretched Indians'.

The authorities were well aware of what was happening. There was no lack of reporting about the overwork and abuse of the Indians of Maranhão and Pará. The Jesuit Luís Figueira wrote in 1637 that the Indians were suffering terrible spiritual and physical privation. Nominally free Indians were forced to labour. The settlers 'oppress the wretches with great violence, forcing them to do very heavy labour such as making tobacco, in which they work seven or eight months on end by day and night. For this they pay them four varas [4.5 metres] of cloth, or three, or two. And, if they fail in this work, the Portuguese put them in the stocks and beat them a number of times. Because of this they flee into the forests and depopulate their villages. Others die of despair in this labour without remedy.' The Crown admitted the terrible situation. In the preamble to a law of 10 November 1647 it acknowledged that pacified Indians entrusted to the care of lay administrators rapidly died of sheer starvation and excessive work. In a provision of the following year, the King blamed the officials in charge of the captaincies of Pará, Cametá and Gurupá for placing factors in each village to force the Indians to produce tobacco. The free Indians were made to work for so many months each year that they could not clear forest plantations to feed their families. Other Indians were made to paddle on the slaving expeditions for two or three years on end, with no chance to communicate with their families; and, when at last they returned home, they were soon sent off again.*

The result of this was the rapid extinction of tribes living near the mouths of the Amazon. Royal laws admitted that 'innumerable heathen have perished or died out in Maranhão'; 'seventeen very populous aldeias have been destroyed'. 'The beaches of Maranhão and Pará were covered with villages of Indians at the first conquest. But, although many, they were not enough to satisfy the administrations of the powerful men.'

It may seem surprising that a few hundred Portuguese could conquer so many warrior tribes with such speed. They had many advantages. They always went to war alongside hundreds of Indian allies – natives who were eager to avenge past feuds with their enemies, and enjoyed fighting alongside the victorious Portuguese and demonstrating their prowess as woodsmen and warriors. The Portuguese went into battle against naked Indians well protected by quilted and leather armour or metal cuirasses and helmets. Their swords were immeasurably superior to the sharpened wooden clubs of their adversaries. But their overwhelming superiority came from firearms, the arquebuses and muskets that emitted such a terrifying booming, smoke and flash and that killed their victims from a distance with deadly magic. By the early seventeenth century firearms were being improved: they were still cumbersome and muzzle-loading, but flintlocks were replacing guns whose powder had to be fired by a lighted length of fuse.

The Portuguese enjoyed the psychological advantage of representing a technology far superior to their adversaries'. The Indians undoubtedly feared and respected them because of their manufactures, and were frightened by first contact with an alien civilisation. The Europeans fought a ruthless war, intent on killing and capturing Indians or occupying their territory. They observed none of the etiquette of inter-tribal fighting, but exploited every possible deception and stratagem of war. They knew what they wanted, whereas the natives were initially unsure of the invaders' origins or intentions. There were undoubtedly tense debates and discussions in each tribe about how best to handle the strangers, and the shamans doubtless employed all the arts of their sorcery to ensure victory. When the Portuguese won, it became clear that their magic was more powerful. Many tribes became resigned to defeat.

In some respects, the forests and rivers of the Amazon favoured an aggressor. The attacking expedition, guided by its native trackers or canoe pilots, could approach its victims' villages unobserved. It could sweep into action in a canoe attack, or could surround a village in darkness to deliver a dawn ambush. The only defence lay in extreme mobility. Tribes like the nomadic Aimoré or the Nheengaíba of Marajó frustrated attempts to destroy their villages by living scattered and on the move. The other recourse of defeated tribes lay in flight. Indians could easily gather up their children and few possessions and migrate far up the rivers to escape the odious foreigners.

Portuguese victories were also the result of their remarkable fighting ability. Many were the product of mixed unions between whites and Indians, and managed to combine the best fighting qualities of both races. They became almost as expert in forest techniques as the Indians themselves. And, whatever their motives, they fought with undoubted determination, skill and courage.

The colonists had an opportunity to demonstrate these abilities against other Europeans immediately after reaching the Amazon. They discovered that Flemings, English and Irish were living among the tribes on the Amazon, and that its Indians were trading cotton, red urucum dye, tobacco and various woods with the Dutch. A Dutch ship was captured there in 1616. But other Dutchmen were soon back, and built forts called Orange and Nassau near the mouth of the Xingu.*

The English also had ambitions on the Amazon. Walter Ralegh had sailed up the Orinoco in 1595 in search of the elusive 'Inca empire of El Dorado'. He wrote a rapturous account of the north coast of South America entitled *The Discoverie of the Large, Rich and Bewtiful Empyre of Guiana*. He assured his compatriots that the wealth of Manoa was such that 'the common soldier shall fight here for gold, and pay himself, instead of pence, with plates of half a foot broad, whereas he breaketh his bones in other wars for provender and penury. . . . To conclude, Guiana is a country that hath yet her maidenhead, never sacked, turned, nor wrought, the face of the earth hath not been torn, nor the virtue and salt of the soil spent by manurance, the graves have not been opened for gold, the mines not broken with sledges, nor their images pulled down out of their temples.' The only trouble was that this legendary empire had not yet been discovered.

Ralegh fell into disgrace, but his writings inspired other ventures to the Guianas. In 1609 Sir Thomas Roe obtained a commission from King James 'to pursue the discoveries of Francis and Walter and to set foot and make a settlement on the great river of the Amazons . . . which was not yet settled by white people'. Ralegh put up £600 towards the cost of the expedition. Roe's objective was to try to discover Manoa from the south, to see whether English conquerors could invade the rich kingdom from the Amazon. Roe sailed from England in February 1610 in a 200-ton ship containing 124 people.

Roe's ship sailed for 200 miles up the Amazon, after which he explored a further hundred miles in his ship's boats. His men 'made divers Journeyes into the mayne among the Indians'. They found the land fertile, but were dismayed by the Indian failure to farm vigorously: 'the natives provide no more than for their necessitie'. Roe left twenty men on the Amazon and went to explore the rivers of the Guiana coast. For thirteen months, he 'entered the Country by Indian Boates, and went over the Chatoracts and hills [and] passed over thirty-two falls . . .'.

The English were convinced that the Amazon was a treasure-house of spices and rare woods. This potential wealth inspired one of Ralegh's captains, Roger North, to take 120 English and Irish colonists to the Amazon in 1620. They sailed upstream for a hundred leagues and settled 'where the sight of the Countrey and people so contented them that never men thought themselves so happy'. The Indians helped them clear tobacco plantations. One Englishman called William White took a pinnace up-river for a further 200 leagues. He found the country delightful – relatively open and well populated. He saw 'greate habitations and manie Nations, and heard a fame of others farr surpassinge them' including the legendary Amazons.

Both English and Dutch settlers loved the way the Indians looked after them. 'The Christians which live in this Countrie take no pains nor labour for anie thing. The Indians both house them, worke for them, [and] bring them victualls and theire Commodities, for a small reward and price, either of some Iron worke or glasse beades and such like contemtible things. . . .'

A charming young Irishman called Bernard O'Brien was on board North's expedition, and he wrote an account of his adventures. The expedition made friends with the Aruak-speaking Sipinipoia Indians some forty miles up the Amazon. They then sailed for a further 200 miles and landed O'Brien at a place called Pataui ('Coconut Grove') in charge of sixteen people: twelve Irishmen and their four English servants. They had plenty of presents to trade with the Indians, and forty muskets with powder and shot. O'Brien built a fort defended by an earth-and-wood rampart and ditch. He learned the language of the local Indians and made good friends with them. He won their admiration, as Anthony Knivet had done with the Tamoio, by leading them into battle against their enemies. They were continuously at war with other tribes, and their weapons were wooden swords, broad-based stone axes, wooden lances the height of a man, wooden shields and arrows tipped with bone or stone heads. 'On various occasions I went out to help those of my district with my musketry and men and won victories for them. With this I won their devotion and obliged them to grow tobacco and cotton and to give us local food and drink.' Some of the Irish also taught the Indians about the Catholic religion, and persuaded two thousand of them of the existence of God, Heaven and Hell.

O'Brien had been promised reinforcements from England or Ireland. When none came, he attempted a voyage of exploration up the river. He took five musketeers and fifty Indians in four canoes and sailed for many hundreds of miles upstream, taking interpreters from one tribe to the next. He finally reached a land where he claimed, with perhaps a touch of blarney, to have contacted the Amazons. When he reached their territory he sent one of his Indian women to their queen Cuña Muchu (the Inca for 'Great Lady'), who happened to be on an island in the river. He sent a mirror, a holland shirt and other merchandise as presents, offered to go and see her if she would send hostages, and promised to obey her orders. She sent three of her most esteemed women as hostages, and young O'Brien went to visit the Amazon queen. 'She asked if it was I who had sent the present and I said yes. She asked me what I wanted, and I said peace and permission to pass through her kingdom and to trade with her. She said she granted it to me, and gave me three of her women slaves in exchange for the merchandise. I dressed her in the Holland shirt, with which she was very haughty. At the end of a week I took my leave, promising to return, and she and her vassals signified that they were sad at my departure.' The only information given by O'Brien about his week's visit was that he saw many women and no men, and that the women had 'their right breasts small like men's, artificially stunted in order to shoot arrows; but the left breasts are broad like other women's'. This anatomical detail came from the well-known Classical legend.

O'Brien's progress up the river was blocked by a fierce tribe who refused all contact with him. He therefore explored another river, conceivably the Trombetas or Paru de Oeste; emerged on to the Atlantic by the Surinam river; thence returned overland to the mouth of the Amazon and back up it to his fort at Coconut Grove.

A Dutch ship appeared and tried to settle near the Irish, but O'Brien threatened to mobilise his four thousand Indian friends to defend his territory. The Dutch therefore sailed downstream and settled on the Gurupá river. In 1624, when no reinforcements had yet reached him, O'Brien sailed back to Europe on a Dutch ship with his tobacco and cotton, leaving an Irishman called Philip Purcell in charge of his fort.†

The Portuguese were alarmed by the sight of rival colonists on the Amazon river. In 1623 the Portuguese–Spanish Government reacted with vigour, sending out a captain to deal with these incursions. He and Bento Maciel Parente mounted an expedition with some seventy white soldiers. The Franciscans in Pará sent Cristóvão de São José, 'who was so respected by the Indians that, during a few days' navigation up the river, forty canoes joined him with over a thousand friendly bowmen. These followed the captain out of goodwill, but were also moved by the many presents he gave to their chiefs and to others who brought offerings of game, fruit and vegetables. He accepted none of these without paying for them in tools, beads, combs, mirrors, fish-hooks and other things, saying that the King had ordered it thus.'

Most of the Portuguese expedition went from Pará to the Amazon in native canoes, through the forested channels west of Marajó. Indian allies of the English and Dutch harassed the approaching expedition. Robert Harcourt wrote that 'many enemies were slaine by ambush in the way'. But the Portuguese landed and soon routed the northern colonists. The English fled inland, 'running up farther into the Countrey' to the protection of friendly tribes. Maciel sailed on and tricked one small Dutch fort into surrendering, by dressing some of the Indians in his canoes in European armour. He moved downstream against another Dutch fort. There was a battle against Aruan Indians, in which many Portuguese were hit by arrows and 'those in the first canoe had their hands so swollen from the heat of the arquebus barrels that they could touch nothing for over twenty days: for each of them fired over forty shots'. The second Dutch fort surrendered and was destroyed. When a Dutch ship appeared, the Portuguese managed to run it aground, hole it, and massacre its 125 crew and passengers.

There was another bout of colonial rivalry in 1625 and 1626. The Dutch destroyed a Portuguese base near Gurupá. But a Portuguese counter-attack wiped out another Dutch fort, some English plantations, and O'Brien's Irish fort.*

All these Portuguese successes did not stop English and Dutch ambitions. A new Guiana Company was formed in London in 1627 with the express purpose of colonising the Amazon. Meanwhile, Bernard O'Brien reappeared in Holland after four years of travels. The Dutch promptly equipped him with 18,000 escudos' worth of trade goods.* He was back on the Amazon by April 1629; but found his former fort destroyed.

O'Brien built another fort in a territory called Toherego or Tauregue on the Manacapuru. He was soon off in the interior, helping his Indian friends fight their enemies. Word came that white men were near his base, killing Indians and burning their villages. O'Brien hurried back with 42 whites and 'ten thousand' Indians and managed to defeat a force of 200 whites and 7000 Indians under the mulatto Pedro da Silva, sent 'to make damage there' by the Governor of Maranhão. At the height of the battle, O'Brien himself fell, wounded by two shots and an arrow. His Indians fled. But his 42 whites fought on and won.

The following September, Pedro Teixeira appeared with a great expedition of 120 Portuguese and 1600 Indians in 98 canoes. He surprised the Irish fort in a night attack. O'Brien was again inland fighting with his Indians. He marched back with sixteen whites and many thousands of Indians. Four English and Dutch ships offered to help him against the Portuguese, but some Irishmen on board the ships wrote to O'Brien (in Irish) that this fleet planned to remove him and his Catholics from the area. Rather than see his beloved Indians taken over by Protestant heretics, O'Brien decided to surrender to the Portuguese. He drew up a solemn treaty with Pedro Teixeira, written in Portuguese and Irish, signed and sealed and sworn 'in the names of His Majesty and the Governor-General of Maranhão and Grão-Pará, in the name of the holy evangels with a missal, on our knees in front of a crucifix'. Some holy symbol must have been missing, for as soon as the fort was surrendered and the Irish were back in the Portuguese settlements 'they removed our possessions, worth 14,000 ducats, from me and my men, and our clothes, tied up some and killed others and mistreated us all. They divided the property among the Governor-General of Maranhão called Francisco Coelho de Carvalho, Captain Pedro Teixeira [and other officials] and forced us to work and do farm labour for the Portuguese, which we have been doing to the present day, without keeping their word or oath.' The Capuchins tried to help the Irish, and there were appeals to the King of Spain and Governor of Brazil.

Eighteen Irish managed to escape to the West Indies. Coelho de Carvalho was furious and imprisoned the rest: he held O'Brien in chains for a year and then exiled him to live among the anthropophagic Cururi Indians. 'In my exile I gained the friendship of the cannibals and learned their language. I went inland over 200 leagues, discovering the rivers, forests, medicines and secrets of the Indians, and reduced a province of them to my devotion. I also taught them a better way to live.' The Governor sent a message begging O'Brien to return with his Indians, which he did. But when Coelho de Carvalho would not allow O'Brien himself to remain in charge of them the Indians ran off. In November 1634 O'Brien finally sailed from Maranhão, taking the son of a powerful Indian chief. He went to appeal to the King of Spain, to whom he addressed the description of his remarkable adventures on the Amazon.†

Pedro Teixeira's expedition of 1629 went on to attack and capture English and Dutch establishments on the island of Tucujus, after disposing of O'Brien's Irish–Dutch fort Tauregue. In one battle a

Potiguar chief from Rio Grande, called Caragataiuba, fought magnificently for the Portuguese. 'He saw three canoes of native Indian allies of the Dutch, took his sword in his mouth and dived in to swim. He went and overturned them one by one, escaped their arrows, and killed many of them.' In another skirmish this chief held off four or five Dutchmen with his shield and then escaped into the undergrowth. 'Throughout this period, the efforts of these Indians for Captain [Teixeira] were remarkable. He let them scale the fort, which they were brave enough to enter. They showed themselves impatient with the delays of war and wanted to come to grips with the enemy at once. But the sad thing is that they received no reward in the name of the King for all this.'

The English were back in 1630, with two hundred men fortified on the Filipe river near Macapá under an old soldier called Thomas Hixson. Jacomé Raimundo de Noronha sailed against them in 1631 with a few white infantry and thirty-six canoes full of warriors from the aldeias of Cametá. The Jesuit leader Luís Figueira appealed to the King on behalf of these mission Indians. 'Your Majesty is under an obligation to the Indians. In the wars against the Dutch and English they helped and always do help the Portuguese, both with their arms and by supplying them with manioc flour, meat and fish, and always paddling the war-canoes. Neither Your Majesty nor the Portuguese have spent anything on them: they provide all these services without reward.' The English were defeated, and surrendered on 1 March 1631. When one group tried to slip away by night in a launch, the Indians allied to the Portuguese 'overtook them and splashed them with their paddles, sending so much water into their boat that they soaked everything. They could no longer use their firearms, so that our Indians entered and slaughtered them all. In short, if we lacked Indians we would have to abandon the land.' Raimundo de Noronha, the expedition's commander, echoed this praise of the Indians. He impressed on the King the need for winning their friendship, 'for if they were against us and some nation came from the north and turned them against us, it would be the total destruction of the Portuguese and of all that state'. The Dutch and English attracted many tribes with boatloads of presents, help in inter-tribal battles, and genuine friendship. But what really mattered was the unbroken record of Portuguese victories. 'All these heathen are subjected by fear and the high opinion they have formed of the valour of the Portuguese.'

With the lower Amazon cleared of rival colonial powers, Portugal was poised to occupy the entire basin of the mighty river. Portugal and Spain had been united under the same kings ever since 1580. This had not greatly reduced the traditional differences between the two Iberian kingdoms. The Portuguese had a far longer history as an independent monarchy, a slightly different racial stock and language, and a subtly different national character – gentler, more pragmatic and adaptable, and with the resilience of a maritime race. The Portuguese were determined not to be swallowed up by their larger neighbour. The area where the two kingdoms were most obviously in confrontation was in the Americas, at the two ends of the Line of Tordesillas, the mouths of the Plate and Amazon. Geography favoured the Portuguese, for the Spaniards approaching from Peru had to confront the barriers of the Andes and the Amazon jungles before penetrating the heart of the continent. The Portuguese brilliantly exploited the union of the two kingdoms to push their conquests far to the west. They seized the heart of South America from its native inhabitants before the Spaniards could do so – and made a dead letter of the Treaty of Tordesillas.

The Spaniards were at first suspicious of the Portuguese move into Pará, for the fort at Belém violated the Line of Tordesillas. But they themselves did nothing to colonise the Amazon. Before long, King Philip was actually writing to encourage the Portuguese to explore the great river. In 1626 he authorised the notorious Indian-killer Bento Maciel Parente to lead an expedition up the river, and when he was too occupied elsewhere to do so the authorisation was repeated in 1633 for another great slaver, Governor Coelho de Carvalho. Bento Maciel Parente was in charge of Ceará in 1626, and his treatment of the Indians was outrageous, even for those lawless times. A Franciscan accused him of 'not allowing Indians who were dying of hunger to clear plantations, paying them nothing although he kept them constantly employed in his mills and on his journeys and similar things, claiming that he could employ them in this way in the name of the King's service. . . . He ordered them to work on Sundays and saints' days. . . . He always keeps various Indian women as concubines, seizing the wives of some Indians and daughters of others, and threatening them all if they spoke about it or failed to bring them. A mission village that is beside his sugar mill seems more like a harem for him and his men than an aldeia of Christians!' But this old libertine was a marvellous fighter, against both Indians and rival European colonists. On 14 June 1637 King Philip IV made Bento Maciel Parente hereditary donatory of the captaincy of Cabo do Norte, and later that year he became Governor of Maranhão. The hereditary captaincy included the north shore of the mouth of the Amazon, upstream as far as the Genipapo (modern Paru) river. All of it lay west of the Line of Tordesillas – and yet the recipient was a Portuguese. The King of Spain and Portugal thus violated the Treaty in favour of Portugal. Bento Maciel was the man who had slaughtered the

Maranhão Tupinambá, and his sons were notorious slavers. By this award, these men obtained a virtual licence to exploit the thousands of Indians living in what is roughly the modern Territory of Amapá, an area the size of France.

In that same year 1637 the colonists of Pará were surprised by the arrival of a canoe containing two Spanish Franciscan friars and half a dozen Spanish soldiers. The Franciscans were from Quito and had been engaged on a mission among tribes on the Napo; their Indians turned hostile and most of the missionaries returned to Quito, but two – Domingo de Brieba and Andrés de Toledo – decided to 'descend the current of the river in a small canoe, with no other purpose than, inspired by divine impulse, to make a discovery of this river in their frail vessel'. The many tribes living on the banks of the Amazon assisted them with food during this prodigious voyage. They arrived in good physical shape, quite prepared to make the return journey if suitably equipped.

The settlers in Belém gave the Spanish explorers an enthusiastic welcome but, when they moved to São Luís in Maranhão, Governor Jacomé Raimundo de Noronha detained them to prevent their discoveries being known in Quito and Peru. Jacomé Raimundo was probably connected with an independence movement in Portugal that was plotting to break the link with Spain and restore a Portuguese king. He was determined to claim the Amazon for Portugal. The Governor rapidly organised an immense expedition of seventy Portuguese soldiers and eleven hundred mission Indians to explore the river. It sailed off, well equipped with arms, ammunition, food and trade goods, in 47 canoes under the command of Captain Pedro Teixeira on 28 October 1637.

The Governor gave Teixeira sealed orders to be opened only after he had passed the territory of the Omagua and was entering the province of Quito. Those orders were to found a Portuguese settlement and to erect boundary markers between the realms of Spain and Portugal. It was a move of breathtaking audacity: the Governor was calmly attempting to claim the vast majority of the Amazon for Portugal, and to violate the Line of Tordesillas by no less than 1500 miles! Jacomé Raimundo was arrested in 1638 and returned to Portugal, but acquitted by a superior court that contained leaders of the independence movement. Portugal managed to break away from Spain two years later, with the acclamation of the Duke of Bragança as King João IV. Pedro Teixeira carried out his instructions, and the boundary between Portuguese- and Spanish-speaking South America has remained high on the upper Amazon, with Brazil occupying roughly half the continent.†

It took Teixeira's expedition eight months to reach the first Spanish settlement. The only fuel to propel the expedition upstream against the current of the Amazon was the muscles of its Indian paddlers. There were delays to explore alternate routes between the islands of the Amazon, and to gather food for such a large force. By the end of 1637 they had only reached the island of Arêas. The Indians were exhausted and longing to return to their families. 'The Tapuia rowers were in despair at their sufferings and determined to desert. But [Teixeira] . . . persuaded them that they had almost conquered the river, when they were in fact only half-way.' Teixeira had to keep rallying his wretched Indians by assuring them that they had almost arrived. 'They were all exhausted by efforts of this magnitude, and congratulated themselves each day because it would be the last of their great exertions.'

The expedition finally reached the upper Amazon, and Teixeira divided his men. Most were left in a camp near the territory of the Omagua. Eight canoes were sent ahead to explore the upper river. Teixeira himself followed. The Portuguese and Indians pushed up the swift Quijos river, and finally scaled the Andes from the east to reach the city of Quito. The explorers were given a tumultuous welcome, with municipal and ecclesiastical ceremonies, many speeches and parties. There were two days of bullfights, in which 'the generosity of the Quitans was so great that they permitted our Indians to kill the bulls with their arrows. They did this most skilfully, and the applause of the crowd multiplied.' The expedition stayed in Quito for many months while the Spanish authorities debated what to do about Teixeira. They decided that he must return, but accompanied by Spanish observers. There were more bullfights, fireworks, and constant parties 'honourable demonstrations . . . that amply publicised the merited glory of the Portuguese nation'.

The return journey left Quito on 16 February 1639, and the chief Spanish observer, the Jesuit Cristóbal de Acuña, wrote a splendid account of the ten-month journey down the Napo and Amazon. He added many details about the tribes along the river to those given by Friar Gaspar de Carvajal a century earlier. He regarded the Omagua (or Cambeba) as the most intelligent and best-governed tribe on the river. One group of Omagua had fled downstream to escape the Spaniards, and had introduced European ideas to the main tribe. Their province was some 500 miles long, and the Omagua inhabited or cultivated all the banks and islands in this stretch of the Solimões (Amazon). 'Their settlements are so close together that one is scarcely lost sight of before another comes into view. . . . It may be imagined how numerous are the Indians who support themselves from so plentiful a country.' Omagua men and women wore cotton robes. They grew their own cotton and were skilful weavers, using different-coloured cottons and finely painted cloths. They practised skull deformation, pressing the heads of infants between two boards at the back and forehead. The front and back thus became as flat as the palm of the hand, and the head bulged to the sides and top. 'It becomes deformed in such a way that it looks more like an ill-shaped bishop's mitre than the head of a human being . . . which causes ugliness in the men, but the women conceal it better with their abundant tresses.'

Acuña was enchanted by the ease with which the Omagua and other tribes existed on the bountiful river. He made their lives sound as idyllic as those of the Indians first encountered on the coast of Brazil. The river islands were very fruitful, with a fertile layer of mud deposited by the river when it rose each year. The Indians planted great quantities of maize and manioc, and had learned that they could bury the manioc roots and recover them after each flood. They made the usual beiju bread and cauin spirit from their manioc, and loved drunken parties as much as any other tribe. 'With the help of this wine they celebrate their feasts, mourn their dead, receive their visitors, sow and reap their crops: indeed on any occasion on which they meet, this liquor is the mercury that attracts them and the riband that detains them.' They grew other plants – sweet potatoes, broad beans, gourds – gathered fruits such as pineapples and guavas, nuts and honey, and obtained salt from the ashes of palm leaves.

Acuña described the Indians pursuing manatees in their light canoes and harpooning them with shell-tipped lances. He also explained how the Omagua stocked the tanks of turtles that Orellana's men had raided so greedily. They would hide near the beaches where the turtles came in their thousands to lay eggs. As the creatures crawled back to the river, the Indians intercepted them and captured hundreds by simply flipping them on to their backs. Holes were then drilled in their shells and the turtles towed back to the villages behind canoes. They were kept in tanks enclosed by wooden railings, were fattened on foliage, and killed when needed. Female turtles produced hundreds of eggs 'almost as good as hen's eggs, though harder of digestion', and full of rich oil that Acuña considered the best possible fat for frying fish. The breastplates of the turtles were sharpened with stones, hardened with fire, and fixed into handles to make hatchets; while the curved jawbones of manatees served as adzes. The Indians gathered turtles in such quantities that every enclosure contained at least a hundred. 'Thus these barbarians never know what hunger is, for one turtle suffices to satisfy the largest family.' But the main food of the Amazon tribes was, of course, fish. The river was teeming with every kind of fish, and the Indians were brilliant fishermen. They shot fish with arrows attached to wooden floats to mark where the fish had dived. When the river subsided and left lakes cut off from the main stream, the Indians beat the water with the poison of timbó lianas, which stunned the fish and brought them floating to the surface.

Acuña gave a good description of the electric eel, long before the discovery of electricity. This fish, which the Indians call paraque, 'is like a conger eel. It has the peculiarity that, when alive, whoever touches it trembles all over his body, while closer contact produces a feeling like the cold shiverings of ague; which ceases the moment he withdraws his hand.'

Not only was the Amazon full of fish, but the forests on its shores also contained all the usual game: tapirs, deer, peccaries, monkeys, coatis, armadillos and every sort of game bird. Whenever Teixeira's expedition camped for the night, its weary Indian rowers cleared the undergrowth and made fires. 'They employed themselves providing for our lodging, which took some time, and then separated – some on land with dogs in search of game, others on the water with only their bows and arrows. In a few hours we saw them return laden with fish and game sufficient to satisfy the hunger of the whole party. This did not happen on any particular day, but throughout the duration of the voyage.' To the Jesuit Acuña this was a manifestation of divine providence comparable with the miracle of the loaves and fishes – rather than a demonstration of Indian skill and endurance.

Every **Omagua** kept at least a couple of canoes for his family, and he did not even have to enter the forest to cut trees to make them. He would wait for a suitable tree, preferably a cedar, to come drifting down from the forests of Peru, lassoed it as it passed, and towed it ashore. When the river fell and the log lay stranded, he would slowly carve his dugout with stone and turtleshell tools. The river Indians moved everywhere by water, 'like Venetians or Mexicans'. Other tribes used light bark canoes so that they could escape enemies by paddling into the shallows and carrying their canoes into tributary lakes.

The river tribes traded with one another: the Omagua produced a surplus of cotton for trade, and the Curucirari, living downstream of the Juruá, traded their magnificent pottery – the polychrome ceramics that had so impressed Carvajal. The Caripuna and Zurina, living on the south side of the Amazon below the Purus, were renowned for making stools carved in animal shapes, and for the excellence of their throwing-sticks. The Manau paddled from the upper Negro to the Japurá and Solimões to trade gold from Colombia with the tribes of the Amazon.

But the tribes were also constantly at war with one another, fighting with throwing-sticks, clubs, arrows and the manatee-hide shields that had often saved the lives of Orellana's Spaniards. The Omagua, for instance, were at war not only with the tribes above and below them on the Amazon, but also with the Ticuna to the north and the Mayoruna in the forests to the south. The last village of each tribal territory was a fortified frontier outpost, filled with warlike Indians, and there was often an unoccupied no-man's-land between one tribe and the next. The deaths in these constant wars seemed to Acuña to be 'the drain provided for so great a multitude, without which the entire land would not be large enough to contain them'. Tribes captured prisoners from one another and kept these as captive workers; but they treated them well, accepting them as part of the tribe and refusing to sell them to the Portuguese. Acuña stressed that almost none of the Amazon tribes ate human flesh. The worst they did to their enemies was to give the most valiant ceremonial executions and exhibit their heads on trophy poles.

By the time of Teixeira's expeditions the tribes of the Amazon were thoroughly terrified of Europeans. Even the most warlike attempted no resistance. Their only defence was in flight, and several riverine tribes abandoned their villages and fled inland as the expedition passed. Most entertained the explorers hospitably. They were impressed that an expedition could travel unharmed up and down the river, moving like lords of the Amazon past its many tribes.

Acuña found the Amazon Indians generally paler than the coastal Tupi, and was impressed by their obvious intelligence and dexterity in manual skills. 'They were meek and gentle . . . conversed confidently with us and ate and drank with us without ever suspecting anything. They gave us their houses to lodge in, while they all lived together in one or two of the largest in the village. And though they suffered much mischief from our Indian allies, with no possibility of avoiding it, they never returned it by evil acts.'

As the expedition sailed down the Amazon, Acuña saw increasing evidence of Portuguese slaving. He refused to erect crosses in native villages, for he knew that it was a slaver's trick to erect these sought-after magic symbols – in return for payment in captives – and then, if the tribe allowed the cross to fall or neglected it, to use this as a pretext for a 'just war' against that tribe for opposing the spread of Christianity. When the expedition reached the mouth of the Negro many of its officers wanted to go up that river in search of slaves. They said that a good cargo of slaves would make them welcome when they reached Belém, whereas without any 'they would be held very cheap for having passed so many different nations and so many [potential] slaves, and yet come back empty-handed'.

But the Jesuits drew up a petition, dated 12 October 1639, begging Teixeira not to go slaving on the Negro. They argued that the expedition was overdue and could not afford this delay, and Teixeira agreed.

Beyond the mouth of the Madeira lay the beautiful great island of Tupinambarana. The expedition discovered to its amazement that this was inhabited by Tupinambá who had migrated from Pernambuco at the time of the Portuguese invasion. Many of Teixeira's men spoke Tupi, so that they could converse freely with these Indians. The Tupinambá told them how, exasperated at their defeat and persecution by the colonists, eighty-four villages had decided to migrate inland. They left simultaneously and took every man, woman and child, from the oldest to the youngest. They travelled up the São Francisco and then across the campo country of northern Mato Grosso, crossing the headwaters of rivers that drain southwards towards the Paraná and Plate. It was a leisurely migration, with delays to force a passage through hostile tribes or to grow crops to continue the journey. Before long, these Tupinambá had marched right across South America until, to their dismay, they met Spanish colonists near the headwaters of the Madeira. They settled there for a while, but were disheartened to encounter more white men. There was friction with the Spaniards and this group of Tupinambá migrated again, descending the entire length of the Madeira to the island where Texeira found them. They had travelled some three and a half thousand miles in their extraordinary exodus – surely one of the largest migrations in history. There must have been some 60,000 people at the outset. But they explained to Acuña that 'with such a multitude of fugitives it was impossible to support them all: they therefore separated over distant tracks . . . some peopling one land, some another'. The Tupinambarana group, although reduced in numbers, were such excellent archers and warriors that they conquered their island in the Amazon, evicting or subduing its inhabitants. Acuña described them as noble-hearted and of good ancestry, and very hospitable towards Teixeira's expedition.

Tupinambá hospitality even included telling the explorers about the Amazons – as with some orientals, many Indians try to gauge what their interrogator wishes to hear, and feel that it is polite to satisfy him by confirming it. The Tupinambá therefore confirmed some of the more exotic medieval legends about Brazil – tribes of pygmies, and the men whose feet were turned backwards so that anyone tracking them went in the wrong direction.

The Tupinambá gave a precise location for the Amazons: they lived high up the Nhamundá or the Trombetas, beyond four other tribes. It was roughly the same location as Carvajal's and O'Brien's: in the dramatic forested hills of Acarai and Tumucumaque that form the watershed between the rivers flowing south into the Amazon or north into the Guianas. The Tupinambá confirmed the usual story about the Amazons preserving their integrity by rearing only female babies and admitting men only once a year for procreation. Acuña concluded that 'time will reveal the truth, and if these are the Amazons made famous by historians they are treasures shut up in their territory'. The tribes which live in the hills of the watershed today, such as the Wai-Wai or Tirió, are somewhat taller, paler and more classically handsome than other Indians. One of the first Portuguese to visit the Amazon remarked on the fine, beardless faces of its peoples. 'The men wear their hair long like women and resemble them from very close. This could have given rise to the deception that is told about Amazons; for nothing more can be discovered about that subject.'

Charles de la Condamine was a French scientist who descended the Amazon a century after Teixeira and Acuña. He was fascinated by the legend of the Amazons. He interrogated various aged Indians about the warrior women. 'All told us that they had heard their fathers talk thus, adding a thousand details too long to repeat, all of which tended to confirm that there had been in this continent a republic of women who lived alone without having men among them.' Various travellers noted that the Tapajós tribe wore brilliant green stones as lip plugs. This tribe told La Condamine that their fathers had obtained the green stones from the 'women-without-husbands'. The French scientist knew that explorers from Cayenne or French Guiana had found many green stones in the Tumucumaque hills. An Indian in the mission village of Mortiguara near Belém offered to guide La Condamine up the Irijó (? Araguari) river, between Macapá and Cabo do Norte, to reach the lands of the Amazons. La Condamine concluded that all the accounts 'concur in placing the common centre . . . in the mountains at the centre of Guiana and in a canton not yet penetrated either by the Portuguese of Pará nor the French of Cayenne'.

La Condamine was impressed by the fact that various Indians had told the first explorers about the Amazons, when they could not possibly have known the Classical legend about them. He decided that they had probably once existed. But he was worried, as a Frenchman and a scientist, about the strain on women living without men. His hypothesis was that, 'either subjugated by another nation or bored by their solitude, the girls finally forgot their mothers' aversion to men. Thus, although we may no longer find actual vestiges of this republic of women, that would not be enough for us to affirm that it never existed.'

The expedition of Teixeira and Acuña also visited the Tapajós tribe.

Its men traded abundant food with the travellers, and even invited them to settle on the Tapajós river. In 1639 the Tapajós were still powerful enough to have escaped the attacks of Portuguese slavers. But, when the expedition reached the fort of Desterro, Acuña was appalled to find Bento Maciel Parente's son of the same name assembling an expedition to raid the Tapajós. The young Bento Maciel assured Acuña that he would not proceed until authorised by the King. 'Yet, scarcely had I turned my back, when [he sailed] in a launch mounting a piece of artillery and other smaller vessels, with as many troops as he could get, and fell upon the Indians with harsh war, when they desired peace.' The Tapajós submitted with goodwill to the Portuguese. Bento Maciel ordered them to surrender their dreaded curare-tipped poisoned arrows. Once this was done, the Portuguese herded the Tapajós warriors into the enclosure under strong guard. They then let their Indian allies loose in the village. Those proceeded to sack the place, pillaging every object, and abusing women before the eyes of their men. 'Such acts were committed that my informant, who is a veteran in these conquests, declared that he would have ceased buying slaves or would even have given the value of those he possessed, not to have beheld them.' Bento Maciel's men then forced the Tapajós to surrender two hundred of their captives, whom they had hidden at the approach of the Europeans. Acuña saw these on their way down to the slave markets of Maranhão and Pará.

Acuña warned the King that it would be difficult to curb the anarchy caused by ransom expeditions on the lower Amazon. This was demonstrated when the expedition reached Cametá, a place that struck Acuña with the great beauty of its views, climate and fertility. In the past it had been famous for the number of its inhabitants and as an assembly point for expeditions up the river. When Acuña saw it in 1639 it was already depopulated and destitute, 'with no one to cultivate the land and nothing besides the ancient site and a few natives'.

Pedro Teixeira returned to Belém to a hero's welcome after his epic ascent and descent of the Amazon. But his brother, Canon Manoel Teixeira, Vicar-General of Maranhão, gave a different impression of the Portuguese impact on the world's greatest river. In a sworn statement on his deathbed, Manoel Teixeira declared that, in the first decades since their arrival in the area, the Portuguese had killed almost two million Indians in Maranhão and Pará. They had destroyed them 'in their violent labour, exhausting discoveries, and unjust wars'. The figure of two million dead was doubtless exaggerated. But the destruction and suffering were real enough.

TWELVE

The Bandeirantes

THERE was a curious and enduring tradition, which began soon after the first discoveries, that Brazil was a great island, enclosed by the river systems of the Amazon and the Plate-Paraná-Paraguay. It was thought that the two rivers rose in the same fabulous lake, which was given various names, including Eupana, Dorado or the Enchanted Lake of Paititi. The Portuguese felt that the Line of Tordesillas ran through the mouths of the Amazon and the Plate. Lopez Vaz declared that 'From the mouth of this river Amazon to the mouth of the river of Plate, is that part of America which the kings of Portugall . . . doe holde.'

Having stated their claim to the coast between the mouths of the Amazon and Plate, the Portuguese then suggested that their share of South America should be the lands enclosed by these two river basins. There is no such lake, but the notion that the two rivers join was not entirely fanciful: Indians such as the Tupinambá who migrated across Brazil and down the Madeira had evidently explained that the Paraguay and Guaporé were separated by only a few miles of watershed. 'Those who navigate upstream on one of these rivers, if they carry their canoes on their backs for that short dividing distance, can return by sailing down the other.' For the two rivers are 'two keys that lock the land of Brazil . . . two giants that defend it and demarcate between us [Portuguese] and Castille'.

The shape of modern Brazil was the result of centuries of penetration along these two axes: westwards to the Plate basin and up into the

A sugar mill and military column during the Dutch wars.

Amazon. In both areas expeditions plunged westwards in search of riches – either precious metals or, failing them, Indian slaves. And in both cases the expeditions were largely manned by Indians serving Portuguese masters. In the south they worked as trackers and porters, and on the Amazon as rowers. Modern Brazil thus owes its vast area, in a sense, to its Indians: it was Indians who provided the skilled manpower for the expeditions into the interior, and Indian slaves were the bait that lured them inland.

The first expedition westwards into southern Brazil came remarkably early. A Portuguese called Aleixo Garcia was shipwrecked off Santa Catarina in southern Brazil, together with a handful of Spaniards. They made friends with the local Guaraní Indians and kept asking for gold or silver. The Indians told about a White King wearing long robes and living in the mountains far to the west. Garcia had the magical advantage of coming from another civilisation, and evidently possessed the personality to inspire Indians. In 1524 he organised an amazing expedition, almost a migration. He moved overland to the Paraná and Paraguay and then with two thousand Guaraní followers plunged across the Paraguayan Chaco to the edges of the Inca empire in modern Bolivia. Garcia's army sacked some Inca towns and returned with a booty of silver and copper objects. He marched for thousands of miles right across South America and back, and was the first white man to see the Inca empire. But, when he sent to urge his original companions to organise another expedition, they refused. And towards the end of 1525 Aleixo Garcia, the first great South American explorer, was killed on the banks of the Paraguay, either by Indians or by Europeans intent on robbery.*

The great Portuguese colonising fleet of Martím Afonso de Sousa reached Brazil five years after Garcia's death. It made an attempt to follow in his footsteps. An expedition of forty arquebusiers and forty crossbowmen was sent inland from Cananéia in September 1531. It was led by Pero Lobo and guided by Francisco de Cháves, who had lived on that coast for some years and who promised 'to return to that port in ten months with 400 slaves loaded with silver and gold'. But it was the intended victims who won. When the Europeans reached one of the great rivers, possibly the Paraná, Carijó Indians invited them to cross in their canoes. The Indians had covered holes and cracks in the canoes with mud. When these were in mid-stream they pulled out these bungs and the canoes sank. The agile, naked Indians swam ashore, but the Portuguese were trapped by the metal armour and weapons that had won them so many battles: most sank and drowned, and those who reached the bank were killed by the Carijó. Martím Afonso ordered two captains to take reprisals on the Carijó, but they were too busy killing Indians on the Iguapé to undertake this additional campaign.

The great achievement of Martím Afonso's voyage was the settlement of São Vicente and, with the help of Chief Tibiriça and his son-in-law João Ramalho, the foundation of São Paulo de Piratininga on the plateau beyond the coastal hills. For the next half-century, the settlers of São Vicente were busy fighting off the Tamoio and establishing their captaincy. It was therefore the Spaniards who explored the basin of the River Plate – explorers such as Sebastian Cabot, Juan de Ayolas, Domingo Martínez de Irala, Álvar Núñes Cabeza de Vaca and Nufrio de Chávez pushed up the river and across the wastes of the Chaco in pursuit of the White King and the treasures reported by Aleixo Garcia's Guaraní. They had many bloody battles against the formidable tribes of the Paraguay, notably the Payaguá and Guaicurú, of whom we shall hear more later. Asunción, which is still the capital of Paraguay, was founded in 1539; and communications with upper Peru were secured by the founding of Santa Cruz de la Sierra in 1561.

It was Spaniards rather than Portuguese who first penetrated much of what are now the Brazilian states of Paraná, Santa Catarina and southern Mato Grosso. This was not unreasonable: these lands lay clearly beyond the Line of Tordesillas and thus in the Spanish sphere of colonisation. But it was not clear where that Line crossed the coast. The southern coasts of what is now Brazil were therefore becoming an area of Spanish–Portuguese rivalry.

Juan Díaz de Solís sailed down the coast in 1516 before being killed by Indians when he landed in the Plate estuary. One of his ships was wrecked near Massiambu at a place they called Puerto de Patos ('Port of Ducks'). Various survivors were later picked up by the Portuguese Cristóvão Jacques – and then imprisoned in Lisbon. The Spanish fleets of Magellan and Francisco García de Loaysa sailed past in 1519 and 1525. Sebastian Cabot, the Genoese who had succeeded Vespucci and Solís as Pilot-Major of Spain, set out in 1526 to search for a passage to the Pacific, but was lured into a hunt for the silver of the Plate river. He landed at the island of Santa Catarina and named it after his wife Catarina Medrano. He then promptly lost his flagship when it ran aground in the strait off the southern tip of the island – now appropriately named Punta dos Naufragados ('Cape of the Ship-wrecked'). When Cabot decided to search for silver some of his officers objected; he marooned them among the Indians of the Lagoon, where they were well received.

Cabot built a fort on the Paraná river and then spent many months exploring upstream in a small boat. His expedition was often saved from starvation by Indian generosity, but responded with the customary brutality of Spanish conquistadores. Relations with the tribes worsened. By mid-1529 the fort on the Paraná was destroyed and its garrison slaughtered, and Cabot's men could land nowhere along the river without being attacked. They decided to sail for home, and tried to recoup some of their losses by seizing fifty Indian slaves at Santa Catarina and São Vicente.

Cabot probably did not sail far enough up the Paraná and Paraguay to reach what is now Brazil. But a later explorer, Juan de Ayolas, spent some years on the rivers, from 1536 to 1539, and almost certainly *did* penetrate Brazilian Mato Grosso. On 2 February 1537 he founded a fort called Candelaria, which may well have been on the site of modern Coimbra or Corumbá. The expedition had a chronicler – the coarse German soldier Ulrich Schmidel. Many groups of Guaraní were encountered. If they brought plenty of food and compliant women, all was well; if not, they were attacked, slaughtered, and their settlements burned. Ayolas was eventually killed by Payaguá Indians who lived in the swamps and creeks of the Paraguay. But one of his captains founded a fort, in August 1537, that he named Asunción. The local Guaraní were excellent farmers who provided plenty of food and enough beautiful girls to provide each member of the expedition with a private harem. Asunción was soon known as 'Mohammed's Paradise'. It flourished and became the main Spanish base in eastern South America. Schmidel accurately recorded the concerns of these Spaniards: much of his narrative dealt with the silver extorted from the natives, the punishments meted out to them, and the beauty and degree of nudity of the women of each tribe.

Spaniards returning from La Plata continued to tell glowing accounts of its riches. King Charles was interested. He appointed a remarkable old explorer as the next governor of Asunción: the sixty-year-old Álvar Núñez Cabeza de Vaca. This formidable man had once been shipwrecked off the southern coast of North America, lived with an Indian tribe there for five years, and in 1533 set out, stark naked, with five companions, to walk right across modern Texas to Mexico, which they reached in 1536. Cabeza de Vaca set off to his new command at the end of 1540. When he reached Santa Catarina he decided to attempt another epic walk – overland from the Atlantic to Asunción on the Paraguay. After careful reconnaissance, and leaving 152 men to claim Santa Catarina for Spain, he set off into the interior on 2 November 1541.

Indians guided Cabeza de Vaca's 250 soldiers through forested hills, and they often had to cut a path for their twenty-six horses. Everyone walked, for the horses were used to carry supplies. Bridges were built for the animals to cross streams. The Spaniards marvelled at the great forests of paraná pines. They were delighted by the monkeys, who would hang by their tails, knock down the pine cones with their feet, and then scramble down to devour them.

At one time the expedition faced starvation but was saved by meeting friendly Guaraní Indians on the Iguaçú river. The Indians were terrified of the horses. They tried to appease them with offerings of meat and fish, and when the horses ignored this they begged the Spaniards 'to tell the horses not to be angry with them'. Cabeza de Vaca's men were the first Europeans to see the stupendous Iguaçú Falls, now the greatest natural tourist attraction in South America. The Spanish explorers were more concerned with the dangers than the beauty of the falls. They had difficulty crossing the river above them and portaging through the forest alongside. Cabeza de Vaca then had to win over a mass of hostile Indians, which he did by gentle talk and presents. This was his secret: he insisted that his men barter for all the food they received from the Indians, and he absolutely forbade them to touch native women. As a result, the Indians helped the expedition to build rafts to cross the mighty Paraná and guided it across the difficult country towards Asunción. It arrived there on 11 March 1542 after making an amazing march without a single fight against Indians or the loss of any men.

Cabeza de Vaca was not the man to relax as Governor of Paraguay. He was soon off, first leading a campaign against the fierce Guaicurú tribe that threatened Asunción. He arranged the construction of ten river-boats, and on 8 September 1543 these sailed upstream with 120 canoes in a gallant flotilla to explore the upper Paraguay. They reached Candelaria after a month. Pressing on up-river, they reached a place that Irala had called Puerto de Los Reyes ('Port of the Magi'). The expedition was now suffering from shoaling of the river, from vampire bats, sting rays and biting ants, and from a plague of mosquitoes that stopped anyone from sleeping by day or night. They were evidently in the Pantanal, one of the world's largest swamps that encloses hundreds of miles of the banks of the upper Paraguay. Los Reyes is thought to have been the site of Corumbá or even Caceres in modern Mato Grosso. Cabeza de Vaca met an Indian who had accompanied Aleixo Garcia's trek across the Chaco to the eastern frontiers of the Inca empire. He turned his expedition westwards, setting off with 300 Spanish soldiers, 700 Guaraní Indians and 10 horses. The hardships of the Chaco proved too great. The expedition stopped short of the Andean foothills. When it returned to the Paraguay, the fort of Los Reyes had to be abandoned because of attack by Guaicurú. This formidable tribe had repelled the first European attempt to invade its territories.*

Cabeza de Vaca's successor Domingo Martínez de Irala explored the Paraná in 1543 as far as the mouth of the Tietê – the river that rises near São Paulo itself. And his lieutenants founded Spanish villages with imposing names on the eastern shores of the Paraná: Ciudad Real del Guairá on the Piquiri river in 1557, and Villa Rica del Espíritu Santo near the junction of the Ivaí and Corumbataí in 1576. These towns were the basis of the Spanish province of Guairá – named after the chief of the Indians living near the Sete Quedas ('Seven Falls') on the Paraná. The province occupied roughly the western half of the modern state of Paraná.

In the wake of the Spanish settlers came Spanish Jesuits, the founders of the famous theocracy of the Paraguayan missions. The black-robed Fathers marched across from Peru and found wonderfully apt converts in the Guaraní. Of all the Brazilian Indians, the Guaraní were the most spiritual, believing in a single creator god and easily led by messianic leaders. One of the first Jesuits in Paraguay, Alonso de Barzana, wrote from Asunción in 1594 that 'all this nation is very inclined to religion, whether true or false. Had the Christians given them a good example, and had various sorcerers not deceived them, they would not only be Christians, but devout Christians. They know all about the immortality of the soul and greatly fear the anguerá, which are souls that have emerged from dead bodies: they say that these go about terrifying people and causing harm. They have the greatest love and obedience for the Fathers if these give them a good example – but the same or more for the sorcerers who deceive them with false religion. . . . This propensity to serve anyone in the name of religion has led many heathen Indians among them to claim to be sons of god and prophets. Indians raised among Spaniards have also escaped and joined hostile [tribes], some calling themselves popes, others Jesus Christ, and for their sensuality they have formed convents of nuns whom they abuse. . . . They have spread thousands of idolatries and superstitions and rites of these shamans, whose chief doctrine is teaching them to dance day and night until they die of hunger, having neglected their crops. These tribes are great farmers: they have vast quantities of food, especially maize, various kinds of manioc and other fine roots, and a great amount of fish.'

When Barzana wrote about the Guaraní in 1594 he reported that the greater part of them had already died of epidemics, ill-treatment and wars, and many more were following their shamans and refusing to admit Jesuits. But the field was extremely fertile for missionaries. They could hardly fail to create flourishing missions among a people that was naturally devout and already settled as skilled farmers.

Barzana wrote that in Guairá alone there were said to be a hundred thousand Guaraní and also the great and valiant tribe of Ibirajara. Two Jesuits, the Portuguese Manoel de Ortega and the Irishman Thomas Fields, opened up the Guairá mission at the end of the sixteenth century. They operated 'roving missions', moving from one village or nomadic group to another. By 1607 they were ready to found permanent mission settlements. These were known as reductions, because the Indians were congregated in them and 'reduced' to a Christian and civilised way of life. Thirteen reductions were created among the Guairá Indians, in the vast, fertile plain east of the Paraná, between the Iguaçú to the south and Paranapanema to the north. They were formed in the face of opposition from the Spanish colonists, who wanted to use Indian labour, either in allotments known as encomiendas or as personal servants called by the Inca word yanacona.

During the years when Spanish Jesuits were crossing the Paraná into Guairá, the settlers of São Paulo, 400 miles to the east, were planning attacks on the Indians living to the south and west of their frontier town. The townsmen of São Paulo – known as Paulistas – called the Guaraní Indians Carijó. In European eyes, the Carijó were the best tribe on the coast of Brazil. 'These are domestic and civilised, for men and women wear cotton sheaths like Moorish loincloths, live in houses, plant manioc and vegetables, have a good appearance and external grace, and some of them are as well proportioned as any Europeans.' 'They go half naked . . . wearing mantles, either of fine matting or skins or featherwork . . . with a form of smock tied above their haunches or falling down to the knees on the men and to mid-leg on the women. . . . The women and girls go bare-headed, with their hair agreeably bound with little ribbons of grasses dyed in lively shining colours.' They were gentler and more apt for conversion than their Tupi enemies – even though the Guaraní and Tupi languages were very similar and the two groups clearly had a common origin.

Nóbrega himself wanted to lead a mission westwards from his new creation of Piratininga: 'My heart always told me that I should send to the Carijó.' Two Jesuits were sent south from São Paulo to the forests of the Carijó in August 1554. They were to make peace between the Carijó (Guaraní) and the Tupi of São Paulo, ensure a safe route from the coast of Santa Catarina to Paraguay, and try to found a great mission among the Carijó. Successful at first, they were soon killed by the Carijó – at the instigation of a Spaniard from Paraguay. These missionaries, Pedro Correia and João de Sousa, thus became the first Jesuit martyrs in

Brazil, and the first victims of the inevitable clash between Portuguese and Spanish colonists in southern Brazil.*

The Paulistas initially had enough local Indians to live comfortably. Nóbrega complained that Paulistas 'can think of nothing but living off the work of their slaves, who fish and collect food for them. Laziness has taken such hold of them, and they are so addicted to sensuality and other vices, that they are not even cured by being excommunicated for possessing these slaves. . . . All or most of the men in this land have consciences weighed down by the slaves they possess against all reason.'

By the 1580s the Indians around São Paulo were becoming extinct and the colonists began to look hungrily towards the populous Carijó. Some sailed down the coast from São Vicente to raid the coastal Carijó of the Lagoon. In 1585 the town council of São Paulo made the first open reference to Indian slavery. It authorised a raid into the sertão in search of Indians. The justification was, quite blatantly, the need for slave labour. 'This land is in great danger of being depopulated because its inhabitants do not have [Indian] slaves as they used to, by whom they have always been served. This is the result of many illnesses . . . from which over 2000 head of slaves have died in this captaincy in the past six years. This land used to be ennobled by these slaves, and its settlers supported themselves honourably with them and made large incomes.'

The Carijó reacted by a half-hearted move against the young settlement of São Paulo itself. They delivered no attack, but the colonists felt threatened by the Carijó in 1590 and again in 1593–4. Whether the threat was genuine or not, it was sufficient justification for the town council to beg the Captain-Major Jorge Correia to do something. He responded by leading another expedition against the Carijó and Tupina. Jerónimo Leitão attacked the Carijó on the coast as far as Paranaguá in 1595–6, and then spent six years assaulting villages along the Anhemby (Tietê) river. Spanish Jesuits claimed that he and his mameluco half-castes destroyed 300 villages, exterminating or enslaving their 30,000 inhabitants. Another official campaign marched north-westwards to the Paranaíba and spent the four years from 1596 to 1600 ravaging Indian tribes. It may have penetrated as far as the Goiás, deep in the heart of Brazil.*

These expeditions were the start of an extraordinary movement of slaving, prospecting, raiding and exploring by the Paulistas. For a century and a half the tiny frontier town of São Paulo – which in 1600 had no more than 2000 inhabitants, and consisted of a hundred rustic houses clustered on a hilltop – sent groups of men plunging into the forests and rivers of central South America. The expeditions have come to be known as bandeiras, and the tough woodsmen who marched on them as bandeirantes. It was a movement that has stirred the imagination of Brazilian historians. There is now a formidable literature about the bandeirantes, inspired by pride at their endurance and achievements as explorers, and by disgust at their slaving and atrocities against the Indians.†

The bandeirantes marched into the forests year after year throughout the seventeenth century. São Paulo was often empty, 'evacuated by its inhabitants finding relief in the sertão' – the sertão was the jungle, the wilderness that stretched interminably across the plateaux to the west of São Paulo, and 'relief' meant the riches to be gained from captive Indian slaves. For a Paulista's prestige lay in his Indian slaves.* The farms around São Paulo were too poor and its frontier was too remote from the sea for the Paulistas to be able to afford many African slaves. The men of São Paulo therefore thrust inland to prey on the Indians. One governor said of them that 'any man too poor to have anyone to serve him would rather submit to travelling for many years in the sertão in search of someone to work for him than to serve someone else for a single day'. And the town council of São Paulo admitted to another governor: 'Your Worship well knows that the Portuguese are not hard workers, especially when they are out of their own country.'

The bandeirantes' treks through the forests and along the rivers were desperately tough. A Portuguese Jesuit marvelled at their misdirected endurance. 'One is astounded by the boldness and impertinence with which, at such great cost, men allow themselves to enter that great sertão for two, three, four or more years. They go without God, without food, naked as the savages, and subject to all the persecutions and miseries in the world. Men venture for two or three hundred leagues into the sertão, serving the devil with such amazing martyrdom, in order to trade or steal slaves.' And a Spanish Jesuit became almost humble when he compared the bandeirantes' hardships with his own. 'These Portuguese do and suffer incomparably more to win the bodies of the Indians for their service than I do to win their souls for heaven. For they are always on journeys on foot that are long and difficult. They lack all necessities of this life, suffering hunger, exhaustion and nakedness, always on guard against a thousand ambushes, with bodies and souls constantly in danger – all to catch four Indians, who run off or die on them next day.'

A bandeirante planning an expedition might obtain the necessary equipment on credit from an outfitter. His expedition would consist of 'sons aged fourteen and upwards, slaves, using muskets, swords, machetes, bows and arrows and other weapons'. He needed many Indians, to act as scouts, porters, paddlers, hunters and soldiers. He carried a formidable armoury of weapons – dozens of shotguns, arquebuses, blunderbusses, powder, shot, ramrods and wicks for the weapons too old to have flintlocks, long pistols, and of course plenty of blades, ranging from swords and daggers to facões – 'big knives' or machetes – that still serve woodsmen for all their needs, from slashing undergrowth to eating, and from carving wooden tools to prising jiggers from between their toes. The firearms were for shooting game and for overpowering the Indian captives that were the objective of the expedition. Bandeirantes also carried plenty of chains, padlocks, iron collars, shackles and rope to tie up their victims. They had objects to trade with the Indians: knives, hatchets, scythes, fish-hooks, red caps, and coloured beads – the same things that have appealed to isolated tribes from Cabral's time to the present. There would be some picks and gold-washing pans in case the expedition came upon precious metal; fishing-hooks, line and nets; and heavy axes, chisels and adzes for clearing forest, felling trees and hollowing out dugout canoes.

The bandeirantes themselves travelled light, with few clothes beyond those they marched in. Their belongings must have become thoroughly worn and torn by the forest, soaked from the rains and the river rapids, and stained from the owner's sweat, food, and the blood of innumerable scratches and insect bites. After a few weeks in the Brazilian forests, everything starts to smell of the mould of dead leaves that thickly carpet the ground. A bandeirante wore a kerchief and an old felt or leather hat, preferably with a brim against the ants, twigs and snakes that tumble out of jungle branches. He was thickly bearded. His shirts and underwear were cotton and his jacket and breeches of baize or coarse cloth. He wore stirrup stockings and tough hide boots. His armour was the padded escaupil that the Spaniards had adopted from the Mexicans – a carapace of raw leather filled with padded cotton and lined with cotton twill. It was light and soft enough to be bearable on long forest marches, and thick enough to withstand most arrows.

The bandeirantes set out with little food, nothing more than some salt in a bamboo tube and a supply of 'war flour' – manioc specially prepared and roasted in the Indian manner to resist ants and mould. They shot the game that abounded in the forests, fished the fertile rivers, and gathered wild honey or the few fruits of the sertão. Some bandeiras paused long enough to grow crops of manioc, or planted roças along their paths for use on the next year's expedition. But one of the main sources of food was provided by the bandeira's terrified victims: the Paulistas stole crops from the Indian villages that were once so numerous in the Brazilian interior. Anyone who has experienced a few months of this forest food will recall the monotony of grilled fish and meat washed down with stream water, and the lack of green vegetables or fresh fruit. Bandeirantes carried few utensils, only a few tin plates, copper pots and drinking-gourds. Some had spoons, but for most a hunting-knife was sufficient to slice off pieces of game. They slept in hammocks, of course, with pillows and a couple of blankets against the cold, wet nights in the forest. Each man had porters carrying his belongings in a leather chest.

Food was the great problem of these tough expeditions that marched for months and years across unexplored wastelands. Bandeiras inevitably struck infertile regions. There were hundreds of miles of campo: dry, open plains covered in coarse grasses, gnarled stunted trees, and towering pink termite-hills. There were swamps flooded by each year's rains; and caatingas – low, dry woods with dense undergrowth. There were great expanses of forest where streams were rare and there was little game.

The Englishman Anthony Knivet marched on many bandeiras, and recalled one large expedition in 1597 led by Martím de Sá, son of the Governor of Rio de Janeiro. One part of the expedition marched inland from Parati, guided by ten lusty young Goiana. They moved up a river for forty days, spending the entire time in the water struggling against endless rapids. The men became very weak from lack of food; many died from disease and intestinal worms. Then came a month in dry campo country. 'The Portugals beganne to despaire, and threw away their peeces [guns], being not able to carry their clothes.' They ate their bucklers made of 'raw hides of buffe; likewise we did eate a Cowes skinne, which the Frier carried with him to cover his things which hee said Masse withall from the raine; happie was hee who could get a Toade or Snake to eate'. The bandeira lost 180 men crossing this campo, but revived when it found honey and palm hearts in the hills beyond. Some Portuguese suspected treachery by their Indian guides – that the 'Canibals did leade them up and downe of purpose to destroy them'.

The interminable march finally brought Knivet's companions to the Javari river and the Tamoio villages they planned to attack. They stealthily approached one village. Some men greedily raided its manioc plantations. 'Wee came before the Towne in the Evening and lay all night in ambush, thinking to take some of them the next morning coming for their meate. That night our men ate so much Mandioco, that when we thought we should have had some skirmish they lay all vomiting that they were not able to stand, and thirteene of them died.' That village proved to be deserted, but the expedition stayed for two months eating its crops. The men then moved on to another village, found freshly planted crops, and stayed for three months eating them. Most members of the bandeira then returned, but Knivet and a dozen others tried to explore a river in search of a mountain of jewels. They were captured by Tamoio and all but Knivet (the only non-Portuguese) were killed and eaten. It was then that Knivet persuaded the tribe to follow him on a disastrous migration to the Atlantic coast. Knivet and all his Indian friends ended as slaves of the Portuguese.

Many bandeirantes failed to return. Sometimes entire expeditions would disappear, and after a few years' absence would be judged to have died. Individuals might die during an expedition and be buried in some distant forest. The expedition's leaders would draw up an inventory of the dead man's effects on some scrap of cloth or hide. They would arrange a funeral ceremony and a sale to other members of the bandeira of the man's worn belongings, 'because of present danger and being in enemy country, where these things could easily be carried off, thus causing his orphans to suffer loss since they have no one to protect their interest'.

Some bandeiras lasted so long that, 'when they returned to their homes, they found new children, born to men who, considering them to be dead, had married their wives. And they themselves brought the children they had engendered in the jungles.'

Most bandeiras contained chaplains. Their function was to administer the last rites to dying bandeirantes – but not to interfere with the business of catching Indians. A Jesuit scornfully called these priests 'wolves in sheep's clothing, hypocrites, who are kept to officiate while the rest are . . . tying up Indians, killing and dismembering children, while they wear long rosaries around their necks . . .'.

Bandeiras were a risky business. Not only was there danger of dying in the forests, there was also the possibility of bringing back few slaves. António Ribeiro, a lady who financed one bandeirante, declared: 'I give as equipment for the sertão: two Indians, a shotgun and 6 pounds of powder and 12 of shot, and all else necessary, on condition that in case of profits I be entitled to half.' The outfitter who provided António Pais and his son with provisions for a bandeira towards Goiás, did so in return for a third of any slaves which 'God might see fit to give him, with their families; and if no slaves be taken they must repay the debt one month after returning – without raising any doubt on this point'.

São Paulo became the bandeirante nucleus because of its relative isolation and inability to grow profitable sugar. The town lay to the west of the coastal hills, at the head of streams flowing westwards towards the Paraná. Its frontiersmen therefore looked westwards for opportunity and adventure, and every young Paulista was lured towards the sertão. This was João Ramalho's city – with his numerous half-caste offspring he was literally the father of São Paulo. Paulistas continued to make unions with Indian women, and the bandeiras were largely led by mamelucos, the sons of Portuguese fathers and Indian mothers. Jacomé Monteiro wrote in 1610 that the citizens of São Paulo were 'mostly mamelucos and rarely Portuguese. . . . They are of terrible condition. Outside the town their dress is to go about like exiled convicts with hood-like halters, bare feet, and bows and arrows which are their normal weapons.'

Bandeiras were an activity where whites and Indians collaborated in harmony. Each bandeira was led by whites and mamelucos but manned by hundreds of their Indians – Tupi, or Carijó after that tribe was subdued and largely enslaved. The Indians contributed their forest skills and geographical knowledge. They soon grasped the purposes of the mission and became expert enslavers of other natives. Although brutalised and worked hard by the captains of the bandeiras, the Indians probably enjoyed service on them. It was quite normal for Tupi warriors to make long marches through the forests to attack enemy tribes. This was an exciting, manly activity – unlike agricultural labour – one in which Indians could make use of their native skills. Portuguese firearms also ensured that the expeditions were successful, so that their Indian members were reasonably sure of victory at the end of their campaigns. The Carijó marching on slaving bandeiras were probably just as happy as their Guaraní cousins in the secure, pious and artificial world of the Jesuit missions. But the victims of the bandeiras suffered appallingly. Torn from their tribal societies, shackled and led off by people from another civilisation, and put to work as slave labour, most died of despair or from alien diseases.

After Jerónimo Leitão's long campaigns against the Carijó and the 'war of the Paranaíba' of 1596 to 1600, bandeiras left São Paulo almost every year. In 1598 Afonso Sardinha took a hundred Christian Indians and marched to the Jeticaí (now Grande) 'to raid and roam the country' or find precious metals.* In 1601 André de Leão marched out in search of the legendary Lake Paraupava, accompanied by the Dutchman Willem Glimmer. The following year it was Nicolau Barreto who led a bandeira, northwards to the Rio das Velhas and on to the São Francisco and Paracatu. He took 300 whites and many Indians – a massive effort that exhausted the Paulistas for a time – and returned after two years and many deaths with some 3000 Temimino and other Indian prisoners.* In 1604 Diogo de Quadros was illegally capturing Carijó, and in 1607 the mameluco Belchior Dias Carneiro took 'forty or fifty white men with whom went a large part of the Indians of this town'. He sent back many contingents of Indian slaves during a two-year bandeira.

This became the pattern throughout the first half of the seventeenth century. Almost every year Paulistas led contingents of their 'domesticated' Indians off on slaving raids. Their attacks fell on tribes near São Paulo – the remnants of the Tupinikin, Tamoio and Goiana – and farther afield against the Tupina, Ibirajara or Bilreiros, Temimino, Puri, Caiapó and Goiá. But the brunt of the slaving was against the Carijó Guaraní, to such an extent that in São Paulo any slave came to be called a Carijó. In 1606 the town council of São Paulo estimated that the Carijó still had up to 200,000 warriors, against whom the five towns of the captaincy of São Vicente could muster 300 Portuguese 'as well as their Indian slaves who probably number over 1500 – men experienced in sertão work, who under good leadership travel as far as Peru, and that is no fable!'

In 1613 the Jesuit Pedro Domingues accompanied a bandeira of thirty Paulistas and as many Indians. They marched northwards on an extraordinary epic journey, for over 800 miles across the unknown forests of what is now Minas Gerais and the desolate campo of Goiás to the headwaters of the Tocantins. They descended the Tocantins for a further 800 miles to its confluence with the Araguaia, and then returned up that river and overland back to São Paulo – a nineteen-month odyssey comparable with the famous African explorations of the nineteenth century.

On the upper Tocantins, this bandeira visited seven large villages of Tupi-speaking Cátinga. These Indians had many iron tools, Rouen shirts, hats and other European goods that they said they had bartered at a French fort which was built years before and lay eleven days' journey downstream. The bandeirantes told the Cátinga of the fine conditions they would find at São Paulo, 'where they would all be together, with their churches and all that was necessary for their salvation. But it was all deceit, the profession of backwoodsmen.' Three thousand people were inspired to migrate by these treacherous stories. A huge quantity of manioc flour was prepared. The emigrants embarked in three hundred of the tribe's many canoes, and the Paulistas persuaded them to leave their weapons behind. The wife of one chief's son was a beautiful half-caste, the daughter of a Frenchman. 'Nature had excelled itself in endowing her with the requisite parts for corporal perfection.' The bandeirantes could not resist her. They could not wait until the tribe was trapped at São Paulo, but gave her to the Paulista captain, and distributed women to the other white men. The tribe began to appreciate its danger. One night its men fell upon the bandeirantes and killed sixteen of the thirty whites and some of their Indians. The other bandeirantes fled to São Paulo; and the Cátinga returned to their villages.

This same Jesuit Pedro Domingues also reported on the tribes living near the headwaters of the São Francisco, north of modern Belo Horizonte. This was the home of the Amoipira, a branch of the Bahia Tupinambá. The Jesuits twice visited them. On one journey the missionaries took four months crossing a thousand miles of sertão, 'suffering great hardship from [lack of] water for four days on end, and of food, passing entire days with only seven grains of corn'. They tried to 'descend' the Amoipira, to settle them in aldeias near Bahia, but the journey across the sertão was so hard that many Indians fled back to their homes. The Amoipira villages were 'always frequented by innumerable Indians, who descend with their families to enjoy the abundance of that river' but could not live on it because of the mosquitoes. The Amoipira also gave refuge to groups of Tupi, fleeing from colonial persecution: the Temimino, who abandoned homes on the Jequitinhonha and came to mingle with the Amoipira; and the Tamoio of Cabo Frio, escaping the destruction of their people in the 1570s, who moved northwards to settle on the Rio Prêto, a tributary of the middle São Francisco.

It was inevitable that the Paulistas, who lived near the source of the Paranapanema, should clash with the Spaniards moving into the province of Guairá at its mouth. In 1607, Manoel Preto raided Guairá and returned with many captives taken near Villa Rica. And in 1611 Governor Luís de Sousa Henriques sent an official raid into Guairá. He wanted Indians to work his mines of Araçoyaba, and persuaded some Guairá chiefs already in São Paulo to send for relatives from their homeland. The expedition reached the Paranapanema and sacked the town of Chief Taubiú. Many captives were being led off to slavery, when the bandeira was attacked and destroyed by António Añasco, the new Spanish governor of Guairá. Next year Sebastião Preto, Manoel's brother, attacked again and captured 900 Guaraní; but was himself attacked by the Governor of Ciudad Real. The Spaniards recaptured 500 Guaraní – although half of these escaped and rejoined the bandeira, thinking that life under the Portuguese might be better than under the Spanish colonists of Guairá.*

In these early years some Paulistas, such as Afonso Sardinha and his sons, found placer gold in the Serra da Mantiqueira and in Guarulhos, Jaraguá and São Roque. Some small gold-mines were also found in the captaincy of São Vicente. But the Paulistas were far more interested in seizing slaves than discovering mines. Governors such as Don Francisco de Sousa, who governed Brazil from 1591 to 1602, were obsessed with the discovery of mines and sent many prospecting expeditions inland from Espírito Santo and particularly from São Paulo. But the Paulistas were afraid that if gold were discovered they would lose their relative independence, and would have-to pay a fifth of any metals as tax to the King – whereas on Indian slaves they paid no tax.*

It was at this time that the Spanish Jesuits started to create their first mission reductions in Guairá. In 1610 Fathers Simón Maceta and José Cataldino founded two large missions on the Pirapó, a tributary of the Paranapanema. These reductions of Our Lady of Loreto and San Ignacio-Mini prospered, and were soon surrounded by great plantations farmed by the industrious Guaraní. The man known as 'the Apostle of the Guairá' was António Ruiz de Montoya, an energetic, passionate and highly literate Jesuit who founded eleven more reductions in the Tibagi and Ivaí valleys of Guairá between 1622 and 1629.

The first Jesuits found the Guaraní thoroughly roused against the Spanish colonists. 'They initially helped the Spaniards and admitted them into their lands as brothers and relatives.' But the Spaniards soon tried to force the Guaraní to work for them. 'The Spaniards kept these Indians in their fields and town houses, with such great power over them that they claimed they were theirs. They used to lend or give them to anyone they wished, for as long as they fancied. They made them work in whatever tasks seemed most useful for their farming. If they fled, they pursued them and whipped them or even put them in chains. . . . These people possessed no land or property, neither horses nor chickens: nothing was theirs, it all belonged to their masters – even their clothes were taken from them and given away.' War broke out between the Guaraní and the Spaniards, and the banks of the Paraná were deserted for hundreds of miles.

The Jesuits had to overcome this hatred and convince the Guaraní that missionaries were not mere agents of the colonists. 'They find the law of God very good, but not the Spaniards. Calling someone a Spaniard among them is to call him a fornicating, adulterous, lying, piratical thief. They therefore hate priests – not because their doctrine seems bad, but because they say that, when [priests] enter, those other evil people come immediately behind them. The abuses and insults of the Spaniards have thus debased the law of God.' But with intelligent and dedicated evangelists like Montoya and Maceta the Jesuits were soon able to create great missions. The Guaraní were relieved to find protectors among the white men. They responded eagerly to the discipline and ceremonial of Christian religion. Their crops flourished as a result of their own farming ability and Jesuit management. Groups of Guaraní volunteers were soon emerging from the forests to join the reductions, or sending to ask the black-robed missionaries to bring them their magic.

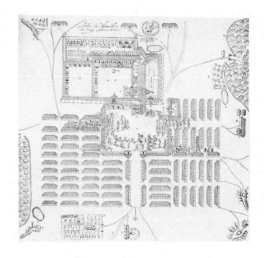

THIRTEEN

Bandeirantes against Jesuits

THE Spanish Jesuits' reductions full of thousands of docile Guaraní were an irresistible temptation to the bandeirantes. The Paulistas were devout Christians after their fashion. They liked to claim that the slaves they brought back were entering the bosom of the Church and were being saved spiritually – even if they suffered and died physically. The bandeirantes were also patriotic, but their nationalism was Portuguese and directed against the Spaniards. They conveniently ignored the fact that the King of Portugal was also King of Spain, just as they ignored Jesuit censure of their slaving. Their patriotism and religion were showy and reactionary, and wholly subordinate to their selfish interests.

It was thus not long before the Paulistas turned against the Spanish Jesuit missions. It was so much easier to attack these great settlements than to chase through the forests after isolated villages or roaming bands of wild Indians. The mission Indians were already disciplined and accultured. The Jesuits had taught them to obey Christian masters and to labour in the mission plantations. They spoke a language akin to Tupi, one that all Paulistas understood. They were hard workers and good woodsmen; and their women were among the most beautiful in Brazil.

Manoel Preto was the first bandeirante to attack Jesuit missions. He led a raid in 1616 and another in 1619 that stole many Indians from the missions of Jesús-María and San Ignacio. On a long bandeira in 1623–4 he brought back over a thousand Christian Indians from Guairá – all of

Portuguese troops enter the mission of San Juan Bautista.

them peaceful and settled subjects of the King of Spain and Portugal. He set them to work as slaves on his sugar and cattle ranch alongside São Paulo. The bandeirantes were back in 1628. António Ruiz de Montoya wrote to his Provincial that the mission of San Xavier, which was recovering from an attack of smallpox, was struck by 'Portuguese pirates, who appear from their evil acts to be more like wild beasts than rational men. . . . Men without souls, they kill Indians as if they were animals, sparing neither age nor sex. They [kill] babies because they impede their mothers' march, and old men and women for the same inconvenience of being unable to march or be useful [workers]. They kill them by hitting them on the head with clubs. They also kill chiefs or braves, because these inspire the rest to return to their homes.'

In desperation, the Jesuits began to arm their parishioners with firearms, even though this violated various royal orders against allowing American natives to have such weapons. The Jesuit in charge of the mission of Encarnación led his Indians in a surprise attack on the bandeirantes and their Tupi followers. They captured 'a good quantity of Tupi, including a very important chief honoured by both the Indians and Portuguese for his bravery. The Father had them flogged, removed [their weapons], and sent them back to their homes. There was such an outcry against this Indian chief in his country because of his flogging that he died of shame.'

The Paulistas had by now overcome any hesitation they may have had about attacking and enslaving peaceful Christian subjects of the King of Spain. They were preparing for a knockout blow on the Guairá missions. Part of the preparation was to suborn a governor of Paraguay. An aged and impoverished gentleman called Don Luís de Céspedes Xeria appeared in Brazil in 1628: he was trying to reach the province he was to govern, but had been provided with no travel allowance to do so. Martím de Sá, the powerful Governor of Rio de Janeiro, had him to stay and then proposed that he marry Sá's niece Victoria. The Spaniard leaped at the opportunity of marrying a beautiful young heiress, and was soon contentedly marching off down the bandeirante trail from São Paulo to Paraguay. Martím's son Salvador followed with his cousin Victoria, the betrothed of the Spanish Governor.

When he was in São Paulo, Céspedes Xeria saw the preparations for an enormous bandeira, and wrote to the King condemning Paulista slaving. But when he reached Paraguay he refused to let the Jesuits arm their Indians, and advised them to abandon the Guairá missions. He did nothing to protect the Jesuit reductions against either Spanish colonists or Portuguese slave-raiders. It was assumed that he was in league with the Paulistas.*

The bandeira that Governor Céspedes Xeria had seen in São Paulo left the town in August 1628. It was a huge undertaking. One report said that it contained 69 whites, 900 mamelucos and over 2000 Indians. The whites included two justices of São Paulo, two aldermen, the public prosecutor, and the son, son-in-law and brother of the senior judge of the town. The leader was a dashing bandeirante and leading citizen of São Paulo called António Rapôso Tavares. He divided the bandeira into four companies, commanded by himself and by Pedro Vaz de Barros, Brás Leme and André Fernandes.

The bandeira avoided the Spanish towns of Villa Rica and Ciudad Real. It took instead a southern route aimed directly at the valleys where the Jesuits were busily founding new missions. The bandeira crossed the Tibagi on 8 September and built a palisade close to a mission village. One Jesuit later claimed that Rapôso Tavares announced: 'We have come to expel you from this entire region: for this land is ours and not the King of Spain's!' Four months of uneasy truce ensued, during which the Paulistas seized roving groups of Guaraní but left the missions unmolested. Jesuit Fathers even entered the bandeirante stockade to baptise and confess the dying.

In January 1629 a very great chief called Tatabrana came to deliver his people to the care of the Jesuit Father Mola in the reduction of San António on the Ivaí. This chief had been captured by the bandeirante Simão Álvares some years before, but had escaped and returned to his home. The Jesuits insisted that Tatabrana's people 'were Christians whom we had won over shortly before the Portuguese entered those parts, by gifts and by celebrations in their honour when they came to visit us in our villages. They were attracted by the good reports that had spread concerning the peace and contentment enjoyed by the Indians who lived in [the reductions] with us.' But the bandeirantes claimed Tatabrana and his people as runaway slaves and demanded that the Jesuits hand them over.†

Whatever the reason, on 30 January 1629 António Rapôso Tavares marched into the mission of San António to seize Chief Tatabrana. His men went on to seize 'all the others whom the Father was instructing. As they themselves admit, they took from it four thousand Indians . . . and they destroyed the entire village, burning many houses, plundering the church and the Father's house, and desecrating an image of Our Lady. With great violence they removed the Indian men and women who had taken refuge in the Father's house and they killed an Indian at the very door of the house, as well as another ten or twelve persons in the same village. They took most of the Father's meagre belongings, including a few shirts, two blankets, shoes, hats, napkins, tablecloths, spoons, knives, ten or twelve iron chisels, and six or seven chickens that he had. They killed one of three cows they found, and took other small things. . . . What is of gravest concern in this whole affair is that . . . the Indians imagine and repeat that we gathered them in, not to teach them the law of God as we told them, but to deliver them to the Portuguese by this subterfuge. They also say that we tricked them by repeatedly assuring them that they were safe with us, and that the Portuguese being Christians and vassals of the same king, would not touch nor harm those who were with the Fathers. . . .'

António Rapôso Tavares dismantled his stockade and burned its huts. Some Jesuits said that aged captives were left to burn in the huts, and were thrown back into the flames when they tried to escape. Another part of the bandeira sacked the mission of San Miguel which the Jesuits had abandoned. A third group went to the mission of Jesús María on the Tibagi. Its Guaraní chiefs received them, but the Paulistas started taking clothing and weapons, and when a chief protested he was shot in the stomach and killed. The bandeirantes then proceeded to shackle the entire mission, taking 1500 men, women and children.

There was much hardship on the forty-day march to São Paulo. The captives had to carry the bandeira's baggage as well as their own children. They were given very little to eat – food stolen from their own plantations – and were not allowed to hunt for more for fear they would run off. At night the Paulistas' Tupi would harangue the column of captives, to persuade them that a good life awaited them at São Paulo, and to warn them of the fate of any who tried to escape.

Two Jesuits, Justo Mancilla and Simón Maceta, were allowed to accompany the bandeira back to São Paulo. They moved on to Bahia and wrote an impassioned protest against the outrage of the Portuguese attack on their missions. They were appalled to see the ease with which the bandeirantes obtained official acquiescence to their illegal raiding. Pedro Vaz de Barros was once given an official licence to enter the sertão to restrain another unlicensed bandeira – but only of course so that he could join it. André Fernandes, a notorious bandeirante, was licensed by the Inquisition to enter the forests in search of a heretic who had taken refuge there. When Rapôso Tavares' bandeira returned, the Jesuits saw its leaders bribe the relevant officials by giving each of them a few Indian captives. 'Thereupon, after committing so many abominations, they were well received. . . . No one who had not seen it with his own eyes could imagine such a thing. The entire life of these bandits is merely going to and returning from the sertão, going and bringing captives with all that cruelty, death and pillage, and then selling them as if they were pigs.'

The two Jesuits noted the various excuses given by the Paulistas. Some tried to claim that King Sebastião's law of 1570 permitted slaving – but that law allowed slaves only in a 'just war'. Others said they were bringing Indians into the Church – a claim that infuriated the Jesuits for its hypocrisy, especially when it was applied to the enslaving of their own catechumens. Some Paulistas justified their slaving by saying that their country needed labour, and that the Indians working there were free men. This was rubbish. 'They go about selling them for a bottle of wine or something else for them or their wives and children to eat or wear, as is common knowledge to everyone of this state. The truth is that the Indians they keep in their houses are free in name only: they are used just as if they were slaves from Guinea. . . . They all wish to be gentlemen, supporting themselves and their wives and children with this infamous merchandise acquired by so much robbery and pillage.'

Once the bandeirantes had destroyed one Jesuit mission with impunity – despite the furious protests of the Jesuit Fathers – nothing could save the remaining Guairá reductions from attacks by the slavers. In 1630 André Fernandes destroyed two more missions, and in 1631 Paulo do Amaral another.

The beleaguered Jesuits were under equally great pressure from Spanish colonists as from Portuguese raiders. The colonists had recently discovered that big profits could be made from extracting herva maté from the forests of the Maracaju hills opposite Guairá across the Paraná. Maté leaves make an aromatic tea that became extremely popular with colonists and Indians – it is still a favourite drink of Argentinian and Brazilian gauchos. The Spanish settlers, backed by their authorities, demanded that the Jesuits release mission Indians to work on maté extraction. Some Guaraní chiefs made a pathetic formal complaint, almost a lament, that despite royal prohibitions 'they have carried off our brothers, sons and subjects repeatedly to the Maracaju [maté forests] where they are all dying and coming to an end. Our subjects have all been consumed there, and not only our subjects but also the sons of leading chiefs and even many chiefs themselves. . . . Those maté forests remained full of the bones of our sons and vassals, and our church is used only to bury the bones of our women. Maracaju is the place where the poor little bones of our poor vassals are piling up. We now have no more sons or vassals because of that Maracaju. It makes us sad. It means that we have no more houses or plantations and it impoverishes and annihilates us. People who used to be here no longer appear and we do not see them. Only our Indian women remain, who never cease to lament the deaths of their husbands and sons. We therefore no longer wish to go to Maracaju or to send our vassals there. . . .'

The Jesuits finally came to the conclusion that their missions in Guairá were untenable. Attacks by Portuguese bandeiras had destroyed five of their seven reductions and tens of thousands of wretched Indians had been led off to slavery. The Spanish colonists were no help. Some of them were in league with the Portuguese, selling them slaves or helping them raid the reductions. Other Spaniards were using mission Indians in the deadly work of maté extraction. The colonists' answer to the bandeirante threat was to suggest that the Jesuits move their reductions close to the Guairá towns – where the converts would be more easily available to work for the settlers. Governor Céspedes Xeria was no help at all. A Jesuit complaint of 1631 accused him of receiving the notorious slaver André Fernandes in Asunción, and of agreeing with the bandeirantes to share their catch of slaves: the Governor received 500 and sent them to work on his Brazilian sugar plantation.* The Jesuits suggested that the Governor be sentenced to six years' service in Chile, or six years in the galleys, for his misconduct.

The Jesuits decided that their only hope lay in flight. António Ruiz de Montoya assembled 10,000 Indians from the two surviving missions of Loreto on the Pirapó and San Ignacio on the Paranapanema. He arranged to move them to safety. It was an extraordinary exodus. The Jesuit Fathers led off their people: men, women and children of all ages with their meagre baggage. They sailed downstream in hundreds of canoes as far as the seven great Guairá waterfalls on the Paraná river. The Guaraní portaged down around the falls, but found their advance checked by a palisade full of Spanish citizens. The colonists demanded that the Indians remain in Guairá, where they could be forced to work in the maté groves. But the Indians and their missionaries resolutely managed to force the passage. They built new canoes and sailed on down the Paraná to new missions a few hundred miles further from the dreaded Paulistas. The long convoy of canoes must have made a dramatic sight as it glided down the broad grey waters of the Paraná, each canoe filled with white-robed Indians, some with a black-gowned Jesuit under an awning amidships, with the congregation breaking into religious song to raise its spirits and inspire the rowers.*

With the Jesuits and their remaining congregations gone, the Spanish province of Guairá collapsed. In 1632 the bandeirantes turned against their former friends in the Spanish towns of Villa Rica and Ciudad Real del Guairá. After a brief defence, the colonists decided that they must follow the mission Indians into exile. The Paulistas let them go. The settlers of Villa Rica and later of Ciudad Real abandoned their towns and moved across the Paraná and south of the Maracaju hills into Paraguay.†

The Jesuits who abandoned Guairá resettled their flocks or started new missions in two new areas. Most moved south and established themselves in the heart of what is now the Brazilian state of Rio Grande do Sul, half-way between the Uruguay river and the Atlantic. Another handful of Jesuits started operating among the Itatín Indians on the east bank of the Paraguay, in what is now southern Mato Grosso.

The Jesuits had been penetrating the upper Uruguay for over a decade before the exodus from Guairá. It had been a confused effort, a mixture of great successes with thousands of converts, and stubborn resistance that amounted almost to a holy war against the Fathers. The penetration began in 1619 when the paramount chief Neenguiru heard of the Jesuits' achievements and sent to invite them to convert his Guaraní-speaking people on the upper Uruguay. The Fathers established the reduction of Concepción on the west bank of the Uruguay, at the point where the river is closest to the Paraná. In May 1620 Father Roque Gonzalez de Santa Cruz paddled far up the Ibicuí into territory that is now Brazilian. He visited the villages of Chief Tabacan, who had been influenced by Neenguiru and received him well.

Farther east, across the watershed in the Jacuí basin, lived the Tape Indians. They were reluctant to admit Father Roque, but relented 'after much persuasion and my citing examples of other chiefs'. The missionary then travelled freely through Tape territory, and left only 'after I had reconnoitred all their lands and looked for a site in which some day to reduce them. . . .'

This same Father Roque founded the first permanent reductions east of the Uruguay: San Nicolás and, on 2 February 1627, Candelaria on the Ijuí. His Indians had the enthusiasm of fresh converts. And yet it was a couple of years before they would freely allow the Fathers to enter their huts to tend the sick, and they were reluctant for them to see their women, who remained inside the huts when the missionaries first appeared. The reduction of San Nicolás flourished, and soon had a population of 2500. The Jesuit Provincial Nicolás Mastrilli Duran described how he was mobbed when he visited the mission in 1628. Duran spent the night before his entry a short distance from San Nicolás, but the new converts 'spent the entire night in festivities and rejoicing that deafened the plains with the noise of their instruments. In the morning they all came out to greet me. They threw themselves forward so precipitously to kiss my hand that I was in danger of being suffocated in the tumult, had not two Fathers who were beside me calmed them.' The Jesuits felt strong enough to attack the Guaraní shamans. Claudio Ruyer wrote in 1627: 'There is a great misery of sorcerers: I have a list of over forty of them. I hope to God that in a short time I will rid [the Indians] of their abuse, and that the sorcerers themselves will help the rest in their conversion. . . .'

When Father Roque moved up the Ijuí to try to convert the Caró Indians, he clashed with their powerful shaman Carupé. Roque had been with the Caró for a fortnight and was starting to build a church. But the tribe's spiritual leader resented the impudent intrusion of this preacher from an alien culture. On 15 November 1628 Father Roque was bending over a beam that was to support the bell of his church. One of Carupé's men smashed his head with a club, and the missionary died instantly. Another Jesuit ran up and was also killed. The chapel and missionary house were burned.

Roque's congregation at Candelaria wanted to go to war to avenge him, but was restrained by other Jesuits. But, when the shaman Carupé led 300 Caró against Candelaria, its newly converted Indians beat them off, with the mounted Father Pedro Romero riding at their head. By 1629 the population of Candelaria had grown to 7000. But in the following year it was struck by the inevitable European epidemic: a thousand Indians died, and the Jesuit Fathers gave frenzied deathbed baptisms to hundreds more.

The killing of two Jesuits dispelled some of the mystique of the black-robed strangers' magic. A federation of chiefs and shamans headed by Chief Nheçu sought to expel the Jesuits altogether. Their army marched towards the mission of San Nicolás. But the Jesuits were saved by Chief Neenguiru, the man who had first invited them into the area: he led 200 warriors across the Uruguay to attack Nheçu's village. Father António Bernal, who had been a professional soldier before joining the Jesuits, accompanied the expedition as a 'strategic auxiliary'. A fierce attack routed the anti-Jesuit federation, with many killed and the assassins of the Jesuit martyrs captured and executed. It was now possible to open a mission among the Caró; many hundreds were baptised or given Christian marriage. But their new reduction was ravaged in the early 1630s by disease and famine.

The last mission in the upper Uruguay region was San Carlos de Caapi, founded early in 1631. Its chief Apicabiyia was 'a terrible Indian, much feared among them for his eloquence and valour'. He threatened the missionaries when they tried to forbid his having eight wives. 'But in the end his hour came, and he changed from a lion to a gentle lamb. He begged with much insistence for holy baptism and said he wanted to be a son of God.' The Jesuits removed seven of his wives and married them to other men, leaving Apicabiyia with one aged wife. 'With the grace of God, who has the power to realise such miracles, he completely left his other women, who were good-looking girls – even one whom he had raised since childhood and loved extremely and by whom he had a one-year-old son.'

The Jesuits now moved eastwards into Tape country. They founded four missions near the headwaters of the Ibicuí between 1632 and 1634. It was all tragically reminiscent of the first missions of the Portuguese Jesuits near Bahia seventy years before. The Tape Indians embraced Christianity with innocent fervour, and were baptised in their thousands. They were a lazy people by European standards, unconcerned with private property and irresponsible when entrusted with cattle – they allowed the animals to die of hunger or thirst, or slaughtered them too soon. They lapsed easily into drunkenness or reverted to their tribal customs. But they were fine musicians and highly skilled at woodwork and ceramics. The Jesuits found that they could copy anything shown to them, and soon had the Tape producing baroque church ornaments. The Fathers imposed iron discipline to make the Tape work their plantations. 'Our Lord God . . . gave these poor Indians a very special respect and obedience towards the fathers. Without this, it would have been impossible to govern them.'

The first Ibicuí mission was Santo Thomás. It grew rapidly and soon had 3000 people baptised and 900 children in its school. But the reduction was then struck by a disease that killed 770 children and 160 adults. This was followed by a plague of jaguars who attacked from all sides and killed dozens of the weakened Indians. After a second wave of jaguar attacks the congregation lost faith in the new religion: most of the survivors fled and reverted to paganism. The second mission was San Miguel, a large Indian village that rapidly grew to a population of 5000. Here a shaman called Tayubai appeared and tried to persuade the people to abandon the Jesuits, who were destroying the old customs and the free life of the Indians. He was betrayed to Father Cristóbal de Mendoza, who imprisoned him briefly and then expelled him. Tayubai retired to the forests of Ibiá and organised another holy federation against the Fathers.

The Indians of the mission of San José were so eager to have missionaries that they themselves built a large church, mission house and cattle corral in anticipation of a Jesuit's arrival. Within a year this village had 'over 600 families, and the children are beginning to read, sing and dance, to their delight and the joy of their parents'. The fourth mission on the Ibicuí was founded in 1634 and soon rose to 2200 families. But tragedy struck it as inevitably as the rest. Ravaged by a terrible epidemic and famine in 1637, many of its Indians died and most of the survivors were persuaded to flee by their shamans. The reduction of Jesús María once had over a thousand Indians matriculated and ready for baptism. But 'at that time the plague entered, and with it the people scattered, so that there were hardly any left in the town. Of some 400 boys who used to come to the church, only ten came after [the epidemic].' The Jesuits cured some people by blood-letting. Others returned to the mission, only to die soon after. 'Our Lord God brought them back so that they could receive holy baptism; and He then took them to Himself as His own elect.' The Fathers were, as always, tireless in seeking out the dying. Pedro Romero described harrowing journeys through forests, rivers, swamps and islands. 'The Father went and found that in a little village of fifteen huts the plague had left none alive. He could find no one near it except two Indians and two boys who were also on the point of death. From thence he returned to other sick persons . . . and after walking for three or four leagues among islands of jungle, full of swamps and streams, he arrived . . . at a place in which he found ten children amid some ferns: three of these were already dying, without strength to support their heads on their shoulders, so that these fell from side to side as if their necks were hinges. And he baptised them with great compassion.'

In 1633, before the ruin of their missions on the Ibicuí, the Jesuits pushed eastwards to the Jacuí valley – almost to the Atlantic coast. They rapidly founded six more missions, filled with thousands of enthusiastic Tape. This expansion was the work of Cristóbal de Mendoza, a South American-born Jesuit who had been active fighting the bandeirantes in Guairá and had taken part in the exodus down the Paraná. With these missions on the Atlantic watershed, the Jesuits had almost completed their dream of a continuous chain of missions, a semi-autonomous theocratic state stretching from the Bolivian altiplano and the fabulous Potosí silver-mines to the Atlantic seaboard.†

Father Cristóbal soon moved north from the Jacuí to organise the Ibirajara of the upper Uruguay-Pelotas to resist a possible Paulista attack. He was returning from this Caagua region on 26 April 1635 when his party was attacked near the Piauí river by Indians under the shaman Tayubai – the holy man he had once humiliated. There was a fierce fight in heavy rain and lightning. Cristóbal's men were hit by a barrage of arrows. The missionary was pulled from his horse, hit by an arrow and stunned by a club. He was stripped and his ear cut off. His men left him on the trail in the pouring rain. The enemy returned next day to burn his body, but followed a trail of blood and found that he had revived and crawled a short distance and was still alive. The Indians demanded why his god had not saved him. Father Cristóbal started to preach to them, but was dragged into the woods and cut to pieces.

The missionary had been well loved by his people, and they soon mustered 1600 catechumens to avenge him. A Christian chief called Guaimica led this force from the mission of Jesús-María. It met the Ibirajara and fought and defeated them, with many killed. Tayubai was captured, and Chief Guaimica dragged him to be clubbed to death at the scene of Cristóbal's martyrdom. The Indians now had their own martyr, and their pagés Chemboabate and Ibapiri sent emissaries to raise the tribes in a holy war against the Christians. Their envoys went singing and dancing from village to village, predicting the destruction of the mission villages. Many converts fled and burned their churches. But other Christians organised armed bands wearing traditional feathers and war paint. These captured some of the pagan envoys and took them to the mission villages to be severely flogged while the Fathers prayed for their souls. The mission Indians then organised a force of over a thousand warriors that marched against a palisade in which the enemy were assembling. The Christian attack was successful; and the chiefs of the Indian alliance were executed.

No sooner had the Jesuits' Tape converts won this victory against the tribal traditionalists than they had to face a more serious threat from Portuguese Christians.

Aggressive Paulistas had been increasingly active against the Carijó living along the coast to the south of their captaincy. During the sixteenth century there had been sporadic attempts to settle the island of Santa Catarina – which Sebastian Cabot had named in 1526 after his wife Catarina Medrano. The Spaniards had attempted short-lived colonies on the island and adjoining mainland and farther south around the Lagoa dos Patos. Portuguese Jesuits were active among these Carijó in Nóbrega's time, then in the 1570s and again in 1616 when two of them settled many Carijó into the aldeias of Barueri and the Reis Magos. But for the first century after their discovery the southern coasts and plains of modern Brazil were relatively unmolested. Their many Indian tribes – reckoned by one Spanish official to number a hundred thousand people – were disturbed only by the visits of occasional slaving ships. Chief Martín of the Santa Catarina Carijó complained to the Spanish authorities in 1576 'about the Portuguese of São Vicente who come once or twice every year to that port of Viaça and, in exchange for iron or some cloth of little value, remove their sons to São Vicente and other parts of Brazil and then to Portugal to be sold as slaves. Those Indians are very terrified by all this.'

Paulista slave-raiding on these southern coasts gathered momentum only after the annihilation or enslavement of other tribes living closer to São Paulo. Manoel Preto – the scourge of the Guairá Indians – decided to try to colonise the island of Santa Catarina with a group of whites, mamelucos and Tupi. He obtained a provision to govern the island in July 1629. But the local Indians evidently managed to destroy this threat from a very experienced bandeirante. For in July 1630 the Spanish Jesuit Simón Maceta was writing jubilantly that Preto had been killed by 'the excellent arrow shots of the Indians. . . . May the Lord provide that he does not inhabit Hell!'

Purchase of slaves was becoming an increasingly organised traffic in Santa Catarina and around the Lagoa dos Patos. Native traders known as 'mus' acted as middlemen. A Jesuit who investigated the Taquarí river in 1635 came across a mu called Parapopi. He had a stockade on the Taquarí near the mouth of the Antas river. 'This one is a very great scoundrel who has sold all that nation. . . . The Portuguese entrust all their ransoming to him. Fleets of miserable captives leave his house every year, and are taken off overland by the Tupi [the bandeirantes' Indians]. It is said that they take only five days to reach the sea from there. I went hoping to bring him by force if he refused to come with me voluntarily, but . . . he was forewarned and fled with some Tupi he had with him. I had his house burned, and destroyed as much of his food as I could, so that he would depart from there.'

In 1635 the Governor of São Vicente licensed an enormous seaborne expedition to the Lagoon. It was an undisguised slave-raid. For many years the Portuguese had peacefully purchased slaves in that area in exchange for trade goods, and even the town council of São Paulo was shocked by this naked aggression. The council wrote that 'those persons took nothing but powder, shot and chains – which are against His Majesty's Law, being an act of war. Over 200 men went to the [Lagoon of] Patos, although the Indians on their part had given no cause for being molested. They had been our friends and the friends of our ancestors for over a hundred years.' The São Paulo council protested to the King in a tone of aggrieved self-righteousness – almost jealousy – about the conduct of the men of São Vicente. It was shocking that the lieutenant had permitted 'ship after ship full of men with powder and shackles and chains to make war on the heathen of the Patos, who had been at peace for so many years, and some of whom were Christians'. A Portuguese Jesuit happened to visit the expedition's base on the Lagoon. He saw fifteen sea-going ships and many large canoes and heard that the Portuguese were hoping for 12,000 Carijó slaves. The slavers even molested a chief called Parrot who had been one of the Paulistas' main agents. 'This Indian had always been a good friend and benefactor of the whites . . . it was he who for twenty years sustained them in everything and gave them free food. . . . But he was held in his principal village like a captive in a prison . . . with a strong guard of Portuguese musketeers placed over him. These, although they had received good treatment from him for so many years, were fleecing him of his vassals. Out of 1200 souls that he used to have in his main village, the one in which he lived, only 150 were left; these were his closest relatives. And yet they even wanted to take [Chief Parrot] himself captive.'

The Spanish Jesuits who had just moved into the Tape and upper Uruguay were naturally alarmed by all this Portuguese activity. Many missionaries had survived the Paulista onslaught on Guairá. They dreaded the destruction of another flourishing missionary field. Their Provincial Diego de Boroa, learned that 'the Brazilians of São Paulo were preparing an invasion of [the missions] so that they could gather up a good haul of captives, as they did recently in Guairá'. Boroa determined to resist. He sent in two young Jesuits, António Bernal and Juan de Cárdenas, who had been soldiers before joining the Society. He gave them full powers to buy arms and ammunition for their Indians – even though it was against the law for natives to have firearms. The next year he reported that the mission Indians 'attend to the military exercises, under the direction of our Brother Bernal, with great enthusiasm. They march out to the fields every day in a troop to train in attacks and counter-attacks, in gymnastics, shooting and fencing. They obey spoken commands and even simple signals.'

The dreaded bandeira arrived soon after: a great force of 150 Portuguese armed with arquebuses and 1500 Tupi. It was led by António Rapôso Tavares, the man whose bandeira had destroyed the first Guairá missions. It moved slowly southwards, capturing many Indians during a seven-month march from São Paulo.

On 2 December 1636 it struck Jesús-María, the most advanced, northernmost of the Tape missions. Rapôso Tavares attacked 'with his army, with drum and battle trumpet, his banners unfurled to the sound of battle. His troops began to fire their arquebuses.' There were two Jesuit fathers and two brothers inside a rampart and palisade. The four led the defenders' firing. Whenever one of them appeared there was a burst of musket and arrow fire. All four Jesuits were wounded, three on the head, but none died. Many of the mission's 1600 Indians were away in the plantations, but the remaining 300 men fought bravely to defend their log rampart. Their women encouraged them. One woman wore a jerkin over her dress and wielded a lance: she managed to kill a Tupi attacker. Five Paulistas and fifty Tupi were killed in the fighting. The battle lasted five hours, and ended when a fire-arrow set fire to the thatch roof of the church. The Indians who had taken refuge inside poured out with 'a chorus of most moving lamentations'. The Fathers surrendered with a white flag. But, although the bandeirantes allowed the Jesuits themselves to leave, they carried off Indian men, women and children to slavery, and stole some of the missionaries' possessions. One version of the battle – probably a Jesuit embellishment – said that when the Indians trooped out of the church like sheep from a corral they were butchered, with arms and legs hacked off and children split in two by the bandeirantes in their padded armour. The great Brazilian historian Capistrano de Abreu asked his readers: 'Are such horrors compensated by the consideration that, thanks to the bandeirantes, the devastated lands now belong to Brazil?'

The Jesuits who left Jesús-María raised an army of 1600 catechumens and managed to hold off a bandeirante attack on the reduction of San Cristóbal. But the bandeira destroyed and burned three other missions. When Diego de Boroa visited them he found only destruction and death. The Tape missions became untenable, and the Jesuits withdrew from their advance towards the Atlantic.

A few months later, in 1637, another bandeira led by Francisco Bueno and André Fernandes struck the missions on the Ibicuí and upper Uruguay. One part of it advanced upon the reduction of Santa Teresa, a magnificent town of 4000 people. This mission surrendered without fighting, and Fernandes herded its Indians into palisades. Since the bandeirantes entered on Christmas Day 1637, they went, candles in hand, to hear no less than three masses in the mission church. The Jesuit Francisco Jiménez berated them from the pulpit for the injustice and cruelty of enslaving Christians. They listened impassively. Then, in a pious gesture, they released the Jesuits' personal acolytes. But they refused to free any other mission Indians.

Such was the bandeirantes' strength that they calmly organised winter quarters at Santa Teresa and made its Indians plant crops for them. André Fernandes sent bands of Paulistas to seize masses of captives, in raids on the Ijuí missions and beyond Candelaria to the recently devastated plains of Caasapamini. The Spanish Governor of Paraguay was too timid to do anything against the Paulistas. The Bishop of Buenos Aires tried issuing an edict of excommunication. In February 1638, when the bandeirantes refused to leave the area or release their Christian captives, an Apostolic Notary marched up to their stockade and, in the presence of a civil notary and three Jesuit witnesses, solemnly read out a proclamation expelling the bandeira's leaders from the bosom of the Church. These merely said they would appeal against the order – and marched off to join Fernandes with 2000 captives. The expedition returned to São Paulo in 1639 with its Christian Indian captives. It left behind devastated reductions and panic-stricken mission Indians.

In 1639 the Spanish authorities at last permitted the Jesuits to arm their Indians with guns – something they had been doing clandestinely for a decade. When the Guaraní could not obtain metal muskets, they improvised: they made guns from heavy bamboo wrapped in layers of raw oxhide, and these contraptions were usually strong enough to withstand the explosion of the gunpowder. The Jesuits organised sentries, drilled their Indians, and promised rewards to wild Indians who warned of a Portuguese approach.

These preparations at last achieved success. The mission Indians began to turn the tables on the bandeirantes. An expedition from São Vicente under Pascoal Leite Paes was defeated in 1639 by the guns of the Indians of Caazapa-Guazu mission.

The next attack came in 1641. The Jesuit Claudio Ruyer described it all, often with unchristian glee at the defeat of his enemies. There was a preliminary skirmish on the Acaragua. The Paulistas attempted a dawn attack on an Indian camp, 'hoping to catch some Indian women whom they greatly desired'. But the camp was empty. There was a river battle between 250 mission Indians in thirty canoes against a hundred bandeirante canoes. The Jesuits' Indians were led by a chief called Ignacio Abiaru, and inspired by a banner of the Society's St Francis Xavier. 'The battle lasted over two hours. One of our musketeers fired, and St Francis Xavier guided the ball, so that it hit a Portuguese on the thigh and broke it, knocking him into the water; another from another canoe hit a Portuguese on the side and felled him; another almost cleared a canoe of enemies with a single musket ball.' But the Jesuits' Indians withdrew to Mbореré under a hail of musket and arrow fire.

The missionaries' main camp was on the Mboreré river ('River of Eleven Bends') that flows into the upper Uruguay. Fathers Pedro Romero and Pedro de Mola had busily assembled 3000 warriors from all their missions. They spent three whole days confessing these men in preparation for battle. They made a hospital, with a fire to cauterise wounds and their own habits for bandages.

The Paulista flotilla appeared on the afternoon of Monday, 11 March 1641. The Indians' captain Ignacio Abiaru 'performed his office excellently, to the applause of the Fathers and Indians . . .'. He attacked at once, with his canoes in a crescent led by an armoured raft containing a cannon. The Jesuits prayed, promising fasts and masses if victory were won. Choirboys sang litanies and, 'at the time when our holy patron

St Francis Xavier was being invoked with great emotion, our Indians fired their volley with such good aim that they killed two Portuguese and capsized three enemy canoes, wounding and killing many [of their] Indians. . . . The battle was waged with great courage on both sides. . . . Our sons loaded and fired so rapidly and with such skill that they seemed like soldiers from Flanders. Our sons retreated, wishing to engage the enemy: they wanted to draw them far from their rabble, in order to shoot them down in safety and put an end to them.'

The bandeirante Captain Pedroso, 'the greatest rascal of them all', jumped ashore with thirty men. They moved through some jungle to attack a contingent of mission Indians on the shore. But these turned and drove them off, wounding Pedroso, 'the man our Indians most wanted to kill, and they almost did so'. Meanwhile three Paulista canoes attacked the Jesuits' palisade, thinking it almost deserted. But it was full of hidden Indians. As the canoes approached, 'our men suddenly fired so many musket shots that the balls seemed to fall on them like hail. All our men showed themselves, rising up and unfurling their banners with great shouting.' The canoes escaped, with their rowers lying prone and paddling with their hands.

The main battle was raging on the river. The Jesuits had only 300 Indians in 70 canoes, against 300 Portuguese and 600 Tupi in 130 canoes. But the Spaniards' Indians were better armed and trained. 'They pressed them so hard that some threw their guns into the water and leaped from the canoes, jumping ashore on the far bank to hide in the jungle. They abandoned some canoes (fourteen of them) with all their equipment – clothing, axes, trade goods and other things – into the hands of our men. Others, to escape, had to leave their guns and take up blades to paddle. Our men pursued them in this way for a long distance, killing and wounding them. Nine Portuguese were killed and very many Portuguese and their Indians wounded, and a banner, powder and shot and a musket were taken from them. . . . In short, we drove them back to . . . their palisade, running and terrified, and our men were victorious, waving their banners, playing their drums and pipes, lords of the battlefield on both land and river!'

The bandeirantes attempted to parley under a flag of truce. The Jesuits and their Indians decided to ignore this. 'Therefore, the reply given to this letter was . . . to send 3000 Indians, who moved through dense jungle and in great silence arrived an arquebus-shot away from the Portuguese palisade. They immediately began to give them a handsome sprinkling of arquebus and arrow fire. They were thrown into confusion', but rallied and fought a fierce three-hour battle at the edge of the stockade. Two later attempts at a truce were similarly rebuffed.

The Spanish Christians saw that they finally had the advantage, and were determined to wreak vengeance for all the destruction and misery caused by the Paulistas.

Father Pedro Romero sent 1200 men to build a stockade at the mouth of the Tabaí to block the escape route from the Mboreré to the Acaragua. Juan de Porras commanded the flotilla of mission canoes. Other Guaraní invested the bandeirante stockade. They would creep up through the forest and fire into the compound. 'One ball entered the hut of a Portuguese who was blowing on his fire, hit him on the mouth and left him dead. Another wretch was in his hammock with an Indian woman (who later left him) beside him, when a musket ball entered between two logs, and also left him dead. Another was dining when a ball landed on the table top, broke the plate from which he was eating, struck him in the navel and immediately killed him.'

There were more battles during the ensuing days. The Paulistas were dismayed by the firearms and fighting qualities of these Indians. They had brought masses of chains and shackles for a rich haul of slaves. They were now furious at having wasted so much money and ammunition, without capturing a single Indian. 'They saw months of effort wasted, and remembered the debts they had incurred for their heavy expenditure on ammunition, powder and other equipment. The repayment for all this was to have been our poor little sons, had not God defended them, their Fathers animated them, and Father Diego de Boroa taken such extraordinary care in increasing their firearms. . . .'

The bandeirantes finally started for home, through dense forests and in torrential rain. They had been refused safe conduct, but begged the mission Indians: '"Do not kill us during Lent", and other words of great submission and pity. But our sons relied on the mercy of Heaven and attacked them more and more. . . . Our sons, valiant soldiers, glory of the Guaraní nation, attacked them intrepidly . . . fighting like demons or cruel tigers.' The pursuit continued furiously through those cold and rain-soaked forests. The Guaraní were 'running through those jungles and hills, falling and picking themselves up on occasion, and doing great damage to the enemy. . . . Finally, seeing all their Indians so terrified and badly wounded, they themselves (I mean the Portuguese) took up their bucklers and machetes and turned to face our sons, while their wounded and the rest of their rabble passed the hills, running forward in full flight. The Portuguese all exerted themselves to the utmost, for their lives depended on it. They wounded over thirty of our men, breaking the arms of some, or piercing their thighs, and they killed three. Our sons then attacked boldly, so that they tangled with the Portuguese themselves, and with clubs and machetes and musket balls killed four Portuguese and so many Tupi that the forests were strewn with their dead bodies.' The Guaraní chiefs led their warriors into battle. Various chiefs had close escapes, being seized or wounded and rescued with difficulty by their men.

The pursuit continued for eight days, with countless skirmishes and acts of heroism. The retreating Paulistas suffered terribly from hunger and exposure. Jesuit Fathers followed their route, gathering up the dead and wounded left in their camp sites. Many were pitifully thin, abandoned without food or fires, shivering with cold and caked in blood from their wounds. Large numbers of Tupi deserted the Paulistas, including one respected slaver who was 'treated as if he were one of them because of his valour and energy. . . . He told us that they were amazed by our strength and impressed by the perseverance of our sons.' This reputation was the most important legacy of the battles of Mbororé. The Paulistas realised that the Guaraní were now well armed and resolute. There were no more easy captives to be seized from the missions. The Jesuits were left relatively unmolested, and could develop a new set of reductions on both banks of the Uruguay.

When the Jesuits were forced to evacuate the Guairá missions in 1632, most fled south to the Uruguay. But one group moved westwards: they crossed the Paraná and the hills of Amambaí and Maracaju and settled on the east bank of the Paraguay. Other Jesuits had sailed up the Paraguay from Asunción and started to convert the Indians of that region, which they named Itatín. Spanish colonists had been in this area for many years, with a settlement called Santiago de Xerez founded in 1580 at the edge of the fertile Bodoquena hills, on the River Mbototeu (Miranda). The local tribes, ancestors of the modern Caiuá, resented the efforts of the Spanish colonists to force Indians to work for them. Their chief Nanduabuçu was assured that, if he received the Jesuits, Spanish settlers would cease to molest his people. In the words of the Jesuit superior Diego Ferrer, Nanduabuçu reasoned: 'Well, that is fine, for this is all that we are seeking. In order that the Spanish [colonists] will not enter, let us send to inform the Fathers that we will receive them well.' The Jesuits welcomed the invitation. Three reductions were soon formed in Itatín.

Although Itatín lay some 300 miles west of Guairá, across a difficult stretch of campo and a range of hills, it was soon attacked by bandeirantes. Itatín was relatively close to Asunción and far to the west of the Line of Tordesillas or of São Paulo; and yet it was invaded and eventually occupied by Paulistas. The colonists of the Spanish settlement of Xerez were largely to blame. They conspired with a Portuguese bandeira to lure Indians away from the Jesuits. Together they managed to persuade one group of Christian Indians that the Jesuits wanted them to attack another group; which the converts did with great gusto. They then invited various chiefs to a meeting, but treacherously seized and shackled them on arrival. They forced the chiefs to summon their people, and disarmed and captured those when they came. Jesuit missionaries were also held, and could not communicate with their Indians. The bandeira led off a thousand Indian converts, including chiefs Nanduabuçu and Paracu. Many of the victims managed to escape during the march toward São Paulo, including some of the chiefs. But those who fled told of a tragedy during the march into captivity. The bandeirantes 'had one entire raft full of chiefs and the most valiant Indians, all with a chain around their necks because they were afraid of them. But the raft capsized and all who were on it were drowned. The weight of the chain pulled them down to the depths, and none could escape because they were chained to one another. We [Jesuits] also learned that the Portuguese returned in extreme exhaustion. They had many misadventures on the journey and even ate frogs and snakes because they could find nothing else on those overland paths.' They even lost some of their own Tupi, who 'left the Portuguese because of the ill-treatment they do them, fleeing from such a cruel and ugly way of life and wishing to remain among our Indians. But [the bandeirantes] pardon none of these [deserters], killing all the Tupi they catch.'

The bandeirantes wiped out the Jesuits' province of Itatín just as thoroughly as they had Guairá. In 1632 the Spanish lieutenant of Xerez helped them to destroy four new reductions. He miscalculated badly – for the bandeirantes then attacked the town of Xerez itself and removed many of its native labourers. The Fathers regrouped the survivors of their congregations into new reductions. But in 1638 another bandeira struck, destroying Iatebo and another mission and carrying off their Indians. The Jesuits withdrew again, forming the mission of Caaguaçu 250 miles north of Asunción, and Tare, nine days' march north of Caaguaçu. There were more disasters. In 1645 Father Pedro Romero and Brother Matheo Fernández were sent across the Paraguay to attract fresh converts. They were opening 'a new conquest, with three reductions', when they were attacked and captured by a federation of uncontacted tribes led by Guaraní shamans. Father Romero had his tongue pulled out and fingers cut off, and was then opened up the middle, and Brother Matheo – who was a smith, shoemaker and saddle-maker – was also killed by these 'sorcerers and ministers of Satan'. The reductions were also continually harassed by the Guaicurú and Paiaguá – the most successful of all Brazilian tribes in fighting white invasion.

The next disaster came on 8 September 1647: a surprise attack on the mission of Tare by a band of Portuguese slavers. The few Indians who survived were regrouped in a new reduction called Mboymboy on the Apa river, the present boundary between Brazil and Paraguay. The following year the formidable old bandeirante António Rapôso Tavares marched through Itatín at the start of the longest and greatest of all the bandeiras – one that was to take him right across South America to the Andes and then down to the mouth of the Amazon. On 1 November 1648 his men fell upon the reduction of Mboymboy. Father Cristóbal de Arenas was shot and captured. When Father Alonso Arias marched to his rescue with a force from Caaguaçu mission, there was a sharp skirmish in which Árias was killed by a musket ball.

The Jesuits' only consolation came from heathen tribes. Rapôso Tavares' bandeira marched on across the Paraguay and into the Chaco, suffering extremes of hunger and sickness. 'In the midst of this weakness and destitution they were continually assaulted by barbarians on foot and horse who shot arrows through them. The difference and superiority of their weapons was of no avail, for there was scarcely anyone fit to wield them.' 'The Paiaguá, infidel Indians and lords of this river [Paraguay], confederated with the Guaicurú nation for this purpose. The Paiaguá came by water and the Guaicurú by land. They attacked them when they were divided and made such a killing and slaughter on them that very few survived and they were almost wholly despoiled of the captive Indians and booty they were taking.' The chastened bandeirantes saw this defeat as divine vengeance for killing a Jesuit. They therefore returned the church ornaments they had stolen – but not the Indians they had seized.

In the 1630s, during which the Jesuits were being evicted from their provinces of Guairá, Tape, Uruguay and Itatín, the Society fought back against the Paulistas. One group of Jesuits armed and trained their catechumens so successfully that they won at Mbororé. Meanwhile, other members of the Society mounted a mighty propaganda campaign. They had an excellent case, and they made the most of it. The Kings of both Spain and Portugal had always justified their American conquests by proclaiming that these colonies brought Christian civilisation to the natives – whether they wanted it or not. Both countries issued a torrent of legislation condemning illegal enslavement of Indians.

Of all the Brazilian tribes, the Guaraní responded to Christianity with most fervour and understanding. The Jesuits were the most determined and intelligent of the missionary orders. Their Paraguayan missions were the most successful attempt at conversion or acculturation of any

South American Indians. Amid all the hypocritical claptrap about the benefits of Christianity, these missions demonstrated that in the right circumstances something could be done. And yet it was against these model missions that the bandeirantes launched their armed raids, and led off thousands of loyal, peaceful, Christian Indians into illegal slavery.

The Jesuits had great influence in Spain and Portugal, and eloquent propagandists in men like Ruíz de Montoya, the 'Apostle of Guairá'. He bombarded the King with memorials about the Paulistas' iniquity, and his *Spiritual Conquest Made by the Missionaries of the Society of Jesus in the Provinces of Paraguay, Paraná, Uruguay and Tape* was a brilliant manifesto. It contained enough exaggeration and embellishment to arouse a reader's full sympathy and indignation, and yet remained essentially accurate. The Jesuits even had it translated into Guaraní to stimulate their native converts.*

Other authorities confirmed the Jesuits' outrage. Don Pedro Estevan Dávila, Governor of Buenos Aires, told the King that in Rio de Janeiro 'before my very eyes they were selling Indians brought to that city by the citizens of São Paulo, as if they were slaves and considered as such by Your Majesty. I made enquiries, and ascertained verbally that between 1628 and 1630 the citizens of São Paulo brought over 70,000 souls from the reductions of the Fathers of the Society of the [Guairá] district of this province of Paraguay. In doing this, those settlers of São Paulo practised such incredible cruelties and inhumanity that by their actions they ceased to be Christian Catholics.'

The Jesuits cleverly introduced a political element into their campaign against the bandeirantes. There was growing unrest among the Portuguese subjects of the King of Spain. Ruíz de Montoya warned the King that the Portuguese planned to rebel and seize much of the Indies for their country. This was why they were so determined to destroy the Spanish Jesuit reductions.*

King Philip IV issued a furious denunciation of the bandeirantes on 16 September 1639 and an edict on 31 March 1640. He accused the Paulistas of destroying, 'according to various authentic reports, over 300,000 souls including captives and dead. With this all those provinces, once so spacious and full of Indians, came to an end.' By 1650 the Jesuits had only twenty-two out of their original forty-eight missions in the provinces of Paraná, Guairá, Uruguay and Itatín. These contained only 40,000 souls, whereas the baptism books showed that 150,000 had been baptised in these provinces. 'Part of these were carried off by the Portuguese enemy, and part died of general plagues of smallpox and typhus and others that have occurred.'

The King sent instructions to his Brazilian governors to arrest Rapôso Tavares and other leading bandeirantes – but advised them to do it by trickery rather than force since these were such tough and powerful men. It was all too late. The Brazilian authorities made no move against the bandeirantes: they were more concerned to enlist their help against the Dutch invasions of north-eastern Brazil. The friction between Spain and Portugal was very real, and it was this that saved the bandeirantes. Portugal broke its subjection to Spain with the proclamation of the Duke of Bragança as King João IV in 1640. And when he was proclaimed King in Brazil on 3 April 1641 the second man to sign the act of acclamation at São Vicente was the great bandeirante António Rapôso Tavares.

The bandeirantes were thus able to continue their expeditions unmolested. They exploited the sixty years of Portuguese subjection to Spain to push Portuguese influence deep into the heart of South America. In their raids against uncontacted or mission Indians, and their later search for gold and silver, they crossed the Paraná and Paraguay, and ranged along the Guaporé, Mamoré and Uruguay. Thanks to them, and to the voyages of Pedro Teixeira and the ransom expeditions up the Amazon, Brazil now occupies half the continent and is one of the world's largest countries.

The town of São Paulo had little to show for the exertions of its citizens. It remained a rural frontier town, without the fine houses or sumptuous churches of the cities of north-eastern Brazil. The municipal authorities were concerned with such problems as cattle knocking over walls in the middle of the town. The bandeirantes had small houses in Sao Pãulo, but their wealth was lavished on fazendas – their estates in the surrounding countryside. It was to these that they took the hundreds of wretched slaves brought back by the bandeiras.

A proud Paulista called Pero Tacques de Almeida Paes Leme recorded the magnificence of the town's leading families. One of the most honoured was Amador Bueno, who 'had a great entourage and opulence. In his administration he dominated many hundreds of Indians. They had been converted from barbarous heathen of the sertão to our holy faith through the industry, valour and force of arms with which Amador Bueno conquered them in their kingdoms and homes. From the labour of these men, employed on broad plantations, every year he had abundant harvests of wheat, corn, beans and cotton' as well as great herds of pigs, cattle, horses and sheep.*

Bueno had various sons, all of them great slave-raiders. One son, Jerónimo, led a large bandeira out of São Paulo in 1644, but he and all his men were killed by Indians – presumably Guaicurú – near the

Paraguay. A descendant called Amador Bueno de Veiga was a leading citizen who held most of the town's elective offices. 'He was potent in archers, for he had numerous Indians in his administration and his fazenda was a populous camp.' And there was Manoel Preto who 'conquered such a mass of Indians that he came to count 999 Indian archers on his fazenda'.

In São Paulo the euphemism for a holding of slaves was an 'administration'. Paes Leme wrote nostalgically in the eighteenth century of the good old days when slaves 'were abundant: there were many who possessed five, six or seven hundred Indians under their administration. These were employed in agricultural labour on copious plantations of wheat, corn, beans, vegetables and cotton.' João do Prado 'came to São Paulo with his wife and established himself there with many Indians whom he had conquered in the sertão. In 1594 he entered the sertão, after making his will, attracted by the greater number of Indians that he wished to conquer that year.' João Pedroso de Moraes earned the nickname 'Terror-of-the-Indians' with his many long raids.

The more successful bandeirantes became chiefs of their clans of captive Indians and used them as private armies. The Indians responded readily to the leadership of the victorious colonists – they preferred marching into battle for their master to labouring in his plantations. Bartolomeo Fernandes de Faria, who 'disposed of a multitude of Carijó', used one of them to commit various murders: he was finally arrested when over eighty and died of disease in prison.* In 1652 two powerful families, the Pires and Camargos, starting feuding. They used their captive Indians to fight one another, and enlisted the help of 'other Paulistas potent in archers'. Such feudal lords led their own Indians on bandeiras, or lent them to the authorities to defend other parts of Brazil against Dutch invasions, pirates, runaway black slaves or independent Indian tribes.

The captive women were also at the disposal of their bandeirante masters. Ruíz de Montoya fulminated that 'with good-looking women captured in this and other towns they destroyed, whether married, single or heathen, the owner shuts them in a chamber with himself, like some billy-goat in a corral of she-goats!'

Some bandeirantes settled their captives in villages that later became towns. The three Fernandes brothers are each credited with founding a modern city in this way: André – the man so hated by the Guairá and Uruguay Jesuits – founded Parnaíba, Baltazar founded Sorocaba, and Domingos founded Itu. Such villages of 'descended' Indians were virtually owned by their administrator, the man who had 'conquered them in their kingdoms and homes'. The administrator controlled their labour and produce, and would bequeath them to his heirs as if they were legally owned slaves. The Marquis de Minas, a governor of Brazil in the late seventeenth century, wrote indignantly to the town council of São Paulo: 'My late father had a deed from the Chief Judge of your district stating that the aldeia of Maruí and its Indians belonged to him. I am now informed that Your Honours have, despite this, taken possession of that aldeia, which cost my great-grandfather so much trouble and personal expense . . . I should have hoped that Your Honours . . . would release to me what directly concerns me: for that aldeia is mine.'

There were also the King's aldeias administered by Portuguese Jesuits. There were four of these near São Paulo, the oldest dating from the days when Nóbrega founded the first mission on the plateau of Piratininga. A law of 1596 had entrusted the administration of aldeias to the Jesuits. It enjoined the Fathers to 'attempt by all good means to persuade the heathen to come and live and communicate with the settlers in places that the Governor will assign them. . . . They will declare to the heathen that they are free and will live in those settlements at liberty, and may own property as they do in the hills. . . .' But, although the Indians of the 'King's aldeias' were free men, they were also forced to work for the settlers at the very low wages fixed by law. The Jesuit Fathers controlled this labour exchange and earned the settlers' hatred by protecting their charges as much as possible. The settlers naturally assumed that the Jesuits were reluctant to hire out Indians because they were using them to enrich their own missions.

There was constant bickering between the Paulistas, the tough bandeirantes who plunged into the forests in search of Indians, and the Portuguese Jesuits trying to protect the nominally free Indians of the aldeias near São Paulo. In 1611 the town council complained that the Jesuits allowed no white man to set foot in their aldeias. The council wanted lay captains put in charge of the aldeias, so that these could supply the settlers with labourers. The following year there was a public meeting at which the settlers lamented their constant need of Indians to relieve their poverty. Each citizen required at least four workers, 'to plant their food to eat, and to go to the mines to extract gold for their support and to pay the royal fifth [tax]'. But when they obtained a licence from the Governor they found no Indians available or willing to work for them. Even when the Indians did go to work for them, they often left too soon, 'leaving the citizens in the mines with their food and persons lost and no one to mine for them. . . . Great damage resulted to the citizens . . . and the Indians made a mockery of them and laughed at them. . . . There should be orders that the heathen work for the citizens for hire and payment, to tend their mines and do their labour. This would result in tithes for God, fifths for the King, and profit for the citizens. It would give [the Indians] and their wives utility and the advantages of clothing themselves by their work. It would remove them from their continual idolatry and drunkenness, from which no service to God can result.' In the settlers' eyes, labour in the mines in return for two yards of cotton cloth a month was a better road to salvation than all the hours spent in mission churches.

With such pressure from the citizens and a constant toll from disease and demoralisation, the São Paulo aldeias rapidly declined. The town council appointed a lay captain in any aldeias not run by the Jesuits, and ordered 'those Indians to obey and respect him as their captain and obey his commands'. The primitive, nomadic Geromimi complained in 1618 'that they were vexed and molested by many white men of this town, who want to take them to their houses by force to work for them and also their sons and daughters against their will'. But the Governor's answer was to put the Geromimi in the care of a neighbouring fazendeiro and order them to obey him.

In an effort to fill the dwindling aldeias, one governor of São Paulo ruled in 1623 that anyone going inland 'to seek Indians' must give a fifth of his captives to the aldeias. Apart from legalising slaving bandeiras, this measure did not save the sad little reservations. Their lands were often very extensive and became too large for their shrinking populations. There was constant invasion of aldeia lands by squatters and settlers' cattle. In 1633 the town council claimed that 'the royal jurisdiction was in danger of being usurped by the Jesuits'. It sent various prominent citizens, including Rapôso Tavares, to expel the Jesuits from the aldeia of Maruí, which was not one of the four originally entrusted to them. These citizens were later excommunicated and deposed from the town council; but they went to Rio de Janeiro and easily obtained full pardon.

The Spanish Jesuits who went to Europe in 1639 to protest against the bandeirantes obtained a Bull from Pope Urban VIII. He reiterated Paul III's Bull of 1537, according to which any form of enslavement of Indians was prohibited on pain of excommunication, and all Indian slaves were to be freed. This Bull was specifically directed at Brazil and Paraguay. Its proclamation in Brazil caused uproar. The citizens of Rio de Janeiro rose and evicted the Jesuits from their college. At São Paulo various religious men tried to calm the hotheads. The Franciscans and Carmelites, women, children and students rallied to the Jesuits. But a meeting of representatives of the various towns was held at São Vicente, and it was decided to expel the Jesuits from the captaincy. The expulsion took place on 13 July 1640, and the aldeia Indians were left to the mercy of the settlers. There was an avalanche of paper – passionate protests for and against the Jesuits. A royal order of 3 October 1643 ordered the town council of São Paulo to restore the Jesuits. Another on 7 October 1647 gave a general pardon to those responsible for the expulsion. But the Jesuits did not return until 1653, and then only on condition that they allowed lay captains to help administer the aldeias.†

The trouble was that the Jesuit system of insulated, paternalistic missions was fine on remote frontiers, but unworkable when surrounded by colonists. The mission villages soon became lay parishes. Mission reservations were encircled by the private property of fazendeiros, and the Indians soon exhausted the game and fish on their land. Mission life was constantly disrupted by settlers' demands for Indian labour. Indians who left the missions were easily debauched with alcohol, and their women were prostituted for lengths of cloth. The Jesuits tried to protect their congregations (as legal minors, which they were in colonial law), but this proved impossible in close proximity with frontier civilisation.

Some Jesuits despaired, and wanted to abandon the thankless task of administering the aldeias. Francisco de Morais begged 'for the love of the holy wounds and precious blood of Our Lord Christ to remove us from these aldeias; for our presence in them serves only to affront and discredit the Society . . . [and leads to] the ignominies and vituperation we suffer'. Instead of working on the mission plantations, the Indians 'are in fact in the sugar mills getting drunk day and night and surrendering their wives and daughters to the masters and factors, as they themselves boast'.

The Portuguese Jesuits wrote to their king in 1646 asking either that he give effective orders that his laws concerning Indians be obeyed, or that he release them from administering the aldeias. The Conselho Ultramarino – the Overseas Council – discussed the issue in July 1647. Salvador de Sá testified to it about the appalling decline in the São Paulo aldeias during the few years since the Jesuits' expulsion. 'Now at a given time there were 1000 families in the village of Marueri, 700 in that of São Miguel, 300 Tupi in that of Pinheiros and more than 800 in that of Guarulhos when the Fathers left these places. When I returned to São Paulo some years later, I found only 120 families in Marueri, 80 in São Miguel, 20 in Pinheiros and 70 in Guarulhos.' The Council decided that the Jesuits must return: 'For if private persons were to continue administering them it would be the total ruin of the heathen, and they would all be lost and destroyed.'

But the aldeias of São Paulo's free Indians had declined beyond redemption. By the end of the seventeenth century they contained only a few hundred Indians. By 1675 they were in such decadence that the Portuguese Government ordered that every possible means be used to avoid their total ruin. A governor of southern Brazil wrote to the King in 1698 that the aldeias would soon disappear. The officials of the town council were depopulating them: they would go and remove men and women that they fancied, and would bequeath those to their heirs when they died. Some forced Indians to marry black slaves, so that the Indians would themselves become slaves. People won and lost Indians at games of chance. The Governor was trying to extract Indians from citizens' houses, to return them to the aldeias. But in the aldeia of Marueri, for instance, where there had once been almost a thousand families, there were now ten adult Indians and a few children. In 1698 the King tried naming one Isidro Tinoco as Captain-Major of the Indians of the São Paulo aldeias, since he was 'a person of talent, valour and aptitude'.

The Jesuits were expelled and returned, the royal aldeias steadily declined, but the bandeiras continued throughout the seventeenth century. They became less frequent only because there were no more Indians within easy reach of São Paulo – such Indians were already captive, or had fled or died out. By the middle of the century the Jesuit provinces of Guairá, Tape, Uruguay and Itatín had all been devastated and abandoned, but the Fathers had demonstrated that they could successfully defend their inner province of Paraguay. The bandeirantes therefore had to range farther from São Paulo.

In 1647 the fifty-year-old António Rapôso Tavares led his bandeira of sixty whites and a few Indians right across South America. This was the group that attacked the Itatín mission of Mboymboy and killed the Jesuit Alonso Arias. It was they who suffered terrible hunger and thirst in the Chaco, and were heavily attacked by the Paiaguá and Guaicurú. But Rapôso Tavares had been commissioned by the Portuguese authorities 'in particular to open a route to Peru'. His bandeirantes therefore pushed on across the terrible Chaco and the great swamps of Izozog and up into the Andes towards the fabulous silver-mines of Potosí. They explored some of the little-known jungle rivers near Santa Cruz de la Sierra. They had made the same amazing crossing of South America as Aleixo Garcia or the Tupinambá who fled from Pernambuco in the mid-sixteenth century. Rapôso Tavares' men then returned to the Atlantic by the same route as the Tupinambá: they descended the Madeira and Amazon, thus confirming that the Plate and Amazon basins link to enclose the 'Island of Brazil'. They were the first whites to journey around the perimeter. Their journey of some 7000 miles is known as 'the greatest bandeira of the greatest bandeirante'. The Jesuit António Vieira met them when they reached Belém do Pará at the mouth of the Amazon. He deplored their cruelty to Indians and their killing of a Spanish Jesuit: but he could not but marvel at their exploit – 'like fables told about the Argonauts, a truly great example of endurance and valour. . . . It was truly one of the most notable [voyages] ever made in the world up to now!' When Rapôso Tavares finally made his way back to São Paulo, he was so disfigured that his own family did not recognise him.

Although Vieira was right in describing this bandeira as one of the greatest explorations of all time, he was impressed by two things told by the bandeirantes: the density of the native populations along the Madeira, and the callous brutality of the explorers towards them. The bandeirantes could only describe the great numbers of natives on the Madeira 'by exclamations of wonder. Fifteen days after embarking on the river they began to see settlements and from then on there was not a day on which they did not see some, and they generally saw many every day. They saw cities in which [they counted] 300 huts . . . in each of which many families live. . . . They reckoned that [one city] contained 150,000 souls.' At one time they travelled for eight days through the territory of a tribe whose villages were almost contiguous along the river banks. The sudden appearance of the bedraggled Europeans caused the usual shock. 'The manner in which these Indians received the Portuguese was normally peaceful – but with signs of great wonder and amazement by the novelty of people whose appearance they had never seen.'

Some of the Madeira tribes took up arms to defend their villages. Vieira asked one of the expedition's leaders how he dealt with such tribes. 'He answered me with great calm and a clear conscience: "We gave this sort a close volley: some fell and others fled. We entered the village, took whatever we needed and placed it in our canoes; and if some of their [canoes] were better than ours we exchanged them and continued our voyage." This captain told me this as if he were telling of a very praiseworthy action. All these men speak like this about the shots they fired, the Indians who fled, those they caught, those who escaped, and those they killed. [It is] as if they were describing the sport of a hunting party and the lives of Indians mattered no more than those of boar or deer. All such killings and robbings have been tolerated in a kingdom as Catholic as Portugal for the past sixty years. . . . [The killers] continue as before without any enquiry or trial or punishment, not even mildly shunned by public disfavour: nothing but total public immunity.' Such was the climate of opinion in seventeenth-century Brazil. The bandeirantes today are honoured as pioneers, explorers and patriots; but their main purpose was the capture of Indians, and they were merciless manhunters.

FOURTEEN

The Dutch Wars

BY the seventeenth century the Atlantic seaboard of Brazil was firmly in Portuguese hands. The French had been expelled and all the great Tupi tribes defeated. The Indians were virtually gone, blown away like the eroded topsoil of the deforested north-east. There was none of the hundreds of populous villages with long-huts full of native families, no flotillas of Indian canoes paddling on the Atlantic, and no great pitched battles between Tupi warriors. Most of the Tupi were dead – killed in their thousands by imported diseases, slaughtered in battle, or worked to death in the plantations. Many had fled inland, like the eighty villages of Tupinambá who marched off simultaneously from Pernambuco. There are no population records for these Indians, but we can suppose that there was a sharp fall in the birth-rate: natives demoralised by cultural shock, with their family and tribal life shattered, expressed their despair by failing to procreate. Hordes of fresh tribes lured to the coast by missionaries or slavers had no chance of forming thriving communities there. They melted away as fast as snow falling on warm earth. The only Indians left near the coast were nomadic bands in a few areas of densely forested hills, such as Espírito Santo; a sprinkling of declining mission villages; and the Indian blood of half-castes, the offspring of white settlers and native women or of Indians and blacks in plantation slave-quarters.

With the Indians gone, the Brazilian coast was developing into a series of flourishing European colonies. Their prosperity was founded on

The fort of Ceará, captured by the Dutch in 1637.

sugar and to a lesser extent cotton, tobacco and hides; and the labour was from Africa. Black slaves had immunity to many diseases that annihilated American Indians. They possessed a moral resilience that enabled them to survive the horrors of the slave ships and the hard labour of the plantations. They held their own in conditions that cast Indians into despair. The result is that, although modern Brazil is a multi-racial nation, the mixture is predominantly between black and white. The Indian element, which numbered several millions when the first whites and blacks landed, has declined catastrophically, while the population of Brazil and the rest of the world has exploded.

The seventeenth-century colonists were building handsome towns at Bahia, Rio de Janeiro, Olinda and Recife, São Luís and many other places. All were ports, for everything depended on trade with Europe. Despite the new towns, a Frenchman described Brazil in 1610 as 'a rather crude and savage country, almost all covered in woods'.

One reason for the extraordinary success of the Portuguese empire – the attempt by a small nation to occupy so much of South America, Africa and Asia – was the mother country's refusal to become involved in European wars. Portugal managed to remain at peace with the rest of Europe throughout the period of its greatest expansion. The English were longstanding allies; France rarely supported its subjects in Brazil, and then only in areas where the Portuguese had failed to establish themselves; and the Dutch maintained a friendly trade. This advantageous neutrality ended in 1580 when Philip II of Spain became King of Portugal.

With Portugal controlled by Spain, Brazil became fair game for Dutch and English corsairs. Their various raids preoccupied colonial governors, but were of little concern to the Indians. Natives occasionally helped these 'pirates', trading with them as they would with any other strangers. More often they fought bravely alongside the colonists, or were enlisted to build fortifications.

In 1609 Spain and Holland made a twelve-year truce, and while it lasted the Portuguese expelled the French from Maranhão and conquered the Tupinambá and other tribes of the lower Amazon. But, when the truce ended in 1621, the Dutch created the Privileged Company of the West Indies, a colonial enterprise with private capital and government military and financial support. Its purpose was colonial conquest, and the coveted area was Brazil. A great fleet was organised, and on 10 May 1624 the Dutch captured the capital of Brazil, Salvador da Bahia, after a brief resistance. Spain's answer was to organise the largest expedition sent to the Americas in the seventeenth century: 12,000 men from the Spanish possessions in Spain, Portugal and Italy, carried in a fleet of 70 ships. Portuguese colonists in Brazil had repelled other Dutch attacks, and they helped this great European army recapture Bahia on 1 May 1625.

One group of Potiguar from the Copaoba hills seized on the Dutch capture of Bahia as an opportunity to rebel. They killed eighteen settlers and captured some of their children, including six girls. When Bahia was recaptured, the Portuguese immediately organised a 'just war' against these rebels. The Potiguar burned their aldeias and churches and retreated for hundreds of miles to seek sanctuary among the Tapuia of the Ceará hinterland. The punitive expedition, under Gregorio Lopes, included many Tobajara, traditional enemies of the Potiguar. It had a hard march into the sertão. At one stage it suffered three days without water. But it survived, discovered the Potiguar, and defeated them after a furious two-day battle. The Tapuia had never before seen white men in their territory, and readily agreed to surrender the Potiguar. Chiefs Cipóuna and Tiquarucu offered to bring all their people back in peace to Copaoba. Gregorio Lopes accepted, because his men were short of food. Hostages were given, and the settlers' children released. But the Portuguese commander 'did not keep this agreement with chief Tiquarucu, who was the most guilty, but ordered him cut to pieces with knives in the presence of all. Nor with Cipóuna . . . who brought all his people. . . . The Governor took none himself, but [ordered] . . . that they be distributed among the soldiers and settlers to serve them as punishment for the crime of rebellion. But many took refuge in the sanctuary of the doctrines of the fathers of the Society [of Jesus], where they were well received. . . .'

The Dutch returned five years later, this time against Pernambuco. A large force captured Olinda and fought its way into Recife in March 1630. The Portuguese colonists fought back with determination under Matias de Albuquerque, a descendant of the first donatory of Pernambuco. One strategic fort was defended by the scourge of the Maranhão Tupinambá, Bento Maciel Parente. There was confused fighting in the sugar mills and hamlets of Pernambuco, and the Dutch were contained inside its coastal cities. Their attempts to land in Paraíba and Rio Grande were repelled. But in 1633 the Dutch began to regain the initiative, with the conquest of Itamaracá island and Rio Grande, whose fort fell in December and whose town of Natal was renamed New Amsterdam. Paraíba held off Dutch attacks for a year, but was finally conquered in December 1634. Throughout these years Matias de Albuquerque and his lieutenants had maintained a defence of the Pernambuco interior, operating from the forts of Arraial do Bom Jesus ('Camp of Good Jesus') and Nazaré ('Nazareth'); but these redoubts

finally fell after repeated attacks and sieges in mid-1634. Many
Portuguese colonists accepted Dutch rule, but some retreated south to
continue the struggle from Alagôas.

This was a white man's war, between two European powers struggling
for possession of a rich colony. It is sometimes known as the Sugar War.
It was fought with guns and warships, and took place amid coastal sugar
plantations, forts and towns where there were few Indians left. Although
the outcome of the war was of little consequence to the Indians, the
tribes of the north-east were inevitably drawn into the fighting. Their
skills as warriors and woodsmen were valued by both sides. Soon after
the capture of Recife, a Dutch commander wrote home describing his
losses from intrepid Indian attacks on his convoys. 'I consider these
people to be a race of spirited and valiant soldiers, who lack nothing but
good command. They are absolutely *not* the "lambs" about which one
reads in histories of the West Indies – and I know this from experience
on various occasions!'

When they conquered the provinces of the north-east, the Dutch took
stock of the land they had seized. They sent back glowing reports of the
wealth and fertility of Pernambuco. But they were shocked by the
condition of the Indians. They learned how badly the native populations
were depleted. In Ceará, where there had once been many villages of
Potiguar capable of raising 8000 warriors, there were now only five
villages and a mere 105 warriors; in Rio Grande and Paraíba there were
ten native villages with a total population of only 3000; in Itamaracá
three villages with 2400 people; and in Pernambuco three villages also
with 2400. In these provinces the number of adult men, or warriors,
varied between a quarter and a third of the population. There were no
other native villages between Ceará and the São Francisco. In 800 miles
of the bulge of the Brazilian coast, the native population had sunk in a
century from many hundreds of thousands to under 9000.†

The Dutch were unaware of the hard fighting by the Potiguar, and
assumed that it had been easy for the Portuguese to conquer 'badly
armed or entirely unarmed Indians' and force them 'immediately to
submit to the yoke'. The newly arrived Dutch witnessed the wretched
condition of the free Potiguar in their few remaining villages. Johannes
de Laet wrote that 'the Portuguese consider them an inconstant people,
unfaithful and ungrateful. But one should not believe this. Each village
has its chief, but the Portuguese generally give them another Portuguese
[captain] to keep them more obedient. He hires them out to work for the
Portuguese. They are supposed to receive five varas [about six yards] of
coarse linen for twenty-five days' work. The captain used to receive one
tostão per month from the hirer for each Indian he hired out. But he was

rarely satisfied with this, and would also keep the poor Indians' linen. Because of this they were very incensed against the Portuguese and immediately passed over to our side. They want no more Portuguese captains.' Conditions were even worse on the Amazon. Gedeon Morris de Jonge reported in 1637 that the Amazon tribes would join anyone who defeated the Portuguese settlers there. 'The labour of these Indians – who are not slaves – is rewarded with a miserly payment; for . . . the Portuguese generally pay them no more than three varas of cloth or an axe, and often give them absolutely nothing.' And in a later letter Gedeon Morris exclaimed that 'those who are free are free in name only and are in fact slaves. For anyone forced to work for a month for three varas of cloth is virtually enslaved; and that is the standard wage here.'

These were first impressions. Before long, the initial enthusiasm and sympathy for the Indians began to turn sour in the face of their indifference to European ways. The industrious Dutch were dismayed by the Indians' unwillingness to work, and shocked by their weakness for alcohol. When a Dutch lieutenant captured the fort of Ceará in November 1637 he was greatly helped by the Tupi of Chief Diogo Algodão. They guided him ashore and helped storm the fort. But when it was taken 'the Indians wanted to kill all [the defenders], and it was not easy to prevent them doing so'. The lieutenant soon became disillusioned by his native allies. 'The men have two or three wives and do nothing but eat and drink. Throughout the year they consume every sort of drink that can make them drunk: namely wine made from cashews and also from sweet potatoes and corn. . . . I cannot obtain the slightest work or help from these Indians without payment. They say that they did absolutely nothing for the Portuguese and it is even less likely that they will do anything for us – even though the land belongs to them.' Adriaan van der Drussen described how the Indians lived in their villages, separated from the Portuguese settlers. Most wore nothing apart from loin-cloths, and they still lived together in palm-thatch houses. 'They stay there day and night, lying in their hammocks. . . . They show no interest in accumulating riches or other goods. They therefore do not work for themselves or for others in order to earn money – except to get something to drink or to acquire a little cloth to make shifts for their women. . . . Money would mean nothing to them, were it not possible to buy alcohol and Spanish wine with it. . . . They go to work as if forced to, and with ill-will. But with alcohol one can get anything out of them.'

The Dutch were determined to be on good terms with the Indians, even if these were so disappointingly apathetic about Dutch civilisation.

The charter of the West Indies Company empowered it to 'contract treaties with native princes and peoples'.

Various important young Indians were taken to Holland from the north-east in 1625. They were to be indoctrinated at the Company's expense, in anticipation of its conquest of Pernambuco. When the conquest took place, these Indians already spoke Dutch and were converted to Calvinism. They were sent back and put to work as interpreters and as witnesses of the power and splendour of Holland. The most famous of them was Pieter Poti, Potiguar chief of the village of Masurepe in Paraíba. He led a contingent of his warriors into battle for the Dutch, and wrote eloquent letters to persuade other chiefs to change sides.* Once Pernambuco was occupied, the Dutch tried sending twenty-five Indian boys to study in Holland, and a similar number of Dutch orphans to Brazil to learn Indian languages. It was an exact repeat of Nóbrega's experiment with Portuguese orphans in the 1550s – and was equally unsuccessful. When the Irish adventurer Bernard O'Brien reached Holland in 1636 after escaping from captivity on the Amazon, he found many Brazilian Indians in Amsterdam, with their own 'synagogue'. They gave him messages to take back to their relatives in Brazil.

The best thing done by the Dutch for the Brazilian Indians was the sending of Count Johan Maurits of Nassau to be governor-general of the provinces they had conquered. Johan Maurits was a 33-year-old German noble, cousin of the Statholder of the Low Countries. He reached Recife in January 1637 and governed the colony for seven years with great brilliance. A veteran of the Thirty Years War, Johan Maurits successfully pursued the invasion of the Portuguese colonies: southwards to the São Francisco river with the capture of Alagôas in 1637, and northwards into Ceará later that year. He failed to capture Bahia, when its citizens repulsed a powerful Dutch expedition in May 1638; but his commanders warded off Portuguese–Spanish attempts to drive the Dutch from Pernambuco. The political climate changed abruptly when Portugal gained its independence from Spain in 1640. Portugal and Holland now had a common enemy in Spain, and they decided on a ten-year truce. Johan Maurits took rather unfair advantage of this truce: while it was being ratified in 1641 he sent forces to occupy Sergipe south of the São Francisco, and fleets to seize São Luís do Maranhão from the aged Bento Maciel Parente, as well as the Portuguese slave base of Luanda in Angola.

Johan Maurits was an intelligent man, enthusiastic about the tropical country he governed. He embellished Recife and Olinda with handsome buildings, and imported savants to study Brazil: the physician Willem

Piso, the botanist and anthropologist Georg Marcgraf, and the painters Frans Post, Albert Eckhout and Zacharias Wagener. These Dutch artists produced the first fine paintings of Brazil, and the most handsome portraits ever done of its Indians. Eckhout painted Indians as dignified individuals rather than exotic curiosities – although he showed one Tapuia woman calmly holding the arm and hand of a victim (Plate 15). Every detail of the Indians' appearance and of the Brazilian scenery was correct. And yet the Dutch painters somehow could not help giving their native models the lumpy figures of well-fed Hollanders: their Indians look like Rubens or Rembrandt subjects surprised in a tropical setting.†

Johan Maurits was also a liberal administrator. He was tolerant towards minorities that he felt could help his administration – the Jews in particular, and native Indians. Although he was keen to introduce Calvinism to the Dutch colony, and expelled the various orders of Catholic friars, he was reasonably tolerant of the settlers' Catholic religion. He arranged a meeting of the municipal officials of the Portuguese towns, at Recife in 1640, in the hope of enlisting their co-operation with Dutch rule. This assembly has sometimes been hailed as the first manifestation of democracy in Brazil – but, although the delegates were allowed to voice their many grievances, nothing was done to remedy them. There was nothing liberal about these settlers' attitudes. The Paraíba delegates, for instance, complained that black slaves were in short supply and asked that Indians be made to work to cut their sugar harvest. They also demanded the removal of Chief Pieter Poti, for 'he is bad and dangerous . . . and it is unwise for such a person to be vested with command'.

For all their liberal intentions, the Dutch ended by administering the Indians in much the same way as the Portuguese. They left them in villages under their own chiefs. But they also saddled each village with a Dutch commandeur 'who rules them and their chiefs. His main task is to animate them to work, and to direct them in improving their plantations. He grants permission for them to work for owners of sugar mills, and ensures that they are not victims of deceit and that their work is paid. They are employed for periods of twenty days at a time, for which they receive $8\frac{1}{2}$ varas of cloth. Once this period is over it is very difficult to make them continue in the work. . . . Since there are now few negroes in this country, the natives are more sought after for work than before. They are well aware of this and refuse to accept work unless paid in advance. If they then get an opportunity they run off, and the master loses his cloth.' Each village also had a Protestant minister for religious instruction, and a Consoler of the Sick, who travelled from village to village. Many of the commandeurs were unqualified men intent on enriching themselves at Indian expense. This was a problem repeated throughout Brazilian history: it was and is almost impossible to find disinterested laymen for the thankless job of administering native villages.

Gedeon Morris de Jonge was an exception – a man who genuinely liked the Indians and did his utmost for them. He wrote to his superiors in Recife: 'I am obliged in conscience to reveal the truth. The origin of all the trouble is simply diabolical greed for temporary riches. Because of greed, the poor Indians were exploited, and men and women were constrained to work for the Portuguese without due remuneration. However, instead of receiving relief from us, they have been subjected to even greater captivity' in the northern conquest of Maranhão.†

Johan Maurits prided himself on his good relations with the Indians. He enjoyed their exotic side, but respected their culture and treated them as equals. He was delighted when they called him their brother, and commissioned a life-size portrait of himself surrounded by Indians. He therefore dismissed some of the worst commandeurs. He even had some tried for abusing the Indians in their care – although, as was inevitable in all colonial régimes and throughout Brazilian history, none was convicted. Johan Maurits decided to appoint a sympathetic protector to be in charge of all the villages in the colony. The protector received a salary of 200 florins a month, and his job was to visit the villages, register their inhabitants, see to their welfare, and in particular to stop any abuse. The first protector was Willem Doncker, who was married to an Indian woman. His successor was Johan Listry, a fine man who administered the villages for many years. The Indians loved him and were overjoyed when, after being captured briefly in 1645, he returned to resume his functions.

When Johan Maurits was recalled in May 1644, he rode to the shore surrounded by burghers and settlers lamenting his departure. But when he reached the sea a crowd of Indians pushed the others aside and carried him shoulder-high through the surf to his boat. Hundreds of them wanted to embark, but he took only six Tapuia sent by their chief to beg him to stay. Back in The Hague, Johan Maurits had his Indians do a war-dance at a party in the Mauritshuis. The sight of stark naked, painted Indians 'caused much amusement and giggling among all sorts of people. . . . But the Dominies, who had come to have a look with their wives, did not find this at all nice.'

Johan Maurits was serious in his concern for the Indians. When he wrote an official report about his years as governor of Dutch Brazil, he added a supplement begging for gentle and just treatment of the Indians. 'The quiet and preservation of the colony of Brazil depends in part on the friendship of the Indians. With this in mind they should be permitted to enjoy their natural freedom. . . . Orders should be issued that they are not outraged by their commandeurs, hired out for money or forced to work in sugar mills against their will. Each [Indian] should, on the contrary, be allowed to live in the way he understands, and to work where he wishes like men of our nation.'

When the Dutch attempted religious instruction, they instinctively followed the Jesuit system. A zealous missionary called David van Doorenslaer set off to preach in the villages, and he was soon followed by others. He taught prayers and hymns, and reported satisfactory progress. His reports became more optimistic. He concentrated on the new village called Mauricia in Paraíba and tried to turn it into a virtual seminary to train native priests. Doorenslaer appeared before the Supreme Council in Recife in 1639 and obtained exemption for his Indians from work in sugar mills or military service. Next year he reported that 'the boys have progressed very regularly in instruction. Some have even made such progress, thanks to daily instruction, that they could have received communion had it not been for the disturbances in the country.'

The Dutch – like the Jesuits – imagined that the way to destroy native cultures and impose Christianity was by indoctrinating the children. In 1636 the Council of Pernambuco reasoned that 'few results are to be hoped for from the adults, since they are stupid and uninterested and are scarcely religious'. The Council proposed a system of compulsory boarding schools in each Indian village. The teachers would be elderly couples sent out from Holland, preferably with children of their own. Classes would be in Dutch or Tupi, but never in Portuguese. The object would be to teach children to read and write, recite Dutch prayers and hymns and learn the Dutch reformed catechism. All children would have to live in these institutions, emerging only to attend church on Sundays and visited once a week by their parents. It was a system strikingly similar to that imposed in the twentieth century by the Italian Salesian missionaries in north-western Amazonas. But it never worked in Dutch Pernambuco. Indian parents absolutely refused to be parted from their children. They had little wish for their offspring to learn an alien culture, religion and language, instead of the skills and lore of their own tribe.

When Doorenslaer and other missionaries faced the failure of their campaign of conversion, they tried to concentrate on the bright Indian children. 'Separated from the adults in schools, these [children] might together study our language, the exercise of arms, and the fundamentals of Christianity. Then, with time, they could accompany us – ignorant since childhood of any form of paganism.' There was a plan to turn a Franciscan convent in Recife into a college for Indian boys. In 1643 the Council ordered lists to be prepared of Indian children who could be brought down for education in Recife – with parental consent. This may have been one reason for an Indian revolt in Ceará, and massacre of the Dutch there.

The Indians were an important factor in the struggles between Dutch and Portuguese. Political expediency won them a measure of self-determination. The Supreme Council wrote back to Holland in 1644 that it was resigned to acquiescing in stubborn native conservatism. The Indians 'generally have no purpose or desire other than to live in liberty and not in servitude. This means that they want an idle and indolent life, consuming any surplus from their plantations and labour in alcohol and not being punished for this. Whichever side gives them most licence in this respect can make them its allies. They have little inclination for their children to be removed and sent to school . . . to be taught Christian religion, useful arts and manual trades. If we wish to create no aversion to our state it is best to leave them as they desire. We can order preachers and nurses in the villages to attempt as far as possible to instruct them in religion and civil life.'

A few weeks later the Supreme Council wrote of the failure of the Indians who had been sent to Holland for special instruction. Having seen what the two societies had to offer, they had evidently chosen to revert to their own culture. The Supreme Council admitted that, 'in truth, we believe that Pieter Poti and António Paraupaba, whose education in Holland cost the Company so much, are more perverse and savage in their way of life than the other Brazilians [Tupi]'. The following year there was an appeal for teachers from Holland – preferably sober people, since the Indians were so prone to alcohol. 'As for the separation of the young from their parents, to educate them from the outset in our language and customs, it is no longer attempted. For we understood that this was contrary to the wishes of the parents.'

Although their religious and educational methods imitated the early Jesuits, the Dutch authorities were generally more sympathetic to the Indians than the Portuguese had been. During the years of Dutch rule the Indians were more highly respected and more free than in any part of Portuguese Brazil. This was partly because there was a war, one in which the Indians had a military value. It was also thanks to Dutch humanism and liberal attitudes. The Dutch had not been in Brazil long enough for their good intentions to evaporate completely in the tropical heat – although when they conquered Maranhão it was sufficiently remote from Recife for the settlers to behave more harshly to the Indians.

Soon after the Dutch reached Maranhão there was a terrible epidemic of smallpox. This started in Paraíba and Itamaracá and spread up the coast to Rio Grande and Ceará. 'The disease of smallpox . . . raged so violently among the Indians that entire aldeias were almost totally extinguished. The survivors retreated into the forests since they no longer dared to remain in their homes.' When the ship *Amsterdam* stopped at the aldeia of Camocim between Maranhão and Ceará it found no single healthy man to help load wood. Thus, when the Dutch invaded Maranhão, they 'brought not only war but also plague. For they brought with them Indians with smallpox which is the plague of that land. They thus killed the majority of the best people in our Indian aldeias, and almost all the settlers' slaves' – an estimated 3000 free and slave Indians in Maranhão alone.

This epidemic led to an acute labour shortage. The Indians were as usual most reluctant to work for the settlers. The supply of slaves had dwindled because of the war: the African slave trade was disrupted, and settlers under Dutch rule could not obtain Indian slaves from the Amazon and Pará. Gedeon Morris de Jonge, who protested about the iniquities of forcing 'free' Indians to work for lengths of coarse cloth, wanted to start salt pans in Maranhão. He became so desperate for labour that he suggested reviving barter for slaves among the Amazon tribes. But Gedeon Morris's letters were generally full of details about illegal enslaving of Indians in Maranhão. The tribes from Marajó island had been enslaved for helping Dutch colonists in the Amazon – but were kept as slaves when the Dutch took Maranhão. Dutch commandeurs took their free Indians off to be sold in the West Indies and, 'instead of finding relief from us Dutch, the Indians are subjected to greater captivity'.

The result of all this was that Indians saw no advantage in a switch to Dutch rule. Many therefore joined a revolt of Portuguese settlers to expel the Dutch from Maranhão. Seeing no difference between the two colonial powers, they supported the side that seemed to be winning. Chief António da Costa Marapirão of the Maranhão Tobajara allied his tribe to the settlers. The Portuguese in Pará also sent help, and in February 1644 they finally drove the Dutch out of São Luís. The Dutch escaped to Ceará, but many were massacred when the Indians of that colony also turned against them. The Dutch authorities sadly concluded: 'We can only infer that the alienation and enmity of the Indians of Ceará and the adjacent coasts against our nation originated in the ill-treatment given to them, above all because they were not

properly paid for their work in the salt flats of Marituba and the loading
of ships at the salt works and other places, even though we occasionally
sent cloth and other merchandise for that purpose.'

Alarmed by the Indian revolt against them in Maranhão and Ceará,
the Dutch decided to treat the Indians better. They demonstrated their
good intentions in April 1645 with an event unique in Brazilian history –
a democratic assembly of representatives of all available Indian
peoples.

The Indian assembly took place in the aldeia of Tapisserica in Goiana.
It was attended by representatives of the twenty aldeias of Indians in all
the provinces under Dutch control. Each sent its chief, deputy chief,
lieutenant, ensign, judge and six or seven adjuncts or councillors. The
meeting was polite and humble enough. It was officially observed by two
Dutch officials, and its product was a series of uncontroversial proposals
that Johan Listry was to present to the Supreme Council. It respectfully
requested that Dutch pastors and schoolteachers be sent to the villages,
and it arranged for certain aldeias to merge. But it was an impressive
show of Indian unity. The assembly left no doubt about the Indians'
determination to be free. The Acts it resolved begin: 'Before all else we
exhibit the Provision that was sent us by the Assembly of the XIX in
Holland, dated Amsterdam, 24 November 1644, referring to the liberty
conceded to us, as to all other inhabitants of Brazil. Item 1: Your
Excellencies should deign to put this law into effect. Liberty should
immediately be conceded to any of our race who might possibly still be
kept as a slave.' The assembly also requested that Indian affairs in the
three Dutch provinces be administered by native councils – and went
ahead with the election of councillors and governors: Domingos
Fernandes Carapeba for Goiana, António Paraupaba for Rio Grande,
and Pieter Poti for Paraíba. Two of these were men whom the Supreme
Council in Recife had so recently described as 'perverse and savage in
their way of life' and whom the settlers condemned as 'bad and
dangerous' and unsuitable for any command.

It was in the fighting between Portuguese and Dutch that the Indians
came into their own. Most initially flocked to the Dutch as the lesser of
two evils, and the only power capable of expelling the Portuguese. But
one Potiguar chief remained stubbornly loyal to the Portuguese. He was
António Poti, and because poti means 'shrimp', he was called by the
Portuguese word for shrimp – António Camarão. His military record
was outstanding: he and his men became expert in all aspects of
seventeenth-century warfare. Camarão himself rose very high in
European esteem, higher than any other pure Brazilian Indian has ever
done. He is the only Indian ever to be the subject of a biography.

When the Dutch first invaded, Camarão brought a force of his warriors and offered to join Matias de Albuquerque. His bowmen were skilful and courageous. In the fierce skirmishes of the first years of fighting, they caused much damage to the Dutch, making full use of their skills as woodsmen and their knowledge of the country. Camarão mounted deadly ambushes, and used 'many stratagems of war'. Although Camarão had relatively few men – only 170 warriors, according to Johannes de Laet, but 'all good musketeers' – he rapidly gained the respect of his friends and enemies. In May 1633 King Philip rewarded his successful commander with a habit of the Order of Christ, a pension of 40,000 reis, and the patent of Commander-in-Chief of the Potiguar Indians. The citation said that all Indians from Pernambuco to Ceará respected Camarão, 'and he has served since the beginning of the war in the most dangerous engagements and near the enemy, fighting on all occasions with much valour; and he is a good Christian'. Camarão adopted the King's name, and became known as Dom António Filipe Camarão.

Later in 1633 a Dutch attack on the island of Itamaracá was beaten off with heavy losses, largely thanks to Camarão. His Indians swam out and attacked the Dutch ships.* By 1635 he was in command not only of 600 Indians, but also of many Europeans. 'Marching through the sertão they went to Goiana and attacked some Indian villages. They razed these and killed any Indian rebels who fell into their hands. Our Indians, many of whom were good musketeers, killed them as if they were their mortal enemies.' They also harassed the Dutch, using classic guerrilla tactics to make a monkey of the veteran Polish commander Crestofle d'Artischau Arciszewsky. 'Camarão always fought with such energy, spirit, valour and military cunning that Artichofsky [sic] . . . was impressed and said that one Indian, namely Camarão, was teaching him a lot and that he could not come to grips with him. At times he attacked from one direction and then from another, then returned to strike again from the first. He mounted many ambushes, exhausting and dis-quieting the Flemings. In one ambush he killed forty-five of them. He took some wagons and used them as a parapet for his musketeers: they caused much damage to the enemy from the top of them.' The bemused Arciszewsky, a veteran of many European wars and commander of 800 men, 'declared that one single Indian had the power to make him retreat on many occasions'.

Camarão then retreated through the forests, rescuing 1600 Portuguese settlers and their families. He led this great column of refugees on a harrowing 150-mile exodus through the Pernambuco interior, in a great arc around the Dutch possessions. They finally reached safety in the walled city of Pôrto Calvo in southern Pernambuco, amid frenetic celebrations.

In 1637 Camarão took the field again with all his Indians, and even 'his wife Dona Clara, riding a horse and with a lance in her hand'. He was one of the Portuguese commanders in a fine retreat south to Sergipe. When the truce of 1641 was negotiated between the two colonial powers, Camarão was left to garrison the interior of Sergipe with his Indians – apparently unpaid, for they were 'to enjoy the fruits of the land and the wild cattle'.

Other groups of Indians fought with the Portuguese at the outset of the war. Some were led by Martím Soares Moreno, the man who became such a close friend and compadre of Chief Jacaúna of the Ceará Potiguar. Martím Soares had returned to Ceará in 1621 after many adventures during the expulsion of the French from Maranhão and capture by French corsairs. He started to found a colony in Ceará, building a large fort 'with the friendship and faith of Jacaúna, whom he persuaded to come and settle with his village half a league from the fort'. He and his Indian friends repulsed Dutch attempts to land in Ceará in 1624 and 1625, and during these years many Potiguar flocked to his captaincy to escape persecution farther south.

When the Dutch took Pernambuco, Martím Soares Moreno called on his Indians to help. He boasted to the King that Chief Algodão 'answered resolutely that both he and his people, and some of the other tribes, would follow me wherever I wished to go'. He soon marched south with the Indians who loved him so dearly. He took part in an attempt to recapture Recife. His men charged a fort at the edge of the city, cut the throats of twelve Dutchmen, captured the sergeant in command, and put the other defenders to flight. The Dutch were terrified by the sight of the Potiguar, 'whom they consider as savages, coming so agilely and fearlessly with ferocious appearance, naked, firing immense arrows, these horrible barbarians with no tapir-hide [shields] other than their own skins'. Martím Soares Moreno continued to fight the Dutch for many years, at the Arraial do Bom Jesus, in attacks on Recife and in campaigns alongside António Camarão on the southern front. He finally relinquished his command in 1648, aged sixty-two and exhausted by incessant adventures, and retired to Portugal. The Dutch intervention gave him no chance to develop his friendship with the Indians of Ceará. He might otherwise have produced a model colony for that century.

The Potiguar of Camarão and other chiefs were already being converted and governed by the Jesuits. The missionary Father who was in charge of the Rio Grande aldeias was called Manoel de Moraes. He

13, 14 Much of the fighting in north-east Brazil was done by mixed-blood mamelucos armed with native or European weapons.

15 A Tapuia woman holding a human hand with a leg in her basket – although her tribe did not in fact eat human flesh. Paintings by Albert Eckhout, c. 1640.

16-17 Sugar was the richest export of sixteenth-century Brazil. Water-wheels and oxen powered a colonial sugar mill but Chavante Indian boys (*left*) still use traditional methods to produce brown sugar on a modern mission.

18 (*below*) A Franciscan missionary supervising the work of his Indians.

19 Firearms against bows and arrows: a battle between bandeirantes and Botocudo Indians. The Paulistas' padded armour protects them from Indian arrows. The fallen Botocudo wears wooden discs in his ear lobes and lower lip.

20 Nothing could resist a charge by Guaicuru, the finest horsemen in South America.

21 Pero Álvares Cabral.

22 António Vieira.

23 Sebastião José de Carvalho e
Mello, Marquis of Pombal.

24 Johan Maurits, Prince of
Nassau.

25 Canela (or Eastern Timbira), a Gê-speaking tribe from Maranhão. (*Left*) a couple seated on the log carried in log-racing. Both sexes have the same hair style, identical with that of Jandui's tribe in the seventeenth century. (*Right*) Canela chief: Jandui must have looked like this old man. (*Below*)two teams of warriors compete in the log race, just as they did when first contacted in the seventeenth century.

26 Gê-speaking Txukarramae
warriors. (*Left*) smoking a pipe and
(*right*) with a Macaw feather at the
nape of the neck. Jarina river,
middle Xingu, Pará.

27 The most aristocratic Brazilian
tribe: Guaicura (Kadiweu),
Bodoquena hills, Mato Grosso.

28 Girl holding a young peccary. Northern Caiapó (Gorotire), Pará.

29 Nambikuara family, Rondônia.

30 (*above left*) A Borôro in full regalia, with feathers in his septum and a mother-of-pearl labret in his lower lip. Mato Grosso.

31 The Carib-speaking Tirió is the tribe that may have inspired the Amazon legend. (*Above right*) Mother and child with facial decoration (*Left*) Tirió warrior. Tumucumaque hills, northern Pará, on the Brazil-Surinam border.

was a good-looking man, thin and dark, with some native blood, and he spoke fluent Tupi. His Jesuit superiors sent him into battle against the Protestants. 'They ordered him to take part in that war because he had much knowledge of the heathen, and [because] these readily obeyed his orders.' Moraes and his Indians fought hard, for six months in Itamaracá and two years in Paraíba. He was finally captured by the Dutch after a stiff fight, near the Rio Grande, in January 1635.

After his capture Moraes amazed the Dutch by offering to serve them. They were at first suspicious of this renegade Jesuit, but soon reported triumphantly that 1600 Rio Grande Indians of all ages had voluntarily passed to their side under the command of Moraes.* The Portuguese were furious: 'Moraes became an apostate and left our Holy Faith and became a public Calvinist, let his beard grow and changed his dress, assembled his Indians and made them join the enemy's side against us. . . .' He went to Holland, wore a sword and civilian clothes, and married a rich Dutch widow. He had children by her, and when she died he married another Dutch woman. The Irishman Bernard O'Brien met Moraes in Amsterdam – the former Jesuit arranged for O'Brien to be pardoned from a death sentence, in the hope that he would lead a Dutch colonisation of the lower Amazon. Moraes tried hard to make O'Brien change religion: 'he molested him to become a heretic and to marry a heretic woman, the daughter of a councillor of the city of Amsterdam'.

Manoel de Moraes returned to Brazil to organise the Indians serving the Dutch. He was captured in December 1643 by Martím Soares Moreno – or, as he himself claimed, he ran away from the Dutch in the forests forty miles from Recife and tried to join the Portuguese settlers. He was shipped off to face the Inquisition in Lisbon. He mounted an eloquent defence. There was an enquiry on his behalf, with Camarão as a leading witness, to stress how hard he had fought the early campaigns and at the time of his capture. Moraes confessed his errors and repented, and his life was spared when most turncoats were executed – although he was excommunicated, defrocked and sentenced to life imprisonment.†

The Dutch thus had many Potiguar and other Tupi, led by Pieter Poti and António Paraupaba or brought to them by the defection of Manoel de Moraes. But the most terrifying of the Dutch native auxiliaries were Tapuia. Tapuia, as has been explained (p. 24), was the Tupi word for tribes speaking other languages: it referred to the tribes of the interior, mostly Gê-speaking, or to those driven inland with the Tupi occupation of the Atlantic seaboard.

A Tapuia chief, Nhandui or Jandui of the Tararyu tribe of the Rio Grande–Ceará hinterland, sent envoys to the Dutch authorities in 1631. Pieter Poti introduced Jandui's envoys to the Dutch, and wrote strongly recommending an alliance with this fierce tribe. Jandui was alarmed by the colonisation of Ceará by Martím Soares Moreno and his Potiguar: he wanted Dutch help to capture Martím Soares' fort. The Dutch were naturally enthusiastic. Embassies were exchanged. Three hundred Tapuia warriors helped the Dutch take Rio Grande; and in March 1634 Chief Jandui himself arrived at the fort there with 1500 of his people, including women and children.†

The trouble with the Tapuia was their inability to distinguish between Portuguese troops and settlers. They could not understand why ordinary Portuguese settlers, members of the enemy tribe, were allowed to continue farming unmolested by the Dutch conquerors. Johannes de Laet wrote that it was dangerous to leave the Tapuia idle, for they wanted to attack any and all Portuguese 'for pillage, which is their principal aim'.

The Tapuia were very tough, muscular and exceptionally fit. They ran as fast as horses, and hunted across their native savannahs by chasing game and clubbing it to death. They could not resist such sport among the settlers' herds of cattle. On one fazenda they killed 200 steers and threw them into a gulley.* They were equally ruthless in hunting down fugitives. When Camarão led off the refugees from Goiana, a Dutch commander called Ipo Eysens led a force of Potiguar and Tapuia to take reprisals on any who had collaborated with Camarão. Settlers were tortured to reveal hidden treasure or fugitive Portuguese troops. Diogo Lopes de Santiago gave grisly descriptions of these horrors. As a settler himself, his greatest fury was against the Indians, who were encouraged to kill Portuguese settlers in full view of the Dutch. The stories were possibly exaggerated, products of war propaganda and the irrational hatred and fear of Indians typical of all frontiersmen. Victims were handed over to the Indians, 'who cut them open from behind while alive with small axes that the Dutch gave them for this purpose'. It was also claimed that Indians had violated European girls and women, which was not typical Indian behaviour, but had a highly inflammatory emotional effect on white readers. The Dutch admitted the barbarity. Herckman wrote that 'after a victory they are very inclined to kill indiscriminately', and the naturalist Georg Marcgraf cautioned that 'it is not convenient to use the help of these Indians except in extreme cases: for they are so inhuman that they kill animals and men and cause great devastation. Besides, our men would never have resorted to them had not the Portuguese also sent savages against us!'

The Dutch employed a German called Jacob Rabe to cement their friendship with the Tapuia. He was extremely successful. He went to them with masses of presents and an open mind; and was soon accepted as a member of the tribe and one of its principal captains. He married a Tapuia woman and, when not with the tribe, used to live with her at Fort Keulen in Rio Grande. Jandui loved him. Years later, when another Dutchman called Roulox Baro visited him, Jandui recalled the good times with Rabe: 'In the past I used to receive from your people lovely trumpets, big halberds, fine mirrors, lovely goblets and beautiful, well-made cups. I keep them in my cupboard to show other Tapuia who come to visit me!' 'When Jacob Rabe was alive he used to take good care of his Tapuia, and descended with them to the Captaincy of Rio Grande. He would say to some [settler] or other: "Give me a beast for my men, or else I will kill one myself." That Jacob had power over his men . . . and made himself feared by the settlers!'

Thanks to Rabe and other observers, the Dutch were able to give a good description of the Tapuia. The main features of their society make it clear that they belonged to the Gê-speaking peoples, a mass of tribes occupying the plateau of central Brazil, from the state of Maranhão in the north to Paraná and Santa Catarina in the south, and from the hinterland of Rio Grande do Norte in the east to central Mato Grosso and Pará in the west.†

Jandui's Tapuia were semi-nomadic hunter-gatherers, great runners, and people for whom roots, wild honey and fieldmice were an important supplement to the usual peccary, deer and other game. Their extraordinary fitness and running ability were demonstrated in frequent log-races. The two halves of the tribe raced against one another, with the men running in relays and carrying a mighty log of buriti palm on their shoulders. This same race is still run by many Gê-speaking tribes: I have seen it done by the Canela in the interior of Maranhão, by the Chavante 900 miles to the south-west of them in Mato Grosso, and by the Krahô in northern Goiás. The log is a couple of feet in diameter and four or five feet long, and very heavy. One runner rolls it off his shoulder on to another man's while they run, and the two packs of runners come pounding round the village in a cloud of dust. When Roulox Baro visited Jandui in 1647 his Tapuia frequently did the log-race. They even chased rats while carrying the logs, and the aged Jandui – whom Baro reckoned to be over a hundred – joined in. On his return Jandui said to Baro: '"What do you say, my son? Doesn't this sport strike you as agreeable?" I answered that it did, and that I was delighted to see him so robust and hearty. He laughed, and then asked why I had not brought him any tobacco. Didn't I know that the tobacco he had planted had been ruined by rain, together with a good part of his corn?' (Plate 25*b, c.*)

Tobacco played an important role in Tapuia ritual. At the marriage ceremony the couple's bodies were covered in gum and a mantle of leaves, and the shaman puffed smoke over them. When, in the darkness of night, the men of the tribe communed with the devil, Houcha, they presented him 'with a big pipe made of a coconut full of tobacco. The young men remained standing . . . and the devil blew the tobacco smoke over them as a blessing. This done, each withdrew except for the most aged, who asked Houcha how they would perform in this war.' When the Tapuia helped the Dutch take Rio Grande, 'various Dutch officers saw and witnessed that they summoned into their presence the Devil, in the guise of a Tapuia, but with only one leg and speaking in a very fine voice like a woman's. He could not be recognised by them. When the spirit disappeared and vanished before their eyes, the women began to weep and scream, which they apparently did to honour him.' The tribe's shamans also used hallucinogens: they dried corpampa seeds, skinned them and drank them mixed with water. After drinking this they immediately began to run about and shout like madmen.

The Tapuia's dance 'is done by singing with a great cry about all that their predecessors and fathers did in time of war, and how many Portuguese they killed and what they suffered from them. Each song thus serves as a memoir, just like our histories.'

Physically, the Tapuia described by the Dutch looked identical to modern Gê-speaking tribes such as the Canela or Krahô. Their skin colour was a slightly yellowish tan. The women were attractive, faithful wives, and noticeably shorter than their men. Both sexes had their hair cut in a curious way: Elias Herckman described it as long behind, but cut level across the front and over the ears, so that it looked like a bonnet (Plate 25b).

When Portugal regained its independence from Spain, Johan Maurits of Nassau staged days of celebrations at Recife, in April 1641. There were horse races, tournaments, jousting, and many parties at which the settlers were shocked to see the most beautiful ladies of Recife – Dutch, French and English women – outdrink the men. One popular spectacle organised by Johan Maurits was a bullfight between a wild bull and two powerful naked Tapuia armed only with bow and arrows. The Indians agilely avoided the bull's charges, and shot their arrows into its flanks. When the bull was weakened from loss of blood, a Tapuia jumped on its back and threw it to the ground. The Tapuia finally killed it and promptly roasted it in a pit to feed their relatives.*

The Dutch celebrated Portugal's break with Spain partly to please the Portuguese settlers, but also because they thought the independent Bragança dynasty too weak to reconquer the lost provinces of Brazil. A young Jesuit missionary called António Vieira was a member of the delegation sent from Brazil to congratulate the new king. King João IV rapidly fell under the spell of the tall, self-assured and dynamic Jesuit. He regarded Vieira as a special expert on Brazil. Vieira became the King's preacher, close friend and leading adviser, and was soon sent on secret diplomatic missions to other European countries, disguised as a layman.

Although Vieira was a fervent Portuguese patriot, he was convinced that Dutch naval superiority was too crushing for his country to oppose them in Brazil. It was better to concentrate on holding Portugal against attempted reconquest by Spain. Vieira's policy was either to buy back Pernambuco, or to make a peace that acknowledged Dutch possession of it. Independent Portugal soon made a truce with the Netherlands, and it looked as though the Dutch were in Pernambuco to stay.

The settlers thought otherwise. They became increasingly restless at the financial exactions of the West Indies Company and its attempts to impose Calvinism on the Catholic population. Discontent began even before Nassau's departure. After he left, it grew into a patriotic popular insurrection among the settlers of Pernambuco. This was a spontaneous patriotic rising: the settlers had no official support from the Portuguese Government or its representatives in Brazil.

The Governor in Bahia wished to help the rebels without breaking the truce between the two colonial powers. During the fighting of the 1630s the Portuguese had formed a regiment of blacks under one Henrique Dias. The Governor now devised a stratagem to help the rebels: he sent Henrique Dias northwards with his Africans, and then sent Camarão off in pursuit of these 'runaway' blacks. The first government troops to join the settlers' rebellion were thus contingents of the two oppressed minorities – Indians and blacks.

The leaders of the settlers' revolt were André Vidal de Negreiros, a powerful sugar-baron, and João Fernandes Vieira, who had made a fortune trading with the Dutch. In all his early speeches Fernandes Vieira promised the conspirators that Camarão's arrival would be the signal for the rebellion. Camarão left Bahia in March 1645, hoping to reach Pernambuco on 10 May. He was delayed by drought in the interior and crossed the São Francisco, high up the river, only in June. The Indians had a gruelling march through the sertão. It was their approach that enabled Vieira on 24 June 1645 to proclaim his 'war of liberty and restoration of Pernambuco' and to call on all settlers to join him. The rebels' morale was raised when seven of Camarão's Indians finally staggered out of the wilderness 'with their Biscayan muskets and a trumpeter playing his trumpet'. They said that Camarão and Henrique Dias would arrive within a week. But, when the two commanders finally appeared, they had only a handful of Indians and blacks. 'The rest of their men, who were many, had died on them for lack of essentials.' The march must have been a nightmarish ordeal to have killed off so many Potiguar veterans.

The Dutch immediately sent off a force of 300 Dutch and 200 Potiguar – 'great enemies of the Portuguese' – to pursue Vieira in the sertão. But on 5 August the insurgents surrounded their pursuers in a fort, captured the Dutch commander and massacred all his Indians. It was a shameful feature of this rebellion that the Pernambucan settlers continually vented their fury on Indians – even though they owed so much to Camarão's alliance. A Pernambucan force surrounded the fort of Serinhaém that contained only eighty Dutch and sixty Indian troops. The Pernambucans offered a truce if the defenders would surrender, and on 2 August 1645 the Dutch commander accepted on behalf of all his men, Dutch and Indians alike. Some Indians tried to flee, but forty-nine were caught. 'Because of [the Indians'] treason and unheard-of tyrannies and cruelties, all the people clamoured that they should be excluded from the quarter granted in the truce. Dr Francisco Bravo da Silva, who was acting as advocate-general, therefore condemned them to death . . . and they were all hanged around the fortress and others killed by the soldiers. But they were first allowed to confess their sins (which they never allowed our people to do) and given holy burial (although *they* gave burial in their stomachs). The Indians' wives and small children were given and divided among the settlers to work for them. . . .' Martím Soares Moreno and André Vidal de Negreiros wrote to the Governor of Brazil the following month to justify this massacre, on the grounds that the Indians had been born as Catholics and subjects of the King of Portugal. 'We therefore condemned thirty-nine of them to death by execution and pardoned the rest because they were minors – which we already regret, for they have fled to Recife.'

The Dutch now unleashed Jacob Rabe and his Tapuia. A Dutchman admitted that 'no quarter is now given: for they will not give it to our Indians, but kill any they catch'. In Rio Grande, the Potiguar and Tapuia 'killed all the Portuguese they could catch within a radius of twenty leagues [seventy miles], so that those places are very desolated. The Tapuia savages now want to do their will cruelly as masters.' Rabe moved across Rio Grande with a force of 160 Dutch and hundreds of Indians. The settlers were terrified: some bought him off; others retreated into stronghouses; many were killed. The settlers regarded Rabe as 'almost as barbaric as those indomitable and cruel heathen. He had lived with them for a long time in the sertão and practised their depraved and brutish customs.' There was an ugly massacre on 29 June at a plantation on the Cunhaú. The Portuguese were herded into the plantation church and then set upon by the Dutch and their Indians, with the Tapuia wielding their war clubs. The ninety-year-old priest told the Tapuia they would shrivel up if they touched him. They hesitated – but the Potiguar had no such scruples and finished him off. Sixty-nine colonists were slaughtered and only three survived by hiding on the roof.

The settlers soon had their revenge for this atrocity. At the beginning of August the Pernambucans won a major victory over a large force of Dutch and Indians at Monte das Tabocas. Most Indians were armed with muskets, others with bows and arrows. But many Indians and 370 Dutch were killed in the battle. The Dutch commanders, Colonels Henrik Haus and Johan Blaar, were pursued to the sugar mill of Ana Pais, now called Casa Forte, almost at the gates of Recife. Camarão and Dias cut off escape from the rear of the plantation. The Pernambucans fought their way in and set fire to the house, despite the presence there of settlers' women held hostage by the Dutch. The Dutch capitulated on 17 August. The surrender document, signed by the leaders of both armies, stated: 'We surrender on the condition and promise that quarter is conceded both to us Dutch and to the Indians, with passage to wherever we approve. Which is confirmed in true faith, with oaths to the Holy Evangels.' This was immediately violated. Once again, the 243 Dutch were taken prisoners of war, but 200 Indians were slaughtered to a man. 'The governors, irritated by so many crimes, ordered them all put to the sword. This sentence was executed immediately and all were beheaded. When they saw that they were to be given no quarter they determined to sell their lives dear and placed themselves on the defensive. But it achieved nothing. They were all killed and strewn on the ground' to be eaten by vultures and dogs.*

The fighting grew in intensity and cruelty. In September 1645 Pieter Poti led a force of 300 Dutch and Indians in an unsuccessful attempt to take the camp of Santo André. In that same month 200 Indians under Jacob Rabe and António Paraupaba did capture the fort of Potengi in Rio Grande. At a signal from the Dutch, the Indians went and surrounded the seventy defenders, who said farewell to one another and commended themselves to God. Diogo Lopes de Santiago wrote detailed descriptions of the grisly deaths given to the settlers and their priest and various women. These were his friends, and he identified each victim by name. Some had their eyes, tongues or genitals cut out while still alive. The wife of one Manoel Rodrigues Moura saw her husband killed, and then had her hands and feet cut off and was left on the ground to die three days later. Eight young men who refused to fight with the Dutch were also killed, even though the Indians wanted to spare them.* It was a fortnight before the widows could return to bury the remains of their husbands.

The atrocities and hard fighting on the field were echoed by passionate rhetoric. João Fernandes Vieira and many other 'afflicted settlers of Pernambuco' wrote to the Portuguese Governor of Bahia to announce their rebellion and beg for his help. They complained bitterly of a German general Sigismund von Schkoppe who 'marched from Serinhaém to Matiope, a distance of thirty leagues, with Tapuia whom he ordered brought down from the sertão for that purpose, killing, beheading and delivering to those Tapuia men, children and women so that they should perform extraordinary excesses in his presence. He behaved in the same way in Goiana, where the heathen Indians and soldiers spent three days destroying the people and doing worse indecencies to married women and maidens than have ever been seen in the world. . . . The Indians want to see us finished and destroyed, for they are enemies of Christianity.' The Portuguese rebel commanders even wrote to the Dutch governors in Recife to protest at these murders of settlers and 'the sighs of noble maidens who were violated and attacked by the heathen and soldiers of Your Lordships, proceeding to deaths and unbridled licentiousness'.

The tragedy for the Indians was that they were being armed and incited against one another by colonial powers fighting for their country. Not only did traditionally hostile groups fight one another, but also tribes normally as cohesive as the Potiguar were violently split by the rival European colonists and religions.

António Camarão tried to reunite the Potiguar by persuading his cousin Pieter Poti to change sides. He had his cousin Diogo Pinheiro Camarão write a series of letters, in Tupi, to Poti and other Indian leaders fighting with the Dutch. These fascinating letters show how thoroughly the missionaries had converted Camarão to Catholicism and persuaded him of the iniquity of Protestantism. 'I must now ask you why you wish to fight us. . . . I sent you a message by God's grace, Mr Pedro Poti, because I am a good relative. Leave that place, which is like the fire of Hell. Don't you know that you are a Christian? Why do you want to pervert yourself? You are a son of God: why do you want to be under the impious? . . . If the Portuguese succeed in this war it is because, being Christians, the Lord God does not permit them to flee or lose. We therefore desire that you pass over to us. . . . I am very amazed to see you alienated from us. Are you not our close relative? Why are you angry with us? We will do you no harm and you should behave in the same way to us.' And in another letter: 'Listen: I, your cousin Pinheiro, advise you that you should pass to our side. Free yourself of those perverse people.' To which old Camarão added that various elders and 'all your other friends say you should change sides. You would be doing a great service to the King and would be no worse off than with that cursed people. Quite the contrary. Therefore believe my word. All the settlers trust me, at which I greatly pride myself.'

Pieter Poti endured these pleas for some weeks, and then wrote a single long reply. It was a far more polished and detailed letter than Camarão's. And it was an eloquent and angry rebuttal. 'I am ashamed of our family and nation at seeing myself so induced, by so many letters from you, to treason and disloyalty: namely, to abandon my legitimate leaders from whom I have received so many benefits. It is folly for you to imagine that you delude us so easily with those vain words. It even leaves me thinking that you use those false impostures because you dare not come to visit us as soldiers. Rest assured that I will remain a soldier loyal to my chiefs until death!

'I am fine here and lack nothing. We live more freely than any of you – for you continue under a nation that has never sought anything but to enslave you. . . .

'Do not believe we are too blind to recognise the advantages we enjoy with the Dutch, among whom I was educated. I have never heard it said that they enslaved any Indian or kept any as [slaves], or that they have at any time killed or mistreated any of our people. They call us brothers and live with us as brothers. We therefore wish to live and die with them.

'On the other side, our people throughout the land find themselves enslaved by the Portuguese, and many would still be so [enslaved] had I not liberated them. The outrages they have done us – more than to the negroes – and the slaughter of our [Potiguar] race committed by them at the Baía de Traição ('Bay of Treason'), are still very fresh in our memory.

'What better demonstrates their tyrannical designs than the cruelty recently committed against our men in Serinhaém after quarter was conceded? That blood cries to God for vengeance – although my cousin António [Paraupaba] has already taken some revenge in Rio Grande.

'No, [António] Filipe, you let yourself be deluded. It is evident that the plan of the Portuguese rascals is simply to gain control of this country and then kill or enslave both you and us.

'So come to our side while there is still time, so that with the help of our friends we can live together in this land which is our home and in the bosom of all our family. We are all agreed about this. Therefore come and join us, and I assure you that the Dutch will give you the same benefits as they do us. Have not the slightest doubt; the Portuguese will slip away; those bandits will disappear like the wind.

'I am a better Christian than you. I believe only in Christ without polluting religion with idolatry as you do in yours. I learned the Christian religion and practise it daily. . . .

'Therefore come over to our side and leave those perjurers and traitors who cannot survive there, for we will soon expel them by force from there and also from Bahia. You should know that their deeds in the south have not the slightest importance. He who has most men is master of the field. . . . You must recognise that the sea dominates Brazil. . . . We are hourly awaiting a great and extraordinarily strong fleet, to which we will add the ships already here and then set to work. In short, the Dutch will seize the initiative to capture all Brazil, for the King of Portugal is without resources or forces. . . .

'Do not talk to me of the weakness of the Dutch. I lived and was educated in that country. They have ships, men, money and everything as abundant as the stars in heaven. Only a fraction of that has come here. Also, it was by means of their ships and troops that King João of Portugal has been supported on the throne for the past four years and was able to reign. . . .

'Therefore, cousin Camarão, abandon these perverse and dangerous Portuguese and come and join us. I guarantee you that you would do well. Together we would form a respectable force, and would expel those swindlers and traitors. Let us remain with the foreigners who respect us and treat our country well. . . .

'We will achieve nothing through letters, so do not write me any more. I do not wish to receive such letters. When you complain about this war you are deluded by that rabble of perjurers and perverse rascals who have so greatly seduced you and all our friends and so tyrannically oppressed our people. Adeus. P. Poti. 31 October 1645.'

Both Potiguar chiefs remained steadfastly loyal to their European allies and religions. The correspondence achieved nothing. The Dutch authorities failed to send the 'extraordinarily strong fleet' on which Poti pinned his hopes. It was the Pernambucan settlers' rebellion that gathered momentum. During the last three months of 1645 another enemy appeared in the shattered colony – a terrible epidemic that ravaged Pernambuco and Goiana. The disease consisted of catarrhs that descended to the base of the lungs, and the victims died of suffocation. An infinite number of whites, Indians and slaves died of it.

At the end of the year Camarão marched north with his regiment of Tupi and a force of 200 Tapuia from the São Francisco river. They punished Indians who were helping the Dutch by burning their villages and capturing their cattle. In January 1646 Camarão invaded Paraíba with a force now increased to 350 Indians and 250 whites. His Tupi were expert musketeers and his Tapuia were armed with bows and arrows. On

27 January Camarão won an impressive victory against a larger force of 500 Dutch and 300 Indians at a position between two rivers in Cunhaú. His Indians defended a trench and earthwork against enemy charges, coolly firing and then retiring to reload while the second line fired. Camarão's archers fought off an attempt by the enemy's Tapuia to turn their flank. His musketeers went on firing until their guns burned their hands and their powder was exhausted. The Dutch finally sounded the retreat, and Camarão's men charged out. The battlefield was soaked in blood and strewn with the bodies of 115 Dutch and their Indian allies; Camarão had only three wounded.

The devout Camarão always prayed before a battle and carried a reliquary containing images of Christ and the Virgin. 'After kissing these holy images with much devotion he made a speech to his soldiers with such effective words that it sounded more like that of a courtly politician than an Indian raised in the wilds of Brazil.' His men then spent four days celebrating their victory – in the customary Indian manner.

The following month Camarão caught a force of sixty Dutch and 160 Indians in one of his brilliant ambushes. The Indians of that force were led by a woman shaman 'who came with a cutlass in her hand, skirmishing and shouting, "I am a jaguar and tiger, and with these claws I will tear apart the flesh of the Portuguese and will eat them roast and boiled!"' Camarão's men killed most of this force with their first volley and the rest as they tried to flee. All sixty Dutch were killed and most of their Indian allies. The sorceress 'was struck by two balls that pierced her breast, and her witchcraft availed her nothing'.

The Dutch were soon forced back into Recife. They were supported by the help and resolution of their Indians, who were now 'the entire remedy of the Flemings. For without the help of the Indians they did not dare emerge into the countryside.' Camarão issued a proclamation calling on Indians to surrender with a white flag and accept his pardon. He stressed the strength of the Portuguese throughout Brazil, and warned that the Dutch would soon sail away and abandon their allies. He tried to dissociate himself from the settlers' massacres of Indians. 'It only remains for me to declare to you that I could not save anyone in the past events of the war. This was a consequence of the war itself. It causes me great grief to see so many of you succumb in different places. Had I been there with only my own people you would not have to lament those events. They must be imputed to the fury of the Portuguese at finding you at the side of the Dutch despite having previously sworn friendship to them.'

The two sides were stalemated. The Dutch still had mastery of the seas, and were occasionally reinforced from the Netherlands. The

Pernambucans held the land. They besieged Recife and the Dutch forts along the coast. Throughout 1646 and 1647 Camarão and his Indians were camped near the Forte dos Afogados ('Fort of the Drowned'), across the Capibaribe river from Recife.

Even the Tapuia were alarmed by the defeats of the Dutch and were starting to change sides. Their beloved Jacob Rabe was murdered by two Dutch officers in April 1646. Jandui demanded that his friend's killer be sent to him to be executed. The Portuguese were now wooing the Tapuia with splendid presents. When the Dutch sent Roulox Baro on an embassy to Jandui in 1647 the old chief received him well and assured him that he was still a friend of the Dutch. But he showed Baro the fine things sent by the Portuguese: 'Look at these axes, these hatchets, these sickles, these knives and other iron tools. The least of these objects is worth more than all your Dutch masters have ever sent me.' And when Baro finally produced his gifts Jandui 'looked at them and shook his head and said to me: "These things are not worth the trouble of being carried from so far. The Portuguese are right to say that Dutch ironware is worthless, and their mirrors are even worse, and their combs. I have never seen anything more wretched."' So Jandui rejected Baro's shoddy presents, and insisted only that he leave behind a couple of fine hunting dogs.

At the beginning of 1648 the Dutch received more reinforcements and decided to try to break the deadlock. They marched out of Recife with 4500 men, hoping to recapture some of the hinterland. They issued a proclamation of pardon to any Indians who would join them, but Camarão's answer was characteristic: 'We are totally resolute and determined to die or win. It is more likely that we will win, for we enjoy divine favour because of the justice of our defence, and human advantage in the greater numbers and valour of our arms.' When the armies met at the hills of Guararapes a few miles south of Recife, on 19 April 1648, António Filipe Camarão commanded one of the four regiments on the Pernambucan side. The Portuguese had only half the strength of the Dutch, and were on the defensive during most of the four-hour battle. Camarão commanded the flank nearest the sea. But the main Dutch attack fell on the other flank, held by Henrique Dias and the regiment of blacks. At one stage there was a charge by sword-wielding Pernambucans that took the Dutch baggage. The Dutch counter-attacked. The Portuguese commander Francisco Barreto wrote: 'There were few of us and we were already exhausted and so we, too, were forced to fall back. I immediately swung into action everywhere in order to prevent the enemy from recovering his artillery, munitions and money that we had already won from him. But I was unable to do so. For with the defeat we had inflicted on the enemy, our troops became more disorganised than the very enemy we had defeated.' The battle raged on across the entire field. But the outnumbered Pernambucans were more determined and more skilful. 'We performed wondrous acts of bravery in which the commanders and other officers distinguished themselves.' 'Dom António Camarão . . . showed in this battle the valour and energy that he always showed on all occasions.' The Portuguese finally won a resounding victory, with 500 Dutch dead and as many wounded, against 80 dead and 400 wounded among the insurgents. The Portuguese gathered up 33 battle standards, 'including the large standard bearing the arms of the United Provinces. . . . The other thirteen flags were destroyed by our negro and Indian soldiers, who saw no value in them except as bright material to tear up for ribbons and other ornaments.' The loot included gold, jewels and food – and shackles and chains intended for the leaders of the rebellion.

Four months after the battle of Guararapes, António Filipe Camarão died of disease on his estate in Pernambuco. His death was a great loss to the Portuguese, for he was a brilliant soldier and a staunch supporter of their cause. He spoke good Portuguese, although he preferred to use an interpreter when talking with important people. He was also a devout Christian, who 'heard mass every day and prayed the office of Our Lady whenever he had time, and made his Indians perform'. He was honoured by all Indians, but especially loved by his own troops, whom he treated with paternal care. Camarão was buried with much honour and funeral pomp in the church at the Camp of Bom Jesus, as befitted the most famous of all Brazilian Indians, and one of the most successful Portuguese military commanders.

The Portuguese victory did not resolve the stalemate. The Dutch were still too powerful at sea and too strong in artillery to be dislodged from their many forts. Ten months after Guararapes, they again tried to march out towards the south. Another major battle was fought on 19 February 1649 on the very same heights of Guararapes. The Pernambucan insurgents again won a great victory after a day of heavy fighting. On this occasion the Indian regiment was commanded by Camarão's cousin or nephew Diogo Pinheiro Camarão. And one of the prisoners was Camarão's opponent Pieter Poti.

António Paraupaba described his friend's agony. 'Pieter Poti, Administrator of our unfortunate nation, fell prisoner of the Portuguese on 19 February 1649 at the second wretched battle of Guararapes. He was barbarously treated by those monsters. What they perpetrated exceeded all the most inhuman cruelties one could imagine.

He was constantly whipped and suffered all manner of tortures. He was dragged to a dark dungeon and imprisoned with iron chains on his feet and hands. He received only bread and water as nourishment and had to perform his natural necessities in that same place for six long months.' Poti was only occasionally allowed out into daylight. He was constantly bombarded by missionaries and other Indians trying to persuade him to change sides and religion. 'When those six months were over those tormentors realised that they could obtain nothing from such a strong spirit by means of martyrdoms or promises of honours, positions and fortune. So they removed him from his dark cellar where he had suffered so, on the pretext of wishing to send him to Bahia; but their plan was to kill him cruelly, which they later did. When he was condemned and imprisoned in the fort at Cape Santo Agostinho, in the company of various Dutch officers, he told them: "I know that they will kill me. I therefore beg you to do me this service: when you return to Recife, tell the members of the Supreme Council what you saw and heard of me – that I died as their loyal subject. And tell the people of my own nation that I exhort them to stay loyal to God and to the States-General for all their lives." '

The situation in Brazil gradually changed. In 1649 the Portuguese King acted on a suggestion by his Jesuit adviser António Vieira and formed the General Company of Trade with Brazil. This eventually provided ships to help the Pernambucan settlers' rebellion. Dutch maritime supremacy was weakened by the war between the Netherlands and Cromwell's England. In January 1654 the Dutch were forced one by one out of the forts defending Recife. On 26 January they finally surrendered, and agreed to withdraw from all their remaining strongholds in north-eastern Brazil. The struggle that had begun twenty-four years before was over; and Portuguese control of Brazil was never again seriously challenged.

The Indians who had sided with the Dutch were in despair. One report said that, in the aftermath of the Dutch occupation, Ceará was a mere desert with nothing but heathen Indians. A Portuguese said that, when the Dutch finally left, some 400 of their Indians avenged themselves for this betrayal by attacking the remaining Dutch and robbing and killing settlers.* But most Indians fled for their lives.

A Dutch observer saw their pathetic exodus. 'The Indians who escaped and retreated from Pernambuco came by land, over 4000 souls in number, from Itamaracá, Paraíba and Rio Grande, to take refuge in Ceará. They said frankly that all Brazil had just been disgracefully lost and handed over virtually without resistance to the Portuguese. They never ceased to curse and vociferate against the Flemings, whom they had served faithfully and helped for a great many years and who now, without daring to confront the enemy, abandoned to them Itamaracá with all its forts, Paraíba and Rio Grande. The only prospect that remained for them was to fall into the clutches of the Portuguese and to suffer perpetual slavery. They were so incensed that they sent messages ahead to the Ceará Indians with orders to massacre the Dutch wherever they found them and to spare none of their lives. They hope to remain sole masters of Ceará and never permit Portuguese or Flemings to establish themselves there. And they plan to make of that captaincy their place of revival and rendezvous.'

The Indians fortified themselves among the Tobajara on the Ibiapaba hills. They called their republic Cambressive. They even made a forlorn attempt to obtain Dutch assistance. António Paraupaba was sent to Holland and presented a moving appeal to the States-General in August 1654. When nothing happened, he tried again with a second appeal in 1656. 'The supplicant is sent by that nation who took refuge with its wives and children in Cambressive in the sertão beyond Ceará in order to escape the ferocious massacres of the Portuguese.' They had been there for two years, but were still loyal to the Dutch Government and religion. 'If help fails them, that people must inevitably finally fall into the clutches of the cruel and bloodthirsty Portuguese, who since the first occupation of Brazil have destroyed so many hundreds of thousands of persons of that nation. . . .' Paraupaba said that he could not believe that the Dutch would fail to help the Indians, to reward their years of loyal service and to protect the Reformed Religion. But he was wrong.

FIFTEEN

António Vieira

THE situation of the Indians in the Portuguese-controlled parts of Brazil may appear to have verged on anarchy, but was in fact subject to legislation from the mother country. The dilapidated mission villages owed their survival to legal protection. In theory, slaving or ransoming expeditions into the interior were regulated by an elaborate code. Although the many laws about Indians were often unrealistic, unenforceable and unenforced, they did carry weight. Any liberal measure favouring Indians provoked an immediate outcry among the settlers, and often led to violence. These reactions show that the laws were taken seriously, even if they were so often flouted. No one would have risked punishment for sedition or rebellion if the laws he was protesting about were meaningless.

All laws concerning Indians were flawed by an insoluble contradiction in the intentions of the legislators. The Iberian monarchs were mindful of their mission to spread Christianity to the American natives. They knew that missionary activity was nullified by abuse and enslavement of Indians. Their consciences told them that slavery and forced labour of Indians were wrong – even if they reconciled themselves to enslaving Africans because their skins were blacker. There was a powerful ecclesiastical lobby, led by the great Dominican Bartolomé de las Casas, to warn the kings of Spain that they risked personal damnation if they permitted illegal and unholy slavery to continue in their colonies.

Settlers expel Jesuits from Amazonia.

But royal good intentions were easily overruled by economic considerations. Portugal's and Spain's immense American territories could only function with the labour of their natives. The European monarchies came to depend on the revenues from the mines and plantations of the New World. The few settlers who were colonising such vast lands remained there only because of the abundance of cheap labour. But the Indians were resolutely determined not to labour for Europeans. They correctly saw that they themselves gained nothing by such work, and easily resisted the lengths of cloth offered them as pay. They had the mentality of hunter-gatherers in a land of plenty – confident that the necessities of life were available whenever required. They might therefore be prepared to work occasionally to earn some tools, alcohol or cloth; but they refused to work regularly or to strive to earn more than their basic needs. They valued their leisure and family life above any considerations of profit, progress, competition or success. No colonists or monarchies could prosper with a labour force so hopelessly devoid of motivation. The laws therefore had to compel the natives to work, or devise situations in which they could be enslaved without excessive violation of Christian ethics.

The insoluble conflict was between the missionaries' attempt to convert the Indians to Christianity and turn them into useful 'civilised' subjects, and the settlers' desperate need for labour. The Crown wanted to favour both missionaries and settlers. Its policies swung from one extreme to the other, from slavery to freedom (on missions, of course) for the Indians. The result was a tangle of contradictory and vacillating legislation.

When the Portuguese throne was occupied by Philip II of Spain, the influence of Las Casas was felt in Brazil. On 24 February 1587 the King confirmed King Sebastião's law of 1570 forbidding slavery of Indians, except in 'just' and officially approved wars. On 11 November 1595 and 26 July 1596 King Philip again affirmed the freedom of Indians, and entrusted aldeias in Brazil to the care of the Jesuits. The law of 1596 described the system of mission reservations: 'Firstly, the [Jesuit Fathers] will attempt by all good means to persuade the heathen to come and communicate with the settlers, in places that the Governor will assign them. . . . They will declare to the heathen that they are free and will live at liberty in those settlements and be owners of their property as they are in the hills . . . so that the heathen cannot claim that they are being made to descend by fraud or against their wills.'

The next king, Philip III of Spain and Philip II of Portugal, was even more concerned about Indian freedom than his father. He pondered the question of Indian slavery and decided that it must be completely abolished, with no loopholes whatsoever. His law of 5 June 1605 explained that 'although there are some legal arguments for introducing captivity [slavery] in certain cases, the arguments to the contrary – especially those concerning the conversion of heathens to our Holy Catholic Faith – are so much more weighty that they must overrule the others . . .'.

The full freedom of Brazilian Indians was proclaimed in the powerful text of the law of 30 July 1609. 'In order to restrain the great excesses that might occur if slavery were permitted in any instance, and to shut the door completely against it, all the Indians of Brazil are declared to be free, according to law and their natural birthright, both those who have been baptised and reduced to our Holy Catholic Faith and also those who still live as gentiles according to their own rites and ceremonies. They will be treated and regarded as free persons, which they are. They will not be compelled to work or do any other thing against their free will. People who employ them on their estates must pay for their labour as they pay all other free persons whom they employ. These heathen may freely and securely possess their lands and property, and live and trade with the settlers of the captaincies.'

Indians already enslaved were to be freed. 'I see fit and order that all be given their liberty, and immediately be removed from the control of any persons in whose power they may be, and sent back to their lands.' The King rejected any 'purchases' or licences that settlers might have for these slaves: 'I declare such bills of sale and licences to be null and void, since they are contrary to law. . . .'

The Indians were still considered as legal minors requiring protection. This was a necessary provision if they were to survive in a land ruled by an alien civilisation, a colony whose European masters had such a radically different society and outlook. The Indians were therefore entrusted to the Jesuits. These missionaries were to seek Indians in the wilds, 'because of the great knowledge and experience they have of these matters and because of the trust and confidence the heathen place in them, to domesticate [the Indians] and assure them of their liberty, and lead them towards salvation, communal society and commerce with the merchants of those parts – but in a manner convenient to the heathen themselves. We decree that these heathen are masters of their estates and villages in which they live, just as they are in the hills. These [lands] may not be taken from them, nor may any injury or injustice of any sort to be done them.'

This was remarkably enlightened legislation. Had it lasted and been enforced, the Indians might have had a chance to experience the advantages of European civilisation, to have learned to co-exist with it and assimilate its peculiar philosophy 'in a manner convenient to the heathen themselves'.

The law of 1609 provoked an explosion of protest among the settlers in Brazil. Much of their fury was directed against the Jesuits, and there was a rising among the colonists in Bahia. Captain Miguel Ayres Maldonado considered the black-robed Fathers as hypocrites intent on self-enrichment. 'It is behind the image of Our Lord Jesus Christ and in its shadow that these ambitious missionaries deploy their precepts and sophistries, cloaked in fraud and malice. . . .' Diogo de Campos Moreno deplored the fact that so much Indian labour was isolated on Jesuit missions. 'The Indians of this land, who would seem easier [to obtain], less costly and more numerous [than African slaves], are lodged with the missionaries. They live subjected to these and adore them . . . and give them marvellous service; but they give no help to laymen, not even a supply of food. Instead, when they are summoned by the poor settlers, it often happens that they take their wage in advance and do nothing for it. . . . Because of this there are great complaints against the missionaries. When these try to . . . punish such behaviour with private prisons or thrashings, however slight, the Indians are such spoiled darlings and so little accustomed to the practice of our justice and obedience that they immediately run off to the forest where they perform abominable practices and rites, joining the Guinea negroes who are also fugitives. The result of all this is deaths, robberies, scandals and violence, so that one cannot cross the sertão comfortably from place to place or extend the settlements inland. . . . The result of these disorders . . . is that no work of public good takes shape. The Indians . . . go wherever they wish, more barbarous and lazy than ever. And the whites are more like guests than settlers all along the coast, isolated from one another, without labour or anyone to work for them . . . plunged into debt in a desert!' The Governor, Diogo de Menezes e Siqueira, joined the settlers in demanding an end to the mission villages. Writing to the King in 1611 he argued that both Indians and the state 'would gain greater advantage if the heathen are introduced into the large towns. Only there can they acquire civilised habits, not isolated in aldeias.'

All this was too much for the King. The royal conscience was smothered by political and economic expediency. On 10 September 1611 a new law cancelled the humanitarian law of 1609. Slavery was reintroduced, for legitimate prisoners in 'just' wars and for ransomed captives of Indian tribes. Lay captains were to administer the civil government of the mission villages. Mission Indians could be forced to work for settlers for fixed wages. The colonists had defeated the Jesuits.

It became common to 'descend' uncontacted tribes – to persuade or force them to descend from the interior to locations conveniently near the coastal towns and plantations. Prominent colonists were given the 'administration' of Indian villages and rewarded by native labour.*

There followed decades of hardship for the Indians. In the south the bandeirantes were hunting Indian slaves with impunity. In the north-east the authorities were fully occupied with the French and Dutch invasions. This may have enhanced the military value of Indians in that area, but it meant that there was scant government control of what happened in Maranhão and Pará. The first settlers to reach the Amazon enslaved its Indians in their thousands. They were acting within the law of 1611, 'ransoming' 'bound Indians' who were supposedly tied up ready to be eaten by other tribes – although the vast majority of Amazon tribes were not cannibalistic. The law of 1611 said that Indians enslaved under its provisions should be slaves for ten years. After a decade had elapsed, the settlers were faced with the prospect of freeing some of their Indian slaves. Therefore, on 29 September 1626 a junta of 'secular and ecclesiastical dignitaries' met in Maranhão and decided that 'slaves who cost more than five axes or an equivalent value . . . should be slaves for all their lives'. It was argued that few slaves would want freedom 'after being in the houses of settlers, looking after their children and developing reciprocal love for one another'. It was not worth a settler's while to plunge into the forests in search of slaves if he lost them after ten years. He would waste a year away from home and, 'if he has not died or fallen sick, he returns bloated and pallid and needs a long time to recuperate'. And he would be lucky if he returned home with half his slaves 'surviving death or flight'.

In 1624 the Jesuits felt that they must do something about the northern provinces of Maranhão and Pará, which were separated from the rest of Brazil with their own royal governor. These were regions filled with innumerable unconverted Indians and a few lawless settlers. The Jesuit Luís Figueira reached Maranhão soon after the expulsion of the French. He was particularly influential with Governor António Moniz Barreiros, who followed his advice and bequeathed a sugar plantation near São Luís to the Fathers. Figueira visited the lower Xingu in 1636 and was impressed by the great number of Indians ripe for missionary activity. He returned to Portugal to recruit more Jesuits for this work. But when he sailed back to Pará his ship foundered in full view of Belém, on 29 June 1643. Many passengers saved themselves, including the Governor Pedro de Albuquerque and his soldiers, but Figueira and eleven fellow-Jesuits clung to a raft made from pieces of the wrecked ship. Winds and current swept them to the far bank of the river, to the island of Joanes (Marajó), where they were all killed by Aruan Indians.*

This was a terrible blow to Jesuit aspirations on the Amazon. Six years later they virtually ceased to operate in the northern provinces. They had two missionaries tending the sugar mill bequeathed to them on the Itapicuru in Maranhão. One of these flogged an Indian slave girl as punishment for sexual promiscuity. She ran off and complained to the Tapuia tribe of Uruati. Indians regard corporal punishment as a terrible insult. 'Being barbarian heathen who do not know how to judge punishments in such matters, since they live without reason like animals of the forests . . . [Chief Patyron of the Uruati] proposed to avenge her by taking the lives of the Fathers.' His Indians appeared at the sugar mill, which they frequented for trading. There were fourteen white men there and two Jesuits. One of the whites fired a gun to frighten off the Indians, but set fire to the thatch roof of a hut. The conflagration emboldened the Indians; the white settlers fled; and the Jesuits were abandoned and clubbed to death, one while kneeling in prayer, the other while trying to escape in a canoe.

The Jesuits' return to the Amazon came in the towering person of António Vieira. Although born of humble parentage in Lisbon in 1608, Vieira was taken to Brazil as a child and educated at the Jesuit college in Bahia. He took his vows to enter the Society a week after the recapture of Bahia from the Dutch in May 1625. Vieira was a brilliant pupil who was only eighteen when he wrote the Jesuit annual letter from Bahia describing the Dutch occupation. His rise was due to his magnificent oratory, in an age when the pulpit was the most powerful medium of communication. The Portuguese were and are a very literary people, proud of their language. They came to acknowledge Vieira as the greatest master of Portuguese prose in his day, and he is still considered second only to Camões. Thomas Maynard, English consul in Lisbon in 1666, described Vieira as 'a Jesuit eminent for his preaching, his sermons being bought up as fast as they are printed and sent for out of all parts of Spain, Italy and France'.

Vieira underwent the full course of Jesuit study and was finally ordained in December 1634. He also took an additional pledge to work as a missionary and learned Tupi-Guaraní and Kimbundu, the language of the Angolan blacks. He did some work among the Indians and black slaves near Bahia. He also became the city's most popular preacher, prominent in its defence against Nassau in 1638, and preacher of the victory sermon.

When Portugal shook off Spanish rule, Vieira was chosen as a member of the delegation sent to congratulate the new Bragança king, João IV. He reached Lisbon in April 1641. As we have seen, Vieira soon became the King's close friend and adviser. He travelled to most European capitals on secret diplomacy for his king. He continued to preach with great effect, for, 'besides his natural eloquence, he has the art of making the scriptures say what he pleases'. Vieira's sermons were fiery, sometimes aggressive and bloodthirsty, sometimes mystical, emotional and intensely patriotic.

With António Vieira so influential at Court, King João issued legislation more favourable to the Indians. An edict of 10 November 1647 described the horrors of work in villages run by lay administrators. The Indians 'either die of hunger or excessive work or flee inland where they perish after a few days' march. For this reason innumerable heathen have perished and ceased in Maranhão and Pará and in other parts of the State of Brazil. . . . [Therefore] since Indians are free, as has been declared by the kings of Portugal and the Supreme Pontiffs, there shall be no more lay administrators . . . and the Indians may freely serve and work for whomsoever they prefer and who pays them best.' The notion that Indians could seek the best market conditions was wishful thinking, for they were powerless to choose or change masters. The King also regulated Indian wages, and insisted that natives were not to be forced to work for more than eight months a year. They were to be allowed home during the four months when forests had to be cleared and manioc planted, so that their families would not starve. Free Indians were not to be employed in the gruelling labour of the tobacco plantations.

António Vieira became so interested in the plight of the Indians that he suddenly declared his intention of returning to missionary work in Brazil. People could scarcely believe that so powerful a figure would return to the wilds. Vieira had a great reputation as a preacher throughout Europe. He controlled Portuguese diplomacy and was a dominant figure at Court. At the last minute even Vieira hesitated to leave; but his rivals called his bluff and ensured that he fulfil his vow and sail for the Amazon. Vieira reached Maranhão in 1653 and began a new career at the age of forty-five. He wrote home to his prince: 'I am now starting to be a missionary!'

Vieira was appalled by what he saw in Maranhão. He wrote to the King of the spiritual plight of Indians working in settlers' houses: 'Many of them live and die as pagans, without their masters or parish priests obtaining baptism for them.' The Indians herded into the aldeias were in even worse condition. 'The Indians who live in aldeias and are nominally free are far more captive than those living in the private houses of the Portuguese. . . . They generally work in tobacco plantations, which is the cruellest of all the work in Brazil. They are forcibly ordered to serve persons and perform work they would not do voluntarily; and they die there from sheer despair. Married women are removed from the aldeias and put to work in private houses . . . to the great distress of their husbands. . . . [Men] are not given time to farm or tend their clearings, as a result of which they and their wives and children suffer and die.' The aldeias were run by tough mameluco captains. Mission Indians were used as personal labourers by each new governor intent on growing rich during his few years in office. Vieira recommended that the villages be run by Indian chiefs rather than administrators appointed by the governors.

Vieira tried to influence the settlers with his famous oratory. He preached a long sermon condemning Indian slavery: 'At what a different price the devil buys souls today compared with what he used to offer for them! There is no market in the world where the devil can get them more cheaply than right here in our own land. . . . In Maranhão . . . all he has to do is offer a couple of Tapuia Indians and he is immediately adored on both knees. What a cheap market! An Indian for a soul! That Indian will be your slave for the few days that he lives; but your soul will be enslaved for eternity, as long as God is God. . . . Christians, nobles, and people of Maranhão . . . break the chains of injustice and free those whom you hold captive and oppressed! . . . All of you are in mortal sin; all of you live in a state of condemnation; and all of you are going directly to Hell!' Vieira compared the settlers with the pharaohs holding captive the children of Israel, and threatened them with the plagues of Egypt. 'Do you know what brought those plagues to the earth? Unjust captivity. Who brought the plague of the Dutch to Maranhão? Who brought the smallpox? Who brought hunger and drought? These captives. . . . If you possessed true faith, if you believed that there is an eternal Hell, you would not take so lightly the captivity of a single Tapuia. . . . Any man who deprives others of their freedom, and being able to restore that freedom does not do so, is condemned!'

Vieira was enough of a politician to anticipate opposition, and to make practical proposals. Later in the sermon he admitted: 'I know what you are going to tell me . . . our people, our country, our government cannot be sustained without Indians. Who will fetch a pail of water for us or carry a load of wood? Who will grind our manioc? Will our wives have to do it? Will our sons? . . . I answer yes and repeat again, yes. You, your wives, your sons, all of us are able to sustain ourselves with our own labour. It is better to live from your own sweat than from the blood of others!' Vieira asked only that the settlers free illegal slaves, and stop illegal slaving. He condemned expeditions up-river to seize free Indians, 'or to "ransom" them, as they say, using the pious verb "to ransom" for a sale so involuntary and violent that it is made at times at pistol point!' Vieira then stressed the laxity of the legislation. Indians who were genuine captives of other tribes could still be ransomed, to save them from death: a tribunal of legal and ecclesiastical judges would decide the merits of each case. Vieira also reminded his congregation that free Indians could still be hired for the ludicrously low wage of a length of cloth, and could be made to work for settlers for six months a year. He urged only that illegal slaves be freed. The advantage would be 'that you will have a clear conscience . . . and will remove this curse from your homes. There is no greater curse on a home or family than to be unjustly supported by the sweat of others!'

For once Vieira's eloquence failed. The settlers of Maranhão had no intention of having their wives fetch water to please the King's preacher. There was no rush to free slaves. When the new governor issued a royal order freeing slaves, 'the effect was for everyone to protest at this law, with public meetings, in the town council, in the square, and everywhere. The shouting, weapons, confusion and perturbation were as great as for the most serious events. All were resolved to lose their lives (and there were some who would sooner lose their souls) than consent that those whom they had purchased with their money be removed from their houses.'

Vieira contemplated a missionary expedition to the Barbados tribe up the Itapicuru. But when he tried to borrow aldeia Indians for the journey, he found all able-bodied men were away working in the Governor's tobacco plantations. 'Thus the zeal and ardent spirit of Vieira were frustrated by the violences of greed and one powerful man.' Thwarted at Maranhão, Vieira sailed on to Belém do Pará, the base for slaving operations on the Amazon and its mighty tributaries.

Things were even worse in Pará. Its lieutenant-governors used free aldeia Indians as if they were personal slaves. Vieira wrote to the King: 'Firstly, none of these Indians goes [to the tobacco plantations] except by violence and force. The work is excessive, one in which many die every year, for the tobacco smoke is very poisonous. They are treated with more harshness than slaves; they are called the most ugly names, which they greatly resent; their food is almost non-existent; their pay is so limited that it does not recompense the smallest part of the time and work involved'; and they have to travel far, for months on end, neglecting crops and families, 'so that the aldeias are always in the greatest hunger and misery'. Nor did they receive any religious instruction. *

The concept of 'just' wars was a cruel farce. Vieira wrote that soon after his arrival in Pará two chiefs arrived from a forest tribe, and accepted an invitation to move their people down to villages near Belém. Nine villages of their tribe were camped on a river bank ready to move. Four other villages decided to stay in the forest and refused to leave their homes. A captain wrote advising the Governor that 'war should immediately be declared on these four "rebel" villages: apart from the service this would do for His Majesty, it would be highly useful to the people who could obtain slaves to serve them in this way'. Vieira commented angrily: 'Thus, when people who are not our subjects do not wish to leave their lands, this is called "rebellion" here. And this crime is considered worthy of punishment by war and enslavement!'

The great preacher decided to make a missionary expedition into the interior immediately after his arrival in Pará at the end of 1653. He took three Jesuit colleagues, all Tupi-speakers, and travelled for 700 miles up the Tocantins. The objective was to persuade the Poquiguara tribe to descend the river and settle in the mission villages near Belém. The Governor of Pará sent a military escort under a Captain Gaspar Gonçalves Cardoso.

Vieira had left the court of Lisbon for just this sort of adventure on the Amazon. He wrote an enthusiastic description of the delights of his first river journey. He was enchanted by the beauty of the Tocantins, with its broad grey waters, pure water and air, the luxuriant foliage of the forest on its banks, and the amazing abundance of its fish. He was impressed by the bounty of God and nature: everything the expedition needed was found along the river banks. The canoes were hollowed-out tree-trunks, the oakum was made from bark, and the pitch from resinous sap. Sails were made of cotton or barkwood, the fibrous layer beneath the bark. Rigging was lianas and creepers that hung from all the trees of the forest. Europeans sat amidships under canopies of broad leaves on a trellis of osiers. The river was a great storehouse of all these supplies. 'Provisions are found with the same facility: for first of all the drinking water is below the keel, and wherever or whenever it is needed it is always fresh and very good.'

The entire expedition was propelled by aldeia Indians. Vieira was shocked by their working conditions, but impressed by their skill and stamina. 'It is the Indians who make the canoes and their awnings, who caulk them, sail them, paddle them; and . . . it is they who often carry them on their backs over portages. It is they who, after rowing for days and nights without end, go out to seek food for themselves and the Portuguese (who always get the most and the best). It is they who build huts for us, and if we have to march along the banks they carry the loads and even the weapons. The poor Indians do all this for no payment other than being called dogs and other more insulting names. . . . There have been expeditions on which more than half the Indians who set out did not return: they died from sheer overwork and harsh treatment.'

Vieira noted that the Tocantins itself 'is named after an Indian nation of this name who inhabited it when the Portuguese came to Pará. But today nothing is preserved but the memory of this tribe, as of so many others, along with many ruins of a small aldeia.' The missionary expedition proved a tragic farce. The Governor of Pará, 'a man without pity for the Indians or respect for his King', regarded the expedition as one to gather slaves rather than souls. He had borrowed some money, and pledged the slaves to be brought from this journey as collateral. He secretly ordered the captain commanding Vieira's escort 'to dispose of those Indians in a manner tantamount to enslaving them'. Eight hundred Indians were gathered up. When the officer began to mistreat them Vieira indignantly left the expedition and returned to Pará to protest. It was all in vain. 'That great Vieira, who had disdained the admiration of the princes of Europe to withdraw to that corner of the world to save souls, found among the Portuguese there nothing but scorn for his person and opposition to his zeal.' Vieira was learning the realities of life on the Amazon.

The Amazon had been depicted as a place of legendary wealth and potential. People forgot all the failures of attempts to colonise it during the past century, and believed the propaganda. It was in reality a tawdry backwater in European terms, with less than a thousand white settlers in both Maranhão and Pará. The towns were clusters of thatched huts, with streets known only by the name of someone who lived on them, or some feature like the local gallows. Sugar did not grow well there, and the only lucrative crops were tobacco, cotton, and a few dyes and medicinal plants gathered in the forests. Movement was entirely by river as the forests were too dense or flooded for roads. The pioneers' farms were clearings on the river banks, and their labour was local Indians – for they were too poor to afford African slaves. There was no minted money until the eighteenth century: the only currency was cotton cloth or barter in other commodities, including Indian slaves. It is awesome to contemplate the destruction caused by those few settlers. The banks of the main stream of the mighty Amazon were almost depopulated and Indians were stripped from the accessible stretches of all its-tributaries. The populous villages seen by Orellana and Acuña were gone, overgrown by jungle, with their tribes fled or annihilated by the white men's diseases and extortions.

With Vieira's arrival in Pará, we suddenly see the place through the eyes of a sophisticated European churchman. It was as if a stone were lifted to reveal the unsavoury activities beneath. A contemporary wrote that Vieira 'pondered that the land was a cesspool of vices, and the truth was that the Portuguese were wolves and the heathen (so often misrepresented for being barbarians) were the sheep. He saw that unlawful enslavements were innumerable and that this sin was taking those settlers to Hell. He found that the self-interest of those in power was so unbridled that they even prevented him harvesting any fruit in the Christian aldeias. For when he sought Indians in them, even during Lent, he found them deserted. For those Indians were forced, with great injustice, to work on tobacco plantations or to be absent from their families in distant forests for eight or nine months, living and dying without sacraments or mass, without doctrine as if they were heathen, and their wives and children dying of hunger because their husbands could not attend to their clearings. . . .'

While Vieira was absent from the Court in Lisbon, the settler lobby was active. The King had sent a new captain-major (governor) to Pará with Vieira, with instructions to free all Indian slaves. There were violent protests, and the royal authorities wrote back that the legislation was unenforceable. The settlers complained that they were too poor to buy black slaves. 'It is deplorable to compare the situation of this captaincy [Maranhão] with that of the State of Brazil, where large numbers of negro slaves enter every month. Here the only help is Indian. New settlements located on the islands and banks of the rivers, widely separated, cannot dispense with the services of these [Indians] as rowers on voyages.' The King yielded completely to the pressure. On 17 October 1653 he admitted that it would be 'most difficult and almost impossible to free all Indians without distinction'. The King therefore reintroduced slavery. He opened the door to slavery so wide that almost any Indian could now be seized. They could 'justly' be enslaved if they raided by land or sea or impeded roads or commerce; failed to pay tribute; failed to obey 'when called upon to work in my service or fight against my enemies'; allied themselves with the King's enemies; ate human flesh after becoming royal subjects; or 'impeded the preaching of the holy evangel'. Anyone could lead a slaving expedition inland, provided only that he obtained permission from a junta and was accompanied by an ecclesiastic. It was an open season on Indians.

Vieira, whose pride was already wounded by the humiliations of his preaching and missionary efforts, was appalled at this betrayal by his friend King João. He decided to return to Portugal in mid-1654. He arrived at an opportune moment; for the King was ill and acceded to many of Vieira's requests, after consulting a panel of lawyers and ecclesiastics of which Vieira was a leading member. A law of 1655 put the Jesuits in full control of all Indian villages, even those long run by other orders. The Jesuit Fathers were to authorise ransom expeditions and to have a say in deciding which Indians legally qualified as slaves. But it was a compromise law; for slavery continued, and Indians judged to be 'justly' captured were slaves for life.*

António Vieira returned to northern Brazil to install his Jesuits in fifty-four aldeias, most of them around the mouth of the Amazon. His biographer boasted that they contained a total of 200,000 souls. He returned accompanied by a new governor, the hero of the Dutch wars, André Vidal de Negreiros. The King ordered the Governor to favour the Jesuits whenever possible.

The next five years were ones of euphoric activity for the Jesuits on the Amazon. They had a vast new field for missionary activity, and the dynamic and influential António Vieira at their head. Royal laws gave them full control of free Indians under Portuguese rule. But they were unable to resolve the fundamental contradiction between Indian conversion and the settlers' demands for labour. In an attempt to compromise and placate the settlers, the Jesuits allowed many expeditions up-river to contact new tribes. They themselves bravely went on these manhunts and used masses of presents to persuade gullible Indians to leave their forest homes and descend to the material and spiritual comforts of Belém do Pará. These descents became murderous deceptions. Even on the journey downstream a large part of each tribe would perish of white men's diseases; and the survivors were placed in aldeias within easy reach of colonial towns, so that they could fulfil the statutory six months a year labour for the foreigners. The Jesuit Fathers consoled themselves that the Indians who died in this way received the all-important deathbed baptism. This ensured them access to Heaven, a blessing denied the unmolested heathen living in tribal homelands. Those who survived were given religious instruction in their new mission villages.

The expeditions took place every year. In 1655 Fathers Francisco Veloso and Tomé Ribeiro went up the Tocantins, taking no military escort but only a Portuguese surgeon and a hundred Indian paddlers. They made peace with the Grajaú, Carajá and Cátinga, and then moved on to contact a group of Tupinambá, 'the most noble and valiant Indians of those sertões'. The missionaries 'proclaimed to them the good news of the new laws of Your Majesty – for preaching these is more effective than preaching the evangel, in persuading them'. A thousand

Tupinambá at once agreed to sail down with the Fathers. They reached the town of Belém in seventy canoes. There were 300 famous warriors among them and these caused consternation when they jumped ashore in full plumage and war-paint. They were welcomed by the Governor and by Vieira, and were soon settled in two aldeias and baptised. But one part of this group of Tupinambá refused to come. They were frightened off by news of the abduction of an Indian woman from the aldeia of Separara by a Portuguese soldier. One shrewd chief or shaman tried to dissuade his fellow-tribesmen from their folly. Vieira's Jesuit biographer described him with grudging admiration: 'There was one among the Indians who had been to Belém. Like some opportune minister of Lucifer, he abhorred the precipitate decision by his people and the ease with which they were going to place themselves among people of whose cruelty infinite tribes complained. . . . This infernal voice obstructed the current of the missionaries' victory. He even tore some souls from their hands, and dissuaded some Indians from leaving their forests. . . .'

Vieira wrote to the King that 'there were many [Tupinambá] who would not come. They said that they were well assured of the good treatment that the Fathers give them, but that they feared only the other Portuguese. Although they had no experience of the functioning of Your Majesty's new laws, about which the Fathers told them, they still did not wish to descend so close to the Portuguese. Many of the oldest members of that tribe said . . . this. They were men who appeared to be the most prudent among them, and their followers obeyed them. But others, apparently selected by God, came very willingly with the Fathers. They reached this city of [Belém do] Pará with seventy canoes filled with these people, of whom over a thousand souls came. Some went to Heaven on the journey. Of the rest, the innocent are already baptised and the adults are being catechised.' On arrival they were alarmed to find many relatives already enslaved by the settlers: these had been seized in 1647 in a raid by Bento Rodrigues de Oliveira accompanied by a friar of another order. Vieira described the tragic hypocrisy of the laws on Indian slavery: 'Children of the same parents are free or enslaved for no reason other than that some were brought down by the Fathers of the Society and others by officers of official ransom troops.'

The Tupi-speaking Cátinga had always been at war with the Portuguese. They attacked some of the missionaries' canoes. But when they learned that the expedition was peaceful, going to tell about God rather than to enslave, they sent canoes upstream to overtake Veloso and Ribeiro and offered to submit to them. Cátinga chiefs were taken down to be received by Governor Vidal de Negreiros and Vieira. They returned to their tribe and persuaded it to descend and settle in Jesuit mission villages near Cametá.

The Grajaú also wanted to descend with the Jesuit Fathers. But these did not have enough manioc or canoes ready for another migration. 'In this fishing for men, the nets were starting to break from the multitude, just as in Saint Peter's fishing for fish.' The missionaries therefore brought down only the chiefs, and persuaded the other Grajaú to wait for a year.

The Juruna were a tribe living on the lower Xingu. They were also known as 'Black Mouths' because of a two-inch band of black genipapo stain across their mouths and up to each temple. The Jesuit Manoel de Sousa descended them to form a group of mission villages near the mouth of the Xingu. They were sufficiently far from the town of Belém to escape the worst ravages of forced labour: as a result a few Juruna still survive, now located far up the Xingu in the sanctuary of the Xingu Indian Park. They were an industrious people, 'never idle, which is a rare thing in this climate'. They took to Christianity with the enthusiasm of converts. André de Barros described a Holy Week procession led by a large cross, with the Juruna men in one column carrying candles in profound silence, followed by the women with equal or greater devotion. Behind came Indians carrying the symbols of the passion, and 'forty Indians dressed in the Portuguese manner, mortifying themselves and drawing blood. . . . Some distinguished Portuguese who were present could not restrain their tears at this spectacle, seeing so much piety and fervour among people so newly come to the faith and to civilisation.'

In his original instructions to António Vieira, the King told him to propagate the Gospel, 'and for this you should erect churches and set up missions in the sertão . . .'. He left it to Vieira's judgement whether to descend Indians from the sertão, or leave them in their villages and send missionaries to instruct them in their own homelands. The tragedy is that Vieira generally chose to descend tribes. His Jesuits persuaded them to move to villages close to the settler towns. They did this for their own convenience and to appease the settlers. But they knew from experience that no tribes survived such moves: they rapidly succumbed to disease, overwork and despair.

Father Manoel Nunes, for instance, heard about some Guajajara living on the Pindaré river between Maranhão and Pará. 'He tried to remove them from the forests, to make them sons of God and to have them more accessible to the settlements of the Portuguese, so that these could employ them for wages whenever they wanted.' They lived for some years at a mission aldeia at Itaqui, three days' journey from São

Luís. Governor Rui Vaz de Siqueira was tempted by the thought of this Indian labour going to waste, and started to plant tobacco plantations to be worked by the Guajajara. 'But the Indians were so scandalised by this that many of them returned to the forests. For they did not on any account wish to work for the whites.' Possibly because of their decision to run back to the forests, the Guajajara have survived as a tribe, still living on the upper Pindaré and Gurupi rivers.

Jesuits also accompanied official ransom expeditions to comply with the legal requirement that an ecclesiastic go to decide which Indians fell within the many categories of 'just' captive. In 1657 Francisco Veloso and Manoel Pires went with a large expedition to the Aruak on the Amazon and Negro. The area was chosen 'because these were the places from which the settlers hoped for the greatest ransom of slaves. And because the Fathers always desired that the settlers should have many, so that they should live assisted and contented . . . Father António Vieira instructed those missionaries . . . to judge with the greatest latitude, as favourably as possible to the settlers. As a result they were highly satisfied and transported many. Justly so, for the wider the gate for legitimate captives, the more slaves would enter the Church and embark on the road to salvation. On that expedition 600 slaves entered through that gate of legitimate captivity. But this did not satisfy those who always wished that there were no gate at all.'

Another powerful ransom troop sailed for the Negro the following year, and spent fifteen months gathering slaves. Vieira again sent two Jesuits: Manoel Pires and the former Provincial of Brazil, Francisco Gonçalves. They explored new territory far up the river and contacted fresh tribes. The missionaries erected crosses in various villages and baptised many natives. Gonçalves made peace between two tribes about to fight one another; and he left many villages of free Indians settled on the banks of the river, 'already domesticated and at peace'. But the canoes sailed back laden with 'over 700 slaves, all examined within the terms of Your Majesty's laws'.

Early in 1656 Father João de Soutomaior accompanied an expedition to the Pacajá river, which flows into the Amazon from the forests between the Tocantins and Xingu. There was a rumour of precious metals on the river, and to deceive the authorities this expedition was announced as the Expedition of Gold. Vieira wrote to the King that it 'had an end that such a bad name prognosticated. Forty Portuguese spent ten months on it, and took 200 Indians, the majority of whom died from hunger and excessive work. Father João de Soutomaior also died after having reduced to the Faith and obedience to Your Majesty 500 Indians . . . of the Pacajá tribe and many others of the Tapirapé tribe who were also persuaded to descend with him. Sire, these are the only certain mines [here].' 'For the expedition's main and true purpose was to capture Indians: to draw from their veins the red gold which has always been the mine of that province!'

There were still some natives near the lower Tocantins, the river emptying closest to Belém. In 1658 Tomé Ribeiro and the Irish Jesuit Richard Carew went up the Tocantins and Araguaia on a mission to the Carajá and Poquiguara. All went well until, on the return journey, a group of Inheiguara attacked the expedition and killed some of its Indian auxiliaries. This was just what the authorities wanted. It was 'an injury that the state would not suffer, and was considered to be an affront to the Faith'. 'The Governor resolved that war be declared on them according to the law, for having impeded the preaching of the evangel.' A punitive expedition of 45 Portuguese troops and 450 Indian bowmen sailed up the Tocantins in 1659, accompanied by the Jesuit superior of Pará, Manoel Nunes. They found the Inheiguara to be 'a people of great resolution and valour, totally impatient of subjection. They had retreated with their weapons to the most hidden and defensible parts of their forests, to a distance of over fifty leagues. They were sought out there, found, surrounded, forced to surrender and almost all taken . . . 240 were taken prisoner. These were judged to be slaves, according to the laws of Your Majesty, for having impeded the preaching of the evangel, and were distributed among the soldiers.'

With this 'impediment' removed, the missionaries travelled overland from the Tocantins for a month of very arduous travel to reach the Poquiguara. The tribe was ready for its exodus. 'Entire villages had to be descended, with their women, children, infants, sick and all the other impedimenta that are found in a transmigration. Finally, after two months of continuous and excessive work and vigilance (which is also necessary), the Fathers reached the river with these people, embarked them on it and descended to the aldeias of Pará a total of about a thousand souls.' Manoel Nunes even went farther upstream to the Tupinambá who had refused to descend with the rest of their tribe in 1655. They now agreed to come. 'These Indians, both Poquiguara and Tupinambá, were all placed in the aldeias closest to the city for the better service of the republic, which in that year was increased by over 2000 Indians, slave and free. But the settlers were not even satisfied by this. For, although the rivers of these lands are the greatest in the world, [settler] greed is greater than their waters.'

Despite the many expeditions to clear Indians from the lower stretches of the great tributaries of the Amazon, there remained the embarrassing fact that the tribes of the island of Marajó, immediately opposite Belém do Pará, were still hostile and unconquered. Marajó is a vast island, the size of Switzerland, lying in the mouth of the Amazon or more correctly between the Amazon and Tocantins-Pará rivers. It is very flat, and its plains now form enormous cattle and buffalo-ranches, but there were also wide areas of forest cut by a labyrinth of meandering rivers, lagoons and swamps. The island was inhabited by many tribes speaking Carib, Aruak and other languages. They were friendly towards the first voyagers to the mouth of the Amazon, and initially welcomed the Portuguese. These called them by the collective term Nheengaíba or Ingaíba – a Tupi name referring to their many incomprehensible languages.

'At first these peoples received our conquerors in good friendship. But long experience showed them that the false claim of peace, with which we entered, was changing into declared captivity. They therefore took up arms in defence of their liberty and everywhere began to make war on the Portuguese.' They dismantled their villages, scattered their houses in the interior of the island, and adopted highly mobile warfare from light canoes in their maze of waterways. They allied themselves to any Dutch and English who ventured into the Amazon. One of their tribes, the Aruan, was responsible for killing Luís Figueira and other Jesuits who escaped the shipwreck off Belém in 1643.

Various punitive expeditions failed to subdue or even chastise the Nheengaíba. In 1654 one of Pará's top soldiers, João Bitancor Moniz, sailed from Belém with a strong force of seventy Portuguese soldiers and 400 Indians. He built a stockade deep in Nheengaíba territory and tried to persuade them to surrender peacefully. They were not deceived, but attacked and mauled the expedition, which was also depleted by disease. Vieira said that the troops suffered unduly because they went 'better equipped with chains and shackles for slaves than with bandages and requisites for the wounded'.

Settlers and soldiers who took part in such campaigns expected to be paid in the Indian slaves they captured. This expedition therefore decided to abandon its attempt on the skilful Nheengaíba, and sailed up the Amazon to seize some easier tribes 'to restock the domestic aldeias, for the public utility in the service of the captaincy and . . . the reduction of many souls to the bosom of the Church'. They sailed up the Jari river opposite the Amazon fort of Gurupá; won the alliance of a powerful tribe of Aruak; and marched with them against the neighbouring tribe of Chief Anybal. There was a stiff fight at a fortified stockade. But the Europeans charged in, stormed the defences, slaughtered many and put the rest to flight. The Aruak were pleased by the Portuguese performance, and the expedition returned to Belém exhausted but 'full of spoils'.

The Nheengaíba problem remained. These Indians were considered almost unconquerable 'because of their daring, caution, astuteness and determination, and above all because of their impregnable location'. The Jesuit João de Soutomaior remained after the 1654 expedition, and managed to convert one group of Nheengaíba after an arduous missionary campaign.* In 1658 Portugal and Holland again went to war. There was a real fear that the Nheengaíba would ally themselves to their Dutch friends from Surinam. If this happened 'they would together be masters of this captaincy: for there were no forces in the state, even if all joined together, to resist them'. A new governor, Pedro de Melo, decided to authorise the largest possible expedition for another attempt to crush the Nheengaíba.

The requisite council meeting was called to approve this campaign as a 'just war'. António Vieira attended, and argued that the Nheengaíba should be given one chance to respond to a peaceful overture. No one believed there was any hope of the ferocious Nheengaíba ending their twenty-year resistance so easily. But Vieira was allowed to try. At Christmas 1658 he sent two Indian chiefs with an open letter to all the Nheengaíba tribes. In it Vieira assured them that the King's new law of 1655 'had ended for ever unjust captivities and all the other wrongs that the Portuguese did to them'. Vieira knew perfectly well that this was nonsense. Royal laws were vacillating and ephemeral: he himself had intervened to have the law of 1655 change that of 1653; and if past history was any guide there would soon be further changes. The law of 1655 put Jesuits in charge of missions, but by no means ended Portuguese abuse of Indians. Vieira's own letters were full of fiery condemnations of his compatriots' misconduct.

To everyone's amazement, the ambassadors were not killed by their fellow-tribesmen, but returned on Ash Wednesday accompanied by a delegation of Nheengaíba. Once again, a gesture of friendship had undermined Indian resistance with pathetic ease. The envoys were given the customary lavish welcome. They delivered a long speech defending their own conduct and 'blaming the past war entirely on the Portuguese, as was true'. But they placed their trust in the tall and powerful António Vieira, 'The Great Father who came in person to our lands, someone of whom we had already heard, who for love of us and of other people of our skin risked his life on the waves of the high seas, and gained good things for us all from the King. We did not understand what this paper said, except by the report on it by these our relatives. But we immediately believed them entirely on this matter. And so, totally forgetting all the wrongs of the Portuguese, we came here to place ourselves in your hands and under the mouths of your cannon. We knew for sure that no one could harm us in the hands of the Fathers; and we call ourselves their sons from today onwards.'

The Nheengaíba returned to their island to prepare an aldeia fit to receive the Jesuits. They reappeared at Belém, as promised, in July 1659 'with seventeen canoes and thirteen more from the Cambocas tribe who also live on that island: thirty canoes in all. In them came as many chiefs accompanied by so many fine men that the city's fortress secretly placed itself under arms.' In mid-August António Vieira set out for Nheengaíba territory. He was finally undertaking a dangerous mission to convert a hostile tribe – the dream for which he had abandoned the Portuguese court and returned to Brazil. He sailed in twelve large canoes taking chiefs from all the Christian tribes, but only six armed Portuguese. After five days they reached the river of the Mapuá tribe. The tribes' chiefs came out in a large canoe handsomely decorated with coloured plumage. They were sounding horns and uttering shouts of joy in unison; Vieira's Indians gave answering salutations. It was found that the Indians had already built a fine, clean thatched church. 'A few yards from the church they brought the Fathers to the house they had prepared for them. It was very well laid out, with a corridor and cubicles and all enclosed round about and with a single door – in short with all the privacy that the missionaries normally maintain among the Indians.'

The Mapuá sent messages to other Nheengaíba tribes. After a week the Mamaianá, people dreaded for their ferocity, began to arrive in their canoes. Portuguese apprehensions were allayed by their 'demonstrations of festivity, trust and true peace'. Vieira said mass before a richly decorated altar. He himself wore full sacerdotal vestments. 'On the right side of the church were the chiefs of the Christian tribes, wearing the best clothes they possessed but with no weapons other than their swords; on the other side the heathen chiefs, naked and plumed in the barbaric manner, with bows and arrows in their hands; and between them the Portuguese.' In his sermon Vieira explained the significance of Christianity and the obligations of subjects of the King of Portugal. He invited each chief to swear allegiance to that crown, and promised that 'if they did this they would enjoy in freedom and security all the possessions and privileges that had been granted to the Indians of this state by Your Majesty in the law of 1655'. The chiefs accepted one by one. Each went up to Vieira to kiss his hand, receive his blessing, and leave his bow and arrows at his feet. Each chief knelt, with his hands in Vieira's, and swore: 'I promise to God and the King of Portugal, in my name and that of my subjects, to believe in our Lord Jesus Christ and to be the vassal of His Majesty. I also promise to keep perpetual peace with the Portuguese, to be a friend to their friends and an enemy to their enemies, and to fulfil these obligations for ever.' The Jesuits gave many presents to the Indians; oaths of allegiance for each tribe were notarised and signed by the chiefs; and there was a disarmament ceremony in which Indians broke their arrows and Portuguese threw their musket balls into the river.

The only discordant – or realistic – note came from a chief called Piye. He silenced everyone by telling Vieira to address his demands and explanations to the Portuguese rather than the Indians. 'We have always been friends and servants of the Portuguese. If this friendship and obedience have been broken it was on the Portuguese side and not ours. It is therefore the Portuguese who must now make or remake the promises they have broken so often – and not I and my people, who have kept them.'

Vieira was justifiably proud of his mission and pacification, which was certainly preferable to the 'just war' that would otherwise have been launched against the Nheengaíba. He boasted to the King that there were 40,000 Indians on Marajó island. They included the Mamaianá, Aruan and Anajá groups, the latter consisting of Mapuá, Paucacá, Guajará, Pixipixi and other subtribes. Most were left in mission villages on their island, and the Jesuits developed vast and successful cattle-ranches there. Nowadays there are plenty of cattle and buffalo on Marajó; but no tribal Indians.

Another Indian stronghold remained sympathetic to the Dutch: the republic of fugitives from the Dutch-occupied provinces who took refuge in the Ibiapaba hills. To Portuguese Catholics, Ibiapaba was full of 'Jews, Calvinists, Lutherans and other monsters of the various northern sects. . . . [It was] an utterly corrupt Geneva, with souls more monstrous than those of the most fearsome beasts that breed in the wastes of vast America. This was the state of deplorable misery in which those aldeias of nominal Christians were living. . . .'

A brave Tobajara named Francisco Mororeiba proposed to the Governor of Maranhão that he attempt an embassy to this 'corrupt Geneva'. Mororeiba set out on the long and difficult journey in May 1655, and to everyone's surprise he was well received in Ibiapaba. The Indians there were disillusioned when their embassy to Holland failed to achieve any support from their former Dutch friends. They therefore sent ten chiefs back to Maranhão with Mororeiba, carrying letters from them written in Indian ink on Venetian paper and sealed in wax – all gifts from the Dutch. The Jesuits Pedro de Pedrosa and António Ribeiro set out immediately. They reached Ibiapaba after a gruelling march from Maranhão in July 1656. Father Pedrosa admitted that 'he could achieve little with the adults who had been with the Dutch. Only one thing gave him more consolation: this was that he baptised 700 children whom God our Lord carried off to himself' in a terrible infant epidemic.†

The Tobajara and other tribes in the Ibiapaba hills were relatively sophisticated from their contact with Europeans during the Dutch wars. They were now sufficiently isolated to be free from settler abuse or demands on their labour. It was a fertile field for the Jesuits, who soon had a large mission called São Francisco Xavier and other mission villages in Ibiapaba. António Vieira was intrigued by what he heard of Ibiapaba: he may have had dreams of creating an isolated Jesuit theocracy in Brazil similar to the Spanish Jesuits' province of Paraguay.

Vieira told the King in 1659 that Chief Simão Tagaibuna of the Ibiapaba Tobajara had sworn to be a faithful vassal and a good Christian, 'and to help . . . in the conquest of all the neighbouring tribes, so that they will all be reduced to faith in God and vassalage to the King'. The King wrote to thank Chief Simão, and sent a solid gold medallion with the arms of Portugal on one side and his own portrait on the other. Vieira decided to deliver these presents in person. So in 1660 the fifty-two-year-old former politician and court preacher set off towards Ibiapaba. It was a tough journey: by sea, up-river, and then for thirty-five days on foot over the dry sertão, under an equatorial sun by day and sleeping on the sand at night. The Tobajara gave the Jesuit Superior a great welcome with music and dances. He delivered the gold medallion to 'the famous Simão, such a civilised and politic Indian . . . that not even the whites themselves were more [civilised] than he'. Vieira was pleased by what he saw of Chief Simão and of the promising Jesuit missions of Ibiapaba. When he left after a short visit he purged the place by expelling most of those who had fought with the Dutch in Pernambuco.

Back in Belém, Vieira was met by a demand from the town council for missionaries to accompany another slaving expedition. Vieira wrote in reply that 'the more slaves are made, there are always more who die, as is shown by experience every day. . . . The Indians of this country are less capable of work and have less resistance against disease [than African slaves]. And because they are near their homelands they flee to them more easily, or die from homesickness for them.' Vieira then listed the expeditions that had been accompanied by Jesuit missionaries during the five years since 1655: 'to the Tupinambá by Father Francisco Veloso; to the Nheengaíba by João de Soutomaior and to the Pacajá by that same Father; to the Aruak by Francisco Veloso; to the Rio Negro by Francisco Gonçalves; to the Carajá by Tomé Ribeiro; to the Poqui by Manoel Nunes; and that of Ibiapaba by António Vieira; and at the present moment there is another on the Amazon river, on which Manoel de Sousa died and Manoel Pires remains. In these expeditions and other lesser ones, over 3000 Indian souls have been descended [to the aldeias] and over 1800 slaves.' Vieira nevertheless agreed to help prepare yet another expedition.

The Jesuits, and António Vieira in particular, have been condemned by modern Brazilian historians, such as João Lucio de Azevedo, Mecenas Dourado, Gilberto Freyre or Jaime Cortesão, for their apparent hypocrisy. They fulminated against the injustices of enslaving Indians, but co-operated in the system by sending missionaries on official ransom or slaving expeditions, and by participating in the screening of slaves after arrival at Belém. They continued the practice of enticing tribes down to their mission villages, even though they saw the mortality this involved and knew that Indians should be left in their homes.

The trouble was that the missionaries were confronting, in the field, the insoluble dilemma between the needs of white settlers and the rights of the natives. Portuguese legislators never resolved this conflict; their laws were either hopelessly ambiguous or swung from extremes of pious liberality to colonial severity. The roots of the conflict lay in the totally different outlook and aspirations of Americans and Europeans. It was intensified by the fact that different diseases had evolved on either side of the Atlantic. As fast as fresh natives appeared on the colonial labour market they were carried off by imported disease. Once European settlers decided to colonise Brazil the Indians were doomed.

Vieira was a politician. He and his Jesuit colleagues reached the Amazon after the settlers had been entrenched there for over three decades, relatively unmolested by sanctions from the other religious orders or royal officials. Vieira evidently felt that his men could function only by some degree of co-operation with the colonists. He needed their military protection: Vieira himself took armed escorts on each of his four expeditions. He deluded himself that the benefits of the Jesuit missions outweighed the sufferings of those who fell foul of the system,

Vieira had no illusions about the illegalities of the Amazon slave trade. He sat on tribunals screening slaves, and had taken part in ransom expeditions. In 1655, for instance, he was one of a junta trying to decide which of 772 captives were 'legitimate' slaves. Vieira wrote a report listing some of the abuses that he witnessed. There was supposed to be only one official ransom expedition each year. Instead, there was 'a procession of many canoes containing private persons leaving for the Amazon river. . . . Each took whatever he pleased, capturing or buying as many as he could find, and returning openly or secretly with canoes loaded with Indians.'

Missionaries were supposed to accompany each expedition to judge whether Indians were captured according to the arcane rules in the royal law. Some missionaries were incompetent. There was a Carmelite called António Nolasco, a former soldier of the Gurupá garrison, 'whose profession is to traffic in slaves. He went on this expedition to take a great quantity of slaves: he brought back thirty-five for his own account and sold them publicly.' He was excessively lenient about judging his companions' captives. At one stage he was sick at the expedition's camp, but issued certificates of captivity, on his oath as a priest, without seeing or hearing the slaves or their captors who were far away up distant rivers.

The first batch of captives brought before the judges at Belém in 1655 were twenty-eight Indians of a Frenchman called Antonio Lemaire, who was captain of the fort of Gurupá. Governor André Vidal de Negreiros decided to question these himself through interpreters. To his surprise, 'they all replied that they were captives: they had been imprisoned in cords, about to be eaten, and their companions had already been eaten. The Governor was amazed by this very uniform response' since it was known that almost no Amazon tribes practised ritual cannibalism. He therefore questioned them one by one in private, but they repeated their stories and Lemaire confirmed them on oath. A week later some chiefs came from the Amazon to protest that Indians had been seized from their peaceful villages, even though they were allies of the Portuguese, had fought the Dutch, and helped build the fortress and church of Gurupá. These proved to be Lemaire's batch of Indians. When the Governor confronted Lemaire with his crime and perjury he answered: 'If others are going to do it, I wanted to do it first.' The Governor then asked the Indians why they had said they were bound prisoners. 'They replied that they said it because their master had taught them that response. He threatened that if they said anything else he would beat them to death.' The Captain of Gurupá had treated one Indian boy so badly that he hanged himself, and had an Indian woman beaten so severely that she died three days later. Because of such cruelties the Indians are 'so terrified of the whites that they do and say whatever they wish, even if it is against themselves'.

The examinations dragged on for two months. At first the Indians gave different replies, 'some saying that they were free; others that they were taken in battle; others that they did not know the origin of their captivity – they had come only because their chiefs had been paid the price; and other similar replies . . .'. But before long all Indians started giving the same answer: that they were tied up about to be eaten. It was obvious that they were being coerced. 'The judges saw it clearly and laughed at the Indians' confessions, and the cunning of their masters. In some examinations, as soon as the judges heard the name of the master presenting the Indians, they at once said, "Then these will certainly all be 'bound' Indians." And so they were. And on that evidence, amid laughter, those same judges condemned all those Indians to be slaves, solely on their own confession and with no other proof.' Antonio Lemaire, a confessed criminal who had earlier perjured himself before the tribunal, appeared later with another batch of captives. These were manifestly not genuine captives; but they confessed and were duly sentenced to slavery. Vieira protested at this and other obvious frauds, but was overruled by the lawyers and ecclesiastics of rival orders on the tribunal.

Vieira was shocked to find in 1655 that many free Poquiguara whom he had descended the previous year were already slaves. Settlers had persuaded their parents to sell them. Free Indian women were married to slave men, so that the women and their children passed into the condition of slavery. 'If these men can commit such crimes here in [Belém do] Pará in the face of the Governor and royal justices, what will they do in the forests and sertão where they are observed only by God whom they do not fear?' Vieira reckoned that, although 772 Indians were presented for examination that year, some 1500 or 2000 had in fact been captured and the rest abducted as illegal slaves.

Vieira had observed the official 'ransom' expeditions in action. The expedition's troops would arrive at an Indian village in its flotilla of canoes. They would show the trade goods they had brought, and say that they were under orders not to leave without that number of captive Indians in exchange. But they made such announcements 'surrounded by muskets and arquebuses and with their interpreters exhorting and menacing. Then the poor Indians, desiring the scythes and axes for their clearings, and far more out of fear that they themselves would be taken captive' went off to catch prisoners from other tribes.*

The victims were herded into riverside corrals called caiçaras – a name that still occurs on maps of Amazonia. For the descent they were thrown into canoes, shackled hand and foot. Many died of exposure and undernourishment. Others tried to escape, still shackled, and drowned or were killed in the forest by other Indians.

A document of 1660 has survived which gives instructions to the military escort accompanying a ransom expedition. The captain of the eight soldiers was told to assist the two Jesuit missionaries in converting Indians, and to observe the various royal laws about ransoming Indians. But he was to seek as many captives as possible within the terms of those laws. The expedition's scrivener had a book in which to record Indians judged as legitimate slaves. He was to 'declare the tribe, age, facial and body marks of those captives, with any other details that can be noted so that no mistakes may occur. . . . A certificate will be registered in the same form for each slave, and will pass with him to his purchaser, so that the legitimacy of his captivity will always be recorded.' The captives were to be divided as follows: of every 52 slaves, $27\frac{1}{2}$ to the Governor, 10 to persons who staked trade goods, $8\frac{1}{2}$ for the soldiers and 6 for the Indian paddlers who formed the bulk of the expedition.

The settlers were not impressed by the Jesuits' co-operation in official ransom expeditions. To them, Vieira and his colleagues were depriving the settlers of slave labour and diverting Indians into mission aldeias. They sent a long complaint to the Queen-Regent in 1659 protesting at the Jesuits' temporal control of aldeias. In January 1661 the town council of Belém sent a strident complaint to Vieira. 'The inhabitants are in the most wretched state. Some noblemen, conquerors and settlers, men who spilled their blood and spent their lives in the service of His Majesty . . . cannot bring their family and children to this city for lack of rowers. . . . During the last Christmas festivity the families of some noblemen did not come to this city because their maiden daughters had nothing to wear to hear mass, and their fathers had no money with which to buy it. Everything stems from not ransoming slaves. Many live in this city with no one to go to fetch a bundle of firewood or a pot of water. Many are perishing in this way because they have no one to work their farms. . . . It all proceeds from a lack of slaves, even though there are quantities of them in many forests where they could be ransomed. There is no doubt that this people in general is suffering great privation. In the sight of everyone . . . honest widows, maiden girls, married women and many orphans are suffering infinite hunger and the greatest abandon one could imagine. . . . All the men, even the most important, go about wearing clothes of coarse cotton dyed black . . .' – and so forth, for page after page.*

Vieira answered as best he could. He blamed the poverty of Pará, the inefficient lack of markets, inflation in Portugal, the remoteness of Belém, and improvident spending by the settlers themselves. He knew that settlers arrived from Europe expecting an easy life in the New World. They had heard wildly exaggerated reports of the wealth of the Amazon. Instead they found a rainy backwater with no lucrative crops. Even had they been prepared to work for themselves, these immigrants would have had difficulty surviving in those harsh tropics. Vieira admitted elsewhere that 'for a man to obtain manioc flour he has to have a small clearing; to eat meat he has to have a hunter; to eat fish a fisherman; to wear clean clothes a washerwoman; and to go to mass or anywhere else a canoe and paddlers.*

'All the labour of the settlers of that state is done by the country's native Indians. Because of [the Indians'] natural weakness, and the idleness, repose and liberty in which they are reared, they are incapable of enduring for long the labour in which the Portuguese make them work – especially that in the cane fields, sugar mills and tobacco [plantations]. For this reason many are continually dying. Since the entire wealth and support of those settlers consists of [Indian] lives, it is very common for [settlers] who were considered to be the richest . . . to fall in a short time to great poverty. For property does not consist of land, which is plentiful, but of the produce of whatever industry each individual works on it. And for this the only instruments are the arms of the Indians.'

Another Jesuit almost blamed the Indians for dying too easily. 'The State is miserably poor, with nothing worthwhile of its own. Those who have a hundred slaves today will not have six left a few days later. The Indians, who are anything but robust, have an incredibly high death rate. Any attack of dysentery kills them; and for any small annoyance they take to eating earth or salt and die.'

Two things now happened to intensify the conflict between Jesuits and settlers: epidemics that ravaged the native population, and the publication of correspondence from Vieira to the King that strongly criticised certain important colonists.

Maranhão was struck by a 'pestilential catarrh' in 1660. Vieira arranged blood-letting and issued sugar to the sick from Jesuit stores. But worse was to come. The Jesuit João Felipe Betendorf gave a harrowing account of an epidemic of smallpox that struck the natives of Maranhão and then Pará. 'Maranhão was burning with a plague of smallpox. The missionary fathers often dug graves with their own hands to bury the dead, for there were aldeias where there were not two Indians left on foot. Parents abandoned their children and fled into the forests in order not to be struck by that pestilential evil.' Stricken Indians changed from reddish to black in colour; their bodies smelt terribly; and some were struck 'with such force that pieces of their flesh fell off'.

The epidemic worsened during the rainy season. Betendorf moved to Belém do Pará and was kept very busy there. 'The smallpox, being contagious, spread throughout the city and captaincies, devastating Indians so terribly that it finished the greater part of them.' One by one the chiefs of the aldeias came to request Jesuits to go and help their people. Betendorf travelled for thirty leagues to a village near Cametá. 'As soon as I reached the aldeia I found it all aflame with smallpox. I immediately ordered all the most dangerous cases gathered into one large hut, so that I could instruct and confess them. You cannot believe the trouble I had to confess one old woman who said she had not sinned. Next day I confessed and gave communion to all whom I found capable of it. Some were missing, having fled into the forests. I ordered that they be summoned. They came and I stayed up most of the night confessing them, greatly irritated by some bugs called tungas that enter one's feet and cause intolerable itching. Only one man was missing. I went to find him, navigating about the islands . . . and finally discovered him by his stench, for he was lying dead and stinking in his hammock.

'From the aldeia of Cametá I went upstream to the Tocantins to exonerate those of that aldeia. Three persons were missing who had fled into the forest. I sent repeatedly to summon them. They delayed, but Our Lord God permitted their enemies to shoot at them with arrows and wound some of their relatives, who then brought them to the aldeia. They were so covered in pox and putridity that they caused horror to their own families. When they saw that a Father wanted to confess them they told me not to approach, for the rotten smell they were giving off was intolerable. I rather feared that I would not hear them well, but it was God's pleasure that I heard them better than the others; and the rotten smell seemed to me like the smell of white bread when it is removed from the oven. To confess them I was forced to put my mouth close to their ears, which were full of nauseating matter from the pox, with which they were entirely covered.'

Impotent medically, the missionaries directed their energies to giving absolution to their dying congregations. They were convinced that they were saving souls by these hasty last rites. The presence of the black-robed strangers – powerful sorcerers – probably *did* give magical consolation to frightened Indians dying in agony of smallpox. Two Jesuits worked very hard at the aldeia of St John the Baptist at Gurupi. 'The pestilential sickness had so thoroughly struck all the Indians in the aldeia that there was none but [the missionaries] who could bury the dead. With repugnance they nursed them, laid them out for burial, dug their graves and interred them, having . . . before all else confessed and administered the sacraments to them.'

Most of the colonists reaching Maranhão and Pará were peasant farmers from the Portuguese mainland and the Azores. They emigrated to the New World with high hopes of improving their social position and becoming prosperous land-owners. But the waters and vegetation of the Amazon were too vast. The immigrants could barely scratch the edges of its rain forests. The Indians, who looked so muscular and physically fit, refused to tolerate the heavy work imposed on them. And they could succumb in a few days to imported diseases.

The colonists were furious to find themselves failing in this difficult environment. They sought scapegoats for their frustration. They found them in the Jesuits, the pious busybodies who warned the colonists that their souls were in danger, and who curbed their pursuit of Indian labour.

While the town councillors of Belém corresponded with Vieira about the need for more ransom expeditions, they also sent a representative to Portugal to lobby on their behalf. Their envoy was the public prosecutor of Maranhão, Jorge de Sampaio. He set out the settlers' grievances in a memorial of twenty-five chapters. Some of the settlers' charges were valid, others unfounded or exaggerated. They protested that the colony faced ruin without more native labour. They were angry that Jesuits controlled not only the spiritual welfare of the Indians, but also ran the administration of the aldeias. The Jesuits were accused of greedily exploiting aldeia Indians for the enrichment of their Society. This was to be a recurring charge during the ensuing decades: by the eighteenth century there was much truth in it, but not in Vieira's day when the Amazon missions were in their infancy.

The settlers accused the missionaries of undue harshness in enforcing their Christian morality on the Indians. Once again the missionary insistence on one-man-one-wife ran counter to the native custom of permitting powerful men several wives. One important chief called António Marapirão had won a knighthood of Christ for his services against the Dutch. But he was an independent chief. When the Jesuits reached Maranhão they found Marapirão in chains in the fortress of Pará for having incited Indians to rebel against the Portuguese. He was saved by a change of governor, and put in charge of a small aldeia called Cojupe. The Jesuits tried to restrain his restlessness by making him marry one wife, but he defied them. In August 1658 Governor Pedro de Melo heard that Marapirão was again planning to rebel and was in contact with the Dutch. He was sent on an expedition up the Amazon, but escaped and reappeared in the forest near his aldeia. Arrested again, he was locked in the guard-house stocks with a shackle on his neck and double grills on his feet. He was sentenced to three years' exile under Jesuit care in Sergipe; but once there he joined settler revolts against the missionaries. The settlers of Pará made a hero of him: they claimed the Jesuits had arranged his arrest 'because he told them he was free and lord of his family and nation, and did not have to obey their orders'.

Another chief who was popular with the settlers – because he was co-operative about supplying Indian labour and a valuable ally in battle – was Lope de Sousa Guaquaiba of the aldeia of Maracanã on the coast east of Belém. He had no use for Jesuit piety and infuriated the missionaries by marrying his widow's sister. Vieira called him 'a most pernicious example, and the greatest rebel against obedience to the Church that has ever existed, not only in Maranhão but in all Brazil. He is taking not only himself but also his entire nation to Hell.' Vieira lured him to Belém with a deceptively friendly letter that ended: 'I will help you in whatever way is necessary. May God guard you with his grace. Nhedenceba' – which is the Tupi for 'your friend'. But, when he arrived, Vieira had him arrested and sent in chains to the fortress of Gurupá.

Another accusation concerned an Indian woman who was living with a white lover. The settler was excommunicated and forced to return the woman to her aldeia. She was then flogged on the orders of Father Francisco Veloso, who watched and said when to stop. She died shortly after. Vieira commented that the thrashing had been neither excessive nor indecent: she might have died by poisoning herself 'because she had been separated from her friend – for she was very obsessed with his company'.

The other accusations were wilder. One was that Vieira was a traitor in league with the Dutch; another that he went on expeditions without an escort in order to capture slaves for himself and his friends. Two officers whose slaving activities were thwarted by the Jesuits retaliated by accusing Vieira of deflowering an Indian maiden. Vieira had his slanderers condemned to penance, stripped to the waist with gags in their mouths; and then had them exiled to Portugal, where they in turn had their sentences quashed, with costs against the Jesuits.

At this time, when tempers were inflamed, a malicious Carmelite published a private letter from Vieira to the King and Queen-Regent. He had obtained the letter two years before, when the ship carrying it was attacked by French pirates. The letter was read out in the town council of Belém and copies were circulated. Vieira's private letter to his sovereigns was highly critical of the settlers and of certain leading colonists in particular. This letter was the match that caused the settlers' fury and frustration to explode.

So in May 1661 the colonists in São Luís do Maranhão rose against the Jesuits. They were encouraged by the other religious orders, jealous of Jesuit power. Even Governor Pedro de Melo, who previously supported the Jesuits, now sided with the colonists against them. He sent envoys to incite the captaincies of Gurupi, Pará and Gurupá. The crowd in Belém do Pará invaded the Jesuit college and took the Fathers to prison. Vieira was held under such close arrest 'that he was not even free for a necessity' but an Indian woman called Marianna Pinta brought him extra food. He was then taken by canoe to Maranhão and embarked, with other Jesuits, on the ship *Sacramento* belonging to the

Governor. An officer called António Arnau owed the Jesuits a lot of money, and 'blindly imagined that by throwing out the Fathers he would acquire treasure for the eleven children he had'. And, as the ship carrying Vieira was about to sail for Portugal, Arnau went in a canoe and shoved at it with both hands, in full view of the city, shouting: 'Out! Out! Out!'

Only a handful of Jesuits escaped the first arrests. One was the German Betendorf. Ordered to hide, he took to the forests with sixteen Indians. After some months their food ran low and they returned to Gurupá. Some settlers tried to arrest Betendorf but were captured by the Gurupá garrison, which remained pro-Jesuit: they were hanged as rebels after confessing to Betendorf. But in 1662 the city council of Belém sent a large force to capture the various Jesuits who had taken refuge at Gurupá. They were then packed off to Portugal in a leaky ship.*

Back in Portugal, Vieira was in familiar waters. On 6 January 1662 he preached a magnificent sermon known as the 'Sermon of the Missions' or 'Sermon of Amazonia' in the court chapel. The Court was stunned. The Queen-Regent Luisa declared herself protector of the missions of Amazonia. But Vieira's success was short-lived. A palace revolution in June 1662 placed the feeble-minded Afonso VI on the throne. The Queen-Mother was relegated to a convent, and Vieira was tried by his enemies in the Dominican-run Inquisition. He was in trouble for the heretical nature of his messianic beliefs about the future of the Portuguese monarchy, and championing Jews or 'New Christians'. His trial lasted two years and he was convicted, but with the light sentence of being confined to a Jesuit college. Vieira's fortunes improved in 1667 with the accession as Regent of Afonso's brother, later King Pedro II. But Vieira never regained his former great influence at Court. He spent six years in Rome and was much in demand as one of the finest preachers in Europe. In 1681 António Vieira returned to his beloved Brazil. He continued to champion the Indians and to write lucid letters, and died at the Jesuit college in Bahia in July 1697.

The eclipse of Vieira and the Queen-Mother brought suffering to the Indians far away in Brazil. Although the Jesuits were restored to Maranhão and Pará, a new law of 12 September 1663 put the Indians at the mercy of the settlers' town councils. Indian chiefs were to run the aldeias, but with a repartidor, or distributor, appointed by the town council to hire out Indian labour. Town councils were also to decide when ransom expeditions would take place and to appoint their leaders. The town councils, which consisted of the richest colonists, thus gained control of the entire pool of Indian labour, both slave and free.

When Vieira regained some influence over the next king, he tried passionately to have Indian slavery stopped. He thundered in 1669: 'Firstly, the so-called expeditions into the sertão must be totally prohibited and stopped, so that the injustice and tyranny cloaked with the name of "ransoms" cease. Under it many thousands of innocent Indians have been enslaved, killed and extinguished. It is the primary origin and cause of all the ruin of that State. The common argument against this proposal is that the State cannot survive without ransoms – as if it were worse to lose it, than to keep it through such unjust and abominable means!'

Vieira's arguments prevailed. King Pedro issued a law favourable to Indians on 1 April 1680. The Jesuits regained control of the aldeias after seventeen years of near-anarchy. Indian slavery was completely forbidden 'to shut the door against the excuses, subterfuges and frauds with which men of evil intent abuse the law'. Indian slaves were freed. Ransom expeditions were stopped, except by missionaries to descend Indians to their aldeias. The Indians were to be given land, since they were the 'original and natural lords of it'.

Vieira's solution to the labour shortage was to import black slaves from Angola, so that native Indians would be left alone. He could not see the absurdity of enslaving one race rather than another. A trading company was created to import African slaves to the Amazon.

But few blacks arrived: the settlers of Pará were too poor to afford them. The Africans were almost as helpless on the Amazon rivers as the white settlers themselves. The inevitable cycle occurred again: within four years there was another settler revolt and the Jesuits were again expelled from Maranhão.

During his time in Brazil, Vieira drew up regulations for the conduct of aldeias. His system of administration lasted for a century. He was very keen that rule of the villages and punishments of Indians should be done by the tribes' own chiefs. 'In the temporal administration . . . it is very important that we proceed paternally and without methods that smell of imperiousness. . . .' He also sought to regulate Indian labour for settlers. Everything possible was to be done to alleviate working conditions, 'for the conversion of the heathen greatly depends on the good treatment done to those already Christian'.

In his writings and sermons, Vieira often praised Indian intelligence. But he was furious when Indians rejected Christian teaching as incomprehensible, alien to their way of life, and irrelevant to their environment. His frustration exploded in one sermon. He complained that highly educated Jesuits had to 'adapt themselves to the most unintelligent and inarticulate people that nature ever created or aborted: to men whose status as men was in doubt, so that the Popes had to define that they were rational and not brutes. . . . [Our teachers] had to return a thousand and one times . . . to teach again what was taught and repeat what was already learned. . . . We perform our missions in poverty and in the wilderness, amid the hardships and miseries of the most uncouth, poorest and most lowly people, the least human people that were ever born in the world!' It was a terrible admission of failure. Many Indians regarded the Jesuit Fathers as mere agents in charge of the settlers' labour pool. They saw that, for all their sanctity, the missionaries were impotent to halt lethal epidemics. In their confusion and despair they clung stubbornly to their own tribal way of life and rejected a genuine conversion to Christianity.

There were many limitations and errors in Jesuit handling of Indians. Vieira's own conduct was open to modern criticism. But with his passing the Indians lost their most powerful and eloquent champion. No one of similar stature and energy concerned himself with Indian welfare during the three centuries of Portuguese colonial rule or the nineteenth-century Brazilian Empire. The tragedy was that the situation was impossible, even for Vieira. Although he established the Jesuit missions of Amazonia, his intervention ultimately did very little to halt the complete disappearance of Indians from the accessible parts of the Amazon basin.

SIXTEEN

Cattle

MOVING inland from the north-eastern bulge of Brazil, the coastal greenery is soon left behind. The plantations of sugar, cotton and tobacco cease as the ground rises and becomes more arid; there are fewer palm trees – cashews, majestic imperial palms or the baroque plumes of babassus. Except for the mighty São Francisco, most rivers peter out and their beds are often dry. There are many woods, but in the open the trees become low and gnarled, pale green, their leaves coated with a sickly glaze. The soil is sandy; dusty pinks and reds interspersed with cement-hard pillars of termite hills. There are lizards and rattlesnakes, and countless ants attacking every crop. The air is more invigorating on the plateau and there are sweeping horizons. Exciting cloud formations race towards the Amazon forests. This is good cattle country; but for tough cattle, preferably zebu able to resist the heat and ticks.

These hills and plateau were the sertão, the dry wilderness inhabited by the Tapuia – a generic Tupi word for all tribes who spoke languages different from theirs. The Indians were handsome people, lean and hard to match their savannahs. They fought and hunted with clubs as much as with bows and arrows, and could outrun their game. Most had no experience of boats. They were less spiritual than the Tupi, less inclined to alcohol. Although semi-nomadic hunter-gatherers, the Tapuia did not migrate as readily as the Tupi: when attacked, they tended to defend their lands rather than escape in despairing exoduses.

Indians fighting.

The sixteenth century saw the conquest of the coastal Tupi; in the seventeenth it was the turn of the tribes further inland. The reactions of most of these tribes followed a similar pattern to that of the Tupi: initial welcome; awe at the strangers' technology, military success and religious conviction; gradual realisation that the settlers' motives were land and labour; armed resistance rather than submission on these terms. But the invasion of the hinterland was different from that of the coast. The land was too weak and remote from Europe to attract many settlers: no cities were founded in the north-eastern interior. Although many Tapuia were lured to the coast in the early days of slaving, black labour had largely replaced Indian by the time the frontier moved inland. It was cattle that led white men into the north-east sertão. A few cattle barons created immense ranches in those thinly populated hills and plains. Some Indians were needed to herd and drive the cattle, but generally the Indians would have been ignored had they willingly surrendered their lands and not interfered in any way with the precious cattle.

One of the first cattle regions was Bahia. At late-sixteenth-century map already marked a corral at the mouth of the Paraguaçu, and during the ensuing decades cattle ranching spread westwards up the Paraguaçu and Itapicuru and across the sertão of Jacobina towards the upper São Francisco river. The Jesuits were powerful cattle-ranchers. But the greatest cattle barons were the descendants of Garcia Dias d'Avila: his seat was a towered house known as the Casa da Torre, and the ranches of the House of Torre eventually covered thousands of square miles. Another cattle baron was ·António Guedes de Brito, and there were many smaller ranchers to whom the Government awarded parcels of former Indian territory. It was a situation very similar to the arrival of cowboys in the American West two centuries later.

Once cattle moved into an area they displaced human beings. The Tapuia tribes were forced to surrender their homes and hunting-grounds to provide grazing for these imported animals. Thomas More wrote in *Utopia*: 'These placid creatures, which used to require so little food, have now apparently developed a raging appetite, and turned into man-eaters. Fields, houses, towns, everything goes down their throats.' The native resistance to this cattle invasion was one of the most important stages in the conquest of the Brazilian Indians. It was also the worst recorded. As always, there is nothing from the Indian side. The natives left no written record and no one recorded their version of the fighting. Most of the tribes displaced by the cattle have disappeared, and those that survive have only vague memories of those remote tragedies. There was no chronicler or historian of these wars from the Portuguese side. The soldiers and bandeirantes who conquered the sertão were often illiterate and left no memoirs. The missionaries wrote little, and by the late seventeenth century there was no flicker of interest in the ethnology of the tribes being destroyed in these campaigns. All that we have are official papers: letters from governors organising expeditions or reporting on their progress. The history that results is patchy and disjointed; but the wars themselves are too important to omit.

The settlers' cattle were terribly tempting to Indian hunters; they had never seen such large animals or game so easy to hunt. In 1612 Indians, probably groups of Aimoré, attacked the Capanema sugar district on the lower Paraguaçu. Ten years later there was a more serious resistance further inland: Indians killed all settlers on the plains of Apora, 'leaving nothing alive', and the area remained uninhabited for years. The natives moved on, to the plains of Itapororocas, forcing settlers there to abandon their farms; and then descended the Paraguaçu to attack Cachoeira and plantations near the Maragogipe, Jaguaripe and Jequiriçá across the Bay from Bahia. The settlers remained on the defensive during the decades of the Dutch wars.

Once the Dutch were gone, the authorities decided to take action. But the conquest of the Bahia interior was slow and halting. It took a quarter of a century to subdue the Tapuia living so close to the capital of Brazil.

In 1651 a governor-general wrote that 'the boldness of the heathen Tapuia obliges us to punish their insolence with all heat'. He ordered the Governor of Ilhéus to 'go up the Maraú river to destroy all the villages from which you suspect they are descending. . . . Try to encourage all [settlers] who want to go with the reward of captives, which I hope will be great. . . .' He also sent a large expedition up the Jequiriçá, but it killed only four Indians, for the tribes had burned their villages and fled into the forest.* The next governor-general tried again, sending an expedition under Gaspar Rodrigues Adorno against the Guerens group of Aimoré. A few Indians remaining in the local mission aldeias were recruited, as well as a force of 400 Tapuia, the private army of one Luís da Silva. Any genuinely friendly Indians were to be descended to coastal aldeias, but all other villages 'will be burned and totally destroyed and all Indian men and women imprisoned'. In the event, the expedition was curiously restrained. It made peace with the Paiaia tribe of the Jacobina sertão, who promised to descend nearer the coast. The Paiaia repeated this promise to later expeditions led by Tomé Dias Laços in 1655 and 1656. But they failed to move. A fort was built on the Urubu ('Buzzard') hills but its lonely garrison died of disease; in 1657 the next governor-general ordered a road built to it.

The Paiaia were a wily tribe, who rapidly understood and exploited white men's thinking. The Paiaia claimed that all the raids were the work of a tribe of Tapuia living beyond them in the Urubu hills. So in 1658 an expedition was sent to help the Paiaia fight this enemy. Its commander was ordered to give food and presents to the Paiaia, and with them as guides 'you will then follow the trail of the Tapuia into their villages of Outinga and Urubu and make war on them, defeating and slaughtering them by every means and effort known to military skill . . . sparing only Tapuia women and children, to whom you will give life and captivity'. A few months later, the punitive expedition had not yet left, and the desperate Governor-General enlisted a force of Paulistas, since the men of São Paulo were famous woodsmen and Indian-fighters. In September 1658 he sent a force of Paulistas inland under Captain Domingos Barbosa Calheiros with the same instructions to favour the Paiaia and smash their enemies.

The expedition finally plunged into the wilds guided by the astute Paiaia. 'These assured them that they would arrive there in five days. But they led them on, deceived, for over sixty days . . . guiding them around in the trackless hills and dense jungles without ever succeeding in reaching the villages they were seeking. One of their tricks was to warn our men not to shoot game or cut wood to extract wild honey, in order to avoid being observed by the Tapuia who were causing us damage. But the Tapuia they described were never found. In fact they never *could* be found, because that tribe was none other than the Paiaia themselves. With this ruse they defeated, exhausted and killed our men by starvation. . . . We abandoned those wildernesses and forests after being consumed and finished by the sickness, misery and hardships of the expedition. . . . Some of our men stayed to guard the munitions in the villages of Tapurice; but [the Indians] killed and ate these. They did the same to others in the village of Camisam, and to all who straggled from exhaustion or strayed. There were no enemies other than them. . . . They did all those excesses under cover of the friendship agreed with us. The few of our men who escaped could take no revenge on them, for those who returned, out of over 200 white men who went on that expedition, were very rare.'

There was a stalemate throughout the 1660s. Some Indians continued to raid, with lightning attacks on isolated farms. Settlers and their slaves were killed, and farms burned. The settlers abandoned the districts of the upper Jequiriça and Jaguaripe and retreated into the Recôncavo farming region alongside Bahia. There were more fruitless expeditions and more attempts to persuade the Paiaia to settle nearer the coast. Every year governors authorised the purchase of presents to lure Indians from the Jacobina hills: eleven suits of clothing in 1663, masses of fish-hooks and six dozen knives in 1664, clothing and tools in 1665. But little was achieved.*

In 1670 there was an incident at Cairu in Ilhéus. The townspeople were celebrating a religious festival with their wives when a horde of Indians appeared in the town. No Indians had previously come that far, so it was assumed this was an attack. The church doors were slammed shut, but an officer called Manoel Barbosa de Mesquita charged out into the thick of the Indians. He fired his two pistols and then hacked at the natives, killing their chief and many others. He and two of his soldiers were finally killed by arrows and the Indians left. But the people of Bahia felt that his death cried for vengeance.*

A belligerent new governor-general, Alexandre de Sousa Freire, was dismayed by the failures of his predecessors. He decided that persuasion was useless. In his view, 'only when they suffer stern discipline do the insolences of conquered barbarians subside. . . . Only after being completely destroyed do they become quiet. . . . All experience has shown that this public nuisance can be checked only at its origin: by destroying and totally extinguishing the villages of the barbarians.' He determined that on the expeditions *he* sent all Indians would be killed or enslaved and their lands divided among colonists. Woe betide friendly Indians who acted as guides but were suspected of encouraging the enemy: they were to be executed as traitors and rebels!

This governor wrote to São Vicente and São Paulo begging for more bandeirantes. In 1671, 400 Paulistas sailed to Bahia under Estevão Ribeiro Baião Parente with a vanguard under Brás Rodrigues de Arzão. They marched inland from the Apora plains with a hundred Indians and plenty of equipment, and established a base at Cachoeira on the Paraguaçu. During the ensuing years they campaigned along the banks of that river, and along the Jacuipe to the north and Jequiriça to the south. They finally managed to locate and defeat some Tapuia at the end of 1672. Their prisoners were led down to Bahia in February 1673. The Governor-General wrote delightedly: 'The leaders of the conquest have arrived with happy results, although with less prisoners than surrendered to them. A form of plague struck these on the journey, so that I understand that over 700 died. They therefore brought down only 750. They lost some of these in this town, and used others to pay private expenses. I have sent the rest with them by ship' back to São Vicente.* Sebastião da Rocha Pitta wrote that the Indians resisted strongly in continuous battles, but eventually suffered many killed and almost all captured. 'The captives were remitted to Bahia where they were sold for such low prices that the best specimens fetched no more than twenty cruzados and the rest far less.'

Another campaign in 1673 found three villages of Maracá Indians containing over 1200 persons. Meanwhile another force located the fires of the villages of the Tapuia who had destroyed the first Paulista expedition. Since this was cattle country, the colonists preferred it cleared of Indians. The Governor therefore reported with pride: 'All the villages are now defeated and the tribes who were most responsible for the violences suffered by the Recôncavo and the neighbouring towns are extinct.' 'With this the area is clear of heathen. The plains and land found there are excellent, and I am very anxious to found two settlements.' Indians who had been brought from São Paulo were told to remain and settle the newly conquered lands. Various Paulistas also chose to remain, and in November 1673 Estevão Ribeiro Baião Parente was authorised to found the town of Santo António da Conquista 260 kilometres from Bahia.†

Some tribes escaped extinction. The Aramaru accepted conversion by the Franciscan Friar Anastacio de Odierne. The wily Paiaia ran off from one expedition in 1672 but were wooed back with presents. The following April the Governor sent '200 axes, 50 scythes for clearing forest, 50 hoes, 100 machetes and 3 sacks full of combs and knives' to persuade the Paiaia to enlist in another expedition.* In 1674 the Paiaia received another consignment that included 616 Flemish knives, 495 combs in a sack and 4000 fish-hooks. They were settled in aldeias run by the Jesuits at the headwaters of the Jacuipe. Later governors often requested that the missionaries send Paiaia on expeditions, for they were considered better scouts than any other tribe.†

The situation in the conquered territories was not a happy one. In January 1677 it was reported that the Indians of Jacobina were on the verge of armed rebellion. For once a governor assumed that settlers were to blame. He sent an officer to 'assure the chiefs that this government greatly regrets that there should be those who have caused this altercation. Punish all [settlers] who have participated in giving [the Indians] the slightest cause for complaint. And . . . so that [the tribes] should see how different our feelings are from what they assume, we order the chiefs from each village . . . to come here, for we wish to give them the presents that most delight them and their wives.'

It then emerged that the Paulista governor of the new region was abusing his mandate to recruit Indians for fresh expeditions. There were repeated complaints of violence. The governors angrily reminded Estevão Ribeiro Baião Parente that 'His Highness does not want . . . Indians treated as slaves. We had charged Captain-Major Gaspar Ruiz Adorno . . . to assemble all scattered Indians into an aldeia. But Your Honour attacked that aldeia, burned the houses and the corn they were harvesting and tied up some Indian men; and when the rest fled you tried to move the women to the town [you are founding]. . . . You are not supposed to make your town by moving peaceful Indians from their aldeias in which they are content. The purpose of your orders was to take men to help you go and conquer wild Indians, whom you were to bring to be sold in the city . . . also to bring them from the sertão to domesticate them and make them Christian. If Your Honour has some other intent, you can immediately resign.'

The authorities did their best to calm the situation and prevent provocation of the Indians. One officer reported that the Jacobina villages were peaceful. But the Captain-Major Agostinho Pereira was killed and, in 1677, there were the inevitable reprisals. In 1678 the Governor-General ordered another commander to stop his troops trying to divide Indian prisoners among themselves – instead, the Governor sent a boat to transport 500 of them down to Bahia so that he could have a share.*

So by 1680 the Tapuia of the Bahia hinterland were finally subdued. Some may have retreated southwards, melting into the forested hills of the interior of Ilhéus; others were settled in aldeias; but many were simply destroyed or sold into slavery in other parts of Brazil. Their lands were now rapidly colonised. Cattle ranches spread westwards to the upper São Francisco, and then north-westwards on the far side of that river. The settlers of this frontier met Paulista bandeirantes moving down the São Francisco in search of slaves, and later met other waves of cattlemen pushing inland from Sergipe, Pernambuco and Rio Grande. The authorities were impressed by the Paulistas' performance. One governor-general wrote in 1699 that 'experience has shown that these men alone are capable of waging war on the heathen. They gave ample proof of this [near Bahia]. In a few years they left this captaincy free of all the tribes of barbarians that oppressed it, extinguishing them so effectively that from then until the present you would not know that there were any heathen living in the wilds they conquered.'

The cattle ranches spread inexorably into the scrublands of the interior, sometimes in chains of sesmarias – a medieval word for land allotments designed to create a land-owning middle class – but often in immense estates of families such as the Dias d'Avila of the House of Torre or Guedes de Brito of the House of Ponte. These mighty pioneers were the poderosos do sertão, the 'great ones of the wilds', whose power caused the Crown to issue edicts to stop their 'oppressing the poor and lowly, who are too frightened to dare complain'. They made life difficult for the few missionaries who penetrated the tough backlands. A French Capuchin, Father Martin de Nantes, wrote an account of his mission among the Cariri, the generic name for a series of Tapuia tribes in the Bahia and Pernambuco hinterland. He described how Francisco Dias d'Avila once launched a punitive raid that captured 500 Indians. They surrendered on promises of pardon from the head of the House of Torre, but he massacred them all two days later. Finally in 1696 the ladies of the House of Torre ordered their cowboys to evict the Jesuits by force from the'r missions and ranches along the São Francisco.†

Anyone who has visited the interior of the Brazilian north-east can easily visualise the hard life of the early cattlemen. This is still dusty and dry country, much of it caatinga, the desperately sparse and arid brushland that can stretch for hundreds of miles between watering-places. A corral or ranch would contain from 200 to 1000 head of cattle and be run by one cattleman. It took a while for newly arrived cattle to grow accustomed to their surroundings, and during that period several stockmen would be employed to help; but from then on the owner would be almost alone. When a number of corrals were grouped together they formed a fazenda or estate, and these might contain from six to twenty thousand head. By 1711 a Jesuit wrote that there were half a million cattle in the interior of Bahia and 800,000 in that of Pernambuco.

The cowboys themselves lived out on the range, sleeping in the open for months on end among their animals. They had plenty of meat and milk, but little else – some wild honey and occasional manioc flour or corn. They used leather for everything – for protective clothing, the doors of their huts, water-carriers, food boxes, bed-rolls, chests, saddles and rope. A cowboy worked for nothing for the first few years, and was then paid in kind; receiving, say, one calf out of four born. He could thus form a herd of his own. These were tough and self-reliant men, proud of the title vaqueiro or cowboy, very skilled at their jobs and scornful of dudes from the coastal towns. There were few men and almost no white women in the backlands. A priest wrote that in Piauí at the end of the seventeenth century there were 129 ranches containing only 441 persons, including 'whites, negroes, Indians, mulattos and half-breeds'. These tough men 'usually roast their meat, as they have no cooking pots. They drink water from wells and lakes, always turbid and impregnated with nitrate. The climate is very stormy and rather unhealthy, so that these wretched men live dressed in hides and look like Tapuias.'

The herds of cattle had to be driven down to the coast. Cattle trails wound across the dry interior, avoiding the forests or the worst deserts, and moving from one watering-place or salt deposit to the next. There were tiny settlements where trails met, or at river fords. The admirable

Jesuit author Andreoni (who used the pseudonym 'Antonil') wrote in 1711 that 'the cattle trains that normally come to Bahia consist of 100, 160, 200 or 300 head of cattle. Some of these arrive almost every week at Capoame, a place eight leagues distant from the city where there is pasture and where the merchants buy them. At some times of year there are weeks when cattle trains arrive every day. Those who drive them are whites, mulattos and blacks, and also Indians, who seek to have some income from this work. They guide themselves, with some going in front singing so that they will be followed by the cattle. Others come behind the beasts, driving them, and ensuring that they do not leave the trail and run wild. Their daily marches are four, five or six leagues [15–22 miles], according to the quality of the pasture where they are to stop. But where water is lacking they continue the march for fifteen or twenty leagues, marching day and night with little rest until they find a stopping-place where they can pause. At the passage of rivers, one of those guiding the train places an ox's horns on his head and, swimming, shows the animals the ford where they must cross.' The cattle that reached Bahia were sadly scrawny. William Dampier was at Bahia in 1699 and saw the slaughterhouses after the Lent fast, with 'men, women, and children flocking thither with great joy to buy, and a multitude of dogs, almost starved, following them; for whom the meat seemed fittest, it was so lean'.

The cattlemen had no sentiment about the moral need to treat Indians well. They helped themselves to Indian lands and, when possible, Indian women. They were ruthless in punishing any tribes who hunted or molested their cattle. But the cowboys' way of life was not too alien to that of the Tapuia, and there was some fellow-feeling between cowboys and Indians. The big cattle-ranchers had private armies of Indians, who followed them willingly because they admired their leadership. Individual Indians did not mind working as cowboys: it was free and virile work that used their skills, unlike the degrading drudgery on the coastal plantations. Martin de Nantes said that when Christian Indians married 'there is always a good number of Portuguese at all such occasions, who bring guitars and violins for the solemnity and sing motets, and who even fire several shots from their guns to enhance the rejoicing'. And the two races mixed amiably at annual religious festivals.

One of the first cattlemen to penetrate the interior of Piauí was Domingos Afonso, known either as 'Mafrense' or simply 'Sertão'. He crossed the São Francisco and descended into the basin of the Parnaíba. 'He entered those lands previously not penetrated by Portuguese and inhabited only by wild heathen, with whom he had many battles, emerging from one dangerously wounded but from all of them victorious, killing many heathen and making the rest retreat to the interior of the sertão.' He reached the Piauí and Canindé rivers, and by the time of his death in 1711 could boast that he was 'lord and owner of half the lands for which I asked in Piauí, with Colonel Francisco d'Avila and his brothers; which lands I discovered and peopled with great danger to my person and at great expense, with the help of my associates' and many lawsuits.* He left his lands to the Jesuits, who thus acquired thirty estates stretching over almost 400 miles and feeding 30,000 cattle and 1500 horses.

A couple of hardy Paulista bandeirantes moved into Piauí at the same time as Mafrense, about 1679. They were a tough rogue called Domingos Jorge Velho and his companion Cristóvão de Mendonça Arrais. Domingos Jorge Velho conquered a territory to the west of Mafrense's, and for a time they fought the local Indians together. Jorge Velho had also come overland from Bahia, moving down the Gurgueia, and he settled on the Poti river. He defeated the Indians of the area and gathered about him a force of the most warlike, mainly Tobajara, Orua and Cupinharuen.

Domingos Jorge Velho boasted to the King about his private army: 'Our militia, Sire, is unlike the regular one found anywhere else. First, our troops, with whom we undertook the conquest of the savage heathen of this very vast sertão, are not made up of people registered in Your Majesty's muster books, nor are they obligated by wages or rations. They are in groups which some of us assemble: each of us joins with the servants he possesses under arms, and together we enter the sertão of this continent – not to enslave (as some hypochondriacs [sic] would have Your Majesty believe), but to acquire Tapuia (a fierce people who eat human flesh) to domesticate them to the knowledge of civilised life and human society and association and rational commerce. In this way they will come to have the light of God and of the mysteries of the Catholic faith which is necessary for their salvation – for anyone who would make them angels before making them men labours in vain. We enlarge our troops from those thus acquired and brought into settlements. And with them we wage war on those who are obstinate and refractory to settlement. If we later use them in our fields we do them no injustice, for this is to support them and their children as much as to support us and ours. Far from enslaving them, we render them a gratuitous service by teaching them to till, plant, harvest and work for their livelihood – something they do not know until the whites teach them. Do you understand this, Sire?'

Domingos Jorge Velho may have considered himself as an altruistic civiliser, evangelist and agricultural instructor. He made a very different impression on the Bishop of Pernambuco: 'This man is one of the worst savages I have ever met. When he came to see me he brought an interpreter, for he cannot even speak correctly. He is no different from the most barbarous Tapuia, except in calling himself a Christian. And, although recently married, seven Indian concubines attend him – from which one can infer his other habits. Until now, ever since he first had the use of reason – if, that is, he ever possessed it, for if he *did* he has lost it and I venture that he will not easily regain it – he has roamed the forests hunting Indian men and women, the latter to exercise his lusts and the former to work on the fields he owns.'

However uncouth, Domingos Jorge Velho was a wonderful woodsman and fighter. In 1685 a governor-general of Brazil therefore decided to enlist this bandeirante to help conquer Palmares, a kingdom of runaway black slaves. This place was a mocambo (the African word for a hideaway or refuge) located in the vast forests of Palmares on the Ipanema river in the interior of Alagôas and Pernambuco, 200 miles south-west of Recife. It had started at the beginning of the seventeenth century, and gathered momentum as more slaves escaped during the Dutch wars. The Dutch tried to suppress Palmares, sending Roulox Baro with his Tapuia to put the place to fire and sword in 1643. He returned after killing about a hundred blacks. Another Dutch expedition of 1645 reached one Palmares town but found that its inhabitants had fled. The town had 220 houses along a broad street, and contained a church, four smithies and a huge council house. The people were fed by extensive fields of cereals, excellently irrigated. A king known as Ganga-Zumba ('Great Lord') ruled Palmares from a fortified compound called Macoco. He was treated with all the deference and obedience due to a powerful monarch, and ruled with iron justice. No sorcery was permitted, and criminals or fugitives were executed. The blacks in Palmares made their own weapons and trained to resist the invasions that they knew were inevitable. But their main defensive tactic was to abandon their stockaded towns and vanish into the forests. Since Palmares remained independent through almost the entire seventeenth century, many of its people were born there; and its warriors often raided Portuguese plantations to liberate slaves. The existence of this sanctuary was an inspiration and magnet to all black slaves suffering cruelties and oppression on the coastal farms.

Many expeditions were sent to extirpate this affront to Portuguese rule. In 1674 there was a proposal to enlist the Tupi of Camarão's successor, Dom Diogo Pinheiro Camarão.* Six costly expeditions marched against Palmares between 1680 and 1686 but achieved nothing. So, when in 1685 the Governor-General received a letter from Domingos Jorge Vẹlho asking for a licence to conquer more Indians, he decided to use the Paulista anḍ his private army against Palmares. He promised the bandeirante that he could keep any slaves and land he conquered. Domingos Jorge Velho accepted and marched off with a thousand native bowmen – 200 of them with firearms – and 84 white men and half-castes. They left their farms in Piauí and embarked on a gruelling march across many hundreds of miles of waterless scrublands. 'This march was made under the worst conditions of toil, hunger, thirst, and destitution that have yet been known and perhaps ever will be known in this sertão . . . 132 persons died because of hunger, thirst and suffering; 63 died of sickness; and over 200 deserted because they could not stand such misery. . . .'

No sooner had the bandeirante and his surviving men reached the Palmares campaign than they were asked to turn round and march urgently against a more serious threat. The Janduin group of Cariri Tapuia had attacked the Portuguese in Rio Grande! It was the start of one of the most serious Indian wars, against a large, warlike and experienced group of tribes.

This conflict had been fermenting for four decades. It involved the tribe of King Jandui that had once been such good allies of the Dutch. When the Dutch were being defeated by the settlers of Pernambuco in 1649, a Tapuia chief was captured at the second battle of Guararapes, and 400 Tapuia changed sides to be with their chief. The Portuguese shrewdly rewarded each man who joined them with an axe, a sickle, and a string of beads for his wife.* These Tapuia then retreated back to the interior of Rio Grande and Ceará, where they remained largely unscathed by the colonisation of the coast.

Cattle-ranching gradually spread inland. There were inevitably some clashes with the Cariri and particularly the warlike Janduin. They were angered by ill-treatment from João Fernandes Vieira, Governor of Paraíba from 1655 to 1657: he arrested the sons of the main Janduin chief and sent them to Portugal. A few years later it was reported that the Janduin 'had rebelled and were declared enemies', and the Queen ordered that they be 'extinguished once and for all'. Little came of that campaign against them. But they responded in the mid-1660s by attacking the domestic Tupi in the mission aldeias: King Panati of the Janduin allied himself with the Paiacú, and together they swept down 'to destroy the countryside and kill and capture the Indians of the [Jesuit] aldeias'. It must have reminded them of the good old days when they had rampaged through Pernambuco with Jacob Rabe. João Tavares de Almeida marched out against them with only 40 soldiers and 170 bowmen, but inflicted a heavy defeat, pursuing them for over a league and killing King Panati and one of his sons.

In 1671 there was further trouble. Chiefs João Algodão and Francisco Aragiba of the Ibiapaba Tobajara and the chiefs of the Jaguaribara all signed a letter complaining that the Paiacú had been killing their wives and children. They asked the Captain-Major of Ceará for help. 'Since we wish to live securely and quietly in our homes and lands . . . we ask Your Honour to give us infantry so that with them, all united and in good order, we can destroy that nation of Paiacú, which would be a great service to God and to His Royal Highness.' Everyone was delighted to help. A junta agreed that a war against the Paiacú was very just. The Commander of Ceará sent thirty Portuguese soldiers to help the Tupí tribes against the Paiacú. He was ordered to attack them by surprise, preferably when they descended to the coast for cashew nuts, and ideally by moonlight, with troops behind to prevent their escape. 'I order that when you catch them you destroy them, putting them to the sword and enslaving the children and women.' As usual, the reprisal against the Indians was out of all proportion to their alleged offence.

There was an uneasy peace for over a decade, but more unrest in the early 1680s when cattle ranches moved up the rivers into the interior of Rio Grande, Paraíba and Ceará. The explosion finally came in 1687. The settlers of Natal sent a desperate appeal for men and ammunition. 'The barbarian heathen has risen and killed over sixty persons, whites and negroes, and is continuing the same ravages.'

The Governor-General sent a force of 300 men from Pernambuco under António de Albuquerque da Câmara. But it ran into a force of 3000 warriors, fought a battle that lasted an entire day, and lost a tenth of its strength. It retreated into a stronghouse on the Açu. A brave old octogenarian called Manoel de Abreu Soares led 120 troops inland from Natal, finding the bodies of settlers and destruction everywhere. He made a fort on the Piranhas and fought a sharp battle on the Salgado. He was soon driven into a stockade where he survived for five months, suffering hunger, desertion, and bold attacks by the Indians who burned part of his camp. The Governor-General wrote in 1688 that 'last year the barbarians of the Rio Grande killed over a hundred people, both whites and slaves, destroying over 30,000 head of cattle. . . . For fear of them the settlers are almost driven to abandon the Captaincy.'

There were the usual desperate appeals for help from the Paulistas, who alone were considered capable of fighting Indians. It was now that Domingos Jorge Velho was asked to break off his attack on the Palmares blacks and march north against the Rio Grande Indians. He was appointed commander of that campaign because of 'his great valour, experience of the heathen, military prudence and other qualities, besides the modesty with which he sought honour for his officers without speaking of his own person'. The colonial treasury was empty, so that Domingos Jorge Velho was to be rewarded by the Indians he captured. The Governor-General told him: 'I hope that you will have not only the glory of slaughtering the barbarians, but also the use of those you capture.' But the aged Governor-General sent even more bloodthirsty instructions to the commander of another large force recruited from Pernambuco. 'Your Honour must be sure not to permit any quarter being given to the barbarians during the fighting. Do not let a desire to take captive slaves mean that they are left alive . . . the little ones and women are sufficient booty. . . .Your Honour is to slaughter [the Indian enemy] and continue until you finally destroy them, giving such punishment that it will lodge in the memory of other tribes and fill them with fear of His Majesty's arms.' But the lesson came from the Indians. Many Pernambucans deserted, and the expedition of 900 men was soon reduced to 200 since most had 'fled blatantly from the barbarians'.

When Domingos Jorge Velho reached Rio Grande with his exhausted army of 600 Indians, he immediately launched an attack on the Janduin. He caught a force of them marching inland with a large haul of cattle, pursued them into the sertão and fought a four-day battle at a lake on the Apodi. Domingos Jorge Velho's men finally exhausted their powder and shot, and had to retreat into the camp on the Açu. During the fighting the Paulistas suffered from 'almost infinite bows and darts' and lost 35 killed and 70 wounded.* They were alarmed to find that the Indians had many firearms – more guns and ammunition than they could have captured from the settlers. It was feared that they were obtaining these by trading with pirates who sailed up the Açu river, or from some traitor in the Portuguese fort of Ceará.†

A terrible epidemic of yellow fever ravaged colonial Brazil at this time. It killed many of the men and officers sailing from São Vicente to help in the Rio Grande war, and on 24 October 1688 it killed the Governor-General Mathias da Cunha. Yellow fever was an American disease to which Indians may have had immunity. Rocha Pitta wrote that, unlike other epidemics, this yellow fever did not strike blacks, mulattos or Indians, who 'may have possessed secret qualities; or else it was God's decree'. When the Governor-General died, the energetic Archbishop of Bahia took over as interim Governor-General. He pursued the Rio Grande war with vigour, but wrote to its commanders, António de Albuquerque and Domingos Jorge Velho to be restrained towards the Indians. 'Do not treat those miserable conquered Indians with cruelties contrary to the law of God or of a just war, for although they look like brutes they are in reality men and descendants of Adam.' But by the end of 1688 the Governor-General wrote that 'the power of the barbarians is now incomparably stronger than that of our arms. From the latest reports I have received from the frontier, not only do our men not dare to invest their villages, but it is they who have succeeded in surrounding our garrisons.'

The authorities in Bahia were increasingly convinced that Paulistas alone were capable of fighting Indians. Appeals went out for more men from São Vicente and São Paulo. Everyone said that the best commander was one Matias Cardoso de Almeida, a Paulista who was forming cattle ranches on the São Francisco river. He agreed to serve, recruited men in São Paulo, and marched his force overland for an amazing 1500 miles to the north-east. Most of his men were half-Indian mamelucos. Another force left São Paulo in June 1689 under João Amaro Maciel Parente, son of the Paulista who had annihilated the Bahia Indians. The two groups joined at a camp at the mouth of the Jaguaribe, and in March 1690 the Governor-General put Matias Cardoso in supreme command of the war to crush the Rio Grande Indians. Line troops were ordered to return to barracks. The strategy changed from holding a line of forts to aggressive bush-warfare by the Paulistas, to search out and destroy Indian villages. The Paulistas were considered 'men accustomed to penetrate the sertão and endure hunger, thirst, and inclemencies of climate and weather. The regular infantry have no experience whatsoever of such conditions; nor do the militia, who lack discipline and endurance.' The idea was that the various Paulista contingents should enter the wilds from different directions 'so that if the barbarians flee from one troop they will fall into the hands of others: with their villages destroyed they will find no food or sustenance for their families'.

The situation was confused. The local settlers were almost more incensed about the presence of so many Paulistas than about the Indian war itself. When Domingos Jorge Velho marched inland with his army of Indians from Piauí, he left their wives, and his various prisoners, in the care of Jesuit missionaries. But the town council of Natal was so jealous of Paulista success in enslaving Indians of their hinterland that they invaded the mission village and seized as slaves 200 Indians. Most of these were the families and dependants of warriors fighting with the Paulistas. The Governor-General furiously ordered the restoration of these women and children. At the same time he wrote to Domingos Jorge Velho: 'I congratulate Your Honour . . . on having slaughtered 260 Tapuia.'

In 1690 the Janduin and their allies decisively gained the initiative.

Matias Cardoso's column of fifty men was twice attacked and defeated. Almost annihilated and with his ammunition exhausted, he was forced to retreat hastily to Fortaleza. He then had to hurry to help Natal itself, which was seriously threatened by Tapuia attack. The Indians had just destroyed a column led by António de Albuquerque, who was wounded. An appeal for urgent help also went to Domingos Jorge Velho, who was quartered on the Açu.

One Paulista commander said that the Tapuia were terrible, astute and treacherous, as numerous as leaves on the trees, and still hankering after their former Dutch friends. Their only inferiority in fighting came from a lack of firearms. But it was this inferiority that gradually gave the advantage to the Portuguese. In one encounter there were ten days of lively firing and skirmishing that ended in an Indian defeat. The Pernambucan António de Albuquerque led a force of 300 horse and foot to the Açu and won a terrible victory: 230 Indians were killed and as many more wounded, and the natives had to retreat rapidly to avoid total defeat. Matias Cardoso once sent his lieutenant Manoel Álvares de Morais Navarro on a raid deep into the interior. After fourteen days' march he discovered a large village, killed its sentries and launched a surprise attack that slaughtered many and yielded fifty-eight prisoners. The Indians attacked his column during the return march, but were beaten off in heavy fighting that lasted from dawn until late afternoon. Soon after, Matias Cardoso feared a Tapuia concentration and sent the same lieutenant with 130 men to counter-attack it. They marched through the night along forest trails and surprised the enemy at dawn; a tough battle lasted until nine in the morning, when the enemy ran off leaving six prisoners.

In 1691 Matias Cardoso's camp was ravaged by measles, a disease that decimated his Indian troops. His white troops were mutinous from lack of pay and supplies. He therefore decided to move his camp to a position a hundred miles from Fortaleza, and to send 3000 head of cattle to Pernambuco. Manoel Navarro led this cattle drive and was repeatedly attacked by Indians during the march. In one battle the Indians killed Navarro's horse and he fought hand to hand with his machete against the Indian warriors; but the cattle were driven to safety. Domingos Jorge Velho chased one group of Indians – possibly peaceful Tupi – who took refuge in the Jesuit mission of Guaraíras. The bandeirante besieged the aldeia until the Fathers surrendered the men in the group. But it was not long before the Tapuia – possibly the same band – returned to ravage the area near Natal. The Jesuits then feared their village would be burned and had to appeal to Matias Cardoso for help. He arrived in time, defeated the Tapuia and killed 600.*

As was usual, much of the Portuguese fighting strength came from other Indians. There were the traditional enemies of the Janduin: the various Tupi groups of the Ibiapaba hills, particularly the Jaguaribara and those under chief Paupina. There were the Paulistas' private armies, recruited along the São Francisco or in Piauí, or brought north from fazendas near São Paulo. And there were the men of the mission villages, nominally free Indians who were continually being recruited to work, for nothing, on some royal project or to fight on some campaign. One regiment of these Christian Indians was still led by a chief called Camarão, a descendant of the hero of the Dutch wars.*

The war gradually turned against the Janduin. Domingos Jorge Velho won an important victory on 10 November 1690, in which his lieutenant Cristóvão de Mendonça Arrais distinguished himself. There was a report that a veritable army of Tapuia was besieging Natal. Matias Cardoso hurried back from Pernambuco by forced marches. He split his force. Manoel Navarro led one column, found the Indians, launched a surprise dawn attack and almost annihilated them. He took 120 captives and recaptured much plunder they were carrying, including two white children. He went on to gain another success, leading 200 men against a concentration on the Açu. After marching for five days and nights he surprised an enemy force and killed or captured them all. Matias Cardoso meanwhile moved up the Jaguaribe against other groups of Janduin, Paiacú and Icó. The climax came in 1691, when Cristóvão de Mendonça won a resounding victory. He captured the King or Paramount Chief of the Janduin, who had been baptised years before as João Fernandes Vieira Canindé. Canindé and 2500 of his people sued for peace. His chief of staff proved to be a baptised pirate, who was brought to Bahia in chains for execution.*

The military prowess of the Janduin – and their political dexterity – gained for them something unique in Brazilian history: recognition as an autonomous kingdom, and a peace treaty with Portugal. This was helped by a timely intervention by the King of Portugal, who wrote on 17 January 1691 that Indians captured in the Rio Grande war should be freed. This remarkable letter revoked a decision by a junta in Brazil declaring that the campaign was a 'just war' whose prisoners would be enslaved. The King proposed that Indians captured by the Paulistas should be purchased from them by the royal treasury as compensation for fighting the war. The prisoners should then be placed as free men in Jesuit mission villages. The new Governor-General Câmara Coutinho (a less militant man than his predecessors) said that the Jesuits in Rio Grande would not dare to take such prisoners for fear that they would run back to their homes. The Governor proposed instead that most of them should be shipped to aldeias near Rio de Janeiro, over a thousand miles to the south; and the King agreed. But the Governor also wrote to provincial officials: 'You can appreciate how sacred is the liberty that my Lord the King wishes observed for the Indians of all Brazil.'

It was in this conciliatory climate that a Janduin delegation arrived in Bahia to sue for a formal peace. The Governor-General was astonished by the idea, but receptive. He wrote to the local officials to ask for more information. 'Will Your Honour immediately advise me of the firmness or mobility that such friendship could have . . . coming from a people who, although they have a king, are not accustomed to keeping faith?' The Janduin delegation consisted of two chiefs and seventy of their followers, and fifteen of these – men and women – had an audience with the Governor-General. He wrote: 'I clothed them in scarlet with staffs, at my expense. Many of them were lords of villages. I at once made peace with them, with signed clauses which I am sending to Your Majesty' for ratification.† And so, on 10 April 1692, a draft treaty was signed at Salvador da Bahia between 'the very powerful Lord Dom Pedro II, by the grace of God King of Portugal and the Algarves, etc., etc., and Canindé, King of the Janduin'.

The Janduin initiative was apparently the idea of a white man, one João Paes Floriano, who was married to Canindé's sister-in-law and had a son by her. He and the other delegates explained that they had travelled 380 leagues to request 'a perpetual peace so that his nation and the Portuguese should live in peace'. The Governor forwarded the draft to the King with a slightly apologetic explanation of why he had treated with a savage monarch. To defend his action, he mentioned the justice of the Janduin claims, the duration and ferocity of the war, the danger of its renewal if the treaty were rejected, the benefit of having the Janduin as allies, and the conversion to Christianity of twenty-two villages containing 13,000–14,000 souls.

In the treaty, Canindé promised that he and his successors would be humble vassals and accept Christian baptism. The Janduin would send 5000 warriors to help the Portuguese against any foreign invader or other Indian tribe; and the Portuguese would help the Janduin against *their* enemies. Janduin were to be guaranteed ten square leagues of land around each village. Their freedom was also guaranteed, and royal officials undertook to protect them from molestation – particularly from the Paulistas. The Janduin would be available to work on settlers' estates, but their own chiefs were to decide the labour quotas. In short, the Portuguese governors undertook not to harm the Janduin, but 'for ever to conserve them in the freedom, peace and quiet in which they wished to live'.

This sort of treaty became fairly frequent between Indian tribes and the British, French or United States governments. Such documents are notorious for their impermanence, for the ease with which they have been broken by colonial powers. The Janduin treaty of 1692 was no exception. There was calm for a few years, during which land was awarded to King Canindé on the Jundiá-Peroba river in Goianinha. Meanwhile, at the King of Portugal's suggestion, villages of friendly Indians were moved into Janduin territory.* The Indians being moved were not consulted: for instance in October 1696 the aldeia of Mamenguape in Paraíba was uprooted and hastily moved with its women and children, but without time to grow crops, to defend the Piranhas river; and it was located in that remote frontier alongside a garrison of twenty-five white soldiers. Also, in violation of the treaty clauses about Indian land rights, the newly won territories were rapidly awarded to settlers and cattlemen.

Although peace had been made with the Janduin, there was continued fighting against other tribes. The Paulistas gradually left the Rio Grande area. Domingos Jorge Velho left in 1694 to resume the attack on the black refuge of Palmares – his men destroyed the redoubt of Macoco after a three-week siege in 1694, and liquidated King Zumba and his staff the following year. Other Paulistas, who had fought hard against the Indians, were now an embarrassment: they made trouble with the Indians and were resented by the settlers. Governors now wrote to the King complaining of Paulista behaviour instead of praising their fighting ability. They received no more pay from the royal treasury and their men were disillusioned and mutinous. Many returned to their estates in the south or tried to establish ranches in the conquered territories. In June 1694 Matias Cardoso was left with only 180 men and suffered a serious defeat on the banks of the Jaguaribe: one of his sons was killed and he himself wounded. He was disgusted by the lack of government support. The following year he angrily returned to his vast ranches on the São Francisco.* Francisco Dias de Siqueira, known as 'the Deaf', moved on to fight the tribes of Piauí where he gained a reputation as a ferocious Indian-fighter. Other Paulistas moved north to fight in the interior of Maranhão.

With the Paulistas gone, there was a period of relative calm. An expedition against the Indians of Ceará in November 1693 led to their begging for peace. The newly peaceful tribes – Paiacú, Janduin and Icó – were formed into a garrison on the Jaguaribe. The officer in charge of the Indians on the Piranhas wrote in 1695 full of optimism about the peace; but the Governor-General urged caution, since the Indians' 'natural inconstancy demands attentive vigilance: for any peace they make with the whites out of fear or self-interest is very suspect'. There were some attacks on cattle on the Piacó (Paraíba) in which twelve settlers were killed and many ranches abandoned; but in October 1696 Theodosio de Oliveira Ledo won a victory there; another peace was made and more mission villages created.* The Captain-Major of Rio Grande from 1694 to 1697 was Bernardo Vieira de Mello, a man of action, but morally very correct and keen on his duty. While he was in charge the conquered tribes were settled on the Jaguaribe, Apodi and Açu, and settlers could occupy the land. When his term of office expired in 1697, the town council of Natal wrote an unprecedented letter to the King asking that he continue in office because he had so successfully 'reduced all the heathen to a universal peace'.

That peace was shattered by a curious and disastrous decision by a new governor-general, João de Lancastro. Towards the end of 1697 he convinced himself that the pacified tribes were still dangerous. One Paulista commander, Manoel Álvares de Morais Navarro, had sent him a long memorandum arguing that the only way to keep the Tapuia subdued was by maintaining a permanent force of 400 Paulistas on their frontier. Navarro was sure that peace through gentleness was impossible. He made a flamboyant offer to act as a hostage 'and if a single Tapuia is reduced to peace I will offer my throat to be cut'. Lancastro was persuaded by this nonsense, and in October 1697 he was writing to São Paulo begging for men to fight under Navarro. His letters were an exact repeat of those of his predecessors a decade earlier: 'Only the valour and great experience of war in the sertão possessed by the Paulistas can destroy and conquer the barbarians: relief depends on Paulista arms, always victorious against the barbarians of Brazil.' It was all sadly familiar. There was an epidemic of smallpox that decimated the aldeia Indians and killed many of the men and officers of the new expedition. Nothing daunted, the Governor-General appointed new officers with orders to 'do everything possible to destroy those barbarians and leave that captaincy free of the violences with which they oppressed it'. He sent manioc flour, powder, shot, flints, pitch, guns, mortars, gunners and plenty of money. He obtained from the King a commission granting the Paulista regiment 'all lands they might conquer from the heathen, and the heathen themselves whom they take prisoner'. And he recruited mission Indians from all parts of Brazil, urging each provincial governor to send the 'most loyal and most war-like' Indians.* But he apologised to Navarro that he could not obtain the chains and neck shackles he had requested to secure his captives.*

Local officials saw the folly of all this. Lancastro's own cousin was governor of Pernambuco, and he wrote suggesting that the presence of

Paulista troops was a provocation that would only make the Indians more hostile. The settlers were violently opposed and tried to release Indians captured by the Paulistas.

The Paulistas were dismayed to find everything quiet when they reached Rio Grande. The Public Prosecutor of Natal, in a sworn deposition of 5 March 1699, accused Navarro and his Paulistas of inciting the tribes to attack one another. Navarro had apparently issued powder and shot to the Janduin and urged them to attack the Paiacú of the Jaguaribe and Apodi rivers. He persuaded them to leave their villages on the Açu and march against the Paiacú, hoping to use this inter-tribal war as a pretext for taking captives. He wanted to make the Janduin 'guilty so that he could wage war on them – without reflecting on the consequences that could result from this: for that nation is the most bellicose and powerful in this captaincy'. But the Janduin saw through his plan and sought protection from the Captain-Major Bernardo Vieira de Mello.

Thwarted by the Janduin, Navarro turned his attention to the Paiacú. Navarro himself gave a detailed account of his own amazing behaviour. He left his camp on the Açu in July 1699 with 130 infantry and 200 pacified Janduin. He hoped to tempt Chief Genipapo-açu of the Paiacú to attack his column by stressing its weakness. 'These barbarians do damage only through treachery. To make this easier for them, I sent to tell them that I was going to visit them in all friendship, and to ask for their assistance in attacking other tribes, since my forces were limited.' But, instead of attacking, the Paiacú chief offered all his men to help Navarro. Navarro sent to tell Genipapo-açu that he would visit him, and reached his village at nine in the morning on 4 August. The Chief said that he wished to celebrate Navarro's arrival with a dance of welcome and a feast. To allay Paiacú suspicions Navarro said that his Janduin auxiliaries would perform a dance first. He had already determined to massacre the Paiacú. 'I placed one of Tapuia to divert [the Chief] and ordered that as soon as the drumming stopped (which was the signal given to the infantry to fire their volley) he should strike him. The Chief's brother came in front of them all, unarmed. As soon as I saw that the time had come, I ordered the drum to cease, and [ordered] them to shoot him, from which he fell dead. At the same time my Tapuia to whom the Chief was entrusted broke his head.' Navarro and a hundred of his infantry then waded into the Paiacú. The remaining thirty infantry kept an eye on the Janduin, fearing that they might turn against the Portuguese; but they cheerfully joined in the slaughter. The village was left strewn with 250 bodies, and more were later found dead in the surrounding woods.

Navarro justified the massacre. He claimed that he was convinced the Paiacú were planning some treachery since they were so well armed. He concluded his report: 'On the fourth of this month [August 1699] God was pleased to grant us a victory so fortunate that, totaliter, it must be attributed to His divine omnipotence rather than to our limited forces.' His only regret was that the tribe's 'baggage' – its women and children – had been waiting in the undergrowth and had time to flee during the massacre of their men. 'When we reached the baggage it was too late. Of those we did catch, the infantry's share was some 230 head, besides those left with the [Janduin] Tapuia.' The expedition had a hard march back: it suffered from lack of water and lost many of its captives from thirst. The terrified Paiacú later told the Jesuit missionary João da Costa that they had lost over 400 people. Another missionary, João Guedes, wrote that he met a 'sad group' of the tribe's women and children on the road to Pernambuco to be sold as slaves.*

Navarro had gone too far. The missionary João da Costa wrote to the Bishop of Pernambuco about the massacre, and the Bishop issued a pastoral letter threatening to excommunicate Navarro unless the Paiacú women were returned to their aldeia within six days. The junta in Pernambuco refused to accept Navarro's captives as slaves taken in a just war. There were violent complaints to the King, particularly by the Captain-Major Bernardo Vieira de Mello. Navarro defended himself by having influential witnesses testify that he had done the right thing. The Paiacú had behaved suspiciously. 'When making war on Tapuia, it is impossible to catch them except by some trick – for they are so fast in flight and carry their food with them.' The Governor-General defended his protégé Navarro. But the King listened to the complaints: in January 1700 he ordered the withdrawal of the Paulista regiment from Rio Grande; and later that year he ordered Navarro's arrest because of 'the repeated complaints made to [me] about the insolences allegedly done by Your Honour and the men of your regiment on the Tapuia of the Paiacú tribe'.

Manoel Navarro was arrested in June 1701. But his eclipse was short-lived. By September 1703 he was free again and being congratulated by the Governor-General. The King wrote in August 1704 praising his services. He returned to the north-east to resume command of the Paulista regiment. He later boasted that he had led his troop for seventeen years 'during which almost all those barbarians were extinguished and that sertão was restored [to cattle ranchers], to the great utility of Brazil'. Navarro died after 1745 as a Knight of Christ and the oldest alderman of Olinda; but the Paiacú ceased as an independent tribe after his massacre.

★

It was always exceptionally difficult to sail along the 'East–West Coast' between Rio Grande and Maranhão. Ships battled against winds and currents and were wrecked on the reefs or driven north to the Caribbean. It was for this reason that Maranhão and Pará were separated from the rest of Brazil and answered directly to Lisbon rather than Bahia. After the defeat of the Rio Grande tribes it became possible to link the two colonies by a land route through the interior of Ceará and Piauí, behind the Ibiapaba hills. But this brought the Portuguese into contact with a new group of Tapuia and opened another round of Indian wars.

The tribes of the Maranhão interior were known to the settlers as 'corso' Indians, which means 'roving' or 'pillaging'. They were naked and always on the move, sleeping under branches. They attacked fast and then disappeared, and posted sentries in tall trees to spy out Portuguese movements. 'The life of these people is amazing in its brutal coarseness, and yet they embrace it as being a most excellent one. . . . Their offensive weapons are arrows, and stone axes fixed into wood and quite sharp, and clubs they call jucar which means "kill". But their defensive [weapons] are their skins. . . .' Corso tribes occasionally raided the sugar mills established along the lower Itapicuru and Mearim rivers in Maranhão after the Dutch wars. But Jesuit missionaries pacified many of these Indians, and the raids were contained by a fort built on the Itapecuru in the 1650s.†

One group of corso Indians, the Tremembé, lived on the coast between Maranhão and Ceará. As one of the last groups of Indians to survive on the Atlantic seaboard they were terribly exposed. Their presence was considered a threat to communication between the two captaincies and to coastal shipping. They used to trade fish, amber and medicinal woods with the Portuguese; but they were accused of continuing this trade with foreign corsairs and pirates who appeared on their coast. They were brilliant swimmers, and it was imagined that they would swim out to cut the anchor ropes of ships anchoring overnight in the shoals off their coast. One ship was wrecked there in the 1670s and the Tremembé took some of the flotsam to barter in São Luís. It was immediately assumed that they had caused the wreck and killed the survivors. The Tremembé who tried to sell 'known pieces of clothing' were promptly executed at the mouths of cannon.* But even this was considered inadequate, for 'the crime was universal and justly required that the severity of the punishment should be [universal] also'. So in April 1679 the Governor of Maranhão sent a punitive expedition of 150 soldiers and 500 Indians in 30 canoes and one large ship. It was led by Vital Maciel Parente, son of the man who had slaughtered the

Maranhão Tupinambá. He tried to emulate his father. The Tremembé survived the first encounters, on one occasion by swimming under-water. But on 6 June they were defeated on land and caught by the expedition's canoes while trying to escape across a river. One commentator was exultant at the victory but deplored the waste of slaves: 'They were almost all consumed by fire and sword without distinction of sex or age: for since slavery is now prohibited (I cannot think why, since the war is a just one) everybody busied himself with killing instead of manacling.' The slaughter was terrible. In one village of 300 Tremembé only thirty-seven survived. The terrified survivors fled to the delta of the Parnaíba and into Ceará. 'Vital Maciel returned to São Luís full of military glory.'

Before returning, Vital Maciel Parente had 'explored' the Paraguaçu (Parnaíba) river, hoping to descend some of its tribes. When these refused to come voluntarily he resorted to violence. But the Indians managed to escape during the descent, possibly after a warning by the expedition's Jesuit missionaries. 'The troop then returned, disgusted at not achieving this important objective for its reputation and profit.'

There were more ransom expeditions, official and clandestine, and attempts to descend the tribes of the Maranhão interior. The settlers used to go inland with their Indians to collect the bark of cravo, a Brazilian cinnamon. Clashes between such gathering parties and the resident tribes were inevitable, and in 1685 the Tacanhape and Gerum tribes of the Urubu and Iluatumá hills attacked cravo collectors and burned their harvests. The King ordered reprisals. Hilario de Sousa d'Azevedo led the expedition against the Tacanhape, which yielded some prisoners. So also did an official campaign against the Amaneju – also guilty of harassing cravo collectors – 'from which many were killed and some taken prisoners, despite their known resistance'. These were 'just wars', whose captives were sold as slaves, and the Crown took its fifth of the proceeds.

There was a spiral of increasing violence on the Maranhão frontier. The settlers of Maranhão were too poor to afford African slaves and were desperate for Indians. Their slaving efforts against the tough tribes of the Maranhão hinterland led inexorably to determined resistance. Indian counter-attacks destroyed and depopulated the sugar mills along the Itapicuru and Mearim, thus further impoverishing the colony. And punitive expeditions against this raiding further escalated the fighting.

In Holy Week 1684 the settlers of Maranhão rebelled under the leadership of a rich planter, Manoel Beckman. They seized the Governor and once again expelled the Jesuits, who were always regarded as the scapegoats for settler miseries. The revolt lost momentum, and a new governor arriving the following year easily restored royal rule: the ringleaders, Beckman and Vieira's old opponent Jorge de Sampaio, were both hanged. But the settlers' revolt did alarm the authorities. The Jesuits became more flexible and the Crown more sympathetic, all at the expense of the Indians.

By 1690 the King was writing to deplore the settlers' poverty from lack of slaves, and encouraged the Governor of Maranhão to send more military expeditions inland to secure Indians. He wrote warm congratulations to one officer who persuaded some tribes to settle on accessible rivers and help him descend more Indians. The King even began to respond favourably to individuals begging for Indians. There was a steady stream of royal letters authorising individuals to ransom Indians. One man was 'a poor gentleman' who needed only twenty Indians to paddle his canoe and forty to tend his plantation; another petitioner was a town that needed a pool of Indian labour; or a Frenchman needing them to extract urucum or anatto, the Indians' beloved red dye, and the medicinal panacea sarsaparilla. Successive governors of Maranhão wrote to the King about 'the miserable state in which those people find themselves from the mortality that occurred among their slaves and the Indians because of smallpox'.

One solution to the attacks of the corso tribes was to import Paulistas to fight them. With the Janduin peace of 1692 the Paulista regiment of Rio Grande became a provocative embarrassment. Its officers were encouraged to lead their men either against the Palmares blacks or north against the Maranhão Indians. One who marched north was Francisco Dias de Siqueira, nicknamed Apuça ('Deaf'). But this notorious Indian-hunter found it difficult to distinguish between wild, hostile tribes and peaceful mission Indians. He marched down-river almost to the city of São Luís ravaging missions along the way. The King had supplied him with stores and ammunition and was furious at Apuça's destructive flouting of his commission. 'It was understood that his purpose would be . . . my royal service and the destruction of the corso heathen. But he did quite the reverse. He caused great destruction and hostilities in the domestic aldeias, using deception to perpetrate this crime. By this action he makes himself worthy of all punishment.' The King ordered exemplary punishment of Francisco Dias de Siqueira as a deterrent to others. But the bandeirante escaped unscathed, went on to slaughter the tribes of Piauí and established a ranch hundreds of miles from the coast. It was alongside Mocha, the first settlement in the interior of Piauí, a place that in 1697 boasted a church of adobe and palm thatch measuring nine by eighteen feet. The Paulista commander was settled at a water-hole nearby 'with a camp of Tapuia, with whom he makes expeditions against the wild heathen and keeps them at bay so that they do not attack the settlement. [His men] have some crops of manioc, rice, corn, beans and fruits such as bananas and potatoes, and everything grows with great abundance, showing the fertility of the land and the negligence of the settlers who from laziness have no fruits on which to live.' The deaf old pioneer died years later at Bahia a rich man with many slaves.

There was a brutal campaign up the Itapecuru in 1697 in which 'the commanders proceeded in a very disorderly manner, killing and imprisoning Indians who came to seek peace'. The captives were sent to the island of Marajó, but most died of smallpox during the journey and the few survivors were distributed to work in settler households. Once again, the King ordered that the Indians be removed to missions and that the guilty commanders be punished; and once again nothing was done.

The Maranhão tribes were now aroused and apparently federated in their war against the whites. In 1698 there were attacks on the settlers of the town of Icatu and along the Mearim and Itapicuru river valleys. The King 'resolved that war be waged on them and that those imprisoned in it be enslaved'. But during the ensuing years there were frequent reports of Indian attacks on plantations in these areas and on the Munim river. Annual expeditions marched against these tribes with little success.

The Crown continued to authorise settlers to obtain more slaves: a typical request in 1700 was for 120 Indian slaves to restock a sugar mill on the Itapecuru, because the area was infested with corso Tapuia and because the mill's existing slaves had been wiped out by smallpox. Another man was authorised to descend a hundred Indian couples: the King felt sorry for him because he had spent eight years as a prisoner of the Moors in Meknès and because he had a wife and seven children. In 1702 the King congratulated a commander who had annihilated a group of Indians he caught raiding a farm near Icatu, and the following year he authorised the citizens of that frontier town to descend the peaceful Anaperu tribe. The Anaperu could make good 'the lack of Indians for work in their plantations, since the majority of those who inhabited their aldeias have died'.

In 1702 an expedition was authorised to explore the mouth of the Parnaíba, but the Captain of Ceará violated his commission and launched a large slaving raid. He sent Colonel Leonardo de Sá up-river with 500 Indians from Ceará and Ibiapaba and orders to capture as many Indians as possible. His victims were the remnants of the Vidal and Axemi tribes living on the Piranji tributary of the Parnaíba. Many were killed or captured, including the chief's wife; the Indians were deeply distressed by her capture and sent to offer two other women in her stead. But when their envoy entered the expedition's hut with these substitutes someone shot him with a pistol, and kept all three women. The furious Vidal and Axemi attacked ranches along the Piracuruça, killing any cowhands, cattle or horses they could catch, and wreaking 150,000 cruzados' worth of damage. One rancher was so angry that he tried to charge his losses to the guilty commander; but the Colonel hid.

The Vidal and Axemi made peace with the settlers by the end of 1704. But the truce was promptly broken. The military commander of Piauí, António da Cunha Souto-Maior, and other whites drew up an indictment of 'false accusations' against these tribes as a pretext for enslaving them; but a wild priest called João da Costa declared that there was no need to sign papers to kill Tapuia – he grabbed a musket and shot the tribe's chief; twelve other Indians were killed in the confused massacre that followed. There was another surrender by the Vidal late in 1705. A cattleman called José Nunes invited them to settle alongside his ranch and provided them with beef to eat. He then sent secretly to bring Ibiapaba Indians to help exterminate these potentially treacherous Tapuia. In the massacre that resulted, Nunes even had women killed so that they could not flee and multiply. The remnants of the Vidal and Axemi were hunted down at the end of 1705 by a troop under Felix da Cunha.†

Cunha's expedition advanced across the Parnaíba and moved on into Maranhão where it struck a mission of the Anaperu Indians. These were abandoned by their missionary, and many were killed or captured. But a half-caste mameluco deserted the expedition and rallied the oppressed tribes. Under his leadership they fought a successful campaign. Many cattlemen, some soldiers and six Carmelite missionaries were killed, and damage was estimated at 200,000 cruzados. On 20 April 1708 the King declared 'the cruellest possible' war to destroy the Anaperu and corso tribes of Maranhão.*

In 1709 António da Cunha Souto-Maior again made peace with the remnants of these various Tapuia tribes. He formed a camp on the Parnaíba and settled ten tribes there. He used them to build roads and corrals and was soon sending great cattle-trains off towards Bahia and the new gold-mines of Minas Gerais. Cunha Souto-Maior's camp was a cruel place. Indian men and women were forced to work without pay. They were also forced to support a garrison of soldiers from Maranhão – 'base and insufferable men' who abused the Indians' wives and daughters. Indian children were sold as slaves and some Indians were killed. Missionaries who tried to intervene were threatened. What most infuriated the Indians was a 'barbarous entertainment' devised by António da Cunha Souto-Maior, his brother Pedro, and Luís Pinheiro, a judge of Maranhão. The three men, mounted on horses, released Anaperu prisoners one by one, galloped after them and chopped off their heads with sabres. One captain, Tomas do Vale Portugal, boasted of being such a good runner that he did *his* pursuits on foot. They ran them down 'like bulls, with sabre thrusts, amid great laughter and gaiety'.

Such atrocities reaped the inevitable reaction. They led to the last great rebellion of the Brazilian north-east. In June 1712 all but two of the tribes in Cunha Souto-Maior's camp rebelled and killed Cunha and most of his officers, twenty soldiers, and some cattlemen. The revolt was led by Mandu Ladino – ladino meant latinised or civilised, for this man had been educated by the Jesuits – an Indian whose sister and brother-in-law were among those killed during Cunha's reign of terror. Mandu's 400 men seized 300 firearms and ammunition in the camp on the Parnaíba, and their rebellion raged through Piauí and Ceará. They had no quarrel against missionaries, sparing a Franciscan and Carmelite who were in Cunha's camp. Although they entered many churches during their campaigns they did not desecrate them, and even preserved holy images when they burned settlers' houses. The only priest they killed was Father Amaro Barbosa, because he was a military chaplain whom they had seen encouraging his men against them and helping to build a fort in their territory.*

The Governor of Maranhão himself led a great punitive expedition against Mandu's tribes. It found a large village and had it surrounded ready for a murderous charge; but someone fired a gun and the Indians had time to escape as night was falling. The expedition returned to São Luís empty-handed. The Indians successfully attacked another punitive expedition as it passed the Fort of Iguará at the mouth of the Piauí. The commander and all but one of his men were killed. In 1716 they destroyed an armed convoy of cattle going to Maranhão.* By 1718 the Colonial Council in Lisbon was seriously worried about Mandu's wars raging in Maranhão, Piauí and Ceará. Over a hundred ranches had been abandoned and destroyed. 'All care is necessary if those regions are not to be lost.'

For a time the peaceful Tupi tribes of Ceará were provoked into joining the Tapuia revolt. One military force 'treacherously killed under peace' over 200 Goianas, including women and children. At the same time soldiers from the fort of Ceará entered an aldeia, beat up its chief and his wife, and abducted many girls. The Tupi therefore joined

Mandu's Tapuia, and in their first fury killed eighty-eight persons, some within a few miles of the fort. They were persuaded to desist only by the arrival of a powerful force from Pernambuco, and much fine talk and presents to 'moderate their just resentment'.

In the end it was other Indians who defeated Mandu Ladino. The Tobajara of the Ibiapaba hills, who had been under Jesuit influence since the departure of the Dutch, were Tupi and traditional enemies of the Tapuia living beyond them. The Tobajara, led by Chief Dom Jacob de Sousa e Castro, moved against the Tapuia 'without any whites whatsoever, who were only an embarrassment to them in the forests'. They defeated Mandu Ladino in a series of engagements, reducing his 400 men to fifty or sixty. And in 1719 they killed the gallant Mandu himself, while he tried to swim to safety across the Poti river. They also killed four of his allied chiefs.† By 1720 a missionary told the King that all these Tapuia were exterminated. Mandu Ladino's rebellion had raged for seven years and cost the Portuguese losses of 500,000 cruzados and many killed among their settlers and the Tobajara who crushed the rebellion.

In 1720 the King called on a number of witnesses – missionaries or former government officers – to advise him about tribes of north-eastern Brazil. He received a series of harrowing reports. There had been a cattle boom in the region, with hundreds of ranches established along the Jaguaribe and in Ceará and Piauí. The result was near-anarchy. Once the cattlemen entered, they destroyed everything with their greed. There had been endless unjust campaigns against Indians throughout the area during the past thirty years. No justice existed to stop frequent murder, robbery and rape of Indians. Soldiers would even enter mission villages at night and seize women at gunpoint 'without fear of God or respect for the missionary'. Indian lands were constantly invaded, even the statutory one square league surrounding each mission. Indians were forced to work on cattle drives, often without pay.

Chiefs suffered from settler aggression: one died and two others were seriously injured by torture and corporal punishment when they refused to provide labourers. In 1707 a chief of Canindé's tribe on the Jaguaribe was killed because he sat in the hammock of a cowboy he was visiting. The same year the 'good chief of the Quixolo Tapuia' was shot by cattlemen at the Ribeira de Jaguaribe because he refused to hand an Indian over to a mulatto – as he died he begged his people not to take revenge, but they did: many battles and deaths ensued, and the Quixolo were exterminated.* Chief Inácio Suassu of the peaceful Caocaya was beaten by ruffians who invaded his village in 1710 and again in 1713. The law imposed a heavy fine and deportation to Angola for anyone who beat Indians, 'but, as with all orders favourable to Indians, this had no effect in Ceará'.

Many convicts had been deported to Ceará, and the cattle lands of the frontier were infested with vagabonds who preyed on the Indians. One of these, a mulatto called Felipe Coelho, actually had himself appointed Administrator of the Ceará Indians: he surrounded himself with Indian girls and produced many offspring, who in their turn became notorious for tyrannising Indians.

But the worst offenders were the senior officers. These would obtain commissions to fight Tapuia (often buying such documents with cattle) and then did so indiscriminately, solely to capture slaves. They attacked tribes whether guilty or not, and made treacherous surprise attacks. One missionary commented that they should learn to fight 'as men fight other men, not men against beasts'. Heathen tribes were sentenced without a hearing, and often killed after surrender. There were unprovoked, treacherous attacks against the Icó of the Jaguaribe in 1704 and again in 1707, 1708 and 1720, with many enslaved on each occasion. Similar raids were made by senior officers on the Cariú in 1704 and 1705, and on the Caratiú in 1708. The deputy Captain-Major of Ceará promised to lead the Jaguaribe to a new aldeia in 1714, but then killed their chiefs and enslaved many; and the same ruse was done against the Anassé of Uruburetama in 1717.

Some tribes in desperation sought the protection of powerful settlers. When a Captain-Major of Ceará sent a force against the Genipapo-açu in 1717, the Indians hid their families in cattlemen's houses and then joined a force of 200 cowboys who rode out to confront the troop, forcing it to retire. The shattered remnants of the Paiacú, Canindé, Genipapo-açu and Cauri were protected by Colonel João de Barros Braga and other well-intentioned settlers. The Colonel had to intervene in 1719 when cowboys tried to provoke the tribes against one another in order to enslave them.†

Another colonel called António da Rocha Bezerra allowed fifty Caboré to settle on his ranch on the Açu after most of their tribe had been killed or imprisoned in 1711. He then led them off to fight in a feud between his Bezerra relatives and the Cavalcantis of Pernambuco; but they killed him and fled back – only to find their wives and families distributed among the Açu cattlemen, who were waiting to kill the Caboré men. The Caboré took to the forests and killed off the offending cowboys one by one in a series of raids. They were attacked by cattlemen in 1718, and in 1720 were reported as being at peace, settled near the church of Açu 'for as long as the cowboys allow them to live'.

More serious fighting continued against the corso tribes of Piauí and

Maranhão during the 1720s. Bernardo Carvalho de Aguiar, the Captain-Major of Piauí, boasted in 1719 that he had already destroyed 'four nations of barbarians' at little cost to the royal treasury. One tribe was wiped out when he killed 400 and captured 25.* But he was still fighting corso tribes in 1725.

One of the most formidable tribes of the Maranhão forests were the Barbados ('Bearded') Indians, probably so called because they dyed their lower faces. The Paulista Francisco Dias de Siqueira had fought them unsuccessfully, and so had the Governor of Maranhão, Cristóvão da Costa Freira, who in 1716 burned a huge aldeia of 291 houses but failed to catch many of its Indians. Bernardo Carvalho de Aguiar now moved against them, 'without motive', and in 1726 they sued for peace, together with the Guanaré and Arua. The Guanaré had been descended by the Jesuits years before, but were struck by smallpox during the move. Fearing enslavement they ran off to the interior. They now sent to Father João de Villar asking him to return to baptise them. He suspected treason but went nonetheless. But, after he had been there a month, other armed Indians appeared and killed the missionary. A punitive expedition under Francisco de Almeida found Villar's naked body on a sandbank with its head smashed.* The Guanaré village was abandoned and burned, but the expedition bravely attempted an attack on the large, populous villages of the Barbados. Previous governors had tried in vain to subdue these warlike Indians, and Almeida's column was heavily attacked. It fought off hordes of Barbados from morning until late afternoon, but managed to enter a large village. During the night Almeida made his Indians sing songs: some were sung by Arua from Piauí, and the familiarity of this music made the related Barbado Arua come next day to ask for peace and friendship. A peace was arranged. The Indians fed the expedition on game meat and manioc cakes and guided it back to the Mearim. Chiefs Proxapay of the Barbados, Anguly of the Arua and Coriju of the Guanaré came to ratify the peace and swear submission to the King of Portugal. The Mission Council in Maranhão voted unanimously to grant the peace and not punish these tribes' 'crimes'. It was delighted to have thousands of new souls reduced to the Christian faith, to add to the colony 'many lands and excellent plains that can be colonised', and to be spared from fighting this difficult conquest, since the state was 'without Indians or forces to carry on a continual war . . . for the aldeias are finished and cannot supply the necessary Indians. . . .' The Council added ominously that, should there by any 'inconstancy' among these tribes, they could be moved down to the city of São Luís or even to Pará 'where they would be safer from returning to their people'.

In 1728 the fighting moved inland, with an expedition against the Timbira, who 'had made the greatest invasions in all that captaincy, and from whom the greatest ruin was feared'. With the Timbira the conquest entered a different phase, for the Timbira were 'superabundantly populous' and still exist as a cohesive tribe in southern Maranhão. But by this time the interior of the North-East was occupied. Portuguese Brazil finally controlled most of the land up to the fifteenth-century Line of Tordesillas. And vast herds of cattle invaded the plateau and hills where the many Tapuia tribes had resisted so stubbornly.

SEVENTEEN

Gold

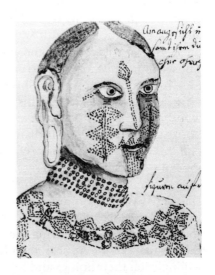

THE Brazilian north-east had its frontier of cowboys and Indians a century and a half before the United States. And at the close of the seventeenth century Brazil produced the other ingredient of the Wild West – a series of gold-rushes.

Ever since the start of Portuguese colonisation there had been hopes of finding precious métals to rival the gold and silver of Spanish America. Many governors sent off adventurers and Indians in search of such riches. Prospecting was the ostensible purpose of many Paulista slaving bandeiras. But it was only at the end of the seventeenth century that important quantities of gold were finally found. By that time there were fewer bandeiras and they had to range further afield in search of captives – the Jesuit missions had trained and armed their congregations and were no longer a source of easy human plunder.

New heroes emerged among the bandeirantes, men whose explorations of the Brazilian interior were as prodigious as their motives were despicable. There was Manoel de Campos Bicudo, who raided on the Guaporé and in central Mato Grosso and then swung back into Goiás. Legend has it that his bandeira met that of Bartolomeu Bueno da Silva in the depths of the forests and scrublands of Goiás in 1682. The meeting of two Paulista expeditions so far from civilisation was as remarkable as an encounter by two ships in an empty ocean.

Bueno da Silva was a tough and wily woodsman who 'made many expeditions into the sertão, conquered many heathen, and was opulent'.

Guaicurú facial decoration.

The Indians called him Anhangüera ('The Old Devil') in grudging admiration for his cunning. It was told that he intimidated the Goiás Indians with a famous trick: he took a bowl of the transparent sugar alcohol cachaça, claimed it was water, set fire to it, and threatened to burn all the tribe's lakes and rivers unless it obeyed his commands. Those commands were to surrender some gold ornaments and to follow him into captivity, so that 'he returned from this conquest without unsheathing his sword, and his name was applauded among all the old woodsmen'. This story appears in modern Brazilian primary-school books, as an example of Indian gullibility and bandeirante cleverness – and this was almost the only reference to Indian history that I could find in textbooks being used on modern Indian reservations.

The bandeirante most admired by his contemporaries was Fernão Dias Pais. With his hundreds of Indian slaves and retainers, he was a leader of the Pires faction in a feud between the Pires and Camargos that split the bandeirantes during the 1650s. He made a great impression on the Goaiana of the Apucarana hills: three groups of them, 5000 strong, willingly left their homes and followed him to a settlement on the Tietê. 'He achieved the success of this reduction without the booming of guns or tyrannies of killing.' In 1671 the Governor-General enlisted Fernão Dias Pais to lead an expedition in search of some legendary emerald deposits. The elderly bandeirante answered the summons by financing a great expedition that included most of his Goaiana followers. He also took his son-in-law Manoel de Borba Gato and Matias Cardoso de Almeida (the man who later commanded the Paulistas in the Rio Grande wars). They marched northwards from São Paulo and roamed for years about the forested valleys of the upper São Francisco, Pardo and Jequitinhonha. They penetrated the wilds of Sabará-bucu and an Indian village known as Casa de Casca ('House of Bark') or Caeté. They even found a few emeralds near Itamarandiba in the territory of the warlike Mapaxó. After seven years the expedition's powder, shot and metal tools were exhausted, most of Dias Pais' Goaiana Indians and many of his soldiers were dead, and in 1681 the old bandeirante himself died somewhere in the interior. His body was embalmed in the bandeirante manner and brought back to São Paulo for burial.

Dias Pais' son-in-law Manoel de Borba Gato settled at the expedition's base camp of Sumidouro near the Rio das Velhas, where there were extensive manioc plantations. In 1682 he was visited by Don Rodrigo de Castel Blanco, an ambitious Spaniard who had persuaded the Portuguese King to name him Administrator-General of the Mines of Brazil. Castel Blanco insisted on taking charge of some of the expedition's emeralds. The circumstances are obscure, but on 28 August someone murdered him. Manoel de Borba Gato felt sure that he would be blamed for a murder done at his camp. He therefore fled to the forests of the Rio Doce, 'and making friends with its savages, whom he tamed to his obedience, he remained among them, respected as a chief and like a sovereign prince among them. He lived there barbarously among them, without communion of any sacrament, in a manner of life without contact with other creatures of our world for sixteen years.'

Fernão Dias Pais' years of fruitless searching had, unknown to him, taken his expedition through areas full of gold. Another bandeirante, António Ruiz de Arzão, raided in the same area during the 1690s and was luckier. His contemporaries described him as 'a woodsman, conqueror of the heathen in the sertão of the Casa de Casca'. He and his force of settlers and 'domesticated Carijó in his keep' camped there for some years, raiding Indians deeper in the forest. But they also managed, without any tools, to pan an ounce of placer gold from streams in the Itaverava hills. Arzão's slaving camp eventually became untenable for 'he was molested by the heathen, who fought him with much fury'. These Indians – presumably Mapaxó – finally forced him to escape by breaking through the dense forests towards Espírito Santo. He arrived with his force terribly depleted from hardships of the forest and Indian wars, 'naked and in rags and without powder or shot, which are the only remedy with which woodsmen made good the lack of food, by hunting the birds and beasts of the sertão with great intelligence in an effort to support themselves'. But he did bring out the precious ounce of gold.

Perhaps the true discoverer of the gold-mines was Ruiz de Arzão's wastrel brother-in-law Bartolomeu Bueno de Siqueira who, having gambled away an inherited fortune, organised a bandeira in 1694. He hoped with a little luck to 'improve his fortunes by work rather than by gambling'. He avoided the Casa de Casca because of its fierce Indians and settled instead in the Itaverava hills; and he found some gold. Other Paulistas began to drift into the area with their contingents of Indian slaves, drawn to the gold like cattle sniffing water. One was Colonel Salvador Fernandes Furtado de Mendonça, whose men soon extracted twelve oitavas (about 1½ ounces) of gold from the streams of the Caeté forests. Another bandeirante badly wanted this first discovery. 'Captain Manoel Garcia Velho had the ambition to be the first possessor of the gold extracted from those mines. He offered to give [the Colonel] for those twelve oitavas of gold the two most beautiful Indian women he chose from those in his band. The Colonel in fact chose a young woman of about twenty-four with a daughter of eleven or twelve. These were catechised and baptised, the mother with the name Aurora and the daughter Celia, and the latter died a few years ago [in the 1740s] in the town of Pitanguí. . . .'

Those first ounces were soon forgotten. For in 1700 the Paulistas discovered the placer deposits they called Our Lady of Carmo, and in 1701 the stream called Our Lady of Good Fortune that led to the fabulous Ouro Prêto ('Black Gold'), the greatest gold-mine in all South America.

There was an immediate gold-rush of epic proportions. Every adventurer in Brazil was soon on his way to the interior of what became known as Minas Gerais ('General Mines'). All the gullies and streams were ransacked by prospectors, and many struck gold. In the excitement no word has come down to us about the fate of the local tribes: they evidently died defending their lands, or were seized to work in the mines, or melted away into forests that did not contain the fatal ore. A governor of São Paulo admitted in 1718 that the entire valley of the long Velhas river had been inhabited by tribes destroyed by the Paulistas. An ungrammatical contemporary account gave a vivid picture of the gold fever: 'Many people died at that time, from diseases and hardships and others who killed to rob on their return anyone bringing gold; and even comrades who went together, when doing their business, or on the return with some gold, killed one another out of ambition to possess it, as happened in many instances.' Men plunged into the forests without thinking about food supplies, and many died of exposure on the journey to the mines. With the sudden inrush of treasure-hunters the region was denuded of game and fish. The gold-mines thus stimulated cattle-ranching and helped provoke the wars against the tribes of Piauí and the São Francisco. Enterprising cowboys drove cattle for hundreds of miles to Ouro Prêto and sold each animal for fabulous sums of gold.

The gold-rush was as disastrous for the Indians who survived near São Paulo as for those in the gold region of Minas Gerais. The desperadoes who hurried off to the mines took any Indians they could lay hands on, to act as porters, hunters and mine-workers. Their victims were the inhabitants of the shabby aldeias near the city, or the groups of Indians living on the estates of bandeirante potentates. In 1700 Manoel de Borba Gato emerged from his years of exile, still leading his adopted tribe from the Rio Doce, and was pardoned by the Governor of São Paulo. The Governor then sent him off to the mines 'with many Indians that the same Governor removed from the domestic aldeias of São Paulo'.

Such forced labour of free Indians was theoretically illegal. The aldeia Indians had an official protector appointed in 1698 – Isidro Tinoco de Sá, 'a person of talent, valour and aptitude'. But he could do little more than protest when his charges were herded off to work at the mines, and when the lands of their denuded villages were then invaded by settlers. Tinoco protested energetically, and the town council ordered the punishment of lawbreakers who removed Indians. But the same town council also wrote to the King complaining that the lack of Indians was hampering the discovery of more gold. It decreed stiff fines for anyone who hired 'Indians for the mines or any other place without first making a petition to us'. In September 1704, Tinoco was replaced as Protector of the Indians by an old man called Pedro Tacques de Almeida, who wrote the usual protests about the wretched state of the Indians and deplored their removal to the mines and the invasion of their lands. But the Vicar of São Paulo accused Tacques de Almeida of serious abuse of the men and women in his charge. He was said to be distributing them among his friends like so many Guinea slaves. When the King ordered an investigation into the widespread sale and dispersal of the lands of the aldeias, forty notable citizens signed a warning to the King to desist from interfering in such a delicate matter. Among the signatures were those of both Isidro Tinoco de Sá and Pero Tacques de Almeida – the past and present administrators of the royal aldeias!* Tacques de Almeida was eventually dismissed in November 1710.

Gold-seekers poured across the Atlantic from Portugal, and from 1708 to 1710 there were revolts and clashes between the Paulistas and these newcomers. Life was very tough on that mining frontier. The first levies of Indian workers did not last long. They were soon replaced by black slaves, who crouched in long rows panning the streams under the eye of armed guards, or sweated underground in the primitive mines. Much of the gold went to Portugal to make João V one of the richest kings of Europe. But enough remained in Minas Gerais to build glorious baroque churches and mansions in towns with resounding names like Vila Rica de Albuquerque (Ouro Prêto), Vila do Ribeirão de Nossa Senhora do Carmo (Mariana), Vila Real de Nossa Senhora da Conceição do Sabará (Sabará), Vila Nova da Rainha (Caeté), Rio das Mortes (São João d'El-Rei) and Vila do Príncipe (Cêrro do Frio), and the very beautiful pilgrimage church of Congonhas.

The search for more mines took bandeirantes deep into the interior of Brazil, on amazing marches across hundreds of miles of campo and forest. These epic journeys – all done on foot or by canoe – are little known outside Brazil, largely because the bandeirantes wrote so little about them. But as feats of exploration and endurance they were just as impressive as Speke's or Livingstone's travels in Africa. In 1722 Bartolomeu Bueno da Silva, son of the old bandeirante Anhangüera, set out to try to find some Indians with gold ornaments that he recalled seeing when he travelled with his father forty years before. The expedition marched from São Paulo to Minas Gerais and then plunged into the wilds to the north-west. What makes this bandeira remarkable is that one of its officers wrote a narrative of the expedition. Bandeirantes were men of action not words. This account by the Ensign José Peixoto da Silva Braga is almost the only surviving eye-witness report out of all the hundreds of expeditions made by Paulistas during the seventeenth and eighteenth centuries. It gives an idea of the hardships of those expeditions, and of their treatment of any natives they met.

The bandeira marched northwards for hundreds of miles. 'We then entered some broad plateaux that lacked all provisions: devoid of forests or food, although there were quite a few streams in which there were some fish. . . . We also found some palm hearts which we ate roasted, and although bitter these sustain one better than maize. Here the men began to collapse completely. Some forty of our people died, whites and blacks, from destitution. I myself stayed alive thanks to my horse. But, to mount it in my extreme weakness, I had to clamber on to it face downwards, raised up on the first termite hill I encountered.'

'When our leader [the younger Anhangüera] saw us in such misery, fearing that all his men would fail and die . . . he called upon Heaven. It was the first time I heard him remember God. He made promises and various novenas to St Anthony, [praying to him] to reveal to us some heathen: we could then conquer them and steal the food we found with them, to remedy the hunger we were suffering.'

'After fifteen days of considerable suffering and effort we struck a path on those campos, and followed it for nine days.' They scouted across some hills and 'on the night of the third day we sighted the huts of the heathen and their fires. We hid in ambush in the bush to attack them at dawn. But we were observed by the many dogs they had, and as we advanced they received us with bows and arrows. On our leader's orders we did not fire a single shot, as a result of which almost all the heathen escaped from us. One of them attacked the leader's nephew, with such spirit that he grabbed his horse's reins, and snatched the gun from his hand and machete from his belt. He gave him a famous blow across one shoulder with it, and another on his left hand, and ran off taking the weapons.

'On this same occasion another Tapuia in a doorway wounded one Francisco Carvalho de Lordello slightly on the chest with an arrow. Another ran up and hit him on the head with a club, from which he fell. And as he fell another Tapuia suddenly appeared and struck him another club blow, leaving him for dead. . . . We reached the huts, thank God, in a hail of arrows and clubs. The Tapuia retired to the woods without losing sight of us. We wanted to bury Carvalho, convinced he was dead. But in two advances against us, they attempted to remove and eat him. When they saw us beaten back they begged us by gesticulations to leave them at least half of him to eat. When we removed Francisco de Carvalho we found his mouth, nose and wounds full of insects. But we saw that his heart was still beating and that he showed other signs of life. We pulled him into one of the huts and cured his wounds with urine and smoke, and bled him with the point of a knife as we had no better lancet. The cure was so successful that Carvalho regained consciousness that night and opened his eyes, but did not speak until the next day.'

The bandeira seized quantities of the Indians' maize and sweet potatoes, and captured seven Indians, whom they chained. They also ate any macaws, parakeets and dogs they found in the village. The tribe they were pillaging were Quirixa, and the Paulistas described them as light-skinned, well built and with both sexes completely naked. There were about 600 living in the village, in nineteen high, round huts covered in palm thatch. They slept on buriti-palm mats and caught plenty of fish in a river alongside their village.

The bandeirantes occupied the Quirixa village for three months. 'During this time the heathen had become more humanised. They sought us out and served us, without their bows and arrows, greatly admiring our weapons. They offered us wood. One day they brought us sixteen Indian women, still girls and very fair and well made, as a sign of friendship: for we were only sixteen white men. Our leader refused to accept them, although all the others opposed him. I was the one who argued hardest to persuade him to accept them. I said we were so few and weak and dying of hunger, while the heathen were so many: we should therefore not offend them. If we placed these girls under guard with the others who were already prisoners, we could easily convert all the rest of the heathen – not only to make peace, but also so that they would give us some [guides] to show us the right road to the Goiás. But none of this moved Anhangüera. . . .' He feared that the girls were a trick to distract the explorers so that the Indians could kill and eat them. But his rejection of the Indians' gesture annoyed the tribe, which disappeared next day.

Anhangüera's expedition now split. The author of this account obtained permission to build canoes and attempt a descent of the Tocantins river. He went with five whites and fourteen Indians and succeeded in reaching Belém do Pará, over 1200 miles away, after many adventures. Anhangüera himself staggered on with the few survivors in search of the chimera of the Goiás gold. Early in 1725 some of his

Indians returned to the coast and reported that his search had failed. Governor Rodrigo César de Meneses wrote to the King that the stubborn bandeirante was determined 'either to discover what he was seeking or die in the attempt'.

In October the explorer reached Cuiabá after having passed through the territory of the Goiá and Araé Indians. The Governor wrote that during over three years of arduous marching, with most of his followers dead or deserted, Anhangüera 'did not slacken in the enterprise. Being a brave, constant and loyal subject of Your Majesty he scorned the evident dangers' of multitudes of Indians and miles of barren wilderness.*

The bandeirante returned to São Paulo long enough to recruit a new expedition, and in 1726 marched off again with the fanatical determination of a Captain Ahab. This time he succeeded thanks to the Goiá Indians. These had fortified themselves near the junction of the Vermelho and Bugres rivers to resist enslavement. But Anhangüera managed to capture their women, 'and by taking these he triumphed and made them show him the places in which they had found the leaves of gold that served as ornaments for their women'. Bartolomeu Bueno da Silva was satisfied that it was the camp he had seen with his father forty-four years before, in 1682. He returned to São Paulo with gold, and another gold rush was launched.

The Goiás camp of Sant' Anna became the town of Vila Boa with Bueno da Silva as its captain-major, and he died there in 1740 aged over seventy. Vila Boa was a particularly wild mining-camp, but gradually evolved into the quiet modern town of Goiás. Once again, the discovery of gold was a disaster for the Indians. Anhangüera took a mass of Carijó Guaraní from near São Paulo to work the mines. These soon ran off and are thought to have established themselves as a fiercely independent and elusive warrior tribe known as Canoeiros ('Canoers') on the Tocantins river. The Goiá, who had the misfortune to have found some gold on their land and revealed it to the strangers, bore the brunt of the mining rush. A historian wrote a century later that 'the Goiá tribe fled from its persecutors: some died, others went away; they were extinguished and exist no longer'. The only memory of them is the name of the town and state of Goiás.

More gold was found a few years before the Goiás discovery, in an even more remote location, deeper in the heart of South America. The ubiquitous Paulistas had roamed westwards to the Paraguay river throughout the seventeenth century. In 1648 António Rapôso Tavares and André Fernandes smashed the missions of the Jesuit province of Itatín and destroyed the town of Jerez on the Mbototeu (Miranda) river.

Later in the century bandeiras raided across the Vacaria sertão, in what is now the south of the State of Mato Grosso. They often clashed with the Spaniards from Paraguay, and in 1682 established a base near the ruins of Jerez on the Mbototeu. A bandeirante called Pascoal Moreira Cabral ran a form of trading-post there, and raided any Indians he could catch. This was no longer very easy, for the Spaniards on the west bank of the Paraguay were well armed, and the tribes of the Paraguay near Mbototeu – the Guaicuru, Paiaguá and Caiapó – were a match for Portuguese and Spaniards alike. The bandeirantes therefore ranged northwards up the Paraguay in search of Indians.

In 1719 Pascoal Moreira Cabral was preying on Indians on the Cuiabá and Coxipó rivers when he saw gold on the river banks. Further up the Coxipó 'he encountered heathen among whom he took prisoners with considerable traces of gold in plugs and other ornaments'. He met another Paulista slaver, António Pires de Campos, a tough and handsome fellow whom a contemporary described as 'in the city square an Adonis, and in the sertão Mars; the scourge of the barbarous heathen Caiapó'. They met on a sandbank called Cuiabá on 8 April 1719 and wrote a report about the discovery of gold. One of their men carried the news back to São Paulo; the Governor jubilantly relayed it to the King; and another gold-rush was launched.

The Cuiabá gold-fields were extraordinarily difficult to reach. It was far easier and faster for a Paulista to travel to Europe than to this remote part of the wilds of Mato Grosso, the aptly named Great or Dense Forest. The fortune-hunters had to travel down or up five formidable rivers – the Tietê, Inhandui, Aquidauana, Paraguay and Cuiabá – to reach their El Dorado. They set out confidently, but often woefully unprepared for the dangers ahead. 'They suffered great destructions: losses of canoes in the rapids for lack of experienced pilots, deaths of men from lack of food, disease, being eaten by jaguars, and many other miseries. They did not know how to fish or hunt, or the practice of carbonising canoes so that [their canoes] all rotted in the rains, or the invention of mosquito nets to defend them against the mosquitoes. . . . There was one convoy in which all died, with no one remaining alive. Those who came behind with the canoes found their rotting belongings and dead bodies on the river banks and redoubts, and hammocks slung with their owners in them, dead. No single person reached Cuiabá that year and there was no news at all.'

From São Paulo a traveller went for 155 kilometres overland to the Tietê; then 1003 kilometres down the turbulent 'poisonous' Tietê, full of 'rapids, tow-lines, races, weirs and waterfalls' at which canoes were lowered by land and 'their cargoes carried on the backs of negroes' during which 'much was lost'. Canoes capsized and people were drowned on almost every journey, and food became a problem as the riverside clearings became less frequent. It was terribly hot by day, and cold and mosquito-infested by night. When the energetic Governor Rodrigo César de Meneses visited the new mines in 1726, this descent alone took his fleet twenty-six days of hard paddling. An expedition then had three days of calm, gliding down 191 kilometres of the broad Paraná. But the ascent of the Pardo was very tough, for like the Tietê it was full of rapids, waterfalls and fallen trees. After 495 kilometres a flotilla reached the famous portage of Camapuã, where there were some fields of manioc and other vegetables. Loads were carried for 13 kilometres across the watershed, and canoes were pulled across on small carts drawn by twenty or thirty black slaves. Gervasio Rebelo called Camapuã 'this portage for canoes and loads, death of whites and blacks, consumer of supplies, and destruction of everything'. There followed eleven days and 374 kilometres down the difficult Camapuã and Coxim with frequent portages around rapids. At one point the Coxim flowed in a gorge between high granite cliffs. This frightened a governor who made the journey in 1751: 'If our enemies the heathen were capable of reasoning, a few of them placed on top of those cliff walls and hurling down stones would be enough to prevent any canoes from passing without being sunk. Their brutality, however, preserves us from this risk.' The flotilla then entered the calmer Taquari and descended 594 kilometres to the Paraguay. The Taquari crosses the Pantanal, possibly the largest swamp in the world, and its mosquitoes 'put everyone in the utmost desperation, but there was no remedy for them'. There followed 844 kilometres of paddling up the hot Paraguay and its tributaries the Porrudos and Cuiabá. It took a flotilla of canoes about five months to make the 3500-kilometre river journey.

Adventurers bound for Cuiabá had to brave more than these natural hazards. Much of their journey was through the territory of the most formidable and resourceful of all Brazilian warrior tribes. The Guaicuru dominated the land on both banks of the Paraguay, and their allies the Paiaguá controlled the river and the labyrinthine waterways of the Pantanal.

The Guaicuru had been in contact with Europeans since the very earliest days of the conquest. It was probably they who killed Aleixo Garcia in 1526, and then traded the silver he had brought back from the Inca empire with Sebastian Cabot, when he sailed up the Plate. It may have been Guaicuru who killed the seventy Portuguese who tried to follow Garcia's route to Peru. The Spanish conquistador Alvaro Núñez Cabeza de Vaca led an expedition of 200 Spaniards and many Guaraní

against the Guaicuru in the 1540s. He launched a dawn attack on the
Guaicuru tents. Although terrified by the horses, which they had never
seen, the Indians managed to set fire to their tents and escape in the
smoke. They even killed some of Cabeza de Vaca's men and severed their
heads 'with singular and barbarous dexterity: they clenched the foe by
the hair, sawed round his neck and twirling the head at the same time, it
came off with inconceivable facility. The instrument with which they
performed this was the jaw of the [piranha].' At that time the Guaicuru
were amazing runners. Cabeza de Vaca said that their speed, wind and
endurance were so strong that they could outrun deer, exhaust them and
catch them by hand.

In many respects the Guaicuru were very conservative. A Franciscan
who lived among them in the eighteenth century wrote: 'One thing they
are very constant about is in maintaining their freedom, and not altering
their customs: no reasoning can persuade them to abandon these. . . .'
But when it came to fighting they could adapt and evolve, and did so
better than any other Brazilian tribe. They took to horses with the skill
and passion of North American plains Indians or Chilean Araucanians.
They lived on relatively open plains where the horses could graze and
could charge and manœuvre in battle. By the time the Paulista
bandeirantes came into contact with the Guaicuru 'they found them
already masters of great herds of cattle, horses and sheep', and because
the Guaicuru had their own words for horse, rather than adapting
European words, there was even a theory that horses were
autochthonous to that part of South America.† One of the first
Portuguese to reach Cuiabá wrote that the Guaicuru 'are so strong that
they win great victories, partly because they are always on their horses,
and because these are Andalusian horses, the finest that can be seen'.

'Their most interesting riches, which they prize most and about which
all Guaicuru care most, consist of their six or eight thousand horses.'
Young and vigorous men did almost nothing all day except tend their
horses, and make canoes, paddles, lances and maces – 'but all without
the slightest exertion'. The entire tribe moved about the plains, living in
hide tents, in order to find pasture for their horses. Francisco Mendes
said that they looked after these very well, apart from exhausting them
'by chasing deer and ostriches in which they place all their glory'.

'They know their horses' diseases better than their own. According to
their knowledge, they bleed them, remove their tumours or deworm
them with such skill that they generally recover. If one has an accident,
the Indians visit it frequently, and bring it into shelter to cure it.'

'They use neither saddles nor stirrups on their horses. They ride
bareback and mount them in a single leap. Even when they are walking

or playing one can see the suppleness of their bodies. They run after their horses to catch or tie them with almost as much agility as the beasts themselves. They use no lassoes or lariats to catch them, or corrals to subdue them. They run after them to mount them, catching the one they want from a herd of other horses. If the horses break and scatter on such occasions, they use their agility to bring them back as before, running to regroup them.'

Another author, Aires do Casal, was more critical of the Guaicuru as horsemen. 'Even though they all ride, because of which they are bow-legged, they are bad horsemen: for they only know how to gallop. They use no saddle or stirrups. . . . Their reins are two cords . . . held in the horse's mouth like a halter. They tame horses in water that comes almost up to their bellies, in order that the horse cannot throw them and any fall will hurt less. Their war-horses are used for no other purpose. The women ride between two bundles of straw on a cloth which also acts as a saddlecloth.'

'The Guaicuru pride themselves on being a mounted nation, on the light and strong horses they always choose for war.' They bred and trained their horses to be faster than those of other tribes, which gave an obvious advantage in battle.

Very cautious, the Guaicuru often paused during a march to scout ahead, climbing tall trees to observe the country. They attacked only when the enemy was weaker, unarmed or unprepared, and 'even then they pursue him in hiding, watching until some carelessness gives them an opportunity to kill as many as they can, without risk or pity, and to capture women and children'. They used to attack Spanish farms in devastating charges, but only to rob cattle and horses, rather than to expel the settlers altogether. They charged into battle naked apart from jaguar skins, crouched low on their horses and wielding lances, clubs or machete cutlasses.

The Guaicuru had no pride about honour: they fought to win. They could be weak and cowardly when caught in the open, and used their fast horses to flee. They tried to kill without themselves suffering injury, and infuriated the Europeans by having no shame about their apparent cowardice. When reproached about this, they sarcastically turned the Christians' religious preaching against them: 'They conclude that . . . since the Portuguese and Spaniards claim they go to heaven when they die, they do well to die quickly. But, since they also claim that the Guaicuru go to hell after death, in that case the Guaicuru want to die as late as possible.'

During much of the sixteenth century the Guaicuru were allies of the Spaniards and helped them subdue other tribes of the Paraguayan

Chaco. But in 1594 there was panic in Asunción when Guaicuru attacked near the city. By 1609 they were friendly again, and Spanish Jesuits were starting to convert them. The Guaicuru were too proud, nomadic and unspiritual to make good converts. By 1633 Father Diego Ferrer said that the various Guaicuru tribes 'are all beasts'. The Guaicuru helped the Jesuits by annihilating a large bandeira led by Jerónimo Bueno on the Paraguay in 1644, and by smashing Rapôso Tavares' bandeira of 1648 after it had destroyed the Itatín missions. But any Jesuit gratitude was short-lived, for in the 1650s Guaicuru occasionally attacked travelling missionaries, and in 1659 they and their Paiaguá allies launched a surprise attack on the mission of Aguaranambi. The nearby mission of Caaguazu hastily sent 300 armed Indians, twenty of them with firearms. But the Guaicuru charged these on their formidable horses and killed sixty. They then rode off with many women and children and all the mission's horses. The Governor of Paraguay organised a great punitive expedition of Spaniards and Indians under General Lázaro Vallejos. Its first attack was successful, but 'next day the barbarian [Guaicuru] avenged themselves on the Spaniards, driving off their three thousand horses and leaving them on foot without a single horse remaining in the army'.

The Jesuits' only answer was to move the missions closer to Asunción to protect them from the Guaicuru. There was an uneasy peace, broken in December 1671 when 500 Guaicuru crossed the Paraguay at different places. They killed thirty persons and burned and looted farms they had visited during the years of peace. They rode on to surprise the towns of Atira and Guarambaré, where they killed the curate and eighty townspeople. There was heavy raiding by the Guaicuru during the following years: towns, farms and churches were sacked, mission Indians reverted to their former tribal customs, and the Spanish colonists lost control of the Paraguay north of Asunción.

When the Portuguese started to pour into the new mines of Cuiabá it came as a shock to them to meet such formidable Indians. Contrary to the normal pattern of South American conquest, the Europeans were on foot and the Indians mounted. 'With their horses [the Guaicuru] terrorised other savages and even the Paulistas, who ventured into the bush only in great bands, and were frightened to meet them on an open plain because of the way they attacked. As soon as the Guaicuru saw [Paulistas] they would join their horses, with oxhides to cover their flanks, and attacked them in such a way that they broke. They trampled their enemy with the violence of their charge and killed with their lances any they caught in their path. The only remedy for the Paulistas was to escape into the forest.'

For all their brilliance in battle, the Guaicuru were very eccentric in their customs. Their most peculiar habit was the refusal of Guaicuru women to have children until nearing their menopause. 'When they feel themselves pregnant they immediately abort the foetus with violent little injuries which they practise once or twice a year. This operation soon makes them look older than they are. It normally leaves them sterile from the age of thirty onwards, which is when they are disposed to rear children and want to conceive – which they rarely succeed in doing.'

This abortion baffled and infuriated any missionaries or administrators who had contact with the Guaicuru. They gave different explanations for it. Francisco Rodrigues do Prado said that a woman returned her husband's tender love with 'an excessive zeal in pleasing him, so much so that when a woman feels pregnant she kills the creature in her womb so as not to inconvenience him by rearing the child'. Ricardo Franco de Almeida Serra thought that the women feared to be abandoned by their husbands if they had children. The Franciscan friar Francisco Mendes thought it might have been to leave women freer to divorce: 'I think that this perverse custom was introduced to be freer to repudiate – not that they consider children an impediment to divorce when it pleases them. . . . Perhaps they cling to this custom because of the great effort that children give them to raise and sustain.' The Jesuit José Sánchez Labrador reckoned that 'the misery in which they wander from place to place, and the licence with which they loose the reins of their brutal passion has obliged them to exterminate even their own loved ones'.

When the Spanish officer Felix de Azara reproached Guaicuru men for this infanticide, they smiled and said it was the women's affair. 'I then went to the women and spoke as energetically as possible to them. After my harangue, to which they listened with scant attention, one said to me: "When we give birth at the end of a pregnancy it mutilates, deforms and ages us – and you men do not want us in that state. Besides, there is nothing more tedious for us than to raise children and take them on our various journeys, during which we are often short of food. This is what decides us to arrange an abortion as soon as we feel pregnant, for our foetus is then smaller and emerges more easily." '

The result of this violent birth-control was depopulation. 'As a result of this cruelty there are few children among the tents of the Guaicuru. In all of them I knew only four married couples who had two children, an exception to the general rule: the rest had one or none.' Rodrigues do Prado declared: 'I know twenty-two captains [nobles] each aged about forty and all married, but only one has a daughter. For this reason I expect that this nation will cease.'

Having so few children of their own, the Guaicuru had to steal boys and girls from other tribes. This became one of the chief motives for their attacks. When they raided they seized children, horses and women; but always killed adult men.

The Guaicuru had chiefs but gave them little real power. There was no purpose or strategy behind their fighting. Objectives were chosen by assemblies of elders, and the Guaicuru raided only one place at a time. When a raid was planned trumpets sounded through the camps and anyone who wished could join. The advance and lightning attack were well co-ordinated, but the raiders returned piecemeal as individuals. This lack of military discipline delighted the Spanish commander Felix de Azara, for 'otherwise there would not now [in 1800] remain a single Spaniard in Paraguay or Portuguese in Cuiabá'. But Rodrigues do Prado, who commanded a fort on the Portuguese side of the Paraguay at that time, said that 'the number of Portuguese killed by them is reckoned at four thousand'.

Another curiosity of the Guaicuru was to keep male transvestites or female surrogates known as cudinhos. These 'act as their women, especially on long journeys. These cudinhos or nefarious demons dress and adorn themselves like women, speak like them, do the same work they do, wear jalatas [women's knickers], urinate squatting, have a "husband" who looks after them and constantly has them in his arms, are very keen to be wooed by the men, and once a month affect the ridiculous pretence of supposing that they are menstruating . . . going to the river daily as the women do with a gourd in the pretended hollow of their jalata.'

Rodrigues do Prado described Guaicuru men as 'tall, so that there are many men among them $6\frac{1}{2}$ feet in height. They are well built, well muscled and with an almost indescribable capacity for enduring hunger, thirst and sustained effort.' Very proud, they considered themselves superior to all other tribes. 'They greatly presume to be noble and valiant; being well set up and tall as they are helps them in this.' 'They count all other tribes as their captives, and do not even judge themselves inferior to Spaniards and Portuguese.' One Governor of Mato Grosso suggested that the Guaicuru should settle down to farm and should intermarry with the Europeans. They held a meeting and decided that all this sounded good, but they sent to ask 'how many slaves was His Excellency going to send to make those plantations, for they themselves were not slaves. They said the same about the houses: the wood for them was very hard and hurt their shoulders; they wanted them very much, but the Portuguese should come and build them for them. With regard to the marriages, they all said that they wanted

Portuguese wives. But they felt it unacceptable to impose the condition that they could not part from these until death. . . . [Such was] the ridiculous pride and vanity of that tribe.' When a Portuguese officer invited the Guaicuru chieftainess Dona Catarina to go to Cuiabá to meet the Governor, 'she consulted her people and gave me this answer: since she was still single she could not go to Cuiabá. For in that state Your Excellency would naturally want to marry her, and being an important lady and daughter of the great Queimá she could not contemplate this.' The Guaicuru considered Portuguese officials to be inferior since to become captains they received a paper commission, baton and braided uniform, whereas the Guaicuru were born as captains in succession to their fathers and grandfathers.

Guaicuru men were naked, apart from a blanket of jaguar skin or wool in broad red, black and white stripes. Both sexes painted their bodies in geometric designs of red urucum and black genipapo. The women tattooed graceful symmetrical designs on their faces with needles. Men and women plucked all their body hair, including eyelashes and eyebrows, and both sexes wore plenty of silver and bead ornament – necklaces, rings, bracelets and girdles. The men pierced their lower lips and inserted bone plugs. They clung to this custom even though it was a 'continual mortification like a thorn that punctures them all their lives'. They wore their hair short, but coated it in a mass of wax mixed with urucum, and sometimes fastened birds' wings to their ears. The Guaicuru generally had irregular teeth, 'but they keep them until death, although blackened by too much pipe smoking. . . . They lose their flesh very early and both men and women reach advanced age with their skin very wrinkled' (Plate 27).

The young men did no work, apart from tending their horses. 'Among these Indians . . . only the aged work. The young men say that their age is suited only to amusing themselves. They in fact spend most of the day in the arms of their wives, and are so inseparable that, even for corporal necessities, for walking or other actions, they do nothing unless the wife and husband do it together.'

Guaicuru women struck the Franciscan friar Mendes as 'generally pale and very good looking; although they immediately lose their [pale] colour because they go about naked from the waist up, and from the abuse of painting their faces and arms. . . . In their speech they are very eloquent and of a happy and joyful nature; but not very docile, although amiable.' Unlike the men, the women were rarely idle. They wove the rugs used by both sexes and the smaller cloths that the women used as breeches to cover themselves from waists to knees. It was the women who set up the tents, cutting and carrying the supports, sticks and rushes, and weaving the sleeping-mats. But it was only the older men and women who did more servile household jobs, such as fetching water and firewood, gathering coconuts or palm-hearts, tending little allotments, and cooking.

Guaicuru women 'are very careful to preserve their chastity and honour until someone of equal rank solicits them as wives: otherwise they do not lose these – except in very illicit ways or during some drinking bout or festival'. A favourite drink was a form of mead: the men gathered honey and made from it 'a terrible wine for their continuous carousing and festivities'. There were ceremonies at fixed seasons such as the rising of the Pleiades in August or the flowering of certain trees, and at the first menstruation of important girls, marriages, or the return of a victorious war-party. In these revels 'they paint, mask and ornament themselves extraordinarily; and the festival ends only when they are all so drunk that they fall. . . . [Parties] always end with everyone going and seeking a companion, with a man forgetting his wife and she her husband. They follow only their inclinations. No one refuses the first request in the hidden places they seek out for these bacchanalian encounters, in the forest or by the river.'

Although husbands and wives treated one another with great affection, it was easy for either sex to divorce a partner if the marriage failed. Francisco Mendes wrote: 'I have seen some women, particularly servants, repudiate three or four husbands in less than a year.' The Guaicuru aristocracy were more sophisticated. 'Every woman, especially the ladies, has one or two eager suitors who constantly go about and sleep at her side. Husbands are not jealous of these, saying that they are there to guard and protect her. One of these braggarts generally sleeps with her when the husband is doing the same with some other woman.' When a woman had a child – a rare event – she would nurse it for five or six years, during which time she and her husband slept with different partners. But she was marked as her husband's wife: 'the women carry, branded on a leg or breast, the same mark that their husbands place with fire and irons indiscriminately on them and on their horses'.

The tribe believed in a creator god, but there was no worship or religious ceremonial. There were shamans, who spoke to the evil spirits amid chanting and rattling of gourds. They cured by sucking their patients and pretending to spit out the infection. But they knew no medicinal plants or poisons; and little respect was paid to them. Guaicuru education was equally casual. Children were never corrected by their parents, 'for the only thing they teach them is to live in absolute and complete freedom'. There was similar freedom in the tribe's attitude to its chiefs. 'They obey him in some matters, but in very many they do whatever they want as if they were independent. It is a government entirely of condescension.' And yet there was great excitement when a son was born to a chief. Women and girls danced around the infant during days of celebration. 'The most exhausted old women, bundles of skin and bones, give their breasts to the infant as a sign of love, as if a parched hide were capable of communicating the snow-white vital juice.'

The Guaicuru impressed, baffled and infuriated Europeans who observed them. Colonel Ricardo Franco de Almeida Serra, an intelligent officer stationed among them, noted some of their idiosyncrasies. 'Their political system – the clinging to inherited customs and abuses; their wandering and libidinous way of life . . . their horror of work, which they consider proper only for slaves and incompatible with their innate pride – for they suppose themselves to be the first and dominant nation of Indians . . . the supreme indifference with which they regard the most obvious sentiments and feelings of religion or natural reason . . . the cruelty with which they annihilate their own race [through abortion], which is incompatible with the exaggerated tenderness and love with which they treat and rear children that they buy or steal from neighbouring tribes'; rivalries between different bands of Guaicuru; lack of interest in material objects or luxuries: 'all, in short, amounts to a confusion of contradictory ideas'.

One Guaicuru trait that fascinated observers was the tribe's relationship to the Guaná tribe. The latter attached themselves to the Guaicuru and worked for them as agricultural and household slaves. 'It is in practice a very gentle slavery, for a Guaná submits voluntarily and abandons it whenever he pleases. Furthermore, his masters give very few orders, never use an imperative or demanding tone, and share everything with the Guaná, even carnal pleasures.' Troops of Guaná would come to serve the Guaicuru, planting crops for them and serving in their tents. Once a year the Guaicuru would descend on the Guaná village, bringing presents but expecting large quantities of food in return. The chiefs of the two tribes intermarried, and many customs were identical. Almeida Serra said that Guaná submission was based on fear, to escape the murderous raids that the Guaicuru inflicted on other tribes: they 'allow themselves to be called their slaves, voluntarily giving them part of their harvests in order to spare the rest and the deaths they regularly used to suffer'. But the relationship became benign enough. It was symbiotic, with the Guaicuru obtaining the agricultural labour they despised, and the Guaná the protection of a powerful warrior tribe.

Although the haughty Guaicuru called the Guaná their slaves, they treated them very well, 'Indeed, these servants are more lords than their masters, who treat them like their children. They rarely reprehend or mistreat them, and . . . are affectionate and affable in their speech, although they always speak with emphasis and arrogance.' Felix de Azara recalled: 'I saw a [Guaicuru] who was cold look for his blanket. But, when he saw that his Guaná slave had taken it before him, he did not remove it or even reveal that he desired it.' Such behaviour towards servants impressed Europeans, probably because it contrasted with their own. But the missionary Francisco Mendes found the Guaná too malleable and weak: 'The Guaná are of an extreme docility which I find very prejudicial to their conversion. They embrace and learn the good today as fast as they forget and abandon it tomorrow, for no reason or motive other than that someone teaches them otherwise. I have had long experience of this. . . . To this one must add that they are very sensual, base, thieving and look equally well upon good and evil.'

Mendes' disapproval of the Guaná included their women, who were 'very facile and amorous, with very good bodies and appearance. They are generally brown, although there are whiter ones and many half-breeds. They are crazy about singing, and this is the reason why they are so prone to becoming healers or soothsayers, in which ministry they have more opportunity to practise singing – if one can give that name to the din they make with a gourd full of shells and pebbles like that of the [Guaicuru] shamans.' In one important respect the Guaná differed from the Guaicuru: 'They do not have the diabolical custom of killing their children in the womb. And for this reason these heathen are so abundant.' The fertility of the Guaná, coupled with their peaceful nature and their agricultural skill, have ensured their survival: their descendants, the Terena, are one of the largest tribes in modern Brazil, and one of the best adapted to Western life. The Guaicuru, on the other hand, are reduced to a small group called Caduveu who live in the beautiful Bodoquena hills and the Pantanal swamps of the Paraguay.†

Another tribe closely related to the Guaicuru were the Paiaguá, a people speaking a similar language and of similar appearance, but a river tribe, as formidable in their canoes as the Guaicuru were on their horses. The Paiaguá had fought intruders ever since the first Spaniards penetrated the upper Paraguay in the sixteenth century. They sometimes opposed the Guaicuru, but were more often their allies: the two tribes fought combined operations by land and river. Throughout the seventeenth century the Paiaguá were described as controlling the Paraguay river. They attacked flotillas of Spanish canoes returning from the maté forests, and they prevented Jesuit advance up the Paraguay. Allied to the Guaicuru, they ravaged Rapôso Tavares' bandeira in 1648 and attacked Jesuit missions during the later decades of the century, sometimes capturing Christian Indians and holding them 'in an oppression no less rigorous than that of [the pirates] of Algeria'. Many expeditions sent against the Paiaguá failed to locate or defeat them. Paulista bandeirantes also failed in attempts to enslave them. A Jesuit in 1703 described the Paiaguá as 'perfidious, rebellious and inconstant', but added: 'What is extraordinary is that they are so proud when they have scarcely 400 or 500 men to bear arms – for every year the mamelucos [bandeirante half-breeds] try to decimate them and they also often destroy themselves by fighting the Guaicuru.'

The bandeirante outpost established on the Mbototeu (Miranda) river in the late seventeenth century preyed on the Paiaguá and roused their fury against the Portuguese. The Paiaguá complained to Spanish Jesuits in 1703 that Paulistas regularly tried to seize their women, children and meagre possessions. In earlier times the slave-raiders dressed as Jesuits and handed out presents of cloth and tools: they deluded tribes into following them, and then chained and shackled them and marched them off into captivity. 'In the end the Portuguese mamelucos have been anti-Christs, like a scorching fire that reduced the numerous tribes that used to inhabit these broad shores almost to a desert. One sees only deserted and destitute villages. Father Juan Manora, who knew them and visited most of these villages, was amazed to see them deserted now.'

The Paiaguá watched the sudden rush of canoe flotillas to the new gold-fields of Cuiabá. They observed from the swamps and inlets of the Pantanal and Paraguay as more and more adventurers paddled past. Their initial reaction must have been relief that they themselves were not the victims of this invasion. But as the influx increased the Paiaguá decided that it represented a threat to their survival along the Paraguay. They determined to resist.

The annual flotillas of gold-seekers were known as monções or monsoons. That of 1725 consisted of twenty canoes carrying 200 people. It struggled up and down the rivers on the journey across Brazil and finally reached the calm waters of the Paraguay. But as it paddled up this last stretch of the journey the Paiaguá suddenly attacked, near the mouth of the Chanes river. They annihilated the convoy. Only one white and one black escaped from the entire monsoon. Another expedition the following year was also attacked by Paiaguá. The battle lasted from early morning until mid-afternoon. The Paulistas fought fiercely, first with firearms, then with swords, and finally grabbing the Indians' lances and turning these against them. But the monsoon's leader Miguel Antunes Maciel was killed fighting, and only part of his flotilla limped into

Cuiabá. Another convoy of 3000 people in 300 canoes reached Cuiabá in November 1726.

One of the discoverers of the Cuiabá gold-fields, the handsome António Pires de Campos, explained how the Paiaguá achieved their devastating victories. 'They were very highly skilled in handling their arrows and lances – they fired several shots during the time the bandeirantes fired a single one. Extraordinary swimmers, they advanced in their canoes and leaped into the water, tipping a side of their boat to act as a shield against bullets. They would suddenly right the canoe again and fire another volley. If they felt they could not overcome the whites' resistance, they submerged their boats, and before long dived and raised them again, and fled with such speed that they seemed to have wings.' Meanwhile the Guaicuru roamed the banks hoping to slaughter any Portuguese who escaped from each river battle.

In 1728 the Governor of São Paulo ordered an enquiry about the various tribes of 'barbarous heathen who have taken up arms to prevent traffic to the mines, killing travellers for no more reason than to give vent to their barbarity'. Some were domestic Indians who had escaped to the forests and were killing those who had pacified them, despite having been 'well treated'. Others were the Caiapó who raided the portage of Camapuã, killing slaves working in its fields. But the worst by far were the Paiaguá canoers and their allies the Guaicuru, 'the most barbaric and ferocious heathen that have been found in Brazil up to now'. A 'just war' must be declared against these tribes.

The Paiaguá continued their successful defence despite these fulminations. In 1728 they attacked a group of bandeirantes coming down-river with a large haul of Paresi captives. The expedition was destroyed, with all its whites either killed or taken prisoner. The following year the Paiaguá attacked a group of colonists trying to establish a settlement on the Coxim river, and few escaped.

The greatest battle of all was on 6 June 1730. That year's annual flotilla left Cuiabá taking 60 arrobas (900 kilos) of gold, with 400 whites, blacks and Indians in its canoes. The Paiaguá waited in ambush in a wooded tributary. Hundreds of them suddenly came skimming out in 83 canoes, manœuvring their craft and fighting with customary skill. The battle raged from nine in the morning until two in the afternoon. 'In each canoe there were ten or twelve savages of gigantic stature, all painted and decorated with feathers. As soon as they came within range, they covered us in such a dense cloud of arrows that it obscured the sun.' The black rowers and their passengers were 'almost ecstatic with terror'. Many black slaves jumped into the river. Their white masters managed to keep the rest paddling only by threatening to kill them if they stopped.

The Paiaguá glided up and killed the panic-stricken with their arrows, lances and clubs. The Portuguese could not help 'admiring the dexterity, courage and spirit, even the desperation of the enemy. They came right up to the mouths of our guns without fear of death, disregarding their own lives while they saw others lose theirs. If they were pursued by one of our canoes, they dived into the water, in which they swam like fishes.' In the heat of battle they calmly felt the pulses of blacks who surrendered, keeping the strongest and killing the weaker. They threw into the Paraguay 'half-living bodies – dead and living were buried in the stomachs of aquatic animals'.

The expedition's leader, Judge António Álvares Lanhas Peixoto, 'performed prodigies of valour and sold his life dearly'. He was alone in a canoe, abandoned by his crew. He managed to fire four arquebuses, but there was no one to reload for him. He disappeared in the mêlée. A few canoes escaped to the bank and launched a counter-attack with thirteen arquebuses; they rescued one canoe from the Indians. But the Paiaguá won a crushing victory. For losses of fifty killed, they annihilated the major part of the flotilla.†

The victors disdainfully threw much of the gold into the river. 'In their barbarity they undervalued this costly metal which would have excited the avarice of Diogenes [*sic*] himself.' They went to the bank and massacred many of the prisoners, sparing only some blacks and white women. They then sailed off down the Paraguay, taking weapons, clothing and some 150 kilogrammes of gold. The Paiaguá chief dressed himself in the Judge's rich clothing, with the Order of Christ around his neck. The white survivors watched him glide past, seated in the poop of a canoe, sheltered by a parasol that also covered 'a wretched eighteen-year-old girl born in Lisbon. She had just married in Cuiabá, and her husband had been slaughtered.' She tried to signal to the survivors on the bank with a handkerchief, but the Paiaguá stopped her. 'She was pregnant, but by divine providence did not give birth among the Indians. She spent three months with them, suffering many martyrdoms, nakednesses, hungers and mockeries. She was unable to use her servant girls, although they were within sight of her, suffering the same as she.' The young widow was called Domingas Ruiz. The Paiaguá shaved her head and plucked her eyebrows and eyelashes in their manner. She had only a torn petticoat to 'cover her private parts'. In September 1730 the Indians took her down to the Spanish town of Asunción. A canoe carrying four Indians 'covered in feathers and armed with arrows and lances, with their faces rouged and dressed in jaguar-skin cassocks', appeared and offered to ransom the white girl, two white boys and some blacks and mestizos. There was hard bargaining. The city's friars contributed church ornaments, and the governor and citizens offered 'things suitable for Indians'. The captives were ransomed. A worthy matron took care of the poor young widow, amid general compassion – she kept bursting into tears and modestly said she was a poor wretch despite her good social position.

The Paiaguá did not know the absurd value that white men attached to gold. They sold it for less than a fifth of its market value. One Spaniard traded a tin plate for six pounds of gold. A lucky citizen called Luís de Torquemada was the first approached by the Paiaguá. He acquired most of their gold, and it formed the basis of one of the town's great fortunes. The Paiaguá chief Cuatiguaçu who commanded this victorious attack lived to be extremely old, dying in Asunción in 1785, fifty-five years after the battle.* The Portuguese were naturally angry at the Spaniards' profiting from their misfortune in this way, and at their harbouring and trading with the victorious Paiaguá.

Another flotilla left Cuiabá soon after that destroyed by the Paiaguá. It found the tragic spectacle of the massacred prisoners, their corpses lying on the ground or thrown into the swamp, some killed by clubs and lances, others disembowelled or hanging from trees. There was a confused mass of broken chests, scattered clothing and torn papers. The Portuguese who survived the battle had decided to attempt to continue their journey to São Paulo, and their escape became an epic of endurance. They paddled up the Porrudos, Piquiri and Pitangui rivers and then marched along the old woodsmen's trail towards Camapuã. They were very short of food, eating only a few beans each day. It took fourteen days to cross the Pantanal swamps, during which 'we had continuous rains, without any hut or place where we could build one; and the mosquitoes in those parts are so many that anyone who does not sleep in a hammock with a well-closed awning cannot relax for a single instant, day or night'. There was continual fear of Indian attack, first from the Paiaguá and Guaicuru, then from the Caiapó and Bororo. All along these rivers the clearings on the banks had been destroyed and their settlers killed, most probably by Caiapó. But the survivors finally reached Camapuã, and then continued to the civilisation of São Paulo.

The Paiaguá victories caused consternation in the remote Cuiabá gold-mines. A large punitive expedition left the town in September 1730 under a Portuguese colonel. He was a veteran of wars in India and the Orient, always boasting of his exploits there. 'He reckoned that he alone possessed all the valour and knowledge needed for this mission: he would adopt the military tactics used in India, of which he was very proud. . . .' But after four months of abortive chasing about the inlets and islands of the Pantanal swamps the Indian Army colonel returned, having found no Paiaguá. He became a laughing-stock among the bandeirante miners, an old fool famous for 'the audacity and arrogance of his departure and the humility of his return'.

The following April Brigadier António de Almeida Lara left Cuiabá with 400 heavily armed men and two bronze trebuchets. They sailed in thirty war-canoes and fifty baggage-canoes. They landed near the mouth of the Mbototeu (Miranda) and were soon attacked by river and land in a joint operation by Paiaguá and Guaicuru. The cannon fired stones and grapeshot into the advancing Indians and killed many; the Indians withdrew. Farther downstream, the expedition tried to negotiate with the Guaicuru. The son of a Guaicuru chief was presented with sumptuous clothing and sent back to his people. He reappeared with a large contingent of mounted warriors. The Portuguese brigadier managed to seize some Guaicuru; he carried a few off to Cuiabá for indoctrination; 'but ordered that the hands and ears be cut off the rest: he told them to go and show themselves to their chiefs and to their Paiaguá friends'. The expedition returned to Cuiabá having achieved nothing.

The Paiaguá continued to harass the Cuiabá miners. They killed or imprisoned a group of Portuguese at Arraial Velho ('Old Camp') in 1731, and destroyed an expedition of fifty people coming from São Paulo in 1733. Letters from Cuiabá told of panic among its settlers, who were doing everything possible to save themselves from Indian attack. Governors in São Paulo wrote to Portugal about the terrible situation, and feverishly tried to organise reluctant Paulistas to march against the Paiaguá. The King issued a series of ferocious proclamations approving 'just war' against these tribes, and the enslavement of any captives.*

It was not until 1734 that a great punitive expedition set sail from Cuiabá under Manoel Ruiz de Carvalho. It was a huge expedition by Brazilian standards: 842 men in 28 war-canoes, 80 baggage-canoes and three fortified rafts – mobile stronghouses mounted on a series of canoes. The flotilla sailed leisurely downstream for a month, feeding itself by fishing and hunting on the river banks. It saw the fires of Paiaguá sentries near Bocaina and managed to surprise these in a night attack: forty were killed and their canoes smashed. The expedition pressed on for four days and nights, and then sighted many Paiaguá fires, burning on the banks of a bay. The expedition silently took up its positions. At dawn the unsuspecting Indians came down to the water. A black soldier sounded his trumpet against orders and the Paiaguá raced for their canoes. They paddled out in a brave attack. But the Portuguese had their canoes arranged in two wings and poured out a deadly fire from 200 muskets. The Paiaguá suffered terrible losses. They were driven back to the sandbank. Ten canoes loaded with men, women and children managed to escape through the smoke of the musket fire. The attackers now landed and advanced, firing furiously into the Indian camp. 'The tumult of the soldiery carried all before it, in a barrage of iron and a din through which nothing could be heard.' One woman screamed out that she was a Spanish prisoner called Josefa Maria, but the officers could not save her in the slaughter. The soldiers started bringing back captives, but were incensed to see their officers divide these spoils among themselves. The soldiers told their officers, 'Come and catch them yourselves if you want them!' and started massacring the Paiaguá rather than bothering to take prisoners.

'The attack was launched in such a way that the enemy could not use their usual tactics, not even for escape. They were so immobile and terrified that they hurt none of our party. That barbarous canaille was totally destroyed, losing all their canoes and people. Only some 240 persons remained alive, and our men took these captive to the mines.' Barbosa de Sá reckoned that 600 were slaughtered. It was a crippling blow to the small Paiaguá tribe. The Governor wrote to the men of Cuiabá that they 'could sing the glory of a triumph achieved miraculously through God. . . . In the fame of these triumphs you leave your names eternalised, emblazoning with them the ever-illustrious and dashing Portuguese nation!'

There was still some fight in the Paiaguá. They attacked a large monsoon of fifty canoes in 1735 and killed or captured all but four of its people. Its commander fought fiercely for two hours. He was helped by a mulatto woman called Maria, a stout matron who fought on until she died from loss of blood, and by a fat black stammerer who felled many Indians with a big club and, when he lost this, knocked them out with his fists. The next year's flotilla was attacked at the same place, Carandá. There was another heroic defence, by the commander, by a Franciscan friar nicknamed Tiger, and by a fat mestizo called Manoel Rodrigues do Prado whose wife loaded his arquebuses and handed them to him at the appropriate moment. Some of this monsoon's canoes dispersed into the swamps and then swept back in a surprise attack that freed some prisoners.

There were more Paiaguá attacks during the following decades, but they were less frequent. The tribe retreated into the depths of its swamps and lakes. It succumbed to punitive expeditions, wars with its former allies the Guaicuru, and the ravages of disease. By the 1780s the Paiaguá were almost annihilated: the few survivors took refuge among the Spaniards, and a pathetic remnant of the tribe now survives on an island reservation at the edge of Asunción. Tourists buy artefacts from the shabby descendants of the warriors who were once the scourge of the Paraguay.†

The Cuiabá gold-rush brought European civilisation to the lands of other tribes besides the Paiaguá and Guaicuru. North-west of Cuiabá lay the mato grosso of the Jauru – the 'dense forest' that gave its name to the entire state – and beyond them the more open, often arid plateaux of the Parecis and Nambiquara that form a watershed between the basins of the Paraguay–Plate and the Amazon. The Parecis were an admirable people: admirable in their way of life, and woefully admirable in the eyes of the bandeirantes, for they were populous, docile and peaceful. António Pires de Campos, the bandeirante Adonis, was one of the first to see the Parecis in their prime in 1718, before the ravages of the slavers. He recalled their great numbers: he used to pass ten or twelve large villages during each day's march. 'They all live from their farming, in which they are tireless. They are sedentary heathen, and the crops they plant most are manioc, some corn and beans, sweet potatoes, many pineapples, and pulses planted in admirable order from which they generally make their wines. . . . These heathen are not warriors: they defend themselves only when they are being procured.'

The Parecis were a religious people, with many idols and shamans. The men used the bull-roarer, a pair of propeller-shaped blades that were twirled to produce an eerie roaring, a male mystery that no woman was allowed to see. Parecis men used a straw penis-sheath and the women wore beautiful feather aprons hanging to mid-leg. 'This feminine heathen is the most attractive that has been seen. For they are very fair, with shapely legs and feet and all their features perfect.' Not only were they beautiful, they were also 'so agile and skilful that they can copy with the greatest perfection anything they are shown, and the men are the same. . . . These heathen make objects of stone like jasper in the shape of Maltese crosses, an insignia that the chiefs alone wear, hanging from their necks. These are as smooth and polished as worked marble. In the same way they carve other curiosities from woods as hard as iron, but without using any iron or steel instruments; and they make stone axes and other objects too difficult to be believed.' The Parecis villages were linked by broad paths, free of leaves. 'This kingdom is so large and widespread that its limit has not been reached. It is filled with heathen and very fertile because of the goodness of the land. The climate is reasonably cool.'

The Parecis were Aruak-speaking, part of the largest linguistic group of all South American Indians – for Aruak tribes are found from Florida around the Caribbean and particularly in the Guianas and forests north of the Amazon. The Parecis had evidently migrated from the Amazon up the Madeira-Guaporé or Tapajós rivers to their present location.

António Pires de Campos hoped that the Parecis would soon be converted to Christianity and become model citizens. The authorities echoed these hopes. If royal laws about good treatment of Indians meant anything, they surely applied to the Parecis, who lived exemplary, industrious lives, and had no vices such as eating human flesh or armed resistance to Christian conversion and Portuguese expansion. The King issued special orders not to molest the Parecis, 'who are of all the heathen of America those who best receive the Holy Faith'. All such edicts were forlorn wishful thinking, patching a dam with elegant parchment. One governor even tried to organise an expedition to return Parecis captives from Cuiabá to their homes! And whenever the authorities issued belligerent declarations of war against the Paiaguá and Guaicuru they tried to exclude the Parecis.

The harsh realities were that the mines of Cuiabá needed labour; it took many months to transport slaves from the coast; the region was far beyond the reach of royal supervision; and the Parecis were perfect slaving-fodder.* They were sought out and brought to Cuiabá in droves. Monsoon flotillas attacked by the Paiaguá always seemed to be carrying some Parecis slaves along with the gold from Cuiabá. Expeditions sent against the Paiaguá had a way of returning with Parecis captives. So many Parecis found their way back to São Paulo that governors were able to coerce citizens to serve against the Paiaguá by threatening to remove all their illegal Parecis. In the letter in which the Governor Count of Sarzedas congratulated the men of Cuiabá on their triumphs over the Paiaguá, he rejected their request to subject the entire Parecis nation to the town's jurisdiction. He reminded them that the Parecis were free people living peacefully in their own lands, 'where our cruelty went and sought them'. It would be a criminal offence to remove their liberty.*

Slaving expeditions against the Parecis were usually disguised as attempts to find more gold deposits. In 1732 there was a famine in Cuiabá that drove many miners off to hunt Parecis – for there was always plenty of food in Parecis villages. Two years later the brothers Artur and Fernão Pais de Barros reached the upper Guaporé with, in the words of a contemporary, 'the energy with which the Paulistas customarily roam the sertão in the conquest of heathen, for whose service they were more ambitious even than for gold. Because of them they went out to explore and settle the innermost wilds of this Brazil. . . .' To their surprise, the Barros brothers actually *did* find gold on the upper Guaporé. The Cuiabá deposits were already becoming depleted, so that the new discovery caused an exodus, a new gold-rush to the camp called Vila

Bela (later Mato Grosso City). This was a further disaster for the Guaporé tribes. Vila Bela had its moment of great wealth; but it was terribly unhealthy, built on a swamp and often flooded, and its gold was soon exhausted. By 1748 its miners had turned to 'hunting heathen, the business of poor men'.

The impoverished miners established themselves at a place called Ilha Comprida ('Long Island') in the Guaporé. A missionary called Agostinho Lourenço was sent in 1752 to make an official report on this Long Island. He was appalled by what he found. 'This settlement was nothing more than a lair of bandits attacking the lives, honour and property of the Indians, on whom they declared war with no motive or authority other than greed. Fifty or a hundred men would arm themselves and, leaving guards on the sandbank, would plunge into the sertão and attack the first Indian village they encountered. They would kill all who seized their bows in just defence. They would put the rest who did not escape into chains and shackles, destroy or burn the houses, ravage the fields, kill the animals and return triumphantly to their Long Island. There they would divide the vanquished among the victors and send them to Cuiabá and Mato Grosso under contract of sale. . . . Many Indians perished here like beasts, felled by an axe or as targets for arrows or guns, and a great multitude from ill-treatment and illness. The women paid with their lives and honour in the same way.'

José Gonçalves da Fonseca, an explorer who made the first ascent of the Madeira and Guaporé in 1749, also found Long Island full of criminals and deserters. He described how its raiders would spy out an Indian village. They attacked when the villagers went out to gather food and would 'terrorise them with shots and take some prisoners'. If the village was small enough, the raiders would charge it in the early hours of the morning 'and, after some killings, tie up those who could not flee, and withdraw with the captives so iniquitously acquired. They keep the best for themselves, and sell the remainder to settlers by means of smugglers who live in the swamps . . . in order to buy food, and powder and shot to repeat new outrages.'

The Long Island den of thieves soon disintegrated from internal quarrels. But by 1797 Ricardo Franco de Almeida Serra wrote that the Parecis 'were almost extinguished by the incursions, slavery and emigration caused by Portuguese. This tribe owed its ruin to its virtue and its peaceful conduct.'

Brazilian tribes could be accused of being too inflexible and conservative. By failing to adapt to the dynamic frontier society that was occupying their country, they doomed themselves to the status of anachronistic outcasts. But it is hard to see what they were supposed to do. The Paiaguá resisted fiercely and were gunned down; whereas the Parecis were too gentle and malleable and were enslaved. The Bororo, who lived to the east of Cuiabá, tried a different policy. The Bororo were formidable warriors living in forests and thick campo. They suffered the initial bandeirante slave-raids; retaliated with sporadic attacks on the mining settlements; and were the object of an official punitive expedition in 1734. Some Bororo then retreated deeper into their forests. But others decided to ally themselves to the Portuguese. The Bororo became 'brave towards other heathen but humble with the whites'.

The man who reduced the Bororo to submission was Manoel Rodrigues de Carvalho, the commander of the expedition that crushed the Paiaguá in 1734. These new allies soon demonstrated their usefulness. An alarming report reached Cuiabá in 1740 that Spanish Jesuits had crossed the Guaporé and were converting the Guaraparé tribe near the headwaters of the Cuiabá river itself. The mining town of Cuiabá was terribly weak at that time – depleted by the exodus of miners to Vila Bela, by years of severe drought and famine, and by losses from Paiaguá attacks. It was therefore decided to try sending friendly Bororo with presents to win over the tribe being converted by the Spaniards. The Bororo were completely successful. The Guaraparé deserted the Jesuits *en masse*, and Spaniards never again penetrated that part of what is now Brazil.*

It was António Pires de Campos who won the affection of the Bororo. He was a formidable woodsman with years of experience as a bandeirante. But he was also sympathetic to Indians. He was remarkable among bandeirantes for writing one of the first attempts at anthropological study of the tribes he discovered. It was Pires de Campos who wrote the panegyric about the Parecis, and who hoped that this admirable tribe could be peacefully converted. The Bororo admired and loved Pires de Campos, and called him Pai Pirá. Their warriors became his private army.

Beyond the Bororo the Gê-speaking Caiapó nation occupied an immense stretch of forest and campo. They raided from the portage of Camapuã in the south to the new mines of Goiás in the north. António Pires de Campos wrote of them: 'They are people [living in] villages. They inhabit much land for they are many people. . . . They live from their plantations, and [the crops] they grow most are sweet potatoes, corn and other vegetables.' They were great raiders of other tribes. Their warriors fought with large bows, and javelins that they threw with great accuracy; and they would boast of the numbers they had killed. 'Their chief interest is to eat those they kill, for they greatly enjoy human meat.

But in their assaults and captures they spare little ones whom they raise as their slaves.' António Rolim, Count of Azambuja, a governor who made the difficult journey to Cuiabá and Vila Bela, described a Caiapó ambush – and his description exactly fits a modern Caiapó ambush I myself have seen: 'They paint themselves in such a way that they become the colour of the forest with black genipapo, and suddenly attack those who pass by. They first fire at them with their arrows, and then break their heads from close range with their clubs. When this is done they at once flee, leaving the weapon with which they did the killing.'

The Caiapó threatened the routes from São Paulo to two separate mining areas: to both Cuiabá and Goiás. They slaughtered 140 slaves at the portage and farm of Camapuã and destroyed many plantations on the banks of the rivers leading to Cuiabá. Their raiding also forced travellers to move in convoys on the road to Goiás. Terror of the Caiapó caused prospectors to abandon the deposits of Pilões near Goiás. There were the inevitable protests to Portugal, and royal orders to destroy the Caiapó.*

António Cabral Camelo said that the main base of the Caiapó was near the mouth of the Rio Verde, a tributary of the Paraná. He described their sudden attacks to kill slaves working in clearings. They used to set fire to undergrowth to destroy whites moving through it. The only defence was to fell trees as a fire-break, or to light counter-fires. Cabral Camelo called the Caiapó 'the most treacherous of all the heathen' because they attacked only the unwary, when they were sure of winning.

Pedro Tacques de Almeida said that the Caiapó threatened hundreds of miles of the road towards Goiás. 'The road was blocked by these barbarians, to the total ruin of commerce and royal rights – all thanks to the repeated assaults of these Indians which have resulted in many deaths, to the horror of humanity.'

Two contingents of troops were sent into the forests to try to catch Caiapó. Their commander 'brought back two heads, which delighted the people, since it was the first time they saw the blood of these heathen'. But it was obvious that regular soldiers were making fools of themselves blundering about the jungles in search of agile and elusive Caiapó. Someone had the inspiration of enlisting António Pires de Campos and his faithful Bororo. The Bororo lived on the far side of the Caiapó and were their traditional enemies. Pires de Campos and his Bororo reached Goiás in August 1742, plunged into the forests, and rapidly destroyed a Caiapó village. 'It is recorded that he did appalling barbarities and a great slaughter. He even reached the main village of the Caiapó which they say lies in the region of Camapuã, but did not dare enter because its inhabitants were innumerable.' The miners were so delighted that they subscribed fifteen kilos of gold to hire him for further clearing operations.

A contract was signed on 12 October 1742 between Governor Luís de Mascarenhas and Colonel António Pires de Campos. Pires de Campos and his Bororo were to spend two years on punitive campaigns. They were to explore a wide area and hunt down any Indians who threatened Goiás. They were to pursue these until they caught them, regardless of distance. The historian Afonso d'Escragnolle Taunay recently found a map in the records of Itamarati, the Brazilian foreign service. It showed the route followed by Pires de Campos and the four Indian villages attacked during his expedition's long marches.†

Violence breeds violence, and the Caiapó reacted fiercely to this invasion. They attacked farms and killed slaves. One farmer marched out against them; but they made a diversion and went and burned the man's fazenda. There was panic. Farmers fled to take refuge in the fortified camp or registro on the Rio Grande, where there were some troops. A certain Manoel Raso marched out against the Caiapó on the Lanhoso. There was a big battle that the Indians won completely: Raso lost many men as well as his horses and baggage, and was forced to flee by night to a fort on the Velhas. The Caiapó won a skirmish against another contingent on the Lanhoso, and all movement on the road to Goiás was paralysed for fear of these 'Bilreiros' or 'club-wielders'. The Caiapó continued to burn farms and kill slaves, horses, pigs, and even children, giving no quarter since none was given to them.

The situation was so serious that the Governor declared another war. This was to continue until the Caiapó were tamed, put to flight or exterminated. He made it an official campaign, offering to pay its members as if they were regular royal troops. The officers were also to enjoy any captives, after the King's fifth had been removed – for in official campaigns the King demanded the same twenty per cent rate of taxation in captive Indian children as he did in mined gold.

António Pires de Campos had returned to fetch the wives and families of his Bororo warriors. He brought them east in 1748 and settled them on the Rio das Pedras, where there was plenty of game and fish. On 15 July 1748 the Governor wrote another contract for Pires de Campos and his private army. The Colonel was to lead his Bororo in frequent raids on the Caiapó and to defend Goiás in case of attack. The royal treasury paid 800 oitavas (6¼ pounds) of gold to establish the Bororo in their new base. If a full year elapsed without any Caiapó|raids, António Pires de Campos was to be made a Knight of the Order of Christ, with a pension of 50,000 reis.*

The Bororo were delighted to be armed and led into battle against their Caiapó enemies. They marched out again and surprised and slaughtered more Caiapó villages. 'In the space of three months [Pires de Campos] took over a thousand prisoners in a radius of 150 leagues (1000 kilometres).'

The Caiapó fought back. In 1751 they bravely attacked Goiás itself, killing some settlers in the town's pasture. Appeals went out to Pires de Campos and his Bororo, and they set out on yet another punitive expedition. They followed the Caiapó's trail and soon caught them. There was another massacre. 'But the triumph cost him dear. For on this occasion a bold Indian attacked him – it was the moment of greatest danger [on his campaigns against] these barbarians – and shot an arrow through his chest on the right side below the shoulder. This misfortune was not enough to prevent him, still pierced by the arrow, from taking [the Indian's] life with his cutlass.' Pires de Campos returned to recuperate at his base. But the Governor begged him to help escort a convoy of gold, for there were rumours of a plot to ambush it. António Pires de Campos marched out with his Bororo, 'excellent arquebusiers', to help the royal dragoons escort the gold. His arrow wound reopened, he became feverish and died in 1751 at Paracatí. He was buried with full military honours; but he also received a month of funeral rites from his Bororo – an elaborate, mysterious ceremonial that the tribe still reserves for its greatest chiefs.

By the middle of the eighteenth century the great Brazilian gold-rushes were over. The discoveries of gold, in quick succession, in Minas Gerais, Goiás, Cuiabá and Mato Grosso extended the settled parts of Brazil deep into the interior. Historians of the bandeirantes divide their activities into three cycles: 'Indian-hunting' chiefly against the tribes around São Paulo and the Spanish Jesuit missions; 'contract wars' against the tribes defending the cattle lands of the North-East; and 'gold', the discovery and exploitation of the new gold-fields. Each phase led to extraordinary feats of exploration and the opening of immense new regions to white settlement. And each led to the contacting and destruction of thousands of native inhabitants of those regions.

EIGHTEEN

Indian Labour on the Amazon

THE man who shouted 'Out! Out!' as he pushed at the ship taking António Vieira away from Brazil in 1661 was Sargento-mor António Arnau. When the Jesuits were gone, the Governor of Pará promptly appointed Arnau to lead an official 'ransom' troop, 'which was his entire ambition, something for which he had been sighing for years. . . . This wretched man decided to go for three whole years into the sertão. He promised great felicity and riches to all who accompanied him, because of which a great mob went in his troop.'

Arnau's men paddled up the Madeira but were frightened by the large numbers of Indians there. They therefore returned to the Urubu river, which flows into the Amazon opposite the mouth of the Madeira. The Aruak-speaking tribes living on the Urubu – the Caboquena and Guanavena – had recently been visited by the Jesuit missionaries Manoel de Sousa and Manoel Pires, who had 'removed their fear of enslavement and promised that under the new laws to be sent by the Most August King, they would have good treatment among the Portuguese, with whom they would live . . . a life of men and not [their present life as] beasts, and after death they would be eternally happy as sons of God. These words moved the Aruak.'

The Aruak of the Urubu became suspicious when Arnau demanded large numbers of prisoners from them. They suspected that he might attempt to capture slaves from their own ninety-six villages. They determined to divide Arnau's force. José de Sousa Ferreira, who was

Indians shooting fish.

with Arnau, recalled that 'the heathen prepared a trap for us. They said they had a village full of captives tied to posts that they wished to give us, but that they needed the help of our arms. . . .' Arnau sent off fifteen white soldiers and a hundred of his Indians. 'These travelled by night, into an ambush, where [the Indians] attacked [and destroyed] them.

'[The Aruak] then came to our camp at daybreak, as if they were peacefully going to sell us some Indian women. They brought these tied with rotten ropes – and by their treatment it was obvious that these were their wives, but we did not realise this. . . .' The Indians went to Arnau's hut, showed him the bound girls, and said: '"Here are the slave girls you wanted." Arnau was delighted. . . . He confidently came to receive the captives they offered him, bringing no weapons at all with him, for he was in a hurry to get out of bed to see the slave girls. As he emerged from the door the Aruak chief struck him with a wooden club, of the sort with which they execute people. He struck one blow on his head that immediately split it into two parts, and another on the mouth that broke his teeth and jaw. . . . He died in the sight of all, without sacraments . . . after lying in pain for three days, moving nothing except that mouth that had spoken so much against the missionaries.' There was a confused battle inside the stockade. The Aruak managed to wound other slavers with their juca-wood clubs and killed a notoriously cruel interpreter called Miranda. 'We retreated under arms from their poisoned arrows, from which few wounded escape. . . . On that occasion the entire troop descended [other rivers] with almost a thousand persons in some twenty canoes. In each canoe there were fifteen or sixteen Indian rowers, three or four Indian officers and as many whites, besides the slaves we were all bringing.'

It was now late 1664. An officer called Pedro da Costa was at the Tapajós aldeia (modern Santarém), accepting the submission of many chiefs terrorised by the same Aruak who had killed Arnau. When he heard of Arnau's death, Costa went and fortified himself near the lands of the Caboquena and Guanavena. The Governor sent reinforcements in 1665, and Costa 'multiplied his devastations, so greatly that the last proud member of those Tapuia wept at the fatal burning of three hundred villages, after the slaughter of seven hundred of the most valiant men of his nation and the captivity of four hundred, who are dragging chains in the city of Belém do Pará as the spoils of victory. . . . All who took part in this expedition so full of dangers gained great credit from its fame.'

The Jesuits returned to the Amazon in 1665, but found Maranhão and Pará devastated by epidemics, of 'smallpox, measles (which is the plague of Brazil), shortage of [manioc] flour and wars with the Aruak tribe. . . . In this way the state gradually has its head forced down, as it is today.'

A new law forbade colonial governors to deal in tobacco or other crops. The governors therefore turned to the forests for quick profits. In those days, 'everyone had his Indian slaver in the sertão . . . and considered best those who sent most slaves to be examined – whether properly or badly ransomed. . . . And there was no lack of examiners, who readily accepted them all [as legitimate slaves], for the thirst of ambition is dangerous in anyone who crosses the ocean, even if he is an ecclesiastic.'

The slavers would herd their captives into corrals for months on end, while they continued their ransoming. 'When they did come to send them back, half were dead or had fled. Of the [remaining] half, less than half arrived down-river, for they were embarked already infected, hostile and exposed like sardines for a month to the rigours of any weather. Anyone who purchased a slave who arrived like this suffered as a result: he was left with a violent thing, badly acquired.'

And so the wretched business went on, year after year. Everyone knew that the Indian slaves were rebellious, intractable and almost useless. They died out pitifully. 'If you put ten slaves in a house, ten years later there would not be one left. But if a married couple flee into the forest they will be found in ten years with ten children.' 'Those who have a hundred slaves one day, will not have six left a few days later. The Indians, who are anything but robust, have an incredibly high death rate. Any attack of dysentery kills them; and for any small annoyance they take to eating earth or salt and die.'

All the accessible parts of the Amazon were being denuded. One man complained in 1693 that it was necessary to go for two months up the Amazon as far as the Omagua to find any slaves. He demanded: 'How far will one have to go seventy years from now to catch any Indians?'

João de Sousa Ferreira was a missionary of the Order of St Peter who kept some slaves. He justified the system, for 'there is no divine or human law that prohibits the possession of slaves', and the Brazilian Indians were barbarous enough 'descendants of the curse of Ham' to qualify as natural slaves. But Sousa Ferreira was aware of the suicidal despair that seized Indians who fell into slavery. 'Among some [Indian] slaves I possessed were girls capable of having offspring. . . . But I noticed that one had already killed four children: the first with earth, which she taught him to eat when he was seven; the second by smashing his head on a log as soon as he was born . . . the third and fourth she aborted before time with a herb she drank. I tried every sort of punishment but to no avail, and finally sold her in Maranhão. The others had been following in her footsteps, showing no improvement, even with punishment. . . . I tried a new agreement with them, declaring that I would give cloth for a skirt to any pregnant Indian woman as soon as she gave birth. . . . This scheme resulted in even the old women making an attempt. One exception was a woman who, because an Indian she wanted to marry did not want her, said to me: "White man, sell me. If you don't, I shall die." I tried to mollify her with words, in order not to have to sell her. But before two months were up she was in the next world.'

The Indians taken by ransom troops were classified either as slaves or free men. The proportion of slaves varied from about a third to the entire haul of Indians brought downstream by the troop. The free Indians were lodged in mission villages, and these aldeias were also stocked by tribes whom the missionaries themselves persuaded to descend.

Slaves, as their name implies, belonged outright to the settler who acquired them. But free Indians formed the missionaries' congregations and were also expected to provide a labour pool for the settlers and for government public works. Jesuits and other missionaries sought to isolate their flocks as much as possible. But they could do this only when the mission was remote from colonial settlements: otherwise the law insisted that they hire out the men of the mission to work for the settlers.

The daily routine of the Amazon missions was laid down by António Vieira in 1660, and continued with little change for almost a century. Each mission was to be self-supporting. Any surplus produce was to be sold in Belém or São Luís, and the proceeds used to buy tools and other things needed by the Indians or for the upkeep of the mission's church and hospital.

There were two missionaries in charge of each village, both among the Jesuits and other orders. They lived in an enclosed house and were permitted four or five household servants and twenty-five labourers each. The missionaries were not to receive anything worth more than one cruzado for themselves, or to accumulate debts of over ten cruzados for the mission. Strangers might visit only with permission from the Superior. There was a guest house for needy travellers, but they were not to stay for long; only important guests might stay in the missionaries' own house.

Religious offices were considered important, and the missionaries must observe their rituals, even on river journeys. The daily routine began with a morning service for everyone. After mass the congregation recited the Lord's Prayer, Ave Maria, Ten Commandments and a shortened Catechism. Most villagers then went out to work in the plantations or workshops. The most intelligent children remained behind to study, and learned reading, writing, scripture, playing musical instruments and singing. At sunset there was another mass, primarily for the children, who then processed around the village square intoning the Creed and Commandments. The villagers were permitted to celebrate traditional dances on Saturday nights and the eves of saints' days. But they were not allowed to dance all night or to consume much alcohol: a bell was rung at 11 p.m. after which the Indians must return to their huts to sleep.

The missionaries were to keep careful record of births, baptisms, marriages and deaths. They could order corporal punishment, but must never inflict it themselves. Women must never be flogged, and men only as sparingly as possible, since the Indians were of limited intelligence and were known to resent physical punishment. Control of the village was by the chief or headman. This was a hereditary position if suitable sons were available; otherwise the missionary might appoint a successor after consulting the village elders.

This routine destroyed native cultures, but it worked reasonably well in the isolated missions. Most tribes accepted missionary supervision passively enough if they saw that it kept their families fed. The trouble was that the system was not allowed to function. If a mission village were within range of white settlements, there were incessant demands on its inhabitants' labour. António Vieira tried to provide some safeguards. Missionaries were urged 'to insist on proper payment for the sweat of these poor wretches, since the conversion of those who are still heathen depends on the good treatment accorded to those who are already Christians'. Women might be employed outside the villages either as wetnurses, or as elderly maidservants for senior officials and impoverished white women, or with their husbands in harvesting manioc – the growing of this staple crop was traditionally women's work in forest Indian villages.

The Indians of the mission villages formed the main labour pool for the settlers and royal authorities of Maranhão and Pará. The law classified all Indian males aged between thirteen and fifty as eligible for labour. The population of the free Indians in the missions fluctuated – it dropped owing to the ravages of epidemics, but was continuously being restocked by fresh descents. There were some 50,000 Indians in the Maranhão and Pará villages in 1686; 54,216 in 1730; and some 25,000 in 1750.* If half these people were men, with a life expectancy of about forty years, the potential labour pool of adult and adolescent Indian men was between seven and fifteen thousand. Many of these lived far from the settlers' towns, far up the Amazon and its tributaries. After 1686 the law stated that half the available Indians might be out working for settlers at any time. This would provide from four to seven thousand labourers. But one governor confessed that he and his predecessors grossly exceeded this proportion: they authorised virtually all available Indians to leave the mission villages and work at all times. The civil authorities thus forced nominally free Indians to labour, at gunpoint if necessary.

There were also many slaves: for the ratio of slave to free Indian taken by ransom expeditions was high, and there is ample evidence in contemporary documents of illegal slaving activity. There could well have been ten thousand Indian slaves in these two states at the turn of the eighteenth century.

When Indians from the mission aldeias went out to work the law considered them to be free men working for hire. In practice they were forced labourers. Their salaries were fixed in 1655 at two varas (2½ yards) of rough cotton cloth for a month's labour. This rate of pay was not changed for almost a century, even though it was scandalously small. Clothing was not a normal need for forest Indians in the tropical climate of the Amazon. In many ways it was a liability: clothes tore in the forests and needed constant repair; clothing was more difficult to wash than human skin; and it could be a health hazard, for Indians bathed frequently, wearing their clothes, and then allowed the wet clothing to dry on their bodies. But Christian Indians were forced to wear clothing. They were punished for going about immodestly and indecently naked. Having imposed this artificial requirement on the Indians, the colonists then used cloth as the standard currency to pay for Indian labour! It was the Indians themselves who produced the cloth with which they were paid. They laboured to grow the cotton, often in mission plantations; and their wives spun and wove the cotton into cloth. After a month of gruelling labour, an Indian obtained none of the few simple things he wanted – an axe, knife, machete or fish-hooks, some alcohol or tobacco, or beads and ribbons for his family. The two yards of cloth had a nominal value of only 200 reis, not enough to purchase any of these things. One can imagine the reception an Indian would have in a colonial town if he tried to exchange his quota of cloth for more useful objects. The system was so grossly unfair that it amounted almost to slave labour.

It was a curious way to attract converts to Christian civilisation. Contemporaries knew very well that the Indians found this forced labour abhorrent. 'There is no doubt whatsoever that if the Indians were not forced to serve whites – neither the men nor their wives, sons and daughters . . . then in a short time many heathen would be converted to our holy faith and would descend from the sertão.'

The Jesuits co-operated with the authorities as best they could. This was partly because their Society was becoming increasingly rich, with large ranches and plantations worked by mission labour. They had more to lose than had Vieira's first missionaries on the Amazon. But it was not easy to keep in step with the laws, which continued to change with bewildering contradictions.

The law of 1680, inspired by Vieira himself, returned to the extremely liberal attitude of the law of 1609. All slavery of Indians was again forbidden. Anyone who captured Indians was to be arrested and exiled, and the victims freed and sent to mission aldeias. Indians captured in battle were to be treated humanely like prisoners of war in Europe. The conversion of Indians was entrusted to missionaries, particularly Jesuits, who were to penetrate the forests without military escorts. But even this liberal law made harsh provisions for mission Indians' labour: at any time, a third were to work for settlers, a third help the missionaries descend more tribes, and a third stay home to feed the mission.*

This left the problem of labour for Maranhão and Pará largely unresolved. The panacea for the area's troubles was to be the importation of African slaves. A government trading monopoly was to import five or six hundred slaves a year to these northern provinces, and sell them cheaply. No one considered that the enslavement of blacks was as unjust as the seizure of native Indians. No Jesuit, not even Vieira, spoke up against this African traffic. In practice it did not work. Black slaves commanded such good prices in the rich sugar-growing parts of Brazil and later in the gold-mines that few reached the impoverished Amazon.

The settlers' reaction was swift – almost as fast as their moves to force repeal of the 1609 or 1655 legislation. In February 1684 there was the revolt led by Manoel Beckman and by Jorge Sampaio, the Public Prosecutor who had led the protest against the 1665 law. The revolt was confined to Maranhão, where the Governor was seized and twenty-seven Jesuits evicted. It was crushed easily enough with the arrival of a new governor, Gomes Freire de Andrade. The ringleaders were hanged.

But the Beckman revolt alarmed the Portuguese Government. Settlers' delegations sailed to Lisbon – one led by Beckman's brother Thomas, and another under Manoel Guedes Aranha, an ardent defender of slavery. They achieved a harsher law of 2 September 1684. This restored private 'administrations' or slaveholdings of Indians, and permitted governors to license individuals to make descents of forest Indians.

The Beckman revolt also frightened the Jesuits. Many of them felt that their attempt to resist enslavement of Indians was hopeless. The Indians were ungrateful and were proving, almost without exception, superficial and unsatisfactory converts. Public opinion among white settlers was convinced that the Jesuits were to blame for the colony's troubles. Some Jesuits therefore wanted to follow the Biblical precept: to shake the dust from their feet and seek easier pastures elsewhere. João Felipe Betendorf, a German-born Jesuit trained at Douai in Flanders, argued that the Society should compromise – it did many good works beside the Indian missions, and should not jeopardise everything by being inflexible on the Indian question.

The Jesuits' compromise resulted in the Regulations of Missions in the State of Maranhão and Grão-Pará (Greater-Pará) of 21 December 1686. The missionaries were confirmed in perpetual control of aldeias, and were granted temporal as well as spiritual control. No outsiders were allowed to enter mission villages or remain in them, on pain of flogging and exile to Angola. The Jesuits yielded many of their villages to missionaries of other orders – the black-robed Fathers kept control only of the south shore of the Amazon as far upstream as the Madeira river.†

In the new regulations, the Jesuits conceded that mission Indians would have to work for settlers for six months each year, instead of the four months of the 1680 legislation. They agreed to keep registers of all eligible males aged from thirteen to fifty. But it was the Governor who apportioned this labour among the settlers. Governor and missionaries were to agree to fix the standard rate of pay for free Indian labour. Government, settlers and missions all had an interest in paying Indians as little as possible. The monthly wage therefore remained at $2\frac{1}{2}$ yards of cloth until 1750 – even though the rate had been as high as ten yards for twenty days' work during the Dutch occupation in 1639.*

A more terrible surrender by the Jesuits concerned the ransoming or enslavement of Amazon Indians. The King bowed to pressure from the colonists, and in decrees of April 1688 reintroduced Indian slavery. A greedy governor of Maranhão had written to tempt the King with the profits he could make from this traffic. 'Each slave can be acquired for four or five milreis – traded for tools, beads and other bagatelles – and can later be sold for thirty! Not only would Your Majesty make a big profit; the settlers would also be helped to put their dismantled mills into operation. . . . Unless slavery is permitted this state can never be anything – although it contains plenty to make it great.'

New decrees therefore revived the annual 'ransoming' expeditions, financed by the royal treasury and each accompanied by a missionary. These expeditions could legally enslave 'bound Indians' (those who had been captured in inter-tribal wars). Captives taken in 'just wars' were also to be slaves. 'Just wars' used to be merely defensive; they were now interpreted to include aggressive attacks on tribes when there was 'certain and infallible fear' that these threatened the Portuguese colonies.* The aged António Vieira, who was in Bahia, protested that the Jesuits would lose all moral authority if they participated in these slaving expeditions. But the missionaries on the Amazon decided that expediency demanded their connivance.

A later governor described how the law worked in practice. 'This royal order was always executed . . . by the formation of expeditions sent into the sertão. The leader was generally a criminal and he was given another of similar origin as his deputy, and . . . a scrivener of similar conscience. At the head of these men, to judge on the [Indians'] liberty or slavery, went a Father called a missionary, who was almost always from the Society [of Jesus]. He judged these important matters with absolute, decisive power. A few soldiers followed these officers, but very few. The rest were a gang of any worthless, licentious men to be found in this state.' This governor described how the expedition would establish itself on some river peopled by Indians. They bribed chiefs with alcohol, beads or knives and persuaded them to seize captives from other tribes. If the chief produced too few such 'bound Indians', 'they would tie up the chiefs themselves, their subjects and families, and bring them down along with the other slaves'. Otherwise they would send out patrols to catch Indians.

'Before presenting these captives to be examined they either flogged them cruelly, or killed one in the presence of his comrades. They told them that the same would be done to them all unless they replied to the missionary as they were taught. . . . The examiners were well aware that such procedures were taking place. But these judges all had a strong interest in that slavery, for the missionary himself was gaining a large number of captives for his Order or for his own interest.' It was usual for *all* captured Indians to be judged as slaves. 'This is how so important a matter was handled. It has made us so irreconcilably hated by the Indians that in many places they go to seek the protection of other European nations bordering with us.'

The new laws about the ransoming of slaves and the hiring out of free Indians were harsh enough. But they failed hopelessly to satisfy the settlers' demands for a labour force large enough to develop profitable exports from the Amazon. The laws were therefore extended, legally and illegally, by settlers, governors and the King himself.

In 1689 the Crown permitted private individuals or groups to make expeditions into the interior, and to bring back 'uncivilised' Indians at their own expense.* This decree piously insisted that the Indians should be persuaded rather than forced to leave their forest homes. It also stipulated that the Indians be resettled close to some European settlement. The persons who financed such resettlements were entitled to hire the labour of these nominally free Indians; but they tended to regard them as private property. One colonist explained, bluntly, that 'expeditions into the sertão to take slaves were resumed. These were not positively conceded by the royal ministers, but were not actually forbidden. The settlers thus recovered and Maranhão improved again during the administrations of three governors.' Anyone who could obtain a licence and gather together enough Indian rowers went paddling eagerly upstream.

Illegal slaving became so widespread that within two years the King admitted the abuse: he issued a pardon for Indians illegally enslaved and fined their masters twice the value of each such slave.* In 1702 a decree clarified the status of private resettlements: a person who descended Indians had the right to their labour during his lifetime, but he could use them only according to the 1686 law, and they were to be under the administration of missionaries.*

Various royal orders told the commanders of the forts along the Amazon to be vigilant against clandestine slaving expeditions. But those commanders were often deeply embroiled in the traffic. The fort of Camutá had an aldeia of Indians who were supposed to work for its settlers. But one commander of the fort sold 'the entire labour of all the Indians of that aldeia for 4000 cruzados' to a local settler, a former chief justice of that captaincy. The judge 'paid this sum immediately, sent someone to take possession of the aldeia, and disposed of all the Indian men (and possibly of the women as well). The settlers of Camutá were deprived of [the labour] designated for them. [The judge] put them into his canoes to go and make descents or raids . . . and completely disposed of them.' These raiders later intercepted a flotilla of Indians being descended by the Jesuits to fill one of their missions. They killed the native bailiff and a Christian Indian canoe-commander. They then tied up the Indians being descended for the missionaries and took them to their master in Belém. He promptly sent them to work on his sugar mill, without the formality of any examination, and kept them as slave labour. By 1705 the King acknowledged that 'all the inhabitants are enslaving Indians against my orders without fear of punishment'. He ordered his legal officers to take action against them.

In 1696 the town council of Belém asked that it be granted the administration of aldeias of Indians descended by settlers at their own expense. The council claimed that this was the only way to make good the miserable state of the colony after a recent epidemic of smallpox. But the King refused. He wrote that abuse by the settlers would only cause the Indians to flee. 'Time has shown that the settlers' ill-treatment consumed the greater part of the people who inhabited the forests surrounding that captaincy.' A few years later the King demanded a report on punishments given to 'the many persons involved in the crime of going to take slaves in the sertão against my orders'. But in 1707 the King admitted the grim reality: that illegal slaving continued 'without fear of God or of the justices. These recognise the impossibility of punishment, not only because of the numbers of the guilty, but also because of the difficulty of proof. For only the poor Indians suffer, and the commanders and officers [of slaving expeditions] stop anyone testifying against them by threatening vengeance.'

The slaving activities that angered the King were private expeditions done without royal licence. But it was easy enough to obtain such a licence. Royal correspondence was full of decrees authorising individual settlers to go into the interior and try to bring back Indians. In 1702 one settler was allowed to hire 20 mission Indians to paddle his canoes, and to descend 20 Indian families to labour on 10,000 feet of cacao he had just planted. Another man was to descend 60 families for his sugar mill. In 1703 the town of Icatu was licensed to descend the entire Anaperu tribe, to make good the losses of its native labourers from smallpox. In 1704 the King felt sorry for the settler who had suffered captivity among the Moors in Meknès and who had seven children; he licensed him to descend a hundred Indian families. Another man was managing a royal indigo factory but was constantly short of labour: many royal decrees authorised him to descend Indians. So it continued, with a stream of licences for a dozen couples, or thirty, fifty, sixty, a hundred or two hundred. In 1708 one Luís Pereira said that he was going to found a colony of settlers on the Xingu river. The King gave him permission to descend 'at his cost all the Indians he can from the Amazon river – Indians who are buried in the forests without the light of the Gospel – so that he can distribute them among the settlers of his new colony . . .'.

In 1718 the cathedral of São Luís needed rebuilding. The King authorised a special ransom expedition to finance the work. He decreed that the expedition's expenses should first be met, from the disposal of its victims. Thereafter 'put up for sale in the city of São Luís 200 ransomed Indians, so that you can undertake the works on that church with whatever is paid for them. . . .' This edict surely set some new record of hypocrisy – a licence to seize and sell Indians to finance the rebuilding of a Christian cathedral!

Free Indians were settled in three types of aldeia. Most were in standard mission villages, known as 'distribution' aldeias because their men were available for hire to local settlers. The legislation of 1686 increased the labour obligation of every free Indian, adolescent and adult, to six months in every year.

Royal governors were to allocate this free labour. In practice they flouted the six-month limit. One governor, João da Maia da Gama, made an extraordinary admission about this. 'I must confess an offence to Your Majesty and lay myself open to the punishment it deserves. I accordingly assure Your Majesty that, during all the time of my government, I exceeded the law of distribution [of Indian labour], because of the utility of the contracts and the urgency for the royal service of the expeditions. On my own head, I assure Your Majesty that in all the "distribution" aldeias, throughout the six years of my government, there remained not half – as Your Majesty orders – nor even a third nor a quarter of the Indians. They were *all* occupied in Your Majesty's service or in the settlers' canoes. I gave them just enough time to leave their clearings planted. My predecessors did not do even that. As a result I found the aldeias diminished and their families dying of hunger.'

Governor Maia da Gama justified his excesses by claiming that he used the mission Indians for royal profit. It was the standard excuse. A typical letter from the King to the previous governor strongly reprimanded him for similar deception. 'Various persons have gone to the aldeias on your orders, to remove Indians on the pretext of royal service. They were in fact for your own labour. They were taken in canoes to extract forest plants, and violence was used to compel the wretched Indians to do this work by force.'

A law of 1718 invited any settlers to petition the King for permission to descend Indians. Each was to state the number of Indian individuals or couples he needed and the purpose. Many settlers had too few Indians to man a canoe: this law advised three or four such poor settlers to pool together to finance the expedition, and then share out the descended Indians among themselves. The distinction between such free Indians and slaves was very tenuous: free Indians had to work only to fifty years of age; their children were nominally free; they received pay of two varas of cloth a month; they could not be bequeathed; and if mistreated or not paid, 'and they complain and are justified, the mission junta and the [Governor-] General may remove them from settlers to whom they are allotted and give them to others who treat them better, which is not done for those in slavery'. There is no record of any such complaint being successfully made by an Indian.

Father Jacintho de Carvalho described a typical expedition by a settler who obtained a licence to descend seventy couples for his sugar mill. 'He reached the Rio Negro, advanced to a village, killed some [Indians], captured others and loaded up the canoes he had brought with them. Many died on the journey – more from starvation and lack of manioc flour and by oppression from the stocks in which they were held than from disease. Many who were still alive but who despaired of life jumped into the water so that those still alive . . . could eat the flour they would have consumed. This may seem to be tyranny, impiety and unheard-of cruelty. But I can affirm in all honesty, as a priest and ecclesiastic, that similar things happen every year in almost all the canoes that go to ransom Indians. That man reached Belém do Pará and took the survivors to his mill. But only for a short time. Within six months he sold them all as slaves, declaring that the Indians would die, but not the money. So much for the need for men to work in the plantations and mills, as it is represented to His Majesty!'

The royal authorities had the right to commandeer aldeia Indians for royal service. They used free Indians to equip the official ransom expeditions, or to build fortifications or roads. In 1722 Governor Maia da Gama obtained eighty mission Indians for two years to open a land route between Maranhão and Pará. When Governor Alexandre de Sousa Freire reached Maranhão in 1728 he promptly 'ordered all the Indians in the aldeias who were capable of working to be removed to go and find some mines that he imagined, for no good reason, to exist in the jungles of the Pindaré. . . . In this way he left the aldeias uninhabited [by men] during the months of July, August and September, the season in which they normally make clearings in this country. There was not one Indian capable of clearing forest. As a result these aldeias have suffered great starvation and have nothing to eat but some forest fruits.'

The authorities would also demand Indians for royal service, but then send them off into the forests to gather cinnamon, sarsaparilla or cacao. Such expeditions plunged deep into the interior and lasted 'over six, seven or eight months. Many [Indians] remain there dead and others almost dead, and those who return are discontented because they are badly rewarded and mistreated.' João Daniel also wrote that it was 'very normal in those Portuguese missions where the men go to work for the whites' for husbands to be absent for from six to eight months. This meant that they could not hunt or fish, and their families had to survive on vegetables.

Some Indian villages were reserved exclusively for royal use, and others – to the fury of the settlers – were for the sole use of the missionary orders. When a governor complained of a lack of labour for the canoe factory on the Moju river near Belém, the Government reserved the men of an entire village for use in that factory. The inhabitants of the village of Moriceira were reserved for work on the fortifications of Pará. Those of Igarapé were put to work for three years on the construction of a jail and municipal buildings for Belém. The Indians of Joannes worked only in nearby salt pans, and those of Maracanã on fishing and salting fish. Twenty-two Indians from Cayá aldeia were allocated to transport meat to the city of Belém, and the city was authorised to descend 150 Indian families to provide a municipal labour force. Similar legislation existed in other parts of Brazil, notably to supply labour for saltpetre workings on the São Francisco river.† Such official demands diminished the inadequate and shrinking pool of Indian labour available to settlers. Desertions and deaths from disease and despair further accelerated the shortage. The colonists clamoured for more labour, but very few of them grew rich in Maranhão or the Amazon.

Governors differed in their attitude to the problem. João da Maia da Gama – the governor who confessed that he and his predecessors regularly exceeded the six-month requirement for each Indian's labour – adminstered Maranhão and Pará from 1722 to 1728. He was one of the ablest governors, and tended to side with the Jesuits against the settlers' most exaggerated demands. His successor Alexandre de Sousa Freire reversed this attitude. He gave any rascal permission to have free Indian labour. The missionaries were powerless to prevent the seizure of all the men in their villages. Sick Indians were hauled from their hammocks and sent to work. Women and children were tortured to discover the whereabouts of their men.

The law required that settlers pay in advance half the cloth that would be earned by an Indian during his six months of labour. The payment was made to the missionary in charge of the aldeia, on behalf of his charge. Once this advance was paid, an employer made very sure that his labourer did not desert, and he extracted the greatest possible labour from the man. 'They took one Indian from Arucara aldeia, and because he was not diligent enough in gathering cacao they tied him to a tree with a rope around his neck, made him stick out his tongue and put it in the lock of a musket. But this was insufficient punishment for his lack of diligence. They therefore began to flog him, so cruelly that the poor Indian lost his life during the flogging.'

An employer of free Indian labour had less concern for the well-being or survival of his labourer than did the owner of a slave. The only slight improvement in this bleak picture of gruelling labour was a shift away from plantation work. Settlers realised that quicker profits could be made by sending Indians to extract forest plants, or up the rivers to catch more Indians. The Indians themselves undoubtedly preferred such expeditions. They performed better on them than they did in humiliating, unmasculine agricultural labour.

The Jesuits were shaken by their expulsions in 1662 and 1684. With António Vieira gone, they no longer had a leader of sufficient stature to defy the settlers in defence of the Indians. The Jesuits returned soon enough, but they became more compromising toward the settlers. The zeal of a new mission was gone. As the years dragged by on the sleepy, isolated Amazon mission stations, the missionaries themselves slackened. Many of them lost the will to continue opposing their compatriots' demands for native slaves or labourers.

The Indians on the missions were docile enough, but there was no real comprehension of Christian teaching. Missionaries were frustrated to see their life's work failing. They made few true conversions based on genuine understanding and acceptance. They found instead that their congregations, although obedient, were sullen and ungrateful, and clung to their ancient ways with stubborn conservatism. Indians still dreaded the coropiras, the evil spirits that chastised them in hostile parts of the forest. Their conversion to Christianity was superficial. 'One can describe the Christian piety and religion of the Indians of the great Amazon river in a few words . . . it is like a dead faith, very unstable . . . not alive nor entrenched in the heart or rooted in the soul.' When questioned about the tenets of the Faith, 'they give one reply to everything, a frivolous, permissive reply, "Aypo", which is like saying "Perhaps; it could be."' They were indifferent to threats of divine retribution, with 'little fear of excommunication, the sword of the Church'. Experienced missionaries had few illusions about Indians' love of church trappings. 'They greatly value veronicas, medallions and images of the saints. But it is for their prettiness and not from the respect and devotion they inspire. They often decorate their monkeys or puppies with them, hanging them about their necks.' Indians failed to understand the purpose of confessions, reciting anything to please the missionary. 'And although they generally hear mass it is from fear of punishment rather than from a desire for spiritual good.'

Music was always a great attraction, a most effective lure for uncontacted tribes. But the missionaries found it impossible to train male choirs or orchestras. They had to use choirs of women, because the men 'are distributed to work for the Portuguese from the age of thirteen onwards'.

Father João Daniel admired the Indians' great powers of endurance when paddling their canoes. He also admired their endemic qualities – 'their disdain for the riches and goods of this world. . . . For if they have enough to eat – game from the forests or fish from the rivers – they are as content as nabobs with their treasures, finery and banquets. . . . They live lightly and without ceremony, clad only in the fine skins their mothers gave them . . . totally naked, like Adam in his state of innocence.' Even the domesticated mission Indians despised possessions. Although they lived near the whites, they acquired none of the settlers' acquisitive ambitions. A mission Indian had little beyond his thin cotton clothing – a little food, bows and arrows, a canoe and paddle, and perhaps an axe and knife. The richest, who worked on expeditions to extract cacao or other forest plants, might have a few yards of linen, a hat, a plate of salt, and a few trinkets for their families. They adored dogs, 'so much so that one could doubt which they loved more, their children or their dogs'.

As a missionary, Daniel approved the marital fidelity of most of his tribes, and the Indians' practice of bathing two or three times a day. But he was dismayed by his inability to stamp out drinking at his tribes' traditional festivities. 'When they laugh in these festivals, their missionaries weep. . . . To avoid such problems some missionaries have forbidden such festivals. Others have the foresight to go through the village and houses on the eve of the festivities, accompanied by officers, to order the breaking of all the vessels they find full [of alcoholic drinks]. This, however, dampens the festivity and makes them melancholy. . . .' Indians who were normally cowed and taciturn forgot themselves when drunk. They no longer cared 'whether people are white, or brown, ecclesiastic or secular' and might even attack their missionary.

The relationship between missionary and flock described by Daniel was one between master and recalcitrant worker. Indians took advantage of newly arrived missionaries, bringing them less fish each day. They 'excused themselves that they could find no fish, or that they had a headache, or other excuses of that type. In this way they often make newcomers fast, for these do not know that a thrashing and beating are the cure for these two excuses. . . . The result of a good thrashing . . . was great abundance of fish from then on.'

João Daniel admired the Indians' medicinal skills and knowledge of herbal cures. But they refused to reveal these to him. 'They are exceedingly tenacious and mysterious in their secrets. When they see some white man wishing to know some useful thing from them, he won't get it out of their traps, no matter how many gifts, enticements or promises he makes them. They always answer, "I don't know", or "Who knows?" and it can be extracted from them only with the cane, and even this generally fails, even if you kill them. Thus, although they know many admirable virtues of herbs, bushes and medicinal plants . . . it is not possible to make them reveal them.' No one ever managed to discover the herbs Indian women took for contraception or abortion.

For all his harshness, the Jesuit Daniel took the Indians' side in the never-ending debate about settlers' abuse of the natives. Daniel was appalled by the cruelty he witnessed. 'They killed them as one kills mosquitoes. In labour they treated them as if they were wild animals or beasts of the forest. Men usually treat their domestic animals with more charity than they treated the poor Indians. But they used, or abused, the feminine sex brutally and lasciviously, monstrously and indecently, without fear of God or shame before men. [They behaved] with such laxity that it seemed as if their consciences were drowned, or vomited into the ocean when they crossed the Line on the voyage to the Americas!'

Sousa Ferreira reckoned that, unlike black slaves, Indians 'are preserved best by affection. Any who does not improve with being treated well will grow more stubborn with punishment.' But the Jesuit João Daniel thought otherwise: 'Fear achieves more with them than respect, a rod than rhetoric, punishment than dissimulation. They generally do no work or any good, except out of fear.' But he was also aware that despairing Indians committed suicide. Some ate earth to die. Others could kill themselves by breathing in violently and sucking their tongues down their throats. 'This method is very dangerous when one is punishing them. It has often happened that, when executioners were about to deliver a thrashing, their victim was already in the other world. Others seem to have such control over death that they say "I die", raise a leg and let themselves fall to the ground, and rapidly go to the other world.' A quick remedy against such suicide was to shove fire into the Indian's mouth to make him gasp with pain.

'It is true that some white men are reprehensible in the cruelty they often use on their Indians. They kill some with the violence of their blows and place others at the gates of death. If they had themselves felt how agonising are the pains of a good thrashing, they might perhaps be less inhuman to their poor Tapuia.' Daniel knew one white man who accidentally received a whip blow on the back in the dark. The pain was so intense that he vowed never again to beat his slaves. Despite this, Daniel himself felt that 'experience has shown that thrashing is the most convenient and appropriate punishment for Indians. All who live and deal with them know that a punishment of only forty strokes is recommended – which is what missionaries customarily give. If the crimes are more atrocious this can be repeated for more days, together with a penalty of imprisonment. They mind this very much, for they find themselves deprived of their hunting, roaming and other entertainments, and especially of their daily bathing, etc. In truth, there is no punishment that tames them better than a long spell of prison, with some good shackles on their feet.'

Just as the ransom troops continued to ply the Amazon rivers, the Jesuits and other missionary orders continued to persuade tribes to descend to their mission aldeias. They were also active in the more humane policy of carrying their mission to the Indians in their own homes.

The German Jesuit João Felipe Betendorf reached Pará in 1661, just before Vieira was evicted. He was soon sent up-river to found a mission among tribes on the Tapajós river. He recorded the simplicity of the preparations for his expedition. The Superior 'gave me a medium-sized canoe, already almost old and with insufficient ribs; a portable altar with all its ornaments; an earthern vat with a year's supply of wine for masses and emergencies; a flask of Portuguese oil; a flagon of three jars of brandy; some alqueires of salt; an axe, a scythe, half a dozen butchers' knives with handles of ordinary white wood: a few fish-hooks, a few needles, some small piles of beads, a few combs and laces from [Portugal]; a sailor's chest containing plates, knives and forks for the table; a wooden set-square to build houses and church; and a little jar of jam. With this he sent me . . . to seek manioc flour for the voyage, and . . . a few turtles to give Father Salvador do Valle, [the missionary at the Tapajós aldeia]'.

Betendorf found that his mission was welcomed, largely thanks to a good Portuguese officer. This was João Corrêa, son of a captain-major of Ceará, who had settled near the Tapajós aldeia with his family and slaves. 'He was a great woodsman and linguist, besides being a bleeder [surgeon] of great charity.' The Tapajós Indians liked Corrêa 'because of the great charity with which he let their blood and cured them of their diseases and ailments. Because of this they called him their atoassana, which means godfather.'

But Betendorf still continued to subscribe to the lethal policy of sending Indians down to live alongside white settlements. He once preached a sermon in the hospital-church of Misericórdia ('Mercy') in Belém. Aware that this hospital foundation was short of funds, Betendorf proposed that a village of Indians be 'descended' to work for it. The Governor applauded the idea. A request was sent to the commander of Fort Gurupá, who sent down a village of eighty households of Taconyape. These were set to work growing sugar and tobacco for the Mercy. Betendorf himself admitted some years later that 'little or nothing was done for them and they therefore diminished. Today [1699] there cannot be a quarter of them left. I happened to be talking to some who had fled. I tried to persuade them to return, but they answered "We want none of your 'mercy'!"'

NINETEEN

The Amazon Frontier

FAR up the Amazon, Spanish Jesuits had crossed the Andes and were steadily bringing their mission down the river. They passed the site of the marker erected by Pedro Teixeira in 1639 to mark the boundary between the possessions of the Kings of Portugal and of Spain. The marker itself was lost, and there were no Portuguese settled this far up the river, but the two colonial empires were destined to clash in these remote forests.†

Father Samuel Fritz, a thirty-five-year-old Jesuit born in Bohemia, was in charge of the Spanish missions on the upper Amazon. He was an energetic, saintly man, well loved by his Yurimagua and Omagua Indians.

In 1689 Father Fritz was staying in a flooded Yurimagua village on the Solimões (the River of Poisons, or upper Amazon) inside what is now Brazil. He was struck, apparently by malaria: 'I fell sick of most violent attacks of fever and dropsy that began in my feet, and other complaints chiefly caused by worms. I was obliged to remain for almost three months shut up day and night in this [bark-roofed] shelter without being able to stir. I felt somewhat easier in day time, but spent the nights in unutterable burnings, for although the river passed only a hand's breadth from my bed, it was out of reach of my mouth.' He could not sleep because of the grunts of crocodiles prowling about the village – one crawled up his canoe, whose prow was drawn up inside the hut, and threatened the prostrate missionary and his boy. The place was infested

Settlers and Indians beside a fort.

with rats, who ate all the food saved from the flood and even gnawed Father Samuel's wooden possessions. News came that a party of Portuguese were gathering sarsaparilla in the territory of the Cuchivara, near the mouth of the Purus. Fritz set off downstream 'in the hope of getting some remedy for my sufferings', since he was too weak to attempt the two-month journey upstream and over the Andes.

It took Fritz about three weeks to reach the mouth of the Negro. He met that year's ransom troop, whose native contingent was commanded by Chief Cumuaru of the Tupinambarana – the section of the Tupinambá tribe that had settled at the mouth of the Madeira after their great migration from Pernambuco to the Andes and back down the Madeira. He was escorted to the Mercedarian mission on the Urubu, and treated with great kindness by its missionary. He was bled against the fevers, fumigated against dropsy, and given other remedies, 'but instead of being benefited, I was made worse than before. Up till then I was able to stand on my feet; but henceforth I had to allow myself to be carried in a hammock. . . .' Portuguese Jesuits took Fritz down-river, pausing at their missions along the way. At Guaricuru (where the Nheengaíba converted by António Vieira had once been settled) Fritz met a military expedition of 80 Portuguese soldiers and two hundred Indian warriors, 'on its way to chastise some natives, for what insolence I know not . . .'.

Fritz recovered his health at the Jesuit college in Belém. But when he wanted to return to his mission the Governor detained him as a potential spy. It all revolved around the location of Teixeira's marker. The Portuguese feared that if they allowed Fritz's mission to continue they would lose control of the upper Solimões. The matter was referred to the King. His reply came in eighteen months: Father Fritz was to be released immediately and returned to his mission at royal expense – but escorted by Portuguese troops to establish the territorial claim.

Fritz's return journey was uneventful, but it gives us a picture of the Amazon at the end of the seventeenth century. Many nights were spent in missions remote from colonial towns, where life continued in a gentle, uneventful rhythm. Fritz was well received at the big fort of Gurupá, and at the Tapajós aldeia where another fort was being rebuilt. But upstream of the Tapajós the expedition travelled for six days without seeing any settlement. João Daniel wrote that when Vieira and his Jesuits were expelled in 1662 'seventeen settlements of Indians between the mouths of the Xingu and Tapajós fled into the forests, disconsolate at the Fathers being removed from them. In all that distance – about four or five days' voyage – there is now hardly a remnant of an Indian.' Daniel also confirmed that the south bank beyond the Tapajós was equally deserted.

Samuel Fritz's expedition paused at the Tupinambarana mission on their island, but then travelled for another six days without seeing any settlement.

At the Urubu mission, Father Fritz discovered that he had become a legendary figure. Amazonian Indians always have, and still do, believe passionately in the powers of messianic figures who pass mysteriously by their settlements. Fritz found that these Indians were convinced that he was immortal: they believed that while detained in Belém he had been cut into pieces by his captors, but immediately reassembled by his soul. They all wanted him to remain as their missionary, and had to be persuaded to touch him to confirm that he was human.

Farther upstream, Chief Carabaina of the Tarumá, who lived at the mouth of the Negro, begged Fritz to stay with them, 'for his people had no love for [the settlers] of Pará'. The chief also promised to stop fighting the Cuchivara, Ybanoma and Yurimagua, all tribes of the Solimões. On the journey upstream, Fritz saw burned and abandoned villages that were a legacy of that inter-tribal fighting.† He moved on and on, for hundreds of miles up the empty, swirling brown waters of the Amazon, and finally reached his base, the mission of La Laguna at the mouth of the Huallaga in February 1692. La Laguna is still a mission today, a humid clearing surrounded by the unbroken line of forest – the same endless forest that carpets the entire Amazon basin and forms the green walls that constantly enclose travellers on its rivers. The modern mission consists of a cluster of thatched huts with walls of vertical palm-slats. It is once again run by the Jesuits, and must look very much as it did in Samuel Fritz's day.

Three years later, Father Fritz returned downstream to resume his mission among the Omagua, inside modern Brazil. He contended that the Portuguese had no right to the Amazon beyond the Line of Tordesillas. He admitted that he alone was the only Spanish representative ever seen by the Omagua tribes, whereas the Portuguese sent regular expeditions up the river. But he insisted that their ransoming expeditions, the purchase of captives and incitement of tribes to attack one another to obtain captives 'is illegitimate and contrary to all right'. In his eyes, such activities did not constitute grounds for claiming *de facto* possession.

When Fritz reached the Yurimagua, their chief told him that a Portuguese expedition had just left, carrying cacao and a few slaves. 'They had departed very annoyed, threatening them [the Yurimagua] and the Aysuares that they would return as soon as possible to carry them all off downstream as prisoners – because they refused to give them their sons to carry away to Pará, or captives to ransom.' Fritz also learned that the Portuguese who had escorted him upstream in 1692 had, on their return, raided on the Coari river, 'where, although they were not opposed, they cruelly killed very many people and took the rest away as slaves'. But he saw other aspects of life on the Amazon. There was the constant threat of inter-tribal war: when he was with one group of Omagua, their settlement was suddenly attacked by wild Cammuri from the depths of the forest. He also found some Portuguese settlers who extracted forest plants without molesting Indians. In 1696, near the mouth of the Juruá, 'I met a Portuguese, Francisco Sousa by name, a peaceful man, who assured me that he had no purpose other than buying a little cacao, and that he would not do the least injury to the Indians; and he acted according to his promise.'

The tribes of the Solimões had great faith in Fritz. They regarded him as immortal, and looked to him as their only protection against European slavers. When he told the Chief of the Aysuare about the after-life, 'the Chief interrupted me, saying: "*You* must not die. For if you should die, who would be our father, lover and protector?"' But, when he tried to persuade them to follow him up-river, they hesitated. They were reluctant to miss their trade with the Manoa tribe from the Rio Negro, who were obtaining marvellous metal tools from the Dutch on the Essequibo.

On 10 April 1697, an international confrontation finally took place at an Aysuare village that Fritz called San Ignacio, on an island some distance upstream of the Tefé. Samuel Fritz met the Provincial of the Portuguese Carmelites, Friar Manoel da Esperança, who had travelled up the Amazon with a small contingent of soldiers to take possession of this stretch of the Solimões. Fritz told them 'that for over eight years I had been in peaceful possession of that mission on behalf of the Crown of Castile. I formed a large part of these heathen Indians into mission settlements, when some were wandering through the forests as fugitives and others living in concealment near the lagoons, because of the murders and enslavements they formerly suffered from the men of Pará. I myself, when I was in that city [Belém], saw many slaves from these tribes.' He argued that the boundary question was something to be settled between the Kings of Portugal and Spain. The Portuguese accepted this, but Fritz had to agree to retreat upstream and abandon this area. The Governor of Pará wrote to the King that, 'after some argument, Father Samuel took his leave, after being formally warned of the manner in which he must conduct himself in these parts'. The King replied that, if Father Fritz were caught again, he was to be brought down to Belém and shipped to Portugal.

The next act in the drama came in September 1700. Twenty-five canoes full of Yurimagua suddenly arrived at the Spanish mission of San Joaquin (Pebas), in modern Peru, 700 miles from their homes downstream in Brazil. The rest of the Yurimagua and Aysuare were following in more canoes. Fritz quickly organised manioc to feed the refugees and had clearings made for them near the mouth of the Napo. They reported that in April a Portuguese Carmelite friar had appeared at their village – one that Fritz called Nuestra Señora de las Niebes ('Our Lady of the Snows') – intending to carry them all downstream. He had a canoe full of shackles and handcuffs for the purpose. The Indians managed to persuade him to wait until the river subsided, so that they could recover their harvest of manioc. Shortly afterwards, another Carmelite had killed Chief Airiparu of the Ybanoma, and then seized all their women and children and embarked them in a canoe to be sold in Belém. When he tried to shackle some men in his canoe, they shouted out, and men of the Wayupe, who lived with the Ybanoma, rushed out and killed the friar and his companions with their clubs. These tribes decided that they must flee up-river to escape the inevitable reprisals.* These Yurimagua became Father Fritz's most loyal followers.

In 1701 the friction was between Spaniards and Indians. Father Fritz went to Quito to request regular military patrols to protect his missions. When he returned to the Marañón in August, he learned that the Omagua were plotting to evict the Spaniards from their lands. They persuaded the wilder Cammuri, Pebas and Ticuna to join them in setting fire to the mission of San Joaquín and killing its Jesuits. Fritz sent for a military force, and travelled down-river with 20 Spanish troops and 200 Indian auxiliaries. They landed, under arms, at San Pablo (modern São Paulo de Olivença), seized the leaders of the suspected rising – chiefs Payoreva and Canuria of the Omagua – and had them flogged and exiled to Spanish prisons. Fritz then went through the huts seizing any idols, scrapers for body paint, and hallucinogenic curupa powder 'with which to deprive themselves of their senses, so that they will perform any evil deed without compunction. After mass, I ordered all this to be placed in a heap and consumed with fire.' But, the following February, Chief Payoreva escaped from captivity at Borja and secretly entered Fritz's mission of San Joaquín. He persuaded all but ten Indians to flee with him deep into the forests, to join the Cammuri and return to destroy the Spaniards and Jesuits. Father Fritz was forced to abandon the mission he had run for sixteen years and take refuge with the Yurimagua.

The Portuguese Carmelites now sent a friar up to Fritz, to try to negotiate the return of the Yurimagua to their former homes. Fritz refused. He said that the Portuguese had no jurisdiction over this tribe, who were free men and had voluntarily come upstream to be with the missionary who first converted them.

But when Fritz went down-river in March he found that his own Omagua had fled back to their former lands near São Paulo de Olivença. He tried to persuade them to return to his mission. He even promised pardon to Chief Payoreva. There were more meetings between the Spanish and Portuguese missionaries, amicable affairs at which the two sides tried to recover their respective Indians in a bizarre tug-of-war. Father Fritz was later elevated to be Provincial, but his successor on the Marañón, the Sardinian Father Juan Baptista Sanna, continued the struggle. 'He protected his mission against the artifices of the Carmelite Friar António de Andrade who, with a military vigour little in keeping with his [religious] condition, was placed in command of some mamelucos and repeatedly tried to make himself master of all the Omagua.' In the end, Father Sanna persuaded most of the Omagua to return upstream – all except Chief Payoreva, who went to Pará, 'either a prisoner or by his own choice'.

The Portuguese Carmelite did not give up. On 10 December 1707 he appeared at the Yurimagua mission near the Napo, leading eleven soldiers and a hundred Indian warriors. They entered the mission with banners flying, and searched the entire region for some fugitive Ybanoma. After a week in which they found no Ybanoma, the Carmelite ordered José de Pinheiro, the officer in charge of his troop, to launch a midnight attack on the Yurimagua huts. 'They seized our friends and carried away eighteen families down the river with them. The three Fathers who were present were unable to prevent it. . . . From the province of the Omagua they carried away for slaves, by armed violence, over a hundred persons; and all but about two of these were Christians.'

Fritz could do nothing and there was a lull until 1709. The new King of Portugal, João V, ordered the Governor of Pará to dislodge the Spanish Jesuits who were converting the Omagua – Cambebas ('Hammerheads') in Portuguese – since these were 'without doubt the most populous of all the heathen of the famous Amazon river, and were located well within the vast dominions of his Crown'. The Governor sent a powerful flotilla under Ignacio Corrêa. On 1 February 1709 Corrêa sent to demand the withdrawal of all the Spanish missionaries from this part of the Marañón and Napo. If they failed to leave within two months, he would take them prisoner to Pará. Father Fritz sent upstream for military help. He wrote to the Portuguese commander: 'Gracious God! Has Portuguese Christianity come to this: to oppress and carry away our toil and labour of so many years for Christ, without taking any account of Pontifical excommunication?' He insisted, again, that the two kings had never ratified the boundary on the Amazon, and that even Pedro Teixeira's marker of 1639 was far downstream. But Corrêa moved on. He reached the Yurimagua mission of San Joaquín and discovered their Indians, whom the missionaries had hidden on Lake Jarapá. All but a few boys were carried away downstream. The Portuguese chronicler Bernardo Pereira de Berredo said that these Indians accepted the change of allegiance quite happily. But the Yurimagua clearly did not: many of them escaped, paddled upstream again, and were settled far up the Huallaga.

Father Fritz sent furious letters to all the available Spanish commanders. Their forces gradually appeared, but Fritz was disgusted by their slovenly appearance and insulting manner toward his Indians. He set off down-river with a large armed force in July 1709. They swept down through the entire province of the Omagua, and on to the former lands of the Yurimagua and Aysuare. Portuguese settlers and missionaries fled downstream. Fritz's expedition reached the last mission before the Rio Negro. They had overtaken many of the Yurimagua, and Fritz persuaded them to come back with him – a migration that almost failed when a Spanish soldier publicly raped the wife of the Aysuare chief. The Indians set fire to three missions they were abandoning. By the end of August the expedition was back upstream, with many Indians, four captured Portuguese slavers, and the Carmelite Friar João da Luz.†

National honour was now at stake. On 24 December the Governor of Pará wrote to his king that he had sent a force of 150 men up the Amazon, with orders to capture Fathers Samuel Fritz and Juan Baptista Sanna 'and to inflict vengeance for the hostilities of the Castilians'. This force moved in ten canoes, guided by the Carmelite António de Andrade. The Jesuit Sanna tried to evacuate his flock from San Joaquín to Jarapá, but the Portuguese caught him at Mayvite. When they were putting the Omagua into fetters, these killed a Portuguese servant. 'And so they slew many of them with shots from swivel-guns, and carried others away as prisoners, together with Father [Sanna] and eight rowers of his company.' The expedition threatened to come to La Laguna to capture Fritz, but it never did. Father Sanna was taken to Portugal and eventually went on a mission to Japan. Friar António de Andrade was killed by Chamas Indians in 1719 when attacking a former Omagua settlement. But the real victims of the dispute were the Indians. 'In April 1710 many Yurimagua and Aysuare sickened of various complaints and died', although the remnants of the tribes survived on the Huallaga. The lands of the populous Omagua were left deserted, a no-man's-land between the two colonial empires. One part of the tribe settled under the

Spaniards on the Ucayali, others in the Portuguese Carmelite missions on the Solimões. And in the Treaty of Madrid of 1750 the boundary was fixed at the Javari river, midway between Fritz's former missions of San Joaquín and San Pablo.

When Charles de la Condamine went down the Amazon in 1743, the Omagua lands were still empty, with no Indians on the 450 miles of river between San Joaquín (Pebas) and São Paulo de Olivença. 'Today there is no warrior nation hostile to Europeans on the banks of the Marañón [Amazon]: all have submitted or retreated far away.' La Condamine visited the six Carmelite missions on the Solimões, five of which were 'formed of the debris of the ancient missions of Father Samuel Fritz and composed of a great number of diverse tribes, most of them transplanted'. But La Condamine was favourably impressed by the missions. He was surprised to find whitewashed stone and brick houses at São Paulo. The Indians seemed richer than their Spanish counterparts, because they went to Pará each year to trade the cacao they gathered in the forests. La Condamine saw 'all the women wearing cotton chemises, and there were chests with locks and iron keys in their houses, and . . . needles, little mirrors, knives, scissors, combs and various other small furnishings from Europe that the Indians procure each year in Pará'. La Condamine was also impressed by a waterproof and remarkably elastic product used by the Omagua. They used it to make unbreakable bottles, boots and hollow bouncing balls; and at their feasts each guest was given a pear-shaped syringe of it for his drink. The Indians called this resin cahout-chou. It was, of course, rubber – the product that was to transform this part of the Amazon at the close of the following century.†

The French scientist La Condamine – who had been sent to Quito by Louis XV to work with the Spaniards in measuring the Equator, a measurement that formed the basis of the metric system – had a jaundiced view of the Indians. He appreciated that it is impossible to generalise about so many different tribes. 'To give an exact idea of the Americans, one would have almost as many descriptions as there are nations among them.' And yet there were basic similarities between them all. La Condamine compared them with the nations of Europe, who differ in language and customs and yet would seem alike to an oriental visitor. 'I believed that I recognised in all of them the same fundamentals of character.'

The Indian character observed by La Condamine was alien to an eighteenth-century European scientist. 'Insensibility is the basis. I cannot decide whether it should be honoured with the name apathy, or debased with that of stupidity. It doubtless arises from their small range of ideas, which do not extend beyond their needs.' The traits that so appealed to the proponents of the noble-savage theory repelled La Condamine. He saw the Indians as 'gluttons to the point of voracity, when they have something with which to satisfy it; but sober when obliged by necessity to be so – they can do without anything and appear to want nothing. Pusillanimous poltroons to excess, unless transported by drunkenness. Enemies of work, indifferent to all motives of glory, honour or gratitude. Solely concerned with the immediate object and always influenced by it; without care for the future; incapable of foresight or reflection. They abandon themselves, if nothing hinders them, to puerile joy which they manifest by leaps and immoderate bursts of laughter without object or design. They spend their lives without thinking, and grow old without emerging from childhood, of which they retain all the defects.' These criticisms applied to both servile, mission Indians and to wilder tribes met by La Condamine.

Some of these comments were true of hunter-gatherer peoples: the ability to gorge after a kill and abstain when necessary; the apparent improvidence of people sure that there is abundant fish and game in the surrounding rivers and forests. But much of La Condamine's condemnation was a comment on the degradation caused by defeat and subjection by Europeans. Early descriptions of tribes like the Omagua showed them as highly efficient farmers with great plantations and tanks of turtles. They were by no means cowardly until confronted by firearms and white men's ruthlessness. And they had a strong code of honour, hospitality and gratitude – even if it differed from that of a French courtier, and was not immediately obvious to a passing traveller. In their lack of philosophic or intellectual curiosity the Amazon Indians were like peasants anywhere, far removed from a French scientist in the Age of Reason.

During the years in which Portuguese Carmelites were taking over the missions on the Solimões, other missionaries were pushing up the main Amazon tributaries.

The Jesuits had a row of prosperous, peaceful missions on the lower reaches of the Xingu. They frequently sent Fathers to accompany ransom expeditions to the Madeira, Trombetas, Negro and other rivers.† Governor João da Maia da Gama praised the Jesuits for their co-operation with the 'continuous and repeated ransom troops' sent out during his six years in office.† 'With these ransom troops, and the zeal, effort and diligence of the Fathers of the Society, over four thousand captives were ransomed, and 3700 slaves entered Pará, yielding duties of three reis per head to the Ransom Treasury' – all during only six years.

One river on which the Jesuits were particularly active was the Madeira, which, despite one bad stretch of rapids, was the most navigable of the mighty southern tributaries of the Amazon. At the beginning of the eighteenth century Father Bartolomeu Rodrigues was in charge of the mission of the Tupinambarana. He wrote to his Provincial in 1714 about the many tribes he had lured down to his mission. 'I will briefly tell of the descents I have made since being in this Tupinambarana mission. . . . The first descent I made to this aldeia was part of the Arerretu tribe. The second was part of the Comandi and Ubucoara. . . . The third was two chiefs of the Andirá with their vassals, who inhabited the headwaters of the Mariacoã river. The fourth was a few Japocu–Abijara who were on the Maués [river] – although this could be called a move rather than a descent. The fifth was the Poraioania tribe and the sixth the Capiurematia tribe, both from the Acoriatos river. The seventh was the entire Mojoaria tribe with part of the Monçaú and Ubucoara tribes from the Maués river. And finally the Sapapé, whose descent is still in progress. To the Andirá aldeia I have descended part of the Amoriat tribe and part of the Acaioniá tribe.

'The effort one suffers in these descents is greatly eased by the consolation . . . of the many souls being gained for Heaven who would otherwise doubtless be lost. [There is] also the sight of how quickly the children of these new peoples, and even some adults, attend the doctrine and are soon instructed and capable of receiving holy baptism – even though they had been raised with so little discipline in the forests. . . .' This missionary listed the tribes he was aware of on the lower Madeira and its affluents. It is a terrifying list of eighty-one tribes. Many were described as 'populous' or 'grandiose'. Yet only one or two of the eighty-one tribes have any survivors today: almost all have vanished without trace in some long-forgotten epidemic or 'descent'.

An admiring Mercedarian praised the Jesuits for their tireless efforts to descend tribes. 'During the four years I was a missionary and neighbour of the Fathers I saw the descents they made for their missions from the heart of the sertão, at a cost of much effort and very heavy expenditure. Father Manoel dos Reis, missionary of the Tupinambarana, made [descents] from the forests of Maué, Andirá, Guabirú and Periquitos; Father Manoel da Motta, missionary of the Abacaxi, removed 624 souls of Arara on one single occasion; Father José da Gama, missionary of the Arapiun, descended and settled many heathen from the Tapajós river. They spent much wealth on all this: canoes, cotton cloth, tools, knives, crockery, beads, made-up clothes, and grandiose presents – without which one cannot convince Indians to leave their lands for the bosom of the Church. And, after these are descended they feed and clothe them for two years. . . . When they descended the Arara heathen in 1724 I saw Father Manoel da Motta dispense 500 varas of cotton cloth in three days' – all cloth made by other mission Indian women.†

Once a tribe made the decision to descend, the flow of enticing presents ceased. And once the period of two years' grace was over the tribe was expected to supply its full quotas of men for river expeditions or as hired labour for settlers.

The most diligent and dedicated of all the Jesuits at the Tupinambarana missions was Father João de Sampaio. So successful was the policy of descents that his aldeia had over a thousand 'serving and fighting' Indians in its heyday.* For a while, Sampaio's progress up the Madeira was obstructed by the hostility of the Tora tribe. These Indians also emerged on to the main Amazon river to harass canoes going upstream to extract cacao from the Solimões. In 1715, therefore, João de Barros da Guerra was appointed to command an expedition against the Tora, 'because of the great damage they have done us, preventing the missionaries from doing the work of God by their hostilities'. Father Bartolomeu Rodrigues described the Tora as 'such a multitude that other tribes call them an anthill'. But preventing the spread of Christianity was considered grounds for 'just war'. The expedition sent against the Tora, in 1719, was a violent affair, and 'the war . . . waged on them left them extinct'.

The removal of the Tora opened the Madeira to exploration and evangelisation. Father Sampaio provided 200 mission Indian rowers, as well as canoes, food and tools, for an expedition up the Madeira under Sargento-mor Francisco de Mello Palheta in 1723. Sampaio himself accompanied the expedition for much of the journey, and helped to pacify mutinous troops and care for the men on their return. Palheta was an experienced woodsman who drove the Indian paddlers hard: during the first ten days the expedition averaged over thirty miles a day against the current. In two years the expedition penetrated as far as the Spanish missions of Santa Cruz de la Sierra in modern Bolivia, and back.*

Father Sampaio also led his own expeditions. His mission Indians paddled him far up the Madeira, and fed his expeditions by fishing and hunting. Sampaio became an experienced woodsman. He travelled with a portable altar and missals, and presents and musical instruments to charm the Indians. In 1723 he led one of the two official ransom expeditions, and did so without any armed escort. This earned the praise of King João V, who noted that Sampaio 'extracted from the River Negro and the River Maués 158 persons, slaves. After these were examined, he sent them to the Governor to distribute.' The Jesuits had various missions on the lower Madeira, notably the large village of Trocano. But Sampaio established an aldeia far up the River Madeira, possibly near the mouth of the Jamari close to the modern city of Pôrto Velho. He called this outpost Santo António das Cachoeiras ('St Anthony of the Rapids') and used it as a base for expeditions into the surrounding forests in search of uncontacted tribes.

Sampaio's missionary campaigns were thwarted by opponents just as formidable as hostile tribes: predatory slavers. On one occasion Sampaio sent a preliminary batch of 400 members of a tribe downstream towards his Abacaxi mission. The migration was caught by Captain Manoel Francisco Tavares, factor of the Governor of Pará. He advanced on the missionary canoes full of potential converts 'and, tying them all up with cords and shackles, threw them into his own canoes'. This same captain once seized six canoe-loads of Aroaxi Indians, took them to Belém and sold eighty as slaves. The worst outrage happened with the powerful Mura tribe. Sampaio contacted them from his advanced village of Santo António. He persuaded one group of Mura to emerge from the forest and come to his main aldeia the following year. He promised to provide tools, clothing and food for them there, while they would prepare clearings for plantations. An unscrupulous Portuguese learned of this plan. He went to the Mura and claimed he was sent by Sampaio, who wanted them to move immediately. They were confused by the change of plan but were persuaded to move. The Portuguese took them all downstream, evading the forts on the Amazon, and sold every man, woman and child in Belém. Their relatives in the forest waited anxiously for news. When they learned of the treachery, the Mura were filled with intense hatred against all whites, including Sampaio and his mission Indians. A nest of hornets – or of painful stinging mutuca of the Amazon forests – had been aroused.

The advent of the Jesuit missions at the mouth of the Madeira, and the zeal of the Fathers themselves, proved powerful magnets for the tribes along the river. They decided, one by one, to move down to this wonderful new society, with its thrilling metal tools, abundant plantations, musical festivities and potent magic. The result was a vacuum, with the banks of the lower Madeira just as empty as the Solimões after the departure of the Omagua. The authorities tried to move settlers into this vacuum, and founded a colony on the right bank. But it was the Mura who moved down from the Jamari to fill the empty spaces not only along the Madeira, but eventually the Solimões as well. They destroyed the new colony on the Madeira. When an expedition under Major João de Sousa d'Azevedo made the first ascent of the

Madeira as far as the Mato Grosso, it had bloody fighting against the Mura. The tribe suffered heavy losses; but it learned not to oppose white gunfire in open combat.

The Mura were fine warriors, proud of their skill as archers and canoers. They fired enormous bows, holding one end to the ground with their toes, and shot long arrows with enough force to pierce an ox or a man. But their greatest military advantage was mobility. Although the tribe preferred to live in high, conical, thatched malocas, they could also live in scattered, temporary shelters, or even sleep in their canoes. They easily defeated the remnants of the Madeira tribes, already weakened by slaving and missionary activity. The Mura then established themselves in the Autaz region, a great wedge of water and forest between the Amazon and Madeira. The Autaz is a region of lagoons, swamps and channels, a labyrinth of islands and waterways that changes with every rainy season. It was a perfect base for the Mura: punitive expeditions floundered in this difficult environment and failed to catch the elusive Indians. So the Mura attacked, raided and robbed settlements and travellers along the Madeira, Solimões and even the Negro. They would ambush travellers at rapids, when they were struggling to drag their canoes through the raging waters. They posted sentries in the tops of ceibas – gigantic silver-barked trees that tower above the rest of the Amazon forests. They ambushed enemies on paths leading to their clearings. The Mura took some prisoners, who were integrated into their own tribe, but they generally killed without distinction of age or sex. They mutilated their victims' bodies, but did not keep trophies and were not cannibals.

The Mura's vengeance on the whites continued for half a century, with 'so many deaths that no single year went by without their killing many, both in sudden attacks on missions, or on canoes going into the sertão either in their depots on land or when they were navigating'. Father Sampaio died in 1742, aged sixty-two, and his missions on the upper Madeira petered out, stricken by disease and the threat of Mura attack. There were soon bitter complaints about the 'cruel and irreconcilable enmity' of the Mura.† Unless there was 'the most furious war . . . to entirely profligate and destroy this tribe' the colonies of the Amazon, Negro, Madeira and Japurá would all be reduced to nothing.

The Rio Negro had long been the most lucrative source of Indian labour. From Vieira's day onwards, the annual ransom camp 'was generally on the Rio Negro, for on it, more than any other river, there were more tribes who ate one another'. Heriarte had written in 1665 that the Negro 'is inhabited by innumerable heathen. It has a chief at its mouth . . . who is like a King, called Tabapari. He has many aldeias of various tribes under his dominion and is obeyed by them with great respect. . . . The aldeias and people of this river are great, and their houses are round, and fortified by stockades like fortresses. If this river were settled with Portuguese we could make an empire, and could dominate all the Amazon and other rivers. . . . The Fathers of the Society of Jesus have begun to extend the faith into these parts with great devotion. And yet they have entered only into the smallest part of one corner, in relation to the multitude that exists there.'

The most famous tribe of the Negro was the Manau. They were great travellers and traders who plied the Negro or cut across to the lagoons of the Japurá by way of the Urubaxi. Cristóbal de Acuña heard that the Manau traded gold objects with the Indians of the upper Amazon. They emerged on to the Solimões from the Japurá, and thus gave rise to Pedro Teixeira's Village of Gold. Father Samuel Fritz met a flotilla of ten canoes of Manau traders when he was lying ill in a Yurimagua village on the Solimões in 1689. He wrote that the Manau lived to the north, on the Urubaxi, and came across to the Solimões during the rainy season, when the forests were flooded. 'They can then go from the [Urubaxi] to the Japurá by canoe. The trade which these Manau have with the Aysuare, Ybanoma and Yurimagua consists of small bars of gold, vermilion and manioc graters. . . .' The combination of gold and mysterious lakes in the depths of the forest had given rise to legends of the Golden City of Manoa on the shores of Lake Parima. Sir Walter Ralegh heard about this when he made his disastrous expedition to the Orinoco in search of El Dorado in 1618–19. Acuña said in 1639 that the Manau obtained their gold from another tribe who 'get a great quantity, so that by heating it they make plates, which they hang to their ears and noses'. This is precisely how Colombian tribes, the Chibcha and Quimbaya, wore their gold ornaments, many of which can be seen in the magnificent Gold Museum in Bogotá. The legend of El Dorado is now thought to have originated in a ceremony among these Colombian tribes. It was possible for the Manau to reach the Chibcha by moving up the Japurá-Caquetá. We also know that they traded with the Dutch by the Rio Branco–Essequibo route, or possibly by the Casiquiare canal to the Orinoco.

At the beginning of the eighteenth century the Manau produced a leader of heroic proportions – the only Indian to emerge as a personality from all the records of European penetration of the Amazon. This leader was Ajuricaba, the paramount chief of the Manau. Francisco Xavier Ribeiro de Sampaio, who was Judge and Lieutenant-General of the Rio Negro later in the eighteenth century, said of Ajuricaba that 'Nature endowed him with a brave, intrepid and warlike spirit. . . . In truth, what is most striking in the story of Ajuricaba is that his subjects and the greater part of his nation showed him the most faithful love and devotion.' Long after his death they believed that he might reappear, just as Portuguese romantics believed in the return of their King Sebastião who disappeared fighting the Moors. 'Throughout the whole course of his life, Ajuricaba was certainly a hero among the Indians.'

Ajuricaba started on good terms with the first missionaries and slavers to penetrate the middle Negro. But for some reason in 1723 he decided to oppose them. Governor João da Maia da Gama wrote indignantly to the King that his official ransom troop had gone up the Negro and established its camp there, when 'a chief of the Manau rebelled and killed another who was our friend, by treason, and for no better reason than that this man was partial to us. He also killed a soldier.' What frightened and infuriated the King of Portugal was that these tribes were communicating with the Dutch by moving up the Rio Branco and down the Essequibo or Courantyne. 'All the tribes of that River [Negro] – except those who are with us and already have missionaries – all the rest have been killers of my vassals and allies of the Dutch! They impede the propagation of the faith, have continually robbed and assaulted my vassals, eat human flesh, and live like brutes, defying the laws of nature. . . . Those barbarians are full of arms and munitions, some of which they were given by the Dutch, and others transmitted to them by men who have hitherto gone to ransom and assault them, contrary to my royal orders. They not only have the use of [fire]arms, but have also entrenched themselves with wood-and-mud stockades, and with watch-towers and defences. Because of this no troop has attacked them up to now, for fear of their arms and courage. Through this dissimulation they have become more proud, and have been emboldened to commit excesses and killings. . . .'

The King authorised his governor to launch a punitive campaign. But the Jesuits argued for a peaceful attempt, and Father José de Sousa went to try to contact Ajuricaba. This chief was now preventing movement by Portuguese ransom troops. He himself was flying a Dutch flag from his canoe, and was trading captured Indians with the Dutch in return for trade goods and firearms. The Governor wrote to the King in 1727 that Father Sousa had sought out and appeased 'the infidel Ajuricaba, a proud, insolent man who called himself governor of all those nations. All the other chiefs respected him and obeyed his precepts with fear and respect. All the insults done to us were on his orders or suggestion. . . .' The Jesuit persuaded Ajuricaba to exchange his Dutch flag for a Portuguese one. Ajuricaba also swore allegiance to the King of Portugal. He was paid fifty ransom payments for fifty slaves. 'The Reverend Father was very content and satisfied. He sent Ajuricaba craftsmen to build him a house, and wrote marvels about him and his great ability and of the great service to Your Majesty that could be done with that Ajuricaba.'

But attacks on the missions continued. Ajuricaba went off with the ransom goods but failed to deliver the promised slaves. Father Sousa became convinced that he had been duped. He angrily ordered the commander of the ransom troop to capture Ajuricaba. The matter was referred to the mission council where everyone but the Jesuit Rector voted in favour of war, and the Governor assembled a powerful punitive force. The expedition moved off in 1728 under Captain João Paes do Amaral. Jesuit missions along the way supplied large contingents of native rowers and warriors.

'It was resolved that they would first seek the barbarian and infidel Ajuricaba. Our people sought him in his aldeia, but he set up a defence before the encirclement was complete. After shots from an artillery piece that our men took there, he resolved to flee and abandon the village with some other chiefs. . . . Our men pursued and sought him during the ensuing days in the villages of his allies. The barbarian ruler and infidel Ajuricaba and six or seven lesser chiefs of his allies were finally captured and two or three hundred prisoners were taken with him. Forty of these will be brought down to pay for the expenditure made by Your Majesty's exchequer, and thirty for the royal fifth [tax].'

Ajuricaba was brought down-river, chained and shackled. He now performed the deed that earned his reputation as a Brazilian hero. 'When Ajuricaba was coming as a prisoner to this city [Belém], and was already within its river [Pará], [he and his men] rose up in the canoe in which they were coming in chains, and tried to kill the soldiers. These seized their arms and smashed some of them and killed others. Ajuricaba then leaped into the sea with another chief and never reappeared dead or alive. Setting aside one's sentiment for the loss of his soul, he did us a great kindness by delivering us from the worry of keeping him.' To modern Brazilians, Ajuricaba has become the symbol of Indian heroism; a chief who preferred death to slavery.

The expedition went on after the rains to attack Ajuricaba's allies, the Mayapena. The Governor was jubilant. 'It seems that God Himself wished it, for that proud chief and his allies were reduced by so few forces and with such good success. . . . With this the passage of the rapids will be unobstructed. A route will be opened for Your Majesty's ransom troops to ransom many captives, and for the missionaries to reduce many thousands of souls. . . .' By chance, the ransom records from this expedition have survived, together with the names of chiefs who furnished prisoners for ransom. A typical entry was: 'Murepana,

Indian of the Manau tribe, aged more or less thirty, with the sign "R" branded above his left breast and another black mark on his left forehead: a principal ally of Ajuricaba, legitimate slave of the war troop, and belonging to the expenses of the royal treasury.'

Once subdued, the Manau became allies of the Portuguese, helping them contact new tribes for the slave trade. The Manau themselves settled in a series of Carmelite missions on the middle Negro. A few families came down the river and settled in the new town of Barra that was growing at the junction with the Amazon. This place became the port city of Manaus, and thus perpetuates the name of the tribe that has otherwise disappeared or merged into the indigenous population.†

The Negro was just as terribly depopulated as the other Amazon tributaries. Father Daniel reckoned that *three million* Indians were descended from the Rio Negro alone in the century up to 1750. 'It is enough to say that some individual [colonists] had over a thousand slaves; and others had so many that they did not know their names.'

TWENTY

Pombal

FATHER JOÃO DANIEL wrote that the Indians of the Amazon basin were reduced to a thousandth part of their former population. 'In truth, arithmetic would be exhausted in trying to count such an innumerable multitude.' The Amazon and all its tributaries 'were peopled by innumerable Indians on both banks. . . . The Indians were as numerous as swarms of mosquitoes, the settlements without number, and the diversity of tribes and languages beyond count.' By the mid-eighteenth century, the Amazon was denuded of Indians.

Nobody wanted the Indians to die out. Land on the Amazon was valueless without people to penetrate its forests or man its canoes. The settlers demanded Indians as hired or slave labour. Missionaries wanted them as Christian converts, to swell and glorify their missions. The royal authorities wanted them as subjects, to be used if necessary on public works or fighting to defend Portuguese possessions against other colonial powers or hostile tribes.

Countless Indians were killed in fighting or through abuse and neglect. But the truly devastating killer, as in other parts of Brazil, was imported disease. Everyone noted how easily Indians fell sick. 'They are also very disheartened. If they fear they will die, death is inevitable.' João Daniel wrote that severe colds – influenza – were a very common form of native sickness. Powerful catarrhs were also prevalent and often fatal. The most notorious scourge was smallpox, regularly imported by African slaves. Thousands of mission Indians died of smallpox and

Spanish troops enter a mission.

many more fled to the forests: they died there in agony and fear, and spread the epidemic to uncontacted tribes. By the eighteenth century, missionaries became aware that even 'measles is equally pestilential for the Indians'.

The Jesuits desperately restocked their missions after each epidemic. Mortigura, near Belém, was originally founded with a Tupinambá congregation, but it and other missions 'have often been restocked with fresh descents of other different tribes, as has happened in all the other missions. For these would all be finished had it not been for these periodic reinforcements of people, through the agency and at the cost of immense fatigues by the Jesuits.' One of the largest missions, at the mouth of the Tocantins, was once struck by a terrible epidemic from which all but one young man died. Contemporary surveys of the missions showed vividly how they became babels, peopled by the remnants of many different tribes from distant parts of the Amazon. Araticu (Oeiras) was initially filled with Nheengaíba, but later replenished with Goiana, Marahanun and many other tribes – 'although each tribe alone used to be enough to make it populous . . . today it is no bigger with so many. Were it not for the many descents made by its missionaries, it would be completely extinct.'

This depopulation brought ruin to the settlers and to the entire colony. Fortifications and public buildings were crumbling, troops unpaid, and the state heavily in debt. A report of 1729 said that São Luís was 'reduced to great poverty and misery, and likewise the other neighbouring towns'. Worse was to come. Smallpox reappeared on the Amazon and caused great slaughter. La Condamine said that it annihilated Indians living near Belém. It struck hardest among Indians newly arrived from the forests, who were still naked. La Condamine recommended the introduction of vaccination, a technique newly discovered in Europe. This was in fact tried by the Carmelite Superior of the Rio Negro missions, Friar José da Magdalena, but the Jesuits were jealous and attacked him for unorthodoxy.†

There used to be a Capuchin mission alongside the fort of Gurupá, but La Condamine found in 1743 that it had 'no Indians other than the inhabitants' slaves', and Gonçalves da Fonseca wrote, six years later, that 'there used to be an ample number of Indians in it, but successive epidemics of smallpox and measles have left it destitute of inhabitants of either sex or any age'.

In 1749 there was a terrible epidemic of measles accompanied by dysentery. It was known as the 'great measles' because of the extent of its destruction. It was particularly virulent among Indians recently descended from the Rio Branco. 'Places were to be seen on that river, formerly inhabited by innumerable heathen, but that now showed no signs of life beyond the bones of bodies that had perished. And those who escaped the contagion did not escape captivity.'

Smallpox struck again in 1750. Governor Francisco Paulo Mendonça Gurjão wrote that 'one could calculate the total loss at 40,000 persons' around Belém alone.* His successor 'was very distressed by [the epidemic's] damage, since the number of servants was greatly diminished, and the rigour of the epidemic struck hardest on that class'. There were further severe epidemics in 1758, 1762, regularly between 1763 and 1772, 1776 and so on through the century.

Faced with such disasters, and a total inability to succeed in the difficult world of the Amazon, the colonists sought scapegoats. Once again, the easiest people to blame were the missionaries. Settlers, whose own Indians died or ran off, were jealous of the relative prosperity of the missions. Despite the constant demands on their labour, the mission Indians were legally free men and they continued to live amid other members of their tribes. They had plantations and a family life. Their villages were administered by missionaries who had devoted their lives to serving the natives' spiritual and physical welfare. It is hardly surprising that the mission villages prospered whereas the settlers had little success with their pathetic contingents of sullen, despondent slaves or reluctant forced labour. Hatred of the missionaries, particularly of the Jesuits, now stemmed from jealousy of their success and imagined wealth even more than from irritation at their protection of the Indians. The situation had many of the classic ingredients to breed intolerance and persecution: the Jesuits were an easily identifiable minority, aloof and secretive, morally and intellectually superior, and manifestly more successful than the rest of the society in which they operated.

There was relative calm for about thirty years after the restoration of Indian slavery in the laws of 1688. There was a flicker of the royal conscience in an edict of 5 July 1715 that expressly prohibited slavery as unjust. But the usual reaction came with the Provision of 9 March 1718. This was more than usually ambiguous. It began by encouraging missionaries to penetrate the wilds to convince Indians of the dangers of remaining free and the advantages of 'living in aldeias with behaviour public and proper to rational men'. There was some moralising about the King of Portugal's reluctance to attack peaceful people outside his domain. But the Provision then proceeded to justify such aggressions, with definitions so absurd and so sweeping that they included almost every Indian in Brazil. Tribes could be attacked if 'they go naked, recognise neither king nor governor and do not live in the form or manner of a republic, trample the laws of nature, make no distinction between mothers and daughters in the satisfaction of their lust, eat one another . . . or are excited by shooting arrows at innocent children'.

The governor who brought this legislation to Maranhão-Pará was Bernardo Pereira de Berredo – a fine chronicler of the history of the province, but no lover of Indians, whom he often referred to as 'rational beasts'. Official ransom expeditions, which had ceased for a few years, were now revived by the new legislation. Berredo convened a Mission Council, which decided that private ransom raids should be permitted. It also suggested that Indians brought down under the new law might go directly to the colonists' plantations without the formality of passing through mission aldeias. The Mission Council even showed concern for settlers too poor to equip a ransom canoe by themselves: it suggested that three or four of them join together to provide the Indian rowers for such a canoe, 'and then divide among them the number of Indians or married couples that is their share'.

Settlers who opposed the Jesuits won relaxations in the Indian laws and often enjoyed the support of local governors. But they were challenging formidable opponents. The Jesuits were brilliant orators and advocates, with seemingly unassailable moral prestige, temporal wealth and power, and profound influence at the royal court. Governors came and went, whereas the Jesuits were constant – and they had a long memory for avenging wrongs. Past opponents such as Beckman or Sampaio were humiliated, or driven to armed revolt and execution as traitors.

But a new opponent arose in the 1720s; and he succeeded where others had failed. He was Paulo da Silva Nunes, Public Prosecutor of Belém. He accumulated documents and made accusations, and for fifteen years conducted a relentless campaign of vilification against the Jesuits in northern Brazil. He attacked on two themes: that the Jesuits were concerned more with material wealth than their spiritual mission – a power-hungry secret society intent on creating a private empire; and that their protégés, the Indians, were neither noble savages nor even useful allies, but subhuman beasts. His ranting propaganda was distorted and often exaggerated. But with repetition it gained credence: many of Silva Nunes' slurs have stuck to the Jesuits' reputation.

It had always been a royal conviction that it was essential to civilise the Indians. 'The security of the sertão and of the very settlements of Maranhão and all America depends on the friendship of the Indians.' The King told his governor to explain 'how useful to my service . . . is the good treatment of [the Indians], since they are the principal defence of that conquest'. Silva Nunes challenged this assumption and openly denigrated the Indians. To him they were 'squalid barbarians, bestial

and abject, like wild beasts in everything except their human appearance
. . . wild brutes incapable of participating in the Catholic faith'. He
even exposed the illogicality of enslaving Africans more readily than
Americans: 'If Ethiopians can be enslaved, why cannot Maranhão
Indians?'

He accused the Jesuits of every conceivable offence: they were despots
who usurped royal authority; they wielded unbridled power on their
missions; excluded whites from the missions and kept prisons in which
they sometimes shut Portuguese; armed their converts with firearms;
obstructed settlers' use of Indian labour to which they were legally
entitled; encouraged slaves to run away from the settlers; dealt
treasonably with the Spanish, Dutch and French; and maintained
massive commercial activities, so that their missions 'look more like
great storehouses than places of prayer'.

Paulo da Silva Nunes was encouraged by Governor Bernardo Pereira
de Berredo. The next governor, João da Maia da Gama, who arrived in
1722, was a Jesuit supporter. There was unrest among the settlers, with
Silva Nunes reading a long dissertation in favour of slavery and against
the Jesuits. He was arrested and briefly imprisoned. He fled to Portugal
and issued more violent accusations. Silva Nunes' campaign was
supported by ex-governor Berredo, and the next governor, Alexandre
de Sousa Freire, was also sympathetic. When Sousa Freire reached
Maranhão he asked the Jesuits for a loan of 4000 cruzados. The Jesuit
Visitor, Jacinto de Carvalho, politely refused, saying that the Society had
too many charitable obligations to be able to discharge the Governor's
private debts. Governor Sousa Freire then proceeded to revive his
fortunes by any possible means – including, of course, energetic
ransoming activity. And, when a new decree of 13 April 1728 said that
descents of Indians could be made only by 'public authority', this
governor interpreted it to mean that any individual could apply to him
for such authority.

The campaign against the Jesuits produced the usual avalanche of
papers – strident manifestos, testimonies, investigations and memorials.
Both sides admitted that they were really fighting about control of the
Indian labour force – even though the Indians themselves were
disappearing so rapidly. In 1734 the King finally sent an official
investigator, and his report was generally favourable to the
missionaries. He found that the benefits of Jesuit protection far
outweighed the partial submission suffered by mission Indians. If
mission villages were transferred to colonists' control, 'in a few years
there would remain only the memory of the aldeias'. He also found the
rumours of vast transatlantic trade by the Jesuits to be exaggerated,

although the missionaries were probably too active in sending Indians inland to extract forest plants. On the whole, the produce of their many farms and ranches went to support and feed their missions. The investigator even suggested that Jesuits might cease commercial activities and receive royal subsidies instead. Horrified Crown officials in Lisbon were unanimous in rejecting this last proposal; and the Jesuits' commercial activities increased.

The Jesuits did not themselves perform manual labour as the Franciscans did. But they were good managers and soon had their missions surrounded by thriving plantations. Each mission village had its own crops of manioc, fruit trees and other indigenous plants. But the wealth of the order came from large-scale farming. One fazenda on Maranhão island possessed machinery for husking rice, a mill for manioc flour, a sugar mill, a still for sugar-alcohol, and a loom: this mission produced rice, manioc, cotton, sugar-cane, corn, sesame, broad beans and tobacco. In the interior of that state there was a big cattle ranch at Maracu (Viana), and nearby a big mill and manioc farm called São Bonifácio. Cacao from the upper Amazon was domesticated and introduced to Maranhão by Father João Felipe Betendorf in 1674: this became a lucrative export when the drinking of chocolate became fashionable in Europe. Many missions grew tobacco and cotton, both plants native to America; and they produced the cotton cloth that was the standard currency for paying Indian labour. Sugar was the Jesuits' greatest export crop, but their largest sugar mills were in the north-east of Brazil rather than in Maranhão and Pará. Father João Daniel described the model sugar plantation Ibirajuba, built in the mid-eighteenth century, a few hours by canoe from the city of Belém. Despite its efficiency, it made almost no profit after supporting the 102 persons who lived there. 'That property, besides having all the usual workshops which make a fazenda renowned – such as a pottery in which much crockery was made, a smith's forge, looms, canoe-building, etc. – also had a sugar press and a still for alcoholic spirits, which are the most profitable produce in that state; it also had some established reed banks and some coffee. Nevertheless, at the end of the year the receipts showed a profit of only 480 reis. Had it not been for the cacao, coffee and workshops, where would the revenue have been, and how high would the expenses have risen?'

The Jesuits' largest industry, after sugar, was cattle. On the island of Marajó opposite Belém they had some 30,000 head on a number of ranches. They exported oxen, steers and horses to other parts of Brazil. They even had their own ships to carry hides across the Atlantic. Mission Indians were trained to be good cowhands.

The missionaries also used the Indians in their care to extract the 'spices of the sertão' – cacao, cinnamon, vanilla, sarsaparilla and other plants. The Indians' great skills as woodsmen, their feel for the forest, the ability to recognise every tree and bush, and the endurance to march for days on end without tiring, all made them far better gatherers than whites or blacks. As early as 1699 the settlers complained that the missionaries 'keep their Indians continually occupied in extracting spices, refusing [Indians] to the settlers or even to the royal service'. The King then ordered the missionaries 'not to use their Indians for temporal purposes in the form of commerce'. The following year, the King reproved the missionaries for being too harsh on their Indians, particularly the chiefs. There had been 'repeated complaints that . . . they are not granted the respect and privileges that were conceded to them with their posts, but are beaten, placed in stocks and other insults, for trivial crimes'. Missionaries other than Jesuits – Franciscans of the orders of Santo António, Conceição and Piedade – were accused of 'using their Indians for their service and convenience, in an impious way, with great dishonour in their behaviour, living very scandalously and abandoned to sensuality, to the great discredit of their [monastic] habits'. Other royal letters reproved the missionaries for giving sanctuary to Indians who fled from the settlers, and then sending them to work on their own estates.

All these complaints were grist for Silva Nunes' anti-Jesuit campaign. By 1729 his accusations were starting to succeed. The King wrote to his governor of Maranhão ordering that missionaries stop enslaving free Indians or using them on sugar and tobacco plantations against their will. The Jesuits were accused of having masses of Indians on their ranches and of monopolising the extraction of forest produce. Their wealth was contrasted with the settlers' poverty. The Governor lamented that colonial towns were being extinguished because their inhabitants 'have not a single Indian man or woman to serve and support them, either in their plantations, or fishing and hunting, or going to the woods to fetch a little wood to roof their houses'. It all seemed to be the fault of the missionaries; and they made easy scapegoats.

The truth was that organised agriculture and trading were necessary to support the mission villages. The Society of Jesus was not growing rich from the labour of its Brazilian Indians. The eighteenth-century attacks on the Society were grossly exaggerated. A modern critic would condemn the missionaries on different grounds. They had no right to impose their religion and strange rules of conduct on tribes that were contented and flourishing with other social customs. And it was criminally irresponsible to keep descending tribes when every missionary knew that this exposed the converts to forced labour and almost certain death from imported disease. But in the eighteenth century all Europeans, of every colonial power, were arrogantly convinced of the rectitude of their religion and the superiority of their culture. Almost no one questioned the need to 'civilise' American natives. And, if the Indians were doomed to incorporation in colonial society, they were vastly better off under missionary protection than adrift in settler society.

By the middle of the eighteenth century, little appeared to have changed on the Amazon. The various missionary orders were presiding over their aldeias. Life in the mission villages continued as calmly as possible, but the pious routine was constantly disrupted by demands for Indian labour from settlers, royal officials and the missionaries themselves. There were frequent deadly epidemics. The missionaries themselves became less zealous and enthusiastic: they seemed resigned to failure, despairing of the physical survival or spiritual conversion of their congregations. The orders became more materialistic with the success of their commercial activities. Ransom expeditions continued unabated, although it was increasingly difficult to catch Indian captives. All the accessible tributaries of the Amazon were denuded by the death, removal or flight of their native inhabitants. And the colonies of Maranhão and Pará that caused all this destruction were in a miserable state of decline.

The stagnation in Brazil was changed by a succession of events in Europe.

King João V, the monarch who embellished Portugal with the wealth of the Brazilian gold-fields, began to have doubts about the treatment of the Indians and about the suitability of Jesuit missionaries. It was at his instigation that Pope Benedict XIV issued an encyclical on 20 December 1741, addressed to the bishops of Brazil, that forbade 'enslaving, selling, buying, exchanging or giving Indians, separating them from their wives and children, despoiling them of their goods, leading them to strange places . . . depriving them of liberty in any way. . . '. The Papal Bull ordered that no one should keep Indian slaves on pain of ex-communication. But it also mentioned the Jesuits and was apparently intended to reduce the activity of the missionaries. The Bishop of Pará prepared to issue the encyclical but desisted; and it was not published in Brazil for sixteen years. It is not clear whether the delay was inspired by fear of a revolt by the Jesuits' settler opponents – or by the opposition of the Jesuits themselves.

The King was sick and dying, but he did issue a resolution on 13 July 1748 that finally ended the official 'ransom' expeditions and declared that all Indians must be freed. This decree admitted that the loopholes in earlier laws had been abused: the only way to protect Indian liberty was to abolish every form of slavery. It was the end of two centuries of legal contradiction.

Before his death in July 1750, King João also achieved a remarkable treaty with King Ferdinand VI of Spain to define the boundaries between their South American empires. The Treaty of Madrid, 13 January 1750, gained for the Portuguese most of the frontiers of modern Brazil. It thus affected the destiny of hundreds of native tribes. The Portuguese now reaped a reward for the arduous expeditions of bandeirantes, Amazon slavers, missionaries and gold prospectors. The Treaty of Tordesillas was scrapped, and Portuguese dominions were extended over half the continent. King João wrote to his delegate that 'since the outset of this negotiation we have adopted as preliminary maxims: firstly, that in lands already peopled by either party each will retain what it may have occupied . . . and secondly we will seek to establish the boundaries along the most conspicuous and obvious landmarks of hills or major rivers, without being bothered about a few leagues of deserted lands, in regions where each Crown will have such an over-abundance that they could not be inhabited for many centuries'.

The Treaty of Madrid came after decades during which the two powers had manœuvred to occupy the unknown heart of the continent. The Spaniards had contemplated invading the mines of Cuiabá and Mato Grosso, and instructed the Jesuits of the Chiquitos and Mojos missions to cross the Guaporé. But the invasion plans came to nothing, because no Spaniards knew the location of the mines or the lie of the lands; and the missions on the Guaporé – San Miguel with 3444 souls, San Simón with 493 and Santa Rosa with 388 – were extinguished when the Bororo allies of the Cuiabá miners lured away their congregations. The Portuguese, for their part, created a new province, which they significantly called Mato Grosso after the gold-field on the Guaporé frontier, rather than Cuiabá after the more populous town. They also established a river route for hundreds of miles from Mato Grosso down the Guaporé, Mamoré and Madeira to the Amazon. Their Indian rowers paddled up and down these rivers in expeditions in 1722–4, 1746–7 and 1749–50. Only someone who has travelled along even part of these rivers can appreciate the magnitude of these expeditions, along seemingly endless stretches of river, between islands and swamps and rapids that thunder for tens of miles on end.†

The former Jesuit provinces of Itatín and Guairá were now in Portuguese hands, on the route from São Paulo to Cuiabá. Farther south, much of the territory once occupied by Carijó Guaraní was now deserted. The cattle from the Jesuit missions of Tape had run wild and multiplied into immense herds. The Portuguese had established some communities along the southern coast: at Paranaguá, and Curitiba farther inland in Paraná; on the islands of São Francisco, Santa Catarina and Laguna in the new captaincy of Santa Catarina; and at Pôrto dos Casais (Pôrto Alegre) and Rio Grande de São Pedro, at either end of the Lagoa dos Patos. These places had once been bases for Paulista slavers. With the Indians gone, they were abandoned for many decades and were reoccupied only in the 1740s by immigrants from the Azores islands.

At the western side of what is now the state of Rio Grande do Sul, Spanish Jesuits had again crossed the Uruguay river. They established seven prosperous missions known as the Sete Povos ('Seven Peoples') to the east of the Uruguay, in the region from which they were driven by bandeirante raids in the 1630s and 1640s. Far to the south, the Portuguese had one more outpost, the Colônia do Sacramento on the northern shore of the Plate estuary, opposite Buenos Aires and upstream of Montevideo. They founded this fortified colony in 1680 in an attempt to control the coastline from the mouths of the Plate to the Amazon – the dream of Portuguese cartographers and statesmen ever since the sixteenth century. Sacramento was a provocation to the Spaniards and the scene of repeated fighting during the eighty years of its control by Portugal.

The Treaty of Madrid of 1750 established all these frontiers in a document ratified by both Crowns. It left the Portuguese with almost half of South America. Thanks to this treaty, Brazil is now one of the world's largest countries, greater in area than the continental United States. The treaty was a triumph for Portuguese diplomats, who established the sensible principles of following natural boundaries and accepting *de facto* occupation. The most brilliant of these statesmen was the Brazilian-born Alexandre de Gusmão. He appreciated the importance of securing the fertile plains of Rio Grande do Sul, the mines of Mato Grosso and the river route from the Guaporé to the Madeira. During the decades before the Treaty itself, Gusmão and the elder statesman Luís da Cunha pressed for exploration and occupation of these regions. And when the time came to negotiate they exchanged the unimportant Colônia do Sacramento for vast territorial concessions along these frontiers.†

It was Portuguese statesmen who won these enormous frontiers. They could do so only because of the prodigious feats of exploration and endurance by the many Portuguese who penetrated the heart of the continent. But it was Indians who provided the original geographical knowledge of those areas. Indians or half-castes formed the greater part of the bandeirante columns, and Indians paddled the canoes that penetrated the Amazonian rivers. Other Indians were the bait – the potential slaves that lured adventurers into these remote forests. And the territories being divided up between the European powers were Indian lands, belonging by natural right to the tribes who had inhabited them for centuries.

Indian tribes adopted the same principles as the royal negotiators in Madrid: tribal territories were divided by natural features, and possession depended on actual occupation. Tribes would resist intruders into their territories, although inter-tribal wars were not normally fought for possession of land, which was so abundant. Wars were rather for vengeance, or for trophies in the form of women or captives. It is not true to say that Indian tribes roamed without fixed territories. They all had well-defined lands, known to themselves and their neighbours. Even semi-nomadic peoples moved within fixed limits. The great migrations were exceptional, and most of those after 1500 were the result of European intrusion – either messianic movements inspired by European adventurers, descents instigated by missionaries, flight from settler abuse, or invasion by tribes such as the Kaingang, Mura or Tikuna of lands whose former inhabitants had been annihilated or removed. Pre-colonial Brazil was a patchwork of tribal states, some of which were densely populated. The European occupation was simply a successful but morally inexcusable invasion of these hundreds of territories.

The Treaty of Madrid had an immediate effect on two groups of mission Indians: those in the Jesuit missions on the Amazon; and the seven Spanish Jesuit missions, the Seven Peoples, east of the Uruguay, that were ceded to Portugal by the treaty.

A new governor was sent to Maranhão-Pará to oversee the demarcation of its new frontiers, and to enforce the decree of 1748 ending Indian ransoms and slavery. This was Francisco Xavier de Mendonça Furtado. His eight years as governor, from 1751 to 1759, were to have a profound effect on the destiny of the Indians of the Amazon basin. For this governor was the stepbrother of Sebastião José de Carvalho e Mello, one of the most powerful personalities in Portuguese history – he governed Portugal from 1750 to 1777, and was virtual dictator from 1755 onwards, as Count of Oeiras and later as Marquis of Pombal.

The royal instructions to Governor Mendonça Furtado told him to end all forms of Indian slavery, to see that Indians were properly paid for their labour and 'treated with humanity, and not with injustice, violent and barbarous rigour, as has been done hitherto'. But he was also ordered to see how many Indians could be removed from mission villages for work in royal service. He was to encourage missionaries to descend more tribes; but he was to improve conditions in the missions, to make them 'an example of care and benevolence that [the Indians] have never experienced'.

The new governor wrote regular letters to his powerful brother. Within a few months of arriving in Belém, he reported the widespread failure to convert or civilise Indians. He blamed this on the use of Tupi-Guaraní (the *lingua geral* that the Jesuits employed throughout their missions), the continuance of pagan rites, and superficial instruction. Instead of converting the Indians, 'many Christians have not only adopted the customs of the heathen but have even followed their rites; and the greatest shame is that many ecclesiastics have entered this number'. He was highly critical of the Jesuits, who ran their missions 'with pride and ambition. ... . They started with general virtue and religious zeal, but have ended in the abominable vice of avarice.' Missionaries quarrelled with one another, confused worship of God with that of their own saints, were disloyal to the King and harsh on their Indians. Mission Indians were 'condemned to the hard yoke of perpetual captivity. . . . Each missionary has twenty-five aldeia Indians for his personal service.' The missionaries forced their congregations into marriages, and punished any who opposed them with thrashing and confinement in private stocks. In their missions, the Jesuits exercised 'an absolute and despotic government in all temporal affairs, with no room for appeal against their injustices ánd violence'.

The Governor reckoned that the various orders had 12,000 Indian men with their families in 63 missions. The Jesuits had nineteen missions, with 475 men working directly for them and thousands more on their plantations and ranches. They paid their labourers with cloth woven by mission Indian women. Their ranches were well stocked. On Marajó island alone, the Mercedarians had between 60,000 and 100,000 head of cattle; the Jesuits had 25,000–30,000; and the Carmelites 8000–10,000.†

The new governor was convinced that the missionaries were intentionally keeping their Indians ignorant. They were taught in *lingua geral* rather than in Portuguese. One chief impressed Mendonça Furtado by telling him how delighted the Indians were that he was 'ending the blind ignorance in which they were reared'. The Governor commented: 'These are the men said to have no judgement and to be capable of nothing! I believe, by God, that if the Fathers applied the methods they ought (which Your Majesty ordered), these people could be turned into a nation like any other. Great benefit could result to Your Majesty's and the public service.'

In January 1752 Father Aquiles Maria arrived in Belém with sixteen canoes loaded with Indians. The Governor reported that this missionary 'has been in the forests for many years engaged in descents, tyrannising Indians'. He brought some 200 Indians for the Jesuits' estates, and thirty-three for the Mercedarians. 'The religious orders are thus publicly stuffing their fazendas with slaves, while the settlers suffer a total prohibition. . . .' 'All the religious orders without exception . . . break faith and capture wretched Indians. They bring them down, bound, on the pretext of ransoming them. This is the truth: every one of the orders steals those it can.'

The Governor was repeating all the accusations made against the missionaries by their most virulent opponents. In November 1752 he wrote to his brother hinting at sexual excesses. 'I have spoken so much to Your Excellency about Indians that it must bore you as much as it does me to hear about this matter. It is, however, so vast that it is never exhausted. There are always new and unimaginable things to tell you about it. . . . The Fathers first extinguished all the men in their aldeias by employing them in their service. They then moved on to the outrage of making the women recluses: they put them into their convents, to do work that should be done by stonemasons' labourers. . . . This year one missionary arrived from the aldeia of Caviana in a canoe manned solely by women, with no man in it other than the missionary himself. On 22 June I met another canoe . . . in which was a lay brother aged about thirty, of those same Fathers of Piedade, with eight girls in his canoe, none of whom was over twenty. They paid their respects to me there – and left me edified! These girls had finished their period of work in the Hospice and had been replaced by a similar number who remained there. In the convent they go about with no covering beyond a poor rag they call a skirt, which does not go below mid-leg, and all the rest of their bodies naked in scandalous indecency. . . . I was in the Carmelite monastery on the day of Our Lady of Carmo, when I saw from the Vice-Provincial's window two scandalous figures of women bathing naked by the well. I told the Fathers that this was indecent. But they replied that it was the custom of Indian women.' The Jesuits were the only order that took care to dress its Indians modestly. The prudish Governor concluded that placing Indians in the care of friars was an invention of the Devil to corrupt them.

In another letter Mendonça Furtado reported that he had tried unsuccessfully to free 'a large band of Tapuia in this city, sculptors and painters, each of whom earns 5 or 6 tostões a day for [the Jesuits], who do big business making use of them in all ways'. The Jesuit rector angrily vetoed the Governor's attempts to free these and other Indians held by his Society. He also sought to prevent the Procurador dos Indios – the Prosecutor who was supposed to protect natives – from investigating whether the Jesuits kept illegal slaves 'until they had finished some building work they were doing on their church'.

Although so passionately critical of the missionaries, Governor Mendonça Furtado was no champion of the colonists. He knew that the new King José I supported his father's decree abolishing Indian slavery. In his letters the Governor therefore condemned the settlers' reliance on Indian slaves. 'In this state a rich man is not one with much land, but one with the greatest quantity of Indians, [who are used] both for agriculture and for the extraction of forest spices.' 'All these people are ignorant to an infinite degree. They imagine that their entire fortune can come from the forests – not from extracting spices, but from imprisoning Indians. With these they propose to make great progress in their factories and plantations.' He feared a violent reaction from the decree abolishing Indian slavery. 'I have no doubt that [the settlers] will entirely abandon this land and go out into the world to beg. . . .' But he told his officials to try to make the settlers less lazy about doing farm labour themselves. He deplored 'the abuse that is so ingrained in this land: that only Indians ought to work, and that it is harmful for any white man to wield a tool for farming the land'.

The Governor's instructions were to stop all forms of Indian slavery. He declared that 'I do not consent to ransom expeditions taking place. I intend to proceed against any who go into the forests to capture Indians – which was a very frequent occurrence in these parts.' He wrote about the terrible abuses that took place in the capture and sham interrogation of Indian prisoners. He mentioned one illegal slaver, Francisco Portilho de Melo, who was operating on a grand scale on the Negro, with many Indian allies and a private dominion of 700 men. Another slaver called António Correa was killed by some Indians who were tied up in his canoe. It transpired that most of the Indians already in this man's service were from tribes of the Solimões and Japurá who, because of their strategic location, 'can in no way be enslaved'. The Governor wanted to free them, but the law officer dealing with Correa's estate insisted on selling them to meet its debts.

Mendonça Furtado was deeply shocked to find that settlers branded Indian slaves that they wanted to punish. 'They order that they be bound, and then, with a red-hot iron or a lancet, they illegally proclaim the name of the supposed master on their chests. This is often done in such large letters that it has to be written on two lines. The wretched

Indians endure this torment without any human remedy. The first time I saw one with this illegal, infamous and scandalous lettering on his chest, it made the appropriate impression on me. . . . This custom originated with the indiscreet zeal of the leader of an official ransom troop. . . . He did not want those that belonged to the royal treasury to be substituted, and therefore ordered them all marked. When these people saw that example, being exceedingly ignorant, they began to imitate it. They exceeded a mere mark by going to a full name. This pernicious custom has spread among the greater part of these settlers: it would therefore be impossible to punish an entire people.'

In 1753 the Governor decided to lead an expedition to define the new boundaries on the upper Negro river. Another expedition was to paddle up the Madeira to dislodge the Spanish Jesuits who were established on the Portuguese side of the Guaporé. Mendonça Furtado recommended that this expedition take the most modern artillery in its canoes, 'to repel any disobedience or insult that those Fathers might attempt. If an occasion arises, I believe that such guns would produce an excellent effect and would terrify those barbarians [the 3000 mission Indians] none of whom would stand firm before them.'

The Governor spent over a year building scores of canoes and recruiting hundreds of Indians for his own expedition. He had the King write to the heads of the missionary orders that he 'would need a great quantity of Indians to conduct the canoes and perform all the other services that may be necessary on that expedition'. Should any mission fail to provide all the Indians demanded by the Governor, 'he may remove them by force'.

Mendonça Furtado clearly anticipated trouble from the missions. He was well aware of the ravages of the recent smallpox epidemics; but nevertheless demanded heavy quotas of native workers. He seemed almost to relish a confrontation, and soon had one. Mission Indians who were forced to build the Governor's canoes ran back to their aldeias. The Governor complained in every letter of hundreds of Indian desertions. He was convinced that Indians were encouraged to flee by their missionaries, and were concealed by them when they returned to their homes.

The Governor's letters to his brother and to the King now turned violently against the missions, and particularly against the Jesuits. In February 1754 he wrote a report on the Jesuit estates in Pará, stressing their wealth and the profits they yielded to the Society. A typical fazenda was Cruça on the island of Marajó. The Jesuits had moved the entire aldeia of Gonçari to this estate, and had added Indians from other missions, who were 'condemned by them to that perpetual exile, in which they remain reduced to the state of indentured labourers. . . . This fazenda is extremely important. In it the Fathers raise cotton, manioc, tobacco, rice and other vegetables. They have great factories of salt fish in it, which make a lot of money for them. They also have some large salt pans that give a considerable profit.' Another nearby fazenda contained two hundred Indians and produced cacao, coffee, manioc, and tobacco. Estates on the Moju river yielded sugar and cacao, and the Jesuits' cattle corrals on the island of Marajó were now said to contain over 30,000 head – an increase on the quantity reported in earlier letters. The situation was even worse in the neighbouring state of Maranhão. 'This [Jesuit] order is lord of almost all the captaincy of Maranhão . . . especially in all the rivers Pindaré, Itapecuru and Iguará, in which they have wide dominions and of which they are absolute masters; also the greater part of the Mearim; and in short of all that miserable captaincy.' The Jesuits had expelled colonists who invaded Indian lands, and encouraged chiefs of tribes under their protection to complain to the Governor about such violations.

Governor Mendonça Furtado was by now convinced that the only way to curb Jesuit power was by removing their jurisdiction over the Indians. He began to describe mission Indians with the emotive word 'slaves'. He wrote that the Jesuits' cattle ranches 'are all inhabited by an infinite number of people whom they consider as slaves'. He told his brother: 'Your Excellency knows very well that in this country wealth is measured in numbers of slaves. Since all the Indians of the mission aldeias, of either sex and of all ages, are the absolute slaves of the monastic orders, it follows logically that these will be masters of all the riches of this state, unless control of the aldeias is removed from them. It is with Indians that they extract the spices of these vast forests, and with Indians that they make turtle butter and extracts of all types of fish that exist here. These are the two most important [products] of this captaincy. Even if their fazendas were removed from them, they could still use their Indians to grow the same crops of manioc, cotton, beans, rice and all the rest that they now grow on their fazendas, on the lands of the mission villages.'

The Governor finally embarked on his expedition up the Amazon and Negro in October 1754. He travelled with twenty-three large canoes. He himself was in a canoe 'equipped like a yacht' with a cabin with four windows, lined in damask. There had been many more desertions by Indian carpenters and labourers during the months of preparation. As the expedition moved up-river there were desertions by Indian paddlers. The Governor kept sending canoes to the missions to seize more rowers. Most of the Jesuit aldeias were deserted, and the Governor was convinced that the Fathers had hidden their congregations in the forests. There were angry clashes with the Jesuits. Mendonça Furtado told his brother about a typical incident at the mission of Guaricuru, which he reached a week after leaving Belém. The mission was deserted. 'As soon as I saw this scandalous disorder, I asked the Father if that was the manner in which the Governor of the State should be received – with the people hidden in the woods to avoid their obligations? . . . He answered a few things that seemed to me insolent, because I scarcely understood a word: for he is a German who has been in this country for only a year. He simply understood the instructions he had received from Father Luís de Oliveira to place the people in the woods.'

The furious Governor never forgave the Jesuits for such obstruction. He contrasted their hostile attitude with the welcome given him at the Carmelite missions on the Negro. At the large Carmelite mission of Mariúa, founded in Manau territory after the suppression of Ajuricaba's revolt, there was an arch of flowers to greet the Governor. A mission Indian read a sonnet in Portuguese congratulating him on the success of his expedition. The Governor then went to the church where a choir of Indian women sang the *Te Deum laudamus*. 'We were all impressed that they could be so well instructed by so few teachers, in a region so far from communication with civilised people.' The Governor was so moved that he paid out of his own pocket for cloth to clothe a number of naked Indian women. He sent to invite Indians from other villages 'who were in the same misery and deprivation' to come and receive free cloth.

All these letters had a profound influence on the Governor's stepbrother, the future Marquis of Pombal. This remarkable man was fifty-one when he became Secretary of State for War and Foreign Affairs for the new King José I in 1750. He was powerfully ambitious, a tall man with an iron constitution, and strikingly handsome. The old King João V had sensed the ruthlessness and sadistic cruelty in Pombal, and denied him a top position in government because he had 'hairs on his heart'. He did, however, send him as diplomatic envoy to London and then to Vienna. Pombal married a young Austrian heiress, and through her obtained the favour of the Austrian-born Queen of Portugal when he returned to Lisbon. It was the terrible Lisbon earthquake of 1 November 1755 that consolidated Pombal's position as virtual dictator of Portugal. The earthquake was an unprecedented catastrophe that destroyed two-thirds of the city and killed between five and fifteen thousand people. There was talk of moving the capital to Coimbra. But Pombal took charge of relief operations and immediately planned the rebuilding of Lisbon with handsome new buildings. The wavering King was impressed by Pombal's resolution, and by his forceful opinions and emphatic, often exaggerated way of expressing his views. For the remaining twenty-two years of his reign, King José entrusted the government of the country to this very capable administrator. And Pombal developed very decided views on the iniquity of the Jesuits, and on the freedom of Brazilian Indians.

TWENTY-ONE

The Expulsion of the Jesuits

DURING the years that the Jesuits appeared to be obstructing the demarcation of the Treaty of Madrid on the Amazon, Spanish Jesuits were causing difficulties 2000 miles away at the southern limit of Brazil.

The Treaty made the middle Uruguay river the new boundary between Spanish and Portuguese possessions. The Seven Peoples, the seven Spanish Jesuit missions that lay to the east of the Uruguay, would have to move across the river. Article 16 of the Treaty ordered that 'the missionaries will leave with all their movable property, taking with them the Indians to settle them in other Spanish territories. The said Indians may also take all their movable goods, and the arms, powder, and ammunition which they possess. In this way the villages, with all their houses, church, edifices and property and ownership of terrain, will be given to the Crown of Portugal. . . .' The same treaty offered compensation for Portuguese settlers who left their homes in Sacramento. In the lands on the Amazon, Guaporé or Pequeri that were also transferred from Spain to Portugal, the Treaty offered local Indians a choice of leaving their homes, without compensation, and moving to Spanish dominions. But with the Guaraní Indians of the seven missions the Treaty offered neither compensation nor choice. It ordered that they leave, taking only movable possessions, and leaving their superb plantations and flourishing villages. Capistrano de Abreu and other leading Brazilian historians have described this clause as 'inhuman'. Luís Gonzaga Jaeger contrasted the treatment given to whites and

Ruins of the Jesuit mission of San Miguel.

Indians who suffered by the Treaty, and called it 'a manifest, intended, and calculated double measure'.

This injustice is inexplicable, for the Indians being victimised were exemplary subjects of the King of Spain. They were Christian, loyal, docile, hard-working and civilised. If any natives of the Americas fulfilled the pious civilising mission of the kings of Spain and Portugal, it was these Tape Guaraní. They possessed special charters, and letters from Spanish kings thanking them for their help in fighting the Portuguese. They could not comprehend that the King of Spain would callously abandon them. And they were determined not to leave their beloved homes, their magnificent churches, the plantations they had developed with so much labour, the plains and rivers inhabited by their forefathers, and the cemeteries containing their ancestors. They were Tape who had always lived east of the Uruguay and had little affinity with the Guaraní west of the river. They could see no reason for such terrible punishment. They had done nothing to deserve banishment and exile or condemnation to create new towns in some hostile wilderness.

There had been a lull in the mid-seventeenth century, after bandeirante raids forced the Spanish Jesuits to abandon their provinces of Tape and Uruguay. But in 1682 the Jesuits began to return, with the creation of the mission of San Borja at a strategic ford on the Uruguay and on its eastern bank. They found the fertile plains to the east largely deserted. Vast herds of wild cattle – imported from Europe by earlier missionaries – roamed across what is now the Brazilian state of Rio Grande do Sul. The local Guaraní-speaking Tape Indians welcomed the return of the black-robed Fathers. By the end of the century there were six more missions to the east of the Uruguay. They were closely grouped for defence. All were located between the Pirantiní and Ijuí tributaries of the Uruguay, with none more than sixty miles from the main river. They were linked by good communications with the twenty-three other missions of the Jesuit province of Paraguay.†

The Guaraní were the most receptive of all Indian tribes to Jesuit teaching. They were an organised, docile people, with a keen spiritual awareness. They followed religious leaders with passionate fervour. A later Portuguese administrator of this area explained how the Jesuits' exemplary behaviour convinced the Guaraní that they were saints. 'It is true that [the Jesuits] abused the vast credulity of the Indians and persuaded them of many superstitions. . . . The Fathers studied the Guaraní character and as a result entertained them with dances, music and many church festivals. They led them to mass, singing and playing music. . . .' They kept the Indians busy working, maintained the populations by insisting on early marriages, provided good houses, hospitals and schools, and kept the people well fed from the produce of their plantations. 'This system convinced [the Indians] that the Fathers, besides feeding and clothing them, were leading them to heaven. It made the people content, with no wish to desert, made them work and even accept violent punishments with such grace that they thanked their directors for them.' The Guaraní loved this simple and uneventful existence. They were pleased to see their families well fed and willingly accepted the missions' strict discipline. Their own culture was obliterated, but they eagerly embraced Christianity and became expert artists in European baroque music, decoration and architecture. No Brazilian Indians have ever been more thoroughly exposed to European civilisation.

A German Jesuit, Anton Sepp, visited these missions at the end of the seventeenth century and in fact founded one of the seven missions now inside Brazil. He wrote a description of his journey that is still the most vivid description of life in this extraordinary theocracy. Father Sepp reached Buenos Aires in 1691 and he and his companions were met by an escort of 300 mission Indians. These lodged at some distance from the wild colonial town 'because the baptised Indians, who are good and simple people, are disgusted and saddened when they see evil among Christians'. The Jesuits embarked on rafts consisting of two tree trunks covered by a bamboo deck, on which were built small huts of straw matting covered in oxhide. Each hut had a door and window, and the Jesuits lived quietly in it while twenty-four Indians paddled each raft up the broad rivers. 'Although this hut is simple . . . one can read one's spiritual books in it, speak silently to one's God, write, eat, sleep and do all one's spiritual exercises. . . . All this can be done without any disturbance, for one hardly notices that the craft is moving. . . . The Indians know how to paddle so carefully that one can scarcely hear the noise of their strokes. They do not speak a single word to one another throughout the day when they are paddling, nor do they shout or sing, in order not to molest the Father in his prayers and devotions.'

Sepp described the missions, many of which were built on banks overlooking the Paraná or Uruguay rivers. All were built on a grid plan, around the vast central square and church. 'The houses form broad streets, as in European cities, but are of different construction. They are very low and do not have wooden floors: the Indians live on the bare earth. . . . The houses have neither windows nor chimneys and are therefore full of smoke all day long [with the walls] blackened. When I visit the sick, which I generally do daily, I am almost asphyxiated by so much smoke. A while ago my eyes hurt so much for fourteen days on end, burning and watering, that I came to fear I would lose my sight.

And, inside the house, where is the hall, where are the bedroom, kitchen, cellar and pantry? Where is the bread in the pantry, the wine and beer in the cellar, the pots and tin basins in the kitchen, the bed in the bedroom? The Indians have gathered all these things into a single room. Their cellar is a hollow gourd, in which they fetch water from the river and from which they drink. Anyone who can hang his hammock . . . between two trees is rich even if he seems poor. Someone with less wealth sleeps on a jaguar skin or cowhide on the flat ground, with a hard block or stone instead of a pillow. The kitchenware consists of one or two pots. Teeth are knives, the five fingers forks, the hand a spoon, and the gourd is cups and glasses. The oven and hearth are beneath the bed, with the hammock slung above. The first stick that comes to hand serves as a spit. On it they roast the meat, which they begin to devour while the other side is still roasting. . . . The door of the house . . . is of oxhide and is never locked for there is nothing in the house that could be stolen. . . . Inside the one room sleep father, mother, brothers and sisters, children and grandchildren, four dogs and three cats, the greatest possible number of vermin and rats, and it is crawling with insects that we call cockroaches and millipedes in the Tyrol. It is easy to imagine the insufferable smell that emanates from all this, in such an enclosed, low and tiny hut.'

The Jesuits insisted on very early marriages. 'When a girl reaches fourteen or fifteen years and a boy sixteen, it is time for holy matrimony. We do not delay over this and thus avoid many evils. No Indian girl reaches a situation of spending some years as a virgin. . . . It is worth noting that, when the Indians wish to marry, it is not the man who goes to ask the hand of the woman but, on the contrary, it is the woman who has to propose holy matrimony to the husband. An Indian girl will come to me and say: "Pai, I wish to marry this or that man, if you agree." I then ask the Indian to come to me and say to him: "My son, this girl wishes to marry you. Do you agree?" If he says yes – and they almost always *do* say yes – nothing more is necessary. I give each of these young couples one of the houses as their palace. I also give them the nuptial vestments, namely five ells of woollen cloth for the husband and the same amount for the wife. . . . I also give them the nuptial banquet consisting of one or more fat cows, just as I give them meat all year long whenever they need it.'

There was certainly no lack of beef on those fertile plains. Father Sepp described the fantastic herds of wild cattle. 'A short while ago my village went out on to the plains to round up cattle for this year's daily food supply. In two months they rounded up fifty thousand head and brought them to my settlement. Had I ordered it they would have brought seventy, eighty or even ninety thousand. These fifty thousand animals didn't cost me a farthing. The greatest effort involved is in the Indians herding the cattle so skilfully that none stampede or run off. What I tell about my village is valid for the other twenty-six reductions. . . . Many more [cattle] still remain on the infinite plains of Paraguay, for necessary breeding. Our three ships took three hundred thousand hides to Spain, and these were not of cows but of mature bulls.'

There was no lack of food. The rivers were teeming with fish. Each mission was surrounded by extensive plantations. There were three types of land: community land which the Indians worked for three days a week, to feed the aged and sick and specialist artisans engaged on mission business, and to grow cotton for the women to spin and weave into cloth; family lands, with each family having a plot from which to feed itself; and church land, worked by boys under fifteen during the hours when they were not busy in religious services or schooling. Surplus produce was sent to Buenos Aires and traded for church ornaments, medicines and fine cloth. One reduction alone produced 2000 tons of cotton. But the greatest export was herva maté. The Indians gathered this herb in the woods or raised it in their plantations. It was used to make maté, the mildly stimulating herb tea that is still a passion among gauchos, the cattlemen of the Argentine and Brazilian plains.

The Jesuits were absolute masters of these missions. Paraguay was very remote, in the heart of the continent, weeks of travel away from the colonial cities. The Spaniards excluded other Europeans from their colonies, and the Jesuits excluded lay Spaniards from their missions. The Indians unquestioningly obeyed the missionary Fathers, who were intellectually ahead of most men of their age and had devoted their lives to missionary work from a strong sense of vocation. There was little need for punishment in the communistic society of the missions. Father Sepp wrote: 'If someone asks, "How do you generally chastise these Indians?" I answer briefly, "As a father punishes the children he loves: that is how we punish those who deserve it!" It is naturally not the Father who wields the cane, but the first Indian who comes to hand – we have no birches or similar things here – and he beats the delinquent just as a father spanks his son or a master his apprentice in Europe. Old and young are punished in this way, and so are women. Punishment in this paternal way gives extraordinary results, even among the most savage barbarians, so that they truly love us, as children love their fathers. In all the world there cannot be a people who love us so much.'

The missionary had a busy daily routine. There were prayers, confessions, visits to the sick and to school classes. Sepp was a keen musician and enjoyed coaching the choirs of tenors and altos. He had an orchestra of 'four trumpets, eight shawm-players and four trumps . . . four harpists, four organists and one lutist'. He taught the little girls to dance. He then visited the various workshops – brickyard, mill, bakery, smiths, carpenters, painters, sculptors, tilers, turners, butchers and kitchen gardeners.

Inside his quarters, the missionary was attended by Indian boys. 'At table the best treble reads to me a chapter of Holy Writ in Latin. Afterwards another small boy reads a passage on the lives of the saints in Spanish, and at the end of the meal reads the passage for the day from the martyrology or calendar of saints. Six other small boys who always live in my house with me wait on table. One brings the dishes, another removes them, one goes to fetch water from the river, another cleans the candles, one serves bread and another brings fruit from the orchard. They all go barefoot with bare heads, very modestly, like novices, ready for any signal. The boys eat after I have finished. I always give them a good piece of white bread, which they appreciate more than anything else, and often a little honey as a sweet, and plenty of meat.'

There were no attacks by Paulistas, who were engrossed in discovering gold-fields. But the Jesuits took no chances. They maintained a large army of mounted Indians, many of them with firearms. They trained their congregations to fear and hate the Portuguese. There is a statue of the Archangel Michael in the Church of Confim at São Gabriel. This is clearly the work of an Indian sculptor: the archangel has a round face, asiatic eyes and an Indian nose, and he wears a cotton cuirass and feather head-dress. And beneath his feet is the prostrate figure of a bearded bandeirante, with the wings of Satan. When the Spanish authorities attacked the Portuguese outpost of Sacramento, opposite Buenos Aires, the Jesuits sent a Guaraní force to help build trenches.

There was one enemy against which the Jesuits were powerless: the terrible European diseases that annihilated so many American Indians. In 1695 the missions were struck by an epidemic of haemorrhagic smallpox. Father Sepp described the symptoms as best he could. 'The force of the disease manifests itself in small pustules, like those that attack children in Europe or those that we develop during a high fever. Here the pustules are a terrible plague that invades the entire body and scarcely leaves any member intact. . . . [The disease] begins by attacking the throat and then the stomach. It burns the intestines with acute pains, and then completely dries the body fluids and causes loss of appetite and weakness in the stomach. Thence comes the continuous flux of blood. With the blood [the disease] finally produces a corruption and evacuation of the intestines themselves. Even the eyes and ears are not spared: some lose their sight, others their hearing. This merciless plague might be just tolerable if it satisfied its fury on the adults alone; but it strikes even unborn children, expelling them with cruel anticipation from the maternal womb, in which nature should give them the right to nine months' shelter.'

'The good mothers surrendered their own lives while trying to give life to their offspring. They were then placed in the same grave. I say grave, but it was an enormous ditch into which the bodies were thrown daily. There were not enough living people to dig graves for the dead, so that death itself assumed the role of gravedigger.'

The Jesuits could do nothing but apply the pathetically inadequate medical knowledge of the seventeenth century. Father Sepp was convinced that bloodletting was the answer. 'As soon as I heard that this epidemic was raging in other reductions, I wanted to let the blood of mine as fast as possible, from children of ten up to old people, so that if the disease attacked it would find the rotten blood eliminated. . . . It was my musicians and smiths who opened the veins – or, rather, miserably pricked the skin with penknives or nails for lack of cutting utensils.' The Indian families were lined up outside their houses. They held out their arms without a murmur while other Indians moved along the line opening veins. 'It was something to see the streets reddened with quantities of spilled blood – a horrible, cruel spectacle that brought tears to the eyes and sighs to the heart.' There were no medicines available. Sepp organised hospitals, separating the men, women and pregnant mothers. The sick lay in rows of hammocks. They received a special diet of half a pound of meat at every lunch and dinner, manioc flour and European wheat, and water sweetened with honey and sugar. There were constant prayers and processions of a replica of the Virgin of Oettingen in Bavaria. And there were deathbed confessions and last rites.

The Christian religion was the inspiration and preoccupation of these missions. The Indians spent hours every day in their devotions. Mission churches were enormous buildings towering over the village and the surrounding countryside. The largest church in the Seven Peoples of Brazil was that of São Miguel. It was designed by the distinguished Milanese architect Giovanni Primoli and took nine years to build, beginning in 1735. Its broad, sober baroque façade was crowned by two great volutes and adorned by two ranks of pilasters. There was a large clock and a gilded cross over the tympanum, and handsome square towers at either end of the façade.

Such was the tranquil theocracy that was to be bisected by the new frontier of the Treaty of Madrid. The missionaries were at first incredulous, until the order to move was confirmed by the Jesuit Provincial in Buenos Aires. The Jesuits were granted three years in which to move the missions. They invited the Indians to inspect new sites west of the Uruguay. But by mid-1752 there was a spontaneous revolt: one by one the missions refused to contemplate a move. They challenged their missionaries: 'Did you not tell us the good tidings that even if Hell rose up against the Church it would not prevail? Well, this is our church. So, even if the Devil and Hell now rise against it they will not prevail.' They were determined to defy the Portuguese army.

The Jesuit Fathers had to use all their authority to change this attitude. But when they persuaded some Indians to move to new locations to the south-west they were frightened by the presence of wild Charrua Indians. They returned to their former homes. In May 1753 the Indians wrote to the Spanish Governor, Don Juan Echevarria, protesting that they were loyal subjects of the King of Spain. 'They could not believe that he wished to punish them for no offence. They had twice delivered the conquered Colonia del Sacramento to him, and if he wished they would bravely serve him again in his conquests. It was incredible to them that he wanted to remove their lands and the work of over a hundred years, causing their children and women and themselves to perish of hunger in other lands.' There was a great assembly of over a thousand Indian leaders from the various missions. They raised an unfurled Spanish flag to show that they were not rebels. The missionaries protested about the impossibility of finding new locations and of moving 29,000 people. They resented the apparent betrayal by their superiors, and at being cast in the role of 'Abrahams who [must] sacrifice their poor Indians and lead them to the slaughterhouse, with both priest and victim with their eyes shut'.

The Portuguese and Spanish crowns established a boundary commission to survey the new frontier. This started its demarcation in what is now Uruguay and moved northwards. They were erecting their markers across a featureless pampa, a prairie of tall grasses. In winter a chill wind called minuano whips across these plains. Ostriches scurry across the grasslands, with the wind ruffling their untidy feathers, and the gaucho cattlemen shelter in mud-and-reed huts or wrap themselves in heavy ponchos. There is a profusion of bird life. This is perfect cattle-country, with vast herds occasionally straying across the artificial frontier. The majestic paraná pine forests are further north, near the Jesuit missions, and covering the neck of land between the Uruguay and Paraná rivers.

By mid-1753 a survey team under Portuguese and Spanish colonels approached the mission territory. They were met by a force of Indians who told them 'to think about an honourable retreat rather than a risky undertaking. For all the lands that they had boldly come to demarcate were neither the dominions of Portugal nor the conquest of Castile. For it was [the Indians] who had preserved themselves, not for years, but for centuries in the peaceful possession of those vast lands. Although they might consider them barbarians in their lack of civilised manners, they should not judge them to be novices in the exercise of arms!' They were determined to fight for their lands and liberty.

The colonels left some presents. But they decided to retreat and report that the affair had become 'more than a demarcation'. The Indians followed the retreating commissioners, and knocked down the boundary markers bearing the royal arms of the two colonial powers.

In August 1753 the Jesuit Visitor addressed a meeting of the missionaries of the Seven Peoples. He regretted the hardship to the Indians, but ordered that the missions must be abandoned by the following August. He also ordered the Indians to stop making powder and lances.

By 1754 the seven missions had not moved. Their Indians openly defied the Jesuits. They stopped all communication across the Uruguay, intercepting messages (even those hidden in lengths of cloth, musical instruments or medicine bottles), and refusing to allow their missionaries to leave. This was now a genuine and spontaneous revolt by the Guaraní. The Jesuit authorities formally surrendered the Seven Peoples missions to the royal government. But no one could force the Indians themselves to comply.*

The authorities decided to enforce the Treaty by military arms. A Spanish army was to move up the Uruguay while the Portuguese under Gomes Freire de Andrade were to advance across country from the Jacuí. The Portuguese base was a fort called Jesus-Maria-José on the Rio Pardo at the northern end of the Lagoa dos Patos. On 29 April 1754 three squadrons of Indians boldly attacked this fort. They attacked from three sides, firing arrows and using four small cannon. It was a heroic but hopeless frontal attack on a fort in broad daylight. A Portuguese captain described it: 'They received the full force of our artillery at a few yards' range. They beat a retreat, already very destroyed. . . .' The prisoners were sent to man the galleys at Rio Grande.

A Spanish army of two thousand men marched north from Buenos Aires, determined 'to wage a war of fire and blood' unless the Indians surrendered and requested full pardon. This force advanced through the swamps of the Uruguay. It was badly organised and badly supplied, and began to suffer terrible hardships. When some mission Indians rode

south to investigate at the end of August 1754, they found fresh graves
and the debris of a retreating army. They saw the corpses of oxen and of
horses with the cuts in their ears that were the mark of royal horses. 'All
were amazed to see how God in His mercy had undone this torment that
threatened their final ruin, and . . . forced the army to retreat amid
miseries, rains, droughts and frosts.'

The other thrust of the royal campaign was the Portuguese advance
inland from the Atlantic coast. In early September, Gomes Freire de
Andrade marched out of the Pardo fort with an army of over 1600 men,
ten cannon, 6000 horses and a thousand oxen. Two weeks later he met
the Guaraní, drawn up on the far side of the Jacuí and protected by a
parapet. The Indians sent Gomes Freire some dried meat and begged
him to leave them their lands. They were terrified of the Portuguese
guns, but remained defiant. They admitted 'that they did not have the
weapons we had: they trusted only in Jesus-Mary-Joseph and Our Lord.
If we had souls, we should consider that they also had them.' A
delegation of Indian chiefs went to see Gomes Freire. 'They told him . . .
that the greatest favour he could do them was to depart immediately
from their lands and from the fortress Jesus-Maria-José, which was
theirs. The Holy Fathers would send him a thousand oxen for his march.
But, if he refused to do this amicably, it would be by force of war, for
they were a great quantity of Indians. Neither the Portuguese nor the
Spaniards could defeat them: only the power of God could do so. If they
were to be saved it could be only in the company of the Holy
Fathers. . . .' There were further parleys during October. The Indians
were drawn up in battle order. The General demanded their surrender.
They sent him a present of tallow fat for his candles and eleven
oxen. They pleaded to be left alone in peaceful possession of their lands.
An embassy led by the chief of the San Miguel mission reasoned with the
Portuguese. 'He told us not to attempt to advance further, for the lands
were his and they had a great force of Indians there. We should not wish
to shed the blood of so many Christians.' Heavy rains soaked the
Portuguese ammunition, and Gomes Freire decided to withdraw. He
gave a banquet for the Indian chiefs and on 14 November signed a treaty
whereby they would keep their own lands but surrender those to the
north. The chiefs were delighted. They asked the Portuguese to say a
mass to celebrate the treaty, and provided triumphal music from their
choirs and orchestras.†

Treaties between colonial powers and American Indians have always
been short-lived. This particular treaty lasted a year. The European
governments refused to accept this obstacle to their Treaty of Madrid.
And so, in December 1755, another joint Spanish–Portuguese army

marched out under the command of Gomes Freire de Andrade and the Spanish Governor of Montevideo.

On 6 February 1756 this army crossed the Jaguari plain and encountered a large force of Indians on the Campo dos Milhos ('Plain of Maize'). 'We reached them at eight o'clock that night, with an excellent moon. We attacked them with such valour that that great mass of Indians all fled after the second volley. Seven of them were left dead, including their great chief Sape [Tiaraju], the best general they had, whom the Governor killed.' Letters were found on the Chief's body, written either by a Jesuit or another chief. These warned him not to trust the Portuguese: 'Remember that in the past they killed our grandfathers, they killed many thousands of them in many places and did not spare innocent creatures. They also made a mockery and derision of the holy images of saints that adorned the altars of Our Lord God in our church. What happened then is exactly what they wish to do to us now. However hard they try, we must not surrender to them. . . .'

The allied army advanced. On 10 February it was stopped by a great force of Indians at Caibaté. There were parleys. General Gomes Freire demanded the surrender of the seven missions to the Crown of Portugal. The Indians requested a delay in which to consult their priests. When this expired, 'the General . . . ordered that all the men in our armies should be absolved by their chaplains in front of each regiment. This was immediately done. We then opened fire on their vanguard with our artillery batteries, at the distance that separated us – roughly an eighth of a league from where they stood with their war banners. They were attacked from the flanks at the same time, by the Spanish cavalry on their left, and by ours with two repeating guns and a company of grenadiers on the right. They were so smothered in gunfire and shot, and the military might of our troops, that they instantly abandoned their battle lines . . . and fled as best they could. But this was of no use to them. For we pursued them with the cavalry, infantry and repeating guns. . . .' 'Our artillery soon had the good fortune to kill the Indians' commander. Since the fire was heavy the Indians broke into precipitate flight. Our men overtook them and were killing them until they entered some gullies that were on either side of their battle corps. They fortified themselves there and fired their arrows. But our infantry forced them out with repeated musketry volleys. The Spanish troops killed all whom they encountered in the other ravines, with gunfire and lances.' 'We killed over fourteen hundred persons. Only a few who were mounted escaped. We captured 127 whom we left alive, in addition to the 1400 dead.' Both armies began with about 1800 men, but the allies lost only three dead and twenty-six wounded during the hour-long battle. The Indians abandoned their banners, drums, and artillery consisting of wooden logs bound with leather. 'On that same afternoon there were many "vivas" to the two sovereigns among the two armies.' They were celebrating the greatest and quickest destruction of an Indian army in Brazilian history.

After the slaughter of Caibaté the allied army advanced across the Jacuí. It was encouraged to receive a letter from the King of Spain saying that, if the missions continued defiant, 'they and the Fathers should be carried by the sword, with all the fire and rigour of war'. The King wrote that he had issued this terrible order to destroy his own Christian subjects only after making confession to an archbishop. The Indians sent another envoy begging the army to turn back. 'Our captain answered that they were all very stupid, barbaric and ignorant: for neither their general nor the Fathers were anything in the eyes of our generals. These carried royal powers to make them all obey and also to raze all their aldeias and settlements, taking the Indians and Fathers by fire. At this reply the Indian was very sad and grave.' The Jesuit missionary of San Luís sent a humble letter to the army. The missionary from San Miguel was more defiant: he wrote that he was already aged seventy and ready to die. The Indians of his mission sent a letter to the allied general saying 'how sad they were at his coming, and how bitterly they were weeping over the loss of so many lives of their relatives who perished in the battle of 10 February'.

The advance continued inexorably throughout March and April. It passed many abandoned farms, houses, chapels and churches. The Indians still had an army of four thousand, all mounted. But when they opposed the allied army they were routed after only eight rounds of artillery fire, with fifty dead. On 17 May the army reached San Miguel, the largest mission. The missionaries and people had fled to the woods after setting fire to the place. But during the ensuing weeks the Jesuit missionaries from other villages gradually came to surrender. Most were cheerful and energetic young men, but their leader, Father Lourenço Baldo, was 'short, thin, ugly and old, with his beard all white'. Gomes Freire called him a rogue and traitor. By 8 June all seven missions had surrendered, and the Indian commanders rode up in a ceremony of submission. The army held a banquet of mission beef to celebrate.

The Jesuits were condemned, by both Spanish and Portuguese authorities, for having incited their Indians to resist. This may not have been a fair criticism: senior Jesuits certainly tried to make the Indians move, although there was a suspiciously large number of Jesuit Fathers in the missions when they were conquered. The Society never contemplated allowing the Indians to remain in their lands, but with Portuguese Jesuits replacing Spaniards.

A new viceroy of La Plata, Don Pedro de Cevallos, was satisfied that the Jesuits had tried to quell the rebellion. It was this viceroy who finally moved the wretched Indians across the Uruguay in August 1758. The Portuguese boundary commission suspected his motives. It refused to accept the seven missions as long as their former Indian inhabitants were camped just across the river. This refusal meant that the Portuguese clung to the Colônia do Sacramento, which was the place being exchanged for the Seven Peoples. The Treaty of Madrid was thus nullified and had to be renegotiated, at the Treaty of Pardo in 1761 and that of Santo Ildefonso in 1777. There was fighting between the two powers at various disputed points along the frontiers. The pragmatic and cordial spirit of the Treaty of Madrid was lost, and the matter became part of European power politics – largely because of the Tape Indians' defiant refusal to leave their traditional homelands.

Whatever the truth of the Jesuits' attitude to the rebellion, most Spanish and Portuguese authorities blamed the Society for the embarrassing Guaraní War. There was growing hostility to the secretive Society of Jesus. The officers of the army that conquered the Seven Peoples made envious reports of the efficiency and luxury of the missions. They contrasted the missionaries' palatial residence with the Indians' simple huts. They described 'all the mills, ovens, factories and everything that those extraordinary men used to have for their convenience and comfort, so that they lived as abundantly as lords'. The Indians' huts were small and uniform. 'Two families live in each house and make their fire in the middle of it. Because of this, these are so blackened that they are worse than negroes' slave quarters. These people are thus placed in the greatest misery that one can imagine, sleeping in hammocks and skins. Their only clothing is a little cotton cloth from which the women make long gowns to their feet. . . . They go about with gowns as dirty as the ground, which is all red clay.' The place was covered in red dust in summer and mud during the rains. 'It is the height of poverty and slavery, a poverty more intense than has been seen or heard of anywhere in the world. The Fathers keep about fourteen hundred families in this way in the mission [of San Miguel]. They give them rigorous punishments using whips . . . with sharp metal points at the ends: each immediately cuts to the bone, leaving them without any flesh; many lose their lives in these punishments. [The Indians] have nothing they can call their own. The Fathers exploit them and all their labour.' The officer who wrote this diatribe went on to describe the magnificent plantations surrounding the mission. He offered no explanation for the Indians' intense loyalty to their missionaries. But the accusations clung to the Jesuits and fuelled the hatred of their Society.

Such lurid accounts inspired the famous epic poem *O Uraguai*, published in Lisbon in 1769. The author was José Basílio da Gama, a senior civil servant and personal friend of Gomes Freire de Andrade. The poem described the war of the Seven Peoples, and depicted the Portuguese as civilising liberators, the Jesuits as greedy villains, and the Indians as innocent pawns. The Indians were shown not as noble savages, but as exotic barbarians who welcomed the advent of Portuguese civilisation. But the poem made a new departure by celebrating the Indians as individual people, some good and others evil, with a powerful moral cause and the victims of deep injustice. The poem's Indian heroes Cepé and Cacambo meet the allied general and give an impassioned plea for him to leave them their lands. Gomes Freire replies: 'The King [of Portugal] is your father: he wishes you to be happy. You are as free as I am. And you will remain free, either here or somewhere else. But you must deliver these lands to us . . . the peace of Europe requires it thus.' Both sides deplore the circumstances that bring them into opposition; but their positions are irreconcilable.

When fighting breaks out, Cepé is soon killed, but Cacambo fights heroically to delay the allied advance. He is in love with Lindoya, a romantic, virginal beauty. The wicked, slothful Jesuit, 'with a heavy, most enormous belly', betroths her to Cacambo's rival, but she conveniently dies from a snake bite before the marriage. The Jesuits arrest Cacambo, who commits suicide. In the end the noble Portuguese conquer the missions and defeat the Jesuits, who are 'ignorant, envious, hypocritical and sowers of discord'. The conquerors contrast the 'miserable huts of the poor Indians . . . and the noble buildings, the delicious habitation of the Fathers'. 'The infamous republic falls to the ground.'

The simple ideas of the poem *O Uraguai* – Indian goodness, Jesuit wickedness, and the virtue of the Portuguese civilising mission – reflected the thinking of Pombal, the man who controlled Portugal. Pombal had become convinced that the Jesuits were intentionally frustrating his policies. He believed the reports from his brother Mendonça Furtado hinting at great wealth on the Jesuit estates. He suspected the diabolical machinations of the Society behind everything that went wrong in his administration. During the decade of the 1750s Pombal's dislike of the Jesuits developed into hatred of their Society and an almost maniacal obsession with destroying it.

In June 1755 Pombal persuaded King José I to issue two laws that completely changed the status of the Brazilian Indians, and that ended two centuries of Jesuit domination of Indian affairs. The Law of 6 June 1755 'restored to the Indians of Greater-Pará and Maranhão the liberty of their persons, goods and commerce'. The text of the law was magnificent, a ringing declaration of Indian freedom. It admitted that 'many thousands of Indians have been descended but are being extinguished, so that the number of villages and their inhabitants is very small; and these few live in great misery'. Indians were declared to be as free as any other citizens. The law of 1611 freeing slaves was repeated. No private colonists were to have control, or 'administration', of Indians: for Indians subjected to such control had 'within a short period of service either died from sheer hunger and excessive work, or fled inland'. Indians were now to enjoy all the rights and privileges of ordinary free citizens. They could work for anyone they chose. The governor and leading officials would establish rates of pay that amply covered Indian labourers' needs. Trade with Indians was to be encouraged, since this was seen as a means of attracting them to European civilisation. Mission aldeias were transformed into towns and were to be given Portuguese place-names. Indians who descended from the forests were to receive ample lands. Indians themselves were to have full control over their villages. No one was to molest Indians or invade their property, and there were special punishments for any who tried to exploit Indian 'simplicity'.

A parallel edict of 4 April 1755 made a valiant attempt to end racial discrimination against Indians. The derogatory word *caboclo* was forbidden. Intermarriage between whites and Indians was to be encouraged. All stigmas were to be removed from half-castes, who were in future to enjoy preference for posts and honours. 'Their children and descendants will be left with no infamy whatsoever, but will rather become more worthy of royal attention and will be preferred . . . for posts and occupations. . . . They will be fit and capable of any employment, honour or dignity.' Pombal hoped, by stimulating miscegenation, to occupy the vast new frontiers gained in the Treaty of Madrid. There was a fear that the Spaniards or even the French or English might attempt to colonise the vacuum on the upper Amazon left by the depredations of 130 years of slaving.

On the day after the Law of Liberties, the King issued an edict that stripped missionaries of temporal power. In future they were to continue evangelical work, particularly in attracting new tribes. But they lost all control over mission villages. These were to be run by the Indians themselves, and settlers were allowed free access to them.*

Pombal anticipated the usual outcry from settlers about the need for Indian labour. His stepbrother Mendonça Furtado suggested the creation of a new trading company 'to import blacks into this state, with whom to develop the excellent and infinite lands that are found in abandon'. Without African slaves 'to cultivate the settlers' estates, it is difficult to restrain and extinguish the illegal contraband in Indians that is rife here'. Pombal agreed. He invited the settlers of Pará and Maranhão to invest in the proposed company, and had the royal treasury provide the balance needed to launch it. A decree of 7 June 1755 created the General Company of Commerce of Greater-Pará and Maranhão. It enjoyed many privileges, and Pombal even lent two royal warships to protect its fleets. A fort was built at Bissau on the Guinea coast to ensure a good flow of African slaves. Blacks proved far better workers than Indians – physically stronger, morally more resilient, less prone to flee to the forests, and with some immunity to the diseases that annihilated American natives. The Company imported 25,365 black slaves to Maranhão and Pará in the twenty-one years from 1757 to 1778. White Carolina rice was introduced in place of yellow native varieties, and rice plantations in Maranhão were remarkably successful. So also were exports of cotton, cacao, coffee, cravo, sarsaparilla, hides and hardwoods. In the twenty-one years of the Company's existence, 138 ships left Belém and 180 ships left Maranhão laden with these exports. The Amazon area enjoyed a revival, almost a boom. European colonisation began to fill the empty river-banks once peopled by Indians; and the black slaves provided a new element in the area's racial mix. Whereas in the early eighteenth century Belém had only 4000 inhabitants and São Luís do Maranhão 3000, each city had about 10,000 after the success of the new company. The fine public buildings still to be seen in those cities date from this period of prosperity. Even on the Amazon, Indians were becoming irrelevant.*

Pombal's Law of Liberties was very sudden. From one day to the next, Indians were expected to enjoy the liberties and accept the obligations of ordinary free citizens. Pombal was aware of the dangers. When he sent the new laws to Mendonça Furtado, he wrote a covering letter discussing the main problems. Some people feared that, once the Indians became truly aware of their new freedom, they might run back to the forests. Pombal hoped that this could be overcome by giving Indians land and by encouraging their commerce. He wrote, optimistically: 'It is not credible that rational men should be so brutish as to flee from those who are doing them so much good.' Another fear was that Indians would refuse to compete in the colonial world. 'It is established that Indians are very inclined to laziness and to live in inaction. Their very barbarity makes them lack the noble and virtuous ambition that makes men work.' Pombal's answers to Indian improvidence were at once naïve and brutal. He suggested that preachers should inveigh against laziness as a moral and political vice, and take every opportunity to mock it. But he also proposed to his stepbrother: 'You should establish houses of correction or public works, where you will force the incorrigibly lazy to work, in such a way that they grow accustomed to work and suffer shame.'

When Mendonça Furtado received the new laws, he was equally afraid of Indian 'laziness'. 'I consider it inevitable that these Indians – being barbaric, rustic and also lazy – as soon as they realise that they are completely free, and that no one can force them to live in the fazendas on which they now are, I am convinced that they will totally abandon the work in that same instant, and run off to mocambos [hideaways in the forest]. This will leave everything in confusion and disorder – for they will admit no half-measure. It is necessary that they be forced to remain orderly.' He suggested that the Indians be obliged to continue working for the settlers for at least six years.

The fears of Pombal and his stepbrother were quickly justified. The mission villages could not function with the missionaries stripped of temporal authority. The more regimented mission Indians were paralysed, like caged birds unable to fly off when their door is opened. But many Indians did return to their former homes. There was no conceivable reason why they would wish to continue working for the settlers in return for lengths of cotton cloth. The system of mission villages along the Amazon rapidly began to crumble.

The decree that stripped missionaries of temporal power was only the opening shot in Pombal's campaign against the Jesuits. The overthrow of the Society accelerated. The King of Portugal persuaded Pope Benedict XIV to issue a Bull, dated 1 April 1758, authorising reform of the Jesuits in Portugal and her dominions. The Fathers were forbidden to engage in commerce, hear confessions, or preach. They reacted furiously. But Pombal had not finished with them. He was convinced that they were immensely rich, with their missions full of treasure. He was even prepared to entertain a French suggestion that the Jesuits were plotting to help the English invade Brazil. When there was an attempt to assassinate Pombal's patron, King José, on 3 September 1758, Pombal suspected the powerful Tavora family and the Jesuits: he systematically and barbarously destroyed the Tavoras and had the mad old Jesuit Father Malagrida garrotted and burned – an act that Voltaire described as 'a supreme combination of the ridiculous and the horrible'. On 19 January 1759 a royal decree ordered the provisional arrest of all Jesuits and confiscation of their property. A decree of 28 June 1759 removed their right to teach. And a law of 3 September 1759 declared the Jesuits proscribed and expelled from all Portugal and her dominions. The law's language was hysterical. It denounced the Jesuits as 'corrupted, deplorably alienated from their saintly vocation, and manifestly unsuitable because of their many, abominable, inveterate and incorrigible vices. . . . They have clandestinely attempted the usurpation of the entire state of Brazil. . . . Notorious rebels, traitors, adversaries and aggressors . . . against my Royal Person . . . by this present law they are denaturalised, proscribed and exterminated. . . . They are to be effectively expelled from all my Kingdom and Dominions, never to return.' This cruel law was enforced in Brazil in 1760. Some 600 Jesuits were forced to evacuate their colleges and mission villages and depart the country.

One of the main reasons for Pombal's destruction of the Jesuits was economic. Portugal enjoyed an export boom during the 1750s, but by the time of the Jesuits' expulsion this was starting to decline. The Guaraní war had been expensive, as had the reconstruction of Lisbon. Pombal was therefore desperately eager for the royal treasury to seize the wealth of the Jesuits. Pombal sent a team of three magistrates headed by Judge Barberino to supervise the confiscation of the Jesuits' assets in Brazil. This team reached Bahia on 28 August 1758 – a few days *before* the assassination attempt on King José, and five months before the decree confiscating Jesuit property. Pombal's agents carefully listed all Jesuit property; but they never discovered the treasures imagined to exist in the missions.

The Jesuits' main functions in the colony had been to educate settlers' children, administer Indian villages, and maintain some of the hospitals. Pombal tried to replace their colleges with 'royal classes'; but there was an acute shortage of teachers, and the result was a near-collapse of education in Brazil. Other missionary orders failed to provide enough dedicated and intelligent friars to fill the vacuum left by the Jesuits' departure. The situation was even worse when lay directors were installed to replace the Fathers in the Indian missions.

It is extraordinary how quickly the Jesuits fell. In 1750 they seemed immensely powerful, entrenched for two centuries throughout the strongly Catholic Portuguese Empire. Pombal's success against them inspired the Spanish King to expel the Society from all his dominions in 1767. The regimented theocracy of the Paraguayan missions now collapsed, and there were emotional scenes when the Guaraní Indians witnessed the departure of their revered Fathers. In that same year Pombal published the *Dedução chronologica*, a historical survey that blamed the Jesuits for all Portugal's economic, political, social and religious problems. The book was an example of extreme prejudice, the sort of hate-propaganda issued by twentieth-century totalitarian régimes. Pombal had it printed in large numbers and disseminated throughout the Empire. It was translated into other European languages. The exaggerations and distortions of this campaign of vilification have had their effect. Partly because of Pombal's anti-Jesuit obsession, the black-robed Fathers now bear the brunt of popular distrust and dislike of the Inquisition (which was run by the rival Dominicans) and of the Papacy in general. Once the kings of Portugal and Spain had expelled the Society of Jesus, it was not long before Pope Clement XIV in 1773 declared its extinction.

The liberation of the Indians that was proclaimed so eloquently in the legislation of 1755 never took place. Governor Mendonça Furtado decided to permit a transitional period of six years before granting the Indians their freedom. He waited until 5 February 1757 to publish the decree removing missionaries from control of the aldeias. Within two months he wrote that he was replacing the missionaries with Portuguese laymen as directors of the mission villages. The law had stipulated that the Indians were to administer their own communities. This bold proposal to give the Indians autonomy and self-reliance might possibly have enabled them to survive the departure of the Jesuits. But the Governor ignored it. On 21 May 1757 he wrote: 'Since it is not possible for [the Indians] to pass from one extreme to the other . . . it occurred to me . . . to place a [white] man in each settlement with the title of director.' He pretended that these 'directors' would be altruistic paragons. 'These would have no form of coercive jurisdiction whatsoever. They would possess only a directive to teach [the Indians], not so much how to govern themselves in a civilised way, but rather how to trade and to cultivate their lands. From such fruitful and beneficial labours [the Indians] themselves would derive the profit that they themselves will doubtless produce. Those profits will make these hitherto wretched men into Christians, rich and civilised. There can be no doubt that this is what will happen if the directors do their duty.'

If Mendonça Furtado really believed all this he was being extraordinarily naïve. No eighteenth-century settlers were going to endure the boredom and hardships of living in Indian villages, solely to give disinterested instruction in how Indians might grow rich. The Governor's earlier letters show that he had no illusions about the rapaciousness of the colonists. The true purpose behind the directors was to ensure that there should be no interruption in the supply of Indian labour to state and settlers. If the Indians were truly freed they would inevitably revert to their primitive 'laziness' – concentrating on feeding their own families instead of labouring for the whites in return for derisory lengths of cotton cloth.

It was obvious to the Governor and his contemporaries that the replacement of Jesuit missionaries – for all their faults – by Portuguese laymen was the substitution of wolves for shepherds. Bento da Fonseca wrote this very clearly in 1755. He reminded the King that the settlers wanted only 'free entry into the sertão to capture Indians, and the free use of Indian men, women, boys and girls from the aldeias. . . . The blood and sweat of the Indians is the insatiable thirst of these settlers.' During earlier periods when the missionaries were absent or royal laws were permissive, settlers had captured wild Indians 'without the slightest impediment, and ruled the Indians of the aldeias, using them all as if they were their slaves, without paying them for their work'. Fonseca asked the King to consider, if laymen were put in charge of the villages, how many Indians they would use for their own service, and that of their wives, relatives and children. How could Portuguese army officers – who had a bad record as persecutors of natives – be expected to defend the Indians and incur the odium of other white settlers? 'If a religious order could scarcely maintain the Indians' defence, it is certain that military captains could not – even if they had any inclination to do so.'

Mendonça Furtado's system of Indian directors, known as the Diretório, was applied to all mission villages on 3 May 1757.† It stated that the director was being appointed to represent the royal government in the aldeia, because of the rusticity and ignorance of the Indians. His duties were to help convert and civilise the Indians, to teach the Portuguese language, try to eliminate drunkenness, encourage mixed marriages, and help the parish priests or missionaries. He was to act with kindness and not frighten the Indians with punishments. But the directors were then given what amounted to a licence to exploit their charges. The directors were to encourage Indians to farm, gather forest plants, and trade in the cities. As their reward, the directors were to receive no less than one-sixth, seventeen per cent of everything grown or gathered by their Indians. The directors were to take charge of Indians' commercial activities, selling their produce for money, from which the director kept his seventeen per cent and the Crown ten per cent. The Indians were still obliged to work for the settlers and of course on public works for the Crown. Their chiefs and the directors were to see that half the eligible Indians, all males aged between thirteen and sixty, were working for the settlers at all times. They were to do this 'even to the detriment of the best interests of the Indians themselves'!

Pombal and King José probably issued their law freeing Indians in a burst of idealism. Their good intentions were immediately nullified by

Pombal's half-brother. For, with his lay directors, Mendonça Furtado introduced one of the worst periods in the history of Brazilian Indians. The new directors had no moral incentive to help Indians. They immediately used their positions to abuse and exploit people they were supposed to help. In all the contemporary writing about the directors, it is hard to find a good word about them. The outcry against them was so great that the Diretório was abolished after some forty years, in 1798.

The directors who replaced Jesuit missionaries are part of a different era. The expulsion of the Jesuits marked the end of the colonial ideal of educating Indians to be Christian subjects of the King of Portugal. With the Treaty of Madrid the conquest of Brazil was essentially over. In two and a half centuries, Portuguese settlers had discovered, explored, penetrated and conquered most of what is now Brazil.

There were still immense areas of plains, scrublands and forests occupied by Indian tribes. Many Brazilian rivers and forests had never been penetrated by whites, and many tribes had had no contact with Europeans. But Brazil was now firmly established as a European colonial country. It had all the ingredients of permanent European civilisation – fine old cities, extensive agriculture, mines, roads, shipbuilding and its own schools of architecture and literature. Brazil's population in the late eighteenth century was reckoned at 3,250,000, of whom over sixty per cent were black slaves or freemen.* During the following centuries there was to be a population explosion, both by European immigration and by a rise in the birth-rate, to bring the country's population to its present hundred million.

White Brazilian citizens of the 1760s lived in a gracious society similar to that of the plantations of the southern states of the United States – and equally based on black labour. Before long they would also be infected with the ideas of the French philosophers, and the inspiration of the American War of Independence. Napoleon's invasion of Portugal accelerated this movement, and in 1822 Brazil became an independent nation ruled by an emperor from the Portuguese royal family.

By Pombal's time the Indians had become irrelevant to the progress of the Brazilian nation. Indians were a vague menace on the western frontiers, far removed from the Brazilian cities. When the first settlers had landed in Brazil over two centuries before, there was real fear of the hordes of native warriors. In those days the Crown and the missionaries were concerned with the transformation of Indians into loyal subjects. European diseases changed all that. The native population was annihilated. European weapons also improved, so that at the battle of Caibaté 1400 Indians could be killed in a matter of minutes. There was now no fear of Indians except among frontier pioneers. There was little interest in Indian labour, which was generally so unsatisfactory, except in impoverished backwaters like the Amazon. There was very little evidence of the Indian heritage along most of the Brazilian coast. All that could be seen was the Indian blood in many half-castes and old settler families; Indian influence in some social customs, foods, hunting and medical lore; and many Tupi place-names.

The Indians completely failed to find any role in the new society that was taking over their lands. This may have been their fault. They emphatically rejected the aggressive, competitive European way of life. Tribe after tribe shrank back upon itself. The Indians repeatedly chose to cling to their own traditions, language and kindred rather than to try to embrace the alien culture. But it is difficult to see what else they could have done. The cultural shock of the European invasion was intense. The two races proved to have radically different attitudes and objectives in life. And the Indians were never given disinterested help in bridging this gulf. They eagerly followed any white adventurer, as is shown by the long list of settlers who led personal bands of Indians. But this trust was invariably abused, if not by the original white chief then by other colonists. Many tribes obeyed missionaries and surrendered their cultural heritages. They clung to missionary protection, only to be betrayed by the settlers' demands for their labour, and the eventual expulsion of their Jesuit protectors. Overriding all else was the decimation from disease. Ravages from unfamiliar epidemics heightened the Indians' fear and bewilderment. And the resulting decline in the native population removed the Indians as a significant element in modern Brazil. With the original natives all but gone, there can never be decolonisation of South America as of Africa. The Brazilian Indians could find no answer to European guns or germs.

Portuguese and Brazilian literature reflected the changing attitude towards Indians. The curiosity of the first discoverers soon ceased. After the sixteenth century there was little praise of the Indians' generosity or lack of greed, none of the admiration that inspired the legend of the noble savage. There was no further interest about Indian customs or ethnology. During the seventeenth century Portuguese historians were more concerned with India than Brazil. It is remarkable how much of the early material on Indians was written by the few foreigners who penetrated Brazil – by the French in Guanabara and Maranhão, German or English adventurers such as Schmidel, Staden or Knivet, and the Dutch during their occupation of the north-east. The Portuguese never recorded conversations by Indians or described individual Indians as interesting personalities. We have to turn to foreign authors for such sympathetic treatment of Indians as living people. During the seventeenth century, when innumerable fresh tribes were contacted and often destroyed, there was no anthropological information of any kind.

All that emerged from those years were generalisations. Governors and military commanders wrote about campaigns to destroy 'heathen'. Missionaries were concerned about the abuse of Indians as a whole, but spoke of individual Indians only with anecdotes about their piety or lack of it. Settlers simply clamoured for ransomed slaves and Indian labour. Indians were either feared, pitied or coveted, but they were invariably scorned as inferior, and the measure of that scorn was the total indifference and ignorance about their way of life.

The only kind things written about Indians during the seventeenth century were legacies from the observations of the early chroniclers. There was the enduring wonder at Indians' lack of ambition. In the *Dialogues about the Grandeur of Brazil*, of 1618, one speaker explained how Indians possess little more than a hammock and a gourd, 'and with just this they consider themselves richer than Croesus with all his gold, living as contentedly and free from ambition as if they were lords of the world'. To which the other speaker answered: 'This custom makes me envious, for it represents to me the golden age.' The eighteenth-century Brazilian historian Rocha Pitta wrote that the Indians' nakedness represented 'the innocence of our first ancestors . . . for these descendants of theirs were ignorant of all that was sin'.

But to Rocha Pitta the Indians were primitive and unworthy recipients of Portuguese civilisation. 'All this immense body [of land] was possessed and inhabited by uncouth heathen, divided into innumerable tribes, some less bestial, but all barbarous. They had no religious doctrine but were greedy idolators. They served their own appetites, with no discipline of law or reason.' Their houses, clothing, food and society were primitive in the extreme. Rocha Pitta contrasted the simplicity of the natives of Portuguese America with the temples and palaces of the Incas and Aztecs of the Spanish colonies. But he noted that, because they were more organised, the great empires proved far easier to conquer: the Portuguese could never seize a country by capturing its ruler as Cortés and Pizarro had done. 'To dominate the natives of Brazil and found the settlements of our provinces, the Portuguese encountered cruel resistance and fierce challenges. [We] spilled much blood and lost many lives to subject them or make them retreat into the interior of the wilds. Innumerable tribes still live there like beasts and have repeatedly come against our plantations and mills causing destruction and death. By comparing [the Spanish and

Portuguese] conquests, one may judge which of them proved more costly or more glorious.'

Rocha Pitta was a good historian of Portuguese Brazil, but he wrote in 1724 at a time when the Indians were still the enemy. He and his contemporaries were convinced of the value of the Christian and Portuguese civilising mission. They were very proud of Portuguese achievements in winning the Brazilian empire. One poet boasted that his compatriots 'polished in battle the barbarous heathen, who were almost ignorant of the laws of nature; broke the savagery of the high crags, explored the jungles, opened up the rivers'. José de Alvarenga Peixoto wrote a poem, *O Sonho* ('The Dream'), in which he imagined the Sugar Loaf of Rio de Janeiro transformed into an Indian who proclaims his loyalty to Portugal. He saw a great future for a race composed of a mixture between Portuguese and Indians.* Another poet glorified São Paulo: 'Here, where with brutal cruelty, human blood once graced the table of the savage chief, whose bestiality was recorded with horror by humanity, here today is an illustrious town which the Portuguese people enjoy in happy tranquillity. By opening the harshness of dense jungles, a rough village became a civilised city!'

One of the most famous eighteenth-century poems was the epic *Caramuru* by the Augustinian friar José de Santa Rita Durão. This poem tells the story of Diogo Álvares Correa, the Portuguese who was shipwrecked near Bahia in the 1520s and adopted by the local tribe. They named him Caramuru and he won the heart of the chief's daughter Paraguassu. The Indians in this poem are capable of great virtue, but only *after* abandoning their customs and becoming Christian. When Caramuru shows an image of the Virgin to chief Gupeva, he immediately becomes 'tame and different to the way he was in his brute savagery'. Before contact with European civilisation, the Indians are the 'horror of humanity' who eat one another's rotting flesh. But after Caramuru takes Paraguassu to France she becomes a perfect European lady, with pale skin and clear eyes and a fine understanding of Christianity.

Other Portuguese and Brazilian authors of this period showed Indians as people with qualities and defects, but profoundly different from Europeans. The Portuguese were as deeply Christian as any other Europeans, and totally convinced of the superiority of their religion and civilisation. They were also particularly proud of their small nation's very great achievements.

Such convictions inspired those authors who mentioned Indians, and they coloured the behaviour of colonial authorities, settlers and even missionaries towards the natives. They explain the complete lack of curiosity about Indian customs. They also explain why the Portuguese, who lived in close proximity to the Indians, and who knew the early reports about them, evolved no notion of the noble savage.

The French meanwhile were developing their theories of natural goodness, with American Indians as the inspiration. The French Jesuit Lafitau wrote a history of the Portuguese conquests in the New World, in which he compared American Indians to ancient Europeans, and concluded that man was naturally good. Another Frenchman, Father Raynal, produced a widely read history of European settlements in the Indies that proclaimed the romantic, innocent vision of Brazilian Indians. Raynal hoped that Europeans would approach the simplicity of Indian life, at the same time as the Indians became more civilised. These ideas became more egalitarian and revolutionary in Montesquieu's *Spirit of Laws.* Montesquieu followed Montaigne in stressing the freedom and equality of Indians: he praised their lack of possessions or greed, and the resulting absence of abuse of the poor for the sake of money. Rousseau refined such thinking into the political theory of the noble savage.* In this way the Brazilian Indians helped indirectly to influence the American and French revolutions.

Portuguese exiles studying in France introduced this novel interpretation of Brazilian Indians into their writings. By the late eighteenth century, in the period after Pombal's eloquent Law of Liberties, such attitudes became acceptable in Brazil and the Indians came to be seen as romantic heroes who had endured terrible injustices. But the reason why Brazilian intellectuals could view even unaccultured Indians with such indulgence was that the Indians had ceased to be a threat to European occupation of Brazil. They had become insignificant, anachronistic and rather pathetic.

Voltaire's hero Candide sailed to South America in a ship carrying troops to fight the Jesuits in the Guaraní War of the Seven Peoples. That same war was the theme of Basílio da Gama's poem *O Uraguai.* That poem viewed the Portuguese as civilising benefactors and the Indians as innocent pawns. But Basílio da Gama could see no way of reconciling the gulf separating the two cultures. Cacambo, the hero of his poem, at one point sighs and declares that the land belonged to his nation: 'Peoples of Europe, if only the sea and wind had never brought you to us! Ah, it was not for nothing that nature extended between us that vast flat expanse of waters.' Once that ocean was crossed, the steady defeat of the American natives became inevitable.

The Population of Brazil in 1500

THERE is no possible way to obtain an accurate count of the Indians living in Brazil in 1500. Even today, when the shattered remnants of the native population are reduced to under 100,000 no one knows exactly how many Indians survive. In one month in 1972, senior officials of the government Indian agency Funai gave three widely differing figures for the current Indian population.

During colonial times, the only attempts at censuses were missionary baptismal records and the survey the Dutch made of the provinces they conquered in north-east Brazil in the 1630s. The missionaries' figures are of interest only when they first established their aldeias. Within a few years the inevitable epidemics, desertions, and changed social patterns made their statistics irrelevant in assessing the original population. Also, missionaries rarely arrived before there had been widespread fighting, enslavement and epidemics. The exceptions were Portuguese Jesuits at Bahia and Piratininga, Spanish Jesuits in Guairá, Tape, Itatín and on the Uruguay, and French missionaries at Guanabara and Maranhão. The Dutch arrived long after the destruction or dispersal of the coastal population, although they did provide information on the Tapuia of the interior.

Early chroniclers give many clues about native population. The first arrivals, such as Vaz Caminha, Vespucci, Paulmier de Gonneville, Vaca de Castro, Schmidel and Lopes de Sousa, spoke of multitudes of Indians. This was confirmed in reports about Caramuru or João

Ramalho. Florestan Fernandes has analysed contemporary reports on the numbers of Tupinambá villages at Guanabara, Bahia and Maranhão. The pages of Staden, Soares de Sousa, Mem de Sá, Knivet and Vicente do Salvador are full of terrible accounts of the numbers of warriors killed or captured in battle. There are occasional precise references to the number of men or war-canoes engaged in battles; and we can assume that a tribe's population was four times the number of its fighting men. Anchieta and other Jesuits wrote of the catastrophic losses from epidemics.

We know from chronicle sources that there were 27 groups or villages of Tupinambá on the small island of Maranhão in 1612, and a further 41 groups on the mainland. Similarly, there were 22 groups on the shores of Guanabara bay, and Thevet's drawing of Governador island shows 36 huts of Maracajá Temimino. We also know that a typical coastal Tupi village contained four or more long-huts, each 100 metres or more in length. According to Léry, each hut contained 500–600 persons, although Cardim, writing somewhat later, gave only 200 persons per hut.

The situation on the Amazon is even more difficult. Carvajal's account of the first Spanish descent told of one populous village after another on the banks of the main river. Orellana's and Aguirre's expeditions were harassed by flotillas of hundreds of canoes and their landings were opposed by hordes of warriors. Bernard O'Brien encountered and boasted that he led large tribes. Decades of anarchy followed the arrival of the Portuguese in the early seventeenth century. By Acuña's time the Amazon was devastated: we have Manoel Teixeira's estimate that two million Indians had already been destroyed on the lower Amazon alone. The first Europeans to penetrate the great tributaries – Rapôso Tavares on the Madeira or Vieira's Jesuits – reported frequent tribes and large villages. In Vieira's time, soon after the Jesuits had started work on the Amazon, they claimed 200,000 converts in their Pará and Maranhão missions.

During almost every year of the century from 1620 to 1720 there were official and unofficial slaving expeditions up the Amazon and its accessible tributaries. An average of perhaps one or two thousand Indians a year passed into the slave markets of Belém and São Luís do Maranhão: a total of 100,000–200,000 during the century. Missionaries 'descended' many other tribes, only to see them rapidly consumed in the disease-ridden mission villages.

On the other hand, the native population was undoubtedly concentrated near the river banks. The annually flooded várzea of the river valleys yielded the best crops, and the river itself provided abundant fish and turtles. Relatively few tribes, such as the Arara, Caiapó, Makú or Cammuri, lived in the expanses of drier forest between the rivers. Estimates of the original population must therefore be based on river basins, not on the vast areas of forest between.

Slavers and missionaries rarely managed to push upstream beyond the rapids that punctuate all Amazonian tributaries. Many tribes successfully escaped upstream to settle on the myriad streams and small rivers that form the headwaters of the great tributaries. There would thus have been far less decline on the upper rivers before their tribes were contacted during this century. We can use figures of surviving populations in these remote regions as a guide to the original numbers.

Destruction and social disruption continued on the Amazon long after the abolition of slavery. There was an appalling succession of epidemics during the eighteenth and nineteenth centuries, and malaria seems to have invaded the region at that time. There were inter-tribal wars between the Mura, Maué and Mundurucú; and there was the Cabanagem rebellion. Malaria decimated settlements along the lower Negro, Tapajós and Madeira. Rubber-tappers carried its ravages into the farthermost recesses of the Amazon basin.

Modern estimates of the pre-conquest native population of Brazil vary wildly. Demographers have behaved like passengers betting on a ship's run: some take the low field, others the high. Carl Sapper in 1924 guessed 3–5 million for non-Andean South America, of which 2–3 million would have been in what is now Brazil. Sapper was a geographer who based his calculations on assumed land-use according to the fertility of each region. In 1939 Alfred Kroeber took the low field. Suspicious of soldiers' and missionaries' claims, ignoring disease, and believing that the introduction of metal tools has tended to increase numbers, Kroeber reckoned the original population of Brazil at well under one million. Ángel Rosenblat in 1945 made accurate calculations by working back through colonial records; but he was more interested in Spanish South America where census records were better than in the Portuguese empire. He calculated 2,035,000 as the population of non-Andean South America: Brazil presumably accounted for about 1.4 million of this. Rosenblat assumed that, beyond the Andes, South America was 'an immense forest or steppe' in which most of the population lived from hunting, fishing or gathering. He chose to ignore the extensive plantations of the Guaraní, Tupi, Omagua and the majority of Brazilian tribes.

Julian Steward in 1949 attempted guesses by tribes or groups of tribes, and reached a figure of some 1.5 million for Indians within Brazil. Steward's method was sensible – it seems better to add the sum of a series of small guesses than to make one sweeping large one. Steward judged the size of each group by calculating the area it occupied and guessing its density of habitation. His densities ranged from 7 per 100 square kilometres for the Timbira of Maranhão to 60 per 100 km² for the coastal Tupi tribes. Some of his estimates seem too high: 139,000 for the Indians of the Juruá and Purús rivers; 36,200 for the Mundurucú; 57,000 for the Carajá. Other estimates seem too low: 16,000 for the Omagua; 72,000 for 'Amazon below Omagua'; and particularly his 189,000 for 'coastal Tupi south of Amazon'.

Pierre Clastres in 1973 deplored the way in which demographers dismiss estimates made by the first eye-witnesses. He noted observations by Léry and Thevet that Tupinambá villages they visited contained between 600 and 6000 persons or that inter-tribal skirmishes involved 10,000–12,000 warriors. Staden wrote that Tupi villages were located 9–12 kilometres from one another. This would mean that each village of, say, 600 people occupied only 150 km² or even less – a density of 400 or more per 100 km², or seven times Steward's calculation of 60 per 100 km² for the coastal Tupi. Abbeville counted 12,000 Tupi living in 27 groups on the crowded island of Maranhão, a density of 1000 per 100 km². Of course, such dense populations existed only close to the sea coast or in particularly fertile areas.

Clastres noted Staden's observation of the distances between villages among the populous coastal Tamoio. From this he proposed a density of 400 per 100 km², and then proceeded to multiply this as though all southern Brazil were similarly populous. He reckoned that there were 1.5 million Guaraní in the rectangle of land between the upper Paraguay and the Atlantic. William Denevan recently increased traditional estimates of the original population of Amazonia. In 1970 he proposed a density of 5.3 per km² for the fertile várzea or floodplain. In a revision of his essay in 1977, he increased these densities to 28 per km² for the floodplains and 1.2 for the upland forest, giving an average of 14.6 per km² for the entire floodplains of Amazonia. He thus arrived at a total of 4,834,000 for the Amazon basin within modern Brazil. In a footnote to his essay, he reduced this by a quarter (to 3,625,000) to allow for unoccupied buffer zones between warring tribes.

Clastres joined Pierre Chaunu in betting the high field. They felt that the aboriginal population of the Americas could have been 80–100 million – one quarter of all humanity at that time, and twice the previous highest guess of 40–50 million by Paul Rivet in 1924. These estimates compare with Kroeber's ultra-conservative 8.4 million for the hemisphere. Such is the spread of educated guesses at native populations.

In my own attempt I have followed Steward's method of building up a total by guessing the original population of each tribe or group of tribes. This is pure guesswork, but I have tried to take into account any clues from eye-witness chronicle reports, from the effort required to subdue each group, from the size of early missions, and particularly from the relative fertility of each region. What matters are rivers and coastlines. I have therefore grouped tribes according to regions or river basins. This departs from the attempts by Sapper, Steward and Clastres to establish a density of land use and then multiply it for large tracts of forest or campo cerrado. By guessing the size of each tribal group, allowance can be made for agricultural efficiency: hunter-gatherers can be distinguished from great farmers such as the Guaraní.

It seems safe to assume that there has been little migration into Brazil during colonial times. Any tribes that survive today were in existence in 1500, even if some large groups (the northern Caiapó, for instance) have fragmented into subtribes. Almost all tribes have been mentioned in some written source during the 450 years since colonisation began – although the same tribe inevitably acquires different names. There has been bewildering movement by some tribes, such as the Tupinambarana or the Juruna, whereas others have remained rooted to their ancestral homelands.

In making these many guesses, I was torn by the same considerations that caused Kroeber to take the low field and Clastres the high field in their estimates. On the low side, there is the modern example of apparently flourishing and well-adjusted tribes that prove to be far smaller than was expected before they were contacted. Neighbouring tribes always tend to exaggerate the numbers of their enemies. Population controls are very strict in some tribes, with regular use of birth-control, abortion, infanticide, or restraints on marriage. If such a tribe is sufficiently isolated and now has 500 members, there is no reason to assume that it was much larger in pre-conquest times. In modern Brazil, 5000 is considered a very large tribe for a forest area – the Yanomani and Tukuna are perhaps the only tribes that large in Brazilian Amazonia. If a given river or stretch of forest now supports a thousand uncontacted Indians, it has presumably never been able to support a greater number. Where we now find a cluster of tribes on the headwaters of an Amazonian tributary, we must allow that some have migrated into the area to escape the advance of the European frontier. Parts of Brazil that now contain Indians may simply have been uninhabited in 1500.

There are, however, strong arguments for giving high estimates of pre-conquest native populations. There is the powerful evidence of chroniclers, explorers and missionaries, already mentioned in this appendix and throughout this book. The devastation caused by disease cannot be overestimated. Portuguese records are filled with reports of epidemics that shattered the native population. Countless tribes have been eliminated by disease, slavery or social disintegration. Darcy Ribeiro has shown that of 230 tribes extant in 1900, over thirty-five per cent were extinct by 1960. When we observe concentrations of tribes on such remote rivers as the Uaupés, upper Purús-Acre, or upper Xingu, we must appreciate that there were once similar concentrations on more accessible rivers that were denuded long ago. We see, time and again, that tribes contacted during recent decades have rapidly been reduced to half, a quarter or less of their original strength by the first onslaught of unknown diseases. This decimation has happened despite the efforts of modern medicine. It therefore seems right to multiply present tribal populations accordingly to arrive at their pre-contact size.

In my list of tribes I have included only the better known or surviving tribes. If my population guesses seem high it is because they are intended to include innumerable other tribes that had only brief historical mention or that were destroyed before their names were recorded.

My estimate is pure guesswork, done on the theory that the sum of dozens of educated guesses is better than one or two sweeping guesses. The total by my method is 2,431,000. There are now about 100,000 Indians in Brazil. The debate about the original native population of Brazil will continue. But there can be no question that an appalling demographic tragedy of great magnitude has occurred.*

	Modern populations (thousands)		1500 estimates (thousands)	
	Dória, Ricardo	Ribeiro, Kietzman	Steward (where directly comparable)	Hemming
1. RIO GRANDE DO SUL				
Timbu (within Brazil)	–	–	–	2
Charrua (within Brazil)	–	–	–	3
Tape, Chane	–	–	–	35
Guaraní, on Uruguai (7 Povos)	–	–	–	30
Carijó on coast and Lagoon	–	–	–	25
			Total	95
2. SANTA CATARINA AND PARANÁ				
Xokleng (Botocudo)	0·4	0·2	–	8
Gualachi				2

	Modern populations (thousands)		1500 estimates (thousands)	
	Dória, Ricardo	*Ribeiro, Kietzman*	*Steward (where directly comparable)*	*Hemming*
Bituruna				5
Guananã				4
Kaingang (Coroado)	6	3–4	17·5	15
Guaraní in Guairá (later missions)				70
Mbuá (Kainguá)				6
Carijó on Paraná plateau and coast				40
Xetá		0·2		2
			Total	152

3. SÃO PAULO STATE

Carijó on Anhembi				25
Goiana on Paraíba				20
Kaingang (Coroado)				25
Southern Caiapó (Bilreiros) in S.P.				12
Oti Chavante		0		4
Tupinikin, Piratininga and coast				35
Tupi on Paraíba, Mantiqueira				15
Tamoio of Iperoig				10
			Total	146

4. SOUTHERN MATO GROSSO

Guaraní (Caiuá, etc.) of Itatín	6·5	3–4		25
Guaná (Terena, Kinikinao, Chané)	4	3–4		35
Guaicurú (Kadiweu, Mbayá)	0·2	0·2		15
Paiaguá				6
Guató		0		4
Southern Caiapó tribes				25
Opaie-Chavante and others				8
			Total	118

	Modern populations (thousands)		1500 estimates (thousands)	
	Dória, Ricardo	*Ribeiro, Kietzman*	*Steward (where directly comparable)*	*Hemming*
5. GUANABARA, RIO DE JANEIRO				
Tamoio of Guanabara				25
Tamoio of Cabo Frio				35
Temimino				8
Purí, Paraíba valley				10
Coropó				6
Cachiné				5
Carayá				8
			Total	97
6. ESPÍRITO SANTO, ILHÉUS				
Waitacá				12
Tupinikin				55
Temimino				10
Papaná				15
Aimoré (Botocudo)				30
Purí				8
Cariri, Gueren, Camuru, etc.				30
			Total	160
7. MINAS GERAIS				
Maxacali, Malali	0·3	0·2		6
Coroado tribes				10
Camacan		0		5
Baenã				5
Cataguá				3
Shacriabá				12
Abaeté				4
Caiapó tribes				10
Caeté, etc., of Casa da Casca				30
Pataxó	0·2	0		6
			Total	91
8. BAHIA				
Tupinambá of Recôncavo, Paraguaçu, etc.				85
Tupinambá of Rio Real, Cirigi				30
Paiaiá				4

	Modern populations (thousands)		1500 estimates (thousands)	
	Dória, Ricardo	*Ribeiro, Kietzman*	*Steward (where directly comparable)*	*Hemming*
Kaimbé	0·5			5
Guerens	2–4			10
Cariri, etc., of Arabó	1			15
			Total	149

9. SÃO FRANCISCO VALLEY

Tupina				10
Chocó		0·2		8
Amoipira				12
Ubirajara				2
Fulniô	1·8	2		10
Pancaruru	2·5	2·2		15
Chucuru		1·5		5
Massacará, Ori				4
Tuxa		0·2		2
Wakoná		1		3
Aticum		1·5		5
Pacarara		0·2		2
Kambiwa				2
Extinct tribes of upper São Francisco				20
			Total	100

10. NORTH-EAST COAST

Caeté, S. Francisco to Sergipe				50
Caeté, C. Sto Agostinho				25
Tobajara of Pernambuco				25
Potiguar, Rio Grande, Paraíba, Ceará		1		90
Tobajara, Potiguar of Ibiapaba				15
Anacé				3
			Total	208

11. NORTH-EAST INTERIOR

Cariri, Caratiú, Caruí, Icó, Panati, etc.				25
Canindé Jandui, Genipapo				20
Guenguen				6

	Modern populations (thousands)		1500 estimates (thousands)	
	Dória, Ricardo	*Ribeiro, Kietzman*	*Steward (where directly comparable)*	*Hemming*
Jucá				2
Paiacú, Tarairu, etc.				12
Poti				3
Jaicó			10	5
Other tribes of Piauí				12
				Total ‾85
12. MARANHÃO				
Tremembé			21	18
Tupinambá on Island				12
Tupinambá of Cumá, Tapuitapera				25
Gamella				4
Barbados				3
Aranhí				2
Guanaré, Vidal, Axemi				8
Eastern Timbira (Canela, Crenyĕ)	0·2	0·5	23·5	20
Tenetehara (Guajajara)	2·5	1–1·5		12
Guajá	0·3	0·2		2
Urubu-Kaapor		1		3
				Total ‾109
13. PARÁ RIVER, MARAJÓ				
Tembé, Turiwara, Jacunda	0·2	0·2		25
Tupinambá in Caeté, Pará				8
Tapuia tribes near Belém				8
Aruan			30	20
Anajá				4
Other Ingaíba on Marajó				12
Pacajá, Uanapú, Camarapin, etc.				10
				Total ‾87
14. TOCANTINS, ARAGUAIA				
Goiá				
Shacriabá, Acroá				5
Akwĕ Shavante	1·5–2		3	10
Sherente	0·3	0·5		15
				5

	Modern populations (thousands)		1500 estimates (thousands)	
	Dória, Ricardo	*Ribeiro, Kietzman*	*Steward (where directly comparable)*	*Hemming*
Canoeiro				3
Krahó	0·6	0·5–1		5
Carajá, Javaé, Xambió	0·9	2·5	57	25
Tapirapé	0·1	0·1	4	2
Caiapó on Araguaia(Dioré, Xikrin, etc.)	0·3	1·5		12
Tacayuna				2
Apinajé	0·3	0·2		3
Gavião, Timbira	0·1	1·5–2		5
Paracanã, Anambé	0·6	0·5		4
Amanayé, etc.		0·1		5
			Total	101

15. XINGU, IRIRI

Xingu headwaters tribes	0·8	1·2	10	11
Bakaïri	0·2	0·2	6	4
Suiá, Manitsauá	0·1	?		2
Northern Caiapó tribes	1·8–2	2·2		25
Asurini, Coani, other Tupi		0·5		5
Tacunyapé				4
Curuaya, Xipaya, others on Iriri		0		5
Arara				4
Juruna	0·1	0·1		6
			Total	66

16. TAPAJÓS BASIN

Apiacá	0·2	0	18	3
Irantxe	0·1	0·2		2
Tapayuna (Beiço-de-Pau)	0·1	?		2
Aripaktsá	0·3			3
Juruena				3
Urupá, Yanahim				5
Kawahib (Kayabí, Parintintin)	0·3	0·5	25·5	8
Mundurucú	1·5	1–1·5	36·2	15
Maué	2	1–1·5		20
Tapajós				25
			Total	86

	Modern populations (thousands)		1500 estimates (thousands)	
	Dória, Ricardo	*Ribeiro, Kietzman*	*Steward (where directly comparable)*	*Hemming*
17. CENTRAL MATO GROSSO, RONDÔNIA, GUAPORÉ				
Bororo, Eastern and Western	0·5	0·5–1	16	12
Umotina		0·2		3
Parecis	0·4	0·5	5	20
Arae				3
Nambikuara	0·7	0·5–1	22	15
Tuparí, Purubora, etc.	0·1	0·2		4
Aruã, Makura, other Tupi	0·1	0		8
Cabixi, Palmela, Cantaro, other Carib				6
			Total	71
18. MADEIRA BASIN				
Suruí, Cinta Larga, etc., of Aripuanã	1·6			8
Cawahib (Tukunafed, Parintintin, Mialat, Kepkiriwat, etc., of Machado)	0·2	0·1		6
Ramarama, Arara	0·6	0		3
Urupá, Jarú, Pakaanova	0·5	1–2		6
Caripuna				7
Karitiana, Arikem, etc., of Jamari	0·1	0		5
Digut, Itogapuk, Diarrói, other Tupi	0·3			8
Tora				15
Mura, Pirahá	0·2	1–1·5	30	20
			Total	78
19. AMAZON, BELOW NEGRO				
Guanavena, Caboquena				
Zurina, Andirá				
Tupinambarana, Arapium				
Conduri, Pauxi				
Maraguá, Curiato				
Tapuiucu, Aracaju, other Aruak				
Arretu, Coani, Apehu				
			all extinct, say 60	

	Modern populations (thousands)		1500 estimates (thousands)	
	Dória, Ricardo	*Ribeiro, Kietzman*	*Steward (where directly comparable)*	*Hemming*
20. AMAPÁ				
Tucujú				12
Paracoto				6
Palicur	0·4	0·5		5
Maraon, Macapá, Mapruan				5
Mayé				3
Wayapí, Emerilon, other Oyapok				10
Karipuna	0·5	0·5		3
Galibí	0·6	0·6		5
			Total	49
21. GUIANA RIVERS, NORTH OF AMAZON				
Apalaí	0·1	0·2		8
Wayana	0·1	0·1		5
Tirió	0·2	2–3		4
Oyampi				2
Katawian				2
Kaxuiana		0·1		3
Parukotó-Xarumá	1·5	1·5		8
Cariguano				2
Warikena	0·3	0		3
Wai Wai		0·2		2
Pianocotó		0·5		5
Arequena, Cashuena				6
Jamundá				3
Apotó				2
			Total	55
22. NEGRO				
Aruaki				15
Pakidái (Surara)				2
Tarumá and other extinct				35
Atroari/Waimiri	2	?		4
Caburicena, Waranacoacena				6
Capueni				1
Yauaperi				2

	Modern populations (thousands)		1500 estimates (thousands)	
	Dória, Ricardo	*Ribeiro, Kietzman*	*Steward (where directly comparable)*	*Hemming*
Baranawa, Carahiahi				3
Manau				8
Makú	0·2	?		3
Baré tribes				17
Mepuri				2
			Total	98
23. BRANCO				
Yanomani (Waika, Guaharibo, Xirianá) in Brazil	3–4	5		9
Pauishana, Paraviyana				2
Mayongong (Maquiritare)	0·1	0·1		3
Makuxí	3	3–5		8
Wapitxana	0·3	1·5		4
Taulipang (Jaricuna)	1	1–1·5		4
Marakanã		0		1
Ingariko	0·1	0·5		2
			Total	33
24. IÇANA, UAUPÉS				
Desana		0·2		1
Baniwa (Hohodene, etc.)	1·4	1·5		6
Tukano tribes				5
Wanana, Waikino		0·5		2
Tariana	0·5	0·5–1		2
Tuyuca		0·1		1
Kobewa	0·5	0·5–1		2
			Total	19
25. IÇA, JAPURÁ				
Kayuishana		0		3
Wainumá		0		1
Yurí		0		5
Tukuna	2·6	1·5–5		8
Pasí, Mirawa		0		2
			Total	19

	Modern populations (thousands)		1500 estimates (thousands)	
	Dória, Ricardo	*Ribeiro, Kietzman*	*Steward (where directly comparable)*	*Hemming*
26. SOLIMÕES (AMAZON ABOVE NEGRO)				
Ybanoma, Soliman				6
Yurimagua				8
Aysuare				5
Cammuri				3
Omagua			16	20
Witoto		0·1		5
			Total	47
27. PURÚS, ACRE				
Purupuru				3
Paumari, Jaruara	0·3	0·4		5
Jamamadi		0·5		4
Marawa, Wainuma, etc.		0		2
Maniteneri, Kulina, Apurinã, and other Aruak	0·8	0·6		5
Daní	0·4	0·3		2
Juma		?		1
Jaminawa		0·2–1		2
Iawano, Amahuaca and other Panoan inside Brazil		1·2		5
Espinho		0		1
			Total	30
28. JURUÁ, JANDITUBA, ITUÍ, JAVARÍ				
Waraicu				2
Catawishí				1
Ipurinan, Kangite		0·5–1		3
Katukina, Culino	0·3	0·5–1		3
Marubo, Maya	1	0·7		2
Tamanaua, Kashinaua, Mayoruna and other Panoan		0		9
Kampa (inside Brazil)		0·1		2
			Total	22

TOTAL FOR BRAZIL 2,431,000

Glossary

ALDEIA: a village, particularly a mission village

ALQUEIRE: a measure of land in Brazil – 48,400 square metres in most states, but half this area in São Paulo

ARROBA: measure of weight, about 15 kilogrammes

BANDEIRA: an expedition into the hinterland in search of Indians or gold, or in exploration

BANDEIRANTE: a member of a bandeira

CABOCLO: slightly offensive term for a Brazilian frontiersman, of Indian or mixed blood

CAIÇARA: palisade fence or the corral enclosed within one

CÂMARA: town council, chamber

CAMPO: prairie, especially the lightly wooded bushlands of the Brazilian plateau

CAPTAINCY (Port. *capitania*): territory awarded by the Portuguese crown to be administered by a donatory and his descendants; colonial administrative unit smaller than a state

CARAÍBA: Tupi word for a legendary hero or prophet; a supernatural being; term used by many modern tribes for 'white man' or 'civilizado'

CAUIN (or CAUIM): refreshing and mildly intoxicating Indian drink made from manioc and other fruits

COMMANDEUR: Dutch term for official in charge of a mission village

COROPIRA (or CURUPIRA): goblin or malevolent spirit that lurked in forests, especially near the crossing of two trails

CORSO: marauding, piratical; applied to Indian tribes of Maranhão and Ceará who resisted Portuguese rule in the seventeenth–eighteenth centuries

CRAVO (DI MARANHÃO): clove cinnamon

CRUZADO: ancient Portuguese gold coin worth 40 centavos

CURUPA: hallucinogenic powder used by Indians on the upper Amazon and Negro

DIRECTOR: lay administrator placed in charge of Indian villages after the expulsion of the Jesuits

DONATORY: recipient of award of a hereditary fief of land to be colonised, in the sixteenth century

ENCOMIENDA: territory whose inhabitants owed tribute in kind and precious metals to the Spanish conquistador to whom it had been awarded

ESCAUPIL: padded or quilted armour, generally of leather filled with cotton; adopted by Spanish conquistadores from the Mexicans

ESCUDO: shield; Portuguese coin and unit of currency

FACÃO (pl. *facões*): large knife, cutlass or machete

FAZENDA: estate, farm or ranch

GAUCHO: cattleman from Argentina or southern Brazil

GENIPAPO: black dye or body paint, from gum of *Genipa americana* tree

MAIR: Tupi word for a heroic, exceptional man; applied to Europeans and particularly to the French, in the sixteenth century

MALOCA: large Indian hut for several families

MAMELUCO: half-caste of Indian and European parentage

MARACÁ: ceremonial rattle, of a pebble-filled gourd mounted on a short handle

MATÉ: aromatic herbal tea, popular in Paraguay, Argentina and southern Brazil

MATO: woods, low forest

MESTIZO: mixed blood

MIL-RÉIS: former Brazilian monetary unit; a thousand réis

MORBICHA: old man, chief

MUTUCA: large, biting horsefly

OITAVA: ancient weight; an eighth of an ounce

PAGÉ: shaman, witch-doctor, medicine-man

PALMO: hand span; lineal measure, a palm

PAI: father, missionary

PAULISTA: inhabitant of São Paulo

PAMPA: savannah, plain

PERO: Tupi word for Portuguese in the sixteenth century

REDUCTION: Spanish Jesuit mission village

REAL (pl. *réis*): royal; former Portuguese silver coin

REGIMENTO: regulations, government, regiment of soldiers

ROÇA: forest clearing, slash-and-burn plantation

SAMBAQUI: low coastal mound, of shells and human remains of ancient Brazilians

SERTÃO: wilderness, wilds, bush, hinterland, backwoods

SESMARIA: allotment of land awarded to colonial settlers

TANGA: curved triangular covering for women's pubic parts, formerly made in the lower Amazon; modern woman's scanty bathing-suit

TIPITI: tubular press for leeching poison out of manioc, made of plaited straw matting

TOSTÃO: Brazilian coin worth 100 réis
URUCUM: anatto, red dye from berries of anatto tree
VAQUEIRO: cowhand, cowboy
VARA: an ell, linear measure of about 1.1 metres
VÁRZEA: floodplain, fertile land on banks of Amazon rivers
VINTÉM: former Brazilian coin
YANACONA: Inca word for personal retainer; Andean Indian who attached himself to Spanish conquistadores as personal servant exempt from other taxes

Bibliography

ABBREVIATIONS

ABAP: *Anais da Biblioteca a Arquivo Público do Pará* (Belém do Pará, 1901–).

ABNRJ: *Anais da Biblioteca Nacional do Rio de Janeiro* (Rio de Janeiro, 1876–).

AEP: *Amazônia na era Pombalina*, ed. Marcos Carneiro Mendonça, 3 vols (São Paulo, 1963).

AI: *América Indígena* (Instituto Indigenista Interamericano, Mexico City, 1941–).

AMN: *Archivos do Museu Nacional* (Rio de Janeiro, 1876–).

BAE: *Biblioteca de autores españoles desda la formación del lenguaje hasta nuestros días*, ed. Manuel Rivadeneira and M. Serrano y Sanz, 71 vols (Madrid, 1846–80); *Continuación*, ed. M. Meléndez Pelayo (Madrid, 1905–).

BMNA: *Boletim do Museu Nacional (Antropologia)*, n.s. (Rio de Janeiro, October 1942–).

BMPEG: *Boletim do Museu Paraense Emílio Goeldi* (Belém do Pará, 1895–1956; n.s., 1957–).

Brasília: periodical published by Universidade de Coimbra (Coimbra, 1942–).

Brasiliana: *Biblioteca Pedagógica Brasileira*, 5th series (Companhia Editôra Nacional, São Paulo, Rio de Janeiro, etc., 1928–).

CA: *Cartas avulsas de Jesuítas (1550–1568)*, ed. Afrânio Peixoto and Alfred do Vale Cabral (Rio de Janeiro, 1931).

CDSP: *Catálogo de Documentos sôbre a História de São Paulo, existentes no Arquivo Histórico Ultramarino, de Lisboa,* RHGB tomo especial, 13 vols (1956–9).

CPJB: *Cartas dos primeiros Jesuítas do Brasil*, ed. Serafim Soares Leite, SJ, 3 vols (São Paulo, 1954). These three volumes, and a fourth covering 1563–8, were also published as *Monumenta Brasilia*, 4 vols (*Monumenta Historica Societatis Iesu* **79–81**, **87**) (Rome, 1956–60).

DH: *Documentos Históricos da Biblioteca Nacional do Rio de Janeiro* (Rio de Janeiro, 1928–).

DHBC: *Documentos para a historia do Brasil e especialmente a do Ceará*, ed. Barão de Studart, 4 vols (Fortaleza, 1908–21).

DI: *Documentos interessantes para a história e costumes de São Paulo*, ed. António de Toledo Piza, 86 vols (Archivo do Estado de São Paulo, 1894–1961).

HAHR: *Hispanic–American Historical Review* (Baltimore, and Durham, NC, 1918–).

HBP: Afonso de Escragnolle Taunay, *Historia das bandeiras paulistas*, 2 vols (São Paulo, 1953). See also HGBP.

HCJB: Serafim Soares Leite, SJ, *História da Companhia de Jesus no Brasil*, 10 vols (Lison/Rio de Janeiro, 1938–50).

HCP: *História da colonização portuguesa do Brasil*, ed. Carlos Malheiro Dias, 3 vols (Pôrto, 1924–6).

HGB: Francisco Adolpho de Varnhagen, Visconde de Pôrto Seguro, *Historia Geral do Brasil*, 3rd ed. (1854–7), annotated by João Capistrano do Abreu and edited by Rodolpho Garcia, 5 vols (São Paulo, 1927).

HGBP: Afonso de Escragnolle Taunay, *Historia geral das bandeiras paulistas*, 11 vols (São Paulo, 1924–50).

HSAI: *Handbook of South American Indians*, ed. Julian H. Steward, Smithsonian Institution, Bureau of American Ethnology, Bulletin 143, 6 vols (Washington, DC, 1946–63), vols 1, *The Marginal Tribes*; 3, *The Tropical Forest Tribes*; 5, *The Comparative Ethnology of South American Indians*; 6, *Physical Anthropology, Lingustics and Cultural Geography of South American Indians*.

JSAP: *Journal de la Société des Américanistes de Paris*, n.s. (Paris, 1903–).

LGM: *Livro grosso do Maranhão*, ed. Artur César Ferreira Reis, 2 Vols (*Anais da Biblioteca Nacional do Rio de Janeiro* **66–7**) (Rio de Janeiro, 1948).

MACC: *Os manuscritos do arquivo da Casa de Cadaval respeitantes ao Brasil*, ed. Virginia Rau and Maria Fernanda Gomes da Silva, 2 vols (Coimbra, 1956–8).

MB: *Monumenta Brasiliae*. Four volumes of the letters of early Jesuits in Brazil, edited by Serafim Soares Leite (*Monumenta Historica Societatis Iesu* **79–81, 87**) (Rome, 1956–60). The first three volumes are identical to CPJB and are cited thus here.

OFM: Order of Minor Friars, or Franciscan. Capuchins were an austere branch of the Franciscan Order.

PAN: *Publicações do Arquivo Nacional, Rio de Janeiro* (1886–).

RH: *Revista de Historia* (São Paulo, 1950–).

RHGB: *Revista do Instituto Histórico e Geographico Brasileiro* (Rio de Janeiro, 1839–). (Formerly *Revista trimensal de historia e geographica* and *Revista trimensal do Instituto Histórico, Geographico e Etnographico do Brasil.*)

RMN: *Revista do Museu Nacional* (Rio de Janeiro).

RMP: *Revista do Museu Paulista* (São Paulo: 1st series, 1895–1942; 2nd series, 1947–).

SJ: Societatis Jesu, or Jesuit.

Studia: *Revista semestral* (Centro de Estudos Históricos Ultramarinos, Lisbon, 1958–).

EARLY SOURCES

D'ABBEVILLE, CLAUDE (Capuchin): *Histoire de la mission des Pères Capucins en l'Isle de Maragnan et terres circonfines, où est traicté des singularitéz admirables et des mœurs merveilleuses des Indiens habitans de ce pais* (Paris, 1614).

— *L'Arrivée des Pères Capucins en l'Isle de Maragnan et la conversion des sauvages à nostre saincte foy* (Paris, 1623).

ACUÑA, CRISTÓBAL DE, SJ: *Nuevo descubrimiento del gran rio de las Amazonas* (Madrid, 1641); trans. Clements R. Markham, in *Expeditions into the Valley of the Amazons*, Hakluyt Society 24 41–134 (London, 1859).

ALMEIDA, GABRIEL RIBEIRO DE: 'Memoria da tomadia dos Sete Povos de Missões . . .' (1806), RHGB 5 3–21, 1843.

ANCHIETA, JOSÉ DE, SJ: *Nuovi avisi delle Indie di Portogallo* (Venice, 1562).

— *Arte de gramática da lingoa mais usada na Costa do Brasil* (Coimbra, 1595; Rio de Janeiro, 1933).

— *Informações e fragmentos históricos do Padre Joseph de Anchieta, 1584–1586* (Rio de Janeiro, 1886).

— *Cartas, informações, fragmentos históricos e sermões*, ed. António de Alcântara Machado (Rio de Janeiro, 1933). Besides various letters, this contains: pp. 301–48, *Informação do Brasil e de suas capitanias* (1584) (also RHGB 6 404–35, 1844); pp. 349–94, *Informacão dos primeiros aldeiamentos da Baía* (c. 1587) (also known as *Breve noticia histórica das missóes dos Jesuítas no Brasil*, and published as 'Trabalhos dos primeiros Jesuítas', RHGB 57 pt 1, 218–47, 1894); pp. 395–408, *Breve narração das coisas relativas aos colegios e residencias da Companhia nesta Provincia Brasilica* (1584); pp. 409–47, *Informação da Provincia do Brasil para nosso Padre* (1585; also published Rio de Janeiro, 1946); pp. 448–56, *Informação dos casamentos dos Indios do Brasil.*

ANON: *Anal de Vila Bela desde o primeiro descobrimento deste sertão do Mato Grosso, no ano de 1734*, in *Congresso do mundo português*, 19 vols (Lisbon, 1940), 10 303–20.

ANON: *Newen Zeytung auss Presillg Landt* (c. 1515), trans. Rodolpho A. Schuller, ABNRJ 33 115–44, 1911; trans. Mark Graubard as *Tidings out of Brazil* (Minneapolis, 1957); ed. Clemente Brandenburger (São Paulo, 1922).

ANON JESUIT: *De algumas coisas mais notáveis do Brasil* (c. 1590), RHGB 94 367–427, 1923.

ANON JESUIT: *Enformação do Brasil e de suas capitanias* (1584), probably by José de Anchieta; RHGB 6 404–35, 1844; and Anchieta, *Cartas, informações* . . . (1933) 301–48.

ANON JESUIT: *Informação dos primeiros aldeiamentos da Baía* (c. 1587), either by José Cristóvão de Gouveia or José de Anchieta, in Anchieta, *Cartas, informações* . . . (1933) 409–47.

ANON JESUIT: *Informação dos primeiros aldeiamentos da Baía* (c. 1587), either by José de Anchieta or Luis da Fonseca. (The manuscript is headed 'Breve noticia

histórica das missões dos Jesuítas no Brasil'.) Anchieta, *Cartas, informações*
. . . (1933) 349–94; also published as 'Trabalhos dos primeiros Jesuítas',
RHGB 57 pt 1, 213–47, 1894; and Rio de Janeiro, 1946.

ANON JESUIT: *Sumário das armádas que se fizeram e guerras que se deram na conquista do Rio Paraíba* (c. 1587), RHGB 36 pt 1, 5–89, 1873. Variously attributed to Fernão Cardim or Vicente do Salvador, but probably by Simão Travassos. The report was addressed to Cristóvão de Gouveia.

ANTONIL, ANDRÉ JOÃO (pseudonym of Giovanni Antonio Andreoni, SJ): *Opulência do Brasil por suas drogas e minas* (Lisbon, 1711; São Paulo, 1923); ed. and trans. into French by Andrée Mansuy (Paris, 1968).

AZARA, MANUEL FELIX DE: *Voyages dans l'Amérique méridionale depuis 1781 jusqu'en 1801*, 4 vols (Paris, 1809); Spanish original (Madrid, 1923).

— *Memorias sobre el estado rural del Rio de La Plata en 1801* . . ., ed. Agustín Azara (Madrid, 1847).

BARLAEUS, CASPAR (Kaspar van Baerle): *Rerum per octennium in Brasilia et alibi nuper gestarum* (Amsterdam, 1647); in German, *Brasilianische Geschichte* . . . (Cleve, 1659); trans. Cláudio Brandão (Rio de Janeiro, 1940).

BARO, ROVLOX (Roclof): *Relation du voyage* . . . *au pays des Tapuies dans la terre ferme du Brésil* (1647), in Augustin Courbe, *Relations véritables et curieuses de l'Isle de Madagascar et du Brésil* (Paris, 1651).

BARROS, ANDRE DE, SJ: *Vida do apostólico Padre António Vieyra* (Lisbon, 1745).

BERREDO, BERNARDO PEREIRA DE: *Annaes historicos do Estado do Maranhão, em que se dá noticia do seu descobrimento e tudo o mais que nelle tem succedido desde o anno em que foy descuberto até o de 1718* (Lisbon, 1749).

BETENDORF, JOÃO FELIPPE, SJ: *Chronica da missão dos Padres da Companhia de Jesus no Estado do Maranhão* (1699), RHGB 72 pt 1, 1–697, 1901.

BRAGA, JOSÉ PEIXOTO DA SILVA: 'Notícias que dá ao Padre Mestre Diogo Soares. Congonhas, 25 Aug. 1734', RHGB 69 pt 1, 219–33, 1908; Afonso de Escragnolle Taunay, *Relatos sertanistas* (1953) 121–37; trans. in E. Bradford Burns (ed.), *A Documentary History of Brazil* (1966) 101–16.

BRANDÃO, AMBROSIO FERNANDES: *Diálogos das grandezas do Brasil* (c.1618), ed. João Capistrano de Abreu (Rio de Janeiro, 1930); ed. Rodolfo Garcia (Rio de Janeiro, 1943); ed. José Antonio Gonsalves de Mello (Recife, 1962).

BRAUM, JOÃO VASCO MANOEL DE: *Descripção chorographica do Estado do Gram-Pará* (1789), RHGB 36 pt 1, 269–322, 1873.

CAIXA, QUIRÍCIO, SJ: *Breve relação da vida e morte do P. José de Anchieta, 5° Provincial que foi do Brasil* (1598), in Serafim Soares Leite, *Páginas de história do Brasil* (São Paulo, 1937) 152–82.

CALADO, MANOEL: *O valeroso Lucideno e triunfo da liberdade* (Lisbon, 1648; Recife, 1942).

CALDAS, JOSÉ ANTONIO: *Notícia geral de tôda esta capitania da Bahia, desde o seu descobrimento até o presente ano de 1759*, 2 vols (Salvador, 1949–51).

CAMINHA, PERO VAZ DE: Letter to King Manoel, Pôrto Seguro, 1 May 1500: *A carta de Pero Vaz de Caminha*, ed. Jaime Cortesão (Rio de Janeiro, 1943); trans. William Brooks Greenlee, *The Voyages of Pedro Álvares Cabral to Brazil and India*, Hakluyt Society, 2nd series, 81 3–33 (London, 1937).

CAMPOS, ANTÓNIO PIRES DE: *Breve noticia que dá . . . do gentio bárbaro que ha na derrota da viagem das minas do Cuyabá e seu reconcavo . . .* (1727), RHGB 25 437–50, 1862.

CARDER, PETER: *The Relation of Peter Carder of Saint Verian in Cornwall* (c.1595), in Purchas, *Hakluytus Posthumus . . .*, Hakluyt Society ed., 16 136–50.

CARDIEL, JOSÉ, SJ: *Declaración de la verdad* (1750; Buenos Aires, 1800).

CARDIM, FERNÃO, SJ: *Do principio e origem dos Indios do Brasil e dos seus costumes, adoração e ceremonias.* First published, in English, in Purchas, *Hakluytus Posthumus . . .* (1625), Hakluyt Society ed., 4 1289–1329.

— *Tratados da terra e gente do Brasil* (1584), ed. Batista Caetano, João Capistrano de Abreu and Rodolfo Garcia (São Paulo, 1939), contains *Do principio . . .*, together with: pp. 29–127, *Do clima e terra do Brasil e de algumas cousas notaveis que se acham assim na terra como no mar*; pp. 247–379, *Narrativa epistolar. Informação da missão do Padre Christóvão de Gouvêa às partes do Brasil* (c.1585).

CARVAJAL, GASPAR DE (Dominican): *Descubrimiento del Río de las Amazonas*, ed. José Toribio Medina (Seville, 1894); trans. Bertram T. Lee and ed. H. C. Heaton, *The Discovery of the Amazon* (New York, 1934).

— *Relación*, in Gonzalo Fernández de Oviedo, *Historia general y natural de las Indias* (Seville, 1535), bk 50, ch. 25.

CARVALHO, JACINTO DE, SJ: *Regimento e leys sobre as Missões do Maranhão e Pará, e sobre a liberdade dos indios* (Lisbon, 1724).

CASAL, MANOEL AYRES DO: *Chorographia Brasílica*, 2 vols (Rio de Janeiro, 1817); ed. Caio Prado, Jr, 2 vols (Rio de Janeiro, 1945).

CHARLEVOIX, P. F. J. DE: *Histoire du Paraguay*, 3 vols (Paris, 1756); trans. (London, 1769).

COELHO, DUARTE DE ALBUQUERQUE: *Memorias diarias de la guerra del Brasil* (Madrid, 1654).

COELHO, FELIPPE JOSÉ NOGUEIRA: 'Memorias chronologicas da Capitania de Mato-Grosso (1718–1779), RHGB 13 137–99, 1850.

COUTO, DOMINGOS DO LORETO: *Desagravos do Brasil e glórias de Pernambuco* (1757), ABNRJ 24, 1902.

CUNHA, JACINTHO RODRIGUES DA: *Diario da expedição de Gomes Freire de Andrade ás Missões do Uruguay* (1756), RHGB 16 139–328, 1853.

DANIEL, JOÃO, SJ: *Thesouro descoberto no maximo rio Amazonas*, RHGB 2, 3, 41, 1840–1, 1878.

DOMINGUES, PERO, SJ: *Relação dada pelo mesmo sobre viagem que de S. Paulo fez ao rio de São Francisco, chamado também Pará*, in Leite, *Páginas de história do Brasil* (1937) 113–16.

— *Informação da entrada que se pode fazer da Vila de S. Paulo ao Grande Pará . . .* (1613), in Leite, *Páginas de história do Brasil* (1937) 103–10.

DRUSSEN, ADRIAEN VAN DER: *Relatório sôbre as capitanias conquistadas no Brasil pelos Holandeses* (1639), trans. António Gonsalves de Mello, Neto (Rio de Janeiro, 1947).

DURÃO, FREI JOSÉ DE SANTA RITA: *Caramuru* (Lisbon, 1781), ed. Francisco Adolfo de Varnhagen (Rio de Janeiro/Paris, n.d.).

D'ÉVREUX, YVES (Capuchin): *Voyage dans le nord du Brésil, fait durant les années 1613 et 1614*, ed. Ferdinand Denis (Leipzig/Paris, 1864).

— *Suite de l'histoire des choses plus mémorables advenues en Maragnan, en années 1613 et 1614* (Paris, 1615).

FERREIRA, ALEXANDRE RODRIGUES: *Diario da viagem philosophica pela capitania de São-José do Rio Negro* (1786), RHGB **48** pt 1, 1–234, **49** pt 1, 123–288, **50** pt 2, 11–142, **51** pt 1, 5–104, 1885–8 ed. Edgard de Cerqueira, 2 vols (São Paulo, 1970).

FERREIRA, JOÃO DE SOUSA: *America abreviada, suas noticias e de seus naturaes, e em particular do Maranhão* . . . (1686), RHGB **57** pt 1, 5–153, 1894.

— *Noticiario Maranhense*, RHGB **81** 289–352, 1917.

FIGUEIRA, LUÍS, SJ: *Informação* (about Ceará and Ibiapaba), Bahia, 26 March 1609, DHBC **1** 1–42, 1908.

— *Relação de algumas cousas tocantes ao Maranhão e Gram Pará* (Lisbon, 1637); RHGB **94** (148) 423–32, 1927; DHBC **2** 245–53, 1909.

FONSECA, BENTO DA: *Noticia do governo temporal dos índios do Maranhão* . . . (1755), in A. J. de Mello Moraes, *Corographia historica* . . . *do Imperio do Brasil* (Rio de Janeiro, 1860) **4** 122–86.

FONSECA, FELIS FELICIANO DA: *Relação do que aconteceu aos demarcadores portuguezes e castellanos no sertão das terras da Colonia, opposição que os indios lhe fizeram* . . ., RHGB **23** 407–11, 1860.

FONSECA, JOSÉ GONÇALVES DA: *Primeira exploração dos rios Madeira e Guaporé em 1749 por ordem do governo*, in Cândido Mendes de Almeida, *Memorias para a historia do extincto Estado do Maranhão* (Rio de Janeiro, 1860) **2** 267–416.

FREYRE, BRITO: *Nova Lusitania, Historia da Guerra Brasilica* (Lisbon, 1675).

FRITZ, SAMUEL, SJ: *Missión de los Omaguas, Jurimaguas, Aysuares, Ibanomas, y otras naciones desde Napo hasta el Rio Negro;* trans. George Edmundson, *Journal of the Travels and Labours of Father Samuel Fritz in the River of the Amazons between 1686 and 1723*, Hakluyt Society, 2nd series, **51**, 1922.

FURTADO, FRANCISCO XAVIER DE MENDONÇA: *Diario da viagem que o Ilmo e Exmo Sr Francisco Xavier de Mendonça Furtado* . . . *fez para o rio Negro à expedição das demarcações dos reais domínios de Sua Majestade* (1755), AEP **2** 615–31 (Rio de Janeiro, 1963).

GAMA, BASÍLIO DA: *O Uraguai* (Lisbon, 1769; Rio de Janeiro, 1941).

GANDAVO, PERO DE MAGALHÃES: *Historia da Provincia de Santa Cruz* (Lisbon, 1576) and *Tratado da terra do Brasil* (1576); both works ed. Rodolfo Garcia and João Capistrano de Abreu (Rio de Janeiro, 1924); trans. John B. Stetson, the Cortés Society, 2 vols (New York, 1922).

— *Tratado da provincia do Brasil*, ed. Emmanuel Pereira Filho (Rio de Janeiro, 1965).

GOIS, DAMIÃO DE: *Crónica do felicíssimo Rei D. Manuel* (1566), 2 vols (Coimbra, 1949–54).

GONNEVILLE, BINOT PAULMIER DE: *Campagne du navie l'Espoir de Honfleur, 1503–1505*, in Armand d'Avezac, 'Relation authentique du voyage du capitaine de Gonneville', extract from *Annales des voyages* (Paris, June–July 1869); also *Mémoire touchant l'établissement d'une mission chrestienne* . . .

(Paris, 1663), in Ch. A. Julien, *Les Français en Amérique* . . . (Paris, 1946).

GUERREIRO, FERNÃO, SJ: *Relação annual dos padres da Companhia de Jesus* (Lisbon, 1605); excerpts about Brazil in Cândido Mendes de Almeida, *Memorias para a historia do extincto Estado do Maranhão*, 2 vols (Rio de Janeiro, 1860), 2 502–56.

HAKLUYT, RICHARD: *The Principall Navigations, Voyages and Discoveries of the English Nation made by Sea or over Land to the most remote and farthest distant quarters of the earth, at any time within the compass of these 1500 years* (London, 1589), Everyman's Library 338, 8 vols (London, 1907; reissued 1962).

HERCKMANS, ELIAS: *Generale Beschrijvinge vande Capitanie Paraiba* (1639), trans. *Revista do Instituto Archeologico e Geographico Pernambucano*, 5 no. 31, 239–88 (Recife, 1886).

IBÁÑEZ DE ECHÁVARRI, BERNARDO: *Reino jesuítico de Paraguay* (Madrid, 1770).

— *La causa jesuítica de Portugal* (Madrid, 1768).

— *Histoire du Paraguay sous les Jésuites* (Amsterdam, 1780).

JABOATAM, ANTONIO DE SANTA MARIA: *Novo Orbe Serafico Brasilico, ou Chronica dos Frades Menores da Provincia do Brasil. Parte primeiro, preambulo* (Lisbon, 1791); 2 vols (Rio de Janeiro, 1859).

— *Catálogo genalógico das principaes familias procedentes de Albuquerque e Cavalcantes em Pernambuco, e Caramurús na Bahia*, RHGB 52 pt 1, 5–489, 1889.

JARQUE, FRANCISCO, SJ: *Ruiz Montoya en Indias: Vida prodigiosa del V.P. Jesuita Antonio Ruiz Montoya* (Madrid, 1662).

— *Insignes missionarios* (Madrid, 1687).

JESUITS: *Cartas avulsas de Jesuítas (1550–1568)*, ed. Afrânio Peixoto and Alfred do Vale Cabral (Rio de Janeiro, 1931). (=CA)

— *Cartas Jesuiticas*, ed. Alfred do Vale Cabral, 3 vols (Rio de Janeiro, 1931).

— *Cartas dos primeiros Jesuítas do Brasil*, ed. Serafim Soares Leite, SJ, 3 vols (São Paulo, 1934). (=CPJB)

— *Novas cartas Jesuítas (de Nóbrega a Vieira)*, ed. Serafim Soares Leite, SJ (São Paulo, 1940).

JONGE, GEDEON MORRIS DE: *Relatorios e cartas no tempo do dominio holandes no Brasil*, RHGB 58 pt 1, 237–320, 1895.

KNIVET, ANTHONY: *The Admirable Adventures and Strange Fortunes of Master Antonie Knivet, which went with Master Thomas Candish on his Second Voyage to the South Seas* (1591), in Purchas, *Hakluytus Posthumus* . . ., pt 2, bk 6, ch.7, Hakluyt Society ed., 16 177–289.

LA CONDAMINE, CHARLES MARIE DE: *Relation abrégée d'un voyage fait dans l'intérieur de l'Amérique Méridionale* (Paris, 1745).

LAET, JOANNES DE: *Novus Orbis, seu descriptionis Indiae Occidentalis* (Leyden, 1633); *Histoire du Nouveau Monde* (Leyden, 1640).

— *Historie ofte Iaerlick Verhael van de Verrichtinghen der Geotroyeerde West-Indische Compagnie* (Leyden, 1644); trans. José Hygino Duarte Pereira and Pero Souto Maior, ABNRJ 30, 1908; 33, 1911; 38, 1916; 41–2, 1919–20.

LÉRY, JEAN DE: *Histoire d'un voyage faict en la Terre du Brésil, autrement dite Amérique*, ed. Paul Gaffarel, 2 vols (Paris, 1880).

— *Le Voyage au Brésil de Jean de Léry, 1556–1558* (La Rochelle, 1578); ed. Charly

Clerc (Paris, 1927); trans. Purchas, *Hakluytus Posthumus* . . ., Hakluyt Society ed., **16** 518–79.

LOZANO, PEDRO, SJ: *Historia de la Conquista del Paraguay, Rio de la Plata y Tucumán* (1754–5), ed. Andrés Lamas, 5 vols (Buenos Aires, 1873–5).

LUÍS, AFONSO: *Naufrágio que passou Jorge d'Albuquerque Coelho, Captão e Governador de Paranambuco (c.* 1580–90), in *História Trágico-Marítima,* ed. Bernard Gomes de Brito, 2 vols (Lisbon, 1735–6); trans. C. R. Boxer, *Further Selections from the Tragic History of the Sea, 1559–1565,* Hakluyt Society, 2nd series, **132** 108–57, 1967.

MACIEL PARENTE, BENTO: *Memorial para conservar y augmentar la conquista y tierra del Marañón,* in Cândido Mendes de Almeida (ed.), *Memórias para a história do extincto Estado do Maranhão* **2** (Rio de Janeiro, 1874).

MADRE DE DEUS, GASPAR DA (Benedictine): *Memórias para a história da Capitania de S. Vicente, hoje chamada de S. Paulo e notícias dos anos em que se descobriu o Brasil* (Lisbon, 1797), ed. Afonso de Escragnolle Taunay (São Paulo/Rio de Janeiro, 1920).

MALDONADO, MIGUEL AYRES: *Descripção* . . . *dos trabalhos e fadigas das suas vidas, que tiveram nas conquistas da Capitania do Rio de Janeiro e São-Vicente com a gentildade e com os piratas n'esta costa* (Rio de Janeiro, 1661), RHGB **56** pt 1, 345–400, 1893.

MARANHÃO: *Livro grosso do Maranhão,* ed. Artur César Ferreira Reis, 2 vols, ABNRJ **66–7**, 1948. (=LGM)

MARCGRAF DE LIEBSTAD, GEORG, and PISO, GULIELMUS: *Historia Naturalis Brasiliae,* ed. Johannes de Laet (Amsterdam/Leiden, 1648); trans. José Procopio de Magalhães (São Paulo, 1942).

MASCARANHAS, JOSEPH FREYRE DE MONTERROYO: *Os Orizes conquistados (c.*1715), RHGB **8** 494–512, 1846.

MENDES, FRANCISCO, OFM: *Carta* . . . *sobre las costumbres, religion, terreno y tradiciones de los Yndios Mbayás, Guanás y demas naciones que ocupan la region boreal del Rio Paraguay* (1772), in Jaime Cortesão, *Do Tratado de Madri à conquista dos Sete Povos* (Rio de Janeiro, 1969) 53–69.

MENDONÇA, HEITOR FURTADO DE: *Primeira visitação do Santo Officio ás Partes do Brasil: Confisões de Bahia, 1591–92,* ed. João Capistrano de Abreu (Rio de Janeiro, 1935).

MOCQUET, JEAN: *Voyages en Afrique, Asie, Indes Orientales et Occidentales* (Paris, 1616).

MONTALBODDO, FRACANZANO DA: *Paesi nuouamente retrouati. Et novo mundo da Alberigo Vesputio Florentino intitulado* (Vicenza, 1507).

MONTEIRO, JÁCOME, SJ: *Relação da Província do Brasil* (1610), in Leite, *História da Companhia de Jesus no Brasil* **8** 393–425 (Lisbon, 1949).

MORAES, FRANCISCO TEIXEIRA DE: *Relação historica e politica dos tumultos que succederam na cidade de S. Luiz do Maranhão* . . . (1692), RHGB **40** pt 1, 67–156, 303–410, 1877.

MORAES, P. JOSÉ DE, SJ: *História da Companhia de Jesus na extinta Província do Maranhão e Pará* (1758), in Cândido Mendes de Almeida, *Memórias para a história do extincto Estado do Maranhão* . . . 2 vols (Rio de Janeiro, 1860), 1;

also Antonio Henriques Leal, *Apontamentos para a historia dos Jesuitas no Brasil*, RHGB 36 pt 2, 101–48, 1873.

— *Memória sobre o Maranhão*, in A. J. de Mello Moraes, *Corografia historica* . . . *do Imperio do Brasil* (Rio de Janeiro, 1860).

MOREAU, PIERRE: *Histoire des derniers troubles du Brésil* (Paris, 1651).

MORENO, DIOGO DE CAMPOS: *Livro que da razão do Estado do Brasil* (1612), ed. Hélio Vianna (Recife, 1955); trans. Engel Sluiter, 'Report on the State of Brazil, 1612', HAHR 29 518–62.

— *Jornada do Maranhão por ordem de Sua Magestade feita no anno de 1614*, in Cândido Mendes de Almeida, *Memorias para a historia do extincto Estado do Maranhão*, 2 vols (Rio de Janeiro, 1860), 2 153–252.

MORRIS, GEDEON: 'Relatorios e cartas no tempo do dominio hollandez no Brasil', RHGB 58 pt 1, 237–320, 1895.

NANTES, MARTIN DE, OFM: *Relation succinte et sincère de la mission du Père Martin de Nantes, Prédicateur Capucin, missionaire apostolique dans le Brésil parmy les indiens appellés Cariris* (1671–88) (Quimper, *c.*1707); ed. F. G. Edelweiss (Salvador, Bahia, 1952).

NÓBREGA, MANOEL DA, SJ: *Cartas do Brasil, 1549–1560*, ed. Serafim Soares Leite, Alfred do Vale Cabral and Rodolfo Garcia (Rio de Janeiro, 1931).

— *Diálogo sôbre a conversão do gentio*, RHGB 43 pt 1, 133–52, 1880; *Cartas do Brasil* 209–45.

— *Informação das terras do Brasil* (possibly by Nóbrega), RHGB 6 91–4, 1844.

NORONHA, JOSÉ MONTEIRO DE: *Roteiro da viagem da cidade do Pará até as ultimas colonias do sertão da provincia* (Barcellos, 1768; Belém do Pará, 1862).

NUNES, PAULO DA SILVA: *Proposta da Camara do Pará a S.M. apresentada pelo Procurador do Estado, Paulo da Silva Nunes, em 1724*, in João Lúcio de Azevedo, *Os Jesuítas no Grão-Pará* 204–8.

NUSDORFER, BERNARDO, SJ: *Relación de todo lo sucedido en estas doctrinas en orden a las mudanzas de los 7 Pueblos del Uruguay* (1750–8), in Jaime Cortesão, *Do Tratado de Madri à conquista dos Sete Povos* (Rio de Janeiro, 1969) 139–300.

OLINDA, BISHOP OF: 'Informações sobre os indios barbaros dos certões de Pernambuco', RHGB 46 103–20, 1883.

PAES LEME, PERO TACQUES DE ALMEIDA: *História da Capitania de S. Vicente desde a sua fundação por Martim Afonso de Sousa* (1772), RHGB 9 137–78, 293–327, 445–75, 1847.

— 'Noticia historica da expulsão dos Jesuitas do collegio de S. Paulo', RHGB 12 5–41, 1849.

— 'Nobiliarchia Paulistana, genealogia das principaes familias de São Paulo', RHGB 32–5, 1869–72.

PAGAN, BLAISE FRANÇOIS, COMTE DE: *Relation historique et géographique de la grande rivière des Amazones* . . . *dans l'Amérique* (Paris, 1655); trans. William Hamilton, *An Historical and Geographical Description of the Great Country and River of the Amazons in America* (London, 1661).

PIGAFETTA, ANTONIO: *Primo viaggio intorno al mundo*. First published in French as *Le Voyage et navigation faicte par les Espaignolz ès Isles de Mollucques* . . . (Paris,

514 *Red Gold*

1522); trans. Lord Stanley of Alderly, Hakluyt Society, 52, 1874; R. A. Skelton, 2 vols (New Haven, Conn./London, 1969); Paula Spurlin Paige (Englewood Cliffs, NJ, 1969); James A. Robertson, 3 vols (Cleveland, Ohio, 1906).

PITTA, SEBASTIÃO DA ROCHA: *História da America Portugueza, desde o anno de 1500 do seu descobrimento até o de 1724* (Lisbon, 1730).

PIZARRO E ARAUJO, JOSÉ DE SOUSA DE AZEVEDO: *Memorias históricas da provincia do Rio de Janeiro* (1820–2), 9 vols (Rio de Janeiro, 1945–8).

PRADO, FRANCISCO RODRIGUES DO: *Historia dos indios Cavalleiros ou da nação Guaycurú* (1795), RHGB 1 21–44, 1839.

PRAZERES, FRANCISCO DE NOSSA SENHORA DOS: 'Poranduba Maranhense ou Relação historica da Provincia do Maranhão . . . até o anno de 1820', RHGB 54 pt 1, 9–184, 1891.

PYRARD DE LAVAL, FRANÇOIS: *Discours du voyage des français aux Indes Orientales . . .* (Paris, 1611); trans. Albert Gray, *The Voyage of François Pyrard de Laval to the East Indies*, 3 vols, Hakluyt Society (London, 1887–9).

PURCHAS, SAMUEL: *Hakluytus Posthumus or Purchas His Pilgrimes* (1625), Hakluyt Society, 20 vols (Glasgow, 1906).

RAMUSIO, GIOVANNI BATISTA: *Navigationi et Viaggi*, 3 vols (Venice, 1550–6).

RAPHAEL DE JESUS: *Castrioto Lusitano* (Lisbon, 1679).

REBELLO E SILVA, THOMAZ DA COSTA CORRÊA: *Memoria sobre a Provincia de Missões*, RHGB 2 157–71, 1840 (3rd ed., 1916).

RENDON, JOSÉ AROUCHE DE TOLEDO: *Memoria sôbre as aldeas de índios da provincia de São Paulo, segundo as observações feitas no anno de 1798*, RHGB 4 295–317, 1842.

— 'Oficio . . . para o Governador de São Paulo, Antonio Manuel de Melo Castro e Mendonça, São Paulo, 10 Nov 1802', CDSP 11 184–91.

RIBEIRO, FRANCISCO DE PAULA: *Roteiro da viagem que fez as fronteiras da Capitania do Maranhão e da de Goyaz no anno de 1815 . . .*, RHGB 10 5–80, 1848.

— *Memoria sobre as nações gentias que habitam o continente do Maranhão* (1819), RHGB 3 184–96, 297–321, 442–56, 1841.

— *Descripção do territorio dos Pastos Bons nos sertões do Maranhão*, RHGB 12 41–86, 1849.

ROLIM, ANTONIO (CONDE DE AZAMBUJA): *Relação da viagem que fez . . . da cidade de S. Paulo para a Villa de Cuyabá em 1751*, RHGB 7 449–74, 1845.

RÓSCIO, FRANCISCO JOÃO: *Breve noticia dos Sete Povos das Missões Guaranís, chamados communamente Tapes Orientaes ao Uruguay* (1802), RHGB 21 271–5, 1858.

RUIZ DE MONTOYA, ANTONIO, SJ. *Conquista espiritual hecha por los religiosos de la Compañía de Jesús en las provincias del Paraguay, Paraná, Uruguay y Tape* (Madrid, 1639); (together with Francisco Xarque, *Ruiz de Montoya en Indias*), Colección de libros españoles raros ó curiosos, 25 vols (Madrid, 1871–96), 16–19, 1890.

RUYER, CLAUDIO, SJ: *Relación de la guerra que tubieron los yndios contra los Portugueses del Brasil* (1641), in Jaime Cortesão. *Jesuítas e bandeirantes no Tape* (Rio de Janeiro, 1969) 345–68.

SÁ, JOSEPH BARBOSA DE: *Relação das povoaçõens do Cuyabá e Matto Grosso de seos principios thé os presentes tempos* (1775), ABNRJ 23 5–58, 1904.

Sá, Mem de: *Documentos relativos a Mem de Sá, governador geral do Brasil* (including his *Instrumento dos serviços*, 1570), ABNRJ 27 129–80, 1905.
— Will, 5 October 1569, HGB 1 445–51.
Saintonge, Jean Alphonse de: *Voyages aventureux* (1528; Poitiers, 1559).
Salvador, Vicente do, OFM: *Historia do Brasil* (1627), ed. João Capistrano de Abreu, ABNRJ 13 1–261, 1885–6; also São Paulo/Rio de Janeiro, 1931.
Sampaio, Francisco Xavier Ribeiro de: *Relação geographica historica do Rio Branco da America Portugueza*, RHGB 13 200–73, 1850.
— *Diario da viagem que em visita e correição das povoações da Capitania de S. Jorge do Rio Negro fez o Ouvidor e Tenente-geral da mesma, Francisco Xavier Ribeiro de Sampaio, no ano de 1774 e 1775* (Lisbon, 1825).
Sánchez Labrador, José, SJ: *El Paraguay católico, con sus principales provincias convertidas a la Santa Fé y vassallage del Rey de España por la predicación de los misioneros celosos de la Compañía de Jesus . . .* (1770), 3 vols (Buenos Aires, 1910–17).
Santa Maria, Agostinho de: *Santuario Mariano* (Lisbon, 1722).
Santiago, Diogo Lopes de: *Historia da guerra de Pernambuco e feitos memoraveis do Mestre de Campo João Fernandes Vieira* (1655), RHGB 38 pt 1, 249–336, 39 pt 1, 97–196, 1875–6.
São José Queiróz, Bishop João de: *Viagem e visita do sertão em o Bispado do Gram-Pará em 1762 e 1763*, RHGB 9 43–106, 179–226, 328–75, 476–526, 1847.
— *Visitas pastorais. Memorias (1761 e 1762–3)* (Rio de Janeiro, 1961).
São Paulo: *Livros de ordens regias* (extracts), RHGB 7 368–86, 1845.
— *Documentos interesantes para a historia e costumes de São Paulo*, 86 vols (São Paulo, 1894–1961). (=DI)
— *Atas da Cãmara da Vila de São Paulo* (Arquivo Publico Municipal de São Paulo, 1914–).
— *Registo geral da Câmara Municipal de São Paulo* (Arquivo Publico Municipal de São Paulo, 1917–).
— *Inventários e testamentos*, 5 vols (São Paulo, 1920).
Schmidel, Ulrich: *Warhaftige Historie einer wunderbaren Schiffart* (Frankfurt-am-Main, 1567); *Reise nach Süd-Amerika in den Jahren 1534 bis 1554* (Tübingen, 1889); ed. Hans Plischke (Graz, 1962); French trans., *Voyage curieux dans l'Amérique ou le Nouveau Monde* (Paris, 1837); trans. Luis L. Dominguez, *The Conquest of the River Plate, 1535–1555*, Hakluyt Society, 1st series, 81, 1889.
Sepp von Reinegg, Anton, SJ: *Viagem às missões Jesuíticas e trabalhos apostólicos* (Nürnberg, 1698); trans. A Reymundo Schneider (São Paulo, 1943); and a poor English translation by Awnsham Churchill, *A Collection of Voyages and Travels* (1732), 4 596–622.
Serra, Ricardo Franco de Almeida: *Parecer sobre o aldêamento dos índios uaicurús e guanás, com a descripção dos seus usos, religião, estabilidade e costumes* (1803), RHGB 7 196–204, 1845; 13 348–95, 1850.
— *Discripção geographica da Provincia de Matto Grosso* (1797), excerpt in RHGB 6 156–96, 1844.
— *Navegação do rio Tapajos para o Pará* (1799), RHGB 9 1–16, 1847.

SERRA, RICARDO FRANCO DE ALMEIDA: *Memoria . . . sobre a Capitania de Mato-Grosso, 31 de Janeiro de 1800*, RHGB 2 19–49, 1840.

SILVA E SOUSA, LUIZ ANTONIO DA: *Memoria sobre o descobrimiento, governo, população e cousas mais notaveis da Capitania de Goyaz* (1812), RHGB 12 429–510, 1849 (2nd ed., 1874).

SILVEIRA, SIMÃO ESTÁCIO DA: *Relação sumária das coisas do Maranhão* (Lisbon, 1624), in Cândido Mendes de Almeida, *Memórias para a história do extincto Estado do Maranhão*, 2 vols (Rio de Janeiro, 1860), 2.

SOARES, DIOGO, SJ: *Notícias práticas* (c. 1732; Évora, 1949).

SOUSA, GABRIEL SOARES DE: *Tratado descriptivo do Brasil em 1587*, ed. Francisco Adolfo Varnhagen, Brasiliana 117 (São Paulo, 1938).

— *Capítulos . . . contra os padres da Companhia de Jesus que residem no Brasil*, ABNRJ 62 337–81, 1940.

— *Derrotero general de la costa del Brasil y memorial de las grandezas de Bahia*, ed. Claudio Ganns (Madrid, 1958).

SOUSA, PERO LOPES DE: *Diario da navegação de Pero Lopes de Sousa* (1530–2), ed. Paulo Prado, 2 vols (Rio de Janeiro, 1927); RHGB 24 9–74, 1861; ed. Eugénio de Castro, 2 vols (Rio de Janeiro, 1940).

STADEN, HANS: *Wahrhaftige Historie und Beschreibung eyner Landtschafft der Wilden, Nacketen, Grimmigen, Menschfresser Leuten, in der Newen Welt America gelegen . . .* (Marburg, 1557); trans. Albert Tootal and Sir Richard F. Burton, Hakluyt Society, 1st series, 51, 1874; trans. Malcolm Letts (London, 1928); *Viagem ao Brasil*, trans. Alberto Löfgren (Rio de Janeiro, 1930).

TECHO, NICOLAU DEL, SJ: *Historia de la Provincia del Paraguay* (Liège, 1673).

TEIXEIRA, DOMINGOS: *Vida de Gomes Freire de Andrada* (Lisbon, 1727).

THEVET, ANDRÉ, OFM: *Les Singularitéz de la France Antarctique* (Paris, 1558), ed. Paul Gaffarel (Paris, 1878).

— *La Cosmographie universelle* (Paris, 1575), in *Les Français en Amérique pendant la deuxième moitié du XVIe siècle: Le Brésil et les brésiliens*, ed. Suzanne Lussagnet (Paris, 1953).

— *Histoire d'André Thevet Angoumoisin, Cosmographe du Roy, de deux voyages par lui faits aux Indes Australes, et Occidentales* (c. 1585), in *Les Français en Amérique* . . . , ed. Suzanne Lussagnet, 237–310.

VASCONCELLOS, SIMÃO DE, SJ: *Das cousas do Brasil*, and *Chronica da Companhia de Jesus do Estado do Brasil e do que obrarão seus filhos nesta parte do Novo Mundo* (Lisbon, 1663; Lisbon, 1865).

— *Vida do Veneravel Padre José de Anchieta* (Lisbon, 1672), ed. Serafim Soares Leite, 2 vols (Rio de Janeiro, 1943).

— *Noticias curiosas e necessarias sobre o Brasil* (Rio de Janeiro, 1824).

VAZ, LOPEZ: *A Discourse of the West Indies and South Sea* (1587), in Hakluyt, *Principall Navigations* 8 153–206.

VESPUCCI, AMERIGO: 'Mundus Novus' letter to Lorenzo di Pier Francesco de' Medici, 1503, published in fifteen editions in five languages between 1503 and 1507. Best known in Fracanzano da Montalboddo, *Paesi nuouamente retrouati* (Vicenza, 1507); RHGB 41 pt 1, 5–32, 1878.

— Letter to Pier Soderini (Gonfaloniere, or Prime Minister, of the Florentine

Republic), Lisbon, 4 Sept 1504, published by Paccini (Florence, 1505–6).

— Letters to Lorenzo di Pier Francesco de' Medici, unpublished until recently: 'Vagliente' letter, 18 July 1500; Cape Verde letter, 4 June 1501; 'Bartolozzi' letter, Lisbon, Sept or Oct 1502; 'Fragmentary' letter, Sept–Dec 1502.

— *Edición facsimilar de las cartas de Vespucio*, ed. Uribe White (Bogotá, 1942).

— *The Letters of Amerigo Vespucci*, ed. Sir Clements Markham, Hakluyt Society, 1894.

— *The Vespucci Reprints*, 5 vols (out of an intended 7 vols) (Princeton University Library, 1916).

VIEIRA, ANTÓNIO, SJ: *Sermoens do Padre António Vieira*, 14 vols (Lisbon, 1679–1710); ed. Gonçalo Alves, 15 vols (Pôrto, 1908).

— *Cartas do Padre António Vieira*, ed. João Lúcio de Azevedo, 3 vols (Coimbra, 1925–8).

— *Padre António Vieira: Obras escolhidas*, ed. António Sérgio and Hernâni Cidade, 12 vols (Lisbon, 1951–4). Vol. 5 deals with Indians and contains: pp. 1–20, *Parecer sobre a conversão e governo dos indios e gentios*; pp. 33–71, *Informação sobre o modo com que foram tomados e sentenciados por cativos os indios do ano de 1655*; pp. 72–135, *Relação da missão da Serra de Ibiapaba*; pp. 174–315, *Resposta aos capitulos que deu contra os religiosos da Companhia, em 1662, o Procurador do Maranhão Jorge de Sampaio*.

— *2,000 trechos selecionados*, ed. Mário Rotter Nunes (Rio de Janeiro, 1958).

WAGENER, ZACHARIAS: *Zoobiblion: Livro de animais do Brasil*, ed. Edgard de Cerqueira Falcão, Brasiliensia Documenta 4 (São Paulo, 1964).

MODERN AUTHORS

ABREU, JOÃO CAPISTRANO DE: *O descobrimento do Brasil* (1883; Rio de Janeiro, 1922).

— *Capítulos de história colonial* (Rio de Janeiro, 1907; 5th ed., Brasília, 1963).

— *Os caminhos antigos e o povoamento do Brasil* (1899; 5th ed., Brasília, 1963).

— *Primeira visitação do Santo Ofício às partes do Brasil* (São Paulo, 1922).

ALCÂNTARA MACHADO, JOSÉ DE: *Vida e morte do bandeirante* (São Paulo, 1930).

ALDEN, DAURIL: *Royal Government in Colonial Brazil* (Berkeley/Los Angeles, 1968).

— (ed.) *Colonial Roots of Modern Brazil* (Berkeley/Los Angeles, 1973).

— 'The Population of Brazil in the Late Eighteenth Century: a preliminary survey', HAHR 43 173–205, May 1963.

ALENCASTRE, J. M. PEREIRA DE: *Annaes da provincia de Goyaz*, RHGB 27 pt 2, 5–186, 229–349, 28 pt 1, 5–186, 229–50; 28 pt 2, 5–167, 1864–5.

ALMEIDA, CÂNDIDO MENDES DE: *Memorias para a historia do extincto Estado do Maranhão*, 2 vols (Rio de Janeiro, 1860).

ALMEIDA, EDUARDO DE CASTRO E: *Inventario dos documentos relativos ao Brasil existentes no Archivo de Marinha e Ultramar de Lisboa*, 3 vols, re Bahia (Rio de Janeiro, 1913–14).

D'AZEVEDO, JOÃO LÚCIO: *Os Jesuítas no Grão-Pará: suas missões e a colonização* (Coimbra, 1930).

— (ed.) *Cartas do Padre António Vieira*, 3 vols (Coimbra, 1925–8).

D'AZEVEDO, JOÃO LUCIO: *História de António Vieira, com fatos e documentos novos*, 2 vols (Lisbon, 1918–20).

— *O Marquez de Pombal e a sua época* (Lisbon, 1922).

AZEVEDO, THALES DE: 'A tuberculose no Brasil pre-cabralino', *Revista do Arquivo Municipal de São Paulo* 75 201–4 (São Paulo, 1941).

— 'Indios, brancos e pretos no Brasil colonial', AI 13 no. 2, 119–32, April 1953.

— *Ensaios de antropologia social* (Salvador, Bahia, 1959); contains: 'Aculturação dirigida', *Trabalhos de Antropologia e Etnologia* 17 491–512 (Pôrto, 1959).

BAIÃO, ANTÓNIO: 'O comércio do pau brasil', HCP 2 317–47, 1923.

BALDUS, HERBERT: *Bibliografia crítica da etnologia brasileira*, 2 vols (Hanover, 1968).

— *Bibliografia comentada da etnologia brasileira* (Rio de Janeiro, 1954).

BOGGIANI, GUIDO: *I Caduvei* (Rome, 1894); trans. Amadeu Amaral Júnior, *Os Caduveo*, ed. Herbert Baldus (São Paulo, 1945).

BOXER, CHARLES RALPH: *Salvador de Sá and the Struggle for Brazil and Angola, 1602–1686* (London, 1952).

— *The Dutch in Brazil, 1624–1654* (Oxford, 1957).

— *A Great Luso-Brazilian Figure, Padre António Vieira, SJ, 1608–1697* (London, 1957).

— *Race Relations in the Portuguese Colonial Empire, 1415–1825* (Oxford, 1963).

— *Um regimento inédito sobre o resgate dos Ameríndios no Estado do Maranhão em 1660* (Coimbra, 1965).

— *The Golden Age of Brazil, 1695–1750* (Berkeley/Los Angeles, 1969).

— *The Portuguese Seaborne Empire, 1415–1825* (London, 1969; Harmondsworth, 1973).

BURNS, E. BRADFORD: (ed.) *A Documentary History of Brazil* (New York, 1966).

CALASANS, JOSÉ: *Fernão Cabral de Ataide e a Santidade do Jaguaribe* (Salvador, Bahia, 1952).

CALMON, PEDRO: *Historia da civilização brasileira*, Brasiliana 14 (Rio de Janeiro, 1933).

— *Espírito da sociedade colonial*, Brasiliana 40 (São Paulo, 1935).

— *História do Brasil, 1500–1800*, 3 vols (São Paulo/Rio de Janeiro, 1939–43).

— *História social do Brasil*, 2nd ed., 2 vols (São Paulo, 1940).

— *História da Casa de Tôrre*, 2nd ed. (Rio de Janeiro, 1958).

CARAMAN, PHILIP: *Lost Paradise* (London, 1975).

CARDOZO, MANOEL: 'The Last Adventures of Fernão Dias Pais', HAHR 26, 1946.

— 'The Brazilian Gold Rush', *The Americas* 3, October 1946.

CARNEIRO, EDISON: *Guerras de los Palmares* (Mexico City, 1946).

CHIMARD, GILBERT: *L'Exotisme américaine dans la littérature française au XVIe siècle* (Paris, 1911).

— *L'Amérique et le rêve exotique dans la littérature française au XVIIe et au XVIIIe siècle* (Paris, 1934).

COHEN, J. M.: *Journeys down the Amazon* (London, 1975).

CORTESÃO, JAIME: *Manuscritos da Coleção De Angelis*:
    1. *Jesuítas e bandeirantes no Guairá (1594–1640)* (Rio de Janeiro, 1951).
    2. *Jesuítas e bandeirantes no Itatim (1596–1760)* (Rio de Janeiro, 1952).
    3. *Jesuítas e bandeirantes no Tape (1615–1641)* (Rio de Janeiro, 1969).

4. *Jesuítas e bandeirantes no Uruguai (1611–1758)*, ed. Hélio Vianna (Rio de Janeiro, 1970).

5. *Tratado de Madri. Antecedentes – Colônia do Sacramento (1669–1749)* (Rio de Janeiro, 1954).

6. *Antecedentes do Tratado de Madri. Jesuítas e bandeirantes no Paraguai (1703–1751)* (Rio de Janeiro, 1955).

7. *Do Tratado de Madri à conquista dos Sete Povos (1750–1802)* (Rio de Janeiro, 1969).

— *A carta de Pêro Vaz de Caminha* (Rio de Janeiro, 1943).

— *Alexandre de Gusmão e o Tratado de Madri*, 8 vols (Rio de Janeiro, 1950–9).

— *Rapôso Tavares e a formação territorial do Brasil* (Rio de Janeiro, 1958).

— 'A maior bandeira do maior bandeirante', RH **22** 3–27, 1961.

— *Introdução à história das bandeiras* (Lisbon, 1964).

COSTA, FRANCISCO AUGUSTO PEREIRA DA: *Anais Pernambucanos* (Recife, 1951).

CUNHA, EUCLIDES DA: *Os sertões* (Rio de Janeiro, 1902); trans. Samuel Putnam, *Rebellion in the Backlands* (Chicago, 1944).

DAVIDSON, DAVID M.: 'How the Brazilian West Was Won: freelance and State on the Mato Grosso frontier, 1737–1752', in *Colonial Roots of Modern Brazil*, ed. Dauril Alden, 61–106.

DENEVAN, WILLIAM M., 'The Aboriginal Population of Amazonia', in *The Native Population of the Americas in 1492*, ed. William Denevan (Madison, Wis., 1977).

DENIS, FERDINAND: (ed.) *Une Fête brésilienne célébrée à Rouen en 1550* (Paris, 1851).

DIAS, CARLOS MALHEIRO: (ed.) *História da colonização portuguesa do Brasil*, 3 vols (Pôrto, 1924–6). (=HCP)

— 'O regímen feudal das donatárias', HCP **3** 219–83, 1926.

DIAS, MANOEL NUNES: 'As frotas do cacau da Amazônia', RH **24** 363–77, 1962.

— 'Fomento ultramarino e mercantilismo: a Companhia do Grão-Pará e Maranhão (1755–1778)', RH **32–41**, 1966–70.

— 'Colonização da Amazônia (1755–1778)', RH **34** 471–90, 1967.

DOMINIAN, HELEN G.: *Apostle of Brazil: the biography of Padre José de Anchieta, SJ, 1534–1597* (New York, 1958).

DOURADO, MECENAS: *A conversão do gentio* (Rio de Janeiro, 1958).

DRIVER, DAVID MILLER: *The Indian in Brazilian Literature* (New York, 1942).

DRUMOND, CARLOS: 'A carta de Diogo Nunes e a migração tupi-guaraní para o Perú', RH **1** 95–102, 1950.

ELLIS, ALFREDO, JR: *Populações paulistas*, Brasiliana **27** (São Paulo, 1935).

— *O bandeirismo paulista e o recúo do meridiano*, Brasiliana 36 (São Paulo, 1938).

FERNANDES, ANTONIO P. C.: *Missionários jesuítas no Brasil no tempo de Pombal* (Pôrto Alegre, 1941).

FERNANDES, FLORESTAN: *Aspectos do povoamento de São Paulo no século XVI* (São Paulo, 1948).

— 'A economia tupinambá', *Revista do Arquivo de São Paulo* **122** 7–77, 1949.

— 'A analise funcionalista da guerra: possibilidades de aplicação à sociedade tupinambá', RMP, n.s., **3** 7–128, 1949.

FERNANDES, FLORESTAN: 'Guerre et sacrifice humain chez les Tupinambá', JSAP, n.s., 40 139–220, 1952.
— *Organização social dos Tupinambá* (1948; São Paulo, 1963).
FREYRE, GILBERTO: *Casa-Grande e senzala. Formação da família brasileira sob o regime de economia patriarcal*, 4th ed., 2 vols (Rio de Janeiro, 1943); trans. Samuel Putnam, *The Masters and the Slaves: a study in the development of Brazilian civilization* (New York, 1946; 2nd ed., 1956).
FURLONG, GUILLERMO: *Misiones y sus pueblos de guaraníes* (Buenos Aires, 1962).
GAFFAREL, PAUL: *Histoire du Brésil français au seizième siècle* (Paris, 1878).
GAMA, FERNANDES: *Memórias históricas de Pernambuco* (Recife, 1844).
GARCIA, RODOLFO: (ed.) *Documentos Holandeses* (Rio de Janeiro, 1945).
GIL MUNILLA, LADISLÃO: *Descubrimiento del Marañón* (Seville, 1954).
GOIÁS: 'Subsidios para a historia da Capitania de Goyaz', RHGB 84 41–294, 1918.
GONÇALVES, MARIA DA CONCEIÇÃO OSORIO DIAS: 'O indio do Brasil na literatura portuguesa dos séculos XVI, XVII e XVIII', *Brasilia* 11 97–209 (Coimbra, 1961).
GONNARD, RENÉ: *La Légende du bon sauvage* (Paris, 1946).
GRAHAM, ROBERT BENTINE CUNNINGHAME: *A Vanished Arcadia, being some account of the Jesuits in Paraguay, 1607 to 1767* (London, 1901).
GWYNN, AUBREY, SJ: 'An Irish Settlement on the Amazon, 1604–1668', *Proceedings of the Royal Irish Academy*, Section C 41, 1932–4.
HAMY, E.-T.: 'Les Indiens de Rasilly: étude iconographique et etnographique', JSAP 5, 1908.
HAUBERT, MAXIME: *L'Église et la défense des sauvages: le Père Antoine Vieira au Brésil* (Brussels, 1964).
HERNÁNDEZ, PABLO: *Missiones del Paraguay: Organización social de las doctrinas guaraníes de la Compañía de Jesús*, 2 vols (Barcelona, 1913).
HOHENTHAL, W. D., JR: 'As tribus indígenas do médio e baixo São Francisco', RMP, n.s., 12 37–86, 1960.
HOLANDA, SÉRGIO BUARQUE DE: *Monções* (Rio de Janeiro, 1945).
— *Raízes do Brasil* (Rio de Janeiro, 1948).
— *Expansão paulista em fins do século XVI e principios do XVII* (São Paulo, 1948).
— 'Índios e mamelucos na expansão paulista', AMP 13 177–290, 1949.
— *Caminhos e fronteiras* (Rio de Janeiro, 1957).
— (ed.) *História geral da civilização brasileira*, 2 vols (São Paulo, 1960).
— *Visão do paraíso: os motivos edénicos no descobrimento e colonização do Brasil* Brasiliana 333 (São Paulo, 1969).
JACOBSEN, JEROME V.: 'Nóbrega of Brazil', *Mid-America* 24 151–87 (Chicago, July 1942).
— 'Fernão Cardim: Jesuit humanist of colonial Brazil', *Mid-America* 24 252–7 (Chicago, October 1942).
— 'José de Anchieta, "Apostle of Brazil"', *Mid-America* 26 40–61 (Chicago, January 1944).
JULIEN, ANDRÉ: *Les Voyages de découverte et les premiers établissements* (Paris, 1948).
— *Les Français en Amérique pendant la première moitié du XVIe siècle* (Paris, 1946).

KIEMAN, MATHIAS C., OFM: 'The Indian Policy of Portugal in America, with special reference to the Old State of Maranhão 1500–1755', *The Americas* 5 no. 4, 131–71, 439–60, April 1949.

— *The Indian Policy of Portugal in the Amazon Region, 1614–1693* (Washington, DC, 1954).

LATHRAP, DONALD W.: *The Upper Amazon* (London, 1970).

LEAL, ANTONIO HENRIQUES: 'Apontamentos para a historia dos Jesuitas extrahidos dos chronistas da Companhia de Jesus', RHGB 34 pt 2–36 pt 2, 1871–3.

LEITE, SERAFIM SOARES, SJ: *História da Companhia de Jesus no Brasil*, 10 vols (Lisbon/Rio de Janeiro, 1938–50). (= HCJB)

— *Páginas de história do Brasil*, Brasilians 93 (São Paulo, 1937).

— *Luís Figueira. A sua vida heróica e a sua obra literária* (Lisbon, 1940).

— *Novas cartas Jesuítas (de Nóbrega a Vieira)* (São Paulo, 1940).

— *Cartas do Brasil e mais escritos do P. Manuel da Nóbrega (Opera omnia)* (Coimbra, 1955).

— (ed.) *Cartas dos primeiros Jesuítas do Brasil*, 3 vols (São Paulo, 1954–8): these three volumes, plus a fourth volume, also published as *Monumenta Brasiliae* (*Monumenta Historica Societatis Iesu* 79–81, 87) (Rome, 1956–60).

— *Suma histórica da Companhia de Jesus no Brasil (Assistência de Portugal) 1549–1760* (Lisbon, 1965).

— *Novas páginas de história do Brasil*, Brasiliana 324 (São Paulo, 1965).

LEVERGER, AUGUSTO (BARÃO DE MELGAÇO): *Apontamentos cronológicos da Província de Mato Grosso* (1856), RHGB 205 208–385, October–December 1949.

— *Roteiro da navegação do rio Paraguay desde a foz do São Lourenço até o Paraná*, RHGB 25 221–84, 1862.

LÉVI-STRAUSS, CLAUDE: *Tristes tropiques* (Paris, 1955); trans. John Russell, *A World on the Wane* (London, 1961); trans. John and Doreen Weightman (London, 1973).

— 'The Use of Wild Plants in Tropical South America', HSAI 6 465–86.

LEVILLIER, ROBERTO: *América la bien llamada*, 2 vols (Buenos Aires, 1948).

— *Amerigo Vespucci – El Nuevo Mundo – Cartas relativas a sus viajes y descubrimientos: textos en Italiano, Español y Ingles* (Buenos Aires, 1951).

— *Amerigo Vespucci* (Madrid, 1966).

— *El Paititi, El Dorado y las Amazonas* (Buenos Aires, 1976).

LINS, IVAN: *Aspectos do Padre António Vieira* (Rio de Janeiro, 1956).

LUNA, LUIS: *Resistência do índio à dominação do Brasil* (Rio de Janeiro, 1965).

MACLACHLAN, COLIN M.: 'The Indian Labor Structure in the Portuguese Amazon, 1700–1800', in *Colonial Roots of Modern Brazil*, ed. Dauril Alden, 199–230.

MADUREIRA, J. M. DE, SJ: 'A liberdade dos índios e a Companhia de Jesus', RHGB, Primeiro Congresso de Historia, Tomo Especial, 4 1–164 (Rio de Janeiro, 1927).

MAGALHAES, BASÍLIO DE: 'A conquista do Nordeste no seculo XVII', RHGB 85 287–310, 1919.

— *Expansão geographica do Brasil colonial*, Brasiliana 45 (Rio de Janeiro, 1935).

MALHEIRO, AGOSTINHO MARQUES PERDIGÃO: *A escravidão no Brasil*, pt 2, *Indios* (Rio de Janeiro, 1867).

MARCHANT, ALEXANDER NELSON DE ARMAND: *From Barter to Slavery* (Baltimore, 1942); trans. *Do escambo a escravidão* (São Paulo, 1943).

— 'Feudal and Capitalistic Elements in the Portuguese Settlement of Brazil', HAHR 22 no. 3, August 1942.

MARTIUS, CARL FRIEDRICH PHILIP VON: *Beiträge zur Etnographie und Sprachenkunde Amerikas zumal Brasiliens*, 2 vols (Leipzig, 1863–7).

MASON, J. ALDEN: 'The Languages of South American Indians', HSAI 6 157–317.

MATTOS, RAYMUNDO JOSÉ DA CUNHA: 'Chorographia historica da provincia de Goyaz', RHGB 37 pt 1, 213–398; 38 pt 1, 5–150, 1874–5.

MAYBURY-LEWIS, DAVID: 'Some Crucial Distinctions in Central Brazilian Ethnology', *Anthropos* 60 340–58 (St Augustin, Germany, 1965).

MEDINA, JOSÉ TORIBIO: *The Discovery of the Amazon* (New York, 1934).

MELLO, JOSÉ ANTÓNIO GONÇALVES DE, NETO: *Tempo dos Flamengos: influência da occupação holandesa na vida e na cultura do norte do Brasil* (Rio de Janeiro, 1947).

— *D. Antonio Filipe Camarão* (Recife, 1954).

— *Confissões de Pernambuco, 1594–1595: primeira visitação do Santo Ofício às partes do Brasil* (Recife, 1970).

MELLO FRANCO, AFONSO ARINOS DE: *O índio brasileiro e a Revolução Francesa* (Rio de Janeiro, 1937).

MELLO MORAES, ALEXANDRE J. DE: *Corografia historica, cronografica, genealogica nobiliaria e politica do Império do Brasil*, 4 vols (Rio de Janeiro, 1872).

— *História dos Jesuitas e suas missões na América do Sul* (Rio de Janeiro, 1872).

MELO-LEITÃO, C. DE: *História das expedições cientificas no Brasil* (São Paulo, 1941).

MENDONÇA, MARCOS CARNEIRO DE: *O Marques de Pombal e o Brasil*, Brasiliana 299 (São Paulo, 1960).

— (ed.) *A Amazônia na era pombalina, 1751–59*, 3 vols (Rio de Janeiro, 1963). (=AEP)

MÉTRAUX, ALFRED: 'Les Migrations historiques des Tupí-Guaraní', JSAP 19 1–45, 1927.

— *La Civilisation matérielle des tribus Tupi-Guaraní* (Paris, 1928).

— *La Religion des Tupinambá et ses rapports avec celle des autres tribus Tupi-Guaraní* (Paris, 1928).

— 'Les Indiens Waitaka', JSAP 21 107–26, 1929.

— 'Un Chapitre inédit du cosmographe André Thevet sur la géographie et l'ethnographie du Brésil', JSAP 25 31–40, 1933.

— 'Le Caractère de la conquête jésuitique', *Acta Americana* 1 no. 1 (Mexico City, 1943).

— 'The Caingang', HSAI 1 445–76, 1948.

— 'The Puri-Coroado Linguistic Family', HSAI 1 523–30, 1948.

— 'The Botocudo', HSAI 1 531–40.

— 'The Paressi', HSAI 3 349–60.

— 'The Guaraní', HSAI 3 69–94.

— 'The Tupinambá', HSAI 3 95–133.

— 'Tribes of the Middle and Upper Amazon River', HSAI 3 687–712.

MOLLAT, MICHEL: 'As primeiras relações entre a França e o Brasil: dos Verrazani a Villegagnon', RH 34 343–58, 1967.

MOOG, CLODOMIR VIANNA: Bandeirantes e pioneiros (Rio de Janeiro, 1954); trans. L. L. Barrett, Bandeirantes and Pioneers (New York, 1964).

— O ciclo do ouro negro: impressões da Amazônia (Pôrto Alegre, 1936).

MORISON, SAMUEL ELIOT: Portuguese Voyages to America in the 15th Century (Cambridge, Mass., 1940).

— The European Discovery of America. The Southern Voyages, 1492–1616 (New York, 1974).

MÖRNER, MAGNUS: The Expulsion of the Jesuits from Latin America (New York, 1965).

— The Political and Economic Activities of the Jesuits in the La Plata Region. The Habsburg Era (Stockholm, 1953).

— 'Os Jesuítas espanhois, as suas missões Guaraní e a rivalidade luso-espanhola pela Banda Oriental, 1715–1737', Revista Portuguesa de História 9 (Coimbra, 1960).

MORSE, RICHARD M.: The Bandeirantes: the historical role of the Brazilian pathfinders (New York, 1965).

NABUCO, JOAQUIM: Limites entre le Brésil et la Guyane Anglaise. Annexes du premier mémoire du Brésil: documents d'origine portuguaise (Rio de Janeiro, 1903).

NASH, ROY: The Conquest of Brazil (New York, 1926); trans. Moacyr N. N. Vasconcellos, A conquista do Brasil (São Paulo/Rio de Janeiro, 1939).

NIMUENDAJÚ (UNKEL), CURT: 'Os índios Parintintín do Rio Madeira', JSAP, n.s., 16 201–78, 1924.

— 'As tribos do alto Madeira', JSAP, n.s., 17 137–72, 1925.

— 'Idiomas indígenas do Brasil', Revista del Instituto de Etnología 2 543–618 (Tucumán, Argentina, 1932).

— Mapa etno-histórico do Brasil e regiões adjacentes (Belém, 1934).

— 'Tribes of the Lower and Middle Xingu River', HSAI 3 213–43.

— 'The Maué and Arapium', HSAI 3 245–54.

— 'The Mura and Pirahá', HSAI 3 255–69.

— 'The Cawahíb, Parintintín and Their Neighbours', HSAI 3 283–97.

— 'The Tucuna', HSAI 3 713–25.

— The Tukuna, trans. William D. Hohenthal, University of California Publications in American Archaeology and Ethnology 45 (Berkeley/Los Angeles, 1952).

— 'Apontamentos sôbre os Guaraní', trans. Egon Schaden, RMP, n.s., 8 9–57, 1954.

NORDENSKIÖLD, ERLAND: 'The Geographical Invasions of the Inca Empire in the Sixteenth Century: an historical Indian migration', The Geographical Review (New York, 1917).

NOWELL, CHARLES E.: 'Aleixo Garcia and the White King', HAHR 26 450–66, 1946.

OLIVEIRA, L. HUMBERTO DE: Coletânea de leis, atos e memorias referentes ao indígena brasileiro (Rio de Janeiro, 1952).

OLIVEIRA, JOSÉ DE ALCÁNTARA MACHADO DE: *Vida e morte do bandeirante* (São Paulo, 1965).

OLIVEIRA, JOSÉ JOAQUIM MACHADO DE: 'Noticia raciocinada sobre as aldêas de indios da provincia de São Paulo', RHGB 8 204–53, 1846.

— 'Os Cayapós', RHGB 24 491–524, 1861.

— 'Notas, apontamentos e noticias para a historia da provincia do Espírito Santo', RHGB 19 161–335, 1856.

OTÁVIO, RODRIGO: *Os selvagens americanos perante o direito*, Brasiliana 254 (São Paulo, 1946).

PASTELLS, PABLO, SJ : *Historia de la Compañía de Jesús en la Provincia del Paraguay*, 8 vols (Madrid, 1912–59).

PEIXOTO, AFRÂNIO: *Martim Soares Moreno* (Lisbon, 1940).

PEREIRA, AMBROSIO: *Anchieta, apóstol del Brasil y taumaturgo de América* (Caracas, 1968).

PINHEIRO, J. C. FERNANDES: 'D. Antonio Filippe Camarão', RHGB 32 201–8, 1869.

PINTO, ESTÊVÃO: 'Introdução à história da antropologia indígena no Brasil (século xvi)', AI 17 no. 4, 341–85; 18 no. 1, 18–49 (October 1957–January 1958).

— *Os indígenas do nordeste*, 2 vols, Brasiliana 44, 112 (São Paulo, 1935–8).

POHL, FREDERICK J.: *Amerigo Vespucci, Pilot Major* (New York, 1944).

PORTO, AURÉLIO: *História das missões orientais do Uruguai* (Rio de Janeiro, 1943).

PRADO, CAIO, JR: *Formação do Brasil contemporâneo. Colônia*, 4th ed. (São Paulo, 1963); trans. Suzette Macedo, *The Colonial Background of Modern Brazil* (Berkeley, 1967).

PRADO, JOÃO FERNANDO DE ALMEIDA: *Historia da formação da sociedade brasileira: Primeiros povoadores do Brasil (1500–1530)*, Brasiliana 37 (São Paulo, 1935).

Pernambuco e as capitanias do Nordeste do Brasil, 4 vols (São Paulo, 1941).

Bahia e as capitanias do centro do Brasil (1530–1626), Brasiliana 247, 3 vols (São Paulo, 1945–50).

São Vicente e as capitanias do Sul de Brasil: As origens (1501–1531), Brasiliana 314 (São Paulo, 1961).

A conquista da Paraíba, Brasiliana 321 (São Paulo, 1964).

QUINTILIANO, AYLTON: *A guerra das Tamoios* (Rio de Janeiro, 1965).

RAMOS, ARTHUR: *Introdução à antropologia brasileira: As culturas indígenas* (Rio de Janeiro, 1971).

RAU, VIRGINIA and GOMES DA SILVA, MARIA FERNANDA: (ed.) *Os manuscritos do arquivo da Casa de Cadaval respeitantes ao Brasil*, 2 vols (Coimbra, 1956–8). (= MACC)

REIS, ARTUR CÉSAR FERREIRA: 'As origens históricas dos Parintintíns', *IX Congresso Brasileiro de Geografia, Anais* 5 (Rio de Janeiro, 1945).

— 'Paulistas na Amazônia e outros ensaios', RHGB 175 233–48, 315–29, 1941.

— *Limites e demarcações na Amazônia brasileira*, 2 vols (Rio de Janeiro, 1947–8).

— *A Amazônia que os Portugueses revelaram* (Rio de Janeiro, 1957).

— *A expansão portuguêsa na Amazônia nos séculos XVII e XVIII* (Rio de Janeiro, 1959).

— *Aspectos economicos da dominação lusitana na Amazônia* (Rio de Janeiro, 1960).

— *A colonização européia nos trópicos* (Manaus, 1966).

— *Roteiro histórico das fortificações no Amazonas* (Manaus, 1966).

REVERDIN, OLIVIER: *Quatorze Calvinistes chez les Tupinambas: histoire d'une mission genevoise au Brésil, 1556–1558* (Geneva, 1951).

RICARDO, CASSIANO: *Marcha para Oeste* (Rio de Janeiro, 1939).

— *O indianismo de Gonçalves Dias* (São Paulo, 1964).

RIBEIRO, SYLVIO SALEMA GARÇÃO: *Um bárbaro e cruel da história do Brasil* (Rio de Janeiro, 1960).

RIVASSEAU, EMILIO: *A vida dos índios Guaicurus*, Brasiliana **160** (São Paulo, 1941).

ROMAG, DAGOBERTO, OFM: *História dos Franciscanos do Brasil* (Curitiba, 1940).

RÖWER, BASÍLIO, OFM: *Páginas de história franciscana no Brasil* (Petrópolis, 1941).

SAMPAIO, THEODORO: *Os naturalistas viajantes e a etnografia indígena* (Salvador, 1951).

SANMARTIN, OLYNTHE: *Bandeirantes no sul do Brasil* (Pôrto Alegre, 1949).

SARAIVA, A. J.: 'Le Père António Vieira, SJ, et la liberté des Indiens', *Travaux de l'Institut d'Études Latino-Américaines de l'Université de Strasbourg,* **3** 85–118 (Strasbourg, 1963).

SCHADEN, EGON: 'O estudo do índio brasileiro: ontem e hoje', RH **5** 385–401, October–December 1952; AI **14** no. 3, 233–52, 1954.

— 'Os primitivos habitantes do território paulista', RH **8** 385–406, 1954.

— *Aspectos fundamentais da cultura Guaraní* (São Paulo, 1954).

— *Aculturação indígena* (São Paulo, 1969).

SILVA, JOAQUIM NOBERTO DE SOUSA: *Memoria historica e documentada das aldêas de indios da provincia do Rio de Janeiro*, RHGB **17** 71–532, 1854.

SILVA, JOSÉ JUSTINO DE ANDRADE E: *Collecão chronológica da legislação portuguesa, compilada e annotada*, 10 vols (Lisbon, 1854–9).

SIMONSEN, ROBERTO C.: *Historia economica do Brasil (1500–1820)* (1937), 3rd ed., Brasiliana, 5th series, **10** (São Paulo, 1957).

SIQUEIRA, JOAQUIM DA COSTA: 'Chronicas do Cuyabá', *Revista do Instituto Histórico a Geográfico de São Paulo,* **4** 4–217, 1898–9.

— *Compendio historico chronologico das noticias de Cuyabá . . .* (1778–1817), RHGB **13** 5–124, 1850.

SOUSA, LUIS ANTONIO DA SILVA E: 'Memoria sobre o descobrimento, governo, população e coisas mais notaveis da capitania de Goyaz', RHGB **12** 429–510, 1849.

SOUSA, TH. O. MARCONDES DE: *Amerigo Vespucci e suas viagens* (São Paulo, 1949).

— *O descobrimento do Brasil. Estudo crítico de acordo com a documentação histórico-cartográfica e a nautica* (São Paulo, 1946).

SOUTHEY, ROBERT: *History of Brazil*, 3 vols (London, 1810–19).

SOUTO MAIOR, PEDRO: *Fastos Pernambucanos* (Rio de Janeiro, 1913), RHGB **76**, 1913.

— 'Nos archivos de Hispanha', RHGB **81** 3–288, 1917.

— 'A arte hollandeza no Brasil', RHGB **83** 101–31, 1918.

SPALDING, WALTER: 'Borges do Canto, o conquistador das missões', RH **34** 165–71, 1967.

STUDART, BARÃO DE: (ed.) *Documentos para a historia do Brasil e especialmente a do Ceará*, 4 vols (Fortaleza, 1908–21). (=DHBC)
— *Documentos para a história de Martim Soares Moreno* (Fortaleza, 1905).
TAUNAY, AFONSO DE ESCRAGNOLLE: *História geral das bandeiras Paulistas*, 11 vols (São Paulo, 1924–50). (=HGBP)
— 'Documentos bandeirantes do Archivo General de Indias em Sevilha', *Annaes do Museu Paulista* 5 5–320 (São Paulo, 1931).
— *A Guerra dos Bárbaros* (separata from *Revista do Arquivo Municipal* 22, São Paulo, 1936).
— *História das bandeiras Paulistas*, 2 vols (São Paulo, 1953). (=HBP)
— *Relatos sertanistas* (São Paulo, 1953).
— *Relatos monçoeiros* (São Paulo, 1953).
THOMAS, GEORG: *Die portugiesische Indianerpolitik in Brasilien, 1500–1640* (Berlin, 1968).
VARNHAGEN, FRANCISCO ADOLFO DE, VISCONDE DE PÔRTO SEGURO: *História geral do Brasil antes da sua separação e independência de Portugal*, 5 vols (São Paulo, n.d., 3rd ed., São Paulo, 1927).
— 'O Caramuru perante a historia', RHGB **10** 109–52, 1848.
— 'Naturalidade de Dom Antonio Felippe Camarão', RHGB **30** pt 1, 501–8, 1867.
VERLINDEN, CHARLES: 'Paulmier de Gonneville e os índios do Brasil em 1504', RH **19** 3–17, 1959.
VIANNA, HÉLIO: *História do Brasil* (1961; 7th ed., São Paulo, 1970).
— *Matias de Albuquerque* (Rio de Janeiro, 1944).
— *Estudos de história colonial* (São Paulo, 1948).
— *História das fronteiras do Brasil* (Rio de Janeiro, 1948).
VIEIRA, HERMES: *Bandeiras e escravagismo no Brasil* (São Paulo, 1968).
WILLEKE, VENÂNCIO, OFM: 'Missão de São Miguel de Una', RH **39** 289–319, 1969.
— 'Frei Cristóvão de Lisboa, OFM, primeiro naturalista do Brasil', *Itinerarium* **17** no. 73, 402–25 (Braga, 1971).
WILLIAMSON, JAMES A.: *English Colonies in Guiana and on the Amazon, 1604–1668* (Oxford, 1923).

Notes and References

Chapter 1   NOBLE SAVAGES

2 *seed pearls.* Pero Vaz de Caminha to King Manoel I, Pôrto Seguro, 1 May 1500. There are many editions of this famous letter, including HCP 2 86–99 (Pôrto, 1923), and Jaime Cortesão, *A carta de Pêro Vaz de Caminha*; and translations by William Brooks Greenlee, *The Voyages of Pedro Alvares Cabral to Brazil and India* 81 3–33, and by Charles David Ley, *Portuguese Voyages 1498–1663* (New York, 1947) 42–59, excerpted in E. Bradford Burns (ed.), *A Documentary History of Brazil* 20–9.

2 *two sticks.'* Greenlee, *Voyages of Cabral* 26.

2 *kiss it.'* Ibid. 29.

2 *much edification.'* Ibid. 30.

3 *Few difficulties.'* Ibid. 29, and Ley in Burns, *Documentary History* 25.

3 *and slept.'* Ibid. 12–13; ibid. 23.

3 *become embarrassed.'* Ibid. 15.

4 *any cloth.'* Ibid. 21.

4 *like hers.'* Ibid. 16; J. F. de Almeida Prado, *Primeiros povoadores do Brasil (1500–1530)* 143–4.

4 *we eat.'* Ibid. 29.

4 *more so.'* Ibid. 23.

4 *respect of modesty.'* Ibid. 30.

5 *off upstream.'* Ibid. 22.

5 *do so.'* Ibid. 30.

5 *with them.'* Ibid. 24.

5 *continental mainland.* Report by Venetian diplomat Giovanni Cretico, 27 July 1501, in Fracanzano de Montalboddo, *Paesi nuouamente retrouati*; Prado, *Primeiros povoadores* 145.

5 *among them.'* Greenlee, *Voyages of Cabral* 28.

5 *great willingness.'* Ibid. 28.

6 *pitied them'.* Ibid. 60: an anonymous narrative, evidently by a Portuguese on Cabral's ship, first published in Montalboddo, *Paesi nuouamente retrouati*, and later in Giovanni Batista Ramusio, *Navigationi et Viaggi* 1.

6 *the world.* João Capistrano de Abreu, *Capitulos de história colonial* 45. Costa Lobo also estimated a population of 1,100,000 (*História da sociedade em Portugal no século XV* (Lisbon, 1903) 32). Other estimates run higher, but none over 2.5 million. Greenlee, *Voyages of Cabral* xvii.

7 *Brazil.* The Papacy had for many years been encouraging Portuguese exploration in Africa. In 1418, Pope Martin V issued a Bull that made a crusade of the Portuguese enterprise in Morocco. Later popes sanctioned the voyages of the Portuguese Order of

Christ and the occupation of the Atlantic islands. The various Bulls reflected the political situation inside Italy: most fifteenth-century popes had reasons for favouring Portugal and being cool towards Spain. This situation changed with the election of the pro-Spanish Rodrigo Borgia as Alexander VI in 1492 and the triumphant return of Columbus in that same year. Columbus called in at Lisbon on his return. When Columbus reported his discovery, the King of Portugal declared that 'this conquest belonged to _him!_' (Martín Fernández de Navarrete, _Colección de los viajes y descubrimientos que hicieron por mar los españoles desde el siglo XV_, 5 vols (Madrid, 1858) 1 310, Diário de Colón, 9 March 1493). The Spanish answer was an appeal to the pro-Spanish pope. Pope Alexander published a Bull awarding Spain all lands and islands to be discovered across the ocean.

The Portuguese protested that this violated some of their earlier concessions. Pope Alexander therefore decided to divide the unknown world between the two Iberian monarchs with a line running 'from the Arctic or North Pole to the Antarctic or South Pole' and located, impossibly, 'distant one hundred leagues to the west and south from any one of the islands commonly called Azores and Cape Verde'. Portuguese protests, threats and counter-proposals led to a more westerly line being agreed between the two kingdoms. It was enshrined in the treaty signed in Tordesillas, near Valladolid in Spain, on 7 June 1494 and later ratified by each country and confirmed by the Papacy in 1506. The new north–south line was located 370 leagues west of the Cape Verde Islands. The Treaty failed to mention which island in that archipelago was to be the starting-point, and there was much confusion in subsequent attempts to draw the Line in South America.

A number of calculations between 1495 and 1545 located the Line of Tordesillas between 42° 30' and 50° West (of Greenwich). But one thing is certain:

only the bulge of Brazil should have been occupied by Portugal. In the most favourable – the most westerly – interpretation the Line bisected the island of Marajó in the mouth of the Amazon and ran down to cross the coast again near the boundaries of the modern states of Santa Catarina and Rio Grande do Sul. The most unfavourable, the Portuguese map of 1502 called 'Cantino', would have placed the future cities of Rio de Janeiro, São Paulo and São Luís do Maranhão all within Spanish South America! During the sixteenth and seventeenth centuries the Portuguese managed to convince themselves that the Line ran from the mouth of the Amazon to the mouth of the Plate. They further believed that those two rivers had a common origin in a great lake in the heart of South America.

7 _was fortuitous._ The arguments about the possible premeditation of Cabral's discovery have been long and heated. The debate began with an article by Joaquim Norberto de Sousa e Silva ('O descobrimento do Brasil por Pedro Álvares Cabral foi devido a um mero acaso ou teve êle alguns indícios para isto?', RHGB 15, 1852). A letter from the surgeon Mestre João to King Manoel, carried in the same ship that took Pero Vaz de Caminha's, made oblique reference to a 'mapa mundi' that already showed Brazil but did not indicate whether it was inhabited or not. A chronicle written between 1505 and 1508 – Duarte Pacheco Pereira's _Esmeraldo de situ orbis_ – mentioned that in 1498 the King of Portugal had sent out a fleet that crossed the ocean to the west and found a great continent full of brazilwood. (Pacheco Pereira, _Esmeraldo de situ orbis_ (London, 1927) 12.)

The arguments in favour of a chance discovery are more impressive. Pero Vaz de Caminha's letter – which was secret and addressed directly to the King – gives no hint that the discovery was foreseen; he indicated that Cabral's fleet followed land birds during the final approach to Brazil, and said that the Admiral summoned a meeting of his captains to decide what to do about the discovery. The King's instructions to Cabral told him to sail well out into the Atlantic to avoid the doldrums near the coast of Africa, but made no mention of finding new land to the west. Cabral's fleet was equipped to trade for produce from India; it was not outfitted as a voyage of exploration. King Manoel described the discovery in a letter of 28 Aug 1501 to his neighbouring monarchs Ferdinand and Isabella, and said that 'It appears that Our Lord miraculously desired that it should be found' (HCP 2 155–68, 1923). He wrote that Cabral had found Brazil 'novamente', but in those days the word meant 'recently' and did not imply 'newly' or 'for a second time'. The voyage of 1498 mentioned by Pacheco Pereira was apparently one by the Cortereal brothers that went to Canada and Newfoundland rather than to Brazil. On the Cantino map of 1502, Newfoundland is marked: 'This land was discovered by order of . . . the King of Portugal. It was found by Gaspar Cortereal.'

The literature on this question includes: the debate in RHGB 15 and 18, 1852 and 1855; João Capistrano de Abreu, *O descobrimento do Brasil* (1929 ed.) 40–6; Duarte Leite, 'Os falsos precursores de Álvares Cabral', HCP 1 107–228, 1921; A. Fontoura da Costa, 'O descobrimento do Brasil', in *História da Expansão Portuguesa no Mundo* (Lisbon, 1940); Prado, *Primeiros povoadores* 37; Hélio Vianna, *História do Brasil* (1970 ed.) 1 44–8.

8 *Line of Tordesillas*. In the years after Columbus' landfall in the West Indies, the Spaniards steadily explored the coasts around the Caribbean. In mid-1499 the navigator Alonso de Hojeda, with the Florentine Amerigo Vespucci in his fleet, sailed south along the Atlantic coastline. Vespucci claimed that they reached latitude 5° South, but the commander of the expedition said that they were 4° 30′ North, and thus outside the boundaries of modern Brazil. It is possible that, having struck the coast of South America near the Oiapoque River (the present boundary between Brazil

and French Guiana), Vespucci parted company from Hojeda. He spent a day investigating the forested coast in his ship's shallops, and then re-embarked. 'We pointed our prows southward . . .' (Vespucci to Lorenzo de' Medici, 18 July 1500, trans. in Frederick Pohl, *Amerigo Vespucci* 77, or J. H. Parry (ed.), *The European Reconnaissance. Selected Documents* (London, 1968) 175–6). They passed two great rivers, the first sixteen miles wide at its mouth, and spent two days rowing up one of these in their small boats. They sailed on in the same direction – presumably south-east – for forty leagues, until stopped by strong adverse currents. Vespucci wrote that they were now beyond the equator. All this could indicate that his ship had passed the mouths of the Amazon and Pará rivers and sailed on until striking the Southern Equatorial Current, which races along the coast of Ceará and Maranhão. In that case, Vespucci was the discoverer of Brazil and of the Amazon.

The next Spanish expedition, commanded by Vicente Yáñez Pinzón, almost certainly *did* reach Brazil. Sailing from the Cape Verde Islands it found a point, now thought to be Santo Agostinho in Pernambuco or Mucuripe or Ponta Grossa in the state of Ceará, and sailed on north-westwards to a 'Sweet Sea' that was evidently the vast expanse of fresh water of the mouth of the Amazon. Pinzón's landfall in Brazil was on 26 Jan 1500 – four months before Cabral's. Another Spanish expedition under Diego de Lepe appears to have followed much the same route, hard on the heels of Yáñez Pinzón. Cabral did not know of these voyages to the northern edge of what is now Brazil: he remains the first Portuguese to reach Brazil and had the inestimable advantage of a superb chronicler, Pero Vaz de Caminha. He was thus the discoverer who revealed Brazil to the Europeans. Visconde de Pôrto Seguro e Rodolfo Garcia, *História Geral do Brasil*, 4th ed. (São Paulo, 1927) 1 79–81, 89–90; Abreu, *O descobrimento do Brasil* 40–6, 224–6; Th. Pompeo Sobrinho, 'Proto-história Cearense', in

História do Ceará (Fortaleza, 1946) 23–4; Vianna, *História do Brasil* 1 39–41; Duarte Leite, 'Os falsos precursores de Álvares Cabral', HCP 1 (Pôrto, 1921).

The Portuguese captain thought to have discovered the River Plate was Esteban Fróes. The *Newen Zeytung auss Presillg Landt* (*c.*1515) said that a Portuguese captain had brought back to the King of Portugal 'a silver axe, similar in shape to their stone axes'. He also heard about a mountain people in the interior who wore gold on their chests and backs – a clear reference to the canipu plates worn by Inca soldiers (Rolando A. Laguarda Trias, *El predescubrimiento del río de la Plata por la expedición portuguesa de 1511–1512* (Lisbon, 1973) 139). The Spaniards then sent a fleet under the Pilot-Major Juan Dias de Solís, who succeeded Vespucci in that post. Solís was killed by Indians in the Plate estuary in 1516.

9 *Land of Brazil.* Luís Vaz de Camões, *Os Lusiadas*, canto 1°, estância 140. Cabral's land or island of the Santa Cruz was first called Terra do Brasil in Pero Lopes de Sousa, *Diario da navegação de Pero Lopes de Sousa* (1530–2). The Indians called the tree *ibira-pitanga* ('red wood'). Monnet de Lamarck gave it the botanical name *Caesalpina echinata*, after Pope Clement VIII's doctor Cesalpino, and *echinata* because of its thorns. António Baião, 'O comércio do pau brasil', HCP 2 317–47; José Bernardino de Sousa, *O pau-brasil na história nacional* (São Paulo, 1939) 64; Bento José Pickel, 'O pau brasil', RH 16 3–8, 1958; Estevão Pinto, 'Introdução à história da antropologia indígena no Brasil (seculo xvi)' 342; Alexander Marchant, *From Barter to Slavery* 28–31; Roberto C. Simonsen, *História econômica do Brasil (1500–1820)* (1937 ed.) 55–6.

Even though the goods traded to the Indians were very cheap, the profit margin for the brazilwood trade was not particularly large. The merchant who financed the voyage received only fifteen per cent of the sale of the wood, the price of which was fixed in 1550 at 80 reis per quintal (about 120 lb). It was not a certain profit, for the risk of losing the entire ship was considerable. The Crown received a share of the proceeds and in later years tried to monopolise some of the brazilwood trade. But its revenue from brazilwood did not equal the cost of defending Brazil and its commerce from rival European traders. Suzanne Lussagnet, in André Thevet, *Les Français en Amérique pendant la deuxième moitié du XVIe siècle: Le Brésil et les brésiliens* 224.

When the Genoese John Cabot sailed from Bristol in the ship *Matthew* and discovered Newfoundland, in June 1497, he called the new continent Brazil or Seven Cities. This may have derived from the Irish word meaning 'fortunate' or 'blessed', since there was no dyewood in Canada. A mythical place called Brasil had been shown, west of Ireland, on maps since 1325. J. A. Williamson, *The Cabot Voyages and Bristol Discovery under Henry VII* (London, 1962) 201; Louis-André Vigneras, *The Discovery of South America and the Andalusian Voyages* (Chicago, 1976) 8. Spanish voyages to northern South America and to the West Indies frequently brought back dyewood that they called brasil.

9 *supply them.'* Thevet, *Le Brésil et les brésiliens* 221; André Thevet, *Les Singularitéz de la France Antarctique* 116–17. Since this is a French quotation I have taken the French measure of some 2·7 miles to the league. A Spanish league was about 4·2 miles.

9 *the whites.'* Anon, *Principio e origem dos indios do Brasil . . .*, RHGB 57 pt 1, 196, 1894.

10 *the Christians'.* Capt. Paulmier de Gonneville, *Déclaration du voyage du capitaine Gonneville et ses compagnons ès Indes* (1505), quoted in Paul Gaffarel, *Histoire du Brésil français au seizième siècle* 45, 35.

10 *eaten prisoners!'* Jean de Léry, *Le Voyage au Brésil de Jean de Léry, 1556–1558* 203.

10 *125 tons.* Many modern authors prefer to call the ship *Bretoa*, although the log says *Bertoa*: 'Llyuro da naoo Bertoa que vay para a terra do Brazyll', HCP 2 343–7; also in Duarte Fernandes, 'Viagem da Náo Bretoa até Cabo Frio em 1511', RHGB 24 96–111, 1861. Apart

from their warehouses at Bahia and Cabo Frio, the Portuguese also had them on the island of Santo Aleixo, at Pernambuco and possibly at Guanabara, the future Rio de Janeiro. A few details of trade during those early years emerge from *Cartas das Ilhas de Cabo Verde de Valentim Fernandes, 1505–1508*, ed. A. Fontoura da Costa (Lisbon, 1939); the anonymous *New Gazette from the Land of Brazil (Newen Zeytung auss Presillg Landt)* of *c.*1515; and the 'Protestation de Bertrand d'Ormesson, Baron de Saint-Blancard' (*c.* 1532), in E. Guénin, *Ango et ses pilotes* (Paris, 1901) 43–7. Marchant, *From Barter to Slavery* 33–6. The French later established themselves more in the Rio de Janeiro–Cabo Frio area, and particularly among the Potiguar on the rivers Paraíba do Norte (then called Santo Domingo), Rio Grande do Norte; on the bays of Traição ('Treason') and Baía Formosa (Aratipicaba); and further south on the Sergipe river. Thevet, *La Cosmographie universelle* 223–4.

Various species of red dyewood were also found in the Caribbean islands. Columbus sent some of this 'brazilwood' back from Española (now the Dominican Republic). On his third voyage of 1498 he found that Francisco Roldán had rebelled and, among other things, had burned the stores of brazilwood ready for shipment (Bartolomé de las Casas, *História de las Indias*, bk 1, chs 159 and 162). Columbus complained bitterly to the King of Spain when the expedition of Alonso de Hojeda and Amerigo Vespucci of 1499 tried to recoup its losses by cutting some of the brazilwood discovered by Columbus. But the King awarded a brazilwood concession to Hojeda (Cédula of 10 March 1501) and another to Columbus (27 Sept 1501).

In his letter of 1502 to Lorenzo de' Medici, Vespucci told about the Portuguese expedition of 1501–2: 'We found infinite quantities of brazilwood of very good quality, [enough] to fill all the ships now at sea and at no cost whatsoever' (Vespucci, *El Nuevo Mundo* (Buenos Aires, 1951) 151–3). The trader Giovanni Francesco Affaitadi wrote to the Venetian ambassador in Spain, Pietro Pasqualigo, 10 Sept 1502: 'The caravels sent last year to explore the Land of Parrots or of Santa Cruz returned on 22 July. The captain reported having discovered over 2500 miles of new coast, without finding any end to it. Those caravels arrived loaded with brazilwood and canafistula wood, but brought no spices' (letter in Trias, *El predescubrimiento* 41).

A letter from Pier Rondinelli, written to Florence from Seville, 3 Oct 1502, described the King's sale of licences to cut brazilwood and fetch slaves to Fernão de Noronha and other 'new Christians' (Jews converted to Christianity). The syndicate sent four ships in 1503, and these returned full of brazilwood and slaves. The Spanish court paid the famous pilot Juan de la Cosa ten gold ducats to spy out information about this voyage; he did so, despite arrest by the Portuguese authorities (Jaime Cortesão, *História do Brasil nos velhos mapas*, 2 vols (Rio de Janeiro, 1965) 1 262–4; Antonio Ballesteros Berreta, *La marina cantabra y Juan de la Cosa* (Santander, 1954) 293–4; Manuel de la Puente y Olea, *Los trabajos geográficos de la Casa de Contratación* (Seville, 1900) 21). The island of Fernando de Noronha still belongs to Brazil, and lies some 200 miles off its north-eastern tip.

11 *promised land.'* Anon, *Newen Zeytung auss Presillg Landt* 119.

11 *those parts.'* Capt.-Gen. Diego García, *Memoria de la navegación que hice*, RHGB 15 10, 1852. Sebastian Cabot was the son of John Cabot, probably a Genoese, and both father and son had sailed to North America for Henry VII of England. Sebastian later moved to Spain, where the King sent him to explore the coast of South America, particularly the River Plate where a silver knife had been found. He sailed far up the Plate and Paraguay and established a fort on the Uruguay called Sancti Spiritus. García later visited the fort and was told that Cabot was upstream and 'reported that he had killed 500 Indians, and was moving up the river with great victories, making war

on the [Guaraní] Indians' (ibid. 11).
11 *an interpreter.* Vespucci letter to Pietro
Soderini, 4 Sept 1504, RHGB 41 pt 1, 11,
1878. Damião de Góes, *Chronica de El Rey
D. Manoel* (Lisbon, 1720), ch. 56, p. 120,
told how Jorge Lopes Bixorda took the
Tupinikin to visit King Manoel. Manuel
Ayres do Casal, *Corografica Brasílica* (1945
ed.) 2 69.
11 *England.* This William Hawkins was
the father of the famous Sir John. He
made several trips to Africa and Brazil in
1530–2. One Martin Cockeram of
Plymouth was left as hostage for the safe
return of the chief. Henry VIII's
courtiers were amazed by the bones
inserted into holes in the chief's cheeks
and lips as a sign of valour. 'All his
apparel, behaviour, and gesture, were
very strange to the beholders.' After a
year Hawkins took the chief back to
Brazil, but 'the said Savage king died at
sea, which was feared would turn to the
losse of the life of Martin Cockeram his
pledge. Neverthelesse, the Savages being
fully perswaded of the honest dealing of
our men with their prince, restored again
the said pledge, without any harme to
him, or any man of the company' ('A
brief relation of two sundry voyages
made by the worshipful M. William
Hawkins of Plymouth . . . in the yeere
1530 and 1532', in Richard Hakluyt, *The
Principall Navigations of the English Nation* 8
14). Other English voyages to Brazil
included one by Robert Reniger and
Thomas Borey of Southampton in 1540
and by one Pudsey of Southampton in
1542.
11 *a country'.* 'Campagne du navie
l'Espoir de Honfleur, 1503–1505', in
Armand d'Avezac, *Relation authentique du
voyage du Capitaine de Gonneville*; Abbé
Binot Paulmier de Gonneville, *Mémoire
touchant l'établissement d'une mission
chrestienne* . . .; André Julien, *Les Français
en Amérique* . . .; Gaffarel, *Histoire du
Brésil français* 33, 47, 53. A descendant of
the Carijó boy and the daughter of Capt.
Gonneville became an abbot in mid-
seventeenth-century Normandy. He sent
an edition of his ancestor's voyage to the
pope and proposed that he should go to

establish a mission in the country visited
in 1503 – but he carefully omitted any
reference to show that it was Brazil. For
years it was thought that the French
might have penetrated the Indian Ocean
or even discovered Australia. The
mystery was solved when the investigator
Pierre Margry discovered Gonneville's
original report in the archives of the
French Navy: it was published in 1869 by
Avezac.
12 *or money.'* Prosper and Mathieu
Paulmier, *Eusebi Caesariensis Chronicon cum
additionibus* (Paris, 1518), quoted in
Gaffarel, *Histoire du Brésil français* 58;
Afonso Arinos de Mello Franco, *O índio
brasileiro e a Revolução Francesa* 66.
12 *American paradise.* Ango's palace was
destroyed in an English bombardment in
1694, but the frieze in the chuch survives.
Gaffarel, *Histoire du Brésil français* 82–3,
108–9; Ferdinand Denis (ed.), *Une Fête
brésilienne célébrée à Rouen en 1550* 26–7.
Another of Ango's houses, the Château
de Varengeville, has survived and there
are medallions of Brazilian Indians in the
corners of its courtyard. The Rouen
Museum also contains woodcut bas-
reliefs taken from a house called Île du
Brésil that was demolished in the mid-
nineteenth century. These panels show
voluptuous women and athletic men,
parrots, monkeys, and scenes of the
brazilwood trade. Pictures of these
Norman scenes of Brazilian Indians are
in Mello Franco, *O índio brasileiro* 105–8.
12 *same country.'* The pageant was officially
recorded: 'La Déduction du sumptueux
ordre . . .', reproduced in Denis, *Une Fête
brésilienne* 13. Gaffarel, *Histoire du Brésil
français* 131–6; Mello Franco, *O índio
brasileiro* 76–9.
13 *water-fowl.'* Denis, *Une Fête brésilienne*
13
13 *ancient monster.'* Simão de Vasconcellos,
*Chronica da Companhia de Jesus do Estado
do Brasil* . . . (1865 ed.) 33.
13 *birds and animals.* 'Carta do piloto
anonymo', published in the collections
of voyages of Montalboddo (*Paesi
nuouamente*, 1507) and Ramusio
(*Navigationi et Viaggi*, 1550, 1). The
Venetian diplomat Giovanni Cretico

reported the discovery of Brazil in 1501 and said that it contained 'naked and beautiful' people (Montalboddo, *Paesi nuouamente* 109). Mello Franco, *O índio brasileiro* 35–6.

14 *property.'* Vespucci to Pier Francesco de' Medici, Lisbon, Sept or Oct 1502 (known as the Bartolozzi Letter after the man who discovered it in 1789; trans. Samuel Eliot Morison, *The European Discovery of America. The Southern Voyages, 1492–1616* 285; or trans. Pohl, *Amerigo Vespucci* 132). Morison gives a masterly summary of the career of the braggart Vespucci and a survey of the immense bibliography of works about the controversial Florentine (*European Discovery* 276–97, 304–12). Vespucci's writings consist of six letters, five of them to the same Medici, his former employer. Only two of these were published during Vespucci's lifetime, but the famous 'Mundus Novus' letter rapidly achieved a remarkable thirty-six imprints in five languages. Roberto Levillier lists these editions in his *Amerigo Vespucci* (Madrid, 1966) 115–16. Vespucci sailed to Brazil in 1501–2 in a fleet of three caravels commanded by the Portuguese Gonçalo Coelho. But he disliked his admiral and never named him in the letters; and the new continent came to be called America, after Vespucci not Coelho.

The Coelho–Vespucci expedition of 1501–2 may well have named many of the famous landmarks of the coast of Brazil. It left Lisbon on 13 May 1501, paused at the Cape Verde Islands, and probably struck Brazil at Cape São Roque near modern Natal. If it named landmarks according to saints' days, its progress was: Cape São Roque, 14 Aug; Cape Santo Agostinho, 28 Aug; a lull during which Vespucci spent twenty-seven days eating and sleeping among the Indians; São Francisco River, 4 Oct; Bahia de Todos Os Santos (All Saints' Bay), 1 Nov. It sailed on to reach a huge estuary, which it called Rio Jordam – possibly the Plate – and Vespucci claimed that it explored 800 leagues of coast, which would have taken it to 40° South in Patagonia. Amerigo Vespucci to Lorenzo

de' Medici, (?) 22 July 1502, *Raccolta de documenti e studi pubblicati della R. Commissione Colombiana*, 14 vols (Rome, 1892–6) 3 i 91; Vigneras, *Discovery of South America* 140–1.

14 *no government.'* Woodcut printed in Nuremburg, *c.*1504, in Rudolph Schuller, 'The Oldest Known Illustration of South American Indians', JSAP, n.s., 16 111, 1924. This unique woodcut was bought by the British Museum at an auction in 1854 for £3 13s 6d (£3.67½). The best-known version of Vespucci's 'Mundus Novus' letter was published by Montalboddo, *Paesi nuouamente*. Vespucci inadvertently won immortality through this letter. In it he wrote that Coelho's fleet of 1501–2 or that of 1503 (of six ships, again commanded by Gonçalo Coelho, financed and sent by the King of Portugal) had sailed for hundreds of miles along the coast of a continent whose existence was unimagined by their ancestors. 'Through my voyage it is proved that their opinion was false and contrary to the truth: for in that southern part I [!] discovered a continent inhabited by more men and animals than our Europe, or Asia or Africa. . . . It is manifest that we have navigated along the fourth part of the world' (*El Nuevo Mundo* (1951 ed.) 172, 190). Some geographers were preparing a new edition of Ptolemy's Geography in Saint-Dié in Lorraine in 1507. Their leader, Martin Waldseemüller, interpreted this letter to mean that Vespucci had discovered the fourth continent – although he had boasted only to have sailed along the equivalent of a quarter of the world. Waldseemüller boldly named the new continent America, after the first name of the Florentine Amerigo Vespucci. The name America was sonorous and easy; and it caught on. Stefan Zweig, *Amerigo Vespucio* (Buenos Aires, 1942); Roberto Levillier, *America la bien llamada* (Buenos Aires, 1948); Morison, *European Discovery* 288–92; Carlos Sanz, *El nombre America*.

14 *sentiments alone.'* Nicolas Barré letter to his friends, Guanabara, 'France

Antarctique', 1 Feb 1555, in Gaffarel, *Histoire du Brésil français* 380.

15 *language and society.* Pero de Magalhães de Gandavo, *The Histories of Brazil* 85, and *Tratado da provincia do Brasil* 181–3; Gabriel Soares de Sousa, *Tratado descriptivo do Brasil em 1587*, ch. 150, p. 364; Vicente do Salvador, *História do Brasil* 53–4; Simão de Vasconcellos, *Das cousas do Brasil*, bk 1, p. 72; Caspar Barlaeus, *Brasilia sub Praefectura Illustrissimi Comitis Mauritii Nassoviae* (Amsterdam, 1647) 21; Mello Franco, *O índio brasileiro* 234–5; Rodrigo Octavio, *Os selvagens americanos perante o direito* 39, 125. It is interesting to note that the Japanese also confuse the letters L and R. Some Brazilian Indians look strikingly Japanese in their skin colour, facial features, hair and physique.

15 *practising evil. . . .'* Pietro Martire d'Anghiera, *Decadas de Orbe Novo* (1500; Milan, 1930) 154, quoted in Sérgio Buarque de Holanda, *Visão do paraíso: os motivos edénicos no descobrimento e colonização do Brasil* 180. This description was about natives in the Caribbean, but it would apply equally to those of Brazil. Sir John Mandeville's *Voyages and Travels* first appeared in French in Lyons in 1480, and is thought to be by the Fleming Jean de Bourgoyne of Liège.

15 *vice and sin'.* Mandeville, quoted in Mello Franco, *O índio brasileiro* 30.

15 *share it.'* Gandavo, *Histories of Brazil* 87; Anon, *Principio e origem dos índios do Brasil* 187; Anon Jesuit, *De algumas coisas mais notáveis do Brasil* 388; Yves d'Evreux, *Voyage dans le nord du Brésil, fait durant les années 1613 et 1614* 74.

16 *laws of nature.'* Gandavo, *Histories of Brazil* 90–1, 92.

16 *Europe.'* Léry, *Voyage au Brésil* 251.

16 *further cares.''* Ibid. 172–3. Evreux, *Voyage* 70. Léry's debate is often quoted: for instance, Florestan Fernandes, *Organização social dos Tupinambá* 94; Darcy Ribeiro, *O índio e a civilização.*

16 *insatiable gluttons!'* Léry, *Voyage au Brésil* 174.

17 *your welcome.'* Thevet, *La Cosmographie universelle* 113–14.

17 *like conies.* Léry, *Voyage au Brésil* 160.

17 *a rein.'* 'Discorso d'un gran capitano di mare Francese del luogo di Dieppa', in Ramusio, *Navigationi et Viaggi* 3 355–6. Paul Gaffarel showed that this 'great sea captain' was Jean Parmentier, who was in northern Brazil in 1525 (*Histoire du Brésil français* 56, 64, 119). Jean Alphonse de Saintonge was a French pilot in the service of the Portuguese. He described his adventures in a rather fanciful book, *Voyages aventureux*, written c.1545 and published in Poitiers in 1559; Pierre Margry, *Navigations françaises* 305. Antonio de Pigafetta, *Le Voyage et navigation faicte par les Espaignolz ès Isles de Mollucques . . .*

17 *in the dark.* Ulrich Schmidel, *Reise nach Süd-Amerika in den Jahren 1534 bis 1554* (first published Frankfurt-am-Main, 1576). Mello Franco, *O índio brasileiro* 42–3.

17 *private parts.'* Thevet, *La Cosmographie universelle* 216. The Jesuit José de Anchieta described a long black insect like a centipede, with a red head and poisonous hairs, that excited the Indians' libido. 'The Indians customarily apply it to the genital parts and thus excite them for sensual pleasure. These swell in such a way that in three days they blister. It often results that the prepuce is split in various places, and the penis itself contracts an incurable corruption. They become ugly from the horrible aspect of the disease, and also stain and infect women with whom they have sexual relations' (Anchieta, *Cartas, informações, fragmentos históricos e sermões* 116, 136; Serafim Soares Leite, *Páginas de história do Brasil* 207). Anchieta's description sounded more like a venereal disease, possibly some form of gonorrhoea, than the effect of an insect bite.

18 *left as eunuchs.'* Vespucci to Piero de' Medici, Lisbon, 1502–3, RHGB 41 pt 1, 25, 23, 1878.

18 *endure it.'* Soares de Sousa, *Tratado descriptivo*, ch. 156, p. 373. Gilberto Freyre, *The Masters and the Slaves: a study in the development of Brazilian civilization* 97.

18 *and laments. . . .'* Evreux, *Voyage* 106–7.

19 *on themselves.'* Léry, *Voyage au Brésil* 159–60.

19 *wearing them.'* Anchieta, *Cartas* 426; Freyre, *Masters and Slaves* 112.

19 *fountain of youth'.* Léry, *Voyage au Brésil* 143–4; Antonio de Pigafetta, *Il primo viaggo intorno al mondo* 83; Vespucci, RHGB 41 pt 1, 25; Henry Vignaud, *Améric Vespuce* (Paris, 1917) 308 ff; Bartolozzi Letter, in Morison, *European Discovery* 286; Anon, *Newen Zeytung auss Presillg Landt* 119; Buarque de Holanda, *Visão do paraíso* 239–43.

19 *five hundred years'.* Fernão Cardim, *Tratados da terra e gente do Brasil* 313.

19 *seven score years.'* Claude d'Abbeville, *Histoire de la mission des Pères Capucins en l'Isle de Maragnan* . . . 264; Buarque de Holanda, *Visão do paraíso* 247.

20 *their lives.'* Anon, *Diálogos das grandezas do Brasil* 100.

20 *of his teeth.'* Léry, *Voyage au Brésil* 242–3.

21 *mother's breast.'* Evreux, *Voyage* 77–8.

21 *own babies.* Mello Franco, *O índio brasileiro* 140, 145–8.

21 *vivre ainsi.'* Pierre de Ronsard, 'Ode contre fortune' (1560), in *Oeuvres complètes*, ed. Elzévirienne, 6 166.

22 *wear breeches!'* Michel de Montaigne, 'Des Cannibales', *The Complete Works of Montaigne*, trans. D. M. Frame (London,

1957). Prado, *Primeiros povoadores* 156–62; Mello Franco, *O índio brasileiro* 167–92; Gilbert Chimard, *L'Exoticisme américaine dans la littérature française au XVIᵉ siècle* 193 ff; René Gonnard, *La Légende du bon sauvage* (Paris, 1946); Dias Gonçalves, *O índio do Brasil na literatura portuguesa* . . . 103–10. M. T. Hogden, *Early Anthropology in the Sixteenth and Seventeenth Centuries* (Philadelphia, 1964); Howard Mumford Jones, *O Strange New World* (London, 1965); John H. Elliott, 'The Discovery of America and the Discovery of Man', *Proceedings of the British Academy* (London) 58 101–25, 1972; Andrew Sinclair, *The Savage: a history of misunderstanding* (London, 1977) 64–80.

22 *their valour.* Montaigne, 'Des Cannibales', quoted in Mello Franco, *O índio brasileiro* 187–8.

23 *poor Indians.'* Paulmier de Gonneville, 'Campagne du navie l'Espoir de Honfleur, 1503–1505'. The evolution of the early accounts of Brazilian Indians into the thinking of the eighteenth-century philosophers was admirably explained by Afonso Arinos de Mello Franco in *O índio brasileiro*.

Chapter 2 FROM BARTER TO SLAVERY

25 *have any.'* Amerigo Vespucci to Lorenzo de' Medici, Lisbon, Sept or Oct 1502, trans. in Samuel Eliot Morison, *The European Discovery of America. The Southern Voyages, 1492–1616* 284.

26 *however small.'* Fernão Cardim, *Do principio e origem dos Indios do Brasil e dos seus costumes, adoração e ceremonias*, RHGB 57 pt 1, 196, 1894.

27 *without eating.'* Ibid. 196. Jaime Cortesão, *Rapôso Tavares e a formação territorial do Brasil* 17; Alfred Métraux, 'The Tupinambá' 100.

27 *his fellows.'* Hans Staden, *The True History of His Captivity*, ch. 7, p. 135.

27 *amass riches'.* Claude d'Abbeville, *História da missão dos Padres Capuchinos na Ilha do Maranhão* . . . (São Paulo, 1945)

236; Florestan Fernandes, *Organização social dos Tupinambá* 84.

27 *few months later.* This burning, called coivara, is a legacy from the Indians that has become a scourge of modern Brazil: farmers in the interior resort to burning on the slightest pretext. The men in an expedition I took part in would light fires that raged for weeks, just to ward off some snake that reared up at them. Flying over central Brazil in a small plane one can be buffeted by hot air and blinded by smoke from hundreds of miles of burning countryside. The ash produces a quick growth of unnaturally bright green grass and a tangle of undergrowth; but repeated burning inevitably exhausts the soil.

27 *with food'*. Staden, *True History*, ch. 20, p. 147.

28 *Brazilian interior*. Tupi expeditions carried a special variety of farinha called 'war flour' that could keep for over a year when carried in waterproof palm-leaf bags. It was a combination of two types of flour made from tubers that had begun to decay: 'water flour' in which the tubers were broken down in running water, and carimã from rotten tubers that were smoked and pounded after soaking. The blend was baked for a long time to achieve the desired hardness that was proof against insects and mould. Métraux, 'Tupinambá' 102. Staden, *True History*, ch. 10, p. 138.

There are a great many varieties of manioc, which is a cultigen – a plant evolved by man. It is called mandioca in Brazil, from the Tupi-Guaraní; yuca in much of Spanish America, from the island language Aruak; and *Manihot utilissima* to botanists. The non-poisonous or sweet variety (*aypi* in Tupi) is more widespread. It is easy to cook – simply boiled or roasted like potatoes. But poisonous or bitter manioc is a better food, higher in starch content and more suitable for making flour and bread. (Gabriel Soares de Sousa, *Tratado descriptivo do Brasil em 1587*, chs 37–43, RHGB 14 pt 2, 1851; Carl O. Sauer, 'Cultivated Plants of South and Central America', HSAI 6 507–8.) The manioc bush has a leafy umbrella of leaves that protects and shades the weak soil.

28 *killing people.'* Pero de Magalhães de Gandavo, *Histories of Brazil* 83–4.

28 *their enemies.'* Yves d'Evreux, *Voyage dans le nord du Brésil, fait durant les années 1613 et 1614* 21.

29 *their wounds.'* Staden, *True History*, ch. 26, p. 153.

29 *natural feathers.'* Jean de Léry, *Le Voyage au Brésil de Jean de Léry, 1556–1558* 190–2; Gandavo, *Histories of Brazil* 94.

30 *the woods'.* Peter Carder, *The Relation of Peter Carder of Saint Verian in Cornwall*, in Samuel Purchas, *Hakluytus Posthumus or Purchas His Pilgrimes* 16 141–2.

30 *with them.'* Anthony Knivet, *The Admirable Adventures and Strange Fortunes*

of Master Antonie Knivet . . ., in Samuel Purchas, *Hakluytus Posthumus or Purchas His Pilgrimes* 16 223.

30 *in peace'.* Ibid. 16 223.

30 *that land'.* Cristóbal de Acuña, *Descobrimentos do Rio das Amazonas* (São Paulo, 1941) 199. The same point was made by Afonso Braz, letter from Espírito Santo, 1551 (RHGB 6 422, 1844).

32 *towards us.'''* Staden, *True History*, chs 20–2, pp. 62–79.

32 *it tastes good.'''* Ibid. bk 1, chs 42–3, pp. 107, 110.

32 *eat it.'* Ibid. bk 2, ch. 28, p. 155. The Tupi tribes believed that a child was related only to its father: the mother was simply the carrier in which it gestated. Because of this belief a man was encouraged to marry his sister's daughter, who was thought to have no consanguinity with him.

32 *still alive'.* Gandavo, *Histories of Brasil* 108.

33 *see it.'* Staden, *True History*, bk 2, ch. 28, p. 155.

33 *my death.'''* Ibid. bk 2, ch. 28, p. 155; Knivet in Purchas 16 222.

33 *to the fire.'* Staden, *True History*, bk 2, ch. 28, p. 155.

33 *a sheep.'* Léry, *Voyage au Brésil* 200.

33 *day and night.'* Knivet in Purchas 16 222.

33 *especially enjoy.'* Staden, *True History*, bk 2, ch. 28, p. 155.

33 *do not touch.'* Léry, *Voyage au Brésil* 201–2. Apart from the sources quoted here, almost every chronicler gave a description of the killing and eating of prisoners: Jácome Monteiro, *Relação da Provincia do Brasil* 409–12; Cardim, *Do principio e origem* 197–203, or his *Tratados da terra e gente do Brasil* 159–68; André Thevet, *La Cosmographie universelle* 191–201; Evreux, *Voyage* 54; Gandavo, *Histories of Brazil* 102–8; Carder in Purchas 16 140; Vespucci, letter to Piero de' Medici, Lisbon, 1502–3, RHGB 41 pt 1, 25, 23, 1878; Antonio de Pigafetta, *Le Voyage et navigation faicte par les Espaignolz ès Isles de Mollucques . . .* ch. 4; Sousa, *Tratado descriptivo*.

34 *human aspect.'* Villegagnon to Calvin,

Fort Coligny, France Antarctique (Rio de Janeiro), 31 March 1557, in Léry, *Voyage au Brésil* 28.

This was the savage aspect of American Indians that inspired Hobbes' famous sentence: 'In such condition there is no place for industry, because the fruit thereof is uncertain, and consequently no culture of the earth; no navigation, nor use of the commodities that may be imported by sea; no commodious building; no instruments of moving, or removing, such things as require much force; no knowledge of the face of the earth; no account of time; no arts; no letters; no society; and, which is worst of all, continual fear, and danger of violent death; and the life of man, solitary, poor, nasty, brutish and short. . . . There are many places, where they live so now. For the savage people in many places of America . . . have no government at all; and live at this day in that brutish manner '. . .' (Thomas Hobbes, *Leviathan* (Oxford, 1955) 82–3). Hobbes was writing to justify the need for authoritarian rule, and to counter the vision of natural goodness of his contemporary John Locke. Both views were equally wide of the complex reality of tribal society. But, as with all other philosophers expounding or debunking the theory of the noble savage, neither Hobbes nor Locke had any direct experience of real Indians.

Michel de Montaigne compared Indian cannibalism favourably with some Christian excesses. 'I think there is more barbarity . . . in tearing by tortures and the rack a body still full of feeling, in roasting a man bit by bit, in having him bitten and mangled by dogs and swine (as we have seen . . . among our neighbours and fellow citizens and, what is worse, on the pretext of piety and religion), than in roasting and eating him after he is dead' ('Des Cannibales', *The Complete Works of Montaigne*, trans. D. M. Frame (London, 1957) 155).

35 *a conquest.* Jean Parmentier, the 'Capitano francese' whose narrative is in Giovanni Batista Ramusio, *Navigationi et Viaggi* 3 352, and quoted in Paul

Gaffarel, *Histoire du Brésil français au seizième siècle* 85–6; also Thevet, *Cosmographie universelle* 224. The known coastguard expeditions were under a captain called Cristóvão Jaques in 1516–19 and 1526–8, but there may well have been others. The French ship was *La Pèlerine*, captured outside Málaga in 1531. It contained a valuable cargo of Brazilian products and belonged to a consortium of powerful Frenchmen. Violent protests ensued, and these led to negotiations for compensation. At other times the Portuguese Crown tried bribing French traders and courtiers to obtain an official halt to French trading in Brazil.

35 *their lord.'* Gonzalo Fernández de Oviedo, *História General y Natural de Las Indias*, BAE, *Continuación* (Madrid, 1959) 118 349–50; J. F. de Almeida Prado, *Primeiros povoadores do Brasil (1500–1530)* 102–3. The name Caramuru may also have meant 'Son of Thunder' because of the arquebus he salvaged from the shipwreck. J. F. de Almeida Prado, *Bahia e as capitanias do centro do Brasil (1530–1626)* 1 37.

35 *ate them.'* Lopes de Sousa, *Diário* 24.

36 *that coast.* Oviedo, *História* 118 350; Prado, *Primeiros povoadores* 102–3. In 1525, Caramuru had interceded with Chief Tinharé and saved four members of the crew of the Spanish ship of Juan de Mori, shipwrecked off Cape Boipeba; the rest were eaten. Mori reported this on his return to Europe. Next year the Spanish ship *San Gabriel* stopped at the Bay to load brazilwood and lost nine men to Indian attack. Its crew reported that a Christian, presumably Caramuru, had been living there for fifteen years: Pilot Francisco de Ávila, in *Colección de los viajes y descubrimientos que hicieron por mar los españoles . . .*, ed. Martín Fernández de Navarrete, 5 vols (Madrid, 1825–39); Prado, *Bahia* 1 38.

36 *sociable life.'* Lopes de Sousa, *Diário* 1 340.

36 *royal monopoly.* A typical grant was that of Pernambuco to Duarte Coelho, 25 Sept 1534: the texts of the documents are translated into English in E. Bradford

Burns (ed.), _A Documentary History of Brazil_ 34–50. A good summary of the donatories' powers is in João Capistrano de Abreu, _Capítulos de história colonial_ 64–6, and Hélio Vianna, _História do Brasil_ 64–5. Also Carlos Malheiro Dias, 'O regímen feudal das donatárias'; H. B. Johnson, 'The Donatory Captaincy in Perspective: Portuguese backgrounds to the settlement of Brazil', HAHR, May 1972, 205–14.

37 _Portugal._ 'Carta da doação' to Martim Afonso de Sousa, DH **13** 144; Sousa, an influential man with a large stretch of land, was allowed as many slaves as he wished in Brazil, but sent home only forty-eight. Duarte Coelho's donation, see Burns, _Documentary History_ 41.

37 _poor people had.'_ Vicente do Salvador, _História do Brasil_ 55–6.

37 _are rebelling.'_ Duarte Coelho to King, Olinda, 20 Dec 1546, HCP **3** 314.

38 _as slaves.'_ Letter from Pero Correia, SJ, São Vicente, 10 March 1553, in Serafim Soares Leite, _História da Companhia de Jesus no Brasil_ **9** 381–2.

38 _so many sins.'_ Cardim, _Tratados_ 283–4.

39 _my life.'_ Evreux, _Voyage_ 55.

39 _they are.'_ Antonio Ponce letter, Archivo General de la Indias, Seville, 144–I–10, quoted in Jaime Cortesão, _Rapôso Tavares e a formação territorial do Brasil_ 59–60.

39 _more prisoners._ Pero de Góis to King, Vila da Raínha, São Tomé, 29 April 1546, HCP **3** 263. Anon Jesuit, _De algumas coisas mais notáveis do Brasil_ 379.

40 _divine justice'._ Pero de Borges to King João III, Pôrto Seguro, 7 Feb 1550, HCP **3** 268.

40 _I saw fit'._ Duarte Coelho to King, Olinda, 20 Dec 1546, ibid. **3** 315–16.

40 _this coast'._ Pero Borges to King, Pôrto Seguro, 7 Feb 1550, ibid. **3** 268.

40 _governor of Brazil._ Regimento of Tomé de Sousa, 17 Dec 1548, ibid. **3** 348.

41 _they are dogs.'_ Manoel da Nóbrega, letter from Pernambuco, 1551, RHGB **6** 106, 1844.

41 _to found.'_ Nóbrega to Mestre Simão, Bahia, 9 Aug 1549, _Cartas Jesuíticas_, ed. Alfredo do Vale Cabral, **1** 79.

41 _married or single.'_ Simão de Vasconcellos, _Chronica da Companhia de Jesus do Estado do Brasil_ . . ., bk 1, p. 61.

41 _her nuns!'_ Pero Correia, letter from São Vicente, 10 March 1553, in Leite, _História da Companhia de Jesus_ **9** 378–9.

42 _children by then.'_ Pero Tacques de Almeida Paes Leme, _História da Capitania de S. Vicente desde a sua fundação por Martim Afonso de Sousa_, RHGB **9** 149. Paes Leme later wrote, mistakenly, that Ramalho arrived with Martim Afonso de Sousa ('Nobiliarchia Paulistana, geneologia das principaes familias de São Paulo', RHGB **33** pt 2, 302).

42 _before dinner.'_ Tomé de Sousa to King, Salvador, 1 June 1553, HCP **3** 365. The name of Tibiriça's tribe is rarely given, although many early documents mention the Goianá as living on the São Paulo plateau. Egon Schaden came to the conclusion that Goianá referred to the Tupinikin, the Tupi nation that became a close ally of the Portuguese. The Tupinikin were normally at war with the Tamoio Tupinambá, who occupied the coast between modern Santos and Rio de Janeiro, and with the Carijó or Guaraní in modern Paraná to the southwest. Egon Schaden, 'Os primitivos habitantes do territorio paulista' 394–5; Plínio Ayrosa, 'Tupi-Guaraní e Guayanás', a series of articles in the _Estado de São Paulo_ between Nov 1938 and Jan 1939.

The problem about the Goianá (or Guayana, Wayanazes, etc.) is that this name appears to have been applied to _two_ distinct tribes living in the São Paulo–Paraná hinterland. One group of Goianá were clearly the ancestors of the modern Kaingang and Xokleng (otherwise known as Coroado and Botocudo). Their language has a few important words related to Gê, and is therefore usually clarified as within the Macro-Gê linguistic family. They lived on the various rivers flowing into the Paraná from the east – Iguaçu, Tibagi, Piquiri, etc. – and on the plains of Guarapuava and forests of the interior of São Paulo state. They were not cannibalistic and were culturally quite distinct from the Tupi-Guaraní. (Hans Staden, _Wahrhaftige Historie und_

Beschreibung eyner Landtschafft der Wilden, Nacketen, Grimmigen, Menschfresser Leuten, in der Newen Welt America gelegen . . . (1925 facsimile ed.) pt 2, ch. 3; Sousa, *Tratado descriptivo*, RHGB 15 99–100, 1851; Rui Diaz de Guzman, *La Argentina* (1612), *Anales de la Biblioteca Nacional, Buenos Aires*, 9 14, 1914; Pedro Lozano, *História de la conquista del Paraguay* . . . (1754) (1873–4 ed.) 1 422.) Lozano described the Goianá as non-Tupi and living on the Iguaçu river and down to the Atlantic. Auguste de Saint-Hilaire, *Voyage dans le district des diamans* (1830–3) 439–61; José Joachim Machado de Oliveira, 'Noticia raciocinada sobre as aldeas de indios da provincia de São Paulo' 248.

Felix de Azara, who lived on the Paraguayan frontier at the start of the nineteenth century, distinguished between two distinct groups of Guayana. One group spoke no Tupi and lived roughly in the former Jesuit province of Guairá. But another tribe known as Guayana lived further north and *did* speak Guaraní. (Manoel Felix de Azara, 'Geografia fisica y esferica de las provincias del Paraguay y misiones guaranies', *Anales del Museo Nacional de Montevideo, Sección Histórico-Filosófica, Montevideo* 1 404–7, 1904; P. F. Vogt, 'Die Indianer des obern Paraná', *Mitteilungen der Anthropogischen Gesellschaft in Wien, Vienna* 34 216–18, 1904; Hermann von Ihering, 'Os Guayanas e Caingangs de São Paulo', RMP 6 23–44, 1904; Benigno F. Martinez, 'Os indios Guayanas', RMP 6 45–52, 1904; Alfred Métraux, 'The Caingang' 445–8; Egon Schaden, 'Xokleng e Kaingang', in *Homem, cultura e sociedade no Brasil* (Petropolis, 1972) 84; J. Alden Mason, 'The Languages of South American Indians', HSAI 6 292–3.

42 *Indians themselves.*' Manoel da Nóbrega, quoted in Prado, *Primeiros povoadores* 93.

42 *Paraíba river.*' Paes Leme, 'Nobiliarchia paulistana' 302; Tomé de Sousa to King, 1 June 1553, HCP 3 365.

42 *two thousand'.* Ulrich Schmidel, *Wahrhaftige Historie einer wunderbaren Schiffart*, quoted in Prado, *Primeiros*

povoadores 92, 185.

43 *Piratininga plateau.* Serafim Soares Leite discovered an important letter from Nóbrega to Luís Gonçalves da Câmara, from the forests of São Paulo, 31 Aug 1553. Nóbrega described Ramalho's offspring among the tribes (with daughters married to many of the most important chiefs) and his great influence. Nóbrega was escorted inland by Ramalho's eldest son 'to give more authority to our ministry' in the interior. He asked his fellow-Jesuit in Portugal to go to Ramalho's homeland of Vouzela near Viseu in central Portugal to see whether his wife was still alive; and, if she was, to seek papal dispensation for him to marry the Indian mother of all his children. Serafim Soares Leite, *Cartas dos primeiros Jesuítas do Brasil* 1 521–7, or his *Cartas do Brasil e mais escritos do P. Manoel da Nóbrega* 183–6. Prado, *Primeiros povoadores* 86–7. Serafim Soares Leite, *Suma histórica da Companhia de Jesus no Brasil (Assistência de Portugal) 1549–1760* 12–13. That letter confirmed the birthplace and the existence of a wife (her full name was Catarina Fernandes das Vacas) mentioned in a will made by Ramalho in 1580 when he was over ninety. A copy of the will appeared among the papers of José Bonifácio de Andrada e Silva, a great statesman of independent Brazil in the early nineteenth century and a champion of the Indian cause. Various Jesuits mentioned the bad relations between their Society and Ramalho: Baltasar Fernandes in a letter of 22 April 1568, quoted in Prado, *Primeiros povoadores* 89; Vasconcellos, *Chronica da Companhia de Jesu*, bk 1, p. 140; Francisco Pires to his Jesuit colleagues in Portugal, 1552, in CA 131.

43 *thirty years'.* Diego García, *Memoria de la navegación*, RHGB 15 10, 1852. The colonising expedition of Martim Afonso de Sousa paused at Cananéia in Aug 1531, on the way back from an exploration of the Plate river. On the advice of the Bacharel of Cananéia, and of the Spanish interpreter Francisco de Chaves, Martim Afonso sent eighty well-

armed men inland in search of treasure.
They were killed by Indians near the
Paraná, and never returned. The
Bacharel may have been Duarte Peres,
mentioned in Ruy Diaz de Guzman,
Argentina, written in 1612.
43 *both races.* The word *mameluco*
presumably derived from the
resemblance of creamy-coloured half-
castes to the Mamelukes of Egypt. The
Portuguese fought the Mamelukes in a
series of naval battles, for control of the
Indian Ocean trade-route to India.
43 *São Vicente.'* Cardim, *Tratados* 170–1;
Sérgio Buarque de Holanda, 'Índios e
mamelucos na expansão paulista' 178;
Schaden, 'Os primitivos habitantes' 393.
43 *Portuguese.'* António Vieira, quoted in
Sérgio Buarque de Holanda, *Raízes do
Brasil* 180.

43 *Christians.'* Anchieta to Diogo Laines,
the Jesuit General, quoted in Gilberto
Freyre, *The Masters and the Slaves: a study in
the development of Brazilian civilization*
85–6. The Portuguese use of
intermarriage as a means of colonising
was praised by Freyre (ibid. 11); Pedro
Calmon, *Espírito da sociedade colonial*
155–6; Caio Prado, Jnr, *The Colonial
Background of Modern Brazil* 107.
43 *their houses!'* Antonio Gonçalves,
Pôrto Seguro, 1556, in Prado, *Bahia* 1
287.
44 *to be seduced.'* Ambrosio Pires, in CA
131.
44 *slaves and mestizos.'* Abreu, *Capítulos de
história colonial* 56.
44 *our children.'* Claude d'Abbeville,
Histoire de la mission des Pères Capucins . . .,
in Prado, *Primeiros povoadores* 137–8.

Chapter 3   ORIGINS AND FANTASIES

46 *not to be believed.'* Hans Staden, *Viagem
ao Brasil* 18–19. The legends of exotic
people occur in many medieval travel
books, such as Brunet Latin's *Li Livres dou
tresor*, in *Jeux et sagesse du Moyen-Age*
(Paris, 1951); *Mandeville's Travels*, ed.
Malcolm Letts, 2 vols, Hakluyt Society
(London, 1953); Edmond Buron, *Ymago
Mundi de Pierre d'Ailly*, 3 vols (Paris,
1930). Sérgio Buarque de Holanda, *Visão
do paraíso: os motivos edênicos no
descobrimento e colonização do Brasil* 19–20;
Afonso Arinos de Mello Franco, *O índio
brasileiro e a Revolução Francesa* 13–21.
Simão de Vasconcellos, *Chronica da
Companhia de Jesus . . .*, bk 1, ch. 31.
References to Amazons will be given at
greater length in the chapter about the
discovery of that river.
47 *Sumé.'* Anon, *Newen Zeytung auss Presillg
Landt*, ed. Clemente Brandenburger, 37;
Buarque de Holanda, *Visão do paraíso*
104–6; Richard Hennig, *Terrae Incognitae*,
4 vols (Leyden, 1936–8), 2 47, 204, 286,
382; San Francisco Xavier, *Cartas y
escritos*, ed. Felix Zubillaga (Madrid,
1953) 102 ff.
47 *when it rises.'* Manoel da Nóbrega,

Informação das terras do Brasil 6 94; Anon
Jesuit, *Enformação do Brasil e de suas
capitanias* 6 433; Manoel da Nóbrega,
Cartas do Brasil, 1549–1560 50, 66;
Francisco S. G. Schaden, 'O mito do
Sumé', *Sociologia* (São Paulo) 6 136;
Buarque de Holanda, *Visão do paraíso*
108.
47 *once preached.* Anthony Knivet, *The
Admirable Adventures and Strange Fortunes
of Master Antonie Knivet . . .*, in Samuel
Purchas, *Hakluytus Posthumus or Purchas
His Pilgrimes* 16 227. The rock was called
Etoaca and was south of Cabo Frio.
Simão de Vasconcellos reported five sets
of footprints along the coast, from
Paraíba to São Vicente (*Chronica da
Companhia de Jesus* 51–2, 111–32), and
Friar Antonio de Santa Maria Jaboatam
saw a set in Pernambuco (*Novo Orbe
Seráfico Brasilico . . .* 2 29).
47 *the apostles.'* Hans Staden, *The True
History of His Captivity*, ch. 15, p. 143.
47 *mock us."'* Jean de Léry, *Le Voyage au
Brésil de Jean de Léry, 1556–1558* 234. Léry
thought that the prophet might have
been St Matthew.
48 *earth divided'.* Genesis, X 25, 29–30.

Gregorio García, *Origen de los indios del Nuevo Mundo e Indias Occidentales* (Valencia, 1607).

48 *were inverted!* Gregorio García in Artur Ramos, *Introdução à antropologia brasileira: As culturas indígenas* 38; Diego Andrés Rocha, *Origen de los indios del Perú, México, Santa Fé y Chile* (1681).

48 *nationalistic pride.* There are many serious surveys of the origin theories, notably by José Imbelloni, 'El poblamiento primitivo de America', *Revista Geografica Americana* 12 no. 70, July 1939; Ramos, *Introdução à antropologia brasileira* 37–54; Annette Laming-Emperaire, 'Les grands théories sur le peuplement de l'Amérique du point de vue de l'archéologie', *Origens do Homem Americano* (Instituto de Pré-História da Universidade de São Paulo, 1964) 210–37, 429–48; P. Bosch-Gimpera, 'La prehistoria y los origenes del Hombre Americano', ibid. 54–131; Lee Eldridge Huddleston, *Origins of the American Indians: European Concepts, 1492–1729* (Austin, Tex., 1967). Some of the protagonists of the different theories were: *Pacific continent* – Charles Reginald Enock, *The Andes and the Amazon* (London, 1908); *Antartida* – Francisco P. Moreno, *Viaje á la Patagonia austral* (Buenos Aires, 1876–7); A. A. Mendes Corrêa, 'Nouvelle hypothèse sur le peuplement primitif de l'Amérique du Sud', *XXII Congress of Americanists* (Rome, 1926); *Carthaginians* – Gonzalo Fernández de Oviedo y Valdés, *História general y natural de las Indias* (Seville, 1535–57); J. de Torquemada, *Monarquia Indiana* (Madrid, 1613); Sir Walter Ralegh, *The Discoverie of the Large, Rich and Bewtiful Empyre of Guiana* (1596); *Scandinavia* – Hugo Grotius, *De Origine Americanorum Dissertatio* (Paris, 1642); *Egypt* – Elliot Smith, *The Migration of Early Culture* (Manchester, 1915), and 'The Origin of the Pre-colombian Civilization of America', *Science* 44 and 45, 1916, 1917, and *The Ancient Egyptians and the Origin of Civilizations* (London, 1923); W. J. Perry, *The Children of the Sun* (New York/London, 1923); *Spain* (by followers of the legendary King Héspero in the seventeenth century B.C.) – Oviedo, *História general y natural; Ophir* (source of King Solomon's gold in III Kings, IX) – Pietro Martire d'Anghiera, *Décadas del Nuevo Mundo* (1500; Buenos Aires, 1944).

48 *America.* Samuel G. Morton, *Crania Americana* (Philadelphia, 1839); F. Ameghino, *La antiguedad del hombre en La Plata*, 2 vols (Paris/Buenos Aires, 1880–1).

50 *and weavers.* Aleš Hrdlička, *Early Man in South America*, Bureau of American Ethnology Bulletin 52 (Washington, DC, 1912); 'The Genesis of the Indian', *XIX International Congress of Americanists* (Washington, 1917); *The Origin and Antiquity of the American Indian*, Report of the Smithsonian Institution (1923, 1928); 'Man's Antiquity in America', *XX International Congress of Americanists* (Rio de Janeiro, 1922), and many other works.

50 *Malay–Polynesian stock.* Early authors who guessed at an Asian origin for American man included: Père Joseph Lafitau, *Mœurs des sauvages américains, comparés aux mœurs des premiers temps* (Paris, 1724), Baron Alexander von Humboldt, and the nineteenth-century Brazilian historian Adolpho de Varnhagen, Visconde de Pôrto Seguro. A. de Quatrefages argued for a New Guinea origin for the Lagoa Santa skeletons in 'L'Homme fossile de Lagoa Santa en Brésil et ses descendants actuels', *Compte-Rendu de l'Académie des Sciences de Paris* 93 no. 22, 1879, and *Introduction à l'étude des races humaines* (Paris, 1883). Herman F. C. Ten Kate saw a Melanesian origin for Lagoa Santa man: 'Sur les crânes de Lagoa-Santa', *Bulletin de la Société d'Anthropologie de Paris*, 3rd series, 8, 1885, and 'Sur la question de la pluralité et de la parenté des races en Amérique', *VIII Congrès Internationale des Américanistes* (Paris, 1890), etc. Paul Rivet's theories were expounded in many articles, notably: 'La Race de Lagoa Santa chez les populations précolombiennes de l'Équateur', *Bulletins et Mémoires de la Société d'Anthropologie de Paris*, 5th series, 9, 1908; 'Les Mélano-Polynésiens et les Australiens en Amérique', *Anthropos* 20, 1925; 'Les Origines de l'homme

américain', *L'Anthropologie* 35 (Paris, 1925); 'Les Malayo-Polynésiens en Amérique', JSAP, n.s., 18, 1926. Others who added or subscribed to these theories included F. Graebner, 'Amerika und die Sudsee Kulturen', *Ethnologica* 2, 1913; Erland Nordenskiöld, in JSAP, n.s., 9, 1912, etc.; José Imbelloni, *La esfinge indiana* (Buenos Aires, 1926), and 'El poblamiento primitivo de América', *Revista Geográfica Americana* 12 no. 70, July 1939, etc.

50 *ten thousand years old.* On Lagoa Santa, in addition to the references to Quatrefages, Ten Kate, Rivet and Nordenskiöld in the previous note, see Sören Hansen, 'Lagoa Santa racen', *Samling af Afhandlinger e Museo Lundii, Copenhagen* 1 no. 5, 1888; H. V. Walter, A. Cathoud and Anibal Mattos, 'The Confins Man – a Contribution to the Study of Early Man in South America', *International Symposium on Early Man* (Philadelphia, 1937); Anibal Mattos, 'Lagoa Santa Man', HSAI 1 399–400; Fernando Altenfelder Silva and Betty Meggers, 'Cultural Development in Brazil', in *Aboriginal Cultural Development in Latin America: an interpretative review*, ed. Betty J. Meggers and Clifford Evans, Smithsonian Miscellaneous Collections, 146 no. 1 (Washington, DC, 1963); Tarcísio T. Messias and Marília C. de Mello e Alvim, 'Contribuições ao estudo do Homem de Lagoa Santa', BMNA 20, 1962. Wesley R. Hurt obtained carbon dates of only 3000 years for remains from one of the Lagoa Santa caves: 'The Cultural Complexes from the Lagoa Santa Region, Brazil', *American Anthropologist* 62, 1960. But Hurt's 'New and Revised Radiocarbon Dates from Brazil', *Museum News* 23 (Vermilion, S. Dak., 1962), recorded far older dates, of some 10,000 years, from objects excavated in another of the caves.

51 *Tupi invasions.* Antonio Serrano, 'The Sambaquís of the Brazilian Coast', HSAI 1 401–7; Wesley R. Hurt, 'Recent Radiocarbon Dates for Central and Southern Brazil', *American Antiquity* 30 no. 1, 25–33, 1964. Also works by J. B. de

Lacerda, Albert Löfgren, Charles Frederick Hartt, Domingos S. Ferreira Penna, Charles Weiner and Josef von Siemiradzki in the nineteenth century; and by Hermann von Ihering, Benedicto Calixto, Everardo Beckheuser, Theodor Bischoff, Sylvio Fróes de Abreu, Léon F. Clérot, José Imbelloni, Ricardo Krone, Antonio Carlos Simões da Silva, and more recently by Marília C. de Mello e Alvim and D. P. de Mello Filho, in the twentieth century.

52 *great beauty.* Betty J. Meggers, 'The Archaeology of the Amazon Basin', HSAI 3 149–66; 'Environment and Culture in the Amazon Basin', in *Studies in Human Ecology* (Pan-American Union, Washington, DC, 1957); Sigvald Linné, 'Les Recherches archéologiques de Nimuendajú au Brésil', JSAP, n.s., 20, 1928; Charles Frederick Hartt, 'The Ancient Indian Pottery of Marajó, Brazil', *American Naturalist* 5, 1871; Betty J. Meggers and Clifford Evans, *Archaeological Investigations at the Mouth of the Amazon*, Bureau of American Ethnology Bulletin 167 (1957); *Archaeological Evidence of Prehistoric Migration from the Rio Negro to the Mouth of the Amazon*, University of Arizona Social Science Bulletin 27 (1958) 9–16; and 'The Reconstruction of Settlement Pattern in the South American Tropical Forest', in *Prehistoric Settlement Patterns in the New World*, ed. Gordon R. Willey (New York, 1956) 156–64; Donald W. Lathrap, 'The Cultural Sequence at Yarinacocha, Eastern Peru', *American Antiquity* 23 379–88, 1958; and *The Upper Amazon* 74–8, 117–21, 145–51; and works by Peter Paul Hilbert, H. A. Torres, Max Uhle, Antonio Mordini, Ladislau Netto, Orville Derby, Heloisa Alberto Torres and others. The best places to see Marajoara pottery are the Museu Paraense Emilio Goeldi in Belém, Pará, and the Museu Nacional in Rio de Janeiro; the Ethnographical Museum, Göteborg, Sweden; and the University of Pennsylvania Museum, Philadelphia. Tangas can still be seen on the beaches of Rio de Janeiro: these are daring bikini bathing-suits called tangas, which consist

of three triangles of cloth held in place by cords.

52 and bosses. Helen C. Palmatary, 'Tapajó Pottery', *Ethnological Studies* **8** 1–138 (Göteborg, 1939); Antonio Serrano in *Revista Geográfica Americana* **9**, 1938, Nimuendajú and others; John H. Rowe, 'Introduction to "The Tapajo" by Curt Nimuendajú', *Kroeber Anthropological Society Papers* **6** (Berkeley, Calif., 1952). Peter Paul Hilbert, 'Archäologische Untersuchungen am Mittleren Amazonas', *Marburger Studien zur Volkerkunde* **1** (Berlin, 1968).

54 fine noses. Imbelloni, Quatrefages, Rivet, etc., already cited; A. C. Haddon, *The Races of Man and Their Distribution* (Cambridge, 1924); Egon von Eickstedt, *Rassenkunde und Rassengeschichte der Menschheit* (Stuttgart, 1937); Clark Wissler, *The American Indian* (New York, 1938); W. Schmidt, 'Kulturkreise und Kulturschichten in Südamerika', *Zeitschrift für Ethnologie* **45** (Berlin, 1913); Maria Julia Pourchet, *Índice cefálico no Brasil* (Rio de Janeiro, 1941).

55 language groups. The most important linguistic classifications of Brazilian Indian languages include works by C. F. P. von Martius, Karl von den Steinen, Paul Ehrenreich, D. G. Brinton, A. T. Chamberlain, Paul Rivet, Rodolfo Garcia, A. Trombetti, Chestmir Loukotka, *Classificación de las lenguas sudamericanas* (Prague, 1935), and 'Linguas indígenas do Brasil', *Revista do Arquivo Municipal de São Paulo* **54** (1939); Curt Nimuendajú, 'Idiomas indígenas del Brasil', *Revista del Instituto de Etnología* **2** (Tucumán, 1932); Norman A. McQuown, 'The Indigenous Languages of Latin America', *American Anthropologist* **57** no. 3, June 1955; J. Alden Mason, 'The Languages of South American Indians', HSAI **6** 157–317 (Washington, DC, 1963); Darcy Ribeiro, 'Culturas e linguas indígenas do Brasil', *Educação e ciências sociais* **2** no. 6 (Rio de Janeiro, 1957), trans. Janice H. Hopper, *Indians of Brazil in the Twentieth Century* (Washington, DC, 1967); Joseph H. Greenberg, 'The General Classification of Central and South American

Languages', *Fifth International Congress of Anthropological and Ethnological Sciences, Selected Papers* (Philadelphia, 1960); Aryon dall'Igna Rodrigues, 'A classificação do tronco lingüístico Tupi', *Revista de Antropologia* **12** (São Paulo, 1964), and 'Grupos lingüísticos da Amazônia', *Atas do Simpósio sôbre a Biota Amazônica* (Rio de Janeiro, 1967); J. Mattoso Câmara, Jnr, *Introdução às línguas indígenas brasileiras* (Rio de Janeiro, 1965).

56 mankind.' André Thevet, *La Cosmographie universelle* 38; Alfred Métraux, *La Religion des Tupinambá et ses rapports avec celle des autres tribus Tupi-Guaraní* 1–51, and 'The Tupinambá' 131; Ramos, *Introdução à antropologia brasileira* 118.

56 and mountains]'. Thevet, *Cosmographie universelle* 39.

56 was extinguished.' Ibid. 39.

56 better men.' Ibid. 40.

57 was consumed.' Ibid. 43.

57 Maira-Monan.' Ibid. 41.

57 ungrateful people. Ibid. 43; Vicente do Salvador, *História do Brasil* 13, 43; Simão de Vasconcellos, *Das cousas do Brasil* 51–2, and *Chronica da Companhia de Jesus . . .*, ch. 61, pp. 111–13; Manoel da Nóbrega, *Informação das terras do Brasil* 94.

58 "Pai Tupan".' Ibid. 92.

58 their enemy.' Thevet, *Cosmographie universelle* 77; Léry, *Voyage au Brésil* 218. This evil spirit was variously spelled by different authors: Añañ, Aignen, Anhangá, etc. It meant the spirit of the woods. Some authors have confused it with Anguera, which means the soul or spirit of the dead.

58 are buried'. Yves d'Evreux, *Voyage dans le nord du Brésil, fait durant les années 1613 et 1614* 349.

59 ('without end'). The Saci's ornithological names are *Tapera naevia* or *Cuculus cayanus*. J. Barbosa Rodrigues, *Poranduba amazonense*, ABNRJ **14**, 1886–7; Ramos, *Introdução à antropologia brasileira* 127; Rodolpho von Ihering, *A vida dos nossos animais* (São Leopoldo, 1953) 90–1.

59 us all.' Evreux, *Voyage* 349. The Tupi were famous for their messianic migrations, which were recorded by

Alfred Métraux ('Les Migrations historiques des Tupi-Guaraní') and by Curt Nimuendajú among the Guaraní of southern Brazil ('Apontamentos sobre os Guaraní').

60 *happen otherwise.*' Thevet, *Cosmographie universelle* 78.

60 *most fortunate.*' Ibid. 78.

60 *a name.*' Ibid. 81.

61 *in there!*"' Ibid. 81.

61 *his duty.*' Ibid. 82.

61 *average pumpkin. . . .*' André Thevet, *Histoire d'André Thevet Angoumoisin . . . de deux voyages par lui faits aux Indes Australes, et occidentales* 51, in *Cosmographie universelle* 82.

61 *die of poison.*' Ibid. 79–80. Thevet described the poisonous ahouai tree as comparable in size with a European pear-tree, with perpetually green leaves, whitish bark, milky sap and a rotten smell when cut. Because his was the first description of the tree, its botanical name is *Thevetia ahouai*.

61 *birds' skins.*' Ibid. 80–1.

62 *the people'.* Evreux, *Voyage* (1874 ed.) 295.

62 *bite them.*' Luís Figueira, letter from Bahia, 26 March 1609, DHBC 1 1–42; João Capistrano de Abreu, 'Tricentenário do Ceará', in *Capítulos de história colonial* 370.

62 *wild honey.*' Figueira letter, 26 March 1609, 35.

62 *causing him harm.*' Ibid. 35; Evreux, *Voyage* 315; Staden, *Viagem ao Brasil* (1942 ed.) 277–8; Heitor Furtado de Mendonça, *Primeira visitação do Santo Officio as Partes do Brasil: Confisões de Bahia, 1591–92* 370; Métraux, 'Tupinambá' 129–30; Ramos, *Introdução à antropologia brasileira* 128–9.

63 *your enemies!*' Léry, *Voyage au Brésil* 194.

63 *must die!*' Gabriel Soares de Sousa, *Tratado descriptivo do Brasil em 1587* 381. Even within the idyllic sanctuary of the Xingu Indian Park, such deaths occur almost every year. I was once fishing with a Mehinaku man accompanied by two boys. He explained that these were not his sons, but the children of men whom the tribe had felt obliged to kill for suspected black magic. He described

exactly how the decisions had been reached, and how the victims were informed of their fate and killed. I later learned that my informant was himself suspect and in danger of a similar accusation.

64 *kill him.*' Fernão Cardim, *Tratados da .erra e gente do Brasil* (1925 ed.) 162–3; Nóbrega, *Informação das terras do Brasil* 92–3; Anon Jesuit, *Enformação do Brasil* 432; Métraux, *Migrations historiques* 12. These despairing migrations, often known as santidades, became more frequent as a reaction against the hardships of colonial conquest.

64 *their ancestors.*' Thevet, *Cosmographie universelle* 49.

64 *position I occupy.*' Evreux, *Voyage* 347; Abbeville, *Histoire de la mission* 254.

64 *the task.*' Sousa, *Tratado descriptivo* 325.

64 *personal valour.*' Abbeville, *Histoire de la mission* 255; Sousa, *Tratado descriptivo* 366; Ambrosio Fernandes Brandão, *Diálogos das grandezas do Brasil* (Rio de Janeiro, 1943) 273–4; Salvador, *História do Brasil*, bk 1, ch. 12, p. 54.

64 *their hammocks.*' Thevet, *Cosmographie universelle* 178.

65 *men's beards.*' Ibid. 124; Jean de Léry, *Histoire d'un voyage faict en la terre du Brésil, autrement dite Amérique* 1 124; Alfred Métraux, *La Civilization matérielle des tribus Tupi-Guaraní* 183.

65 *hog's tongue.*' Thevet, *Cosmographie universelle* 126; Pero de Magalhães Gandavo, *Histories of Brazil* 2 88–9; Hans Staden, *Vera historia* (Buenos Aires, 1944) 118; Léry, *Histoire* 1 126–7. The most important men had up to nine of these stones in their lips and cheeks. The lip plugs, or labrets, would be of green or white stone: beryl, amazonite, chrysoprase, chalcedony, quartz or crystal.

65 *stockings. . . .*' Thevet, *Cosmographie universelle* 128.

67 *silk thread.*' Ibid. 162, and *Histoire d'André Thevet* 277; Evreux, *Voyage* 23. The anonymous *Vocabulário na lingua brasílica* says that a wax-and-feather bonnet placed on condemned prisoners was called tobapigaba; whereas the ordinary

feather bonnet was called acojaba. Thevet called the round ostrich-feather ornament amonas, whereas Staden called it enduap. Both authors included fine engravings of Tupinambá wearing these plumes. The Dutch also brought back magnificent Brazilian feather cloaks and headdresses. Some of these are in the National Museum in Copenhagen – presumably sent to the King of Denmark by Prince Johan Maurits of Nassau.
67 *palme tree leaves'.* Peter Carder, *The Relation of Peter Carder of Saint Verian in Cornwall*, in Samuel Purchas, *Hakluytus*

Posthumus or Purchas His Pilgrimes 16 140; Knivet in ibid. 16 248.
67 *among them.'* Cardim, *Tratados* 272.
67 *share it.'* Gandavo, *Histories of Brazil* 2 87; Thevet, *Cosmographie universelle* 116–17, 251; Léry, *Histoire* 2 95; *Informação da provincia do Brasil para nosso Padre*, in José de Anchieta, *Cartas, informações, fragmentos históricos e sermões*; Ferdinand Denis (ed.), *Une Fête brésilienne célébrée à Rouen en 1550* 16.
67 *call of nature.'* António Blásques, in Serafim Soares Leite, *Páginas de história do Brasil* 22.

Chapter 4   THE FIRST COLONIES

71 *its own accord.'* Pero de Magalhães Gandavo, *Tratado da provincia do Brasil* 147–9.
71 *Tupinambá women.'* Gabriel Soares de Sousa, *Tratado descriptivo do Brasil em 1587* 342. Gilberto Freyre, *The Masters and the Slaves: a study in the development of Brazilian civilization* 86. João Fernando de Almeida Prado, *A conquista da Paraíba* 64–5. The historian João de Barros had written a chronicle of the reign of King João II and the *Decadas da India* about Portuguese exploits in India. He was also Factor and Treasurer of the Casa da India. Vicente do Salvador said that some survivors of Barros' expedition found refuge among the Gê-speaking Tapuia tribes of the interior – enemies of the Tupi who had destroyed the Portuguese colony. When the Portuguese finally conquered Maranhão in 1614 the bearded descendants of these Portuguese–Tapuia unions welcomed their Portuguese relatives. Salvador also stated that the Tapuia inhabited the island of São Luís in the 1530s. It is therefore possible that the settlers were destroyed by the same Tupinambá invasion that evicted the Tapuia from the island. But it seems more likely that the Tupinambá were already in possession of most of Maranhão at the time of the arrival of the Europeans. Vicente do Salvador, *História do Brasil*, bk 2, ch. 13, p. 130.

71 *Brazil'.* Anon Jesuit, *Sumário das armadas que se fizeram e guerras que se deram na conquista do Rio Paraíba*, addressed to the Jesuit Superior Cristóvão de Gouvêa, perhaps by Vicente do Salvador or Fernão Cardim, 8.
71 *very valiantly.'* Antony Knivet, *The Admirable Adventures and Strange Fortunes of Master Antonie Knivet . . .*, in Samuel Purchas, *Hakluytus Posthumus or Purchas His Pilgrimes* 16 246. The Potiguar wore green stone plugs in their lower lips. On the march they chewed a wad of tobacco held between the lip and teeth. Knivet observed that 'as they goe the rume runneth out of the hole that they have in their lippes'.
72 *the sea.'* André Thevet, *La Cosmographie universelle* 223–4; Anon Jesuit, *Sumário das armadas* 14.
72 *one another.'* Ibid. 8.
72 *French.* The Portuguese donatory Pero Lopes de Sousa conquered Itamaracá island from the French, who had a fort on it armed with artillery and manned by over a hundred soldiers. Pero Lopes captured two French ships in the Atlantic, and sent Tupi-speaking agents to persuade the Indians to change sides. The French surrendered Itamaracá, dismayed by these reverses and by the strength of the Portuguese expedition. But Pero Lopes later hanged many of them after someone had tried to

assassinate him. He returned to Portugal and was drowned while sailing to India in 1539. Salvador, *História*, bk 2, ch. 11, pp. 122–5; Sousa, *Tratado descriptivo* 25; Alexander Marchant, *From Barter to Slavery* 77; Hélio Vianna, *História do Brasil* 68–9. The settlement of Conceição on Itamaracá has now vanished, but the place had a few sugar estates during the sixteenth century. During its brief period of prosperity in the 1540s Itamaracá was managed by João Gonçalves, who tried to keep on good terms with the Indians.

72 *generally victorious.* Anon Jesuit, *Sumário das armadas* 12–13. Various letters to the King mentioned the slave raids on the Potiguar coast: Duarte Coelho, Olinda, 20 Dec 1546, HCP 3 316; Afonso Gonçalves, Olinda, 10 May 1548, HCP 3 317; Duarte Coelho, Olinda, 14 April 1549, HCP 3 319.

72 *Caeté.'* Sousa, *Tratado descriptivo* 28. Duarte Coelho was the son of Gonçalo Coelho, commander of the fleets that explored the coast of Brazil in 1501–2 and 1503. Amerigo Vespucci sailed on those voyages and usurped the entire credit for them through his letters.

72 *enslave them'.* Salvador, *História*, bk 2, ch. 8, p. 108.

73 *such spirit.'* Ibid. bk 2, ch. 8, p. 110.

73 *grows there'.* Hans Staden, ch. 4, HCP 3 317. André Thevet mentioned that the Tamoio used similar pepper mixed with 'a certain grease' to smoke the Portuguese out of their houses at São Vicente (*Histoire d'André Thevet Angoumoisin, Cosmographe du Roy, de deux voyages par lui faits aux Indes Australes, et Occidentales* 299). The Tupinambá of Bahia also tried to repel smallpox in 1562 by sprinkling their houses with pepper.

73 *great sorcerer'.* Salvador, *História*, bk 2, ch. 9, p. 112.

73 *the siege.* Ibid. bk 2, ch. 9, p. 113.

74 *the roads'.* Ibid. bk 2, ch. 9, p. 116.

74 *Brazil.'* Ibid. bk 2, ch. 9, p. 117.

74 *their enmity.'* Ibid. bk 2, ch. 9, p. 118.

74 *by leagues'.* Robert Southey, *History of Brazil* 1 54, quoting Sebastião da Rocha Pitta, *Historia da America Portugueza, desde o anno de 1500 do seu descobrimento ate o de 1724*, bk 2, p. 108; Oliveira Lima, *A Nova*

Lusitania, HCP 3 292; Jerônimo de Albuquerque to King, Olinda, 28 Aug 1555, HCP 3 380–1.

75 *would camp.'* 'História do naufrágio do Nau São Paulo', from *História Tragica Maritima*, in Antonio da Santa Maria Jaboatam, *Nove Orbe Serafico Brasilico . . .* 2 144, and C. R. Boxer, *Further Selections from the Tragic History of the Sea*, Hakluyt Society, 2nd series, 132 115, 1968.

75 *make ready.'* Jaboatam, *Novo Orbe Serafico Brasilico* 2 145.

75 *Brazil.* Salvador, *Historia*, bk 3, ch. 15; Francisco da Costa, *Anais Pernambucanos* 1 328, 353, 398–9. Jerônimo de Albuquerque was a leading figure of Pernambuco and all Brazil for almost half a century. His Tobajara wife was christened Maria do Espírito Santo Arcoverde ('Mary of the Holy Spirit Green Bow'). Their daughter Catarina married the Florentine Cavalcante, and was the ancestor of a powerful family. Jerônimo's nephew Jorge returned to Portugal in 1565, but sailed back to govern the captaincy from 1572–6. Jaboatam, *Novo Orbe* 2 145–6, and *Catálogo genealógico das principaes familias . . .*; Antonio Borges da Fonseca, 'Nobiliarchia Pernambucana', ABNRJ 48 354–463, 1926. The Cape of Santo Agostinho is some 40 kms south of Recife and Olinda, and Serinhaém is 80 kms south.

76 *others came.'* Salvador, *Historia*, bk 3, ch. 15, p. 204; Sylvio Salema Garçao Ribeiro, *Um bárbaro e cruel da história do Brasil* 55–6; Fernão Cardim, *Tratados da terra e gente do Brasil* 171–2; Costa, *Anais Pernambucanos* 1 394–5.

76 *him.'* Salvador, *Historia*, bk 3, ch. 15, p. 204.

76 *ten leagues.'* Anon Jesuit, *Enformação do Brasil e de suas capitanias* 408–9.

77 *or more.'* Pero de Magalhães Gandavo, *Histories of Brazil* 2 41; and *Tratado* 69–71. Lopes Vaz said that by 1587 Pernambuco had over 3000 houses (*A Discourse of the West Indies and South Sea*, in Richard Hakluyt, *The Principall Navigations of the English Nation . . .* 8 172).

77 *all things.'* Ambrosio Fernandes

Brandão, *Diálogos das grandezas do Brasil* (1943) 142.

77 *spend lavishly.*' Cardim, *Tratados* 320; Pedro Calmon, 'Espírito da sociedade colonial' 39–40.

77 *in Lisbon.*' Cardim, *Tratados* 295–6; Sousa, *Tratado descriptivo*, bk 1, ch. 16, pp. 28–9.

78 *lobsters, sardines. . . .*' Francisco Martins Coutinho, Relação about the Captaincy (1536), in João Fernando de Almeida Prado, *Bahia e as capitanias do centro do Brasil (1530–1626)* 1 60.

78 *and conspiracies. . . .*' Pero Borges to King João III, Pôrto Seguro, 7 Feb 1550, HCP 3 268; Prado, *Bahia* 1 69.

78 *to return.* Pero de Campo Tourinho to King, Pôrto Seguro, 28 July 1546, HCP 3 266–7. Caramuru warned his compatriots that Bahia was about to fall to the French. A French ship had gone to seize the guns abandoned there by the fleeing Portuguese. It had agreed with the Tupinambá to return in a few months' time with more ships for a permanent occupation.

79 *had killed.* Pero de Campo Tourinho to King João III, Pôrto Seguro, 28 July 1546, HCP 3 266–7; Regimento de Tomé de Sousa, 17 Dec 1548, HCP 3 345; Salvador, *Historia* (1931 ed.) p. 44; Sousa, *Tratado descriptivo*, bk 1, ch. 28, p. 52. Anon Jesuit, *De algumas coisas mais notaveis do Brasil*, RHGB 94 374, 1923.

79 *brought them.* Caramuru's voyage to France was related by Salvador, *Historia* (1931 ed.) p. 60 (who said she was baptised Luiza) and repeated in Simão de Vasconcellos, *Chronica da Companhia de Jesus* . . . 38–9, and Rocha Pitta, *História da America Portuguesa* (Lisbon, 1880) 30. The great nineteenth-century historian Francisco Adolpho de Varnhagen, Visconde de Pôrto Seguro, sought to disprove this journey to France and carefully failed to cite Salvador's account of it ('O Caramuru perante a historia'). Afonso Arinos de Mello Franco, *O índio brasileiro e a Revolução Francesa* 73–5.

79 *done to them.*' Regimento de Tomé de Sousa, Lisbon, 17 Dec 1548, HCP 3 347.

79 *up to now.*' Ibid. 347–8.

80 *were chiefs.*' Ibid. 345.

80 *their customs'.* King João III to Diogo Álvares, Lisbon, 19 Nov 1548, in Jaboatam, *Catálogo* 7–8.

81 *European man-at-arms.* Prado, *Bahia* 1 93.

81 *for a while.*' Duarte da Costa to King, Salvador, 10 June 1555, HCP 3 377.

81 *in the woods.*' Ibid. 378.

82 *bishop of Brazil.*' Vasconcellos, *Chronica*, bk 2, p. 186.

82 *not counting slaves'.* Sousa, *Tratado descriptivo*, bk 1, ch. 18, p. 33.

82 *and children!*' Nóbrega to the former Governor Tomé de Sousa, Bahia, 5 July 1559, in CPJB 72–3, 82. The Bishop had also quarrelled with the Jesuits, who had originally welcomed his arrival. They had hoped that he would help them defend the Indians, but the Bishop tended to side with the colonists. The city council of Salvador da Bahia, which consisted of the most powerful settlers, regarded the Bishop as their spokesman in complaining about Duarte da Costa to the King: Câmara of Salvador to King, 18 Dec 1556, HCP 3 381.

83 *Potiguar.*' Sousa, *Tratado descriptivo*, bk 1, and bk 17, chs 13, 19, pp. 20, 34–5, 409–10. The locations of these tribes were somewhat confused, since the tribal nations split up, migrated and fragmented. Gabriel Soares de Sousa said that Tupinambá and Caeté lived at the mouth of the São Francisco, and that up the river were various Tapuia nations – Tupina, Amoipira, Ubirajara and Amazons. The Spaniard Luis Ramírez had mentioned some Tupinambá on the coast of Pernambuco, in a letter written from the Plate river on 10 July 1528, RHGB 15 17, 1852. A Jesuit, Pedro Domingues, visited the Amoipira in the early seventeenth century: 'Relação . . . sôbre a viagem que de São Paulo fez . . .', in Serafim Soares Leite, *Páginas de história do Brasil* 113–14. Cardim, *Tratados* 172; Salvador, *Historia* (1931 ed.) p. 52; Jaboatam, *Novo Orbe* 1 14–21; Simão de Vasconcellos, *Notícias curiosas e necessarias sobre o Brasil* 29–33. For modern discussions of the distribution of these

tribes, see Alfred Métraux, *La Civilization matérielle des tribus Tupi-Guaraní* 13, and 'The Tupinambá' 95–7, 'Les Migrations historiques des Tupi-Guaraní' 4–6; Aires do Casal, *Corografia Brasilica* 1 84; Florestan Fernandes, *Organização social dos Tupinambá* 33–40; Artur Ramos, *Introducão à antropologia brasileira: As culturas indígenas* 75–8.

83 *noble actions!'* Vasconcellos, *Chronica*, bk 2, p. 210.

83 *native fantasies!'* Ibid. bk 2, p. 211. The chief's tribe lived on the island of Curupeba. After being defeated, it was assembled in one aldeia under the Jesuits.

84 *with blood'.* Ibid. bk 2, p. 213.

84 *be counted.'* Ibid. bk 2, pp. 215–16.

84 *160 villages.* Sousa, *Tratado descriptivo* (1938 ed.) 132; Salvador, *Historia* (1931 ed.) p. 67; Anon jesuit, *Enformação do Brasil* 406; Gandavo, *Tratado* (1924 ed.) 48–9; Vasconcellos, *Chronica* 126.

84 *word of God.'* Letter from an unknown Jesuit, Bahia, 19 July 1558, published in E. Bradford Burns, 'Introduction to the Brazilian Jesuit Letters', *Mid-America*, July 1962, 181–6, and his *Documentary History of Brazil* 63, 62.

85 *and children.'* José de Anchieta, *Cartas, informações, fragmentos historicos e sermões* 374–5; Fernandes, *Organização social* 38; Sousa, *Tratado* (1938 ed.) 132; Anchieta and Cardim said that the Tupinambá fled for 200–400 leagues into the interior: Anchieta, *Cartas* 378, 435; Cardim, *Tratados* (1939 ed.) 171.

85 *of the Indians.* Nóbrega, quoted in Prado, *Bahia* 2 65; Nóbrega letter, Bahia, Aug 1549, in Serafim Soares Leite, *Suma histórica da Companhia de Jesus no Brasil* . . . 4.

85 *and interpreter.* Francisco Pires letter, Bahia, 1552, CA 131; Prado, *Bahia* 2 64–5.

85 *works of piety.'* Salvador, *Historia* (1931 ed.) p. 60. Letter from Francisco Pires, SJ, to Brothers in Portugal, 1552, CA 131; Anon, *Santuario Marianno* (Lisbon, 1723) 9 9 and 12. Jaboatam, *Catálogo* 84–102, 138–44, lists the succession of Caramuru's fifteen legitimate and many illegitimate children. Henriques Leal,

RHGB 36 pt 2, 69–70, 1873; Southey, *History of Brazil* 1 38–9; T. C. Accioly, *Memorias historicas e politicas da Provincia da Bahia* (Bahia, 1835) 205; João Fernando de Almeida Prado, *Primeiros povoadores do Brasil (1500–1530)* 103–8; Alexandre J. de Mello Moraes, *Corografia historica, cronografica, genealogica nobiliaria e politica do Império do Brasil* 1 126.

86 *these people.'* Sousa, *Tratado descriptivo*, bk 1, ch. 19, p. 35.

86 *with them'.* Ibid. bk 1, ch. 19, p. 36; Anchieta, *Cartas* 355, 356–7; CA 358.

86 *Brazil.* François Pyrard de Laval, *Discours du voyage des français aux Indes orientales* . . . (Paris, 1611) 281–9; Thales de Azevedo, 'Indios, brancos e pretos no Brasil colonial' 88; Marchant, *From Barter to Slavery* 132.

87 *Tupinikin.* Regimento de Tomé de Sousa, HCP 3 346–7; Sousa, *Tratado descriptivo*, ch. 30, p. 57; Salvador, *Historia* (1931 ed.) p. 42. This group of Tupinikin lived between the rivers São Mateus (Cricaré) and Camamu; another tribe with the same name lived near São Vicente and Santos. The name probably meant simply 'neighbouring Tupi'.

87 *turned to ashes.'* Vasconcellos, *Chronica* 243–4. Vasconcellos said that this campaign was against the Aimoré, but other writers show that Mem de Sá fought a rising of the Tupinikin and that the Aimoré attacks on Ilhéus came later.

88 *on their heads'.* Ibid. 244.

88 *killing them there.'* Manoel da Nóbrega to Tomé de Sousa (then returned to Lisbon), Bahia, 5 July 1559, in Leite, *Cartas dos primeiros Jesuítas* 3 100; Vasconcellos, *Chronica* 244.

88 *his new city.* Regimento de Tomé de Sousa, 17 Dec 1548, HCP 3 345.

88 *did so. . . .'* Mem de Sá, *Documentos relativos a Mem de Sá, governador geral do Brasil* 133.

88 *colour of blood'.* Vasconcellos, *Chronica* 245.

89 *naked people.'* Manoel da Nóbrega to Tomé de Sousa, Bahia, 5 July 1559, Leite, *Cartas dos primeiros Jesuítas* 101.

89 *depopulated of them'.* Vasco Fernandes Coutinho to King Sebastião, Ilhéus, 22 May 1558, 'Documentos historicos

extrahidos da Torre do Tombo', RHGB
49 pt 1, 587, 1886. Coutinho was, in fact,
Donatory of Espírito Santo, but wrote
from Ilhéus. The Donatory of Ilhéus
never went in person to Brazil, and the
area tended to be administered by royal
governors from Bahia.

89 *best captaincy!'* Manoel da Nóbrega to
Tomé de Sousa, Bahia, 5 July 1559, Leite,
Cartas dos primeiros Jesuítas 77, 78–9.

89 *other captaincies.* Sousa, *Tratado
descriptivo* 77–8, 81–2; Salvador, *Historia*
(1931 ed.) p. 40. The donatory Vasco
Fernandes Coutinho quarrelled with the
largest landholder in his area, Duarte de
Lemos. Although he abandoned the
captaincy, it was reoccupied by his son of
the same name.

90 *many heathen. . . .'* Instrumento de
Mem de Sá, in *Documentos relativos* 132–3;
Francisco Adolpho de Varnhagen,
Visconde de Pôrto Seguro, RHGB **1** 397;
Luis Norton, *A dinastia dos Sás no Brasil*
(Lisbon, 1965) 5–6.

90 *their heads'.* Queen-Regent to Mem de
Sá, in Varnhagen, RHGB **1** 381.
Salvador, *Historia* (1931 ed.) p. 68;
Vasconcellos, *Chronica*, bk 2, pp. 280–1;
Casal, *Corografia* **2** 57; Southey, *History of
Brazil* **1** 299; Prado, *Bahia* **2** 80.

90 *more peaceful than ever'.* Mem de Sá,
Documentos relativos 136.

91 *Brazil.'* Jean de Léry, *Histoire d'un
voyage faict en la terre de Brésil, autrement
dite Amérique* **1** 78. Waitacá is a modern
phonetic spelling of the tribe's name:
the chroniclers called it Goaytaca, Goya-
taka, Waitacazes, Ouetacazes, etc. The
neighbours with whom the Waitacá
were at war were: to the north, the
Tupinikin and Temimino; to the south,
the Tamoio Tupinambá of Cabo Frio
and Guanabara; to the east, the Puri of
the upper Paraíba, and the Ocauan and
Caraia; to the north-east the Papana.

Alfred Métraux saw the Ocauan,
Caraia, Ouanem, Guarus, Guarulhos,
Sacarus and Papana as precursors of the
tribes known to later travellers as
Coroado ('Crowned Indians') because of
the tufts of hair on the tops of their
heads. The Puri were closely linked with
the Coroado, although Knivet, who

visited the Puri in about 1600, said that
they had adopted many Tupi customs,
such as the use of hammocks and
tobacco. But other Puri were very similar
to the Coroado, and came to form a
linguistic group related to Gê, known as
Puri-Coroado. These Indians survived
until the early nineteenth century in the
dense forests of eastern Minas Gerais.
They therefore became a favourite
attraction for visiting scientists such as
Spix and Martius, Saint-Hilaire, Wied-
Neuwied, Rugendas, Debret, etc.
Métraux, however, does not follow other
ethnologists in assuming that the
Waitacá also merged with these other
Coroado tribes. Nor does he assume that
the Waitacá were Gê-speaking, even
though their way of life was similar to
other Gê tribes. The fact is that the
Waitacá are extinct and nothing is known
about their language. Alfred Métraux,
'Les Indiens Waitaká' 108, 118–21.

91 *all other meats'.* André Thevet, *Histoire*
296; Léry, *Histoire* **1** 79; Sousa, *Tratado
descriptivo*, ch. 45, p. 83.

91 *were eaten.'* Knivet in Purchas **16** 252.
Thevet and Léry both located the
Waitacá as living between Maguehay
(Macaé) and the Paraíba; Thevet, *Le
Grand Insulaire*, in *Les Français en Amérique
pendant la deuxième moitié du XVIe siècle: Le
Brésil et les brésiliens*, ed. Suzanne
Lussagnet, 293; Léry, *Histoire* **1** 78–80
and **2** 130; Vasconcellos said they were
between Cape São Tomé and the
Itabapoana river, but Soares de Sousa
gave a far greater area, between Cape São
Tomé and the Cricaré (now São Mateus)
river in northern Espírito Santo. All
agree that they lived at the mouth of the
Paraíba, and near Lagoa Feia ('Ugly
Lagoon') on the Campos dos
Guaitacazes ('Plain of the Waitacá').

91 *my own eyes!'* Thevet, *Histoire* 296.

91 *my enemy's.''* Ibid. 293–5.

91 *surround it.'* Ibid. 296; Knivet in
Purchas **16** 252.

92 *their bows'.* Simão de Vasconcellos,
Vida do Veneravel Padre José de Anchieta,
bk 4, ch. 11. Thevet said that the Waitacá
had to obtain wood for their bows by
trading with the forest-dwelling Ocauan

(?Puri) who lived higher up the Paraíba.
92 *their houses.'* Knivet in Purchas **16** 252.
92 *country wasted.'* Pero de Góis to King
João III, Vila da Rainha, São Tomé, 29
April 1546, HCP **3** 263. Pizarro e Araújo,
Memórias históricas do Rio de Janeiro **2**
119–20. Pero de Góis had sailed with
Martim Afonso in 1531 and had been a
settler in São Vicente before being
awarded the captaincy of São Tomé. He
had two peaceful years there, followed by
five years of war against the Waitacá.
93 *Irish'.* Knivet in Purchas **16** 250.
93 *any other nation'.* Jacome Monteiro,
Relação da Província do Brasil, in HCJB **8**
407.
94 *wilde Beasts'.* Knivet in Purchas **16** 250.
94 *in the ashes.'* Ibid. **16** 250.
94 *arrows to match.'* Gandavo, *Histories of
Brazil* **2** 109.
94 *forest floor.* Monteiro, *Relação* 407.
94 *great runners'.* Sousa, *Tratado descriptivo,*
bk. 1, ch. 30, p. 57.
94 *people or weapons'.* Monteiro, *Relação*
406.
94 *with a Target.'* Knivet in Purchas **16** 250.
94 *hit by arrows.'* Fernão Guerreiro, *Relação
anual das cousas* . . . (Évora/Lisbon,
1603–8), entry for 1605, in Prado, *Bahia* **1**
199–200.

94 *even of water.'* João Azpilcueta, Pôrto
Seguro, 24 June 1555, CA 147; Prado,
Bahia **1** 292–3.
95 *captaincy's defence.* Apothecary Felipe
Guillen to Queen, Pôrto Seguro, 1561,
in Prado, *Bahia* **1** 312. A Jesuit report of
1573 noted nine aldeias of Tupinikin
containing 4000 persons within thirty
miles of the town of Pôrto Seguro. There
were then about 120 whites and 800
slaves in three small towns on its coast,
and the Aimoré seemed to have acquired
a fear of the Portuguese (ibid. **1** 289–90).
95 *almost all lost.'* Guerreiro, *Relação,* entry
for 1605, in Prado, *Bahia* **1** 200.
95 *three thousand slaves.'* Sousa, *Tratado
descriptivo,* bk 1, chs 30 and 32, pp. 57,
59–60. One of the Ilhéus sugar
plantations to be abandoned in the face
of Aimoré attack had once been the pride
of Governor Mem de Sá. It covered 60
kms of land and was worked by masses of
Indians and negro slaves.
95 *submission to captivity.'* Gandavo,
Histories of Brazil **2** 110, 111.
95 *three times.* Cardim, *Tratados* (1925 ed.)
297; Anchieta, *Cartas* 308, 417–19.
96 *round his waist.* Petition by Diogo
Botelho, Bahia, 19 Jan 1606, RHGB **73**
pt 1, 217, 219, 1910.

Chapter 5   *THE ARRIVAL OF THE JESUITS*

98 *by the ground.* . . . .' Ambrosio Pires to
Diego Morin, Pôrto Seguro, *c.*1555,
CPJB **2** 150, quoting what he had been
told by a settler of São Vicente. Serafim
Soares Leite, HCJB **9** 422; Estevão Pinto,
'Introdução à história da antropologia
indígena no Brasil (século xvi)' 352.
Nóbrega's thinness was the result of his
diet – of African pumpkin boiled in
water, 'and when they make a celebration
for him they serve some oranges' (Pires,
CPJB **2** 150).
98 *ethnology.* These various Jesuit works
are listed in the Bibliography. Anchieta's
report on Brazilian flora and fauna was
first published in Venice in 1562 as *Nuovi
Avisi delle Indie di Portogallo* and later

published in Latin and Portuguese:
Serafim Soares Leite, HCJB **10** 86. His
*Arte de Gramatica da Lingoa mais usada na
costa do Brasil* was written when he was
among the Goianá in 1555 but published
in Coimbra only in 1595. Fernão
Cardim's book on natural sciences was
*Do clima e terra do Brasil e de algumas cousas
notaveis que se acham assim na terra como no
mar,* and his ethnological work was *Do
principio e origem dos Indios do Brasil.* This
was first published, in English, by
Samuel Purchas in 1625 and in
Portuguese only 300 years later, when
Capistrano de Abreu discovered the
original manuscripts at Évora.
98 *creatures of his.'* Nóbrega, letter from

Bahia, 10 Aug 1549, *Cartas do Brasil* 94.

99 *continual converse.*' Nóbrega to King, 1551, ibid. 125.

99 *their customs.*' Nóbrega letter from Pernambuco, 1551, RHGB 6 104, 1844.

99 *law better'.* Nóbrega to Mestre Simão, Bahia, 9 Aug 1549, *Cartas Jesuíticas*, ed. Alfredo do Vale Cabral, 1 81.

99 *we order.*' Nóbrega to Dr Navarro of Coimbra, Salvador, Bahia, 10 Aug 1549, *Cartas Jesuíticas* 1 91–2.

99 *they accept.* . . . ' Antonio Rodrigues to the Fathers of Bahia, Aldeia do Bom Jesus, Aug 1561, CPJB 3 388–9.

99 *a thousand souls'.* Luís de Grã to Miguel de Torres, Bahia, 22 Sept 1561, CPJB 3 430.

100 *soon founded.*' Simão de Vasconcellos, *Chronica da Companhia de Jesus* . . ., bk 2, p. 175.

100 *like horses.*' Vicente do Salvador, *Historia do Brasil* 169.

100 *about it'.* Leonardo do Vale to Diego Laynes in Rome, Bahia, 23 Sept 1561, CPJB 3 440.

100 *it was a novelty'.* Antônio Pires, Bahia, 19 July 1558, E. Bradford Burns (ed.), *A Documentary History of Brazil* 59–60.

101 *good ones.*' Letter from anonymous Jesuit, Bahia, 12 Sept 1558, in ibid. 61–2. The governor in question was in fact Mem de Sá's predecessor, the second governor Duarte da Costa.

101 *no one died.*' João de Azpilcueta, Pôrto Seguro, 24 June 1555, CA 146–7; Anchieta to Loyola, Piratininga, July 1554, CPJB 2 79.

101 *the more.*' Vasconcellos, *Chronica*, bk 1, p. 83.

102 *much trouble.*' Pedro Correia, São Vicente, 1551, CA 94; Mecenas Dourado, *A conversão do gentio* 63–4.

102 *so fickle.*' Afonso Braz, Espírito Santo, 1551, CA 88.

102 *ancient customs'.* Anchieta to Loyola, São Paulo de Piratininga, 1 Sept 1554, CPJB 2 107.

102 *human flesh'.* Ibid.

102 *their customs.*' José de Anchieta, *Cartas, informações, fragmentos historicos e sermões* 97.

102 *divine instruction.*' Ibid. 145.

103 *primitive bestiality.*' Manoel da Nóbrega, *Diálogo sobre a conversão do gentio* 133–4.

103 *is worthless.*' Nóbrega, *Diálogo*, in Serafim Soares Leite, *Cartas do Brasil e mais escritos do P. Manoel da Nóbrega* 229.

103 *Christian children.*' Nóbrega, *Diálogo* 143, 146.

103 *is preferable.* The Jesuits also experimented successfully with sending Portuguese boys to mingle with and instruct the Indians. The first batch reached Brazil in 1550, and groups of about twenty a year were sent out until 1557. They were 'lost boys, thieves and bad boys whom we call rascals here'. (Pero Domenech to Loyola, Almeirim, Portugal, 7 Feb 1551, quoted in Serafim Soares Leite, 'O primeiro embarque de órfãos para o Brasil', in *Páginas de história do Brasil* 71–80. Letters from Vicente Rodrigues and Francisco Pires, in 1552, told of the successes of the orphans in explaining Christianity to the natives and teaching them European singing, CPJB 1 320–1, 376–89.) Anchieta wrote to Loyola, on behalf of Nóbrega, that Brazilian-born mestizos were useless in helping to spread Christianity unless sent to Portugal for thorough indoctrination (Piratininga, July 1554, CPJB 2 76). The first twenty Indian boys, aged ten and eleven, were admitted to the Jesuit college in Bahia in 1557.

103 *these heathen',* João de Azpilcueta, Pôrto Seguro, 24 June 1555, CA 146; Dourado, *A conversão do gentio* 66.

104 *way of life.* Luís de Grã to Loyola, 1553, in Serafim Soares Leite, *Novas cartas Jesuítas (de Nóbrega a Vieira)* 166–7.

104 *things of God.*' Antonio Pires, Pernambuco, 5 June 1552, CA 122.

104 *South America.* Nóbrega had explained his intention of segregating converted Indians in missionary settlements in a letter to King João III in 1552 (*Cartas do Brasil* 112–17); the foundation of Piratininga was described by Nóbrega (ibid. 163–70, 181–2, or CPJB 1 489–504, 522–3; Serafim Soares Leite, *Suma histórica da Companhia de Jesus no Brasil* . . . 12–13).

104 *inconveniently located.*' Antonio Pires,

Bahia, 19 July 1558, Burns, *Documentary History* 57–8.

105 *as savages.'* Anon Jesuit, *Enformação do Brasil e de suas capitanias* 435.

105 *also helps'.* Nóbrega, *Cartas do Brasil* 75.

105 *by love.'* Ibid. 140.

105 *and arguments.'* Ibid. 159.

106 *this land.'* Manoel da Nóbrega, 'Apontamentos das coisas do Brasil', 8 May 1558, in Leite, *Novas cartas Jesuítas* 77–8; Dourado, *A conversão do gentio* 77–8.

106 *brutish people.'* Nóbrega to ex-Governor Tomé de Sousa, Bahia, 5 July 1559, in Serafim Soares Leite, *Cartas dos primeiros Jesuítas do Brasil* 3 71–2.

106 *come in.'* Luke, XIV 23. This is from the parable of the rich man whose guests did not appear and who therefore sent servants out to round up beggars and passers-by. The same text was used by the Spanish Franciscan Gerónimo de Mendieta (1525–1604) as the basis for his book *Historia eclesiástica indiana* (first published Madrid, 1870). He compared the Spanish monarchy with the host in the parable.

106 *compelling them to come in.'* Anchieta, letter of 16 April 1563, HCJB 1 291; Dourado, *A conversão do gentio* 26–7; C. R. Boxer, *Race Relations in the Portuguese Colonial Empire, 1415–1825* 92.

106 *all mankind.'* Nóbrega, 1557, CPJB 2 448–9, trans. Boxer, *Race Relations* 91.

106 *great harvest.* . . .' Anon Jesuit, Bahia, 12 Sept 1558, CA 205, and Burns, *Documentary History* 63.

107 *propagation of the Faith.'* Leite, *Suma histórica* 70; the aldeia near the town was São Sebastião and that on the Rio Vermelho was Nossa Senhora (Nóbrega, *Cartas do Brasil* 202–3). After founding the large aldeia of São Paulo near Bahia in 1558, Nóbrega made it his normal residence and it became the effective centre of Jesuit government in Brazil for a number of years. Alexander Marchant, *From Barter to Slavery* 107–8. HCJB 2 49–58.

107 *accept the Faith.'* António Blásques, Bahia, 1558, CA 188–9.

107 *spiritually.'* Antonio Pires, 2 Oct 1559,

CA 247–8; Dourado, *A conversão do gentio* 92.

107 *royal regulation.'* Pero Rodrigues, HCJB 2 59–60.

108 *diabolical customs.* . . .' Anchieta to Diego Laynes, the Jesuit General in Rome, São Vicente, 30 July 1561, CPJB 3 370.

108 *those of God.'* Anchieta to Diego Laynes, Piratininga, March 1562, CPJB 3 454–5.

109 *the Fathers.'* Gabriel Soares de Sousa, *Tratado descriptivo do Brasil em 1587* (1938 ed.), bk 1, ch. 25, p. 47; Dourado, *A conversão do gentio* 99–100.

109 *have nothing.'* Ruy Pereira, Bahia, 1560, CA 261; Marchant, *From Barter to Slavery* 111.

110 *their language.* . . .' Vasconcellos, *Chronica*, bk 2, pp. 177–8.

111 *firm and constant.'* Nóbrega to Jesuits in Portugal, Pernambuco, 1551, *Cartas Jesuítas* 1 115.

111 *glory to God'.* Nóbrega, *Cartas do Brasil* 300–1; Leite, *Suma histórica* 19, 22, 24–5, etc. The Jesuit Constitution did not permit boys to live in the same house as the Fathers. They were therefore housed immediately alongside, under the care of a lay master.

111 *singing matins'.* CPJB 3 144, and Leite, *Suma histórica* 25. Gilberto Freyre roundly condemned the exploitation of the young and the resulting destruction of tribal cultures (*The Masters and the Slaves: a study in the development of Brazilian civilization* 163–4).

111 *heaven-sent.'* Vasconcellos, *Chronica*, bk 1, p. 45.

111 *with boughs.'* Ibid. bk 1, p. 125; Freyre, *Masters and Slaves* 164.

112 *love of God.'* António Blásques to Diego Laynes, Bahia, 10 Sept 1559, CPJB 3 133.

112 *poor old man.'* Ibid. 3 133–4.

112 *with this.'* Manoel da Nóbrega, *Informação das terras do Brasil* 93.

112 *they had.* . . .' Nóbrega to Miguel de Torres, Bahia, 5 July 1559, in Leite, *Cartas dos primeiros Jesuítas* 3 53.

112 *Christian.'* Baltasar Telles, *Chronica da Companhia de Jesus*, bk 3, ch. 7, in Antonio Henriques Leal, 'Apontamentos para a

historia dos Jesuitas extrahidos dos chronistas da Companhia de Jesus', RHGB 34 pt 2, 77, 1871.

112 *in prison.*' Leite, *Cartas dos primeiros Jesuítas* 3 53.

112 *good convert.* Nicolau del Techo, *Historia de la Provincia del Paraguay de la Compañía de Jesus*, trans. M. Serrano y Saenz (Madrid, 1897) 17–18; Jaime Cortesão, *Rapôso Tavares e a formação territorial do Brasil* 139.

113 *save him.* Letter by Francisco Dias Taño, Tape, 6 Sept 1635, in ibid. 139.

113 *missionaries' cook.* Ruiz de Montoya, *Manuscripto Guaraní*, ABNRJ 6 250; Freyre, *Masters and Slaves* 165.

113 *instruct them.*' Manoel da Nóbrega, 'Lei que se deve dar aos índios', in Leite, *Cartas do Brasil* 277–92, and CPJB 2 445–59; Leite, *Suma histórica* 22; Thales de Azevedo, *Ensaios de antropologia social, Catequese e aculturação* 48.

113 *French'.* Anon Jesuit, *Enformação do Brasil*, RHGB 6 430, 1844; Baldus and Willems, *Dicionário de Etnologia e Sociologia*, entry for 'Antropofagia'.

115 *honoured among them.*' António Blásques to Diego Laynes, Bahia, 10 Sept 1559, CPJB 3 137; Nóbrega to Dr Navarro, Salvador, 10 Aug 1549, *Cartas Jesuíticas* 1 92.

115 *right gallantly.*' José de Anchieta, *Informações e fragmentos historicos do Padre Joseph de Anchieta, 1584–1586* 47, or *Cartas* 426.

115 *immodestly nude'.* Simão de Vasconcellos, *Vida do Veneravel Padre José de Anchieta*, quoted in Freyre, *Masters and Slaves* 111.

116 *populations of savages. . . .*' Ibid. 112.

117 *music and singing'.* CPJB 2 351; Leite, *Suma histórica* 64.

117 *Holy Faith.*' Manoel Gomes, 'Informação . . . do Maranhão e Pará', Lisbon, 22 Jan 1621, HCJB 3 429.

117 *very adequately.*' Anon Jesuit, *Informação da Provincia do Brasil para nosso Padre*, HCJB 2 100; Leite, *Suma histórica* 67; Anchieta, *Cartas* 416.

117 *they consider bravery.*' Salvador, *Historia*, bk 4, ch. 39, p. 393.

117 *for the festival.*' Ibid. bk 3, ch. 39, pp. 393–4. Friar Vicente was a Franciscan, an Order that allowed more exuberant festivals than the Jesuits.

118 *may have possessed.*' Freyre, *Masters and Slaves* 109, 110.

Chapter 6 ANTARCTIC FRANCE

120 *Portuguese.*' Jean Crespin, *Histoire des martyrs persécutez et mis à mort pour la vérité de l'Évangile*, in Paul Gaffarel, *Histoire du Brésil français au seizième siècle* 445–6. André Thevet said (*La Cosmographie universelle* 36–7) that the Portuguese had once maintained a trading-post at Cabo Frio, north of Rio de Janeiro. But the Tupinambá unexpectedly attacked it, in order to seize its stock of trade goods, and massacred every man, woman and child. It is not clear when the Portuguese tried to colonise Guanabara. Norman traders from Honfleur were active there in 1525, so that Gaffarel thought that the attempt was before that date. Amerigo Vespucci wrote that the expedition of 1503–4 spent five months in a port on the Brazilian coast building a fortress storehouse. They left twenty-four men and twelve pieces of artillery in it when they sailed back to Portugal. (Amerigo Vespucci, *El Nuevo Mundo* (Buenos Aires, 1951) 264–6; Alonso de Santa Cruz, *Islario general de todas las islas del mundo* (c. 1541) (Madrid, 1918) 346.) Rolando A. Laguarda Trias argued strongly in favour of Rio de Janeiro as the location of this early tower (*El predescubrimiento del río de la Plata por la expedición portuguesa de 1511–1512* (Lisbon, 1973) 43). The Portuguese certainly did have a fortified trading-post at Cabo Frio, not far north of Rio de Janeiro. The ship *Bertoa* or *Bretoa* loaded wood there in June and July 1511. Its pilot was João Lopes de Carvalho. He was later enlisted by Magellan (or, to give him his Portuguese

name, Fernão de Magalhães) to guide the circumnavigation fleet. He directed it to the Bay of Guanabara or Rio de Janeiro, where Magellan's fleet spent an idyllic two weeks in December 1519. Carvalho arranged that the local Indians (Tamoio or possibly Tupinikin) would let their girls sleep with the sailors in exchange for German knives 'of worst quality'. There were nightly revels under a waning moon with the Sugar Loaf and Corcovado as dramatic backdrops. Carvalho himself was greeted by an Indian woman who showed him their seven-year-old son, conceived on the *Bertoa* voyage. (Antonio de Pigafetta, *Il primo viaggio intorno al mondo*; Samuel Eliot Morison, *The European Discovery of America. The Southern Voyages, 1492–1616* 361.)

Jean Crespin may, however, have been referring to the voyage of Martim Afonso de Sousa, who landed there in April 1530. He built a stronghouse and remained for three months while his men built two brigantines. The Indians provided his 400 men with food for a year, and he described them as identical to the Tupinambá of Bahia, but more gentle. His expedition was also among them for three months on its return in 1531 (Pero Lopes de Sousa, *Diario da navegação de Pero Lopes de Sousa* 185–7, 349–50.) The Temimino chief Arariboia was the godson of Martim Afonso de Sousa and took his name – as did Tibiriça of the Piratininga Tupinikin.

120 *no abuse'.* José de Anchieta, *Cartas, informações, fragmentos historicos e sermões* 310–11; Simão de Vasconcellos, *Vida do Venerável Padre José de Anchieta*, bk 2, ch. 1, pp. 68, 83; Florestan Fernandes, *Organização social dos Tupinambá* 27.

120 *lacked water.* Simão de Vasconcellos, *Chronica da Companhia de Jesus do Estado de Brasil . . .* 2 77; Mem de Sá, *Documentos relativos a Mem de Sá, governador geral do Brasil* 134–5; Francisco Adolpho de Varnhagen, Visconde de Pôrto Seguro, *HGB* 1 385. The island itself was called Fort Coligny but is now known as the Ilha de Villaganhon. It is a small, low island alongside the domestic airport Santos Dumont.

121 *human shapes.'* Villegagnon to Calvin, France Antarctique, 31 March 1557, in Jean de Léry, *Le Voyage au Brésil de Jean de Léry, 1556–1558* (1927 ed.) 28; also Nicolas Barré letter, 1 Feb 1955, in Gaffarel, *Histoire* 380.

121 *his service.'* Thevet, *La Cosmographie universelle* 112; Léry, *Voyage au Brésil* 158, 261–2.

121 *seek it.'* Villegagnon to Calvin, 31 March 1557, in ibid. 28.

121 *pain of death'.* Nicolas Barré to his friends, Guanabara, 26 May 1556, in Gaffarel, *Histoire* 383.

121 *on your errands.'''* Thevet, *La Cosmographie universelle* 137; Jean Alphonse de Saintonge, *Voyages aventureux*, in Pierre Margry, *Navigations françaises* 305; Léry, *Voyage au Brésil* 203; Yves d'Evreux, *Voyage dans le nord du Brésil, fait durant les années 1613 et 1614* 94.

121 *seven years'.* Barré, in Gaffarel, *Histoire* 383.

122 *strike me down'.* Villegagnon to Calvin, 31 March 1557, in Léry, *Voyage au Brésil* 30. These mercenaries were also disaffected by the poor food, lack of water, rough country 'and the incredible labour they were given' (Barré letter, May 1556, in Gaffarel, *Histoire* 383). The Norman interpreter, whose punishment by Villegagnon led to the plot, managed to escape to the mainland. He turned all the other Norman interpreters against the colonists, who thus lost contact with the Indians.

122 *Espírito Santo.* Luís de Grã letter, in HCJB 1 233. Maracajá is the Tupi for the large jungle wildcat now called Jaguatirica *(Felis pardalis chipiguazou).* The French referred to their enemies as Margageat (Thevet) or Margaïas (Léry). Léry wrote that there was a group of them in Espírito Santo when he and his Calvinist friends sailed out in Feb 1557: either the people transported from Governor's Island or Temimino already resident on that coast near Angra dos Reis and inland near the Paraíba. Léry also confirmed that there were some of these Maracajá Temimino living on Ilha Grande in 1557, but they were attacked and largely exterminated by the Tamoio

soon after. (Léry, *Voyage au Brésil* 183; Fernandes, *Organização social* 27.) The Tamoio Tupinambá even tried to attack the Temimino who found refuge in Espírito Santo. Luís de Grã, in Serafim Soares Leite, *Novas cartas jesuítas (de Nóbrega a Vieira)* 180; Alfred Métraux, *La Civilization matérielle des tribus Tupi-Guaraní* 14; HCJB 1 233, 363; Suzanne Lussagnet, in André Thevet, *Les Français en Amérique pendant la deuxième moitié du XVIe siècle: Le Brésil et les brésiliens*, ed. Suzanne Lussagnet, 17. The Ilha do Governador now contains the international airport of Rio de Janeiro. Its original Indian name was Paranapecu, but it became known as Governor's Island because half of it was awarded by Mem de Sá to his nephew Salvador Corrêa de Sá, who was twice Governor of Rio de Janeiro. The award was confirmed in Lisbon, 13 Feb 1576. HGB 1 415. Thevet produced a fine map of Governor's Island, showing no less than thirty-six native long-huts on this island alone. The map was with the manuscript known as 'Le Grand Insulaire' discovered by Alfred Métraux; it is reproduced in Lussagnet's edition of Thevet's *Le Brésil et les brésiliens* 294.

123 *called that!'''* Léry, *Voyage au Brésil* 254-5.

123 *our defence.'* Thevet, *La Cosmographie universelle* 89; Gabriel Soares de Sousa also wrote that the Tamoio were 'large of body and robust' (*Tratado descriptivo do Brasil em 1587*, ch. 68, p. 102). They fought all their neighbours except the related Tupinambá – Temimino, Tupinikin and Goianá to the south, Waitacá to the north.

124 *his suite.'* Thevet, *La Cosmographie universelle* 92. The chief's name was appropriate: it apparently meant 'He Who Talks Slowly'. One Portuguese killed and eaten by Cunhambebe was Rui Pinto: the Tamoio chief kept this man's habit and cross of the Order of Christ among his trophies.

124 *above all else.'* Ibid. 232. In his *Histoire d'André Thevet Angoumoisin . . .*, Thevet described other occasions on which Indians used arquebuses. They would not be content with the standard charge of powder, but would fill the barrel with it, so that the guns often blew up, wounding those who fired them. A valiant nephew of Quoniambec was killed in this way.

124 *wherever they go.'* Sousa, *Tratado descriptivo*, ch. 68, p. 103.

125 *of the coast.'* Mem de Sá to Queen Catarina, São Vicente, 16 June 1560, RHGB 27 pt 1, 14, 1864.

125 *day or night. . . .'* Ibid. 13–14; Anchieta to Jesuit General, São Vicente, 1 June 1560, *Cartas* 159. Vicente do Salvador said that Mem de Sá wrote to Bois-le-Comte to try to persuade him to surrender. He claimed that the King of Portugal had protested about Antarctic France to the King of France, and that the latter had 'replied to him that if [Villegagnon] was there he should make war on him and throw him out, for he had gone without his [royal] commission' (*Historia*, bk 3, ch. 8, p. 172). Bois-le-Comte refused to surrender his uncle's colony.

125 *fought fiercely'.* Mem de Sá, *Documentos relativos* 134.

125 *on land.'* Anchieta, 1 June 1560, *Cartas* 159. Vicente do Salvador tells the story of the two soldiers capturing the powder – one of whom was a 'brown man' (*Historia*, bk 3, ch. 8, p. 173).

125 *Fort Coligny.* Mem de Sá, *Documentos relativos* 135; and the testimony of Sebastião Álvares, ibid. 152; Anchieta letter of 1 June 1560, *Cartas* 159.

125 *to fight'.* Mem de Sá to Queen Catarina, 16 June 1560, 14; ten years later in his 'Instrumento' he increased the enemy to 120 Frenchmen and 1500 Indians.

126 *our men.'* Mem de Sá to Queen Catarina, 16 June 1560, 14.

126 *Indian allies.* Anchieta, 1 June 1560, *Cartas* 159; Sousa, *Tratado descriptivo*, ch. 53, p. 95; Salvador, *Historia*, bk 3, ch. 8, p. 173.

126 *in this land. . . .'* Mem de Sá to Queen Catarina, 16 June 1560, 14.

126 *stay here longer.'* Gabriel Soares de Sousa said that the Queen was annoyed that Mem de Sá destroyed the French fort

and did not occupy it (*Tratado descriptivo*, ch. 53, p. 95; Thevet, *La Cosmographie universelle* 14–15). Thevet, who was not present, wrote that the defenders surrendered after agreeing to an armistice, but that this was violated and they were enslaved. Villegagnon's Scotsmen and some of the French happened to be away in Cabo Frio enjoying themselves among the native women. They remained there to continue the war. HGB 1 385, 402; Ch.-A. Julien, *Les Voyages de découverte et les premiers établissements* (Paris, 1948) 206–10; A. Heulhard, *Villegagnon, roi d'Amérique* (Paris, 1897) 200–2.

126 *rather than soldiers'*. Nóbrega to Cardinal Infante Enrique, *Cartas do Brasil* 175, 227; Serafim Soares Leite, *Páginas de história do Brasil* 217. Rio de Janeiro replaced Bahia as capital of Brazil in the eighteenth century, and remained capital until the building of Brasília.

126 *Indians.'* Mem de Sá, *Documentos relativos* 135.

126 *fire and blood'*. Anchieta, *Cartas* 235; Leonardo do Vale, CA 339–40, 362–4; Leite, *Páginas de história* 217–18.

127 *were killed.'* Town council of São Paulo de Piratininga to King, 20 May 1561, HGB 1 401; Anon Jesuit, *Enformação do Brasil e de suas capitanias* 409.

127 *Easter 1561.* Anchieta letter of 12 June 1561, HGB 1 387. The expedition left in canoes during Lent and destroyed a village on Good Friday. Vasconcellos, *Chronica* 140. There is some confusion about this group of Tupinikin. All the chroniclers agree that there were Tupinikin at Bahia when the Portuguese first arrived there, and also on the coast of Ilhéus and Pôrto Seguro. Only Hans Staden and Fernão Cardim mention another group of Tupinikin on the coast at São Vicente and inland to Piratininga and beyond for some distance down the Tietê (Staden, *Duas viagens* (1942) 154; Cardim, *Tratados da terra e gente do Brasil* 173; Fernandes, *Organização social* 26; J. F. de Almeida Prado, *Primeiros povoadores do Brasil (1500–1530)* 128; Artur Ramos, *Introdução à antropologia*

brasileira: As culturas indigenas 77; Alfred Métraux, 'The Tupinambá' 96). Anchieta explained the politics between the Tamoio and Tupinikin in his letter of 8 Jan 1565, MB 4 126–7. The Tupinikin were probably descendants of the first wave of Tupi to migrate along the Brazilian coast. By the mid-sixteenth century they were being overrun or evicted by invasions of other Tupi such as the Tupinambá.

There is also the problem of the Goianá or Goianazes. Various early chroniclers mention them as living on the Piratininga plateau, and Knivet visited them at the end of the century, when they were still firm friends of the Portuguese. Egon Schaden decided that Goianá was another name for the Tupinikin themselves ('Os primitivos habitantes do territorio paulista' 395; Plinio Ayrosa, 'Tupi-Guaranís e Guyanás', articles in *Estado de São Paulo*, Nov 1938–Jan 1939).

128 *their own people.'* Anchieta, letter to Diego Laynes in Rome, São Vicente, 16 April 1563, CPJB 3 550; *Cartas* 184.

128 *was invincible.'* Robert Southey, *History of Brazil* 1 298.

128 *iron rod'*. Anchieta to Laynes, São Vicente, 16 April 1563, CPJB 3 553–4.

128 *eating us all.'* Ibid. 3 556.

128 *His Church.'* Ibid. 3 555.

128 *Brazilian'*. Ibid. 3 555.

128 *our lives'*. Ibid. 3 556. Vasconcellos, *Chronica* 274–7, and *Vida do Anchieta*, bk 2, ch. 14, 1 81–2; Pedro Tacques de Almeida Paes Leme, *Historia da Capitania de S. Vicente desde a sua fundação por Martim Afonso de Sousa* 150.

128 *possession of it.'* Vasconcellos, *Chronica*, bk 3, pp. 284–5.

128 *cruel business'*. Anchieta to Laynes, São Vicente, 8 Jan 1565, MB 4 123.

129 *intimidate them.'* Vasconcellos, *Chronica*, bk 3, p. 280. Vasconcellos tells of various Indian women whose Christian convictions were so strong that they preferred death to dishonour after capture by the Tamoio (bk 3, pp. 258–9); Câmara of São Paulo to Estácio de Sá, 12 May 1564, MB 4 49–51; Anchieta to Laynes, São Vicente, 16 April 1563, CPJB

3 563, or *Cartas* 184. Salvador, *Historia*, bk 3, ch. 10, p. 178.

129 *trust in us'*. Anchieta to Laynes, São Vicente, 8 Jan 1565, MB 4 126.

129 *way of life.'* Ibid. 4 129.

129 *even see.'* Ibid. 4 130.

129 *and swords.'* Ibid. 4 126.

129 *without reason.'* Ibid. 4 127.

130 *to love.'* Ibid. 4 128.

130 *harsh things'*. Ibid. 4 133.

130 *we all die!'* Ibid. 4 134.

130 *very cruel'*. Ibid. 4 134.

130 *Pindobuçu's men.* This canoe was commanded by Pindobuçu's son Paranapuçu ('Wide Ocean'). Ibid. 4 142–3; Vasconcellos, *Chronica*, bk 3, p. 291, and *Vida do Anchieta*, bk 2, ch. 6, 1 88–9.

131 *reduced in strength'*. Vasconcellos, *Chronica*, bk 3, p. 288, and *Vida do Anchieta*, bk 2, ch. 5, 1 85.

131 *on the other.'* Anchieta to Laynes, 8 Jan 1565, MB 4 146. There is some confusion about whether this Tamoio chief Cunhambebe was the same as the Quoniambec who travelled to Rio de Janeiro to visit Villegagnon's island colony. Thevet wrote that the Quoniambec he knew had died in an epidemic in 1556 (*La Cosmographie universelle* 88). Two distinguished Brazilian historians, João Capistrano de Abreu and José de Alcantara Machado, both felt that the two chiefs must be different. Hans Staden had mentioned a 'supreme king' of the Tamoio of Ubatuba called Konyan Bebe, 'a great man, but also a very cruel one when it came to eating human flesh'. This Konyan Bebe told Staden: 'I have already helped to catch and eat five Portuguese, who claimed they were Frenchmen but who all lied' (*The True History of His Captivity* 78–9). It seems impossible that two equally important chiefs with such similar names could have been in the same area during that decade. Thevet does not mention Cunhambebe's death in other works in which he describes that chief: *Les Singularitez de la France antarctique* 273, and the unpublished 'Les vrais pourtraicts et vies des hommes illustres'. Serafim Soares Leite and

Suzanne Lussagnet therefore think that Thevet was mistaken when he said that the chief died in 1556: Anchieta, *Cartas* 243; MB 4 145; *Brésil et les brésiliens* 88–9.

132 *for you there."'* Vasconcellos, *Chronica*, bk 3, p. 62, quoting Anchieta; Antonio de Matos, *De prima Colegii Fluminensis Januarii Institutione* (Rome, 16th cent.) 21; Anon Jesuit, *De algumas coisas mais notáveis do Brasil* 378; Anchieta, *Cartas* 235–6; Anon Jesuit, *Enformação do Brasil* 410; Paes Leme, *História* 321; Leite, *Páginas* 218–19; Leonardo do Vale, CA 451; Anchieta, letter to Diogo Mirão, 9 July 1565, *Cartas* 249; HGB 1 427–9; HCJB 1 382–3; Leite, *Suma histórica* 34; Salvador, *Historia*, bk 3, ch. 10, p. 181.

133 *as the others."'* Thevet, *La Cosmographie universelle* 208; Gaffarel, *Histoire* 88.

133 *customary way.'* Léry, *Voyage au Brésil* 206–7.

133 *three days!'* Ibid. 170.

134 *on it. . . ."'* José Pizarro Araujo, *Memórias históricas da provincia do Rio de Janeiro* 1 40. Soares de Sousa wrote, however, that the Tamoio fought very well with French arquebuses, and were well supplied with powder and shot (*Tratado descriptivo*, ch. 54, p. 96).

134 *any labours.'* Anchieta letter to Diogo Mirão, Bahia, 9 July 1565, *Cartas* 253; Luis Norton, *A dinastia dos Sás no Brasil* (Lisbon, 1965) 14.

134 *upon them'*. Vasconcellos, *Chronica* 354–5; Salvador, *Historia*, bk 3, ch. 10, pp. 182–3. St Sebastian himself was said to have appeared as a gentleman soldier who jumped into the Tamoio canoes and frightened them into fleeing. The victory was commemorated by an annual parade of canoes on St Sebastian's Day.

134 *very rigorous.'* Anon Jesuit, *De algumas coisas* 381; HGB 1 416; Mem de Sá, *Documentos relativos* (testimony of Vicente Monteiro) 200; Salvador, *Historia*, bk 3, ch. 12, p. 191; Paes Leme, *Historia* 321; Vasconcellos, *Chronica* 357; Anon Jesuit, *Enformação do Brasil* 410–11; Leite, *Páginas* 224. Estácio was buried in the camp and later reburied by his cousin Salvador Corrêa de Sá in a special chapel in the church of St Sebastian in 1583. His tomb was opened in 1862 and found to

contain three bodies: one body, of a sturdy man 1·74 metres tall, was identified as his. When the church was demolished in 1921 to make way for the Esplanada do Castelho, the body of Estácio de Sá was moved to a modern Capuchin convent church in the Rua Haddock Lobo in Tijuca.

135 *I granted it them. . . .'* Mem de Sá, *Documentos relativos* 135–6. The third fortified village was near the mouth of the Carioca river.

135 *great creation.'* Ibid. 136; Salvador, *Historia,* bk 3, ch. 12, pp. 191–2. The new city had only 150 settlers, but its foundation was of great significance to the Portuguese. In a spectacle presented for King Sebastião at Coimbra in 1570, the figures of three rivers came to request the blessing of Portuguese dominion: the Ganges, the Nile, and the January river of Brazil (even though it was a bay, and not a river at all). HCJB 2 600. Vicente do Salvador said that Mem de Sá originally built his town on a hill, for easy defence, 'but later, when the land was at peace, it extended into the valley alongside the sea, in such a way that the beach serves it as a main street. . . . Canoes that come from the townspeople's plantations and orchards remain there, with each man disembarking at his door or near it with what he brought, and not requiring the effort of carts needed [to climb] the slope. They themselves would not have gone up there throughout the year, and their wives even less, had the cathedral and the church of the Fathers of the Society not been up there. . . .'

135 *entire world.'* Anchieta quoted in Leite, *Suma histórica* 34–5.

135 *Rio de Janeiro.'* Ibid. 35–6.

135 *banquet of him'.* Vasconcellos, *Chronica* 383. Arariboia had been christened in 1530 and took the name of the first lord of São Vicente, Martim Afonso de Sousa, who acted as his godfather: Salvador, *Historia,* bk 3, ch. 14, p. 197.

136 *his own body'.* Vasconcellos, *Chronica,* bk 3, p. 385; Anon Jesuit, *De algumas coisas* 379; Salvador, *Historia,* bk 3, ch. 14, pp. 198–9; Sousa, *Tratado descriptivo,*

ch. 56, p. 100.

136 *greater good.'* Gonçalo de Oliveira letter from Rio de Janeiro, 1570, in Leite, *Páginas* 142; Fernandes, *Organização social* 31. In Salvador's attack on Cabo Frio, a French ship was captured when an arrow went through the visor in its captain's helmet: Vasconcellos, *Chronica;* HGB 1 420–1.

136 *to your court."'* Salvador, *Historia* (1931 ed.) p. 98.

136 *after him'.* Sesmaria grant, 16 March 1568, RHGB 17 301, 1854. The old chief was still alive in 1583: he was seated in one of the twenty decorated canoes that paddled out to greet the Jesuit Visitor Cristóvão de Gouveia. He was greatly honoured and was still receiving his pension as a Commander of the Order of Christ. Cardim, *Tratados* 305; J. da Cunha Barbosa wrote a biography of Arariboia in RHGB 4 207–9, 1842.

136 *arquebuses and cannons'.* Anon Jesuit, *Enformação do Brasil* 407.

137 *without battle.'* Ibid. 408, 425; Sousa, *Tratado,* ch. 55, pp. 88–9; Luís da Fonseca letter, Bahia, 17 Dec 1577, in DHBC 2; João Capistrano de Abreu, 'Gravetos da historia patria', *Gazeta de Noticias,* Rio de Janeiro, 6 Nov 1882; Sylvio Salema Garção Ribeiro, *Um bárbaro e cruel da história do Brasil* 34; Eduardo Tourinho, 'A cruel Expedição Salema', *Revista da Semana,* Rio de Janeiro, May 1957.

137 *oppose us.'* Miguel Ayres Maldonado, *Descripção . . . dos trabalhos a fadigas das suas vidas, que tiveram nas conquistas da Capitania do Rio de Janeiro* 346.

137 *the north'.* Ibid. 346. Sousa, *Tratado descriptivo,* ch. 55, p. 99.

137 *no trace of them'.* Jácome Monteiro, *Relação da Provincia do Brasil* (1610), HCJB 8 400. Anchieta had written earlier that some Tamoio were still alive in the 1580s; and so had the anonymous Jesuit author of the *Enformação do Brasil* of 1584 (p. 408). Maldonado remembered rushing to arms in the late 1580s to defend São Vicente from an attack by a hundred Tamoio canoes: many were slaughtered, and the rest fled to the south. Some Tamoio were added to the

Jesuit aldeias of São Barnabé and São Lourenço near Rio de Janeiro – alongside their enemies the Temimino. But by 1584 there were only 3000 Indians of any tribe left in these two aldeias. The Tamoio soon ceased to be mentioned as a separate group among the tribes in these mission villages.
137 *America'*. Anthony Knivet, *The Admirable Adventures and Strange Fortunes of Master Antonie Knivet* . . ., in Samuel Purchas, *Hakluytus Posthumus or Purchas His Pilgrimes* 16 208.
138 *for shame'*. Ibid. 16 224.

138 *very well.'* Ibid. 16 262.
138 *Rio de Janeiro*. Ibid. 16 225–7, 287. One group of Tamoio fled north-westwards from Cabo Frio, and spent six months among the Amoipira tribe on the Rio Prêto, a tributary of the upper São Francisco in the barren sertão between the modern states of Bahia and Goiás. This group may well have moved on westwards to the Araguaia or beyond. They were mentioned by Pero Domingues, *Relação . . . sôbre a viagem . . .*, in Leite, *Páginas* 114.

Chapter 7 DISEASE AND SLAVERY

139 *contain them.'* Afonso Braz, Espírito Santo, 1551, RHGB 6 442, 1844. Amerigo Vespucci had written, in his letter to Pietro Soderini, 4 Sept 1504: 'We indeed found the land populous . . .' (RHGB 41 pt 1, 8, 1878).
139 *slaughterhouses'*. Tomé de Sousa, quoted in J. F. de Almeida Prado, *Bahia e as capitanias do centro do Brasil (1530–1626)* 1 90.
139 *the interior . . .'*. Pero de Magalhães Gandavo, *Tratado da 'terra do Brasil*, quoted in Rodrigo Otávio, *Os selvagens americanos* 22–3.
139 *find the land'*. Gaspar de Carvajal, *The Discovery of the Amazon* 202.
140 *to carry you. . . .'* Antony Knivet, *The Admirable Adventures and Strange Fortunes of Master Antonie Knivet* . . ., in Samuel Purchas, *Hakluytus Posthumus or Purchas His Pilgrimes* 16 288–9.
140 *[venereal disease].'* Manoel da Nóbrega, Pôrto Seguro, 1550, *Cartas do Brasil, 1549–1560* 111, CPJB 1 168; Serafim Soares Leite, *Páginas da história do Brasil* 208. It is not yet certain on which side of the Atlantic venereal disease originated – possibly different types came from each hemisphere. Syphilis seems to have had more drastic effects in Europe in the early sixteenth century than in the Americas: it presumably originated in the Americas, whose

natives may have had some immunity. But European archaeologists have found traces of syphilis in ancient Roman skeletons. José de Anchieta treated an old Indian woman, married for many years to a Portuguese: 'Her secret parts were corrupted: this was her disease, one that is very common among these Brazilian women, even the virgins' (Anchieta to Padre Geral, São Vicente, 31 May 1560, *Cartas, informações, fragmentos históricos e sermões* 111). André Thevet blamed the wanton Indian women: 'For these people, being savage, are very given to debauchery, especially the women who seek and practise all means they can to arouse their husbands. Which makes me think . . . that this malady originated from such corruption and over-frequent intercourse with women thus heated. It is none other than that lovely pox which is at present so widespread throughout Christianity. . . .' Thevet wrote that the Spaniards brought it back from Jamaica and that it spread through Europe from Naples northwards. It was particularly virulent in France. Various members of Villegagnon's expedition to Guanabara in 1555–60 caught it from native women, and three Scotsmen were left permanently afflicted. Thevet claimed that the natives cured themselves with sarsaparilla bark. Thevet and Anchieta also described genitals that were probably swollen from a venereal disease, but which they thought had been done on purpose by an insect bite: see note to p. 17 above. (André Thevet, *La Cosmographie universelle* ch. 10; note by Suzanne Lussagnet in Thevet, *Les Français en Amérique pendant la deuxième moitié du XVIᵉ siècle: Le Brésil et les brésiliens* 142. Sérgio Buarque de Holanda, *Visão do paraíso: os motivos edénicos no descobrimento e colonização do Brasil* 272–3; J. P. Leite Cordeira, *A terapeutica da sifilis desde o mercurio até a penicilina*(São Paulo, 1948).

140 *all the world'.* Thevet, *La Cosmographie universelle* 86. Thevet also noticed that there were no cripples, hunchbacks, blind people or deformities among the Indians. He did not realise that tribes would kill any member with such defects, on suspicion of sorcery.

140 *the children were saved.'* Francisco Pires to Brothers in Portugal, Bahia, 1552, CA 129.

140 *to the grave.'* Simão de Vasconcellos, *Chronica da Companhia de Jesus* . . . 138.

140 *infinite number of savages.'* Thevet, *La Cosmographie universelle* 86. Nicolas Barré wrote that over 800 Indians died of this epidemic (Barré letter to his friends, Guanabara, 26 May 1556, in Paul Gaffarel, *Histoire du Brésil français au seizième siècle* 384).

140 *with them'.* Thevet, *La Cosmographie universelle* 86.

140 *at once ceased'.* Pero Correia to Brás Lourenço, São Vicente, 18 July 1554, CPJB 2 70–1.

140 *eat us.'* Thevet, *La Cosmographie universelle* 87. Thevet, writing some years after Barré's letter, raised the number of victims from 800 to 8000. He and Villegagnon were visiting a powerful village of Tamoio when its chief and four of his children fell ill. The Frenchmen escaped being lynched only because an Indian warned them to flee.

141 *like twigs.'* Francisco Pires letter, Bahia, 1552, CA 129–30.

141 *do die.'* Ibid. 129.

141 *mortal catarrh'.* Vasconcellos, *Chronica* 103.

141 *struck them down'.* António Blásques to

Diego Mirón, Bahia, 31 May 1564, MB 4 54; Anchieta to Diego Laynes in Rome, São Vicente, 12 June 1561, 30 July 1561, CPJB 3 379, *Cartas* 173; Antoñio de Sá to Fathers in Bahia, Espírito Santo, Feb 1559 and 13 June 1559, CPJB 3 18–19, 38–9; anonymous letter from Espírito Santo, *c.*1559, CA 207.

141 *by the dying.'* António Blásques, Salvador da Bahia, 23 Sept 1561, CA 312–13.

142 *evil-smelling beasties.'* Vasconcellos, *Chronica*, bk 3, p. 283.

142 *too strong to endure.'* Leonardo do Vale, HC 2 575–6; Serafim Soares Leite, *Suma histórica da Companhia de Jesus no Brasil* . . . 170.

142 *were healed.'* Anchieta, *Cartas* 239–40; Leite, *Páginas* 198, 202.

142 *pharmacists and nurses.'* Anchieta, *Cartas* 239–40.

142 *who saw them.'* António Blásques to Diego Mirón, Bahia, 31 May 1564, MB 4 55.

143 *from the spring.'* Leonardo do Vale to Gonçalo Vaz de Melo, Bahia, 12 May 1563, MB 4 10.

143 *they died'.* Ibid. 4 11.

143 *routed them up.'* Ibid. 4 11.

143 *fetch water.'* Ibid. 4 12.

143 *punishes them.'* Ibid. 4 9.

143 *already in irons.'* Ibid. 4 10.

144 *their own children.'* Vasconcellos, *Chronica*, bk 3, p. 312; Francisco Augusto Pereira da Costa, *Anais Pernambucanos* 1 359; J. F. de Almeida Prado, *Bahia e as capitanias do centro do Brasil (1530–1626)* 1 220.

144 *the missionaries.* Leonardo do Vale to Gonçalo Vaz de Melo, Bahia, 12 May 1563, MB 4 12 or CA 385; António Blásques, CA 406.

144 *only 300 men.* Anon Jesuit, *De algumas coisas mais notaveis do Brasil* 382; Gabriel Soares de Sousa, *Tratado descriptivo do Brasil em 1587*, bk 1, ch. 25, p. 47, said that by 1587 this surviving aldeia had only 300 fighting men: Anchieta, *Cartas* 377. Anchieta calculated that Portuguese colonists brought down 20,000 from the sertão of Arabó, and that annual slaving raids from 1568 onwards added 2000–3000 more – a further 20,000 or

more by 1580; Heitor Furtado de Mendonça, *Primeira visitação do Santo Offício às Partes do Brasil: Confisões de Bahia, 1591–92* 168–9; Vasconcellos, *Chronica*, bk 3, p. 283; Robert Southey, *A History of Brazil* 1 299, 306; João Capistrano de Abreu, *Capitulos de história colonial* 79; Florestan Fernandes, *Organização social dos Tupinambá* 39–40; Alexander Marchant, *From Barter to Slavery* 116–17; Serafim Soares Leite, HCJB 2 575–6, and *Suma histórica* 170.

144 *so short a time.'* Anchieta, *Cartas* 377; Abreu, *Capitulos de história colonial* (1954 ed.) 115.

144 *tears of compassion.'* António Blásques to Diego Mirón, Bahia, 31 May 1564, MB 4 55.

144 *now be twenty.'* Prado, *Bahia* 1 219.

145 *ravaged and abandoned.'* Vasconcellos, *Chronica*, bk 3, pp. 335–6.

145 *with them.'* Certidão by Bishop of Brazil, Bahia, 26 March 1582, HCJB 2 629.

145 *against this.'* Anon Jesuit, *Informação dos primeiros aldeiamentos da Bahia* (or 'Trabalhos dos primeiros Jesuitas'), Anchieta, *Cartas* 377.

146 *its victims.* Vasconcellos, *Chronica*, bk 3, p. 346.

146 *Protestant propagandists.* Sérgio Buarque de Holanda, *Visão do paraíso* 301; Lewis Hanke, *The Spanish Struggle for Justice in the Conquest of America* (Philadelphia, 1949; John Hemming, *The Conquest of the Incas* (London, 1970) 129–30, on Spanish morality to the Indians; or the writings of Las Casas himself.

146 *reduced to slavery'.* Simão de Vasconcellos, *Das cousas do Brasil*, bk 2 (in *Chronica* 101–2), quotes this Bull in Latin. Rodrigo Otávio, *Os selvagens americanos perante o direito* 47; Afonso Arinos de Mello Franco, *O índio brasileiro e a Revolução Francesa* 38. An earlier papal grant, the Padroado Real, or Royal Patronage, had given the kings of Portugal complete control of the Church in their dominions, but with a duty to support the Church and its missions.

147 *Brazilian Indians.* Regimento de Tomé de Sousa, HCP 3 345–50; Mathias C.

Kieman, *The Indian Policy of Portugal in the Amazon Region, 1614–1693* 145–6; Otávio, *Os selvagens* 83–4; Georg Thomas, *Die portugiesische Indianerpolitik in Brasilien, 1560–1640* 198–9.

147 *to the Indians.* Mem de Sà to D. Sebastião, 31 March 1560, *Documentos relativos a Mem de Sá, governador geral do Brasil* 228; Anchieta, *Cartas* 157–60.

148 *too late.* Anon Jesuit, *Informação* 355–6.

148 *their lands.'* Queen-Regent to Câmara of Salvador (Bahia), 1558, in Francisco Adolpho de Varnhagen, HGB 1 383; Luis Norton, *A dinastia dos Sás no Brasil* (Lisbon, 1965) 6.

148 *newly converted. . . .'* King to Mem de Sá, 1556, in HGB 1 423–4, or Anchieta, *Cartas* 359–60.

148 *Prosecutor for the Indians.* António Blásques said that the Governor 'has placed in every settlement an honoured man who should have the title of captain, to act as a protector of them, defending them from the injuries and oppressions of the Christians' (letter to Diego Mirón, Bahia, 31 May 1564, MB 4 65). The Procurador dos Indios was a thirty-six-year-old Spaniard, Diego Zorrilla, who had fought for ten years, chiefly at sea as Alcalde do Mar ('Marine Commander') of Bahia. His daughter married the powerful plantation-owner Antonio Dias Adorno. There is little record of his having done anything to help the Indians. Anon Jesuit, 'Trabalhos dos primeiros Jesuitas', RHGB 57 pt 1, 226, 1884; Mendonça, *Primeira visitação* 389.

148 *the sale price'.* Pereira da Costa, *Anais Pernambucanos* 1 359. The Mesa da Consciência ('Tribunal of Conscience') was founded in 1532 by King João III after a Papal decree awarded the Portuguese Crown the mastership of the three military orders – of Christ, Santiago da Espada and São Bento de Avis. The Mesa advised the King on all ecclesiastical affairs that involved royal power, and also on the administration of the Orders. Its Regulations were confirmed by Papal brief in 1563 and redefined by Philip III in 1608.

149 *freed if not.* Nóbrega cited a dozen

authorities to support his case, including Thomas Aquinas and Duns Scotus: Serafim Soares Leite, *Novas páginas de história do Brasil* 120–4 and MB 4 387–415, and *Suma histórica* 80–1; Anon Jesuit, 'Trabalhos dos primeiros Jesuitas', RHGB **57** pt 1, 226. The Junta's resolution of 30 July 1566 is in Anchieta, *Cartas* 360–6. It was signed by Mem de Sá and Bishop Pedro Leitão of Bahia.

149 *to the Indians.* Mendonça, *Primeira visitaçao*; Prado, *Bahia* **2** 114–15, 120. Mem de Sá's will was dated Bahia, 5 Oct 1569. Wanderley Pinho, 'Testamento de Mem de Sá', *Anais do III Congresso de História Nacional*, 9 vols (Rio de Janeiro, 1941–4), **3** 56–7; José António Gonçalves de Mello, *Confissões de Pernambuco, 1594–1595* . . . 11.

149 *to be preserved.'* Mem de Sá to Queen, 30 March 1570, HGB **1** 436.

150 *unjust wars.'* Anon Jesuit, *Informação*, in Anchieta, *Cartas* 378, quoted by Capistrano de Abreu in HGB **1** 459.

151 *be enslaved'.* Law of 20 March 1570; in Francisco Correa, *Leys e provisões que El-Rey Dom Sebastião . . . fez depois que começou a governar* (Lisbon, 1570) 238 ff; Humberto de Oliveira, *Coletânea de leis, atos e memorias referentes ao indigena brasileiro* 57; Kieman, *Indian Policy* 147; Thomas, *Indianerpolitik* 199–200; Leite, HCJB **2** 206–7, and *Suma histórica* 81; Pereira da Costa, *Anais Pernambucanos* **1** 389–90.

151 *other Indians'.* Ibid. **1** 389–90.

151 *Cabo Frio.* Sylvio Salema Garção Ribeiro, *Um bárbaro e cruel da história do Brasil* 22, 33–5; Eduardo Tourinho, 'A cruel expedição Salema', *Revista da Semana*, Rio de Janeiro, May 1957. Domingos Fernandes revealed that he had gone slaving on the Governor's orders in 1576, 1577 and 1578–9, in his confession to the Inquisition in Bahia, 11 Feb 1592, in Mendonça, *Primeiro visitação* 168–9. Leite, HCJB **2** 207–9, and *Suma histórica* 82.

152 *Jesuits.* Antonio Barreiros, Bishop of Bahia, 'Certidão por que o bispo da Bahia certifica o que os padres da Companhia fasem na conversão dos indios e em outras cousas do serviço de Deus e de El-Rei', Bahia, 26 March 1582, in HCJB **2** 629; 'Lei . . . sobre os indios do Brasil que não podem ser captivos e declara o que podem ser', 24 Feb 1587, in Thomas, *Indianerpolitik* 79–80; and 'Lei sobre se não poderem captivar os gentios das partes do Brasil, e vivarem em sua liberdade . . .', 11 Nov 1595, in ibid. 200–3.

Governor-General Barreto demonstrated his pro-colonist bias in various ways. In 1584 the settlers of Ilhéus complained that the Jesuits were holding back the progress of the colony by denying Indian labour. They were furious against Father Diogo Nunes, and even arrested the overseer of the Jesuits' Indians at Boipeba. The Governor sided with the settlers. He also destroyed Jesuit missionary efforts in Sergipe by authorising its occupation by colonists.

152 *use them as slaves'.* Alvitre ('opinion') of Francisco Bruza de Espiñosa, CPJB **2** 382.

152 *sell them as slaves'.* Nóbrega to Tomé de Sousa, Bahia, 5 July 1559, ibid. **3** 79.

152 *infinite heathen'.* Vicente do Salvador, *Historia do Brasil*, bk 3, ch. 20, p. 220.

152 *price of a sheep.'* Ibid. bk 3, ch. 20, p. 85.

153 *wives and children'.* Knivet in Purchas **16** 197. Knivet's master was Martim de Sá, son of Mem de Sá's nephew Salvador Corrêa de Sá, who governed Rio de Janeiro twice, 1567–72 and 1578–98. Knivet was captured after shipwreck in 1592, and as a former corsair was under a virtual death-sentence.

153 *I was sure of blowes.'* Ibid. **16** 201.

153 *I did of him.'* Ibid. **16** 203.

153 *themselves and me.'* Ibid. **16** 204.

154 *their enemies.'* Ibid. **16** 205.

154 *Portugals.'* Ibid. **16** 206.

154 *Ilha Grande.'* Ibid. **16** 207. This Ilha Grande is off Angra dos Reis, south-west of Rio de Janeiro. Knivet had been betrayed by the Puri and brought before Martim de Sá near the island of São Sebastião, some 100 kms east of Santos. The Puri later fled from the Paraíba and were found on the upper Rio Doce, inland from Espírito Santo, in later centuries.

154 *restrained by anyone.'* Pero de Magalhães Gandavo, *Histories of Brazil* 2 114.

154 *steal slaves.'* Anon Jesuit, *Sumário das armádas que se fizeram e guerras que se deram na conquista do Rio Paraíba* 13–14.

155 *in a desert.'* Salvador, *Historia* (1931 ed.) p. 92.

155 *sustain themselves.'* Anon Jesuit, *Informação*, in Anchieta, *Cartas* 378.

155 *heathen slaves'.* Mendonça, *Primeira visitação* 94, 96, 97–8, 103, 104; Confessions of Rodrigo Martins, Manoel Branquo, Thomas Ferreira and João Gonçalves.

156 *in good spirits.* Prado, *Bahia* 1 316, quoting Vicente do Salvador. Dias Adorno was one of Caramuru's grandsons.

156 *in the Indian manner.'* Mendonça, *Primeira visitação* 168–9. It was a Tupi and Gê practice to glue feathers to the skin with gums and resins. Tomacauna confessed that he had progressively more wives on each expedition – evidently as his reputation grew he was given more of them. The seven wives were on the expedition of 1578–9 in Ilhéus.

156 *paying attention'.* Mendonça, *Primeira visitação* 172.

157 *for them to eat'.* Confession of Luisa Barbosa, 23 Aug 1591, in ibid. 65.

157 *became their slaves'.* Confession of Gonçalo Fernandes, 13 Jan 1592, in ibid. 87.

157 *Christians.'* Confession of Fernão Cabral de Tayde, 2 Aug 1591; of Dona Margarida da Costa (his wife), 30 Oct 1591; of Domingos Fernandes 'Tomacauna', 11 Feb 1592, in ibid. 28, 79, 170. Prado, *Bahia* 1 209; Thales de Azevedo, *Ensaios de antropologia social* 57; José Calasans, *A Santidade de Jaguaripe* (Bahia, 1952).

157 *on his head'.* Confession of Domingos

Fernandes Nobre, in Mendonça, *Primeira visitação* 171.

158 *has been informed.'* Diogo de Campos Moreno, *Livro que da razão do Estado do Brasil* 155.

158 *in 1629.* King Philip III to Governor Gaspar de Sousa, 19 Jan 1613, in unpublished collection of 'Cartas de El-Rei a Gaspar de Sousa', in Itamarati Library, Brasília. Moreno, *Livro que da razão* 154–5, and note by Hélio Vianna. The Adornos were daring mameluco raiders who specialised in expeditions into the sertão. Vicente do Salvador told how Álvaro Rodrigues Adorno managed to pacify a group of Aimoré by befriending a captured girl. He also helped to conquer Sergipe from the French and fought the Dutch in 1599. His son Afonso helped fight the Indians of Pôrto Seguro, marched against the Santidade in 1629, and later conquered the Paiaiá and the Indians of the Jacobina sertão. Prado, *Bahia* 1 217.

158 *trade goods.* Confession of Lazaro da Cunha, 21 Jan 1592, in Mendonça, *Primeira visitação* 108.

158 *white slavers.* Ibid. 107–8.

158 *for ever'.* Mello, *Confissões de Pernambuco* 28.

159 *in great necessitie'.* Knivet in Purchas 16 224.

159 *thirty thousand of us.'* Ibid. 16 224.

159 *their slaves'.* Ibid. 16 226–7. Knivet's figures are inflated, but the story seems accurate in other respects.

159 *to keep them.'* Certidão by Bishop of Brazil, Bahia, 26 March 1562, HCJB 2 629.

160 *our own people despise'.* Pero Correia, São Vicente, 10 March 1553, HCJB 9 378.

160 *can never escape!'* Nóbrega to Provincial in Portugal, São Vicente, 1553, CPJB 1 455–6.

Chapter 8   THE POTIGUAR

161 *warlike and treacherous.'* Gabriel Soares de Sousa, *Tratado descriptivo do Brasil em 1587*, chs 12–13, pp. 23–4; Anthony

Knivet, *The Admirable Adventures and Strange Fortunes of Master Antonie Knivet . . .*, in Samuel Purchas, *Hakluytus*

Posthumus or Purchas His Pilgrimes **16** 248.

162 *frontier wars.* Vicente do Salvador, *Historia, do Brasil,* bk 3, ch. 22, pp. 225–6.

162 *as before.'* Ibid. bk 3, pp. 110 and 96; J. F. de Almeida Prado, *A conquista da Paraíba* 70; Anon Jesuit, *Sumário das armadas que se fizeram e guerras que se deram na conquista do Rio Paraíba* 15. The expedition was led by the corregidor Fernão da Silva.

163 *Potiguar.* Ibid. 17–18; Salvador, *Historia* (1931 ed.) pp. 111–12; Prado, *A conquista da Paraíba* 72–3; Sousa, *Tratado descriptivo,* chs 11–12, pp. 20–2; Lopez Vaz, *A Discourse of the West Indies and South Sea,* in Richard Hakluyt, *The Principall Navigations of the English Nation . . .* **8** 172.

163 *instinct of nature'.* Francis Fletcher, *The World Encompassed: Sir Francis Drake His Voyage about the World* (London, 1628), in John Hampden, *Francis Drake – Privateer* (London, 1972) 137.

163 *lay upon them. . . .'* Ibid.

163 *São Vicente.* In this battle waged in torrential rain at São Vicente, on 24–5 Jan 1583, English gunfire sank the second largest Spanish ship. Edward Fenton was in command of the 400-ton galleon *Leicester,* and was accompanied by the 300-ton *Edward Bonaventure* under Capt. Luke Ward. Ward described the battle in his narrative *The Voyage Intended towards China . . . Begun Anno Dom. 1582,* in Hakluyt, *Principall Navigations* **8** 125–6. Fenton's ships later had a skirmish with Indians when trying to load water and lost five dead to Indian arrows. But they returned to England in late May 1583.

An Englishman called John Withal was then in Santos, married to the heiress of the Genoese José Adorno (whom Withal called Signor Ioffo Dore and whose real name was, I suppose, Giuseppe Doria), who had been with Nóbrega and Anchieta among the Tamoio of Iperoig and had acted as emissary to the French at Rio de Janeiro. John Withal wrote to his friend Richard Stapler boasting that 'This my marriage will be worth to me two thousand duckets, little more or lesse', because his wife's inheritance consisted of a sugar plantation with 60–70 slaves. He strongly

urged his friends to send a ship laden with trade goods, promising that 'this voyage is as good as any Peru-voyage' (Withal to Stapler, Santos, 26 June 1578, in Hakluyt, *Principall Navigations* **8** 16). They responded promptly by sending the ship *Minion.* This ship reached Santos in February 1581 and was 'well received and intertained of the Captaine, the kings officers, and all the people' (Thomas Grigs, Purser, *Certain Notes of the Voyage to Brasill with the Minion of London, in the yere 1580,* in ibid. **8** 22). The authorities sent to Bahia to ask whether they might trade with the English; but news then arrived that the King of Spain had become King of Portugal. The English were no longer welcome.

When Fenton reached Brazil in 1582, he tried to rouse Portuguese nationalist sentiment against Spain. He 'proclaimed that the Catholic King was dead and that Don Antonio [the pretender, the Prior of Crato] held the Kingdom of Portugal, offering great things on behalf of the Queen of England' (Salvador, *Historia* (1918 ed.), bk 4, ch. 1, pp. 268, 270–1). From then onwards, English voyages to Brazil were privateering raids against King of Spain. In 1587, Robert Withrington and Christopher Lister took their ships *The Red Dragon* and *Clifford* to attack shipping in Bahia and along the coast of Pernambuco (*The voyage of M. Robert Withrington and M. Christopher Lister intended for the South Sea, with two tal ships set forth at the charges of . . . the Earle of Cumberland . . .,* in Hakluyt, *Principall Navigations* **8** 146). Thomas Cavendish surprised the port of Santos at Christmas 1591 and burned and looted some plantations; but his fleet was repulsed at Santos and at Espírito Santo on its return in 1592 (John Jane, *The last voyage of M. Thomas Candish intended for the South sea . . .,* in ibid. **8** 289–90). James Lancaster's fleet of three ships seized the port of Olinda in Pernambuco and held it for a month, in March–April 1595 (*The prosperous voyage of Master James Lancaster to the towne of Fernambuck in Brasil* (1594), in ibid. **8** 30–43). In all these raids, and in those of French and Dutch corsairs, the

Brazilian Indians fought with distinction to help the Portuguese repel the intruders (Anon Jesuit, *Informação dos primeiros aldeiamentos da Baía*, in José de Anchieta, *Cartas, informações, fragmentos historicos e sermões* 379, or RHGB **57** pt 1, 244; Fernão Guerreiro, in Cândido Mendes de Almeida, *Memorias para a historia do extincto Estado do Maranhão* **2** 509).

163 *our camp.*' Anon Jesuit, *Sumário das armadas* 25; Salvador, *Historia*, bk 4, ch. 3, pp. 275–6.

163 *in the open.*' Anon Jesuit, *Sumário das armadas* 26.

164 *were slaves'.* Ibid. 25.

164 *to survive.* José de Anchieta, *Breve narração das coisas relativas aos colegios e residencias da Companhia nesta Provincia Brasilica* (28 Dec 1584), in *Cartas* 404.

164 *'Fin')*. Alfred Métraux thought that the word 'Tobajara' meant simply 'enemy' in Tupi. He cited various tribes with this name, and concluded that they were all tribes of the interior referred to as 'the enemy' by the coastal Tupi. Many of his references, however, referred to Piragiba's Tobajara, who migrated north-westwards from the São Francisco towards the Ibiapaba hills and thus appeared in different locations. Alfred Métraux, 'The Tupinambá' 96–7.

164 *as well.*' Salvador, *Historia*, bk 3, ch. 20, p. 220.

164 *their homes.*' Ibid. bk 3, ch. 20, pp. 220, 291; the author of the *Sumário das armadas* was sure that the King would have punished the treacherous slavers, had they lived: *Sumário das armadas* 37; Prado, *Conquista da Paraíba* 74–5.

164 *see the like'.* Salvador, *Historia* (1931 ed.) p. 117.

165 *first attack.*' Anon Jesuit, *Sumário das armadas* 36; Salvador, *Historia* (1931 ed.) p. 118.

165 *worth seeing!*' Anon Jesuit, *Sumário das armadas* 51.

165 *for a storehouse'.* Ibid. 53.

166 *chance to worry. . . .*' Ibid. 55–6.

166 *"be at them!"*' Ibid. 62.

166 *dead bodies.*' Ibid. 62.

166 *destroying them.*' Ibid. 62.

166 *any in Brazil.*' Ibid. 63.

166 *with the other.*' Ibid. 68.

167 *to kill them.*' Ibid. 69.

167 *this one'.* Ibid. 69.

167 *no one knew'.* Ibid. 71.

167 *villages we take'.* Ibid. 72.

167 *in any direction.*' Ibid. 75–6.

167 *at every step.*' Ibid. 76.

168 *in such crises'.* Ibid. 79.

168 *had done them'.* Ibid. 79.

168 *great disaster . . .'.* Ibid. 87.

168 *raising of cattle'.* Sousa, *Tratado descriptivo* 321; Gilberto Freyre, *The Masters and the Slaves: a study in the development of Brazilian civilization* 161.

169 *women and labour.* Prado, *Conquista da Paraíba* 76, 82–3. The Jesuit who wrote the splendid *Sumário das armadas* praised Martim Leitão, a good friend of the Jesuits, and branded Fructuoso Barbosa as a coward – possibly because Barbosa preferred Franciscans to Jesuits.

There were some confusing name-changes on the Paraíba. The river itself was called São Domingos or St-Dominique by the first Portuguese and French colonists, but it is now known as the Paraíba do Norte to distinguish it from the southern Paraíba that runs inland of Rio de Janeiro. The first Portuguese fort at the mouth of the river was called São Filipe (in honour of King Philip I of Portugal and II of Spain); it was later called Santa Catarina; and is now Fort Cabedelo. The town a few miles upstream was founded as Filipeía de Nossa Senhora das Neves ('Philippi of Our Lady of the Snows'), became Paraíba, and is now the city of João Pessoa, capital of the state of Paraíba. João Pessoa was a governor of Paraíba assassinated in 1929 when he was candidate for Vice-President of Brazil.

169 *Big Thistle'.* Salvador, *Historia* (1931 ed.), bk 4, ch. 31, p. 360.

169 *[of the stockade].*' Ibid. bk 4, ch. 31, p. 361.

169 *sight of blood'.* Ibid. bk 4, ch. 31, p. 361.

169 *of the river'.* Ibid. bk 4, ch. 31, p. 363.

170 *exhort them to work.*' Ibid. bk 4, ch. 31, p. 364.

170 *smallpox epidemic.*' Ibid. bk 4, ch. 31, p. 364.

170 *cowardly and timorous.'* Ibid. bk 4, ch. 32, pp. 366–7.
170 *Magi.* This mameluco (half-caste) Jerônimo de Albuquerque was the son of the first Jerônimo de Albuquerque and his Indian wife Maria do Espírito Santo Arco Verde. The first Jerônimo de Albuquerque was the brother-in-law of Duarte Coelho, Donatory of Pernambuco. Vicente do Salvador told how, in the 1530s, he was hit by an arrow and captured by the Tobajara. He was prepared for execution when Muira Ubi, daughter of Chief Arco Verde ('Green Bow'), fell in love with him, like Pocahontas for John Smith. She was baptised as Maria do Espírito Santo, and the children she had by Jerônimo de Albuquerque were legitimised by a royal decree of 1561. In all, twenty-four children were attributed to him, and he became known as 'the Adam of Pernambuco.' The son Jerônimo who became the first capitão-mor of Rio Grande and later of Maranhão, was born at Olinda in 1548 and died at São Luis in 1618. Mário Severo de Albuquerque Maranhão, 'Os Albuquerque Maranhão', RH 39 203–7, 1969.
171 *by the artillery.'* Salvador, *Historia*, bk 4, ch. 33, pp. 370–1.
171 *surprise attacks.'* Ibid. bk 4, ch. 33, p. 371.
171 *solemnity of law'.* Ibid. bk 4, ch. 33, p. 371.
171 *among them'.* Ibid. bk 4, ch. 33, p. 360.
171 *in the way'.* Knivet in Purchas 16 241.
171 *that were slaine.'* Ibid. 16 242. Knivet had heard the name of Pirajiba, meaning 'the finne of a fish', and mistakenly reported that he was chief of the Potiguar besieging Rio Grande.
172 *King of Spaine'.* Ibid. 16 242.
172 *like them.* Salvador, *Historia* (1931 ed.) p. 161.
172 *good treatment of them'.* Report by Manoel Mascarenhas Homem, Olinda, 29 June 1603, RHGB 73 pt 1, 38, 1910.
172 *they succeeded.* Royal enquiry into achievements of Diogo Botelho, Olinda, 6 Sept 1603, para 14, RHGB 73 pt 1, 62, 70–1, 78, 85, 94, 104, 111, 116, 121, etc., 1911; Petition by Diogo Botelho, 8 Feb

1608, ibid. 185, 194, 196, 198, etc.; Petition by Diogo Botelho, 19 Jan 1606, ibid. 217, 219; Testimony of Câmara of Salvador, 20 Dec 1607, ibid. 30.
172 *in the mirror.'* Salvador, *Historia* (1931 ed.) p. 162. Fernão Guerreiro, in Almeida, *Memorias* 2, or ABNRJ 26 346.
173 *gave them things'.* Salvador, *Historia* (1931 ed.) p. 162.
173 *into his land.'* Ibid. (1931 ed.) p. 170. Zorobabe wanted the aged Pirajiba ('Fish Fin') to come and greet him at the entrance to his village. But Pirajiba replied that, 'except in wartime, he only waited on the road for women. Since Zorobabe was neither a lady nor coming to fight, he would not rise from his hammock.'
173 *which was innumerable'.* Salvador, *Historia* (1931 ed.) p. 170.
173 *he might rebel.'* Ibid. p. 174.
174 *fighting-men.'* Jácome Monteiro, in HCJB 8 405.
174 *with deceptions'.* Anon Jesuit, *Informação dos primeiros aldeiamentos da Baía*, in Anchieta, *Cartas* 372; Inácio Tolosa letter, Bahia, 7 Sept 1575, in Felisbello Firmo de Oliveira Freire, *História de Sergipe* (Rio de Janeiro, 1891) 6–13, or HCJB 1 440–2. Surubi's village was possibly on the site of the modern town of Itaporanga. An anonymous Jesuit (who may well have been Anchieta) wrote that the Sergipe tribes had 'always been at war with the Portuguese because of the raids and aggression done to them, and had killed some Portuguese in self-defence' (*Informação*, in Anchieta, *Cartas* 371). And Inácio Tolosa wrote that the slaves had fled back to Sergipe because they had been seized from there.
174 *Portuguese arrive!'"* Ibid. 375.
174 *when he comes?'"* Ibid. 375.
175 *were enslaved.'* Sousa, *Tratado descriptivo*, ch. 23, pp. 43–4; Salvador, *Historia*, bk 3, ch. 19, p. 216.
175 *slaves for life.'* Anon Jesuit, *Informação*, in Anchieta, *Cartas* 376. The Jesuit who described the campaign recorded that the church smelled so badly after its use as a prison that the filthy floor had to be dug out before it could again be used for mass.
175 *until now [1587].'* Ibid. 376.

175 *against the enemy'*. Inácio Tolosa letter, 7 Sept 1575, HCJB 1 444.

175 *used as slaves'*. Official enquiry, Lisbon, 1576, HCJB 1 445.

176 *successfully colonised.* The Sergipe war of 1590 was launched in the instructions to Governor-General Francisco Giraldes: he was to eliminate the Indians impeding land communications between Pernambuco and Bahia, 9 March 1588, RHGB 67 pt 1, 224. Freire, *Historia de Sergipe* 418. Barros' thousands of captives were put to work clearing ranches for Barros and other new colonists. Basilio de Magalhães, *Expansão geographica do Brasil colonial* 33; HCJB 1 447. In an enquiry about the war in Lisbon, Gabriel Soares de Sousa testified against the Jesuits. But the decision went against Governor Brito de Almeida. J. F. de Almeida Prado, *Bahia e as capitanias do centro do Brasil (1530–1626)* 2 133–5.

176 *in the aldeia'*. André de Almeida to Governor-General Luís de Sousa, Cabo Frio, 4 Aug 1620, *Livro primeiro do governo do Brasil, 1607–1633* (Ministerio das Relações Exteriores, Rio de Janeiro, 1958) 305. This aldeia at Macaé was created on the advice of Martim de Sá in 1617; AMN 3 pt 2, 33–4, 1927.

176 *amazed and delighted.'* Capitão Miguel Ayres Maldonado, *Descripção . . . dos trabalhos e fadigas das suas vidas . . .* (1661) 352.

176 *highly satisfied.'* Ibid. 355.

176 *an abundance!'* Ibid. 357.

177 *Paraíba.'* Ibid. 371.

177 *in this.'* Ibid. 387.

177 *one heifer.'* Ibid. 391–2. The Governor was the highly respected Salvador Corrêa de Sá, a descendant of Mem de Sá, and this episode was in 1647.

177 *fraud and malice. . . .'* Ibid. 396–7.

177 *now tractable'*. Conde de Attouguia to King, Bahia, 25 Jan 1656, DH 4 282.

177 *become quiet.'* Report by Alexandre de Sousa Freyre and others, Bahia, 4 March 1669, DH 5 213–14.

178 *number of white immigrants.* Afonso de Escragnolle Taunay, *Subsídios para a história do tráfico Africano no Brasil* (São Paulo, 1941) 305; Luis Viana Filho, 'Rumos e cifras do tráfico baiano', *Estudos Brasileiros* (Rio de Janeiro) 15 357–8, Nov–Dec 1940; Thales de Azevedo, 'Indios, brancos e pretos no Brasil colonial'; Artur Ramos, *O negro brasileiro* (São Paulo, 1940); and many other studies by such authors as Roberto Simonsen, Pedro Calmon, Hélio Vianna, João Capistrano de Abreu, Rocha Pombo, Nina Rodrigues, Gilberto Freyre, etc.

178 *a mill running.'* Antonil-Adreoni, *Cultura e opulência do Brasil* (1923 ed.) 91.

179 *without exception.'* Confession of João Remirão, Bahia, 2 Feb 1592, Mendonça, *Primeira visitação* 145.

179 *in favour of whiteness.* Caio Prado, Jr, *The Colonial Background of Modern Brazil* 121; C. R. Boxer, *Race Relations in the Portuguese Colonial Empire* 93, etc.; Freyre, *Masters and Slaves* 13–14.

179 *mission aldeias.* The *Informação da provincia do Brasil para nosso padre*, dated 31 Dec 1585 and probably by Anchieta, gave a summary of Jesuit missions. Pernambuco had three (São Tomé, Nossa Senhora da Escada, Gueena); Sergipe three (São Tomé, Santo Inácio, São Paulo); Bahia was reduced to only 'three aldeias of Christian Indians with some 2500 persons'; Espírito Santo was now the best province, 'for it still has many heathen and is not too scandalised by the Portuguese' – its ten aldeias included São João, Nossa Senhora da Conceição and Santo Inácio dos Reis Magos; Rio de Janeiro had two (São Lourenço in Niterói and São Barnabé near Itaboraí, with almost 3000 Indians in the two villages); at São Vicente there were four (Maniçoba and Jaraïbatiba) with two of 1000 Indians each alongside São Paulo (Nossa Senhora dos Pinheiros and São Miguel de Uraraí). *Informação*, in Anchieta, *Cartas* 419. Estêvão Pinto, 'Introdução à história da antropologia indígena no Brasil (século xvi)' 351.

180 *his remote grandmother.'* Freyre, *Masters and Slaves* 87.

181 *did likewise'*. Sousa, *Tratado descriptivo* 170.

181 *attached to it.'* Yves d'Evreux, *Voyage dans le nord du Brésil, fait durant les années 1613 et 1614* 111.

Chapter 9 THE DISCOVERY OF THE AMAZON

183 Brazil. Inspired by the discoveries of Columbus, Yáñez Pinzón obtained a licence to discover new lands provided his discoveries were not those of the Admiral Columbus and provided they did not infringe on the Portuguese sphere of the Line of Tordesillas. Yáñez had been captain of one of the ships on Columbus' first voyage. (Yáñez Pinzón, Capitulación, Seville, 6 June 1499, in Antonio Muro Orejón, 'La primera capitulación con Vicente Yáñez Pinzón para descubrir en las Yndias', *Anuario de Estudios Americanos* 4 (Seville, 1947) 741–56). He sailed from Spain with four ships in mid-November 1499, paused in the Cape Verde Islands, and sailed south-south-west. In late Jan 1500, Yáñez and his men were amazed to strike land only 300–400 leagues from the Cape Verdes. Yáñez called the new land Rostro Hermoso ('Beautiful Face'). (Testimony of Manoel de Valdovinos, *De los Pleitos de Colón* (1512), vols 7 and 8, 1892, 1894, of *Colección de documentos inéditos relativos al descubrimiento . . . de las antigas posesiones españolas de ultramar*, 25 vols (Madrid, 1885–1932).) The expedition was described by Francisco López de Gómara, *Historia general de las Indias* (1552), ch. 36, 2 vols (Madrid, 1922), 1 83 ff; Pietro Martire d'Anghiera, *Décadas del Nuevo Mundo*, decade 2, bk 9, ch. 3, trans. F. A. MacNutt, *De Orbe Novo: the eight decades of Peter Martyr D'Anghera*, 2 vols (New York, 1912), 1 158; Antonio de Herrera, *Historia general de los hechos de los Castellanos en las islas y tierra firma del Mar Océano* (1601–15), decada 1, bk 4, ch. 6; Antonio Leon Pinelo, *El Paraíso en el Nuevo Mundo* (Madrid, 1656), ed. Raúl Porras Barrenechea (Lima, 1943) 2 444. See also: José Hernandez-Pinzón y Ganzinotto, *Vicente Yáñez Pinzón, sus viajes y descubrimientos* (Madrid, 1920); Ladislão Gil Munilla, *Descubrimiento del Marañón* 19–50; Roberto Levillier, *América la bien llamada* 1 114–23; Gaspar de Carvajal, *The Discovery of the Amazon* 153–4; Louis-André Vigneras, *The Discovery of South*

America and the Andalusian Voyages (Chicago, 1976) 69–76.

This would have been the first expedition to see part of Brazil, unless Amerigo Vespucci did so a few months earlier, in late 1499. Vespucci separated from Alonso de Hojeda, probably off the coast of Amapá or French Guiana. He then sailed south past two great rivers (the Amazon and the Pará?) until his progress was barred by strong currents along the coast of Ceará. Vespucci to Pier Francesco de' Medici, Seville, 1500, trans. in Frederick J. Pohl, *Amerigo Vespucci* 78.

183 Germans'. Herrera, *Historia general*, decada 1, bk 4, ch. 6. Virtually no one doubts that Yáñez Pinzón's men saw what is now Brazil. Some Brazilians do, however, dispute whether his landfall was the Cape of Santo Agostinho in Pernambuco, or whether it was some cape further north such as Cape São Roque, or Mucuripe in Ceará (HGB 1 79–81; João Capistrano de Abreu, *O descobrimiento do Brasil* (1929 ed.) 30–46; Th. Pompeu Sobrinho, *Proto-história Cearense* (Fortaleza, 1946) 23–4).

183 all their lives'. Herrera, *Historia general*, decada 1, bk 4, ch. 5. The Spaniards also had a stiff battle with some Indians. They tried to trade, throwing the natives a hawkbell and receiving in return a gilded club. The Indians tried to grab a Spaniard, and in the ensuing battle a shower of arrows killed about ten Europeans – the first to die in Brazil. The Indians tried to seize the Spaniards' boats, killing their guardian; but they were driven off with heavy losses from European spears and swords. Pietro Martire trans. MacNutt, *De Orbe Novo* 1 159; Vigneras, *Discovery of South America* 72. Yáñez Pinzón's capitulación authorised him to bring back 'black or mulatto slaves', but he was not supposed to bring American Indian slaves, nor brazilwood, which was a royal monopoly in Spain.

183 the Amazon itself. Another Spanish

expedition led by Diego de Lepe went to Brazil, hard on the heels of Yáñez Pinzón. Lepe, an Andalusian and a relative of Yáñez Pinzón, probably reached Brazil on 12 Feb 1500, because he named a river there after St Julian, whose saint's day was on that date. His two ships sailed a short distance southwards, rounding Cape Santo Agostinho south of Recife before turning northwards. Diego de Lepe had a battle with Indians who killed eleven of his men, but he also brought back native captives and handed them over to the powerful Bishop Juan Rodríguez de Fonseca. Bartolomé de las Casas was disgusted that the prelate accepted this illegal human booty (Las Casas, *Historia de las Indias* (1552–61), ed. A. Millares Carlos, 3 vols (Mexico, 1951), 2 159).

Lepe sailed up a river whose water was less fresh than that of Yáñez Pinzón's, and that the natives called Marañón – possibly the Pará, the river that forms the southern shore of the huge island of Marajó. The problems of who discovered which river were investigated very thoroughly by Gil Munilla in his *Descubrimiento del Marañón* 29–33, 41–2. He showed convincingly that Lepe left Spain six to eight weeks after Yáñez Pinzón, at the end of 1499. By carefully examining the testimonies of members of both expeditions (in *De los Pleitos de Colón*) he noticed that the name Marañón occurred only in relation to Lepe's expedition and never in the descriptions of Yáñez'. The men who sailed on the two voyages (which met off the coast of Guiana) differentiated between the freshwater river (Santa Maria de la Mar Dulce) explored by Yáñez Pinzón, and the Marañón explored by Lepe. It is significant that the waters of the Pará are more saline than those of the main Amazon, and do not carry fresh water out to sea. It therefore seems that Yáñez Pinzón discovered the main Amazon, and Lepe the Pará, which he called Marañón. The name Marañón first appeared in the testimonies of 1512–13 and was first shown on the map of Maggiolo in 1519, then on that of

Salviati, and on all later maps. It came to be identified with the territory to the south-east of Marajó that is now the Brazilian state of Maranhão. It was also applied by some cartographers to the main Amazon, which is why the upper part of that river, the branch that rises in the Peruvian Andes not far from Lima, is called the Marañón.

No one knows the exact origin of the name Marañón. It was probably a corruption of some native name, for the prefix *mara* also occurs in the island of Marajó: Spaniards tended to change native words to correspond to towns in Spain. Pietro Mártire d'Anghiera said that it was a native name. Other versions were: that it was named after some of Yáñez Pinoñs sailors from Marañón in Navarre; that his men were not sure whether they were sailing on a sea or not – 'por un mar o non'; that Lope de Aguirre's expedition lost itself in a great entanglement (*maraña*) of waterways – hence a *marañón* (Manuel Rodríguez, *El Marañón y Amazonas* (Madrid, 1684) 18); or that it was named after a later explorer called Marañón. Gil Munilla, *Descubrimiento del Marañón* 45–6.

184 *Treaty of Tordesillas.* The Treaty signed at Tordesillas in Spain on 7 June 1494 divided the spheres of exploration of Spain and Portugal by a line from pole to pole 370 leagues west of the Cape Verde Islands. It failed to specify which of the many Cape Verde Islands was the starting-point, and did not define how many leagues were in a degree. Geographers of the early sixteenth century struggled with the problem. They located the Line of Tordesillas at different points between about 42° 30′ and 49° 45′ west of Greenwich, or roughly between the Parnaíba river and the Tocantins. Even the most westerly interpretation, the most favourable to Portugal (by Duarte Pacheco Pereira in his *Esmeraldo de Situ Orbis* (1505) or by Diego Ribeiro in 1529), left the mouths of the main Amazon inside the Spanish sphere. Jaime Cortesão, 'Relações entre a geografia e a história do Brasil', in *História da Expansão Portugêsa no Mundo* 2

22–3; Henry Harrisse, *The Diplomatic History of America* (London, 1897); Hélio Vianna, *História diplomática do Brasil* (São Paulo, 1958) 13–22, and *História do Brasil* (1970 ed.) 36–7.

184 *Indians*. Diego de Ordaz sailed with 400 men in three ships, in search of El Dorado. His own ship was deflected to Trinidad by currents, but the other ships under Captain Juan Cornejo were apparently wrecked on the Amazon. Oviedo wrote: 'It is believed that these Spaniards . . . were subjected by the Amazons and married them.' Royal licence to Diego Ordaz to explore and conquer the Marañón, 20 May 1530; letter from the Archbishop of Santo Domingo to the King, 11 Aug 1531, about its failure; enquiry on services of a nephew of Ordaz, Nov 1533; legal action by Francisco Pereira against Ordaz over the boundaries between their respective provinces of Paria and Marañón, Nueva Cádiz (Cubagua), 23 June 1531 – all quoted in Carvajal, *Discovery* 156–8; the expedition was described in Herrera, *Historia general*, decada 4, bk 10, ch. 9; Juan de Castellanos, *Elegías de varones ilustres de Indias* (Madrid, 1589), elegy 9, canto 1; Oviedo, *Historia general*, bk 49, ch. 1. Orellana's expedition down the Amazon in 1542 heard reports of Christians living among the Indians, and assumed that they were some of the survivors of Ordaz' venture. Carvajal, *Discovery* 211, 241–2; Roberto Levillier, *El Paititi, El Dorado y las Amazonas* (Buenos Aires, 1976) 53–4.

184 *against the current*. Pero de Magalhães de Gandavo wrote that colonists sailed upstream for 250 leagues, or almost 800 miles, which would have taken them as far as the mouth of the Rio Negro. Antonio de León Pinelo, *El Paraíso en el Nuevo Mundo* (Lima, 1943 ed.) 2 450; Vicente do Salvador, *Historia do Brasil*, ABNRJ 13 56; Gabriel Soares de Sousa, *Tratado descriptivo do Brasil em 1587*, chs 4, 5, 10, pp. 9, 11, 18–19. The Spaniards rescued a boatload of starving Portuguese sailors who became separated from the expedition. The Audiencia of Santo Domingo wrote to the King, 12 Feb 1536, that the expedition contained 1500 men and 120 horsemen in twelve ships, and that it intended to colonise the Marañón/ Amazon river 'within the territory marked off for Your Majesty'; Carvajal, *Discovery* 159.

185 *the upper Amazon. Apontamentos de Diogo Nunes das suas viagens na America* (c.1554), HCP 3 367–8; Marcos Jiménez de la Espada, 'La jornada del capitán Alonso de Mercadillo a los indios Chupachos e Iscaicingas', *Boletin de la Sociedad Geográfica, Madrid* 38 217–18, 1895; Jaime Cortesão, *Rapôso Tavares.e a formação territorial do Brasil* 23; Carlos Drumond, 'A carta de Diogo Nunes e a migração tupi-guaraní para o Perú'.

185 *great treasures . . .'*. Gonzalo Pizarro to King Charles, Tumibamba, 3 Sept 1542, in Carvajal, *Discovery* 245. Gonzalo Pizarro's was by no means the first or the only expedition into the Amazonian forests. Francisco Pizarro's Greek artilleryman Pedro de Candía had led a great – and disastrous – expedition into the forests east of Cuzco; Pedro de Ansurez marched into the lands of the Mojos near what is now the Brazilian state of Acre; Alonso de Mercadillo and Alonso and Hernando de Alvarado had penetrated to the lands of the Motilones on the Huallaga and down the upper Amazon to the Omagua near the frontier of modern Brazil. Sebastián de Benalcázar, the conqueror of Quito, was also obsessed with the idea of discovering La Canela or El Dorado – he had descended the Cauca river in Colombia towards the Amazon, told the historian Gonzalo Fernández de Oviedo about his plans in 1540, and on 31 May 1540 obtained from the Emperor Charles a monopoly of the cinnamon he might discover (Marcos Jiménez de la Espada, 'Primeros descubrimientos del país de La Canela', *El Centenário* (Madrid) 2 442–3, 1892; Oviedo, *Historia general*, bk 49, ch. 1) and was still writing to the Emperor about it, from Cali on 20 Sept 1542. Hernán Pérez de Quesada also marched out of Bogotá on 1 Sept 1541 with 260 Spaniards and 200 Indians and

plunged deep into south-eastern Colombia in search of the river full of riches, about which there had been so many reports (letter of Pérez de Quesada, Cali, 16 May 1543, in Gil Munilla, *Descubrimiento del Marañón* 174).

186 *[the Atlantic]'*. Gonzalo Pizarro to Emperor Charles, Tumibamba, 3 Sept 1542, in Carvajal, *Discovery* 247. In that same month, Sebastián de Benalcázar also wrote to the Emperor. Benalcázar said that he planned to sail down the rivers rising in what is now Colombia, 'and I plan to correspond with the North Sea [Atlantic] and to discover a port on it. . . .' Benalcázar to Emperor, Cali, 20 Sept 1542, in Gil Munilla, *Descubrimiento del Marañón* 193.

186 *the whole expedition.'* Pizarro to Emperor Charles, Tumibamba, 3 Sept 1542, Carvajal, *Discovery* 248. Pizarro's men had by then eaten over a hundred horses and 'more than a thousand dogs' (dogs to which Pizarro occasionally fed Indians that he wished to punish) and were reduced to eating palm hearts, nuts and forest grubs. They seized some canoes and followed Orellana's trail for a time. They were saved by finding natives with plenty of food, precisely at the river where Orellana was supposed to have found it. They had a harrowing journey back to Quito, and arrived there with no horses, porters, dogs or equipment whatsoever, 'with only our swords and each with a staff in his hand'.

Gonzalo found that in 1541 his brother Francisco had been murdered in his palace in Lima by the followers of his former partner Diego de Almagro. His other brother Hernando was imprisoned in Spain for having executed Almagro. Gonzalo himself retired to his estates in the altiplano of what is now Bolivia. Three years later he emerged to lead the settlers of Peru in a revolt against laws that they considered far too liberal towards the Indians. Gonzalo pursued the King's Viceroy to Quito and killed him in battle, and for three years Gonzalo himself ruled Peru as uncrowned King. It was a reign of terror in which hundreds of colonists were

executed and the natives suffered terribly. The King of Spain repealed his liberal legislation, and sent a cleric, Pedro de la Gasca, to reconquer Peru. The settlers flocked back to their allegiance to the Crown. The handsome, cruel young Gonzalo Pizarro was defeated outside Cuzco in 1548 and promptly hanged and quartered as a rebel.

187 *without sense.'* Carvajal, *Discovery* 71, 172.

187 *emptied into it. . . .'*. Ibid. 171.

187 *too strong. . . .'* Question 17 of an official enquiry held on Margarita Island in the Caribbean, for Cristóbal de Segovia (one of Orellana's men), Oct 1542, in ibid. 269. The various witnesses naturally confirmed this version of what had happened.

187 *miles of river.* Gonzalo Fernández de Oviedo interviewed members of the expedition when they reached the Caribbean, and also published the first version of Friar Gaspar de Carvajal's famous eye-witness account of it. Oviedo wrote that, having become separated from Gonzalo Pizarro, 'this captain [Orellana] and his companions decided to proceed forwards with the current in search of the North Sea [the Atlantic] to escape alive. This is what they gave me to understand. . . .' Oviedo, *Historia general*, bk 49, ch. 2; Herrera, *Historia general*, decada 6, bk 9, ch.2. trans. Clements Markham, *Expeditions into the Valley of the Amazons*, Hakluyt Society (London, 1859), 24 23–4; Garcilaso de la Vega, *Comentarios reales de los Incas*, pt 2 (1617), bk 3, chs 2–3, trans. Markham, *Expeditions* 12; Pedro de Cieza de León, *Guerra de Chupas, Chronica del Perú*, pt 4, bk 2, chs 18–22 and 81, trans. Markham, Hakluyt Society, 2nd series, 42 54–77, 189–92 (London, 1917); Francisco López de Gómara, *Historia general de las Indias* (1552); Agustín de Zárate, *Historia del descubrimiento y conquista de la provincia del Perú* (1555), bk 4, chs 2–5; Toribio Ortigüera, *Jornada del rio Marañón* c.1581), BAE (*Continuación*) 15 (*Historiadores de Indias 2*) 329, trans. in Carvajal, *Discovery* 310–20.

It is clear that Gonzalo Pizarro knew that the river led to the Atlantic, from an award of an encomienda he made to Gonzalo Diaz de Pineda just before leaving Quito on 4 Jan 1541, in which he mentioned that Diaz had been on an expedition 'towards the North Sea, which is the entry towards La Canela' (quoted in Gil Munilla, *Descubrimiento del Marañón* 208). Immediately after returning to Quito, Gonzalo Pizarro wrote to Sebastián de Benalcázar that 'a captain had rebelled on a river . . . with all the supplies, arms and guns of the expedition in order to emerge down the river on to the North Sea . . .' (Benalcázar to Emperor Charles, Cali, 20 Sept 1542, in Marcos Jiménez de la Espada, 'La traición de un tuerto', *La Ilustración Española y Americana* (Madrid, 22 Aug 1894) 107).

Orellana behaved with the correctness of a guilty man before setting off down the river with his new boat. His men presented him with a petition begging him not to attempt to sail back upstream towards Pizarro (text and trans. in Carvajal, *Discovery* 258–61). Then, on 1 March 1542, Orellana resigned his commission as Pizarro's lieutenant and was elected as their captain by the forty-seven men of the expedition, with the two friars serving as witnesses and the scrivener administering Orellana's oath of acceptance (ibid. 77–8). Various judicial enquiries were later held on behalf of different members of the expedition, to clear their conduct in continuing downstream (ibid. 266–310). Orellana himself appeared before the Council of the Indies in Seville in 1543. He reiterated that after being swept downstream for over 200 leagues it was impossible for him to return. He had heard about the wealth of the lands that lay ahead, and determined 'to explore those vast provinces' in order to serve God and King by bringing Christianity to their natives and by claiming them for Spain (ibid. 321). The Council was sympathetic, and issued Orellana with a licence to return and colonise the Amazon. His capitulación, dated Feb

1544, made Orellana Governor and Captain-General of the south bank of the Amazon for 200 leagues inland from its mouth. He left Spain in May 1545.

188 *Amazon.* Toribio Medina, in ibid. 98; Gil Munilla, *Descubrimiento del Marañón* 301.

188 *find the land'.* Carvajal, *Discovery* 202.

188 *towards them.'* Ortiguëra, *Jornada*, in ibid. 317–18.

188 *two dead.* Ortiguëra, in ibid. 318; ibid. 190–3. Francisco Vázques, who recorded the voyage of Lope de Aguirre down the Amazon in 1561 also mentioned these tanks of turtles: *Relación verdadera de todo lo que sucedió en la jornada de Omagua y Dorado*, BAE *(Continuación)* 15 432. Gil Munilla argues convincingly that the village of Machiparo or Machifaro was close to the mouth of the modern Tefé, which flows into the Solimões from the south, roughly mid-way between the Negro and the frontier with Peru and Colombia (*Descubrimiento del Marañón* 320).

188 *fruitful land.'* Carvajal, *Discovery* 200.

189 *Toribio de Ortigüera.* Ibid. 317; Cristóbal de Acuña, *Nuevo descubrimiento del gran rio de las Amazonas*, trans. Markham, *Expeditions* 101–2.

189 *twenty villages.'* Carvajal, *Discovery* 203; Acuña, who travelled down the Amazon a century later, said that a great multitude of Paguana lived on the Tefé river: *Nuevo descubrimiento*, ch. 59, in Markham, *Expeditions* 104. Acuña reported that the longest village seen by his expedition was 1¼ leagues long and belonged to the Yoriman (Yurimagua?) tribe living on the south bank of the Amazon downstream of the Tefé; Acuña, ch. 62, in ibid. 106.

191 *manly fashion'.* Carvajal, *Discovery* 204.

191 *survived.* The transparent, dark-blue waters of the Negro carry very little sediment. They drain the Guiana highlands, an area that has been tectonically stable and subjected to extreme erosion for millions of years. The remaining surface is generally an ancient pre-Cambrian mass of granitic and gneissic rocks. In places this is still capped by layers of slightly younger, but

still very ancient, sedimentary rocks. These form sandstone table-lands with sheer cliffs and spectacular waterfalls – the most famous of which are 8000-foot (2600-metre) Roraima and the Pacaraima hills to the west. The Rio Negro is noted for being free of mosquitoes, possibly because of some chemical property of its waters. The main Amazon is a 'white river', turbid from millions of tons of sediment carried down from the largely unconsolidated slopes of the Andes. South of the Amazon, the pre-Cambrian shield ends at the Madeira river, above which are meandering white rivers such as the Purús and Juruá. Rainfall tends to be greater on the upper Amazon – abundant throughout the year, and ranging up to 120 inches a year. On the middle and lower Amazon, the rain is concentrated between October and May, and is generally less than seventy inches a year.

191 *prepared an attack.* Carvajal, *Discovery* 207.

191 *attack us.'* Ibid. 208.

192 *'like wounded dogs'.* Ibid. 210.

192 *of the Amazons'.* Ibid. 212.

192 *to the Amazons'.* Ibid. 213.

192 *the end of me.'* Ibid. 214.

193 *ten Indian men.'* Ibid. 214.

193 *their caprice'.* Ibid. 220.

193 *arts of war'.* Ibid. 221.

193 *quick to comprehend'.* Ibid. 222.

194 *Amazons''.'* López da Gómara, *Historia general de las Indias*, BAE 22 210, trans. in Carvajal, *Discovery* 26; Herrera (*Historia general*, decada 6, bk 9, ch. 4) believed that women had fought at the head of this tribe, but criticised Orellana for assuming on such slim foundation that they were Amazons. José Toribio Medina agreed with that judgement, but stressed that Carvajal made it clear that he was repeating what they understood the Indian to have told them, and not what they observed themselves.

194 *suffering or pain.'* Carvajal, *Discovery* 216.

194 *miraculous event'.* Oviedo, *Historia general*, bk 50, ch. 24, trans. in Carvajal, *Discovery* 405. Orellana cleared himself of the charge of treason against Gonzalo

Pizarro, and obtained a licence to return and colonise the Amazon (13 Feb 1544). His colony was to be called New Andalusia. It consisted of the south bank of the Amazon for 200 leagues from its mouth. After many tribulations, Orellana sailed with four badly equipped ships and some 400 colonists. By the time they reached Brazil in Dec 1545, half the people were already dead of disease, or had deserted in the Cape Verde Islands or been lost at sea. Everything went wrong: after months of searching Orellana failed to find the main channel of the Amazon, his expedition scattered, many died of hunger and others were killed by Indians. Orellana himself died of disease and despair late in 1546. José Toribio Medina wrote a fine account of this sad expedition, trans. in Carvajal, *Discovery* 124–52.

195 *Omagua.'* Marquis of Montesclaros, Viceroy of Peru, to King, Callao, 12 April 1613, in Marcos Jiménez de la Espada, *Relaciones Geográficas de Indias* 4, BAE *(Continuación)* 135 233, 1965. Pedro de Cieza de León, who wrote in 1551, said that 200 Indians reached Chachapoyas: Many more had been killed by other tribes during their journey. Various Spanish captains were eager to lead expeditions to conquer the rich lands described by these Indians (*Cronica del Perú*, pt 1, ch. 78).

195 *perpetual ease'.* Pero de Magalhães de Gandavo, *Historia da Provincia de Santa Cruz* ch. 14; Diego de Aguilar y Córdoba, *Marañón* (1578) chs 5 and 6, in Jiménez de la Espada, *Relaciones Geográficas* 237–9; Toribio de Ortigüera, *Jornada del Marañón* (1585), in ibid. 239–41; Francisco López de Caravantes, *Noticia general del Perú, Tierra-Firme y Chile* (c.1610), vol. 1, disc. 2, in ibid. 241. The arrival of the Brazilian Indians at Chachapoyas in 1550 was recorded by: Pedro de Cieza de León, *Crónica del Perú*, pt 1, ch. 78; Antonio de la Calancha, *Cronica moralizada del orden de San Agustín en el Perú* (Barcelona, 1639); Juan Cristóbal Calvete de Estrella, *Rebelión de Pizarro en el Perú y vida de D. Pedro Gasca*, bk 4, ch. 14, BAE *(Continuación)* 167–8,

1964–5; and the accounts of the Ursúa–
Aguirre expedition by Gonzalo de
Zúñiga and Francisco Vázquez, cited
later. Magalhães de Gandavo said that
the Brazilian Tupi travelled through
forests for some years before striking the
Amazon, which they then ascended in
two years. Ortigüera said that
13,000–14,000 of them started the
migration, under Chief Curaraci and
accompanied by two Portuguese, one of
whom was called Matheo. Alfred
Métraux, 'Les Migrations historiques des
Tupi-Guaraní' 21–2.
195 *in the world'*. Captain Altamirano of
Chachapoyas (who was on the
exploratory party) quoted by Antonio
Vázquez de Espinosa, (*Compendio y
descripción*) *Description of the Indies*, bk 4,
ch. 11, p. 413. Altamirano's is one of the
best accounts of the famous
Ursúa–Aguirre expedition (in ibid. bk 4,
chs 10–16, pp. 410–25). Other accounts
were: Toribio de Ortigüera, *Jornada del
rio Marañón* (1581), in *Historiadores de
Indias* 2 305–422. BAE *(Continuación)*15
(Madrid, 1909); Diego de Aguilar y
Córdoba, *El Marañón* (Madrid, 1578);
Gonzalo de Zúñiga, 'Jornada de Pedro
de Ursúa', *Colección de Documentos Inéditos
del Archivo de Indias* 4 215, and report by
Pero de Monguía, ibid. 4 191 ff, and
Aguirre's letter to King Philip, ibid. 4
274; Francisco Vázquez, *Relación
verdadera do todo lo que sucedió en la jornada
de Omagua y Dorado*, BAE *(Continuación),
Historiadores de Indias*, 2 (Madrid, 1909)
431 ff; Lopez Vaz, *Discourse*, in Hakluyt 8
166–70. Other historians told the story,
based on these sources: Inca Garcilaso
de la Vega, *Comentarios reales de los Incas*,
pt 2 (1617), bk 8, ch. 14; Herrera, *Historia
general*, decada 6, bk 9, ch. 6; Juan
Meléndez, *Tesoros verdaderos de las Indias*
(Rome, 1681); Juan de Castellanos,
Elegías de varones ilustres de Indias (Madrid,
1589). Also the letter from Marques de
Montesclaros, Viceroy of Peru, to King
Philip, Callao, 12 April 1613, in Jiménez
de la Espada, *Relaciones Geográficas* 3,
BAE *(Continuación)* 185 (Madrid, 1965)

233–4. Pedro Simón, *Noticias historiales
(sexta noticia) de las conquistas de Tierra
Firme* (Cuenca, 1626) ch. 1, trans.
William Bollaert, Hakluyt Society 28,
1861.
196 *to labour.'* Lopez Vaz, *Discourse*
167.
196 *to conquer that. . . .'* Ibid. 167.
196 *Peru'*. Capt. Altamirano, in Vázquez
de Espinosa, *Description of the Indies*, bk 4,
ch. 12, p. 414.
197 *unto you.'* Lopez Vaz, *Discourse* 169.
197 *his death. . .'*. Ibid. 169.
197 *of a traytor'*. Ibid. 170.
197 *that cursed river.'* Lope de Aguirre to
King Philip, in Markham, *Expeditions* xii.
Sir Clements Markham followed
Cristóbal de Acuña and José de Acosta
(*Historia natural y moral de las Indias*, bk 2,
ch. 6) in thinking that Aguirre travelled
up the Negro, through the Casiquiare
canal and down the Orinoco to reach
Margarita, an island near Trinidad.
There seems to be little to justify this
complicated route. Acosta may have
thought that the Amazon had two
mouths, one of which was the Orinoco.
Altamirano, Lopez Vaz and Pedro
Simón, who copied from Francisco
Vázquez, all said that Aguirre's
expedition descended the main Amazon
river until it met the ocean tides, and that
it made the sea voyage to Margarita in
under three weeks. This was quite
possible, since currents and winds often
swept shipping from the mouth of the
Amazon to the Caribbean. Orellana's
expedition of 1540 had also ended by
sailing up the coast to the island of
Margarita.

Some modern accounts of Aguirre's
extraordinary adventure are: Emiliano
Jos, *La Expedición de Ursúa al Dorada y la
rebelión de Lope de Aguirre* (Huesca, 1927);
and *Ciencia y osadía sobre Lope de Aguirre el
Peregrino* (Seville, 1950); Juan B. Lastres
and C. Alberto Seguin, *Lope de Aguirre, el
rebelde* (Buenos Aires, 1951); Robin
Furneaux, *The Amazon* (London, 1969)
41–8; J. M. Cohen, *Journeys down the
Amazon* (London, 1975).

Chapter 10 MARANHÃO

198 *Brazil.* The corsair was Jacques Riffault. The man who promoted the idea was Charles des Vaux, and the head of the colonial company was Daniel de la Touche, Sieur de La Ravardière. He was joined in it by François de Rasilly, Sieur des Aumels and Nicolas de Harlay de Sancy, Baron de la Molle et de Gros-Bois. The charter was granted in 1610 by Marie de' Medici as regent for the young Louis XIII. On Riffault, see: Vicente do Salvador, *Historia do Brasil*, bk 4, ch. 30, pp. 357–8; Claude d'Abbeville, *Histoire de la Mission des Pères Capucins* . . . 12; letter from Feliciano Coelho de Carvalho, Paraíba, 20 Aug 1597, and Richard Hakluyt, *The Principall Navigations of the English Nation* . . . 2 43–7.

199 *nothing worth while.'* Yves d'Evreux, *Voyage dans le nord du Brésil, fait durant les années 1613 et 1614* 16, 132. These Caeté lived on the coast roughly halfway between Maranhão and Pará. They should not be confused with the Caeté of the São Francisco river. Capistrano de Abreu thought that the name of the chief taken to France, whom Abbeville called Ouyrapiue, meant 'Dry Wood' (note in Salvador, *Historia* (1931 ed.) p. 243. The fort was named after the saintly King Louis IX, and the name has survived in the city of São Luís do Maranhão.

199 *our enemies."'* Evreux, *Voyage* 17.

199 *French.'* Ibid, 64, 65, 41.

200 *a sign of joy.'* Ibid. 219.

200 *good friends to us!"'* Ibid. 220, 222.

200 *excels them.'* Abbeville, *Histoire* 311.

220 *they see done.'* Ibid. 313.

200 *bothering to work'.* Ibid. 299.

201 *live fatly'.* Evreux, *Voyage* 73.

201 *in the sand.'* Ibid. 71.

201 *said or done.'* Ibid. 70–1.

201 *a good smell.'* Ibid. 89–90.

201 *watching them.'* Monsieur de Manoir, 'Sommaire relation de quelques autres choses plus particulières qui ont esté dictes de bouche aux Pères Capucins', in Claude d'Abbeville, *L'Arrivée des Pères Capucins en l'Isle de Maragnan et la conversion des sauvages à nostre saincte foy* 15–16.

201 *such an affront?'* Ibid. 16–17.

201 *mass.'* Évreux, *Voyage* 30.

202 *strong and valiant!"'* Ibid. 31.

202 *prophets of God.'* Abbeville, *L'Arrivée* 9.

202 *hundred thousand men'.* Ibid. 9.

202 *over there.'* Evreux, *Voyage* 322.

203 *such a fine nag.'* Ibid. 326.

203 *gestures and speech."'* Ibid. 327.

203 *than I was."'* Ibid. 327.

203 *be with you."'* Ibid. 328–9.

204 *exchange for tools.'* Ibid. 330.

204 *very handsomely."'* Ibid. 333.

204 *fish for them.'* Ibid. 355–6.

205 *spoke the truth.'* Ibid. 60.

205 *capture slaves.'* Ibid. 21.

206 *avenge our deaths!"'* Ibid. 28–9. The Camarapin presumably lived on Marajó island in the mouth of the Amazon. They might have been one of the tribes that the Portuguese knew by the collective Tupi name Nheengaíba or Ingaíba. These included the Comboca and Aruan.

207 *gold garnishing.'* Diogo de Campos Moreno, 'Jornada do Maranhão', in Cândido Mendes de Almeida, *Memorias para a historia do extincto Estado do Maranhão* 2 250. By the time Campos Moreno saw these Tupinambá in Dec 1614 another had died, leaving only two survivors. Abbeville, *Histoire* (Paris, 1922 ed.) 334–81; Bernardo Pereira de Berredo, *Annaes historicos do Estado do Maranhão* . . ., bk 2, pp. 73–4, bk 4, p. 160; Francisco Teixeira de Moraes, *Relação historica e politica* . . . 78–84; testimony by Antonio Landuzeo Gascon, a French carpenter captured by the Portuguese in Maranhão in 1614, ABNRJ **26** 271, 1904; Jean Mocquet, *Voyages en Afrique, Asie, Indes Orientales et Occidentales* 81; Charles de la Roncière, *Histoire de la Marine Française* (Paris, 1910) 4 354; Afonso Arinos de Mello Franco, *O índio brasileiro e a Revolução Francesa* 93–6. Abbeville described how one ship carrying Tupinambá back to France was forced by bad weather to spend six weeks

at Falmouth in England. The Indians were appalled to see English merchants bargaining for their goods. 'They therefore took such an aversion to that people that they at once called them "worthless white enemies" and said in their language that ... they are extremely stingy and mean' (Abbeville, *Histoire* 298). One Indian wanted to buy oysters from the English fishermen, and offered a round, black stone as payment. He was told that only yellow or silver metal coins would do. He therefore took chalk and whitened his stone, at which the fishermen roared with laughter and gave him the oysters.

207 *Rio Grande*. Diogo de Campos Moreno, *Livro que da razão do Estado do Brasil* (1612) 204, 208–11; royal alvará of 1614, awarding 185 lots of land in Rio Grande, DHBC 2 115–54. Only two awards mentioned the fact that these lands had once belonged to Indians. Both noted that the recipient's cattle had destroyed the plantations of the Indians, who complained: ibid. 135. The name Poti means 'Shrimp' in Tupi, which is why the Portuguese translated the name of the chief as Camarão. He was the father or uncle of the famous chief Don Felipe Camarão, a great ally of the Portuguese against the Dutch.

207 *they went.'* Salvador, *Historia*, bk 4, ch. 38, p. 387.

207 *to comfort the soldiers.'* Ibid. bk 4, ch. 38, p. 388.

208 *the French fought'.* Ibid. bk 4, ch. 38 p. 389.

208 *dangers and victories'.* Berredo, *Annaes*, bk 2, p. 44; Salvador, *Historia*, bk 4, ch. 38, p. 390; Diogo Botelho, Instructions to Pero Coelho de Sousa, Olinda, 21 Jan 1603, and Report, 26 Jan 1603; Enquiry about the conduct of the expedition, 26 March 1605, all in 'Correspondencia de Diogo Botelho', RHGB 73 pt 1, 42–3, 44–6, 51–5, 187, 1910. Salvador said that the expedition had 65 whites, Berredo said 80 and Botelho said 200. Claude d'Abbeville wrote that the expedition had 800–10,000 whites and Indians; but it had been swollen by the 5000 Ceará Indians.

208 *hate so much'.* King to Diogo Botelho, 22 Sept 1605, DHBC 4 7–8; Justification by Diogo Botelho, Bahia, Feb 1608, RHGB 73 pt 1, 184–212, 1910.

208 *soldiers had begun. . . .'* · Salvador, *Historia*, bk 4, ch. 43, p. 409.

208 *the company of her children.'* Ibid. bk 4, ch. 43, p. 410.

209 *Brazil'.* Ibid. bk 4, ch. 44, p. 412.

209 *to the barbarians'.* Ibid. bk 4, ch. 44, p. 412.

209 *blood and mud'.* Ibid. bk 4, ch. 44, p. 414; Figueira, letter of 26 March 1609, DHBC 1 1–42; P. José de Moraes, *História da Companhia de Jesus na extinta Provincia do Maranhão e Pará*, bk 1, ch. 6; João Felippe Betendorf, *Chronica da missão dos Padres da Companhia de Jesus no Estado do Maranhão* 41–2; Antonio Henriques Leal, 'Apontamentos para a historia dos Jesuitas extrahidos dos chronistas da Companhia de Jesus', RHGB 36 pt 2, 104–5, 1873.

210 *as they say'.* Diogo de Campos Moreno, *Jornada*, in Almeida, *Memorias* 163; Afrânio Peixoto, *Martim Soares Moreno* 8.

210 *of his fortress'.* Campos Moreno, *Livro que da razão* 211. Diogo de Campos Moreno was a senior officer, Sargento-Mor of the state of Brazil, and was the uncle of Martim Soares Moreno.

210 *Mocuripe.* Campos Moreno, *Jornada*, in Almeida, *Memorias* 164; Diogo de Meneses letter, 1 March 1612, documents published by Barão de Studart in DHBC 1 1908, and 'Documentos para a historia de Martim Soares Moreno', *Revista da Academia Cearense* (Fortaleza) 14 2, 1910; Salvador, *Historia*, bk 5, ch. 1, p. 465; João Capistrano de Abreu, 'Tricentenário de Ceará', *Revista do Instituto do Ceará, Fortaleza* 18, 1904, and in *Capítulos de história colonial* (1963 ed.) 363–5; Peixoto, *Martim Soares Moreno* 15. The fort on the Ceará was called Fort St Sebastian, and the fort further west was Nossa Senhora do Rosário ('Our Lady of the Rosary') at Jericoacoara ('Bay of Turtles'), some forty miles east of the Camocim river. Martim Soares Moreno maintained his friendship with the Potiguar and

Tobajara throughout his life: it was of great help at the time of the Dutch invasions.

211 *Rio Grande.'* Salvador, *Historia*, bk 5, ch. 2, p. 466. The Franciscan friar Manoel da Piedade was the brother of Frei Bernardino das Neves, who had helped convert the Rio Grande Potiguar, and the son of João Tavares, who had fought them. Albuquerque had far more difficulty recruiting white settlers. Most hid on their plantations, and the Governor had to order that each planter send a younger son – knowing that he would also send at least one white and two black servants to attend the boy. Second-in-command was Diogo de Campos Moreno, who had fought in France and Flanders and was uncle of Martim Soares Moreno. Campos Moreno, *Jornada*, in Almeida, *Memorias* 242–4; Regimento by Gaspar de Sousa to Jerônimo de Albuquerque, 22 June 1614, DHBC 1 83–92; Testimony by Alexandre de Moura, 20 Oct 1620, about the help given to him by the Jesuits, DHBC 2 194–5; Berredo, *Annaes*, bk 2, p. 94; Francisco Teixeira de Moraes, *Relação* 82.

211 *those barbarians'.* Berredo, *Annaes*, bk 3, pp. 93, 96–7. The Portuguese of the fort of Jericoacoara had already sent two men to help Juripari-guaçu defeat some of his enemies, but 'he not only fed his brutal appetite at length with the abominable fodder of the conquered, but reserved for the final dish his benefactors' – the two Portuguese. Nevertheless, Albuquerque made an alliance with this 'rational beast' as Berredo called him. Albuquerque also made contact with the Tupinambá of Maranhão, but without much success. On 19 June 1614, 38 Portuguese, reinforced by Manoel de Sousa d'Eça, repelled an attack by the powerful French ship *Régente* on their fort at Jericoacoara.

212 *from Brazil for ever.* The battle of Guaxenduba was on 19 Nov 1614 and the truce on 27 Nov. Campos Moreno, *Jornada*, in Almeida, *Memorias* 206–17; Manoel de Sousa d'Eça, *Breve relación de la jornada de la conquista del Marañón*,

ABNRJ 26 285, 1904; interrogation of French prisoners taken at the battle: replies of Étienne Maréchal, Noël de la Motte and Jean Pache, 'Documentos sobre a expedição de Jerônimo de Albuquerque ao Maranhão', ABNRJ 26 265, 268, 275, 1904; Salvador, *Historia*, bk 5, ch. 3, p. 472; Berredo, *Annaes*, bk 4, pp. 119–30; Teixeira de Moraes, *Relação histórica* 82–4; José de Moraes, *Historia*, in Leal, 'Apontamentos', RHGB 36 pt 2, 107, 1873.

During the year's truce both sides sent envoys to their home governments to negotiate a peace settlement. Berredo quoted the instructions of Jerônimo de Albuquerque to his envoy to France, his cousin Gregorio Fragoso (*Annaes*, bk 4, p. 160). Diogo de Campos Moreno took the news to Spain. But King Philip III refused to sanction a French settlement in lands claimed by Portugal. The Portuguese built a fort, São José de Itapari, on the island of Maranhão itself and brought up reinforcements under Alexandre de Moura from Pernambuco. These were about to attack the French fort when La Ravardière capitulated and withdrew.

212 *over a hundred.'* Letter from Manoel Gomes to Jesuit Provincial, Maranhão, 1616, ABNRJ 26 329, 1904.

212 *in their language.'* Ibid.

212 *were exhausted.'* Agostinho de Santa Maria, *Santuario Mariano* 9 376–7, quoted in Capistrano de Abreu's 1931 edition of Vicente do Salvador's *Historia* 617–18. The *Santuario Mariano* was generally copied from Salvador's *Historia*. The decision to send Francisco Caldeira was taken at a meeting in Maranhão on 15 Dec 1615 and he left on the twenty-fifth. ABNRJ 26 86–90, 99, 1904; Manoel Barata, *A jornada de Francisco Caldeira* (Belém, 1916) 58. This first expedition to Pará contained two Franciscans of Santo Antonio, including the fine missionary Frei Cristóvão de São Joseph.

213 *from his command.* The Regimento naming Martim Soares captain of the lands from Cumá (Tapuitapera or Alcântara) to Caeté was dated 2 Jan 1616, ABNRJ 26 83–5, 1904. He had amazing

adventures after leaving Maranhão. The
ship taking him south was driven by
storms and currents north to the West
Indies. Martim Soares then sailed for
Spain in a Spanish fleet, but his small
ship parted company in a storm, 'and I
met a [French] pirate ship of eighteen
guns with which I fought, and it killed all
my crew, who were nineteen men, there
remaining only three men and a boy all
in pieces, and I myself had twenty-three
wounds with a cut hand and a dagger
slash on my face. As soon as I reached
France and they found that I had killed
Frenchmen from Dieppe, [my victims']
widows and orphans assembled, and at
their insistence I was arrested and
sentenced to death and held for ten
months in rigorous captivity' (Martim
Soares Moreno, *Relação do Seará* (1618),
in Studart, 'Documentos para a historia
de Martim Soares Moreno' 71; Eugène
Guénin, *Ango et ses pilotes* (Paris, 1901)
24–5). Martim Soares was finally freed
after the intervention of the Spanish
ambassador to France. He was heavily in
debt from ruinous legal fees over his
many appeals. He was given a ten-year
patent to colonise Ceará, and returned to
Brazil. The King gave him the habit of a
Knight of Santiago, but very little money.
Vicente do Salvador said he had to 'stave
off hunger by finding amber', with a pun
on the Spanish words *hambre* and *ambar* –
for the coasts of Ceará produced
valuable grey amber (*Historia*, bk 5, ch. 8,
pp. 611–12).

213 *bosom of the Church'*. Berredo, *Annaes*,
bk 5, p. 180.
213 *defended them.'* Santa Maria, *Santuario
Mariano* (1722) 9 377, in Salvador, *Historia*
(1931 ed.) 618.
213 *a close siege.'* Ibid. 619.
214 *sold as slaves.* Berredo, *Annaes*, bk 5,
p. 188; Simão Estacio da Silveira, *Relação
summaria das cousas do Maranhão* (1624), in
Almeida, *Memorias* 2 16; João de Sousa
Ferreira, *America abreviada* . . . (1693),
RHGB **57** pt 1, 50–1, 1894; Betendorf,
Chronica 45–6.
214 *seen in it'.* Berredo, *Annaes*, bk 5,
p. 190.
214 *virtually impossible.'* Ibid. bk 6, p. 198.
The feuds between Portuguese, French
and Dutch must have seemed equally
absurd to the Indians.
214 *mouth of a cannon.'* Ibid. bk 6,
pp. 198–9.
214 *savage breast. . . .'* Teixeira de
Moraes, *Relação historica*, RHGB **40** pt 1,
88, 1877.
215 *too bloody.* Governor Luís de Sousa,
appoint of Bento Maciel Parente,
Recife, 22 March 1619, DHBC **4** 13–22.
215 *in that area'.* Berredo, *Annaes*, bk 6,
p. 207; Ferreira, *America abreviada* 50–1.
215 *to do it'.* Berredo, *Annaes*, bk 6,
p. 207; Ferreira, *America abreviada* 50–1.
Carvalho, *Chronica da Companhia de Jesus*,
quoted in J. Lucio d'Azevedo, *Os Jesuitas
no Grão-Pará: suas missões e a colonização*
157.
216 *his own life.'* Berredo, *Annaes*, bk 6,
p. 211.

Chapter 11 ANARCHY ON THE AMAZON

217 *São Luís.* The new State of Maranhão
was created as early as 1621. It included
Maranhão, Grão-Pará and Ceará, and
each of the latter two captaincies had its
own capitão-mor or captain-major. The
first governor was empowered to create
hereditary captaincies within these areas.
Six such captaincies were created:
Tapuitapera on the Cumá coast north-
west of São Luís in 1633; Caeté or

Gurupi, further along the coast, between
the Turiaçu and Caeté (modern
Bragança) rivers, also in 1633; Cametá,
on the left bank of the lower Tocantins,
in 1636; Cabo do Norte, modern Amapá
and the north shore of the lower
Amazon, granted to Bento Maciel
Parente, the man who destroyed the
Maranhão Tupinambá, in 1637; the Ilha
Grande de Joanes, or Marajó Island, in

1665; and Xingu, the right bank of that river near its mouth, in 1685. Ceará was transferred from dependency on Maranhão to Pernambuco, in 1652, after the expulsion of the Dutch. By the eighteenth century the Amazon had gained in importance. The capital of the state was therefore moved from São Luís to Belém do Pará in 1737. In that century two new royal captaincies were created within what was by then called Grão-Pará e Maranhão: Piauí, in the barren hinterland between Maranhão and Ceará; and São José do Rio Negro on the basin of the Negro and Solimões rivers.

217 *repose.'* Francisco Teixeira de Moraes, *Relação historica e politica dos tumultos que succederam na cidade de S. Luiz do Maranhão* . . . (1692), RHGB 40 pt 1, 89, 95, 1877.

218 *difficulty.'* Ibid. 130.

218 *arms.'* Simão Estácio da Sylveira, *Intentos da jornada do Pará,* Lisbon, 1618, ABNRJ 26 364, 1904.

218 *distress'.* Jácome Raimundo de Noronha, *Relação sobre as cousas pertenecentes a conservação e aumento do Estado do Maranhão* (1638), ABNRJ 26 437, 1904. Capuchins called Antonio da Merciana and Cristóvão de São Joseph sailed to Pará in the first expedition of 1616. But the Capuchins' later leader was Frei Cristóvão de Lisboa. He sailed from Portugal with Francisco Coelho de Carvalho, who was appointed first governor of Maranhão in 1623, but reached São Luís only in 1626.

219 *slaves.* Bernardo Pereira de Berredo, *Annaes historicos do Estado do Maranhão* . . ., bk 7, p. 245.

219 *service'.* Ibid. bk 7, p. 247.

219 *wilds'.* Ibid. bk 7, p. 252.

219 *paganism!'* Ibid. bk 7, p. 253.

220 *all.'* Jácome Raimundo de Noronha and João Pereira de Cáceres, Informação, 23 May 1637, ABNRJ 26 418, 1904, DHBC 3 46; Bernardo O'Brien del Carpio petition to Spanish King, Archivo General de Indias, Seville, estante 147, caja 5, legajo 21.

220 *Indian villages.* Bernard O'Brien told the story of the shooting of the Capuchin in his petition to the King of Spain in the Archive of the Indies in Seville:

Informação by Jácome Raimundo de Noronha, ABNRJ 26 418, 1904; Teixeira de Moraes, *Relação historica* 130. Frei Cristóvão de Lisboa was forty-one when he took charge of the Franciscan mission in Maranhão in 1624. He had already written to the King deploring the excesses of the laymen who were in charge of Indian aldeias. 'They have their eyes only on temporal profit, for which they exploit the captaincies [of Maranhão and Pará] without any control whatsoever. They abuse the Indians in various ways. They hire them and make them work to excess. They take from them their daily wages and sometimes even take their wives and daughters, treating them all with immoderate harshness and rigour. They take no care to assist them or provide for their wants; but instead do not even give them time to make their own plantations from which to support both themselves and the Portuguese' (Archivo Historico Ultramarino (Lisbon), Maranhão, Papéis avulsos, 17 Oct 1623, quoted in Venâncio Willeke, 'Frei Cristóvão de Lisboa, O.F.M.', *Itinerarium,* Braga, 17 no. 73, 402–25, 1971). Frei Cristóvão worked at the Franciscan mission of Una, two miles east of Belém, among the Tupinambá. He also visited many rivers of Pará, and wrote a description of the animals, plants and natives of Maranhão, now lost.

220 *inhabited villages.'* Teixeira de Moraes, *Relação historica* 92.

221 *Tapuitapera.'* João Felippe Betendorf, *Chronica da missão dos Padres da Companhia de Jesus no Estado do Maranhão,* ch. 4, p. 97; DHBC 1 223. The expedition to 'appease' the Pacaja was led by Pedro da Costa Favela in 1638.

221 *Indians'.* António Vieira, *Resposta aos capítulos que deu . . . Jorge de Sampaio* (1662), *Obras escolhidas* 5 279.

221 *remedy.'* Luís Figueira, *Memorial sobre as terras e gentes do Maranhão e Grão-Pará e rio das Amazonas,* Lisbon, 10 Aug 1637, RHGB 94 (vol. 148) 431, 1923; also comments on this report by Manuel de Vasconcellos e Brito, DHBC 3 29.

222 again. João de Sousa Ferreira, *America abreviada . . .* 84–5.

222 destroyed'. Law of 10 Nov 1647 and Provisão of 9 Sept 1648, in Artur Cesar Ferreira Reis (ed.), *Livro grosso do Maranhão*, pt 1, ABNRJ **66** 17–18, 19, 1948.

222 men.' Sousa Ferreira, *America abreviada* 84.

223 Xingu. The Dutch ship of 1616 was the *Golden Cock* that sailed from Flushing under Pieter Adriaansz with 130 Dutch and English settlers, including a few women and children. They took supplies for one year – bread, pease, beef, pork, bacon, oatmeal, vinegar – and twenty hogsheads of brandy. They built a fort on the north shore of the Amazon and established excellent relations with the Supanes tribe. They helped the Supanes against their rivals, the Percotes. In return, the Indians helped them plant tobacco and the red dye anatto. The colony lasted for six years until abandoned in 1623.

An account of this Dutch colony was in John Scott, 'History and Description of the River Amazones' (Bodleian Library, Oxford, Rawlinson MS. A175, f. 355, quoted in James A. Williamson, *English Colonies in Guiana and on the Amazon, 1604–1668* (Oxford, 1923) 68–9; Aubrey Gwynn, SJ, 'An Irish Settlement on the Amazon (1612–1629)', *Proceedings of the Royal Irish Academy*, Section C, **41** 6, 1932–4. 'Colonel' Scott was a rather disreputable adventurer of the Restoration period who never visited the Amazon. But his account of Adriaansz' expedition was based on the testimony of a Fleming called Mathias Matteson and it is considered reliable.

Scott located Adriaansz' fort near the mouth of the Genipapo (Paru) river. Charles de la Condamine, a French scientist who sailed down the Amazon in 1743, wrote that he stayed at Fort Paru, at the mouth of the Paru and on the ruins of a former Dutch fort (*Relation abrégée d'un voyage fait dans l'intérieur de l'Amérique Méridionale* 145). Scott may have been confused about the name of the tribe that helped the Dutch. The Supanes appear to

have been located closer to the mouth of the Amazon. Early maps show villages called Sapno, Sapanopoko, Sapanow and Sipinipoia on the shore or islands near the Atlantic.

Early cartographers of the mouth of the Amazon include: (1) Gabriel Tatton, map made for Matthew Morton in Radcliffe, 1615, now owned by the Duke of Northumberland in Alnwick Castle; (2) a French expedition of 'pères de famille' led by Jesse de Forest of Avesnes, who visited the Amazon in 1623 (British Museum, Sloane MS. 179B, published in Mrs Robert de Forest, *A Walloon Family in America*, 2 vols (Boston/New York, 1914), 2 189–279); (3) Jan de Laet, map in his *Beschryvinghe van West-Indien* (Leiden, 1625); (4) Henrik Hondius, map of Guiana and the Amazon Region (Amsterdam, 1631); (5) William Blaeuw, map of Guiana almost identical to Hondius', 1631; (6) Johannes Vingboons, 'Vatican' Atlas (*c.*1637), vol. 2, map 3, 'Bocas del Pará', reproduced in F. C. Wieder, *Monumenta Cartographica*, 5 vols (The Hague, 1925–33), **4**, plate 82.

The two Dutch forts on the Xingu were probably established by a trading company run by one Joon Moor. Fort Nassau was probably at a place called Materou on early maps, which became the Jesuit mission Maturá and is now the town of Pôrto de Moz. Fort Orange may have been upstream on the right bank of the Xingu at a place called Gormoarou, possibly the later mission Itacuruça, now Veiros.

223 temples.' Sir Walter Ralegh, *The Discoverie . . . of Guiana* (London, 1596), in D. B. Quinn, *Raleigh and the British Empire* (Harmondsworth, 1973) 149–50.

223 white people'. Petition by Bernardo O'Brien 'del Carpio' to King Philip of Spain (*c.*1637), MS. in Archivo General de Indias, Seville, est. 147, caja 5, legajo 21.

224 among the Indians'. John Stow, *The Annals or General Chronicle of England*, revised by Edmund Howes (London, 1615) 946; John Smith (the Virginia pioneer), *True Travels, Adventures and Observations* (London, 1630), 2 vols

(Edinburgh, 1910), 2 894–5; Williamson, *English Colonies* 53; Gwynn, 'Irish Settlement' 4–5.

224 *necessitie'.* Ibid.

224 *thirty-two falls . . . '.* Ibid. Howes mentioned the twenty men left on the Amazon by Roe, in his revision of Stow's *Annals.* In March 1617, Lord Carew wrote to Roe (who was then on an embassy to the Great Moghul in India) that four or five of his men had returned from the Amazon and sold their tobacco crop for the handsome sum of £2300 (*State Papers Domestic, James I* 95 no. 22, 15). A Spanish agent in The Hague reported to the Council of the Indies in Madrid in April 1615 that Roe had left a 'notable fort' at the mouth of the Amazon (*Documentos para a historia da conquista e colonização do Brasil* (Rio de Janeiro, 1905) 175–7). Sir Thomas Roe himself described his exploits in a letter to Robert Cecil, Earl of Salisbury, Port of Spain, Trinidad, 28 Feb 1611, Public Record Office, C.O. 1/1 no. 25, and *Colonial Calendar, 1574–1660* 11. George Edmundson, 'The Dutch on the Amazon', *English Historical Review* 18 644–6, 1903; Williamson, *English Colonies* 55; Gwynn, 'Irish Settlement' 56–7.

224 *so happy.'* John Smith, *True Travels, Adventures and Observations* (1630), ed. Edward Arber and A. G. Bradley, 2 vols (Edinburgh, 1910), 2 894–5. Roger North had been with Ralegh on his ill-fated Orinoco expedition of 1617 and was one of the last to remain loyal to his leader. He organised the Amazon Company immediately after his return. It received the Great Seal on 5 Sept 1619, and its subscribers included the earls of Warwick, Arundel, Rutland and Dorset as well as other nobles and gentlemen from the City of London. The Spanish ambassador, Count Gondomar, was alarmed at the prospect of English colonists on the Amazon. He protested vigorously to King James and for a time succeeded in delaying North's departure. North finally sailed, in April 1620, with a ship, a pinnace and two shallops. He reached the Amazon in June and recruited some English and Irish who

had been there since 1612 to join his colony. He himself returned to England later in 1620, bringing a cargo of tobacco, but was imprisoned and had his cargo confiscated because of the machinations of the pro-Spanish faction at Court. North left 100 men on the Amazon under Captain Charles Parker, brother of a royal councillor called Lord Mounteagle.

224 *farr surpassinge them'.* Robert Harcourt, *A Relation of a Voyage to Guiana*, 2nd ed. (1626), ed. Sir C. Alexander Harris, Hakluyt Society, 2nd series, 60 144, 1928. Jan de Laet mentioned this exploration by 'a trustworthy Englishman', presumably White, who reached a great lake of green and brackish water, and saw a native village of 300 houses and 1000 inhabitants. The lake may have been Grande near the mouth of the Maicuru or Itandeva opposite the Tapajós. Laet, *Histoire du Nouveau Monde* (Leiden, 1640) 571.

224 *contemtible things . . . '.* Statement of 1622–3, Public Record Office, C.O. 1/2 no. 18, in Williamson, *English Colonies* 88.

225 *drink.'* Petition by Bernardo O'Brien del Carpio to King Philip of Spain (*c.*1637), MS. in Archivo General de Indias, Seville, estante 147, caja 5, legajo 21. Carlos de Araújo Moreira Neto of Rio de Janeiro kindly lent me a copy of this unpublished document, which was written in Spanish. O'Brien said that he was related to the Earl of Thomond, but that his father had had three castles confiscated by the English in 1621 because of his Catholicism. Donough O'Brien, 4th Earl of Thomond from 1581–1624, was a staunch supporter of the English and Protestants in Ireland. His youngest brother, Daniel O'Brien, who later became 1st Viscount Clare, started pro-Protestant but became a champion of the Catholics in the Irish Parliament. He was reprimanded in England in 1613 for forcibly trying to keep a Catholic Speaker in that chamber. The middle brother, Teige, is the most likely to have been Bernard's father. He joined Tyrone's rebellion in 1595 and was continually involved in Catholic

opposition to the English. Bernard O'Brien claimed that all his efforts on the Amazon were done to raise money to redeem his father's confiscated estates.

O'Brien wrote that he was seventeen in 1621 when he met 'Henry' Roe 'who had sailed with Drake and Ralegh'. He presumably meant Thomas Roe, who led the 1610 expedition and was behind North's venture in 1620. After his Amazon expedition, Sir Thomas Roe had gone to lead an embassy to the Great Moghul; he was back in London in 1619, but left for an embassy to Turkey in late 1621. It is curious that another Irishman, known to Spaniards as Gaspar Chillan (? Jasper Dillon, Collins or Sean), who also addressed a petition to the King of Spain, in 1632, also said that this expedition was led by 'don Thomas Rodriguez'. The Jesuit Luís Figueira, who was in Pará at the time, wrote that it was led by 'don Tomas Ro'. Chillan's petition is also in the Archivo General de Indias, estante 71, caja 3, legajo 18. Aubrey Gwynn published the full text of Chillan in 'Documents Relating to the Irish in the West Indies', *Analecta Hibernica* (Dublin) 4 139–286, 1932, and a translation in 'Irish Settlement' 40.

Both O'Brien and Chillan agree that the English sailed on up the Amazon after leaving the Irish. Chillan complained that the Irish were virtually marooned to make room on the ship, which was overcrowded after taking on the survivors of a shipwreck. There is a Portuguese account of a large English ship that tried to grow tobacco near the lower Tapajós. The Tapajós tribe received them well at first, but then attacked those who tried to settle. The ship hoisted its sails in a hurry to escape. João Felippe Betendorf, *Chronica da missão dos Padres da Companhia de Jesus no Estado do Maranhão*, bk 2, ch. 2, RHGB 72 pt 1, 59, 1909; Cristóbal de Acuña, *Nuevo descubrimiento del gran río de las Amazonas* (1641) ch. 75, trans. Clements Markham, *Expeditions into the Valley of the Amazons*, Hakluyt Society 24 127, 1859. Blaise, comte de Pagan, *Relation . . . de la grande rivière des Amazones* (Paris, 1655) 99.

225 *departure.'* O'Brien petition. O'Brien wrote that he sailed 700 leagues upstream from his fort before reaching the Amazons. He presumably meant up the main Amazon and then up the Jari, or the Paru. Both rivers have broad mouths where they join the Amazon, and might have been mistaken for the main river.

225 *women's.'* O'Brien petition.

225 *fort.* Ibid. When he finally reached England, O'Brien found that his father was imprisoned in Ireland for *lèse majesté* and spent a quarter of his Amazonian fortune buying his pardon. Even so, 'they did not return his three castles to him, and only a sixth part of his lands'.

O'Brien's account of the return voyage from the land of the Amazons is very confused. He said that he sailed *down* another river that 'emerges from that river' and runs through a country called Haravaca full of crystalline stones. Where this river flowed into the Atlantic it was called Sarenam. It would have taken many months to sail up the Jari, Paru or other rapid-infested rivers north of the Amazon, cross the watershed, and descend the equally steep Surinam or Marowijne. And a land journey from Surinam to the Amazon, across what are now French Guiana and Amapá, would also be a formidable achievement. O'Brien insisted that when he sailed from Pará to Caracas in 1635 he passed the mouth of the Surinam, the river he had descended. It is conceivable that O'Brien travelled up the Jari, Paru or even *Trombetas* rather than the main Amazon. This would explain his meeting Amazons in the area where both Carvajal and Acuña located them. He would then have crossed the watershed to the Courantyne or the Surinam river. It would also tally with Roe's objective of exploring the rivers flowing into the Amazon from the Guiana highlands. The tribe now living on this watershed, the Tumucumaque hills, is the Carib-speaking Tirió.

O'Brien then spent four years wandering: 'I wanted to see lands, and travelled in Denmark, Moscow, Poland, Germany, Italy and Portugal.'

226 *thus.*'Vicente do Salvador, *Historia do Brasil*, bk 5, ch. 20, p. 500. André Pereira, *Relaçam do que ha no grande rio das Amazonas novamente descoberto* (1616), ABNRJ **26** 256, 258, 1904; Berredo, *Annaes*, bk 6, pp. 217–20, 229–32. Henrique Santa Rosa, *Historia do rio Amazonas* (Belém, 1926) 154; Anisio Jobim, *O Amazonas, sua historia*, Brasiliana **29** 24 (São Paulo, 1957).

226 *way.*' Robert Harcourt, *A Relation of a Voyage to Guiana* (1616, revised 1626), ed. Sir C. Alexander Harris, Hakluyt Society, 2nd series, **60** 146, 1928; Gwynn, 'Irish Settlement' 18. Harcourt wrote that the Portuguese had 300 European soldiers and 1500 Indians in canoes.

226 *countrey.*' Harcourt, *Relation* **60** 146.

226 *shots.*' Salvador, *Historia*, bk 5, ch. 20, p. 502. The Dutch ship belonged to Pieter Adriaansz. It tried to intervene when Bento Maciel was moving to attack the English trading post of Sapanapoko on Tucujus island (Ilha Grande de Gurupá). The Portuguese and their Indians attacked the ship with reckless courage, holing it, causing it to run aground, and eventually setting it on fire at the mouth of the Okiari river. Most of its crew perished, including six Englishmen, one of whom was Captain Charles Parker. Luis Aranha de Vasconcellos, Petition, 12 May 1625, *Documentos para a historia da conquista e colonização do Brasil* (Rio de Janeiro, 1905) 232; Berredo, *Annaes*, bk 6, p. 220; Smith, *True Travels* (Edinburgh, 1910) **2** 899; French pères de famille, Sloane MS. 179B, f. 8; Harcourt, *Relation* 146.

226 *Irish fort.* These skirmishes between the colonial powers had only an indirect bearing on the Indians. Bento Maciel left a small garrison at Gurupá, but Pieter Janss told the French 'pères de famille' on 6 January 1624 that he had just burned this (Sloane MS 179B, f. 8). A newly arrived Dutch expedition of 200 men under Nicolas Hofdan joined O'Brien's friend Philip Purcell in an attempt to occupy a fort called Mandiutuba near Gurupá.

The Portuguese counter-attack was led by Pedro Teixeira. It consisted of 50 Portuguese and 500 Indians with the Franciscan Friar Antonio da Marciana. It attacked Fort Mandiutuba near Gurupá on 23 May 1625. After a fierce fight, the Dutch and Irish slipped away by night during a storm. They crossed the Amazon to join some English plantations (called Tilletille and Warmeonaka by the French who were there in 1624) on the Okiari river (? modern Cajari). Teixeira attacked both these stronghouses, but both were abandoned by their settlers. The ensuing pursuit ended in a sharp battle some distance inland. Sixty English, Dutch and Irish were killed, including Nicolas Hofdan and Philip Purcell, both of whom were covered in wounds; the remaining settlers fled into the forest (Berredo, *Annaes*, bk 6, pp. 227–31; Gwynn, 'Irish Settlement' 24–5). Gaspar Chillan wrote that 70 Irish surrendered on the basis of 'feigned letters from the King' carried by Teixeira, and 54 of them were then treacherously killed.

Teixeira completed his victorious campaign by obtaining the surrender of a small fort 15 leagues away that contained only 20 men. This may have been O'Brien's Irish fort. In December 1626 and January 1627, Marciana and Teixeira swore affidavits to confirm that one Irishman called Stephen Corse (? Courcey) had surrendered voluntarily without any resistance. A new captain-general of Pará, Manoel de Sousa d'Eça, allowed three Irishmen to leave for Europe in 1627. Their names emerge from various sources as Stephen Corse, James Purcell (brother of Philip) and 'Mortoni mor' (? Morton Moore). Bento Maciel Parente, the previous captain-general, was alarmed that these men should be allowed to leave, since they knew so much about the Amazon and its tribes. Maciel obtained the permission of the Governor of Maranhão to sail in pursuit. He chased them to the Antilles but failed to prevent their sailing to Europe. His suspicion was justified, for they were back on the Amazon within two years. Luis Figueira, *Relação de algumas coisas tocantes ao Maranhão e Gram-Pará*, DHBC 2 251; Diogo de Castro, *Informação sobre cousas do Maranhão*, Lisbon, 12 Nov 1630, in *Documentos para a historia da conquista e colonização do Brasil* 191.

226 *trade goods*. O'Brien petition, Archivo General de Indias, Seville. The new Guiana Company was formed by a merger of the interests of Roger North and Robert Harcourt. Its patent passed the Great Seal in May–June 1627 and its governor was the Duke of Buckingham, with a galaxy of peers, noblemen, clergy and businessmen as its backers. Its full title was: The Governor and Company of Noblemen and Gentlemen of England for the Plantation of Guiana.

The Company sent out four ships and some 200 people during 1628 and 1629. The first ship arrived safely in 1628 with 112 men. The Jesuit Luís Figueira reported that the adventurers arrived on the island of Tucujus (Ilha Grande de Gurupá) and built a rectangular fort, in April 1628. O'Brien's ship was evidently one described by John Smith, writing in the summer of 1629: 'And since January is gone from Holland 100 English and Irish, conducted by the old Planters.' Portuguese sources do not mention O'Brien as one of these 'old Planters' – they name James Purcell and Morton Moore as the Irish leaders. Luís Figueira, *Relação*, in Marcos Jiménez de la Espada, *Viaje del Capitán Pedro Teixeira* (Madrid, 1889) 127–8; Diogo de Castro, *Informação*, 12 Nov 1630, in *Documentos para a historia da conquista e colonização do Brasil* (Rio de Janeiro, 1905) 191; Smith, *True Travels* 2 898.

226 *damage there'*. O'Brien petition. O'Brien's new fort, Tauregue or Torego, had been occupied by the Dutch and the Irish until 1623 or 1625. The fort was shown on the map of Johannes Vingboons, Vatican Atlas of *c*.1637, vol. 2, map 3. Vingboons evidently obtained his information from an earlier Dutch route plan showing navigators how to reach Fort Tauregue. The fort was located far up a tributary, apparently either the modern Amaverapucu or the Preto, just south of the equator and north of the Okiari (F. C. Wieder, *Monumenta cartographica*, 5 vols (The Hague, 1925–33), 4, plate 83). Blaeuw's map showed Tauregue with less precision, but also placed it up a small tributary to the north of the River Okiari, which contained the plantations Tilletille and Warmeonaka.

O'Brien wrongly wrote that the mulatto commanding the expedition from Pará was Pedro da Silva. It was Pedro da Costa, who left Belém do Pará on 21 June 1629 with 70 Portuguese and many Indians. The description of the campaign by Portuguese authors (Figueira and Berredo) tallies reasonably well with O'Brien's. When Costa saw that his force was too weak to defeat the northern colonists, he withdrew to Mariocay near Gurupá and sent for reinforcements. Figueira described the Irish fort Tauregue as square and built of logs, with an outer wall 9 feet high and almost 12 feet thick, surmounted by a parapet 3 feet high and 3 feet thick, with a moat in front 15 feet deep.

226 *crucifix'*. O'Brien petition. O'Brien wrote that Teixeira attacked Fort Tauregue by night. Luís Figueira, a leading Jesuit who was with the Portuguese expedition, agreed with O'Brien that the attack occurred in Sept 1629, but he described a siege that began on 28 Sept and lasted for thirty days. On 17 Oct three Irishmen (Figueira wrongly called them Scots) appeared in front of the fort, with a Portuguese interpreter, to attempt a surrender on the grounds that they were fellow-Catholics. One of these envoys was a cavalier, booted and spurred in the manner of his country and speaking excellent Latin. Teixeira was desperate to conclude the surrender because of the approach of English ships. He therefore offered apparently generous terms. Eighty survivors of the garrison marched out on 23 Oct, with the honours of war but surrendering their arms and their fort. O'Brien multiplied the numbers of attackers: the Portuguese from 120 to 300, and the Indians from

1600 to 15,000. He also mentioned the appearance of three ships from England and one from Zealand, which sound very like the vessels that John Smith described in his *True Travels* of 1629. Figueira, *Relação*, in Jiménez de la Espada, *Viaje del Capitán Pedro Teixeira* 128; Berredo, *Annaes* 256; Gwynn, 'Irish Settlement' 32–4; Williamson, *English Colonies* 115–19.

226 *oath.'* O'Brien petition.

227 *live.'* Ibid. Figueira confirmed that Pedro Teixeira sent the Irish prisoners to live in the sertão of Cametá on the lower Tocantins. Later the Governor of Maranhão ordered that they be scattered throughout the province, with some working near Belém and others at Caeté between Pará and Maranhão. All of this tallies exactly with O'Brien's account. O'Brien also correctly named the Capuchins who helped the Irish as Friars Luís da Asunção and Cristóvão de São José, and the officials who robbed them as Governor Francisco Coelho de Carvalho, Captain Pedro Teixeira, Ouvidor (Judge/Councillor) Antonio de Basbaro, and the Chief Treasurer.

227 *Amazon.* O'Brien had many more adventures: his ship reached Venezuela, where he used his knowledge of Indian medicine to cure people of the buboes; he sailed from Caracas in March 1635 but his ship was captured by the Dutch; and he spent some months with them, raiding in the Atlantic and visiting the pirate haven of Tortuga off the north coast of Haiti.

Back in The Hague in late 1635 or early 1636, O'Brien met the Brazilian Jesuit renegade Manuel de Moraes, who had once been in charge of the Indians of Pernambuco and Rio Grande do Norte. Moraes was captured by the Dutch in January 1635, changed sides and was now a Protestant and ally of the Dutch. O'Brien was under sentence of death by the Dutch for having surrendered their Fort Tauregue, but Moraes obtained his pardon so that he could lead another colonial enterprise on the Amazon. Moraes wanted to convert O'Brien to Protestantism and marry him to the

daughter of an Amsterdam burgher – a prospect that caused O'Brien to flee through Flanders and back to London. O'Brien claimed that the Guiana Company then paid him a salary and planned to have him lead 400 men and women in three ships to colonise the Amazon. O'Brien wrote that he recruited 200 soldiers, 150 of them Irish, and including William Howard, second son of the Earl of Arundel. O'Brien was presumably referring to a son of Thomas Howard, Earl of Berkshire, who had organised English efforts at the mouth of the Amazon between 1631 and 1633 (see note to p. 228 below). The Guiana Company promised to send many more settlers from their islands in the West Indies, and to pardon any Catholics, pirates, convicted debtors or other prisoners who might wish to join the colony. But on the day that O'Brien was to swear allegiance to the King of England, he and his faithful Indian boy escaped to Dover and thence to Spain, with the help of the Spanish ambassador. He warned the King of Spain of the urgent need to colonise the Amazon before the heretic English and Dutch did so.

227 *them.'* Figueira, *Relação*, DHBC **2** 251; Berredo, *Annaes*, bk 7, pp. 254–7. Acuña wrote that the Tucujus were on the north bank of the Amazon, near the mouth, downstream of the Paru river: *Nuevo descubrimiento*, ch. 77, in Markham, *Expeditions* 129.

227 *this.'* Figueira, *Relação*, DHBC **2** 251. In that same year, 1629, Francisco Coelho de Carvalho expelled some Dutch ships who were 'very boldly going along the River burning the villages of our heathen friends who refused to follow them, and obliging others to do so with the usual presents and arrogances': Consulta of the Council, 12 Nov 1630, DHBC **4** 38.

227 *reward.'* Luís de Figueira, Memorial, 10 Aug 1637, DHBC **2** 28 and RHGB **94** (vol. 148) 430, 1923; Berredo, *Annaes*, bk 8, pp. 262–5.

228 *land.'* Figueira, Memorial. The English fort among the Tucujus was known to the English as Pattacue or North's Fort and was near modern Macapá on the north shore of the Amazon. It was established by an expedition that left England in about Aug 1629 with 200 men in two ships, a pinnace and some shallops. It was led by William Clovell and Thomas Hixson, who had previously been in charge of the Company's operations on the Wiapoco in Guiana. The English hoped to carry the mouth of the Amazon by weight of numbers, and the Company's promoters were more enthusiastic about settling the Amazon than the Guianas. A relief ship called the *Exchange* reached the new colony in 1630, but another ship called *Hopewell* capsized on a sandbank near Cabo do Norte and most of its passengers drowned. The fort was taken after fierce fighting. Hixson was killed, and William Clovell surrendered on 1 March 1631. Six Englishmen led by Henry Clovell escaped and were sheltered by the Indians for six months before being picked up by an English ship. Williamson, *English Colonies* 125–7; High Court of Admiralty, Examinations no. 50, evidence of Henry Clovell, Roger Glover and John Barker, 18 Oct 1633.

228 *state.'* Jácome Raimundo de Noronha, *Relação sobre as cousas pertenecentes à conservação e aumento do Estado do Maranhão* (1638), ABNRJ 26 435, 1904.

228 *Portuguese.'* Ibid. 436. The English made one last attempt on the Amazon, but were defeated by Indian hostility – the natives had learned from cruel Portuguese reprisals not to back the ineffectual northerners. Thomas Howard, Earl of Berkshire, sent Captain Roger Fry to Dunkirk in May 1631 to buy a 160-ton ship, which they renamed *Bark Andevor (Andover)*. In July 1631 the Privy Council authorised Berkshire to buy 50 guns for his 'Plantation in the Southerne Continent of America' (*Acts of the Privy Council, Colonial Series*, ed. W. L. Grant and J. Munro (London, 1908), 1 277). Captain Fry established himself at a place called Fort Cumaú in the Tucujus – a place called Comoo was shown near

modern Macapá on Gabriel Tatton's map of 1615. In 1632 the Earl of Berkshire published a pamphlet about his colony: *A Publication of Guiana's Plantation . . . and Company for that most famous River of the Amazons in America*, written by 'I.D.', presumably John Day. The author describes the cannon and other defences of the new fort and says that 'I also purpose (God willing) to goe with my wife and friends, to inhabit some part of that spacious and goodly countrie' (Williamson, *English Colonies* 137–8). But the new Fort Cumaú did not last long enough to receive more colonists. Jácome Raimundo de Noronha and Feliciano Coelho led an expedition that stormed the fort in late 1631 or early 1632, killing 86 defenders including Roger Fry. They then massacred or enslaved the Indian allies of the English.

When a fresh English ship arrived in 1632, it found Cumaú a ruin. The local Indians were too frightened to help the English, who were soon starving. After two months, 28 of the original 40 Englishmen were dead of starvation and the rest surrendered to the Portuguese. A letter of 22 June 1633 from Lord Cottington to Sir John Coke spoke of the destruction of a fort near Mocapo (? Macapá) and the hostility of the natives. Statements by Noronha and João Pereira de Cáceres, *Documentos para a historia da conquista e colonização do Brasil* 260–1, 275; Berredo, *Annaes*, bk 8, pp. 268–70; Williamson, *English Colonies* 140–1.

The Dutch also tried again in 1639 but were thrashed by João Pereira de Cáceres, commandant of Fort Gurupá. In the mid-1640s a Dutch corsair, called Ubandregos or Baldregues by the Portuguese, established himself among the Ingaíba. He and his son were captured by Sebastião de Lucena de Azevedo. Lucena de Azevedo to King, Belém, 1 Jan 1647, and Jorge de Albuquerque and others to King, Lisbon, 18 Sept 1647, ABNRJ 26 457, 460, 476, 1904.

228 *Carvalho*. Acuña, *Nuevo descubrimiento*, chs 50 and 51, and Memorial to Council

of the Indies, 1641, in Markham, *Expeditions* 50–1, 138. The Spanish Council of War discussed the new Portuguese fort in Pará as early as 1617; but by 1623 funds were being sent to help Bento Maciel Parente expel foreigners from the Amazon: Souto Maior, *Nos archivos de Hispanha*, RHGB 81 32, 1917.

229 *Christians!'* Frei Cristóvão de Lisboa to Brother Manoel Severim de Faria, Ceará, 2 Oct 1626, DHBC 2 200, 1909.

229 *vessel'*. Acuña, *Nuevo descubrimiento*, ch. 7, in Markham, *Expeditions* 53; Berredo, *Annaes*, bk 9, pp. 289–90.

230 *continent*. Acuña, *Nuevo descubrimiento*, ch. 10, in Markham, *Expeditions* 55; Berredo, *Annaes*, bk 9, p. 292. Acuña said that the expedition also contained hundreds of Indian women and boys (which seems improbable) so that the total of persons was almost two thousand. Berredo said that it had 70 whites and over 900 Indians. Jaime Cortesão has shown the connections between Teixeira's expedition and the Portuguese independence movement. He cited a secret report of 1634 by the Count-Duke of Olivares to the Spanish King about unrest in Portuguese Brazil, and a letter by Alonzo Perez de Salazar, President of the Audiencia of Quito, to King Philip on 19 May 1639 in which he suspected Teixeira's intentions. The Viceroy of Peru, the Count of Chinchón, wrote to Perez de Salazar from Lima on 10 Nov 1638 to be sure to send Spanish observers with Teixeira on his return journey. They were to give a reliable account of all they saw to the authorities in Spain – the Council of the Indies in Seville and the King in Madrid. The chief observer, Cristóbal de Acuña, mentioned this assignment no less than three times in his *Nuevo descubrimiento* (chs 11, 14, 16). In his Memorial to the King in 1641, Acuña strongly urged Spanish occupation of the Amazon. He warned that 'the Portuguese of the coast of Maranhão and Pará intend to attempt communication [with Peru]. I can positively affirm this, and having heard it discussed among them many times can assert it to be an undoubted fact. . . . If the Portuguese who are at the mouth of the river should attempt, with the aid of warlike tribes that are subject to them, to penetrate by the river as far as Perú or the kingdom of New Granada [Colombia] – which is likely, given their small degree of Christianity and less of loyalty –. . . these disloyal vassals of your Majesty would pillage those lands and cause very great damage' (Acuña, Memorial of 1641, in Markham, *Expeditions* 138, 140). Acuña failed to mention that on 16 Aug 1639 Teixeira had obeyed his instructions by taking possession in the name of the King of Portugal of a place he called Franciscana opposite the mouth of the Rio de Oro high up the Amazon (Berredo, *Annaes*, bk 10, pp. 310–12). The Council of the Indies in Madrid was furious about Teixeira's expedition, and determined that Spain should occupy the Amazon and fortify it against any intruders – including the Portuguese. But nothing was done by the Spanish court, beyond the absurd gesture of trying to destroy every copy of Acuña's *Nuevo descubrimiento* shortly after its publication in 1641, so that its information would not fall into the wrong hands. Jaime Cortesão, 'O significado da Expedição de Pedro Teixeira, à luz de novos documentos', *Anais do IV Congresso de História Nacional* (Rio de Janeiro, 1949) 3 169–209, and his *Rapôso Tavares e a formação territorial do Brasil* (Rio de Janeiro, 1958) 238–46.

230 *half way.'* Berredo, *Annaes*, bk 9, p. 297; Acuña, *Nuevo descubrimiento*, ch. 10, in Markham, *Expeditions* 55.

230 *exertions.'* Berredo, *Annaes*, bk 9, p. 297.

230 *multiplied.'* Ibid. bk 9, p. 298.

231 *nation'*. Ibid. bk 9, p. 301; Acuña, *Nuevo descubrimiento*, chs 13–16, in Markham, *Expeditions* 57–60.

231 *country.'* Acuña, *Nuevo descubrimiento*, ch. 51, in Markham, *Expeditions* 95. Berredo reported that Teixeira paused for a time at a village of the Omagua (or Cambeba as the Portuguese called them, because, after deformation, their heads were shaped like hammerhead sharks') which became the Carmelite mission of

São Paulo de Olivença in Berredo's time, the beginning of the eighteenth century (*Annaes*, bk 10, p. 315). Acuña wrote that the Omagua territory was 200 leagues long, and ended 54 leagues upstream of the mouth of the Jurua. Below them lived the Curis and Guayrabas to the north of the river, and Cachiguaras and Tucuriyus to the south; but all these tribes set their villages back from the river so that Teixeira's expedition saw none of them.

231 *tresses.'* Acuña, *Nuevo descubrimiento*, ch. 51, in Markham, *Expeditions* 96.

231 *detains them.'* Acuña, ch. 23, in ibid. 67.

232 *digestion'.* Acuña, ch. 26, in ibid. 70.

232 *family.'* Acuña, chs 26, 39, in ibid. 70, 82.

232 *voyage.'* Acuña, ch. 28, in ibid. 72.

233 *Mexicans'.* Acuña, ch. 37, in ibid. 81.

233 *them'.* Acuña, ch. 36, in ibid. 80.

234 *acts.'* Acuña, ch. 43, in ibid. 86.

234 *empty-handed.'* Acuña, ch. 66, in ibid. 112.

235 *another'.* Acuña, ch. 70, in ibid. 118. Alfred Métraux reckoned that they probably left Pernambuco in the 1530s and migrated for fifty or sixty years before settling on the Amazon ('Les Migrations historiques des Tupi-Guaraní' 23–4). Yves d'Evreux learned about the Amazons from a Tupinambá who lived 'two moons' journey away from Maranhão – possibly one of these Tupinambarana.

235 *territory'.* Acuña, *Nuevo descubrimiento*, ch. 72, in Markham, *Expeditions* 123. The Tupinambá called the river on which the Amazons lived the Cunuris, and named the tribes on it as Cunuri, Apanto (who spoke Tupi), Tagua and Guacará, beyond whom lived the Amazons.

235 *subject.'* Capt. André Pereira, *Relaçam*

do que ha no grande rio das Amazonas novamente descuberto (1616), ABNRJ **26** 258, 1904. Sérgio Buarque de Holanda, *Visão do paraíso: os motivos edénicos no descobrimento e colonização do Brasil* 27–30. Sir Richard Schomburgk dismissed the Amazons as a fable, while Alfred Wallace agreed that men with long hair, earplugs and necklaces might have been mistaken for women. Robert Southey agreed with Alexander von Humboldt and La Condamine that they probably did exist.

235 *them.'* Charles Marie de La Condamine, *Relation abrégée d'un voyage fait dans l'intérieur de l'Amérique Méridionale* 102.

236 *Cayenne'.* Ibid. 107, 143. Earlier on his voyage, La Condamine talked to a seventy-year-old chief at Coari on the Solimões who told him that his grandfather had met a canoe-full of Amazon women crossing the main river, travelling from the area between the Tefé and Coari rivers northwards to the Negro (ibid. 103).

236 *existed.'* Ibid. 108.

236 *peace.'* Acuña, *Nuevo descubrimiento*, ch. 75, in Markham, *Expeditions* 125. The Desterro fort lay on the north bank of the Amazon, 20 miles below the mouth of the Paru, and thus within the captaincy recently awarded to Bento Maciel the elder. It was abandoned soon after.

236 *them.'* Acuña, ch. 75, in ibid. 126.

237 *natives.'* Acuña, ch. 80, in ibid. 131. Teixeira's expedition made a triumphant entry into Belém do Pará on 12 Dec 1639 after its journey to the Andes and back. Berredo, *Annaes*, bk 10, p. 323.

237 *wars'.* António Vieira, *Resposta aos capítulos que deu . . . Jorge de Sampaio* (1662), reply to ch. 24, *Obras escolhidas* 5 280; Betendorf, *Chronica*, ch. 7, p. 72.

Chapter 12 THE BANDEIRANTES

238 *doe holde.'* Lopez Vaz, *A Discourse of the West Indies and South Sea*, in Richard Hakluyt, *The Principall Navigations of the English Nation . . .* 8 166. Vicente do

Salvador said (*Historia do Brasil*, bk 1 ch. 3, p. 19) that the famous cosmographer Pero Nunes reckoned that the Line of Tordesillas crossed the coast near the Oiapogue river, 2° North, and at the Gulf of San Matias in southern Argentina. 'But in practice Brazil reaches only as far as the River Plate.' Salvador very aptly described the bulge on the coast of Brazil as harp-shaped.

238 *and Castille'*. Simão de Vasconcellos, *Chronica da Companhia de Jesus . . .*, quoted in Jaime Cortesão, *Rapôso Tavares e a formação territorial do Brasil* 39. The French pilot Jean Alphonse de Saintonge, who worked for the Portuguese, said in his *Voyages aventureux*, written in 1528 and published in 1559, that the two rivers rose in the same lake. This lake appeared on the map of André Homem in 1559 and that of Bartolomeu Velho in 1562, and all subsequent Portuguese maps until the mid-eighteenth century. Sixteenth-century authors such as Gabriel Soares de Sousa, Pero de Magalhães Gandavo and the seventeenth-century *Diálogos das grandezas do Brasil* also said that the São Francisco river rose in a similar lake.

239 *intent on robbery*. Luis Ramírez letter from Rio de la Plata, 10 July 1528, RHGB 15 14–41, 1852; Ruy Diaz de Guzmán, *La Argentina* (c.1610), bk 1, ch. 5, ed. Paul Groussac, *Anales de la Biblioteca de Buenos Aires* 9 34–41, 1911; Diego García, *Memoria de la navegación que hice . . . en la parte del ·Mar Océano . . .* (1526), mentioned that the expedition had been done by 'one of my men', RHGB 15 387, 1852; Sebastiano Caboto, *Probanza*, in F. Tarducci, *Di Giovanni e Sebastiano Caboto* (Venice, 1892) 387; Alvaro Núñez Cabeza de Vaca, *Naufragios y comentarios* (Madrid, 1922) 271 ff; and various letters by Governor Domingo Martínez de Irala, published in R. de Lafuente Machaín, *El Gobernador Domingo Martínez de Irala* (Buenos Aires, 1939). Erland Nordenskjöld, 'The Guaraní Invasion of the Inca Empire in the Sixteenth Century', *Geographical Review* (New York) 4 103–21, 1917, and *Comparative Ethnographical Studies* (Göteborg) 3 80, 1924; Alfred Métraux, 'Les Migrations historiques des Tupi-Guaraní' 19–20; Charles E. Nowell, 'Aleixo Garcia and the White King',

HAHR 26 450–66, 1946; Sérgio Buarque de Holanda, *Visão do paraíso: os motivos edénicos no descobrimento e colonização do Brasil* 72 ff; Cortesão, *Rapôso Tavares* 53–4. If not on Diego Garcia's voyage of 1525, Aleixo Garcia may have been on Cristóvão Jacques' 'coastguard' expedition of 1521. Métraux felt that he had struck the Inca empire between Tomina and Mizque, near Cochabamba in central Bolivia. His Guaraní had cheerfully pillaged the area until driven off by Charcas Indians.

239 *silver and gold'*. Pero Lopes de Sousa, *Diário da navegação de Pero Lopes de Sousa*, ed. Eugénio de Castro, 1 211. Other references to this expedition are: Cabeza de Vaca, *Naufragios* 182; Guzmán, *Argentina* (1943 ed.) 37, who described a similar Portuguese expedition under someone called Capt. Sedeño. The town council of São Paulo, in its session of April 1585, mentioned the expedition and said that Martim. Afonso left two captains with instructions to punish the Carijó, which they failed to do: *Atas da Câmara da Vila de São Paulo* 1 276. Holanda, *Visão do paraíso* 80–2.

243 *territories*. The main sources for the early Spanish explorations of the Plate–Paraguay–Paraná are: Ulrich Schmidel's *Wahrhaftige Historie einer wunderbaren Schiffart*; Alvaro Núñez Cabeza da Vaca, *Relación de los naufragios y comentarios* (Valladolid, 1555), ed. M. Serrano y Sanz, 2 vols (Madrid, 1906); Gonzalo Fernándes de Oviedo y Valdés, *Historia general y natural de las Indias* (1535–57), bk 23, BAE *(Continuación)* 121 vol. 2, 351–85; letter by Francisco de Villalta, Asunción, 22 June 1556; Antonio de Herrera, *Historia general de los hechos de los Castellanos en las Islas y Tierrafirme de Mar Océano* (Madrid, 1610–15), decada 6, bk 7, ch. 5, ed. Miguel Gómez del Campillo (Madrid, 1954) 13 101–4. Good modern works are: Paul Groussac, 'La expedición de Mendoza', *Anales de la Biblioteca Nacional* (Buenos Aires) 8, 1912; Enrique de Gandia, *Historia de la conquista del Río de la Plata y del Paraguay* (Buenos Aires, 1932); Julio Cesar Chaves, *Descubrimiento y*

conquista del Río de la Plata y del Paraguay (Asunción, 1968). Cabeza de Vaca's name – 'Cow's Head' – derived from the exploit of an ancestor who guided a Christian army through a pass in the thirteenth century by marking it with a cow's skull. The Governor's strict morality soon infuriated the settlers of Asunción. They refused to be parted from their harems of Guaraní girls and instead decided to dispense with the censorious Cabeza de Vaca. He was ousted, in the name of 'Liberty', and sent in irons to Spain. The reward for all his explorations and good treatment of the Indians was a further six years in prison on trumped-up charges.

When the Spaniards were first exploring the Paraguay, their compatriots on the western side of the continent were just beginning to penetrate the Bolivian Altiplano. Diego de Almagro crossed it on the way to Chile in 1535; Hernando and Gonzalo Pizarro first fought their way into the eastern foothills of the Bolivian Andes in 1538; and various later expeditions sought to find a route from upper Peru to the Paraguay. The effort was intensified when a mountain of silver was discovered at Potosí in 1545.

Samuel Eliot Morison, *The European Discovery of America. The Southern Voyages, 1492–1616* 568 ff; Goodman, *The Explorers of South America* 59–62.

243 *a great amount of fish.*' Alonso de Barzana to Juan Sebastián, Asunción, 8 Sept 1594, in Marcos Jiménez de la Espada, *Relaciones Geográficas de Indias*, BAE *(Continuación)* **184** 85 (Madrid, 1965).

244 *Europeans.*' Jácome Monteiro, *Relação da Provincia do Brasil*, in HCJB **8** 396.

244 *shining colours.*' Binot Paulmier de Gonneville, 'Relation authentique du voyage du capitaine de Gonneville', in Charles Verlinden, 'Paulmier de Gonneville e os índios do Brasil em 1504' 6. Modern editors of Gonneville – Avezac, Julien and Métraux – all assume that this French captain lived among the Carijó during his visit to Brazil in 1504. I am not so sure. Gonneville's descriptions

of his tribe's villages, with many huts in a circle and without any vegetable crops, the long-hair styles, and the status of the chiefs, sound more like a Gê-speaking tribe than Guaraní. They might have been Ibirajara.

244 *Carijó.*' Nóbrega quoted in Serafim Soares Leite, *Novas páginas de história do Brasil* 9; Manoel da Nóbrega, *Informação das terras do Brasil* 91; Nóbrega to King João III, Piratininga, Oct 1553, CPJB **2** 16; Anchieta to Ignatius Loyola, São Paulo de Piratininga, 1 Sept 1554, CPJB **2** 116–17; Loyola to Pedro de Ribadeneira, Rome, 3 March 1556, CPJB **2** 265. The Ibirajara lived near the mouth of the Tietê and along the Paraná and Jeticahy (modern Grande). Simão de Vasconcellos said their name was distorted to Bilreiros, because they fought with round pieces of wood (*bilros* in Portuguese), which they fired with great accuracy, and barbed lances like harpoons (Monteiro, *Relacão* 395–6). It is more probable that the 'wooden discs' referred to their lip-plugs. Taunay said they were part of the southern Cayapó, which would tally with characteristics noted by Nóbrega (HGBP **1** 189–90). When Spanish Jesuits moved into what is now the Brazilian state of Rio Grande do Sul in the 1620s, they found Ibirajara living to the north of them, near the headwaters of the Uruguay or Pelotas river. The Ibirajara were then allied to the Portuguese against the Guaraní-speaking Tape. These Ibirajara could well have been on the coast a century earlier, in Paulmier de Gonneville's day.

245 *Brazil.* Anchieta, Feb 1555, CPJB **2** 201. Because they were killed at the instigation of another Christian, the two Jesuits could not be officially beatified as martyrs of the Faith. They were two of the earliest victims of Spanish–Portuguese rivalry in South America. Serafim Soares Leite, *Suma histórica da Companhia de Jesus no Brasil (Asistência de Portugal) 1549–1760* 16.

245 *reason.*' Nóbrega to Simão Rodrigues, Pôrto Seguro, 6 Jan 1550, *Cartas jesuíticas* **1** 110. HGBP **1** 67.

245 *large incomes.'* Atas da Câmara de São Paulo, 1585, in HGBP **1** 156.

245 *heart of Brazil.* This 'war of Paranaíba' began under Captain-Major João Pereira de Souza Botafogo. Pero Tacques de Almeida Paes Leme, 'Nobiliarchia paulistana . . .', RHGB **33** pt 1, 82, 1870, and his *História da Capitania de S. Vicente* . . ., RHGB **9** 145, 1847; José de Anchieta, *Cartas, informações, fragmentos históricos e sermões* 268–70, 293; HGBP, **1** 173, 176–7; São Paulo, *Inventários e testamentos* 335, 339, 340, all refer to men who were off fighting on the Paranaíba campaign. Myriam Ellis, in Richard M. Morse, *The Bandeirantes: the historical role of the Brazilian pathfinders* 49.

246 *Indians.* The word *bandeira* may have derived from a bandeira or flag carried by the expeditions; or from the name of a small company of troops raised by a captain; or from a raiding party detached from the main expedition; or from medieval municipal militias. The term *bandeira* was first used to describe one of these Brazilian expeditions in about 1635. But the word *bandeirante* to describe one of its members appeared only in the mid-eighteenth century. Cortesão, *Rapôso Tavares* 69; Morse, *Bandeirantes* 22–3, 74. The literature on the bandeirantes is led by Afonso de Escragnolle Taunay's rambling but comprehensive eleven-volume *História geral dos bandeiras Paulistas.* The main sources used by Taunay were Paes Leme's eighteenth-century 'Nobiliarchia paulistana', a glorification of the leading families of São Paulo and the deeds of their forebears; the municipal records of the town council (Câmara) of São Paulo, and the wills and testaments of its citizens; and the few surviving descriptions of journeys or routes into the Brazilian interior, notably those collected by Diogo Soares in the early eighteenth century. Pablo Pastells and Jaime Cortesão have edited collections of documents by the Paraguayan Jesuits, many of which were irate attacks against the bandeirantes. Historians of the bandeirantes include: João Capistrano de Abreu, Basílio de Magalhães, José de Alcântara Machado, Alfredo Ellis, Jr, Washington Luís Pereira de Sousa, Francisco de Assis Carvalho Franco, Sérgio Buarque de Holanda, Jaime Cortesão, Clodomir Viana Moog, Magnus Mörner, Cassiano Ricardo, Hélio Vianna, Myriam Ellis and Richard M. Morse.

246 *Indian slaves.* Municipal act of 1625 quoted by José de Alcântara Machado, *Vida e morte do bandeirante* (São Paulo, 1930), trans. in Morse, *Bandeirantes* 68.

246 *a single day'.* Governor Paes de Sande, 1692, quoted by Pedro Calmon, *Espírito de sociedade colonial* 24.

246 *their own country.'* Câmara of São Paulo to donatory Count of Monsanto, Jan 1606, quoted in C. R. Boxer, *The Golden Age of Brazil, 1695–1750* 33.

246 *steal slaves.'* Anon Jesuit, *Sumário das armadas . . .*, RHGB **36** pt 1, 13–14, 1873. This description was about the northeast of Brazil (where slaving expeditions were known as *entradas*), but it could equally well refer to Paulista bandeiras.

246 *next day.'* Diego Ferrer, Anua of 21 Aug 1633, in Jaime Cortesão, *Jesuítas e bandeirantes no Itatim (1596–1760)* 45, or *Rapôso Tavares* 158–9.

246 *other weapons'.* Act of 20 Feb 1610, São Paulo, *Atas da Câmara da Vila de São Paulo* **2** 123.

248 *their clothes.'* Anthony Knivet, *The Admirable Adventures and Strange Fortunes of Master Antonie Knivet*, in Samuel Purchas, *Hakluytus Posthumus or Purchas His Pilgrimes*, pt 2, bk 6, ch. 7, Hakluyt Society ed., **16** 213.

248 *to eate'.* Ibid. **16** 213.

248 *destroy them'.* Ibid. **16** 213.

248 *thirteene of them died.'* Ibid. **16** 214. The men who died evidently did not know about the need to leach poisonous prussic acid out of some types of manioc.

249 *their interest'.* Inventory of Brás Gonçalves, who died in Temimino territory on 31 July 1603, quoted in Alcântara Machado, *Vida e morte do bandeirante* 267, trans. in Morse, *Bandeirantes* 76.

249 *in the jungles.'* Antonio Ruiz de Montoya, *Conquista espiritual* (Madrid,

1639) 45; João Capistrano de Abreu, *Capítulos de história colonial* 123.

249 *around their necks. . . .'* Ruiz de Montoya, *Conquista espiritual* 46.

249 *entitled to half.* Will of Antônia Ribeiro quoted in Alcântara Machado, trans. Morse, *Bandeirantes* 69.

249 *on this point'.* Ibid.

250 *normal weapons.'* Monteiro, *Relação da Província do Brasil,* HCJB, **8** 395. Children that were half white and half Indian were mamelucos; those who were half white and half black were mulattos. The word *mameluco* probably derived from the similarity in appearance of these half-castes with the Mamelukes of Egypt. The Portuguese were fighting a fierce naval war against the Mamelukes in the Indian Ocean during the sixteenth century.

250 *precious metals.* São Paulo, *Atas da Câmara* **2** 47; HGBP **1** 177–8.

250 *Indian prisoners.* Taunay thought Barreto's bandeira was to the Paraná and Piquiry, HGBP **1** 185–8, but Orville Derby argued for the more northern route, and his interpretation is accepted by Buarque de Holanda (*Visão do paraíso* 53). Orville Derby, 'Roteiro de uma das primeiras bandeiras paulistas', *Revista do Instituto Historico e Geographico de São Paulo,* **4** 129 ff, and 'As bandeiras paulistas de 1601 a 1604', ibid. **8** 399 ff. Basílio de Magalhães, *Expansão geographica do Brasil colonial* 112. Justo Mansilla van Surck, 1629, in Pablo Pastells, *Historia de la Compañia de Jesús* . . . **1** 191; Letter of 13 Jan 1606, São Paulo, *Atas da Câmara* **2** 497–500. Glimmer described his adventures in the bandeira into what is now Minas Gerais, in Georg Marcgraf, *Historiae rerum naturalium Brasiliae* 263–4. Orville Derby deduced that he had been on the bandeira of André de Leão.

250 *this town'.* São Paulo, *Atas da Câmara* **2** 223, 151, 169; São Paulo, *Registo geral da Câmara Municipal de São Paulo* **7** 151; HGBP **1** 188.

251 *no fable!'* Câmara of São Paulo to the donatory of São Vicente, 13 Jan 1606, Magalhães, *Expansão geographica* 112–13.

251 *backwoodsmen.'* Pero Domingues, 'Informação da entrada que se pode

fazer da Vila de S. Paulo ao Grande Pará . . . ' (part of a report by Antonio de Araújo), in Serafim Soares Leite, *Páginas de história do Brasil* 105. The French fort was presumably that of St Louis at Maragnan, or possibly that of Sergipe. The Cátinga also volunteered, 'without being asked', the information that a tribe of Amazons, 'whom they call Camaïma or women without breasts', lived eleven days' journey away on another branch of the Pará. The Tocantins was variously known as the Pará, Urubu, Alma or Maranhão.

251 *corporal perfection.'* Ibid. 106.

252 *grains of corn'.* Pero Domingues, *Relação . . . sobre a viagem que de São Paulo fez ao rio de S. Francisco, chamado tambem Pará,* in Leite, *Páginas de história* 114. Domingues was, of course, wrong to say that the São Francisco was also called the Pará. But he correctly pointed out that it was possible to reach the upper São Francisco from São Paulo, with much of the journey by canoe; whereas travel up the São Francisco itself was blocked by rapids.

252 *that river'.* Ibid.

252 *Guairá.* São Paulo, *Atas da Câmara* **2** 184; HGBP **1** 188, 191; Magalhães, *Expansão geographica* 115; Pastells, *Historia de la Compañia* **1** 188–9, 222–4; Cortesão, *Rapôso Tavares* 134–5.

253 *paid no tax.* São Paulo, *Atas da Câmara* **2** 267; Buarque de Holanda, *Visão do paraíso* 54.

253 *brothers and relatives.'* Anon Jesuit, *Relación en que se da cuenta de las ciudades de la Governación del Paraguay y de sus indios* (December 1620), in Jaime Cortesão, *Jesuítas e bandeirantes no Guairá (1594–1640)* 167. The Spanish authorities supported the Jesuit missionary efforts in Guairá and Jerez (Itatín), paying for them out of treasury funds: Provision of 7 Sept 1600, and letter to King from Antonio de Anasca, Lieutenant-Governor of Paraguay and Río de la Plata, 1609, in Pedro Souto Maior, 'Nos archivos de Hispanha', RHGB **81** 27–8, 1917.

253 *given away.'* Cortesão, *Jesuítas e bandeirantes no Guairá* 167.

253 *law of God.'* Ibid. 168.

Chapter 13 BANDEIRANTES AGAINST JESUITS

255 *to their homes.*' Ruiz de Montoya to Nicolas Duran, Carta Anua of 1628, in Jaime Cortesão, *Jesuítas e bandeirantes no Guairá (1594–1640)* 269, 270; Jaime Cortesão, *Rapôso Tavares e a formação territorial do Brasil* 167; Basílio de Magalhães, *Expansão geographica do Brasil colonial* 116. Manoel Preto's ranch was in the Terras da Expectação, now the São Paulo suburb of Nossa Senhora do O.

255 *he died of shame.*' Ruiz de Montoya, in Cortesão, *Jesuítas e bandeirantes no Guairá* 276–7.

255 *Paulistas.* Someone wrote an account of the Governor's journey, illustrated with the first maps of the interior of São Paulo State: *Relación de los sucesos ocorridos durante el viaje que hizó el governador del Paraguay Don Luis Céspedes Xeria desde Madrid hasta llegar a la cuidad de la Asunción*, in AMN 2 15–221, 1925; Afonso d'Escragnolle Taunay, 'A viagem de Dom Luís de Cespedes Xeria', RHGB 84 449–78, 1918.

256 *King of Spain's!*' Antonio Ruiz de Montoya, *Conquista espiritual* (Madrid, 1639) 35; Magalhães, *Expansão geographica* 121. The Paulistas liked to think of the Paraná river as their western boundary. But the Guairá region lay to the west of the Line of Tordesillas, and thus fell within the Spanish sphere of that treaty.

256 *with us.*' Justo Mancilla and Simón Masseta, *Relación de los agravios que hicieron algunos vecinos y moradores de la Villa de S. Pablo de Piratininga . . . saqueando las aldeas de los Padres de la Compañía de Jesus en la misión de Guairá y campos del Yguaçu*, Bahia, 10 Oct 1629, Cortesão, *Jesuítas e bandeirantes no Guairá* 314–15, trans. in Morse, *Bandeirantes* 85.

256 *hand them over.* There had been an attempt by the Jesuits and their Indians to evict the Paulistas from their stockade and release some of their captives. This battle took place the previous October. A mission army of over a thousand Indians, some armed with firearms, attacked the bandeirantes and drove them into their stockade many miles from the reductions. One white man and forty Indians were killed on the Paulista side, according to a letter from Governor Céspedes Xeria to the King from Ciudad Real. Jesuit letters shortly after the battle boasted of it as a victory. But the Fathers later decided not to mention their attack. They later described it as an attempt to parley that was greeted by a hail of arrows and gunfire. Cortesão, *Rapôso Tavares* 169–73.

257 *Fathers. . . .*' Mancilla and Masseta, *Relación de los agravios*, in Cortesão, *Jesuítas e bandeirantes no Guairá* 315, trans. in Morse, *Bandeirantes* 85–6.

257 *as if they were pigs.*' Mancilla and Masseta, *Relación* 335–6, trans. in Morse, *Bandeirantes* 88–9. The two Jesuits wrote an eloquent, dramatised version for propaganda purposes, and a more restrained account to their own Jesuit Provincial. They obtained a decree against the Paulistas from the Governor of Brazil in Bahia, and returned to Guairá in 1630. Nothing was done to restrain the bandeirantes.

258 *robbery and pillage.*' Mancilla and Masseta, *Relación* 336, trans. in Morse, *Bandeirantes* 89.

259 *our vassals there. . . .*' Chiefs of the mission of San Ignacio del Ipaumbucu on the Paraná to Don Diego Luís de Oliveira, Governor of Brazil, San Ignacio, 14 Aug 1630, in Cortesão, *Jesuítas e bandeirantes no Guairá* 354–5. This protest was a reply to the Governor's request for more information about Paulista raiding, dated 4 Dec 1629 (ibid. 339–41). At this time the Jesuits were condemning maté, partly because its use made Indians urinate too frequently so that they kept leaving mass. In June 1619, Cardinal Frederico Borromeo, having consulted leading doctors in Milan, recommended to the Jesuit Provincial that he do his utmost to eradicate this pernicious evil. But the Jesuits later came to adopt maté on a grand scale. Their missions derived

much of their income from the extraction and sale of maté. And the Fathers adapted a Tupi legend that a great shaman called Sumé had taught them the use of herva-maté: the missionaries claimed that Sumé was Thomé or St Thomas, who had reached Brazil to preach the gospel centuries before their arrival. They thus claimed maté as a Christian discovery, and attracted many converts to their missions by its widespread use there. See Egon Schaden's 'A erva do diabo', AI **8** no. 3, 165–9, July 1948.

259 *sugar plantation*. Complaint by Father Francisco Dias Taño against Don Luis de Céspedes Xeria, 1631, in Cortesão, *Jesuítas e bandeirantes no Guairá* 399–408, and another legal complaint of sixty-two charges against the Governor, 1631, ibid. 409–24. Requerimiento by citizens of Villa Rica, 23 Nov 1630, ibid. 361–3, and by those of Ciudad Real de Guairá, 24 May 1631, ibid. 363–9; Report by Antonio Ruíz de Montoya, Córdoba, Tucumán, 22 Jan 1632, in Hélio Vianna (ed.) *Jesuítas e bandeirantes no Uruguai* 320.

259 *inspire the rowers*. Various participants described this exodus, in ibid. 317 ff.

260 *Paraguay*. The Spaniards founded a new town called Villarica in a new province called Guairá, eighty miles south-east of Asunción in Paraguay. Manoel Ayres do Casal wrote in 1817 that he had visited the ruins of the first Villa Rica, eight days' journey up the Ivaí in an area then occupied by wild Indians, presumably Kaingang. He also reported that in 1773 the Portuguese tried to rebuild Ciudad Real del Guaira at the mouth of the Piquiry, but desisted when the colonists all died of malaria (*Chorografia Brasílica* 1 214). See also: Virginia D. Watson, 'Ciudad Real: a Guaraní-Spanish site on the Alto Paraná river', *American Antiquity* 13, 1947.

260 *other chiefs'*. Roque Gonçalvez de Santa Cruz, Reduction of Los Reyes, 15 Nov 1627, in J. M. Blanco, *Documentos para la Historia Argentina* (Buenos Aires, 1929) **20** 373, and Aurélio Pôrto, *História das missões orientais do Uruguai* 49.

260 *reduce them.* . . .' Blanco, in Pôrto, *História* 50.

261 *calmed them.'* Mastrilli Duran, Anua of 12 Nov 1628, Pôrto, *História* 52.

261 *their conversion.* . . .' Claudio Ruyer, Carta anua, Mission of Santa Maria del Iguassu, 9 Nov 1627, Vianna, *Jesuítas e bandeirantes no Uruguai* 71.

261 *eloquence and valour'*. Anua of Father Romero, in Pôrto, *História* 58–9.

262 *one-year-old son.'* Romero, in Pôrto, *História* 59.

262 *to govern them.'* José Cardiel, *Relación verídica de las Misiones de la Compañia de JHS en la Provincia que fué del Paraguay* (Faenza, 1722) 52; Pôrto, *História* 45.

262 *their parents'*. Anua of Father Romero, 1633, in ibid.

263 *[the epidemic].'* Pedro Romero, Anuas from Paraná and Uruguay missions, Santos Martires de Caro, 21 April 1635, Vianna, *Jesuítas e bandeirantes no Uruguai* 139.

263 *His own elect.'* Ibid. 139.

263 *with great compassion.'* Ibid. 142.

263 *the Atlantic seaboard*. Jaime Cortesão, who tended to regard bandeirantes as Portuguese patriots resisting Jesuit imperialism, noted that Nóbrega had envisaged a link between the Portuguese and Spanish Jesuits, and that Diego de Torres, first Provincial of the Jesuit province of Paraguay, saw his province as the hub of Jesuit land communications running east–west and north–south across South America: Anua of Diego de Torres, 17 May 1609, in Cortesão, *Rapôso Tavares* 126–8.

264 *by all this.'* Hernando de Montalvo, Treasurer of Río de la Plata, to King Philip II, Asunción, 29 March 1576, HGBP 1 171–2, and 8 348. Hernando de Montalvo, Treasurer of Río de la Plata, to King Philip II, Asunción, 29 March 1576, HGBP 1 171–2 and 8 348. After Aleixo Garcia had been on the coast of Santa Catarina, Sebastian Cabot visited it after 1526. The Spanish governor of Asunción, Álvaro Núñes Cabeza de Vaca, set out from there in 1540, and left a settlement of 140 men on the coast: these had vanished by 1547. Another Spanish attempt by Juan de Senabria, sent by

Charles V, failed when the Carijó stopped supplying food to the colony: the German gunner Hans Staden (the man who later lived among the Tupinambá) was with a group of these colonists who spent two years on São Francisco Island in Santa Catarina. The last Spanish endeavour in Santa Catarina was in the 1570s, when Philip II appointed Hernandarias de Saavedra to conquer the Guairá area. It was intended that he should also settle Santa Catarina as a port for Potosí silver. It was Saavedra who wrote that there were 100,000 Indians in Santa Catarina and Rio Grande.

Nóbrega sent Leonardo Nunes, nicknamed Abarebebe or the Flying Father, to convert the Carijó south of São Vicente. In the 1570s the Portuguese Jesuit Domingos Garcia appeared among the Indians of the Lagoon and tried to restrain the excesses of his compatriots in their slaving activities there. In 1616 the Portuguese Fathers João Fernandes and João de Almeida settled some of the Carijó of Santa Catarina into mission villages; and a few years later the Spanish Paraguayan Jesuits moved into Rio Grande do Sul from the west. The Jesuit João de Almeida was in fact an Englishman called John May, born in London in 1571. He had been apprenticed to a trader and gone to Pernambuco in 1588, joining the Jesuits four years later. He was regarded as a particularly saintly figure in Rio de Janeiro, and worked among the Indians of Espírito Santo and São Paulo as well as the Patos. C. R. Boxer, *Salvador de Sá and the Struggle for Brazil and Angola, 1602–1686* 87.

265 *inhabit Hell!'* Simón Masseta to the Jesuit Procurator of Portugal, July 1630, HGBP 8 350.

265 *depart from there.'* Francisco Ximenes to Jesuit Provincial, 1635, in Cortesão, *Rapôso Tavares* 194–5.

265 *a hundred years.'* São Paulo, *Atas da Câmara* 4 252–3.

265 *Christians'.* São Paulo, *Registo geral* 1 500.

266 *himself captive.'* Inácio de Sequeira

letter, 1635, HCJB 6 504–5; Cortesão, *Rapôso Tavares* 201; HGBP 8 350. The seaborne expedition of 1635 was commanded by Luiz Dias Leme and Fernando de Camargo.

266 *Guairá'.* Diego de Boroa, Carta anua of 1635, J. M. Blanco, *Documentos para la Historia Argentina, Iglesia* (Buenos Aires, 1929) 2 549–50; Aurélio Pôrto, *História das missões orientais do Uruguai* 84.

266 *simple signals.'* Diego de Boroa, Anua, 13 August 1637, Blanco, *Documentos para la Historia Argentina, Iglesia* 20 549.

266 *their arquebuses.'* Diego de Boroa, Santa Fé, 10 April 1637, HGBP 8 396.

267 *moving lamentations'.* Ibid. 397; Cortesão, *Rapôso Tavares* 423.

267 *Brazil?'* João Capistrano de Abreu, *Capítulos de história colonial* (1934 ed.) 115–16. This terrible account was based on Antonio Ruiz de Montoya's *Conquista espiritual.* The Anua (an annual letter written for other officials of the Society of Jesus) by the Provincial Diego de Boroa was more restrained: it said that the bandeirantes had asked the Fathers for peaceful passage on the eve of the attack. It also omitted the slaughter of the refugees who emerged from the church. This slaughter was improbable, since the Paulistas tended to keep their victims alive for enslavement. Pôrto, *História* 90 ff; Cortesão, *Rapôso Tavares* 141–4, 223–4, 423; HGBP 8 396–8.

268 *greatly desired'.* Claudio Ruyer, *Relación de la guerra que tubieron los yndios contra los Portugueses del Brazil*, Reduction of San Nicolás, 6 April 1641, in Jaime Cortesão, *Jesuítas e bandeirantes no Tape (1615–1641)* 349.

268 *musket ball.'* Ibid. 349.

268 *Indians . . .'.* Ibid. 351.

269 *an end to them.'* Ibid. 353.

269 *of them all'.* Ibid. 353.

269 *they almost did so'.* Ibid. 353.

269 *with great shouting.'* Ibid. 353.

269 *land and river!'* Ibid. 354.

269 *into confusion'.* Ibid. 356.

270 *killed him.'* Ibid. 357.

270 *their firearms. . . .'* Ibid. 359.

270 *cruel tigers.'* Ibid. 360–1.

271 *dead bodies.'* Ibid. 361.

271 *our sons.'* Ibid. 366.

271 *receive them well.'* Diego Ferrer, 21 Aug 1633, Jaime Cortesão, *Jesuítas e bandeirantes no Itatim (1596–1760)* 37. Leading Jesuits who went from Guairá to Itatín included Inácio Martinez, Justo Mansilla, Diego Ferrer and Nicolás Henarico: Manuel Berthod, *Testemunho sôbre a história das reduções de Itatim,* 20 March 1652, in Cortesão, *Jesuítas e bandeirantes no Itatim* 100.

272 *overland paths.'* Diego Ferrer, to the Provincial, Itatín, 21 Aug 1633, in ibid. 45.

272 *they catch.'* Ibid. 42.

272 *three reductions'.* Antonio Ruiz Montoya to Diego de Chaves, Lima, 17 Nov 1645, in ibid. 69.

272 *Satan'.* Juan Baptista Ferrufino, Carta anua for the Province of Paraguay for 1645 and 1646, in ibid. 79.

273 *to wield them.'* Antonio Vieira to Provincial of Brazil, Pará, *c.*Jan 1654, *Cartas Jesuiticas* 1 411.

273 *they were taking.'* Diego Francisco de Altamirano, Anua of years 1653–4, Córdoba, 31 Dec 1654, Cortesão, *Jesuítas e bandeirantes no Itatim* 198, and *Rapôso Tavares* 357, 441. Bandeiras later/in the seventeenth century attacked the Spaniards and Jesuits inside what is now Paraguay. On 14 Feb 1676, Francisco Xavier Pedroso surprised the town of Villa Rica del Espíritu Santo on the Jejuy, founded by colonists who had abandoned Villa Rica in Guairá. He sacked the town and removed Indians from four nearby Jesuit missions. Don Juan Diaz de Andino, Governor of Paraguay, marched out of Asunción with 400 Spanish horsemen and 600 Indians. Pedroso awaited him on the Maracaju hills. He routed the Spaniards, capturing 300 horses and leading 4000 Indians off to captivity, along with booty from sacked towns and churches. Magalhães, *Expansão geográfica* 131; Carta régia of Regent Dom Pedro, 23 March 1679, including letters of protest from the Spanish ambassador in Lisbon, 1 Jan 1679, and from the Governor of Río de la Plata, 1677, all in Brazilian National Archive.

274 *native converts.* The *Conquista espiritual* was published in Madrid in 1639 and also in Guaraní in Paraguay itself. Jaime Cortesão, one of the bandeirantes' most determined apologists, called the Spiritual Conquest 'that evangel of hatred translated into Guaraní' (*Rapôso Tavares* 137).

274 *Christian Catholics.'* Pedro Estevan Dávila to King Philip IV, Buenos Aires, 12 Oct 1637, in Cortesão, *Jesuítas e bandeirantes no Itatim* 61; Pierre François-Xavier de Charlevoix, *Histoire du Paraguay* 3 vols (Paris, 1761), 1 433–4; Magalhães, *Expansão geográfica* 123–4.

274 *Spanish Jesuit reductions.* Ruiz de Montoya said that he had given this warning as early as 1638, in his memorial to the King of 1643. Pablo Hernández, *Organización social de las doctrinas guaraníes de la Compañía de Jesús* (Barcelona, 1913) 1 630; Cortesão, *Rapôso Tavares* 251.

274 *came to an end.'* Royal cédula, 17 Sept 1639, in Cortesão, *Jesuítas e bandeirantes no Itatim* 279; 'Real cédula . . . para remedio y castigo de los Portugueses de San Pablo de Brasil', 16 Sept 1638, in Georg Thomas, *Die portugiesische Indianerpolitik in Brasilien, 1500–1640* 214–20. This edict named Federico del Melo (sic) and particularly Antonio Rapôso Tavares, who led away 40,000 of 100,000 souls captured from the missions. This figure was increased to over 300,000 in later royal edicts.

274 *that have occurred.'* Información by Francisco Diaz Taño, 1650, in Vianna, *Jesuítas e bandeirantes no Uruguai* 168; and Taño, *Informe acerca de las cosas tocantes a las doctrinas que estaban a cargo de la Compañía,* Asunción, 30 April 1657, in ibid. 334–41. The King of Spain had been issuing denunciations of Paulista raids on the missions ever since 1628, and the Spanish governors had frequently joined the Jesuits in impassioned protests: Souto Maior, 'Nos archivos de Hispanha' 35, 43, 47 ff.

275 *horses and sheep.* Pero Tacques de Almeida Paes Leme, 'Nobiliarchia Paulistana...', RHGB 32 pt 1, 179, 1869. Jean de Laet wrote in 1640 that the town of São Paulo 'contains more or less a hundred houses and about two hundred

inhabitants, both Portuguese and mestizos. It has one parish church, two monasteries – Benedictine and Carmelite – and a house of the Fathers of the Society [of Jesus]. Their principal revenue comes from sheep and farm labour.' (Laet, *L'Histoire du Nouveau Monde* (Leiden, 1640), bk 15, ch. 17, p. 516.)

276 *populous camp.'* Ibid. RHGB 33 pt 2, 104, 1870.

276 *his fazenda'.* Ibid. RHGB 33 pt 2, 184.

276 *vegetables and cotton'.* Ibid. RHGB 33 pt 1, 226, 1870.

276 *conquer that year.'* Ibid. RHGB 33 pt 2, 82.

276 *in prison.* Ibid. RHGB 33 pt 2, 98.

276 *potent in archers'.* Ibid. RHGB 34 pt 1, 31, 1871.

276 *she-goats!'* Antonio Ruiz de Montoya, *Conquista espiritual* (Madrid, 1639) 93.

277 *kingdoms and homes'.* The towns being founded in the interior of São Paulo were clustered along the Tietê and Paraíba. The dates of their charters as towns (often some years after their origins) were: Moji das Cruzes, 1611; Parnaíba, 1625; Taubaté, 1650; Jacareí, 1653; Jundiaí, 1655; Guaratinguetá, 1657; Itu, 1657; Sorocaba, 1661; Pindamonhangaba, 1705. M. E. Azevedo Marques, *Apontamentos históricos, geográficos . . . da Provincia de São Paulo* (Rio de Janeiro, 1879): João Capistrano de Abreu, *Capítulos de história colonial* 130.

277 *that aldeia is mine.'* Marquis de Minas to Câmara of São Paulo, Bahia, 3 Aug 1685, DH 11 119–20.

277 *in the hills. . . .'* Law of 26 July 1596, HC 2 623–4.

278 *can result.'* Declaration of meeting of 10 June 1612, São Paulo; and resolution of Câmara of 15 Aug 1611, in Pero Tacques de Almeida Paes Leme, 'Noticia histórica da expulsão dos Jesuítas do Collegio de S. Paulo,' RHGB 12 9, 7–8, 1849.

278 *obey his commands'.* Provision of João Soares as captain of the aldeia of Guarapiranga by Magistrate João Peres Canhamares, São Paulo, 17 Nov 1607, *Registo geral* 1 150–1, and other similar appointments, ibid. 239–40, etc.

278 *against their will'.* Gonçalo Correia de Sá, São Paulo, Aug 1618, *Registo geral* 1 277–8. The Geromimis or Moromomins lived in the forests along the Paraíba before being settled near São Paulo. Jácome Monteiro described them as sleeping on the ground (in the manner of Gê-speaking rather than Tupi tribes) and not planting manioc. Unlike other Indians, they played games of chance and gambled bows, arrows, etc. (Monteiro, *Relação da Provincia do Brasil* (1610), HCJB 8 395–6). Egon Schaden thought it conceivable that the Moromomins were part of the Kaingang (also called Coroado because of their crown of hair, shaved round the sides of their heads). Schaden, 'Os primitivos habitantes do território paulista' 395.

278 *Indians'.* Ruling of 18 Oct 1623 in J. J. Machado de Oliviera, 'Noticia raciocinada sobre as aldêas de indios da provincia de São Paulo', RHGB 8 219, 1846.

278 *Jesuits'.* São Paulo, *Atas da Câmara* 4 172; Cortesão, *Rapôso Tavares* 89.

279 *administer the aldeias.* Urban VIII Bull Commissum Nobis, 22 April 1639, in HCJB 6 569–71, 244–93; Leite, *Suma histórica* 84–6; Paes Leme, 'Noticia historica da expulsão' 18–33. Leite felt that the Papacy's interdict against the expulsion, and the confirmation of this in 1651, were decisive in shaming the Paulistas into allowing the Jesuits' return. Various important advisers, such as Jorge Mascarenhas, Marquis of Montalvão, and Martim de Sá, Governor of Rio de Janeiro, urged the King to restore the Jesuits (Martim de Sá affidavit, Rio de Janeiro, 20 April 1630, in Boxer, *Salvador de Sá* 126). Martim de Sá greatly praised the Jesuits, who 'generally act as if they were their fathers, and are in fact so regarded and appreciated by the Indians'. But other Paulistas wrote fiery denunciations of the Jesuits and protested that their return would mean the ruin of the captaincy, loss of mines, etc.

279 *we suffer'.* Memo from Francisco de Morais to Simão de Vasconcellos, in HCJB 6 97.

279 *they themselves boast'*. Ibid.

279 *Guarulhos.'* Salvador de Sá testimony, 1647, in HCJB 6 239–40, trans. Boxer, *Salvador de Sá* 126–7.

279 *lost and destroyed.'* Carta regia, 6 Dec 1647, HCJB 6 102.

280 *valour and aptitude'*. King to Artur de Sá e Menezes, 22 Jan 1700, HGBP 9 297; Artur de Sá to King, 22 May 1698, ibid. 296.

280 *Peru'*. Anon Jesuit account of the attack on Mboymboy, in Cortesão, *Jesuítas e bandeirantes no Itatim* 91, or *Rapôso Tavares* 285. Rapôso Tavares had just returned from Portugal, and according to this Jesuit he was armed with seven small cannon and financed by the Duke of Revelado to explore a route to Peru. It was eight years since Portugal had regained her independence from

Spain, and when the bandeirantes captured the mission they raised the national standard and shouted 'Long live the King of Portugal D. João IV!' (ibid. 91).

281 *up to now!'* António Vieira to Provincial of Brazil, Pará, *c.*Jan 1654, *Cartas Jesuiticas* 1 411; Cortesão, *Rapôso Tavares* 443, 445. Cortesão summarised his information and theories about this bandeira in: 'A maior bandeira do maior bandeirante', RH 22 no. 45, 3–27, Jan–March 1961, which is translated into English in Morse, *Bandeirantes* 100–13.

281 *150,000 souls.'* Vieira letter, *c.*Jan 1654, *Cartas Jesuiticas* 1 413; Cortesão, *Rapôso Tavares*, 446.

281 *had never seen.'* Vieira in *Cartas Jesuiticas* 414.

282 *public immunity.'* Ibid. 414–15.

Chapter *14* THE DUTCH WARS

284 *covered in woods'*. François Pyrard de Laval, *Discours du voyage des françois aux Indes Orientales* (Paris, 1911) 281.

285 *well received. . . .'* Vicente do Salvador, *Historia*, bk 5, ch. 44, p. 594.

286 *on various occasions!'* Governor Colonel Diederik van Weerdenburch to States General, Olinda, 27 July 1630, in Rodolfo Garcia (ed.), *Documentos Holandeses* 1 50; and also to the Council of the XIX (the 19 Directors of the West Indies Company), 23 July 1630, in José António Gonçalves de Mello, *Tempo dos Flamengos* . . . 234.

286 *under 9000*. Johannes de Laet, *Historie ofte Iaerlijck Verhael* . . ., ABNRJ 41–2 8, 86, 90–1, 1919–20. There is a slight contradiction in Laet's survey: at one point he said that in 1635 there were seven villages in Paraíba, with 1500 people in the largest, Pinda-una, and about 300 each in the others – 3300 in Paráiba; but he said later that there were only four villages in Paraíba, and that Paráiba and Rio Grande (where there were six villages) had only 3000 natives between them. Adriaen van der Drussen gave an even worse picture. He wrote in

1639 that there were 4 villages in Pernambuco, 5 in Goiana (the region between Pernambuco and Rio Grande), 5 in Rio Grande and 5 in Paraíba. But he said that they contained a total of only 1923 men of all ages, of which a thousand were fighting men. Even allowing for a preponderance of women and children, this would give a total of some five thousand for these areas – to which could be added some 1500 to 2000 for Ceará. (Adriaen van der Drussen, *Report on the Captaincies Conquered in Brazil by the Dutch*, trans. Gonçalves de Mello, 90–1.) This decline was confirmed by Domingos da Veiga, in 1627, who said that Rio Grande had 'little more than 300 bowmen divided among four villages. There used to be such a quantity of them here that their numbers were not known. But they are fleeing to Ceará every day because of the rotten treatment given them by the captains here, and the good that Captain Martim Soares [Moreno] does them in Ceará' (description of Rio Grande by Domingos da Veiga, DHBC 4 35). Laet confirmed this. He wrote that, when the Dutch withdrew in 1625, Chief Jaguarari of the village of Taboussouram, inland of the Bay of Treason, fled to the Tapuia for fear of Portuguese reprisals. When the Dutch took Rio Grande in 1631 they found that 'few savages live there, for many have been killed in various encounters. The rest have gone off to the Tapuia, because of their hatred of the Portuguese. They are hidden among the Tapuia, awaiting an opportunity to return to their people' (Laet, *L'Histoire du Nouveau Monde ou description des Indes Occidentales* (Leiden, 1640), chs 4, 5, pp. 540–1).

286 *to the yoke'.* Johan van Walbeeck to Directors of West Indies Company, 2 July 1633, in Garcia, *Documentos Holandeses* 1 122.

287 *Portuguese captains.'* Laet, *Histoire*, ABNRJ 41–2 86, 1919–20.

287 *absolutely nothing.'* Gedeon Morris de Jonge to the Directors of the West Indies Company, Middleburg, 22 Oct 1637, RHGB 58 pt 1, 246–7, 1895.

287 *standard wage here.'* Gedeon Morris to City Council of Zeeland, São Luís do Maranhão, 7 April 1642, RHGB 58 pt 1, 292, 1895.

287 *doing so'.* Lieut. van Ham letter of 13 Jan 1638, RHGB 58 pt 1, 267, 1895. This Potiguar chief was called Algodão (Cotton) possibly because his Tupi name meant 'Cotton'.

287 *belongs to them.'* Lieut. van Ham letter to Supreme Council, Ceará, 19 April 1638, RHGB, 58 pt 1, 268–9, 1895. He also reported that a dozen Indians used to maintain a manioc plantation to feed the fort, and were paid three varas of cloth a month each by the Portuguese. They refused to work for the Dutch for less.

287 *out of them.'* Adriaen van der Drussen, *Report on the Captaincies . . .* 87.

288 *princes and peoples'.* Estates General's charter to the Privileged West Indies Company, 1621, in Capistrano de Abreu, *Capítulos de história colonial* (1954 ed.) 145; Hélio Vianna, *História do Brasil* 1 149.

288 *change sides.* Hessel Gerritsz mentioned Pieter Poti and other Indians as his informants, in his *Journaux et nouvelles* of 1628. So also did Johannes de Laet, *Histoire du Nouveau Monde* (Leyden, 1640) and his *Historie*, ABNRJ 30 96, 1908. J. A. Gonçalves de Mello, Neto, *Tempo dos Flamengos* 37, 231–3, 255. C. R. Boxer, *The Dutch in Brazil, 1624–1654* 135. It was Boudewijn Hendricksz who attacked the Portuguese near the Bay of Treason, twenty miles north of Pernambuco, in 1625, and then took some Indians back to Holland.

289 *tropical setting.* The German scientist Georg Marcgraf of Liebstadt (1610–44) died of fever aged thirty-four. But for this and for the loss of much of his work, he might have been the greatest naturalist since Aristotle. His *Historia Naturalis Brasiliae* was the first truly scientific study of the flora and fauna of Brazil, with 200 accurate woodcuts of plants, 222 of animals, birds, fish and insects, and details of meteorology and the ethnography of the Indians of Pernambuco.

Johan Maurits maintained six artists, the most famous of whom were the landscape artist Frans Post of Leiden (1612–80) and Albert Eckhout, who preferred to paint people and animals. Johan Maurits later became Prince of Nassau, but he parted with many of his artistic treasures. He sent some of Eckhout's finest paintings to King Frederick III of Denmark in 1654; and was rewarded with the Order of the White Elephant. Some of these paintings survive in the National Museum and the Ethnographical Museum in Copenhagen. Others were burned in a fire at Christiansborg. Watercolour copies of them were sent to the English philosopher John Locke in 1697 and are now in the British Museum Manuscripts Department. Eckhout's originals were almost life-sized.

Forty pictures were also sent to Louis XIV in 1678, with a covering letter in which Prince Maurits suggested that they would make fine subjects for tapestries. They were exhibited in the Louvre in 1679 and the nakedness of the Indians caused a great impression among the French courtiers. And they *did* appear on Gobelin tapestries for many years. Pedro

Souto Maior searched for them in the 1920s and found six landscapes by Post in the dusty vaults of the Louvre. There is also a painting of a Brazilian aldeia by Post in Hampton Court palace.

Zacharias Wagener was a soldier from Dresden who went to Brazil in 1634 and impressed Johan Maurits with his drawing ability. The Governor helped him produce an album of 109 coloured drawings of people and animals (closely similar to Eckhout's) known as the *Zoobiblion* or *Thierbuch*. Wagener later served the Dutch in Canton, Nagasaki and as governor of Cape Colony. Pedro Souto Maior, 'A arte hollandeza no Brasil', RHGB 83 101–31, 1918, and *Fastos Pernambucanos* 195; Alfredo de Carvalho, 'Zoobiblion de Zacharias Wagener', *Revista do Instituto Archeologico Pernambucano*, 1903–4; Boxer, *Dutch in Brazil* 150. There was an exhibition of these works, called 'Maurits de Brazilaan' in the Mauritshuis in The Hague in April–May 1953, with a useful catalogue. Joaquim de Sousa Leao, *Os pintores de Mauricio de Nassau* (Rio de Janeiro, 1968) and *Frans Post, 1612–1680* (Amsterdam, 1973); Erik Larsen, *Frans Post, Interprète du Brésil* (Amsterdam/Rio de Janeiro, 1962); P. J. P. Whitehead, 'The Marcgrave Drawings', *Bulletin of the British Museum (Natural History), Zoology*, Supplement 5 (London, 1973), 187–219.

289 *vested with command'*. Acts of General Assembly, Mauricia (Recife), 27 Aug 1640, *Revista do Instituto Archeológico e Geographico Pernambucano* 5 no. 31, 229, Oct 1886.

289 *loses his cloth.'* Van der Drussen, *Report* 88; Elias Herckman, *General Description of the Captaincy of Paraíba* (1639) 259. The commandeur of one new village called Mauricia, for the Indians of Paraíba, was an Englishman named John Harrison.

290 *Maranhão.* Gedeon Morris to Count Johan Maurits, São Luís do Maranhão, 29 Jan 1643, in Gonçalves de Mello, *Tempo dos Flamengos* 245.

290 *at all nice.'* *Brierwisseling van Constantijn Huyghens, 1608–1687*, 6 vols (The Hague, 1913–15), 4 52, trans. in C. R. Boxer,

Dutch in Brazil 157. Johan Nieuhof, *Gedenkweerdige Brasiliaense Zee- en Lant-Reize* (Amsterdam, 1682) 57.

291 *of our nation.'* Johan Maurits of Nassau, report to States General, 27 Sept 1644, in Gonçalves de Mello, *Tempo dos Flamengos* 234–5.

291 *in the country.'* Van Doorenslaer, Mauricia, 1640, quoted in ibid. 258. Van der Drussen, *Relatório* 89.

291 *scarcely religious'.* Political Council's instructions to Gervaes Carpentier, Recife, 20 Feb 1636, in Gonçalves de Mello, *Tempo dos Flamengos* 249.

292 *any form of paganism.'* General Missive, Recife, 28 Feb 1642, in ibid. 260.

292 *civil life.'* Supreme Council general missive to Council of XIX, Recife, 5 April 1644, DHBC 3 90–1; Gonçalves de Mello, *Tempo dos Flamengos* 262–3.

292 *[Tupi]'.* Supreme Council general missive, Recife, 10 May 1644, in ibid. 263.

292 *of the parents.'* Supreme Council, general missive, Recife, 13 Feb 1645, in ibid. 263.

293 *in their homes.'* Supreme Council of Brazil to Directors of the West Indies Company, Recife, 18 Feb 1642, in Gedeon Morris de Jonge, *Relatorios e cartas . . .*, RHGB 58 pt 1, 288, 1895, and Gedeon Morris to City Council of Zeeland, São Luís, 7 April 1642, ibid. 291.

293 *settlers' slaves'.* Report by Antonio Teixeira de Mello, Capitão-mor of Maranhão, to King, São Luís, 14 March 1645, DHBC 3 129.

293 *greater captivity'.* Gedeon Morris de Jonge to Supreme Council, São Luís do Maranhão, 29 Jan 1643, RHGB 58 pt 1, 307. The Dutch authorities did finally free any Indians whom the Portuguese had enslaved for having sided with the Dutch: Council of the XIX to Supreme Council, 18 April 1642. They later abolished all slavery in Maranhão and ruled that 'the Indians and natives of Maranhão should be considered free, as are the Brazilians [Tupi]' (Council of XIX to Count Johan Maurits and Supreme Council, 10 Oct 1642, in Gonçalves de Mello, *Tempo dos Flamengos* 242–3).

294 *for that purpose.'* Notulen of 21 March 1644, RHGB **58** pt 1, 317, 1895. Chief Antonio da Costa Marapirão had a curious saga. His father Marcos da Costa was a staunch supporter of the Portuguese and received the habit of the Order of Christ from them. After the Dutch took Maranhão, they sent the two Tobajara chiefs, father and son, by ship to Pernambuco. The chiefs later claimed that they were being sent as prisoners; but others claimed that they were being sent to receive honours. The ship landed on the coast of Ceará and Marapirão and his son escaped. They returned overland towards Maranhão, but the father was killed by a shark when crossing a river. His son Antonio returned in time to help Portuguese settlers evict the Dutch from Maranhão. He later went to Portugal to visit the King. Various dignitaries recommended that he be honoured, and the King made him chief of all the Tobajara and a Knight of Christ, and authorised that 30 milreis be spent on clothing for Antonio and his wife and on twelve habits of chivalry for other Maranhão chiefs. (Petition by Antonio da Costa, Lisbon, 3 Oct 1648, and royal order, 11 Oct 1648, DHBC **3** 177–80). Two years later the Portuguese decided that they had made a big mistake. It appeared that Marapirão had been helping the Dutch, and had in fact caused the execution of a dozen settlers by betraying them to the Dutch. When the son went to see the Portuguese governor of Maranhão in 1650, 'this Antonio da Costa [Marapirão] stayed with the other Indians behind the Church of Our Lady of Mount Carmo. He made speeches to [the other Indians] of such hatred against us that the ecclesiastics and the friars' servants heard them and came . . . to tell me of the rotten speeches he made to the rest' (Governor Luis de Magalhães, São Luís, 30 Nov 1650, DHBC **3** 188). The truth was that Antonio Marapirão had written to the King to complain of the ill-treatment given to the Indians by Governor Magalhães. Among other things the Governor had ordered him to lead a canoe-full of his Indians on a slaving expedition up the Amazon. The Governor wrote to the King in a tone of injured innocence: '. . . the Indians are so well treated by me that the settlers are amazed by their idleness resulting from the good treatment I give them. If any settler needs one [as a labourer], I make him pay in advance the usual wage, which is two varas of cloth a month. And, Sire, there is nothing else to be said against this truth' (Magalhães to King, ibid.).

294 *kept as a slave.'* Acts of Assembly of Indians in the aldeia of Tapisserica, Tuesday, 11 April 1645, from *Notulen van Brazilië*, Royal Archive, The Hague, in Souto Maior, *Fastos Pernambucanos* 164. The full text of the assembly's acts are published, in Portuguese, in ibid. 160–72.

294 *their way of life'.* Supreme Council to Council of the XIX, Recife, 10 May 1644, Gonçalves de Mello, *Tempo dos Flamengos* 263.

295 *'many stratagems of war'.* Diogo Lopes de Santiago, *Historia da guerra de Pernambuco . . .*, RHGB **38** pt 1, 283, 1875.

295 *'all good musketeers'.* Laet, *Historie*, ABNRJ **41–2** 90, 1919–20. Camarão's village was São Miguel in Pernambuco. He had 600 Potiguar there, and shared it with a similar number of Tobajara under a chief called Estevão or Tebu. The biography of Camarão was by José Antonio Gonsalves de Mello in 1954, and there was also a biographical article by J. C. Fernandes Pinheiro in 1869. Camarão was baptised as a child in the aldeia of Igapó on 4 March 1612. He was therefore about eighteen when he first started to fight the Dutch in 1630. He once testified that he had been taught in the aldeia of Meretibi by the Jesuit missionary and later turncoat, Manoel de Moraes, in about 1629 (RHGB, **70** pt 1, 119–20). Many Brazilians with Indian blood, such as Marshal Rondon, have been the subjects of biographies. But I can think of no pure Indian other than Camarão to achieve this distinction.

295 *Christian'.* King to Mathias de Albuquerque, Lisbon, 14 May 1633, DH

17 290. At the outset of the fighting, the King had sent Albuquerque twenty suits of green and red cloth bordered with hollanderie, and fifty machetes to be distributed among friendly Indians – trinkets to make them fight the Dutch (King to Mathias de Albuquerque, Madrid, 21 April 1631, Archive of Simancas, Secretarías Provinciales, bk 1523, p. 37, in Souto Maior, 'Nos archivos de Hispanha' 40). The King later sent more rewards to Camarão: a further 40,000 reis, and in 1639 a vacant sinecure and a gold chain and medallion of himself (King to Conde de Torre, DH 17 291–3).

295 *the Dutch ships*. Lopes de Santiago, *Historia*, RHGB **38** pt 1, 310–11, 1875; J. C. Fernandes Pinheiro, 'D. Antonio Filippe Camarão, RHGB **32** pt 1, 204, 1869. After a Dutch defeat near Recife in October 1633, Camarão's Indians killed 390 out of 400 fugitives: Raphael de Jesus, *Castrioto Lusitano*, pt 1, bk 3, p. 87.

295 *their mortal enemies.'* Lopes de Santiago, *Historia*, RHGB **39** pt 1, 129, 1876. Laet, *Historia*, ABNRJ **41–2** 149, 1919–20. Raphael de Jesus, *Castrioto Lusitano*, pt 1, bk 3, p. 138. Laet said that Camarão commanded 2000 European *soldiers* but this must have been a mistake as there were scarcely that many on the Portuguese side. He probably meant the refugees led to safety by Camarão.

295 *the top of them.'* Lopes de Santiago, *Historia* 129–30. This was the battle of Terra Nova, 16 Aug 1636.

295 *on many occasions'.* Ibid. 283. Raphael de Jesus, *Castrioto Lusitano* 138–9.

296 *in her hand'.* Lopes de Santiago, *Historia* 138; Raphael de Jesus compared the mounted Dona Clara with Zenobias or Semiramis: *Castrioto Lusitano* 143.

296 *the wild cattle'.* Lopes de Santiago, *Historia* 168.

296 *the fort'.* Diogo de Campos Moreno, *Jornada do Maranhão . . .,* in Cândido Mendes de Almeida, *Memorias . . . do extincto Estado do Maranhão* **2** 163–4; Afrânio Peixoto, *Martim Soares Moreno* 16.

296 *I wished to go'.* Martim Soares Moreno to King, Ceará, 8 Jan 1631, DHBC **2** 258. In this letter Martim Soares said that he was fighting various groups of nomadic Tapuia, but held them off easily since he had won the friendship of the Potiguar, of seven Tapuia tribes, and of the Tobajara of the Ibiapaba hills.

296 *their own skins'.* Brito Freyre, *Nova Lusitania, Historia da Guerra Brasilica* (Lisbon, 1675) 203–4, bk 4; Rodolfo Garcia note to Varnhagen, HGB **2** 341; DHBC **2** 260. Martim Soares Moreno was the subject of a good biography by Afrânio Peixoto, and he also inspired the romantic novel *Iracema* by José de Alencar. In this a Tobajara virgin called Iracema – her name is an anagram of America, and she symbolised the innocent new continent – fell in love with a 'White Warrior', a virile Portuguese captain, and had a son by him and saved his life.

297 *obeyed his orders.'* Processo de Manoel de Moraes (1647), RHGB **70** pt 1, 56, 1907.

297 *the command of Moraes.* Laet, *Historia*, ABNRJ **41–2** 89, 1919–20; *Processo de Manoel de Moraes* 32.

297 *against us. . . . '* Ibid. 16.

297 *Amsterdam'.* Bernardo O'Brien del Carpio, Petition to King of Spain, c.1637, AGI est. 147, caj. 5, leg. 21. Moraes told O'Brien why he had changed sides. He said that Mathias de Albuquerque had once called him a Jew in Pernambuco. He had gone to Portugal to protest, but had received no satisfaction in this or over some money he was owed. His revenge was to change sides and religion.

297 *life imprisonment.* Manoel de Moraes' confession was delivered at Lisbon on 23 April 1646 and the sentence was delivered on 15 Dec 1647. *Processo de Manoel de Moraes* 56, 94, 159, etc. His conversations with O'Brien show that Moraes (or possibly O'Brien himself) tended to exaggerate: he claimed that he had been procurator and chief interpreter for all the Brazilian Indians, that he had guided the Dutch in the capture of Pernambuco and Paraíba, and that he intended to marry the sister of the Dutch governor of Brazil.

298 *women and children.* The Tapuia had

first become aware of the Dutch when a Dutch ship cruising off the coast of Ceará captured a Portuguese and released 25 Tapuia men, women and children he was taking to be sold as slaves in Rio Grande. The Tapuia had for some years been trading with the Portuguese, exchanging captives for trade goods. Jandui's envoys to the Dutch in 1631 were sent home with presents, and accompanied by the Dutchman Elbert Smient and a Portuguese Jew called Samuel Cohen. Most were killed or captured by the Portuguese during the journey: one was freed when the Dutch took the Fort on the Rio Grande in February 1634, and was sent to tell Jandui. Laet, *Historie*, ABNRJ 38 225, 344, 1916, and **41-2** 8–9, 1919–20; Pieter Poti to Supreme Council, 1631, ABNRJ, 1907, Souto Maior, *Fastos pernambucanos* 145; Gonçalves de Mello, *Tempo dos Flamengos* 233; Boxer, *Dutch in Brazil* 52, 135.

The Dutch gave Nhandui the good Flemish name of Jandui or even 'King Jan Duwy'. His warriors helped Arcizcewsky take the bar of Cunhaú on the Rio Grande, and were rewarded with a banner that they prized. The Tararyu (or Tatairyou and other spellings) were led by Jandui and a lesser chief called Caracara (Elias Herckmans, *General Description of Paraíba* 279; Roulox Baro, *Relation du voyage . . .* 253; Laet, ABNRJ **41-2** 37, 1919–20). His tribe had 1600 members, but there were five other allied or subordinate groups. They lived inland from Rio Grande: five days' march by men alone, or ten days by the entire tribe with its women and children. The other Tapuia tribe to join the Dutch was a group of Cariri under Chief Keri-oukeiou or Oquenou.

298 *principal aim'.* Laet, *Historie*, bk 11, p. 9.

298 *gulley.* Ibid. bk 11, pp. 33–4.

298 *for this purpose'.* Lopes de Santiago, *Historia da guerra de Pernambuco*, RHGB 39 pt 1, 123, 130, 156, 1876. Frei Raphael de Jesus said that the Dutch tortured settlers with burning oil, hot nails on their genitals, and sexual deviation with their women in full view of the men:

Castrioto Lusitano, pt 1, bk 3, pp. 135–6, 189–92.

298 *to kill indiscriminately'.* Herckmans, *General Description of Paraíba* 281.

298 *against us!'* Georg Marcgraf, *Historiae rerum naturalium Brasiliae*, bk 8, ch. 4, trans. José Procopio de Magalhães, 269.

299 *to visit me!'* Baro, *Relation du voyage* 218–19.

299 *by the settlers!'* Ibid. 222.

299 *in the west.* The nineteenth-century German ethnologist Carl Friedrich Philip von Martius proposed that the language be called Gê, which is a suffix among them meaning 'chief', 'father' or 'ancestor'. He also proposed that they might be called Cran or Kren, which means 'son', 'descendant' or 'people' (von Martius, *Beiträge zur Ethnographie . . .* (Leipzig, 1867) 1 257–8). Von Martius was the first to demonstrate that many tribes in this immense area of central Brazil share a common language and form a linguistic group. Von Martius reckoned that the Tapuia of the early chroniclers were the same as his Gê. This was disputed by Rudolf Schuller in 1912 on the grounds that the Gê are always shy of water, and never use horses, whereas the Tapuia described by Barlaeus swam and sent mounted warriors to meet Roulox Baro (Schuller, 'Zur Affinität der Tapuyer-Indianer des Theatrum Rerum naturalium Brasiliae', *Internationales Archiv für Ethnographie* 21 79–98, 1912). David Maybury-Lewis disputes both reasons: the Gê are *not* shy of water – they swim well, even if few have boats – and Jandui's horsemen were clearly a piece of showmanship to impress his visitor. Maybury-Lewis shows that in most respects the Dutch Tapuia were similar to modern Gê. But they differed in some essential ways: the use of hammocks and of alcohol made from honey; the real temporal and spiritual power of the chief, who as a shaman used tobacco in a rite, and who ceremonially deflowered girls at puberty. Maybury-Lewis concluded that these Tapuia 'were not identical with the Gê, though they shared a large number of cultural traits with them' (Maybury-

Lewis, 'Some Crucial Distinctions in Central Brazilian Ethnology', *Anthropos* **60** 343, 1965). Maybury-Lewis also agreed with Curt Nimuendajú (and disagreed with Lévi-Strauss and others) that the Gê have always been a savannah people, who intensely dislike the forest. As savannah people they were *not* recent migrants driven from the coastal forests to the savannahs of the plateau by the Tupi invasion.

Personally, I think that von Martius was right after all. The similarities between the Dutch Tapuia and modern Gê are far more striking than the differences. The log race is a very curious custom peculiar to the Gê. It is still being performed almost exactly as it was described by the Dutch who visited Jandui. The haircut of Jandui's Indians was also identical to that of modern Timbira (Canela and Krahô): an important similarity, not noted in Maybury-Lewis' list of common features. Maybury-Lewis felt that the Tapuia were people driven inland from the coast, and living between the Tupi and the then virtually unknown Gê of the savannahs. I think they were more probably Gê closely related to the modern Timbira, but who lived close enough to the coast to have learned about hammocks and honey alcohol from the Tupi. They used to descend to the coast between November and January each year, but did so to gather cashew nuts rather than for any reason connected with the sea. (Herckmans, *General Description of Paraíba* 279.)

299 *his corn?'* Roulox Baro, *Relation du voyage* 220–1, 224, 223, 228. Herckmans, *General Description of Paraíba* 283.

300 *in this war.'* Baro, *Relation du voyage* 237, 240–1.

300 *honour him.'* Herckmans, *General Description of Paraíba* 280.

300 *our histories.'* Maurits of Nassau to Louis XIV, letter accompanying paintings of Brazil, in Souto Maior, 'A arte hollandeza no Brasil', RHGB **83** 122, 1918.

300 *their relatives.* Frei Manoel do Salvador 'Calado', *Valeroso Lucideno*,

quoted by Souto Maior, *Fastos Pernambucanos* 62.

301 *Pernambuco'.* Diogo Lopes de Santiago, *Historia da guerra de Pernambuco*, RHGB **39** pt 1, 379, 1876. This writer, himself a settler and participant in the war, left no doubt that the rebels awaited Camarão's arrival as the signal for revolt: ibid. 347–8, 370.

301 *playing his trumpet'.* Ibid. 401–2.

302 *lack of essentials.'* Lopes de Santiago, *Historia da guerra*, RHGB **40** pt 1, 441, 1877.

302 *Portuguese'.* Ibid. 391. The Potiguar tribe was split: some with the Dutch, and others with Camarão and the Portuguese.

302 *work for them. . . . '* Lopes de Santiago, *Historia da guerra*, RHGB **40** pt 1, 40, 1877.

302 *Recife'.* Martim Soares Moreno and André Vidal de Negreiros to Antonio Telles da Silva, Governor of Brazil, 6 Sept 1645, RHGB **69** pt 1, 188, 1906.

302 *as masters.'* Anon, *Diary or Brief Discourse about the Rebellion . . . of the Portuguese in Brazil . . .* (Arnhem, 1647), trans. in *Revista do Instituto Archaeologico e Geographico Pernambucano* 6 no. 32 (Recife, April 1887), 151. This observer wrote that 700 or 800 Potiguar and Tapuia were fighting for the Dutch in 1645.

302 *brutish customs.'* Lopes de Santiago, *Historia da guerra*, RHGB **39** pt 1, 404, 1876.

303 *Holy Evangels.'* Surrender document, signed by André Vidal de Negreiros and João Fernandes Vieira, 17 Aug 1645, in Souto Maior, *Fastos Pernambucanos* 104.

303 *vultures and dogs.* Lopes de Santiago, *Historia da guerra* 40 pt 1, 456, 1877; Manoel do Salvador Calado, *Valeroso Lucideno* 323.

304 *to spare them.* Lopes de Santiago, *Historia da guerra* 41 pt 1, 171–4, 177–8, 1878.

304 *Christianity.'* Traslado do assento que se fez sobre as cousas de Pernãobuco (1645), RHGB **69** pt 1, 170, 1906.

304 *unbridled licentiousness'.* Martim Soares Moreno and André Vidal de Negreiros to Dutch Governors of Recife, Serinhaem (August) 1645, RHGB **69** pt 1, 195, 1906.

305 *pride myself.'* Diogo Pinheiro

Camarão to Pieter Poti, 22 Oct 1645, and Diogo Pinheiro and Antonio Felipe Camarão to Pieter Poti, undated, in Souto Maior, *Fastos Pernambucanos* 149–50, 150–1. Pedro Souto Maior found Dutch translations of these letters in the volumes for 1645–6 in the Rijks Archief in The Hague. Besides these two, there was one from the Indian envoy Diogo da Costa to Pieter Poti, Friday 17 Oct 1645; Diogo Pinheiro Camarão to Captain Itaque and other Indian captains, 27 Oct 1645; Camarão to all Indian officers serving the Dutch, 19 Aug; Camarão to Antonio Paraupaba, 4 Oct; all in *Fastos Pernambucanos* 149–53.

306 *31 October 1645.* Pieter Poti to Antonio Felipe Camarão, 31 Oct 1645, ibid. 153–6.

307 *Brazil.'* Lopes de Santiago, *Historia da guerra*, RHGB 41 pt 1, 411, 1878.

307 *roast and boiled!"'* Ibid. 422–3.

307 *availed her nothing'.* Ibid. 423. The Timbira are often inspired by women shamans. I have seen women busy with rituals in many huts of the Canela. It was a woman with magical powers who led the tribe in a disastrous onslaught on the cattle encroaching on their reserve near Barra do Corda as recently as 1963. The cattlemen retaliated with a murderous night attack on the village that left six dead, eight wounded, the village in flames and the tribe in flight into the wilds. See William H. Crocker, 'The Canela Messianic Movement, an Introduction', *Atas do Simpósio sôbre a Biota Amazônica*, 2 vols (Rio de Janeiro, 1967), 2 69–83.

307 *the countryside.'* Lopes de Santiago, *Historia da guerra*, RHGB 42 pt 1, 167, 1879.

307 *friendship to them.'* Proclamation by Camarão, 28 March 1646, in Souto Maior, *Fastos Pernambucanos* 159.

308 *anything more wretched."'* Roulox Baro, *Relation du voyage* 216–17, 218. Jacob Rabe was shot when walking home from dinner with a friend near his home at Fort Keulen in Rio Grande, on 5 April 1646. It was immediately assumed that he was shot on the orders of a Lt-Col. George Garsman. The motive was either

that Rabe suspected Garsman of planning to desert, or Garsman and his accomplices may have been after Rabe's reputed treasure. Rabe was in fact found to have a chest full of objects looted from settlers' farms: books, mirrors, ribbons, children's clothing and so forth, possibly intended as presents for the Tapuia. After a confused trial it was decided that Garsman and his ensign Jacques Boulan had conspired to have two of their soldiers murder Jacob Rabe. The accused merely had their goods confiscated and were deported to Holland. The Tapuia were furious and vowed that the Dutch would regret their lenience. Roulox Baro, *Relation du voyage* 222–3; Souto Maior, *Fastos Pernambucanos* 118–21; Gonçalves de Mello, *Tempo dos Flamengos* 240.

The Tapuia chief from the São Francisco who fought with Camarão in early 1646 was known to the Portuguese as A Rodela, or 'The Target' or 'Shield'. The leaders of the insurrection complained as late as May 1646 that many settlers refused to join them for fear of the Dutch Tapuia: Martim Soares Moreno and André Vidal de Negreiros to Antonio Telles da Silva, 28 May 1646, DHBC 4 59.

308 *of our arms.'* Camarão to Dutch governors in Recife, April 1648, in Lopes de Santiago, *Historia da guerra* 43 pt 1, 22–3, 1880.

309 *we had defeated.'* Report on the battle by Mestre-de-Campo-General Francisco Barreto, in *Documentos dos Arquivos Portugueses que importam ao Brasil* (Lisbon, 1944–5) 2 2–3, trans. in E. Bradford Burns (ed.), *A Documentary History of Brazil* 78.

309 *distinguished themselves.'* Ibid.

309 *on all occasions.'* Lopes de Santiago, *Historia da guerra*, RHGB, 43 pt 1, 61, 1880.

309 *other ornaments.'* Barreto report, in Burns, *Documentary History* 79.

309 *his Indians perform'.* Lopes de Santiago, *Historia da guerra* 43 pt 1, 77, 1880.

310 *six long months.'* Appeal by Antonio Paraupaba to the States General, The

Hague, 1656, in Souto Maior, *Fastos
Pernambucanos* 176.
310 *all their lives.*"' Ibid. 177–8. Lopes de
Santiago said that Pieter Poti was held in
irons for $2\frac{1}{2}$ years, and then died at sea
while being shipped to Portugal (*Historia
da guerra*, RHGB 43 pt 1, 216, 1880).
310 *killing settlers.* Francisco de Brito
Freire, *Relação da restauração de*

Pernambuco (Feb 1654), in MACC 1 130;
Duarte Correia de Albuquerque report,
Lisbon, 27 Feb 1646, in MACC 1 45.
311 *revival and rendezvous.*' Letter from
Becx, Barbados, 8 Oct 1654, Souto
Maior, *Fastos Pernambucanos* 191.
311 *of that nation. . . . .*' Appeal by Antonio
Paraupaba, The Hague, 6 Aug 1654, in
ibid. 175.

Chapter 15   ANTÓNIO VIEIRA

313 *against their wills.*' Lei . . . *sobre a
liberdade dos indios*, 26 July 1596, HCJB 2
623–4, 2 211–14; Mathias C. Kieman, *The
Indian Policy of Portugal in America* 147;
Georg Thomas, *Die Portugiesische
Indianerpolitik in Brasilien, 1500–1640*
203–4.
314 *overrule the others . . . .*'. Law of 5 June
1605, J. J. de Andrade e Silva, *Colleção
chronológica da legislação portuguesa . . .* 1
129; A. M. Perdigão Malheiro, *A
escravidão no Brasil*, pt 2, *Indios* 46;
Kieman, *Indian Policy* 149.
314 *settlers of the captaincies.*' Alvará,
'Gentios da terra são livres . . .', 30 July
1609, Andrade e Silva, *Colleção* 1 271–3;
Perdigão Malheiro, *Escravidão* 46–8;
Kieman, *Indian Policy* 149; Serafim Soares
Leite, *Suma histórica da Companhia de Jesus
do Brasil . . .* 83; Thomas, *Indianerpolitik*
205.
314 *their lands.*' Ibid.
314 *contrary to law. . . . .*' Ibid.
314 *done them.*' Ibid.
315 *fraud and malice. . . . .*' Miguel Ayres
Maldonado and José de Castilho Pinto,
*Descripção . . . dos trabalhos e fadigas das
suas vidas*, RHGB 56 pt 1, 397, 1893.
315 *debt in a desert.*' Diogo de Campos
Moreno, *Livro que da razão do estado do
Brasil* (1612) 113–14.
315 *isolated in aldeias.*' Diogo de Menezes
to King, 7 Feb 1611, Perdigão Malheiro,
Escravidão 2 49.
316 *native labour.* Carta de lei, 10 Sept
1611, 'Declara a liberdade dos gentios do
Brazil, exceptuando os tomados em
guerra justa . . .', Andrade e Silva,

Colleção 1 309; Perdigão Malheiro,
Escravidão 2 50–1; Kieman, *Indian Policy*
151; Thomas, *Indianerpolitik* 207–11; São
Paulo, *Registo geral da Câmara Municipal de
São Paulo* 1 326–35; *Livro primeiro do
governo do Brasil* (Ministerio das Relações
Exteriores, Rio de Janeiro, 1958) 71–5;
HCJB 5 3–8; Leite, *Suma histórica* 84.
316 *all their lives'.* João de Souza Ferreira,
America abreviada . . ., RHGB 57 pt 1, 54,
1894.
316 *one another'.* Ibid.
316 *death or flight'.* Ibid.
317 *Aruans Indians.* Three Jesuits survived,
and one of these, Nicolau Teixeira,
described the shipwreck, DHBC 3 ; José
de Moraes, *Historia da Companhia de Jesus
na extincta Provincia do Maranhão e Para*, in
Antonio Henriques Leal, 'Apontamentos para a historia dos Jesuitas . . .',
RHGB 36 pt 2, 127–9, 1873; João
Felippe Betendorf, *Chronica da missão
dos Padres da Companhia de Jesus . . .*
bk 2, ch. 4, RHGB 72 pt 1, 66, 1909;
António Vieira, *Resposta aos capitulos que
deu contra os religiosos da Companhia . . .
Jorge de Sampaio*, in *Obras escolhidas* 5 237;
João Lúcio de Azevedo, *Os Jesuítas no
Grão-Pará . . .* 48.
317 *Fathers.*' Betendorf, *Chronica*, bk 2,
ch. 6, p. 70; Moraes, *Historia da Companhia*
131. The Jesuit who flogged the girl was
Francisco Pires, one of the three
survivors of the shipwreck at Belém. The
missionary in charge was Manoel Moniz.
The Jesuits were receiving the mill's
profits only during the minority of
Antonio Moniz Barreiros' son.

317 *France'*. Public Record Office, London, State Papers Portugal, 89/7, fol. 350, quoted by C. R. Boxer, *A Great Luso-Brazilian Figure, Padre António Vieiro, SJ, 1608–1697* 4. Boxer's work is easily the best short life of Vieira, and there is another fine summary in his *The Dutch in Brazil, 1624–1654* 271–3.

318 *what he pleases'*. Comment by a British envoy in Lisbon, 1668, Public Record Office, State Papers Portugal, 89/11, fol. 206, quoted by Boxer, *Great Luso-Brazilian Figure* 12.

318 *pays them best.'* Álvara of 10 Nov 1647, Perdigão Malheiro, *Escravidão* 2 60; *Livro Grosso do Maranhão*, pt 1, ABNRJ 66 17–18, 1948; Kieman, *Indian Policy* 157–8; the decrees regulating Indian pay and periods of labour were: Álvara of 12 Nov 1647, repeated 5 and 29 Sept 1649, decree of 5 Sept 1648, provision of 29 May 1649, in ibid. 57–8; MACC 1 69; Azevedo, *Os Jesuítas* 57; *Livro Grosso do Maranhão*, pt 1, ABNRJ 66 19, 1948; Souza Ferreira, *America abreviada* 61.

318 *to be a missionary!'* Vieira to Prince Teodósio, Maranhão, 25 Jan 1653, *Cartas* 1 301.

318 *baptism for them.'* Vieira to King João IV, São Luís do Maranhão, 20 May 1653, ibid, 1 308.

319 *suffer and die.'* Vieira to King, ibid. 1 311.

319 *directly to Hell!'* Vieira's sermon, Maranhão, first Sunday in Lent 1653, HCJB 9 211; trans. in E. Bradford Burns (ed.), *A Documentary History of Brazil* 82–9.

319 *is condemned!"'* Ibid. 84–5.

319 *the blood of others!'* Ibid. 86.

320 *at pistol point!"'* Ibid. 87.

320 *the sweat of others!"'* Ibid. 88.

320 *from their houses.'* Vieira to Jesuit Provincial of Bahia, São Luís do Maranhão, 22 May 1653, *Cartas* 1 331.

320 *one powerful man.'* André de Barros, *Vida do apostólico Padre António Vieyra* 141.

320 *any religious instruction.* Vieira to King João IV, Maranhão, 4 April 1654, *Cartas* 1 418.

321 *in this way'.* Vieira to Jesuit Provincial, Belém do Pará, c.Jan 1654, ibid. 1 356.

321 *war and enslavement!'* Ibid. 1 356.

321 *fresh and very good.'* Vieira to Jesuit

Provincial, ibid. 1 373–4; trans. C. R. Boxer, *The Golden Age of Brazil, 1695–1750* 273.

322 *harsh treatment.'* Vieira to Jesuit Provincial, *Cartas* 1 374–5; trans. Boxer, *Golden Age* 22.

322 *a small aldeia.'* Vieira, *Cartas* 1 376. The Tocantins had been 'reduced to peace with the Portuguese' by the Franciscan Frei Cristóvão Severim in 1625. 'Scandalised by the oppressions done to them, they were almost in rebellion. He took with him the sons of the chiefs to indoctrinate and domesticate them. He prohibited under pain of excommunication that the free Indians should be sold, as was being done on the pretence that they were selling only their labour.' He also confiscated books left by French heretics, playing cards, and the native concubines of the settlers of Pará. Vicente do Salvador, *Historia do Brasil,* bk 5, ch. 39, p. 537.

322 *his King'.* Barros, *Vida* 143.

322 *enslaving them'.* Ibid.; Moraes, *Historia,* chs 2–3, pp. 449–70.

322 *to his zeal.'* Barros, *Vida* 144–5.

323 *to their clearings. . . .'* Ibid. 145.

323 *rowers on voyages.'* Settler complaint to King, 1653, in Roberto C. Simonsen, *Historia economica do Brasil (1500–1820)* 2 122, trans. Kieman, *Indian Policy* 159.

323 *without distinction'.* Bernardo Pereira de Berredo, *Annaes historicos do Estado do Maranhão . . .* bk 13, 427; Andrade e Silva, *Collecão* 4 292.

323 *my enemies'.* Ibid.; LGM 1 20.

323 *the holy evangel'.* Ibid.

324 *slaves for life.* Law of 9 April 1655, LGM 1 25–8; Kieman, *Indian Policy* 160–1; Azevedo, *Os Jesuítas* 76–7.

324 *those sertões'.* Barros, *Vida* 191.

324 *persuading them'.* Vieira, *Resposta aos capitulos,* in *Obras escolhidas* 5 268.

325 *their forests. . . .'* Barros, *Vida* 191–2.

325 *being catechised.'* Vieira to King João IV, Pará, 8 Dec 1655, *Cartas Jesuiticas* 1 450.

325 *official ransom troops.'* Vieira to King, ibid. 1 451.

326 *fishing for fish.'* Barros, *Vida* 197.

326 *this climate'.* Ibid. 205.

326 *and to civilisation.'* Ibid. 206.

326 *in the sertão.* . . . .'. King João to Vieira, Lisbon, 21 Oct 1652, Berredo, *Annaes*, bk 13, p. 423.

326 *whenever they wanted '* Betendorf, *Chronica*, ch. 10, p. 80.

327 *for the whites.'* Ibid. 81.

327 *no gate at all.'* Vieira, *Resposta aos capitulos*, in *Obras escolhidas* 5 271–2. Vieira wrote this to rebut settlers' protests that the Jesuits were obstructing their slaving activities: hence his apparent approval of legally enslaving as many as (legally) possible. If the Jesuits were to operate in Maranhão and Pará at all, they had to compromise with the settlers' insatiable need for labour.

327 *at peace'.* Betendorf, *Chronica*, bk 3, ch. 14, p. 133.

327 *Your Majesty's laws'.* Vieira, *Resposta aos capitulos*, in *Obras escolhidas* 5 272; Barros, *Vida* 260–1; HCJB 7 25; Betendorf, *Chronica*, bk 3, ch. 14, pp. 133–4. Francisco Gonçalves died at Cameté during the return journey.

328 *certain mines [here].'* Vieira to King Afonso VI, São Luís do Maranhão, 20 April 1657, *Cartas* 1 462.

328 *of that province.'* Vieira, *Resposta aos capitulos*, in *Obras escolhidas* 5 269. Father Souto Maior walked across country from the Pacajá to the Tapirapé on the Tocantins – a remarkable expedition over some fifty miles of rain forest. But on the return journey, after making contact with the Tapirapé, the thirty-two-year-old Jesuit stumbled and fell fatally on to a rock. The Pacajá carried him back to their village and buried him, but the Jesuits later exhumed him for a martyr's burial – his body in Belém and head in Lisbon (Barros, *Vida* 209–13; Betendorf, *Chronica*, bk 3, ch. 5, p. 100).

As for the Pacajá (who had suffered a slaughter by the 1628 expedition of Pedro da Costa Favella), they were dispersed to distant missions. The last seen of them was in 1763 when they were one of thirteen tribes making up the population of 400 Indian remnants in the Jesuit mission of Portel (João Daniel, *Thesouro descoberto no maximo rio Amazonas*, RHGB 3 182, 1841; João de São José,

Viagem e visita do sertão . . ., RHGB 9 490, 1847; Curt Nimuendajú, 'Little-known Tribes of the Lower Tocantins River Region', HSAI 3 203). According to Betendorf, the Pacajá were Tupi-speaking. The Parakana are a Tupi tribe now living near the headwaters of the Pacajá river, who came into permanent contact when the Transamazônica highway was cut near their villages in 1971.

328 *to the Faith'.* Barros, *Vida* 262.

328 *preaching of the evangel.'* Vieira, *Resposta aos capitulos*, in *Obras escolhidas* 5 273.

328 *among the soldiers.'* Vieira to King Afonso VI, São Luís do Maranhão, 28 Nov 1659, *Cartas* 1 554. In this letter Vieira called the tribe Inheiguara, as did Betendorf (*Chronica*, bk 3, ch. 8, p. 113). In the Resposta aos capitulos written in 1662, Vieira said that the tribe being punished were 'some of the wilder Pochiguaras' (*Obras escolhidas* 5 273) and Vieira's biographer André Barros called them Poquiguaras (*Vida* 262, 264). The Inheiguara may well have been a subtribe of the Poqui (variously spelled Poquiguara, Pochiguara, Potyguara, etc.).

328 *a thousand souls.'* Betendorf, *Chronica* bk 3, ch. 8, p. 113.

328 *their waters.'* Vieira to King Afonso VI, Maranhão, 28 Nov 1659, *Cartas* 1 555; Betendorf, *Chronica*, bk 3, ch. 8, p. 114. Betendorf reported that the earlier batch of 1200 Tocantins Tupinambá were moved to the Island of the Sun or Island of the Tupinambá, after a brief stay near Belém. When the German Jesuit Betendorf was in Portugal in 1684–7 he told the King about the plight of the valiant Tupinambá, and King Pedro ordered that those on this island be left alone by the settlers. Despite this, Betendorf wrote that there were very few Tupinambá left when he wrote his *Chronica* in 1699.

329 *Portuguese.'* Vieira to King Afonso VI, São Luís do Maranhão, 28 Nov 1659, *Cartas* 1 556. Marajó was then called Joannes island.

329 *for the wounded'.* Vieira, *Resposta aos*

capítulos, para. 25, in *Obras escolhidas* 5 224; Azevedo, *Os Jesuítas* 84.

329 *the Church'*. Berredo, *Annaes*, bk 13, p. 433.

329 *'full of spoils'*. Ibid. 434.

330 *impregnable location'*. Vieira to King, 28 Nov 1659, *Cartas* 1 557.

330 *an arduous missionary campaign*. Betendorf, *Chronica* 91-4. Betendorf, who was Jesuit Superior of Maranhão and Grão-Pará from 1668 to 1674, gave credit to Soutomaior for this difficult conversion; whereas Vieira tended to claim that he himself had first won over the Nheengaiba.

330 *to resist them'*. Vieira to King, *Cartas* 1 559. Vieira said that the Dutch used to come every year to Cabo Norte, the northern shore of the mouth of the Amazon, to trade with the Indians. They would fill twenty ships with sea-cows or manatees – which are now a threatened species.

330 *did to them'*. Vieira, *Cartas* 1 560.

330 *as was true'*. Ibid. 1 560.

331 *from today onwards.'* Ibid. 1 560-1.

331 *under arms.'* Ibid. 1 561.

331 *among the Indians.'* Ibid. 1 563.

331 *true peace'*. Ibid. 1 563-4.

331 *Portuguese.'* 1 564.

331 *law of 1655'*. Ibid. 1 565.

332 *these obligations for ever.'* Ibid. 1 566; Barros, *Vida*, bk 3, pp. 287-8.

332 *kept them.'* Vieira, *Cartas* 1 565.

332 *were living. . . .'* Barros, *Vida*, bk 2, p. 317.

333 *infant epidemic*. Betendorf, *Chronica*, bk 3, ch. 3, p. 96. Vieira also noted that in the four years between 1656 and 1660 'the fathers had buried over five hundred innocents, whom they themselves baptised, but very few adults . . .' (*Resposta aos capítulos*, in *Obras escolhidas* 5 274).

333 *to the King'*. King to Simão Tagaibuna, Lisbon, 1659, DHBC 3 226-7. In 1658 Jorge Gomes Ticuna from Ibiapaba, son of Chief Domingos Ticuna of the aldeias of the Camocim river in Ceará, sailed to Portugal at Vieira's suggestion. He forgot his letters of introduction, but the Count of Odemira looked after him and presented him to the King on 1 Aug 1569.

He petitioned for favours because of his father's capture of the fort of Ceará from the Dutch in 1644. The Royal Council refused him the Order of Christ, but sent red costumes complete with the usual ornaments, sword, hat and stockings for him and his father. They also sent two gold medallions with the King's effigy: DHBC 3 222-4; Barros, *Vida*, bk 2, pp. 256-7.

333 *more [civilised] than he'*. Betendorf, *Chronica*, bk 3, ch. 11, p. 123. Vieira was escorted by an Indian musketeer called Cristóvão. This man had shown so much spirit in the wars against the Dutch that he was enlisted as a King's soldier. Betendorf said that 'although he took up his guard in a shirt without drawers or doublet, with his musket on his back, he was esteemed not only by the Fathers but by all Portuguese soldiers as if he were one of them' (*Chronica*, bk 3, ch. 11, p. 122). Vieira described his mission to Ibiapaba: *Relação da missão da Serra de Ibiapaba*, in *Obras escolhidas* 5 72-134; Barros, *Vida*, bk 2, p. 225. Barros tried to claim that his hero Vieira made the initial journey to Ibiapaba in 1656, whereas Vieira himself correctly said that he went only in 1660.

334 *over 1800 slaves.'* Vieira to Câmara of Pará, 12 Feb 1660, *Cartas* 1 581-2.

334 *loaded with Indians.'* Vieira, *Informação sobre o modo com que foram tomados e sentenciados por cativos os índios do ano de 1655*, in *Obras escolhidas* 5 40.

335 *sold them publicly.'* Ibid. 5 41.

335 *do it first.'* Ibid. 5 46.

335 *beat them to death.'* Ibid. 5 46.

335 *against themselves'*. Ibid. 5 49.

336 *no other proof.'* Ibid. 5 53-4.

336 *do not fear?'* Ibid. 5 47.

336 *from other tribes*. Ibid. 5 54.

337 *will always be recorded.'* Regimento issued by Governor Dom Pedro de Melo to Ajudante Baltasar Fernandes, Maranhão, 1660, in C. R. Boxer, *Um regimento inédito sobre o resgate dos Ameríndios no Estado do Maranhão em 1660* (Coimbra, 1965) 8.

337 *for page after page*. Belém Câmara to Vieira, 15 Jan 1661, Berredo, *Annaes*, bk 14, pp. 449-50.

337 *a canoe and paddlers.'* Vieira, *Resposta aos capítulos*, in *Obras escolhidas* 5 269; Vieira to Belém Câmara, 12 Feb 1661, Berredo, *Annaes*, bk 14, pp. 451–5; Vieira, *Representação to Belém Câmara*, 21 June 1661, in *Obras escolhidas* 5 140–50.

338 *arms of the Indians.'* Vieira, *Resposta aos capítulos*, in ibid. 5 298.

338 *salt and die.'* Betendorf, letter, 20 July 1673, HCJB 7 295; trans. in Boxer, *Golden Age* 278.

338 *'pestilential catarrh'.* Barros, Vida, bk 5, p. 569.

338 *that pestilential evil.'* Betendorf, *Chronica*, bk 4, ch. 11, p. 203.

338 *their flesh fell off'.* Ibid. bk 4, ch. 11, p. 203.

338 *greater part of them.'* Ibid. bk 4, ch. 12, p. 213.

339 *were entirely covered.'* Ibid. bk 4, ch. 12, pp. 215–16.

339 *sacraments to them.'* Ibid. bk 4, ch. 12, p. 216.

340 *obey their orders'.* Jorge de Sampaio e Carvalho, Representação against the Jesuits, 1661, DHBC 4 113. Vieira did not deny this charge, but argued that the fiercely independent Marapirão was an improbable martyr for the settlers to champion: *Resposta aos capítulos*, ch. 17, *Obras escolhidas* 5 211–12; Alexandre J. de Melo Morais, *Corografia historica* . . . 4 213; Azevedo, *Os Jesuítas* 95; Mecenas Dourado, *A conversão do gentio* 134–5.

341 *Hell.'* Vieira, *Resposta aos capítulos*, ch. 18, in *Obras escolhidas* 5 213–14. In his letter to the King from the beaches of Cumá (22 May 1661, DHBC 4 122–3), Vieira said that, apart from marrying irregularly, this chief allowed his village to live as heathen, captured and sold Indians, and refused to obey the Fathers. In that letter Vieira called him Lope de Sousa Guarapauba; in the *Resposta aos*

capítulos (which may not have been written by Vieira himself) he is called Capaúba; and when Vieira wrote to him from Mortigura aldeia on 21 Jan 1661 he called him Guaquaiba or Lope de Sousa (*Cartas* 1 577–8); he is called Acapuava in Sampaio's Representação, DHBC 4 113–14.

341 *'your friend'.* Vieira to Lope de Sousa Guaquaiba, Mortigura, 21 Jan 1661, *Cartas Jesuiticas* 1 578.

341 *with his company'.* Vieira, *Resposta aos capítulos* ch. 24, *Obras escolhidas* 5 222; Sampaio, Representação 115. Sampaio further charged that Father Veloso refused permission to a judge to visit the aldeia to investigate the death.

341 *for a necessity'.* Betendorf, *Chronica*, bk 4, ch. 4, p. 177.

342 *eleven children he had'.* Ibid. bk 4, ch. 11, p. 204.

342 *a leaky ship.* Ibid. bk 4, chs 5–6, pp. 179–91; Barros, *Vida*, bk 3, pp. 312–42; Beredo, *Annaes*, bk 15, pp. 493–519.

343 *abominable means!'* Vieira Opinion to the Prince Regent, *c.*1669, *Obras escolhidas* 5 316–17, trans. Boxer, *Great Luso-Brazilian Figure* 22. Vieira's sermon of January 1662 is in HCJB 9 216.

343 *the law'.* Law of 1 April 1680, Perdigão Malheiro, *Escravidão* 2 70; Francisco Adolpho de Varnhagen, *História geral do Brasil* . . . (1926–36 ed.) 3 339–41; Kieman, *Indian Policy* 166; Azevedo, *Os Jesuítas* 135; HCJB 4 63–4.

343 *natural lords of it.'* Ibid.

343 *that smell of imperiousness. . . .'* Regulamento das Aldeias, 1658–60, para. 38, Leite, *Suma histórica* 74; HCJB 4 119–21.

343 *in the world!'* Vieira, *Sermões* 4 (Lisbon, 1685) paras 550–1; Dourado, *Conversão* 127–8.

Chapter 16 CATTLE

347 *'leaving nothing alive'.* Report by Alexandre de Sousa Freyre and others, Bahia, 4 March 1669, DH 5 208. Aporá was eighteen leagues (seventy miles) inland from the city of Salvador da ⌐ .ia.

347 *will be great. . . .'* Conde de Castelmelhor to Governor of Ilhéus,

Bahia, 20 June 1651, DH 3 113–14.
347 *fled into the forest.* Patents to Gaspar
Rodrigues Adorno to command this
campaign and to his officers, Bahia, 4
Sept 1651, DH 31 96–105; Report by
Alexandre de Sousa Freyre, Bahia, 4
March 1669, DH 5 209.
347 *imprisoned'.* Conde de Atouguia
instructions to Capitão-mor Gaspar Roiz
Adorno, Bahia, 24 Dec 1654, DH 4 40, 5
232–7; orders to chiefs of aldeias, 1 Oct
1654, DH 3 217–18, and to Jesuit
superior of Camamú, 16 Oct 1654, DH 3
228–9; patents to expedition's officers,
24 Dec 1654, DH 31 153–7.
348 *life and captivity'.* Francisco Barreto
instructions to Bernardo Bartolomeu
Aires, Bahia, 1 Feb 1658, DH 4 71–2, 5
285–96; for the previous campaigns, see
the instructions to Thomé Dias Laços, 9
Oct 1656, DH 5 245–50, 31 191–4, 21
Dec 1657, DH 4 57–9, 5 276–7; Report by
Alexandre de Sousa Freyre, Bahia, 4
March 1669, DH 5 210–11.
348 *very rare.'* Report by Alexandre de
Sousa Freyre, Bahia, 4 March 1669, DH 5
211–12; Francisco Barreto instructions
to Capt. Domingos Barbosa Calheiros,
Bahia, 5 Sept 1658, DH 5 321–7.
349 *little was achieved.* Francisco Barreto
instructions to Thomé Dias Laços, Bahia,
14 Feb 1662, DH 5 338–41, 31 270–4;
Conde de Óbidos instructions to Gaspar
Roiz Adorno, Bahia, 23 Sept 1664, DH 5
402–5; Conde de Óbidos, portaria, 8
Nov 1663, DH 7 127–8, 19 Sept 1664,
DH 7 193, 3 Jan 1665, DH 7 208.
349 *cried for vengeance.* Sebastião da Rocha
Pitta, *Historia da America Portugueza . . .,*
bk 6, pp. 380–4.
349 *villages of the barbarians.'* Alexandre de
Sousa Freire report, 4 March 1669, DH 5
213–14.
349 *São Vicente.* Afonso Furtado de Castro
do Rio de Mendonça, Visconde de
Barbacena, to Town Council of São
Paulo, Bahia, 11 Feb 1673, DH 6 239–40,
and to Governor of Rio de Janeiro, 10
Dec 1672, DH 6 239; Sousa Freire
appeals to São Vicente and São Paulo, 18
Sept 1670, DH 6 148–52; issue of six suits
with habits of Christ and six hats for
chiefs of São Francisco river Indians to

enlist their help on expedition, 4 Jan
1670, DH 7 430; Furtado de Castro do
Rio de Mendonça appoints officers for
expedition from Cairú, 29 May 1671, DH
8 28–9; to Governor of Pernambuco
about departure of expedition, 5 Sept
1671, DH 9 434; punishment of aldeia
Indians who ran off from expedition, 10
Dec 1671, DH 8 73–4; authorises
treasury to re-equip Paulistas and aldeia
Indians going on a second expedition, 11
Feb 1672, DH 8 78–9; instructions to
Gaspar Roiz de Adorno, 20 April 1672,
DH 8 87; decrees about equipping the
ship to take slaves back to São Vicente, 19
Jan, 13 Feb 1673, DH 8 134–6, 146; lists
of ammunition and supplies taken by
expedition, 22 April and 8 May 1673, DH
8 180–1; congratulations to Brás Ruiz de
Arzão, 5 and 11 Nov 1672, and to Estevão
Ribeiro Bayão Parente, 14 July 1573, DH
8 310–13, 373–4; report on success of
campaign, 9 Feb 1673, DH 8 343–4;
letters to Jesuits to furnish Indian rowers,
6 and 18 March 1673, DH 8 356–8.
349 *far less.'* Rocha Pitta, *Historia,* bk 6,
p. 390. Rocha Pitta gave the main credit
for the campaign to Parente's son João
Amaro Parente.
350 *are extinct.'* Mendonça to São Paulo
town council, 11 Feb 1673, DH 6 240.
350 *two settlements.'* Mendonça to
Capitão-Mor of São Vicente, 10 July
1673, DH 6 249.
350 *Bahia.* This commander's son João
Amaro Maciel Parente gave his name to
the sertão of João Amaro and later
opened a route from Ilhéus to the upper
São Francisco. Rocha Pitta said that João
Amaro later returned to São Paulo and
sold the town and all his lands in the
sertão that bears his name to Col.
Manuel de Araújo de Aragão (*Historia,*
bk 6, p. 391). Mendonça, portaria,
22 Sept 1673 about Indians remaining,
DH 8 170–1; foundation of Santo
Antonio da Conquista, 5 Nov 1673,
DH 8 184; royal portaria, 19 March
1674, Afonso de Escragnolle Taunay,
A Guerra dos Bárbaros 90–1.
350 *another expedition.* Mendonça, 22 April
1673, DH 8 181; 23 Oct 1672, DH 8 117;
14 Nov 1672, DH 8 126.

350 *any other tribe.* On one occasion the
Jesuits refused to send all the Paiaia men
on an expedition. The Governor-
General wrote furiously to the Jesuit
superior: 'You limit your offer to twenty
Paiaia when all of them are needed. They
are free vassals of His Highness and not
slaves of your College and at its disposal.
Your Paternity says that the Society has
few [Indians] in Brazil; but it is notorious
to everyone that they are very many, even
if they may seem few to the Society.'
Antonio Guedes de Brito to the Jesuit
Provincial, José de Seixas, Bahia, 6 July
1676, DH 9 24; Roque da Costa Barreto
to João Peixoto Viegas, 26 Oct 1678, DH
9 75, 77; Afonso Furtado de Castro do
Rio de Mendonça, portaria, 22 April
1674, DH 8 190–1.

350 *their wives.'* Antonio Guedes de Brito
to Capitão-Mor Agostinho Pereira, 4 Jan
1677, DH 9 34–5.

351 *immediately resign.'* Agostinho de
Azevedo Monteiro and Antonio Guedes
de Brito to Estevão Ribeiro Baião
Parente, Bahia, 25 May 1677, DH 9 41.
The Orders were issued on 14 July 1676,
to crush some villages that had been
raiding and frightening settlers on the
Guairaru hills and the interior of
Maragogipe, Jaguaripe and Cachoeira,
DH 8 252–7.

351 *have a share.* Roque da Costa Barreto,
letters of 3 Feb, 17 March, 4 April and 26
Oct 1678, DH 8 281 and 9 60–1, 75.

351 *they conquered.'* João de Lancastro to
Fernando Martins Mascarenhas de
Lancastro, Governor of Pernambuco,
Bahia, 11 Nov 1699, DH 39 88–9.

351 *to dare complain'.* Edict of 19 Jan 1699,
in C. R. Boxer, *The Golden Age of Brazil,
1695–1750* 229.

352 *São Francisco.* Once the tribes of the
Bahia hinterland were subdued, cattle
moved in to their former homes. A
similar movement had been taking place
on both banks of the São Francisco river
ever since the conquest of Sergipe at the
end of the sixteenth century. The first
settlers avoided cátinga, the dense, dry
and low woods, full of thorn-trees, that
covered much of the lands near the São
Francisco. But later pioneers came to

terms with it: they learned how to clear
or burn cátinga, and found that it was
often interspersed with stretches of good
open pasture. Water was always a
problem. Most of the rivers in this part of
Brazil dried up during part of the year.
Water-holes and natural deposits of salt
became important landmarks, and
ranches tended to develop along the
large, permanent rivers.

Cattle ranches spread up both banks of
the São Francisco, and up the other rivers
between it and Bahia: Vasa Barris, Real,
Itapicurú and Jacuípe. A cattle trail ran
from the middle São Francisco to Bahia.
It passed close to various Indian aldeias:
from the islands of Pambú and Uacapara
on the São Francisco itself, to that of
Jeremoabo on the Vasa Barris and
Canabrava (Pombal) and Sahy (Jacobina)
on the Itapicurú. These mission villages
were inhabited by various Cariri tribes:
Pancaruru at Pambú; Caimbé and
Massacará farther south. Upstream of
the Pancaruru were the Ocren, and
beyond them the Tupi-speaking Tupina
and Amoipira. At the headwaters of the
Itapicurú were the Orí, not pacified until
the early eighteenth century.

The French Capuchin Martin de
Nantes was active at Pambú between
1672 and 1683, and the missions on this
part of the river remained under
Franciscan jurisdiction. At the end of the
century Governor João de Lancastro
founded the settlement of Barra, some
600 miles up the river and due west of
Bahia, as a protection against the Acroa,
a warrior tribe related to the formidable
Chavante. There were old seventeenth-
century missions at Sahy and Jeremoabo,
both of which evolved into frontier
towns; at Massacará, where in 1687 the
mighty cattle baron Garcia d'Avila kept a
contingent of his private army; Natuba
and Inhambupe, founded by the Jesuits;
and along the course of the São
Francisco itself, from Barra downstream: the missions of Our Lady
of Pilar, Sorobabé, Pambú, Aracapá,
Pontal and Pajehú. By 1705, an author
wrote that there were cattle ranches and
missions for 600 leagues (2000 miles)

along both banks of the São Francisco, from the sea to the bar of the Velhas: in all this distance, 'there was no uninhabited or deserted part in which it would be necessary for travellers to sleep or lodge in the open, for they could repair to the houses of cattlemen, as they normally do, for the good welcome they find in them' (*Informação sobre as minas do Brasil*, 1705, ABNRJ **57** 179–80, 1939; João Capistrano de Abreu, *Capítulos de história colonial* 153–4). The big cattle barons were Garcia d'Avila, with an empire eighty leagues wide between the São Francisco and Parnaíba that stretched inland for 260 leagues (210 by 960 miles): Antonio Guedes de Brito with 160 leagues (590 miles) of the right bank of the river from the morro do Chapeu (Hat Hill) to the Velhas; João Peixoto Viegas on the upper Paraguaçu; the Paulistas Matias Cardoso and Figueira who controlled the passages for cattle moving from Piaú to the gold mines of Minas Gerais; the Franciscans, with their many missions; and the Jesuits, who inherited the Sobrado Ranch of Domingo Afonso 'Mafrense' or 'Sertão' (Capistrano de Abreu, *Capítulos* 146–7; Basílio de Magalhães, *Expansão geographica . . .* 236; André João Antonil, *Opulência do Brasil . . .* 186; Anon, *Roteiro do Maranhão a Goiás pela Capitania do Maranhão*, RHGB **62** pt 1, 60–161, 1900; Euclides da Cunha, *Rebellion in the Backlands* 79–82).

At the start of the eighteenth century, saltpetre or nitrate was found on the river now called Salitre. The authorities were eager to exploit this valuable ingredient of gunpowder. There were frequent letters from the Governor-General to Franciscan missionaries or Indian chiefs, refusing to exempt mission Indians from labour in the saltpetre works. And when a missionary complained that the cattle of Garcia d'Avila were destroying his Indians' plantations – they were too poor to fence their land, and too busy in the saltpetre to protect it – the Governor sided with the head of the House of Torre, because he did so much for the King (Rodrigo da Costa to Garcia d'Avila Pereira, 19 March 1705, DH **41** 12; also DH **40** 162, 165, 335, **41** 20, 72, 121, 164–9, etc.).

In 1704 Bernardo Cardoso de Macedo was given permission to capture any roaming Indians he caught along the São Francisco. The following year the newly pacified Araquens and Tamanquin were given temporary exemption from saltpetre work; but the Paiaia and Sacuriú and the men of the Sahy, Jacuípe and Rio Real (Sergipe) aldeias all had to do this work. In 1710 Colonel Garcia d'Avila Pereira was congratulated for descending scattered groups of Ocren and settling them in a mission on the São Francisco near the Salitre (DH **41** 245–6, **42** 336–7). They were soon working on the saltpetre. In 1713 the wild, nomadic Orí were pacified. They lived in the densely forested Cassuca hills at the headwaters of the Vasa Barris and Itapicurú, and often raided settlements along these rivers. The Christianised Caimbé captured a hunting party of nineteen Orí, a local priest stopped the Caimbé killing their captives, he indoctrinated these instead, and then returned them to their people dressed in Portuguese clothes. The Orí were so delighted that they readily accepted peace and Christianity. 'They applauded the arrival of the happy day of their baptism with songs and universal festivities, playing flutes which they use a lot . . . and all crowned with chaplets woven of various flowers that they picked in their fields. Among them everything was joy and jubilation.' 3,700 Orí were baptised in one session, and the authorities were pleased to see 'the greatest enemies of Portuguese rule joined to them in such great friendship' (Joseph Freyre de Monterroyo Mascarenhas, *Os Orizes conquistados* (1713), RHGB **8** 511, 1846). In 1728 the Italian Capuchin Frei Domingos de Cesena descended two tribes of Gren and Pocurunché (letter by Fathers of Hospicio de N. S. da Piedade da Bahia, 10 Dec 1757, in Eduardo de Castro e Almeida, *Inventario dos documentos relativos ao Brasil . . .* **1** 323).

The authorities promoted a Cariri chief, Francisco Dias Mataroa of Pontal aldeia, to be Governor of the Indians of the São Francisco. He was routed by the Orí in 1705, but led a contingent in the campaigns against Mandu Ladino in Piauí in 1715–18, and in 1720 was ordered to force married 'volunteers' to leave their villages on the São Francisco and occupy a new aldeia in Piauí (DH 42 334–5, 339, 43 171, 362–3, 44 5, etc.).

There was frequent unrest in these missions. In 1705 there were complaints that the Franciscans were using all their Indians to drive cattle to the gold mines. In August that year there was a dispute between these missionaries and Garcia d'Avila Pereira over ownership of their missions' lands and islands – a dispute which the missionaries won. In 1709 the Indians of the aldeia of the Rio Real da Praia (Royal Beach River) complained of overwork and financial extortion by their missionary; in 1711 the Italian Capuchin of the aldeia of Pacatuba was ordered to be less harsh on his Indians; in 1714 that of the aldeia of Santo Antonio of the Upper Itapicurú treated his Indians in a way that the Governor found 'contrary to all reason'; and in 1715 Chief Mataroa's aldeia of Pontal was in 'near revolt' against the harshness of its Franciscan (DH 41 21, 107, 238, 354, 42 183, 274–5, 330). The Royal authorities often intervened to tell the missionaries to be more gentle. There was a violent condemnation of the Franciscans in a report by Jeronimo Mendes da Paz in 1761. He cited the killing of the Indian João da Costa by Frei Posidonio da Mirandula at Pambú in 1717, by beating and castration while he was in the stocks; and of two Indian women and three girls, all of whom died after several beatings. Frei Posidonio left, and there were no further killings until 1753. But between 1753 and 1757 there was a rash of beatings, several of which led to the deaths of the victims. When Chief Bernardino da Cruz of Axará aldeia complained that a missionary had stolen 60 cattle and 4 mares from him, the missionary Frei

João Baptista de Cramanico defied all the legal authorities, claiming that 'in his missions he was Pope, cardinal, bishop, emperor, king, governor, councillor, judge and executioner!' (Mendes da Paz, *Parallelos dos missionarios Capuchinos e Jesuitas do Bispado e Capitania de Pernambuco*, 3 April 1761, in Castro e Almeida, *Inventario* 1 447). An official enquiry in 1762 failed to find evidence of Capuchin cruelty, beyond the killing of two Indians at Pacatuba aldeia (ibid. 2 12–13). A report by the priest of the parish of Jeremoabo in 1759 mentioned that it included the missions of Massacará, with 100 families of Caembé and Cariri under the Franciscans, and that of Saco dos Morcegos with 800 Kiriri under the Jesuits. But the area was full of cattle ranches run by lazy, tough, violent and rebellious people. The parish was the worst of any in Brazil: cattle convoys had to cross it armed as if they were moving through the territories of hostile Indians. (Padre Januário José de Sousa Pereira, *Relação da Freguezia de S. João Baptista do Jerimuabo do Certão de Cima*, Bahia, 29 Dec. 1759, in ibid. 1 229–31).

Some of these tribes still survive. There are about a thousand Kiriri at the former Jesuit mission of Saco dos Morcegos ('Sack of Bats') now Posto Kiriri near the town of Mirandela; some Massacará (or Kamakan) are on the Indian Service (Funai) post Paraguaçu or Caramuru near the town of Itaquira; about 500 Kaimbé live at a Funai subpost in Massacará, some twenty-five miles from Mirandela; on the São Francisco itself, over two thousand Pankararú live on the four square miles of Posto Pancararus, twenty miles from Petrolândia, Pernambuco, and there are more people called Panakaré near Santo António da Glória (former Curral dos Bois), Bahia; upstream of these are two hundred Tuxá or Rodela at Posto Rodelas on the river bank; some 250 Xokó and Xukurú live on Pôsto Alfredo Damaso at Pôrto Real do Colégio, Alagoas, not far from the mouth of the river. All these groups are highly acculturated, almost mestizo, with little or no memory of their tribal languages or cultures, only the vestige of a tribal identity. (W. D. Hohenthal, Jr, *As tribos indígenas do médio e baixo São Francisco*, RMP, n.s. **12**, 1960; Estevão Pinto, *Os indígenas do nordeste*, Brasiliana **44** (São Paulo, 1935); Th. Pompeu Sobrinho, 'Tapuias do Nordeste', *Revista do Instituto do Ceará*, Fortaleza, **53** 1939; Robert H. Lowie, 'The "Tapuya", the Cariri, and the Pancararú', HSAI **1** 553–61.)

352 *half-breeds'.* Miguel de Carvalho, Report to Bishop of Pernambuco, Piauí, 2 March 1697, in E. Ennes, *Os Palmares, Subsídios para a sua história* (Lisbon, 1937) 148–71, trans. in Boxer, *Golden Age* 235. Capistrano de Abreu, *Capítulos de História Colonial* (1934 ed.) 140–4. Antonil, *Cultura e opulência do Brasil* (1711) (São Paulo, 1923) 262–5.

352 *Tapuiás.'* Miguel de Carvalho, Report, in Boxer, *Golden Age*.

353 *they must cross.'* Antonil, *Cultura e opulência do Brasil* (1923 ed.) 268–9.

353 *it was so lean'.* William Dampier, *A Voyage to New Holland in 1699* (London, 1939) 41; Boxer, *Golden Age* 232.

353 *the rejoicing'.* Martin de Nantes, *Relation succinte et sincère de la mission . . . dans le Brésil . . .* (1707) (Salvador, Bahia, 1952) 35–6; Boxer, *Golden Age* 233.

354 *the sertão.'* Rocha Pitta, *Historia*, bk 6, p. 385. Domingos Afonso already had a ranch called the Sobrado ('Big House') on the far side of the São Francisco. He sent men ahead to explore Piauí and then followed himself with his band of retainers.

354 *many lawsuits.* Domingos Afonso's will, June 1711, RHGB **20** 144 ff; HCJB **5** 550–65; Boxer, *Golden Age* 234.

354 *Sire?'* Domingos Jorge Velho to King, Serra da Barriga ('Belly Mountain'), Palmares, 15 July 1694, Ernesto Ennes, *As guerras nos Palmares*, Brasiliana **127** (São Paulo, 1938) 204–7, trans. in Richard M. Morse, *The Bandeirantes: the historical role of the Brazilian pathfinders* 118, or C. R. Boxer, *Race Relations in the Portuguese Colonial Empire, 1415–1825* 94–5. On the first penetration of Piauí, see: Rocha Pitta, *Historia* bk 6; Francisco Augusto

Pereira da Costa, *Chronologia Histórica do Estado do Piauhy* (Recife, 1909); Barbosa Lima Sobrinho, *O devassamento do Piauí* (Rio de Janeiro, 1946); Carlos Eugênio Porto, *Roteiro do Piauí* (Rio de Janeiro, 1955); HGBP **4**; Boxer, *Golden Age* 233–5. A damaged document relating to a sesmaria, of 1705, mentioned that the previous year Domingos Jorge Velho's widow Jerônima Cardim Frois had petitioned, together with Cristóvão de Mendonça Arrais, claiming that they had been in Piauí for twenty-four or twenty-five years. There is some confusion about this: some historians think that she meant twenty-five years before 1687 (a date also mentioned in the petition), rather than before 1704. Hélio Vianna, *História do Brasil* **1** 221–2.

355 *fields he owns.'* Letter by Bishop of Pernambuco to Junta das Missões, 18 May 1697, quoted in Junta's Opinion of October 1697, Edison Carneiro, *Guerras de los Palmares* (Mexico, 1946) 133–4; Ennes, *As guerras nos Palmares* 353; Boxer, *Golden Age* 233–4; Morse, *Bandeirantes* 125.

355 *Dom Diogo Pinheiro Camarão.* Portaria, 11 April 1674, DH **8** 187–8. There is an extensive biography about Palmares, notably the studies by Ernesto Ennes and Edison Carneiro, already cited, and Stuart B. Schwartz, 'The Mocambo: Slave Resistance in Colonial Bahia', *Journal of Social History* **3** 1970; R. K. Kent, 'Palmares: an African State in Brazil', *Journal of African History*, **6**, Cambridge, 1965.

356 *such misery. . . .'* Petition on behalf of Domingos Jorge Velho and his men, Ennes, *As guerras nos Palmares* 317–44, trans. in Morse, *Bandeirantes* 119–20. João da Cunha Souto Maior to King, Bahia, 7 Nov 1685, ibid. 116–17; the Patent to Domingos Jorge Velho was dated 12 March 1695; HBP **1** 174.

356 *his wife.* Governor of Brazil to King, 8 Oct 1649, DHBC **3** 183–4.

356 *for all'.* Queen-Regent Luiza de Gusmão to Governor-General Francisco Barreto, 9 Jan 1662, in Taunay, *A Guerra dos Bárbaros* 19–20. The Queen feared that the Janduins might become indomitable

enemies like the Araucanians of southern Chile.

356 *[Jesuit] aldeias'.* Royal appointment of João Tavares de Almeida as Capitão-Mór of Ceará, Lisbon, 2 Oct 1673, DHBC 4 182.

357 *His Royal Highness.'* Petition by Chiefs Algodão, Aragiba, Cachoe and Maxure, aldeia of Parangava, 10 Aug 1671, DHBC 4 174–5. Chief Algodão, or his father, had been a close friend of Martim Soares Moreno, the first Portuguese coloniser of Ceará. He was with the tribes that took sanctuary in Ibiapaba. In 1656 he turned against his Portuguese friends and marched his tribe to the Camocim River, then called Rio da Cruz: a fort was built there to intimidate his Tobajara (André Vidal de Negreiros to King, 8 July 1656, DHBC 3 199). Two years later he was corresponding with António Vieira and asking for more Jesuit missionaries: Vieira to Father Provincial, Maranhão, 10 June 1658, DHBC 3 211. In 1661 he was back in favour, appointed Capitão-Mór of the Indians of Ceará and rewarded with fine clothing: Francisco de Brito Freire, Recife, 11 April 1661, DHBC 4 120–1, and Francisco Barreto, Recife, 17 April 1662, ibid. 4 136.

357 *children and women.'* Capitão-Mór Jorge Correa da Silva instructions to Francisco Martins, Ceará, 11 Oct 1671, DHBC 4 177.

357 *the same ravages.'* Mathias da Cunha to Goyernor of Pernambuco, Bahia, 17 June 1687, DH 10 245; Taunay, *Guerra dos Barbaros* 31. The first appeal from Natal was dated 23 Feb 1687.

357 *abandon the Captaincy.'* Mathias da Cunha to Câmara of São Paulo, Bahia, 10 March 1688, DH 11 139–40, and to Domingos Jorge Velho, 8 March 1688, DH 10 262; Taunay, *Guerra dos barbaros* 31–3, and HBP 1 170.

358 *his own person'.* Mathias da Cunha patent to Domingos Jorge Velho, HBP 1 171; DH 10 312–15.

358 *those you capture.'* Mathias da Cunha to Domingos Jorge Velho, Bahia, 8 March 1688, DH 10 262. Cunha also ordered the mission aldeias in every province to send all able-bodied Indians on the campaign. As was customary, these men were not paid for their service, which was considered their duty to the King: DH 10 263–76.

358 *His Majesty's arms.'* Mathias da Cunha to Col. Antonio de Albuquerque da Camara, 14 March 1688, DH 10 280, 277–8.

358 *the barbarians'.* Mathias da Cunha to Bishop of Pernambuco, 29 Sept 1688, DH 10 306.

358 *70 wounded.* D. Frei Manuel da Ressureição, Archbishop-Governor, to Col. Antonio Cubas, 22 March 1689, Taunay, *Guerra dos bárbaros* 93; Carneiro, *Guerras de los Palmares* 121.

358 *Ceará.* Mathias da Cunha to Bishop-Governor of Pernambuco, 29 Sept 1688 and 12 Oct 1688, DH 10 306, 326, and various letters by him contrasting the success of the Paulistas with the cowardice of the Pernambucans, DH 10 315–23. Domingos Jorge Velho's four-day battle was fought in late Aug 1688: two Indians travelled for twenty-nine days to take news of it to the Governor. The suspicion about pirates was later confirmed when one was captured among the Janduin. The settlers and troops of Ceará resented Paulista intrusion so greatly that they were considered capable of supplying arms to the Indians to defeat Domingos Jorge's men.

358 *God's decree'.* Rocha Pitta, *Historia*, bk 7, p. 434.

359 *Adam.'* Archbishop-Governor, Bahia, 30 Nov 1688, DH 10 349.

359 *our garrisons.'* Archbishop-Governor Frei Manoel to Câmara of São Paulo, 30 Nov 1688, DH 11 142.

359 *discipline and endurance.'* Archbishop-Governor Frei Manoel to Camara Coutinho, Governor of Pernambuco, HBP 1 175; Pero Tacques de Almeida Paes Leme, 'Nobiliarchia Paulistana . . .', RHGB 33 pt 2, 54–5, 146, 165–6, 1870, 34 pt 1, 225, 1871; Archbishop-Governor to Câmara de São Paulo, asking for help, Bahia, 30 Nov 1688, DH 11 142–5, and to Matias Cardoso, 9 Dec 1688, DH 11 146–9, to Capitão-Mór de São Vicente, 1 Sept 1689, DH 11 158,

and to Agostinho Cesar de Andrade, Capitão-Mór of Rio Grande, 10 March 1690 sacking Antonio Albuquerque da Camara and appointing Matias Cardoso de Almeida, DH 10 383; Patents to Matias Cardoso and his officers, 6–12 April 1690 and 19–29 July 1690, DH 30 7–35, 99–114.

359 *their families'*. Archbishop-Governor to Governor of Pernambuco, 9 March 1690, DH 10 391.

359 *Tapuiá.'* Archbishop-Governor Frei Manoel to Domingos Jorge Velho, 27 Aug 1689, DH 10 373, and to Câmara of Natal, same date, ibid. 10 365–7. The Jesuit aldeia was Guariri, which became the town of Estremoz.

360 *killed 600.* Memorandum by Manoel Alvares de Morais Navarro to João de Lancastre, 26 July 1694, and Petition by him to King, 15 Nov 1696, Taunay, *Guerra dos bárbaros* 143–51, 163–71, or HGB 1 176–80. The aldeia of Guaraíras became the town of Arês.

361 *Dutch wars.* Camara Coutinho to thank Chief Paupina, 30 Jan 1692 – he told the chief that the King of Portugal would 'probably' reward him for his tribe's alliance, DH 10 422–4; Archbishop-Governor Frei Manoel to Governor of Pernambuco, 9 March 1690, DH 10 391, about the role of Camarão's Indians. Many letters refer to levies of mission Indians, DH 11 148, 10 336, etc. In 1693 Sebastião Pinheiro Camarão replaced Diogo Pinheiro Camarão as Governor of the Indians, DH 38 299.

361 *chains for execution.* Antonio Luiz Gonçalves da Camara Coutinho, Governor-General, to Agostinho Cesar de Andrade, Capitão-Mór of Rio Grande, Bahia, 2 April 1691, DH 10 408–9, and congratulations to Cristóvão de Mendonça, 3 April 1691, ibid. 10 412–13; Taunay, *Guerra dos bárbaros* 110, 117–18.

362 *Brazil.'* Antonio Luiz Gonçalves da Camara Coutinho to officials of Espírito Santo, Bahia, 15 Dec 1691, DH 11 179; Camara Coutinho to King, 19 June 1691, DH 33 340: the King had written that every aldeia must have a missionary but no secular administrators. DH 33 344–6, about buying freedom of Rio Grande captives and sending them to Rio de Janeiro, to which the King agreed on 16 Feb 1692, Camara Coutinho to King, 4 July 1692, DH 34 61. The Governor-General had written, shortly before receiving the King's letter, that the Janduin captives, the people of King Canindé, should be given to Domingos Jorge Velho for use in a campaign against the black mocambo of Palmares (Camara Coutinho to Agostinho Cesar de Andrade, Capitão-Mór of Rio Grande, 2 April 1691, DH 10 409); but on 11 Dec 1691 he sent the same Capitão-Mór a copy of the King's decree on the liberty of Indians, and deplored Domingos Jorge Velho's abuse and sale of his prisoners, DH 10 414.

362 *keeping faith?'* Camara Coutinho to Agostinho Cesar de Andrade, 17 April 1692, DH 10 425, and to Constantino de Oliveira, same date, ibid. 10 426–7.

362 *for ratification.* Camara Coutinho to King, 4 July 1692, DH 34 64. Two weeks later the Governor wrote to the King recalling that when he had been Governor of Pernambuco, in 1686 or 1687 – before the Rio Grande war – two envoys had come from King Canindé requesting peace from the King of Portugal; which Camara Coutinho had granted (Camara Coutinho to King, 18 July 1692, DH 34 42). The delegation was also received by the Secretary of State for War, Bernardo Vieira Ravasco, who was the brother of the great Jesuit António Vieira.

362 *King of the Janduin'.* HGBP 8 287–8, HBP 1 176; Taunay, *Guerra dos bárbaros* 130–4; Ennes, *A Guerra nos Palmares* 472.

362 *live in peace'.* Treaty of 10 April 1692, HGBP 8 290. Camara Coutinho to Capitão-Mór of Rio Grande, 17 April 1692, DH 10 425. Nothing is known about João Paes Floriano except that he was married to the daughter of chief Nhonguge, who was also father of Canindé's wife. The other chiefs leading the delegation were called by their baptismal names: Joseph de Abreu Vidal and Miguel Pereira Guajeru Pequeno.

362 *wished to live'.* Ibid.; HGBP **8** 291.

363 *Janduin territory.* João de Lancastre to Matias Cardoso de Almeida, Bahia, 4 June 1694, DH **38** 304; the King had written on 6 March 1694 ordering that six such villages be created along the Açu, Jaguaribe and Piranhas rivers. Various letters of 1694 and 1695 relate to these moves: DH **38** 315, 338, 346–7, 408. The aldeia of Jundiá was later merged with that of Guaraíras (modern Arês). In 1696 an aldeia of tame Cariri and the aldeia of Mamanguape were moved to Janduin territory on the Piranhas river.

363 *São Francisco.* Letter from Capitão-Mór Fernão Carrilho, 26 June 1694, Taunay, *Guerra dos bárbaros* 151, 171–2, HBP **1** 179. His lieutenant Mançel Álvares Morais Navarro was sent south in 1694 to help Domingos Jorge Velho against the Palmares: Petition by Navarro, 15 Dec 1696, HBP **1** 182. His other lieutenant João Amaro Maciel Parente also petitioned for rewards, 12 Jan 1696; Taunay, *Guerra dos bárbaros* 173–9; Paes Leme, 'Nobiliarchia Paulistana,' RHGB **33** pt 2, 168, 1870, and **34** pt 1, 226, 1871.

364 *very suspect'.* João de Lancastro to Bernardo Vieira de Mello, Capitão-Mór of Rio Grande, 14 July 1696, DH **38** 400; Paes Leme, 'Nobiliarchia Paulistana,' RHGB **33** pt 2, 167–8, 1870.

364 *mission villages created.* João de Lancastro to Capitão-Mór of Paraíba, 21 May 1695, and to Bernardo Vieira de Mello, 26 Nov 1695 and 2 Nov 1696, DH **38** 338, 378–80, 411–13; Taunay, *Guerra dos bárbaros* 187–8.

364 *a universal peace'.* Natal Câmara to King, ibid. 201. The king granted their request, 18 Nov 1697.

364 *to be cut'.* Manoel Álvares de Morais Navarro to João de Lancastro, 26 July 1694; ibid. 147.

364 *Brazil.'* João de Lancastro to Câmara of São Paulo, 19 Oct 1697, HBP **1** 183. He sent money to recruit and transport men, and a force left Santos and reached Bahia in August 1698. DH **38** 444–8.

364 *oppressed it'.* Lancastro to Navarro, 21 Jan 1699, DH **39** 6.

364 *they take prisoner'.* Lancastro to Fernando Martins Mascarenhas de Lancastro, Governor of Pernambuco, 11 Nov 1699, DH **39** 87.

364 *Indians.* Lancastro to Capitão-Mór of Ceará, 21 Jan 1699, DH **39** 21.

364 *secure his captives.* Lancastro to Navarro, 2 Aug 1699, DH **39** 72–3.

365 *in this captaincy'.* Gonçalo Ferreira da Ponte deposition to Câmara of Natal, 5 March 1699; Taunay, *Guerra dos bárbaros* 205.

365 *forces were limited.'* Manoel Álvares de Morais Navarro to João de Lancastro, 29 Aug 1699; ibid. 224.

365 *broke his head.'* Navarro, in ibid. 225.

366 *limited forces.'* Ibid. 222–3.

366 *Tapuia.* Ibid. 226.

366 *sold as slaves.* João Guedes report, undated, Ibiapaba, MACC **2** 398. Guedes said that the first volley killed eighty-five Paiacu.

366 *with them.'* Taunay, *Guerra dos bárbaros* 238. Navarro said that the Paiacu had helped the Uriús Grandes when they were attacked by Constantino de Oliveira Ledo in 1697. João da Costa, Jesuit missionary of the aldeia on the Jaguaribe, admitted to an ecclesiastical enquiry that Navarro had consulted him before attacking the Paiacu. Costa asked Navarro only that he spare converted Indians. Asked if he felt the massacre would damage his mission, Costa 'replied that he had no scruples about it: only if Indians were well punished could he reap any harvest with them'. He told Navarro that if Indians refused to submit 'he should make them burn'; but the Paulista had 'burned the dry wood with the green', or the heathen with the baptised (Enquiry by Padre Pero Fernandes, in Taunay, *Guerra dos bárbaros* 233). The massacre took place on the site of the modern town of Limoeiro, between the Jaguaribe and Banabiú in Ceará. The Bishop of Pernambuco was Dom Frei Francisco de Lima, and his pastoral condemning Navarro was issued on 19 Sept 1699. João de Lancastro wrote him an angry letter on 11 Nov 1699 because his junta had ruled against the Paulistas and believed João

da Costa rather than Navarro: DH 39 93. Navarro also charmed a German Jesuit, João Guinzel, sent to investigate. Guinzel wrote to the Governor-General Lancastro on 29 Oct 1699 praising Navarro's endurance and patience: 'I confess that when I heard news of the slaughter done to these people I was seriously disconsolate. However, when I later heard of the reasons that obliged [Navarro] to make war on them, I had no course but to confirm God's will.' Only with the Paulista regiment camped on the Açu could the Tapuia tribes 'be kept in the subjection necessary to achieve the desired fruits with them' (Taunay, *Guerra dos bárbaros* 242).

366 *Paiacú tribe'.* Lancastro to Navarro, 8 April 1701, DH 39 141. Lancastro wrote on the same date ordering the Ouvidor-Geral of Paraíba to go to Navarro's camp and arrest him with a minimum of uproar. He also wrote to appoint José de Morais Navarro to command the Paulista regiment; DH 39 138. Lancastro had written to King Pedro II on 7 Jan 1700 defending Navarro, who himself wrote to the King on 11 May saying how useful the massacre had been. The King was unimpressed: he ordered the Paulistas to march north against Ceará and Maranhão Indians, 13 Jan 1700, DH 39 114; he then ordered Navarro's arrest. The King was influenced by a campaign led by a missionary, Father Miguel de Carvalho, and a letter of 29 June 1700 from the Bishop Frei Francisco de Lima violently condemning the slaughter as unchristian and illegal and Navarro himself as a man of 'scandalous life'.

366 *Brazil'.* Navarro petition, 1732; Taunay, *Guerra dos bárbaros* 238. The report of Navarro's arrest was sent to Lancastro by Cristóvão Soares Reimão, Paraíba, 8 July 1701, DH 39 153. Lancastro wrote to Navarro commiserating about it, 21 June 1701, DH 39 146–7. The next Governor-General Rodrigo da Costa wrote congratulating him on regaining his freedom, 17 Sept 1703, ibid. 39 187. Many governors wrote letters about the

pay of the Paulista regiment. Luís César de Meneses said on 12 Sept 1707 that he considered the men receiving pay in it were 'almost all fantastic', DH 39 237; but it was still being paid in 1715, DH 40 71.

367 *skins. . . .'* Francisco Teixeira de Moraes, *Relação historica e politica . . .*, RHGB 40 pt 1, 150–1, 1877.

367 *in the 1650s.* The fort was called São João Baptista. Its first commander was Pascoal Paes Parente, who spent eight years there, repelling Corso raids and recapturing prisoners they carried off; Petition for rewards, Lisbon, 11 Aug 1674, DHBC 4 184. Teixeira de Moraes, *Relação historica* 151–2. The fort was abandoned because of Indian attack, and the King wrote to the Governor of Maranhão, 2 Sept 1684, suggesting that it be rebuilt: LGM 1 65.

367 *the mouths of cannon.* Teixeira de Moraes, *Relação historica* 154; João Felippe Betendorf, *Chronica da missão dos Padres de Jesus . . .*, 319–20; Bernardo Pereira de Berredo, *Annaes historicos do Estado do Maranhão . . .*, bk 18, pp. 578–9.

367 *[universal] also'.* Ibid. bk 18, p. 579. The campaign of 1679 violated a peace made three years earlier with the Tremembé; Report by Father Pero de Pedrosa, São Luís do Maranhão, 25 Aug 1682, DHBC 4 232.

368 *instead of manacling.'* Teixeira de Moraes, *Relação historica* 154; Berredo, *Annaes*, bk 18, pp. 579–80. HGB 3 298; HGBP 8 282.

368 *military glory.'* Berredo, *Annaes*, bk 18, p. 581. Some Tremembé later returned to the Jesuit mission of Tutóia on the coast of Maranhão. In 1720 Father Domingos Ferreira Chaves complained that the Capitão-Mór of Ceará kept forcing them to go for months on end, with their women and children, to gather turtles for him on the Jaguaribe (MACC 2 404). In 1730 King João V ordered the Governor of Maranhão to arrest three Lopes brothers and their cousin, an escaped murderer, who had been molesting the Tremembé (LGM 2 246–7).

368 *reputation and profit.'* Teixeira de

Moraes, *Relação historica* 155. The King had written to the Governor of Maranhão, 1 Dec 1677, encouraging him to continue exploring the Paraguaçu, because of its many tribes, 'in whose conversion you could do great service to God and could augment that State' (LGM 1 41–2).

368 *their known resistance'.* King to Governor of Maranhão, Lisbon, 8 Feb 1691, LGM 1 114. Also ibid. 72, 110, 112–13, 139.

369 *because of smallpox'.* King to Câmara of Pará, Lisbon, 10 Jan 1697, LGM 1 166, and to Câmara of Maranhão, 10 Dec 1695, ibid. 1 155. On the Beckman rebellion, see Berredo, *Annaes*, bks 18–19, pp. 588–625, or Teixeira de Moraes, *Relação histórica*, RHGB 40 pt 1, 303–410, 1877. That rebellion was fought as much by pen as by sword, and there were volumes of protests by impoverished settlers and outraged Jesuits.

369 *all punishment.'* King Pedro II to Câmara of São Paulo, 2 Nov 1693, in Paes Leme, 'Nobiliarchia Paulistana', RHGB 34 pt 1, 13, 1871.

370 *on which to live.'* Miguel de Carvalho report to Bishop of Pernambuco, Piauí, 2 March 1697, in Ernesto Ennes, *Os Palmares. Subsídios para a sua história* (Lisbon, 1937) 148–71; HGBP 7 chs 35–6, HBP 1 188. Mocha with its tiny church was known by the resounding name 'Parish of Our Lady of the Victory of the Swamp of Mocha of the Sertão of Piauí', and is now the remote town of Oeiras on the Canindé tributary of the Parnaíba.

370 *to seek peace'.* King to Ouvidor-Geral of Maranhão, Lisbon, 28 Nov 1697, LGM 1 172. Earlier that year Domingos Jorge Velho offered to extinguish all the hostile Maranhão Indians, but it came to nothing since he was too busy fighting the Palmares and because 'there are no Indians in that State, and the aldeias are almost depopulated by smallpox' (King to Antonio d'Albuquerque Coelho de Carvalho, 17 Jan 1697, ibid. 1 167).

370 *be enslaved'.* King to Antonio d'Albuquerque Coelho de Carvalho, 10 Feb 1699, ibid. 1 186.

370 *have died'.* King to Manuel Rolim de Moura, 29 Jan 1703, ibid. 1 234. There had been wars against the Anaperu in Piauí in 1701 and 1702, but the white commander had treated them gently after surrender because of a request by the Jesuits of the Ibiapaba missions (Report by Father Antonio de Sousa Leal, *c.*1721, MACC 2 384).

371 *Felix da Cunha.* Report by Father Antonio de Sousa Leal, 1720, MACC 2 384–6, and by Father João Guedes, ibid. 2 395–6. These were both experienced and responsible missionaries: Sousa Leal had worked in the area for eighteen years. They pointed out that the Tapuia tribes living to the west of the Serra da Ibiapaba had long been on good terms with the missionaries there, and were at peace when attacked. The royal order to sound the bar of the Parnaíba in 1702 had insisted that there be no provocation of its Indians.

371 *tribes of Maranhão.* King to Cristóvão da Costa Freire, Lisbon, 9 April, 16 April, 15 Aug 1709, LGM 2 39, 52–3, 59; Marquis of Angeja to Lourenço de Almeida, Bahia, 9 Dec 1715, DH 40 67; Memorandum by Cristóvão de Caldas, Lisbon, 2 Feb 1721, MACC 2 299.

371 *insufferable men'.* Report to João Guedes, *c.*1720, MACC 2 396.

372 *laughter and gaiety'.* Antonio de Sousa Leal report, MACC 2 386, João Guedes report, ibid. 2 396–7.

372 *in their territory.* Father Domingos Ferreira Chaves, Missionary-General of Brazil, to King, Ceará, 23 Nov 1719, MACC 2 248–9; João Guedes report, ibid. 2 397. Anti-Indian propagandists claimed that the rebels desecrated churches and tore out the heart of Father Barbosa: Bernardo de Carvalho e Aguiar to King, undated, and Cristóvão de Caldas, Lisbon, 2 Feb 1721, MACC 2 299, 380. King João V to Bernardo Pereira de Berredo, Governor of Maranhão, Lisbon, 20 Oct 1718, LGM 2 162–3. The missionaries said this was untrue: Barbosa was shot by a musket and his body was not desecrated.

372 *going to Maranhão*. King to Cristóvão da Costa Freire, Governor of Maranhão, Lisbon, 17 Dec 1712, LGM **2** 110; Berredo, *Annaes* 675–6, 678. The expedition was led by Thomas do Valle, and had 'destroyed the greater part of the heathen inhabiting the forests of Iguará and Parnaíba' before being attacked by them. Bernardo de Carvalho e Aguiar to King, undated, MACC **2** 380. The authorities were still trying to fill the Fort of Iguará with mission Indians from Ceará in mid-1715; DH **40** 43–4. They also enlisted the help of Garcia de Ávila of the Casa da Tôrre against the Maranhão Indians in 1715: DH **40** 67, **42** 247. Frei Francisco de N. S. dos Prazeres, *Poranduba Maranhaense* (1826), RHGB **54** pt 1, 99, 1891. 'Volunteer' Indians from the São Francisco were forced to settle in Piauí, as a base against its tribes (DH **42** 334–5, 339, **43** 171, 362, etc.).

372 *not to be lost.'* Consultation of Conselho Ultramarino, Lisbon, 6 Oct 1718, MACC **2** 207; royal order to recruit 400 Indians from Camarão's aldeias and those of Ceará, 20 Oct 1718, ibid. **2** 210.

373 *their just resentment.'* João Guedes report, MACC **2** 397; Representação by Câmara of Ceará, 6 Nov 1719, ibid. **2** 240–3.

373 *in the forests'.* Father Domingos Ferreira Chaves to King, Ceará, 23 Nov 1719, MACC **2** 248–9.

373 *his allied chiefs.* Salvador Álvares da Silva, Capitão-Mór of Ceará, to King, Ceará, 15 Nov 1719, MACC **2** 244–7; Representação by Câmara of Ceará, São José de Ribamar, 6 Nov 1719, ibid. **2** 240–3; Consultation by Conselho Ultramarino, 16 Oct 1720, ibid. **2** 282–7. In a census of Jesuit missions in 1702 it was reported that four aldeias had been joined to form one containing 4000 persons: João Perreira, *Informação para a Junta das Missões de Lisboa*, Bahia, 5 July 1702, HCJB **5** 571. The Governor-General wrote to Chief Jacob de Sousa e Castro, 25 Feb 1715, thanking him for leading all his men against the Tapuia, DH **40** 10. Later that year the Jesuit superior of Ibiapaba tried to avoid sending Indians to fight in Piauí and

Maranhão, because his mission had suffered 160 killed by rebel Ceará Indians, King to Governor of Maranhão, 18 June 1715, LGM **2** 131. After their successes against Mandu Ladino, the Tobajara went on to fight the Anaú in late 1719. Chief Jacob de Sousa e Castro then went to Lisbon with his son to protest against a proposal to move his aldeia in Ibiapaba from the jurisdiction of Ceará to that of Maranhão. He asked that his men be armed by the Crown with firearms, and promised to defeat any rebellious Tapuia if so armed, ibid. **2** 253.

373 *the missionary'.* Father Francisco de Araújo, missionary of the Ribeira do Apodi mission, 20 March 1720, MACC **2** 266–7.

373 *were exterminated.* Report by Antonio de Sousa Leal, *c.*1720, MACC **2** 389.

374 *Ceará'.* Ibid. **2** 392.

374 *against beasts'.* Antonio Rodrigues da Costa to King, Lisbon, 20 Oct 1720, MACC **2** 279.

374 *to enslave them.* Report by Antonio de Sousa Leal, MACC **2** 391. A commentary on the terrible diminution of these tribes came from Father Domingos Ferreira Chaves, Visitor-General of the tribes of northern Ceará. He suggested in 1720 the formation of one mission for the Paiacu of the Jaguaribe, two missions for the Genipapo-açu (Paiacu) and Canindé, and one for the Cariri and 'what was left of the Icó, Quixolo, Cariú, Caratiú, Curiú and Iocás' (MACC **2** 401).

374 *allow them to live'.* Report by Antonio de Sousa Leal, MACC **2** 393.

375 *captured 25.* Carvalho de Aguiar to King, MACC **2** 380–1; King to Cristóvão da Costa Freire, 28 Oct 1717, to Bernardo Pereira de Berredo, 20 Oct 1718, and to João da Maia da Gama, 2 March 1725, LGM **2** 150–1, 162, 210. One group of Indians under Chief Mataroa went from the São Francisco river to help fight the Piauí Indians, and fought many battles and took many prisoners during six years of fighting: King to João da Maia da Gama, 30 Oct 1724, ibid. **2** 205–7.

375 *without motive'.* Antonio de Sousa

Leal report, MACC 2 384; King to Governor of Maranhão, 19 Dec 1716, LGM 2 146. The King said that the Barbados had done much damage on the Itapecuru, Mearim and Munim rivers. Berredo, *Annaes* 679.

375 *its head smashed*. Antonio Franco, *Synopsis annalium Societatis Jesu in Lusitania* (1726), in Antonio Henriques Leal, 'Apontamentos para a historia dos Jesuitas . . .', RHGB 36 pt 2, 268–9, 1873; Decision of Junta das Missões, São Luís do Maranhão, 30 March 1726, HC 3 439. The punitive expedition consisted of 60 or 70 paid soldiers, 14 settlers, 40 or 50 mission Indians, and 35 Caicais who wanted vengeance on the Barbados.

375 *that can be colonised'*. Decision of Junta da Missões, ibid, 3 442.

375 *necessary Indians. . .'*. Junta das Missões, ibid. 3 442.

375 *to their people'*. Junta das Missões, ibid. 3 443.

376 *was feared'*. King to Alexandre de Sousa Pereira, Lisbon, 23 Dec 1728, LGM 2 226–7. As a defensive measure against the Timbira, some Ibiapaba Indians were moved across to occupy an abandoned fort.

376 *'superabundantly populous'*. Francisco de Paula Ribeiro, *Memória sôbre as nações gentias que presentemente habitam o continente do Maranhão* (1819), RHGB 3 4, 1841; Curt Nimuendajú, *The Gamella Indians* 3.

Chapter 17   GOLD

377 *was opulent'*. Pero Tacques de Almeida Paes Leme, 'Nobiliarchia Paulistana . . .', HBP 1 111.

378 *old woodsmen'*. Paes Leme ('Nobiliarchia Paulistana . . .', RHGB 35 pt 1, 313, 1872) in fact tells the story about one Francisco Pires Ribeiro, but in modern legend it was Anhangüera's trick. Two early historians of Goiás both attributed it to Anhangüera: Father Luiz Antonio da Silva e Sousa, *Memoria . . .*, RHGB 12 432, 1849; J. M. Pereira de Alencastre, *Annaes da Provincia de Goyaz*, RHGB 27 pt 2, 29, 1864.

378 *tyrannies of killing.'* Paes Leme, 'Nobiliarchia Paulistana' RHGB, 35 pt 1, 106–9, 1872; HBP, 1 108. The Guayaña (or Goiana, Wayana, etc.) cleared great stretches of forest for Dias Pais, and were content with the abundant fish in the Tietê. Franciscan friars were brought to convert them, and their chief Tombu requested a death-bed baptism.

379 *sixteen years.'* Bento Fernandes Furtado de Mendonça, *Noticias dos primeiros descubridores das primeiras minas de ouro . . .*, in Afonso de Escragnolle Taunay, *Relatos sertanistas* 49.

379 *Casa de Casca'*. Ibid. 21.

379 *with much fury'*. Ibid. 49.

379 *support themselves'*. Ibid. 21–2.

379 *by gambling'*. Ibid. 22.

380 *Pitanguí. . . .'* Ibid. 24; the author was the son of the Colonel in the story, and claimed that in 1701 he discovered the stream of Nossa Senhora do Bom Sucesso, which was the source of the streams of Ouro Prêto. There were other versions of the discovery of the Ouro Prêto mines: the Camp Master José Rebelo Perdigão said that one Duarte Lopes found gold near what became Mariana when he was on Fernão Dias Pais' bandeira: *Noticia que dá ao R. P. Diogo Soares o Mestre-de-Campo José Rebello Perdigão*, in Taunay, *Relatos sertanistas* 172; Paes Leme attributed the discovery to Carlos Pedroso da Silveira and Bartolomeu Bueno de Siqueira; and João António Andreoni 'Antonil' said that the first gold was found by a mulatto from Taubaté who told Miguel de Sousa how to find the site of the deposit. Caeté (which means tall rain-forest, as opposed to smaller forest interspersed with campo) is a town on the site of the Casa de Casca, a few miles east of the booming modern city of Belo Horizonte.

380 *many instances.'* Anon, *Relação do principio descoberto destas Minas Gerais*, quoted in HBP 1 217, 2 301.

380 *São Paulo'*. Furtado de Mendonça,

Noticias 52. Borba Gato made a fortune mining gold on the Rio das Velhas, and his friend Governor Artur de Sá e Meneses persuaded the King to name him Admiral of a naval squadron. He never put to sea, but retired to a farm on the Parauvupeba river when his mines were exhausted. He died there in 1734, aged over ninety, and rather poor, 'which is the customary conclusion for those of this land'. Ibid. 54.

380 *and aptitude'*. Royal decree naming Tinoco as Capitão-mor of the Indians of the São Paulo aldeias, 22 Jan 1700, HGBP 9 297; he had been named as Procurator-General of the Indians on 2 Jan 1698.

381 *petition to us'*. Decree of São Paulo Câmara, 19 Jan 1705, HGBP 9 305. Carta regia, Lisbon, 18 Jan 1701, DI 51 10, thanking Tinoco de Sá for his efforts to return Indians to aldeias. Artur de Sá e Meneses, Minas Gerais, 26 Nov 1701, DI 51 50, orders that Indians working in mines return to their aldeias. The King wrote for comment on the Câmara's complaint of lack of Indians, 9 Dec 1701, DI 51 51, but Governor Álvaro da Silveira de Albuquerque wrote back, 20 Aug 1702, that the complaint was 'untimely'. In 1701 the chiefs of the aldeia of São Miguel appeared before the Câmara begging for a missionary because their village was infested with measles and Tinoco was failing to help. Tinoco attacked those who took Indians to the mines, on 4 March 1703; and on 3 Nov 1704 he tried to refuse an order from the Governor to furnish Indians to a priest called Joseph Dendon who was organising a gold prospecting expedition.

381 *royal aldeias!* King to Governor of Rio de Janeiro, 12 July 1706, DI 51 34; HGBP 9 306–8. Taunay, the great historian of the bandeirantes, was shocked at the 'many outrages and violences committed against the elementary rights of the poor Indians in the question of conceding sesmaria allotments' in flagrant violation of royal orders: ibid. 9 308.

383 *the next day.'* *Notícias que dá ao Padre Mestre Diogo Soares o Alferes José Peixoto da Silva Braga do que se passou na primeira bandeira que entrou no descobrimento das minas dos Guaiazes até sair na cidade de Belém do Grão Pará*, HGBP 11 56–7; also in Taunay, *Relatos sertanistas* 121–37. Diogo Soares was a Jesuit who reached Brazil in 1729, charged by King João V to make maps of the coast and interior. He diligently questioned bandeirantes and assembled a valuable collection of travellers' reports on the Brazilian interior, which he called *Notícias práticas*. For further information about him, see: Serafim Soares Leite, *Diogo Soares, SJ, matemático, astronomo e geógrafo da sua Magestade no Estado Brasil* (Lisbon, 1947). Diogo Soares' *Notícias práticas* has been published, in Évora in 1949.

383 *Anhangüera....'* José Peixoto da Silva Braga, in HGBP 11 58.

384 *in the attempt'.* Rodrigo César de Meneses to King, 24 April 1725, DI 32 136; HGBP 11 pt 1, 79. The Tocantins was called Paraupava at that time. The bandeirantes who escaped by descending the Tocantins saw frequent traces of Indian settlement along the upper river. When they reached a new Jesuit mission on the Tocantins below the confluence of the Araguaia, they frightened the mission Indians by appearing naked and with firearms. The Jesuit missionary feared that they were Manaus Indians, who obtained guns by trading with the Dutch and were fighting the missionaries on the Tocantins, not so far from Dutch Surinam (Peixoto da Silva Braga, in E. Bradford Burns (ed.), *A Documentary History of Brazil* 114).

384 *barren wilderness*. Rodrigo César de Meneses to King, São Paulo, 27 Oct 1725, in J. M. Pereira de Alencastre, *Annaes*, RHGB 27 pt 2, 40–1, 1864; Silva e Sousa, *Memoria*, RHGB 12, 433–6, 1849.

384 *their women'.* Ibid. 12 436. The itinerary of Anhangüera's bandeiras has been studied in depth by João Pandiá Calógeras, *Reconstituição dos roteiros de Silva Braga e Urbano do Couto*, and by Taunay, HBP 2 197–211.

384 *no longer'.* Silva e Sousa, *Memoria* 438;

José de Sousa de Azevedo Pizarro e Araújo, *Memorias historicas da Provincia do Rio de Janeiro* 9 217. The theory that runaway Carijó were the origin of the Canoeiros, who lived on the Tocantins and the Serra Dourada, was advanced by Raymundo José da Cunha Mattos, *Chorographia historica da provincia de Goyaz* (c.1825), RHGB 38 pt 1, 19, 1875. The town of Goiás still has some eighteenth-century architecture. It has not developed like other cities in the State of Goiás – Goiânia, Anápolis or the federal enclave of Brasília.

385 *other ornaments'*. Joseph Barbosa de Sá, *Relação das povoaçõens do Cuyabá e Mato Grosso . . .*, HGBP 10 pt 3, 5.

385 *Caiapó'*. Paes Leme, 'Nobiliarchia Paulistana', RHGB 34 pt 1, 190, 1871.

385 *at all.'* Barbosa de Sá, *Relação*, HGBP, 10 pt 3, 7.

386 *'much was lost'*. Gervasio Leite Rebelo, *Relação verdadeira da derrota e viagem que fez de São Paulo para as minas do Cuyabá o Exmo. Sr. Rodrigo César de Menezes . . .* (c.1727), HGBP 11 pt 2, 35, 109.

386 *destruction of everything'*. Ibid. 11 2, 40.

386 *this risk.'* Antonio Rolim de Moura, Count of Azambuja, *Relação da viagem que fez . . . da cidade de S. Paulo para a Villa de Cuyaba em 1751*, RHGB 7 464, 1845.

386 *remedy for them'*. Rebelo, *Relação* 42.

387 *of the [piranha].'* Robert Southey, *History of Brazil* (1817–22 ed.) 1 131; Cabeza de Vaca, *Naufragios y comentarios* (Madrid, 1922 ed.) 201.

387 *abandon these. . . .'* Francisco Mendes, *Carta . . . sobre las costumbres, religion, terreno y tradiciones de los Yndios Mbayás . . .*, Jaime Cortesão, *Do Tratado de Madri à conquista dos Sete Povos (1750–1802)* 62.

387 *horses and sheep'*. Francisco Rodrigues do Prado, *Historia dos indios Cavalleiros ou da nação Guaycurú*, RHGB 1 35, 1839.

387 *South America.* The theory of indigenous horses was not as absurd as it might appear. There had in fact been prehistoric horses in South America: their bones were found by the early conquistadores and by Charles Darwin and later palaeontologists. But these horses (and the giant ostriches and other beasts) had died out long before horses

were reintroduced by the sixteenth-century European colonists.

387 *can be seen'*. António Pires de Campos, *Breve noticia . . . do gentio bárbaro que ha na derrota da viagem das minas do Cuyabá e seu reconcavo . . .* (1727) RHGB 25 440, 1862.

387 *six or eight thousand horses.'* Ricardo Franco de Almeida Serra, *Parecer sobre o aldêamento dos indios uaicurús e guanás . . .*, RHGB 7 202, 1845.

387 *slightest exertion'*. Ibid. 7 354.

387 *all their glory'*. Mendes, *Carta* 61.

387 *cure it.'* José Sánchez Labrador, *El Paraguay católico* (1770) 1 298; Guido Boggiani, *Os Caduveo,* introduction by Herbert Baldus 18.

388 *regroup them.'* Labrador, *El Paraguay católico* 1 245.

388 *a saddlecloth.'* Manoel Ayres do Casal, *Chorografia Brasílica* (1817) 1 279. Riding in the Paraguayan Chaco, one is often in water up to the horse's girth: the Guaicuru could easily have found such places to break in their horses.

388 *for war.'* Almeida Serra, *Parecer*, RHGB 13 368, 1850.

388 *women and children'*. Ibid. 13 368–9.

388 *as late as possible.'* Ibid. 13 370.

389 *'are all beasts'*. Carta annua by Diego Ferrer, Itatín, 21 Aug 1633, Jaime Cortesão, *Jesuítas e bandeirantes no Itatim (1596–1760)* 46; Alonso de Barzana letter, 1594, in Jiménez de la Espada, *Relaciones Geográficas de Índias*, BAE (Continuación) 184 83, 1964; Andrés de Rada replies to questions by royal ouvidor, 23 Oct 1644. Cortesão, *Jesuítas* 279.

389 *in the army'*. Father Pero de Lascamburu, *Dificultades para un viage a Chiquitos,* in Cortesão, *Itatim* 306–7; Andrés de Rada answers, ibid. 280–1; Frei Gabriel de Valencia to Governor of Tucumán, 8 May 1657, ibid. 256.

389 *into the forest.'* Prado, *Historia* 20.

390 *in doing.'* Almeida Serra, *Parecer*, RHGB 13 357, 1850.

390 *rearing the child'*. Prado, *Historia* 22.

390 *raise and sustain.'* Mendes, *Carta,* in Cortesão, *Do Tratado de Madri* 61; Almeida Serra, *Parecer* 357.

390 *loved ones'*. Labrador, *El Paraguay*

católico 2 31; Baldus introduction to Boggiani, *Os Caduveo* 22.

390 *more easily.'''* Manuel Felix de Azara, *Viajes por la America Meridional* (Madrid, 1923) 66–7. Azara commanded the Spanish frontier in Paraguay from 1781 to 1801.

390 *one or none.'* Labrador, *El Paraguay católico* 2 31.

390 *will cease.'* Prado, *Historia* 26.

391 *Cuiabá'.* Azara, *Viajes* 65.

391 *four thousand'.* Prado, *História* 23–4.

391 *their jalata.'* Almeida Serra, *Parecer* 358.

391 *sustained effort.'* Prado, *Historia*, RHGB 1 23; Labrador, *El Paraguay católico* 1 244–5; Kalervo Oberg, *The Terena and the Caduveo of Southern Mato Grosso, Brazil* (Washington, DC, 1949) 5.

391 *in this.'* Mendes, *Carta* 62.

391 *Portuguese.'* Almeida Serra, *Parecer*, RHGB 7 196, 1845.

392 *that tribe.'* Ibid., RHGB 13 349, 1850.

392 *contemplate this.'* Ibid. 13 349–50.

392 *all their lives'.* Mendes, *Carta* 62. The French traveller Francis de Castelnau, comte de Laporte, described the women's facial decoration being done with a stick dipped in a mixture of charcoal and genipapo, or printed on with a seal: *Expédition dans les parties centrales de l'Amérique du Sud*, 6 vols (Paris, 1850–9) 2 472. Claude Lévi-Strauss has photographs of women's faces decorated with these arabesques, in his *Tristes tropiques*.

392 *very wrinkled.'* Ayres do Casal, *Chorografia brasílica* (1945 ed.) 1 277–8.

392 *do it together.'* Almeida Serra, *Parecer*, RHGB 13 353–4. Antonio Vázquez de Espinosa wrote, in about 1630, that young Guaicuru warriors were initiated in an agonizing ceremony during which their penises were pierced with the serrated tails of sting-rays and their faces and chests smeared with the resulting blood. He also wrote that the Guaicuru 'act like stallions with mares with their young women to debauch them': *Compendio y descripción de las Indias Occidentales*, bk 5, ch. 42, trans. Charles Upson Clark (Washington, DC, 1968) 684.

392 *although amiable.'* Mendes, *Carta* 64.

393 *bout or festival'.* Ibid. 63.

393 *carousing and festivities'.* Almeida Serra, *Parecer*, RHGB 13 354.

393 *river.'* Ibid. 13 354–5, 357.

393 *less than a year.'* Mendes, *Carta* 60.

393 *other woman.'* Almeida Serra, *Parecer*, RHGB 13 356.

393 *their horses.* Ricardo Franco de Almeida Serra, *Discripção geográphica da Província de Matto Grosso* (1797), RHGB 6 179, 1844.

393 *complete freedom'.* Mendes, *Carta* 59.

394 *condescension.'* Labrador, *El Paraguay católico* 1 273.

394 *vital juice.'* Ibid. 2 14.

394 *contradictory ideas'.* Almeida Serra, *Parecer*, RHGB 7 197, 1845.

394 *carnal pleasures.'* Azara, *Viajes* (1809) 2 96–7; Roberto Cardoso de Oliveira, *O processo de assimilação dos Terena* (Rio de Janeiro, 1960) 30–7; Baldus introduction to Boggiani, *Os Caduveo* 26. The Alsatian Ulrich Schmidel first recorded the relationship between the two tribes in the mid-sixteenth century.

394 *used to suffer'.* Almeida Serra, *Parecer* 199.

395 *emphasis and arrogance.'* Mendes, *Carta* 62.

395 *desired it.'* Azara, *Viajes* (1923) 56.

395 *good and evil.'* Mendes, *Carta* 67.

395 *so abundant.'* Ibid. 68.

395 *Paraguay.* The Guaicuru language is now considered separate from other language groups. Tribes that spoke Guaicuru included the Mbaiá (the people described by Francisco Mendes and others, of whom one branch are the modern Caduveu of southern Mato Grosso); the Guatchi (who lived on the Miranda river, Mato Grosso, in the nineteenth century but are now extinct); the Paiaguá (the fierce Canoeiros of the Paraguay river); the Toba (or Tokoit or Frontones) who now live on the banks of the Pilcomayo; the Mokovi, who mingled with the Toba and whose descendants live in the Argentine province of Santa Fé; and the Abipon or Callaga, now extinct, who used to roam the Chaco.

The Caduveu were special favourites

of the Brazilian Emperor Dom Pedro II. When they helped Brazil repel the Paraguayan invasion of Mato Grosso in 1865, the Emperor rewarded the tribe with a vast stretch of land in the Pantanal and Serra da Bodoquena. Almost all this land is now leased to cattle ranchers, and the few surviving Caduveu live very simply at a remote Funai (Indian Service) post. Their huts are scattered in woods around a grassy open space ringed by beautiful forested cliffs. These huts have a nomadic look, consisting only of two pitched thatch roofs supported by poles and with both ends open. The Caduveu now sleep in hammocks, but their floors are covered with the traditional matting and skins, and the women make pottery decorated with the cursive geometric designs that used to adorn their faces. The Caduveu long ago abandoned the Guaicuru practice of abortion, but the tribe is still under 200 persons. Many of these are elderly, thin and wrinkled, but with a dignity worthy of their proud ancestry.

396 *Algeria'*. Father Diego Francisco de Altamirano, Annua of 1653–4, Cordova, 31 Dec 1654, in Cortesão, *Itatim* 199. Ulrich Schmidel had first mentioned the Paiaguá, who lured the early sixteenth-century conquistador Juan de Ayolas into a swamp and killed him and all his men: Southey, *History of Brazil* 1 84; Diego de Boroa Annua of 1614, in Cortesão, *Itatim* 25, and Diego Ferrer Annua of 1633, ibid. 47; Letter from Frei Gabriel de Valencia, 8 May 1657, ibid. 257, and other similar references, ibid. 280, 288, 302, 303–4; Vázquez de Espinosa, *Compendio*, bk 5, ch. 43, trans. Clark, 686.

396 *Guaicuru.'* Report on a journey to discover a link between the Paraguay and Chiquitos missions, 1703, Cortesão, *Jesuítas a bandeirantes no Paraguai (1703–1751)* 21.

396 *deserted now.'* Father Bartolomé Ximenez, Report on journey from Paraguay to Chiquitos, 1703, ibid. 53.

397 *to have wings.'* Pires de Campos, *Breve noticia* RHGB 25 440, 1862; HGBP 10 pt 3, 35, 168–9; Augusto Leverger, Barão

de Melgaço, *Apontamentos cronológicos da Provincia de Mato Grosso* (1856), RHGB 205 217–18, Oct–Dec 1949.

397 *their barbarity'*. Rodrigo César de Meneses to Ouvidor-Geral of Câmara of São Paulo, 10 Feb 1728, DI 13 135. This governor had actually made the difficult journey to Cuiabá, arriving in Nov 1726. On New Year's Day 1727 he elevated the mining-camp of 148 hearths to the status of royal town: Vila Real do Senhor Bom Jesus do Cuyabá. He imposed some order on the place in a series of edicts, in one of which he declared the need for wild Indians to be left in their precious natural liberty – an edict that Taunay, the historian of the bandeirantes, called 'delicious hypocrisy'. He also 'held consultations for a war against the Paiaguá – consultations that culminated in wind, vapour, nothing!' in the words of Barbosa de Sá, who hated Rodrigo Cesar de Meneses. HBP 2 60–1.

397 *up to now'*. Rodrigo César de Meneses, DI 13 135.

397 *the sun.'* João Antonio Cabral Camelo, Account of destruction of monção of Ouvidor Antonio Álvares Lanhas Peixoto, HGBP 11 pt 2, 50.

397 *with terror'*. Barbosa de Sá, *Relação*, HGBP 10 pt 3, 254.

398 *like fishes.'* Domingo Lourenço de Araújo, in Diogo Soares, *Notícias práticas*, HGBP 11 pt 2, 58–9.

398 *aquatic animals'*. Barbosa de Sá, *Relação*, HGBP 10 pt 3, 254.

398 *sold his life dearly'*. Leverger, *Apontamentos cronológicos* 222.

398 *the flotilla.* Rodrigues do Prado said that the Paiaguá attacked with over 500 men, losing 50; but Barbosa de Sá said they had only 300. Rodrigues do Prado wrote that they killed over 400 Christians and that only eight survived; but João Antonio Cabral Camelo, one of the survivors, said that 83 survived – 23 whites and 60 blacks – and 107 were killed.

398 *Diogenes himself.'* Barbosa de Sá, *Relação*, HGBP 10 pt 3, 254. The Paiagúa were not the only threat to the gold of Cuiabá. The King was entitled to a fifth of any gold mined there. His share of the

consignment of 1726 travelled in sealed chests, covered in locks, up and down the rivers and rapids of Mato Grosso. It reached São Paulo after months of travel, and then went to Rio de Janeiro in three large chests, escorted by a squadron of cavalry. It was shipped across the Atlantic in a heavily armed fleet, and ceremoniously opened by King João V in the presence of many of his courtiers. The locks and seals appeared to be intact. But when the King opened his chests they were found to contain no gold, but only lead shot! There was furore in Brazil. One official in São Paulo was arrested on suspicion of this appalling *lèse-majesté*; he was found to have false keys and, despite his protests, was imprisoned and had his huge fortune confiscated.

398 *had been slaughtered.'* Domingos Lourenço de Araújo report to Diogo Soares, HGBP **11** pt 2, 59; Cabral Camelo, Account of destruction of monção of Ouvidor Antonio Álvares Lanhas Peixoto, HGBP **11** pt 2, 52.

398 *the same as she.'* Letter by Don Carlos de los Reyes Valmaseda, Asunción, 4 Nov 1730, in Diogo Soares, *Notícias práticas*, HGBP **11** pt 2, 65.

398 *private parts'.* Ibid., 65.

398 *jaguar-skin cassocks'.* Ibid. 63.

399 *after the battle.* Juan Francisco Aguirre said that he met Cuatiguaçu at Asunción in 1783, *Noticia del Reino y Estado del Brasil*, quoted in Afonso de Escragnolle Taunay, *Ensaios de história paulista* 53, HGBP **10** pt 3, 254–5. Aguirre inserted into his *Noticia* a letter of about 1750 by Manoel de Flores to the Marquis of Valdelirios, which told about the arrival of the Paiaguá with their captured gold.

399 *day or night'.* Cabral Camelo report, HGBP **11** pt 2, 56. It is worth noting that, although mosquitoes were a plague, there was no mention of fevers or malaria on the Paraguay at that time. The same is true of eighteenth-century accounts of the Amazon. Malaria evidently arrived in the nineteenth century, after which there are frequent reports of fever.

399 *very proud. . . .'* Barbosa de Sá, *Relação*, HGBP **10** pt 3, 257.

400 *his return'.* Ibid.; Leverger, *Apontamentos cronologicos* 223.

400 *Paiaguá friends'.* Ibid. 224; Cabral Camelo, RHGB **4** 494, 1842; HGBP **10** pt 3, 263–5. Governor Antonio Luis de Tavora, Count of Sarzedas, to King, São Paulo, 6 Feb 1734, CDSP **2** 331.

400 *any captives:* Some of these letters and edicts can be found in: DI **13** 135, **22** 12, **24** 27, **40** 8, **41** 40–1, 51–2, 84; CDSP **2** 178–80, 184, 218–19, 241–2, 331–2, **3** 43, 61–3; HGBP **10** pt 3, 271–80.

401 *could be heard.'* Barbosa de Sá, *Relação*, HGBP **10** pt 3, 282.

401 *want them!'* Ibid.

401 *the mines.'* Governor Count of Sarzedas to Conselho Ultramarino, São Paulo, 24 Dec 1734, CDSP **3** 59–60, DI **40** 161.

401 *Portuguese nation!'* Count of Sarzedas to Câmara of Cuiabá, 31 March 1735, DI **41** 257.

402 *Paraguay.* José Gonçalves da Fonseca reported the Paiaguá's weakness in 1740 (*Noticia da situação de Mato-Grosso e Cuyabá*, RHGB **29** pt 1, 365, 1866) and Francisco José de Lacerda e Almeida said that in 1788 they were almost annihilated, largely by the Guaicuru (*Diario da viagem pelas capitanias do Pará, Rio Negro, Mato Grosso, Cuyabá e São Paulo, nos anos de 1760 a 1790* (São Paulo, 1841) 69). Later actions by the Paiaguá included the destruction of a camp on the Saipe in 1743; an attack on a flotilla in 1744 and on a fortified settlement on the Paraguay; and some attacks on isolated settlers near Cuiabá in 1753, 1770 and 1771 (Leverger, *Apontamentos cronológicos* 244, 267; HGBP **10** pt 3, 311). The Portuguese built forts at Coimbra in 1775 and Corumbá (then called Albuquerque) in 1778 to dominate the Paraguay river in what had been Paiaguá territory.

By the 1860s a few Paiagúa were living in filthy hide tents on the beaches of Asunción, peddling fish, firewood, canoe paddles and straw mats to the citizens, and getting drunk on the proceeds (Sérgio Buarque de Holanda, *Monções* 183). The Paiaguá were divided into two bands, the northern called

Saringué and the southern Maca (or Magatch, Agaces or Siakuá). Some Maca now live on an island up the river from the botanical gardens of Asunción, and can be visited on payment of an entrance fee.

402 *being procured.*' Pires de Campos, *Breve noticia*, RHGB **25** 443, 1862.

402 *features perfect.*' Ibid. **25** 444.

402 *to be believed.*' Ibid.

402 *reasonably cool.*' Ibid.

403 *Holy Faith*'. Provision by King João V, Lisbon, 11 March 1732, CDSP **2** 233.

403 *slaving-fodder.* It was the Count of Sarzedas who tried to organise the Parecis repatriation, São Paulo, 20 Sept 1732, CDSP **3** 62. Other orders relating to the Parecis: DI **13** 135, **20** 301–2, **22** 12, **41** 40–1, 84, 257; Leverger, *Apontamentos cronológicos* 223, 225; HGBP **10** pt 3, 259, 274, 287, etc.

403 *their liberty.* Sarzedas to Câmara of Cuiabá, 31 March 1735, DI **41** 257. Diogo Soares, the Jesuit who collected so many geographical accounts, cited the Parecis as a fine example of natural Indian liberty, in a letter to the town council of Taubaté, Santos, 12 Dec 1735, DI **2** 93.

The distinguished Argentinian historian Roberto Levillier argued that the Parecis region was El Paititi, the legendary refuge of the last Incas. Some Incas could have escaped from Cuzco eastwards down the Madre de Dios river and then up the Guaporé to reach the Parecis hills. Pizarro's Cretan gunner Pedro de Candia led a large expedition down the Madre de Dios in 1538 in search of this El Dorado. Juan Álvarez Maldonado followed the same route with an expedition in 1568. Both ventures failed miserably, defeated by the hardships of the forest and the hostility of its tribes (Levillier, *El Paititi, El Dorado y las Amazonas* (Buenos Aires, 1976) 85–112).

Other Spaniards approached this area from a different direction. Álvar Núñez Cabeza de Vaca left Asunción on 8 Sept 1543, sailing north up the Paraguay with 400 Spaniards and 800 Indians in ten brigantines and 120 canoes. At the end of

that year, having reached the upper Paraguay, Cabeza de Vaca sent out two reconnaissance expeditions. One of these, under Francisco de Ribera, took a brigantine upstream for 50 leagues. They reached a great lake – presumably Lake Uberaba or Lake Mandioré, then known as the lakes of Xarayes (Jerús). There the local Jerús Indians told them about a rich land inhabited by Amazons that lay ten days' journey to the north-west, which would be near the Parecis hills. Ribera's men tried to reach this land, but the journey was too hard. One soldier described it, in a passage that could apply to almost any exploration of central Brazil: '. . . we hacked through to the limit of our endurance for most of the time. We marched across that land to explore it, barefoot and naked, for many thousands of miles, with a bag of roast manioc flour over our shoulders and a gourd of water at our waists, carrying our weapons and opening a trail along which to travel, under rains falling on our heads, with nowhere to lodge other than in the shadow of some tree trunk' (Ambrosio Eusebio letter to Aretino, in Levillier, *El Paititi* 190; Ulrich Schmidel, *Wahrhaftige Historien einer Wunderbaren Schiffart*, chs 34–40; Padre Francisco González Paniagua, Memorial of 3 March 1545, *Revista de la Biblioteca Nacional de Buenos Aires* **1** 429–73, 1937). Nuflo de Chaves left Asunción in Feb 1558 to colonise the Xarayes lakes. But, although well received by the Indians there, he pressed on westwards and founded Santa Cruz de la Sierra in 1561.

403 *Brazil. . . .*' Anon, *Anal de Vila Bela desde o primeiro descobrimento dêste sertão de Mato Grosso, no ano de 1734* (c.1755), ed. Artur da Mota Alves, *Anaes do Museu Paulista* **10** HBP **2** 101.

404 *poor men*'. Barbosa de Sá, *Relação*, HGBP **10** pt 3, 312. Mato Grosso City was abandoned in the late eighteenth century but revived in the rubber boom. It is now a dismal, lawless backwater with crumbling buildings and balustrades along the river, and a population largely of descendants of runaway black slaves.

In the early 1960s the state police tended to avoid Mato Grosso City.

404 *in the same way.'* Agostinho Lourenço, *Relação de uma viagem que fêz em 1752 de ordem do Capitão-general Dom Antonio Rolim de Moura*, in Leverger, *Apontamentos cronológicos*, RHGB **205** 232, Oct–Dec 1949.

404 *some prisoners'.* José de Gonçalves da Fonseca, *Primeira exploração dos rios Madeira e Guaporé em 1749* . . ., in Cândido Mendes de Almeida, *Memorias* . . . **2** 392.

404 *new outrages.'* Ibid. **2** 393.

404 *peaceful conduct'* Almeida Serra, *Discripcão geográphica*, RHGB **6** 195, 1844. Almeida Serra said that some Parecis (now written Paresi) escaped and intermingled with the Mambaré (Waimaré) and Cabixi. Pires de Campos had written in 1723 that the Mahibarez (Mambaré) had their ears pierced with enormous holes. They lived to the north of the Paresi, had similar customs, and 'in quantity they are infinite, so that they cannot be counted' (*Breve noticia* 444). His description reminds one of the Erigpactsa, who live north of the Paresi, between the junctions of the Juruena, Sangue and Arinos rivers in northwestern Mato Grosso. This isolated tribe came into contact with missionaries and Indian Service agents during the 1960s. Its men are remarkable for wearing enormous discs in their ear-lobes. Pires de Campos also described a visit to an anthropophagous tribe living beyond the Paresi: its huts were full of grisly pieces of human meat. These were the Cavihi or Cabishi. They may have been part of the Paresi: a tribe known as Paresi-Cabishi or Kozarine lives in the forests of the upper Guaporé, Juba and Jaurú. Otherwise the name Cabishi is sometimes given to groups of Nambikuara absorbed by the Aruak.

This is a part of Brazil that is only just being finally opened to settler penetration; in 1971 I saw a group of Nambikuara from forests near the Cabixi River who had had no previous contact with the rest of Brazil.

The Paresi refer to themselves as Ariti, and are divided into the subgroups Paresi, Kaxiniti, Waimaré and Kozarine. The tribe was helped by Colonel Cândido Rondon in the early days of the Indian Protection Service, and by 1928 was well acculturated and flourishing. Since then its numbers have declined seriously, probably from disease. There are now only a few hundred Paresi, mostly living in small communities near the Cuiabá–Porto Velho road. About half the tribe lives in a large new Paresi Reserve on barren country north of this road. Its southern edge runs along the road for about 100 kms.

405 *with the whites'.* Cardoso de Abreu (1783) in HGBP **11** pt 2, 167. Bororo living on the São Lourenço and Cuiabá rivers were being hunted by the Paulistas who first found the Cuiabá gold deposits. On 22 Nov 1734 Brigadier Antonio de Almeida Lara issued orders for a bandeira from Cuiabá against the Bororo, who were accused of having killed some slaves near the town: he promised that any caught in battle would be divided among the members of the expedition; CDSP **3** 45–6. Another group of Bororo called Aravira lived west of Cuiabá, on the Cabaçal river between Cuiabá and Vila Bela (Mato Grosso). Almeida Serra reported that four of these appeared at Vila Bela in 1797 to seek friendship, but were very timorous despite being given presents by the Governor (*Descripção geographica* 163, 178).

405 *Brazil.* Leverger, *Apontamentos cronológicos* 229; HBP **2** 95. The Conselho Ultramarino in Lisbon discussed, 17 April 1742, a request for financial help from Carvalho for having reduced the Bororo; CDSP **3** 347.

405 *other vegetables.'* Pires de Campos, *Breve noticia* 437.

406 *their slaves,'* Ibid. Modern Caiapó are never anthropophagous and this is unusual for Gê-speaking tribes, although it was also said of the Botocudo Aimoré. The eating of human flesh by these southern Caiapó was evidently done for enjoyment of the meat, with none of the ritual killing and vendettas of the coastal Tupi.

406 *the killing.*' Antonio Rolim, *Relação da viagem que fez . . . da cidade de S. Paulo para a Villa de Cuyabá em 1751*, RHGB 7 466, 1845. The Kren-Akoro, related to the northern Caiapó, killed the English explorer Richard Mason in exactly this way. He was leading an expedition to explore the Iriri river (on the Pará–Mato Grosso border in the Cachimbo hills) in September 1961. The eleven-man expedition, of which I was a member, was backed by the Instituto Brasileiro de Geografia e Estatística and the Royal Geographical Society. Mason was ambushed while walking along a path we had cut in the forest. He was struck at very close range by arrows and clubs. The Indians left seventeen clubs and over forty arrows alongside the body.

406 *Caiapó.* Rodrigo César de Meneses to Câmara of Cuiabá, 10 Feb 1728, HGBP 10 pt 3, 211, DI 13 135; King to Caldeira Pimentel, 8 Aug 1730, HGBP 10 pt 3, 261; Conde de Sarzedas to King, 17 Aug 1732, HGBP 10 pt 3, 271; DI 13, 135, 22 120, 24 27, 40 8; Cabral Camelo, HGBP 11 pt 2, 53; Câmara of São Paulo to King, 14 July 1736, CDSP 3 134; King to Gomes Freire de Andrade, 12 April 1738, CDSP 4 35; Royal order of open war on Caiapó, 5 March 1732, Arquivo Municipal de São Paulo. *Livro de ordens regias* 255, HGBP 11 pt 1, 238–9.

406 *all the heathen'.* Cabral Camelo, HGBP 11 pt 2, 163.

406 *horror of humanity.*' Paes Leme, 'Nobiliarchia Paulistana', RHGB 34 pt 1, 191, 1871.

406 *these heathen'.* Conselho Ultramarino meeting, 25 Feb 1743, CDSP 4 35.

406 *were innumerable.*' Luiz Antonio da Silva e Sousa, *Memoria*, RHGB 12 447, 1849.

407 *long marches.* The first village was on the upper Anicuns, a tributary of the Rio dos Bois, 150 kms south of Goiás. The route then led south to a village 'attacked on 14 August 1753' (presumably 1743, since Pires de Campos died in 1751), between the Verde and Pardo rivers, not far from Camapuã. The route then turned east to the Paranaíba to attack another village near the Mineiro triangle. The fourth village was between the Bonito and Caiapó rivers on the headwaters of the Araguaia. HGBP 11 pt 1, 243–4.

407 *50,000 reis.* Luiz de Mascarenhas, Conde de Alva, *Regimento que há de observar o Coronel Antonio Pires de Campos*, 15 July 1748, CDSP 4 362, HGBP 11 pt 1, 252–3, HBP 2 255–6; various letters during the preceding years, in DI 22 185, 50 169, 66 182, 215. The main Bororo village was Lanhoso, some 15 kms from the left bank of the Paranaíba, on the Goiás-Araxá road, almost 600 kms south-east of the town of Goiás. There is still a town there, near Araguari, called Indianapolis.

408 *(1000 kilometres).*' Alencastre, *Annaes*, RHGB 27 pt 2, 77, 1864.

408 *his cutlass.*' Paes Leme, 'Nobiliarchia paulistana', RHGB 34 pt 1, 192, 1871.

408 *'excellent arquebusiers'.* Ibid.

Chapter 18   INDIAN LABOUR ON THE AMAZON

409 *his troop.*' João Felippe Betendorf, *Chronica da missão dos Padres da Companhia de Jesus no Estado do Maranhão*, RHGB 72 pt 1, 204–5, 1901.

409 *Aruak.*' André de Barros, *Vida do apostólico Padre Antonio Vieyra*, bk 3, pp. 305–6.

410 *this. . . .*' João de Sousa Ferreira, *America abreviada . . .*, RHGB 57 pt 1, 132, 1894.

410 *the missionaries.*' Betendorf, *Chronica* 206; Bernardo Pereira de Berredo, *Annaes . . .*, bk 16, pp. 524–6.

410 *all bringing.*' Sousa Ferreira, *America abreviada* 132–3.

410 *its fame.*' Berredo, *Annaes*, bk 16, p. 537. Betendorf told of a large expedition against the Aruak led by Governor Rui Vaz de Siqueira. He set out with forty-eight large war-canoes full of

soldiers and Indians, amid 'great festivities and firing of artillery' (*Chronica,* ch. 17, p. 233). They found seventeen villages of peaceful Aruak all abandoned because their people had fled from abuse by the Captain of the Gurupá fort. They also counted 98 deserted villages of unconquered Aruak, whose inhabitants had fled deep into the forests. The expedition lost its boat full of food and trade goods, and had to subsist for three months on manioc. After many expeditions deep into the forests, the expedition returned with only 300 prisoners, mostly old people and children. But it did catch and execute the brave old chief Caytabuna of the Aruak, who had lost the sight of both eyes and been abandoned by his people. Betendorf noted that the Aruak loathed captivity, and preferred death by poison to enslavement by the whites.

411 *it is today.'* Sousa Ferreira, *America abreviada* 62.

411 *an ecclesiastic.'* Ibid. 57, 65.

411 *badly acquired.'* Ibid. 57.

411 *ten children.'* Ibid. 117.:

411 *and die.'* Father João Betendorf letter, 20 July 1673, HCJB **7** 295, trans. in C. R. Boxer, *The Golden Age of Brazil, 1695–1750* 278.

411 *Indians?'* Sousa Ferreira, *America abreviada* 117.

411 *curse of Ham'.* Ibid. 56, 101.

412 *the next world.'* Ibid. 121–2.

413 *Christians'.* António Vieira, *Regulamento das aldeias,* 1660, HCJB **4** 106–24, Serafim Soares Leite, *Suma histórica* . . . 88, summary and translation in Boxer, *Golden Age* 283.

413 *in 1750. Regimento das missões do Estado do Maranhão e Grão-Pará,* 1686; Mathias C. Kieman, *The Indian Policy of Portugal in the Amazon Region, 1614–1693* 439, 442; A. L. Monteiro Baena, *Ensaio corográfico sobre a Provincia do Pará* (Pará, 1839) 23; Barão de Guajará, *Catechese dos indios no Pará,* ABAP **2** 132, 1902; Manoel Nunes Dias, 'Colonização da Amazônia (1755–1778)', RH **34** 475–6; Mendonça Furtado to Pombal, 21 Nov and 30 Dec 1751, AEP **1** 72, 153; João Lúcio d'Azevedo, *Os Jesuítas no Grão-Pará* . . . 229,

reckoned a total of about 30,000; Colin M. MaLachlan, 'The Indian Labor Structure in Portuguese Amazon' 1700–1800' 208.

414 *the sertão.'* Anon, *Do modo de fazer as missões no Maranhão,* in Alexandre J. de Mello Moraes, *Corografia historica* . . . **4** 258–9.

415 *feed the mission.* Provision and Law of 1 April 1680, LGM **1** 51–6, 57–9; HGB (1926–36 ed.) **3** 339–41; L. Humberto de Oliveira, *Coletânea de leis, atos e memorias referentes ao indígena brasileira* 59; Kieman, *Indian Policy* 166–7; A. M. Perdigão Malheiro, *A escravidão no Brasil* **2** 70–1; Azevedo, *Os Jesuítas no Grão-Pará* 189.

416 *Madeira river.* The Jesuits kept Marajó island, the missions around Belém city, and 'all that lies to the south of the Amazon river . . . without limit towards the interior' (King to Antonio de Albuquerque Coelho de Carvalho, 19 March 1693, LGM **1** 142–3). This included the lower reaches of the Tocantins, Xingu, Tapajós and Madeira rivers. The north shore of the Amazon was divided as follows: from Cabo do Norte on the Atlantic to the Jari and Paru rivers, Franciscan Capuchins of Santo Antonio; the shore opposite Gurupá fort as far as the Trombetas and Gueribi rivers, Franciscans of Piedade and of Conceição or Santa Bonaventura; between the Urubu and Negro rivers, Mercedarians. The Negro itself was offered to both the Jesuits and Mercedarians, but later fell to Carmelite missionaries. The Jesuits briefly had a mission for the Tarumás, near modern Manaus, where the Crown also had a fort. Jesuits did not penetrate the Solimões (the Amazon upstream of the Negro), apart from a mission on the frontier with Spanish America, at modern Tabatinga, that they founded in mid-eighteenth century. The Solimões was also left to the Carmelites. The other missionary orders were less determined than the Jesuits in opposing Indian slavery.

416 *Dutch occupation in 1639.* Adriaen van der Drussen (*Relatório sôbre as capitanias conquistadas* . . . 88) recorded this wage of

8 varas. The Dutch were trying to woo the Indians, and there was a serious shortage of black slaves during the Dutch occupation. Johannes de Laet said that even the Portuguese paid 5 varas for free labour in Pernambuco in 1633 (*Historie . . .* 86). Wages tended to be lower in Maranhão and Pará, where there were more Indians and the settlers were poorer. The wage there was 2 varas in 1650 (DHBC 3 188). A vara was about 1.10 metres, or 43 inches.

416 *make it great.'* Gomes Freire de Andrade to King, 13 Oct 1685, in Oliveira, *Coletânea* 60.

417 *Portuguese colonies.* Álvaras of 1, 24 and 28 April 1688, LGM 1 97–101; Perdigão Malheiro, *Escravidão* 2 82–3; Kieman, *Indian Policy* 442; Oliveira, *Coletânea* 60.

417 *this state.'* Francisco Xavier de Mendonça Furtado to his brother the Marquis of Pombal, Pará, 10 Nov 1752, AEP 1 290.

417 *other slaves'.* Ibid. 1 291.

417 *with us.'* Ibid. The neighbouring nations were the Dutch, English and French in the Guianas and the Spaniards further up the Amazon or on the Orinoco. Mendonça Furtado sent his brother Pombal blank certificates of slavery signed by the missionary Father Aquiles Maria Avogadre. These were to have been used on a ransom expedition to the Negro.

417 *own expense.* Carta regia of 2 Sept 1689, McLachlan, 'Indian Labor' 203.

418 *three governors.'* Francisco Teixeira de Moraes, *Relação histórica . . .* 140–1.

418 *each such slave.* Álvara of 6 Feb 1691, Oliveira, *Coletânea* 60; Perdigão Malheiro, *Escravidão* 2 84.

418 *administration of missionaries.* King Pedro II to Junta of Maranhão, 21 April 1702, MacLachlan, 'Indian Labor' 203.

418 *disposed of them.'* João da Maia da Gama to King, Lisbon, 28 Feb 1730, Mello Moraes, *Corografia* 4 266, and another letter by him, ibid. 269.

418 *fear of punishment'.* King Pedro II to Ouvidor-geral of Maranhão, 24 Dec 1705, LGM 1 264–5.

419 *that captaincy.'* King to Câmara of Pará, Lisbon, 10 Jan 1697, LGM 1 166.

419 *against my orders'.* King to Ouvidor-geral of Pará, Lisbon, 6 May 1703, LGM 1 249.

419 *threatening vengeance.'* King to Ouvidor-geral of Pará, Lisbon, 16 Dec 1707, LGM 2 23.

419 *his new colony. . . .'.* King to Cristóvão da Costa Freire, Lisbon, 5 Oct 1708, LGM 2 28. The *Livro Grosso do Maranhão* is full of royal licences to descend Indians – for instance, LGM 1 199–200, 214, 217, 234, 242, 256, 266–7, etc. etc.

419 *paid for them . . .'.* King to Governor of Maranhão, 30 May 1718, LGM 2 156.

420 *dying of hunger.'* João da Maia da Gama to King, Lisbon, 28 Feb 1730, in Mello Moraes, *Corografia* 4 264. He was governor in the 1720s. The text of the *Regimento das Missões do Estado do Maranhao e Pará,* 1 Dec 1686, is in HCJB 4 369–75. Also: Azevedo, *Jesuítas* 188–9; Boxer, *Golden Age* 279–81; DH 10 402, 11 179, 189; Oliveira, *Coletânea* 59; Kieman, *Indian Policy* 439–41; Perdigão Malheiro, *Escravidão* 2 75–8; Jacinto de Carvalho, *Regimento e leys sobre as Missões do Maranhão e Pará, e sobre a liberdade dos indios* (Lisbon, 1724); report by Betendorf to King on Beckman revolt, Mello Moraes, *Corografia* 4 199–241, and for the settlers' point of view Francisco Teixeira de Moraes, *Relação historica,* and to some extent Berredo, *Annaes* bk 18.

420 *by force.'* King to Manoel Rolim de Moura, Lisbon, 14 Nov 1703, LGM 1 273.

420 *those in slavery'.* Decision of Junta das Missões, Belém, 20 March 1719, implementing Law of 9 March 1718, in Mello Moraes, *Corografia* 4 305.

421 *His Majesty!'* Jacintho de Carvalho to Jesuit Procurador, Belém, 16 Dec 1729, ibid. 4 329–30.

421 *forest fruits.'* Representation by Maranhão Jesuits about vexations since the arrival of Alexandre de Sousa Freire, *c.*1732, Mello Moraes, *Corografia* 4 393.

421 *and mistreated.'* Testimony of Frei João de São Diogo (Minister-Provincial of Capuchins of Santo Antonio in Portugal), in Mello Moraes, *Corografia* 4 284.

421 *for the whites'*. João Daniel, *Thesouro descoberto no maximo rio Amazonas*, pt 2, ch. 19, RHGB 3 290, 1841.

422 *São Francisco river*. Conselho Ultramarino to Bishop Frei Miguel de Bulhões, 26 May 1756, in MacLachlan, 'Indian Labor' 206; Cartas régias in LGM 1 217, 223, 2 200, 269, and in ABAP 2 193.

There was an ugly incident in 1701. A Capuchin of Santo Antonio, Frei José de Sta Maria, had persuaded the Aruan (or Aruã) of Marajó island to settle in three villages on the Paraguari (Soure) stream near Belém. But Governor Fernão Carrilho of Pará broke promises to them, and forced them to work continuously building the fortifications of the city. They fled to their former homes. Frei José and his companion Frei Martinho went by canoe to visit them. They warned the missionaries that they 'would never return to be under the halberds of the sergeants of Belém, who had abused them with starvation, work and beatings' (Francisco de N. S. dos Prazeres, 'Poranduba Maranhense . . .', RHGB 54 pt 1, 96, 1891; Berredo, *Annaes*, bk 20, p. 659; King to Manoel Rolim de Moura, 6 May 1703, LGM 1 247). The missionaries tried to land, but were both riddled by arrows.

The inevitable reprisal expedition of 60 soldiers and 200 Indians left Belém in 1702. An old woman told them that those responsible for the killings had fled to the French in Cayenne. Despite this, the expedition returned with fifty captive Aruan and the bodies of the two missionaries, who were given martyrs' burials. 'But the Commandant Manoel Cordeiro did not feel that he had yet obtained sufficient satisfaction for such an ugly crime. He therefore continued . . . the fatal devastations until the end of May, when he returned to [Belém do] Pará full of just glory' (Berredo, *Annaes*, bk 20, pp. 659–60). The injustice of these reprisals was so manifest that the King wrote in May 1703 ordering an enquiry and the release of any wrongly enslaved. But some Aruan had already been executed by firing from cannon.

These were the same Aruan who had been friends of Bernard O'Brien in 1621 on Caviana or Sipinipoco Island and on the north-eastern part of Marajó. They were the tribe blamed for the killing of the Jesuits shipwrecked off Belém in 1643, and their chief Piyé was one who surrendered to António Vieira in 1659. The tribe lived all along the coast stretching towards Cabo do Norte and French Cayenne (Guiana), and many were migrating to Guiana before the killings of 1701.

Portuguese policy was to prevent a link between the Aruan and French. Those in the village of Ganhoão on the north coast of Marajó were transferred up the Amazon in 1702 to the declining Aruak Mission on the Urubu; other Aruan were brought south from Cabo do Norte and settled near Belém, in the village of Caiá. Most escaped to French Guiana.

In 1722 the Aruan tried to regain their former homes, attacking the Portuguese under a chief called Guayamã of Guamã. They occupied the village of Moribira, thirty miles north of Belém, for a year, and the fighting continued until 1727. In 1793 more Aruan were forced to move from the north coast of Marajó to a village called Murú created for them on the lower Tocantins; and the entire Atlantic coast of Amapá was stripped of Aruan by the authorities at the end of the eighteenth century. In the mid-eighteenth century a Father Lombard gathered some Maraón and Aruan fugitives into Ouanari mission in Cayenne. Another group of Aruan were settled on the Uaçá river, near the frontier between Brazil and Cayenne: they were mentioned by Father Dabbadie in 1854 and Henri Coudreau in 1891, and were visited by Curt Nimuendajú in 1926, by which date none could recall the Aruan language (Henri Coudreau, *La France equinoxiale*, 2 vols (Paris, 1886–7), 1 220–4; Barão de Rio-Branco, *Frontières entre le Brésil et la Guyane française, Seconde mémoire* (Bern, 1899) 2 53, 90, 101; Curt Nimuendajú, 'The Turiwara and Aruã', HSAI 3 197).

There was another incident involving the killing of missionaries. In 1708 Periquis Indians killed two Capuchins of Piedade at a mission on the Uatumã river (a northern tributary of the Amazon, between the Trombetas and Negro). The missionaries, Antonio de Vila Viçosa and Pero de Évora, were killed while preaching. The authorities demanded that the Periquis chiefs surrender the killers. When they refused, a punitive expedition was sent. The tribe resisted, and the soldiers went into action, killing forty and enslaving many more (King to Cristóvão de Costa Freire, 9 April 1708, 26 Aug 1709, LGM 2 26, 61).

422 *the flogging.* Representation by Jesuits of Maranhão, *c.*1732, Mello Moraes, *Corografia* 4 394–5.

423 *in the soul.'* Daniel, *Thesouro descoberto,* pt 2, ch. 11, p. 485.

423 *their necks.'* Ibid. pt 2, ch. 11, pp. 485–6.

423 *spiritual good.'* Ibid. pt 2, ch. 11, p. 490.

423 *thirteen onwards.'* Ibid. pt 2, ch. 11, 492.

424 *state of innocence.'* Ibid. pt 2, ch. 1, RHGB 2 340, 1840.

424 *their dogs'.* Ibid. pt 2, ch. 1, p. 347.

424 *ecclesiastic or secular'.* Ibid. pt 2, ch. 1, pp. 362–3.

424 *from then on.'* Ibid. pt 2, ch. 5, 458–9.

424 *reveal them'.* Ibid. pt 2, ch. 5, p. 459.

425 *Americas!'* Ibid. pt 2, ch. 1, 330.

425 *with punishment.'* Ibid. pt 2, ch. 11, p. 122.

425 *out of fear.'* Ibid. pt 2, ch. 5, p. 456.

425 *Tapuiá.'* Ibid. pt 2, ch. 14, pp. 46–7.

426 *their feet.'* Ibid. pt 2, ch. 14, p. 48.

426 *Tapajós aldeia].'* Betendorf, *Chronica,* bk 4, ch. 1, p. 159.

426 *which means godfather.'* Ibid. bk 4, ch. 1, pp. 162, 164.

426 *your 'mercy'!'''* Ibid. bk 4, ch. 13, p. 219.

Chapter 19   THE AMAZON FRONTIER

427 *forests.* The Portuguese call the main stream of the Amazon above the confluence of the Negro the Solimões or 'River of Poisons' – probably because its tribes used curare and other poisons on their arrows. The Spaniards call the main river Marañón.

Charles de la Condamine, a French scientist who descended the Amazon in 1743, found what he was sure was Teixeira's marker. It was at the Paraguari mission, a few miles upstream of the mouth of the Tefé tributary of the Solimões. La Condamine thus concluded that Teixeira's Rio de Ouro was the Japurá, which enters from the north-west opposite that mission (Condamine, *Relation abrégée* . . . 100–1). This agrees with Cristóbal de Acuña, who came downstream with Teixeira in 1639 (Clements R. Markham, *Expeditions into the Valley of the Amazons,* Hakluyt Society, 24 102). This interpretation was hotly disputed by the Portuguese, who had since established the Brazilian-

Peruvian frontier 350 miles further west. Father Samuel Fritz, who descended the Amazon in 1689, claimed that the marker was a large tree trunk on elevated ground at the Cuchivara (Purús) River, not far upstream of the Rio Negro – but Fritz had a strong motive for placing the boundary far downstream, so that his mission among the Omagua (Cambeba) would fall in Spanish territory: *Journal of the Travels and Labours of Father Samuel Fritz* . . . 67–8, 89.

427 *my mouth.'* Ibid. 60.

428 *my sufferings'.* Ibid. 63.

428 *in a hammock.* . . . .' Ibid. 65. That year's official ransom troop was led by Captain-Major André Pinheiro and accompanied by the Jesuit João Maria Garzoni; it went to the Rio Negro.

428 *I know not* . . . '. Ibid. 66.

428 *Indian.'* João Daniel, *Thesouro descoberto no maximo rio Amazonas,* ch. 15, 51; Fritz, *Journal* 71.

429 *Pará'.* Ibid. 73. Many recent travellers on the Amazon and Solimões have

described the passage of messianic figures. When I was on the Solimões in 1971 I found all the settlements transformed by the preachings of such a man, João da Cruz, who had passed by, erecting crosses, establishing his own cult, forbidding alcohol, opposing the Christian missionaries, threatening floods, and leaving with his flotilla of canoes loaded with gifts (Edwin Brooks, René Fuerst, John Hemming, Francis Huxley, *Tribes of the Amazon Basin in Brazil, 1972* 52–3).

429 *inter-tribal fighting.* The main tribes mentioned by Fritz were the Cuchivara, living on the south bank between the Madeira and Purús; the Ybanoma, also on the south bank, between the Purús and Juruá; the Aysuares and Yurimagua opposite these on the north bank, around the mouth of the Japurá. The Yurimagua language was quite different from the Omagua (Fritz, *Journal* 92). On his map, Fritz showed the great Omagua nation occupying the entire north shore from the Japurá up to the Napo. Yurimaguas is the name of a modern Peruvian town on the Huallaga, indicating the place where this tribe was finally settled by the missionaries. Fritz marks very many other tribes on his map, including the Ticuna, some distance up the Içá-Putumayo. The Ticuna have since moved down to occupy the vacuum left when the Omagua fled upstream. They are now the only pure Indian tribe living on the main stream of the Amazon-Solimões anywhere in Brazil.

429 *all right'.* Ibid. 89.

429 *to ransom.'* Ibid. 91.

430 *as slaves'.* Ibid. 94.

430 *his promise.'* Ibid. 96. Fritz' easternmost mission was San Inacio of the Aysuares, on an island between the Juruá and Tefé; upriver of it was Nuestra Señora de las Niebes (inappropriately named 'Our Lady of the Snows', perhaps out of homesickness for the snows of Bohemia). It was located on an island near the modern village of Foz do Mamoriá, between the Jutaí and Juruá. The other missions marked on his map were: Cuatinavates, just east of the mouth of the Jutaí; San Pablo, modern São Paulo de Olivença; N. S. de Guadelupe, among the Mayoruna in what is now Peru, roughly opposite Leticia; and San Joaquín, modern Pebas in Peru.

430 *lover and protector?"'* Ibid. 97.

430 *these parts'.* Antonio de Albuquerque Coelho de Carvalho to King, Belém, 29 July 1697, in ibid., app. 3, 151; ibid. 101–2; King's reply to Albuquerque Coelho de Carvalho, Lisbon, 10 Dec 1697, LGM, 1 pt 1, p. 173.

431 *inevitable reprisals.* Fritz, *Journal* 107.

431 *with fire.'* Ibid. 110.

432 *the Omagua.'* Ibid. 114.

432 *own choice'.* Ibid. 114.

432 *Christians.'* Ibid. 118.

432 *Crown'.* Bernardo Pereira de Berredo, *Annaes . . .* 670.

432 *Pontifical excommunication?'* Fritz, *Journal* 120.

433 *Frei João da Luz.* Ibid. 124–5. The slavers were members of the punitive expedition and included its leader Ignacio Corrêa. He was held captive in Quito, but when an exchange of prisoners was finally arranged, five years later, it was found that Corrêa had gone to Lima and was married to a Peruvian lady.

433 *Castilians'.* King to Governor Cristóvão da Costa Freire, Lisbon, 13 May 1710, in Fritz, *Journal* 155, also 126; Berredo, *Annaes* 672; José de Moraes, *Historia da Companhia de Jesus . . .,* in Candido Mendes de Almeida, *Memorias . . .* 1 539–40; Roberto Cardoso de Oliveira, *O índio e o mundo dos brancos* 48.

433 *his company.'* Fritz, *Journal* 126. The expedition was led by Joseph Antunes da Fonseca who had been sent in 1697 to claim the Solimões formally for Portugal.

433 *and died'.* Ibid. 126. The Omagua who opted for Spanish Jesuit rule settled at San Joaquín de Omaguas, and in 1732 helped repel another major Portuguese invasion. In 1734 the Jesuit Visitor-General of Quito, Andrés de Zárate, wrote to the Governor of Pará threatening to train and arm an army of Indians on the Maynas missions unless

Portuguese aggressions ceased. But in 1735 'squadrons of Portuguese and robbers' again came upstream and attacked the Spanish missions on the Marañón. They destroyed houses and churches, seized some Indians and carried them off to Pará, and forced the Jesuits to withdraw the remainder of their congregations. There was now a no-man's-land of hundreds of miles between the two countries' missions on the upper Amazon (Francisco de Figueroa, *Relación de las misiones de la Compañia de Jesús en el país de los Maynas* (Madrid, 1904), app., 294, 331–2, 367–70; J. Fred Rippy and Jean Thomas Nelson, *Crusaders of the Jungle* (Chapel Hill, NC, 1936) 247–8).

The great Omagua tribe was badly decimated by disease. By 1737 there were only 522 inhabitants in San Joaquín, and in 1751 there was a further epidemic of smallpox. There are now only a few Omagua left in the villages of San Salvador de Omagua and San Joaquín, and they have been absorbed by the numerous Cocama tribe of the Huallaga. (On Fritz' mission, see: Pablo Maroni, *Noticias auténticas del famoso rio Marañón y misión apostólica de la Compañhía de Jesús de la Prov. de Quito en los dilatados bosques de dicho rio . . .* (1738), ed. Marcos Jiménez de la Espada (*Boletín de la Sociedad Geográfica Nacional,* Madrid, 26–30, 1889–92) 30 227–35; José Chantre y Herrera, *Historia da las misiones de la Compañia de Jesús en el Marañón español, 1637–1767* (Madrid, 1901) 284, 297, 313–15.) The Omagua who chose Portuguese rule survived for a time at São Paulo de Olivença and on some islands in the Solimões. They have now vanished into the mestizo population of the Amazon (Alfred Métraux, 'Tribes of the Middle and Upper Amazon River' 690).

434 *far away.'* La Condamine, *Relation abrégée* 88.

434 *transplanted'.* Ibid. 94. The missions were: São Paulo, Yviratuha, Traquatuha, Paraguari, Tefé and Coari – all on the south bank. After the Treaty of Madrid, Portuguese Jesuits were asked to plant a

mission at the new frontier, and a fort was built at Tabatinga, opposite the mouth of the Javari (King José I, instructions to Francisco Xavier de Mendonça Furtado, 31 May 1751, AEP 1 32). João Daniel, who left the Amazon in 1757, wrote that in the hundreds of miles of the Solimões between the Madeira and Javari there was not a single settlement of whites or Indians apart from two or three tiny Carmelite missions – yet this was the river once teeming with village after village of natives (*Thesouro descoberto* 441). Tabatinga is now a large and efficient Brazilian army camp, and there is an Indian Foundation post for the Ticuna a short distance downstream. On the south shore is the squalid town of Benjamin Constant, much of it built over mudflats on rotting wooden jetties.

434 *Pará'.* La Condamine, *Relation abrégéé* 90.

434 *following century.* Ibid. 78–9. He also commented on the Omaguas' love of the hallucinogenic visions they obtained by blowing powdered curupá leaves *(Mimosa acacioides)* up one another's nostrils with Y-shaped reeds. Shamans also had visions by drinking ayahuasca or floripondia *(Datura arborea).*

434 *among them.'* Ibid. 51.

434 *fundamentals of character.'* Ibid. 51.

435 *their needs.'* Ibid. 52.

435 *all the defects.'* Ibid. 52–3.

435 *other rivers.* Some of the Jesuits who accompanied such expeditions were: Jódoco Peres to the Iruris of the Madeira, 1683; José Barreiro and João Ângelo Bonomi to the Iruris again, 1688; João Maria Gorzoni to the Negro, 1689; another to the Trombetas, 1689; João Justo Pfeil to the Negro, 1692; another to the Jari, 1709, and many more in the early eighteenth century.

435 *in office.* Maia da Gama to King, Lisbon, 28 Feb 1730, in Alexandre J. de Mello Moraes, *Corografia historica* 4 261. His ransom troops were: Thomas Teixeira to the Tapajós, 1722; Francisco de Mello Palheta to the Madeira, 1722, accompanied by the Jesuit João de Sampaio; another by this missionary in 1723; João Paes do Amáral in 1723

accompanied by Jesuits; Sampaio to the Negro, 1724; Estevão de Albuquerque to the Tapajós, 1724. There were also troops to the Xingu, 1726, with the Jesuit Francisco Cardoso; and to the Negro with José de Sousa, 1727, etc. Serafim Soares Leite lists no less than 160 expeditions made by Jesuits, most of them during the century in which the Society was active on the Amazon, in the General Index of his monumental *História da Companhia de Jesus no Brasil* **10** 79–83.

435 *Ransom Treasury'*. Maia da Gama, in Mello Moraes, *Corografia* **4** 261.

436 *in the forests. . . .'* Bartholomeu Rodrigues, Tupinambarana aldeia, 2 May 1714, ibid. **4** 365–6.

437 *Indian women*. Testimony by Frei Diogo da Trinidade, Lisbon, 16 July 1729, ibid. **4** 282. The Arapiun were thought by both Martius and Métraux to be the same as the Maué. This was because João Daniel described their girls' puberty rite of being bled from head to foot with a cutia tooth, and the boys' ordeal of having their arms tied in gourds full of extremely painful biting sauba ants. Both these rituals were practised by the Maué (*Thesouro descoberto* 168–71, 478). But Curt Nimuendajú pointed out that the Arapiun had other customs different from the Maué – their eating of dead people's flesh by their relatives, and reverence for the new moon – which made him think that they were part of the Tapajós tribe. They lived at the Arapiun mission and some crossed to the north bank of the Amazon, to the Pauxis mission (Óbidos); but there are no mentions of the Arapiun after about 1750. When Nimuendajú explored the Arapiun river (between the Tapajós and Madeira) in 1924, he found many old Indian dwelling-places with pottery similar to that of the Tapajós; 'The Maué and Arapiun', HSAI **3** 253–4.

437 *its heyday*. José Gonçalves da Fonseca, *Primeiro exploração . . .* 292.

437 *their hostilities'*. King to Capitão-mór of Pará, 4 July 1716, and to Governor Cristóvão da Costa Freira, 6 Feb 1717, LGM **2** 137, 147–8.

437 *an anthill'*. Rodrigues, 2 May 1714, Mello Moraes, *Corografia* **4** 363.

437 *left them extinct'*. Gonçalves da Fonseca, *Primeira exploração* 304. João de Barros was killed when returning from the expedition, by a falling tree that crushed his canoe – a normal hazard in Amazon forests during the rains.

437 *and back*. Maia da Gama to King, 28 Feb 1730, in Mello Moraes, *Corografia* **4** 260; Testimony of Mercedarian Frei Diogo da Trinidade, Lisbon, 16 July 1729, ibid. **4** 282; Vitor Hugo, *Desbravadores* **1** 29.

438 *to distribute.'* King to Visitador-geral of Jesuit missions, 6 Feb 1726, LGM **2** 213; Maia da Gama to King, 28 Feb 1730, Mello Moraes, *Corografia* **4** 261; Bento da Fonseca, SJ, letter, Lisbon, 4 June 1749, HCJB **9** 395.

438 *his own canoes'*. Testimony of Frei Diogo da Trinidade, Lisbon, 16 July 1729, Mello Moraes, *Corografia* **4** 282–3; Hugo, *Desbravadores* **1** 34. King to Ouvidor-geral of Pará, 11 Feb 1730, LGM **2** 243. Manoel de Seixas, SJ, *Informação do Maranhão, Pará e Amazonas para El-Rei*, 13 June 1718, HCJB **4** 388; the tribe seized by Captain Tavares were Iaraguaris.

439 *were navigating'*. Daniel, *Thesouro descoberto* (c.1760), pt 2, ch. 17, RHGB **3** 167, 1841; Hugo, *Desbravadores* **1** 60; Francisco Xavier Ribeiro de Sampaio, *Diario da viagem . . . no ano de 1774 e 1775*; Curt Nimuendajú, 'The Mura and Pirahá', HSAI **3** 256, 262; Alexandre Rodrigues Ferreira, *Diario da viagem philosophica . . .* (1786), RHGB **50** pt 2, 69–70, 1887.

439 *Mura:* Francisco Xavier Ribeiro de Sampaio, quoted in ibid. **50** pt 2, 70, 1887; Antonio José Pestana da Silva, *Meios de dirigir o governo temporal dos indios* (c.1788) 141. The mission of Santo Antonio was moved in 1739 to a place called Camuan (now Missões de São Francisco) on the Madeira upstream of the mouth of the Jiparaná.

Events on the Tapajós river were somewhat similar to those on the Madeira. Early travellers were impressed by the size, fighting ability and sophistication of the Tapajós tribe living near the river's mouth. By Acuña's time the Tapajós were being attacked and enslaved by Bento Maciel Parente's son, and they formed the original inhabitants of the Tapajós aldeia (modern Santarém). The Jesuit Betendorf was with the Tapajós in 1660, when he opposed the union between the tribe's 'princess' or chief soothsayer, Maria Moacara, and a Portuguese lover. Betendorf found the couple together in a hammock and cut its rope, telling them they were committing an offence against God. He advised Maria to remain celibate as an honoured widow (João Felippe Betendorf *Chronica . . .*, ch. 3, p. 172). Heriarte said that in 1665 Tapajós was the largest aldeia, able to muster 60,000 bowmen (*Descrição do Estado do Maranhão, Pará . . .*, in HGB, 7th ed., 3 179, 1962).

Beyond the Tapajós, in the area west of the river's mouth, lay the Andirá and Maué. They were shown on Samuel Fritz' map of 1691, and Betendorf wrote that the Andirá welcomed Father João Valladão, a missionary from the Tupinambarana mission, in 1698 (*Chronica* 36). The Maraguá group of Maué lived on a lake opposite the eastern end of Tupinambaranas Island. They killed some whites, and in 1692 a punitive expedition was sent against them. They were forewarned and scattered into the forests. The Jesuits took up residence among them in 1696, and soon persuaded them to descend to live in the mission of Guamá close to Belém. They either died from disease or merged into the native population near the city; for they were not mentioned again.

The Maué managed to stop Portuguese advance up the Tapajós. In 1724 and 1725 Governor Maia da Gama sent strong expeditions under Estevão de Albuquerque 'to make war and open up an entry to that river, which had always been obstructed up to that time' (Report by Maia da Gama, 28 Feb 1730, Mello Moraes, *Corografia* 4 261). He had received a royal order to attack the Indians at the river's first rapids, because they habitually harassed Portuguese canoes (*Carta régia*, 17 Feb 1724 and 6 Feb 1726, LGM 2 194–5, 213). After these campaigns, the Maué settled in the Jesuit missions on the lower Tapajós. But the tribe took up arms again in the later eighteenth century, and there was much fighting in the century after the scope of this book. In 1746 the famous explorer João de Sousa Azevedo pioneered a descent of the Arinos and Tapajós, and made contact with many more tribes on the upper river, such as the Apiacá and Cawahíb. Ricardo Franco de Almeida Serra also wrote about a possible river route down these turbulent rivers, in 1797 (RHGB 9 1–16, 1847).

On the Xingu, it is not certain which tribes were first contacted by the Jesuits of Luis Figueira and the Capuchins in the early seventeenth century. Heriarte, Fritz and Betendorf mentioned the Coani, Guahuara and Guayapi, the last two of which were Tupi-speaking. Nimuendajú noted that Betendorf implied that the Guahuara (who had 22 villages in the interior between the Xingu and Tapajós in 1688) were related or identical to the Curubare or Curuaya, a tribe that may have given its name to the Curuá river on the upper Iriri. The Coani and Guayapí lived on the west bank of the lower Xingu. According to Nimuendajú they made an extraordinary migration northwards probably up the Jari, to settle on the Oyapock (the boundary between Brazilian Amapá and French Cayenne). (Curt Nimuendajú, 'Tribes of the Lower and Middle Xingu River, HSAI 3 217.)

The tribe that was dominant in the lower Xingu was the Juruna, who still exist as a coherent tribe, now far up the Xingu near the Villas-Boas' post of Diauaram. Juruna was a Tupí name for them, meaning 'Black Mouths'. One branch of the tribe called itself Shipaya, and lived on the lower Iriri. One Captain of Gurupá Fort led a powerful expedition of 100 musketeers and 3000 Indian allies against the Juruna in about 1660. But the Juruna, allied to other tribes, cleverly mounted ambushes and retreated into the forest, so that the expedition did little damage. They had previously annihilated a group of Paulista bandeirantes – either part of Rapôso Tavares' great bandeira, or some unknown group of pioneers that made the first descent of the Xingu. Jesuit missionaries then succeeded where armed force had failed: they persuaded the Juruna to settle for a time in an aldeia on the Xingu and at Maturá (Pôrto de Mós) where there were still some in 1699 (Betendorf, *Chronica*, bk 3, ch. 9, pp. 116–17; Andre de Barros, *Vida do apostólico Padre António Vieyra*, 204–5). The Juruna later objected when the Jesuits tried to send their children to Belém for education – and as hostages for the good behaviour of their parents. Their missionary suspected a rising, and fled. The Juruna then retreated up the Xingu, and together with the Tacunyape, successfully repelled an expedition led by Gonçalves Paes de Araújo in about 1685. (Daniel, *Thesouro descoberto*, pt 2, ch. 17, RHGB 3 172–3, 1841; Nimuendajú, 'Tribes of the Lower and Middle Xingu' 218; Orlando and Cláudio Villas Boas, 'Os Juruna no Alto Xingu', *Reflexão*, University of Goiás, 1 no. 1). Some, however, remained under the Jesuits, in missions on the lower Xingu and in others created in the eighteenth century near modern Altamira. Bishop João de São José mentioned 500 Juruna and Guayapí living at Aricari (Sousel), Piraviri (Pombal) and Itacuruçá (Veiros) in 1762: (*Viagem e visita do sertão . . .* 372–3).

The Juruna's allies the Tacunyape lived between the lower Xingu and Tocantins. Vieira's Jesuits made strenuous efforts to bring the Tacunyape into their missions, in 1662–3, 1667 and in 1668 by Fathers Pedro de Pedrosa and Antonio Ribeiro. Many followed the missionaries and settled for a time in the mission of Itacuruçá (Veiros). When the Jesuit Betendorf suggested that Indians be drafted to help work for the impoverished church of the Misericordia in Belém, the Captain of Gurupá sent 80 families of Tacunyape (*Chronica*, bk 4, ch. 13, p. 219). This and other abuse made the tribe flee, up the Xingu and back to their forest homes. They helped the Juruna against Gonçalves Paes in 1685. An expedition under Hilario de Sousa de Azevedo moved against them in 1686 (LGM 1 72, 112–13). The Jesuit José Maria Gersoni reassembled some Tacunyape and other Indians at Itacuruçá in 1692; but intervention by the Captain of Gurupá again forced the tribe to flee. Some were in the Jesuit mission of Tauaquera (Tacuana) near Altamira in the early eighteenth century.

439 *this tribe*'. Ribeiro de Sampaio, *Diario da viagem*.

439 *one another*'. Daniel, *Thesouro descoberto*, pt 2, ch. 8, RHGB 2 469, 1840.

440 *exists there*.' Heriarte, *Descrição*, 182, 183, 190. Heriarte was the first author to note that the Negro is free of insects. Some decaying vegetation in its black waters is an insecticide that prevents the growth of insect larvae.

440 *manioc graters. . . .*' Fritz, *Journal* 40, 62; Acuña, in Markham, *Expeditions* 102; the editor of Fritz' *Journal*, Rev. George Edmundson, quotes José Monteiro de Noronha's *Roteiro da viagem* (1768) and an anonymous manuscript, *Synopse de algumas noticias geographicas* (1766), both of which confirm that these two rivers connect during the rainy season, and that the Manaus used them to bring gold from the upper Negro. Acuña called the Manaus Managus, and Fritz called them Manaves. La Condamine also confirmed these stories, and it was he who found what he took to be Teixeira's marker – opposite the mouth of the Japurá: *Relation abrégée* 100–1, 129.

440 *ears and noses*'. Acuña, in *Expeditions* 102.

441 *Indians*.' Ribeiro de Sampaio, quoted in Fritz, *Journal* 42–3. In a boundary dispute between Brazil and British Guiana at the beginning of the twentieth century, both governments quoted Ajuricaba in support of their respective cases. The British sought to show him as a patriotic hero, and the Brazilians countered by revealing him as a slave-trader. *British Guiana – Brazilian Boundary Arbitration, Appendix to British Case*, i, 114;

Joaquim Nabuco, *O direito do Brasil –
Primeira Memória* (Paris, 1903) and *Limites
entre le Brésil et la Guyane Anglaise. Annexes
du premier mémoire du Brésil*, vol. 1,
Documents d'origine Portuguaise (Rio de
Janeiro, 1903).

441 *a soldier.'* King to Maia da Gama, 17
Feb 1724, in ibid. 34.

441 *excesses and killings. . . .'* King to Maia
da Gama, ibid. 35.

441 *orders or suggestion. . . .'* João da Maia
da Gama to King, Belém, 26 Sept 1727,
ibid. 37. Ribeiro de Sampaio, *Diário da
viagem* 110.

442 *Ajuricaba.'* Nabuco, *Limites* 37.

442 *royal fifth [tax].'* Maia da Gama, ibid.
38, or in *O direito do Brasil* 107–11; King
to Maia da Gama, 23 Jan 1728, LGM 2
219; testimony by Miguel de Siqueira
Chaves and by Leandro Gemac de
Albuquerque (both officers of the
campaign), Belém, Sept 1728, in Mello
Moraes, *Corografia* 4 276, 279. HCJB 3
378–9. Artur Reis, *História do Amazonas*
85–6. Dutch documents have confirmed
that slaves from the Negro were being
received from the Manaus through
another intermediary tribe. In 1714 the
Dutch West India Company sent
Commander Pieter van der Heyden to
explore in search of the fabulous Lake
Parima – which Walter Ralegh and
others had sought on the upper Rio
Branco (then called Parima). The
Manaus were always identified with
legends of El Dorado and rich lakes,
doubtless because they were the tribe that
traded Chibcha gold with the Omagua
and other tribes of the Solimões. The flat
plain around the modern city of Boa
Vista on the upper Branco may have been
flooded when first seen by sixteenth-
century Spanish explorers. This would
explain why Lake Parima was shown
there on the maps of Hondius, Blaeu
and other seventeenth-century cartographers.

Van der Heyden probably made
contact with the Manaus in 1714. In
1722, the Dutch reported the appearance
of Maganouts (Manaus) on the
Essequibo. Their return there in 1723
frightened the Dutch settlers; but the

authorities established that the Manaus
had come to trade in slaves and with no
warlike intentions. Forty years later the
Dutch governor, Storm van's
Gravesande, heard that the Manaus were
dissatisfied with their treatment by the
Portuguese and eager to trade with the
Dutch. But nothing came of it, to Van
Gravesande's regret. He felt it was
because in 1722 the Manaus 'were so
injudiciously and childishly driven away,
badly treated and forever estranged from
us, that all efforts to enter into
communication with them have hitherto
proved fruitless'. C. A. Harris and J. A. J.
de Villiers, *Storm van's Gravesande: the rise
of British Guiana*, 2 vols, Hakluyt Society,
2nd series, 26–7, 1911, 1 25, 187–8, 2
414–15, 464; Minutes of the Court of
Policy, Essequibo, in Rijksarchief, The
Hague, 5 Jan, 10 April, 20 Sept and 4 and
19 Oct 1723; *British Guiana – Brazilian
Boundary Arbitration, Appendix to British
Case*, i 20; Marcos Jiménez de la Espada
(ed.), 'Noticias auténticas del famoso Río
Marañón' (1738), *Boletín de la Sociedad
Geográfica de Madrid* 26 262.

442 *keeping him.'* Maia da Gama to King,
in Nabuco, *Limites* 37.

442 *thousands of souls. . . .'* Ibid. 37.

443 *royal treasury.'* Record of ransom
troops accompanied by Father José de
Sousa, HCJB 3 377.

443 *indigenous population.* La Condamine,
Relation abrégée 126–7. It is important to
realise that the Manaus' homeland was
300–400 miles upstream of the modern
city of Manaus. Acuña and Fritz located it
on the Urubaxi river. An anonymous
report on the Rio Negro of about 1755
said of the Daraá river (which enters the
Negro opposite the mouth of the
Urubaxi, near the modern Salesian
mission of Tapurucuara): 'today there
are no people on it. The Indians who
used to frequent it were Manaus. Those
who survive are either settled in the
mission aldeias or are slaves in Pará and
Maranhão' (*Relação dos rios que desaguam
no rio Negro*, AEP 2 684). The largest
mission on the Negro was Mariúa
(Barcelos), which was founded by the
Carmelites and the punitive expedition

against Ajuricaba: Rodrigues Ferreira, *Diário da Viagem philosophica*, RHGB **49** pt 1, 183–5, 1886. Antonio José Pestana da Silva wrote, in about 1788, that Mariúa was founded by the Carmelite Friar Mathias, who persuaded a chief from the upper Negro to settle there with 20,000 Indians. (*Meios de dirigir o governo temporal dos indios*, Mello Moraes, *Corografia* **4** 122–85). Ribeiro de Sampaio said that the 'Court of the Manaus' was at Tomar, sixty miles below the mouth of the Urubaxi. João Vasco Manoel de Braum, who was Governor of Macapá in 1789, mentioned Manaus among the babel of other tribes in various towns along the middle Negro from Barcelos to Lamalonga. *Descripção chorographia do Estado do Gram-Pará*, RHGB **36** pt 1, 269–322, 1873.

A Manau chief called Theodosio was arrested in 1729 for fear that he was going to try to 'substitute the place of the dead Ajuricaba': he was sent to Portugal with a recommendation that he be sentenced to the galleys for life – but the King felt there was insufficient evidence for such a brutal punishment. Alexandre de Sousa Freire to King, Belém, 6 Oct 1729, Nabuco, *Limites* 50. In 1757 a Manau Indian from Lamalonga led a rebellion that destroyed Lamalonga and Moreira; he occupied the island of Timoní and formed a federation with other forest tribes. Métraux, 'Tribes of the Middle and Upper Amazon', HSAI **3** 707–8. Manaus appear for a while among the tribes descended to the aldeias near the city of Belém do Pará (João de São José, *Viagem e visita do sertão* 490). By 1743 Charles de la Condamine therefore wrote that the Manaus had been 'transplanted and dispersed' (*Relation abrégée* 129).

443 *their names.'* Daniel, *Thesouro descoberto*, pt 2, ch. 8, RHGB **2** 472, 1840.

Chapter 20 POMBAL

444 *beyond count.'* João Daniel, *Thesouro descoberto no maximo rio Amazonas*, pt 2, ch. 15, RHGB **3** 50, 1841.
444 *death is inevitable.'* Ibid. pt 2, ch. 20, RHGB **3** 290, 1841.
445 *Indians'.* Ibid. **3** 295.
445 *Jesuits.'* Ibid. pt 2, ch. 21, **3** 428.
445 *completely extinct.'* Ibid. **3** 429.
445 *neighbouring towns'.* Report of Sept 1729, Document 300, ABAP **4** 58, 1905.
445 *for unorthodoxy.* Alexandre Rodrigues Ferreira, *Diário da viagem philosophica . . .*, RHGB **48** pt 1, 29, 1885; Charles de la Condamine, *Relation abrégée . . .*, 183–5. It is true that La Condamine was impressed by the civilised appearance of the city of Belém when he arrived there in 1743. He had just completed an arduous descent of the Amazon, so that any city would seem a miraculous return to civilised comforts. Belém today, with its tree-lined avenues, wooded parks, and bustling port and market, is a delightful place with an invigorating climate in the dry season. But most of the baroque buildings that survive were rebuilt in the mid-eighteenth century, during the boom of the 1750s and 1760s.

445 *inhabitants' slaves'.* Ibid. 149.
445 *any age.'* José Gonçalves da Fonseca, *Primeira exploração . . .* 274.
446 *escape captivity.'* Rodrigues Ferreira, *Diário da viagem*. Gonçalves da Fonseca said that two epidemics of measles and smallpox struck between 1743 and 1749, killing two-thirds of the Indians in the missions near the mouth of the Madeira: *Primeira exploração* 292.
446 *Belém alone.* Mendonça Gurjão to Conselho Ultramarino, Belém, 15 Aug 1750, in Manuel Núñes Dias, *Colonização da Amazônia* (1755–1778), RH **34** 475, 1967.
446 *that class'.* Rodrigues Ferreira, *Diário da viagem*, 30. The King's instructions to Francisco Xavier de Mendonça Furtado, 31 May 1751, AEP **1** 28, referred to the many Indians killed in the epidemic, and told the new governor to ensure that 'the few Indians who survived this contagion should enjoy their liberty'.
446 *rational men'.* King to Cristóvão da

Costa Freire, 9 March 1718, LGM 2 152; A. M. Perdigão Malheiro, *A escravidão no Brasil* 2 87; L. Humberto de Oliveira, *Coletânea de leis* . . . 61; Mathias C. Kieman, *The Indian Policy of Portugal in the Amazon Region, 1614–1693* 444.

447 *innocent children'*. Ibid.

447 *their share'*. Decision by Junta das Missões do Maranhão, Belém, 20 March 1719, regarding application of Law of 9 March 1718, Alexandre J. de Mello Moraes, *Corografia historica* . . . 4 304. The suggestion that descended Indians should pass directly to settlers' farms was approved by local ecclesiastics; but the Conselho Ultramarino in Lisbon suspended a decision on this for a decade.

447 *Indians.'* Royal letter of 1685, LGM 1 71, quoted in C. R. Boxer, *The Golden Age of Brazil, 1695–1750* 288.

447 *that conquest'*. King to Albuquerque Coelho de Carvalho, 3 Dec 1692, LGM 1 134.

448 *Catholic faith'*. Paulo da Silva Nunes, *Capitulos sobre os maus procedimentos do Governador General do Estado do Maranhão*, in João Lúcio d'Azevedo, *Os Jesuítas no Grão-Pará* . . . 206.

448 *Maranhão Indians?'* Ibid. 206.

448 *places of prayer'*. Ibid. 203.

448 *the aldeias*. Anon, *Chronica da Companhia de Jesus na Vice-Provincia do Maranhão*, bk 3, ch. 26, in Azevedo, *Jesuítas* 220. Some of the arguments for and against the Jesuits are in: ibid. 212–15; HCJB 8 150–3; F. A. Oliveira Martins, *Um heroi esquecido, João da Maia da Gama*, 2 vols (Lisbon, 1944) 1 106–13; Mello Moraes, *Corografia* 2 474–84 (Anon, *Cálculo do importantissimo cabedal que embolçarão os Rvms missionarios* . . .), 4 122–86 (Bento da Fonseca, *Noticia do governo temporal dos indios do Maranhão*), 4 258–74 (Report by João da Maia da Gama, 28 Feb 1730), 4 276–84 (various pro-Jesuit testimonies), 297–300 (Silva Nunes, *Representação*, Lisbon, 12 April 1729), 329 (Jacinto de Carvalho, Belém, 16 Dec 1729); LGM 2 232–5.

449 *have risen?'* Daniel report, 1757, in Leite, HCJB 4 175, or Serafim Soares Leite, *Suma histórica* . . . 185. Also HCJB 3

140, 191.

450 *royal service'*. King to Antonio d'Albuquerque Coelho de Carvalho, 20 Nov 1699, LGM 1 194.

450 *form of commerce'*. Ibid. 1 194.

450 *trivial crimes'*. King to Albuquerque Coelho de Carvalho, 11 Jan 1701, LGM 1 204.

450 *[monastic] habits'*. King to Cristóvão da Costa Freire, 17 July 1710, LGM 2 81.

450 *their houses'*. King to Alexandre de Sousa Pereira, 27 Sept 1729, LGM 2 233–4.

451 *any way*. . . .' Encyclical, 'Immensa', 20 Dec 1741, Petrus Card. Gasparri, (ed.), *Cordicia juris canonici fontes* (Rome, 1926) 1 710; Kieman, *Indian Policy*, 447; Perdigão Malheiro, *A escravidão* 2 94; João Capistrano de Abreu, *Capítulos de história colonial* (Brasília, 1963 ed.) 187.

452 *many centuries'*. Instructions to Tomás da Silva Teles, Visconde de Vila Nova de Cerveira, 1749, *Documentos sôbre o Tratado de Madrid de 1750*, ABNRJ 52 1930, 18–19 (Rio de Janeiro, 1939); Hélio Vianna, *História do Brasil* 1 324.

452 *miles on end*. The populations of the Jesuit missions are from a catalogue of 1748 in Pablo Pastells, *Historia de la Compañia de Jesús* . . . 7 748. The Madeira expeditions were: Francisco de Melo Palheta and Father João de Soutomaior in 1722–4; some little-known expeditions between 1744 and 1746; the first upstream voyage all the way from Belém do Pará to Mato Grosso in 1748–9 by the woodsman-trader João de Sousa Azevedo – who had already made a descent of the Tapajós from Mato Grosso to Pará in 1746–7; and an official mission upstream from Belém that left in July 1749 under Sargento-mór Luís Fagundes Machado and the secretary of the Pará government, José Gonçalves da Fonseca, who wrote an account of the journey – the expedition reached Mato Grosso after nine months, and descended again in three months at the end of 1750. David M. Davidson, 'How the Brazilian West Was Won . . .' 65–6, 98–9, 103. Virgilio Corfêa Filho, 'João de Sousa Azevedo', *Revista do Instituto Histórico de Mato Grosso* 13–14, 39–60, 1941–2;

Ricardo Franco de Almeida Serra, *Noticia da viagem de João de Sousa de Azevedo*, in João Severiano da Fonseca, *Viagem ao redor do Brasil*, 2 vols (Rio de Janeiro, 1888–1) 1 68–72; Gonçalves da Fonseca, *Navegação . . .*, passim.

453 *these frontiers*. The frontiers agreed at the Treaty of Madrid in 1750 were: from the south of Lagoa Mirim (in modern Uruguay), along the inner shore of that Lagoon and the Negro river to the Ibicuí; down the Ibicuí to the Uruguay; along the Uruguay upstream to the Pepiri-Guaçu; north to the Iguaçu and down this, past the famous falls, to the Paraná; up the Paraña to the Igureí; up this river and across the watershed to descend to the Paraguay along the Apa; up the Paraguay to the mouth of the Jauru thence in a line to the Guaporé; down the Guaporé and Mamoré and Madeira to a point midway between the mouths of the Mamoré and of the Madeira; thence a line westwards to the source of the Javari; down the Javari to the Amazon (Solimões) and down it to the mouth of the Japurá (so that for some 400 miles the south bank was Portuguese and the north bank Spanish); north to the Rio Negro and up it to the watershed of the Orinoco and Negro–Branco basins as far as the Pacaraima hills, the limit with Dutch Guiana. Brazil later added to these boundaries. There were some extensions in Rio Grande do Sul and along the Paraguay frontier. Some land around the upper Guaporé and the large Acre territory were gained from Bolivia. The north bank of the Solimões up to Tabatinga opposite the Javari was gained from the Spaniards of what is now Colombia. Otherwise the modern boundaries of Brazil are those of the Treaty of Madrid.

455 *done hitherto.*' King José I, instructions to Mendonça Furtado, 31 May 1751, AEP 1 28.

455 *never experienced*'. Ibid. 1 29.

455 *this number*'. Mendonça Furtado to Oeiras, Belém do Para, 21 Nov 1751, AEP 1 64.

455 *vice of avarice.*' Ibid. 1 66.

455 *personal service.*' Ibid. 1 67–8.

455 *injustices and violence*'. Ibid. 70.

455 *8000–10,000*. Mendonça Furtado to King, Pará, 23 Dec 1751, ibid. 1 132. A week later, he wrote that there were 63 mission aldeias – 19 Jesuit, 15 Carmelite, 9 Franciscans of Santo Antonio, 7 Franciscans of Conceição, 10 Franciscans of Piedade, and 3 Mercedarian. He did not know their populations, but reckoned that none had less than 150 persons and some had 800 or more: letter to King José, 30 Dec 1751, ibid. 1 153.

455 *were reared*'. Mendonça Furtado to King, 8 Jan 1752, ibid. 1 166.

456 *public service.*' Ibid. 1 166.

456 *Indians*'. Mendonça Furtado to King, 26 Jan 1752, ibid. 1 212.

456 *total prohibition. . . .*' Ibid. 1 212.

456 *those it can.*' Mendonça Furtado to Oeiras (Pombal), 1 Feb 1752, ibid. 1 237.

456 *Indian women.*' Mendonça Furtado to Oeiras (Pombal), 2 Nov 1752, ibid. 1 259–60.

457 *all ways*'. Mendonça Furtado to Oeiras (Pombal), Belém do Pará, 8 Nov 1752, ibid. 1 275.

457 *their church*'. Ibid. 1 277.

457 *forest spices.*' Mendonça Furtado to Oeiras (Pombal), 21 Nov 1751, ibid. 1 77.

457 *factories and plantations.*' Mendonça Furtado to Oeiras (Pombal), 30 Nov 1751, ibid. 1 84.

457 *world to beg. . . .*' Ibid. 1 84.

457 *the land*'. Mendonça Furtado instructions to Capitão-mór João Batista de Oliveira for founding a town at Macapá, 18 Dec 1751, ibid. 1 116.

457 *these parts.*' Mendonça Furtado to Oeiras (Pombal), 30 Nov 1751, ibid. 1 86.

457 *be enslaved*'. Mendonça Furtado to King, 13 Nov 1752, ibid. 1 300.

458 *entire people.*' Mendonça Furtado to King, 16 Nov 1752, ibid. 1 304–5.

458 *before them.*' Mendonça Furtado to Oeiras (Pombal), 9 Nov 1752, ibid. 1 282.

458 *that expedition*'. King to prelates of religious orders, Lisbon, 18 May 1753, ibid. 1 396.

458 *by force*'. Ibid. 1 396.

459 *considerable profit.*' Mendonça Furtado report on estates of the Jesuits in Pará, Belém, 8 Feb 1754, ibid. 2 485–6.

459 *miserable captaincy.'* Mendonça Furtado to Pombal, Belém, 22 Feb 1754, ibid. **2** 512.

459 *as slaves'.* Mendonça Furtado, Report on Jesuit estates in Pará, 8 Feb 1754, ibid. **2** 487.

459 *mission villages.'* Mendonça Furtado to Pombal, 18 Feb 1754, ibid. **2** 503.

459 *a yacht'.* Anon, *Diario da viagem que o Ilmo. e Exmo. Sr. Francisco Xavier de*

Mendonça Furtado . . . fez para o rio Negro à expedição das demarcações dos reais domínios de Sua Majestade, ibid. **2** 615.

460 *the woods.'* Mendonça Furtado to Pombal, Mariúa (Barcellos), 6 July 1755, ibid. **2** 703.

460 *civilised people.'* Anon, *Diario da viagem . . .,* AEP **2** 630.

460 *misery and deprivation'.* Ibid.

Chapter 21 THE EXPULSION OF THE JESUITS

462 *Portugal. . . .'* Treaty of Madrid, 1750, Article 16, quoted in Luís Gonzaga Jaeger, *A expulsão da Companhia de Jesus do Brasil em 1760* (Pôrto Alegre, 1960), in Magnus Mörner, *The Expulsion of the Jesuits from Latin America* (New York, 1965) 119.

463 *double measure'.* Ibid.

463 *Paraguay.* Three of the seven missions in Brazil are still quite important towns: São Borja on the Uruguay, Santo Ângelo and São Luís Gonzaga. The other four were São João Batista, São Nicolau, São Miguel das Missões and São Lourenço. The dates of foundation, and populations in 1750 were: São Nicolau (1687) 3940, São Luís Gonzaga (1687) 2350, Santo Ângelo (1706) 1960, São Miguel das Missões (1687) 1900, São João (1698) 1600, São Francisco de Borja (1682) 1300, São Lourenço (1691) 960. Total population: 14,000.

Of the twenty-three other Jesuit missions from this period of greatest prosperity, fifteen are in the Argentine province of Misiones, and eight in southern Paraguay between Asunción and Encarnación. Ruins of many of the missions survive, but the easiest for a modern visitor to see are those of San Ignacio Miní, north-east of Posadas in Argentina; São Miguel in Rio Grande do Sul; and Trinidad and Jesús north-west of Encarnacíon in Paraguay.

The ruins of San Ignacio Miní consist of a grass-covered plaza a hundred metres square, flanked on either side by arcaded streets of single-storey houses.

Most of these are roofless, but their massive reddish stone walls are in good condition. There were thirty blocks of these dwellings, with ten one-room units in each block. On the south side of the plaza are the ruins of the splendid baroque church finished in 1724. Beside it are the ruins of the missionaries' house, school, cloisters, workshops and cemetery. The site is well maintained as a national monument, and is a popular tourist attraction. Trinidad in Paraguay also has a vast ruined church and a small museum of religious ornaments and sculptures, but it is a wilder place, more overgrown and less visited. The great cathedral of São Miguel in Brazil was ruined, overgrown and pillaged by local people seeking building stone. It was cleaned and restored in 1940. Parts of the old streets were restored by the Carioca architect Lúcio Costa, the future planner of Brasília. One Indian residence became a museum.

463 *playing music. . . .'* Thomaz da Costa Corrêa Rebello e Silva, *Memoria sobre a Provincia de Missões,* RHGB **2** 161, 1840.

464 *for them.'* Ibid. **2** 162.

464 *Christians'.* Anton Sepp, *Viagem às missões Jesuiticas e trabalhos apostólicos* 98.

464 *prayers and devotions.* Ibid. 98.

465 *tiny hut.'* Ibid. 119–20.

465 *need it.'* Ibid. 121–2.

466 *mature bulls.'* Ibid. 131.

466 *so much.'* Ibid. 137.

467 *one lutist'.* Ibid. 140.

467 *plenty of meat.'* Ibid. 141.

468 *nine months' shelter.'* Ibid. 170.

468 *role of gravedigger.*' Ibid. 170.
468 *to the heart.*' Ibid. 171–2.
469 *not prevail.*' Bernardo Nusdorfer, *Relación de todo lo sucedido en estas doctrinas en orden a las mudanzas de los 7 Pueblos del Uruguay* . . . 154.
469 *other lands.*' Ibid. 190.
469 *eyes shut*'. Ibid. 203.
470 *exercise of arms!*' Felis Feliciano da Fonseca, *Relação do que aconteceu aos demarcadores portuguezes e castelhanos no sertão das terras da Colonia* . . . (1753), RHGB 23 409, 1860.
470 *a demarcation*'. Ibid, 23 411.
470 *to comply.* Letter from Jesuit Provincial to missionaries, Córdoba, 19 Jan 1753; Renunciation of powers over 7 Missions, by Provincial Joseph de Barreda to Governor of Buenos Aires, Córdoba, 2 May 1753; Barreda to King, 13 May; all in Jaime Cortesão, *Do Tratado de Madri a conquista dos Sete Povos (1750–1802)* 119–24, 127–38.
470 *very destroyed. . . .*' Capt. Jacintho Rodrigues da Cunha, *Diario da expedição de Gomes Freire de Andrade as missões do Uruguay*, RHGB 16 168, 1853. The Jesuit Bernardo Nusdorfer gave a different account of these events. According to him, there was an earlier attack on the fort, on 22 February, which failed when the Indians started to plunder captured arms and tools. 'It failed because of great greed, little reasoning, and excessive confidence – all natural traits of the Guaraní' (Nusdorfer, *Relación* 246). The second attack succeeded in capturing all the fort's horses and cattle. The Portuguese in the fort showed a white flag. Fifty-three Indians entered the fort to parley, led by Chief Joseph of San Miguel Mission. These envoys were treacherously seized and sent south as prisoners. Those who reached Rio Grande were, however, freed and repatriated by Gomes Freire, who was 'possibly aware of and did not approve the treachery by his people' (ibid. 252–3, 264).
470 *fire and blood*'. Ibid. 260.
471 *droughts and frosts.*' Ibid. 272. Before retreating, the Spanish army slaughtered 6000 head of cattle from the Yapeyu

mission, and mauled the mission Indians when they pursued too closely, killing 120 in several volleys.
471 *had them.*' Ibid. 191.
471 *Holy Fathers. . . .*' Ibid. 192.
471 *Christians.*' Ibid. 198.
471 *choirs and orchestras.* The Treaty was with the Indians of the Missions of San Luis, San Lorenzo and Santo Angelo, and was signed for them by Don Martin Chauri. The Indians tried demanding that the Portuguese abandon their fort on the Pardo, at which Gomes Freire banged the table and refused. The Jesuit Nusdorfer could not understand why the Portuguese withdrew, even though they had lost many stores in the Indian attack on their fort. He speculated that Gomes Freire might have received a letter from his King telling him to favour the Indians (ibid. 280–1). The Indians remained calm but defiant. In mid-1755 the Jesuits attempted to read out an open letter from the Jesuit Visitor telling the Indians that they must move. But the letter was burned in each mission before it could be read out (ibid. 293).
472 *Governor killed.*' Ibid. 233.
472 *to them. . . .*' Ibid, 235.
472 *repeating guns. . . .*' Ibid. 239.
472 *gunfire and lances.*' Anon, *Diario da marcha dos exercitos de suas Magestades Fidelissima e Catholica, do dia 1 de fevereiro de 1756 em diante, e successos della*, in Eduardo de Castro e Almeida, *Inventario dos documentos relativo ao Brasil* . . . 1 146.
472 *1400 dead.*' Rodrigues da Cunha, *Diario da expedição de Gomes Freire de Andrada* 239.
473 *two armies.*' Ibid. 239.
473 *rigour of war*'. Ibid. 249.
473 *sad and grave.*' Ibid. 254.
473 *10 February*'. Ibid. 267.
473 *all white*'. Ibid. 310.
474 *their labour.*' Ibid. 299–300. The French admiral and explorer Louis de Bougainville paused at Montevideo in 1763. He recorded an arrogant remark about the recent war by a Jesuit leader: 'I have reason to be surprised that these two kings should make dispositions to divide a country which does not belong to them. We Jesuits alone have

conquered it; we alone have the right to
dispose of it, to keep and defend it, from
all and against all! It is certain that the
Indians of Paraguay are the subjects of
this Society, both at home in their
families and when they go out to battle'
(Antoine Joseph Pernety, *Histoire d'un
voyage fait aux Iles Malouines*, 2 vols (Paris,
1770); trans. into English as *The History of
a Voyage to the Malouine (or Falkland)
Islands, made in 1763 and 1764 under the
Command of M. de Bougainville ...*
(London, 1771) 167).
475 *it thus.'* José Basílio da Gama, *O
Uraguai*, canto II (Rio de Janeiro, 1941)
31). Maria da Conceição Osório Dias
Gonçalves, 'O índio do Brasil na
literatura portuguesa ...' 167. David
Miller Driver, *The Indian in Brazilian
Literature* 391. Afrânio Coutinho, *A
literatura portuguesa ...*, 2 vols (Rio de
Janeiro, 1956), 1 137, 165.
475 *enormous belly'. O Uraguai* canto III.
475 *sowers of discord'.* Ibid. canto III.
475 *Fathers'.* Ibid. canto IV, 85.
475 *the ground.'* Ibid. canto V, 101.
476 *goods and commerce'. Ley porque V.
Magestade ha por bem restituir aos indios do
Grão-Pará e Maranhão a liberdade das suas
pessoas, e bens, e commercio, na forma que nella
se declara*, in A. M. Perdigão Malheiro, *A
escravidão no Brasil* 2 99, 102: L.
Humberto de Oliveira, *Coletânea de leis
...* 63–4; Mathias C. Kieman, *The Indian
Policy of Portugal in the Amazon Region,
1614–1693* 452.
476 *great misery'.* Ibid.; Malheiro,
Escravidão 2 99.
476 *fled inland'.* Kieman, *Indian Policy* 452.
476 *honour or dignity.'* Álvara of 4 April
1755, *Ley sobre os casamentos com as Indias*.
Even the title of this law envisaged white
men taking Indian women – but not the
reverse.
476 *to them.* Álvara of 7 June 1755. *Álvara
com forca de ley, porque V. Magestade ha por
ben renovar a inteira e inviolavel observancia
da Ley de 12 de Setembro de 1653.*
477 *in abandon'.* Mendonça Furtado to
Pombal, 18 Jan 1754, doct. 119, ABAP 3
207, 1904; Nunes Dias, *Colonização da
Amazônia*, RH 34 478, 1967.
477 *rife here'.* Ibid. **34** 478.

477 *becoming irrelevant.* Manoel Nunes
Dias, 'Colonizacão da Amazônia' 480–9;
Aroldo de Azevedo, *Vilas e cidades do
Brasil colonial* (São Paulo, 1956) 49;
Francisco D. F. C. Trancoso, 'Os
arquivos das Companhias Gerais do
Grão-Pará e Maranhão, e de
Pernambuco e Paraíba, in *Ocidente*,
Lisbon, 33 nos 113–14, Sept–Oct 1947;
J. Lúcio de Azevedo, *Os Jesuitas no Grão-
Pará ... 294*, and *Estudos Paraenses* (Pará,
1893); Armando Gonçalves Pereira,
'Relações econômicas Luso-Brasileiras',
Brasília, Coimbra, 2 333, 1943.
477 *so much good.'* Pombal to Mendonça
Furtado, 4 Aug 1755, AEP 2 794.
477 *men work.'* Ibid. 2 794.
478 *suffer shame.'* Ibid. 2 795.
478 *remain orderly.'* Mendonça Furtado to
Pombal, Mariúa, 12 Nov 1755, AEP 2
824.
478 *the horrible'.* Voltaire quoted in C. R.
Boxer, *The Portuguese Seaborne Empire
1415–1825* 187. Pombal's sentence on
the Távoras, issued on 12 Jan 1759, was
of unprecedented brutality: the Duke of
Aveiro and Marquis of Távora were both
'rolled alive' by being churned on a
wheel and beaten to death with clubs; the
Marchioness of Távora was beheaded,
and her sons, the Marquis of Távora and
Count of Atouguia, were hanged along
with four servants. The King fully
supported his Minister and now made
him Count of Oeiras. He became
Marquis of Pombal in 1770.
479 *never to return.'* Law of 3 Sept 1759, in
Marcos Carneiro de Mendonça, *O
Marquês de Pombal e o Brasil* 59–63; partly
trans. in Mörner, *Expulsion of the Jesuits*
127.
480 *title of director.'* Mendonça Furtado to
King, 21 May 1757, in João Capistrano
de Abreu, *Capítulos de história colonial*
(1963 ed.) 185.
480 *their duty.'* Ibid. 185.
481 *their work'.* Bento da Fonseca, *Noticia
do governo temporal dos índios do Maranhão
... 165, 167*.
481 *do so.'* Abreu, *Capítulos* 185.
481 *3 May 1757.* The first director was
installed in the mission of Trocano,
renamed Vila de Borba-a-Nova, on the

Madeira, on 6 Jan 1756. These instructions, of 95 clauses, were confirmed by royal decree of 7 July 1757. The system of directors was extended to all aldeias in Pará and Maranhão on 3 May 1757 and approved by an álvara of 17 Aug 1758. Pombal's legislation freeing Indians and removing the temporal power of missionaries initially applied only to the Grão-Pará and Maranhão. It was extended to all Brazil on 8 May 1758, as was the diretorio.

481 *Indians themselves'!* Diretorio regimento, 3 May 1757, Perdigão Malheiro, *Escravidão* 2 110.

482 *slaves or freemen.* Dauril Alden, 'The Population of Brazil in the Late Eighteenth Century: a preliminary survey', HAHR 43 173–205, May 1963.

484 *golden age.'* Ambrósio Fernandes Brandão, *Diálogos das grandezas do Brazil*, ed. João Capistrano de Abreu, 271. There are six dialogues in this book, between an experienced colonist and a curious newcomer. The second dialogue compares negroes and Indians, and the sixth is about Indian customs. The author is now known to have been Ambrósio Fernandes Brandão.

484 *was sin'.* Sebastião da Rocha Pitta, *História da America Portugueza . . .* 49.

484 *law of reason.'* Ibid. 48.

485 *more glorious.'* Ibid. 52–3.

485 *the rivers'.* Claudio Manoel da Costa, poem 'Vila-Rica', in *Obras* 181–263. Costa was born in the gold-mining town of Mariana in 1729 and died in 1789 after taking part in the Mineiro conspiracy for independence from Portugal; Dias Gonçalves, 'O índio do Brasil' 163–4.

485 *Indians.* Alvarenga Peixoto was born in Rio de Janeiro in 1748, but became a magistrate of an area of Minas Gerais.

He also joined the Mineiro conspiracy led by 'Tiradentes' ('Tooth-puller'), the dentist Ensign Joaquim José da Silva Xavier. Some authors who believed in the benefits of Portuguese supremacy were: the Franciscan Frei Francisco de São Carlos (1763–1829) in his poem, *A Assunção*; Bento de Figueiredo Tenreiro Aranha, in his poetic drama *A felicidade do Brasil*; Joaquim José Lisboa, in his *Descrição curiosa*. Dias Gonçalves, 'O índio do Brasil' 182–5.

485 *civilised city!'* António Dinis da Cruz e Silva (1731–99), Sonnet 47, *Poesias de António Dinis da Cruz e Silva*, 6 vols (Lisbon, 1807–17), 1 249; Dias Gonçalves, 'O índio do Brasil' 186.

485 *brute savagery'.* Santa Rita Durão, *Caramuru* (1781), ed. F. A. de Varnhagen, (Rio de Janeiro/Paris), canto II, 59. Dias Gonçalves, 'O índio do Brasil' 178–82; this fine essay demonstrates that the most famous eighteenth-century poets – Santa Rita Durão and Basílio da Gama – did *not* depict Indians as noble savages or naturally virtuous. Both authors regarded Indians as savage until improved by Portuguese civilisation. The 'noble savage' interpretation of their writing was given by Coutinho, *A literatura no Brasil* 1 137, 165.

486 *noble savage.* Joseph François Lafitau, *Mœurs des Sauvages Amériquains comparés aux Mœurs des Anciens Temps* (1724), and *Histoire des Découvertes et Conquêtes des Portugais dans le Nouveau Monde* (Paris, 1773); G. T. Raynal, *Histoire Philosophique et Politique des Établissements et du Commerce Européens dans les deux Indes*, 4 vols (Geneva, 1780), vol. 2, bk 9, about Brazilian Indians.

486 *expanse of waters.'* Basílio da Gama, *O Uraguai*, canto II (1941 ed.), 33.

Appendix   THE POPULATION OF BRAZIL IN 1500

492 *has occurred.* Brave authors who have attempted the impossible task of guessing the pre-conquest population of Brazil include, in chronological order: Paul Rivet, 'Langues de l'Amérique du

Sud et des Antilles', in A. Meillet and Marcel Cohen (eds), *Les Langues du monde* (Paris, 1924) 16 639–712; Carl Sapper, 'Die Zahl und Volksdichte der indianischen Bevölkerung in Amerika vor der Conquista und in der Gegenwart', *International Congress of Americanists, The Hague, 1924* 95–104; Alfred L. Kroeber, 'Cultural and Natural Areas of Native North America', *University of California Publications in American Archeology and Ethnology. Berkeley, Calif.,* 38 1939; Ángel Rosenblat, *La población indígena de América desde 1492 hasta la actualidad* (Buenos Aires, 1945); Julian H. Steward, 'The Native Population of South America', NSAI 5 655–68, 1949; Thales de Azevedo, 'Panorama demográfico dos grupos étnicos da América Latina', AI **17** no. 2, 121–39, 1957; Julian H. Steward and Louis C. Faron, *Native Peoples of South America* (New York, 1959) 51–60; Pierre Chaunu, 'La Population de l'Amérique indienne: nouvelles recherches', *Revue Historique* (Paris), 1 1963; Pierre Clastres, 'Éléments de démographie amér-indienne', *L'Homme* (Paris), **13** no. 1–2, 1973, or in his *La Société contre l'état* (Paris, 1974) 69–87; William M. Denevan, 'The Aboriginal Population of Amazonia', in Denevan (ed.), *The Native Population of South America in 1492* (Madison, Wis., 1977) 205–34.

There are some useful general surveys of modern Indians in Brazil: Kenneth G. Grubb, *The Lowland Indians of Amazonia* (London, 1927); Cândido M. da S. Rondon, *Índios do Brasil*, 3 vols (Rio de Janeiro, 1946); Curt Nimuendajú's many articles in the NSAI and elsewhere, and his splendid ethnographic maps in NSAI 1 382 and 3 284 and 800; José M. da Gama Malcher, *Índios: grau de integração, grupo linguístico, localização* (Rio de Janeiro, 1962); Arthur Ramos, *As culturas indígenas* (*Introdução à antropologia brasileira* 2) (Rio de Janeiro, 1971); Julio Cezar Melatti, *Índios do Brasil* (Brasília, 1970).

Statistics on numbers of present-day tribes can be found in: Dale W. Kietzman, 'Indians and Culture Areas of Twentieth Century Brazil', in Janice H. Hopper (ed.), *Indians of Brazil in the Twentieth Century* (Washington, DC, 1967) 1–51; Darcy Ribeiro, 'Culturas e linguas indígenas do Brasil', *Educação e Ciências Sociais* **2** no. 6, Rio de Janeiro, 1957, trans. in Hopper, *Indians of Brazil* 77–165; Carlos Alberto Dória and Carlos Alberto Ricardo, 'Populations indigènes du Brésil: perspectives de survie dans la région dite "Amazonie légale"', *Bulletin de la Société Suisse des Américanistes* **36** 19–35, 1972; A. Robin Hanbury-Tenison, *Report of a Visit to the Indians of Brazil on Behalf of . . . Survival International* (London, 1971); Edwin Brooks, René Fuerst, John Hemming, Francis Huxley, *Tribes of the Amazon Basin in Brazil, 1972* (London, 1973).

Index

53180